LIFT EVERY

VOICE

STUDIES IN RHETORIC AND COMMUNICATION

General Editors:
E. Culpepper Clark
Raymie E. McKerrow
David Zarefsky

LIFT EVERY

VOICE

African American Oratory, 1787–1900

Edited by PHILIP S. FONER

and ROBERT JAMES BRANHAM

THE UNIVERSITY OF ALABAMA PRESS

Tuscaloosa and London

∞

The paper on which this book is printed meets the minimum requirements of American National Standard for Information Science-
Permanence of Paper for Printed Library Materials, ANSI Z39.48-1984

Library of Congress Cataloging-in-Publication Data

Lift every voice : African American oratory, 1787–1900 / edited by
   Philip S. Foner and Robert J. Branham.
      p. cm. — (Studies in rhetoric and communication)
   Includes index.
      ISBN 0-8173-0848-2 (cloth : alk. paper). — ISBN 0-8173-0906-3
(paper : alk. paper)
      1. Afro-Americans—History—18th century—Sources. 2. Afro-
Americans—History—19th century—Sources. 3. Political oratory—
United States—History—18th century. 4. Political oratory—United
States—History—19th century. 5. Speeches, addresses, etc.,
American—Afro-American authors. I. Foner, Philip Sheldon, 1910–
. II. Branham, Robert J. III. Series.
   E185.18.L54 1998
   973'.0496073—dc21   97-21268

British Library Cataloguing-in-Publication Data available

Publication

of this book

was made possible in part

by subventions from

THE NATIONAL ALUMNI ASSOCIATION

OF THE UNIVERSITY OF ALABAMA *and*

BATES COLLEGE.

CONTENTS

LIFT EVERY
VOICE

INTRODUCTION

In his 1852 address "Orators and Oratory," William Grant Allen advised his student listeners, "Cultivate the oratorical, do it diligently and with purpose, remembering that it is by the exercise of this weapon perhaps more than any other that America is to be made a free land, not in name only, but in deed and truth."[1] Allen, one of the first African American members of a college faculty, believed the study of oratory to be essential to the pursuit of liberal education and social justice. To study great speeches, he reasoned, was to learn the most influential ideas of the day in their most eloquent expressions; to learn to speak well oneself was to prepare for participation in civic life and reform. These ideas were matters of faith to most nineteenth-century Americans, whose public lives consisted largely of occasions for oratory.[2]

Although oratory is no longer the popular entertainment it was in the nineteenth century, and training in rhetorical practice and criticism no longer occupies a central place in American education,[3] oratory remains a pervasive and important practice in American political and social life. Oratory is still the basic tool of organizing, the crown of ceremonial observance, the currency of advocacy and deliberation. It is the means by which group interests are publicly identified and action is mobilized; it is the means by which individual voices are brought together and purpose forged in common bond. It is also a means by which profound differences may be understood and through which grievances and dissent may be brought face-to-face with audiences responsible for injustice.

Historically, oratory has occupied a significant place in African American life as a set of rhetorical practices and values forged not only in America but also in Africa. The earliest known writings on rhetorical theory and practical instruction are Egyptian. Formal oratory and debate have occupied central roles in many African cultures and continue to do so.[4] As Ethel Albert observed in Burundi, "Speech is explicitly recognized as an important instrument of social life; eloquence is one of the central values of the cultural world-view; and the way of life affords frequent opportunity for its exercise."[5] In both speaking practices and the power and respect accorded oral eloquence, African American oratory reveals its African, as well as its American, roots. "African American oratory," writes Molefi Asante, is "the totalization of the Afrocentric experience," in which "the African person finds the ability to construct a discourse capable of calling forth *nommo,* the generative and productive power of the spoken word."[6] The rhetoric of African Americans continues to reflect, in part, the great and diverse oratorical traditions of Africa.[7]

For over two hundred years, oratory has been an essential element in African American self-expression, community life, and negotiation with whites. Nineteenth-century African American communities conferred extraordinary importance upon the development and use of oratorical skills as a means by which to achieve both social reform and individual advancement. Early African American rhetoricians, including William G. Allen, Newell Houston Ensley, and Hallie Quinn Brown, worked to extend opportunities for training in public speaking, imagining

> the day when a Kindergarten shall be established by the side of every school house, when the trident of oratory shall be added to the curriculum of every school in the land, that it may be taught in every town, village and hamlet.
> When no teacher may enter the temple without its refining influence.
> When no student shall face life's stern realities without the proper study of this theme.[8]

Throughout the nineteenth century, African Americans developed institutions to promote training in public speaking, to develop its free exercise, and to preserve and disseminate the works of black orators.

This collection focuses on the use of oratory in the struggle that, from the early national period to the present, black Americans have waged for liberation. African American orators provided leadership in the struggle against slavery before the Civil War and in the battle for civil rights and meaningful freedom that has characterized black protest from before emancipation to the present day. The vast majority of the speeches we have included address the problems of African Americans in a profoundly racist society and the various possible ways of dealing with these problems. Some of these orations and orators are well known, at least to scholars; most, however, have long languished in obscurity—unpublished, out of print, or uncollected.

The great treasury of African American oratory from the eighteenth and nineteenth centuries exists against all odds. For the millions of African Americans enslaved during this period, public speeches, with the exception of sermons by slave preachers, were almost entirely prohibited. Nominally "free" black Americans were systematically excluded from the practice of law, from the professoriate, from political office, and from much of the ministry, those professions whose members made speeches that commanded the greatest public attention and were most likely to be preserved. The lyceum movement, which dominated the organization of community lectures and the training of orators in the nineteenth-century United States, was almost entirely segregated. "American colorphobia is never more rampant towards its victims," wrote African American historian and orator William C. Nell in 1855, "than when one would avail himself of the facilities for mental improvement, in common with the more favored dominant party,—as if his complexion was, indeed, prima facie evidence that he was an intruder within the sacred portals of knowledge." In his own home city of Boston, Nell wrote, "the so-called 'Athens of America,' large audiences have been thrown almost into spasms by the presence of one colored man in their midst."[9]

African American speakers were rarely invited to address major municipal and national civic ceremonies in the nineteenth century, and when they were, their speeches were less likely to be published than those of their white fellow orators. During the national centennial celebration of 1876, for example, in which most cities and towns held commemorative ceremonies marked by public address, most Americans heard nothing of the contributions of African Americans to the creation of the nation.[10] Similarly, African Americans were almost entirely excluded from participation in Chicago's Columbian Exposition of 1893 and from the World's Congress of Representative Women convened in conjunction with it.[11] Barred from speaking in most integrated settings, African Americans created their own occasions, organizations, and venues for speech. The earliest surviving speech by an African American, reprinted here, is Cyrus Bustill's 1787 address to slaves in Philadelphia.[12] This was by no means, however, the first African American public address. The earliest known African American orators were exhorters and preachers. Some of them turned their pulpits into platforms for social activism and political organization, while others, particularly those who ministered to the enslaved, sought to "provide the basis of hope which would allow one to endure another week."[13] The Great Awakening of the mid-eighteenth century led to the rise of itinerant lay preachers and exhorters, including African American men and women, who preached before both black and white audiences in open-air revivals or other unconventional settings.[14] Black preachers, despite severe denominational restrictions on their activities,[15] achieved considerable fame before the American Revolution. Harry Hosier, a traveling black Methodist preacher thought to have been born in slavery around 1750, was said by influential contemporaries to be "the greatest orator in America"[16] and was also one of the most popular.[17] George Liele preached in Augusta, Georgia, as early as 1773 and, like Andrew Bryan a few years later, sought to establish separate black churches.[18] Yet no texts of their speeches are known to survive.

Most early African American sermons were delivered extemporaneously, a practice that Richard Allen and many of his contemporaries believed best, as it combined "the speaker's intuition in a fortuitous blend with the congregation's reaction."[19] With neither speaking manuscripts nor active reporting or transcription of sermons when delivered, few texts of African American sermons survive from the period, and those that do often lack attribution; an identified author would run the risk of personal attacks from disapproving whites.[20] Speeches by African American preaching women have been especially prone to disappear. The sermons of itinerant A.M.E. preacher and later Shaker eldress Rebecca Cox Jackson were said to have "touched off responsive waves of revivalistic fervor, among whites at least as much as among blacks, wherever she spoke" in the 1830s but appear not to have been recorded.[21] Similarly, although some autobiographical writings survive from such early black women preachers of the A.M.E. Church as Jarena Lee and Zilpha Elaw, the sermons by which they came to fame appear lost, unrecorded in official annals of the church.[22]

Yet as the sermons that do survive make clear, black churches provided important venues for political oratory and organizing that placed the locus of control over moral and social reform within black communities.[23] African American ministers were often community leaders and political activists of great influence who, when speaking in black churches, enjoyed considerable independence and immunity from backlash.[24] Safer than most public gathering places and more susceptible to black control than most other venues for speech, black churches offered consistent audiences for speakers promoting social organization and reform. As Joseph C. Price, the "World's Orator" and founder of Livingstone College, observed, "The popular lecture-room may be poorly attended; the political mass-meeting may be thin. . . . But the Negro church will be packed."[25] For African Americans denied access to public parks, meeting halls, and theaters, black churches provided essential space for both secular and religious gatherings.

Free African Americans created their own mutual benefit and fraternal organizations at least as early as 1787 and marked their gatherings with oratory. Meetings at the Prince Hall Masonic lodges and other black organizations in the early republic provided venues, audiences, and occasions for sermons and speeches that considered a broad range of social issues. African Americans also organized to broaden opportunities for instruction and practice in public speaking and debate. Between 1828 and 1846, African Americans responded to their exclusion from white-dominated lyceums by establishing more than forty literary and debating societies.[26] When African Americans were denied admission to the lyceum in abolitionist New Bedford, for example, they established "an independent Lyceum, where men, irrespective of accidental differences, could freely assemble, and have dispensed to them the precious stores of knowledge."[27] Such societies were viewed as essential instruments of educational, moral, and social advancement, providing knowledge and developing skills in a weekly "mental feast."

The greatest impetus for the surge in African American organization, speech training, and oratory in the early nineteenth century was the campaign of the American Colonization Society to promote the emigration of free blacks to Africa. Although initially supported by some African Americans who despaired of ever gaining equality and justice in their homeland, the schemes of the Colonization Society were soon understood as rooted in prejudice and damaging to the position and progress of blacks in the United States. The colonization movement, which spurred political organization and protest oratory among African Americans, culminated in the creation of the black convention movement and active black participation in the newly formed antislavery societies of the 1830s. The convention movement, beginning in regional conferences in 1817, expanded to include representatives from throughout the northern and border states by 1830. In these congresses, black men (and later women) debated colonization and other major issues, such as temperance, education, slavery, and racial prejudice, affecting African Americans.[28]

The explosion of organized antislavery activity in the 1830s also brought significant numbers of black political speakers before predominantly white audiences. By the early 1840s, lectures by fugitive slaves and free black abolitionists were common features at antislavery gatherings. American Anti-Slavery Society agent John A. Collins wrote to William Lloyd Garrison in 1842 that "the public have itching ears to hear a colored man speak, and particularly a *slave*. Multitudes will flock to hear one of this class speak." Oral testimony by former slaves proved a popular and convincing component of antislavery meetings. "Drawing on the black oral tradition, the fugitives delighted their audiences," writes John Blassingame, and "elicited sympathy, tears, and increased interest in abolition."[29] Black abolitionists brought an understanding and commitment born of personal experience that no white orator could fully share. "Most free blacks," writes Shirley Yee, "were former slaves themselves, had relatives and friends who were still enslaved, and encountered racism in their daily lives."[30] Black abolitionists, especially those who had personally experienced the bitter yoke of slavery, understood themselves to occupy a special place in the abolitionist movement. Who else could refute so effectively those who argued that slaves actually benefited from their bondage and were happy to be human property?

Frederick Douglass, Charles Lenox Remond, Sojourner Truth, William Wells Brown, Frances E. Watkins, Sarah Parker Remond, and many others traveled throughout the northern states and to other countries in order to gain support for the abolitionist cause. Black abolitionist orators often described the sense of responsibility they felt to speak for those who had no voice and to disprove, through their own words and deeds, prejudicial notions of racial inferiority that forged the chains of slavery. In his address to the 1848 black national convention in Cleveland, Frederick Douglass told his listeners:

> In the Northern states, we are not slaves to individuals, not personal slaves, yet in many respects we are the slaves of the community. We are, however, far enough removed from the actual condition of the slave to make us largely responsible for their continued enslavement, or their speedy deliverance from chains. For in the proportion which we shall rise in the scale of human improvement, in that proportion do we augment the probabilities of a speedy emancipation of our enslaved fellow-countrymen. It is more than a figure of speech to say, that we are as a people, chained together. We are as one people—one in general complexion, one in a common degradation, one in popular estimation. As one rises, all must rise, and as one falls all must fall.[31]

Even within the major antislavery societies, speaking opportunities and leadership roles for African Americans were limited. When former slaves such as Douglass sought to move beyond autobiographical narratives to broader considerations of politics and social prejudice, they often met opposition from their presumed allies. Douglass was advised by his Garrisonian colleagues not to sound too "learned," because people might not "believe you were ever a slave."[32]

Douglass and others sought not only to raise their own voices, but to gain control of the forums and media in which their voices would be heard and reprinted. Black Americans created their own newspapers and publishing firms through which to disseminate their opinions. "We wish to plead our own cause," wrote the editors of *Freedom's Journal* in their inaugural issue of 1827: "Too long have others spoken for us." Many of the speeches that appear in this collection were first published by black-owned presses or in black-edited newspapers, including *Freedom's Journal*, the *Provincial Freeman*, the *Christian Recorder*, the *New York Age*, and the *Colored American*, which sought to bring the important addresses of African Americans to extended audiences.

Black abolitionist orators redefined the scope and objectives of the movement, linking slavery, segregation, prejudice, and inequality as mutually reinforcing practices that must all be attacked if meaningful change was to be achieved. Moreover, African Americans proclaimed, by the act of speaking for themselves as well as by their words, the right of self-determination. "Coming to voice is an act of resistance," writes bell hooks. "Speaking becomes both a way to engage in active self-transformation and a rite of passage where one moves from being object to being subject. Only as subjects can we speak. As objects, we remain voiceless—our beings defined and interpreted by others."[33] Oratory is only one means through which African Americans have come to voice, but it is a singularly important one.

All known African American speeches published in the antebellum period were delivered in the North or abroad. The slaves of the South could not, of course, use the platform to voice their feelings, and even free blacks were generally forced to maintain public silence south of the Mason-Dixon Line.[34] The mere possession of a copy of *Uncle Tom's Cabin* by a free black in Maryland brought ten years in prison; any African American who voiced public opposition to slavery risked enslavement.

African Americans, North or South, who dared to speak to unconverted audiences on behalf of abolition or civil rights risked ridicule, harassment, and injury. John Marrant's first sermons in Massachusetts in 1789 were broken up by mobs of club-wielding whites; Charles Lenox Remond dodged eggs and stones while speaking in northern Maine in the 1830s; Sojourner Truth and Frances E. Watkins were routinely threatened and heckled; Frederick Douglass was assaulted on the speaker's platform in Boston. To many African Americans, such assaults and proscriptions on black orators confirmed the power and importance of oratory. A practice so feared and persecuted by the enemies of freedom, they reasoned, was a mighty force indeed. "Slavery cannot tolerate free speech" by abolitionist orators, Frederick Douglass told a Boston audience in 1860 after he had been beaten and thrown from the stage during an earlier address: "Five years of its exercise would banish the auction block and break every chain in the South." Although all abolitionist speakers faced danger, black abolitionists faced far greater hazards. As Theodore Wright told his abolitionist audience in 1836: "The whole land has been raised up against you, because you have labored to convince the oppressor, that he should no longer oppress." In addition to the hostility occasioned by their remarks, black lecturers faced the daily indignities of discrimination in transportation, accommodations, and social affairs that were not endured by their white allies and too often were supported by them.

Black abolitionist women who dared mount the public platform faced a double burden of prejudice. Although women had spoken publicly during the revivalist movement of the mid-eighteenth century, their speaking had been widely viewed as transgressive. As itineracy was tamed through regulation and licensure, women speakers became quite rare. The reemergence of black women speakers in the abolitionist movement of the 1830s challenged prevailing notions of womanhood. Speaking in public was generally regarded in early nineteenth-century America as a violation of "woman's essential nature," threatening to her physical well-being and reproductive capacity.[35] Women speakers who addressed "promiscuous" mixed-sex audiences were especially scandalous. Itinerant preacher Rebecca Cox Jackson, for example, was rebuked by the leadership of the A.M.E. Church for "aleading the men."[36] Maria Stewart, the first American-born woman to leave extant texts of public speeches she had written, was pelted with tomatoes by black men in her audience when she criticized them.[37] Yet despite some initial resistance, black males proved more willing than whites to accept women as orators.[38] As Shirley Yee concludes, "The act of public speaking and writing among black women, by defying racist expectations of black docility and intellectual inferiority, led black male leaders as well as many white abolitionists to accept black women writers and speakers as symbols of black success and resistance."[39]

The earliest surviving speeches by African American women, including those by Margaret Odell, Maria Miller Stewart, and Sarah Mapps Douglass, are reproduced here. Yet the lost speeches for social justice by poet Lucy Terry Prince (c. 1730–1821) and others were legendary long before these women spoke. When her eldest son was denied admission to Williams College because of his color, Prince reportedly delivered a brilliant but futile three-hour speech, laced with biblical allusions and legal citations, to the college's board of trustees. Later she gained national attention through her courtroom arguments in a Vermont land claims case. Presiding justice Samuel Chase is said to have pronounced Prince's speech "a better argument than he had heard from any lawyer at the Vermont bar," but no transcript or detailed description of her remarks has been found.[40]

For both male and female African American orators of the nineteenth century, when public speaking was prized as the highest achievement of human intellect, proficiency at the public platform was frequently used to refute notions of race and gender inferiority. Referring to two speeches delivered by African Americans the previous year, William Hamilton exclaimed in an 1809 address to the New York African Society for Mutual Relief that "if we continue to produce specimens like these, we shall soon put our enemies to the blush; abashed and confounded they shall quit the field, and no longer urge their superiority of souls." Black students at the New York African Free School offered public exhibitions of speaking skills that drew visitors from around the world in the 1820s and were cited in the school's fundraising campaigns as proof of black educability. The skill and evident intelligence of former slaves who recounted the stories of their bondage and escapes were cited at antislavery gatherings as proof of the slave's full humanity, capacity for learning, and entitlement to citizenship rights. After Frederick Douglass's first antislavery speech in New Bedford in 1841, William Lloyd Garrison rose on the stage and asked: "Have we been listening to a thing, a chattel personal, or a man?" "A man! A man!" the audience shouted.[41] Throughout the nineteenth century, the exhibition of eloquence by African American orators was cited by both black and white advocates as carrying a double message, pressing the case for equality and respect through oratorical achievement as well as through explicit argument.[42]

The passage of the Fugitive Slave Act of 1850 made slavery, as William Wells Brown would lament, coterminous with the borders of the nation and placed all black Americans, no matter their status or location, in jeopardy of enslavement. African American orators renewed debates over emigration, disunion, and armed resistance, particularly through the state convention movement initiated by African Americans in this period. At the same time, they helped turn the nation's attention to the inevitable conflict that lay ahead.

During the Civil War, African American orators again made a special contribution. The United States entered the war with the avowed object of preserving the Union and only that. Gradually, a fundamental change occurred in the thinking of many Americans, including President Lincoln, regarding the mission of the war. From a confused and somewhat timid hope that slavery might die of its own weight if only it were held to the South, the lessons of the war brought to the majority of the northern population the realization that slavery had been at the root of the conflict, and the end of slavery and arming of black soldiers were essential to victory and a stable peace. The shift in popular thought regarding the purposes of the war was the result, in large measure, of patient and persistent efforts of the abolitionists. The contributions of black abolitionist orators to this shift were enormous, as they redefined "The Mission of the War," as one of Frederick Douglass's stock wartime lectures was titled and rallied the black enlistment and support of the war effort on which the Union cause ultimately depended. Black abolitionists also acted, in Benjamin Quarles's words, as "ministers without portfolio" whose public lectures and private lobbying abroad played a crucial role in keeping England from supporting the Confederacy.[43] From the outset of the conflict, African American orators urged the government of the United States to arm blacks and abolish slavery. In due time they were to see this program adopted as the policy of the Lincoln administration. Lincoln himself agreed with his field commanders that "the emancipation policy and the aid of colored troops constituted the heaviest blow yet dealt to the rebellion."[44]

Following the Civil War, the Reconstruction era marked the entrance of African Americans into national and state elective offices, where their voices at long last joined in legislative deliberations over public policy. Black elected officials, however, produced but a fraction of the notable oratory by African Americans of the period. African American missionaries, teachers, and lecturers, for example, toured the South for the first time to address and organize newly freed men and women. Black lecturers such as Frances E. Watkins Harper and James Lynch played a vital role in the education and political mobilization of freedpersons and in the raising of funds to support these efforts. Black orators reminded white audiences that through their direct participation in the Civil War, African Americans had helped save the Republic and were entitled to all rights of citizenship in that government. Anything less than full and complete freedom and equality, they warned, would again endanger the life of the nation. Harper, Douglass, Sojourner Truth, Robert Purvis, Mary Ann Shadd Cary, and other African American orators were also active during the Reconstruction era in efforts to secure the franchise and full citizenship rights for women.

When the Thirteenth, Fourteenth, and Fifteenth Amendments to the Constitution were adopted, there were those who believed that the need for antislavery organizations no longer existed. The American Anti-Slavery Society, among others, disbanded in the belief that its mission was now complete. But events soon demonstrated that this belief had no basis in reality. A new pattern of oppression, replacing the old slave system, grew up in the South; and in the North, the problems of prejudice and a caste society still prevailed. "Press, platform, pulpit," Frederick Douglass wrote in July 1870, "should continue to direct their energies to the removal of the hardships and wrongs which continue to be the lot of the colored people of this country because they wear a complexion which two hundred and fifty years of slavery taught the great mass of the American people to hate and which the Fifteenth Amendment has not yet taught the American people to love."[45]

African Americans mounted the speaking platform to fight for civil and political equality, particularly the Civil Rights Act of 1875, in the South as well as the North. The first black representatives in the U.S. Congress made plain in their speeches that while constitutional amendments guaranteeing equality and citizenship rights looked fine in print, the practices of the nation and the experiences of African Americans were quite a different matter. What, they asked, were the Fourteenth and Fifteenth Amendments worth to the victims of Ku Klux Klan terror? What did the ballot mean to those reduced to a state of peonage?

These questioning voices were not heeded. The hopes and opportunities raised by the outlawing of slavery and the granting of citizenship rights and the franchise were relentlessly diminished by various acts, legal and illegal.

Promised reparations for slavery and land reform never materialized. Amnesty for ex-Confederate soldiers reempowered the rebels; the withdrawal of federal troops from the South in 1877 gave white supremacists a free hand; land and wealth were returned to antebellum slaveholders. A resurgence of racial prejudice and racial violence swept the nation. "The Red Record," as Ida B. Wells termed it, of lynching and other forms of terrorism reinforced segregation and second-class citizenship for African Americans. By the 1890s, disfranchisement of black Americans had begun in earnest, and by 1910 it was an established fact through most of the South. A second Jim Crow society was firmly entrenched in both North and South. White liberals in the North who had demanded equal rights for African Americans were largely silent by 1900. The northern press had for the most part ceased to criticize southern treatment of African Americans; federal courts nullified much of the Fourteenth and Fifteenth Amendments and ruled that "separate but equal" facilities were constitutional. Economic inequity was institutionalized.

Competing black leaders and ideologies of the late nineteenth century offered very different responses to the resurgence of racial prejudice, inequality, and violence. Some, led by Booker T. Washington, urged African Americans to learn trades and improve their minds and morals while waiting patiently for full citizenship rights to be awarded at some future date. At the same time, however, more militant voices organized for social change. The demand for full citizenship was asserted by Ida B. Wells, Francis Grimké, Bishop Henry M. Turner, and others who spoke directly and passionately to black Americans, whose resistance they helped mobilize, and to white Americans, whose inaction, they charged, meant death and despair.

A vast array of new African American political and social organizations responded in various ways to the needs and opportunities of the late nineteenth century, yet all relied upon oratory to deliberate over policies, to attract and inspire members, and to represent their interests and positions before other groups. The African American women's club movement organized for social justice and mutual aid; black intellectuals created their own academies and journals. "Local churches, associations, conventions, and conferences," according to Benjamin Mays and Joseph Nicholson, became "the Negro's Democratic and Republican Conventions, his Legislature and his Senate and House of Representatives."[46] African American business leaders created self-sufficient trade and lending institutions. Still other black Americans, however, renewed the call to abandon the "white man's country" and emigrate to Africa or the Caribbean. As the nineteenth century drew to a close and America extended the global reach of empire, democracy at home was denied even to those African Americans who had distinguished themselves in the war with Spain. African Americans vanished from the halls of Congress and from state legislatures across the land. Once again denied both legal protection and political power in white-dominated institutions, African Americans urgently organized as never before and employed oratory to advance and critique these new efforts.

Although many of the speeches in this volume are devoted to the great issues of slavery and racial prejudice, these were far from the only concerns addressed by African American orators, and we accordingly include speeches on a broad range of other topics. African Americans played significant roles in most of the important social and political movements of the nineteenth century, including temperance, suffrage, socialism, anarchism, unionism, anti-imperialism, and educational reform. Black orators frequently approached these issues and movements with distinctive perspectives and concerns. Even when excluded from white-dominated national reform organizations or relegated to "auxiliary" status, African Americans helped shape the national debate on each issue, often through speeches included in this volume.

These orations offer indispensable access to the actual voices of the historical actors, set in the context of those occasions when they believed their words might be instrumental and transformative. The speeches in this collection offer a variety of perspectives on the conditions that have faced African Americans at different stages of American history and represent a shared belief in the value of oratory as a means to challenge and change these conditions, even though many spoke with knowledge of a battle being waged against tremendous odds. "While oratory has brought its costliest, golden treasures, and laid them on the altar of God and of freedom, it has aimed its fiercest lightning and loudest thunder at the strongholds of tyranny, injustice, and despotism," declared Henry Highland Garnet in his great 1865 address to the U.S. House of Representatives: "The orators and statesmen of our own land, whether they belonged to the past, or to the present age, will live and shine in the annals of history, in proportion as they have dedicated their genius and talents to the defense of justice and man's God-given rights." Each of these speeches represents a moment at which the speaker sensed some opportunity for raising consciousness or advancing the cause of social justice, a conjunction of occasion and audience that called forth speech.[47]

Each speaking situation presents its own problems and possibilities. Many of these speeches—such as Douglass's "What, to the Slave, Is the Fourth of July?" Lucy Parsons's "I Am an Anarchist," and Maria W. Stewart's "What If I Am a Woman?"—include explicit criticism of the speaking situation itself: of the audience's problematic expectations for the speech and predisposition toward the speaker, of the occasions for their remarks, and of the institutions that have sponsored them. Such speeches are acts of rhetorical criticism designed to transform the contexts in which they are understood and interpreted. They expose what Asante has termed "the subtle machinations of power" that frame the speaking event, and they assert a critical authority in the act of speaking.[48] Particularly for African Americans addressing predominantly white audiences, the rhetorical situation itself may be an exigence, in Bitzer's terms, "an imperfection marked by urgency" that the orator seeks to ameliorate, in part, by "making it plain."[49]

These speeches are the expressions of women and men from all walks of life who for more than two centuries knew daily the bitter ironies of having been born black in a land that prided itself as the symbol of hope for the world's oppressed peoples. Whatever their immediate occasions and topics, most of the speeches in this collection are concerned with the paradoxes associated with being black in America and with charting the prospects for change through what was perceived to be the most powerful available medium: oratory.

Very few of the speeches gathered in this collection have ever appeared in a general anthology or survey course of American public address.[50] Of the thousands of speeches published in *Vital Speeches of the Day*, published before 1970, less than one-tenth of 1 percent were by African Americans.[51] The massive fifteen-volume collection of *American Eloquence* (1925), billed as "a library of the world's best spoken thought," includes only two speeches by African Americans, both by Booker T. Washington, while devoting over fifty pages to racist anecdotes about black people, culled from the works of white after-dinner speakers.[52] African American oratory receives little more consideration in contemporary anthologies of American public address. Washington's Atlanta Exposition Address, Sojourner Truth's "Ar'n't I A Woman?" and an excerpted version of Douglass's "What, to the Slave, Is the Fourth of July?" are still too often the only representations of African American oratory from the nineteenth century in survey courses and anthologies of American public address.

As important as these speeches may be, they represent but a few of the orations by African Americans that should be a part of the education of any serious student of American public address or history. Although this collection includes the best-known and most-studied speeches by African Americans, we have devoted much of the anthology to speeches that have been unjustly neglected, unpublished, or long out of print and thus denied the critical attention they deserve.

Recent years have witnessed the invaluable publication of writings and speeches by many individual black orators, including the papers of Maria Miller Stewart, Frederick Douglass, Ida B. Wells-Barnett, Frances E. W. Harper, Henry Highland Garnet, Booker T. Washington, Marcus Garvey, Malcolm X, and Martin Luther King, Jr. Furthermore, most documentary histories of African Americans, such as Herbert Aptheker's *Documentary History of the Negro People in the United States*, Dorothy Porter's *Early Negro Writing, 1760–1837*, C. Peter Ripley's *Black Abolitionist Papers*, Gerda Lerner's *Black Women in White America*, Loewenberg and Bogin's *Black Women in Nineteenth Century Life*, Dorothy Sterling's *We Are Your Sisters*, and Beverly Guy-Sheftall's *Words of Fire*, pay significant attention to speeches. We have drawn upon these collections and discoveries in assembling this anthology but have endeavored to provide greater comprehensiveness in the coverage of orators, topics, and periods. *Lift Every Voice* is also exclusively devoted to oratory as a unique form of literature and political activity with particular significance in African American history. Its traditions and developments may best be understood when many of its greatest practitioners and examples are seen together.

The anthology of African American oratory has a long and distinguished tradition in African American letters. In 1896, Miles V. Lynk, M.D., a cofounder of the American Medical Association of Colored Physicians and Surgeons, published *The Afro-American School Speaker and Gems of Literature* at his own publishing house in Jackson, Tennessee. Lynk's reader collects recent speeches by Booker T. Washington, John Mercer Langston, T. Thomas Fortune, and others and combines them with poems and other "lofty, soul-inspiring, and in many instances, classic utterances" of the "noble sons and daughters of Ham." In his preface to the reader, Lynk explains that "if the colored youths of the country become imbued with these exalted ideas, no power on earth can prevent their rapid rise and keep them from occupying a position in line with that of the foremost races of the world." "The way to inculcate them with such loftiness," Lynk concludes, "is to place these gems into a school speaker and let our young people recite them at their rhetoricals, social circles, lyceums, debating clubs, school and college commencements." For schools lacking such organizations, Lynk appends a model constitution of a speech and debate society.[53]

Lynk's reader was perhaps the first of many important collections of speeches by African Americans. When Daniel Alexander Payne Murray, an African American staff member at the Library of Congress, assembled a collection of eleven hundred books and pamphlets by black authors for the celebrated American Negro Exhibit at the Paris Exposition in 1900, he included numerous printed speeches and speech collections. Most of the speakers and many of the individual speeches he assembled appear in the present collection.[54] Twentieth-century anthologies of African American oratory include Alice Ruth Moore Dunbar's *Masterpieces of Negro Eloquence* (1914), Carter G. Woodson's *Negro Orators and Their Orations* (1925), Roy L. Hill's *Rhetoric of Racial Revolt* (1964), Jamye Williams and McDonald Williams's *The Negro Speaks* (1970), Arthur Smith (Asante) and Stephen Robb's *Voice of Black Rhetoric: Selections* (1971), and the direct predecessor to this collection, Philip S. Foner's two-volume *Voice of Black America.* All are now out of print. More recent anthologies, such as Warren J. Halliburton's *Historic Speeches of African Americans* (1993), Robbie Jean Walker's *The Rhetoric of Struggle: Public Address by African American Women,* and Shirley Wilson Logan's *With Pen and Voice* (1995), are valuable but more narrowly focused.

By its size and diversity, this collection of speeches makes clear both continuities and differences in African American thought, politics, oratorical practices, and strategies. As these speeches demonstrate, African Americans were far from seeing eye to eye on all major issues of the nineteenth century. Questions of emigration, assimilation, women's rights, the advisability of armed resistance, and political party affiliation, to name but a few, deeply divided African Americans and produced passionate debates and orations.

Speeches well known in isolation, such as Washington's Atlanta Exposition Speech, are here presented in the context of heated debates among African Americans regarding the best response to racist terrorism, disfranchisement, and economic oppression.

This collection necessarily includes only a fraction of the surviving African American speeches from the eighteenth and nineteenth centuries that deserve attention. Moreover, for every great speech included here, others of equal merit have doubtless disappeared. Too often, our efforts to locate the lost works of prominent orators met with frustration, compounded by surviving words of praise for the vanished works, as when the correspondent for the *Liberator* was so impressed by the speech of Harriet Tubman to the New England Colored Citizens' Convention in 1859 that he declined to reprint it: "The mere words could do no justice to the speaker, and therefore we do not undertake to give them; but we advise all our readers to take the earliest opportunity to see and hear her."[55] As Alice Moore Dunbar lamented in the preface to *Masterpieces of Negro Eloquence*, "Much of the best is lost; much of it is hidden away in forgotten places."[56]

Surviving texts from speakers before the era of electronic recording should be understood as bearing an indeterminate relationship to the speech as first presented to its immediate audience.[57] Many of the speeches included in this volume were delivered extemporaneously, without a prepared manuscript. What survives may be the result of a speaker's later recollection and writing, as in the case of George White's 1809 "Substance of a Funeral Sermon," or, in most cases, the report of a journalist or other member of the audience. Such transcriptions, as recent controversy over differences among the surviving accounts of Sojourner Truth's famous Akron speech of 1851 makes clear, are of varying reliability and usually paraphrase the speaker's actual words. Alterations in the transcription may be inadvertent or, as in the case of Booker T. Washington's National Peace Jubilee address (1898) when Washington omitted from later printings a line that had offended his white southern backers, deliberate. In some instances, the newspaper or other account in which the speech text appears is openly hostile toward the speaker. Even where a manuscript exists, its relationship to the speech actually presented may be unclear. Hallie Quinn Brown, professor of elocution at Wilberforce, recalls listening to the speech of Frederick Douglass during the Emancipation Day observance at the 1893 Chicago World's Fair:

> Thunderous applause greeted Mr. Douglass as he walked to the front and laid his written speech on the desk. He had not proceeded far when a remarkable thing occurred. He paused, stood very erect, brushed aside his manuscript, stepped to the front and delivered the most powerful speech of his life. He seemed a very god come to avenge a defenseless people. With flashing eyes and shaking his heavy mane, he recounted the inequalities, the slanders, the outrages heaped upon the Negro race.
> His invective was so strong, his arguments so convincing, his ora-

tory so scathing, as he hurled blast after blast against the white race who fostered and propagated prejudice, intolerance and hatred—that the audience was keyed to the highest point of excitement and enthusiasm. They laughed, they cried, they shouted, men and women jumped to their feet, clapped, hats and handkerchiefs were waved as the people cheered and yelled. It was the most disorderly, orderly mass of humanity one ever saw, as those present can testify.

I looked, and not one reporter was taking notes. It was a scene long to be remembered. For the next two days, the press commented on the remarkable speech delivered. Several voiced the opinion that not since the famous speech of Patrick Henry had the like been heard and I wish to affirm this fact *that speech was never reported!* The historian has recorded the written speech Douglass *discarded.*[58]

We have also certainly, if inadvertently and unavoidably, reprinted some speeches from which the orators deviated in their actual presentations. We have endeavored to provide the most authoritative texts available for the speeches included, to note questions regarding the authenticity of particular speeches insofar as we are aware of them, and to cite discrepancies between the texts as published here and other extant versions. Many of the speeches as printed here were first published in pamphlets and newspapers and reached far larger contemporary audiences in this form than in their original presentations.[59]

Most of the speeches in the first volume of the original *Voice of Black America* have been reprinted in this collection. Over sixty additional speeches have been included, reflecting recent discoveries, the opening of new archives, and the publication of collected works, particularly those of African American women. Certain categories of oratory—notably slave testimonies, school speeches and lectures, club talks, and sermons—are also more fully represented in this collection. Most of the speeches have been reprinted in their entirety. In a few instances, however, we have chosen to excerpt lengthy speeches (nineteenth-century orations routinely exceeded two hours in length) in the interest of including a broader range of texts and speakers and of reducing repetitive material. On the other hand, many speeches presented in excerpted form in the original *Voice of Black America* have been restored to their full texts in this collection. In many instances the speeches presented here were delivered and printed without a descriptive title. We have taken the liberty of providing titles where none appeared, drawing these titles from the texts of the speeches themselves.

Each speech text is introduced by a brief essay that sets the speech in its historical context, draws attention to strategies and features of critical interest, and provides biographical information regarding the speaker. Annotative notes to the speech text are offered to clarify historical and literary references. Biographical information has been compiled primarily from the following sources: William J. Simmons, *Men of Mark: Eminent, Progressive and Rising* (1887); L. A. Scruggs, *Women of Distinction: Remarkable in*

Works and Invincible in Character (1892); Hallie Q. Brown, *Homespun Heroines and Other Women of Distinction* (1926; reprint, New York: Oxford University Press, 1988); Rayford W. Logan and Michael Winston, eds., *Dictionary of American Negro Biography* (New York: Norton, 1982); Sidney Kaplan and Emma Nogrady Kaplan, *The Black Presence in the Era of the American Revolution* (Amherst: University of Massachusetts Press, 1989); C. Peter Ripley, ed., *The Black Abolitionist Papers* (Chapel Hill: University of North Carolina Press, 1991); Jessie Carney Smith, ed., *Notable Black American Women* (Detroit: Gale Research, 1992–1996); and Darlene Clark Hine, ed., *Black Women in America* (Brooklyn: Carlson, 1993). Other sources specific to the individual speaker are noted when they were used. Richard Leeman's *African-American Orators: A Bio-Critical Sourcebook* (Westport, Conn.: Greenwood, 1996) offers valuable information on several of the speakers in this collection.

We deeply appreciate the help of staff members at the libraries, archives, and historical societies that greatly contributed to this work. They include: the Schomburg Research Center, the Moorland-Spingarn Research Center at Howard University, the New York Historical Society, the Library of Congress, the State Historical Society of Wisconsin, the Historical Society of Pennsylvania, the Lincoln University Library, the New York Public Library, the National Archives, the Library of Bowdoin College, the Princeton University Library, the Boston Public Library, the American Antiquarian Society, the Tamiment Institute Library of New York University, the Library of Atlanta University, and the Library of Fisk University. We wish to thank Bishop John D. Bright, Sr., of the A.M.E. Church, First Episcopal District, and the Reverend Mr. Harry J. White, Sr., of the Mother Bethel African Methodist Episcopal Church in Philadelphia for permission to use the files of the *Christian Recorder* in the church archives.

Special thanks are due to the members of the interlibrary loan and reference staff of the Ladd Library at Bates College—Laura Juraska, Tom Hayward, Sandra Groleau, LaVerne Winn, and Elaine Ardia—for their extraordinary patience, persistence, and resourcefulness and to Sylvia Deschaine, Syvia Hawks, Joyce Caron, Nancy Lambert, Sallie Hackett, Clementine Brasier, Liam Clarke, and Quoc Tran for their careful work in typing and manuscript preparation. Bates colleagues Charles Nero, Marcus Bruce, and Hilmar Jensen provided valuable suggestions and encouragement. In innumerable ways, Celeste Branham made it possible to complete this work.

NOTES

1. William Grant Allen, "Orators and Oratory," *Liberator* (November 1852), 176; Allen's speech is reproduced elsewhere in this volume.

2. Nan Johnson, *Nineteenth-Century Rhetoric in North America* (Carbondale: Southern Illinois University Press, 1991); Kenneth Cmiel, *Democratic Eloquence: The Fight over Popular Speech in Nineteenth-Century America* (New York: William Morrow, 1990).

3. Jay Heinrichs, "How Harvard Destroyed Rhetoric," *Harvard Alumni Magazine* (July–August 1995), 37–43.

4. Giles Wilkeson Gray, "The 'Precepts of Kagemni and Ptah-Hotep,'" *Quarterly Journal of Speech* 32 (December 1946), 446–54; Michael V. Fox, "Ancient Egyptian Rhetoric," *Rhetorica* 1 (Spring 1983), 9–22.

5. Ethel M. Albert, "'Rhetoric,' 'Logic,' and 'Poetics' in Burundi: Cultural Patterning of Speech Behavior," *American Anthropologist*, pt. 2, 66 (December 1964), 35.

6. Molefi Kete Asante, *The Afrocentric Idea* (Philadelphia: Temple University Press, 1987), 17.

7. Adetokunbo F. Knowles-Borishade, "Paradigm for Classical African Orature: Instrument for a Scientific Revolution?" *Journal of Black Studies* 21 (June 1991), 488–500; Viv Edwards, *Oral Cultures Past and Present: Rappin' and Homer* (London: Basil Blackwell, 1990), 14–35; Ruth Finnegan, *Limba Stories and Story-Telling* (New York: Oxford University Press, 1967), 13; Roger D. Abrahams, *The Man-of-Words in the West Indies: Performance and the Emergence of Creole Culture* (Baltimore: Johns Hopkins University Press, 1993), 21–39.

8. Hallie Quinn Brown, quoted in Annjennette Sophie McFarlin, "Hallie Quinn Brown—Black Woman Elocutionist (1845?–1949)" (Ph.D. diss., Washington State University, 1975), 171–72.

9. William C. Nell, *Colored Patriots of the American Revolution* (Boston: Robert F. Allcut, 1855), 113.

10. Philip S. Foner, "Black Participation in the Centennial of 1876," *Phylon* 39 (Winter 1978), 283–96.

11. Hazel V. Carby, *Reconstructing Womanhood: The Emergence of the Afro-American Woman Novelist* (New York: Oxford University Press, 1987), 3–6.

12. At least two earlier published sermons by African Americans are known to exist: "A Sermon on the Present Situation of Affairs of America and Great Britain, Written by a Black" (Philadelphia: Bradford and Hall, 1782) and "A Sermon on the Evacuation of Charlestown, By an Aethiopian" (Philadelphia: Woodhouse, 1783). Both, however, appear to have been written for publication rather than orally presented to specific audiences.

13. Grace Sims Holt, "Stylin' Outta the Black Pulpit," in Thomas Kochman, ed., *Rappin' and Stylin' Out: Communication in Urban Black America* (Urbana: University of Illinois Press, 1972), 195–96. See also Eugene Genovese, "Black Plantation Preachers in the South," *Southern Studies* (1972–1991), 203–29; and Norrece T. Jones, Jr., "Slave Religion in South Carolina—A Heaven in Hell?" *Southern Studies* (1990), 5–32.

14. Timothy D. Hall, *Contested Boundaries: Itineracy and the Reshaping of the Colonial American Religious World* (Durham: Duke University Press, 1994); Graham Hodges, ed., *Black Itinerants of the Gospel: The Narratives of John Jea and George White* (Madison, Wis.: Madison House, 1993).

15. William D. Pierson, *Black Yankees: The Development of an Afro-American Subculture in Eighteenth-Century New England* (Amherst: University of Massachusetts Press, 1988), 71–72.

16. W. P. Harrison, *The Gospel Among the Slaves* (Nashville: Publishing House of the M.E. Church, 1893), 127, quoted in Warren Thomas Smith, "Harry Hosier: Black Preacher Extraordinary," *Journal of the American Theological Center* 7 (1980), 114.

17. James Weldon Johnson, *God's Trombones: Seven Negro Sermons in Verse* (New York: Viking Press, 1927), 3.

18. John W. Davis, "George Liele and Andrew Bryan, Pioneer Negro Baptist Preachers," *Journal of Negro History* 3 (April 1918), 119–27.

19. Carol V. R. George, *Segregated Sabbaths: Richard Allen and the Emergence of Independent Black Churches, 1760–1840* (New York: Oxford University Press, 1973), 161.

20. Ibid., 163.

21. Jean McMahon Humez, ed., *Gifts of Power: The Writings of Rebecca Jackson, Black Visionary, Shaker Eldress* (Amherst: University of Massachusetts Press, 1981), 21.

22. Jualynne Dodson, "Nineteenth-Century A.M.E. Preaching Women," in H. F. Thomas and R. S. Keller, eds., *Women in New Worlds* (Nashville: Abingdon, 1981), 276–89.

23. Hortense J. Spillers, "Moving on Down the Line," *American Quarterly* 40 (March 1988), 86.

24. James Oliver Horton and Lois E. Horton, *Black Bostonians: Family Life and Community Struggle in the Antebellum North* (New York: Holmes & Meier Publishers, 1979), 50.

25. Quoted in William Jacob Walls, *Joseph Charles Price: Educator and Race Leader* (Boston: Christopher Publishing House, 1943), 413.

26. Dorothy B. Porter, "The Organized Educational Activities of Negro Literary Societies, 1828–1846," *Journal of Negro Education* 5 (October 1936), 555–76.

27. William C. Nell, *Colored Patriots of the American Revolution*, 114.

28. John W. Cromwell, *The Early Negro Convention Movement* (Washington, D.C.: American Negro Academy, 1904).

29. John W. Blassingame, *Slave Testimony: Two Centuries of Letters, Speeches, Interviews, and Autobiographies* (Baton Rouge: Louisiana State University Press, 1977), 123.

30. Shirley J. Yee, *Black Women Abolitionists: A Study in Activism, 1828–1860* (Knoxville: University of Tennessee Press, 1992), 3.

31. "An Address to the Colored People of the United States," in C. Peter Ripley, ed., *Witness for Freedom: African American Voices on Race, Slavery, and Emancipation* (Chapel Hill: University of North Carolina Press, 1993), 127.

32. William McFeely, *Frederick Douglass* (New York: W. W. Norton, 1991), 95.

33. bell hooks, *Talking Back: Thinking Feminist, Talking Black* (Boston: South End Press, 1989), 12.

34. Free African Americans of the antebellum South did, however, form private literary societies for speech and debate. See, for example, Michael P. Johnson and James L. Roark, " 'A Middle Ground': Free Mulattoes and the Friendly Moralist Society in Antebellum Charleston," *Southern Studies* 21 (1982), 246– 65; and Robert L. Harris, Jr., "Charleston's Free Afro-American Elite: The Brown Fellowship Society and the Humane Brotherhood," *South Carolina Historical Magazine* 82 (October 1981), 289–310.

35. Kathleen Hall Jamieson, *Eloquence in an Electronic Age: The Transformation of Political Speechmaking* (New York: Oxford University Press, 1988), 67–79; Doris G. Yoakam, "Woman's Introduction to the American Platform," in William N. Brigance, ed., *A History and Criticism of American Public Address* (New York: Russell & Russell, 1943); Lillian O'Connor, *Pioneer Women Orators: Rhetoric in the Antebellum Reform Movement* (New York: Columbia University Press, 1954).

36. Jean McMahon Humez, ed., *Gifts of Power*, 20.

37. Shirley J. Yee, *Black Women Abolitionists*, 115. See also Marilyn Richardson, *Maria W. Stewart: America's First Black Woman Political Writer* (Bloomington: Indiana University Press, 1987), 3–27.

38. Paula Giddings, *When and Where I Enter: The Impact of Black Women on Race and Sex in America* (New York: William Morrow, 1984), 59.

39. Shirley J. Yee, *Black Women Abolitionists*, 127.

40. Bernard Katz, "A Second Version of Lucy Terry's Early Ballad?" *Negro History Bulletin* 29 (1966), 183–84.

41. William McFeely, *Frederick Douglass*, 88.

42. Robert James Branham, "Emancipating Myself: Mays the Debater," in Lawrence E. Carter, Sr., ed., *Walking Integrity: Benjamin E. Mays, Mentor to Generations* (Atlanta: Scholars Press, 1996); Robert James Branham, " 'I Was Gone On Debating': Malcolm X's Prison Debates and Public Confrontations," *Argumentation and Advocacy* 31 (Winter 1995), 117–37.

43. Benjamin Quarles, "Ministers Without Portfolio," *Journal of Negro History* 39 (January 1954), 27–42.

44. Letter to J. C. Conkling, August 26, 1863, *Lincoln's Complete Works*, vol. 9 (New York: Francis D. Tandy, 1905), 99.

45. Letter to Charles Sumner (July 6, 1870), quoted in Philip S. Foner, *Frederick Douglass* (New York: Citadel Press, 1964), 276.

46. Benjamin E. Mays and Joseph W. Nicholson, *The Negro's Church* (New York, 1933; rpt. New York: Arno Press and New York Times, 1969), 9.

47. Marcus Boulware, *The Oratory of Negro Leaders, 1900–1968* (Westport, Conn.: Negro Universities Press, 1969), 12.

48. Molefi Kete Asante, *The Afrocentric Idea* (Philadelphia: Temple University Press, 1987), 24–27.

49. Lloyd Bitzer, "The Rhetorical Situation," *Philosophy and Rhetoric* 1 (1968), 8; Robert James Branham and W. Barnett Pearce, "Between Text and Context: Toward a Rhetoric of Contextual Reconstruction," *Quarterly Journal of Speech* 71 (February 1985), 19–36; Robert James Branham, "Speaking Itself: Susan Sontag's Town Hall Address," *Quarterly Journal of Speech* 9 (August 1989), 259–76.

50. For a review of the representation of works by African Americans in public address anthologies, see Charles I. Nero, " 'Oh, What I Must Tell This World!': Oratory and Public Address of African-American Women," in Kim Marie Vaz, ed., *Black Women in America* (Thousand Oaks: Sage, 1995), 266–69.

51. Jamye Coleman Williams and McDonald Williams, *The Negro Speaks: The Rhetoric of Contemporary Black Leaders* (New York: Noble and Noble, 1970), xii.

52. Ashley Thorndike, ed., *Modern Eloquence: A Library of the World's Best Spoken Thought* (New York: Lincoln Scholarship Fund, 1928).

53. Miles V. Lynk, *The Afro-American School Speaker and Gems of Literature* (Jackson, Tenn.: M. V. Lynk, 1896).

54. Daniel Murray, *Preliminary List of Books and Pamphlets by Negro Authors* (Washington, D.C.: Library of Congress, 1900). See also Dorothy B. Porter, "Preface," *The Negro in the United States: A Selected Bibliography* (Washington, D.C.: Library of Congress, 1970), v.

55. "New England Colored Citizens' Convention," *Liberator* (August 26, 1859), quoted in Earl Conrad, *Harriet Tubman* (Washington, D.C.: Associated Publishers, 1943), 108–9.

56. Alice Moore Dunbar, ed., *Masterpieces of Negro Eloquence* (New York: Bookery, 1914), 7.

57. Such discrepancies between published speech texts and speeches delivered orally persist today. See, for example, Haig Bosmajian, "The Inaccuracies in the Reprintings of Martin Luther King's 'I Have a Dream' Speech," *Communication Education* 31 (April 1982), 107–14. On the challenges posed for the critic and student of public address by textual inaccuracies, see Lester Thonssen and A. Craig Baird, *Speech Criticism: The Development of Standards for Rhetorical Appraisal* (New York: Ronald, 1948), 297–311.

58. Hallie Quinn Brown, quoted in Annjennette Sophie McFarlin, "Hallie Quinn Brown," 53.

59. Genevieve Fabre, "African-American Commemorative Celebrations in the Nineteenth Century," in Genevieve Fabre and Robert O'Meally, eds., *History and Memory in African-American Culture* (New York: Oxford University Press, 1994), 73.

1

I SPEAK TO THOSE
WHO ARE IN SLAVERY

Cyrus Bustill

The Bustill family records have been remarkably well preserved, and a sketch of the family history was published by Anna Bustill Smith in the Journal of Negro History *in 1925 (638–49). Cyrus Bustill was born in slavery in Burlington, New Jersey, on February 2, 1732. Bustill learned bread making from his third slaveholder, Quaker Thomas Prior (Pryor) and was greatly influenced by Quaker teachings. He "early became convinced of the rectitude of Friends' (Quakers') principles and conformed to their mode of garb and speech," according to Smith (639). Freed from slavery in 1769, Bustill soon established his own bakery. During the American Revolution, Bustill supplied bread to the Continental Army and was later recognized by Washington for his contributions to the war effort.*

Despite the conciliatory tone of the address here reprinted, Cyrus Bustill was a committed abolitionist and refused to marry in his early adult life because "he would not perpetuate a race of slaves." He eventually married Elizabeth Morey and moved to Philadelphia, where he again established a successful bakery and was also engaged in the building construction business. In 1796 he became the first African American schoolteacher in the city. He was an active member of the Free African Society, founded on April 12, 1787, a mutual aid group that Dorothy Porter has identified as the first organized African American society. Bustill died in 1806.

On September 18, 1787, Bustill addressed a group of slaves in Philadelphia. The manuscript of the speech is in the Historical Society of Pennsylvania and was published in the William and Mary Quarterly *for January 1972. It is reprinted here with permission of the* William and Mary Quarterly.

The speech is representative of the viewpoint of many in the free black community of Philadelphia of the time. While making clear his opposition to slavery, Bustill insisted that slaves must take no action to liberate themselves. In due time, he argued, God, in his mercy, would liberate all the slaves. African American preachers, particularly those ministering to slaves, had to walk a rhetorical tightrope by speaking defiantly enough to engage their listeners yet not so as to alarm slaveholders or the authorities.

The notes are reprinted as they appeared in the William and Mary Quarterly, *where they were furnished by Melvin H. Buxbaum, who discovered the speech. References to scriptural passages indicated by superscript letters were added by another hand and are appended here as they*

appear on the manuscript ("J" and "V" are omitted on the manuscript).
Other editorial changes presumably made by the same person have not
been retained.

M Y BROTHERIN and Fellow men, as Love to one Another Seemes to
have been the way to all happyness, formerly in the Early Ages of the
world, when our Lord was on the Earth So it Seemes to Remain in this our
Day. I am thinking it will Remain So to the End of time. Our Lord and master, Seemes to Confirm it when he [en]joyns on his People to this affact,
when he was about to Leave the world in So Solum and Prassing a maner
Saying[a] a new Comandment I Give unto you, that ye Love one another as I
have Loved you, that ye also Love one another by this Shall men know that
you are my Disciples; and he further injoyns it with a veraily I Say unto you
Love one another, now we find theirs a Repeitasien [Repetition] of the wards
and yet he Does not Leave it here neither, but he Still Carrys it on further,
as if to make it more binding and by wards Like thess, by this Shall all men
know that ye are my Disciples or Followers. If ye Love one another, now here
[is] a mark of Distinksion a Qiutt Differant mark from that which the kings
and Great men of the Earth Put on their Soldiers and officers, and the Reason
is, because theirs are marks of Blood, of war, Contension and Such Like, but
my Bretherin his are not So, for we find his are marks of Peace and Love,
kindness, Respect, Regard, Gratatued, forbearonce, Long Suffurance, mod-
orasion And Gentelness, Soboriety and meetness, and Such Like, theses are
the uniforms that his Soldiers are [Clad] with for they are All Clad upon by
him, and they are Pretty much in a Livery too, it may be Scen to Whose
Rigment they beLong, and he gives them all their accuterements from the
head to the foot, meals [males] and females, but they are Ginerly volenteers,
for it Seem theirs but few Presst men, now a Days he is Grand Capt. a very
Grand Ginoral, And Comands the hearts of his People and the very thoughts
of those that are Lead by him, he is [a] Prince too, the Prince of Peace and
king of kings. Then how is it that So few of us, Dare Enter the Roles and
apear in his Sarvice? is it because we [are] Cowards, no, but because [we] are
trators, to him, and to ourselves to. I Reather think, [illegible] then my Fellow men Resolve to Doe Better for the fewter, Since theirs no Better Coman-
der nor no kinder master, Let us endeavour to Serve him with Loyalty and
faithfulness or other wise we Shall not be accounted worthy, he Disers no
Person to go further then he Leads the way, then my Bretherin Let us [Pay]
Due, Respect to his Precepts, for [no] Soldier may Disobey orders, then Let
us take heed that we Do not trenccgress [transgress] the Lawes of his Disci-
plin, for it will be very Disagreable to him and will not be Consistent with
his Love and justice which Run Parallel and theirfour my Bretherin Let me
injoyn this once more that we Pay a Particulor Regard to his Lawes. Whin I
think of the wonderful Love of the Great Marter, of the univerice, and his

[a]John XIII. 34. 35.

unbounded Condiscnding and unspeakable Regard, toward the Children of men, I am the more Eranstly moved in that Love, to enteurt [intreat] my Fellow men that they may Learn to Love and fear him and by Steady Complince to his will they may Learn to know by Exsperience that[b] God is no Respector [of] Persons, but in Every Natison, he, that fearth him and workth Righteousness, is Excepted with him, and now my Fellow men here is encouragment for us in Perticulor to keep that in our favour which he hath So Boundtyfully bestoued on us. I Speak to thoss Who are in Slavery, because I was Born So and Remaind untill I was almost 37 years of age, when it Pleased him out of his Great Marcey and his Still abounding Goodness, Towards me, to Plock me out of the hands of unseasonable men, and that at a time when I Little Exspected it, I Shall here Relate the maner in which he Delivered [me] from that Estate in which I was Born, then understand I Came into the world belonging [to] the Estate of Samuel Bustill of the City of Burlington, but he Dying when I was Young I was Sold to John Allen of the Same City who had a Son of the Same Name who, Resided at Trenton, with his familey, the father had often told me, that I should never Serve any man, after his Death, but that I Should be free, my mistress was willing and tryed all the ways that Lay in her Power to have [it] So, but Son Resolved to thought [thwart] all her Disigns, the which he affactuly Did, the father Diing in the Yeer 1752 the Son Binding, the Mother to a Subsisance which was Partly to Com of my Earnings She [Could] very ill afford it, but Did try more then once, but She Ding about the [year] 1756, the Son Sold me in 1762 to Thomas Pryor junr. for the sum of one Hundred pounds Down, befour they agree, my friend having Ofered 80 Pounds for 4 yeers Service of me, but Refowsed [Refused] Saying Slavery, was his Determinasion, my friend then Payd Down the money, and I became a Sarvent to one of those friendly People Called Quakers, of happy Memorry to Such as we are, I Servcid him Seven Yeers According to the agreement he made with me and at the End, of which he Gave me, aful Discharge. I Could not forbaer, to mension this [in] Gratitude to that People, and to my master, and his familey, who was as insteriments [instruments], in the Divin hand to help me *and* that People who are still endeavouring to bring us to the fear and knowledge, of that being who, made the world, and [all] that it Contains, whom to know is Life Eternal. My Bretherin Let us edeavour to Learn to[c] fear the Lord it is the begining of wisdom and will to us [be] a Good understanding, if we will but Depart from Evill, you being in bondage in Particular, I would that [ye] take heed that afend not with your toungue, be ye wiss [wise] as Serpants and harmless as Doves, that he may take with you, when you are wrong'd. Other ways, you Cannot Exspect him to side with you nor to Soport your Cause, no not at any time or Place, I would my Bretherin that ye be faithful to your masters, at all times and on all ocasions, too, for this is Praise worthy, be honst and true to their intrust.

[b]Acts X. 34. 35.
[c]Proverbs IX. 10.

Sappose they Do not See it the Great Master will See it and give Cradit for it too, and therefore I would that ye Doe their business [with] Chairfulness[d], not with Eye Sarvice, but willingly and with Singleness of heart as unto God, and not unto men, knowing this also, that Sarvent which know his masters will, and PrePared not himself, neither [nor did] According to his will Shall be beat with many Strips, but on the other hand they that Continues faithful to the End, Shall be Rewarded, my Bretherin the encouragments to well do-ing are many. Remember, if the Son make you free, you Shall be free indeed; for myselfe I can safely say, I fand no satisfactsion, Like unto that which arise from that of well Doing, tis Like [an] anchor in a Storm, on which all may Depend and Safly Reily, and firmly Trust and is Surly [illegible] let the winds blow as they will, and it was Said by one formerly,[e] if our heart Con-demn us, God is greater than our heart, and knowth all things. If our heart Condemn us not, then have we Confidence towards God, and he Seeing into the very inermost Recess of the heart, there Can be no Securits [secrets] hid from him, or Escape his notice; besides, their is that unering Guide that is Placest in the hearts of Every individual of us, that is Come to the Years of Discrasion and that to Profat with all, now if we do not Profat, the fault is our own, for[f] Light is Come into the world and men Loved Darkness Rather then Light because their Deeds were Evill, now Let us, endeavour to make our Calling, and Election Sure, by a Steady Adherence to his holy Law writin in our hearts, for they are Sure Giude to them and to Every of [them] that are made willing to be Giuded by him, whose Right it tis to Rule, in the hearts of the Children of men, now this is a Great Steap on [the] way, only to be Lead by him, it tis undoutedly his Right to Rule and Riegn in our hearts, but alis [alas] my Bretherin[g] we would not have this man to Raign over us, theirfore it [was] Said[h] away with him, now I would that we Could under-stand this, my Fellow men it tis not our will, but his will that is to be Done, and therfore we ought not to Consult, ourselves on these maters, but Refear all to him who is all our Stranth, if we Could only Trust to him, I believe would [be] more So and would Do more, and Better for us, if [we] Could Re-member to keep his enstructisons in veiw and Practice we Should Come much higher the Mark and Patrein [Pattern] he hath Set and So Lovingly enjoyn'd on us, when he Said[i] Thou Shalt Love the Lord thy God, with all thy heart, And with All [thy] Soul, and with all [thy] Mind. This is [the] first and Great Comandment, and the Second is Like unto it Thou Love thy Naigh-bour as thyself, On thess tow [these two] Comandments hang all the Law and the Prophats, now my Bretherin this is a Great and fondemental Rule, whereby we may Square our Acctions at All times and in All the Saveral

[d]Ephesians VI. 6. 7.
[e]1st John. III. 20. 21.
[f] John III. 19.
[g]Luke XIX. 14.
[h]Acts XXI. 36.
[i] Matthew XXII. 37. 38. 39. 40.

Stations of life the which it has Pleased him, to Place us only Let's Remember to keep this in our veiw, as the Pole Star whereby we may Steer, in the Darkest Night. Prehaps Some may Say they Cannot Read, but my friends this needs no humain Learning, to Read our own hearts, tis Given from above, and Cannot be taken away, but by our own wickedness, theirs but few needs be a Loss I must Repeat it agin, Love the Lord thy God with all [thy] heart, and with all [thy] Soul, and thy Naighbour as thyself for in this is Contained the Grand Scope of All Religion, thairs Nothing Done, without Charity towards God and our Naighbours, Lets Remember Charity begins at home, we must Examine ourselves, theirfore, and endeavour to get in order here as much as Possable, and I am Persuaed Shall find the Adventage of it, and by this Practice we Shall be Come wise unto Salvasion. If we Could only Observe to Put in Practice this Duty, it [will] make us wise here, and happy here after, now my Bretherin Let us One and All resolve newness of Life, in All holy Conversasion Soberiety and Godly fear, Redeeming the time, because of the Evill of the Day; and here Let [me] Caution you, my Bretheirin, Against that Crying Sin of Drunkinness that is So much in Fashion, that Abominable Practice of Rum-Drinking to Excess, and So hurtful to men of our Colour yea, and women too are too fond of it. Remember that kind invitasion Given by our Lord and master and the vast encouragment, held up to them, as it were, for them that [were] Gro[w]n old in ill Practices, how he Received them that Came in at the[k] Elevnth hour of the Day, how he, Gave them waggens Equil with them that [had] Born the Burden and the heat of Day this, me thinks might, encourage men to Put away that Sin that Doth Esily beset them, I Raily belive therirs more Damage Done by that one Liquiour then by all the Rest Put togather, that we have in the Country.

My Fellow men I would wish us, to Remember no [Drunkard] Can enter the kingdom no nor unClean Person, therfore Let us endeavour to walk worthy, and avoid that Sin which Doth Esasily besoten us, Surly in vain is the net Sprad in the Sight of the Bird, but aliss [alas] we Seem to go into this Net willingly and with our Eyes opon, and at all time of the Day, And in the face of the Sun, as if in defienc to Every thing that is [good] and Reasonable. I think it one of the Adversary's most aluring Baits where with he tempts many to their own Ruin, I believe I have Seen more then one, who have Shortind their Days by this Dradful Practice, I am not a young man, I am in the 56 Yeer of my age, and have had time to Reflact on things Passt, I have Seen Numbers Laid in Graves, I belive at a time when Som of them little Exspected, and it may be as Little Prepared, I know not how Soon it may be my turn, I would therfore that we work while its Called to Day, for[l] the [night] Cometh wherin no man Can work, and where Shall we Look or which way Shall [we] turn ourselves but unto the Lord that made us, and

[k]Matthew XX. 6 to 14.
[l]John IX. 4.

will most asuredly help us, if we walk in his Pathes, which [he] hath Set
before us, theirfore we may Depend opon the Lord as a Sure Guide in all
times of need, he will be[friend] us to [the] last Degree of friendship, he will
be a[m] Lamp unto my feet, and a Light unto my Paths therfore we may Trust
him, with Confidence, none of them that Trust in him Shall be Desolat,[n] he
that Trusteth in the Lord, marcey Shall Compass him about, this is encouragement for us to Passaveer [persevere] in well Doing, if we Could but Con-
fide in him[o] he hath not Dealt with us after our Sins, nor Rewarded us, According to our iniquitys, for as the Heavens is high above the Earth, So Great
is his marcey toward them that fear him, as far as the East is from the west,
So far hath he Removed our Transgrasions from us, Like as [a] father Pititith
his Childrin So the Lord Pititith them, that fear him for he knoweth our
fram[e], he Remembereth we are but Dust my friends he hath Given us, All
that we Can Reasonabely Exspect, or Even Disire, by way of encouragement,
but if he had only once Speak the word it would have been Soficent, for us
to Rely and Trust to, for all that we have, or Can hope to have, well then my
friends, Sceing the Great kindness of the heavenly father, toward them that
Love and fear him, and keep his Comandments, Let us keep our hearts, with
all the Dilegence that in us Lays, Aways looking op unto that unering Guide
which is Given to Every of us, to Profat with all, [illegible] Shall a man Profat if he Should Gain the whole world and Loose his Soul,[p] where Can be his
Profat, well my Fellow men, Let us, endeavour to walk worthy of the vocation where with we are Calld, and endeavour to love the Lord our God with
hearts, and with all our Soul and our Naighbour as ourselves, and then we
sh[a]ll be on the way to happyness Depend on it, and we may with his halp
Continue, then Let us endeavour, by a Frugil Steady indostry [illegible] to
Procure an honst Living for ourselves And famileys with all Soberiety, for
this is Comendable to All, keep a Particulor Grad [Guard] Against All, bad
Compainy, keeping, knowing[q] Evill Comunicasion Corupps Good maners,
theirfore Let us conduct ourselves as men, who Are to Give An account, for
the deeds Done in the Body, Let us Strive to Enter in at the Stright Gate for,
maney are Called but few Chosen and yet God is no Respector of Persons,
for in Every Nasion kindred and Toungue, they that Love honour and Obay
him is Exccepted [Accepted] of him all this not for [any] thing that [they]
have Done, or Can do for him no, but out of his Great Love and unbonded
kindness and Regard toward the Chidren of men, now the thoughts of this
Great Love and Condisending Marcey, me thinks aught to Constrain men to
endeavour, to walk in his Preceepts, And the more Espesaly when we See
him So engaged and on our behalf, to Deliver from the bond of Slavery, both,

[m]Psalm CIX. 105.
[n] Psalm XXXII. 10.
[o] Psalm CIII. 10. 11. 12. 13. 14.
[p] Mark VIII. 36.
[q] 1st Corinthians XV. 33.

in [this] world and [that] which is to Come And [not] Only encouraging us, by the Saaft [Soft] Admonision, of his holy Spirit, at many times And in many Places, but is Calling an us alound, in and thro the voice of his People, who Seem to Spear [Spare] no Pains to bring us to the true, and Saving knowlege of the Living God, we may See if we take but a Little notice Look which we will, we may see Somthing that tends to Call on us, if we would but endeavour to understand it So, how Ever their is no wont [of] teachings, tis very Plain and Clair to me, And to be Disobaydent when we are Calld opon by them, is a Dangerus Setouasion [Situation], thin how mach more So, to Ridicul and Laugh them to Scorn,[r] who so Dispiseth the Ward, Shall be Destroyed, but he that feareth the Comandment Shall be Rewarded, and much more might be Said, but I Rather Persuade men, I would not wish to apear as an accuser, but Rather I Say, Persuade men to Pertake of his marcey and Goodness and to Passaver [persevere] in the Practice of well Doing it tis said[s] are not Five Sparrawes Sold for tow farthings and not one of them is forgoten before God, And here tis to be noticest they did not Pass unRegarded by him, for he in his wonted Goodness was Pleasd to make a very Grasius Speach and ful of love to men, and Speakes in this maner[t] are not tow Sparraws Sold for a farthing Ye are of more [value] then many Sparraws then Since he was Grasiusly Pleased to value men more then many Sparraws Let us Strive to be As inosent as one of them, this [is] my Diser [desire?] that we may be harmliss and atentive to his Grasius invitason and be hold him Calling on us,[u]

Come unto me all ye that Labour and are havy Laden and I will Give you Rest, take my Yoke opon you and Learn of me for I am meek And Lowly in heart, And ye Shall find Rest unto your Souls, for my yoke is Easey and my Burden is Light, now [to] me [illegible] this is a most Gloriyus invitasion and very Extinsive, for All are Calld opon to Pertake of his Goodness And marcey, then my Brethren who Can Refaus to the Grasious and many fold ofars [manifold offers] of So Loving a father who Can but be willing, to Comply with his marceyful invitasions,[w] behold I Stand at the Door and [knock], if Any man hear my voice And opon the door, I will Come in to him And Sup with him And he with me, then here we are invited to Sup with the king of kings, O the Stupendeous Love and Condescending marcey, of the heavenly father toward the Chirldlren of men, having Droped a few hints Respecting the Love of our heavenly father if it be kindly Receivd I Shall think myself amply Reward,∎

—Cyrus Bustill

[r] Proverbs XIII. 13.
[s] Luke XII. 6.
[t] Matthew X. 29. 31.
[u] Matthew XI. 28. 29. 30.
[w] Revelation III. 20.

2

YOU STAND ON THE LEVEL WITH THE GREATEST KINGS ON EARTH

John Marrant

The extraordinary, if brief, life of John Marrant, perhaps the first ordained black minister to preach in the United States, began in New York on June 15, 1755. Following the death of his father four years later, Marrant and his mother moved first to St. Augustine and then settled in Georgia. Marrant learned to read and write before he left school at age eleven. He also became an accomplished musician and performed locally on the violin and French horn. His musical proficiency brought him a steady income but also led him to a life of intemperance that he would later repent. He recounts in his 1785 autobiography, A Narrative of the Lord's Wonderful Dealings With John Marrant, A Black (London: Gilbert and Plummer): "I was now in my thirteenth year, devoted to pleasure and drinking in iniquity like water, a slave to every vice suited to my nature and years" (7).

According to his autobiography, when Marrant was passing by a crowded meetinghouse where the famous British itinerant George Whitefield was preaching, he was struck "speechless and senseless" to the ground. Later, Whitefield came to him and said, "JESUS CHRIST HAS GOT THEE AT LAST." Marrant remained steadfast in his conversion, despite the disapproval of his family. He contemplated and rejected suicide, then ran away to the wilderness. After spending a few days near starvation, Marrant met and befriended an Indian hunter. When they visited a large Cherokee settlement, however, Marrant was taken prisoner and sentenced to torture and death. According to his own account, his spoken prayers, first in English and then in the Cherokee language, so moved his appointed executioner that he was brought before the king of the Cherokees, whom he subsequently converted. Marrant and the Cherokee king visited the nearby Catawar and Housaw Nations in what proved to be far less successful missionary efforts. Finally, Marrant felt the "invincible desire of returning home" (19). Dressed in animal skins and Indian headdress, he emerged from the woods into the settlements and rejoined his family, who had presumed him dead.

At the outbreak of the American Revolution, Marrant was pressed into service as a musician aboard the British sloop Scorpion. He remained in the British service for nearly seven years and participated in the Battle of Charleston. After he was seriously wounded and hospitalized, Marrant was discharged from the navy. Working for a cotton merchant in London, Marrant felt the call to preach "for the salvation of my

*countrymen." With the support of the abolitionist Countess of Hunting-
don, he was ordained by Calvinist Methodists in 1785 and began preaching in Bristol and Bath. He accepted an invitation from his brother to
preach in Nova Scotia, where many African Americans who had supported the British had settled. In August 1785 he sailed to Nova Scotia,
where he preached for four years to whites and Indians as well as to
black settlers. In 1789, Marrant moved to New England. His sermons
were at first disrupted by armed mobs, but he persisted and preached in
communities throughout Massachusetts. He befriended Prince Hall, a respected leader of Boston's African American community and grand master of Boston's African Lodge of the Honorable Society of Free and Accepted Masons, the first black masonic lodge in the United States.
Marrant accepted Hall's invitation to serve as chaplain of the lodge.*

*On June 24, 1789, Marrant delivered an eloquent sermon to the mem-
bers of the lodge. His sermon proclaims the greatness of Africa and Africans and rejects the notion that slavery is a sign of racial inferiority: "For
if we search history, we shall not find a nation on earth but has at some
period or other of their existence been in slavery, from the Jews down to
the English nation." Marrant's indictment of white prejudice in Massachusetts occurred against the backdrop of the previous year's ruling by
the Commonwealth's General Court that required black residents to produce a certificate of citizenship from any previous state in which they
had resided. Those who could not produce such a certificate were threatened with jail, whipping, and deportation.* Here Marrant uses black Masonic membership as a basis from which to argue for black entitlement
to civil rights and social justice. Six months after delivering this sermon,
Marrant sailed back to England, where he died in 1791 at the age of
thirty-five.*

*The text of the speech was published as a pamphlet. Copies survive
in the collections of the American Antiquarian Society and the Schomburg Research Center.*

R OMANS XII., 10. "Be kindly affectioned one to another, with brotherly
love, in honor preferring one another."

In this chapter, from whence my text is taken, we find the Apostle Paul
laboring with the Romans to press on them the great duties of Brotherly
Love.

By an entire submission and conformity to the will of God, whereby are
given to us exceeding great and precious promises, that by these we might
be made partakers of the divine nature, having escaped the corruption that
is in the world through lust—That being all members of the body of Christ
with the Church, we ought to apply the gifts we have received to the advan-

*Sidney Kaplan and Emma Nogrady Kaplan, *The Black Presence in the Era of the
American Revolution*, rev. ed. (Amherst: University of Massachusetts Press, 1989).

tage of our brethren, those of us especially who are called to any office in the church, by discharging it with zeal and integrity and benevolence, which is the most important duty, and comprehends all the rest, and particularly the following—which the apostle here sets down—which are to love one another sincerely, to be ready to all good offices—to sympathize in the good or evil that befalls our brethren, to comfort and assist those that are in affliction, and to live together in a spirit of humility, peace and unity. Benevolence does yet further oblige Christians to love and bless those who hate them and injure them, to endeavor to have peace with all men, to abstain from revenge, and to render them good for evil; these are the most essential duties of the religion we profess; and we deserve the name of Christians no further than we sincerely practise them to the glory of God and the good of our own souls and bodies, and the good of all mankind.

But first, my brethren, let us learn to pray to God through our Lord Jesus Christ for understanding, that we may know ourselves; for without this we can never be fit for the society of man; we must learn to guide ourselves before we can guide others, and when we have done this we shall understand the apostle, Romans xii. 16. "Be not wise in your own conceits," for when we get wise in ourselves we are then too wise for God, and consequently not fit for the society of man—I mean the Christian part of mankind. Let all my brethren Masons consider what they are called to—May God grant you an humble heart to fear God and love His commandments; then and only then you will in sincerity love your brethren: And you will be enabled, as in the words of my text, to be kindly affectioned one to another, with brotherly love in honor preferring one another. Therefore, with the Apostle Paul, I beseech you therefore, brethren, by the mercies of God, that ye present your bodies a living sacrifice, holy, acceptable unto God, which is your reasonable service—let love be without dissimulation, abhor that which is evil, cleave to that which is good. These and many other duties are required of us as Christians, every one of which are like so many links of a chain, which when joined together make one complete member of Christ; this we profess to believe as Christians and as Masons.—I shall stop here with the introduction, which brings me to the points I shall endeavor to prove.—

First, the anciency of Masonry, that being done, will endeavor to prove all other titles we have a just right as Masons to claim—namely, honorable, free and accepted: To do this I must have recourse to the creation of this our world—After the Grand Architect of the Universe had framed the heavens for beauty and delight for the beings he was then about to make, he then called the earth to appear out of darkness, saying, let there be light, and it was so; He also set the sun, moon and stars in the firmament of heaven, for the delight of His creatures—He then created the fishes of the sea, the fowls of the air, then the beasts of the earth after their various kinds, and God blessed them.

Thus all things were in their order prepared for the most excellent accomplished piece of the visible creation, Man.—The forming this most excellent creature Man, was the close of the creation, so it was peculiar to Him to have a solemn consultation and decree about His making, and God said, let us make Man.—Seneca says, that man is not a work huddled over in haste, and done without fore-thinking and great consideration, for man is the greatest and most stupendous work of God.—Man hath not only a body in common with all inferior animals, but into his body was infused a soul of a far more noble nature and make—a rational principle to act according to the designs of His creation; that is, to contemplate the works of God, to admire His perfections, to worship Him, to live as becomes one who received his excellent being from Him, to converse with his fellow creatures that are of his own order, to maintain mutual love and society, and to serve God in consort. Man is a wonderful creature, and not undevedly [sic] said to be a little world, a world within himself, and containing whatever is found in the Creator.—In him is the spiritual and immaterial nature of God, the reasonableness of Angels, the sensitive power of brutes, the vegetative life of plants, and the virtue of all the elements he holds converse with in both worlds.—Thus man is crowned with glory and honor, he is the most remarkable workmanship of God. And is man such a noble creature and made to converse with his fellow men that are of his own order, to maintain mutual love and society, and to serve God in consort with each other?—then what can these God-provoking wretches think, who despise their fellow men, as tho' they were not of the same species with themselves, and would if in their power deprive them of the blessings and comforts of this life, which God in His bountiful goodness hath freely given to all His creatures to improve and enjoy? Surely such monsters never came out of the hand of God in such a forlorn condition.—Which brings me to consider the fall of man; and the Lord God took the man and put him into the garden of Eden, to dress it and to keep it, and freely to eat of every tree of the garden; here was His delightful employ and bountiful wages, and but one tree out of all that vast number he was forbidden to eat of. Concerning this garden, there have been different opinions about it by the learned, where it was, but the most of them agree that it was about the center of the earth, and that the four rivers parted or divided the four quarters of the world. The first was Pison, that was it which compasseth the land of Havilah; this river Pison is called by some Phasis, or Phasi Tigris, it runs (they say) by that Havilah whither the Amalekites fled, see 1 Sam. xv. 7, and divides it from the country of Susianna, and at last falls into the Persian Gulf, saith Galtruchius and others; but from the opinions of Christian writers, who hold that Havilah is India, and Pison the river Ganges. This was first asserted by Josephus, and from him Eustubius, Jerom, and most of the fathers received it, and not without good reason; for Moses here adds as a mark to know the place by, that there is gold, and the gold of that land is good; now it is confessed by all, that India is the most noted for gold, and of the best sort. It is added again, a note whereby to discover that place, that there is bedellium and the onyx stone—and India is famous for precious stones and pearls.—The name of the second river is Gihon, the same is it which compasseth the whole land of Ethiopia (or Cush as it is in the original) there is reason to believe that this Gihon is the river of Nile, as the forenamed Josephus and most of the ancient writers of the church hold, and by the help of the river Nile, Paradise did as it were border upon Egypt, which is the principal part of the African Ethiopia, which the ancient writers hold is meant there: The name of the third river is Hiddekel, that is it which goeth toward the east of Assyria, ver. 14. That it was a river belonging to Babylon is clear from Dan. x. 4; this is concluded to be the river Tygris, which divides Mesopotamia from Assyria, and goeth along with Euphrates, this being the great middle channel that ran through Edom or Babylon, and may be thought to take its name from its fructifying quality. These are the four grand landmarks which the all-wise and gracious God pleased to draw as the bounds and habitation of all nations which he was about to settle in this world; if so, what nation or people dare, without highly displeasing and provoking that God to pour down His judgments upon them.—I say, dare to despise or tyrannize over their lives or liberties, or encroach on their lands, or to enslave their bodies? God hath and ever will visit such a nation or people as this.—Envy and pride are the leading lines to all the miseries that mankind have suffered from the beginning of the world to this present day. What was it but these that turned the devil out of heaven into a hell of misery, but envy and pride?—Was it not the same spirit that moved him to tempt our first parents to sin against so holy and just a God, who had but just (if I may use the expression) turned his back from crowning Adam with honor and glory?—But envy at his prosperity hath taken the crown of glory from his head, and hath made us, his posterity, miserable.—What was it but this that made Cain murder his brother, whence is it but from these that our modern Cains call us Africans the sons of Cain? (We admit it if you please) and we will find from him and his sons Masonry began, after the fall of his father. Altho, Adam, when placed in the garden, God would not suffer him to be idle and unemployed in that happy state of innocence, but set him to dress and to keep that choice piece of earth; here he was to employ his mind as well as exercise his body; here he was to contemplate and study God's works; here he was to enjoy God, himself and the whole world, to submit himself wholly to his divine conduct, to conform all his actions to the will of his Maker; but by his sudden fall he lost that good will that he owed to his God, and for some time lost the study of God's works; but no doubt he afterwards taught his sons the art of Masonry; for how else could Cain after so much trouble and perplexity have time to study the art of building a city, as he did on the east of Eden, Gen. iv. 17, and without doubt he teached his sons the art, ver. 20, 21.

But to return, bad as Cain was, yet God took not from him his faculty of studying architecture, arts and sciences—his sons also were endowed with the same spirit, and in some convenient place no doubt they met and communed with each other for instruction. It seems that the all-wise God put this into the hearts of Cain's family thus to employ themselves, to divert their minds from musing on their father's murder and the woeful curse God had pronounced on him, as we don't find any more of Cain's complaints after this.

Similar to this we have in the 6 Gen., 12 & 13, that God saw that all men had corrupted their way, and that their hearts were only evil continually; and 14, 15, 16 verses, the great Architect of the universe gives Noah a complete plan of the ark and sets him to work, and his sons as assistants, like deputy and two grand wardens. One thing is well known, our enemies themselves being judges, that in whatsoever nation or kingdom in the whole world where Masonry abounds most, there hath been and still are the most peaceable subjects, cheerfully conforming to the laws of that country in which they reside, always willing to submit to their magistrates and rulers, and where Masonry most abounds, arts and sciences, whether mechanical or liberal, all of them have a mighty tendency to the delight and benefit of mankind; therefore we need not question but the all-wise God by putting this into our hearts intended, as another end of our creation, that we should not only live happily ourselves, but be likewise mutually assisting to each other. Again, it is not only good and beneficial in a time of peace, in a nation or kingdom, but in a time of war, for that brotherly love that cements us together by the bonds of friendship, no wars or tumults can separate; for in the heat of war if a brother sees another in distress he will relieve him some way or other, and kindly receive him as a brother, prefering him before all others, according to the Apostle's exhortation in my text, as also a similar instance you have 1 Kings, x, from 31st to 38th verse, where you find Benhadad in great distress, having lost a numerous army in two battles, after his great boasting, and he himself forced to hide himself in a chamber, and sends a message to Ahab, king of Israel, to request only his life as a captive; but behold the brotherly love of a Mason! no sooner was the message delivered, but he cries out in a rapture—is he alive—he is my brother! Every Mason knows that they were both of the craft, and also the messengers. Thus far may suffice for the anciency of this grand art; as for the honor of it—it is a society which God himself has been pleased to honor ever since he breathed into Adam the breath of life, and hath from generation to generation inspired men with wisdom, and planned out and given directions how they should build, and with what materials. And first, Noah in building the ark wherein he was saved, while God in his justice was pleased to destroy the unbelieving world of mankind. The first thing Noah did upon his landing was to build an altar to offer sacrifice to that great God which had delivered him out of so great a deluge; God accepted the sacrifice and blessed him, and as they journey from the east towards the west, they found a plain in the land of Shinar and dwelt there, and his sons.

Nimrod the son of Cush, the son of Ham, first founded the Babylonian monarchy, and kept possession of the plains, and founded the first great empire at Babylon, and became grand master of all Masons, he built many splendid cities in Shinar, and under him flourished those learned mathematicians, whose successors were styled in the book of Daniel, Magi, or wise men, for their superior knowledge. The migration from Shinar commenced fifty-three years after they began to build the tower, and one hundred and fifty-four years after the flood, and they went off at various times and traveled east, west, north and south, with their mighty skill, and found the use of it in settling their colonies; and from Shinar the arts were carried to distant parts of the earth, notwithstanding the confusion of languages, which gave rise to Masons faculty and universal practice of conversing without speaking, and of knowing each other by signs and tokens; they settled the dispersion in case any of them should meet in distant parts of the world who had been before in Shinar. Thus the earth was again planted and replenished with Masons the second son of Ham carried into Egypt; there he built the city of Heliopolis—Thebes with an hundred gates—they built also the statue of Sphynx, whose head was 120 feet round, being reckoned the first or earliest of the seven wonders of arts. Shem, the second son of Noah, remained at Ur of the Chaldes in Shinar, with his father and his great-grandson Heber, where they lived in private and died in peace: But Shem's offspring traveled into the south and east of Asia, and their offspring propagated the science and the art as far as China and Japan.

While Noah, Shem and Heber diverted themselves at Ur in mathematical studies, teaching Peleg, the father of Rehu, of Sereg, Nachor, and Terah, father of Abram, a learned race of mathematicians and geometricians; thus Abram, born two years after the death of Noah, had learned well the science and the art before the God of glory called him to travel from Ur of the Chaldes, but a famine soon forced him down to Egypt; the descendants of Abram sojourned in Egypt, as shepherds still lived in tents, practiced very little of the art of architecture till about eighty years before their Exodus, when by the overruling hand of providence they were trained up to the building with stone and brick, in order to make them expert Masons before they possessed the promised land; after Abram left Charran 430 years, Moses marched out of Egypt at the head of 600,000 Hebrews, males, for whose sakes God divided the Red Sea to let them pass through Arabia to Canaan. God was pleased to inspire their grand master Moses, and Joshua his deputy, with wisdom of heart; so the next year they raised the curious tabernacle or tent; God having called Moses up into the mount and gave him an exact pattern of it, and charges him to make it exactly to that pattern, and withal gave him the two tables of stone; these he broke at the foot of the mount; God gave him orders to hew two more himself, and after the likeness of the former. God did not only inspire Moses with wisdom to undertake the oversight of the great work, but he also inspired Bezaleel with knowledge to do all manner of cunning workmanship for it.—Having entered upon the Jewish dispensation, I must beg leave still to take a little notice of the Gentile nations, for we have but these two nations now to speak upon, namely, the Gentiles and the Jews, till I come to the Christian era.

The Cananites, Phenicians and Sidonians, were very expert in the sacred architecture of stone, who being a people of a happy genius and frame of mind, made many great discoveries and improvements of the sciences, as well as in point of learning. The glass of Sidon, the purple of Tyre, and the exceeding fine linen they wove, were the product of their own country and their own invention; and for their extraordinary skill in working of metals, in hewing of timber and stone; in a word, for their perfect knowledge of what was solid in architecture, it need but be remembered that they had in erecting and decorating of the temple at Jerusalem, than which nothing can more redound to their honor, or give a clearer idea of what this one building must have been.—Their fame was such for their just taste, design, and ingenious inventions, that whatever was elegant, great or pleasing, was distinguished by way of excellence with the epithet of Sidonian.—The famous temple of Jupiter Hammon, in Libian Africa, was erected, that stood till demolished by the first Christians in those parts; but I must pass over many other cities and temples built by the Gentiles.

God having inspired Solomon with wisdom and understanding, he as grand master and undertaker, under God the great architect, sends to Hiram, king of Tyre, and after acquainting him of his purpose of building a house unto the name of the Lord his God, he sends to him for some of his people to go with some of his to Mount Lebanon, to cut down and hew cedar trees, as his servants understood it better than his own, and moreover he requested him to send him a man that was cunning, to work in gold and silver, and in brass, iron, purple, crimson and in blue, and that had skill to engrave with the cunning men, and he sent him Hiram, his name-sake; this Hiram, God was pleased to inspire with wisdom and understanding to undertake, and strength to go through the most curious piece of workmanship that was ever done on earth.—Thus Solomon as grand master, and Hiram as his deputy, carried on and finished that great work of the temple of the living God, the inside work of which, in many instances as well as the tabernacle, resembles men's bodies; but this is better explained in a well-filled lodge; but this much I may venture to say, that our blessed Saviour compared His sacred body to a temple, when he said, John ii, 19: Destroy this temple and I will raise it up again in three days; and the Apostle, 1 Peter, i, 14, says that shortly he should put off this tabernacle. I could show also that one grand end and design of Masonry is to build up the temple that Adam destroyed in Paradise— but I forbear. Thus hath God honored the Craft, or Masons, by inspiring men with wisdom to carry on his stupendous works.

It is worthy our notice to consider the number of Masons employed in the work of the Temple: Exclusive of the two Grand Masters, there were 300 princes, or rulers, 3300 overseers of the work, 80,000 stone squarers, setters, layers or builders, being able and ingenious Crafts, and 30,000 appointed to work in Lebanon, 10,000 of which every month, under Adoniram, who was the Grand Warden; all the free Masons employed in the work of the Temple was 119,600, besides 70,000 men who carried burdens, who were not numbered among Masons; these were partitioned into certain Lodges, although they were of different nations and different colors, yet were they in perfect harmony among themselves, and strongly cemented in brotherly love and friendship, till the glorious Temple of Jehovah was finished, and the cape-stone was celebrated with great joy—Having finished all that Solomon had to do, they departed unto their several homes, and carried with them the high taste of architecture to the different parts of the world, and built many other temples and cities in the Gentile nations, under the direction of many wise and learned and royal Grand Masters, as Nebuchadnezar over Babylon—Cyrus over the Medes and Persians—Alexander over the Macedonians—Julius Caesar over Rome, and a great number more I might mention of crowned heads of the Gentile nations who were of the Craft, but this may suffice.—I must just mention Herod the Great, before I come to the state of Masonry from the birth of our Saviour Jesus Christ.—This Herod was the greatest builder of his day, the patron and Grand Master of many Lodges; he, being in the full enjoyment of peace and plenty, formed a design of new building the Temple of Jerusalem. The Temple built by the Jews after the captivity was greatly decayed, being 500 years standing, he proposed to the people that he would not take it down till he had all the materials ready for the new, and accordingly he did so, then he took down the old one and built a new one.—Josephus describes this Temple as a most admirable and magnificent fabric of marble, and the finest building upon earth.—Tiberius, having attained the imperial throne, became an encourager of the fraternity.

Which brings me to consider their freedom, and that will appear not only from their being free when accepted, but they have a free intercourse with all Lodges over the whole terrestial [sic] globe; wherever arts flourish a man hath a free right (having a recommendation) to visit his brethren, and they are bound to accept him; these are the laudable bonds that unite Free Masons together in one indissoluble fraternity—thus in every nation he finds a friend, and in every climate he may find a house—this it is to be kindly affectioned one to another, with brotherly love, in honor preferring one another.

Which brings me to answer some objections which are raised against the Masons, and the first is the irregular lives of the professors of it.—It must be admitted there are some persons who, careless of their own reputation, will consequently disregard the most instructive lessons—Some, I am sorry to say, are sometimes to be found among us; many by yielding to vice and intemperance, frequently not only disgrace themselves, but reflect dishonor on Masonry in general; but let it be known that these apostates are unworthy of their trust, and that whatever name or designation they assume, they are in reality no Masons: But if the wicked lives of men were admitted as an argument against the religion which they profess, Christianity itself, with all its divine beauties, would be exposed to censure; but they say there can be no good in Masonry because we keep it a secret, and at the same time these very men themselves will not admit an apprentice into their craft whatever, without enjoining secrecy on him, before they receive him as an apprentice; and yet blame us for not revealing our's.—Solomon says, Prov. xi. 12, 13, He that is void of wisdom despiseth his neighbour but a man of understanding holdeth his peace; a tale-bearer revealeth secrets, but he that is of a faithful spirit concealeth the matter. Thus I think I have answered these objections. I shall conclude the whole by addressing the Brethren of the African Lodge.

Dear and beloved brethren, I don't know how I can address you better than in the words of Nehemiah (who had just received liberty from the king

Artaxerxes, letters and a commission, or charter, to return to Jerusalem) that thro' the good hand of our God upon us we are here this day to celebrate the festival of St. John—as members of that honorable society of free and accepted Masons—as by charter we have a right to do—remember your obligations you are under to the great God, and to the whole family of mankind in the world—do all that in you lies to relieve the needy, support the weak, mourn with your fellow men in distress, do good to all men as far as God shall give you ability, for they are all your brethren, and stand in need of your help more or less—for he that loves everybody need fear nobody: But you must remember you are under a double obligation to the brethren of the craft of all nations on the face of the earth, for there is no party spirit in Masonry; let them make parties, who will, and despise those they would make, if they could, a species below them, and as not make of the same clay with themselves; but if you study the holy book of God, you will there find that you stand on the level not only with them, but with the greatest kings on the earth, as Men and as Masons, and these truly great men are not ashamed of the meanest of their brethren. Ancient history will produce some of the Africans who were truly good, wise, and learned men, and as eloquent as any other nation whatever though at present many of them in slavery, which is not a just cause of our being despised; for if we search history, we shall not find a nation on earth but has at some period or other of their existence been in slavery, from the Jews down to the English nation, under many Emperors, Kings and Princes; for we find in the life of Gregory, about the year 580, a man famous for his charity, that on a time when many merchants were met to sell their commodities at Rome, it happened that he passing by saw many young boys with white bodies, fair faces, beautiful countenances and lovely hair, set forth for sale; he went to the merchant, their owner, and asked him from what country he brought them; he answered from Britain, where the inhabitants were generally so beautiful. Gregory (sighing,) said, alas! for grief, that such fair faces should be under the power of the prince of darkness, and that such bodies should have their souls void of the grace of God.

I shall endeavor to draw a few inferences on this discourse by way of application.—

My dear Brethren, let us pray to God for a benevolent heart, that we may be enabled to pass through the various stages of this life with reputation, and that great and infinite Jehovah, who overrules the grand fabric of nature, will enable us to look backward with pleasure, and forward with confidence—and in the hour of death, and in the day of judgment, the well-grounded hope of meeting with that mercy from our Maker which we have ever been ready to show to others, will refresh us with the most solid comfort, and fill us with the most unspeakable joy.

And should not this learn us that new and glorious commandment of our Lord Jesus Christ to his disciples, when he urges it to them in these words—Love the Lord thy God with all thy heart, and thy neighbor as thyself.—Our Lord repeats and recommends this as the most indispensable duty and necessary qualification of his disciples, saying, hereby shall all men know that ye are my disciples, if ye have love one to another.—And we are expressly told by the Apostle, that charity, or universal love and friendship, is the end of the commandment.

Shall this noble and unparalleled example fail of its due influence upon us—shall it not animate our hearts with a like disposition of benevolence and mercy, shall it not raise our emulation and provoke our ambition—to go and do likewise.

Let us then beware of such a selfishness as pursues pleasure at the expense of our neighbor's happiness, and renders us indifferent to his peace and welfare; and such a self-love is the parent of disorder and the source of all those evils that divide the world and destroy the peace of mankind; whereas Christian charity—universal love and friendship—benevolent affections and social feelings, unite and knit men together, render them happy in themselves and useful to one another, and recommend them to the esteem of a gracious God, through our Lord Jesus Christ.

The few inferences that have been made on this head must be to you, my worthy brethren, of great comfort, that every one may see the propriety of a discourse on brotherly love before a society of free Masons—who knows their engagements as men and as Christians, have superadded the bonds of this ancient and honorable society—a society founded upon such friendly and comprehensive principles, that men of all nations and languages, or sects of religion, are and may be admitted and received as members, being recommended as persons of a virtuous character.

Religion and virtue, and the continuance and standing of this excellent society in the world—its proof of the wisdom of its plan—and the force of its principles and conduct has, on many occasions, been not a little remarkable—as well among persons of this, as among those of different countries, who go down to the sea and occupy their business in the great waters, they know how readily people of this institution can open a passage to the heart of a brother; and in the midst of war, like a universal language, is understood by men of all countries—and no wonder.—If the foundation has been thus laid in wisdom by the great God, then let us go on with united hearts and hands to build and improve upon this noble foundation—let love and sincere friendship in necessity instruct our ignorance, conceal our infirmities, reprove our errors, reclaim us from our faults—let us rejoice with them that rejoice, and weep with those that weep—share with each other in our joys, and sympathize in our troubles.

And let the character of our enemies be to resent affronts—but our's to generously remit and forgive the greatest; their's to blacken the reputation and blast the credit of their brethren—but our's to be tender of their good name, and to cast a veil over all their failings; their's to blow the coals of contention and sow the seeds of strife among men—but our's to compose their differences and heal up their breaches.

In a word, let us join with the words of the Apostle John in the 19th chapter of Revelations, and after these things I heard a great voice of much people in heaven, saying, Alleluia, salvation and glory, and honour, and power, unto the Lord our God; for true and righteous are his judgments—and the four beasts, fell down and worshipped God that sat on the throne, saying, Amen; Alleluia; and a voice came out of the throne, saying, praise our God, all ye his servants, and ye that fear him, both small and great.

To conclude the whole, let it be remembered; that all that is outward, whether opinions, rites or ceremonies, cannot be of importance in regard to eternal salvation, any further than they have a tendency to produce inward righteousness and goodness—pure, holy, spiritual and benevolent affections can only fit us for the kingdom of heaven; and therefore the cultivation of such must needs be the essence of Christ's religion—God of his infinite mercy grant that we may make this true use of it. Unhappily, too many Christians, so called, take their religion not from the declarations of Christ and his apostles, but from the writings of those they esteem learned.—But, I am to say, it is from the New-Testament only, not from any books what-soever, however piously wrote, that we ought to seek what is the essence of Christ's religion; and it is from this fountain I have endeavored to give my hearers the idea of Christianity in its spiritual dress, free from any human mixtures—if we have done this wisely we may expect to enjoy our God in the world that is above—in which happy place, my dear brethren, we shall all, I hope, meet at that great day, when our Great Master shall sit at the head of the great and glorious Lodge in heaven—where we shall all meet to part no more for ever and ever—Amen.■

3

A CHARGE DELIVERED TO THE BRETHREN OF THE AFRICAN LODGE

Prince Hall

A leading organizer of Boston's eighteenth-century black commu-nity, Prince Hall (1735–1807) left an enduring institutional legacy. Little of his early life, however, can be recounted with certainty. Per-haps born in Barbados, he was enslaved by William Hall of Boston, a leather dresser, for twenty-one years and was finally manumitted in 1770.

On March 6, 1775, Hall and fourteen other free blacks were inducted into the order of Free and Accepted Masons by British soldiers stationed near Boston. With the departure of the British less than two weeks later, Hall and the other black members were permitted to continue meeting and on July 3 formed the provisional African Lodge No. 1, the first black Masonic lodge in the United States. After the war (in which Hall is believed to have fought), Hall as grand master of the lodge petitioned for and received a permanent charter, authorized in April 1787. African lodges were soon formed in other cities and joined with Boston's lodge in the Prince Hall Solidarity. By 1977, Hall biographer Charles Wesley notes, there were more than fifty-five hundred lodges with over half a million members organized under the Prince Hall designation.

*Hall and other African Americans saw in Masonry an institution with great political power in the early republic, a society for mutual aid and benefit, and a platform for appeals to social justice. Hall and three fellow Masons were among those African Americans who petitioned the Massachusetts state legislature in 1777 to abolish slavery. In 1787, in the midst of Shays's Rebellion and a new wave of discrimination against Boston's black residents, Hall and other African lodge members again petitioned the legislature but this time asked the state to support the voluntary return of black citizens to Africa, "where we shall live among our equals, and be more comfortable and happy, than we can be in our present situation." Hall's appeal constituted the "first major statement on the subject in Afro-American history," according to Kaplan and Kaplan (*The Black Presence, *207). When no action was taken on his back-to-Africa proposal, Hall renewed his efforts to combat slavery and racial discrimination in Massachusetts.*

On June 25, 1792, Hall delivered the speech reprinted below at the Charlestown meeting hall of William Smith. In it he identifies the principles of Masonry and duties of membership in the lodge. Hall praises the principles of Masonry but also alludes to his anger and dismay at the continuing segregation of Masonic lodges and at the discriminatory attitudes and practices of white Masons toward the members of the African lodges. Near the end of his speech, Hall wonders aloud whether the medieval Masonic order was segregated even after the spread of Christianity to Africa: "whether, if they were all whites, they would refuse to accept them as their fellow Christians and brother Masons; or whether there were any so weak, or rather foolish, as to say, because they were blacks, they would make their lodge or army too common or too cheap?" The Prince Hall Grand Lodge did not gain full recognition from the English Grand Lodge until 1996.

*Hall's speech was printed and sold at the Bible and Heart in Boston; it was reprinted in Dorothy Porter, ed., *Early Negro Writing, 1700–1837 *(Boston: Beacon Press, 1991). For additional biographical material on Hall, see Charles Wesley, *Prince Hall: Life and Legacy *(Washington, D.C.: United Supreme Council, 1977); and Sidney Kaplan and Emma Nogrady*

Kaplan, The Black Presence in the Era of the American Revolution *(Amherst: University of Massachusetts Press, 1989), 203–14.*

Dearly and well beloved Brethren of the African Lodge, as through the goodness and mercy of God, we are once more met together, in order to celebrate the Festival of St. John the Baptist; it is requisite that we should on these public days, and when we appear in form, give some reason as a foundation for our so doing, but as this has been already done, in a discourse delivered in substance by our late Reverend Brother *John Marrant,* and now in print,

I shall at this time endeavour to raise part of the superstructure, for howsoever good the foundation may be, yet without this it will only prove a Babel. I shall therefore endeavour to shew the duty of a Mason; and the first thing is, that he believes in one Supreme Being, that he is the great Architect of this visible world, and that he governs all things here below by his almighty power, and his watchful eye is over all our works. Again we must be good subjects to the laws of the land in which we dwell, giving honour to our lawful Governors and Magistrates, giving honour to whom honour is due; and that we have no hand in any plots or conspiracies or rebellion, or side or assist in them: for when we consider the blood shed, the devastation of towns and cities that hath been done by them, what heart can be so hard as not to pity those our distrest brethren, and keep at the greatest distance from them.* However just it may be on the side of the opprest, yet it doth not in the least, or rather ought not, abate that love and fellow-feeling which we ought to have for our brother fellow men.

The next thing is love and benevolence to all the whole family of mankind, as God's make and creation, therefore we ought to love them all, for love or hatred is of the whole kind, for if I love a man for the sake of the image of God which is on him, I must love all, for he made all, and upholds all, and we are dependant upon him for all we do enjoy and expect to enjoy in this world and that which is to come.—Therefore he will help and assist all his fellow-men in distress, let them be of what colour or nation they may, yea even our very enemies, much more a brother Mason. I shall therefore give you a few instances of this from Holy Writ, and first, how did Abraham prevent the storm, or rebellion that was rising between Lot's servants and his? Saith Abraham to Lot, let there be no strife I pray thee between me and thee, for the land is before us, if you will go to the left, then I will go to the

---

*Hall may be referring here to Shays's Rebellion, which ignited western Massachusetts in 1786 and 1787. Revolutionary War veteran Captain Daniel Shays led a revolt of indebted farmers and others. Prince Hall offered the assistance of the African lodge in helping to quell the rebellion, but this offer was refused by Governor Bowdoin. See Sidney Kaplan and Emma Nogrady Kaplan, *The Black Presence in the Era of the American Revolution* (Amherst: University of Massachusetts Press, 1989), 258–59. Hall may instead be referring to recent slave uprisings in Louisiana and Virginia. See Herbert Aptheker, *American Negro Slave Revolts* (New York: International Publishers, 1943), 209–14.

right, and if you will go to the right, then I will go to the left. They divided and peace was restored. I will mention the compassion of a blackman to a Prophet of the Lord, Ebedmelech, when he heard that Jeremiah was cast into the dungeon, he made intercession for him to the King, and got liberty to take him out from the jaws of death. See Jer. xxxviii, 7–13.

Also the prophet Elisha after he had led the army of the Eramites blind-fold into Samaria, when the King in a deriding manner said, my *Father* (not considering that he was as much their Father as his) shall I smite, or rather kill them out of the way, as not worthy to live on the same earth, or draw the same air with himself; so eager was he to shed his brethren's blood, that he repeats his blood-thirsty demand, but the Prophet after reproaching him therefore, answers him no, but set bread and water before them; or in other words, give them a feast and let them go home in peace. See 2 Kings vi, 22–23.

I shall just mention the good deeds of the Samaritan, though at that time they were looked upon as unworthy to eat, drink or trade with their fellow-men, at least by the Jews; see the pity and compassion he had on a poor dis-trest and half dead stranger, see Luke x. from 30 to 37. See that you endeav-our to do so likewise.—But when we consider the amazing condescending love and pity our blessed Lord had on such poor worms as we are, as not only to call us his friends, but his brothers, we are lost and can go no further in holy writ for examples to excite us to the love of our fellow-men.—But I am aware of an objection that may arise (for some men will catch at any thing) that is that they were not all Masons; we allow it, and I say that they were not all Christians, and their benevolence to strangers ought to shame us both, that there is so little, so very little of it to be seen in these enlight-ened days.

Another thing which is the duty of a Mason is, that he pays a strict re-gard to the stated meetings of the Lodge, for masonry is of a progressive na-ture, and must be attended to if ever he intends to be a good Mason; for the man that thinks that because he hath been made a Mason, and is called so, and at the same time will wilfully neglect to attend his Lodge, he may be assured he will never make a good Mason, nor ought he to be looked upon as a good member of the craft. For if his example was followed, where would be the Lodge; and besides what a disgrace is it, when we are at our set meet-ings, to hear that one of our members is at a drinking house, or at a card table, or in some worse company, this brings disgrace on the Craft: Again there are some that attend the Lodge in such a manner that sometimes their absence would be better than their Company (I would not here be understood a brother in disguise, for such an one hath no business on a level floor) for if he hath been displeased abroad or at home, the least thing that is spoken that he thinks not right, or in the least offends him, he will raise his temper to such a height as to destroy the harmony of the whole Lodge; but we have a remedy and every officer ought to see it put in execution. Another thing a Mason ought to observe, is that he should lend his helping hand to a brother in distress, and relieve him; this we may do various ways—for we may sometimes help him to a cup of cold water, and it may be better to him than a cup of wine. Good advice may be sometimes better than feeding his body, helping him to some lawful employment, better than giving him money; so defending his case and standing by him when wrongfully accused, may be better than clothing him; better to save a brother's house when on fire, than to give him one. Thus much may suffice.

I shall now cite some of our fore-fathers, for our imitation: and the first shall be Tertullian, who defended the Christians against their heathen false accusations, whom they charged with treason against the empire and the Emperor, because of their silent meetings: he proved that to be false for this reason, for in their meetings, they were wont to pray for the prosperity of the Empire, of Rome, and him also; and they were accused of being enemies to mankind, how can that be, said he, when their office is to love and pray for all mankind. When they were charged with worshipping the Sun, because they looked towards the East when they prayed; he defended them against this slander also, and proved that they were slandered, slighted and ill-treated, not for any desert of theirs, but only out of hatred of them and their profession. This friend of the distrest was born in Carthage in Africa, and died Anno Christi 202.

Take another of the same city, Cyprian, for his fidelity to his profession was such, that he would rather suffer death than betray his trust and the truth of the gospel, or approve of the impious worship of the Gentiles: He was not only Bishop of Carthage, but of Spain and the east, west and northern churches, who died Anno Christi 259.

But I have not time to cite but one more (out of hundreds that I could count of our Fathers, who were not only examples to us, but to many of their nobles and learned); that is, Augustine, who had engraven on his table these words

> He that doth love an absent Friend to jeer,
> May hence depart, no room is for him here.

His saying was that sincere and upright Prayer pierceth heaven, and returns not empty. That it was a shelter to the soul. A sacrifice to God and a scourge to the Devil. There is nothing, said he, more abateth pride and sin than the frequent meditation on death; he cannot die ill, that lives well, and seldom doth he die well, that lives ill: Again, if men want wealth, it is not to be unjustly gotten, if they have it they ought by good works to lay it up in heaven: And again he that hath tasted the sweetness of divine love will not care for temporal sweetness. The reasonable soul made in the likeness of God may here find much distraction, but no full satisfaction; not to be without afflictions, but to overcome them, is blessedness. Love is as strong as death; as death kills the body, so love of eternal life kills worldly desires and affections. He called Ingratitude the Devil's sponge, wherewith he wipes out all the favours of the Almighty. His prayer was: Lord give first what thou requirest, and then require of me what thou wilt. This good man died Anno Christi 430.

The next is Fulgentius, his speech was, why travel I in the world which can yield me no future, nor durable reward answerable to my pains? Thought it better to weep well, than to rejoice ill, yet if joy be our desire, how much more excellent is their joy, who have a good conscience before God, who dread nothing but sin, study to do nothing but to accomplish the precepts of Christ. Now therefore let me change my course, and as before I endeavoured amongst my noble friends to prove more noble, so now let my care and employment be among the humble and poor servants of Christ, and become more humble that I may help and instruct my poor and distrest brethren.

Thus, my brethren, I have quoted a few of your reverend fathers for your imitation, which I hope you will endeavour to follow, so far as your abilities will permit in your present situation and the disadvantages you labour under on account of your being deprived of the means of education in your younger days, as you see it is at this day with our children, for we see notwithstanding we are rated for that, and other Town charges, we are deprived of that blessing. But be not discouraged, have patience, and look forward to a better day; Hear what the great Architect of the universal world saith, *Aethiopia shall stretch forth her hands unto me.* Hear also the strange but bold and confident language of *J. Husk,* who just before the executioner gave the last stroke, said, *I challenge you to meet me an hundred years hence.* But in the mean time let us lay by our recreations, and all superfluities, so that we may have that to educate our rising generation, which was spent in those follies. Make you this beginning, and who knows but God may raise up some friend or body of friends, as he did in *Philadelphia,* to open a School for the blacks here, as that friendly city has done there.

I shall now shew you what progress Masonry hath made since the siege and taking of Jerusalem in the year 70, by Titus Vespasian; after a long and bloody siege, a million of souls having been slain or had perished in the city, it was taken by storm and the city set on fire. There was an order of men called the order of St. John, who besides their other engagements, subscribed to another, by which they bound themselves to keep up the war against the Turks. These men defended the temple when on fire, in order to save it, so long, that Titus was amazed and went to see the reason of it; but when be came so near as to behold the *Sanctum Sanctorum,* he was amazed, and shed tears, and said, no wonder these men should so long to save it. He honored them with many honors, and large contributions were made to that order from many kingdoms; and were also knighted. They continued 88 years in Jerusalem, till that city was again retaken by the Turks, after which they resided 104 years in the Cyrean city of Ptolemy, till the remains of the Holy Conquest were lost. Whereupon they settled on the Island of Cyprus, where they continued 18 years, till they found an opportunity to take the Island Rhodes; being masters of that, they maintained it for 213 years, and from thence they were called knights of Rhodes, till in the year 1530 they took their residence in the Island of Malta, where they have continued to this day, and are distinguished by the name of the knights of Malta. Their first Master was Villaret in the year 1099. Fulco Villaret in the year 1322, took the Island of Rhodes, and was after that distinguished by the title of Grand Master, which hath devolved to his Successors to this day.

Query, Whether at that day, when there was an African church, and perhaps the largest Christian church on earth, whether there was no African of that order; or whether, if they were all whites, they would refuse to accept them as their fellow Christians and brother Masons; or whether there were any so weak, or rather so foolish, as to say, because they were blacks, that would make their lodge or army too common or too cheap? Sure this was not our conduct in the late war; for then they marched shoulder to shoulder, brother soldier and brother soldier, to the field of battle; let who will answer; he that despises a black man for the sake of his colour, reproacheth his Maker, and he hath resented it, in the case of Aaron and Miriam. See for this Numbers xii.*

But to return: In the year 1787 (the year in which we received our charter) there were 489 lodges under charge of his late Royal Highness the Duke of Cumberland; whose memory will always be esteemed by every good Mason.

And now, my African brethren, you see what a noble order you are members of. My charge to you is, that you make it your study to live up to the precepts of it, as you know that they are all good; and let it be known this day to the spectators that you have not been to a feast of Bacchus, but to a refreshment with Masons; and see to it that you behave as such, as well at home as abroad; always to keep in your minds the obligations you are under, both to God and your fellow men. And more so, you my dear brethren of Providence, who are at a distance from, and cannot attend the Lodge here but seldom; yet I hope you will endeavour to communicate to us by letters of your welfare; and remember your obligations to each other, and live in peace and love as brethren.—We thank you for your attendance with us this day, and wish you a safe return.

If thus, we by the grace of God, live up to this our Profession; we may cheerfully go the rounds of the compass of this life, having lived according to the plumb line of uprightness, the square of justice, the level of truth and sincerity. And when we are come to the end of time, we may then bid farewell to that delightful Sun and Moon, and the other planets, that move so beautifully round her in their orbits, and all things here below, and ascend to that new Jerusalem, where we shall not want these tapers, for God is the Light thereof; where the Wicked cease from troubling, and where the weary are at rest.

>   *Then shall we hear and see and know,*
>   *All we desir'd and wish'd below,*

---

*When Aaron and Miriam denounce Moses for having "married an Ethiopian woman," they are stricken with leprosy in God's wrath.

And every power find sweet employ,
   In that eternal world of joy.
Our flesh shall slumber in the ground,
   Till the last trumpet's joyful sound,
Then burst the chains with sweet surprize,
   And in our Saviour's image rise.■

4

PRAY GOD GIVE US THE STRENGTH TO BEAR UP UNDER ALL OUR TROUBLES

Prince Hall

On June 24, 1797, Prince Hall delivered a Masonic sermon to the African lodge at Menotomy (later West Cambridge), Massachusetts, in which he strongly denounced the African slave trade and the shameful abuse of people of color in Boston and expressed faith that God would soon end these and other evils. Boston society was thoroughly segregated in the last decade of the eighteenth century. Racial hostility and discrimination were rampant in every sphere of the city's economic and social life. Hall's 1797 address catalogs some of the daily insults and risks of physical assault to which African Americans in Boston were subjected "at such a degree that you may truly be said to carry your lives in your hands." As in his 1792 address, Hall draws upon the Bible for examples of interracial tolerance and respect and upon the Haitian Revolution as a beacon of hope.

Self-educated, Hall was particularly outraged by the complete denial of formal education to black residents, although he is careful to explain in this speech that unschooled blacks may be intelligent, wise, and knowledgeable. Blacks were taxed to support educational institutions whose services they were denied, he argued in his 1787 petition to the Massachusetts state legislature for educational funding. Hall's petition was denied. In 1796, the year before the speech that appears below, Hall had appealed to the selectmen of the city of Boston to establish a school for black children. The selectmen agreed in principle but said there was no building in which such a school might be held. In 1800, with funding from the city selectmen, Hall started the school in his own home, employing Harvard students as instructors. Hall died on December 4, 1807.

The text of the speech was published as a pamphlet and is reprinted in Dorothy Porter, ed., Early Negro Writing, 1760–1837 *(Boston: Beacon Press, 1971), 70–78. An alternate version, previously reprinted in* Voice of Black America, *appears in William Nell's* Colored Patriots of the American Revolution *(1855).*

Beloved Brethren of the African Lodge,'Tis now five years since I deliver'd a Charge to you on some parts and points of Masonry. As one branch or superstructure on the foundation; when I endeavoured to shew you the duty of a Mason to a Mason, and charity or love to all mankind, as the mark and image of the great God, and the Father of the human race.

I shall now attempt to shew you that it is our duty to sympathise with our fellow men under their troubles, the families of our brethren who are gone: we hope to the Grand Lodge above, here to return no more. But the cheerfulness that you have ever had to relieve them, and ease their burdens, under their forrows, will never be forgotten by them; and in this manner you will never be weary in doing good.

But my brethren, although we are to begin here, we must not end here; for only look around you and you will see and hear of numbers of our fellow men crying out with holy Job, Have pity on me, O my friends, for the hand of the Lord hath touched me. And this is not to be confined to parties or colours; not to towns or states; not to a kingdom, but to the kingdoms of the whole earth, over whom Christ the king is head and grand master.

Among these numerous sons and daughters of distress, I shall begin with our friends and brethren; and first, let us see them dragg'd from their native country by the iron hand of tyranny and oppression, from their dear friends and connections, with weeping eyes and aching hearts, to a strange land and strange people, whose tender mercies are cruel; and there to bear the iron yoke of slavery & cruelty till death as a friend shall relieve them. And must not the unhappy condition of these our fellow men draw forth our hearty prayer and wishes for their deliverance from these merchants and traders, whose characters you have in the xviii chap. of the Revelations, 11, 12, & 13 verses, and who knows but these same sort of traders may in a short time, in the like manner, bewail the loss of the African traffick, to their shame and confusion: and if I mistake not, it now begins to dawn in some of the West-India islands;* which puts me in mind of a nation (that I have somewhere read of) called Ethiopeans, that cannot change their skin: But God can and will change their conditions, and their hearts too; and let Boston and the world know, that He hath no respect of persons; and that that bulwark of envy, pride, scorn and contempt, which is so visible to be seen in some and felt, shall fall, to rise no more.

When we hear of the bloody wars which are now in the world, and thou-

*The slave insurrection on the French colony of Saint Domingue began in August 1791 and led to the establishment of the Republic of Haiti.

sands of our fellow men slain; fathers and mothers bewailing the loss of their sons; wives for the loss of their husbands; towns and cities burnt and destroy'd; what must be the heart-felt sorrow and distress of these poor and unhappy people!* Though we cannot help them, the distance being so great, yet we may sympathize with them in their troubles, and mingle a tear of sorrow with them, and do as we are exhorted to—weep with those that weep.

Thus my brethren we see what a chequered world we live in. Sometimes happy in having our wives and children like olive branches about our tables; receiving the bounties of our great Benefactor. The next year, or month, or week we may be deprived of some of them, and we go mourning about the streets, so in societies; we are this day to celebrate this Feast of St. John's, and the next week we might be called upon to attend a funeral of some one here, as we have experienced since our last in this Lodge. So in the common affairs of life we sometimes enjoy health and prosperity; at another time sickness and adversity, crosses and disappointments.

So in states and kingdoms; sometimes in tranquility, then wars and tumults; rich today, and poor tomorrow; which shews that there is not an independent mortal on earth, but dependent one upon the other, from the king to the beggar.

The great law-giver, Moses, who instructed by this father-in-law, Jethro, an Ethiopean, how to regulate his courts of justice and what sort of men to choose for the different offices; hear now my words, said he, I will give you counsel, and God shall be with you; be thou for the people to Godward, that thou mayest bring the causes unto God, and thou shall teach them ordinances and laws, and shall shew the way wherein they must walk, and the work that they must do: moreover thou shall provide out of all the people, able men, such as fear God, men of truth, hating covetousness, and place such over them, to be rulers of thousands, of hundreds and of tens.

So Moses hearkened to the voice of his father-in-law, and did all that he said. Exodus xviii. 22–24.

This is the first and grandest lecture that Moses ever received from the mouth of man; for Jethro understood geometry as well as laws, *that* a Mason may plainly see: so a little captive servant maid by whose advice Nomen, the great general of Syria's army, was healed of his leprosy; and by a servant his proud spirit was brought down: 2 Kings v. 3–14. The feelings of this little captive for this great man, her captor, was so great, that she forgot her state of captivity, and felt for the distress of her enemy. Would to God (said she to her mistress) my lord were with the prophets in Samaria, he should be healed of his leprosy: So after he went to the prophet, his proud host was so haughty that he not only disdain'd the prophet's direction, but derided the good old prophet; and had it not been for his servant he would have gone to his grave with a double leprosy, the outward and the inward, in the heart, which is the worst of leprosies; a black heart is worse than a white leprosy.

How unlike was this great general's behaviour to that of as grand a char-

*England and France had been at war since 1793.

acter, and as well beloved by his prince as he was; I mean Obadiah, to a like prophet. See for this 1st Kings xviii. from 7 to the 16th.

And as Obadiah was in the way, behold Elijah met him, and he knew him, and fell on his face, and said, Art not thou, my Lord, Elijah, and he told him, Yea, go and tell thy Lord, behold Elijah is here: and so on to the 16th verse. Thus we see that great and good men have, and always will have, a respect for ministers and servants of God. Another instance of this is in Acts viii. 27 to 31, of the European Eunuch, a man of great authority, to Philip, the apostle: here is mutual love and friendship between them. This minister of Jesus Christ did not think himself too good to receive the hand, and ride in a chariot with a black man in the face of day; neither did this great monarch (for so he was) think it beneath him to take a poor servant of the Lord by the hand, and invite him into his carriage, though but with a staff, one coat, and no money in his pocket. So our Grand Master, Solomon, was not asham'd to take the Queen of Sheba by the hand, and lead her into his court, at the hour of high twelve, and there converse with her on points of masonry (for if ever there was a female mason in the world she was one) and other curious matters; and gratified her, by shewing her all his riches and curious pieces of architecture in the temple, and in his house: After some time staying with her, he loaded her with much rich presents: he gave her the right hand of affection and parted in love.

I hope that no one will dare openly (tho' in fact the behaviour of some implies as much) to say, as our Lord said on another occasion, Behold a greater than Solomon is here. But yet let them consider that our Grand Master Solomon did not divide the living child, whatever he might do with the dead one, neither did he pretend to make a law to forbid the parties from having free intercourse with one another without the fear of censure, or be turned out of the synagogue.

Now my brethren, as we see and experience that all things here are frail and changeable and nothing here to be depended upon: Let us seek those things which are above, which are sure, and stedfast, and unchangeable, and at the same time let us pray to Almighty God, while we remain in the tabernacle, that he would give us the grace of patience and strength to bear up under all our troubles, which at this day God knows we have our share. Patience I say, for were we not possess'd of a great measure of it you could not bear up under the daily insults you meet with in the streets of Boston; much more on public days of recreation, how are you shamefully abus'd, and that at such a degree that you may truly be said to carry your lives in your hands, and the arrows of death are flying about your heads; helpless old women have their clothes torn off their backs, even to the exposing of their nakedness; and by whom are these disgraceful and abusive actions committed, not by the men born and bred in Boston, for they are better bred; but by a mob or horde of shameless, low-lived, envious, spiteful persons, some of them not long since, servants in gentlemen's kitchens, scouring knives, tending horses, and driving chaise. 'Twas said by a gentleman who saw that filthy behaviour in the common, that in all the places he had been in, he never saw so cruel behaviour in all his life, and that a slave in the West-Indies, on Sunday or holidays enjoys himself and friends without any molestation.* Not only this man, but many in town who hath seen their behaviour to you, and that without any provocation—twenty or thirty cowards fall upon one man—have wonder'd at the patience of the Blacks: 'tis not for want of courage in you, for they know that they dare not face you man for man, but in a mob, which we despise, and had rather suffer wrong than to do wrong, to the disturbance of the community and the disgrace of our reputation: for every good citizen doth honor to the laws of the State where he resides.

My brethren, let us not be cast down under these and many other abuses we at present labour under: for the darkest is before the break of day. My brethren, let us remember what a dark day it was with our African brethren six years ago, in the French West-Indies. Nothing but the snap of the whip was heard from morning to evening; hanging, broken on the wheel, burning, and all manner of tortures inflicted on those unhappy people for nothing else but to gratify their masters pride, wantonness, and cruelty: but blessed be God, the scene is changed; they now confess that God hath no respect of persons, and therefore receive them as their friends, and treat them as brothers. Thus doth Ethiopia begin to stretch forth her hand, from a sink of slavery to freedom and equality.

Although you are deprived of the means of education, yet you are not deprived of the means of meditation; by which I mean thinking, hearing and weighing matters, men, and things in your own mind, and making that judgment of them as you think reasonable to satisfy your minds and give an answer to those who may ask you a question. This nature hath furnished you with, without letter learning; and some have made great progress therein, some of those I have heard repeat psalms and hymns, and a great part of a sermon, only by hearing it read or preached and why not in other things in nature: how many of this class of our brethren that follow the seas can foretell a storm some days before it comes; whether it will be a heavy or light, a long or short one; foretell a hurricane, whether it will be destructive or moderate, without any other means than observation and consideration.

So in the observation of the heavenly bodies, this same class without a telescope or other apparatus have through a smoak'd glass observed the eclipse of the sun: One being ask'd what he saw through his smoaked glass, said, Saw, saw, de clipsey, or de clipseys. And what do you think of it?—Stop, dere be two. Right, and what do they look like?—Look like, why if I tell you, they look like two ships sailing one bigger than tother; so they sail by one another, and make no noise. As simple as the answers are they have a meaning, and shew that God can out of the mouth of babes and Africans shew

*For a description of racial intolerance in Boston, see John Daniels, *In Freedom's Birthplace: A Study of the Boston Negroes* (New York: Negro Universities Press, 1914); and James Horton and Lois Horton, *Black Bostonians: Family Life and Community Struggle in the Antebellum North* (New York: Holmes and Meier, 1979).

forth his glory; let us then love and adore him as the God who defends us and supports us and will support us under our pressures, let them be ever so heavy and pressing. Let us by the blessing of God, in whatsoever state we are, or may be in, to be content; for clouds and darkness are about him; but justice and truth is his habitation; who hath said, Vengeance is mine and I will repay it, therefore let us kiss the rod and be still, and see the works of the Lord.

Another thing I would warn you against, is the slavish fear of man, which bringest a snare, saith Solomon. This passion of fear, like pride and envy, hath slain its thousands.—What but this makes so many perjure themselves; for fear of offending them at home they are a little depending on for some trifles: A man that is under a panic for fear, is afraid to be alone; you cannot hear of a robbery or house broke open or set on fire, but he hath an accomplice with him, who must share the spoil with him; whereas if he was truly bold, and void of fear, he would keep the whole plunder to himself: so when either of them is detected and not the other, he may be call'd to oath to keep it secret, but through fear, (and that passion is so strong) he will not confess, til the fatal cord is put on his neck; then death will deliver him from the fear of man, and he will confess the truth when it will not be of any good to himself or the community: nor is this passion of fear only to be found in this class of men, but among the great.

What was the reason that our African kings and princes have plunged themselves and their peaceable kingdoms into bloody wars, to the destroying of towns and kingdoms, but the fear of the report of a great gun or the glittering of arms and swords, which struck these kings near the seaports with such a panic of fear, as not only to destroy the peace and happiness of their inland brethren, but plung'd millions of their fellow countrymen into slavery and cruel bondage.

So in other countries; see Felix trembling on his throne. How many Emperors and kings have left their kingdoms and best friends at the sight of a handful of men in arms: how many have we seen that have left their estates and their friends and ran over to the stronger side as they thought; all through the fear of men, who is but a worm, and hath no more power to hurt his fellow worm, without the permission of God, than a real worm.

Thus we see, my brethren, what a miserable condition it is to be under the slavish fear of men; it is of such a destructive nature to mankind, that the scriptures every where from Genesis to the Revelations warns us against it; and even our blessed Saviour himself forbids us from this slavish fear of man, in his sermon on the mount; and the only way to avoid it is to be in the fear of God: let a man consider the greatness of his power, as the maker and upholder of all things here below, and that in Him we live, and move, and have our being, the giver of the mercies we enjoy here from day to day, and that our lives are in his hands, and that he made the heavens, the sun, moon and stars to move in their various orders; let us thus view the greatness of God, and then turn our eyes on mortal man, a worm, a shade, a wafer, and see whether he is an object of fear or not; on the contrary, you will think him in his best estate to be but vanity, feeble and a dependent mortal, and stands in need of your help, and cannot do without your assistance, in some way or other; and yet some of these poor mortals will try to make you believe they are Gods, but worship them not. My brethren, let us pay all due respect to all whom God hath put in places of honor over us: do justly and be faithful to them that hire you, and treat them with that respect they may deserve; but worship no man. Worship God, this much is your duty as christians and as masons.

We see then how becoming and necessary it is to have a fellow feeling for our distres'd brethren of the human race, in their troubles, both spiritual and temporal—How refreshing it is to a sick man, to see his sympathising friends around his bed, ready to administer all the relief in their power; although they can't relieve his bodily pain yet they may ease his mind by good instructions and cheer his heart by their company.

How doth it cheer up the heart of a man when his house is on fire, to see a number of friends coming to his relief; he is so transported that he almost forgets his loss and his danger, and fills him with love and gratitude; and their joys and sorrows are mutual.

So a man wreck'd at sea, how must it revive his drooping heart to see a ship bearing down for his relief.

How doth it rejoice the heart of a stranger in a strange land to see the people cheerful and pleasant and are ready to help him.

How did it, think you, cheer the heart of those our poor unhappy African brethren, to see a ship commissioned from God, and from a nation that without flattery faith, that all men are free and are brethren; I say to see them in an instant deliver such a number from their cruel bolts and galling chains, and to be fed like men and treated like brethren. Where is the man that has the least spark of humanity, that will not rejoice with them; and bless a righteous God who knows how and when to relieve the oppressed, as we see he did in the deliverance of the captives among the Algerines; how sudden were they delivered by the sympathising members of the Congress of the United States, who now enjoy the free air of peace and liberty, to their great joy and surprize, to them and their friends.* Here we see the hand of God in various ways bringing about his own glory for the good of mankind, by the mutual help of their fellow men; which ought to teach us in all our straits, be they what they may, to put our trust in Him, firmly believing that he is able and will deliver us and defend us against all our enemies; and that no weapon form'd against us shall prosper; only let us be steady and uniform in our walks, speech and behaviour; always doing to all men as we wish and desire they would do to us in the like cases and circumstances.

Live and act as Masons, that you may die as Masons; let those despisers see, altho' many of us cannot read, yet by our searches and researches into

---

*From 1786 to 1797, Congress signed a series of treaties with the Barbary states pledging annual payments of tribute in exchange for a halt to piracy and the release of Americans taken prisoner by Barbary pirates.

men and things, we have supplied that defect; and if they will let us we shall call ourselves a charter'd lodge of just and lawful Masons; be always ready to give an answer to those that ask you a question; give the right hand of affection and fellowship to whom it justly belongs; let their colour and complexion be what it will, let their nation be what it may, for they are your brethren, and it is your indispensable duty so to do; let them as Masons deny this, and we & the world know what to think of them be they ever so grand: for we know this was Solomon's creed, Solomon's creed did I say, it is the decree of the Almighty, and all Masons have learnt it: tis plain market language, and plain and true facts need no apologies.

I shall now conclude with an old poem which I found among some papers:

> Let blind admirers handsome faces praise,
> And graceful features to great honor raise,
> The glories of the red and white express,
> I know no beauty but in holiness;
> If God of beauty be the uncreate
> Perfect idea, in this lower state,
> The greatest beauties of an human mould
> Who most resemble Him we justly hold;
> Whom we resemble not in flesh and blood,
> But being pure and holy, just and good:
> May such a beauty fall but to my share,
> For curious shape or face I'll never care.■

5   ADDRESS TO THE PEOPLE OF COLOR

Abraham Johnstone

In 1745, a broadside was issued entitled The Declaration and Confession of Jeffrey, Negro, who was executed in Worcester, October 17, 1745, for the Murder of his Mistress Tabitha Sanford, at Mendon, the 12th of September. *A notice of the broadside was published in the* Boston Evening Post *of October 28, 1745, but there does not appear to be in existence any copy of the sheet itself or the "Declaration and Confession."*

Early in 1797, Abraham Johnstone, a free African American who had

*been born in slavery in Delaware and later manumitted, was convicted
by a jury of having murdered Thomas Read, also black. He was sentenced to be hanged. When asked by the court for a statement, Johnstone
delivered a long address to "the people of color," much of it devoted to
advice on how to conduct themselves in American society. Sections of
the address, which are printed below, were evidently intended for white
listeners, despite its title. The speech was later published in Philadelphia
as "The Address of Abraham Johnstone . . . to the People of Colour," and
there were added "The Dying Words of Abraham Johnstone" and his letter to his wife, both written in Woodbury jail, July 8, 1797. The anony-
mous printer of the pamphlet in an address "To the Public," which appeared as a foreword, questioned Johnstone's guilt and pointed out that
he had been convicted on very flimsy evidence. "Juries," he warned,
"ought to be extremely cautious how they admit evidence founded solely
on presumption to affect the life of a fellow creature and deprive society
of a member: Proof of so vague and indeterminable a nature, being too
dangerous to be admitted in this country where I am sorry to say there
is but too little regard paid to oaths; and the most glaring perjuries are
suffered to pass with impunity."*

*The excerpts here presented were taken from a pamphlet in Rutgers
University Library—*The Address of Abraham Johnstone, A Black Man,
Who Was hanged at Woodbury in the County of Glocester, and State of
New Jersey, on Saturday the 8th day of July last; to the People of Colour
(Philadelphia, 1797.)

I MOST EARNESTLY EXHORT and pray you to be upright and circumspect in your conduct; I must the more earnestly urge this particular from
a combination of circumstances that at this juncture of time concur to make
it of importance to our color for my unfortunate unhappy fate, however unmerited or undeserved, may by some ungenerous and illiberal-minded persons, but particularly by those who oppose the emancipation of those of our
brethren who as yet are in slavery, be made a handle of in order to throw a
shade over or cast a general reflection on all those of our color, and the keen
shafts of prejudice be launched against us by the most active and virulent
malevolence. But such general reflections or sarcasms will be only made by
the low-minded illiberal and sordid persons who are the enemies of our
color, and of freedom; and to them I shall simply answer that if the population throughout the United States be then taken, and then a list of all the
executions therein be had, and compared therewith impartially, it will be
found that as they claim a preeminence over us in every thing else, so we
find they also have it in this particular, and that a vast majority of whites
have died on the gallows when the population is accurately considered. A
plain proof that there are some whites (with all due deference to them) ca-

pable of being equally as depraved and more generally so, than blacks or people of color. . . .

From the first bringing of our color into this country they have been constantly kept to the greatest toil and labor, to drudge incessantly yet without the smallest hopes of a reward, and oftentimes denied a sufficient portion of food to suffice the cravings of nature, or raiment sufficient to hide their nakedness or shield them from the inclemency of the weather. Yet, laboring under all those hardships and difficulties, the most unheard of cruelties and punishments were daily inflicted on us. For what? For not performing impossibilities, for not doing what was impossible for human nature or strength to have done with in the time allotted. And if the most pressing hunger should compel us to take from that master by stealth what were sure to be denied if we asked, to satisfy our craving appetites, the most wanton and dreadful punishments were immediately inflicted on us even to a degree of inhumanity and cruelty. That I do not exaggerate is, I dare say, known to many of ye that hear me, or that may hereafter read this address to you, and therefore I appeal to ye, as personal knowledge of the facts I have here stated, I declare myself that I speak from experience. . . .

And here, my dear brethren, I think it necessary to take notice of the cavils raised by some against us, and the foolishly chimerical notion that prevails with such, to say because we are black, we are not to enjoy a future state, not to be admitted to inherit the kingdom of God, and that our Saviour did not die for us, therefore we cannot hope a redemption; while some other speaking idiots would have us to be the seed of Cain* all equally fallacious and ridiculous; and indeed is enough to make any unconcerned or disinterested person merry to hear such foolishly frivolous arguments adduced with such solemnity against us. However, that I should not be wanting in respect to the whites, nor in justice to my own color, I shall make such objections to those arguments as will, I pledge myself, fully and completely refute them.

As to the first, I shall content myself with making one general observation, namely, that God is neither a respecter of persons, nor colors, be they white, black or mulatto, but respects them merely from their deeds and observance of His divine commands, and I humbly but confidentially insist that no one living can produce a scriptural or even respectably rational authority in support of such a vague and nonsensical opinion, therefore that argument fails.

As to the second, that we shall not inherit the kingdom of God, or enjoy a future state, I wonder where such chimerical notion exists, except in their heated brains or childishly prejudiced imaginations; for Scripture tells us ex-

---

*A racist justification for enslavement of Africans alleged that blacks were descendants of Cain, who had been cursed by God for having killed Abel. A poem entitled "Africa," published in the *Literary Digest* of March 5, 1904, contained the lines: "She to whom fell the dark disgrace, / Cain's evil brood to bear!"

In the Mormon Church blacks were long excluded from the priesthood because they were believed to be descended from Cain.

pressly, "That all that believe shall be saved," but to go a step farther and reason the matter candidly and without prejudice, I am confident that the odds will be considerably in our favor. And first, I will ask all those persons seriously, how the economy of divine providence with respect to us, can be made reconcilable with our conceptions of the nature of the divine Supreme Being and his attributes, upon the supposition of this being the first and final stage of our existence? That we are endowed with reason and reflection, and a sensibility of pain as well as pleasure, is acknowledged to be an incontestable truth, neither can it be denied by any one. Nor is it less evident and unquestionable that the latter is oftentimes more than overbalanced by the former. To instance only in our poor brethren at this moment in slavery in the Southern states, what exquisite, what affecting tortures do many of them endure (tho some few of them perhaps meet a more friendly fate) from some merciless callous-hearted monster of a master? How frequently to the pangs of hunger and a distempered body are there added the most cutting stripes and scourges most liberally and as wantonly dealt out to them by their inhuman masters or drivers, and all this merely for their not effecting perhaps impossibilities! But wherefore all these agonizing pains and miseries heaped on an offspring of divine Providence? And why because our color happens to be black? Are we not a living animated part of the creation? Are we not flesh and blood? Do we not as well as they know what sorrow means? Yes; and for them only, their use, or accidentally their pride, their wantonness, their cruelty were we brought into a sensible existence! Shall one being be created, but even under the bar possibility of being made miserable (more or less) solely for the use and service of another? Lord, what is man? Or rather what are not brutes? The unmerited sufferings among whites urged with are great strength of reasoning, in proof of a recompense reserved for them hereafter. And must a being that happens to move in low and humble sphere in society be at once pronounced unworthy of the like provision? But wherefore this partiality to their noble selves? Why must they plead a right to be dealt with on the part of justice by the Almighty, and yet think it no injury done to us, if our sufferings in a state we are forced into by our common Lord and Creator, meet not from him an hereafter some similar tokens of an universal and impartial goodness toward his creatures so necessary and essential to the divine nature. But to bring it more closely home to these our enemies. I will ask them, if they would think it just or equitable for the Moors in Algiers to deny a salvation or a recompense in an hereafter to those of this country who are there kept in slavery; and whose color is white?* Oh, they surely would not, they would laugh at the absurdity of the idea and treat it with all the ridicule it justly deserved.■

*Pirates from Tripoli and Algiers attacked American vessels and enslaved American seamen, practices that led to a war with Tripoli and the signing of a treaty.

6 EULOGY FOR WASHINGTON

Richard Allen

Richard Allen (1760–1831), activist and founder of the African Methodist Episcopal Church, was born in slavery in Philadelphia and sold along with his family to the Stokeleys of Delaware. He converted to Methodism in 1777 and joined other slaves in attending the biweekly meetings of the Methodist Society. Allen was able to purchase his freedom through work as a brick maker and wood splitter, occupations he continued after gaining his release. He also became an itinerant preacher, often speaking to mixed or white audiences along his stops as a wagon driver for the Continental Army during the American Revolution. In late 1784, he is believed to have attended the founding conference of American Methodism. Two years later, he returned to Philadelphia to preach.

Allen preached not only to his assigned flock at St. George's Methodist Episcopal Church but also throughout the city, sometimes several times a day, to different groups of "my African brethren, who had been a long forgotten people and few of them attended public worship." But by 1792, when black worshipers had been pulled off their knees during prayers at St. George's and instructed to move to a segregated pew, the necessity of a separate black church had become painfully clear to Allen and others.

These plans were delayed by the yellow fever epidemic of 1793, which killed thousands of Philadelphians. Allen and Absalom Jones organized the black community to fight the epidemic and in 1794 published A Narrative of the Proceedings of the Black People, During the Late Awful Calamity in Philadelphia, *which detailed African American contributions to the city's recovery during the crisis and refuted false charges of their inactivity.*

At last, in July 1794, Allen's dream of a separate black church became reality with the opening of Mother Bethel, complete with pulpit carved by Allen's own hands. Although many before him had sought in vain to establish such an institution, writes Carol George in Segregated Sabbaths, *it was Allen who proved able to "manipulate the winds of social change that whirled about him to achieve a relatively safe and theologically satisfying spiritual home for Black people" (7). In 1816 Allen was ordained as the first bishop of the African Methodist Episcopal Church.*

Allen was also an activist in spheres beyond the church. In 1787, Allen and Absalom Jones founded the Free African Society, perhaps the earliest African American mutual aid organization in the United States, and he opened a school for African American children in 1795. Allen campaigned vigorously against slavery and the schemes of the American Colonization Society.

Allen spoke extemporaneously, believing that "reading sermons will never prove so beneficial to the colored people as spiritual or extempore preaching." Such a preaching style was adapted to the occasion and "at its best," writes George, "combined the speaker's inspiration in a fortuitous blend with the congregation's reaction" (161).

On Sunday, December 29, 1799, Allen delivered a eulogy of George Washington to the congregation of the Philadelphia's African Methodist Episcopal Church. A sketch of Allen's address was published two days later in the Philadelphia Gazette. *On the same page as Allen's eulogy appears an advertisement for sale of "The TIME of a NEGRO MAN, who has 6 years to serve." The white editor of the* Gazette *introduced Allen's eulogy by pronouncing that "it will show that the African race participate in the common events of our country—that they rejoice in our prosperity, mourn in our adversity, and feel with other citizens the propriety and necessity of wise and good rulers, of an effective government, and of submission to the laws and government of the land."*

But Allen's eulogy does much more. Allen uses the occasion of Washington's death, a time when his ideals and achievements were subjects of national contemplation, to focus on Washington's eventual opposition to slavery. Although a slaveowner himself, Washington had written as early as 1786 of his desire "to see some plan adopted by which slavery may be abolished by law."* Some of Washington's actions as president, however, seem in conflict with this belief. In 1793, for example, he signed into law the first federal law requiring the return of fugitive slaves. Yet upon his death, Washington's will set free his enslaved companion William Lee and provided for the emancipation of his other slaves following his wife's death. The memory of Washington, Allen argues, can best be served by abiding by his principles, "for you cannot honour those who have loved you and been your benefactors more than by taking their council and advice."

The speech text is taken from the Philadelphia Gazette *of December 31, 1799. For further information on Allen, see Carol George,* Segregated Sabbaths: Richard Allen and the Emergence of Independent Black Churches, 1760–1840 *(New York: Oxford University Press, 1973);* Charles H. Wesley, Richard Allen: Apostle of Freedom *(Washington, D.C.: Associated Publishers, 1969); and Richard Allen,* The Life Experience and Gospel Labors of Richard Allen *(Philadelphia: Martin and Boden, 1833).*

A t this time it may not be improper to speak a little on the late mournful event—an event in which we participate in common with the feel-

---

*Quoted in James Thomas Flexner, *George Washington: Anguish and Farewell, 1793–1799* (Boston: Little, Brown, 1972), 121.

ings of a grateful people—an event which causes "the land to mourn" in a season of festivity. Our father and friend is taken from us—he whom the nations honoured is "seen of men no more."

We, my friends, have particular cause to bemoan our loss. To us he has been the sympathising friend and tender father. He has watched over us, and viewed our degraded and afflicted state with compassion and pity—his heart was not insensible to our sufferings. He whose wisdom the nations revered thought we had a right to liberty. Unbiased by the popular opinion of the state in which is the memorable Mount Vernon—he dared to do his duty, and wipe off the only stain with which man could ever reproach him.

And it is now said by an authority on which I rely, that he who ventured his life in battles, whose "head was covered" in that day, and whose shield the "Lord of hosts" was, did not fight for that liberty which he desired to withhold from others—the bread of oppression was not sweet to his taste, and he "let the oppressed go free"—he "undid every burden"—he provided lands and comfortable accommodations for them when he kept this "acceptable fast to the Lord"—that those who had been slaves might rejoice in the day of their deliverance.

If he who broke the yoke of British burdens "from off the neck of the people" of this land, and was hailed his country's deliverer, by what name shall we call him who secretly and almost unknown emancipated his "bondmen and bondwomen"—became to them a father, and gave them an inheritance!

Deeds like these are not common. He did not let "his right hand know what his left hand did"—but he who "sees in secret will openly reward" such acts of beneficence.

The name of Washington will live when the sculptured marble and statue of bronze shall be crumbled into dust—for it is the decree of the eternal God that "the righteous shall be had in everlasting remembrance, but the memorial of the wicked shall rot."

It is not often necessary, and it is seldom that occasion requires recommending the observance of the laws of the land to you, but at this time it becomes a duty; for you cannot honour those who have loved you and been your benefactors more than by taking their council and advice.

And here let me intreat you always to bear in mind the affectionate farewell advice of the great Washington—"to love your country—to obey its laws—to seek its peace—and to keep yourselves from attachment to any foreign nation."

Your observance of these short and comprehensive expressions will make you good citizens—and greatly promote the cause of the oppressed and shew to the world that you hold dear the name of George Washington.

May a double portion of his spirit rest on all the officers of the government in the United States, and all that say my Father, my Father—the chariots of Israel, and the horsemen thereof, which is the whole of the American people.■

7 UNIVERSAL SALVATION

Lemuel Haynes

Lemuel Haynes (1753–1833), believed to be the first African American ordained by a Protestant church in the United States, was born to a black father and a white mother in West Hartford, Connecticut. Abandoned by his mother, he was bound out to the Rose family of Granville, Massachusetts, and was indentured until the age of twenty-one. Soon after his release, he volunteered as a minuteman and later fought as a member of the Continental Army under Ethan Allen.

In 1776, Haynes was preoccupied with the conflict between the stated principles of the revolution and the continued existence of slavery and racial discrimination among its patriots. In his ballad "The Battle of Lexington," composed one year after the events of April 1775, Haynes insists that

> *For liberty each Freeman strives*
> *As its a Gift of God*
> *And for it, willing yield their Lives*
> *And Seal it with their Blood.*
>
> *Twice happy they who thus resign*
> *Into the peacefull Grave*
> *Much better those in Death Consign*
> *Than a Surviving Slave.*

Also in 1776, Haynes composed the remarkable if unfinished essay "Liberty Further Extended; or, Free thoughts on the illegality of Slave-keeping," the manuscript of which was discovered in 1983 by Ruth Bogin. Its title page reprints the newly issued Declaration of Independence. To be consistent with its principles, Haynes argues, the emerging nation must "let the oppressed go free" and recognize "that an African, or, in other terms, that a Negro . . . has an undeniable right to his Liberty: Consequently, the practice of Slave-keeping, which so much abounds in this Land is illicit."

After the war, Haynes studied for the ministry. He learned Latin and Greek while supporting himself as a teacher. In 1785, he was ordained in the Congregational ministry in Torrington, Connecticut. Soon after, he journeyed as a missionary to the Vermont frontier and in 1788 became second pastor in Rutland, where he would preach for thirty-four years. Haynes's sermons became justly famous, and the number of his congregants multiplied several fold. During his tenure in Rutland, Haynes delivered more than five thousand sermons. He possessed an astonishing memory and was able to recite Milton's Paradise Lost *and much of the Bible with uncanny accuracy. Haynes's sermons ranged widely in theme; he often wrote and spoke of national and international affairs. He condemned the French Revolution and opposed the War of 1812, for example. In March 1804, Haynes was awarded an honorary M.A. degree from Middlebury College. He was probably the first African American to be recognized in this way.*

The most famous of Haynes's sermons was "Universal Salvation," delivered extemporaneously in June 1805. Hosea Ballou, a prominent Unitarian theologian, preached in West Rutland and expounded the belief that all people might gain salvation through adherence to the gospel. These views were anathema to Haynes, who attended Ballou's sermon. Haynes was an evangelical Calvinist, "consistently indicating," writes Helen MacLam, "an unwavering belief in predestination and personal election." When Ballou finished speaking, he invited comments from Haynes, who rose to deliver the witty and stinging rebuke that follows. "Universal Salvation" was reprinted in over seventy editions in Europe and the United States during the sixty years following its delivery. It is, among other things, a treatise on the ethics of persuasion, in which Haynes attributes his adversary's persuasiveness to Ballou's diabolical character and to the gullibility of listeners.

This sermon spread Haynes's already considerable fame. Yet in March 1818, his Rutland church voted not to renew his contract. An unknown contemporary offered a possible reason: "The people in Rutland, where he preached thirty years, at length began to think they would appear more respectable with a white pastor than a Black one, and therefore, or at least measurably on that account, dismissed him." Haynes himself explained that "he lived with the people in Rutland thirty years, and they were so sagacious that at the end of that time they found out that he was a nigger, *and so turned him away" (quoted by MacLam in Newman, xxxiv). At the age of sixty-five, Haynes was again reduced to itineracy. He died in 1833.*

The text of the speech comes from Richard Newman, ed., Black Preacher to White America: The Collected Writings of Lemuel Haynes *(Brooklyn: Carlson, 1990), which includes an excellent introductory biographical essay by Helen MacLam.*

Genesis 3, 4, And the serpent said unto the woman, ye shall not surely die.

The holy scriptures are a peculiar fund of instruction. They inform us of the origin of creation; of the primitive state of man; of his fall, or apostacy from God. It appears that he was placed in the garden of Eden, with full liberty to regale himself with all the delicious fruits that were to be found, except what grew on one tree—if he eat of that, that he should surely die, was the declaration of the Most High.

Happy were the human pair amidst this delightful Paradise, until a certain preacher, in his journey, came that way, and disturbed their peace and tranquility, by endeavoring to reverse the prohibition of the Almighty; as in our text, ye shall not surely die.

> *She pluck'd, she ate,*
> *Earth felt the wound; nature from her seat,*
> *Sighing through all her works, gave signs of woe,*
> *That all was lost.*

Milton

We may attend,—To the character of the preacher; to the doctrines inculcated; to the hearer addressed; to the medium or instrument of the preaching.

I. As to the preacher, I shall observe, he has many names given him in the sacred writings; the most common is the devil. That it was he that disturbed the felicity of our first parents, is evident from 2 Cor. 11:3, and many other passages of Scripture. He was once an angel of light and knew better than to preach such doctrine; he did violence to his own reason.—But to be a little more particular, let it be observed:

1. He is an old preacher. He lived above one thousand seven hundred years before Abraham; above two thousand four hundred and thirty years before Moses; four thousand and four years before Christ. It is now five thousand eight hundred and nine years since he commenced preaching. By this time he must have acquired great skill in the art.
2. He is a very cunning, artful preacher. When Elymas the sorcerer, came to turn away people from the faith, he is said to be full of all subtlety, and a child of the devil, not only because he was an enemy to all righteousness, but on account of his carnal cunning and craftiness.
3. He is a very laborious, unweried preacher. He has been in the ministry almost six thousand years; and yet his zeal has not in the least abated. The apostle Peter compares him to a roaring lion, walking about seeking whom he may devour. When God inquired of this preserving preacher, Job 2:2, From whence camest thou? He answered the Lord, and said, From going to and fro in the earth, and from walking up and down in it. He is far from being circumscribed within the narrow limits of parish, state, or continental lines; but his haunt and travel is very large and extensive.*

---

*Haynes here condemns itinerant preachers, like Ballou, who "usurped" the established congregations of established ministers.

4. He is a heterogeneous preacher, if I may so express myself. He makes use of a Bible when he holds forth, as in his sermon to our Savior; Matt. 4:6. He mixes truth with error, in order to make it go well, or to carry his point.

5. He is a very presumptuous preacher. Notwithstanding God had declared, in the most plain and positive terms, Thou shalt surely die, or In dying, thou shalt die, yet this audacious wretch had the impudence to confront omnipotence, and says ye shall not surely die!

6. He is a very successful preacher. He draws a great number after him. No preacher can command hearers like him. He was successful with our first parents, with the old world. Noah once preached to those spirits who are now in the prison of hell; and told them from God, that they should surely die; but this preacher came along and declared the contrary, ye shall not surely die. The greater part it seems believed him and went to destruction. So it was with Sodom and Gomorrah. Lot preached to them; the substance of which was, up, get ye out of this place, for the Lord will destroy this city. Gen. 19:14. But this old declaimer told them, no danger, no danger, ye shall not surely die. To which they generally gave heed, and Lot seemed to them as one who mocked; they believed the universal preacher, and were consumed. Agreeably to the declaration of the apostle Jude, Sodom and Gomorrah and the cities about them, suffering the vengeance of eternal fire.

II. Let us attend to the doctrine inculcated by this preacher; ye shall not surely die. Bold assertion! without a single argument to support it. The death contained in the threatening was doubtless eternal death,— as nothing but this would express God's feelings towards sin, or render an infinite atonement necessary. To suppose it to be spiritual death, is to blend crime and punishment together; to suppose temporal death to be the curse of the law, then believers are not delivered from it, according to Gal. 3:13. What Satan meant to preach, was that there is no hell, and that the wages of sin is not death, but eternal life.

III. We shall now take notice of the hearer addressed by the preacher. This we have in the text, And the serpent said unto the woman, etc. That Eve had not so much experience as Adam, is evident; and so was not equally able to withstand temptation. This doubtless was the reason why the devil chose her, with whom he might hope to be successful. Doubtless he took a time when she was separated from her husband.

That this preacher has had the greatest success in the dark and ignorant parts of the earth, is evident: his kingdom is a kingdom of darkness. He is a great enemy to light. St. Paul gives us some account of him in his day, 2 Tim. 3:6. For of this sort are they which creep into houses, and lead captive silly women, laden with sin led away with divers lusts. The same apostle observes, Rom. 16:17, 18. Now I beseech you, brethren, mark them which cause divisions and offences, contrary to the doctrine which ye have learned, and avoid them. For they that are such serve not the Lord Jesus Christ, but their own belly; and by good words and fair speeches deceive the simple.

IV. The instrument or medium made use of by the preacher will now be considered. This we have in the text: And the serpent said etc. But how came the devil to preach through the serpent?

1. To save his own character, and the better to carry his point. Had the devil come to our first parents personally and unmasked, they would have more easily seen the deception. The reality of a future punishment is at times so clearly impressed on the human mind, that even Satan is constrained to own that there is a hell; altho' at other times he denies it. He does not wish to have it known that he is a liar; therefore he conceals himself, that he may the better accomplish his designs, and save his own character.

2. The devil is an enemy to all good, to all happiness and excellence. He is opposed to the felicity of the brutes. He took delight in tormenting the swine. The serpent, before he set up preaching Universal Salvation, was a cunning, beautiful, and happy creature; but now his glory is departed; for the Lord said unto the serpent, because thou hast done this, thou art cursed above all cattle, and above every beast of the field, upon thy belly shalt thou go, and dust shalt thou eat all the days of thy life. There is therefore, a kind of duplicate cunning in the matter, Satan gets the preacher and hearers also.

> *And is not this triumphant flattery,*
> *And more than simple conquest in the foe?*
>
> *Young*

3. Another reason why Satan employs instruments in his service is, because his empire is large and he cannot be every where himself.

4. He has a large number at his command, that love and approve of his work, delight in building up his kingdom, and stand ready to go at his call.

Inferences

1. The devil is not dead, but still lives; and is able to preach as well as ever, ye shall not surely die.

2. Universal Salvation is no new fangled scheme, but can boast of great antiquity.
3. See a reason why it ought to be rejected, because it is an ancient devilish doctrine.
4. See one reason why it is that Satan is such an enemy to the Bible, and to all who preach the gospel, because of that injunction, And he said unto them, go ye into all the world, and preach the gospel to every creature. He that believeth and is baptized shall be saved; but he that believeth not shall be damned.
5. See whence it was that Satan exerted himself so much to convince our first parents that there was no hell; because the denunciation of the Almighty was true, and he was afraid they would continue in the belief of it. Was there no truth in future punishment, or was it only a temporary evil, Satan would not be so busy, in trying to convince men that there is none. It is his nature and his element to lie. When he speaketh a lie, he speaketh of his own; for he is a liar, and the father of it.
6. We infer that ministers should not be proud of their preaching. If they preach the true gospel, they only, in substance, repeat Christ's sermons; if they preach ye shall not surely die, they only make use of the devil's old notes, that he delivered almost six thousand years ago.
7. It is probable that the doctrine of Universal Salvation will still prevail, since this preacher is yet alive, and not in the least superannuated; and every effort against him only enrages him more and more, and excites him to new inventions and exertions to build up his cause.

To close the subject: As the author of the foregoing discourse has confined himself wholly to the character of Satan, he trusts no one will feel himself personally injured by this short sermon: But should any imbibe a degree of friendship for this aged divine, and think that I have not treated this Universal Preacher with that respect and veneration which he justly deserves, let them be so kind as to point it out, and I will most cheerfully retract; for it has ever been a maxim with me, render unto all their dues.

The following Hymn, taken from the Theological Magazine, was repeated after the delivery of the preceding discourse.

A late writer in favor of Universal Salvation, having closed his piece with these lines of Pope's Messiah:

> The seas shall waste, the skies in smoke decay,
> Rocks fall to dust, and mountains melt away;
> But fix'd his word, his saving pow'r remains,
> Thy realm forever lasts, thy own Messiah reigns.

His antagonist made the following addition to them:

Universalism Indeed.

"When seas shall waste, and skies in smoke decay,
Rocks fall to dust, and mountains melt away;
In adamantine chains shall death be bound,
And hell's grim tyrant feel th' eternal wound."

But all his children reach fair Eden's shore,
Not e'er to see their father Satan more.
The tot'ring drunkard shall to glory reel,
And common strumpets endless pleasure feel.

Blest are the haughty who despise the poor,
For they're entitled to the heav'nly store:
Blest all who laugh and scoff at truth divine,
For bold revilers endless glories shine.

Blest are the clam'rous and contentious crew,
To them eternal rest and peace is due:
Blest all who hunger and who thirst to find,
A chance to plunder and to cheat mankind,
Such die in peace—for God to them has giv'n,

To be unjust on earth, and go to Heav'n:
Blest is the wretch whose bowels never move,
With gen'rous pity or with tender love;

He shall find mercy from the God above.
Blest all who seek to wrangle or to fight,
Such mount from seas of blood to worlds of light:
Go riot, drink, and every ill pursue,
For joys eternal are reserv'd for you;
Fear not to sin, till death shall close your eyes;
Live as you please, yours is th'immortal prise.
Old serpent hail! thou mad'st a just reply
To mother Eve, "ye shall not surely die!"

But reader stop! and in God's holy fear,
With sacred truth, these tenets first compare;
Our Saviour's sermon on the mount peruse—
Read with attention, and the bane refuse!■

8 ABOLITION OF THE SLAVE TRADE

Peter Williams, Jr.

At the Constitutional Convention in 1787, the delegates agreed that no law could be passed prohibiting the African slave trade until the first day of 1808. On December 2, 1806, President Thomas Jefferson, responding to the pressure of antislavery forces in the United States, among whom free blacks were especially active, urged Congress to outlaw the external slave trade, and on March 2, 1807, a bill to that end was passed, with the prohibition to become effective on January 1, 1808 (England abolished its traffic in slaves on March 25, 1807). Weak enforcement of the law, however, prevented total abolition of the slave trade in America for many years.

African Americans throughout the North celebrated the closing of the African slave trade. In New York City, the Reverend Peter Williams, Jr. (1780?–1840), son of one of the founders of the African Methodist Episcopal Zion Church, delivered an address in the New York African Church hailing the abolition of the slave trade.

Williams had been educated at the New York African Free School and later tutored by Episcopalian clergy. He was licensed as a lay reader in 1812 and led the drive to establish a separate black Episcopalian church. On July 3, 1819, St. Philip's African Church was consecrated, and seven years later, Williams was ordained as its priest. His congregation included such future leaders as Alexander Crummell and James McCune Smith. Williams was a leader of the New York black community and an ardent campaigner for the extension of full citizenship rights to African Americans. He was a cofounder of the first black-edited U.S. newspaper, Freedom's Journal, *in 1827 and of various mutual aid and educational programs.*

Williams's denunciation of the slave trade sometimes relies upon strategies problematic for modern readers. He portrays African people and society before the slave trade as simple, uncivilized, and content. But Wiliams's re-creation of the destruction of Africa is powerful and moving, and he draws upon the living memories of his audience to "bring to view these scenes of bitter grief." Williams celebrates the abolition of the slave trade as testimony to the power of the ideas expressed in the Declaration of Independence.

The text of the address is taken from Peter Williams—An Oration on the Abolition of the Slave Trade; Delivered in the African Church, in the City of New York, January 1, 1808 *(New York, 1808).*

Fathers, Brethren, and Fellow Citizens: At this auspicious moment I felicitate you on the abolition of the Slave Trade. This inhuman branch of commerce, which, for some centuries past, has been carried on to a considerable extent, is, by the singular interposition of Divine Providence, this day extinguished. An event so important, so pregnant with happy consequences, must be extremely consonant to every philanthropic heart.

But to us, Africans and descendants of Africans, this period is deeply interesting. We have felt, sensibly felt, the sad effects of this abominable traffic. It has made, if not ourselves, our forefathers and kinsmen its unhappy victims; and pronounced on them, and their posterity, the sentence of perpetual slavery. But benevolent men have voluntarily stepped forward to obviate the consequences of this injustice and barbarity. They have striven assiduously, to restore our natural rights; to guaranty them from fresh innovations; to furnish us with necessary information; and to stop the source from whence our evils have flowed.

The fruits of these laudable endeavors have long been visible; each moment they appear more conspicuous; and this day has produced an event which shall ever be memorable and glorious in the annals of history. We are now assembled to celebrate this momentous era; to recognize the beneficial influences of humane exertions; and by suitable demonstrations of joy, thanksgiving, and gratitude, to return to our heavenly Father, and to our earthly benefactors, our sincere acknowledgments.

Review, for a moment, my brethren, the history of the Slave Trade. Engendered in the foul recesses of the sordid mind, the unnatural monster inflicted gross evils on the human race. Its baneful footsteps are marked with blood; its infectious breath spreads war and desolation; and its train is composed of the complicated miseries of cruel and unceasing bondage.

Before the enterprising spirit of European genius explored the western coast of Africa, the state of our forefathers was a state of simplicity, innocence, and contentment. Unskilled in the arts of dissimulation, their bosoms were the seats of confidence; and their lips were the organs of truth. Strangers to the refinements of civilized society, they followed with implicit obedience the (simple) dictates of nature. Peculiarly observant of hospitality, they offered a place of refreshment to the weary, and an asylum to the unfortunate. Ardent in their affections, their minds were susceptible of the warmest emotions of love, friendship, and gratitude.

Although unacquainted with the diversified luxuries and amusements of civilized nations, they enjoyed some singular advantages from the bountiful hand of nature and from their own innocent and amiable manners, which rendered them a happy people. But alas! this delightful picture has long since vanished; the angel of bliss has deserted their dwelling; and the demon of indescribable misery has rioted, uncontrolled, on the fair fields of our ancestors.

After Columbus unfolded to civilized man the vast treasures of this western world, the desire of gain, which had chiefly induced the first colonists of America to cross the waters of the Atlantic, surpassing the bounds of reasonable acquisition, violated the sacred injunctions of the gospel, frustrated the designs of the pious and humane, and enslaving the harmless aborigines, compelled them to drudge in the mines.

The severities of this employment was so insupportable to men who were unaccustomed to fatigue that, according to Robertson's "History of America," upwards of nine hundred thousand were destroyed in the space of fifteen years on the island of Hispaniola. A consumption so rapid must, in a short period, have deprived them of the instruments of labor, had not the same genius which first produced it found out another method to obtain them. This was no other than the importation of slaves from the coast of Africa.

The Genoese made the first regular importation, in the year 1517, by virtue of a patent granted by Charles of Austria to a Flemish favorite; since which, this commerce has increased to an astonishing and almost incredible degree.

After the manner of ancient piracy, descents were first made on the African coast; the towns bordering on the ocean were surprised, and a number of the inhabitants carried into slavery.

Alarmed at these depredations, the natives fled to the interior, and there united to secure themselves from the common foe. But the subtle invaders were not easily deterred from their purpose. Their experience, corroborated by historical testimony, convinced them that this spirit of unity would baffle every violent attempt; and that the most powerful method to dissolve it would be to diffuse in them the same avaricious disposition which they themselves possessed; and to afford them the means of gratifying it, by ruining each other. Fatal engine: fatal thou hast proved to man in all ages: where the greatest violence has proved ineffectual, their undermining principles have wrought destruction. By the deadly power, the strong Grecian arm, which bid the world defiance, fell nerveless; by thy potent attacks, the solid pillars of Roman grandeur shook to their base; and, Oh! Africans! by this parent of the Slave Trade, this grandsire of misery, the mortal blow was struck which crushed the peace and happiness of our country. Affairs now assumed a different aspect; the appearances of war were changed into the most amicable pretensions; presents apparently inestimable were made; and all the bewitching and alluring wiles of the seducer were practiced. The harmless African, taught to believe a friendly countenance, the sure token of a corresponding heart, soon disbanded his fears and evinced a favorable disposition towards his flattering enemies.

Thus the foe, obtaining an intercourse by a dazzling display of European finery, bewildered their simple understandings and corrupted their morals. Mutual agreements were then made; the Europeans were to supply the Africans with those gaudy trifles which so strongly affected them; and the Africans in return were to grant the Europeans their prisoners of war and convicts as slaves. These stipulations, naturally tending to delude the mind, answered the twofold purpose of enlarging their criminal code and of exciting incessant war at the same time that it furnished a specious pretext for the prosecution of this inhuman traffic. Bad as this may appear, had it prescribed the bounds of injustice, millions of unhappy victims might have still been spared. But, extending widely beyond measure and without control, large additions of slaves were made by kidnapping and the most unpalliated seizures.

Trace the past scenes of Africa and you will manifestly perceive these flagrant violations of human rights. The prince who once delighted in the happiness of his people, who felt himself bound by a sacred contract to defend their persons and property, was turned into their tyrant and scourge: he, who once strove to preserve peace and good understanding with the different nations, who never unsheathed his sword but in the cause of justice, at the signal of a slave ship assembled his warriors and rushed furiously upon his unsuspecting friends. What a scene does that town now present, which a few moments past was the abode of tranquillity. At the approach of the foe, alarm and confusion pervade every part; horror and dismay are depicted on every countenance; the aged chief, starting from his couch, calls forth his men to repulse the hostile invader: all ages obey the summons; feeble youth and decrepit age join the standard; while the foe, to effect his purpose, fires the town.

Now, with unimaginable terror the battle commences: hear now the shrieks of the women, the cries of the children, the shouts of the warriors, and the groans of the dying. See with what desperation the inhabitants fight in defense of their darling joys. But, alas! overpowered by a superior foe, their force is broken; their ablest warriors fall; and the wretched remnant are taken captives.

Where are now those pleasant dwellings, where peace and harmony reigned incessant? where those beautiful fields, whose smiling crops and enchanting verdure enlivened the heart of every beholder? Alas! those tenements are now enveloped in destructive flames; those fair fields are now bedewed with blood and covered with mangled carcasses. Where are now those sounds of mirth and gladness, which loudly rang throughout the village? where those darling youth, those venerable aged, who mutually animated the festive throng? Alas! those exhilarating peals are now changed into the dismal groans of inconceivable distress; the survivors of those happy people are now carried into cruel captivity. Ah! driven from their native soil, they cast their languishing eyes behind, and with aching hearts bid adieu to every prospect of joy and comfort.

A spectacle so truly distressing is sufficient to blow into a blaze the most latent spark of humanity; but, the adamantine heart of avarice, dead to every sensation of pity, regards not the voice of the sufferers, but hastily drives them to market for sale.

Oh Africa, Africa! to what horrid inhumanities have thy shores been witness; thy shores, which were once the garden of the world, the seat of almost paradisiacal joys, have been transformed into regions of woe; thy sons, who were once the happiest of mortals, are reduced to slavery, and bound in weighty shackles, now fill the trader's ship. But, though defeated in the contest for liberty, their magnanimous souls scorn the gross indignity, and choose death in preference to slavery. Painful; ah! painful, must be that existence which the rational mind can deliberately doom to self-destruction.

Thus the poor Africans, robbed of every joy, while they see not the most transient, glimmering, ray of hope to cheer their saddened hearts, sink into the abyss of consummate misery. Their lives, embittered by reflection, anticipation, and present sorrows, they feel burthensome; and death (whose dreary mansions appall the stoutest hearts) they view as their only shelter.

You, my brethren, beloved Africans, who had passed the days of infancy when you left your country, you best can tell the aggravated sufferings of our unfortunate race; your memories can bring to view these scenes of bitter grief. What, my brethren, when dragged from your native land on board the slave ship, what was the anguish which you saw, which you felt? what the pain, what the dreadful forebodings which filled your throbbing bosoms?

But you, my brethren, descendants of African forefathers, I call upon you to view a scene of unfathomable distress. Let your imagination carry you back to former days. Behold a vessel, bearing our forefathers and brethren from the place of their nativity to a distant and inhospitable clime; behold their dejected countenances, their streaming eyes, their fettered limbs; hear them, with piercing cries, and pitiful moans, deploring their wretched fate. After their arrival in port, see them separated without regard to the ties of blood or friendship: husband from wife; parent from child; brother from sister; friend from friend. See the parting tear rolling down their fallen cheeks; hear the parting sigh die on their quivering lips.

But let us no longer pursue a theme of boundless affliction. An enchanting sound now demands your attention. Hail! hail! glorious day, whose resplendent rising disperseth the clouds which have hovered with destruction over the land of Africa, and illumines it by the most brilliant rays of future prosperity. Rejoice, Oh! Africans! No longer shall tyranny, war, and injustice, with irresistible sway, desolate your native country; no longer shall torrents of human blood deluge its delightful plains; no longer shall it witness your countrymen wielding among each other the instruments of death; nor the insidious kidnapper, darting from his midnight haunt, on the feeble and unprotected; no longer shall its shores resound with the awful howlings of infatuated warriors, the deathlike groans of vanquished innocents, nor the clanking fetters of woe-doomed captives. Rejoice, Oh, ye descendants of Africans! No longer shall the United States of America, nor the extensive colonies of Great Britain, admit the degrading commerce of the human species; no longer shall they swell the tide of African misery by the importation of slaves. Rejoice, my brethren, that the channels are obstructed through which slavery, and its direful concomitants, have been entailed on the African race. But let incessant strains of gratitude be mingled with your expressions of joy. Through the infinite mercy of the great Jehovah, this day announces the abolition of the Slave Trade. Let, therefore, the heart that is warmed by the smallest drop of African blood glow in grateful transports, and cause the lofty arches of the sky to reverberate eternal praise to his boundless goodness.

Oh, God! we thank Thee, that thou didst condescend to listen to the cries of Africa's wretched sons, and that Thou didst interfere in their behalf.

At Thy call humanity sprang forth and espoused the cause of the oppressed; one hand she employed in drawing from their vitals the deadly arrows of injustice; and the other in holding a shield, to defend them from fresh assaults; and at that illustrious moment, when the sons of '76 pronounced these United States free and independent; when the spirit of patriotism erected a temple sacred to liberty; when the inspired voice of Americans first uttered those noble sentiments, "We hold these truths to be self-evident, that all men are created equal; that they are endowed by their Creator with certain unalienable rights; among which are life, liberty, and the pursuit of happiness"; and when the bleeding African, lifting his fetters, exclaimed, "Am I not a man and a brother"; then, with redoubled efforts, the angel of humanity strove to restore to the African race the inherent rights of man.

To the instruments of divine goodness, those benevolent men who voluntarily obeyed the dictates of humanity, we owe much. Surrounded with innumerable difficulties, their undaunted spirits dared to oppose a powerful host of interested men. Heedless to the voice of fame, their independent souls dared to oppose the strong gales of popular prejudice. Actuated by principles of genuine philanthropy, they dared to despise the emoluments of ill-gotten wealth, and to sacrifice much of their temporal interests at the shrine of benevolence.

As an American, I glory in informing you that Columbia boasts the first men who distinguished themselves eminently in the vindication of our rights and the improvement of our state.

Conscious that slavery was unfavorable to the benign influences of Christianity, the pious Woolman* loudly declaimed against it; and, although destitute of fortune, he resolved to spare neither time nor pains to check its progress. With this view he traveled over several parts of North America on foot and exhorted his brethren, of the denomination of Friends, to abjure the iniquitous custom. These, convinced by the cogency of his arguments, denied the privileges of their society to the slaveholder, and zealously engaged in destroying the aggravated evil. Thus, through the beneficial labors of this pattern of piety and brotherly kindness, commenced a work which has since been promoted by the humane of every denomination. His memory ought therefore to be deeply engraven on the tablets of our hearts; and ought ever to inspire us with the most ardent esteem.

Nor less to be prized are the useful exertions of Anthony Benezet.† This inestimable person, sensible of the equality of mankind, rose superior to the illiberal opinions of the age; and, disallowing an inferiority in the African genius, established the first school to cultivate our understandings and to better our condition.

Thus, by enlightening the mind and implanting the seeds of virtue, he

---

*John Woolman (1720–1772) was a Quaker and tailor in Mt. Holly, New Jersey, who devoted most of his life to the campaign against slavery through his writings and sermons.

†Benezet (1713–1784) was a Philadelphia Quaker, schoolteacher, and antislavery campaigner.

banished, in a degree, the mists of prejudice, and laid the foundations of our future happiness. Let, therefore, a due sense of his meritorious actions ever create in us a deep reverence of his beloved name. Justice to the occasion, as well as his merits, forbid me to pass in silence over the name of the honorable William Wilberforce. Possessing talents capable of adorning the greatest subjects, his comprehensive mind found none more worthy his constant attention than the abolition of the slave trade. For this he soared to the zenith of his towering eloquence, and for this he struggled with perpetual ardour. Thus, anxious in defense of our rights, he pledged himself never to desert the cause; and, by his repeated and strenuous exertions, he finally obtained the desirable end. His extensive services have, therefore, entitled him to a large share of our affections, and to a lasting tribute of our unfeigned thanks.

But think not, my brethren, that I pretend to enumerate the persons who have proved our strenuous advocates, or that I have portrayed the merits of those I have mentioned. No, I have given but a few specimens of a countless number, and no more than the rude outlines of the beneficence of these. Perhaps there never existed a human institution which has displayed more intrinsic merit than the societies for the abolition of slavery.

Reared on the pure basis of philanthropy, they extend to different quarters of the globe, and comprise a considerable number of humane and respectable men. These, greatly impressed with the importance of the work, entered into it with such disinterestedness, engagedness, and prudence, as does honor to their wisdom and virtue. To effect the purposes of these societies no legal means were left untried which afforded the smallest prospects of success. Books were disseminated, and discourses delivered, wherein every argument was employed which the penetrating mind could adduce from religion, justice or reason, to prove the turpitude of slavery, and numerous instances related calculated to awaken sentiments of compassion. To further their charitable intentions, applications were constantly made to different bodies of legislature, and every concession improved to our best possible advantage. Taught by preceding occurrences, that the waves of oppression are ever ready to overwhelm the defenseless, they became the vigilant guardians of all our reinstated joys. Sensible that the inexperienced mind is greatly exposed to the allurements of vice, they cautioned us, by the most salutary precepts and virtuous examples, against its fatal encroachments; and the better to establish us in the paths of rectitude they instituted schools to instruct us in the knowledge of letters and the principles of virtue.

By these and similar methods, with divine assistance they assailed the dark dungeon of slavery; shattered its rugged wall, and enlarging thousands of the captives, bestowed on them the blessings of civil society. Yes, my brethren, through their efficiency, numbers of us now enjoy the invaluable gem of liberty; numbers have been secured from a relapse into bondage, and numbers have attained a useful education.

I need not, my brethren, take a further view of our present circumstances, to convince you of the providential benefits which we have derived from our patrons; for if you take a retrospect of the past situation of Africans, and descendants of Africans, in this and other countries, to your observation our advancements must be obvious. From these considerations, added to the happy event which we now celebrate, let ever entertain the profoundest veneration for our munificent benefactors, and return to them from the altars of our hearts the fragrant incense of incessant gratitude. But let not, my brethren, our demonstrations of gratitude be confined to the mere expressions of our lips.

The active part which the friends of humanity have taken to ameliorate our sufferings has rendered them, in a measure, the pledges of our integrity. You must be well aware that notwithstanding their endeavors, they have yet remaining, from interest, and prejudice, a number of opposers. These, carefully watching for every opportunity to injure the cause, will not fail to augment the smallest defects in our lives and conversation; and reproach our benefactors with them as the fruits of their actions.

Let us, therefore, by a steady and upright deportment, by a strict obedience and respect to the laws of the land, form an invulnerable bulwark against the shafts of malice. Thus, evincing to the world that our garments are unpolluted by the stains of ingratitude, we shall reap increasing advantages from the favors conferred; the spirits of our departed ancestors shall smile with complacency on the change of our state; and posterity shall exult in the pleasing remembrance.

May the time speedily commence when Ethiopia shall stretch forth her hands; when the sun of liberty shall beam resplendent on the whole African race; and its genial influences promote the luxuriant growth of knowledge and virtue.■

9 A THANKSGIVING SERMON

Absalom Jones

 Absalom Jones, the first African American priest of the Episcopal Church, was born in slavery on November 6, 1746, in Sussex, Delaware. At the age of sixteen, he was moved to Philadelphia, where he worked in his slaveholder's store. In the evenings, he attended school and did independent work for hire. By 1784, he was able to purchase his freedom and enter business for himself.

Along with Richard Allen, Jones became a lay preacher for the African American members of St. George's Methodist Episcopal Church. Under their ministry, black attendance increased to an extent that alarmed

the white clergy. One day in November 1787 Jones and other African American worshipers were pulled from their knees during prayers by a trustee of the church and were ordered to move to a segregated pew. Jones and the other black parishioners walked out of the church. Seven months later, Jones and Allen drafted the preamble for the Free African Society, a nondenominational religious and mutual aid organization. They began holding Sunday services in 1791 and soon after began to plan the construction of a church. The African Episcopal Church (St. Thomas's), a separate institution that was accepted in the Pennsylvania Diocese yet placed under the control of its African American members, was dedicated in 1794, with Absalom Jones as its licensed lay reader. He was ordained as deacon in 1794 and as priest in 1804.

Jones was a social and political activist who saw these concerns as inextricably related to the life of the church and to his role as minister. He was an ardent abolitionist and an early supporter of the black convention movement. In 1799, he drafted a petition, signed by seventy-three other African Americans, "to the President, Senate and House of Representatives" urging the immediate abolition of slavery.

On January 1, 1808, in Philadelphia's St. Thomas's African Episcopal Church, Jones delivered the following sermon, "On Account of the Abolition of the African Slave Trade." Jones's sermon, like many later African American texts, develops a parallel between American slavery and the bondage of the Jews in Egypt and Babylon. Just as God delivered the Jews from captivity, Jones reasons, so too will He intervene on behalf of black Americans. Jones argues that the suffering of blacks has been part of God's divine plan, designed to instruct and prepare them for holy work. He insists that African Americans must "publickly and privately" acknowledge "that an African slave, ready to perish, was our father or our grandfather." "Sermons like those of Jones," writes Carol George in Segregated Sabbaths, *"interpreted the past in terms of the present needs of the community; an example, perhaps, of a black hermeneutic" (166).*

The text of the speech was printed as a pamphlet and appears in Dorothy Porter, Early Negro Writing, 1760–1837 *(Boston: Beacon Press, 1971).*

E XODUS, iii. 7, 8: And the Lord said, I have surely seen the affliction of my people which are in Egypt, and have heard their cry by reason of their task-masters; for I know their sorrows; and I am come down to deliver them out of the hand of the Egyptians.

These words, my brethren, contain a short account of some of the circumstances which preceded the deliverance of the children of Israel from their captivity and bondage in Egypt.

They mention, in the first place, their affliction. This consisted in their privation of liberty: they were slaves to the kings of Egypt, in common with their other subjects; and they were slaves to their fellow slaves. They were compelled to work in the open air, in one of the hottest climates in the world; and, probably, without a covering from the burning rays of the sun. Their work was of a laborious kind: it consisted of making bricks, and travelling, perhaps to a great distance, for the straw, or stubble, that was a component part of them. Their work was dealt out to them in tasks, and performed under the eye of vigilant and rigorous masters, who constantly upbraided them with idleness. The least deficiency in the product of their labour, was punished by beating. Nor was this all. Their food was of the cheapest kind, and contained but little nourishment: it consisted only of leeks and onions, which grew almost spontaneously in the land of Egypt. Painful and distressing as these sufferings were, they constituted the smallest part of their misery. While the fields resounded with their cries in the day, their huts and hamlets were vocal at night with their lamentations over their sons; who were dragged from the arms of their mothers, and put to death by drowning, in order to prevent such an increase in their population as to endanger the safety of the state by an insurrection. In this condition, thus degraded and oppressed, they passed nearly four hundred years. Ah! who can conceive of the measure of their sufferings, during that time? What tongue, or pen, can compute the number of their sorrows? To them no morning or evening sun ever disclosed a single charm: to them, the beauties of spring, and the plenty of autumn had no attractions: even domestick endearments were scarcely known to them: all was misery; all was grief; all was despair.

Our text mentions, in the second place, that, in this situation, they were not forgotten by the God of their fathers, and the Father of the human race. Though, for wise reasons, he delayed to appear in their behalf for several hundred years, yet he was not indifferent to their sufferings. Our text tells us that he saw their affliction, and heard their cry: his eye and his ear were constantly open to their complaint: every tear they shed was preserved, and every groan they uttered was recorded, in order to testify, at a future day, against the authors of their oppressions. But our text goes further: it describes the judge of the world to be so much moved, with what he saw and what he heard, that he rises from his throne—not to issue a command to the armies of angels that surrounded him to fly to the relief of his suffering children—but to come down from heaven in his own person, in order to deliver them out of the hands of the Egyptians. Glory to God for this precious record of his power and goodness: let all the nations of the earth praise him. Clouds and darkness are round about him, but righteousness and judgment are the habitation of his throne. O sing unto the Lord a new song, for he hath done marvelous things: his right hand and his holy arm hath gotten him the victory. He hath remembered his mercy and truth toward the house of Israel, and all the ends of the earth shall see the salvation of God.

The history of the world shows us that the deliverance of the children of Israel from their bondage is not the only instance in which it has pleased God to appear in behalf of oppressed and distressed nations, as the deliverer of the innocent, and of those who call upon his name. He is as unchangeable in his nature and character as he is in his wisdom and power. The great and blessed event, which we have this day met to celebrate, is a striking proof that the God of heaven and earth is the same, yesterday, and today, and forever. Yes, my brethren, the nations from which most of us have descended, and the country in which some of us were born, have been visited by the tender mercy of the Common Father of the human race. He has seen the affliction of our countrymen, with an eye of pity. He has seen the wicked arts, by which wars have been fomented among the different tribes of the Africans, in order to procure captives, for the purpose of selling them for slaves. He has seen ships fitted out from different ports in Europe and America, and freighted with trinkets to be exchanged for the bodies and souls of men. He has seen the anguish which has taken place when parents have been torn from their children, and children from their parents, and conveyed, with their hands and feet bound in fetters, on board of ships prepared to receive them. He has seen them thrust in crowds into the holds of those ships, where many of them have perished from the want of air. He has seen such of them as have escaped from that noxious place of confinement, leap into the ocean, with a faint hope of swimming back to their native shore, or a determination to seek an early retreat from their impending misery, in a watery grave. He has seen them exposed for sale, like horses and cattle, upon the wharves; or, like bales of goods, in warehouses of West India and American sea ports. He has seen the pangs of separation between members of the same family. He has seen them driven into the sugar, the rice, and the tobacco fields, and compelled to work—in spite of the habits of ease which they derived from the natural fertility of their own country—in the open air, beneath a burning sun, with scarcely as much clothing upon them as modesty required. He has seen them faint beneath the pressure of their labours. He has seen them return to their smoky huts in the evening, with nothing to satisfy their hunger but a scanty allowance of roots; and these, cultivated for themselves, on that day only, which God ordained as a day of rest for man and beast. He has seen the neglect with which their masters have treated their immortal souls; not only in withholding religious instruction from them, but, in some instances, depriving them of access to the means of obtaining it. He has seen all the different modes of torture, by means of the whip, the screw, the pincers, and the red-hot iron, which have been exercised upon their bodies, by inhuman overseers: overseers, did I say? Yes: but not by these only. Our God has seen masters and mistresses, educated in fashionable life, sometimes take the instruments of torture into their own hands, and, deaf to the cries and shrieks of their agonizing slaves, exceed even their overseers in cruelty. Inhuman wretches! though You have been deaf to their cries and shrieks, they have been heard in Heaven. The ears of Jehovah have been constantly open to them: He has heard the prayers that have ascended from the hearts of his people; and he has, as in the case of his ancient and chosen people the Jews, *come down to deliver* our suffering countrymen from the hands of their oppressors. He *came down* into the United States, when they declared, in the constitution which they framed in 1788, that the trade in our African fellowmen should cease in the year 1808: He *came down* into the British Parliament, when they passed a law to put an end to the same iniquitous trade in May, 1807: He *came down* into the Congress of the United States, the last winter, when they passed a similar law, the operation of which commences on this happy day. Dear land of our ancestors! thou shalt no more be stained with the blood of thy children, shed by British and American hands: the ocean shall no more afford a refuge to their bodies, from impending slavery: nor shall the shores of the British West India islands, and of the United States, any more witness the anguish of families, parted for ever by a publick sale. For this signal interposition of the God of mercies, in behalf of our brethren, it becomes us this day to offer our united thanks. Let the song of angels, which was first heard in the air at the birth of our Savior, be heard this day in our assembly: Glory to God in the highest, for these first fruits of peace upon earth, and good-will to man: O! let us give thanks unto the Lord: let us call upon his name, and make known his deeds among the people. Let us sing psalms unto him and talk of all his wonderous works.

Having enumerated the mercies of God to our nation, it becomes us to ask, What shall we render unto the Lord for them? Sacrifices and burnt offerings are no longer pleasing to him: the pomp of public worship, and the ceremonies of a festive day, will find no acceptance with him, unless they are accompanied with actions that correspond with them. The duties which are inculcated upon us, by the event we are now celebrating, divide themselves into five heads.

In the first place, Let not our expressions of gratitude to God for his late goodness and mercy to our countrymen, be confined to this day, nor to this house: let us carry grateful hearts with us to our places of abode, and to our daily occupations; and let praise and thanksgivings ascend daily to the throne of grace, in our families, and in our closets, for what God has done for our African brethren. Let us not forget to praise him for his mercies to such of our colour as are inhabitants of this country; particularly, for disposing the hearts of the rulers of many of the states to pass laws for the abolition of slavery; for the number and zeal of the friends he has raised up to plead our cause; and for the privileges we enjoy, of worshiping God agreeably to our consciences, in churches of our own. This comely building, erected chiefly by the generosity of our friends, is a monument of God's goodness to us, and calls for our gratitude with all the other blessings that have been mentioned.

Secondly, Let us unite, with our thanksgiving, prayer to Almighty God, for the completion of his begun goodness to our brethren in Africa. Let us beseech him to extend to all the nations in Europe, the same humane and just spirit towards them, which he has imparted to the British and American nations. Let us, further, implore the influences of his divine and holy Spirit, to dispose the hearts of our legislatures to pass laws, to ameliorate the condition of our brethren who are still in bondage; also, to dispose their masters to treat them with kindness and humanity; and, above all things, to favour them with the means of acquiring such parts of human knowledge, as will enable them to read the holy scriptures, and understand the doctrines of the Christian religion, whereby they may become, even while they are the slaves of men, the freemen of the Lord.

Thirdly, Let us conduct ourselves in such a manner as to furnish no cause of regret to the deliverers of our nation, for their kindness to us. Let us constantly remember the rock whence we were hewn, and the pit whence we were digged. Pride was not made for man, in any situation; and, still less, for persons who have recently emerged from bondage. The Jews, after they entered the promised land, were commanded, when they offered sacrifices to the Lord, never to forget their humble origin; and hence, part of the worship that accompanied their sacrifices consisted in acknowledging, that a Syrian, ready to perish, was their father: in like manner, it becomes us, publickly and privately, to acknowledge, that an African slave, ready to perish, was our father or our grandfather. Let our conduct be regulated by the precepts of the gospel; let us be sober-minded, humble, peaceable, temperate in our meats and drinks, frugal in our apparel and in the furniture of our houses, industrious in our occupations, just in all our dealings, and ever ready to honour all men. Let us teach our children the rudiments of the English language, in order to enable them to acquire a knowledge of useful trades; and, above all things, let us instruct them in the principles of the gospel of Jesus Christ, whereby they may become wise unto salvation. It has always been a mystery, why the impartial Father of the human race should have permitted the transportation of so many millions of our fellow creatures to this country, to endure all the miseries of slavery. Perhaps his design was that a knowledge of the gospel might be acquired by some of their descendants, in order that they might become qualified to be the messengers of it, to the land of their fathers. Let this thought animate us, when we are teaching our children to love and adore the name of our Redeemer. Who knows but that a Joseph may rise up among them, who shall be the instrument of feeding the African nations with the bread of life, and of saving them, not from earthly bondage, but from the more galling yoke of sin and Satan.

Fourthly, Let us be grateful to our benefactors, who, by enlightening the minds of the rulers of the earth, by means of their publications and remonstrances against the trade in our countrymen, have produced the great event we are this day celebrating. Abolition societies and individuals have equal claims to our gratitude. It would be difficult to mention the names of any of our benefactors, without offending many whom we do not know. Some of them are gone to heaven, to receive the reward of their labours of love towards us; and the kindness and benevolence of the survivors, we hope, are recorded in the book of life, to be mentioned with honour when our Lord shall come to reward his faithful servants before an assembled world.

Fifthly, and lastly, Let the first of January, the day of the abolition of the slave trade in our country, be set apart in every year, as a day of publick thanksgiving for that mercy. Let the history of the sufferings of our brethren, and of their deliverance, descend by this means to our children to the remotest generations; and when they shall ask, in time to come, saying, What mean the lessons, the psalms, the prayers and the praises in the worship of this day? let us answer them, by saying, the Lord, on the day of which this is the anniversary, abolished the trade which dragged your fathers from their native country, and sold them as bondmen in the United States of America.

Oh thou God of all the nations upon the earth! we thank thee, that thou art no respecter of persons, and that thou hast made of one blood all nations of men. We thank thee, that thou hast appeared, in the fullness of time, in behalf of the nation from which most of the worshipping people, now before thee, are descended. We thank thee, that the sun of righteousness has at last shed his morning beams upon them. Rend thy heavens, O Lord, and come down upon the earth; and grant that the mountains, which now obstruct the perfect day of thy goodness and mercy towards them, may flow down at thy presence. Send thy gospel, we beseech thee, among them. May the nations, which now sit in darkness, behold and rejoice in its light. May Ethiopia soon stretch out her hands unto thee, and lay hold of the gracious promise of thy everlasting covenant. Destroy, we beseech thee, all the false religions which now prevail among them; and grant, that they may soon cast their idols, to the moles and the bats of the wilderness. O, hasten that glorious time, when the knowledge of the gospel of Jesus Christ, shall cover the earth, as the waters cover the sea; when the wolf shall dwell with the lamb, and, the leopard shall lie down with the kid, and the calf and the young lion and the fatling together, and a little child shall lead them; and, when, instead of the thorn, shall come up the fir tree, and, instead of the brier, shall come up the myrtle tree: and it shall be to the Lord for a name and for an everlasting sign that shall not be cut off. We pray, O God, for all our friends and benefactors in Great Britain, as well as in the United States: reward them, we beseech thee, with blessings upon earth, and prepare them to enjoy the fruits of their kindness to us, in the everlasting kingdom in heaven; and dispose us, who are assembled in thy presence, to be always thankful for thy mercies, and to act as becomes a people who owe so much to thy goodness. We implore thy blessing, O God, upon the President, and all who are in authority in the United States. Direct them by thy wisdom, in all their deliberations, and O save thy people from the calamities of war. Give peace in our day, we beseech thee, O thou God of peace! and grant, that this highly favoured country may continue to afford a safe and peaceful retreat from the calamities of war and slavery, for ages yet to come. We implore all these blessings and mercies, only in the name of thy beloved Son, Jesus Christ, our Lord. And now, O Lord, we desire, with angels and arch-angels, and all the company of heaven, ever more to praise thee, saying, *Holy, holy, holy, Lord God* Almighty: *the whole earth is full of thy glory.* Amen.■

10 MUTUAL INTEREST, MUTUAL BENEFIT, AND MUTUAL RELIEF

William Hamilton

On January 1, 1809, New York African Americans held three separate celebrations of the first anniversary of the abolition of the
slave trade. "These 1809 celebrations were the high point," writes
Benjamin Quarles in Black Abolitionists. "Within three years the January 1 observances would be discontinued. For by then Negroes had unhappily taken note that the law prohibiting the foreign slave trade had
become almost a dead letter, being blatantly flouted" (119).

One of the primary orators of the occasion was William Hamilton
(1773–1836). President and cofounder of the New York Society for Mutual
Relief, Hamilton was a carpenter and leader of New York's black community, rumored to be the son of Secretary of the Treasury Alexander
Hamilton. Like many abolitionist orators, Hamilton makes explicit reference in his speech to the rhetorical paradox he faces: antislavery orators
must somehow acknowledge and raise awareness of the horrors of slavery, yet no words are adequate to do so: "Who can recount half their sufferings, where is the artist that can delineate a full picture of their miseries?" asks Hamilton. "Their wretched situation baffles description; let us
then withdraw from, and at once acknowledge our inability to the task."

Whatever its limitations, oratory is an act of great significance for
Hamilton. He addresses allegations of racial inferiority based on the supposed dearth of black poets, mathematicians, and scientists partly by
holding aloft a printed copy of orations presented by African Americans
(presumably including that of Peter Williams, Jr., who was seated in
Hamilton's audience) at the January 1, 1808, celebrations. "If we continue to produce specimens like these," he insists, "we shall soon put our
enemies to the blush; abashed and confounded they shall quit the field,
and no longer urge their superiority of souls."

Hamilton devotes the bulk of his address, presented in the Universal-
ist Church on January 2, 1809, to an explanation of the aims of the New
York African Society for Mutual Relief, an important and enduring institution designed to enlist African American support for mutual aid to widows, orphans, and the sick. A copy of Hamilton's address is in the Schomburg Collection of the New York Public Library.

My Brethren and Fellow Members of the New York African Society, for
Mutual Relief, I congratulate you on this first anniversary of a day
which has produced an event that, for its importance to Africans and descendants, stands unrivaled; an event that long and arduous have been the exer-

tions of many philanthropic characters to bring forth; an event that every benevolent mind rejoices to see. This day we are met with hearts big with gratitude, to celebrate an act of congress of the United States of America, which for its justice and humanity, outstrips any that have ever passed that honorable body; by an act bearing date March the second, eighteen hundred and seven, and which became an effectual law, January the first, eighteen hundred and eight, that species of commerce designated the slave trade was abolished.

This abominable traffic, the most execrable and inhuman that ever was practiced, had been carried on for olympiads and centuries, and the tide of misery flowing through this channel had arisen to an incalculable height. The wretched victims of the trade were not only deprived of life's first and most valuable jewel and best blessing, their liberty, not only were they torn from their native land, and all they held delightful and dear; but they were likewise doomed to pass through a train of as severe inflicted miseries as could be devised, such as at the bare recital of, the heart of sensibility sickens.

The country of our forefathers might truly be called paradise, or the seat of ease and pleasure, until the foul fiends entered—fiends did I say? yes, the name is too sacred an appellation for the base ravagers of the African coast: Until the man-stealing crew entered, peace may be said to be within her borders, and contentment in her dwelling, but the dealers in human flesh, not contented with setting the nations on to fierce, bloody, and incessant contests—not contented with making Africa groan from its sea line to its centre; but as if to be the more immediate instruments of cruelty, they obtain the captives taken in war, they kidnap thousands, they sever them from all their enjoyments! handcuff, brand, chain, clog, and scourge them, but why do we enumerate, who can recount half their sufferings, where is the artist that can delineate a full picture of their miseries—their wretched situation baffles description; let us then withdraw from, and at once acknowledge our inability to the task; but we stand confounded at the reflection that there should be found any of the human family so lost to their nature and the fine feelings of man, as to commit, unprovokedly commit, such acts of cruelty on an unoffending part of the human family.

But my Brethren, however this may be, it is for us to rejoice that the cause or source from whence these miseries sprang are removing; it is for us to rejoice not only that the sources of slavery are dying away, but that our condition is fast ameliorating; it is for us to rejoice that science has began to bud with our race, and soon shall our tree of arts bear its full burthen of rich and nectarious fruit, soon shall that contumelious assertion of the proud be proved false, to wit, that Africans do not possess minds as ingenious as other men.

The proposition has been advanced by men who claim a preeminence in the learned world, that Africans are inferior to white men in the structure both of body and mind; the first member of this proposition is below our notice; the reasons assigned for the second are that we have not produced any poets, mathematicians, or any to excel in any science whatever; our being oppressed and held in slavery forms no excuse, because, say they, among the Romans, their most excellent artists and greatest scientific characters were frequently slaves, and that these, on account of their ascendant abilities, arose to superior stations in the state; and they exultingly tell us that these slaves were white men.

My Brethren, it does not require a complete master to solve this problem, nor is it necessary in order (like good logicians) to meet this argument, that we should know which is the major and the minor proposition, and the middle and extreme terms of syllogism, he must be a willful novice and blind intentionally, who cannot unfold this enigma.

Among the Romans it was only necessary for the slave to be manumitted, in order to be eligible to all the offices of state, together with the emoluments belonging thereto; no sooner was he free than there was open before him a wide field of employment for his ambition and learning and abilities with merit, were as sure to meet with their reward in him, as in any other citizen. But what station above the common employment of craftsmen and labourers would we fill, did we possess both learning and abilities; is there aught to enkindle in us one spark of emulation: must not he who makes any considerable advances under present circumstances be almost a prodigy: although it may be true we have not produced any to excel in arts and sciences, yet if our situation be properly considered, and the allowances made which ought to be, it will soon be perceived that we do not fall far behind those who boast of a superior judgment, we have produced some who have claimed attention, and whose works have been admired, yes in despite of all our embarrassments our genius does sometimes burst forth from its incumbrance. Although the productions of Phillis Wheatly may not possess the requisitions necessary to stand the test of nice criticism, and she may be denied a stand in the rank of poets, yet does she possess some original ideas that would not disgrace the pen of the best poets.—Without naming others who have appeared in the interim of her and the present time, I hold in my hand a specimen of African genius; African I term it because in the position that the present argument is offered, it makes no kind of difference whether the man is born in Africa, Asia, Europe or America, so long as he is proginized from African parents.

This book contains an introductory address and an oration on the abolition of the slave trade, delivered in the African Church, the first of January eighteen hundred and eight, by two young men whom you are generally acquainted with: the address or frontispiece to the work is a flow of tasteful language, that would do credit to the best writers; the oration or primary work is not a run of eccentric vagaries, not now a sudden gust of passionate exclamation, and then as sudden calm and an inertness of expression, but a close adherence to the plane of the subject in hand, a warm and animating description of interesting scenes, together with an easy graceful style. If we continue to produce specimens like these, we shall soon put our enemies to the blush; abashed and confounded they shall quit the field, and no longer urge their superiority of souls.

You my Brethren have formed yourself into an association for the purpose of protecting each other from indigency, as far as in your power lies, conscious that deep poverty and distress is the bane of improvement, conscious, too, that our advancement in every point of view depends much on our being united in social bodies.

Man in the abstract is subject to almost every inconvenience that can be named, his hand is feeble, his sight short, his movements slow; but united with his fellow man he is strong, he is vigorous, he turns the channel of mighty rivers, throws down huge mountains, removes thick forests, builds great cities, pushes on the great machine of trade, his arm is next omnipotent, not only so he is formed for social life, the gloomy hermit we pity, and the snarling cynic we despise, these are men who appear to be rubbed off the list of men, they appear to have lost the fine fibres of the mind, on which it depends for expansion and growth, they appear to be sunk into a state of insensibility of the extreme happiness growing out of social life.

But my Brethren, mere socialities is not the object of our formation, but to improve the mind, soften the couch of the sick, to administer an elixir to the afflicted, to befriend the widow, and become the orphan's guardian, and is this not a noble employment, can there be found a better, you ought to be proud to be engaged in such an exercise. It is employment of this kind that raises the man up to the emperium, or highest heaven.—But in order that an association of this kind may appear to better advantage, let us take a view of the situation of man, precarious indeed, subject to continual vicissitudes.—This day strong and active, tomorrow, feeble and decripped, today healthful and vigourous, tomorrow lifeless and entombed. See the rich and lordly owner of a manor, now rolling in his gilded chariot, or now sitting beneath his stately dome, surrounded by his wife and children, his hall crowded with a retinue of servants, his fine-wrought board covered with costly viands and full-flowing bowls of delicious cordials, his walls revibrating with the loud cheer of convivial friends, his sun of bliss shines clear, not a cloud to intercept its rays, but suddenly storms and tempest arise, and thick clouds overspread his horizon, he is driven as by a torrent of misfortune, and as by a whirlwind his riches all flee away, and with them, as is common, flee his friends; he is turned from his stately dwelling to give room to some hard-hearted creditor, and from a reverse of fortune, now takes up his abode in some low hovel; But does the scenes of distress close here, he must not only suffer the mortification of his loss of property, friends, and pleasures, but he must likewise be subject of affliction and death, pale sickness astrides him, he is rid until his enfeebled body can sustain the pressure no longer, then Death, but oh! with what horror, what ghastly horror does he attack the man, Oh! Death thou cruel monster, thou does not appear half so dreadful when in the field of battle, where blood and carnage spread the ground, and where from the mouth of ordnance as from a vulcano fierce flaming fire issues forth, spreading destruction in every direction, or where the battle pushes on by furious leaders to the foul entrance of a fortress kept by tube behind tube, and thou Oh! Death, standing in dread array forwarning the presumptuous invader of his fate; or when the furious tempest howls, and the angry ocean convulsed to its low foundation, swells and lifts its head as to make war with heaven, and the fierce lightning's vivid flashes, darting from the clouds, accompanied with the loud roar of thunder, the affrighted mariner in his crazy bark, dished about from wave to wave, expecting momently the sea to be his tomb.—No, thou fell monster, thou does not appear half so terrible in scenes like these, as to the man about to be torn from his wife and children by thy cruel fangs; at thy approach his eyes start inward, his blood retreats back to its reservoir, an icy coldness takes possession of the vacuated parts of his body, he heaves a languishing look at his family, and with his cold quivering lips, feebly exclaims, oh! my family, most merciful God, what shall be the fate of my family, gracious heaven protect my wife—my children!

But my Brethren, are scenes of distress confined to the rich made indigent by misfortune, are they the only depressed by affliction; happy indeed were this the case, would it be for the human family, but the wretched of this class stand as a mere cypher compared with the poor of mankind, the labouring part of the community, who depend on their daily earnings for their substance, each winter brings to these its anxieties, but let affliction attack them when it may, it is sure to bring with it additional sorrows; here then arises the necessity of societies to lessen the miseries of mankind, to participate in their sorrows and to reciprocate joy and happiness as extensively as their mutual endeavours at relief will admit.

Happy for these United States that the spirit of Liberty, improvement, and philanthropy pervades the people; societies for the purpose of spreading useful knowledge, diffusing virtuous principles, or for ameliorating the condition of man are amply encouraged; this state, and particularly this city, has produced its full proportion of useful institutions; without naming a long list of excellent associations, I shall take the liberty to mention one to which we are extremely indebt, as Africans, and their descendants, I here mean the Manumission Society: this institution was established in or about the year one thousand seven hundred and eighty-four, by a number of gentlemen of the first respectability, who were strongly possessing the true spirit of patriotism, felt for the honor of their country; they saw that while the siren song of liberty and equality was sang through the land, that the groans of the oppressed made the music very discordant, and that America's fame was very much tarnished thereby; they were not contented with barely planning the means of the emancipation of large numbers of the enslaved, but they likewise established a seminary of learning, and so spirited were they in our cause, that in the year one thousand eight hundred, when, from the inadequacy of their funds to the accumulated expenses of the society, they had incurred a debt of twelve hundred dollars and upwards, the trustees of their school pledged themselves to each other to raise the just mentioned debt, by subscription, or defray the same from their own private funds.— Thou source of Benevolence, and first and main spring of all good actions, be not jealous of us, but next to thee, we owe to these men our highest tribute of gratitude, but to them as to thee, we can render nought but unprofitable thanks.

My Brethren, many and repeated attempts have been made in this city, to establish societies of various kinds among the people of colour, but whether from the impolicy of the plans, our unripeness for those institutions, we will not say, but they have always soon perished or dwindled away to a number so small as scarcely to deserve the name of society; whether this will be the case with this institution or not, remains for futurity to say; but if we may judge from appearances, we shall predict that its standing shall be long, and that the rays of its beneficence shall make the hearts of thousands of yet unborn members dilate by its cheering effulgence and effusions of benefits in seasons of sickness and distress.

This society has not been formed three quarters of a year, and the number of its members exceed by three times the number of any civil institution yet attempted among us.

The principles on which this institution is founded are congenial not only with the wish, but likewise with the interest of its members; its principles forbid the idea of its members becoming beggars to the society for relief in times of sickness, but it is the pledge, the agreement, and the duty of this institution to pay the sums specified by its Constitution to its sick members, and the widows and orphans of deceased members who have stood as such the limited time. So long as the principles of this society remain unchanged, so long shall its limbs remain unwithered and its trunk uncorrupted, its boughs shall never refuse to bear fruit for want of nutriment in the tree; never can you, my Brethren, be so infatuated as to shake off this institution, except by the over-persuasion of some foul daemon. Guard against the enemy, for enemies we have that would make merry at our overthrow; but above all things let our meetings be conducted with order and propriety, let order be our guide and peace our way mark; let friendship and good will be our atmosphere, be attentive to the sick members, never let it justly be said that we assumed the name of Mutual Relief for nought.

To you, my Brethren, the Standing Committee, let me address myself. Your's is truly an exalted station in which there is much confidence and trust reposed, with you rests the credit of this society, her fame shall spread through your vigilance, it is for you to immortalize her name by your active attention to the duties imposed on you; be then attentive to the sick members, and the widows and orphans of deceased members. If there should be found any one among you who should refuse to do his duty, let him be set aside as an unfit character to have such high trust reposed in him; but surely, my Brethren, there is not one of you who would be so forgetful of his honor and the solemn pledge he has given of the strict performance of the duties assigned him.

The other Officers are no less bounden and no less responsible, and in them is reposed equal trust, and from them is expected an equal attention to their duties.

Let us all be united, my Brethren, in rearing this edifice—steady to our several departments—and so on shall be raised a wide spreading dome that shall stand the admiration and praise of succeeding generations, and on its front shall be eternally engraven

> *MUTUAL INTEREST,*
> *MUTUAL BENEFIT,*
> *AND MUTUAL RELIEF.*∎

11 A SERMON PREACHED ON THE FUNERAL OCCASION OF MARY HENERY

George White

George White (1764–1836) was born in slavery in Accomack, Virginia, and had been sold twice by the age of six. After he was released from bondage by a dying slaveholder in the early 1780s, White spent several years in a futile search for his mother, then journeyed north to New York City. White converted to abolitionist Methodism but bridled at the church's segregationist practices and, with other black Methodists, left to build a separate church. In 1804, he felt the call to preach and served as an itinerant exhorter for black camp meetings in New Jersey and on Long Island, though he was repeatedly denied a license to preach by the white Methodist elders. He was finally approved in 1807 and appointed a deacon (the highest office then open to a black Methodist) in 1815. In 1820, he joined Richard Allen's breakaway Bethel African Methodist Episcopal Church.

Black preachers delivered tens of thousands of funeral sermons in the early republic, but very few have survived. In his autobiographical narrative, one of the first published by an African American, White includes the following text of a sermon delivered at the funeral of Mary Henery. White returned from a preaching tour of Long Island in 1809 to discover that Henery, an enslaved twenty-year-old whom White had converted at a New York camp meeting, was deathly ill and calling for him. "With loud shouts of joy and praise to God, White sat at Henery's bedside until

she died. "As God had made me instrumental in the awakening and con-
version of this young sister, and being present at her death," White
writes, "her parents requested me to preach her funeral sermon, the sub-
stance of which, at their desire, I shall here insert." It is in his funeral
sermon for Mary Henery, writes biographer Graham Russell Hodges, that
"White's theology is best expressed" (14). White exalts Henery as a
model of faith, repentance, self-denial, and chastity.

The speech text was published in A Brief Account of the Life, Experi-
ence, Travels and Gospel Labours of George White, An African *(New*
York: John C. Totten, 1810) and was reprinted and analyzed in Graham
Russell Hodges, ed., Black Itinerants of the Gospel: The Narratives of
John Jea and George White *(Madison, Wis.: Madison House, 1993).*

From *"Strive to enter in at the strait gate, for many I say unto you shall
seek to enter in, and shall not be able."* Luke xiii. 34

The occasion on which we are assembled this day, is truly solemn, interesting and alarming; being met together to pay our last respects to the
remains of our departed sister, who but recently filled her usual seat in this
house; and rejoiced, on all religious occasions, to unite with you, my brethren, in chanting the songs of Zion, with an heart filled with the love of
Christ, and exulting in the joys of his salvation.

But she is now no more: and though called to lament the loss of so worthy a member of the Church of Christ; yet we do not mourn as those without
hope, for, "Them that sleep in Jesus, God will bring with him," at the last
day; and our Saviour says, he "came to seek and save that which was lost:"
and in the chapter of which our text is a part, he intimates, that the chief
of sinners may be saved who will repent; by preaching the doctrine of repentance, from the circumstance of the Gallaleans, whose blood Pilate mingled
with their sacrifices; and that without repentance, none can be saved. But
this blessing our departed sister had no doubt attained, with whom we hope
to join in strains of immortal praise hereafter, when our bodies shall have
endured the original sentence denounced against us for sin, "Dust thou art,
and unto dust shalt thou return." For like her, through Jesus Christ we may
obtain victory over death, hell and the grave, by complying with the terms
of our text, which says "Strive to enter in at the strait gate, for many I say
unto you, shall seek to enter in, and shall not be able."*

From which I shall take the liberty briefly to shew,

First, What we are to understand by the strait gate, and how we are to
enter in thereat.

Secondly, Why it is called strait. And,

Thirdly, Who they are that shall seek to enter in, and shall not be able.
And,

I. I am to shew what we are to understand by the strait gate, and how

*Luke 13:24.

we are to enter in thereat. By their strait gate we are undoubtedly to understand, Jesus Christ himself, who has said, "I am the way, and the truth, and
the life; no man cometh unto the Father but by me." And again: "Strait is
the gate and narrow is the way that leadeth to life, and few there be that find
it." "I am," says he, "the door, by me if any man enter in he shall be saved,
and go in and out and find pasture."

Christ then being "the strait gate," and his doctrines the narrow way,
and himself the only door of admission to the favour of God, and salvation;
the scripture directs us how we are to enter in thereat, that is, by repentance,
and faith in the merits of the atonement he has made for sinners, by the once
offering of himself to God without spot.

By faith, then, we are to enter in at this gate: for although it is said,
"strive to enter in at the strait gate," yet we are to place no dependance upon
our labours or strivings; for we can do nothing effectual in our own salvation, only as far as we are assisted by the all-sufficient grace of God; for it
is written, "By grace are ye saved, through faith, and that not of yourselves,
it is the gift of God."*

Yet although our strivings alone cannot prove effectual to our salvation,
in this way, however, we must come to Christ, and receive him into our
hearts. Therefore, "Strive to enter in at the strait gate, for many I say unto
you shall seek to enter in, and shall not be able." But,

II. Why is this gate called strait? I answer: from the example Christ has
left us, that we should follow his steps, which is directly contrary to the
corruptions of our own natures; and because repentance and faith, by which
we must enter in thereat, are crossing, humbling and self-renouncing; in the
attainment of which, the soul is brought into great inward straits of fear,
terror and difficulty, but is always accompanied with hope of mercy, and followed with a revelation of Jesus Christ, as the all-sufficient Savior, to such
as commit the care of their souls to him, trusting in his mercy alone for
pardon and eternal salvation; and if adhered to, will lead to that eternal rest
of glory, which our departed sister this day enjoys, in the presence of God
and the Lamb. Therefore, "Strive to enter in at the strait gate, for many I say
unto you shall seek to enter in, and shall not be able."

I am 3dly, and lastly to shew, who they are that shall seek to enter in,
and shall not be able.

There is no impediment to our entering in at the strait gate, but what
originates in ourselves; for Christ has said, "He that cometh unto me, I will
no wise cast out:" and assigns it as the only reason why men are not saved,
that they will not come unto him, that they might have life. And they do
not come to Christ, because their hearts are opposed to his government, and
his ways too crossing to their carnal inclinations.

But says, the text, "Many shall seek to enter in, and shall not be able:"
either because they do not seek aright, or in good earnest, by forsaking all

*Ephesians 2:8.

their sins, resisting evil of every kind and degree; and by an agonizing, wrestling spirit, which refuses to be comforted, till Christ is formed in the heart the hope of glory.

Or lastly, because they seek too late; which is the reason Christ assigns in the words immediately following the text, "Strive to enter in at the strait gate, for many I say unto you shall seek to enter in, and shall not be able;" for, "When once the master of the house is risen up, and hath shut to the door, and ye begin to stand without, and to knock at the door, saying, Lord, Lord, open unto us; and he shall answer and say unto you, I know you not whence you are, depart from me all ye workers of iniquity." How sad the disappointment, to seek for mercy too late to find it; even at the hand of him, who now says, "Behold, I stand at the door and knock; if any man hear my voice, and will open the door, I will come in to him, and will sup with him, and he with me.[*]

Improvement.

Whoever would go to heaven then, must repent, and believe in Jesus Christ, who is the only door of salvation, the way, the truth, and the life; and as our Lord said to Nichodemus, must be born again, or they cannot see the kingdom of God: for except renewed by the grace of God, in the very nature of things, no man can be happy; for the very nature of sin prevents the enjoyment of God, the only source and fountain of all happiness; so that, whoever dies without being renewed, must meet the just reward of their ungodliness, in the awful day of judgment, when the secret of all hearts shall be revealed.

As this change of heart is called entering in at the strait gate, because it implies self-denial, mortification, self-renunciation, conviction and contrition for sin; and as all this is directly contrary to the dispositions of corrupt nature, it requires great and constant exertions, and mighty struggles of soul, under the influence of divine grace, to attain the blessing. For let none vainly imagine, that barely wiping their mouth will excuse them from damnation, or answer as a substitute for inward and outward holiness, in the great day of the wrath of God Almighty, when he shall come to judge the world in righteousness: therefore, "Seek ye the Lord while he may be found, call ye upon him while he is near: let the wicked forsake his way, and the unrighteous man his thoughts, and let him turn unto the Lord, who will have mercy upon him, and to our God, for he will abundantly pardon."[†]

And in this great and important work there is no time for delay; for life, the utmost extent of the day of grace, is uncertain; which is not only proved by the common occurrences of every day, but particularly by the instance of mortality which has occasioned our convention at this time; which speaks to you in the most pathetic language: "Be ye also ready, for in such an hour as ye think not the Son of man is risen up, and shut to the door, and ye begin

---

[*]Revelations 3:20.
[†]Isaiah 55:6–7.

to stand without, and to knock, saying, Lord, Lord, open unto us;" you will be only be answered with "depart from me all ye that work iniquity:" therefore now return unto the Lord from whom you have departed, by sincere repentance, that your souls may live. Secure a supply of the oil of grace; trim your lamps, and prepare to meet the bridegroom at his coming, that ye may enter in to the marriage supper of the Lamb, before the door of mercy is forever shut.

I see before me a large number of mourners, whose showering tears bespeak the anguish of heart excited by the death of her, whose relics we have so recently followed to the house appointed for all the living. But hush the heaving sigh, and dry the briny tear, for your deceased relative, and our much-loved Christian sister, has, no doubt, found a safe passage through the strait and narrow gate to the blissful regions of eternal day; where she now joins the Church triumphant, around the dazzling throne of God, in songs of praise and shouts of victory.

And while you, with the rest of the congregation, have the offers of mercy yet held out to you in the name of Jesus Christ, who stands knocking at the door of your hearts for entrance; embrace it, and bid him welcome, that you may be prepared when death shall call you hence, to join the jubelant throng with our departed sister, and chant the wonders of redeeming grace forever.

But to you, especially, who are in the bloom of youth, this instance of mortality calls aloud to prepare for death; remember your all is at stake; death is at your door, and will shortly summon you to appear at the bar of God, who will assuredly bring you into judgement for living after the desires of your own wicked hearts. Reflect then for a moment, how awful it will be to die in your sins, strangers to God, and meet the awful Judge of quick and dead, to hear the sentence pronounced upon your guilty souls, "Depart ye cursed into everlasting fire, prepared for the devil and his angels."* To avert this dreadful doom delay no longer; but now, even now, embrace the offers of mercy tendered to you by the gospel of Jesus Christ, and experience his great salvation.

And finally, brethren, let us all consider our ways, turn to the Lord, and strive to enter in at the strait gate, that we may not be found among the number of those, who by seeking too late, shall not be able to enter in; that when we are called to lie upon our death bed, we may have the same ravishing views of heaven, our departed sister had two days before her death, who said, she "saw heaven opened, and heard the saints in glory sing:" and like her, leave the world, crying glory! glory! glory! even so, Lord Jesus. Amen! and Amen!■

*Matthew 25:41.

12 O! AFRICA

William Hamilton

Hamilton's oration in observance of the seventh anniversary of the ostensible abolition of the U.S. slave trade was delivered on January 2, 1815, in the Episcopal Asbury African Church on Elizabeth Street in New York. The speech consists of three main sections, beginning with an evocation of the African past, prior to the onset of the slave trade. Ancient Africa is described as an idyllic and peaceful land, the "first fair garden of God's planting." From the African Eden, Hamilton argues, "fair science first descended and the arts began to bud and grow," particularly in Egypt, which he describes as the point of origin for both African and Asian peoples.

In Hamilton's account, the wisdom, kindliness, and accomplishments of the Africans are shattered by the introduction of the slave trade. In the second and longest section of the speech, Hamilton not only describes the horrors of slavery but also contrasts an essentially moral character of African peoples with that possessed by those of European descent. Hamilton disputes "their boasted superiority" by claiming that there is a "low, sly, wicked, cunning, peculiar to the Europeans." "Some nations have painted their devil in the complexion of a white man," he observes. "View the history of the slave trade, and then answer the question, could they have made choice of a better likeness to have drawn from?"

In the concluding section of his remarks, Hamilton makes an abrupt transition from the graphic description of the lashing of a woman slave with infant strapped to her back to an acknowledgement of the ceremonial occasion at which he speaks. "But, my brethren," Hamilton explains, "we are this day called on to rejoice."

Hamilton's address was published in 1815 by C. W. Bunce for the New York African Society and is reprinted in Dorothy Porter, Early Negro Writing, 1760–1837 *(Boston: Beacon Press, 1971), 391–99.*

It may not be amiss, my brethren, to commence this part of the exercise of this day, with a description of the country of our parents.

Here let me observe, that when I first turned my mind on the subject of this day, I had intended instead of what would be in me, a vain attempt at oratory, or rhetorical flourishes, to have given as far as in my power lay, a plain instructive address; but I am sorry to say, the resources from whence I intended to draw materials for such an address were entirely without my reach. I am therefore obliged to content myself with what I shall now offer.

We shall first give the geographical situation of Africa, that is, its place in this globe or earth. Its latitude is 37 deg. north and 34 deg. south of the equator, or the middle distance of the sun's perigrination north and south, so that the sun, its extreme distance never stretching beyond 23.5 deg. north or south of the equator, it never reaches beyond the boundaries of Africa.

We hereby see that Africa lies immediately under the influence of the sun, for its rays fall obliquely, when at its greatest distance, north on Africa's extreme northerly line, only about 13.5 deg. and southerly only 10.5. (We shall make some use of this directly.) Its longitude is 17 deg. west, and 51 deg. east of London, that is, when the sun is at its meridian, or it is noon at London, from that place in Africa the sun is at its meridian at the same time to Africa's extremely westerly line, is 17 deg. and extremely easterly line is 51 deg.

The form of Africa is a three-sided figure; its northerly side is bounded by the Mediterranean Sea, which separates it from Europe; its easterly side, by a neck of land called the Isthmus of Suez, which separates it from Asia, by the Red Sea, and by the Indian or Southern Ocean; its westerly side, is bounded by the great Atlantic Ocean, which separates it from America.

Of this description we shall make the following use: first, that Africa, being situated in the middle of the Globe, surrounded by the other continents, to wit, Asia, Europe, and America, in case of an universal Empire, she would make a grand eligible situation for the seat of Authority, and who knows—as she has descended to the ultimate point of degradation—but she may ascend to the zenith of glory and aggrandizement.

Next, as the nations of the Earth generally agree that mankind had an original, and as our religion teaches the same, would not Africa have made (she lying immediately under the fostering care of the sun) an eligible situation for the growth of man in his first state of existence? Let each study the nature of man, and answer the question for himself.

From these speculative thoughts, we turn to give a short account of the history of Africa; here were we disposed to dwell, we have an ample field before us; for Africa has a long, and in some parts, a proud account to give of herself. She can boast of her antiquity, of her philosophers, her artists, her statesman, her generals; of her curiosities, her magnificent cities, her stupendous buildings, and of her once widespread commerce. Our account shall be as plain and as simple as we can give.

That part of the continent known by the name of Egypt is the part that history gives its first account of; and is divided into what is called upper and lower Egypt—the one the Southern, the other the Northern division—of the origin of this settlement we have no authentic account: that natives claim an antiquity beyond what we are willing to believe, but of so ancient a date it is, that some of the most learned believe, for reasons it would be out of our way to give, that China, that very ancient settlement, was originally a colony peopled from Egypt; perhaps we cannot do better than here to introduce an account given by a nation found in the interior of the country (which account agrees with that given by the most learned), who say they were originally of that part of Egypt where the magnificent City of Thebes was built, which is described as having its hundred gates.

They tell us that Egypt was anciently settled by an honest, industrious, peaceable and well-disposed people; that they were divided into distinct parts, or hordes, with a father or chief to each horde, and one general, chief, or father to the whole, that each horde followed come useful employment, and that some of each horde made the science their particular study, and that these became the teachers of the youth, that they were all rich alike, for the one common storehouse clothed and fed them, that they lived in peace and quietness, until a wicked nation entered and laid waste their country, making slaves of some of the inhabitants, and put to death others, and that as many of the hordes as escaped, chose rather to leave the country in the possession of this savage people, than shed the blood of their fellow men; of these each family or horde, went to seek a place for themselves in the interior of the country. The name given to their invaders is one that agrees with Josephuses, king's shepherds, or king's beasts.

They further state that this wanton people were driven out by a hero of mixed blood by the name of Sos (or perhaps the great Sesostris, famous in the history of Egypt), under whose wise laws Egypt again enjoyed prosperity and peace; and after a lapse of time, Egypt was again overrun by a nation more wicked than the first, and who committed greater enormities; and again the inhabitants sought an asylum in the interior. The last, my brethren, may be the people driven out of Canaan by Joshua; for it is said of a people that invaded Egypt, when they were asked of what country they were, we are of Canaan driven out by Jesus or Joshua the Robber. From this account, we shall draw the following inferences.

First, that those inhabitants that occupy the country from the tropic of Cancer to the cape of Good Hope were originally from Egypt.

Secondly, that they were an industrious, honest, peaceable people.

Thirdly, as it was an attachment to a peaceable life that made them leave their native soil and seek an asylum in another clime, they must have remained the same peaceable, just, and honest, people for a long series of time.

And as Africa, with the exception of her sandy deserts, is very fertile, producing its fruits with very little labour of the husbandman, and as virtue carries with it no corroding thoughts, they must have been a very happy people.

But O! Africa, thou first fair garden of God's planting, thou once delightful field and original nursery for all those delicious fruits, tasteful herbage, and fragrant plants, that man highly prises, thou tract of earth over which the blest luminary, the sun, delights to make his daily splendid pass, thou spot of earth, where fair science first descended and the arts first began to bud and grow; how art thou chang'd and fallen.

Yes, my brethren, from once perhaps the most happy people the earth ever knew, to the most miserable under heaven. But such is the nature of the case, that to them that forc'd on her the cup of misery, to them shall be dealt an equal cup of bitterness.

Look at the present state of the present inhabitants of Egypt. Sunk, and they shall continue to sink, until they are on a level with the worm they crush beneath their feet; no effort can save them.

Look at the Portuguese, the first traders in African blood and sinews, and the Spaniards, the base followers of so base an example: have they not for more than a century been sinking into a state of effeminacy, weakness and degradation, do they hold the proud standing in the rank of nations they did two centuries ago? No, and they shall continue to sink, altho they may, like a dying man, sometimes seem to revive, until they are below the Africans they have so debased, or until the memory of them is obliterated from the nations of the earth. It is fortunate for England that she is making something like an atonement for her more than base treatment of the African people.

We would here proceed to give the origin of that trade whose character is marked with African gore, and carried with it rapine and murder, only that its origin has been treated of by those who have addressed us heretofore on these occasions.

I shall content myself with observing that the trade was began by white men, and by Europeans, by men who boast of the proud trust they put in the book that tells us, "with what measure you mete to others, shall be meted to you again." By men who boast of their superior understanding, their superior genius, their superior souls.

Their boasted superiority was set to work at the basest employment. When they first explored the western, and eastern shores of Africa, they found the natives a peaceable, simple, unsuspicious people.

They set to work that low, sly, wicked, cunning, peculiar to the Europeans, to the creating of jealousies and animosity, one horde or nation with another. To those princes who were proof against their vile craftiness they administered draughts of their intoxicating spirituous liquor and then distilled in them their base purposes.

Thus they laboured until Africa became one continued scene of suspicion, mad jealousy, confusion, war, rapine, blood and murder.

No longer was the banjo and the drum the call to the dance and to glee, but the signals to the work of destruction; no sooner does those instruments that used to be the call to pleasure strike the ear, than the mother clasps her infant in her arms and flies to the thicket for shelter to hide from the foe: the father and the sons grasp the weapons of defense, and prepare to meet the attack.

O! Africa, what carnage hast thou witnessed; thy flesh, thy bones, thy very vitals have been torn from thee.

The question will hardly arise, what was all this butchery set on foot for? if it should, I will tell you my brethren; for sordid gain, the white man's God.

They purchased the captives taken in war for gewgaws and for draughts of that intoxicating liquor that is sometimes the bane of the peace of families among themselves, and sold them again at an advanced price.

Other base modes were set on foot besides that of war. One of which was they sent out parties, who hid themselves in the thicket by day, and night, surrounded the peaceful hamlet, and made prisoners of its inhabitants.

The Europeans were not satisfied with making slaves of them in their own country, and enjoying the benefit of their labour on their own soil.

They were not contented with this, they must prepare their floating dungeons, or rather floating hells manned with fiends. Yes, my brethren, hells manned with fiends, I will not retract, not ask pardon for the warmth of expression, for they deserve no better name, and it would be impossible for me to talk coolly, when the slave trade is the subject.

Some nations have painted their devil in the complexion of a white man. View the history of the slave trade, and then answer the question, could they have made choice of a better likeness to have drawn from? All that low, sly, artful, wicked, cunning attributed to him, was practised by them. All the insulting scorn, savage cruelty, and tormenting schemes, practised by him, were executed by them.

Yes, my brethren, I repeat it; they prepared their floating hells manned with fiends, to carry the Africans across a wide ocean, to a new-explored continent, to wit, America. Would to God that Columbus with his exploring schemes had perished in Europe ere he touched the American Isles; or that Americus had perished in the ocean ere he explored the southern parts of the Continent; or rather that the hateful Cortes, with his murderous band, had been swallowed by an earthquake ere he reached the City of Mexico. Then might Africa been spared the terrible calamity she has suffered; pardon me my brethren I seem to wander.

On ship-board in their passage from Africa, they were treated with the most horrible cruelty that the imagination can conceive of.

The murderous scenes on Africa were delightful, compared with these. But we will spare your ears the recital of a tale that would curdle your blood, and the wish you had been there with an arm strong enough to have dashed the perpetrators to death, would stiffen your sinews, and like the citizens gathered around Mark Antony, make you mad for revenge on the murders of your brethren.

Permit me to relate one of the lightest scenes of this tragical drama. An infant of ten months old, had taken sulk on board of a slave ship, that is, refused to eat; the savage captain with his knotted cat whipped it until its body and legs had much swollen, he then ordered it in water so hot, that its skin and nails came off; he then bound it in oilcloth; he after a few days whipped it again, swearing he would make it eat or kill it; in a few hours after it expired, he then ordered the mother to throw her murdered infant overboard, she refused, he beat her until she took it up, turned her head aside, and dropped it into the sea. Now tell me my brethren, is there in God's domain other and worse fiends than these?

But we will hasten. Our parents were brought originally to this country to supply the place of the aborgines; the Spanish had found that these could not bear the burden they had put on them. The Indians were fast dwindling away: they thought that Africans would make better beasts of burden, yes, my brethren, beasts of burden they were, and such they still are.

The European with his bloated pride, conceives himself an order of being above any other order of men, and because ye have found out their vein and sometimes fawn on and flatter them, and call them master, a name they ought to despise, for the odium it carries with it when used between men. They think you have really given into their whim, and acknowledge them a superman, or demigod. But still I wander, yes my brethren, the Africans were brought over to supply the place of Indians, or native Americans, to do the drudgery of the new-found world, as it is sometimes called by way of eminence, but to them a new-found place of misery. Soon were the extensive shores of America covered with the best sons and daughters of Africa; toiling as slaves for men to whom they had never forfeited their right to freedom, and who had no better claim to them than the thief, or the purchaser of stolen goods, knowing them to be such, have to their booty; (and if it was not stepping out of our way we would prove they have not half the right) but the labouring was not all, the more than cruel barbarous treatment they underwent, such as the mind sickens at first glance at; it was not enough that in Africa they should set on foot wars, rapine, and murder! it was not enough to tear from her, her sons and her daughters? it was not enough that on shipboard they should be confined in stenchful holes, crowded together like common lumber, fettered with irons, tortured with thumb-screws and other instruments of cruelty: it was not enough they should be slaves in a foreign country, far from all that was dear to them, and there made to toil and labour and face a scorching sun each day, with a very scanty miserable meal. All this, and the picture is not half drawn. But still, like Shylock, "nothing but the pound of flesh nearest the heart;" nothing would satiate but that an iron-hearted fellow must be placed over them, with his knotted scourge to quicken them with the smart thereof to labour: it was not enough that the father whose heart writhing with anguish, being torn from his loving wife, and dear prattling infants, he should be awakened from his reverie by the whip from the driver, making long furrows in his back: it was not enough that the lad who had been the hope of his father and pride of his mother, when casting a wishful thought toward home, should forget for the moment to work the hoe; should be startled to sense of his neglect, by the flesh-cutting stroke of the driver's whip: it was not enough that the tender girl, once the pleasure of her mother, and darling of her father, who had stopped to wipe away a fallen tear, at the supposed anguish of her parents, should receive from an arm that ought to have been palsied at the stroke, the heart-stinging lash of the driver, but still the pound of flesh nearest the heart: the mother! the tender mother, with her more tender infant lashed to her back, and her feet clogged with weights. Because, with a mind torn with anguish, her thoughts had turned on him she had each day hailed with joy, the partner of her better days.

She had dropped her hoe; the cruel driver with his lacerating stroke; but we will turn from the scene, it is too disgusting. We seem to catch the blow to save the victim.

If these are some of the marks of superiority may heaven in mercy always keep us inferior: go, proud white men, go, boast of your superior cunning; the fox, the wolf, the tyger, are more cunning than their prey. But my brethren, we are this day called on to rejoice: to rejoice that the sadness of a long gloomy night is passed away, and that the fair opening for a better day is before us. To rejoice that the venomed monster, that Hydra with seven heads, is expiring. To rejoice that the slave trade, that cursed viper that fed on Africa's vitals; from the Danish, the British, and the American commerce, is swept away. To rejoice, that the friends of humanity have triumphed over our foes. Yes my brethren; among white men, are found, after all this shocking picture of their wickedness, men who are indeed the friends of humanity. Such was the good Anthony Benezet,* such is the great, good, and immortal Mr. Wilberforce;[†] and such is that angelically good man, Mr. Tho. Clarkson,[‡] whose name ought never to be pronounced by us but with the highest esteem and gratitude. Our children should be taught in their little songs, to lisp the name of Clarkson: he laboured in the field for the abolition of the slave trade, literally day and night, with very little time to refresh himself with sleep. Twenty years did Mr. Clarkson labour for the abolition of the slave trade. His labours were finally successful: too much cannot be said in his praise. In the British Parliament, long and hard was the struggle for the destruction of this trade: and it was shameful for Britain, who boasts so much of her strong attachment to liberty, and humanity that the struggle should be so long.

Of the Danish nation we can say nothing; except their having agreed to abolish the trade ten years after they passed a law to that effect.

In Congress of these United States, the motion for the abolition of the slave trade was brought on by a Mr. Bradley,[§] a gentleman from Vermont: among our other friends from this State, was that excellent gentlemen, and friend of man, Dr. Mitchell a member from this city; the motion was opposed by members from the southern section of these United States. Why they opposed, we know not: except their guilty souls, fearful that it would bring on Mr. Jefferson's doomsday, that made him tremble for the fate of his country, when he reflected that God was just; and had no attribute wherewith to favour their cause. But they writhed and twisted as long as they could; but the friends of humanity triumphed: it was the Lord's doing, and it is marvelous in our eyes.

To him be the praise, we add no more.■

---

*Abolitionist Anthony Benezet (1713–1784) was a Philadelphia Quaker and prolific author of works on social issues, including *A Caution and Warning to Great Britain and Her Colonies on the Calamitous State of the Enslaved Negroes,* published in 1766.

[†]As a member of the House of Commons, William Wilberforce (1759–1833) was a leader in the campaign for the abolition of West Indian slavery.

‡Thomas Clarkson (1760–1846) was a prominent English abolitionist and wrote a history of the slave trade.

[§]In December 1805, Senator Stephen R. Bradley (1754–1830) introduced a bill to end the slave trade after January 1, 1808. See Donald L. Robinson, *Slavery in the Structure of American Politics, 1765–1820* (New York: Harcourt Brace Jovanovich, 1970), 332–35.

13 VALEDICTORY ADDRESS

Margaret Odell

The New York African Free School was founded in 1787 by the New York Manumission Society, which was devoted to three objectives: to lobby for the legislative abolition of slavery; to secure the protection of free blacks and fugitive slaves in New York from kidnapping by slave-dealers; and "to provide means for educating children of color of all classes," both slave and free. Denied admission to existing New York schools, forty children enrolled during the Free School's first year of operation. By 1828, the affiliated schools' enrollments had grown to more than three hundred male and female students.

For most of their history, the schools received substantial support from New York's black community. Samuel E. Cornish, editor of Freedom's Journal *and later of the* Colored American, *worked as a home agent for the school in the late 1820s. The African Free School's distinguished graduates included Peter Williams, Jr., James McCune Smith, and Ira Aldridge (who played Othello at the Royal Theater in London), but few of the perhaps thousands of students who had passed through the school had been able to secure positions commensurate with their education and talents, as Charles C. Andrews, teacher and principal at the school, noted in his history of the institution in 1830. "In almost every instance," Andrews laments, "difficulties have attended them on account of their color, either in their obtaining a thorough knowledge of the trades, or, after they have obtained them, in finding employ in good shops; and a general objection is made, by white journeymen to working in the same shop with them" (*History, *122).*

Margaret Odell was among five graduates of the school listed in Andrews's 1830 History *as having obtained positions commensurate with their education. But Odell's employment as a teacher at the Hudson School for black children was short-lived, as she soon quit in protest over inadequate funding, enrollment, and community support.*

The teachers and friends of the African Free School mounted an ambitious public relations campaign, Andrews explains, "in order, that a more correct idea may be formed, by strangers, of the practicability of imparting the useful branches of education to the descendants of Africans." Central to this effort were the public graduation examinations administered to students in order to exhibit their knowledge of various fields of instruction, including spelling, needlework (for female students only), reading, writing, arithmetic, grammar, geography, and elocution. Members of the public, especially civic leaders and journalists, were invited to attend the examinations so that they might see for themselves that "they are as susceptible of mental cultivation as the children of white parents."

The examinations drew many distinguished visitors, including General Lafayette.

Students' delivery of public speeches written for the occasion by faculty or friends of the school was a highlight of the public examinations, which were designed to demonstrate elocutionary skills in the vocalization, memory, and bodily movement esteemed by nineteenth-century Americans as hallmarks of learnedness. Female students were admitted to the African Free School soon after its founding, and a female teacher was added to the staff in 1791. Like their male counterparts, female students participated in graduation examinations that offered public exhibition of their accomplishments.

The following speech by Margaret Odell, delivered on April 18, 1822, is among the earliest known texts of a public speech by an American-born woman. An entry in the records of the school housed at the New York Historical Society describes the speech as having been "written for the occasion by C.C.A.," presumably school principal Charles C. Andrews. It is nonetheless quite personal in its tenor, concerns, and outlook and should be viewed as reflecting a collaboration between speaker and speechwriter.

In her valedictory address of 1822, Margaret Odell makes clear the conclusion that she hopes her audience will draw from her performance: "That the African race, though by too many of their fellow men, have long been, and still are, held in a state most degrading to humanity, are nevertheless endowed by the same Almighty Power that made us all, with intellectual capacities not inferior to any people on earth." She directs the attention of the audience to her brother John and contrasts their imminent voluntary parting with the forcible sundering of slave families. She then addresses him as an audience of one, offering advice and encouragement designed to be "overheard" by others. As writer, Andrews also uses Odell to indulge in self-promotion, crafting the sentiments toward the school that he wishes his students to proclaim.

Black support for the school plummeted in 1830, when principal Andrews, the author of the history of the African Free Schools in which racial prejudice is condemned, was accused of reprimanding a student for using the term "gentleman" to refer to an African American. Black protests and boycotts forced the resignation of Andrews and the hiring of a black replacement, under whose direction black enrollments soared until the absorption of the schools by the public school system in 1834.

The text of the speech is taken from the appendix to Charles C. Andrews, The History of the New-York Free-Schools *(1830), 133–34. For additional information on the education of African American females in the early nineteenth century, see Shirley Yee,* Black Women Abolitionists: A Study in Activism, 1828–1860 *(Knoxville: University of Tennessee Press, 1992), 40–59; and Dorothy Sterling, ed.,* We Are Your Sisters: Black Women in the Nineteenth Century *(New York: Norton, 1984). Historical information on the African Free Schools is available in John L. Rury,*

"The New York African Free School, 1827–1836: Conflict Over Community Control of Black Education," Phylon 44 (1983), 187–97; and Carleton Mabee, Black Education in New York State *(Syracuse: Syracuse University Press, 1979), 19–25.*

RESPECTED FRIENDS AND PATRONS, I appear before you, as it regards myself, under very interesting circumstances. It is to take my leave of my schoolmates, and my much endeared teachers. In doing this, I feel it difficult to suppress those feelings which such an occasion is calculated to produce on a heart sensible of obligations so numerous as those which I am under to the gentlemen who support, and the teachers who have the immediate superintendence of this institution.

The advantages which this school is calculated to afford to the children of color, have, on former occasions, been presented to your view. I therefore shall be excused from repeating them; I need only to point you to these specimens, and remind you of those exercises this day exhibited before, to demonstrate a truth, which must, at no distant period, find its way to the breasts of the now most incredulous; viz. That the African race, though by too many of their fellow men, have long been, and still are, held in a state the most degrading to humanity, are nevertheless endowed by the same Almighty Power that made us all, with intellectual capacities, not inferior to any people on earth.

In looking round on my schoolmates, I see one among them who excites my most tender solicitude,—It is my brother. John, this I feel to be an occasion, which calls up all those tender emotions that Heaven has designed should be felt by brother and sister towards each other. What shall I say to you! O, if I were called to part with you, as some poor girls have to part with their equally dear kindred, and each of us, like them, were to be forcibly dragged away into wretched slavery, never to see each other again—But I forbear: thank heaven, it is not, no, it is not the case with us; nor have I even the anxiety which the circumstances of leaving you under the care of strangers would produce. No, I leave you to receive instruction from well known and long tried friends; be obedient, diligent, and studious; and, when the period shall arrive for you to take leave of this school, I trust it will be under circumstances no less affecting to you, that the present is to me.

Before I conclude my address, I must indulge myself in the pleasure of thanking my teachers for all the kindness which they have shown me.

To you, my instructress, I am indebted for what I know of the use of the needle. Allow me, if you please, to leave with you a small piece of my humble performance; it will serve as a testimony of my affectionate regard, and also, as an example to others of my dear schoolmates under the direction, to follow with something in the same way, but I hope, more meritorious.■

14 THE CONDITION AND PROSPECTS OF HAITI

John Browne Russwurm

No event of the late eighteenth century alarmed the slaveholders of the United States and aroused the enthusiasm of black Americans, free and slaves, as much as the insurrection of the slaves in the French island of Saint Domingue. The revolt began in August 1791 and, after a decade of bloody conflict, ended with the expulsion of the French, the defeat of Napoleon's crack army of 25,000 soldiers under General Le Clerc, and the establishment on January 1, 1804, of the Republic of Haiti—the first black republic in the world, the first independent country in Latin America, the second independent nation in the hemisphere, and the one land in which black slaves defeated those who had enslaved them.

It is not surprising then, that when the second black college graduate in the United States delivered his commencement address, he should have chosen the Haitian revolution and the future of Haiti as his subject.* The graduate was John Browne Russwurm; the institution, Bowdoin College, in Brunswick, Maine, and the date September 6, 1826. Russwurm was born in Port Antonio, Jamaica, October 1, 1799, of a black mother and a white father who was an English merchant in the West Indies. At the age of eight, Russwurm was sent to school in Quebec. When the elder Russwurm moved into the District of Maine a few years later, he brought his son with him. Russwurm entered Bowdoin College in the fall of 1824 and graduated in 1826. In March 1827, he became coeditor and copublisher with Samuel B. Cornish of Freedom's Journal, *the first black newspaper published in the United States. But Russwurm soon became convinced that because of the strength of racism here no black man could really live a life of freedom and dignity in the United States. He turned to colonization and in 1829 went to Africa as superintendent of public schools in Liberia. In 1836 he was appointed governor of the Cape Palmas district of Liberia, and he continued in his position until his death on June 17, 1851.*

Russwurm's commencement address at Bowdoin College aroused some interest at the time it was delivered. An extract from the speech was published in the Portland Eastern Argus *of September 12, 1826;[†] this*

---

*The first black college graduate was Edward Jones, who received his degree from Amherst College on August 23, 1826.

[†]The Eastern Argus also published the following interesting report of the commencement: "The Commencement of the Bowdoin College took place on Wednesday last, (Sep-

was reprinted two days later in the Boston Courier, *and somewhat later in the* National Philanthropist *and the* Genius of Universal Emancipation. *The last, an early antislavery journal published in Baltimore by Benjamin Lundy, headed the extract "African Eloquence." The full text of Russwurm's commencement address is presented here with the permission of the Library of Bowdoin College, where the original, in Russwurm's handwriting, is kept.*

THE CHANGES which take place in the affairs of this world show the instability of sublunary things. Empires rise and fall, flourish and decay. Knowledge follows revolutions and travels over the globe. Man alone remains the same being, whether placed under the torrid suns of Africa or in the more congenial temperate zone. A principle of liberty is implanted in his breast, and all efforts to stifle it are as fruitless as would be the attempt to extinguish the fires of Etna.

It is in the irresistible course of events that all men who have been deprived of their liberty shall recover this precious portion of their indefeasible inheritance. It is in vain to stem the current; degraded man will rise in his native majesty and claim his rights. They may be withheld from him now, but the day will arrive when they must be surrendered.

Among the many interesting events of the present day, and illustrative of this, the Revolution in Haiti holds a conspicuous place. The former political condition of Haiti we all doubtless know. After years of sanguinary struggle for freedom and a political existence, the Haitians on the auspicious day of January first, 1804, declared themselves a free and independent nation. Nothing can ever induce them to recede from this declaration. They know too well by their past misfortunes, by their wounds, which are yet bleeding, that security can be expected only from within themselves. Rather would they devote themselves to death than return to their former condition.

Can we conceive of anything which can cheer the desponding spirit, can reanimate and stimulate it to put everything to the hazard? Liberty can do this. Such were its effects upon the Haitians—men who in slavery showed

tember 6). Thirty-one gentlemen received the degree of Bachelor of Arts, of whom twenty-four were selected to take parts in the exhibition. . . . One circumstance was peculiarly interesting and we believe it was a perfect novelty in the history of our Colleges. Among the young gentlemen who received the honors of the College, and who had parts assigned to them, was a Mr. Russwurm, a person of African descent. He came on the stage under an evident feeling of embarrassment, but finding the sympathies of the audience in his favor, he recovered his courage as he proceeded. He pronounced his part in a full and manly tone of voice, accompanied with appropriate gestures, and it was received by the audience with hearty applause. Altogether it was one of the most interesting performances of the day. His subject was happily selected. It was the condition and prospects of *Hayti.* Believing our readers would feel an interest in a literary performance so novel under all its circumstances, we have obtained the extracts which we subjoin" (September 12, 1826).

neither spirit nor genius: but when Liberty, when once Freedom struck their astonished ears, they became new creatures, stepped forth as men, and showed to the world, that though slavery may benumb, it cannot entirely destroy our faculties. Such men were Toussaint L'Ouverture, Desalines and Christophe!*

The Haitians have adopted the republican form of government; and so firmly it is established that in no country are the rights and privileges of citizens and foreigners more respected, and crimes less frequent. They are a brave and generous people. If cruelties were inflicted during the revolutionary war, it was owing to the policy pursued by the French commanders, which compelled them to use retaliatory measures.

For who shall expostulate with men who have been hunted with bloodhounds, who have been threatened with an auto-da-fé, whose relations and friends have been hanged on gibbets before their eyes, have been sunk by hundreds in the sea—and tell them they ought to exercise kindness toward such mortal enemies? Remind me not of moral duties, of meekness and generosity. Show me the man who has exercised them under these trials, and you point to one who is more than human. It is an undisputed fact, that more than sixteen thousand Haitians perished in the modes above specified. The cruelties inflicted by the French on the children of Haiti have exceeded the crimes of Cortes and Pizarro.

Thirty-two years of their independence, so gloriously achieved, have effected wonders. No longer are they the same people. They had faculties, yet were these faculties oppressed under the load of servitude and ignorance. With a countenance erect and fixed upon Heaven, they can now contemplate the works of divine munificence. Restored to the dignity of man and to society, they have acquired a new existence; their powers have been developed; a career of glory and happiness unfolds itself before them.

The Haitian government has arisen in the neighborhood of European settlements. Do the public proceedings and details of its government bespeak an inferiority? Their state papers are distinguished from those of many European courts only by their superior energy and nonexalted sentiments; and while the manners and politics of Boyer emulate those of his republican neighbors, the court of Christophe had almost as much foppery, almost as many lords and ladies of the bedchamber, and almost as great a proportion of stars and ribbons and gilded chariots as those of his brother potentates in any part of the world.†

---

*Toussaint L'Ouverture, a former slave, was the great leader of the Haitian revolution, and Henri Christophe and Jean-Jacques Dessalines, also former slaves, were his chief generals. Toussaint L'Ouverture was tricked by Napoleon into visiting France for negotiations; there he was imprisoned, and there he died in 1803.

†After the elimination of the French, Dessalines was assassinated by the followers of Alexandre Pétion. Thereafter the island was divided during fourteen years of civil war between Pétion and Christophe. The latter ruled the north almost like a feudal monarchy, and Pétion ruled the south. In 1822, after the death of both Christophe and Pétion, the latter's protégé, Jean-Pierre Boyer, ruled the whole island for twenty-five years.

(Placed by divine providence amid circumstances more favorable than were their ancestors, the Haitians can more easily than they, make rapid strides in the career of civilization—they can demonstrate that although the God of nature may have given them a darker complexion, still they are men alike sensible to all the miseries of slavery and to all the blessings of freedom.)

May we not indulge in the pleasing hope, that the independence of Haiti has laid the foundation of an empire that will take rank with the nations of the earth—that a country, the local situation of which is favorable to trade and commercial enterprise, possessing a free and well-regulated government, which encourages the useful and liberal arts, a country containing an enterprising and growing population which is determined to live free or die gloriously will advance rapidly in all the arts of civilization.

We look forward with peculiar satisfaction to the period when, like Tyre of old, her vessels shall extend the fame of her riches and glory, to the remotest borders of the globe—to the time when Haiti treading in the footsteps of her sister republics, shall, like them, exhibit a picture of rapid and unprecedented advance in population, wealth and intelligence.■

15 TERMINATION OF SLAVERY

Austin Steward

The Fourth of July, Howard Martin has written, was "the most important national ceremonial during the last century." Community ceremonies across the nation were marked by orations that characteristically looked back to the American Revolution as having achieved those principles of liberty and equality set forth in the Declaration of Independence. In slave-holding Charleston, South Carolina, five years before Denmark Vesey's revolt, John J. Mauger's oration on July 4, 1817, noted (without conscious irony) the assembly of "millions of freemen" to celebrate the "Birth Day of American Freedom."

With three million Americans in chains, such pronouncements struck many as the height of hypocrisy. "What, to the American slave, is your Fourth of July?" Frederick Douglass would ask his predominantly white audience of July 5, 1852: "A day that reveals to him, more than all the other days in the year, the gross injustice and cruelty to which he is the constant victim." (His speech is included elsewhere in this volume.) Many African Americans observed the occasion as a time of protest.

When on July 4, 1827, the State of New York emancipated its slaves, many black American communities marked the occasion with speeches and ceremonies. In Rochester, where twenty-five years later Douglass would offer his famous rebuke of Independence Day celebrations, Austin Steward (1793–1865) was selected to deliver the principal oration.

Born in slavery in Prince William County, Virginia, Steward was moved to New York, where he escaped in 1813. He opened a grocery store in Rochester and was subjected to violent abuse by local whites. He became active in the antislavery and temperance movements and served as vice president of the first black national convention, held at Philadelphia's Bethel A.M.E. Church in 1830. The following year, Steward left the United States to direct the Wilberforce Colony in Canada. He returned to Rochester in 1837 and resumed his active participation in the black convention movement and antislavery politics.

Reporting on the activities of African Americans on July 4, 1827, the Rochester Daily Advertiser *observed:*

The extinction of that curse by the laws of our State was marked by appropriate rejoicings on the part of the African race of the neighborhood. A procession of considerable length and respectable appearance, preceded by a band of music, moved from Brown's Island through the principal streets to the public square, yesterday forenoon, where a stage and seats were erected for the speakers and audience. The throne of Grace was addressed by the Rev. Mr. Allen, a colored clergyman. The act declaring all slaves free in this State, on the fourth day of July, 1827, was read, which was succeeded by the reading of the Declaration of Independence and delivery of an oration by Mr. Steward. We have heard but one opinion from several gentlemen who were present, and that was highly complimentary to the composition and delivery of the same.

Steward's oration is a searing mix of praise and blame, of celebration and sadness, of jubilation and anger. "We will rejoice, though sobs interrupt the songs of our rejoicing," he tells his listeners, "and tears mingle in the cup we pledge to freedom." Reminding his audience that the nation's hypocrisy on this "civil holy day" continues, his "celebration" of the day invokes those countrymen who, in "this boasted land of civil and religious liberty" are "writhing under the lash and groaning beneath the grinding weight of Slavery's chain." Steward also exhorts his black audience to industry and upright living in emancipation, anticipating the many African American orators who took up this theme in the late nineteenth century. Steward stresses the need for black business and economic advancement as a key for social power: with money, "you may direct as you will the actions of your pale, proud brethren."

The speech text is taken from Steward's autobiography, first pub-

lished in 1856, Twenty-Two Years a Slave and Forty Years a Freeman, *reprinted in 1968 by Negro Universities Press (New York).*

T HE age in which we live is characterized in no ordinary degree, by a certain boldness and rapidity in the march of intellectual and political improvements. Inventions the most surprising; revolutions the most extraordinary, are springing forth, and passing in quick succession before us,—all tending most clearly to the advancement of mankind towards that state of earthly perfection and happiness, from which they are yet so far distant, but of which their nature and that of the world they inhabit, are most certainly capable. It is at all times pleasing and instructive to look backward by the light of history, and forward by the light of analogical reasoning, to behold the gradual advancement of man from barbarism to civilization, from civilization toward the higher perfections of his nature; and to hope—nay, confidently believe, that the time is not far distant when liberty and equal rights being everywhere established, morality and the religion of the gospel everywhere diffused,—man shall no longer lift his hand for the oppression of his fellow man; but all, mutually assisting and assisted, shall move onward throughout the journey of human life, like the peaceful caravan across the burning sands of Arabia. And never, on this glorious anniversary, so often and so deservedly celebrated by millions of free men, but which we are today for the first time called to celebrate—never before, has the eye been able to survey the past with so much satisfaction, or the future with hopes and expectations so brilliant and so flattering; it is to us a day of two-fold joy. We are men, though the strong hand of prejudice and oppression is upon us; we can and we will rejoice in the advancement of the rapidly increasing happiness of mankind, and especially of our own race. We can, and we will rejoice in the growing power and glory of the country we inhabit. Although Almighty God has not permitted us to remain in the land of our forefathers and our own, the glories of national independence, and the sweets of civil and religious liberty, to their full extent; but the strong hand of the spoiler has borne us into a strange land, yet has He of His great goodness given us to behold those best and noblest of his gifts to man, their fairest and loveliest forms; and not only have we beheld them, but we have already felt much of their benignant influence. Most of us have hitherto enjoyed many, very many of the dearest rights of freemen. Our lives and personal liberties have been held as sacred and inviolable; the rights of property have been extended to us, in this land of freedom; our industry has been, and still is, liberally rewarded; and so long as we live under a free and happy government which denies us not the protection of its laws, why should we fret and vex ourselves because we have had no part in framing them, nor anything to do with their administration. When the fruits of the earth are fully afforded us, we do not wantonly refuse them, nor ungratefully repine because we have done nothing towards the cultivation of the tree which produces them. No, we accept them with lively gratitude; and their sweetness is not embittered by reflecting upon the manner in which they were obtained. It is the dictate of sound wisdom, then, to enjoy without repining, the freedom, privileges, and immunities which wise and equal laws have awarded us—nay, proudly to rejoice and glory in their production, and stand ready at all times to defend them at the hazard of our lives, and of all that is most dear to us.

But are we alone shut out and excluded from any share in the administration of government? Are not the clergy, a class of men equally ineligible to office? A class of men almost idolized by their countrymen, ineligible to office! And are we alone excluded from what the world chooses to denominate polite society? And are not a vast majority of the polar race excluded? I know not why, but mankind of every age, nation, and complexion have had lower classes; and, as a distinction, they have chosen to arrange themselves in the grand spectacle of human life, like seats in a theater—rank above rank, with intervals between them. But if any suppose that happiness or contentment is continued to any single class, or that the high or more splendid order possesses any substantial advantage in those respects over their more lowly brethren, they must be wholly ignorant of all rational enjoyment. For what though the more humble orders cannot mingle with the higher on terms of equality. This, if rightly considered, is not a curse but a blessing. Look around you, my friends: what rational enjoyment is not within your reach? Your homes are in the noblest country in the world, and all of that country which your real happiness requires, may at any time be yours. Your industry can purchase it; and its righteous laws will secure you in its possession. But, to what, my friends, do you owe all these blessings? Let not the truth be concealed. You owe them to that curse, that bitter source of Africa, whose partial abolishment you are this day convened to celebrate. Slavery has been your curse, but it shall become your rejoicing. Like the people of God in Egypt, you have been afflicted; but like them too, you have been redeemed. You are henceforth free as the mountain winds. Why should we, on this day of congratulation and joy, turn our view upon the origin of African Slavery? Why should we harrow up our minds by dwelling on the deceit, the forcible fraud and treachery that have been so long practiced on your hospitable and unsuspecting countrymen? Why speak of fathers torn from the bosom of their families, wives from the embraces of their husbands, children from the protection of their parents; in fine, of all the tender and endearing relations of life dissolved and trampled under foot, by the accursed traffic in human flesh? Why should we remember, in joy and exultation, the thousands of our countrymen who are to-day, in this land of gospel light, this boasted land of civil and religious liberty, writhing under the lash and groaning beneath the grinding weight of Slavery's chain? I ask, Almighty God, are they who do such things thy chosen and favorite people? But, away with such thoughts as these; we will rejoice though sobs interrupt the songs of our rejoicing, and tears mingle in the cup we pledge to Freedom; our harps though they have long hung neglected upon the willows, shall this day be strung full high to the notes of gladness. On this day, in one member at least of this mighty Republic, the Slavery of our race has ceased forever! No more shall the insolent voice of a master be the main-spring of our actions, the sole guide of our conduct; no more shall their hands labor in degrading and profitless servitude. Their toils will henceforth be voluntary, and be crowned with the never failing reward of industry. Honors and dignities may perhaps never be ours; but wealth, virtue, and happiness are all within the compass of our moderate exertions. And how shall we employ a few moments better than in reflecting upon the means by which these are to be obtained. For what can be more proper and more profitable to one who has just gained an invaluable treasure, than to consider how he may use it to the best possible advantage? And here I need not tell you that a strict observance to all the precepts of the gospel ought to be your first and highest aim; for small will be the value of all that the present world can bestow, if the interests of the world to come are neglected and despised. None of you can be ignorant of what the gospel teaches. Bibles may easily be obtained; nor can there be a greater disgrace, or a more shameful neglect of duty than for a person of mature age, and much more, for any father of a family to be without that most precious of all books—the Bible. If, therefore, any of you are destitute of a Bible, hasten to procure one. Will any of you say that it can be of no use to you, or that you cannot read it? Look then to the noblest of all remedies for this evil, the Sunday School—that most useful of all institutions. There you may learn without loss of time or money, that of which none should be ignorant—to read.

Let me exhort you with earnestness to give your most sincere attention to this matter. It is of the utmost importance to every one of you. Let your next object be to obtain as soon as may be, a competency of the good things of this world; immense wealth is not necessary for you, and would but diminish your real happiness. Abject poverty is and ought to be regarded as the greatest, most terrible of all possible evils. It should be shunned as a most deadly and damning sin. What then are the means by which so dreadful a calamity may be avoided? I will tell you, my friends, in these simple words—hear and ponder on them; write them upon the tablets of your memory; they are worthy to be inscribed in letters of gold upon every door-post— "industry, prudence, and economy." Oh! they are words of power to guide you to respectability and happiness. Attend, then, to some of the laws which industry impose, while you have health and strength. Let not the rising sun behold you sleeping or indolently lying upon your beds. Rise ever with the morning light; and, till sun-set, give not an hour to idleness. Say not human nature cannot endure it. It can—it almost requires it. Sober, diligent, and moderate labor does not diminish it, but on the contrary, greatly adds to the health, vigor, and duration of the human frame. Thousands of the human race have died prematurely of disease engendered by indolence and inactivity. Few, very few indeed, have suffered by the too long continuance of bodily exertion. As you give the day to labor, so devote the night to rest; for which that has drunk and reveled all night at a tippling shop, or wandered about in search of impious and stolen pleasures, has not by so doing not only committed a most heinous and damning sin in the sight of Heaven, but rendered himself wholly unfit for the proper discharge of the duties of the coming day. Nor think that industry or true happiness do not go hand in hand; and to him who is engaged in some useful avocation, time flies delightfully and rapidly away. He does not, like the idle and indolent man, number the slow hours with sighs—cursing both himself and them for the tardiness of their flight. Ah, my friends, it is utterly impossible for him who wastes time in idleness, ever to know anything of true happiness. Indolence, poverty, wretchedness, are inseparable companions,—fly them, shun idleness, as from eminent and inevitable destruction. In vain will you labor unless prudence and economy preside over and direct all your exertions. Remember at all times that money even in your own hands, is power; with it you may direct as you will the actions of your pale, proud brethren. Seek after and amass it then, by just and honorable means; and once in your hand never part with it but for a full and fair equivalent; nor let that equivalent be something which you do not want, and for which you cannot obtain more than it cost you. Be watchful and diligent and let your mind be fruitful in devises for the honest advancement of your worldly interest. So shall you continually rise in respectability, in rank and standing in this so late and so long the land of your captivity.

Above all things refrain from the excessive use of ardent spirits. There is no evil whose progress is so imperceptible; and at the same time so sure and deadly, as that of intemperance; and by slow degrees it undermines health, wealth, and happiness, till all at length tumble into one dreadful mass of ruin. If God has given you children, he has in so doing imposed upon you a most fearful responsibility; believe me, friends, you will answer to God for every misfortune suffered, and every crime committed by them which right education and example could have taught them to avoid. Teach them reverence and obedience to the laws both of God and man. Teach them sobriety, temperance, justice, and truth. Let their minds be right instructed—imbued with kindness and brotherly love, charity, and benevolence. Let them possess at least so much learning as is to be acquired in the common schools of the country. In short, let their welfare be dearer to you than any earthly enjoyment; so shall they be the richest of earthly blessings.

My countrymen, let us henceforth remember that we are men. Let us as one man, on this day resolve that henceforth, by continual endeavors to do good to all mankind, we will claim for ourselves the attention and respect which as men we should possess. So shall every good that can be the portion of man, be ours—this life shall be happy, and the life to come, glorious.■

16

THE NECESSITY OF A GENERAL UNION AMONG US

David Walker

The moderate, passive approach to slaves set forth in Cyrus Bustill's speech was shattered in September 1828 by David Walker when he published at his own expense his revolutionary pamphlet: Walker's Appeal, in Four Articles: together with a preamble, to the coloured Citizens of the World, but in Particular and Very expressly to those of the United States of America. *More commonly known as* David Walker's Appeal, *the twenty-six-page pamphlet warned America that blacks "must and shall be free" and asked the slaveholders if they wished to risk having the slaves take their freedom by force. Should the slaveholder fail to respond, those enslaved had only one course to follow: begin a bloody insurrection against their oppressors. While Walker cautioned against such action until the way was clear, he rejected the idea of waiting for heaven to redeem the enslaved from under their "cruel oppressors and murderers." Walker stressed that so long as slavery existed in America, no African American would ever be accepted on an equal basis with any white man. For this reason every free African American had to support the overthrow of slavery immediately and by force if necessary, including insurrections among those enslaved.*

David Walker was freeborn in Wilmington, North Carolina, and moved to Boston, where he was the proprietor of a new and used clothing store from 1825 to his death in 1830. (Whether his death was caused by poison administered by agents of the slaveholders who hated and feared him, as has been frequently charged, or was due to natural causes is a question that has never been answered).

Walker's Appeal *is well known and has recently been reprinted in several editions. His speeches, however, are less well known. He delivered this address in December 1828 before the Massachusetts General Colored Association, founded in 1826 in Boston to oppose slavery and restrictions on the freedom of free blacks. Walker was a member of the association and was hopeful that it would serve to unite African Americans in a common struggle for liberty and equality. Walker's speech offers a fascinating look at the ways in which he sought to forge the organization and unity he describes in the* Appeal.

Although Walker rejected the view that slaves should wait until God liberated them, he was a very religious man and believed that there was no doubt that once they rose up, God would be on their side. This religious influence is also reflected in the speech.

Walker's speech is reprinted from Freedom's Journal *of December 19, 1828.*

MR. PRESIDENT,—I cannot but congratulate you, together with my brethren on this highly interesting occasion, the first semi-annual meeting of this Society. When I reflect upon the many impediments through which we have had to conduct its affairs, and see, with emotion of delight, the present degree of eminency to which it has arisen, I cannot, sir, but be of the opinion, that an invisible arm must have been stretched out in our behalf. From the very second conference, which was by us convened, to agitate the proposition respecting the society, to this final consolidation, we were by some, opposed, with an avidity and zeal, which, had it been on the opposite side, would have done great honor to themselves. And, sir, but for the undeviating, and truly patriotic exertions of those who were favorable to the formation of this institution, it might have been this day, in a yet unorganized condition. Did I say in an unorganized condition? Yea, had our opponents their way, the very notion of such an institution might have been obliterated from our minds. How strange it is, to see men of sound sense, and of tolerably good judgment, act so diametrically in opposition to their interest; but I forbear making any further comments on this subject, and return to that for which we are convened.

First then, Mr. president, it is necessary to remark here, at once, that the primary object of this institution, is, to unite the colored population, so far, through the United States of America, as may be practicable and expedient; forming societies, opening, extending, and keeping up correspondences, and not withholding anything which may have the least tendency to ameliorate our miserable condition—with the restrictions, however, of not infringing on the articles of its constitution, or that of the United States of America. Now, that we are disunited, is a fact, that no one of common sense will deny; and, that the cause of which, is a powerful auxiliary in keeping us from rising to the scale of reasonable and thinking beings, none but those who delight in our degradation will attempt to contradict. Did I say those who delight in our degradation? Yea, sir, glory in keeping us ignorant and miserable, that we might be the better and the longer slaves. I was credibly informed by a gentleman of unquestionable veracity, that a slaveholder upon finding one of his young slaves with a small spelling book in his hand (not opened) fell upon and beat him almost to death, exclaiming, at the same time, to the child, you will acquire better learning than I or any of my family.

I appeal to every candid and unprejudiced mind, do not all such men glory in our miseries and degradations; and are there not millions whose chief glory centres in this horrid wickedness? Now, Mr. President, those are the very humane, philanthropic, and charitable men who proclaim to the world, that the blacks are such a poor, ignorant and degraded species of beings, that, were they set at liberty, they would die for the want of something to subsist upon, and in consequence of which, they are compelled to keep them in bondage, to do them good.

O Heaven! what will not avarice and the love of despotic sway cause men to do with their fellow creatures, when actually in their power? But, to return whence I digressed; it has been asked, in what way will the *General Colored Association* (or the Institution) unite the colored population, so far, in the United States, as may be practicable and expedient? to which enquiry,! I answer, by asking the following: Do not two hundred and eight years very intolerable sufferings teach us the actual necessity of a general union among us? Do we not know indeed, the horrid dilemma into which we are, and from which, we must exert ourselves, to be extricated? Shall we keep slumbering on, with our arms completely folded up, exclaiming every now and then, against our miseries, yet never do the least thing to ameliorate our condition, or that of posterity? Shall we not, by such inactivity, leave, or rather entail a hereditary degradation on our children, but a little, if at all, inferior to that which our fathers, under all their comparative disadvantages and privations, left on us? In fine, shall we, while almost every other people under Heaven, are making such mighty efforts to better their condition, go around from house to house, enquiring what good associations and societies are going to do us? Ought we not to form ourselves into a general body, to protect, aid, and assist each other to the utmost of our power, with the before mentioned restrictions?

Yes, Mr. President, it is indispensably our duty to try every scheme that we think will have a tendency to facilitate our salvation, and leave the final result to that God, who holds the destinies of people in the hollow of his hand, and who ever has, and will, repay every nation according to its works.

Will any be so hardy as to say, or even to imagine, that we are incapable of effecting any object which may have a tendency to hasten our emancipation, in consequence of the prevalence of ignorance and poverty among us? That the major part of us are ignorant and poor, I am at this time unprepared to deny. But shall this defer us from all lawful attempts to bring about the desired object? nay, sir, it should rouse us to greater exertions; there ought to be a spirit of emulation and inquiry among us, a hungering and thirsting after religion; these are requisitions, which, if we ever be so happy as to acquire, will fit us for all the departments of life; and, in my humble opinion, ultimately result in rescuing us from an oppression, unparalleled, I had almost said, in the annals of the world.

But some may even think that our white brethren and friends are making such mighty efforts, for the amelioration of our condition, that we may stand as neutral spectators of the work. That we have many good friends yea, very good, among that body, perhaps none but a few of these who have ever read at all will deny; and that many of them have gone, and will go, all lengths for our good, is evident, from the very works of the great, the good, and the godlike Granville Sharpe, Wilberforce, Lundy, and the truly patriotic and lamented Mr. Ashmun, late Colonial Agent of Liberia, who, with a zeal which was only equalled by the goodness of his heart, has lost his life in our cause,* and a host of others too numerous to mention: a number of private gentlemen too, who, though they say but little, are nevertheless, busily engaged for good. Now, all of those great, and indeed, good friends whom God has given us, I do humbly, and very gratefully acknowledge. But, that we should co-operate with them, as far as we are able by uniting and cultivating a spirit of friendship and of love among us, is obvious, from the very exhibition of our miseries, under which we groan.

Two millions and a half of colored people in these United States, more than five hundred thousand of whom are about two-thirds of the way free. Now, I ask, if no more than these last were united (which they must be, or always live as enemies) and resolved to aid and assist each other to the utmost of their power, what mighty deeds would be done by them for the good of our cause?

But, Mr. President, instead of a general compliance with these requisitions, which have a natural tendency to raise us in the estimation of the world, we see, to our sorrow, in the very midst of us, a gang of villains, who, for the paltry sum of fifty or a hundred dollars, will kidnap and sell into perpetual slavery, their fellow creatures! and, too, if one of their fellow sufferers, whose miseries are a little more enhanced by the scourges of a tyrant, should abscond from his pretended owner, to take a little recreation, and unfortunately fall in their way, he is gone! for they will sell him for a glass of whiskey!† Brethren and fellow sufferers, I ask you, in the name of God, and of Jesus Christ, shall we suffer such notorious villains to rest peaceably among us? Will they not take our wives and little ones, more particularly our little ones, when a convenient opportunity will admit, and sell them for money, to slave holders, who will doom them to chains, handcuffs, and even unto death? May God open our eyes on those children of the devil and enemies of all good!

But, sir, this wickedness is scarcely more infernal than that which was attempted a few months since, against the government of our brethren, the Haytiens, by a consummate rogue, who ought to have, long since, been haltered, but who, I was recently informed, is nevertheless, received into com-

---

*Jehudi Ashmun (1794–1828), perhaps more than any other person, was responsible for whatever success the entire enterprise of Liberia, in Africa, and of the American Colonization Society, in America, may be said to have achieved. He died in New Haven on August 10, 1828, at the age of thirty-five from a fever contracted in Africa. It was for Ashmun that Lincoln University was first named when it was established in 1854 as Ashmun Institute. It is interesting that Walker, who made clear his bitter opposition to the American Colonization Society and emigration to Liberia in his pamphlet, had high respect for Ashmun for his selfless work for the cause of colonization.

†Walker is referring to actual incidents that had occurred only a few months before in Boston in which some African Americans were kidnapped and sold to slaveowners. The incidents enraged Walker as they did others in the black community.

pany among some of our most respectable men, with a kind of brotherly affection which ought to be shown only to a gentleman of honor.*

Now, Mr. President, all such mean, and more than disgraceful actions as these, are powerful auxiliaries, which work for our destruction, and which are abhorred in the sight of God and of good men.

But, sir, I cannot but bless God for the glorious anticipation of a not very distant period, when these things which now help to degrade us will no more be practiced among the sons of Africa,—for, though this, and perhaps another, generation may not experience the promised blessings of Heaven, yet, the dejected, degraded, and now enslaved children of Africa will have, in spite of all their enemies, to take their stand among the nations of the earth. And, sir, I verily believe that God has something in reserve for us, which, when he shall have parceled it out upon us will repay us for all our suffering and miseries.■

17 SLAVERY AND COLONIZATION

Peter Williams, Jr.

On December 28, 1816, the American Society for Colonizing the *Free People of Colour of the United States (popularly known as the American Colonization Society) was organized. The Society, supported by influential groups, aimed to colonize free blacks overseas and thus rid the United States of a "troublesome presence." Although some leading African Americans supported voluntary emigration, believing that black people could never achieve freedom and dignity in the United States, most opposed the scheme from its inception. They were convinced that the promoters of the Society wished to get rid of free blacks in order to make slavery secure, and they were repelled by the racist arguments directed by the Society against African Americans as a inferior, degraded class who should be removed from the United States. They charged, furthermore, that the Society, by encouraging anti-black prejudice, was responsible for the deprivation of rights already enjoyed by free blacks.*

On July 4, 1830, the Reverend Peter Williams, Jr., delivered a sharp

---

*For the honor of our city, we are proud in stating that the individual referred to is tolerated in but one or two families, who, according to Major Noah, are styled "good society." [Note by Editor of *Freedom's Journal.*]

indictment of the Colonization Society in an address at St. Philip's Prot-
estant Episcopal Church, of which he was pastor. Williams was a mem-
ber of the Board of Managers of the New York Anti-Slavery Society, but
in 1834 was forced to resign under pressure from his white bishop.

Williams uses the occasion of "Independence Day" to highlight na-
tional hypocrisies. He dismantles the claims of the colonizationists, some
of whom concealed their true objectives and prejudices with pretensions
to charity and social improvement. Williams brilliantly exposes their con-
tradictory premises and actions. At the same time, Williams endorses the
purchase of a tract of land in Canada for use as an asylum if African
Americans are forcibly driven from their native country, and he urges his
audience to support a colony of blacks forced to flee there after the Cin-
cinnati riots.

The speech text has been taken from Carter G. Woodson, Negro Orators and Their Orations *(Washington, D.C.: Associated Publishers, 1925),*
77–81.

On this day the fathers of this nation declared, "We hold these truths to be self-evident, that all men are created equal, that they are endowed by their Creator with certain unalienable rights, among which are life, liberty, and the pursuit of happiness."

These truly noble sentiments have secured to their author a deathless fame. The sages and patriots of the Revolution subscribed them with enthusiasm and "pledged their lives, their fortunes, and their sacred honour" in their support.

The result has been the freedom and happiness of millions, by whom the annual returns of this day are celebrated with the loudest and most lively expressions of joy.

But although this anniversary affords occasion of rejoicing to the mass of the people of the United States, there is a class, a numerous class, consisting of nearly three millions, who participate but little in its joys, and are deprived of their unalienable rights by the very men who so loudly rejoice in the declaration that "all men are born free and equal."

The festivities of this day serve but to impress upon the minds of reflecting men of colour a deeper sense of the cruelty, the injustice, and oppression, of which they have been the victims. While others rejoice in their deliverance from a foreign yoke, they mourn that a yoke a thousandfold more grievous is fastened upon them. Alas, they are slaves in the midst of freedom; they are slaves to those who boast that freedom is the unalienable right of all; and the clanking of their fetters, and the voice of their wrongs, make a horrid discord in the songs of freedom which resound through the land.

No people in the world profess so high a respect for liberty and equality as the people of the United States, and yet no people hold so many slaves, or make such great distinctions between man and man.

From various causes (among which we cheerfully admit a sense of justice to have held no inconsiderable rank) the work of emancipation has within a few years been rapidly advancing in a number of States. The State we live in, since the 4th of July, 1827, has been able to boast that she has no slaves, and other States where there still are slaves appear disposed to follow her example.

These things furnish us with cause of gratitude to God, and encourage us to hope that the time will speedily arrive when slavery will be universally abolished. Brethren, what a bright prospect would there be before us in this land had we no prejudices to contend against after being made free.

But, alas! the freedom to which we have attained is defective. Freedom and equality have been "put asunder." The rights of men are decided by the colour of their skin; and there is as much difference made between the rights of a free white man and a free coloured man as there is between a free coloured man and a slave.

Though delivered from the fetters of slavery, we are oppressed by an unreasonable, unrighteous, and cruel prejudice, which aims at nothing less than the forcing away of all the free coloured people of the United States to the distant shores of Africa. Far be it from me to impeach the motives of every member of the African Colonization Society. The civilizing and Christianizing of that vast continent, and the extirpation of the abominable traffic in slaves (which notwithstanding all the laws passed for its suppression is still carried on in all its horrors), are no doubt the principal motives which induce many to give it their support.

But there are those, and those who are most active and most influential in its cause, who hesitate not to say that they wish to rid the country of the free coloured population, and there is sufficient reason to believe, that with many, this is the principal motive for supporting that society; and that whether Africa is civilized or not, and whether the Slave Trade be suppressed or not, they would wish to see the free coloured people removed from this country to Africa.

Africa could certainly be brought into a state of civil and religious improvement without sending all the free people of colour in the United States there.

A few well-qualified missionaries, properly fitted out and supported, would do more for the instruction and improvement of the natives of that country than a host of colonists, the greater part of whom would need to be instructed themselves, and all of whom for a long period would find enough to do to provide for themselves instead of instructing the natives.

How inconsistent are those who say that Africa will be benefited by the removal of the free people of colour of the United States there, while they say they are the *most vile and degraded* people in the world. If we are as vile and degraded as they represent us, and they wish the Africans to be rendered a virtuous, enlightened and happy people, they should not *think* of sending *us* among them, lest we should make them worse instead of better.

The colonies planted by white men on the shores of America, so far from benefiting the aborigines, corrupted their morals, and caused their ruin; and yet those who say *we* are the most vile people in the world would send us to Africa to improve the character and condition of the natives. Such arguments would not be listened to for a moment were not the minds of the community strangely warped by prejudice.

Those who wish that that vast continent should be *compensated* for the injuries done it, by sending thither the light of the gospel and the arts of civilized life, should aid in sending and supporting well-qualified missionaries, who should be wholly devoted to the work of instruction, instead of sending colonists who would be apt to turn the ignorance of the natives to their own advantage, and do them more harm than good.

Much has also been said by Colonizationists about improving the character and condition of the people of colour of this country by sending them to Africa. This is more inconsistent still. We are to be improved by being sent far from civilized society. This is a novel mode of improvement. What is there in the burning sun, the arid plains, and barbarous customs of Africa, that is so peculiarly favourable to our improvement? What hinders our improving here, where schools and colleges abound, where the gospel is preached at every corner, and where all the arts and sciences are verging fast to perfection? Nothing, nothing but prejudice. It requires no large expenditures, no hazardous enterprises to raise the people of colour in the United States to as highly improved a state as any class of the community. All that is necessary is that those who profess to be anxious for it should lay aside their prejudices and act towards them as they do by others.

We are NATIVES of this country, we ask only to be treated as well as FOREIGNERS. Not a few of our fathers suffered and bled to purchase its independence; we ask only to be treated as well as those who fought against it. We have toiled to cultivate it, and to raise it to its present prosperous condition; we ask only to share equal privileges with those who come from distant lands, to enjoy the fruits of our labour. Let these moderate requests be granted, and we need not go to Africa nor anywhere else to be improved and happy. We cannot but doubt the purity of the motives of those persons who deny us these requests, and would send us to Africa to gain what they might give us at home.

But they say the prejudices of the country against us are invincible; and as they cannot be conquered, it is better that we should be removed beyond their influence. This plea should never proceed from the lips of any man who professes to believe that a just God rules in the heavens.

The African Colonization Society is a numerous and influential body. Would they lay aside their *own* prejudices, much of the burden would be at once removed; and their example (especially if they were as anxious to have *justice done us here* as to send us to Africa) would have such an influence upon the community at large as would soon cause prejudice to hide its deformed head.

But, alas! the course which they have pursued has an opposite tendency.

By the *scandalous misrepresentations* which they are continually giving of our character and conduct we have sustained much injury, and have reason to apprehend much more.

Without any charge of crime we have been denied all access to places to which we formerly had the most free intercourse; the coloured citizens of other places, on leaving their homes, have been denied the privilege of returning; and others have been absolutely driven out.

Has the Colonization Society had no effect in producing these barbarous measures?

They profess to have no other object in view than the colonizing of the free people of colour on the coast of Africa, with their *own consent;* but if our homes are made so uncomfortable that we cannot continue in them, or, if like our brethren of Ohio and New Orleans, we are driven from them, and no other door is open to receive us but Africa, our removal there will be anything but voluntary.

It is very certain that very few free people of colour *wish* to go to that *land.* The Colonization Society *know* this, and yet they do certainly calculate that in time they will have us all removed there.

How can this be effected but by making our situation worse here, and closing every other door against us?

God in His good providence has opened for such of us as may choose to leave these States an asylum in the neighbouring British Providence of Canada.

There is a large tract of land on the borders of Lake Huron, containing a million of acres, which is offered to our people at $1.50 per acre. It lies between the 42nd and 44th degrees of north latitude. The climate is represented as differing but little from this; the soil as good as any in the world; well timbered and watered. The laws are good, and the same for the coloured man as the white man. A powerful sympathy prevails there in our behalf, instead of the prejudice which here oppresses us; and everything encourages the hope, that by prudence and industry we may rise to as prosperous and happy a condition as any people under the sun.

To secure this land as a settlement for our people it is necessary that a payment of $6,000 be made on or before the 10th of November next.

This sum it is proposed to lay out in the purchase of 4,000 acres, and when paid will secure the keeping of the remainder in reserve for coloured emigrants ten years. The land so purchased is to be sold out by agents, or trustees to emigrants, and the moneys received in return to be appropriated to a second purchase, which is to be sold as at first, and the returns again laid out in land, until the whole tract is in their possession; and then the capital so employed is to be expended on objects of general utility.

The persons who have bargained for the land have found it necessary to apply to the citizens of the United States to aid them by their donations in raising the amount necessary to make their first purchase, and also to aid a number of emigrants who were driven away in a cruel manner, and in a destitute condition from Cincinnati, to seek a home where they might, and who have selected the Huron tract as their future abode.*

Each of these particulars present powerful claims to your liberality. "Cast thy bread upon the waters," says the wise man in the text, "and thou shalt find it after many days. Give a portion to seven and also to eight, for thou knowest not what evil shall be upon the earth." Oh! truly we "know not what evil shall be upon the earth."

When we look at the course of events, relative to our people in this country, we find reason to conclude that it is proper we should provide a convenient asylum to which we and our children may flee in case we should be so oppressed as to find it necessary to leave our present homes. The opinion is daily gaining ground, and has been often openly expressed, that it would be a great blessing to the country if all its free coloured population could be removed to Africa. As this opinion advances, recourse will naturally be had to such measures as will make us feel it necessary to go. Its operation has been already much felt in various States.

The coloured population of Cincinnati were an orderly, industrious and thriving people, but the white citizens, having determined to force them out, first entered into a combination that they would give none of them employment; and finally resorted to violent measures to compel them to go. Should the anxiety to get rid of us increase, have we not reason to fear that some such courses may be pursued in other places.

Satan is an inventive genius. He often appears under the garb of an angel of light, and makes religion and patriotism his plea for the execution of his designs. Our Lord foretold His disciples that "the time cometh, when whosoever killeth you, will think that he doeth God service." Brethren, the time is already come when *many* think that whosoever causeth us to remove from our native home does service to his country and to God.

Ah! to many in other places beside Cincinnati and New Orleans the sight of *free* men of colour is so unwelcome that we know not what they may think themselves justifiable in doing to get rid of them. Will it not then be wise for us to provide ourselves with a convenient asylum in time. We have now a fair opportunity of doing so; but if we neglect it, it may be occupied by others, and I know of none likely to be offered which promises so many advantages. Indeed, I feel warranted in saying, that if they are not

---

*On June 29, 1829, officials of Cincinnati issued a proclamation announcing their intention to enforce the 1804–1807 "black laws," requiring any black resident to produce a legal certificate of freedom and to post a bond of $500, signed by two white men, guaranteeing good behavior. By enforcing the law, whites sought to force the city's more than two thousand black residents to flee. African American workers were fired from their jobs and began to plan a migration to Canada. After white mobs attacked black residents in their homes for three days beginning on August 22, over twelve hundred African American residents fled for Canada West, Indiana, and Illinois. See Marilyn Baily, "From Cincinnati, Ohio to Wilberforce, Canada: A Note on Antebellum Colonization," *Journal of Negro History* 58 (October 1973), 427–40.

speedily secured, attempts will be made to prevent our securing them here-after, and that propositions have *actually* been made, by influential men, to purchase them, in order that the coloured people may not get them in their possession.

It is true that Africa and Hayti, and perhaps some other countries, will still afford us a place of refuge, yet it will not certainly be amiss to have Canada also at our choice. Some may prefer going there to any other place. But suppose we should never stand in need of such an asylum (and some think that our having provided it will make it less necessary, an effect we should all rejoice in, as we have no wish to go if we can stay in comfort); suppose we should never stand in need of such an asylum, still the amount required to secure it is so small that we can never regret parting with it for such an object. What is $6,000 to be raised by the coloured people through-out the United States? How few are so poor that they cannot give a few shil-lings without missing it? Let it have the amount which is usually spent by our people in this city on the Fourth of July in celebrating the national in-dependence, and it will make up a very considerable part of it.

I have been informed that at the suggestion of one of our coloured cler-gymen the members of one of the societies who intended to dine together tomorrow have agreed to give the money which would have been paid for dinner tickets to this object. This is truly patriotic. I would say to each of you, brethren "go and do likewise." Give what you would probably expend in celebrating the Fourth of July to the colony of your brethren in Canada; and on the birthday of American freedom secure the establishment of a col-ony in which you and your children may rise to respectability and happiness. Give it, and you will be no poorer than if you gave it not; and you will secure a place of refuge to yourselves in case of need. "Give a portion to seven and also to eight, for thou knowest not what evil shall be upon the earth."

You are strongly urged to liberality on this occasion by a regard to your future welfare. No scheme for our colonization that has ever yet been at-tempted has so few objections, or promises so many advantages; but if you withhold your aid until every imaginable objection is removed, you will never effect any object beneficial to yourselves or to your brethren.

Brethren, it is no time to cavil, but to help. If you mean to help the col-ony, help now. The amount of the first purchase must be paid by the 10th of November, or not at all. Brethren, this scheme of colonization opens to us a brighter door of hope than was ever opened to us before, and has a peculiar claim upon our patronage, because it has originated among our own people. It is not of the devising of the white men, nor of foreigners, but of our own kindred and household. If it succeeds, ours will be the credit. If it succeeds not, ours will be the fault. I am happy, however, to find that it meets the approbation of most, if not of all, of those wise and good men who have for many years been our most zealous and faithful friends, and it evidently ap-pears to be specially favoured by Providence. But the occasion has not only an appeal to your interest, but to your charity.

Your brethren exiled from Cincinnati for no crime but because God was pleased to clothe them with a darker skin than their neighbours cry to you from the wilderness for help. They ask you for bread, for clothing, and other necessaries to sustain them, their wives and their little ones, until by their industry they can provide themselves the means of support. It is true, there are some among them that are able to help themselves; but for these we do not plead. Those who can help themselves, will; but as the ablest have been sufferers in the sacrifice of their property, and the expenses and dangers of their forced and hurried removal, they are not able to assist their destitute brethren.

Indeed, most of the wealthy men of colour in Cincinnati arranged so as to remain until they could have a chance of disposing of their property to advantage; but the poor were compelled to fly without delay, and consequently need assistance. Brethren, can you deny it to them? I know you too well to harbour such a thought. It is only necessary to state to you their case to draw forth your liberality. Think then what these poor people must have suffered in being driven with their wives and their little ones from their comfortable homes late in autumn to take up their residence in a wide and desolate wilderness. Oh, *last* winter must have been to them a terrible one indeed! We hope that they, by their own efforts, will be better prepared for the next; but they must yet stand in need of help. They have the rude forest to subdue, houses to build, food to provide. They are the pioneers for the establishment of a colony, which may be a happy home for thousands and tens of thousands of our oppressed race. Oh, think of the situation of these, your brethren, whom the hand of oppression has driven into exile, and whom the providence of God has perhaps doomed, like Joseph, to suffering, that at some future day *much people may be saved alive.* Think of them, and give to their relief as your hearts may dictate. "Cast thy bread upon the waters," etc.■

18 THE CAUSE OF THE SLAVE BECAME MY OWN

Sarah M. Douglass

Sarah Mapps Douglass (1806–1882) was an active participant in the antislavery movement and was among the organizers of the Philadelphia Female Anti-Slavery Society and the Female Literary Society of Philadelphia. She wrote political essays for the Liberator *and the*

Anglo-African Magazine *and was a frequent lecturer. She opened and directed her own high school for African American women and later served as an instructor in physiology and hygiene at the Institute for Colored Youth.*

Douglass was a Quaker, attending the Arch Street Friends Meetinghouse in Philadelphia. Despite the Friends' staunch commitment to abolitionism, Douglass and other African Americans found themselves seated on segregated "Negro pews" when they attended Quaker meetings. Her explanation was characteristically direct: "I believe they despise us for our color." As with Maria Stewart, Douglass believed that social activism must be grounded in religious faith, and her speeches are replete with religious references. "We can do nothing for ourselves," she insisted, urging her listeners to place their "whole dependence on God."

Born to an affluent family and speaking to an audience composed primarily of Philadelphia's black elite, Douglass emphasized the need for the fortunate to look beyond their own lives to the misery of others. As she acknowledged, it was the experience of seeing the oppressor "lurking on the border of my own peaceful home" that induced her empathy, probably referring to recent initiatives in the Pennsylvania legislature to return fugitive slaves and restrict the rights of free blacks.

The following address was delivered to the recently formed Female Literary Society of Philadelphia in late June 1832. It appears in volume 3 of C. Peter Ripley, ed., The Black Abolitionist Papers (Chapel Hill: University of North Carolina Press, 1991), 116–17.

M Y FRIENDS—MY SISTERS: How important is the occasion for which we have assembled ourselves together this evening, to hold a feast, to feed our never-dying minds, to excite each other to deeds of mercy, words of peace; to stir up in the bosom of each, gratitude to God for his increasing goodness, and feeling of deep sympathy for our brethren and sisters, who are in this land of christian light and liberty held in bondage the most cruel and degrading—to make their cause our own!

An English writer has said, "We must feel deeply before we can act rightly; for that absorbing, heart-rendering compassion for ourselves springs a deeper sympathy for others, and from a sense of our weakness and our own upbraidings arises a disposition to be indulgent, to forbear, to forgive." This is my experience. One short year ago, how different were my feelings on the subject of slavery! It is true, the wail of the captive sometimes came to my ear in the midst of my happiness, and caused my heart to bleed for his wrongs; but, alas! the impression was as evanescent as the early cloud and morning dew. I had formed a little world of my own, and cared not to move beyond its precincts. But how was the scene changed when I beheld the oppressor lurking on the border of my own peaceful home! I saw his iron hand stretched forth to seize me as his prey, and the cause of the slave became my own. I started up, and with one mighty effort threw from me the lethargy which had covered me as a mantle for years; and determined, by the help of the Almighty, to use every exertion in my power to elevate the character of my wronged and neglected race. One year ago, I detested the slaveholder; now I can pity and pray for him. Has not this been your experience, my sisters? Have you not felt as I have felt upon this thrilling subject? My heart assures me some of you have.

And now, my sisters, I would earnestly and affectionately press upon you the necessity of placing your whole dependence on God; poor, weak, finite creatures as we are, we can do nothing for ourselves. He is all power-ful; He is waiting to be gracious to us as a people. Do you feel your inability to do good? Come to Him who giveth liberally and upbraideth not; bring your wrongs and fears to Him, as you would to a tender parent—He will sympathize with you. I know from blessed, heart-cheering experience the ex-cellency of having a God to trust to in seasons of trial and conflict. What but this can support us should the pestilence which has devastated Asia be born to us by the summer breezes? What but this can uphold our fainting footsteps in the swellings of Jordan? It is the only thing worth living for—the only thing that can disarm death of his sting. I am earnestly solicitous that each of us may adopt this language:

> *"I have no hope in man, but much in God—*
> *Much in the rock of ages"*

In conclusion, I would respectfully recommend that our mental feast should commence by reading a portion of the Holy Scriptures. A pause should pro-ceed the reading for supplication. It is my wish that the reading and conver-sation should be altogether directed to the subject of slavery. The refresh-ment which may be offered to you for the body, will be of the most simple kind, that you may feel for those who have nothing to refresh body and mind.■

19 IT IS TIME FOR US TO BE UP AND DOING

Peter Osborne

 The contradiction between the existence of slavery and the princi-ples enunciated in the Declaration of Independence caused many African Americans to refuse to celebrate the Fourth of July until after the Emancipation Proclamation. Most black Americans held their obser-

vance on July 5, and the speeches generally dealt with the need to apply the Declaration of Independence to all people, regardless of color. Some have praised Abraham Lincoln's Gettysburg Address for transforming America and the mission of the Civil War by rhetorically elevating the Declaration of Independence to constitutional status.* But Lincoln's actions were anticipated by Osborne and other black abolitionists who had seized upon the abolitionist implications and sacred status of the Declaration for decades before the Civil War.

In Osborne's jeremiadic vision, the Declaration is a compact for all Americans, including those of African descent, whose "forefathers fought, bled, and died to achieve the independence of the United States." Osborne urges black political unity to "contend for the prize" in America and resist the efforts of the emigrationists to foreclose their birthrights here.

The following speech was delivered by Peter Osborne, a Connecticut community leader, in the New Haven African Church on July 5, 1832. The address as presented here was taken from the Liberator *for December 1, 1832.*

FELLOW CITIZENS, on account of the misfortune of our color, our Fourth of July comes on the fifth. But I hope and trust that when the Declaration of Independence is fully executed, which declares that all men, without respect to person, were born free and equal, we may then have our Fourth of July on the fourth. It is thought by many that this is as impossible to take place, as it is for the leopard to change his spots; but I anticipate that the time is approaching very fast. The signs in the North, the signs in the South, in the East and West, are all favorable to our cause. Why, then, should we forbear contending for the civil rights of free countrymen? What man of national feeling would slumber in content under the yoke of slavery and oppression, in his own country? Not the most degraded barbarian in the interior of Africa.

If we desire to see our brethren relieved from the tyrannical yoke of slavery and oppression in the South, if we would enjoy the civil rights of free countrymen, it is high time for us to be up and doing. It has been said that we have already done well, but we can do better. What more can we do? Why, we must unite with our brethren in the North, in the South, and in the East and West, and then with the Declaration of Independence in one hand and the Holy Bible in the other, I think we might courageously give battle to the most powerful enemy to this cause. The Declaration of Independence has declared to man, without speaking of color, that all men are born free and equal. Has it not declared this freedom and equality to us too?

What man would content himself and say nothing of the rights of man with two millions of his brethren in bondage? Let us contend for the prize.

*See, for example, Garry Wills, *Lincoln at Gettysburg: The Words That Remade America* (New York: Simon and Schuster, 1992), 38–39.

Let us all unite and with one accord declare that we will not leave our own country to emigrate to Liberia,* or else, to be civilized or Christianized. Let us make it known to America that we are not barbarians; that we are not inhuman beings; that this is our native country; that our forefathers have planted trees in America for us, and we intend to stay and eat the fruit. Our forefathers fought, bled and died to achieve the independence of the United States. Why should we forbear contending for the prize? It becomes every colored citizen in the United States to step forward boldly and gallantly defend his rights. What has been done within a few years, since the union of the colored people? Are not the times more favorable to us now, than they were ten years ago? Are we not gaining ground? Yes—and had we begun this work forty years ago, I do not hesitate to say that there would not have been, at this day, a slave in the United States. Take, courage, then, ye Afric-Americans! Don't give up the conflict, for the glorious prize can be won.■

20 WHY SIT YE HERE AND DIE?

Maria W. Stewart

▥ *Maria W. Stewart was among the first native-born American women to leave extant copies of their public speeches. Speaking in public was widely regarded as unwomanly in the nineteenth century, and women's political opinions were both devalued and proscribed by law and social practice. Stewart resisted these pressures, asking, "What if I am a woman!" in her Boston farewell address of 1833. A person of deep religious conviction, she believed that the injustices to which she responded would have led even St. Paul to relent in his proscription of women's speech. If he knew "of our wrongs and deprivations," she argued, "he would make no objection to our pleading in public for our rights."*

Maria Miller was born in Hartford, Connecticut, in 1803. Orphaned at the age of five, she was "bound out in a clergyman's family" as a servant until the age of fifteen. In 1826, she married James W. Stewart, a shipping agent, in Boston, a center for black political activity. The Massachusetts General Colored Association, dedicated to agitation on both lo-

---

*In 1821, the American Colonization Society purchased land in Africa for the establishment of a colony that was named Liberia from the Latin word *liber,* meaning "free." Monrovia, its capital, was named in honor of President James Monroe (1758–1831), a member of the society.

cal and national issues, was founded in the year of their marriage. Locally produced black publications, such as Freedom's Journal, *offered their readers news of "whatever concerns us as a people . . . interwoven with all the principal news of the day." Boston's David Walker (1785–1830), whose 1829 tract,* Walker's Appeal, *called for armed self-defense and militant resistance to slavery and oppression, was a friend and mentor to Maria Stewart. James Stewart died in 1829, and Walker followed him (perhaps by poisoning) the following year. Grief-stricken, Maria Stewart underwent a powerful religious experience. Rooted in her newly deepened faith were a sense of "holy indignation" at the plight of African Americans and a commitment to speak out in public against the injustices that beset them. In the fall of 1831, Stewart approached William Lloyd Garrison, editor of the* Liberator, *with a manuscript urging African Americans to "sue for your rights and privileges" and to "know the reason that you cannot attain them." Writing shortly before the execution of Nat Turner, she stated defiantly, "We are not afraid of them that kill the body and after that can do no more."**

Highly unusual for her time, Stewart spoke in public on political topics before "promiscuous" audiences composed of both men and women. Black males in one of her audiences reportedly threw tomatoes at her when she upbraided them for failure to adhere to Christian principles (Yee, Black Women Abolitionists, *115). In her four Boston addresses of 1832 and 1833, Stewart denounced colonization schemes ("Before I go, the bayonet shall pierce me through") yet invoked pride in the African heritage (Richardson,* Maria W. Stewart, *17).*

The following speech was her second public lecture in Boston, delivered on September 21, 1832, at Franklin Hall, the meeting site of the New England Anti-Slavery Society. She offers poignant description of black women's labors and frustrations in domestic service, grounded in her own experience. She also makes it clear that black women labored under a double burden of racism and sexism. Denied education and prohibited from occupational advancement, she argues, African American women in the North were generally relegated to menial servitude that was little better than slavery.

The text comes from Marilyn Richardson, Maria W. Stewart: America's First Black Woman Political Writer *(Bloomington: Indiana University Press, 1987), 45–49. See also Shirley Yee,* Black Women Abolitionists: A Study in Activism, 1828–1860 *(Knoxville: University of Tennessee Press, 1992), 112–16.*

W hy sit ye here and die? If we say we will go to a foreign land, the famine and the pestilence are there, and there we shall die. If we sit

---

*Maria Stewart, Religion and the Pure Principles of Morality (1831), quoted in Richardson, *Maria W. Stewart,* 40.

here, we shall die. Come let us plead our case before the whites: if they save us alive we shall live—and if they kill us, we shall but die.

Methinks I heard a spiritual interrogation—'Who shall go forward, and take off the reproach that is cast upon the people of color? Shall it be a woman?' And my heart made this reply—'if it is thy will, be it even so, Lord Jesus!'

I have heard much respecting the horrors of slavery; but may Heaven forbid that the generality of my color throughout these United States should experience any more of its horrors than to be a servant of servants, or hewers of wood and drawers of water [Joshua 9:23]! Tell us no more of southern slavery; for with few expectations, although I may be very erroneous in my opinion, yet I consider our condition but little better than that. Yet, after all, methinks there are no chains so galling as those that bind the soul, and exclude it from the vast field of useful and scientific knowledge. O, had I received the advantages of an early education, my ideas would, ere now, have expanded far and wide; but, alas! I possess nothing but moral capability—no teachings but the teachings of the Holy Spirit.

I have asked several individuals of my sex, who transact business for themselves, if providing our girls were to give them the most satisfactory references, they would not be willing to grant them an equal opportunity with others? Their reply has been—for their own part, they had no objection; but as it was not the custom, were they to take them into their employ, they would be in danger of losing the public patronage.

And such is the powerful force of prejudice. Let our girls possess whatever amiable qualities of soul they may; let their characters be fair and spotless as innocence itself; let their natural taste and ingenuity be what they may; it is impossible for scarce an individual of them to rise above the condition of servants. Ah! why is this cruel and unfeeling distinction? Is it merely because God has made our complexion to vary? If it be, O shame to soft, relenting humanity! "Tell it not in Gath! publish it not in the streets of Askelon!" [2 Samuel 1:20]. Yet, after all, methinks were the American free people of color to turn their attention more assiduously to moral worth and intellectual improvement, this would be the result: prejudice would gradually diminish, and the whites would be compelled to say, unloose those fetters!

> *Though black their skins as shades of night*
> *Their hearts are pure, their souls are white.*

Few white persons of either sex, who are calculated for anything else, are willing to spend their lives and bury their talents in performing mean, servile labor. And such is the horrible idea that I entertain respecting a life of servitude, that if I conceived of their [*sic*] being no possibility of my rising above the condition of servant, I would gladly hail death as a welcome messenger. O, horrible idea, indeed! to possess noble souls aspiring after high and honorable acquirements, yet confined by the chains of ignorance and poverty to lives of continual drudgery and toil. Neither do I know of any who have enriched themselves by spending their lives as house-domestics, washing windows, shaking carpets, brushing boots, or tending upon gentlemen's tables. I can but die for expressing my sentiments; and I am as willing to die by the sword as the pestilence; for I am a true born American; your blood flows in my veins, and your spirit fires my breast.

I observed a piece in the Liberator a few months since, stating that the colonizationist had published a work respecting us, asserting that we were lazy and idle. I confute them on that point. Take us generally as a people, we are neither lazy or idle; and considering how little we have to excite or stimulate us, I am almost astonished that there are so many industrious and ambitious ones to be found; although I acknowledge, with extreme sorrow, that there are some who never were and never will be serviceable to society. And have you not a similar class among yourselves?

Again. It was asserted that we were "a ragged set, crying for liberty." I reply to it, the whites have so long and loudly proclaimed the theme of equal rights and privileges, that our souls have caught the flame also, ragged as we are. As far as our merit deserves, we feel a common desire to rise above the condition of servants and drudges. I have learnt, by bitter experience, that continual hard labor deadens the energies of the soul, and benumbs the faculties of the mind; the ideas become confined, the mind barren, and, like the scorching sands of Arabia, produces nothing; or like the uncultivated soil, brings forth thorns and thistles.

Again, continual and hard labor irritates our tempers and sours our dispositions; the whole system becomes worn out with toil and fatigue; nature herself becomes almost exhausted, and we care but little whether we live or die. It is true, that the free people of color throughout these United States are neither bought nor sold, nor under the lash of the cruel driver; many obtain a comfortable support; but few, if any, have an opportunity of becoming rich and independent; and the enjoyments we most pursue are as unprofitable to us as the spider's web or the floating bubbles that vanish into air. As servants, we are respected; but let us presume to aspire any higher, our employer regards us no longer. And were it not that the King eternal has declared that Ethiopia shall stretch forth her hands unto God, I should indeed despair.

I do not consider it derogatory, my friends, for persons to live out to service. There are many whose inclination leads them to aspire no higher; and I would highly commend the performance of almost anything for an honest livelihood; but where constitutional strength is wanting, labor of this kind, in the mildest form, is painful. And doubtless many are the prayers that has ascended to Heaven from Afric's daughters for strength to perform their work. Oh, many are the tears that have been shed for the want of that strength! Most of our color have dragged our as miserable existence of servitude from the cradle to the grave. And what literary acquirement can be made, or useful knowledge derived, from either maps, books, or charts, by those who continually drudge from Monday morning until Sunday noon? O, ye fairer sisters, whose hands are never soiled, whose nerves and muscles are never strained, go learn by experience! Had we had the opportunity that you have had, to improve our moral and mental faculties, what would have hindered our intellects from being as bright, and our manners from being as dignified as yours? Had it been our lot to have been nursed in the lap of affluence and ease, and to have basked beneath the smiles and sunshine of fortune, should we not have naturally supposed that we were never made to toil? And why are not our forms as delicate, and our constitutions as slender, as yours? Is not the workmanship as curious and complete? Have pity upon us, have pity on us, O ye who have hearts to feel for other's woes; for the hand of God has touched us. Owing to the disadvantages under which we labor, there are many flowers among us that are

> ... *born to bloom unseen*
> *And waste their fragrance on the desert air.*

My beloved brethren, as Christ had died in vain for those who will not accept his offered mercy, so will it be vain for the advocates of freedom to spend their breath in our behalf, unless with united hearts and souls you make some mighty efforts to raise your sons and daughters from the horrible state of servitude and degradation in which they are placed. It is upon you that woman depends; she can do but little besides using her influence; and it is for her sake and yours that I have come forward and made myself a hissing and reproach among the people [Jeremiah 29:18]; for I am also one of the wretched and miserable daughters of the descendants of fallen Africa. Do you ask, why are you wretched and miserable? I reply, look at many of the most worthy and most interesting of us doomed to spend our lives in gentlemen's kitchens. Look at our young men, smart, active and energetic, with souls filled with ambitious fire; if they look forward, alas! What are their prospects? They can be nothing but the humblest laborers, on account of their dark complexions; hence many of them lose their ambition, and become worthless. Look at our middle-aged men, clad in their rusty plaids and coats; in winter, every cent they earn goes to buy their wood and pay their rent; the poor wives also toil beyond their strength, to help support their families. Look at our aged sires, whose heads are whitened with the frosts of seventy winters, with their old wood-saws on their backs. Alas, what keeps us so? Prejudice, ignorance and poverty. But ah! methinks our oppression is soon to come to an end; yea, before the Majesty of heaven, our groans and cries have reached the ears of the Lord of Sabaoth [James 5:4]. As the prayers and tears of Christians will avail the finally impenitent nothing; neither will the prayers and tears of the friends of humanity avail us anything, unless we possess a spirit of virtuous emulation within our breasts. Did the pilgrims, when they first landed on these shores, quietly compose themselves and say, "The Britons have all the money and all the power, and we must continue their servants forever?" Did they sluggishly sigh and say, "Our lot is hard, the Indians own the soil, and we cannot cultivate it?" No; they first made powerful efforts to raise themselves and then God raised up those illustrious patriots, WASHINGTON and LAFAYETTE, to assist and defend them. And, my brethren, have you made a powerful effort? Have you prayed the legislature for mercy's sake to grant you all the rights and privileges of free citizens, that your daughters may rise to that degree of respectability which true merit deserves, and your sons above the servile situations which most of them fill?■

21 LET US ALONE

Nathaniel Paul

Born in New Hampshire, Paul (c. 1793–1839) assumed the pastorate of Albany's First African Baptist Church in 1820. He campaigned both against slavery and against racial discrimination while arguing that blacks could diminish white prejudice through temperance, educational achievement, and diligent labor.

But in 1830, frustrated with black progress and prospects in the United States, Paul emigrated to the Wilberforce Colony in Upper Canada. Two years later, he was sent to England to raise funds. In 1833–1834, Paul and William Lloyd Garrison toured Britain to campaign against the efforts and claims of the American Colonization Society, whose representative, Elliot Cresson, was then engaged in a British fundraising tour.

*On July 13, 1833, Paul appeared with Garrison at an anticolonization meeting in London's Exeter Hall, where he delivered the following address. Through the persuasive efforts of Paul and other visiting black American lecturers who soon followed him, writes Peter Ripley, "British antislavery leaders came to recognize that a black abolitionist presence was essential to the development of British abolitionism" (*Witness for Freedom, *44).*

The text of Paul's speech was published in Speeches Delivered at the Anti-Colonization Meeting in Exeter Hall, London *(Boston: Isaac Knapp, 1833), 12–15, and was reprinted in Dorothy Porter,* Early Negro Writing, 1760–1837 *(Boston: Beacon Press, 1971), 286–91. See also C. Peter Ripley,* Witness for Freedom: African American Voices on Race, Slavery, and Emancipation *(Chapel Hill: University of North Carolina Press, 1993).*

In rising to address an audience of this description, I shall not offer an apology, because I consider it to be unnecessary. Nature has furnished me with an apology in the complexion that I wear, and that shall speak in my behalf. (Cheers.)

Allow me to say that Mr. Garrison* has, for many years past, devoted himself exclusively to the interests of the slaves and the free people of color in the United States of America. He requires, however, no commendation from me, or from any other gentleman whatever; "the tree is known by its fruits," and "out of the abundance of the heart, the mouth speaketh." But if there be any necessity for calling evidence in favor of that gentleman, there is an abundance, demonstrating that he has acted a most disinterested part on behalf of those whose cause he has espoused. It has been his lot to make large sacrifices, in order that he might be enabled to pursue the object of his heart's desire. He might have swum upon the tide of popular applause, and have had the great and the noble of our country on his side, who would now have been applauding him, instead of persecuting him as the disturber of the peace and tranquility of the nation, if he had not lifted up his voice on behalf of the suffering slaves. (Hear, hear.) To my certain knowledge, when he commenced his career, it was under the most unfavorable circumstances. No one stood forward in his defense, and he was under the necessity of adopting and pursuing a system of the most rigid economy, in order that he might be sustained while he was engaged in the important work he had undertaken.

But it is not merely the sacrifice that Mr. Garrison has made, or the rigid system of economy that he has adopted, that speaks on his behalf; but the sufferings that he has endured likewise recommend him to the attention of every philanthropist. This gentleman has suffered forty-nine days incarceration in a prison in the city of Baltimore, in the State of Maryland, because he had the hardihood to engage in defense of the suffering slaves in that State. The fact of Mr. Garrison's imprisonment has been loudly sounded throughout this country. The agent of the American Colonization Society has seen fit to represent Mr. Garrison as a mere pamphleteer, as the editor of a Negro newspaper in the United States, and as a convicted libeller. This is the manner in which this gentleman has been spoken of in this country, by the agent of the American Colonization Society. And does that agent suppose that by such mere slang he can lower Mr. Garrison in the estimation of the British public? The simpleton reminds me of another of whom I have heard, who, for some cause or other, became exceedingly exasperated at the moon, and stood the whole night angrily shaking his fist at it, but could not reach it. (Cheers.)

I make no complaint against the agent of the American Colonization Society for stating the fact that Mr. Garrison was convicted, and thrown into prison in the United States; it is a fact, and he had a right to the advantage of it whenever he saw fit. I only blame him because, in stating it, he did not tell the cause why—who the persons were at whose instigation it was done—

---

*Abolitionist William Lloyd Garrison (1805–1879) was editor of the *Liberator* and a founder of the American Anti-Slavery Society.

or the character of the court that condemned him. Inasmuch as that gentleman did not perform that part of his duty, if you will allow me I will undertake to discharge it for him.

Perhaps it is not generally known that in the United States of America—that land of freedom and equality—the laws are so exceedingly liberal that they give to man the liberty of purchasing as many negroes as he can find means to pay for (hear, hear), and also the liberty to sell them again. In consequence of this, a regular system of merchandise is established in the souls and bodies of our fellow creatures. It so happened that a very large number of mercantile gentlemen resided in the city of Baltimore and its vicinity, who were engaged in this traffic; and Mr. Garrison had the impudence, the unblushing effrontery to state, in a public newspaper, that this traffic was a direct violation of the laws of God, and contrary to the principles of human nature. (Cheers.) This was the crime of which he was convicted. And now I will tell you the character of the judicial tribunal before which the conviction took place. Allow me to say, and let that suffice, that the judges of the court were slaveholders (hear, hear), and the jury likewise. Had it been the case that such men as William Wilberforce, Thomas Clarkson, Thomas Fowell Buxton,[*] James Cropper,[†] and in addition to these, the honorable gentleman who sits on my right (Mr. O'Connell)[‡] (cheers), and had these gentlemen in the place where Mr. Garrison resided pursued the course they have adopted in this country, they would have been indicted, convicted, and thrown into prison. In regard to my friend on my right, (Mr. O'Connell,) I know not what they would have done with him: he could have expected no quarters whatever. (Laughter and cheers.) I believe he has more than once arraigned the American Republic before the British community, before God, and before the world, as the most detestable political hypocrite in the world. And this is not all. I may say, in addition, that that Court and that jury would have convicted the whole Anti-Slavery Society of this country, and would have transported them all to Liberia as the punishment of their crimes. (Laughter and loud cheers.)

These are the causes and these the reasons why our friend, Mr. Garrison, was imprisoned; and as I said before, tho' I have no complaint to make against the agent of that benevolent institution, as it is called—the American Colonization Society—for stating that Mr. Garrison was cast into prison; yet I submit that, in connection with it, he ought to have told the reason why it took place. But I shall leave this Garrison to itself. It possesses, I believe, ammunition enough to defend itself from any attack that may be made upon

---

[*]Buxton (1786–1845) led the antislavery party in the House of Commons and founded the African Civilization Society.

[†]Cropper (1773–1841) was an antislavery pamphleteer and philanthropist.

[‡]Daniel O'Connell (1775–1847), Irish member of Parliament, supported the abolition of the West Indian slave trade.

it, either by the agent of that Society, or the gentleman who has appeared here to plead on its behalf this morning. (Loud applause.)

I now come directly to express my views in relation to the American Colonization Society.

As a colored man, and as a citizen of the United States, it necessarily follows that I must feel more deeply interested in its operation, than any other individual present. In relation to the Society, I know not which is the most detestable in my view—its cruelty, or its hypocrisy. Both of these are characteristics of its whole operation.

I brand it as a cruel institution, and one of the most cruel that has ever been brought into existence by the ingenuity of man. If I am asked, why it is cruel? I answer, in the first place, because it undertakes to expel from their native country hundreds of thousands of unoffending and inoffensive individuals, who, in time of war, have gone forth into the field of battle, and have contended for the liberties of that country. Why does it seek to expel them? Because the God of heaven has given them a different complexion from themselves. (Cheers.) I say it is a cruel institution, because it seeks to rob the colored men in that country of every right, civil, political or religious, to which they are entitled by the American Declaration of Independence. It is through the influence of that Society, to the everlasting disgrace of a land boasting of liberty and equality, that there are laws enacted which absolutely forbid the instruction of the slave, or even the free person of color, in the use of letters. I say it is a cruel institution, because in addition to this, it has also been the means of having laws enacted which prevents them from meeting together to pay homage to their Creator, and worship the God who made them. I might go on enumerating instances of cruelty, and show to this meeting that even combinations have been formed in what are called the free States, under the influence of this Society, not to give to the colored man employment, but to rob him of the means of gaining his livelihood, that he may thereby be compelled to leave the land of his nativity, and go to Africa.

In the next place, I condemn the Society on account of its hypocrisy; and this, I believe, will be detested wherever it appears, by every honest man. And wherein does that hypocrisy consist or appear? I mean more particularly in regard to the representations which have been made of the Society in this country. It comes to Great Britain, and begins to talk about the evils of slavery, pitying the condition of the unhappy victims of cruelty and oppression in the United States of America; and it tells the British public that its object is to do away with slavery, and to emancipate those who are in bondage. What Briton's heart is there but responds to such a sentiment as this? (Cheers.) Englishmen are seeking for the liberation of the slaves; and, giving credit to the reports which they have heard respecting the American Colonization Society, without examining its principles, many benevolent individuals in this country have come forward and freely contributed to its funds. But instead of the institution being the enemy of slavery; instead of its being formed for the purpose of annihilating the system; its object is to perpetuate it, and render more secure the property of man in man. I will show to the meeting, in a few words, that its object cannot be the abolition of slavery, because through a hundred of its organs it has over and over again denounced the proposition of liberating the slaves, except on condition of their being transported to Africa. And now let the audience understand that, at the present time, there are upwards of 2,000,000 of slaves in the United States, and that their annual increase is more than 60,000. If slavery, therefore, is to be abolished only as those who shall be emancipated are transported from the United States to Africa, we ask, when is slavery to cease in that country? The Colonization Society, with all the efforts that it can bring to bear, cannot transport the annual increase of the slaves (hear, hear), and, therefore, if no other means be adopted for the abolition of slavery in America, its extinction will not take place until the last trumpet shall sound. (Immense applause.)

Again I repeat it, it is hypocritical, because it professes to be the friend of the free people of color, and to pity their present condition; and hence it says, "It seeks to promote their welfare." That gentleman (Mr. Abrahams) tells us that he is acquainted with the people of North America, and that this Society is formed, in part, for the benefit of the free people of color. Does that gentleman know that when an effort was made at New Haven, two or three years since, to establish a College for the instruction of the free people of color,—notwithstanding New Haven is within the boundaries of that part of the country which is called the "free States," yet the supporters of the Society came forward, held a meeting, and passed the most spirited resolutions against the establishment of that institution in the city? (Hear, hear!) Does that gentleman know that in the same State, a white female, in endeavoring to establish a school for the instruction of colored females,* has been most inhumanly assailed by the advocates of the Colonization Society, who, in town meetings, passed resolutions against her benevolent object, as spirited as if the cholera were about to break out in the village, and they by a single effort of this kind could hinder its devastations? They could not have acted with more promptness, and energy, and violence, than they did in persecuting this excellent lady, because her compassion led her to espouse the cause of the suffering blacks. (Cheers.) They were ready to expel her from the country. I could relate many facts with regard to that part of the country for which the Rev. gentleman contends, and show that, instead of the American Colonization Society seeking the welfare of the free people of color, it is their most bitter enemy. Whenever it speaks of this class, both in public and in private, it calumniates and abuses them in the most extravagant manner, as its reports will abundantly show.

Wishing to be brief, and knowing that there are gentlemen present who

---

*When Prudence Crandall's school for girls in Canterbury, Connecticut, admitted a black student in 1832, it was forced to close. The following year Crandall opened a boardingschool for black girls and was arrested and convicted of violating the state's newly passed law prohibiting education of nonresident blacks.

will address you with more interest than I can (hear, hear), I will make but one remark more, and that respects the designs of this Society with regard to Africa. O, bleeding, suffering Africa! We hear of the sad condition which that country is in; it is enveloped in darkness infinitely deeper than the sable hue of its degraded sons. The vilest superstition there abounds; and hence this Society represents it as their object to let in the rays of the gospel, and enlighten the people. But, according to their own reports, whom do they select as instruments to spread civilization and christianity? People not fit to live in America—people who are a disgrace to that country. (Hear, hear.) I pity Africa as much as any man; I want her to be enlightened; but let us send men who are enlightened themselves. If we mean to evangelize Africa, let us at least send Christians there to do the work. (Cheers.)

Mr. Garrison has well remarked that the free people of color in the United States are opposed to this Society. I will venture to assert that I am as extensively acquainted with them, throughout both the free and slave States, as any man in that country; and I do not know of a solitary colored individual who entertains the least favorable view of the American Colonization Society; but, in every way they possibly could, they have expressed their disapprobation of it. They have said to the Society, *"Let us alone."*

The argument which is brought by the friends of the Society in favor of colonization is, that the white population of America can never amalgamate or live on terms of equality with the blacks. Be it so. Let it be admitted that their prejudices are strong. All that I will say is, that if such be the case, they ought not to send an agent to this country to ask assistance to enable them to gratify a prejudice of which they ought to be ashamed.■

22 WHAT IF I AM A WOMAN?

Maria W. Stewart

This speech contains Stewart's most comprehensive discussion of the need for women—and especially African American women—to participate in politics and social change. She draws inspiration from the past achievements of women in many nations and ages, asking: "What if such women as are here described should rise among our sable race?"

In her farewell address, delivered on September 21, 1833, Stewart alludes to the difficulties she had faced in Boston, which remained a segregated city. "During the short period of my Christian warfare," she la-

ments, "I have indeed had to contend against the fiery darts of the devil." Scorned and jeered for the advocacy of her beliefs, she nonetheless persisted in speaking out, convinced that her God was speaking through her: "He hath unloosed my tongue, and put his word in my mouth, in order to confound and put all those to shame that have rose up against me." Stewart justifies her violation of proscriptions against public speaking partly in the same way that black American women did decades earlier in the Great Awakening as itinerant exhorters: God commands me to speak and His is a higher law.

But Stewart goes far beyond this argument. Her speech is significant because she not only pleads for the slave and calls upon African Americans to live in greater righteousness but also firmly defends her right as a woman to do so. Stewart was a pioneer advocate of women's rights. In a speech to the Female Literary Association of Philadelphia, published in the Liberator *of June 9, 1832, she had touched on this theme. But here she really developed it "in words," according to Eleanor Flexner, "that heralded the arguments the Grimkés were to use a few years later" (*Century of Struggle, 44*). She describes women's accomplishments in the public sphere and decries the barriers that prevent other women from realizing their ambitions and abilities.*

After leaving Boston, Stewart moved to New York, where she became a teacher and eventually assistant principal at the Williamsburg school. She wrote for Frederick Douglass's paper, the North Star, *and remained an active participant in the antislavery movement. Stewart died in December 1879, shortly after the publication of* Meditations, *her collected works.*

The speech is reprinted from Meditations from the Pen of Mrs. Maria W. Stewart *(Washington, D.C., 1879), 74–82. See also Marilyn Richardson,* Maria W. Stewart, America's First Black Woman Political Writer *(Bloomington: Indiana University Press, 1987); and Eleanor Flexner,* Century of Struggle: The Woman's Rights Movement in the United States *(Cambridge, Mass.: Belknap Press, 1959).*

> "Is this vile world a friend to grace,
> To help me on to God?"

Ah, no! For it is with great tribulation that any shall enter through the gates of the holy city [Acts 14:22].

My Respected Friends, You have heard me observe that the shortness of time, the certainty of death, and the instability of all things here, induce me to turn my thoughts from earth to heaven. Borne down with a heavy load of sin and shame, my conscience filled with remorse; considering the throne of God forever guiltless, and my own eternal condemnation as just, I was at last brought to accept of salvation as a free gift, in and through the merits of a crucified Redeemer. Here I was brought to see,

'Tis not by works of righteousness
That our own hands have done,
But we are saved by grace alone,
Abounding through the Son.

After these convictions, in imagination I found myself sitting at the feet of Jesus, clothed in my right mind. For I had been like a ship tossed to and fro, in a storm at sea. Then was I glad when I realized the dangers I had escaped; and then I consecrated my soul and body, and all the powers of my mind to his service, and from that time henceforth; yea, even for evermore, amen.

I found that religion was full of benevolence; I found there was joy and peace in believing, and I felt as though I was commanded to come out from the world and be separate; to go forward and be baptized. Methought I heard a spiritual interrogation, are you able to drink of that cup that I have drank of? And to be baptized with the baptism that I have been baptized with [Matthew 20:22]? And my heart made this reply: Yea, Lord, I am able. Yet amid these bright hopes, I was filled with apprehensive fears, lest they were false. I found that sin still lurked within; it was hard for me to renounce all for Christ, when I saw my earthly prospects blasted. O, how bitter was that cup. Yet I drank it to its very dregs. It was hard for me to say, thy will be done; yet I was made to bend and kiss the rod. I was at last made willing to be anything or nothing, for my Redeemer's sake. Like many, I was anxious to retain the world in one hand, and religion in the other. "Ye cannot serve and God and mammon [Matthew 6:24]," sounded in my ear, and with giant-strength, I cut off my right hand, as it were, and plucked out my right eye, and cast them from me, thinking it better to enter life halt and maimed, rather than having two hands or eyes to be cast into hell [Mark 9:43]. Thus ended these mighty conflicts, and I received this heart-cheering promise, "That neither death, nor life, nor principalities, nor powers, nor things present, nor things to come, should be able to separate me from the love of Christ Jesus, our Lord [Romans 8:38,39]."

And truly, I can say with St. Paul that at my conversion I came to the people in the fullness of the gospel of grace [Romans 15:29]. Having spent a few months in the city of ———, previous, I saw the flourishing condition of their churches, and the progress they were making in their Sabbath Schools. I visited their Bible classes, and heard of the union that existed in their Female Associations. On my arrival here, not finding scarce an individual who felt interested in these subjects, and but few of the whites, except Mr. Garrison, and his friend, Mr. Knapp; and hearing that those gentlemen had observed that female influence was powerful, my soul became fired with a holy zeal for your cause; every nerve and muscle in me was engaged in your behalf. I felt that I had a great work to perform; and was in haste to make a profession of my faith in Christ, that I might be about my Father's business [Luke 2:49]. Soon after I made this profession, The Spirit of God came before me, and I spake before many. When going home, reflecting on what I had said, I felt ashamed, and knew not where I should hide myself. A something said within my breast, "Press forward, I will be with thee." And my heart made this reply, Lord, if thou wilt be with me, then I will speak for thee as long as I live. And thus far I have every reason to believe that it is the divine influence of the Holy Spirit operating upon my heart that could possibly induce me to make the feeble and unworthy efforts that I have.

But to begin my subject: "Ye have heard that it hath been said, whoso is angry with his brother without a cause, shall be in danger of the judgment; and whoso shall say to his brother, Raca, shall be in danger of the council. But whosoever shall say, thou fool, shall be in danger of hell-fire [Matthew 5:22]." For several years my heart was in continual sorrow. And I believe that the Almighty beheld from his holy habitation, the affliction wherewith I was afflicted, and heard the false misrepresentations wherewith I was misrepresented, and there was none to help. Then I cried unto the Lord in my troubles. And thus for wise and holy purposes, best known to himself, he has raised me in the midst of my enemies, to vindicate my wrongs before this people; and to reprove them from sin, as I have reasoned to them of righteousness and judgment to come. "For as the heavens are higher than the earth, so are his ways above our ways, and his thoughts above our thoughts [Isaiah 55:9]." I believe, that for wise and holy purposes, best known to himself, he hath unloosed my tongue, and put his word into my mouth, in order to confound and put all those to shame that have rose up against me. For he hath clothed my face with steel, and lined my forehead with brass. He hath put his testimony within me and engraved his seal on my forehead. And with these weapons I have indeed set the fiends of earth and hell at defiance.

What if I am a woman; is not the God of ancient times the God to these modern days? Did he not raise up Deborah to be a mother and judge in Israel? Did not Queen Esther save the lives of the Jews? And Mary Magdalene first declare the resurrection of Christ from the dead? Come, said the woman of Samaria, and see a man that hath told me all things that ever I did; is it not this the Christ? St. Paul declared that it was a shame for a woman to speak in public, yet our great High Priest and Advocate did not condemn the woman for a more notorious offense than this; neither will he condemn this worthless worm. The bruised reed he will not break, and the smoking flax he will not quench till he send forth judgment unto victory. Did St. Paul but know of our wrongs and deprivations, I presume he would make no objection to our pleading in public for our rights.

Again: Holy women ministered unto Christ and the apostles; and women of refinement in all ages, more or less, have had a voice in moral, religious, and political subjects. Again: Why the Almighty hath imparted unto me the power of speaking thus I cannot tell. "And Jesus lifted up his voice and said, I thank thee, O Father, Lord of heaven and earth, that thou hast hid these things from the wise and prudent and hast revealed them unto babes: even so, Father, for so it seemed good in thy sight."

But to convince you of the high opinion that was formed of the capacity and ability of woman by the ancients, I would refer you to "Sketches of the Fair Sex." Read to the fifty-first page, and you will find that several of the northern nations imagined that women could look into futurity, and that they had about them an inconceivable something approaching to divinity. Perhaps the idea was only the effect of the sagacity common to the sex, and the advantages which their natural address gave them over rough and simple warriors. Perhaps, also, those barbarians, surprised at the influence which beauty has over force, were led to ascribe to the supernatural attraction a charm which they could not comprehend. A belief, however, that the Deity more readily communicates himself to women, has at one time or other prevailed in every quarter of the earth: nor only among the Germans and the Britons, but all the people of Scandinavia were possessed of it. Among the Greeks, women delivered the oracles. The respect the Romans paid to the Sybils is well known. The Jews had their prophetesses. The prediction of the Egyptian women obtained much credit at Rome, even unto the emperors. And in most barbarous nations all things that have the appearance of being supernatural, the mysteries of religion, the secrets of physic, and the rights of magic, were in the possession of women.

If such women as are here described have once existed, be no longer astonished, then, my brethren and friends, that God at this eventful period should raise up your own females to strive by their example, both in public and private, to assist those who are endeavoring to stop the strong current of prejudice that flows so profusely against us at present. No longer ridicule their efforts, it will be counted for sin. For God makes use of feeble means sometimes to bring about his most exalted purposes.

In the fifteenth century, the general spirit of this period is worthy of observation. We might then have seen women preaching and mixing themselves in controversies. Women occupying the chair of Philosophy and Justice; women haranging in Latin before the Pope; women writing in Greek and studying in Hebrew; nuns were poetesses and women of quality divines; and young girls who had studied eloquence would, with the sweetest countenances and the most plaintiff voices, pathetically exhort the Pope and the Christian princes to declare war against the Turks. Women in those days devoted their leisure hours to contemplation and study. The religious spirit which has animated women in all ages showed itself at this time. It has made them, by turns, martyrs, apostles, warriors, and concluded in making them divines and scholars.*

*Stewart is here reporting information gleaned from her reading of John Adams, *Woman, Sketches of the History, genius, Disposition, Accomplishments, Employment, Customs and Importance of the Fair Sex in all Parts of the World* (London, 1790). For an account of the influence of this work on Stewart's thought, see Marilyn Richardson, " 'What If I Am A Woman?': Maria W. Stewart's "Defense of Black Women's Political Activism," in Donald M. Jacobs, ed., *Courage and Conscience: Black and White Abolitionists in Boston* (Bloomington: Indiana University Press, 1993), 201–3.

Why cannot a religious spirit animate us now? Why cannot we become divines and scholars? Although learning is somewhat requisite, yet recollect that those great apostles, Peter and James, were ignorant and unlearned. They were taken from a fishing-boat, and made fishers of men.

In the thirteenth century, a young lady of Bologne devoted herself to the study of the Latin language and of the laws. At the age of twenty-three she pronounced a funeral oration in Latin in the great church of Bologne; and to be admitted as an orator, she had neither need of indulgence on account of her youth or of her sex. At the age of twenty-six she took the degree of doctor of laws, and began publicly to expound the Institutes of Justinian. At the age of thirty, her great reputation raised her to a chair, where she taught the law to a prodigious concourse of scholars from all nations. She joined the charms and accomplishments of a woman to all the knowledge of a man. And such was the power of her eloquence, that her beauty was only admired when her tongue was silent.

What if such women as are here described should rise among our sable race? And it is not impossible; for it is not the color of the skin that makes the man or the woman, but the principle formed in the soul. Brilliant wit will shine, come from whence it will; and genius and talent will not hide the brightness of its lustre.

But to return to my subject. The mighty work of reformation has begun among this people. The dark clouds of ignorance are dispersing. The light of science is bursting forth. Knowledge is beginning to flow; nor will its moral influence be extinguished till its refulgent rays have spread over us from East to West and from North to South. Thus far is this mighty work begun, but not as yet accomplished. Christians must awake from their slumbers. Religion must flourish among them before the church will be built up in its purity or immorality be suppressed.

Yet, notwithstanding your prospects are thus fair and bright, I am about to leave you, perhaps never more to return; for I find it is no use for me, as an individual, to try to make myself useful among my color in this city. It was contempt for my moral and religious opinions in private that drove me thus before a public. Had experience more plainly shown me that it was the nature of man to crush his fellow, I should not have thought it so hard. Wherefore, my respected friends, let us no longer talk of prejudice till prejudice becomes extinct at home. Let us no longer talk of opposition till we cease to oppose our own. For while these evils exist, to talk is like giving breath to the air and labor to the wind, Though wealth is far more highly prized than humble merit, yet none of these things move me. Having God for my friend and portion, what have I to fear? Promotion cometh neither from the East or West; and as long as it is the will of God, I rejoice that I am as I am; for man in his best estate is altogether vanity. Men of eminence have mostly risen from obscurity; nor will I, although a female of a darker hue, and far more obscure than they, bend my head or hang my harp upon willows; for though poor, I will virtuous prove. And if it is the will of my

Heavenly Father to reduce me to penury and want, I am ready to say: Amen, even so be it. "The foxes have holes, and the birds of the air have nests, but the Son of man hath not where to lay his head."

During the short period of my Christian warfare, I have indeed had to contend against the fiery darts of the devil. And was it not that the righteous are kept by the mighty power of God through faith unto salvation, long before this I should have proved to be like the seed by the wayside; for it has actually appeared to me, at different periods, as though the powers of earth and hell had combined against me, to prove my overthrow. Yet amidst their dire attempts, I found the Almighty to be "a friend that sticketh closer than a brother." He never will forsake the soul that leans on him; though he chastens and corrects, it is for the soul's best interest. "And as a father pitieth his children, so the Lord pitieth them that fear him."

But some of you said: "Do not talk so much about religion; the people do not wish to hear you. We know these things; tell us something we do not know." If you know these things, my dear friends, and have performed them, far happier and more prosperous would you now have been. "He that knoweth his Lord's will, and obeyeth it not, shall be beaten with many stripes." Sensible of this, I have, regardless of the frowns and scoffs of a guilty world, plead up religion and the pure principles of morality among you. Religion is the most glorious theme that mortals can converse upon. The older it grows the more new beauties it displays. Earth, with its brilliant attractions, appears mean and sordid when compared to it. It is that fountain that has no end, and those that drink thereof shall never thirst; for it is, indeed, a well of water springing up in the soul unto everlasting life.

Again: Those ideas of greatness which are held forth to us are vain delusions—are airy visions which we shall never realize. All that man can say or do can never elevate us; it is a work that must be effected between God and ourselves. And how? By dropping all political discussions in our behalf; for these, in my opinion, sow the seed of discord and strengthen the cord of prejudice. A spirit of animosity is already risen, and unless it is quenched, a fire will burst forth and devour us, and our young will be slain by the sword. It is the sovereign will of God that our condition should be thus and so. "For he hath formed one vessel for honor and another for dishonor." And shall the clay say to him that formed it: Why hast Thou formed me thus? It is high time for us to drop political discussions; and when our day of deliverance comes, God will provide a way for us to escape, and fight his own battles.

Finally, my brethren, let us follow after godliness, and the things which make for peace. Cultivate your own minds and morals: real merit will elevate you. Pure religion will burst your fetters. Turn your attention to industry. Strive to please your employers. Lay up what you earn. And remember that the grave distinction withers and the high and low are like renowned.

But I draw to a conclusion. Long will the kind sympathy of some much-loved friend be written on the table of my memory, especially those kind of individuals who have stood by me like pitying angels and befriended me when in the midst of difficulty, many blessings rest on them. Gratitude is all the tribute I can offer. A rich reward awaits them.

To my unconverted friends, one and all, I would say, shortly this frail tenement of mine will be dissolved and lie mouldering in ruins. O, solemn thought! Yet why should I revolt, for it is the glorious hope of a blessed immorality beyond the grave that has supported me thus far through this vale of tears. Who among you will strive to meet me at the right hand of Christ? For the great day of retribution is fast approaching; and who shall be able to abide his coming? You are forming characters for eternity. As you live, so you will die; as death leaves you, so judgment will find you. Then shall we receive the glorious welcome: "Come, ye blessed of my Father, inherit the kingdom prepared for you from before the foundation of the world." Or hear the heartrending sentence: "Depart, ye cursed, into everlasting fire prepared for the devil and his angels." When thrice ten thousand years have rolled away, eternity will be but just begun. Your ideas will but just begin to expand. O, eternity, who can unfathom thine end or comprehend thy beginning?

Dearly beloved, I have made myself contemptible in the eyes of many, that I might win some. But it has been like labor in vain. "Paul may plant and Apollos water, but God alone giveth the increase."

To my brethren and sisters in the church I would say, be ye clothed with the breast-plate of righteousness, having your loins girt about you with truth, prepared to meet the bridegroom at his coming: for blessed are those servants that are found watching.

Farewell! In a few short years from now we shall meet in those upper regions where parting will be no more. There we shall sing and shout, and shout and sing, and make heaven's high arches ring. There we shall range in rich pastures and partake of those living streams that never dry. O, blissful thought! Hatred and contention shall cease, and we shall join with redeemed millions in ascribing glory and honor and riches and power and blessing to the Lamb that was slain and to Him that sitteth upon the throne. Nor eye hath seen nor ear heard, neither hate it entered into the heart of man to conceive of the joys that are prepared for them that love God. Thus far, has my life been almost a life of complete disappointment. God has tried me as by fire. Well was I aware that if I contended boldly for his cause I must suffer. Yet I chose rather to suffer affliction with his people than to enjoy the pleasures of sin for a season. And I believe that the glorious declaration was about to be made applicable to me that was made to God's ancient convent people by the prophet: "Comfort ye, comfort ye, my people; say unto her that her warfare is accomplished, and that her inequities are pardoned. I believe that a rich reward awaits me, if not in this world, in the world to come. O, blessed reflection. The bitterness of my soul has departed from those who endeavor to discourage and hinder me in my Christian progress; and I can now forgive my enemies, bless those who have hated me, and cheerfully pray for those who have despitefully used and persecuted me.

Fare you well! farewell!■

23 EULOGY ON WILLIAM WILBERFORCE

William Whipper

Upon the death of William Wilberforce, the great British opponent of the slave trade, in late July 1833, black Americans exhibited profound grief. The members of the Phoenix Society of New York, a black self-improvement organization, wore badges of mourning for a month, and memorial services were held in several cities. In the 1850s one of the two colleges founded for African Americans before the Civil War was named in his honor.

On December 6, 1833, African Americans in Philadelphia met in the Second African Presbyterian Church for the purpose "not only of commemorating the disinterested labors of that great and good man, William Wilberforce, Esq., but the noble and dignified course which he so eminently and availingly advocated,—viz., the glorious cause of Freedom." At the invitation of a committee representing the "colored citizens of Philadelphia," William Whipper delivered the eulogy.

William Whipper was born about 1801 and was a leading figure in the national and state conventions of African Americans of the 1830s. He was a founder, in 1835, of the short-lived American Moral Reform Society, which emerged from the convention movement, and he edited the National Reformer, *the society's organ. In Columbia, Pennsylvania, where he was engaged in the lumber business, Whipper was a conductor on the Underground Railroad and a supporter of Canadian emigration.*

In his eulogy, Whipper traces the long and persistent struggle Wilberforce waged in Parliament to achieve abolition of the slave trade. Following are concluding portions of the address, taken from a pamphlet in the collection of the Historical Society of Pennsylvania, Eulogy on William Wilberforce, Esq., Delivered at the Request of the People of Color of the City of Philadelphia, in the Second African Presbyterian Church on the Sixth Day of December, 1833, by William Whipper. *For further information, see Thomas Lessl, "William Whipper," in Richard Leeman, ed.,*

African-American Orators: A Bio-Critical Sourcebook *(Westport, Conn.: Greenwood, 1996), 375–83.*

W hen we speak of America, we do it with those feelings of respect that are due to it as our country—not as the land of our adoption, nor with the alienated breath of foreigners, but with the instinctive love of native-born citizens. We look upon her as favored by Providence above all other for the geniality of her climate and fruitfulness of her soil and, in the language of Dr. Rush,* as possessing "a compound of most climates of the world"—a country said to be the "freest on the globe," where not only the liberty of the press is guaranteed, but the Christian and the infidel, the Mohammedan and pagan, the deist and the atheist, the Jew and Gentile are not only protected in their faith, but may propagate their doctrines unmolested—a country where the oppressed of all nations and castes seek shelter from oppression and become incorporated into the spirit of her laws and rally round her standard of liberty, *except those of African origin.*

We admire her declaration of rights, and worship it as our holy creed; but we mourn over its fallen spirit as we would over some ancient ruin whose splendor and magnificence had attracted the gaze of an admiring world. We point to the graves of our relatives and immediate ancestors as the graves not of departed Africans, but of American citizens; many of whom have *fallen in battle* with the revolutionary fathers in their arduous struggle for liberty; whose blood has moistened this sacred soil, and whose tombstones, if erected, would not only direct us to the depositories of departed heroes, but would light our path to a patriot's grave. There are yet many of our aged fathers who were scions of the British colonies that have survived the struggle and have been incorporated in that bond of union that forms the national standard and have grown up through American liberty, but who have never enjoyed the glorious privilege of citizenship. They have *weakened* with her *strength,* and their heads that are now blossomed for a future world, stand as evidence against American cruelty, the injustice of her policy, and the spirit of her laws. . . .

My friends, of the millions who sound forth his [Wilberforce's] praises, probably there are only thousands who do him honor. Those who advocate slavery and perpetual servitude are unworthy of kneeling at his sacred shrine; those who are opposed to the natural elevation of the man of color to the rights and privileges of free citizens, are unworthy of paying him devotion; those who have not adopted for the line of their conduct toward their fellow men, the golden rule—"do unto others as you would they should do unto you"—are unfit to utter forth his name. As well might an angel of darkness bow down and worship the prince of light and glory, as for men pos-

*Benjamin Rush (1775–1813) was a prominent physician, temperance advocate, and abolitionist. He served in the Continental Congress and was cofounder of the Pennsylvania Abolition Society.

sessing such a motley of inconsistencies to attempt to pay tribute to his memory. But his fame is fixed, the influence of his extensions is felt, and the news that a *great and good man is fallen* has been uttered in such pathetic strains that babes have caught the sound, and are beginning to lisp forth his name, which must be transmitted to posterity enrobed in the mantle of Christian virtue that nothing can tarnish but our degeneracy. If we should fail to render ourselves worthy of so powerful an advocate, we shall retard the influence of those virtues. If we shall fail to walk in those paths of elevation, marked out for us by the laws of our country and the achievements of philanthropy, we shall not only destroy the prospects of those who come after us, but will weaken the cause of those who come forward for our support. Let that not be our course. Let us march forward with a firm, unvarying step, not only occupying every inch of ground acquired by those philanthropists who are laboring in our behalf, but let the strength of our characters, by the influence of their examples, acquire for us new territory, and the name of William Wilberforce will not only burnish into brighter fame, but will serve as a lamp, the light of whose blaze will grow broader and higher, until it shall have not only warmed the most remote regions, by "encircling the globe we inhabit," but, by its revolutionary power, *we,* in our ascent upward, shall be lost in the regions of the skies.■

24 THE SLAVERY OF INTEMPERANCE

William Whipper

African Americans played significant roles in most of the major reform movements that swept the United States in the 1830s and particularly in the temperance movement. Resolutions against the intemperate consumption of alcohol (and sometimes in support of total abstinence) were issued at all national black conventions beginning in 1830. At the second national convention, the members authorized the formation of the Coloured American Conventional Temperance Society. By 1840, most black communities had some form of temperance society and many had temperance boardinghouses, stores, restaurants, and newspapers. Black community leaders in the temperance movement argued that the use of alcohol, while understandable as an act of despair over thwarted aspirations and limited opportunities, was a destructive force akin to slavery. They also urged temperance in the hope that self-improvement and moral uplift would lessen racial prejudice.

*The abolition and temperance movements were very closely linked. As Benjamin Quarles notes, "a supporter of abolition was likely to be a supporter of temperance" (*Black Abolitionists, *93). The ranks of prominent temperance lecturers included such black abolitionists as Daniel A. Payne, Theodore S. Wright, Frances E. W. Harper, Frederick Douglass, William Wells Brown, David Ruggles, J. W. Loguen, and the Philadelphia business leader and activist William Whipper (c. 1804–1876). These orators linked the abolitionist and temperance movements both politically and rhetorically.*

In his presidential address to the Colored Temperance Society of Philadelphia on January 8, 1834, Whipper develops a richly detailed analogy, likening chattel slavery and the "tyranny of intemperance" while acknowledging that "probably to no people on earth would this language be more objectionable than to the present audience." Whipper also warns his audience that if the temperance reform movement is "left to the whites, we shall be as widely separated in morals as complexion." He advocates both temperance and the temperance movement as means of racial advancement.

The speech text appeared in the Liberator *on June 21–28 and July 5, 1834. It was previously reprinted in C. Peter Ripley, ed.,* The Black Abolitionist Papers *(Chapel Hill: University of North Carolina Press, 1991). For more information on the role of black abolitionists in the temperance movement, see Benjamin Quarles,* Black Abolitionists *(New York: Oxford University Press, 1969), 92–100.*

FELLOW MEMBERS: Having been so highly honored by your suffrages, as to be elevated to the distinguished situation of presiding over this institution, the claims of duty require of me the arduous task of explaining the motives and considerations that should actuate us in promoting its objects.

Those who associate themselves for the improvement of their moral condition, are exercising the highest order of legislation. The present is an era for us to notice the evils, and mark the moral depravity, that have afflicted the human family since they have fallen from the holy estate that our first parents enjoyed.

Intemperance, the blighting monster, that extirpator of the human species, has slain mankind with a power that can only be likened unto the *axe,* which in the march of civilization is rapidly clearing our native forests. It is an evil for magnitude unexcelled, and in the history of the world must stand without a parallel. Every negro slavery, horrible as it is, painted in its most ignominious colors, and ferreted out in all its degrading consequences, is but a concomitant. Probably to no people on earth would this language be more objectionable than to the present audience; yet I firmly believe it to be strictly true. To a people like ours, whose whole history is wrapt in the most obsequious degradation, multiplied injuries and tyrannical barbarity, from the effects of domestic slavery, they might be inclined to suppose that no human scourge had ever surpassed it in the enormity of its inflictions. But a still greater tyrant reigns. It fills a more extensive range—it occupies a higher seat; and swells its influence over the dominions of our world. It is found in the palace; it exists in the forum; it mingles with society; its abode is by the fireside; it is felt in the sanctuary; it despises the prejudices of caste; it seeks its victims alike among the learned and ignorant, the poor and the rich; it confines itself neither to the geographical lines of state or territory, of nation or continent; but disdaining all local attachments, it claims for its domain the map of the universe.

It is not my intention, on the present occasion, to delineate its features. You all, probably, have seen the base original revelling in all its loathsomeness, defying alike the imagination of the poet, and the pencil of the artist, to describe its ghastly countenance and destructive mien. The time may come when my limits may allow me to enter into the economy of the subject; but for the present, I must only refer to the able speeches and writings of the temperance reformers, that are now so successfully revolutionizing public opinion on this important question. I could quote from ecclesiastical history, and prove that the voluntary use of "ardent spirits" is inconsistent with the spirit of the gospel and our holy religion. I could refer to medical authority to prove its deleterious effect on the human system. I claim not the high privilege of being a pioneer in this cause. But I hold it to be my duty to pass by all these, and approach the subject on new grounds; and I am proud to say that years have elapsed since I adopted the following sentiments, viz:

That the people of color, in these United States, (above any other class of citizens) are morally, politically and religiously bound to support the cause of temperance, as advocated and supported in our country.

We are indebted to the ingenuity of man for the two greatest evils that ever scourged the human family, viz. Intemperance and Slavery. I mean by the former, that intemperance which has arisen from the use of ardent spirits. By the latter we are to consider that species of slavery, generally termed negro slavery. I cannot probably better call your attention to the subject, than by presenting for your consideration the comparative evils they inflict, and the forcible claims their very existence has upon the wise and the good, for their total extermination from the face of the earth. If I shall be able to convince those who hear me, that the former is as wicked and heinous as the latter, I feel confident that they will lend their influence to exterminate its roots from the soil of society.

The principal effects of these evils on the character and interests of mankind you are familiar with. I need only present you with a few facts, asking leave to place them in the scales of justice, regulated by right and reason, and suffer you to form your own conclusions.

We shall begin with negro slavery.

What have been its effects on society and mankind generally?

Why, it has made the master (though of human form, and bound by christian obligations to love and seek the welfare of himself and those around him) a tyrant—a murderer of this species—an earthly demon, pouring out his wrath on the innocent and unoffending, inflicting torments and stripes on the aged and infirm, separating husband and wife, parents and their offspring, like cattle and beasts of burden; and to communicate the same wicked lesson to his children and survivors who visit on unborn generations the same penalties; and society around him copies his example. Although born in the image of his Maker, his life and acts bear the impress of Satan. He dies, and leaves his country taxed with national cruelty—his heirs in the possession of God's creatures, with their multiplied increase.

Now, what are its effects on the slave? Why, the dense fog of slave-holding cruelty, falling like mildew, smites the earliest dawn of his intellect, and destroys it in the bud. His mind, that was formed to soar into infinite space, and there admire and explore the beauties of creation, and the splendor of worlds—scarcely moves beyond the measure of his chains. His body, unlike the animals of the forest, is without the natural covering to shelter his person from the pitiless storm; yet like them, he seldom receives protection from the burning suns and chilling snows. Though born and reared in the image of man, he walks to and fro with the taciturnity of the brute. His mind not being permitted to expand he remains destitute of that compound that God intended for his creatures, vis. a union of mind and body; but in the stature of the latter he roams over the earth a walking animal.

It is of materials like these, that the ligaments of society in slaveholding counties are formed. While the oppressor deserves the condign punishment of an insulted Providence, and the just execration of the wise and good, the prayers of the righteous ought to ascend upwards, in torrents of supplication and appeal to Heaven for their deliverance. Who will charge me with injustice in this description?

But it now becomes our duty to describe the *tyrant* intemperance—a *demon* more ferocious in his character and despotic in the cruelty of his infliction and the destructiveness of his sway. All that I have said, or that can be said against slavery, is truly applicable to intemperance. It is happy for mankind and the glory of humanity, that the wickedness of the former is confined to Africa and her descendants; while the latter abhorring all national distinctions, spreads its "wide wasting calamity" over the great family of nations. It far surpasses the former in the cruelty of its depredations, the number of its victims, and its deathless ignominy. If their afflictions were equal, the ratio of numbers alone would turn the scale. But we shall exhibit some of its destructive feats, that the former, with all its atrocities, is incapable of achieving. The slave is only kept in subjection because his mind remains stupefied; for both the security of the master and contentment of the slave forbid its expansion, because no large number of intelligent beings can remain enslaved—for light and knowledge would dissolve the compact, melt the bands, and burst the chains asunder. The tyrant Elrius makes no such limited pretensions to the perpetuity of power; but, as if determined to keep mankind in awe, and subject the world to his control, he frequently reaches after the mightiest intellect, makes him bow his haughty head, bend his knee, fall down and worship the god Bacchus, and lay his trophies at his feet. So that in the possession of intelligence and learning, there is no safe retreat from his grasp. If the slave has wealth, he may purchase his freedom. But to the subject of intemperance, wealth only strengthens his chains; for it furnishes him with materials to revel in his guilt, and fans the flames of his destruction. The slave hates his situation, and only remains in it because his bonds are forcible. The other loves it, because having slain his reason and self-respect, it promotes his animal luxury.

The slaveholder dreads rebellion and insurrectionary movements; but the tyrant intemperance fears them not, for those whom he oppresses most, love him best. He is an able ruler, alike skillful in the cabinet and the field; though a murderer and a despot, he reigns in the hearts of his subjects. He is the prince of tacticians, heads a large army, and when he desires the acquisition of numbers to procure new territory, he martials his soldiers, and stretches his magic wand, possessing in himself the power of the magnet. Thousands follow after him, and join the train; few desert his camp; and when arrayed for combat, are seemingly invulnerable; but *all fall in battle.*

The slave may escape from the rule and presence of his master, by flying to a land of freedom; but the subject of intemperance finds that *his* master is almost omnipresent. He may leave his state or country, and become adopted in another realm, but even there he finds the omniscient eye of his master is upon him, and the same consequences await him. The odiousness of the traffic is far more desperate in its extent and cruelty, owing to the limited value of the subject, and the protection given to the trade. Slaves generally command such a price, that none but capitalists can engage in its guilt, or reap its gains. But the intemperance traffic is so republican in its nature, that every person, who can buy a glass of liquid poison, can purchase a subject—can rob and deprive a family of their protector or slay on the funeral pyre some unguarded young man, or some unfortunate female. The facilities for its perpetuation are superior to that of either the slave trade or domestic slavery: for in connection with the heavy purchases of the one, there is to be added the expense of rearing and supporting the slave—but the other, as the advocate of intemperance would say, "enjoying an uncontrollable liberty," supports himself, and bestows his profits to the cause, and thus perpetuates the misery of millions.

I could extend the chain of comparison much further; but I am willing to submit it to your consideration without further comment, trusting that you will regulate your decision by the weight of the evidence.

But I have said that negro slavery is but a concomitant of intemperance. Do you desire the proof? I refer you to Clarkson, and other historians on the slave trade, and you will discover that I am borne out in the assertion, that one of its earliest achievements (although then in its infant state)—like the tempter in Eden—was to secure the "slave trade" by inducing the native Africans to sell their brethren while under its influence, and by the artifice it was effected. Is there a person of color in these United States, calling into recollection the features of that abominable trade—its murderous effect on our mother country, and our very existence in this country—our paternal relation to Africa, to humanity and religion—and its excruciating effects on upwards of two millions of our brethren in this our native land; is there one who is not equally ready to denounce the tyranny of the one, and the guilt of the other? Shall we, by the flood of our indignation, bear the names of the perpetrators of that trade into the pit of infamy, without accompanying with them the means by which their designs were executed? Is not ardent spirit susceptible of the same power in like hands? If our hostility to slavery arises, as it justly should, from its deleterious and demoralizing effects on the human family; ought not our hatred to intemperance be founded on the same principles? Can we consistently support the vices of the one, while we detest the vices of the other? Are not both obnoxious in the sight of heaven? If the slaveholder merits the indignation of the christian public, for perpetuating his system of crime and oppression, is not the retailer of ardent spirits equally culpable? Are we prepared to send forth our denunciations against American slavery, while we are nurturing and supporting a like system, and one that I have said is pregnant with and inflicts greater evils on the human race?

But having already given you the parallel, I ask you to draw your own conclusions. Have we not reason to fear that they will reflect back our language, and tell us "to remove the mote from our own eyes?" Is not that system of society that justifies each equally base? Are not the supporters of each individually guilty of a gross violation of public morals, nay, even virtue and religion? I propound these questions for your consideration: weigh them.

I will leave you in possession of these facts, while I pass on the consideration of the following question, viz. this being the present state of things, is not every man of color in these United States morally, politically and religiously bound to support the temperance reform, as advocated in our country?

To assert that we are normally bound to support the cause, is only to say that our obligations to our Maker and society impose upon us the duty of promoting the welfare of our species. Though the doctrine of the immorality of the "traffic in ardent spirits" is of modern origin, yet its legality has been sanctioned by men we readily believe, when they place the same stigma on domestic slavery; and it is still advocated, and has become adopted into the creed of the ablest reformers of the age. That it promises the moral purity of society, all must admit. But what says the objector? Why, its laws are too binding. We want the liberty of drinking when we please, and then letting it alone. We want no control in this matter. We abhor binding force. But what is the amount of these objections? Why, uncontrollable liberty would be the most despotic tyrant that ever existed; it would gratify an absolute and unconditional lust of the human passions; it would dethrone all power, destroy our institutions, and overthrow the foundations of all government; it would leave mankind without protection for either their property or persons. It is a liberty that was never intended for man; it was forbidden by our Creator, when He pointed to the "forbidden fruit" and said, "the day thou eatest thereof, thou shalt surely die."

Yet I firmly believe that if the three hundred thousand free colored people possessed such a character, the moral force and influence it would send forth would disperse slavery from our land. Yes, it would reserve the present order of things; it would reorganize public opinion, dissolve the calumnies of our enemies, and remove all the prejudices against our complexion; for there is nothing in the ordination of Providence calculated to degrade us in the eyes of the world, or prevent our occupying the highest situation in the order of intellectual beings. And when the nations of the earth can point to our whole people, and find them possessing a character, the christian base of which is as broad and high as that of the individual I have exhibited in miniature, it will be then that they will regard us as virtuous ornaments—that our sable hue will be changed from a badge of degradation to a badge of honor—that the more dark the complexion, the more frizzled the hair, the most illustrious the personage. It will be then, even in this country, that that glorious achievement will be completed, which has been asserted by a distinguished divine to be beyond the powers of humanity, legislation or religion to control. It will be then that when our brethren are visiting our mother country on errands of mercy, to christianize and evangelize that benighted continent, they will carry with them the materials for rearing up free institutions and the blessings of civilization. It will be then that the whole christian world, disdaining to count what they now term a homely visage and black complexion, will rise up and call her blessed. Is there not chivalry enough in us to accomplish this moral enterprise? Let every one answer for himself—not for another. If our enemies should reply in the negative, we should scout the idea. Would it not be equally offensive coming from any other source? Is there any too poor to purchase it, any too rich to enjoy it, any too wise to apply it, or any too ignorant to profit by it? I am positively not aware of any method so well calculated to effect this desirable result as the *temperance reform.* I wish not to be understood to insinuate, that we are more intemperate than the whites, for I do not believe it; but that we must be more pure than they, before we can be duly respected, becomes self-evident from the situation we at present occupy in our country.

Ardent spirit is so fruitful in iniquity, that the reformers of the present day regard it as the forbidden fruit. But the doctrine of the objectors might be pursued still further. The primary object of this institution is to harmonize, bless and elevate mankind.

In all great causes, there must be pioneers, who will breast the storm, and bear the burden. These have gone before, and it now becomes our duty to sustain them. The icy obstacles that have beset their path have been melted in the crucible of truth; and a glorious prospect is before us. Though a chance cloud may interpose itself, and darken our meridian way, it will be our duty *still to preserve.* It is our duty to inform and enlighten public opinion on this subject. Let us aim at a correct public opinion, and cease to regard who frames the laws; for it is on this basis that all laws are founded.

Hence that legislation that fixes the morals, must ever be regarded supreme; and thus all "uncontrollable liberty" is checked by governmental power.

But we are particularly called upon to support the temperance cause, for the single reason that if we neglect it, the very temperance reformation in this country will prove to us the greatest *curse*. If it be left to the whites, we shall be as widely separated in morals as complexion; and then our elevation is scarcely to be hoped for. To succeed and be respected, we must be superior in morals, before the balance of power will allow us to be admitted as their equals.

Show me the man of color in this country who possesses an unquestionable character for piety, morality and probity, and I will point you to a truly noble being. He stands alone on his own merits, clothed, it is true, in the badge of complexional degradation—without the title of citizenship—without the enjoyment of a participation in the affairs of his government—without any share in the administration of its laws—without the hope of earthly reward or future fame; yet, under all these disadvantages, his virtues are seen embellishing his character, and encircling his name. He lives a model for the world—an honor to his country, but a slave to its laws.

But if we believe that there is no present necessity for this reform; that this "uncontrollable liberty," with regard to the voluntary use of ardent spirits, needs no check, let us go on and fill up the measure of our iniquity. Let us ask the monster to extend still further his blessings of human misery on our world—let us solicit him to add to his hundreds of millions of murdered victims, thousands of millions in order that our voracious appetites may be satisfied at the slaughter-house of his vengeance; hoping that the summit of his ambition may be achieved, and the vortex of his misery filled. Let us view the present state of things and survey our peculiar situations; and then let me ask you, if the voice of public opinion was ever needed to sustain a reform; is it not now, and are we not bound, both by precept and example, to hasten the cause?

But the question may be asked, "Can a radical change be achieved?" I answer in the affirmative. We must have our institution placed on a pure moral basis, and we must plead for the natural, moral and political elevation of our whole people. We must earnestly remonstrate against their present course; and then if there be those who are deaf to all the appeals of reason, our institution must rise in its power and denounce the traffic. The grog-shops and taverns must be termed nuisances and disturbers of public peace and private enjoyments. If we cannot invoke their reason, we must provoke their passions; and this will bring forth retort; and retort will lead to discussion; and discussion will elicit enquiry; and enquiry will beget truth; and truth will bring conviction; and thus the reform will be completed. It will never do to content ourselves with crying out against the taverns and grog-shops; that will never bring about a reform; their *political action* is too powerful to be overcome. If I wished to rule an intemperate community, powerful as the press is acknowledged to be, I would choose their influence as preferable; for they in part control the latter, and their power is strongly felt in our legislative assemblies; and they more than partially rule our government. They are founded on the faith of public morality, and are suffered to exist only by the impurity of public opinion; and they flourish in proportion to the liquid cravings of the community. And it would be of little consequence to remove these while that opinion exists; because those whom they accommodate would be left to get the liquid poison elsewhere. They were erected to supply the public wants; and many of them by men, who, when separated from the traffic, are honorable and praiseworthy citizens. These, like other industrious men, have sought that employment which they consider most profitable. Therefore it becomes our duty to undermine the interests of this traffic by moral action; and then these will be induced to relinquish the trade and convert their establishments into merchandise more profitable to themselves and certainly less destructive to their fellow citizens. There must be inns, hotels and boarding houses for the accommodation of travellers and the public; but these should not be suffered to sell "ardent spirits."

The time is already come when we should all stand united as one man in this great moral contest, holding the high and invincible ground, that intemperance is an enemy to our civil and political improvement; and that we must oppose its advocates and supporters without distinction of color.

When the advocates of slavery cry out "How is the evil to be removed?" we tell them to "quit stealing"—"destroy the market, and render the whole system worthless." Can we say otherwise to the advocates of intemperance than to quit "poisoning," and the trade will die of itself? There are probably no two evils so closely allied, that the cure for the one is applicable to the other; and just so in their perpetuation. And the guilt of each is shrouded in the corruption of public opinion.

The slaveholder who says that he desires slavery to be abolished, and will not manumit his slaves; we doubt the sincerity of his assertions. The moderate drinker, who says he wishes drunkenness swept from the land, and still keeps on drinking—shall we believe him? He, like the former, says that "I am strictly in favor of temperance, but I hate your fanatical denunciations, your cold water societies for reform. Let every man be his own guardian. I hate both drunkards and drunkenness. I like moderation in every thing." So says the moderate drinker. But yet, under his very system of self-government, has the evil arisen with all its accumulated power. Will the same evil or the same legislation cure itself? Certainly not. And if this "uncontrollable liberty" is to be the ruling monitor, it will be impossible to fix a moral boundary. The man who drinks his small glass of brandy in a day or a week, will infringe on another's rights, if he reproves him who drinks his quart in a day or an hour—for each, in the exercise of this guaranteed liberty, only satisfied his own thirst. We should despise neither the drunkard or those engaged in the traffic; we should hate their ways, and our admonitions should flow from a love to their welfare. These moderate men appear to be true *facsimiles* of another class of citizens, called colonizationists. They both cry out against the evil, and propose their remedies; but figures, "which cannot lie," prove the inefficiency of their plans; for their application has only op-erated like extinguishing fire with oil; for both intemperance and slavery have flourished under their cure. The superiority of associated bodies over isolated individuals, in expressing their disapprobation of any measure, is so self-evident, that I would not insult your senses by adducing proof. Mark the revolution in public opinion produced in the Eastern States, in regard to the use and sale of ardent spirits; and then mark the consequence. In that same region have risen up our most powerful friends, who wish to elevate our moral and political condition; and wherever we see what we term a true abo-litionist, he is invariably a friend of the temperance cause. It is their enlight-ened views of human good that lead them to advocate the exalted principles of human rights. And shall we condemn their exertions by our principles and practices? Can there be any of our people, who advocate our improve-ment, and view drunkenness as an evil, who will not lend their aid and influ-ence to stay it? Can they be so blind to their dearest interests, and those of posterity? Let their acts answer! We are certainly bound to prepare the way for the rising generation. No doubt the present race of drunkards will live out their days in their own way; but let us rescue posterity from the evils that intemperance inflicts on the present race.■

25 WHY A CONVENTION IS NECESSARY

William Hamilton

In 1830, partly in response to the Cincinnati riots, a convention of free black delegates from New York, Delaware, Pennsylvania, Mary-land, and Virginia met in Philadelphia to "devise ways and means for the bettering of our condition." The convention met annually for six years and other such gatherings were held throughout the antebellum pe-riod. At these meetings, the free black population asserted its demands for full rights in American society and for the abolition of slavery.

At the fourth annual Convention of the Colored People, held in New York City from June 2 to June 13, 1834, there were fifty delegates and two visitors from Canada and Haiti. The chief address was delivered by William Hamilton of New York. The 1834 convention was less concerned than previous gatherings with opposition to colonization or with the es-tablishment of a national black university. Instead, the convention was largely devoted to broader campaigns for social and economic advance-ment. Hamilton recounts in detail the chains of prejudice and discrimina-

tion that continued to bind nominally "free" African Americans, whether in the North or South.

The text of this address comes from A Documentary History of the Negro People in the United States edited by Herbert Aptheker (New York: Citadel Press, 1951), 154–57. See also Howard Holman Bell, A Survey of the Negro Convention Movement, 1830–1861 (New York: Arno Press, 1953–69).

GENTLEMEN: It is with the most pleasing sensations, that I, in behalf of my colored fellow citizens of New York, tender you of the delegation to this convention, a hearty welcome to our city. And in behalf of the Conventional Board, I repeat the welcome. And, gentlemen, with regard to myself, my full heart vibrates the felicitation.

You have convened to take into consideration what may be the best means of the promotion of the best interest of the people of color of these United States, particularly of the free people thereof. And that such convention is highly necessary, I think a few considerations will amply show.

First, the present form of society divides the interest of the community into several parts. Of these, there is that of the white man, that of the slave, and that of the free colored man. How lamentable, how very lamentable, it is that there should be, anywhere on earth, a community of castes, with separate interests! That society must be the most happy, where the good of one is the common good of the whole. Civilization is not perfect, nor has reason full sway, until the community shall see that a wrong done to one is a wrong done to the whole; that the interest of one is or ought to be the common interest of the whole. Surely that must be a happy state of society where the sympathies of all are to all alike.

How pleasing, what a compliment to the nation, is the expression of Monsieur Vallier, a celebrated traveler in Africa, where, speaking of the Hottentots, he says, "There none need to offer themselves as objects of compassion, for all are compassionate." Whatever our early-tutored prejudice may say to the contrary, such a people must be happy. Give me a residence in such a society, and I shall fancy myself in a community the most refined.

But alas for the people of color in this community! Their interest is not identified with that of other men. From them, white men stand aloof. For them the eye of pity hath scarcely a tear.

To them the hand of kindness is palsied, to them the dregs of mercy scarcely are given. To them the finger of scorn is pointed; contumely and reproach is continually theirs. They are taunt, a hissing, and a byword. They must cringe and crouch and crawl and succumb to their peers. Long, long, long has the demon of prejudice and persecution beset their path. And must they make no effort to throw off the evils by which they are beset? Ought they not to meet to spread out their wrongs before one another? Ought they not to meet to consult on the best means of their relief? Ought they not to make one weak effort—nay, one strong, one mighty moral effort—to roll off the burden that crushes them?

Under present circumstances it is highly necessary the free people of color should combine and closely attend to their own particular interest. All kinds of jealousy should be swept away from among them and their whole eye fixed, intently fixed, on their own peculiar welfare. And can they do better than to meet thus, to take into consideration what are the best means to promote their elevation, and after having decided, to pursue those means with unabating zeal until their end is obtained?

Another reason why this convention is necessary is that there is formed a strong combination against the people of color, by some who are the master spirits of the day, by men whose influence is of the strongest character, to whom this nation bow in humble submission and submit to their superior judgment, who turn public sentiment whichever way they please.

You cannot but perceive that I allude to the Colonization Society. However pure the motives of some of the members of that society may be, yet the master spirits thereof are evil-minded toward us. They have put on the garb of angels of light. Fold back their covering, and you have in full array those of darkness.

I need not spread before you the proof of their evil purposes. Of that you have had a quantity sufficient; and were there no other good reason for this convention, the bare circumstance of existence of such an institution would be a sufficient one. I do hope, confidently hope, that the time will arrive and is near at hand when we shall be in full possession of all the rights of men.

But as long at least as the Colonization Society exists, will a convention of colored people be highly necessary. This society is the great Dragon of the land, before whom the people bow and cry, Great Johovah, and to whom they would sacrifice the free people of color. That society has spread itself over this whole land; it is artful, it suits itself to all places. It is one thing at the South, and another thing at the North; it blows hot and cold; it sends forth bitter and sweet; it sometimes represents us as the most corrupt, vicious and abandoned of any class of men in the community. Then again we are kind, meek and gentle. Here we are ignorant, idle, a nuisance and a drawback on the resources of the country. But as abandoned as we are, in Africa we shall civilize and Christianize all that heathen country. And by thus preaching continually they have distilled into the minds of the community a desire to see us removed.

They have resorted to every artifice to effect their purposes—by exciting in the minds of the white community the fears of insurrection and amalgamation; by petitioning state legislatures to grant us no favors; by petitioning Congress to aid in sending us away; by using their influence to prevent the establishment of seminaries for our instruction in the higher branches of education.

And such are the men of that society that the community are blind to their absurdities; contradictions and paradoxes. They are well acquainted with the ground and the wiles by which to beguile the people.

It is therefore highly necessary we should meet, in order that we may confer on the best means to frustrate the purpose of so awful a foe.

I would beg leave to recommend an attentive consideration to this matter. Already you have done much toward the enervation of this giant: he begins to grow feeble; indeed he seems to be making his last struggle, if we may judge from his recent movements. Hang around him, assail him quickly. He is vulnerable. Well-pointed darts will fetch him down, and soon he breathes no more.

Cheer up my friends! Already has your protest against the Colonization Society shown to the world that the people of color are not willing to be expatriated. Cheer up. Already a right feeling begins to prevail. The friends of justice, of humanity, and of the rights of man are drawing rapidly together and are forming a moral phalanx in your defense.

That hitherto strong-footed but sore-eyed vixen, prejudice, is limping off, seeking the shade. The Anti-Slavery Society and the friends of immediate abolition are taking a noble, bold and manly stand in the cause of universal liberty. It is true they are assailed on every quarter, but the more they are assailed the faster they recruit. From present appearances the prospect is cheering, in a high degree. Antislavery societies are forming in every direction. Next August proclaims the British dominions free from slaves.

These United States are her children, they will soon follow so good an example. Slavery, that Satanic monster, that beast whose mark has been so long stamped on the forehead of the nations, shall be chained and cast down into blackness and darkness for ever.

Soon, my brethren, shall the judgment be set. Then shall rise in glory and triumph, reason, virtue, kindness and liberty, and take a high exalted stand among the sons of men. Then shall tyranny, cruelty, prejudice and slavery be cast down to the lowest depths of oblivion—yea, be banished from the presence of God and the glory of his power forever. Oh blessed consummation; and devoutly to be desired!

It is for you, my brethren, to help on in this work of moral improvement. Man is capable of high advances in his reasoning and moral faculties. Man is the pursuit of happiness. And reason—or experience, which is the parent of reason—tells us that the highest state of morality is the highest state of happiness. Aside from a future day of judgment and retribution, there is always a day of retribution at hand. That society is most miserable that is most immoral; that most happy that is most virtuous. Let me therefore recommend earnestly that you press upon our people the necessity and advantage of a moral reformation. It may not produce an excess of riches, but it will produce a higher state of happiness and render our circumstances easier.

You, gentlemen, can begin here. By managing this conference in a spirit of good will and true politeness; by constantly keeping in view and cultivating a spirit of peace, order and harmony, rather than satire, wit and eloquence; by putting the best possible construction on each other's language, rather than charging each other with improper motives. These dispositions will bespeak our character more or less virtuous and refined, and render our setting more or less pleasant. I will only now add, that the report of the Conventional Board will be submitted at your call; and my earnest hope is that you may have a peaceful, pleasant sitting.■

26 PUT ON THE ARMOUR OF RIGHTEOUSNESS

James Forten, Jr.

James Forten, Jr. (1817–?), was the son of Charlotte and James E. Forten, prominent Philadelphia abolitionists. James Forten, Sr., served in the Revolutionary War and helped found several of the first African American organizations in Philadelphia, including the Free African Society (1787) and the African Masonic Lodge (1797). He was an ardent Garrisonian and among the organizers of the American Anti-Slavery Society in 1833. The Fortens were one of the most affluent and influential of Philadelphia's black families and their home was regularly visited by African dignitaries, abolitionist leaders, and fugitive slaves.

Raised in this extraordinary family, James Forten, Jr., became politically active at an early age. While still a teenager, he wrote for the Liberator *and was an active member of the Young Men's Anti-Slavery Society in Philadelphia and of the American Moral Reform Society. At the age of nineteen, on the evening of April 14, 1836, he presented the following address to the Ladies' Anti-Slavery Society in Philadelphia. In the introductory and concluding sections of the speech reprinted here, Forten discusses the relationships between male and female abolitionists and the role of women in the movement. When confronted with the dedicated political work of women, he argues, man "feels an innate disposition to check the modest ardour of her zeal and ambition, and revolts at the idea of her managing the reigns of improvement." Forten predicts that women's participation in the abolitionist movement will revolutionize public opinion regarding the political abilities and rights of women. At the same time, his speech also surveys the difficulties faced by abolitionist orators: public scorn and the constant threat of violence.*

The full text of the speech may be found in James Forten, Jr., An Address Delivered Before the Ladies' Anti-Slavery Society of Philadelphia, On the Evening of the 14th of April, 1836 *(Philadelphia, Pa., 1836), 3–16; the speech is reprinted in volume 3 of C. Peter Ripley, ed.,* The Black Abolitionist Papers *(Chapel Hill: University of North Carolina Press, 1991),* *154–65.*

L ADIES—There is nothing that could more forcibly induce me to express my humble sentiments at all times, than an entire consciousness that is the duty of every individual who would wish to see the foul curse of slavery swept forever from the land—who wishes to become one amongst the undaunted advocates of the oppressed—who wishes to deal amongst the undaunted advocates of the oppressed—who wishes to deal justly and love mercy. In a word, it is my indispensable duty, in view of the wretched, the helpless, the friendless condition of my countrymen in chains, to raise my voice, feeble though it be, in their behalf; to plead for the restoration of their inalienable rights. As to the character of the ANTI-SLAVERY-SOCIETY, it requires but one glance from an impartial eye, to discover the purity of its motives—the great strength of its moral energies; its high and benevolent— its holy and life giving principles. These are the foundations, the very architecture of Abolition, and prove its sovereignty. In fact, all associated bodies which have for their great aim the destruction of tyranny, and the moral and intellectual improvement of mankind, have been, and ever will, considered as bearing a decided superiority over all others. And how well may this Association, before which I now have the honor to appear, be deemed one of that description; and still more is its superiority increased from a knowledge of the truth that it is composed entirely of your sex. It stands aloof from the storms of passion and political tumult, exhibiting in its extended and Christian views a disposition to produce an immediate reformation of the heart and soul. Never before has there been a subject brought into the arena of public investigation, so fraught with humanity—so alive to the best interest of our country—so dear to all those for whose benefit it was intended, as the one which now calls you together. How varied and abundant—how eloquent and soul-thrilling have been the arguments advanced in its defence, by the greatest and best of the land; and yet, so boundless is the theme—so inexhaustible the fountain, that even the infant may be heard lisping a prayer for the redemption of the perishing captive.

LADIES—The task you are called upon to perform is certainly of vital importance. Great is the responsibility which this association imposes upon you; however, I need scarcely remind you of it, feeling confident that long before this you have made a practical and familiar acquaintance with all its bearings, and with every sentence contained in your society's sacred declaration; ever remembering that in it is concentrated one of the noblest objects that ever animated the breast of a highly favored people—*the immediate and unconditional abolition of Slavery.* It is the acknowledgement of a broad principle like this, and recommending it to a prejudiced public, who have been all along accustomed to reason upon the dangerous doctrine of gradualism, viewing it as the only safe and efficient remedy for this monstrous evil which has brought about such an excitement, and convulsed our country from North to South; an excitement which I have every reason to believe will prove a powerful engine towards the furtherance of your noble cause. As to this opposition now arrayed against you, terrible as it appears, it is no more than what you might anticipate; it is a fate which, in this age of iniquity, must inevitably follow such a change as your society proposes to effect. For what else is to be expected for a measure the tendency of which is to check the tide of corruption—to make narrower the limits of tyrannical power—to unite *liberty and law*—to save the body of the oppressed from the blood-stained lash of the oppressor—and to secure a greater respect and obedience to Him who wills the happiness of all mankind, and who endowed them with life, and liberty, as conducive to that happiness? What else, I repeat, can be expected but opposition, at a time like this, when brute force reigns supreme; when ministers of the Gospel, commissioned to spread the light of Christianity among all nations are overleaping the pale of the church, forsaking the holy path, and sowing the seeds of discord where they should plant the "olive branch of peace." When liberty has dwindled into a mere shadow, its vitality being lost, shrouded in darkness, swallowed up as it were in the eternal dumbness of the grave. This, my friends, is the present situation of things, and warns you that the desperate struggle has commenced between *freedom* and *despotism—light and darkness.* This is the hour you are called upon to move with a bold and fearless step; there must be no lukewarmness, no shrinking from the pointed finger of scorn, or the contemptuous vociferation of the enemy; no withholding your aid, or concealing your mighty influence behind the screen of timidity; no receding from the foothold you have already gained. To falter now, would be to surrender your pure and unsullied principles into the hands of a vicious and perverted portion of the community, who are anxiously waiting to see you grow weak and fainthearted; you would be casting the whole spirit and genius of patriotism into that polluted current just described. To falter now would retard the glorious day of emancipation which is now dawning, for years, perhaps forever. But why should you pause? It is true that public opinion is bitter against you, and exercises a powerful influence over the minds of many; it is also true that you are frustrated in nearly every attempt to procure a place to hold your meetings, and the hue and cry is raised, "Down with the incendiaries—hang all who dare to open their mouths in vindication of equal rights;" still, this would be no excuse for a dereliction of duty; you are not bound to follow public opinion constantly and lose sight of the demands of justice; for it is plain to be seen that public opinion, in its present state, is greatly at fault; it affixes the seal of condemnation upon you without giving you an opportunity to be fairly heard; therefore I think the obligation ought to cease, and you pursue a more natural course by looking to your own thoughts and feeling as a guide, and not to the words of others. Again—in order to promote your antislavery principles you should make it the topic of your conversation amidst your acquaintances, in every family circle, and in the shades of private life. Be assured that by acting thus, hundreds will rise up to your aid. . . .

I rejoice to see you engaged in this mighty cause; it befits you; it is your province; your aid and influence is greatly to be desired in this hour of peril; it never was, never can be insignificant. Examine the records of history, and you will find that woman has been called upon in the severest trials of public emergency. That your efforts will stimulate the men to renewed exertion I have not the slightest doubt; for, in general, the pride of man's heart is such, that while he is willing to grant unto woman exclusively many conspicuous and dignified privileges, he at the same time feels an innate disposition to check the modest ardour of her zeal and ambition, and revolts at the idea of her managing the reins of improvement. Therefore, you have only to be constantly exhibiting some new proof of your interest in the cause of the oppressed, and shame, if not duty, will urge our sex on the march. It has often been said by anti-abolitionists that the females have no right to interfere with the question of slavery, or petition for its overthrow; that they had better be at home attending to their domestic affairs, &c. What a gross error—what an anti-christian spirit this bespeaks. Were not the only commands, "Remember them that are in bonds, as bound with them,"* and "Do unto others as ye would they should do unto you,"† intended for women to obey as well as man? Most assuredly they were. But from whom does this attack upon your rights come? Not, I am confident, from the respectable portion of our citizens, but invariably from men alienated by avarice and self-importance from the courtesy and respect which is due to your sex on all occasions; such "men of property and standing" as mingled with the rank, breath, and maniac spirit, of the mob at Boston,‡ men (I am sorry to say) like the Representative from Virginia, Mr. [Henry] Wise, who, lost to all shame, openly declared you to be devils incarnate. And for what? Why, because the ladies in the several states north of the Potomac, in the magnitude of their philanthropy, with hearts filled with mercy, choose to raise their voices in behalf of the suffering and the dumb—because they choose to raise their voices in behalf of the suffering and the dumb—because they choose to exercise their legal privileges, and offer their time and talents as a sacrifice, in order that the District of Columbia may be freed, and washed clean from the stains of blood, cruelty and crime. It is for acting thus that you received so refined a compliment. Truly, some of our great men at the South are hand and hand in inequity: they are men after the heart of the tyrant Nero, who wished that all the Romans had but one neck that he might destroy them all at a single blow. This is just the position in which these Neros of a modern mould would like to place all who dare to utter one syllable against the sin of slavery—that is if they had the power.

But, Ladies, I verily believe that the time is fast approaching when thought, feeling and action, the three principal elements of public opinion,

---

*Hebrews 13:3.
†Matthew 7:12.
‡Garrison had been set upon by a mob of one hundred on October 21, 1835, and narrowly escaped lynching.

will be so revolutionized as to turn the scale in your favor; when the prejudice and contumely of your foes will be held in the utmost contempt by an enlightened community. You have already been the means of awakening hundreds from the deep slumber into which they have fallen; they have arisen, and put on the armour of righteousness, and gone forth to battle. Yours is the cause of Truth, and must prevail over error; it is the cause of sympathy, and therefore it calls aloud for the aid of woman.

> *Sympathy is woman's attribute,*
> *By that she has reign'd—by that she will reign.*

Yours is the cause of Christianity; for it pleads that the mental and physical powers of millions may not be wasted—buried forever in ruins; that virtue may not be sacrificed at the altar of lasciviousness; making the South but one vast gulf of infamy; that the affections of a parent may not be sundered; that hearts may not be broken; that souls, bearing the impress of the Deity— the proof of their celestial origin and eternal duration—may not be lost. It is for all these you plead, and you must be victorious; never was there a contest commenced on more hallowed principles. Yes, my friends, from the height of your holy cause, as from a mountain, I see already rising the new glory and grandeur of regenerated—Free—America! And on the corner stone of that mighty fabric, posterity shall read your names. But if there be the shadow of a doubt still remaining in the breasts of anyone present as to your success, I would beg them to cast their eyes across the broad bosom of the Atlantic, and call to mind the scenes which transpired a short time since. (There shone the influence of a woman!) Call to mind the 1st of August,* a day never to be forgotten by the real philanthropist; when *justice,* mantled in renovated splendour, with an arm nerved to action—her brow lighted up by a ray from Heaven, mounted on the car of *Freedom,* betook her way to the spot were *Slavery* was stalking over the land, making fearful ravages among human beings. There the "lust of gain, had made the fiercest and fullest exhibition of its hardihood." There, Justice looked, on the one hand, to the "prosperity of the lordly oppressor, wrung from the sufferings of a captive and subjugated people;" and on the other, to the "tears and untold agony of the hundreds beneath him." There, was heard the sighs and stifled groans of the once happy and gay; hopes blighted in the bud. There, cruelty had wrought untimely furrows upon the cheek of youth. She saw all this; but the supplicating cry of mercy did not fall unheeded upon her ear. No. She smote the monster in the height of his power; link after link fell from the massive chain, and *eight hundred thousand human beings sprung into life again.*

It was WOMAN who guided that car! It was woman who prompted Justice to the work. Then commenced the glorious Jubilee; then the eye, once dim, was seen radiant with joy.■

---

*The anniversary of the British Empire's abolition of slavery in 1834.

27

THE SLAVE HAS A FRIEND IN HEAVEN, THOUGH HE MAY HAVE NONE HERE

Theodore S. Wright

Born in New Jersey, Theodore Wright (1797–1847) attended the African Free School in New York City. His teachers included Samuel Cornish, founder of Freedom's Journal, *who became Wright's lifelong mentor and collaborator. Together they composed a powerful anticolonization manifesto,* The Colonization Scheme Considered *(1840). After attending Princeton Seminary, Wright succeeded Cornish as pastor of New York City's First Colored Presbyterian Church. Wright was a founding member of the American Anti-Slavery Society and an active campaigner for black suffrage in New York State.*

In Boston on May 24, 1836, Wright delivered the following address at the convention of the New England Anti-Slavery Society. Formed in 1832, the society was dedicated to the immediate and complete abolition of slavery, opposed to gradual emancipation and to colonization schemes. The 1836 convention was the largest to date, drawing over five hundred delegates from every state in New England.

Wright rose to speak on behalf of the resolution, "That in carrying forward this great work, we must strive to act in accordance with the will of God." Wright speaks of the promise of liberty in heaven, where at last "the chains of the slave will be knocked off" and the prejudice that afflicts free blacks on earth "will not exclude us." Not content to wait for freedom in the afterlife, however, Wright urges his "down-trodden brethren to stand up and be free," even if their "blood may be spilt." A few months after this speech was delivered, Wright himself was assaulted by a southern student while visiting Princeton Seminary, his alma mater.

The text of the speech is taken from the Proceedings *of the New England Anti-Slavery Convention (Boston: Isaac Knapp, 1836), 20–22. The preceding year, Wright was among the first African Americans to have addressed an integrated antislavery society meeting. Such speeches were still unusual, as is evident from the following editorial comment through which Wright's 1836 speech is introduced in the* Proceedings:

Rev. Theodore S. Wright, of New York, (an educated black gentleman, the pastor of a Presbyterian church in the city of New York) seconded the resolution. We give his language, as near as possible, precisely as he spoke, in order that those who doubt the capacity of the colored

*man, may, if they are candid, judge from the effects of a limited edu-
cation, in the case of Mr. Wright, judge what might be done, if the
colored race enjoyed the same means and incentives for intellectual
culture as the whites. Mr. Wright is not merely a colored man, but a
black man.*

Mr. President, were it not the fact that humanity is suffering, and suffering in the race to which I belong—fellow-men of my own color;
and were it not that I had been requested to speak, I should not venture to
open my mouth in an assembly, where there are so many of my friends, so
much better able to plead the cause of humanity. Sir, I am identified with
two millions and a half of men, women, and children, whose minds, as well
as their bodies are chained down by slavery, and who have no power to speak
for themselves. Every one of them, if their voice could reach my ears, would
say 'Speak for us!—Oh, plead for us!' They would say, 'Oh, if I were in your
place, how I would speak and plead for myself, and for my fellow-sufferers.'
Let me then, sir, say a few words.

If the two millions and a half slaves in these United States, could lift
up their heads, bowed low, and look upon this assembly, and see the noble
spirits that are laboring in the cause of humanity, with the spirit of the gospel, they would exclaim, go on; go on, in the spirit of the resolution, and as
the big tears rolled down their cheeks, they would praise God for what he
was doing for them, and learn to pray for grace to wait patiently till the time
of their deliverance shall come. They would say to you, not to be discouraged—they would say to the professing Christians of this land, not to reproach them, but they would say, 'the spirit of Christianity is the love of
God, and God tells you, if you love him, to love your neighbor. We are your
neighbors, and you see us down-trodden and poor, and blind, and naked: you
see the spirit of oppression abroad, crushing our souls and bodies to the dust,
and you hear God commanding you to go to the oppressors, and in his name
to call upon them to undo the heavy burdens, and let the oppressed go
free. We can't do it. You have the laws in your hands. We must suffer and be
silent—you can speak and undo the heavy burden.' Yes, sir, this would be
their language. I see their tears flow in gratitude, as you are ready to answer
them, and tell them you are hastening to undo their heavy burdens. Yes, sir,
it is true, thanks be to God. We hope much from your agents, from the press,
from your conventions, from all you are doing for us, but we hope more from
God! The cause of emancipation is identified with prayer. Did you ever see
an abolitionist without prayer? You have gone forth armed with prayer, in
the spirit of the Prince of Peace. The whole land has been raised up against
you, because you have labored to convince the oppressor, that he should no
longer oppress. You have had to contend with a world in arms. Talent, power,
wealth, the Government and the Church have all been roused against you.
But, though you be persecuted even unto death, God is on your side, and he

is stronger than them all. Christianity has gone forth, though Stephen was stoned, though Paul was imprisoned and mobbed, and the city in commotion. It cost life to spread the gospel, but blessed be God, life has not been taken here, in the cause of abolition. Yes, the friend of the colored man lives—blessed to God, GARRISON *lives!** To the uttermost parts of the earth, where ever the colored man can hear this, he will raise his hands to heaven, and say blessed to God, Garrison lives! I am speaking the language of the slave. I pray to be excused, if I am trespassing on any of the customs of society in saying this, in the presence of my friend, but I cannot help it. I know how the colored man feels. God has raised up Garrison for him, and blessed be God, he lives to plead his cause. Oh, it is impossible for you to tell how the heart of the colored man yearns toward those who plead in his cause. You have never felt the oppression of the slave. You have never known what it is to have a master, or to see your parents and children in slavery. I was born in New Jersey. I knew a woman, the slave of the richest man in the place, and he was one of the judges of the land. He despised her entreaties, and would not let her go free. I pity him. They are both dead. I believe she is in heaven, but where he is God knows.

The slave has a friend in heaven, though he may have none here. There the chains of the slave will be knocked off, and he shall enjoy the liberty of the sons of God. We know that the influence of prejudice, and the love of power and avarice will oppress us here, and exclude us from privileges, on account of our color; but we know it will not exclude us from heaven, for God is no respecter of persons. Though we must be despised here, we know that our Redeemer liveth. We trust in God, who is able to save, all that come unto him. God speed you on! Go forward in his name, and you will prosper. I listen, and I think I hear the trump of jubilee sounding—I hear the voice of emancipation proclaiming to my down-trodden brethren, to stand up and be free! The strong efforts that are making, throughout the whole world, to abolish the slavery of my race, shall be accomplished. What do we hear from Europe, from South America, from every part of the world? The cry is, *emancipation!* it is liberty! and I as much believe the work will be accomplished, as if I now saw it with my own eyes. I want to see my brethren prepare for this. Slavery will be abolished, and I feel a great anxiety to prepare by [my?] brethren, by moral and religious instruction for this great change. Go on! If you suffer martyrdom, you will suffer in a glorious cause. Did not all the pioneers of Christianity suffer martyrdom but one? Some of you may be called to suffer martyrdom—your blood may be spilt, but I repeat it, it will be shed in a glorious cause. It will be like the blood of the martyrs. That was the seed of the Church, and this shall be the seed of liberty to the captive. I will detain you no longer. [The resolution passed.]■

*Abolitionist William Lloyd Garrison (1805–1879) barely escaped lynching when he was attacked by a mob on October 21, 1835.

28 ON THE IMPROVEMENT OF THE MIND

Elizabeth Jennings

Founded in 1834, the Ladies' Literary Society of New York was an organization of the city's elite black women that was devoted to reading, discussion, self-instruction, and political activism. In May 1837, the society sent a delegation to the First Anti-Slavery Convention of American Women.

Elizabeth Jennings, a schoolteacher and member of the society, is best remembered today for her celebrated suit against New York's Third Avenue Railroad Company. In 1854, Jennings refused a conductor's order to move to a separate car.

> I answered again and told him I was a respectable person, born and raised in New York, did not know where he was born, that I had never been insulted before while going to church, and that he was a good for nothing impudent fellow for insulting decent persons while on their way to church. He then said I should come out and he would put me out. I told him not to lay his hands on me; he took hold of me and I took hold of the window sash and held on; he pulled me until he broke my grasp and I took hold of his coat and held on to that, he also broke my grasp from that (but previously he had dragged my companion out, she all the while screaming for him to let go). He then ordered the driver to fasten his horses, which he did, and come and help him put me out of the car; they then both seized hold of me by the arms and pulled and dragged me flat down on the bottom of the platform, so that my feet hung one way and my head the other, nearly on the ground. I screamed murder with all my voice, and my companion screamed out "you'll kill her; don't kill her." The driver then let go of me and went to his horses; I went again in the car, and the conductor said you shall sweat for this; then told the driver to drive as fast as he could and not to take another passenger in the car; to drive until he saw an officer or a Station House.

Taunted by the police and the officer to "get redress if she could," Jennings did just that, winning $225 in damages, legal protection for black passengers, and national attention.

But Jennings's eloquent activism had begun long before. A group of male abolitionists attended the third anniversary meeting of the Ladies' Literary Society in August 1837 and reported its program and their impressions of it to the editors of the Colored American. The "admirable dis-

*play of female talent," they wrote, "consisted of original composition,
oratory, dialogues on temperance, propriety of conduct, &c. such as are
rarely to be met with." Jennings's speech was the seventh item on the
program and was preceded and followed by musical performances.
"Truly it was a* mental feast," *the visitors concluded: "Indeed, we were
not only amused, but what was of much greater importance we were
edified." They recommended that parents enroll their daughters in the society, agreeing with Jennings' message that to do so would cultivate their
minds and diminish racial prejudice against them.*

*Jennings portrays education as a means through which women might
better meet what she regards as their intended roles: "To make ourselves
useful and pleasing to others." She also, however, rejoices in the personal
rewards of the edifying company and mission of the women's society:
"Let us accord with that voice which we hear urging us and resolve to
adorn our minds with a more abundant supply of those gems for which
we have united ourselves."*

The text of Jennings's speech comes from the Colored American *of
September 23, 1837. Jennings's story of her confrontation with the conductor was published in the* New York Tribune, *19 July 1854, and is reprinted in C. Peter Ripley,* Witness for Freedom *(Chapel Hill: University
of North Carolina Press, 1993), 60–61. For more information on the Ladies' Literary Society of New York, see Anne M. Boylan, "Antislavery Activity Among African American Women," in Jean Fagan Yellin and
John C. Vanhorne, eds.,* The Abolitionist Sisterhood: Women's Political
Culture in Antebellum America *(Ithaca: Cornell University Press, 1994),
127–29.*

Friends, in appearing before you this evening, I find words inadequate to
express my feelings, for the honor conferred on me of addressing you, in
the celebration of this anniversary. I am conscious of my incapacity to do
justice to the task allotted me. But as our object is improvement, and feeling
that yours is the same, we have but to solicit your kind indulgence.

It is now a momentous time, a time that calls us to exert all our powers,
and among the many of them, the mind is the greatest, and great care should
be taken to improve it with diligence. We should cultivate these powers and
dispositions of the mind, which may prove advantageous to us. It is impossible to attain to the sphere for which we were created, without persevering.
It is certain we were formed for society, and it is our duty and interest to
cultivate social qualities and dispositions to endeavor to make ourselves useful and pleasing to others—to promote and encourage their happiness—to
cherish the friendly affections, that we may find in them the source of the
greatest blessings this world can afford.

But, alas! society too often exhibits a far different scene, and this is in
consequence of neglect of cultivation, which certainly is much more fatal
than we can imagine. Neglect will plunge us into deeper degradation, and

keep us grovelling in the dust, while our enemies will rejoice and say, we do not believe they (colored people) have any minds; if they have, they are unsusceptible of improvement. My sisters, allow me to ask the question, shall we bring this reproach on ourselves? Doubtless you answer NO, we will strive to avoid it. But hark! methinks I hear the well known voice of Abigail A. Matthews, saying you can avoid it. Why sleep thus? Awake and slumber no more—arise, put on your armor, ye daughters of America, and start forth in the field of improvement. You can all do some good, and if you do but little it will increase in time. The mind is powerful, and by its efforts your influence may be as near perfection, as that of those which have extended over kingdoms, and is applauded by thousands.

Let us accord with that voice which we hear urging us and resolve to adorn our minds with a more abundant supply of those gems for which we have united ourselves—nor let us ever think any occasion too trifling for our best endeavors. It is by constant aiming at perfection in every thing, that we may at length attain to it.■

29 PREJUDICE AGAINST THE COLORED MAN

Theodore S. Wright

As abolitionist societies and ranks grew more numerous in the mid-1830s, serious rifts formed over issues of racial prejudice and social equality. Many who opposed slavery also insisted upon segregation and maintained beliefs in white supremacy.* Black abolitionists spoke out against racism within the movement, especially at antislavery conventions where the nature and purposes of the organizations were under discussion.

At the convention of the New York State Anti-Slavery Society, held in Utica, September 20, 1837, the Reverend Theodore S. Wright, pastor of the First Presbyterian Church in New York City, made two dramatic speeches condemning racial prejudice. In the first he attacked racist thinking present within the abolitionist movement and made it clear that it was not enough just to be against slavery. The second speech followed the introduction of a resolution saying that prejudice against col-

*See Leon F. Litwack, "The Abolitionist Dilemma: The Antislavery Movement and the Northern Negro," *New England Quarterly* 34 (March 1961), 50–73.

ored people was "nefarious and wicked and should be practically repro-
bated and discountenanced." Below are an extract from the first speech
and the complete text of the second.

The extract from the first speech is taken from the Colored American
[New York], October 4, 1837; the second speech is taken from the Liberator, *October 2, 1837.*

THREE YEARS AGO, when a man professed to be an Abolitionist we knew where he was. He was an individual who recognized the identity of the human family. Now a man may call himself an Abolitionist and we know not where to find him. Your tests are taken away. A rush is made into the Abolition ranks. Free discussion, petition anti-Texas, and political favor converts are multiplying.* Many throw themselves in, without understanding the breadth and depth of the principles of emancipation. I fear not the annexation of Texas. I fear not all the machination, calumny and opposition of slaveholders, when contrasted with the annexation of men whose hearts have not been deeply imbued with these high and holy principles. Why, sir, unless men come out and take their stand on the principle of recognizing man as man, I tremble for the ark, and I fear our society will become like the expatriation society—everybody an Abolitionist. These points which have lain in the dark must be brought out to view. The identity of the human family, the principle of recognizing all men as brethren—that is the doctrine, that is the point which touches the quick of the community. It is an easy thing to ask about the vileness of slavery at the South, but to call the dark man a brother, heartily to embrace the doctrine advanced in the second article of the Constitution, to treat all men according to their moral worth, to treat the man of color in all circumstances as a man and brother—that is the test.

Every man who comes into this society ought to be catechized. It should be ascertained whether he looks upon man as man, all of one blood and one family. A healthful atmosphere must be created in which the slave may live when rescued from the horrors of slavery. I am sensible, I am detaining you, but I feel that this is an important point. I am alarmed sometimes when I look at the constitutions of our societies. I am afraid that brethren sometimes endeavor so to form the constitutions of societies that they will be popular. I have seen constitutions of abolition societies, where nothing was said about the improvement of the man of color! They have overlooked the giant sin of prejudice. They have passed by this foul monster, which is at

---

*The reference is to those who joined the antislavery cause primarily in opposition to the annexation of Texas and the assault on freedom of speech and press. The petition issue refers to the "gag rule" adopted by Congress in 1836 on the motion of John C. Calhoun. It provided that all antislavery petitions thenceforth submitted to Congress be laid on the table without action. The struggle against the rule, led by John Quincy Adams, forced its repeal in 1844. The rule was attacked during this eight-year period as an unconstitutional deprivation of the right of petition.

once the parent and offspring of slavery. Whilst you are thinking about the annexation of Texas, whilst you are discussing the great principles involved in this noble cause, remember this prejudice must be killed or slavery will never be abolished. Abolitionists must annihilate in their own bosoms the cord of caste. We must be consistent—recognize the colored man in every respect as a man and brother. In doing this we shall have to encounter scorn; we shall have to breast the storm. This society would do well to spend a whole day in thinking about it and praying over it. Every Abolitionist would do well to spend a day in fasting and prayer over it and in looking at his own heart. Far be it from me to condemn Abolitionists. I rejoice and bless God for this first institution which has combined its energies for the overthrow of heaven-daring, this soul-crushing, prejudice.

The successors of Penn, Franklin and Woolman* have shown themselves the friends of the colored race. They have done more in this cause than any other church, and they are still doing great things both in Europe and America. I was taught in childhood to remember the man of the broad-brimmed hat and drab-colored coat and venerate him. No class have testified more to the truth on this subject. They lifted up their voices against slavery and the slave trade. But, ah, with but here and there a noble exception, they go but halfway. When they come to the grand doctrine, to lay the ax right down at the root of the tree and destroy the very spirit of slavery—there they are defective. Their doctrine is to set the slave free, and let him take care of himself. Hence, we hear nothing about their being brought into the Friends' church, or of their being viewed and treated according to their moral worth. Our hearts have recently been gladdened by an address of the annual meeting of the Friends' Society in the city of New York, in which they insist upon the doctrine of immediate emancipation. But that very good man who signed the document as the organ of that society within the past year, received a man of color, a Presbyterian minister, into this house, gave him his meals alone in the kitchen, and did not introduce him to his family. That shows how men can testify against slavery at the South, and not assail it at the North, where it is tangible. Here is something for Abolitionists to do. What can the friends of emancipation effect while the spirit of slavery is so fearfully prevalent? Let every man take his stand, burn out this prejudice, live it down, talk it down, everywhere consider the colored man as a man, in the church, the stage, the steamboat, the public house, in all places, and the death blow to slavery will be struck.

Mr. President, with much feeling do I rise to address the society on this resolution, and I should hardly have been induced to have done it had I not been requested. I confess I am personally interested in this resolution. But were it not for the fact that none can feel the lash but those who have it upon

---

*John Woolman, Quaker antislavery agitator, was the author of a popular journal and a series of pamphlets exposing slavery and the slave trade. The inclusion of Penn is not clear, since William Penn owned slaves and did not manumit them on his death.

them, that none know where the chain galls but those who wear it, I would not address you.

This is a serious business, sir. The prejudice which exists against the colored man, the free man is like the atmosphere, everywhere felt by him. It is true that in these United States and in this State, there are men, like myself, colored with the skin like my own, who are not subjected to the lash, who are not liable to have their wives and their infants torn from them; from whose hand the Bible is not taken. It is true that we may walk abroad; we may enjoy our domestic comforts, our families; retire to the closet; visit the sanctuary, and may be permitted to urge on our children and our neighbors in well doing. But sir, still we are slaves—everywhere we feel the chain galling us. It is by that prejudice which the resolution condemns, the spirit of slavery, the law which has been enacted here, by a corrupt public sentiment, through the influence of slavery which treats moral agents different from the rule of God, which treats them irrespective of their morals or intellectual cultivation. This spirit is withering all our hopes, and ofttimes causes the colored parent as he looks upon his child, to wish he had never been born. Often is the heart of the colored mother, as she presses her child to her bosom, filled with sorrow to think that, by reason of this prejudice, it is cut off from all hopes of usefulness in this land. Sir, this prejudice is wicked.

If the nation and church understood this matter, I would not speak a word about that killing influence that destroys the colored man's reputation. This influence cuts us off from everything; it follows us up from childhood to manhood; it excludes us from all stations of profit, usefulness and honor; takes away from us all motive for pressing forward in enterprises, useful and important to the world and to ourselves.

In the first place, it cuts us off from the advantages of the mechanic arts almost entirely. A colored man can hardly learn a trade, and if he does it is difficult for him to find any one who will employ him to work at that trade, in any part of the State. In most of our large cities there are associations of mechanics who legislate out of their society colored men. And in many cases where our young men have learned trades, they have had to come to low employments for want of encouragement in those trades.

It must be a matter of rejoicing to know that in this vicinity colored fathers and mothers have the privileges of education. It must be a matter of rejoicing that in this vicinity colored parents can have their children trained up in schools.—At present, we find the colleges barred against them.

I will say nothing about the inconvenience which I have experienced myself, and which every man of color experiences, though made in the image of God. I will say nothing about the inconvenience of traveling; how we are frowned upon and despised. No matter how we may demean ourselves, we find embarrassments everywhere.

But sir, this prejudice goes further. It debars men from heaven. While sir, slavery cuts off the colored portion of the community from religious privileges, men are made infidels. What, they demand, is your Christianity? How do you regard your brethren? How do you treat them at the Lord's table?

Where is your consistency in talking about the heathen, transversing the ocean to circulate the Bible everywhere, while you frown upon them at the door? These things meet us and weigh down our spirits.

And, sir, the constitution of society, molded by this prejudice, destroys souls. I have known extensively, that in revivals which have been blessed and enjoyed in this part of the country, the colored population were overlooked. I recollect an instance. The Lord God was pouring out His Spirit. He was entering every house, and sinners were converted. I asked, Where is the colored man? who is weeping for them? who is endeavoring to pull them out of the fire? No reply was made.—I was asked to go round with one of the elders and visit them. We went and they humbled themselves. The Church commenced efficient efforts, and God blessed them as soon as they began to act for these people as though they had souls.

And sir, the manner in which our churches are regulated destroys souls. Whilst the church is thrown open to everybody, and one says come, come in and share the blessings of the sanctuary, this is the gate of heaven—he says to the colored man, *be careful where you take your stand.* I know an efficient church in this State, where a respectable colored man went to the house of God, and was going to take a seat in the gallery, and one of the officers contended with him, and said, "you cannot go there, sir."

In one place the people had come together to the house of the Lord. The sermon was preached—the emblems were about to be administered—and all at once the person who managed the church thought the value of the pews would be diminished if the colored people sat in them. They objected to their sitting there, and the colored people left and went into the gallery, and that, too, when they were thinking of handling the memorials of the broken body and shed blood of the Savior! And, sir, this prejudice follows the colored man everywhere, and depresses his spirits.

Thanks be to God, there is a buoyant principle which elevates the poor down-trodden colored man above all this:—It is that there is society which regards man according to his worth; it is the fact, that when he looks up to Heaven he knows that God treats him like a moral agent, irrespective of caste or the circumstances in which he may be placed. Amid the embarrassments which he has to meet, and the scorn and contempt that is heaped upon him, he is cheered by the hope that he will be disenthralled, and soon, like a bird set forth from its cage, wing his flight to Jesus, where he can be happy, and look down with pity on the man who despises the poor slave for being what God made him, and who despises him because he is identified with the poor slave. Blessed be God for the principles of the Gospel. Were it not for these, and for the fact that a better day is dawning, I would not wish to live.—Blessed be God for the antislavery movement. Blessed be God there is a war waging with slavery, that the granite rock is about to be rolled from its base. But as long as the colored man is to be looked upon as an inferior caste, so long will they disregard his cries, his groans, his shrieks.

I rejoice, sir, in this Society; and I deem the day when I joined this Society as one of the proudest days of my life. And I know I can die better, in more peace to-day, to know there are men who will plead the cause of my children.

Let me, through you, sir, request this delegation to take hold of this subject. This will silence the slave holder, when he says where is your love for the slave? Where is your love for the colored man who is crushed at your feet? Talking to us about emancipating our slaves when you are enslaving them by your feelings, and doing more violence to them by your prejudice, than we are to our slaves by our treatment. They call on us to evince our love for the slave, by treating man as man, the colored man as a man, according to his worth.■

30 SLAVERY BRUTALIZES MAN

Daniel A. Payne

A militant anecdotal speech against slavery was delivered in June 1839 by Daniel A. Payne (1811–1893) at Fordsboro, New York, on the occasion of his ordination by the Franckean Synod of the Lutheran Church. The speech was delivered in support of a synodical report to end slavery in America, and it was influential in achieving the acceptance of that report. Although never a slave himself, Payne uses his knowledge of those enslaved and their religious life to great effect: "I speak not of what others have told me, but of what I have both seen and heard from the slaves themselves."

Payne was born February 24, 1811, in Charleston, South Carolina, the son of free blacks. Educated at a local school established by free blacks and by a private tutor, he mastered mathematics, Greek, Latin, and French. In 1826 he joined the Methodist Episcopal Church and three years later opened a school for African American children, which he conducted until the South Carolina legislature passed a law on December 17, 1834, imposing a fine and whipping on free persons of color who kept schools to teach slaves or free blacks to read or write. Forced to abandon his school, Payne entered the Lutheran Theological Seminary at Gettysburg, Pennsylvania, and became a Lutheran preacher. Later, he left the Lutheran Church, joined the African Methodist Episcopal Church in 1841, and in May 1852 was elected a bishop. In 1863 he became president of Wilberforce University, an Ohio institution established for the education of African Americans in 1856, and served in that office for thirteen years.

The speech appeared in the Lutheran Herald and Journal of the Fort Plain, N.Y., Franckean Synod *1:15 (August 1, 1839), 113–14. It is published here with permission of the Lutheran Theological Seminary, Abdel Ross Wentz Library, Gettysburg, Pennsylvania. William J. Simmons includes a biographical sketch of Payne in* Men of Mark: Eminent, Progressive and Rising *(1887), 1078–85.*

MR. PRESIDENT: I move the adoption of the Report, because it is based upon the following propositions:

American Slavery brutalizes man—destroys his moral agency, and subverts the moral government of God.

Sir, I am opposed to slavery, not because it enslaves the black man, but because it enslaves *man.* And were all the slaveholders in this land men of color, and the slaves white men, I would be as thorough and uncompromising an abolitionist as I now am; for whatever and whenever I may see a being in the form of a man, enslaved by his fellow man, without respect to his complexion, I shall lift up my voice to plead his cause, against all the claims of his proud oppressor; and I shall do it not merely from the sympathy which man feels towards suffering man, but because God, *the living God,* whom I dare not disobey, has commanded me to open my mouth for the dumb, and to plead the cause of the oppressed.

Slavery brutalizes man. We know that the word *man*, in its primitive sense, signifies ———.* But the intellectual and moral structure of man, and the august relations which he sustains to the Deity, have thrown around the name, and being designated by it, a halo of glory, brightened by all the ideas, that are ennobling on earth, and blessed in eternity. This being God created but a little lower than the angels, and crowned him with glory and honor; but slavery hurls him down from his elevated position, to the level of brutes, strikes this crown of glory from his head and fastens upon his neck the galling yoke, and compels him to labor like an ox, through summer's sun and winter's snow, without remuneration. Does a man take the calf from the cow and sell it to the butcher? So slavery tears the child from the arms of the reluctant mother, and barters it to the soul trader for a young colt, or some other commodity! Does the bird catcher tear away the dove from his mate? So slavery separates the groaning husband from the embraces of his distracted and weeping wife! And are the beasts of the forest hunted, tortured and slain at the pleasure of the cruel hunter? So are the slaves hunted, tortured and slain by the cruel monster slavery! To treat a man like a brute is to brutalize him. We have seen that slavery treats man like a brute, therefore slavery brutalizes man! But does slavery stop here? Is it content with merely treating the external man like a brute? No, sir, it goes further, and with a heart as brazen as that of Belshazzar and hands still more sacrilegious, it lays

---

*The blank space is the original report of the speech.

hold of the *immortal mind, seizes the will, and binds that which Jehovah did not bind—fetters that which the Eternal made as free to move and act as the breath of Heaven. "It destroys moral agency!"* To destroy moral agency is to fetter or obstruct the will of man. Now let us see if slavery is innocent of this. The very moment that a man conceives the diabolic design of enslaving his brother's body, that very moment does he also conceive the still more heinous design of fettering his will, for well does he know that in order to make his dominion supreme over the body, he must fetter the living spring of all its motions. Hence, the first lesson the slave is taught is to yield his will unreservedly and exclusively to the dictates of his master. And if a slave desire to educate himself or his children, in obedience to the dictates of reason or the laws of God, he does not, he cannot do it without the consent of his master. Does reason and circumstances and the Bible command a slave to preach the gospel of his brethren? Slavery arises, and with a frown, an oath and a whip, fetters or obstructs the holy volition of his soul! I knew a pious slave in Charleston who was a licensed exhorter in the Methodist Episcopal Church; this good man was in the habit of spending his Saturday nights on the surrounding plantations, preaching to the slaves. One night, as usual, he got into a canoe, sailed upon James' Island. While in the very act of preaching the unsearchable riches of Christ to dying men, the patrols seized him and whipped him in the most cruel manner, and compelled him to promise that he would never return to preach again to those slaves. In the year 1834, several colored brethren, who were also exhorters in the Methodist Episcopal Church commenced preaching to several *destitute white families,* who gained a subsistence by cultivating some poor lands about three or four miles from Charleston. The first Sunday I was present; the house was nearly filled with these poor white farmers. The master of the house was awakened to a sense of his lost condition. During the following week he was converted. On the third Sunday from the day he was convinced of sin he died in the triumphs of faith, and went to heaven. On the fourth Sunday from the time the dear brethren began to preach, the patrols scented their tract, and put them to chase. Thus, an end was put to their labors. Their willing souls were fettered, and the poor whites constrained to go without the preaching of the gospel. In a word, it is in view of man's moral agency that God commands him to shun vice, and practice virtue. But what female slave can do this? I lived twenty-four years in the midst of slavery and never knew but six female slaves who were reputedly virtuous! What profit is to the female slave that she is disposed to be virtuous? Her will, like her body, is not her own; they are both at the pleasure of her master; and he brands them at his will. So *it subverts the moral government of God.*

In view of the moral agency of man, God hath most wisely and graciously given him a code of laws, and certain positive precepts, to control and regulate moral actions. This code of laws, and these positive precepts, with the divine influence which they are naturally calculated to exert on the mind of man, constitutes his moral government.

Now, to nullify these laws—to weaken or destroy their legitimate influence on the human mind, or to hinder man from yielding universal and entire obedience to them is to subvert the moral government of God.

Now, slavery nullifies these laws and precepts—weakens and destroys their influence over the human mind, and hinders men from yielding universal and entire obedience to them; therefore slavery subverts the moral government of God. This is the climax of the sin of slavery! This is the blackest, foulest, and most horrid feature of the heaven-daring *Monster!* He stretcheth out his hand against God, and strengtheneth himself against the Almighty—he runneth on him, even on his neck, upon the thick bosses of his buckler. Thus saith the Lord, "Thou shalt not commit adultery." But does the man who owns a hundred females obey the law? Does he not nullify it and compel the helpless woman to disobey God? Concerning the religious instruction of children, thus saith the Lord, "Bring them up in the nurture and admonition of the Lord." But what saith slavery? "They are my property, and shall be brought up to serve me." They shall not *even learn to read his word,* in order that they may be brought up in his nurture and admonition. If any man doubts this, let him read the slave code of Louisiana and see if it is not death to teach slaves. Thus saith the Lord, "Remember the Sabbath day, to keep it holy." Does not slavery nullify this law, and compel the slave to work on the Sabbath? Thus saith the Lord, "Obey thy father and thy mother." Can the slave children obey this command of God? Does not slavery command the children to obey the master and let him alone? Thus saith the Son of God, "What God hath joined together let no man put asunder." Does not slavery nullify this law, by breaking the sacred bands of wedlock, and separating the husband and wife forever? Thus saith the Son of God, "Search the Scriptures." Does not slavery seal up the word of God and make it criminal for the slave to read it? In 1834, the legislature of South Carolina enacted a law prohibiting the instruction of any slave; and Mr. Lawrence in a pamphlet which he published in 1835, to defend this law, declared that if the slaves were permitted to read the Bible, ninety of them would become infidels, like Voltaire, where ten would become Christians. "Go ye into all the world, and preach the Gospel unto every creature," saith the Son of God. Does slavery permit it? In 1835, a minister of the Episcopal Church, in the city of Charleston, appealed to the civil authority for permission to preach to the free population of an evening, but they would not permit him.

The objector may reply, that at the present moment there are four Methodist missionaries, and one Lutheran, laboring among the slave population of South Carolina. We answer, that this is true, and we are glad of it; but this fact does not overthrow our proposition, nor falsify what we have stated, for although a few planters have permitted the Gospel to be preached to their slaves, the majority of them prohibit it, and this permission is extraneous to slavery and is no part of its creed or code. Slavery never legislates for the religious instruction of slaves, but, on the contrary, legislates to perpetuate their ignorance; and there are laws this very moment in the statute books of South Carolina and other states, prohibiting the religious instruction of slaves. But this is not all that slavery does to subvert the moral government of God. The slaves are sensible of the oppression exercised by their masters; and they see these masters on the Lord's day worshiping in his holy Sanctuary. They hear their masters professing Christianity; they see their masters preaching the Gospel; they hear these masters praying in their families, and they know that oppression and slavery are inconsistent with the Christian religion; therefore they scoff at religion itself—mock their masters, and distrust both the goodness and justice of God. Yes, I have known them even to question His existence. I speak not of what others have told me, but of what *I have both seen and heard from the slaves themselves.* I have heard the mistress ring the bell for family prayer, and I have seen the servants immediately begin to sneer and laugh; and have heard them declare they would not go in to prayers, adding, if I go in she will only just read, "Servants obey your masters"; but she will not read, "Break every yoke, and let the oppressed go free." I have seen colored men at the church door, *scoffing at the ministers,* while they were preaching, and saying, you had better go home, and set your slaves free. A few nights ago between ten and eleven o'clock a runaway slave came to the house where I live for safety and succor. I asked him if he was a Christian. "No sir," said he, "white men treat us so bad in Mississippi that we can't be Christians."

Sir, I taught school in Charleston five years. In 1834 the legislature of our state enacted a law to prohibit colored teachers. My school was filled with children and youth of the most promising talents; and when I looked upon them and remembered that in a few more weeks this school shall be closed and I be permitted no more to teach them, notwithstanding I had been a professor seven years, I began to question the existence of the Almighty and to say, if indeed there is a God, does he deal justly? Is he a just God? Is he a holy Being? If so, why does he permit a handful of dying men thus to oppress us? Why does he permit them to hinder me from teaching these children, when nature, reason and Revelation command me to teach them? Thus I began to question the divine government and to murmur at the administration of His providence. And could I do otherwise, while slavery's cruelties were pressing and grinding my soul in the dust, and robbing me and my people of those privileges which it was hugging to its breast, and giving thousands to perpetuate the blessing which it was tearing away from us? Sir, the very man who made the law alluded to, did that very year, increase the property of South Carolina College.

In a word, slavery tramples the laws of the living God under its unhallowed feet—weakens and destroys the influence which those laws are calculated to exert over the mind of man, and constrains the oppressed to blaspheme the name of the Almighty. For I have often heard them sneeringly say, that *"The Almighty made Charleston on Saturday night, when he was weary, and in a great hurry." O, Brethren of the Franckean Synod! awake! Awake to the battle and hurl the hottest thunders of divine truth at the head of this cruel monster, until he shall fall to rise no more, and the groans of the enslaved are converted into the songs of the free!!*■

31

WE MEET THE MONSTER PREJUDICE EVERY WHERE

Clarissa C. Lawrence

*On May 1–3, 1839, the third national women's antislavery convention was held in Philadelphia at the Pennsylvania Riding School, "no better place being available for so unpopular a gathering," writes Quarles (*Black Abolitionists, *28). At the previous year's convention, white mobs outraged at the gathering of black and white women "sitting together in amalgamated ease" had disrupted the speeches at Pennsylvania Hall, then burned down the building. The mayor of Philadelphia asked Lucretia Mott to ensure that those attending the 1839 convention "avoid unnecessary walking with colored people" and conclude their business as soon as possible.*

On May 3, 1839, the last day of the convention, Clarissa C. Lawrence, the president of the Colored Female Religious and Moral Society of Salem (formed by black women in 1833), addressed the gathering. Lawrence had also served as vice president of the Salem Female Anti-Slavery Society, a reorganized and racially integrated version of the Female Anti-Slavery Society of Salem, the earliest known antislavery organization formed by black women, founded February 22, 1832.

Lawrence rose to second the resolution "that henceforth we will increase our efforts to improve the condition of our free colored population, by giving them mechanical, literary, and religious instruction, and assisting to establish them in trades, and such other employments as are now denied them on account of their color." The motion was adopted. The 1839 convention was the last held by the antislavery women, "the time having come for their admission to the hitherto all-male societies" (Quarles, Black Abolitionists, *28).*

While returning from New York on an overnight packet, Lawrence broke the color bar by sharing a cabin with a white woman. A vote taken among the passengers the next day condemned their actions, and proslavery forces created a scandal from the incident, citing it as proof that abolition would promote integration. For an account of the controversy, see the Liberator, *May 24 and 31, 1839.*

The text of the speech is taken from the Proceedings of the Third Anti-Slavery Convention of American Women, Held in Philadelphia, May 1, 2, 3, 1839 *(Philadelphia: Merrihew and Thompson, 1839), 8–9. See also Benjamin Quarles,* Black Abolitionists *(New York: Oxford, 1969), 28–29; Dorothy Sterling, ed.,* We Are Your Sisters: Black Women in the Nineteenth Century *(New York: Norton, 1984), 115–17; and Shirley Yee,* Black

Women Abolitionists: A Study in Activism, 1828–1860 *(Knoxville: University of Tennessee Press, 1992), 82–89.*

W̶e meet the monster prejudice every where. We have not power to contend with it, we are so down-trodden. We cannot elevate ourselves. You must aid us. We have been brought up in ignorance; our parents were ignorant, they could not teach us. We want light; we ask it, and it is denied us. Why are we thus treated? Prejudice is the cause. It kills its thousands every day; it follows us every where, even to the grave; but, blessed be God! it stops there. You must pray it down. Faith and prayer will do wonders in the anti-slavery cause. Place yourselves, dear friends, in our stead. We are blamed for not filling useful places in society; but give us light, give us learning, and see then what places we can occupy. Go on, I entreat you. A brighter day is dawning. I bless God that the young are interested in this cause. It is worth coming all the way from Massachusetts, to see what I have seen here.■

32 SLAVERY PRESSES DOWN UPON THE FREE PEOPLE OF COLOR

Andrew Harris

Most black abolitionists sought to emphasize the connectedness of "free" blacks and slaves, and the relationships between the institution of slavery and the systematic discrimination experienced by African Americans in the North. Andrew Harris (1810–1841) graduated from the University of Vermont in 1838, having been refused admission to Union and Middlebury Colleges on the basis of race. In his address delivered to nearly five thousand abolitionists at New York City's Broadway Tabernacle on May 7, 1839, Harris argues that the existence of slavery in the South fuels racial prejudice in the North. It is the dissemination of slavery's "deadly poison," he suggests, that leads the northern "lords of these institutions" of higher education to "rise up and shut the door" when African American students apply for admission.

Harris poignantly observes the dilemma facing free blacks when "wrongs are inflicted upon us that are grievous and heavy to be borne." If they remained silent in the face of oppression ("fold our arms and bear it"), this silence was used to rationalize the oppression; if, on the other hand, they spoke out in protest, they risked mob violence. Harris offers no answer but makes clear his determination to endure whatever might be inflicted upon him in America rather than emigrate to colonize another land.

The text of the speech is taken from The Sixth Annual Report of the Executive Committee of the American Anti-Slavery Society *(New York: William S. Dorr, 1839).*

It is with no pleasant feeling, said he, that I stand here to speak in relation to the wrongs of a portion of the inhabitants of this country, who, by their complexion, are identified with myself. It is with feeling of great responsibility that I stand here as their representative.

Who of our Pilgrim fathers, when they entered ship, and committed themselves to the waves—when the breeze carried back the echo of their songs, ever thought the day would come, when an assembly like this would meet on the island of Manhattan, for such an object? Who would then have supposed, that the oppression and wrongs of millions in this country, would have been so great as to call together an audience like this? If an inhabitant of another world should enter one of these doors, and look abroad upon these thousands, and ask, "For what are you assembled?" and the voice of this multitude should be heard in answer, "We have come to hear and converse about the wrongs of our fellow men;" would he esteem it a light or trifling thing, which has brought this audience together?

But from whence spring these wrongs? The original source from which they spring, is the corruption of the human heart. The beginning of its development is *slavery.* Shall I again point to the South, and depict the sufferings of the slave? If the groans and sighs of the victims of slavery could be collected, and thrown out here in one volley, these walls would tremble, these pillars would be removed from their foundations, and we should find ourselves buried in the ruins of the edifice. If the blood of the innocent, which has been shed by slavery, could be poured out here, this audience might swim in it—or if they could not swim they would be drowned. If the tears that slavery has caused to be shed, were poured out here, there might be a sea on which to ply the oar in exercise of sport and diversion. But this is not all—the anguish produced by separation of husband and wife, children and parents, and the scourges of the defenseless and unoffending slave, are a fathomless sea, and an ocean without a shore.

But slavery does not stop here. It presses down upon the free people of color. Its deadly poison is disseminated from the torrid regions of the South to the frigid North. We feel it here. Yet, with all this, if the colored man is vicious, or if he is not elevated, it is set down to his natural stupidity and depravity, and the argument is raised that he belongs to an inferior race. The colored people are also charged with want of desire for education and improvement; yet, if a colored man comes to the door of our institutions of learning, with desires ever so strong, the lords of these institutions rise up and shut the door; and then you say we have not the desire nor the ability to acquire education. Thus, while the white youth enjoy all these advantages, we are excluded and shut out, and must remain ignorant. It is natural to suppose, then, that there should be more crime among us. But is this crime properly chargeable to the colored man, as evidence of the vicious propensities of his race?

Again, in the social relations of life, wrongs are inflicted upon us that are grievous and heavy to be borne, and we must fold our arms and bear it. But even this is thrown out as a taunt against us, that we do not speak of our wrongs, as evidence that we are too stupid and degraded to feel them: while, if we rise to defend ourselves and to plead our cause, the torch and the brick-bat are poured out as arguments on the other side. As a specimen, I will mention what I experienced in my passage to this city, from the city of "brotherly love," so called; but as to the claim it has upon that title, I leave the ruins of Pennsylvania Hall to answer.* On the way, they refused to give the colored man a seat, but put him up in boxes, as they would monkeys or wild geese. And why was this? Was it because he had no money? No. Was it because he was not decently clad? No. Was it because he was an idiot, and they feared he would annoy the company with his foolishness? No—it is because he has *the complexion which God has given him.* The bible says the love of money is the root of all evil; and if the love of money is a predominant passion anywhere, it is in this land. Yet, without disputing the correctness of the declaration, it seems to me that slavery had developed a passion in the human heart that is stronger than the love of money; for they refuse to gratify this disposition which the bible says is the root of all evil, through the influence of that still deeper root of evil, *prejudice.*

Again: the colored man is deprived of the opportunity of obtaining those situations in society which his enemies say he ought to hold, if capable. If he wishes to be useful as a professional man, a merchant or a mechanic, he is prevented by the color of his skin, and driven to those menial employments which tend to bring us more and more into disrepute.

The church itself was not free from participation in the general guilt of oppressing the black man. He feared that some of her pastors would in the great day, have the Judge say to them, "though ye have cast out devils in my name, yet this devil of prejudice you have not cast out of your own hearts—and though you may have done many wonderful works, one great work, that of emancipating the slave, ye have left undone."

Time would fail me, said he, to depict all these wrongs. Yet, with all the oppression and odium that is heaped upon us here, I for one would rather stand and endure it all, choosing rather to suffer affliction with my people, than to emigrate to a foreign shore, though I might there enjoy the pleasures of Egypt. And while I live, let my prayer be, that the same soil which cher-

---

*Philadelphia's Pennsylvania Hall was burned by an antiabolitionist mob on May 17, 1838.

ished my father may cherish me; and when I die, that the same dust may cover me that covered the ashes of my father.■

33 LET US DO JUSTICE TO AN UNFORTUNATE PEOPLE

Thomas Paul

The following speech by Thomas Paul, who was described as "a Colored Student of Dartmouth College," was delivered before the Massachusetts Anti-Slavery Society on January 27, 1841. Paul was the son of the pastor of the African Baptist Church in Boston, and when Garrison first published the Liberator, *young Paul assisted him as an apprentice. He had been a student at the antislavery academy at Canaan, New Hampshire, until its building had been dragged away by farmers protesting its interracial character. Later, he became the first African American graduate of Dartmouth College. In 1849, Paul was appointed as the first African American headmaster of the Smith School in Boston, following protests about the racist behavior of the school's all-white staff toward black pupils. Paul and the Smith school became focal points for the Massachusetts struggle over segregated education. Black boycotts of the school continued after Paul's appointment and it closed after the state passed an integrated education law in 1855.*

Paul begins this speech with a reflexive analysis of the rhetorical situations facing himself and other abolitionist speakers—the burdens of proving the self-evident, of undermining the prejudices that obscure sound judgment, and of revealing horrors denied or obscured by others. Directed to fellow antislavery activists, Paul's address is a good example of the intraorganizational appeals necessary to sustain a social or political movement.

The speech is reprinted from the National Anti-Slavery Standard *of April 1, 1841. For more information on Paul and the battle over school segregation in Boston, see James O. Horton and Lois E. Horton,* Black Bostonians: Family Life and Community Struggle in the Antebellum North *(New York: Holmes and Meier, 1979), 70–75.*

MR. PRESIDENT: I have often asked myself, what posterity would think of the strange contest in which the abolitionists are engaged.

Here we meet, time after time, newspapers are printed and speeches delivered, to prove—what? Why, that a man is a man, and that he is the only human possessor of himself. But these propositions are self-evident propositions, and self-evident propositions we all know, though the most difficult to be proved, are the most easily understood, because they need no proof. The mind sees their truth intuitively, without the aid of reasoning. The attempt to prove them, therefore, would be ridiculous, were it not for the consideration of the amazing state of delusion and vassalage to which prejudice reduces the mind when unenlightened by reason.

The history of every age shows the truth of this assertion. At one time, we see Galileo thrown into prison by the Inquisition, because he had made some discoveries tending to confirm the Copernican system, and forced to purchase his liberty by retracting his opinions. Again, before the sacred page was punctuated, some of the Alexandria fathers placed a punctuation mark in one of the chapters of St. John's Gospel, Chrysostom, alarmed at this terrible innovation, denounced it as a heresy; and Epiphanius declared it blasphemous, and the sin against the Holy Ghost. When, therefore, we see the control which prejudice, aided by circumstances and encouraged by self-interest, has in times past exercised over the human mind, and the tenacity with which it has held its deluded victims, stopping up the avenues of improvement, clipping the wings of genius, and retarding the progress of truth—when we see the minds whose energies have been crippled, and whose spheres of action have been curtailed by its influence—when we see the tremendous power which reformers have brought to bear against the prevailing sins of the ages in which they lived, the firm opposition they encountered, and the long and arduous struggles which preceded a better state of things— we are led, by analogical reasoning, to believe, that the contest in which we are engaged is not an unnatural one—that it is not so dissimilar in its character and measures to others which have been carried triumphantly through—that the modern champions of freedom do not savor so much of quixotism as their traducers have represented—and that the unfortunate men, whose cause they have espoused, have as just a claim to humanity as their oppressors, and like them have been created a little lower than the angels.

In all moral reforms, too, there is a striking similarity in the various passions, qualities and traits of character called forth. The same zeal and boldness of the reformer—the same caution, distrust and timidity of the conservative, wincing at this phrase, trembling at that expression, and whining about ultraism—the same headlong fury of the rabble, who, for want of something better, would fain

'Prove their doctrines orthodox
By mobocratic blows and knocks'—

the same rapid speed of truth when once elicited by reason and argument— and the same general results.

How was it five years ago in regard to the question of slavery! A gloom hung over the moral atmosphere, which nothing seemingly could dissipate, save a miracle from God himself. All saw it, but no one durst expose his own breast to the pitiless peltings of the gathering storm. The pulpit and the press, instead of being faithful to their trust, were the panders to the general lust. But mind, like matter, must have its legitimate scope. How absurd was the attempt of the ancient king to chain the Hellespont! And yet not more so than the attempt of modern republicans to bridle the human mind. There are always some spirits who will resist such unnatural domination. And such a spirit was found in the father of American anti-slavery. In that dark hour, he arose to cheer us on our gloomy pathway. The shafts of criticism, and sarcasm, and denunciation, which rang against his buckler, told only where he stood up unscathed, in his moral and intellectual might, and bearing down all opposition. The result is well known, nor does Mr. Garrison need any eulogy from me.

The task of a reformer is far from being an agreeable one. The hidden springs which are to be touched by him, and set into motion, are not discernible to common eyes; and, if they were, few would know how to approach or dare to meddle with them. He scatters his truths among the body politic, and the effect is electrical. He is greeted at once with smiles and frowns, with blessing and cursing, with eulogy and abuse. Now he is almost stifled with the caresses of devoted friends, and anon he is exposed to the fury of a blood-thirsty mob. But, if it is melancholy to see some run mad, we have the gratification to behold others restored to their reason. Much may depend upon accidental circumstances for the success of the reformer, but more depends upon himself. In him are found the great qualities of the head and heart. For the burden of proof is upon him, and he is to answer cavils, refute sophistry, and prove his propositions, while slanderers are crucifying his reputation, and assassins are aiming deadly daggers at his heart. All moral reformations have been attended with more or less persecution; but the American abolitionists stand preeminently distinguished in this respect. Not that those of their ranks, who have been imprisoned and murdered, can bear comparison numerically with other reformers. But the light of religious toleration had not dawned upon the Inquisition; and the dogma, that all men are created equal, is a newly discovered truth. But the Americans, with the moral and intellectual light of the nineteenth century, should have known better than to shoot down a man for his faithful advocacy of those burning truths enunciated by their own great apostle of democracy. They present the rare spectacle of a nation boasting of equal rights, while a large part of the population are the most oppressed and degraded beings that crawl on the face of the earth. If they have fled from the fire of tyranny in the old world, it is to light up a still more horrid one in the new, whose lurid glare serves only to show more distinctly the hollow mockery of their hypocritical professions. If they have driven the poor Indian, who 'sees God in clouds, or hears him in the wind,' from the home of his fathers, it is only to make room for the still more imbruted slave, and to introduce a civilization which has been a curse to half of mankind. And thus they have become guilty of the double atrocity of immolating two races of men upon the bloody altars of their avarice and ambition. The red men are fast disappearing from our midst, and soon the halloo of their hunters, long since heard upon every margin of our lakes and rivers, will be succeeded only by the mournful winds as they sigh through their forests, and sing their requiem. But the place of the Indian is being fast supplied by that of the slave, upon whose devoted head all that can torture the body or enfeeble the intellect is pouring out. The wretched alternative even of removing to the far west is denied him. The wide world, with its joys and sorrows, its pleasures and pains, its paths to wealth and poverty, to distinction and disgrace, is limited to the plantation on which he toils the livelong day.

But why attempt to portray the atrocities of American slavery? The isolated facts of murder and violence that, ever and anon, come to our ears, are but whispers in that whirlwind that rages at the South. We read of deeds of barbarity, but they come mostly from the perpetrators of them, or from persons entrusted in stripping them of their terrors. If the victims themselves, who have been whipped and burnt to death, could break the silence of the grave, they "could a tale unfold whose lightest word would harrow up the soul." If the abominations of that system could be exposed to the eye, well might we thank Heaven that *we* are removed from scenes so petrifying to the moral feelings, and that *we* do not behold a picture too appalling for human sight, and too shocking to the sensibilities of our nature. If the monster herself could become visible to our natural as well as to our mental sight, and stalk into the midst of this assembly reeking with the tears and blood of her victims, well might she exclaim, as she lifted the veil from her horrid features, well might she exclaim in the language of the veiled prophet of Khorassan—

> "Here, judge if hell, with all its powers to damn,
> Can add one curse to the foul thing I am."

But, sir, the great characteristic of American slavery, and that which distinguishes it from all other species of oppression, is that hatred of the free colored man which makes his condition little superior to that of servitude itself. The slave escapes from the southern to the northern States, and just begins to congratulate himself upon his good fortune, as he beholds the same dreaded form, though dressed in different habiliments, baffling all his schemes and enterprises. Though his flesh is not bared to receive the lash, and his limbs are unfettered, yet he feels his immortal mind dragged to the dust by a weight far more galling than chains, and more torturing than fetters. The gates that lead to intemperance, licentiousness and death are unbound, and he is permitted to enter them and die; but the road to the hill of science is guarded by a fiend, who sits at the entrance, hissing and gnashing his teeth upon him. The distant view is all that blesses his longing sight. The fragrance of the enamelled fields comes floating to him on every breeze, and he has the mortification to behold others plucking the flowers, and revel-

ling in the sunny pastures. All the motives that excite in the citizen enterprise, virtue and patriotism, lies dormant in his breast. These inestimable
qualities are to him mere words "full of sound and fury, signifying nothing,"—the theoretical emanations of minds with whose emotions he knows
not how to sympathize. As if he were a mere beast, his animal powers alone
are strengthened and indulged; but when he has once tasted the proffered
cup of intemperance, licentiousness and crime, like other rational and ac-
countable beings, he becomes responsible for his acts, and dearly pays the
penalty of violated law. Is it strange, then, that he does not stand out in
the dignity of his nature when so many of the attributes of humanity and
the springs of human action are enfeebled by disease, and palsied by neglect?
Is it strange that he does the State so little service, when the doors to honorable and profitable occupation are bolted and barred against him? Is it
strange that, goaded to madness by his accumulated wrongs, he sometimes
lays aside his pacific character, and turns upon his tormentors and rends
them? Surely not. His patient endurance, under such provocations, ought to
be a passport to public favor; and though he seldom indulges in retaliation,
it argues not that he is insensible to his degradation, but that he is actuated
by a manly and Christian forbearance.

But it is not the colored man alone, who is to be benefitted by the abolition of slavery. Its effects will be most salutary upon the white population,
and particularly upon the slaveholder. I speak not of the deleterious influence
of slavery upon the morals of the South—that is too well known—but the
dispositions of the slaveholders are spoiled by it. Accustomed to the implicit
obedience of their slaves, they cannot bear contradiction from freemen; and
the signal vengeance which they take upon the abolitionists caught within
the precincts of their States, shows how little restraint they exercise over
their passions. See how they burnt a free man of color by slow fire in St.
Louis, merely because, in a paroxysm of rage, he stabbed a white man to
facilitate the escape of a runaway slave! In their fiendish exultation, they
mocked the dying man's agonies while the hot blood was boiling out of his
mouth! And because Lovejoy* called this a cruel act, they destroyed his
press; and when he sought protection from the laws of a non-slaveholding
State, they pursued him, and deliberately shot him down, to show in what
contempt they hold the laws and liberties of the free States. And they may
tell us of their happiness and security, and that the slaves do not want their
freedom; but we know nothing of the hours when they are visited by the
most horrible spectres that the imagination of a guilty man can conjure up.
They dare not tell us how, in the silent hour of midnight, their fitful slumbers are broken by the forms of their murdered victims, as they glide by their
aching vision, and every murmur of the wind is the cry of the wronged slave
cheering on his fellows to revenge and slaughter!

It is, then, to stay this torrent of vice that is rushing over us, and threat-

---

*Newspaper editor Elijah Lovejoy (1802–1837) was killed by a mob in Alton, Illinois,
while defending his press.

ening to sweep away every vestige of that edifice the revolutionary fathers constructed with so much care and art, that we have formed the anti-slavery society. It is to lift up our perishing countrymen from the horrible state into which they are plunged by a despotism unparalleled in the history of nations. It is to give opportunity for the development of the moral and intellectual powers of man, to save woman from the bloody lash that is raised above her shrinking form, and to restore the babe to its bereaved mother. It is to save our churches and ministers from the awful charge of fostering and maintaining a sin, against which the great Author of our religion has denounced the most fearful penalties. It is to wipe a foul blot from our country, that her guilty, cowering form may stand erect, no longer the butt of merited ridicule and sarcasm, to save her from the horrors of a servile war, and render her more secure against the foreign harpies who are ready to pounce upon her. And call you this treason? And do the friends of the slave deserve hanging for such motives and purposes?

Nor need we be despondent. A voice comes on every wind of heaven encouraging to us, but full of terrible warning to the oppressor. The genius of British liberty, with a consciousness of being ever foremost in the cause of the slave, shows us the broken chains which fell from eight hundred thousand human beings, and tells us to go and do likewise. The voices of our revolutionary fathers, who fought long and hard for the freedom of their country, are heard repeating the same words that startled their armies of yore, 'Give us liberty, or give us death.' The free Haytien's voice is heard above the roar of the Atlantic, telling us, if we would avoid the horrors of a servile war, we must let the oppressed go free. The ancient as well as modern nations tell us of the impossibility of always holding men in bondage. Greece, though dead, yet speaketh. Though the vile herd have long since mangled her carcass, and 'strewed her ashes on the wind,' yet still her 'spirit walks abroad,' and points to Thermopylae, and Marathon, and Salamis, as beaconfires to light the oppressed to freedom.

But, *abolition is dying away*, cry the assassins of Lovejoy, and the incendiaries of Pennsylvania Hall.* Dying away? As is the torrent, when swollen by rains and increased by tributary streams, it sweeps on with greater strength against the barriers that are opposed to its impetuous course. Dying away? As is the sun, when new risen it 'looks through the horizontal misty air, shorn of its beams,' but soon to dissipate the gloom, and smile unclouded upon the glad earth. Dying away? Impossible! *Truth* never dies. Her course is always onward. Though obstacles may present themselves before her, she rides triumphantly over them; and the more formidable the enemy, the more terrible the encounter, and the more glorious the victory. No—

---

*As more and more owners of assembly halls closed their doors to abolitionists, Philadelphia antislavery groups decided to build an auditorium of their own. Construction of Pennsylvania Hall was completed in the spring of 1838, and on May 14, 1838, the doors were thrown open. An antislavery meeting addressed by William Lloyd Garrison was held in the hall, and during the third day of the meeting, mobs attacked the hall, wrecked the interior, and burned the building to the ground.

though abolition is covered with scars, and bleeds at every pore, and has been often thrown to the ground, yet, like the fabled giant, she always wakes with renewed strength and vigor to the attack; and while her infatuated enemies are singing her funeral dirge, she will rise before their scared visages, and make them cry out with Macbeth—

'The times *have been*
That when the brains were out, the man would die,
And there an end: but *now* they rise again
With twenty mortal murders on their crowns,
And push us from our stools.'

I am aware, sir, that many of the suggestions and arguments that have been used this evening, have been repeated again and again by others who are better able than myself to explain and defend the doctrines of the abolitionists. But I plead the necessity of the case. New truths, though as clear as the light of the sun, must be repeated often, and enforced and illustrated in a thousand different ways. But this only shows the difficulty of proving self-evident propositions when obscured by prejudice and preconceived opinions. Again, the nice discriminations and hair-splitting distinctions, in which this controversy is involved, serve to confuse the mind and obscure the truth. Some philosophers have attempted to prove the non-existence of the world and all within it. But, if we cannot prove by mathematical demonstration the absurdity of this theory, we can tell them that we feel conscious of our own existence, and this is all the refutation such rhapsodies deserve. Some men have also endeavored to prove the inferiority of one race of men to another upon no better grounds than a dissimilarity in their outward conformation. But this, I apprehend, is as difficult a task as the other, and merits as little notice—though it is always amusing to see the ingenuity of some abstract reasoners. And both these theories would be equally amusing, were they equally harmless. Suppose we should see a dog, or any other quadruped, remarkable for his sagacity, and his master, by some unaccountable conceit, should come to the conclusion that he belonged to the human family, and gravely demand his admission to the society of bipeds. Would you not think this person a fit subject for the insane hospital, and that you would indeed prefer the society of the dog to that of such a man, lest he should be seized with some other hallucination that might perhaps be equally amusing, but at the same time a little more dangerous to personal safety? I, for one, should prefer to keep at a respectable distance from him. And yet there *are* men, who, with the full knowledge of the disabilities under which some of their fellow creatures labor, because they do not, with a supernatural effort, throw off the weight that presses them to the earth, have the impious effrontery to insult their Maker by classing them with brutes. Yet they are not accounted insane! But where is the difference! If you cannot metamorphose a brute into a man, can you make a man a brute? Why then *treat* him as such?

Let us, then, do justice to an unfortunate people. Let the wings of the American eagle be extended wider and wider, till they cover the oppressed

of every clime who seek refuge beneath them, and afford protection and security alike to patrician and plebeian, to freeman and slave.—Let the efforts
of our statesmen be directed to the removal of every source of discontent
from among the people, by abrogating oppressive and injurious laws, instead
of seeking offices of preferment and personal aggrandizement. Let our private citizens, instead of suffering themselves to be hoodwinked and cajoled
by ambitious demagogues and designing politicians, sustain those only by
their votes who give proof of integrity and disinterested love of liberty.—Let
us all work for the common good, and strive to make the government what
the great Solon would call the most perfect—where an injury done to one
individual is the concern of all. "Then shall our light break forth as the
morning, and our health spring forth speedily," and peace and happiness
bless the nation.■

34 THE RIGHTS OF COLORED CITIZENS IN TRAVELING

Charles Lenox Remond

*Charles Lenox Remond (1810–1873) was an active abolitionist and
served for many years as an agent of the American Anti-Slavery
Society. Remond was the first black abolitionist speaker to address large
integrated audiences. In 1840 he attended the World Anti-Slavery Convention in London. After spending two years lecturing in Great Britain
and Ireland, he returned to the United States in 1842 and became involved in the campaign to end segregation on the railroads of Massachusetts. In February 1842, he testified before a legislative committee of the
Massachusetts House of Representatives that was then holding hearings
on the issue. As Remond notes in his introduction, this was the first
speech delivered by an African American before the all-white body.
Legal segregation was finally abolished in April 1843, and six years
later, Frederick Douglass proclaimed in Faneuil Hall that "not a single
railroad can be found in any part of Massachusetts where a colored
man is treated and esteemed in any other light than that of a man and
a traveller."* *

Recruited by friends to testify on short notice, Remond offers a

---

*Frederick Douglass, "The Colonization Revival: An Address Delivered in Boston,
Massachusetts, May 31, 1849," in John W. Blassingame, ed., *The Frederick Douglass Papers*, vol. 2 (New Haven: Yale University Press, 1982), 212.

*highly personal and anecdotal speech. He details some of the indignities
that he has recently suffered in segregated transportation and, like many
African Americans who traveled to Europe, reports on the vastly different
treatment he received there. "I never felt to loathe my American name so
much as since my arrival," he tells the committee.*

*Following is the address Remond delivered before the legislative com-
mittee. It is taken from the* Liberator *for February 25, 1842.*

MR. CHAIRMAN and gentlemen of the Committee: In rising at this
time, and on this occasion, being the first person of color who has
ever addressed either of the bodies assembling in this building, I should, perhaps, in the first place, observe that, in consequence of the many miscon-
structions of the principles and measures of which I am the humble advocate, I may in like manner be subject to similar misconceptions from the
moment I open my lips in behalf of the prayer of the petitioners for whom I
appear, and therefore feel I have the right at least to ask, at the hands of this
intelligent Committee, an impartial hearing, and that whatever prejudices
they may have imbibed be eradicated from their minds, if such exist. I have,
however, too much confidence in their intelligence and too much faith in
their determination to do their duty as the representatives of this Commonwealth, to presume they can be actuated by partial motives. Trusting, as I
do, that the day is not distant, when, on all questions touching the rights of
the citizens of this state, men shall be considered great only as they are good,
and not that it shall be told and painfully experienced that, in this country,
this state—aye, this city, the Athens of America—the rights, privileges and
immunities of its citizens are measured by complexion or any other physical
peculiarity or conformation, especially such as over which no man has any
control. Complexion can in no sense be construed into crime, much less be
rightfully made the criterion of rights. Should the people of color, through a
revolution of Providence, become a majority, to the last I would oppose it
upon the same principle; for in either case it would be equally reprehensible
and unjustifiable, alike to be condemned and repudiated. It is justice I stand
here to claim, and not favor for either complexion.

    Our right to citizenship in this state has been acknowledged and secured
by the allowance of the elective franchise and consequent taxation;* and I
know of no good reason, if admitted in this instance, why it should be denied
in any other.

    With reference to the wrongs inflicted and injuries received on railroads
by persons of color, I need not say they do not end with the termination of
the route, but in effect tend to discourage, disparage and depress this class
of citizens. All hope of reward for upright conduct is cut off. Vice in them

---

*The right of African Americans in Massachusetts to vote was established in the case
of Paul Cuffe in 1778. It was fully settled in the Body of Liberties of 1790, which guaranteed men suffrage without regard to race.

becomes a virtue. No distinction is made by the community in which we live. The most vicious is treated as well as the most respectable, both in public and private.

But it is said we all look alike. If this is true, it is not true that we all behave alike. There is a marked difference; and we claim a recognition of this difference.

In the present state of things, they find God's provisions interfered with in such a way, by these and kindred regulations, that virtue may not claim her divinely appointed rewards. Color is made to obscure the brightest endowments, to degrade the fairest character, and to check the highest and most praiseworthy aspirations. If the colored man is vicious, it makes but little difference; if besotted, it matters not; if vulgar, it is quite as well; and he finds himself as well treated, and received as readily into society, as those of an opposite character. Nay, the higher our aspirations, the loftier our purposes and pursuits, does this iniquitous principle of prejudice fasten upon us and especial pains are taken to irritate, obstruct and injure. No reward of merit, no remuneration for services, no equivalent is rendered the deserving. And I submit, whether this unkind and unchristian policy is not well calculated to make every man disregardful of his conduct and every woman unmindful of her reputation.

The grievances of which we complain, be assured, sir, are not imaginary, but real—not local, but universal; not occasional, but continual, everyday matter-of-fact things—and have become, to the disgrace of our common country, matter[s] of history.

Mr. Chairman, the treatment to which colored Americans are exposed in their own country finds a counterpart in no other; and I am free to declare that, in the course of nineteen months' traveling in England, Ireland and Scotland, I was received, treated and recognized, in public and private society, without any regard to my complexion. From the moment I left the American packet ship in Liverpool, up to the moment I came in contact with it again, I was never reminded of my complexion; and all that know anything of my usage in the American ship, will testify that it was unfit for a brute, and none but one could inflict it. But how unlike that afforded in the British steamer *Columbia!* Owing to my limited resources, I took a steerage passage. On the first day out, the second officer came to inquire after my health; and finding me the only passenger in that part of the ship, ordered the steward to give me a berth in the second cabin; and from that hour until my stepping on shore at Boston, every politeness was shown me by the officers, and every kindness and attention by the stewards; and I feel under deep and lasting obligations to them, individually and collectively.

In no instance was I insulted or treated in any way distinct or dissimilar from other passengers or travelers, either in coaches, railroads, steam packets, or hotels; and if the feeling was entertained, in no case did I discover its existence.

I may with propriety here relate an accident, illustrative of the subject now under consideration. I took a passage ticket at the steam-packet office in Glasgow, for Dublin; and on going into the cabin to retire, I found the berth I had engaged occupied by an Irish gentleman and merchant. I inquired if he had not mistaken the number of his berth. He thought not. On comparing tickets, we saw that the clerk had given two tickets of the same number; and it appeared I had received mine first. The gentleman at once offered to vacate the berth, against which I remonstrated and took my berth in an opposite stateroom. Here, sir, we discover treatment just, impartial, reasonable; and we ask nothing beside.

There is a marked difference between social and civil rights. It has been well and justly remarked by my friend Mr. Phillips* that we all claim the privilege of selecting our society and associations; but, in civil rights, one man has not the prerogative to define rights for another. For instance, sir, in public conveyances, for the rich man to usurp the privileges to himself, to the injury of the poor man, would be submitted to in no well-regulated society. And such is the position suffered by persons of color. On my arrival home from England, I went to the railway station, to go to Salem, being anxious to see my parents and sisters as soon as possible, asked for a ticket, paid fifty cents for it, and was pointed to the American designation car. Having previously received information of the regulations, I took my seat peaceably, believing it better to suffer wrong than do wrong. I felt then, as I felt on many occasions prior to leaving home, unwilling to descend so low as to bandy words with the superintendents or contest my rights with conductors or any others in the capacity of servants of any stage or steamboat company or railroad corporation, although I never, by any means, gave evidence that by my submission I intended to sanction usages which would derogate from uncivilized, much less long- and loud-professing and high-pretending America.

Bear with me while I relate an additional occurrence. On the morning after my return home, I was obliged to go to Boston again, and on going to the Salem station I met two friends, who inquired if I had any objection to their taking seats with me. I answered, I should be most happy. They took their seats accordingly, and soon afterward one of them remarked to me, "Charles, I don't know if they will allow us to ride with you." It was some time before I could understand what they meant, and, on doing so, I laughed, feeling it to be a climax to every absurdity I had heard attributed to Americans. To say nothing of the wrong done those friends, and the insult and indignity offered me by the appearance of the conductor, who ordered the friends from the car in a somewhat harsh manner. They immediately left the carriage.

On returning to Salem some few evenings afterward, Mr. Chase, the superintendent on this road, made himself known to me by recalling bygone days and scenes, and then inquired if I was not glad to get home after so long

---

*Wendell Phillips (1811–1884), Boston bred and Harvard educated, was one of the greatest of the abolitionist leaders associated with William Lloyd Garrison. He fought against discrimination as well as against slavery.

an absence in Europe. I told him I was glad to see my parents and family again, and this was the only object I could have, unless he thought I should be glad to take a hermit's life in the great pasture; inasmuch as I never felt to loathe my American name so much as since my arrival. He wished to know my reasons for the remark. I immediately gave them, and wished to know of him, if, in the event of his having a brother with red hair, he should find himself separated while traveling because of this difference, he should deem it just. He could make no reply. I then wished to know if the principle was not the same; and if so, there was an insult implied by his question.

In conclusion, I challenged him as the instrument inflicting the manifold injuries upon all not colored like himself to the presentation of an instance in any other Christian or unchristian country, tolerating usages at once so disgraceful, unjust and inhuman. What if some few of the West or East India planters and merchants should visit our liberty-loving country, with their colored wives—how would he manage? Or, if R. M. Johnson,* the gentleman who has been elevated to the second office in the gift of the people, should be traveling from Boston to Salem, if he was prepared to separate him from his wife or daughters.

Sir, it happens to be my lot to have a sister a few shades lighter than myself; and who knows, if this state of things is encouraged, whether I may not on some future occasion be mobbed in Washington Street, on the supposition of walking with a white young lady!

Gentlemen of the Committee, these distinctions react in all their wickedness—to say nothing of their concocted and systematized odiousness and absurdity—upon those who instituted them; and particularly so upon those who are illiberal and mean enough to practice them.

Mr. Chairman, if colored people have abused any rights granted them, or failed to exhibit due appreciation of favors bestowed, or shrunk from dangers or responsibilities, let it be made to appear. Or if our country contains a population to compare with them in loyalty and patriotism, circumstances duly considered, I have it yet to learn. The history of our country must ever testify in their behalf. In view of these and many additional considerations, I unhesitatingly assert their claim, on the naked principle of merit, to every advantage set forth in the Constitution of this Commonwealth.

Finally, Mr. Chairman, there is in this and other states a large and growing colored population, whose residence in your midst has not been from choice (let this be understood and reflected upon), but by the force of circumstances over which they never had control. Upon the heads of their oppressors and calumniators be the censure and responsibility. If to ask at your hands redress for injuries and protection in our rights and immunities, as

*Richard Mentor Johnson (1780–1850) of Kentucky served as vice president of the United States under Martin Van Buren. In about 1812, he openly adopted Julia Chinn, a slave, as his mistress. Johnson treated their two girls as his legal daughters and expected his community to accept his family as peers. Chinn died in 1833.

citizens, is reasonable and dictated alike by justice, humanity and religion, you will not reject, I trust, the prayer of your petitioners.

Before sitting down, I owe it to myself to remark, that I was not appraised of the wish of my friends to appear here until passing through Boston, a day or two since; and having been occupied with other matters, I have had no opportunity for preparation on this occasion. I feel much obliged to the Committee for their kind, patient, and attentive hearing.■

35 WE MUST ASSERT OUR RIGHTFUL CLAIMS AND PLEAD OUR OWN CAUSE

Samuel H. Davis

The National Convention of Colored Citizens met in Buffalo, New York, August 15 to 19, 1843. Although the highlight of the convention was Henry Highland Garnet's militant appeal to the slaves, the opening address of Samuel H. Davis of Buffalo, the chairman, was also noteworthy.

Davis sets the keynote for the convention by raising fundamental questions about the rhetorical strategies of those who have assembled. The goal of black abolitionists, Davis insists, must be to "make known our wrongs to the world and to our oppressors," primarily by demonstrating to these "slaves of slavery" that slavery is against their self-interest. The more difficult questions raised by Davis are: to whom should these appeals be directed, and what form should they take? Davis rejects most of the standard outlets—petitions to legislatures, appeals to the church, alliance with political parties, but insists that whatever rhetorical action is taken, African Americans should "lead our own cause." After Davis's keynote, the convention voted to urge the abandonment of any church— white or black—that practiced racial discrimination or refused to assist the antislavery cause.

Below are excerpts from that address, reprinted from Minutes of the National Convention of Colored Citizens held at Buffalo on the 15th, 16th, 17th, 18th, and 19th of August, 1843 *(Albany, N.Y.), 4–7.*

GENTLEMEN: I consider this a most happy period in our history, when we as a people are in some degree awake to a sense of our condition

and are determined no longer to submit tamely and silently to wear the galling yoke of oppression, under which we have so long suffered—oppression
riveted upon us, as well by an unholy and cruel prejudice, as by unjust and
unequal legislation. More particularly do I consider it ominous of good,
when I see here collected, so much of wisdom and talent, from different
parts of this great nation, collected here to deliberate upon the wisest and
best methods by which we may seek a redress of those grievances which
most sorely oppress us as a people.

Gentlemen, in behalf of my fellow citizens of Buffalo, I bid you welcome,
from the East and West, the North and South, to our city. Among you are
the men who are lately from that part of our country where they see our
brethren bound and manacled, suffering and bleeding, under the hand of the
tyrant, who holds in one hand the Constitution of the United States, which
guarantees freedom and equal rights to every citizen, and in the other "the
scourge dripping with gore," drawn from the veins of his fellow man. Here
also are those who live in my native New England, among the "descendants
of the pilgrims," whose laws are more in accordance with the principles of
freedom and equal rights, so that but few laws are found recorded on their
statute books of which we need complain. But though their laws are not
marked with such palpable and flagrant injustice toward the colored man as
those of the South, yet there we are proscribed, by a fixed and cruel prejudice
little less oppressive. Our grievances are many and great, but it is not my
intention to enumerate or to enlarge upon them. I will simply say, however,
that we wish to secure for ourselves, in common with other citizens, the
privilege of seeking our own happiness in any part of the country we may
choose, which right is now unjustly and, we believe, unconstitutionally denied us in a part of this Union. We wish also to secure the elective franchise
in those states where it is denied us, where our rights are legislated away,
and our voice neither heard nor regarded. We also wish to secure, for our
children *especially,* the benefits of education, which in several States are entirely denied us, and in others are enjoyed only in name. These, and many
other things, of which we justly complain, bear most heavily upon us as a
people; and it is our right and our duty to seek for redress, in that way which
will be most likely to secure the desired end.

In your wisdom, you will, I doubt not, take into consideration these and
the many other grievances which we suffer, and form such organizations and
recommend such measures as shall, in your wisdom, seem most likely to
secure our enfranchisement, the benefits of education to our children, and
all our rights in common with other citizens of this republic.

Two objects should distinctly and constantly be borne in mind, in all
our deliberations. One is the diffusion of truth, and the other the elevation
of our own people. By the diffusion of truth I mean that we must take a bold
and elevated stand for the truth. We must determine, in the strength of God,
to do everything that will advance the great and holy cause of freedom, and
nothing that will in the least retard its progress. We must, by every means
in our power, strive to persuade the white people to act with more confi-

dence in their own principles of liberty—to make laws just and equal for all the people.

But while the color of the skin is made the criterion of the law, it is our right, our duty and, I hope I may say, our fixed determination, to make known our wrongs to the world and to our oppressors; to cease not day nor night to "tell, in burning words, our tale of woe," and pour a flood of living light on the minds and consciences of the oppressor, till we change their thoughts, feelings, and actions toward us as men and citizens of this land. We must convince our fellow men that slavery is unprofitable; that it is for the well-being and prosperity of this nation, the peace and happiness of our common country, that slavery and oppression be abolished within its borders, and that laws be enacted equal and just for all its citizens.

Proscription is not in accordance with equal rights, no more than is oppression with holy freedom, or slavery with the spirit of free institutions. The present system of laws, in this our country, enacted in reference to us, the oppressed and downtrodden descendants of Africa, do, and will continue to, operate like the canker worm in the root of the tree of liberty, preventing its growth and ultimately destroying its vitality. We may well say, in the language of a distinguished statesman and patriot of our own land, "We tremble for our country when we reflect that God is just, and that his justice will not always sleep."* By the example of other nations, who have gone before, whose history should be a warning to this people, we learn that slavery and oppression has nowhere prospered long; it blasts a nation's glory and prosperity, divides her power, weakens her strength, and grows like a corroding consumption in her very vitals. "God's judgments will not sleep forever, but he will visit the nations of the earth in justice." We love our common country—"With all her faults, we love her still." This is the land where we all drew our first breath; where we have grown up to strength and manhood. "Here is deposited the ashes of our fathers"; here we have contracted the most sacred engagements, the dearest relations of life; here we have found the companions of our childhood, the friends of our youth, the gentle partners of our lives; here are the haunts of our infancy, the scenes of every endearing hour—in a word, this is our own native land. I repeat it, then: We love our country, we love our fellow citizens—but *we love liberty more.* . . .

It is time that we were more awake to our own interests, more united in our efforts, and more efficient in our measures. We must profit by the example of our oppressors. We must act on their principles in resisting tyranny. We must adopt their resolutions in favor of liberty. "They have taught us a lesson, in their struggle for independence, that should never be forgotten. They have taught the world emphatically that a people united

---

*This is one of Thomas Jefferson's most famous statements regarding slavery. He wrote it at the time of the battle in Congress over the Missouri Compromise.

in the cause of liberty are invincible to those who would enslave them, and that heaven will ever frown on the cause of injustice, and ultimately grant success to those who oppose it." Shall we, then, longer submit in silence to our accumulated wrongs? Forbid it, heaven, that we should longer stand in silence, "hugging the delusive phantom of hope," when every gale that sweeps from the South, bears on its wings, to our ears, the dismal sound of slavery's clanking chains, now riveted on three millions of our brethren, and we ourselves are aliens and outcasts in our native land.

Is the question asked, what shall we do? Shall we petition for our rights? I do not pretend to dictate the course that should be pursued; but I have very little hope in petitioning longer. We have petitioned again and again, and what has been the result? Our humblest prayers have not been permitted a hearing. We could not even state our grievances. Our petitions were disregarded, our applications slighted, and we spurned from the mercy seat, insulted, abused and slandered. And this day finds us in the same unhappy and hopeless condition in which we have been for our whole lives; no other hope is let us, but in our own exertions and an "appeal to the god of armies." From what other source can we expect that help will come? Shall we appeal to the Christian community—to the church of our own land? What is her position? Behold her gigantic form, with hands upraised to heaven! See her increased and made rich by the toil and sweat and blood of slaves! View her arrayed in her pontifical robes, screening the horrid monster, slavery, with her very bosom—within her most sacred enclosures, that the world may not gaze on its distorted visage or view its hellish form! Yes, throwing around this accursed system, the very drapery of heaven, to cover this damning sin and give it character and respectability in the eyes of the country and in the eyes of the world. We cannot, therefore, look to her for help, for she has taken sides against us and on the side of slavery. Shall we turn to either of the great political parties of the day? What are our prospects there? Is there any hope of help? No, they are but the slaves of slavery, too, contending which shall be most faithful in supporting the foul system of slavery, that they may secure the vote of the slaveholder himself, and of his scores of human cattle. Shall we, then, look to the abolitionists and wait for them to give us our rights? I would not say a word that would have a tendency to discourage them in their noble efforts in behalf of the poor slave, or their exertions to advance the cause of truth and humanity. Some of them have made great sacrifices and have labored with a zeal and fidelity that justly entitle them to our confidence and gratitude. But if we sit down in idleness and sloth, waiting for them—or any other class of men—to do our own work, I fear it will never be done. If we are not willing to rise up and assert our rightful claims, and plead our own cause, we have no reason to look for success. We ourselves must be willing to contend for the rich boon of freedom and equal rights, or we shall never enjoy that boon. It is found only of them that seek.■

36 AN ADDRESS TO THE SLAVES OF THE UNITED STATES OF AMERICA

Henry Highland Garnet

Henry Highland Garnet (1815–1881) was born in slavery in Maryland, escaped with his parents in 1824 and settled in New York City. Garnet was educated in the African Free School No. 1 and at Oneida Institute. A brief stay at the Canaan Academy in Canaan, New Hampshire, in 1835 was interrupted when the academy was destroyed by an infuriated mob opposed to the education of black students. Garnet prepared for the ministry, and in 1842 was licensed to preach. He became pastor of the Liberty Street Presbyterian Church in Troy, New York, and later of the Shiloh Presbyterian Church in New York City, a pastorate he held for more than forty years, during which time he became the foremost African American clergyman in the city.

In 1843, Garnet attended the National Convention of Negro Citizens at Buffalo, New York, and on August 16 delivered a militant speech calling for slave rebellions as the surest way to end slavery. It was perhaps the most radical speech by a black American during the antebellum period. The proposal stirred the delegates and failed by one vote of being adopted. After he had read the speech, John Brown, the martyr of Harper's Ferry, had it published at his own expense in 1848.

Garnet's speech is ostensibly addressed to an audience not present to hear it. Garnet speaks "to" the enslaved "on behalf of" the assembled conventioneers. Apologizing for the timidity and ineffectiveness of abolitionist efforts, Garnet encourages slaves to "Arise! Strike for your lives and liberties." For Garnet's immediate audience, the conventioneers who "overhear" Garnet's address to slaves not present, his message is one of anger, frustration, and a call for greater militancy.

Garnet's address is published in A Memorial Discourse by Rev. Henry Highland Garnet, Delivered in the Hall of the House of Representatives, Washington, D.C., on Sabbath, February 12, 1865, *with an introduction by James McCune Smith, M.D. (Philadelphia, 1865), 44–51. For further infromation on Garnet's oratory, see Cynthia P. King, "Henry Highland Garnet," in Richard Leeman, ed.,* African-American Orators: A Bio-Critical Sourcebook *(Westport, Conn.: Greenwood, 1996), 143–50.*

BRETHREN AND FELLOW CITIZENS: Your brethren of the North, East and West have been accustomed to meet together in national conventions, to sympathize with each other, and to weep over your unhappy condition. In these meetings we have addressed all classes of the free, but we have never, until this time, sent a word of consolation and advice to you. We have been contented in sitting still and mourning over your sorrows, earnestly hoping that before this day your sacred liberties would have been restored. But we have hoped in vain. Years have rolled on, and tens of thousands have been borne on streams of blood and tears to the shores of eternity. While you have been oppressed, we have also been partakers with you; nor can we be free while you are enslaved. We, therefore, write to you as being bound with you.

Many of you are bound to us, not only by the ties of a common humanity, but we are connected by the more tender relations of parents, wives, husbands and sisters and friends. As such we most affectionately address you.

Slavery has fixed a deep gulf between you and us, and while it shuts out from you the relief and consolation which your friends would willingly render, it afflicts and persecutes you with a fierceness which we might not expect to see in the fiends of hell. But still the Almighty Father of mercies has left to us a glimmering ray of hope, which shines out like a lone star in a cloudy sky. Mankind are becoming wiser, and better—the oppressor's power is fading, and you every day are becoming better informed and more numerous. Your grievances, brethren, are many. We shall not attempt in this short address to present to the world all the dark catalogue of this nation's sins which have been committed upon an innocent people. Nor is it indeed necessary, for you feel them from day to day, and all the civilized world looks upon them with amazement.

Two hundred and twenty-seven years ago the first of our injured race were brought to the shores of America. They came not with glad spirits to select their homes in the New World. They came not with their own consent, to find an unmolested enjoyment of the blessings of this fruitful soil. The first dealings they had with men calling themselves Christians exhibited to them the worst features of corrupt and sordid hearts, and convinced them that no cruelty is too great, no villainy and no robbery too abhorrent for even enlightened men to perform, when influenced by avarice and lust. Neither did they come flying upon the wings of Liberty to a land of freedom. But they came with broken hearts from their beloved native land and were doomed to unrequited toil and deep degradation. Nor did the evil of their bondage end at their emancipation by death. Succeeding generations inherited their chains, and millions have come from eternity into time, and have returned again to the world of spirits, cursed and ruined by American Slavery.

The propagators of the system, or their immediate successors, very soon discovered its growing evil and its tremendous wickedness, and secret promises were made to destroy it. The gross inconsistency of a people holding slaves, who had themselves "ferried o'er the wave" for freedom's sake, was too apparent to be entirely overlooked. The voice of Freedom cried, "Emancipate your slaves." Humanity supplicated with tears for the deliverance of the children of Africa. Wisdom urged her solemn plea. The bleeding captive pleaded his innocence and pointed to Christianity who stood weeping at the cross. Jehovah frowned upon the nefarious institution, and thunderbolts, red with vengeance, struggled to leap forth to blast the guilty wretches who maintained it. But all was vain. Slavery had stretched its dark wings of death over the land, the Church stood silently by, the priests prophesied falsely, and the people loved to have it so. Its throne is established, and now it reigns triumphantly.

Nearly three millions of your fellow citizens are prohibited by law and public opinion (which in this country is stronger than law) from reading the Book of Life. Your intellect has been destroyed as much as possible, and every ray of light they have attempted to shut out from your minds. The oppressors themselves have become involved in the ruin. They have become weak, sensual and rapacious; they have cursed you; they have cursed themselves; they have cursed the earth which they have trod.

The colonies threw the blame upon England. They said that the mother country entailed the evil upon them, and they would rid themselves of it if they could. The world thought they were sincere, and the philanthropic pitied them. But time soon tested their sincerity. In a few years the colonists grew strong and severed themselves from the British government. Their independence was declared, and they took their station among the sovereign powers of the earth. The declaration was a glorious document. Sages admired it, and the patriotic of every nation reverenced the Godlike sentiments which it contained. When the power of government returned to their hands, did they emancipate the slaves? No; they rather added new links to our chains. Were they ignorant of the principles of Liberty? Certainly they were not. The sentiments of their revolutionary orators fell in burning eloquence upon their hearts, and with one voice they cried, "Liberty or death." Oh, what a sentence was that! It ran from soul to soul like electric fire and nerved the arms of thousands to fight in the holy cause of Freedom. Among the diversity of opinions that are entertained in regard to physical resistance, there are but a few found to gainsay that stern declaration. We are among those who do not.

Slavery! How much misery is comprehended in that single word. What mind is there that does not shrink from its direful effects? Unless the image of God be obliterated from the soul, all men cherish the love of liberty. The nice discerning political economist does not regard the sacred right more than the untutored African who roams in the wilds of Congo. Nor has the one more right to the full enjoyment of his freedom than the other. In everyman's mind the good seeds of liberty are planted, and he who brings his fellow down so low as to make him contented with a condition of slavery commits the highest crime against God and man. Brethren, your oppressors aim to do this. They endeavor to make you as much like brutes as possible. When they have blinded the eyes of your mind; when they have embittered the sweet waters of life; when they have shut out the light which shines from the word of God—then, and not till then, has American slavery done its perfect work.

To such degradation it is sinful in the extreme for you to make voluntary submission. The divine commandments you are in duty bound to reverence and obey. If you do not obey them, you will surely meet with the displeasure of the Almighty. He requires you to love Him supremely, and your neighbor as yourself, to keep the Sabbath day holy, to search the Scriptures, and bring up your children with respect for His laws, and to worship no other God but Him. But slavery sets all these at nought and hurls defiance in the face of Jehovah. The forlorn condition in which you are placed does not destroy your moral obligation to God. You are not certain of Heaven, because you suffer yourselves to remain in a state of slavery, where you cannot obey the commandments of the Sovereign of the universe. If the ignorance of slavery is a passport to heaven, then it is a blessing, and no curse, and you should rather desire its perpetuity than its abolition. God will not receive slavery, nor ignorance, nor any other state of mind, for love and obedience to Him. Your condition does not absolve you from your moral obligation. The diabolical injustice by which your liberties are cloven down, neither God nor angels, nor just men command you to suffer for a single moment. Therefore it is your solemn and imperative duty to use every means, both moral, intellectual and physical, that promises success. If a band of heathen men should attempt to enslave a race of Christians, and to place their children under the influence of some false religion, surely Heaven would frown upon the men who would not resist such aggression, even to death. If, on the other hand, a band of Christians should attempt to enslave a race of heathen men, and to entail slavery upon them, and to keep them in heathenism in the midst of Christianity, the God of heaven would smile upon every effort which the injured might make to disenthrall themselves.

Brethren, it is as wrong for your lordly oppressors to keep you in slavery as it was for the man thief to steal our ancestors from the coast of Africa. You should therefore now use the same manner of resistance as would have been just in our ancestors when the bloody footprints of the first remorseless soul thief was placed upon the shores of our fatherland. The humblest peasant is as free in the sight of God as the proudest monarch that ever swayed a scepter. Liberty is a spirit sent out from God and, like its great Author, is no respecter of persons.

Brethren, the time has come when you must act for yourselves. It is an old and true saying that, "if hereditary bondsmen would be free, they must themselves strike the blow."* You can plead your own cause and do the work of emancipation better than any others. The nations of the Old World are moving in the great cause of universal freedom, and some of them at least will, ere long, do you justice. The combined powers of Europe have placed their broad seal of disapprobation upon the African slave trade. But in the slaveholding parts of the United States the trade is as brisk as ever. They buy and sell you as though you were brute beasts. The North has done much; her opinion of slavery in the abstract is known. But in regard to the South, we adopt the opinion of the *New York Evangelist*—"We have advanced so far, that the cause apparently waits for a more effectual door to be thrown

---

*Paraphrased from Lord Byron, *Childe Harold's Pilgrimage* (1818).

open than has been yet." We are about to point you to that more effectual door. Look around you and behold the bosoms of your loving wives heaving with untold agonies! Hear the cries of your poor children! Remember the stripes your fathers bore. Think of the torture and disgrace of your noble mothers. Think of your wretched sisters, loving virtue and purity, as they are driven into concubinage and are exposed to the unbridled lusts of incarnate devils. Think of the undying glory that hangs around the ancient name of Africa—and forget not that you are native-born American citizens, and as such you are justly entitled to all the rights that are granted to the freest. Think how many tears you have poured out upon the soil which you have cultivated with unrequited toil and enriched with your blood; and then go to your lordly enslavers and tell them plainly that you *are determined to be free.* Appeal to their sense of justice and tell them that they have no more right to oppress you than you have to enslave them. Entreat them to remove the grievous burdens which they have imposed upon you, and to remunerate you for your labor. Promise them renewed diligence in the cultivation of the soil, if they will render to you an equivalent for your services. Point them to the increase of happiness and prosperity in the British West Indies since the Act of Emancipation.* Tell them, in language which they cannot misunderstand, of the exceeding sinfulness of slavery and of a future judgment and of the righteous retributions of an indignant God. Inform them that all you desire is freedom, and that nothing else will suffice. Do this, and forever after cease to toil for the heartless tyrants, who give you no other reward but stripes and abuse. If they then commence the work of death, they, and not you, will be responsible for the consequences. You had far better all die—*die immediately*—than live slaves and entail your wretchedness upon your posterity. If you would be free in this generation, here is your only hope. However much you and all of us may desire it, there is not much hope of redemption without the shedding of blood. If you must bleed, let it all come at once—rather *die freemen than live to be slaves.* It is impossible, like the children of Israel, to make a grand exodus from the land of bondage. The Pharaohs are on both sides of the blood-red waters! You cannot move *en masse* to the dominions of the British Queen, nor can you pass through Florida and overrun Texas and at last find peace in Mexico. The propagators of American slavery are spending their blood and treasure that they may plant the black flag in the heart of Mexico and riot in the halls of the Montezumas.[†] In the language of the Reverend Robert Hall, when addressing the volunteers of Bristol who were rushing forth to repel the invasion of Napoleon, who threatened to lay waste the fair homes of England, "Religion is too

---

*Slavery was abolished in the British West Indies by an act of Parliament in 1833.

[†]American-Mexican relations deteriorated after the annexation of Texas in December 1845. American troops had moved into territory claimed by Mexico in July 1845, and when the Mexicans entered this territory, President Polk requested a declaration of war, which Congress made on May 12, 1846. The war was basically the result of the drive by the slaveowners to acquire new land for cotton.

much interested in your behalf not to shed over you her most gracious influences."

You will not be compelled to spend much time in order to become inured to hardships. From the first moment that you breathed the air of heaven, you have been accustomed to nothing else but hardships. The heroes of the American Revolution were never put upon harder fare than a peck of corn and few herrings per week. You have not become enervated by the luxuries of life. Your sternest energies have been beaten out upon the anvil of severe trial. Slavery has done this to make you subservient to its own purposes. But it has done more than this; it has prepared you for any emergency. If you receive good treatment, it is what you can hardly expect; if you meet with pain, sorrow, and even death, these are the common lot of the slaves.

Fellow men, patient sufferers, behold your dearest rights crushed to the earth! See your sons murdered, and your wives, mothers and sisters doomed to prostitution. In the name of the merciful God, and by all that life is worth, let it no longer be a debatable question, whether it is better to choose liberty or death.

In 1822, Denmark Veazie, of South Carolina, formed a plan for the liberation of his fellow men.* In the whole history of human efforts to overthrow slavery, a more complicated and tremendous plan was never formed. He was betrayed by the treachery of his own people, and died a martyr to freedom. Many a brave hero fell, but history, faithful to her high trust, will transcribe his name on the same monument with Moses, Hampden, Tell, Bruce and Wallace, Toussaint L'Ouverture, Lafayette and Washington. That tremendous movement shook the whole empire of slavery. The guilty soul thieves were overwhelmed with fear. It is a matter of fact that at this time, and in consequence of the threatened revolution, the slave states talked strongly of emancipation. But they blew but one blast of the trumpet of freedom, and then laid it aside. As these men became quiet, the slaveholders ceased to talk about emancipation; and now behold your condition to-day! Angels sigh over it, and humanity has long since exhausted her tears in weeping on your account!

The patriotic Nathaniel Turner† followed Denmark Veazie. He was goaded to desperation by wrong and injustice. By despotism, his name has

---

*Denmark Vesey (or Veazie) was a slave in Charleston, South Carolina, who bought his own liberty after he won a fifteen-hundred-dollar raffle. Once free himself, he was determined to aid others in gaining their freedom, and for four years he planned a vast slave plot. The slaves involved had hidden away weapons and ammunition. In 1822 the plot was uncovered when two house slaves turned informers, and the authorities arrested 131 suspects. Federal troops were present to protect Charleston against further revolts as the leaders of the revolt were hanged.

†The Turner revolt in Virginia in 1831 was the greatest slave revolt in American history. At the head of a small band of slaves, Turner moved from plantation to plantation, murdering slaveholding families. Some sixty whites were killed, and in retaliation, more than one hundred blacks, innocent and guilty, were murdered before the rebellion was crushed. Turner was later captured and executed.

been recorded on the list of infamy, but future generations will remember him among the noble and brave.

Next arose the immortal Joseph Cinque, the hero of the *Amistad.* * He was a native African, and by the help of God he emancipated a whole shipload of his fellow men on the high seas. And he now sings of liberty on the sunny hills of Africa and beneath his native palm trees, where he hears the lion roar and feels himself as free as the king of the forest.

Next arose Madison Washington, that bright star of freedom, and took his station in the constellation of true heroism.† He was a slave on board the brig *Creole,* of Richmond, bound to New Orleans, that great slave mart, with a hundred and four others. Nineteen struck for liberty or death. But one life was taken, and the whole were emancipated, and the vessel was carried into Nassau, New Providence.

Noble men! Those who have fallen in freedom's conflict, their memories will be cherished by the true-hearted and the God-fearing in all future generations; those who are living, their names are surrounded by a halo of glory.

Brethren, arise, arise! Strike for your lives and liberties. Now is the day and the hour.‡ Let every slave throughout the land do this, and the days of slavery are numbered. You cannot be more oppressed than you have been; you cannot suffer greater cruelties than you have already. *Rather die freemen than live to be slaves.* Remember that you are three *millions!*

It is in your power so to torment the God-cursed slaveholders that they will be glad to let you go free. If the scale was turned, and black men were the masters and white men the slaves, every destructive agent and element would be employed to lay the oppressor low. Danger and death would meet with plagues more terrible than those of Pharaoh. But you are a patient people. You act as though you were made for the special use of these devils. You act as though your daughters were born to pamper the lusts of your mas-

---

*In 1839, Joseph Cinque, son of an African king, led fifty-four slaves in a revolt aboard the *Amistad* off the coast of Cuba. Cinque and his men seized the ship and attempted to sail it back to Africa, but the slave dealers, whose lives had been spared, landed the vessel on the Connecticut coast. Defended by abolitionists, the case went all the way up to the Supreme Court with ex-President John Quincy Adams acting as the lawyer for the Africans. On March 9, 1841, the Supreme Court ordered Cinque and his fellow Africans freed. They returned to Sierra Leone in 1842.

†In 1841 a mutiny broke out aboard the *Creole,* sailing from Virginia for New Orleans. On the high seas 130 slaves, led by Madison Washington, rebelled, killed a slaveowner and guided the ship into the harbor of Nassau, where, under British law, they would be free. Over the objections of the U.S. Department of State, the British allowed them to go free, although the British government finally agreed to pay an indemnity for not returning the slaves.

‡In an alternate version of the speech, published in C. Peter Ripley, ed., *The Black Abolitionist Papers,* vol. 3 (Chapel Hill: University of North Carolina Press, 1991), vol. 3, the first three sentences of this paragraph are omitted and instead the following appear: "We do not advise you to attempt a revolution with the sword, because it would be inexpedient. Your numbers are too small, and moreover the rising spirit of the age, and the spirit of the gospel, are opposed to war and bloodshed. But from this moment cease to labor for tyrants who will not remunerate you" (410).

ters and overseers. And worse than all, you tamely submit while your lords tear your wives from your embraces and defile them before your eyes. In the name of God, we ask, are you men? Where is the blood of your fathers? Has it all run out of your veins? Awake, awake; millions of voices are calling you! Your dead fathers speak to you from their graves. Heaven, as with a voice of thunder, calls on you to arise from the dust.

Let your motto be Resistance! *Resistance!* RESISTANCE! No oppressed people have ever secured their liberty without resistance. What kind of resistance you had better make you must decide by the circumstances that surround you, and according to the suggestion of expediency. Brethren, adieu! Trust in the living God. Labor for the peace of the human race, and remember that you are three millions!■

37 FOR THE DISSOLUTION OF THE UNION

Charles Lenox Remond

Adopting the slogan "No Union with Slaveholders" at their convention on May 7, 1844, members of the American Anti-Slavery Society urged that the North and South be divided and that the Constitution of the United States be denounced as a "covenant with death and an agreement with hell" because of its use to support slavery. As a practical matter, they believed that dissolution of the union would cut off economic support for slavery and avoid the otherwise inevitable intersectional conflict. On a theoretical level, dissolution of the union was felt to be the necessary response to a government unable to secure fundamental rights for African Americans. Abolitionists urging dissolution accepted the southern view that the Constitution supported slavery. "Slavery was in the understanding that framed it," Charles Lenox Remond insisted. "Slavery is in the will that administers it."

A few weeks later, the New England Anti-Slavery Society took up the question of disunion at its convention. Among the speakers was Remond, who on May 29 rose in opposition to Dr. Walter Channing's defense of the Constitution. The resolution favoring disunion was subsequently adopted by a margin of 252 to 24.

The text of the speech was published in the National Anti-Slavery Standard, *July 18, 1844, and is reprinted in volume 3 of C. Peter Ripley, ed.*, The Black Abolitionist Papers, *vol. 3 (Chapel Hill: University of North Carolina Press, 1991), 442–45. For further information on the disso-lution movement, see Walter M. Merrill,* Against Wind and Tide *(Cam-bridge, Mass.: Harvard University Press, 1963), 204–11.*

I do not intend, Sir, even to attempt an answer to the respected friend who has just taken his seat. My point of view is too distant from his to leave me the vantage-ground for doing so. But I feel a deep interest in the question, and the present moment is perhaps the most fitting one for the expression of my humble views. I cannot expect them to make much impression upon the many—upon the body of this nation, for whose benefit the Constitution was made; but they will meet a response from the few whom it entirely over-looks, or sees but to trample upon, and the fewer still, who identify them-selves with the outcast, by occupying this position, of a dissolution of their union with Slaveholders.

It does very well for nine-tenths of the people of the United States, to speak of the awe and reverence they feel as they contemplate the Constitu-tion, but there are those who look upon it with a very different feeling, for they are in a very different position. What is it to *them* that it talks about peace—tranquillity—domestic enjoyments—civil rights? To them it is no such union; and resting, as it does, upon all their dearest and holiest rights, I cannot but express surprise that there are so many to wonder that they, and those who feel with them, should look upon this Union as one that ought to be dissolved. Oh, Sir! look at them as they are falling, generation after generation, beneath the sway of the Union, sinking into their ignomini-ous graves unwept, uncared for, unprayed for, enslaved, and say what has the Union been to them that they should look upon it with filial reverence! There was McIntosh, of St. Louis.* He raised his dark, fettered hand, in de-fence of the chastity of his wife, as it is claimed that a *white* man ought to do, and he was burned in a slow fire! What was the Union to him? What was it to Turner of Southampton, than whom a nobler soul has never risen upon the human race in all the long line of its prophets and its heroes! The Union does not even preserve his name. *He* had no place in life under its protecting aegis—in history he is only Nat Turner, the miserable negro. Sir, *I* will never contemptuously call him *Nat* Turner, for had he been a white man, Massachusetts and Virginia would have united to glorify his name and to build his monument; and is it strange, seeing all these things, that I should feel them too, and act upon the feeling? Yet, when such thoughts as these get such imperfect utterance as I am able to give them, men say to me, "Remond! you're wild! Remond! you're mad! Remond! you're a revolu-tionist!" Sir, in view of all these things, ought not this whole assembly—this whole nation to be revolutionists too?

*Arrested while breaking up a fight on April 28, 1836, Francis J. McIntosh was burned to death and his body decapitated by a mob that broke into the jail.

I belong to that class of persons called women's rights men; and I look upon this matter in the light of my principles on that subject. Do you not all recollect the case of the woman in Maryland, which went the round of the papers not long since? She was endeavoring to make her escape to the land of Victoria—she was pursued and overtaken, and was about to be returned to her home of whips, and chains, and fetters, and of the American Constitution. She sprang into the Potomac, and sank from the clutch of her pursuers. As her condition was, then, stands that of one million of American women today! And when she was seized, I well remember that it was pleaded in favor of her savage pursuers, that, by the provisions of the American Constitution, she must be returned!—that all their proceedings were legal!

What if the word "slave" is not in it? It does not matter to me nor mine. Slavery was in the understanding that framed it—Slavery is in the will that administers it. If there were nothing but Liberty in it, would there be two and a half millions ground to the dust beneath it this day?

If any authority besides this fact were needed, I might cite the words of John Quincy Adams to the people of color, when we applied to him in the case of Latimer.* He said his opinion should be forthcoming, *subject to the provisions of the American Constitution.*

With all my knowledge of the origin and the progress, and my experience of the present practical workings of the American Constitution, shall I be found here advocating it as a glorious means to a glorious end? No! my fellow countrymen, I am here to register my testimony against it! Not because I do not feel how valuable it might be, were its provisions secured to the few as they are to the many—not because I wish to claim anything more for the few than an equality of privileges—not because I am not ready to "yield everything to the Union *but* Truth—Honor—Liberty" [*pointing to a banner inscribed with those words of Dr. Channing*]†—but because (and I regret to say it) we have, as a people, yielded even these; and with such a people, I feel that I must not, an individual, be numbered.

I have spoken of particular instances in illustration of the nullity of the Union. How is it with every colored man and woman in Boston? Can one of you plead its provisions at the South? No! It will be with you there even as it was with Nat Turner, and the Fugitive of the Potomac. If I am wronged, I may appeal, and I may go on appealing and appealing till I am grey-headed—in vain! Go the rounds of the Union, and tell me at what tribunal the man of color can have justice? Court, Judge, Jury—all are against him; and to what is it owing? Why, as an honest Buckeye (for he was fond of calling himself so) told me in Cincinnati, "it is this everlasting yielding to Slavery," which always must take place, when Freedom yields the first step, by

*George Latimer was an escaped slave arrested in Boston in 1842. Adams refused to serve as counsel and warned that any legal advice he offered would be restricted by his pledge to support the Constitution.

†"Language cannot easily do justice to our attachment to the Union. We will yield every thing to it but truth, honor, and liberty. These we can never yield" (*The Works of William E. Channing, D. D.* [Boston, Mass., 1882], 739).

coming into union with it. If the Union had been formed upon the supposition that the colored man was a *man,* a man he would have been considered, whether in New Hampshire or Kentucky. But under the Union as it was, and as it is, he is kicked, stoned, insulted, enslaved, and the public sentiment that does it, falls back upon the Constitution for support, and will turn its back upon you, wherever you may be, if you deny that instrument to be obligatory as the paramount law.

I need not say how greatly I am troubled whenever a difference of opinion exists in the minds of those who love the cause of Freedom. I have tried in my own mind to make out a case for those who do not see eye to eye with us in this matter. But the more I have labored at it, the stronger becomes my conviction of duty in calling for a dissolution of the union between Freedom and Slavery. I speak after long thought, free and full discussion, and the clearest view of all the consequences and all the obstacles. I have taken all things into consideration; and in view of each and of all, I say here, as I did in New York, that if I can only sustain the Constitution, by sustaining Slavery, then—"live or die—sink or swim—survive or perish," I give my voice for the dissolution of the Union.■

38 I AM FREE FROM AMERICAN SLAVERY

Lewis Richardson

Many fugitive slaves appeared before northern abolitionist society gatherings to tell the stories of their bondage and escape. These firsthand testimonies offered dramatic proof of the terrible conditions of slavery and convincing rebuttal to the claims by some defenders of slavery that slaves were contented and well-treated. As historian John Blassingame has noted, these addresses by "men and women fresh from slavery" drew on black oral traditions, were often "filled with pathos and humor" and "elicited sympathy, tears, and increased interest in abolition."

The speech of Lewis Richardson attracted particular attention because he had escaped from Ashland, the Kentucky plantation of prominent U.S. senator, former U.S. secretary of state, and presidential candidate Henry Clay (1777–1852). Richardson spoke to a large interracial audience in Union Chapel, Amherstburgh, Canada West, on the evening of March 13, 1846. The speech text was published in the Signal of Liberty, *March 30, 1846, and was reprinted in* Slave Testimony, *edited by*

John W. Blassingame (Baton Rouge: Louisiana State University Press, 1977), 164–66.

Dear Brethren, I am truly happy to meet with you on British soil (cheers), where I am not known by the color of my skin, but where the Government knows me as a man. But I am free from American slavery, after wearing the galling chains on my limbs 53 years 9 of which it has been my unhappy lot to be the slave of Henry Clay. It has been said by some, that Clay's slaves had rather live with him than be free, but I had rather this day, have a millstone tied to my neck, and be sunk to the bottom of Detroit river, than to go back to Ashland and be his slave for life. As late as Dec. 1845, H. Clay had me stripped and tied up, and one hundred and fifty lashes given me on my naked back: the crime for which I was so abused was, I failed to return home on a visit to see my wife, on Monday morning, before 5 o'clock. My wife was living on another place, 3 miles from Ashland. During the 9 years living with Mr. Clay, he has not given me a hat nor cap to wear, nor a stitch of bed clothes, except one small coarse blanket. Yet he has said publicly his slaves were "fat and slick!" But I say if they are, it is not because they are so well used by him. They have nothing but coarse bread and meat to eat, and not enough of that. They are allowanced every week. For each field hand is allowed one peck of coarse corn meal and meat in proportion, and no vegetables of any kind. Such is the treatment that Henry Clay's slaves receive from him. I can truly say that I have only one thing to lament over, and that is my bereft wife who is yet in bondage. If I only had her with me I should be happy. Yet think not that I am unhappy. Think not that I regret the choice that I have made. I counted the cost before I started. Before I took leave of my wife, she wept over me, and dressed the wounds on my back caused by the lash. I then gave her the parting hand, and started for Canada. I expected to be pursued as a felon, as I had been before, and to be hunted as a fox from mountain to cave. I well knew if I continued much longer with Clay, that I should be killed by such floggings and abuse by his cruel overseer in my old age. I wanted to be free before I died—and if I should be caught on the way to Canada and taken back, it could but be death, and I might as well die with the colic as the fever. With these considerations I started for Canada.

Such usage as this caused me to flee from under the American eagle, and take shelter under the British crown. (Cheers.) Thanks be to Heaven that I have got here at last: on yonder side of Detroit river, I was recognized as property; but on this side I am on free soil. Hail, Britannia! Shame, America! (Cheers.) A Republican despotism, holding three millions of our fellow men in slavery. Oh what a contrast between slavery and liberty! Here I stand erect, without a chain upon my limbs. (Cheers.) Redeemed, emancipated, by the generosity of Great Britain. (Cheers.) I now feel as independent as ever Henry Clay felt when he was running for the White House. In fact I feel better. He has been defeated four or five times, and I but once. But he was running for slavery, and I for liberty. I think I have beat him out of sight. Thanks be to God that I am elected to Canada, and if I don't live but one night, I am determined to die on free soil. Let my days be few or many, let me die sooner or later, my grave shall be made in free soil.■

39 UNDER THE STARS AND STRIPES

William Wells Brown

William Wells Brown (1815–1884) was born in slavery in Kentucky. He escaped to the North and became an effective antislavery speaker, a novelist (author of Clotel; or, The President's Daughter, *among the first novels published by African Americans), a playwright, and a historian. In 1854, years after he had escaped from slavery, his English friends, worried for his safety under the Fugitive Slave Act of 1850, purchased Brown's freedom for three hundred dollars. Besides being one of the most active abolitionist lecturers, Brown was deeply involved in the temperance, woman suffrage, prison reform, and peace movements.*

On November 4, 1847, Brown delivered a lecture on slavery and its influence upon the morals and character of the American people before the Female Anti-Slavery Society of Salem, Massachusetts. The lecture was later published in pamphlet form by the Massachusetts Anti-Slavery Society.

Brown discusses the effect of slavery on America's standing in the world and employs the opinions of other nations as a mirror through which to examine American affairs. He strikingly transforms the American flag from an emblem of liberty into a symbol of cruel slavery, which wherever unfurled means the end of liberty to those of African descent.

Parts of this lecture are presented here; they were taken from William Wells Brown, A Lecture Delivered before the Female Anti-Slavery Society of Salem, at Lyceum Hall, Nov. 4, 1847, by William W. Brown, a Fugitive Slave, Reported by Henry M. Parkhurst *(Boston, 1847).*

IT IS DEPLORABLE to look at the character of the American people, the character that has been given to them by the institution of slavery. The profession of the American people is far above the profession of the people of any other country. Here the people profess to carry out the principles of Christianity. The American people are a sympathizing people. They not only profess, but appear to be a sympathizing people to the inhabitants of the whole world. They sympathize with everything else but the American slave. When the Greeks were struggling for liberty, meetings were held to express sympathy.* Now they are sympathizing with the poor downtrodden serfs of Ireland, and are sending their sympathy across the ocean to them.†

But what will the people of the Old World think? Will they not look upon the American people as hypocrites? Do they not look upon your professed sympathy as nothing more than hypocrisy? You may hold your meetings and send your words across the ocean; you may ask Nicholas of Russia to take the chains from his poor downtrodden serfs, but they look upon it all as nothing but hypocrisy. Look at our twenty thousand fugitive slaves, running from under the stars and stripes, and taking refuge in the Canadas; *twenty thousand*, some leaving their wives, some their husbands, some leaving their children, some their brothers, and some their sisters—fleeing to take refuge in the Canadas. Wherever the stars and stripes are seen flying in the United States of America, they point him out as a slave.

If I wish to stand up and say, "I am a man," I must leave the land that gave me birth. If I wish to ask protection as a man, I must leave the American stars and stripes. Wherever the stars and stripes are seen flying upon American soil, I can receive no protection; I am a slave, a chattel, a thing. I see your liberty poles around in your cities. If tomorrow morning you are hoisting the stars and stripes upon one of your liberty poles, and I should see the man following me who claims my body and soul as his property, I might climb to the very top of your liberty pole, I might cut the cord that held your stars and stripes and bind myself with it as closely as I could to your liberty pole. I might talk of law and the constitution, but nothing could save me unless there be public sentiment enough in Salem. I could not appeal to law or the Constitution; I could only appeal to public sentiment; and if public sentiment would not protect me, I must be carried back to the plantations of the South, there to be lacerated, there to drag the chains that I left upon the Southern soil a few years since.

This is deplorable. And yet the American slave *can* find a spot where he may be a man—but it is not under the American flag. Fellow citizens, I am the last to eulogize any country where they oppress the poor. I have nothing to say in behalf of England or any other country, any further than as they extend protection to mankind. I say that I honor England for protecting the black man. I honor every country that shall receive the American slave, that shall protect him, and that shall recognize him as a man.

---

*During the Greek struggle for independence from Turkey, there was widespread sympathy for the Greek cause in the United States. Webster, Clay, and other leading Americans favored American acknowledgment of the independence of the Greeks, and in 1823 President James Monroe at first recommended this course, but was persuaded by Secretary of State John Quincy Adams to abandon it.

†During the famine in Ireland in 1847, relief supplies were sent from the United States to aid the starving.

I know that the United States will not do it; but I ask you to look at the efforts of other countries. Even the Bey of Tunis, a few years since, has decreed that there shall not be a slave in his dominions; and we see that the subject of liberty is being discussed throughout the world. People are looking at it; they are examining it; and it seems as though every country and every people and every government were doing something, excepting the United States. But Christian, democratic, republican America is doing nothing at all. It seems as though she would be the last. It seems as though she was determined to be the last to knock the chain from the limbs of the slave. Shall the American people be behind the people of the Old World? Shall they be behind those who are represented as almost living in the dark ages?

> Shall every flap of England's flag
> Proclaim that all around are free,
> From farthest Ind to each blue crag
> That beetles o'er the western sea?
> And shall we scoff at Europe's kings,
> When Freedom's fire is dimmed with us;
> And round our country's altar clings
> The damning shade of Slavery's curse?*

Shall we, I ask, shall the American people be the last? I am here, not for the purpose of condemning the character of the American people, but for the purpose of trying to protect or vindicate their character. I would to God that there were some feature that I could vindicate. There is no liberty here for me; there is no liberty for those with whom I am associated; there is no liberty for the American slave; and yet we hear a great deal about liberty! How do the people of the Old World regard the American people? Only a short time since, an American gentleman, in traveling through Germany, passed the window of a bookstore where he saw a number of pictures. One of them was a cut representing an American slave on his knees, with chains upon his limbs. Over him stood a white man, with a long whip; and underneath was written, "the latest specimen of American democracy." I ask my audience, Who placed that in the hands of those that drew it? It was the people of the United States. Slavery, as it is to be found in this country, has given the serfs of the Old World an opportunity of branding the American people as the most tyrannical people upon God's footstool.

Only a short time since, an American man-of-war was anchored in the bay opposite Liverpool. The English came down by the hundreds and thousands. The stars and stripes were flying; and there stood those poor persons that had never seen an American man-of-war, but had heard a great deal of American democracy. Some were eulogizing the American people; some were calling it the "land of the free and the home of the brave." And while

---

*From John Greenleaf Whittier, "Stanzas" ("Our Fellow-Countrymen in Chains").

they stood there, one of their number rose up, and pointing his fingers to the American flag, said:

> United States, your banner wears
> Two emblems,—one of fame;
> Alas, the other that it bears,
> Reminds us of your shame.
> The white man's liberty entyped,
> Stands blazoned by your stars;
>
> But what's the meaning of your stripes?
> They mean your Negro scars. *

What put that in the mouth of that individual? It was the system of American slavery; it was the action of the American people; the inconsistency of the American people; their profession of liberty, and their practice in opposition to their profession.■

40 I HAVE NO CONSTITUTION, AND NO COUNTRY

William Wells Brown

Brown was one of twenty American delegates to attend the Paris Peace Congress in August 1849, where he encouraged the assembly to denounce slavery as a form of violence against blacks. After the Congress, he embarked upon an antislavery lecture tour in Britain and, on September 27, spoke to a meeting held at the Concert Rooms on Store Street in London. The meeting had been interrupted by a confrontation between abolitionist George Thompson, who was introducing Brown, and a member of the audience who disputed Thompson's claim that prejudice against African Americans in the northern United States was "quite as galling" as slavery in the South.

Brown's response on behalf of Thompson's claim spoke to his own experience as a person without a country, a fugitive from his native nation, not simply one region. "Slavery," he reminded his audience, "is a na-

*Thomas Campbell, "To the United States of North America," in W. Alfred Hill, ed., *The Poetical Works of Thomas Campbell* (London: George Bell and Sons, 1891), 261.

tional *institution," economically supported and legally enforced (by fugitive slave laws) in all sections of the country. For Brown to set foot in any part of the United States, he noted, could have doomed him to return to slavery. Although Brown professed his love for the country to which he could not then return, he made clear that he hated "those laws and institutions of America, which consign three millions of my brethren and sisters to chains for life."*

Abolitionist speakers could expect to be challenged by members of their audiences. The success of their speeches sometimes depended upon their effectiveness in meeting these challenges to the satisfaction of their listeners.

The speech text was published in the Liberator, *November 2, 1849.*

Sir, I wish to make a remark or two in seconding the resolution which is now before the meeting. I am really glad that this meeting has produced this discussion, for I think it will all do good; in fact, I know it will, for the cause of truth. Reference has been made to slavery having been carried to America by the sanction of this country. Now, that is an argument generally used in America by slaveholders themselves. (Hear, hear.) Go to the United States; talk to slaveholders about the disgrace of slavery being found in a professedly Christian republic, and they will immediately reply, "England imposed it upon us; Great Britain was the cause of it, for she established slavery in America, and we are only reaping the fruits of her act." Now, gentlemen, I would reply to our friend here* as I have replied to Americans again and again—If you have followed England in the bad example of the institution of slavery, now follow her in the good example of the abolition of slavery. (Cheers.) Some remarks were also made by that gentleman respecting the Americans having abolished the slave trade. It is true that they did pass a law, but not in 1808, that the slave trade should be abolished: they passed a law in 1788 that they would only continue the slave trade for twenty years longer and at the end of that period there should not be any more slaves imported into the United States. They said, "We will rob Africa of her sons and daughters for twenty years longer, and then stop." (Hear and laughter.) But why did they determine that the slave trade should be put an end to? The honorable gentleman has not told you that. Why, it was to give to Virginia, Kentucky and Maryland a monopoly in the trade of raising slaves to supply the Southern market. (Cheers.) That was the reason, and the only reason, why they abolished the foreign slave trade in America. They allowed the foreign slave trade to be carried on for twenty years from that time, and during the whole of that period made those who were engaged in the internal slave traffic pay a duty of ten dollars for every slave brought into the country, the whole of the money going into the exchequer of the United States. The Gov-

*George Jones of Boston, the audience member who had spoken out against Thompson's claim.

ernment said, "We will have a tariff of so much per head upon God's children that are stolen from Africa, and the revenue derived therefrom shall be the support of the republican institutions of the United States." (Hear, hear.) Do the Americans claim credit for an act like that? Claim credit for abolishing the foreign slave trade, in order that they might make a lucrative domestic slave trade! (Cheers.) Why, ladies and gentlemen, only a few years since, 40,000 slaves were carried out of the single State of Virginia, in one year, and driven off to the far South, to supply the market there. Claim credit for abolishing the slave trade! Claim credit for husbands torn from their wives, and children from their parents! Claim credit for herds of human beings carried off in coffle gangs, and to be worked to death in the rice and cotton fields! That is the character of the domestic slave trade now carried on, even in the capital of America. No, no; the people of the United States can claim no credit on that score. They can find no apology in the fact of slavery being a domestic institution. A pretty "domestic institution," truly! (Hear, hear.) Why, in 1847, only two years since, a woman and her daughter were sold in the very capital of America, in the very city of Washington, by the U.S. marshal, on the 3d day of July, the day before the national anniversary of the glorious Declaration of Independence, by which all men were declared free and equal, and the product of the sale of these immortal beings was put into the treasury of the United States. That is one specimen among many of the working of the "domestic institution" of America. (Cheers.) It dooms me, for example, to be a slave as soon as I shall touch any part of the United States. (Hear, hear.) Yes, Sir, it is indeed domestic enough; it is domesticated all over the country; it extends from one end of America to the other, and is as domesticated as is the Constitution of the United States itself; it is just as domesticated as is the territory over which the United States Government have jurisdiction. Wherever the Constitution proclaims a bit of soil to belong to the United States, there it dooms me to be a slave the moment I set my foot upon it; and all the 20,000 or 30,000 of my brethren who have made their escape from the Southern States, and taken refuge in Canada or the Northern States, are in the same condition. And yet this American slavery is apologized for as a "domestic institution"! I am glad that our eloquent friend, Mr. Thompson, has impressed the fact upon your minds, that slavery is a *national institution,* and that the guilt of maintaining it is *national guilt.* I am anxious that that circumstance should be understood, and that Englishmen should know, that the slave is just as much a slave in the city of Boston; of which this gentleman is just as much a citizen as he is in Charleston, South Carolina: he is just as much a slave in any of the Eastern States as he is in the Southern States. If I am protected in my person in the city of Boston, and if I have been protected there for the last two or three years, and the slaveholder has not been able to catch me and carry me back again into slavery, I am not at all indebted for that privilege to the Constitution of the United States, but I owe it entirely to that public sentiment which my friend Mr. Thompson, at the peril of his life, so nobly helped to create in America. (Loud cheers.) I am indebted to the anti-slavery sentiment, and that alone, when I am in Boston itself, for the personal protection I enjoy. I cannot look at the Constitution or laws of America as a protection to me; in fact, I have no Constitution, and no country. I cannot, like the eloquent gentleman who last addressed you say—"I am bound to stand up in favor of America." (Hear.) I would to God that I could; but how can I! America has disfranchised me, driven me off, and declared that I am not a citizen, and never shall be, upon the soil of the United States. Can I, then, gentlemen, stand up for such a country as that? Can I have any thing to say in favor of a country that makes me a chattel, that renders me a saleable commodity, that converts me into a piece of property? Can I say any thing in favor of a country, or its institutions, that will give me up to the slave-holder, if he can only find out where I am, in any part of America? Why I am more free here tonight, in monarchical England, than I should be in my own republican country! Whatever our friend from Boston may do, I would that I could say with him, "I must, in honor, stand up in favor of America." And yet I love America as much as he does. I admire her enterprising and industrious people quite as ardently as he can; but I hate her hideous insti-tution, which has robbed me of a dear mother, which has plundered me of a beloved sister and three dear brothers, and which institution has doomed them to suffer, as they are now suffering, in chains and slavery. Whatever else there may be to admire in the condition of America, at all events, I hate that portion of her Constitution. I hate, I fervently hate, those laws and in-stitutions of America, which consign three millions of my brethren and sis-ters to chains for life. Talk about going to the slaveholders with money! Talk about recognizing their right to property in human beings! What! property in man! property in God's children! I will not acknowledge that any man has a right to hold me as property, till he can show his right to supersede the prerogative of that Creator whose alone I am. (Cheers.) Just read the letter which you will find in the preface to my narrative, where my own master has very kindly offered to sell me to myself for half price. (Laughter.) He imagines that the anti-slavery movement has depreciated his property in me, and therefore he offers to take half price for his runaway property. (Renewed laughter.) My answer to him was, that he should never receive a single dollar from me, or any one else in my behalf, with my consent. (Cheers.) I said so, because I am not willing to acknowledge the right of property in man under any circumstances. I believe that the same God who made the slaveholder made the slave (hear, hear) and that the one is just as free as the other.

Before resuming my seat, I would say to our friend from Boston, as I said to another gentleman a short time before I left America, who talked in a similar manner about the slave States, and the good treatment the slaves re-ceived, and so forth. At the close of a meeting, that gentleman rose, and re-quested permission to ask me some simple questions, which were as follows: Had I not enough to eat when I was in slavery? Was I not well clothed while in the Southern States? Was I ever whipped? and so forth. I saw that he only wanted a peg on which to hang a pro-slavery speech, but I answered his ques-tions in the affirmative. He immediately rose and made a speech, in which he endeavored to make his audience believe that I had run away from a very good place indeed. (Laughter.) He asked them if they did not know hundreds and thousands of poor people in America and England, who would be willing to go into the State of Missouri and there fill the situation I had run away from. (Cries of Oh, Oh!) A portion of the assembly for a moment really thought his plea for slavery was a good one. I saw that the meeting was anxious to break up, in consequence of the lateness of the hour, and therefore that it would not do for me to reply at any length, and I accordingly rose and made a single remark in answer to this pro-slavery speech. I said, the gentleman has praised up the situation I left, and made it appear quite another thing to what it ever appeared to me when I was there; but however that may be, I have to inform him that that situation is still vacant, and as far as [I] have any thing voluntary to do with it, it shall remain so; but, nevertheless, if that gentleman likes to go into Missouri and fill it, I will give him a recommendation to my old master, and I doubt not that he would receive him with open arms, and give him enough to eat, enough to wear, and flog him when ever he thought he required it. (Loud cheers and laughter.) So I say to our friend from Boston, to-night, if he is so charmed with slavery, he shall have the same recommendation to my old master. (Loud cheers.)■

41 THE FUGITIVE SLAVE BILL

Samuel Ringgold Ward

One of the provisions of the Compromise of 1850 designed to settle the sectional controversy arising from the Mexican War called for the enactment of a stricter fugitive slave law. The proposed bill was denounced by black and white abolitionists, and by none more vigorously than by Samuel Ringgold Ward (1817–c. 1865). Brought to New York at the age of three by his parents, who escaped from slavery in Maryland, Ward received an education, taught school, and became a preacher, ministering to a predominantly white congregation in Cortlandville, New York. A leading antislavery agent, he became famous as an orator. After the fugitive slave bill became law, Ward spoke out so vehemently against it that he was forced to flee to Canada. He never returned to the United States but continued to lecture in Canada and England. He died in Jamaica.

The following is a speech Ward delivered in Boston on March 25, 1850, at an anti-Webster meeting in Faneuil Hall. In his speech in the Senate on March 7, 1850, Daniel Webster had indicated his support for stricter enforcement of the fugitive slave law, and the Boston abolition-

ists gathered to condemn the senator from Massachusetts. Ward denounced Webster and James M. Mason, Senator from Virginia and author of the bill. He concluded his speech with a call for resistance by all means necessary.

The speech here presented is taken from the Liberator, *April 5, 1850.*

I AM HERE TONIGHT as a guest. You have met here to speak of the sentiments of a Senator of your state whose remarks you have the honor to repudiate. In the course of the remarks of the gentlemen who preceded me, he has done us the favor to make honorable mention of a Senator of my own State—William H. Seward.[*]

I thank you for this manifestation of approbation of a man who has always stood head and shoulders above his party and who has never receded from his position on the question of slavery. It was my happiness to receive a letter from him a few days since, in which he said he never would swerve from his position as the friend of freedom.

To be sure, I agree not with Senator Seward in politics, but when an individual stands up for the rights of men against slaveholders, I care not for party distinctions. He is my brother.

We have here much of common cause and interest in this matter. That infamous bill of Mr. Mason of Virginia proves itself to be like all other propositions presented by Southern men. It finds just enough of Northern doughfaces[†] who are willing to pledge themselves, if you will pardon the uncouth language of a backwoodsman, to lick up the spittle of the slavocrats, and swear it is delicious.

You of the old Bay State—a state to which many of us are accustomed to look as to our fatherland, just as we look back to England as our mother country—you have a Daniel who has deserted the cause of freedom. We, too, in New York, have a "Daniel who has come to judgment," only he don't come quite fast enough to the right kind of judgment. Daniel S. Dickinson[‡] represents some one, I suppose, in the State of New York; God knows, he doesn't represent me. I can pledge you that our Daniel will stand cheek by jowl with your Daniel. He was never known to surrender slavery, but always to surrender liberty.

The bill of which you most justly complain, concerning the surrender of fugitive slaves, is to apply alike to your state and to our state, if it shall ever apply at all. But we have come here to make a common oath upon a common altar, that that bill shall never take effect. Honorable Senators may record their names in its behalf, and it may have the sanction of the House of Representatives; but we, the people, who are superior to both House and

---

[*]Seward, senator from New York, opposed the Compromise of 1850 and upheld the principle of a "Higher Law" under which slavery could never be justified.

[†]"Doughfaces" were Northerners with southern principles.

[‡]Daniel Stevens Dickinson (1800–1866) was a leader of the Democratic Party in New York state and was elected U.S. senator in 1844 after serving as lieutenant governor.

the Executive, too, we, the people, will never be human bipeds, to howl upon the track of the fugitive slave, even though led by the corrupt Daniel of your state, or the degraded one of ours.

Though there are many attempts to get up compromises—and there is no term which I detest more than this, it is always the term which makes right yield to wrong; it has always been accursed since Eve made the first compromise with the devil. I was saying, sir, that it is somewhat singular, and yet historically true, that whensoever these compromises are proposed, there are men of the North who seem to foresee that Northern men, who think their constituency will not look into these matters, will seek to do more than the South demands. They seek to prove to Northern men that all is right and all is fair; and this is the game Webster is attempting to play.

"Oh," says Webster, "the will of God has fixed that matter; we will not reenact the will of God." Sir, you remember the time in 1841, '42, '43 and '44, when it was said that Texas could never be annexed. The design of such dealing was that you should believe it, and then, when you thought your-selves secure, they would spring the trap upon you. And now it is their wish to seduce you into the belief that slavery never will go there, and then the slaveholders will drive slavery there as fast as possible. I think that this is the most contemptible proposition of the whole, except the support of that bill which would attempt to make the whole North the slave catchers of the South.

You will remember that that bill of Mr. Mason says nothing about color. Mr. [Wendell] Phillips, a man whom I always loved, a man who taught me my hornbook on this subject of slavery, when I was a poor boy, has referred to Marshfield. There is a man who sometimes lives in Marshfield, and who has the reputation of having an honorable dark skin. Who knows but that some postmaster may have to sit upon the very gentleman whose character you have been discussing to-night? "What is sauce for the goose is sauce for the gander." If this bill is to relieve grievances, why not make an application to the immortal Daniel of Marshfield? There is no such thing as complex-ion mentioned. It is not only true that the colored men of Massachusetts—it is not only true that the fifty thousand colored men of New York may be taken—though I pledge you there is one, whose name is Sam Ward, who will never be taken alive. Not only is it true that the fifty thousand black men of New York may be taken, but any one else also can be captured. My friend Theodore Parker alluded to Ellen Craft.* I had the pleasure of taking tea with her and accompanied her here tonight. She is far whiter than many who come here slave-catching. This line of distinction is so nice that you cannot tell who is white or black. As Alexander Pope used to say, "White and black soften and blend in so many thousand ways, that it is neither white nor black."

This is the question. Whether a man has a right to himself and his chil-

---

*Ellen Craft and William Craft, her husband, escaped from slavery in Georgia by dis-guising themselves. Ellen Craft posed as a white gentleman and her husband as her slave. They traveled through the slave states and gained freedom in the North.

dren, his hopes and his happiness, for this world and the world to come. That is a question which, according to this bill, may be decided by any backwoods postmaster in this state or any other. Oh, this is a monstrous proposition; and I do thank God that if the Slave Power has such demands to make on us, that the proposition has come now—now, that the people know what is being done; now that the public mind is turned toward this subject; now that they are trying to find what is the truth on this subject.

Sir, what must be the moral influence of this speech of Mr. Webster on the minds of young men, lawyers and others, here in the North? They turn their eyes toward Daniel Webster as toward a superior mind, and a legal and constitutional oracle. If they shall catch the spirit of this speech, its influence upon them and upon following generations will be so deeply corrupting that it never can be wiped out or purged.

I am thankful that this, my first entrance into Boston and my first introduction to Fanueil Hall, gives me the pleasure and privilege of uniting with you in uttering my humble voice against the two Daniels, and of declaring, in behalf of our people, that if the fugitive slave is traced to our part of New York State, he shall have the law of Almighty God to protect him, the law which says, "Thou shalt not return to the master the servant that is escaped unto thee, but he shall dwell with thee in thy gates, where it liketh him best." And if our postmasters cannot maintain their Constitutional oaths and cannot live without playing the pander to the slave hunter, they need not live at all. Such crises as these leave us the right of Revolution, and if need be, that right we will, at whatever cost, most sacredly maintain.■

42 A PLEA FOR THE OPPRESSED

Lucy Stanton

Lucy Stanton was probably the first African American woman to complete a four-year collegiate course of study. Stanton's stepfather, John Brown, was a Cleveland barber active in the Underground Railroad who founded a school for the city's black children. Lucy graduated from her father's school and enrolled at the nearby Oberlin Collegiate Institute, noted for its abolitionist politics and admission of both male and female African American students in significant numbers. In 1850, she completed the "ladies' course," which, unlike the B.A. program, required no Greek, Latin, or higher mathematics.

As president of the Oberlin Ladies Literary Society, Stanton was invited to offer a graduation address at the commencement exercises on Au-

gust 27, 1850. Delivered just two weeks before the enactment of the Fugitive Slave Act, Stanton's speech offers a stirring portrayal of slavery as bloody warfare. She appeals to her fellow women students to embrace the cause of the slave and to work in the service of emancipation and uplift. She offers vivid, present-tense vignettes of women's life in slavery, appealing to the women in her audience to see themselves in the place of the enslaved and act on their behalf: "Mother, sister, by thy own deep sorrow of heart; by the sympathy of thy woman's nature, plead for the downtrodden on thy own, of every land."

The text of Stanton's speech was published in the Oberlin Evangelist *of December 17, 1850, whose editors praised her "charming voice, modest demeanor, appropriate pronunciation and graceful cadences." A trustee of the college rose after she finished her address and cited Stanton's performance as proof of the desirability of admitting black students, whereupon the audience reportedly erupted in a "swelling burst of applause." The speech was reprinted with a biographical sketch of Stanton in Ellen NicKenzie Lawson,* The Three Sarahs: Documents of Antebellum Black College Women *(New York: Edwin Mellen Press, 1984).*

W hen I forget you, Oh my people, may my tongue cleave to the roof of my mouth, and may my right hand forget her cunning!* Dark hover the clouds. The Anti-Slavery pulse beats faintly. The right of suffrage is denied. The colored man is still crushed by the weight of oppression. He may possess talents of the highest order, yet for him is no path of fame or distinction opened. He can never hope to attain those privileges while his brethren remain enslaved. Since, therefore, the freedom of the slave and the gaining of our rights, social and political, are inseparably connected, let all the friends of humanity plead for those who may not plead their own cause.

Reformers, ye who have labored long to convince man that happiness is found alone in doing good to others, that humanity is a unit, that he who injures one individual wrongs the race;—that to love one's neighbor as one's self is the sum of human virtue—ye that advocate the great principles of Temperance, Peace, and Moral Reform will you not raise your voice in behalf of these stricken ones!—will you not plead the cause of the Slave?

Slavery is the combination of all crime. It is War.

Those who rob their fellow-men of home, of liberty, of education, of life, are really at war against them as though they cleft them down upon the bloody field. It is intemperance; for there is an intoxication when the fierce passions rage in man's breast, more fearful than the madness of the drunkard, which if let loose upon the moral universe would sweep away everything pure and holy, leaving but the wreck of man's nobler nature. Such passions does Slavery foster—yea, they are a part of herself. It is full of pollution.

*Stanton paraphrases Psalm 137: "If I forget thee, O Jerusalem, let my right hand forget her cunning / If I do not remember thee, let my tongue cleave to the roof of my mouth."

Know you not that to a slave, virtue is a sin counted worthy of death? That many, true to the light within, notwithstanding the attempts to shut out the truth, feeling that a consciousness of purity is dearer than life, have nobly died? Their blood crieth to God, a witness against the oppressor.

Statesmen, you who have bent at ambition's shrine, who would leave your names on the page of history, to be venerated by coming generations as among those of the great and good, will you advocate the cause of the down-trodden, remembering that the spirit of liberty is abroad in the land? The precious seed is sown in the heart of the people, and though the fruit does not appear, the germ is there, and the harvest will yet be gathered. Truly is this an age of reform. The world is going on, not indeed keeping pace with the rapid tread of its leaders, but none the less progressing. As the people take a step in one reform, the way is prepared for another. Now while other evils in man's social and political condition are being remedied, think you that Slavery can stand the searching test—an enlightened people's sense of justice? Then speak the truth boldly; fear not loss of property or station. It is a higher honor to embalm your name in the hearts of a grateful people than to contend for the paltry honors of party preferment.

Woman, I turn to thee. Is it not thy mission to visit the poor? to shed the tear of sympathy? to relieve the wants of the suffering? Where wilt thou find objects more needing sympathy than among the slaves!

Mother, hast thou a precious gem in thy charge, like those that make up the Savior's jewels? Has thy heart, trembling with its unutterable joyousness, bent before the throne of the Giver with the prayer that thy child might be found in his courts? Thou hast seen the dawning of intelligence in its bright eye, and watched with interest the unfolding of its powers. Its gentle, winning ways have doubly endeared it to thee. Death breathes upon the flower, and it is gone. Now thou canst feel for the slave-mother who has bent with the same interest over her child, whose heart is entwined around it even more firmly than thine own around thine, for to her it is the only ray of joy in a dreary world. She returns weary and sick at heart from the labors of the field; the child's beaming smile of welcome half banishes the misery of her lot. Would she not die for it? Ye who know the depths of a mother's love, answer! Hark! Strange footsteps are near her dwelling! The door is thrown rudely open! Her master says—"There is the woman!" She comprehends it all—she is sold! From her trembling lips escape the words—"my child!" She throws herself at the feet of those merciless men, and pleads permission to keep her babe, but in vain. What is she more than any other slave, that she should be permitted this favor? They are separated.

Sister, have you ever had a kind and loving brother? How often would he lay aside his book to relieve you from some difficulty? How have you hung upon the words of wisdom that he has uttered? How earnestly have you studied that you might stand his companion—his equal. You saw him suddenly stricken by the destroyer. Oh! How your heart ached!

There was a slave-girl who had a brother kind and noble as your own. He had scarcely any advantages: yet stealthily would he draw an old volume from his pocket, and through the long night would pore over its contents.

His soul thirsted for knowledge. He yearned for freedom, but free-soil was far away. That sister might not go, he staid with her. They say that slaves do not feel for or love each other; I fear that there are few brothers with a pale face who would have stood that test. For her he tamed the fire of his eye, toiled for that which profited him not, and labored so industriously that the overseer had no apology for applying the lash to his back. Time passed on: that brother stood in his manhood's prime as tenderly kind and as dearly beloved as ever. That sister was insulted;—the lash was applied to her quivering back; her brother rushed to save her! He tore away the fastenings which bound her to the whipping post, he held her on his arm—she was safe. She looked up, encountered the ferocious gaze of the overseer, heard the report of a pistol, and felt the heart's blood of a brother gushing over her. But we draw the veil.

Mother, sister, by thy own deep sorrow of heart; by the sympathy of thy woman's nature, plead for the downtrodden of thy own, of every land. Instill the principles of love, of common brotherhood, in the nursery, in the social circle. Let these be the prayer of thy life.

Christians, you whose souls are filled with love for your fellow men, whose prayer to the Lord is, "Oh! that I may see thy salvation among the children of men!" Does the battle wax warm? dost thou faint with the burden and heat of the day? Yet a little longer; the arm of the Lord is mighty to save those who trust in him. Truth and right must prevail. The bondsman shall go free. Look to the future! Hark! the shout of joy gushes from the heart of earth's freed millions! It rushes upward. The angels on heaven's outward battlements catch the sound on their golden lyres, and send it thrilling through the echoing arches of the upper world. How sweet, how majestic, from those starry isles float those deep inspiring sounds over the ocean of space! Softened and mellowed they reach earth, filing the soul with harmony, and breathing of God—of love—and of universal freedom.■

43 I WON'T OBEY THE FUGITIVE SLAVE LAW

Reverend Jermain Wesley Loguen

A month after the infamous Fugitive Slave Act was passed, the eloquent voice of Reverend J. W. Loguen, thundering defiance of the law, moved the city of Syracuse, New York, to declare that city a refuge for liberated slaves. On October 4, 1850, the people of Syracuse filled

city hall to hear a discussion of the recently passed law. The unintended
result, as Loguen later observed, was an increase in public interest in
the antislavery cause. Samuel Ringgold Ward, the distinguished orator,
spoke in opposition to the act, and he was followed by Reverend J. W.
Loguen (1813–1872). A fugitive slave himself, Loguen appealed to his fellow citizens to honor the Constitution by dishonoring the law that
would reenslave him and others. As Loguen observes, his continued freedom depended upon the willingness of his white fellow citizens to resist
the law and protect him if he were threatened. Following his plea that
Syracuse be made an "open city" for fugitive slaves, the meeting voted
395 to 96 in favor of his proposal. But soon after, he was forced into hiding when informed that the marshal held papers for his capture.

A prominent abolitionist and a leader of the Underground Railway,
Loguen became a bishop of the African Methodist Episcopal Zion
Church. He is said to have helped over fifteen hundred fugitives and participated in the famous rescue of William "Jerry" Henry in Syracuse on
October 1, 1851. Loguen pursued political paths in abolition, presiding at
the Liberty Party convention in 1853 and participating in the Radical
Abolitionists Party in 1855–1856. Disillusioned with the prospects for political action, he later supported armed resistance and helped recruit
black volunteers for John Brown.

The speech is reprinted from The Rev. J. W. Loguen, As a Slave and
As a Freeman: A Narrative of Real Life (Syracuse, N.Y., 1859), 391–94.
See also Clara Merritt DeBoer, Be Jubilant My Feet: African American
Abolitionists in the American Missionary Association, 1839–1861 (New
York: Garland, 1994), 217–20.

I WAS A SLAVE; I knew the dangers I was exposed to. I had made up my
mind as to the course I was to take. On that score I needed no counsel, nor
did the colored citizens generally. They had taken their stand—they would
not be taken back to slavery. If to shoot down their assailants should forfeit
their lives, such result was the least of the evil. They will have their liberties
or die in their defense. What is life to me if I am to be a slave in Tennessee? My neighbors! I have lived with you many years, and you know me. My
home is here, and my children were born here. I am bound to Syracuse by
pecuniary interests, and social and family bonds. And do you think I can be
taken away from you and from my wife and children, and be a slave in Tennessee? Has the President and his Secretary sent this enactment up here, to
you, Mr. Chairman, to enforce on me in Syracuse?—and will you obey him?
Did I think so meanly of you—did I suppose the people of Syracuse, strong
as they are in numbers and love of liberty—or did I believe their love of liberty was so selfish, unmanly and unchristian—did I believe them so sunken
and servile and degraded as to remain at their homes and labors, or, with
none of that spirit which smites a tyrant down, to surround a United States
Marshal to see me torn from my home and family, and hurled back to bond-

age—I say did I think so meanly of you, I could never come to live with you. Nor should I have stopped, on my return from Troy, twenty-four hours since, but to take my family and movables to a neighborhood which would take fire, and arms, too, to resist the least attempt to execute this diabolical law among them. Some kind and good friends advise me to quit my country, and stay in Canada, until this tempest is passed. I doubt not the sincerity of such counsellors. But my conviction is strong, that their advice comes from a lack of knowledge of themselves and the case in hand. I believe that their own bosoms are charged to the brim with qualities that will smite to the earth the villains who may interfere to enslave any man in Syracuse. I apprehend the advice is suggested by the perturbation of the moment, and not by the tranquil spirit that rules above the storm, in the eternal home of truth and wisdom. Therefore I have hesitated to adopt this advice, at least until I have the opinion of this meeting. Those friends have not canvassed this subject. I have. They are called suddenly to look at it. I have looked at it steadily, calmly, resolutely, and at length defiantly, for a long time. I tell you the people of Syracuse and of the whole North must meet this tyranny and crush it by force, or be crushed by it. This hellish enactment has precipitated the conclusion that white men must live in dishonorable submission, and colored men be slaves, or they must give their physical as well as intellectual powers to the defense of human rights. The time has come to change the tones of submission into tones of defiance,—and to tell Mr. Fillmore and Mr. Webster, if they propose to execute this measure upon us, to send on their bloodhounds. Mr. President, long ago I was beset by over-prudent and good men and women to purchase my freedom. Nay, I was frequently importuned to consent that they purchase it, and present it as evidence of their partiality to my person and character. Generous and kind as those friends were, my heart recoiled from the proposal. I owe my freedom to the God who made me, and who stirred me to claim it against all other beings in God's universe. I will not, nor will I consent, that anybody else shall countenance the claims of a vulgar despot to my soul and body. Were I in chains, and did these kind people come to buy me out of prison, I would acknowledge the boon with inexpressible thankfulness. But I feel no chains, and am in no prison. I received my freedom from Heaven, and with it came the command to defend my title to it. I have long since resolved to do nothing and suffer nothing that can, in any way, imply that I am indebted to any power but the Almighty for my manhood and personality.

Now, you are assembled here, the strength of this city is here to express their sense of this fugitive act, and to proclaim to the despots at Washington whether it shall be enforced here—whether you will permit the government to return me and other fugitives who have sought asylum among you, to the Hell of slavery. The question is with you. If you will give us up, say so, and we will shake the dust from our feet and leave you. But we believe better things. We know you are taken by surprise. The immensity of this meeting testifies to the general consternation that has brought it together, necessarily, precipitately, to decide the most stirring question that can be presented, to wit, whether, the government having transgressed Constitutional and natural limits, you will bravely resist its aggressions, and tell its soulless agents that no slaveholder shall make your city and county a hunting field for slaves.

Whatever may be your decision, my ground is taken. I have declared it everywhere. It is known over the state and out of the state—over the line in the North, and over the line in the South. I don't respect this law—I don't fear it—I won't obey it! It outlaws me, and I outlaw it, and the men who attempt to enforce it on me. I place the governmental officials on the ground that they place me. I will not live a slave, and if force is employed to reenslave me, I shall make preparations to meet the crisis as becomes a man. If you will stand by me—and I believe you will do it, for your freedom and honor are involved as well as mine—it requires no microscope to see that—I say if you will stand with us in resistance to this measure, you will be the saviors of your country. Your decision to-night in favor of resistance will give vent to the spirit of liberty, and it will break the bands of party, and shout for joy all over the North. Your example only is needed to be the type of popular action in Auburn, and Rochester, and Utica, and Buffalo, and all the West, and eventually in the Atlantic cities. Heaven knows that this act of noble daring will break out somewhere—and may God grant that Syracuse be the honored spot, whence it shall send an earthquake voice through the land!■

44 AR'N'T I A WOMAN?

Sojourner Truth

Sojourner Truth (c. 1797–1883), one of the most celebrated orators of the nineteenth century, was born in slavery in New York and freed in 1827 with the state's emancipation. She did domestic work and after a period of religious revivalism became an active abolitionist, exchanging her name Isabella for the name Sojourner Truth. Although she remained illiterate all her life, she was a brilliant and eloquent advocate for the antislavery and women's rights causes.

The speech reproduced here was delivered at the Woman's Rights convention in Akron, Ohio, on May 29, 1851. Some of the delegates to the convention urged that she not be allowed to speak, fearing that the abolitionists would harm their cause. But Frances Dana Gage, who was presiding, invited her to address the convention. Sojourner Truth directed her re-

marks against a previous speaker, a clergyman who had ridiculed the weakness and helplessness of women and argued that they should not be entrusted with the vote. Her eloquence and wit captured the gathering.

Truth's 1851 address to the Akron convention is among the most widely reprinted, anthologized, and quoted African American speeches. Yet the familiar text of the speech has been strongly disputed by recent historians. Most reports of the speech are taken from the account written by Truth's friend Frances Gage, the presiding officer of the Akron convention. This version was reproduced in the 1875 edition of Truth's Narrative and in Elizabeth Cady Stanton et al., History of Woman Suffrage (1881). But Gage took no notes during Truth's speech and did not write her "faint sketch" of the speech until twelve years later. The four extant contemporary transcriptions of Truth's speech differ substantially from Gage's text; none of the four, most notably, includes the famous phrase "Ar'n't I a Woman?" (changed to "A'n't" by Stanton) by which the speech has come to be known, although all contain similar sentiments, and Truth may have used the phrase in reference to the familiar abolitionist slogan, "Am I not a woman and a sister?"

However inaccurate in its transcription of Truth's own words, Gage's account (which, after all, Gage never claimed to be more than an approximation) has become such a widely used and inspirational text that we have reproduced it here, along with the contemporary text from the Salem, Ohio, Anti-Slavery Bugle of June 21, 1851, which has gained favor among some recent historians.

Sojourner Truth's speech is reproduced without the "plantation" dialect in which it was recorded in E. C. Stanton, S. B. Anthony, and M. J. Gage, History of Woman Suffrage (Rochester, N.Y., 1887), vol. 1, p. 116. Truth's speech patterns were complex and varied (she spoke Dutch until the age of ten, for example), but unlikely to have conformed to the stereotypical dialect of Gage's account (Stetson and David, Glorying in Tribulation, 112). On the controversy over various accounts of Truth's speech, see Jeffrey C. Stewart's introduction to Narrative of Sojourner Truth (New York: Oxford, 1991), xxxiii–xxxv; Erlene Stetson and Linda David, Glorying in Tribulation: The Lifework of Sojourner Truth (East Lansing: Michigan State University Press, 1994); Carleton Mabee and Susan Mabee Newhouse, Sojourner Truth: Slave, Prophet, Legend (New York: New York University Press, 1993); and Nell Irvin Painter, Sojourner Truth: A Life, a Symbol (New York: W. W. Norton, 1996).

Well, children, where there is so much racket there must be something out of kilter. I think that 'twixt the negroes of the South and the women at the North, all talking about rights, the white men will be in a fix pretty soon. But what's all this here talking about?

That man over there says women need to be helped into carriages, and lifted over ditches, and to have the best place everywhere. Nobody ever helps me into carriages, or over mud-puddles, or gives me any best place! And arn't I a woman? Look at me! Look at my arm! I have ploughed, and planted, and gathered into barns, and no man could head me! And arn't I a woman? I could work as much and eat as much as a man—when I could get it—and bear the lash as well! And arn't I a woman? I have borne thirteen children, and seen them most all sold off to slavery, and when I cried out with my mother's grief, none but Jesus heard me! And arn't I a woman?

Then they talk about this thing in the head; what's this they call it? ["Intellect," whispered someone near.] That's it, honey. What's that got to do with women's rights or negro rights? If my cup won't hold but a pint, and yours holds a quart, wouldn't you be mean not to let me have my little half-measure full?

Then that little man in black there, he says women can't have as much rights as men, because Christ wasn't a woman! Where did your Christ come from? From God and a woman! Man had nothing to do with Him. . . .

If the first woman God ever made was strong enough to turn the world upside down all alone, these women together ought to be able to turn it back, and get it right side up again! And now they are asking to do it, the men better let them.

FROM THE *ANTI-SLAVERY BUGLE:*

One of the most unique and interesting speeches of the Convention was made by Sojourner Truth, an emancipated slave. It is impossible to transfer it to paper, or convey any adequate idea of the effect it produced upon the audience. Those only can appreciate it who saw her powerful form, her whole-souled, earnest gesture, and listened to her strong and truthful tones. She came forward to the platform and addressing the President said with great simplicity:

May I say a few words? Receiving an affirmative answer, she proceeded; I want to say a few words about this matter. I am a woman's rights [sic]. I have as much muscle as any man, and can do as much work as any man. I have plowed and reaped and husked and chopped and mowed, and can any man do more than that? I have heard much about the sexes being equal; I can carry as much as any man, and can eat as much too, if I can get it. I am strong as any man that is now.

As for intellect, all I can say is, if woman have a pint and man a quart— why can't she have her little pint full? You need not be afraid to give us our rights for fear we will take too much—for we won't take more than our pint'll hold.

The poor men seem to be all in confusion and don't know what to do. Why children, if you have woman's rights give it to her and you will feel better. You will have your own rights, and they won't be so much trouble.

I can't read, but I can hear. I have heard the Bible and have learned that Eve caused man to sin. Well if woman upset the world, do give her a chance to set it right side up again. The lady has spoken about Jesus, how he never spurned woman from him, and she was right. When Lazarus died, Mary and Martha came to him with faith and love and besought him to raise their brother. And Jesus wept—and Lazarus came forth. And how came Jesus into the world? Through God who created him and woman who bore him. Man, where is your part?

But the women are coming up blessed be God and a few of the men are coming up with them. But man is in a tight place, the poor slave is on him, woman is coming on him, and he is surely between a hawk and a buzzard.■

45 ORATORS AND ORATORY

William G. Allen

 Many black abolitionists regarded oratory as a most powerful instrument for the promotion of social justice. As African Americans gained increasing access to the public lectern and fame in its use, many offered reflections upon the importance of oratory to the quest for freedom. In his June 22, 1852, oration to the Dialexian Society of New York Central College, William Grant Allen insists that the greatest oratory always has human liberty as its central concern and crisis and tumult as its backdrop. He argues "that orators worthy the name must originate in the nation which is in a transition state, either from slavery to freedom or from freedom to slavery." Allen was among the first African American college professors and is the earliest known to have taught rhetoric.

Allen was one of three black American professors employed at New York Central College, a predominantly white institution in McGrawville. He created a furor when he married a white student at the school. In 1853, the year following this speech, the couple fled to England, narrowly escaping a mob that sought to tar and feather Allen. In England, Allen published an account of his travails, The American Prejudice Against Color: An Authentic Narrative, Showing How Easily the Nation Got Into an Uproar *(London, 1853). He spoke on the lecture circuit and gave lessons in elocution. He was later appointed headmaster of the Caledonia Training School at Islington.*

In this speech, Allen not only considers the component qualities of oratorical greatness but evaluates noted orators of the day—including black abolitionist speakers—according to these standards. One month after this address, Frederick Douglass came to the campus for a series of

*four lectures, and Douglass and Allen attended the 1852 organiza-
tional meeting of the Women's State Temperance Convention in Rochester.*

The speech text is taken from the Liberator, *October 29, 1852. Ex-
cerpts were previously anthologized in Otelia Cromwell, Lorenzo Dow
Turner, and Eva B. Dykes, eds.,* Readings from Negro Authors *(New York:
Harcourt, Brace, 1931). For more information on Allen, see Benjamin
Quarles,* Black Abolitionists, *114, 138–39.*

Gentlemen and Members of the Dialexian: My subject is ORATORS
AND ORATORY.

It is not only true, that "the mind is the only medal of honor—the only
badge of distinction—the only measure of the man"—but it is also true, that
he that thinks the largest thought is the ruler of the world. Such a ruler may
not sit upon the throne, nor may occupy the President's chair, nor the Governor's seat; nevertheless, he is the ruler of the world, and that by reason of
his superior and God-given powers. Accustomed as the world now is, to regard shadows as substances, and shows as realities, it is unable to recognize
its true rulers; but as it moves onward and upward to God—as the *merely*
intellectual shall give place to the moral AND the intellectual, usurpers will
be dethroned, rulers attain their proper places, and be known and read of
all men.

Is Fillmore the *rightful* ruler of this nation?* No more necessarily so
that I would be a dentist, because all the people of McGrawville should get
together and vote me such. That was a sagacious boy who would not: admit
that the calf's tail *was* a leg, merely because it was *called* such. Solomon
has written the following: "This wisdom have I seen under the sun, and it
seemed great to me. There was a little city, and few men within it; and there
came a great king against it, and besieged it, and built great bulwarks against
it. Now there was found in it, a poor wise man, and he, by his wisdom, delivered the city; and yet no man remembered that same poor man." This is
admirable, and to the point. If he be not the *rightful* ruler of a city, who, "by
his wisdom," delivers it, then what claim hath Wisdom over Folly, Virtue
over Vice, Power over Weakness. I repeat the idea he is the ruler of a nation
or the world, who is superior to his fellows in the capacity to rule—who
thinks the largest thoughts, performs the greatest deeds, and takes good care
that these thoughts, and these deeds, and the law of Rectitude shall be in
perfect harmony.

Nothing is easier, as, indeed, nothing is more common, than to call both
persons and things by improper names. Toussaint figures less largely on the
pages of history than Napoleon; and, yet in every element of the *rightful*

---

*Millard Fillmore (1800–1874) had succeeded to the presidency in 1850 following the
death of Zachary Taylor. Fillmore signed the Compromise of 1850, including the Fugitive
Slave Law.

ruler, Toussaint was the superior.* If results are in any degree an exponent of character, they who judge righteous judgment, will judge this judgment true. I will not say that Napoleon was less intellectual than Toussaint—I will not say that Toussaint was as intellectual as Napoleon; but I will say that he had character more symmetrical by far, and an ambition more worthy of beings who were made to look upward.

After the thinker, the next in order is the orator. Indeed, the consummate orator is thinker, speaker, and righteous man combined. The world has seen but few such; but wherever and whenever seen, they have represented the "highest style of men"—the most perfect specimens of intellectual and moral grandeur.

The art of oratory is consequent upon the introduction of sin. Had there been no disturbing force, all men would have been poets. Do you ask why? Because poetry is the natural language of the sinless heart. The Bible is the most poetic of books, because most conformable to nature. The Hebrew language is the most poetic of languages, because spoken before sin had been wrought into a science. Even the sounds of this language are prayerful and poetic.

Had there been no disturbing force, all would have been harmony;—and what need, therefore, would there have been of logic, since there would have been nothing to correct? What need of rhetoric, since no art of persuasion would have been necessary to impress men with either the beauty or the holiness of virtue? Our outward world is an expression of our interior life. Not the Psalmist alone, therefore, but all men would have exclaimed, and the exclamation would have been spontaneous,

> *The Heavens declare the glory of God.*
> *And the Firmament sheweth his hand work*
> *Day unto day uttereth speech.*
> *And night unto night sheweth knowledge.*

The whole universe would have been to all mankind a paradise, and creation holy ground. Had there been disturbing force, there would have been thought, but no reflection; no casting of the mind backward, but ever forward, onward and upward.

> *The meanest flower that blows*
> *Can give thoughts that do often lie too deep for tears.*

Since, then, the art of oratory is consequent upon the introduction of sin; and since the sin of sins is the oppression of the weak by the strong, it follows that no other subject can beget the highest efforts of oratory than that of personal or political liberty. Liberty is the first condition of human

---

*Toussaint L'Ouverture, a former slave, led the Haitian revolution and the defeat of Napoleon's troops.

progress. Whoso does not admit this, is irredeemably dull of comprehension. It follows, also, that orators worthy the name must originate in the nation that is a transition state, either from slavery to freedom, or freedom to slavery. I was about to say, that orators worthy the name, must originate among the oppressed races, but on turning to the pages of history, I was reminded of the fact, that all races, with scarcely an exception, had, at some period of their existence, been in a state of thraldom. In the veins of English and Americans; the freest of men—flows the blood of slaves. At the Norman Conquest, and close to the Saxon Heptarchy, two-thirds of the population of England were held and in different degrees of servitude. One person in every seven was an absolute slave, and a marketable commodity in every sense of the word. Slaves and cattle were legal tender; and the law was, that one slave should be held in value as equivalent to four oxen. A little consolation is better than none; so I would say to the black man, therefore—*Take courage, friend, you are only taking your turn.*

But to return and repeat. Orations worthy the name must have for their subject personal or political liberty; and orators worthy of the name must necessarily originate in the nation that is on the eve of passing from a state of slavery into freedom, or from a state of freedom into slavery. How could this be otherwise? Where there is no pressure, the highest efforts of genius must lie undeveloped.

The celebrated Demosthenes arose at a period when Athens was passing into a state of thraldom under Philip. Cicero, when Rome was in a transition state from a Commonwealth to an Empire. Patrick Henry, when the colonies were passing from the darkness of British tyranny into the light of American freedom. And certainly none need be told, when Ireland produced her O'Connell, the dark-skinned American his Douglass, the Hungarian his Kossuth.

I proceed now to illustrate. The most distinguished of ancient orators are Demosthenes and Cicero. Julius Caesar, too, was one of Rome's greatest orators; and had he given his attention exclusively to the art, would doubtless have surpassed him whose name sheds so much lustre on Roman history. Caesar was a man of wonderful genius. Romans thought him a God; and, I was about to say—well they might; for judged in the light of mind, as comprehensive as flexible, as flexible as comprehensive, and as intense as both—Rome never produced his equal.

Of the personal history of Demosthenes and Cicero, I have not time to speak, nor is it important to consider it in such a lecture as this. All know something more or less of the early life of Demosthenes—how he was hissed from the stage because of his ungainly appearance, and indistinct articulation—how he shaved his head that he might not go abroad—how he hung a sword before his mirror, that if he should gesticulate awkwardly, it might give him friendly admonition—how, at last, to correct his enunciation, he practiced with pebbles in his mouth, and, to accustom himself to the clamor of the multitude, declaimed upon the sea-shore taking for his audience the roaring and dashing of the billows—how, in short, he gave himself to the intensest application in the art in which he was determined to excel. All know, also, who know anything of his history, what the result was of such persevering efforts.

Caesar, also, in early life, labored under disadvantages not a few; being less formidable than those of Demosthenes, they were, of course, more easily overcome.

Demosthenes' most celebrated oration is his "Oratio De Coron." It was delivered about 329 B.C.; and in connection with Ctesiphon, with whom the great orator was an associate. The indictment was moved by Aschines—a man of great power, and especially remarkable for his personal and political hatred of Demosthenes. Ctesiphon had proposed that Demosthenes be crowned for his services to the State. The ceremony was to be performed in the Theatre of Bacchus, during the festival held in honor of that god, and the crown, as usual, to be a chaplet of olive, interwoven with gold. Aschines opposed the measure. He had great powers of oratory; and in addition thereto, the weight and influence of character which attached themselves to the leader of a powerful Grecian faction. But, with all these, he was unable to stand the fire of Demosthenes. The result is known. He was overwhelmed with disgrace, and compelled to submit to exile.

The plan of this masterpiece of Demosthenes, as given synoptically by Champlin, is as follows:-

(1) Exordium.
(2) Refutation of charges foreign to the indictment.
    (a) Of a private nature.
    (b) Of a public nature.
(3) Reply to the charges contained in the indictment.
(4) Strictures upon the character, and of course of his antagonist, compared with his own.
(5) Peroration.

Cicero's orations are more numerous than those of Demosthenes. He was a man of more varied and extensive attainments, and of greater versatility of talent. Among the most famous productions of Rome's greatest orator, are his speeches on the injustice of Verres, and the conspiracy of Cataline. It would be well to enter into detail here, were it not that in such an Institution as this, the work would be one of supererogation.

Demosthenes and Cicero are the opposites in style. If Demosthenes be the prince of orators, then one may obtain to the highest position in the art, and yet be almost entirely deficient in ideality. Demosthenes deals in logic and facts. His argumentation is iron linked; and when he smites, it is as though he wielded one of the thunder-bolts of Jove. Cicero, on the other hand, is less strong, but more graceful, grander, and more magnificent. The one speaks in sentences, short, vivid, and of lightning stroke; the other, in sentences long, easy, flowing and majestic. The State endangered, or in emergencies generally, Demosthenes is superior to Cicero, because more vehement and rapid. He so constructs his sentences, also, as to demolish as with a consuming fire every thing which opposes him. He is vindictive, sarcastic, severe, terrible. Take the following from his oration on the crown:

> "Aschines hearest thou this?***Why, then, accused wretch, hast thou reproached me so wantonly on this head? Why has thou denounced against me that which the gods in justice can denounce only on thee, and thy vile associates?***He accuses me of favoring Philip! Heavens, and earth,, what would not this man assert?"*****"Wretches, flatterers, miscreants, tearing out the vitals of their country, and tendering its liberties first to Philip, and then to Alexander! Was it thus with me? By no means, my countrymen. My conduct throughout has been influenced by a spirit of rectitude, justice, and integrity. I have been engaged in affairs of greater moment than any statesman of my time; and I have administered them with an exact fidelity, and uncorrupted faith; and these are the merits on which I claim this honor."

Take the following from Cicero's oration, in favor of Milo—a candidate for the consulship:

> Indeed, if I imagined it (a guard) was stationed there in opposition to Milo, I should give way to the times, and conclude there was no room for an orator in the midst of such an armed force. But the prudence of Pompey, a man of such distinguished wisdom and equity, whose justice will never permit him to leave exposed to the rage of soldiery, a person whom he has delivered up to legal trial, nor his wisdom to give the sanction of public authority to the outrage of a furious mob, both cheers and relieves me. Wherefore, those centurions and cohorts, so are from threatening me with danger, assure me of protection; they not only banish my fears, but inspire me with courage, and promise that I shall be heard not only with safety, but with silence and attention.

By this comparison of extracts, you will perceive that in beauty and harmony of diction, Cicero is superior to Demosthenes. There is about the Roman a power of insinuation, a worming of one's self into the affection, which the great Grecian does not possess. To sum up in a few words the comparison between these two lights of ancient history, it may be said that Cicero *wins*, Demosthenes *compels*.

I come now to modern times and in doing so, shall be compelled by want of time, to pass over the names which form so brilliant a galaxy on the pages of English and Irish history. I should be glad to speak of Burke, of Curran, of Fox, of Pitt, of Sheridan, of Erskine, of Mansfield, of Grattan, of Brougham, of Shiel; but glad though I be to do it, yet to night, at least, time tells me to forbear. I come, then, at once to America.

The most eminent orator which America in her prosperous days has produced, is unquestionably Daniel Webster; and the greatest speech, viewed artistically, which has ever been delivered on the American Continent is his reply to Hayne.* Though this speech (or, I should say, parts of it) is repeated at almost every school-room declamation, yet, to me, at least, it has lost none of its freshness and its vigor. The origin of this most celebrated oration is well known to all who are in the least acquainted with American history. For my present purpose, it is sufficient to say, that the body of the speech is an exposition of constitutional law, and an argument against nullification. Though necessarily abounding in abstract reasoning, it, by no means, lacks that vitality which stirs the blood, and arouses to the highest possible excitement every faculty of the human soul. One who was present says, that where the orator reached the point where he concluded the encomium upon the land of his nativity—New England—no one who was not present, could possibly understand the excitement of the scene; and no one who was present could give an adequate description of it. No word painting could convey the intense, deep enthusiasm—the reverential attention of the vast assembly, nor transfer to canvass their earnest, eager, awe-struck countenances. As he stood sawing his arm like a huge tilt hammer up and down—his swarthy countenance lighted up with excitement—he appeared amid the smoke, the fire, the thunder of this eloquence, like Vulcan in his armory, forging thoughts for the gods. The speech was delivered on the 26th of January, 1830. I need not give extracts. It is sufficient to say that throughout the entire production is a ponderousness of argument, together with a massiveness of style, which belittles some men, enviable for their talents, into dwarfs of very small dimensions. His speech on Plymouth Rock is all a-glow with the might and majesty of intellectual and moral grandeur. It is in the light of this speech and his present character that the words of the Poet fall upon our ears in sounds which send deep sadness to the inner heart.

> So fallen' so lost, the light withdrawn
>   Which once he wore!
> The glory from his grey hairs gone
>   For evermore!
> Scorn! Would the angels laugh to mark
>   A bright soul driven
> Fiend-goaded down the endless dark,
>   From hope of heaven!
> All else is gone; from those great eyes
>   The soul has fled

*Webster debated with Senator Robert Hayne of South Carolina on the floor of the U.S. Senate, January 19–27, 1830, on tariffs. Hayne argued that the constitution was a compact among the states and could be nullified; Webster held the floor for two days in his response, proclaiming "Liberty and Union, now and Forever, one and inseparable!" (Charles M. Wiltse, ed., *The Papers of Daniel Webster: Speeches and Formal Writings*, vol. 1 [Hanover, N.H.: University Press of New England, 1974–1989], 348.

> *When faith his lost, when honor dies,*
>   *The man is dead!*

Compared with Clay, Webster is less a genius, so far as genius lies in contrivance and the ability to lead, but a man of more magnificent talent. This superlatively great and superlatively bad man of America, is eminently an expounder and defender, not a leader and aggressor.

The speeches of Webster are destined to fill a large and important place in the history of American literature; and not only so, some hundred years hence will be read with more eagerness than now. In reading, we may separate the thought and the man, but the human mind is so constituted that it cannot thus deal with the speaker who lives his history amongst us. As models of a style uniting beautifully the simple and the majestic, the speeches of Webster are unsurpassed, and, I believe, unsurpassable.

As an offset to Webster, I will now introduce to you the celebrated John B. Gough.* Though in mental energy vastly inferior to Webster, he has nevertheless produced results which Webster could not achieve. Who believes that Webster could deliver one hundred eighty lectures on the same topic, to the same audience, and, to the last, keep his audience in ecstacies of delight? And, yet John B. Gough has done this—in no less a city than Boston—the most enlightened in the Union, and consequently, the most difficult to speak in. This is an intellectual phenomenon, and needs to be explained. Demosthenes tell us, "that which is called eloquence, depends no less upon the audience than upon the speaker." Here, then, is the unravelling of the mystery. Between the speaker and the audience there must exist a sympathy, which sympathy being wanting, and though the speaker should be, as Dr. Beecher said Theodore D. Weld was, "as eloquent as an angel, and as powerful as thunder," he would, nevertheless, be tame to those who heard him. "Put your soul in my soul's stead," contains a world of philosophy. Webster appeals more directly to the logical and reasoning faculties, and these are active in comparatively few. Gough appeals more directly to the sympathies, and touches the chords which vibrate most readily in the deep depths of the human heart. And in no respect does he more completely show his ability in adapting means to ends than in the fact that while he comes down to the level of audience, he keeps just far enough above them to inspire them with respect. In style, he is dramatic in the extreme. He is, in fact, a consummate actor, every limb speaking a distinct and emphatic language. He is witty, and his wit is always fresh. He is humorous, and his humor is always genial. He is pathetic, and his pathos always touching. He is benevolent and sarcastic, insinuating and compulsive. His logic lies in facts, not in form, and his rhetoric is a sincere love of the drunkard, and a straightforward endeavor to

---

*John Bartholomew Gough (1817–1886) was a popular professional lecturer on temperance and other subjects. He is estimated to have delivered over three thousand public lectures from 1842 to 1852 and to have induced more than 140,000 of his audience members to sign temperance pledges.

inspire the same degree of love and earnestness in others. His language is chaste; and though a consummate actor, his general appearance, paradoxical as it may seem, is still quite dignified and impressive. Having heard Gough several times, these are the opinions which I entertain of his oratory.

I come now to the latest and the greatest of orators, whether of ancient or moderate date—I mean Louis Kossuth.* Partaking somewhat of the prevailing spirit of excitement, I, too, travelled some ninety miles to get a sight of the lion. Be it understood that my travel was to see Louis Kossuth, "the world's Apostle of Liberty." This latter title I have never awarded him, and I am less inclined to do it now than at any former period. I do not design to discuss his principles or his policy. These have no relation to this lecture, and with regard to these, men may be innocently permitted to cherish different opinions. And, were I disposed to discuss his principles or his policy at length, I should defer to do so, at least at present, as I do not regard myself as competent to the task. This much I know, however, and this much I will say, that nations are but conveniences, and were never designed to abrogate the great law of equal brotherhood.—He, therefore, that would appropriate to himself the title of "Apostle of Liberty," must have a heart not circumscribed by national lines, and sympathies which can grasp the entire human family. Kossuth has no such heart, and no such sympathies; or, if he has them, what is quite as bad, he has failed to give them expression. Not a word in reference to the wrongs of the American slave has he ever dropped in this country. He has not even called him by name; thereby giving the impression to those who might not know the contrary, that not a slave walked over all this fair America. Before his countrymen, before the world, and before his God, I charge him with the utterance of statements which are not only false; but which he could not, by any possibility, have failed to know were such. "A great, a glorious, a FREE people," said he, at the editorial banquet in New York;—"a great word this, gentlemen, but it is LITERALLY (!) true!" LITERALLY true that we are a *free* people! Heavens! was ever irony so severe?

Now, be it understood, that Kossuth is not asked to leave his Hungary, and adopt the cause of the American slave; or to divide his energies between the one cause and the other. Nobody would ask that unless he be a fool. He is simply asked to be truthful, to abide by the law of Rectitude, and to leave his country in the hands of the great God, who holdeth *all* nations in his hands, even as a very little thing. He is asked, and ye shall be the judges, whether it be not right that he should thus be asked, to be a Philanthropist, not a Politician—a Christian, not a Patriot. That Hungary may be free, must be the prayer of every true and generous heart. Let evil, and only evil, be my portion, should I offer a different prayer from this.

*Louis Kossuth was a leader of the Hungarian Independence movement who, forced into exile in 1848, toured the United States as a popular lecturer in 1849 and 1851. Abolitionists denounced him when he failed to endorse the antislavery struggle. See Donald S. Spencer, *Louis Kossuth and Young America: A Study of Sectionalism and Foreign Policy, 1848–1852* (Columbia, Mo., 1977).

I shall not enter into historical detail. All know that Hungary now lies in the jaws of the Austrian tyrant, and that Kossuth is the length and the breadth, the height and the depth of the movement that has for its object her complete and entire release. For the energy, the self-sacrifice, and patriotism which he has displayed in behalf of his bleeding Hungary, let honor crown him with a golden crown; but forbear to call him "the World's Apostle of Liberty."

The Hungarians, or, to speak more specifically, the Magyars, are descendants of a very feeble race of Northern Asiatics. They were driven about a thousand years ago, by the Turkish invasion, into Hungary; and, finding that part of Hungary to which they were driven to be an exceedingly fertile spot, they changed entirely their former mode of life. In Asia, they were wanderers from pillar to post; in Europe they adopted a settled manner of life. The result of this was a continual going upward in intellectual and moral improvement. The Magyars are also a mixed race. In the sixth century they became mixed with the Persians on the shores of the Baltic; and in the ninth century with the Hunns. It is, doubtless, owing to this mixture, and their favorable climate, that the Magyars are not only among the finest looking, but are also among the most intellectual of men. They have the cool logic of the European, and the glowing fancy of the Asiatic. Brace tells us that they are positively a nation of orators—even the waiter addresses you and answers your commands in speeches most remarkable for their brilliancy. It is not to be supposed, however, that all Magyars are Kossuths. In exigencies, the superior man necessarily and inevitably gets jostled into his position. Kossuth's superior position, therefore, may, in some degree, be taken as an index of this intellectual advance of his countrymen.

I now introduce Kossuth to you as an orator. Judging him from the speeches which I have read, and those which I have heard, I should regard him, as I have already said, superior to any orator who has ever spoken, whether of ancient or modern date. True, he does not thunder like Demosthenes, nor does he link his logic with such iron as the Grecian; nor does he smite with so terrible a bolt. He has not the swelling flow, nor the grandeur, nor the magnificence of Cicero; nor is he as massive or as ponderous as Webster. But he has enough of all these qualities to constitute a symmetry which is far better than any exclusive prominence of any of the faculties of either rhetoric or logic, while in exuberance of fancy and glowing indignation, he certainly never had an equal. The following is from his last speech delivered in New York City. It is not equal, in the qualities of mind in which he is pre-eminent, to the exordium of his speech delivered in Louisville, Kentucky, but it will answer as a substitute, inasmuch as I have lost the extract which I intended to present:

How great is the progress of Humanity! Its steps are counted by centuries; and, yet while countless millions stand almost at the same point where they stood, and some have even declined since America first emerged out of an unexploded darkness, which had covered her for thousands of years, like the gem in the sea; while it is but yesterday, a few pilgrims landed on the wilds of Plymouth, flying from causeless oppression—seeking but for a place of refuge and of rest, and for a free spot in the wilderness to adore the Almighty in their own way; still, in such a brief time—shorter than the recorded genealogy of the noble horse of the wandering Arab—yes, almost within the turn of the hand—out of the unknown wilderness, a mighty empire arose, broad as an ocean, solid as a mountain rock, and upon the scarcely rooted roots of the primitive forest, proud cities stand, teeming with boundless life—growing like the prairie's grass in spring—advancing like the steam engine—baffling time and distance like the telegraph—and spreading the pulsation of their life tide to the remotest parts of the world; and in those cities, and on that broad land, a nation, free as the mountain air, independent as the soaring eagle, active as nature, and powerful as the giant strength of millions of freemen.

How wonderful! What a present, and what a future yet! Future?—then, let me stop at this mysterious word—the veil of unrevealed eternity!

The shadow of that dark word passed across my mind, amid the bustle of this gigantic bee hive—there I stood with meditation alone.

And the spirit of the immovable Past rose before my eyes, unfolding the misty picture-rolls of vanished greatness, and of the fragility of human things.

And among their dissolving views, there I saw the scorched soil of Africa, and upon that soil Thebes, with its hundred gates, more splendid than the most splendid of all the existing cities of the world; Thebes, the pride of old Egypt, the first metropolis of arts and sciences, and mysterious cradle of so many doctrines which still rule mankind in different states, though it has long forgotten their source. There I saw Syria, with its hundred cities—every city a nation—and every nation with an empire's might. Baalbee, with its gigantic temples—the very ruins of which baffle the imagination of man—as they stand like mountains of carved rocks in the desert, where, for hundreds of miles, not a stone is to be found, and no river flows, offering its tolerant back to a mountain's weight, and there they stand, those gigantic ruins; and as we glance at them with astonishment, though we have mastered the mysterious elements of nature, and know the combination of levers, and how to catch the lightning, and command the power of steam, and of compressed air—and how to write with the burning fluid out of which the thunderbolt is forged—and how to drive the current of streamers up the mountain's top—and how to make the air shine in the night, like the light of the sun—and how to drive to the bottom of the deep ocean—and how to rise up to the sky—though we know all this, and many things else, still, looking at the temple of Baalbee, we cannot forbear to ask what people of giants was that, which could do what neither the efforts of our skill, nor the ravaging hand of unrelenting time can undo, though thousands of years. And then, I saw the dissolving picture of Ninevha, with its ramparts covered with mountains of sand, where Layard is digging up colossal-winged bulls, huge as a mountain, and yet carved with the nicety of a cameo; and then Babylon, with its wonderful walls; and Jerusalem, with its unequalled Temple; Tyrus, with its countless fleets; Arad, with its wharves; and Sydon, with its Labyrinth of workshops and factories, and Askelon, and Gaza, and Beyrout, and farther off, Persepolis, with its world of palaces.

All these passed before my eyes, as they have been; and again they pass, as they now are, with no trace of their ancient greatness, but here and there a ruin, and everywhere the desolation of tombs. With all their splendor, power, and might, they vanished like a bubble, or like the dream of a child, leaving but for a moment, a drop of cold sweat upon the sleeper's brow, or a quivering smile upon his lips; then, this wiped away, dream, sweat, smile, all is nothingness!

Cicero says (De Oratore) that "no man can be an accomplished orator who has not a fund of universal knowledge, and a thorough knowledge of all the affections which nature has implanted in the human soul." Certainly no one approaches nearer this definition than does the illustratious Kossuth. His knowledge of history is profound, and so indeed even of local circumstances. During his stay in this country, nothing has surprised the people more than he should know almost everybody, and literally almost everything. He is, in his knowledge, as expansive as profound, and as profound as expansive. Antiquity, the laws of nations, of states, of empires, of kingdoms, of races, and even municipal law, are at his tongue's end, to be used just when and where he wishes. It is amazing that one head so small can carry so great a weight. His wonderful knowledge also is not more remarkable than his skill in its application. Herein also lies a high evidence of his genius. To know the when and the where—ah! this it is that brings a man to greatness.

His knowledge of all the affections which nature has implanted in the human soul, is also as thorough as Cicero would have it.—When the Austria-Russian army were on the borders of Hungary, Kossuth employed himself, body and soul of Hungary as he was, in addressing assemblies of his countrymen. In a few days the Austrians, Russians, Sclavonians, Croats, Serbs and Wallachians were expected to come down like a crushing avalanche upon doomed and unhappy Hungary. There was but a moment left him, so the historian tells us; and that moment was to leave behind it either liberty or annihilation. I give the words of the narrator:

Rising to make a speech, after passing deliberately through a long array of facts and arguments by which he carried conviction into every heart, he ceased to speak, but still maintained his position. Raising his large and now watery eyes to Heaven, he seemed to be making his last petition at the throne of Eternal Justice. A cloud passed over his brow, as if he then saw by prophetic illumination a revelation of the future. Then lowering his aspect a little, and looking abroad, through the open windows of the building, upon the grand and historical scenery about him—the river, the plains, the mountains—he then again raised his eyes and withered hands on high, exclaiming with that emphasis of his which no words can represent, "O, Hungary! Hungary! Hungary! how can I give thee up? O, bury me, Hungarian earth, within thy holy bosom, or be to me a land of freedom!" At this pathetic appeal, every representative before him, even the iron-hearted generals, hearing the tones of his voice, and seeing the tears rolling down his face, wept even as children weep!

Here is emphatically a master's power. Here is the man who can find his way without effort into the deep depths of the human heart.

In style, if I may use the expression, Kossuth is aromatic and luxuriant. As a declaimer, he is inferior to Thompson; and this, no doubt, arises from the fact, that while the one deals largely in denunciation, the other entirely discards it. Nothing in Kossuth's speeches, in the line denunciatory, equals the denunciation of America delivered by George Thompson,* one year ago, in the city of Syracuse. The denunciation was embodied in a comparison of America with Russia. Those who were present on the occasion referred to, will remember the comparison, and its startling effects; effects rendered, none the less startling by the speaker's emphatic gesticulations, and the prodigious opening of his mouth. The power to denounce is a great power to him that useth it well. Some sins are to be reasoned out, some are to be ridiculed out, and some are to be denounced out of the world.

In personal appearance, Kossuth is dignified and impressive. He has not the colossal look of Webster, but his manners are certainly much more insinuating and graceful. He is of medium height, and most superb gait. His smile is the most winning—most fascinating—that I have ever encountered in mortal man—not woman. His eyes express dreaminess, rather than energy of character; though this latter trait is certainly his, by way of preeminent right. His voice is deep-toned, and sepulchral; and well calculated to produce oratorical effort. I should regard him as Democratic in all his thoughts and feelings. Certainly, if he is not so, he has consummate ability to adapt himself to circumstances. At the various depots at which the cars stopped on his way from Syracuse to Utica, he mingled as freely with the multitude as his hurried circumstances would permit; and always had a fitting reply to the various remarks of which he was the recipient. To a question put by a codger in the crowd, as to what were the prospects for Hungary, he made the reply, not so remarkable for its words as its manner.—"Ah,"

---

*George Thompson (1804–1878) was a prominent English abolitionist who made antislavery lecture tours of the United States in 1834–1835 and again in 1851.

said he, "that is a long tale.—We must fight a little, and leave the rest with the Almighty God." If I were an ultra peace man, I should be disposed to criticize this remark, but as I am not, I pass it without comment.

Having said thus much, I now take my leave of the exile, the patriot, and the orator: and, could I in conscience do it, would gladly add the Philanthropist and the Christian.

I can not close this lecture without a tribute to the colored people of this country.—Already have they done something to achieve a place among those who have written their names in large letters upon the pages of the orator's history; and, being yet in a transition state, we may expect developments in the oratorical art which shall surpass anything which ever yet they have made.

Ward,* as a stump orator, has certainly few superiors. A friend writing from New York city in reference to his celebrated speech in reply to Dr. Grant, said he could no more report that speech than he could the coruscations of lightning. The Doctor attempted to prove scientifically that the African was but a connecting link between the man and the monkey. Douglass was also present, and, of course, made such a reply as Frederick Douglass *can* make. The Doctor, however, rejected the reply of Douglass, on the ground that he was no African, but was full one-half white. At this jumped up Ward; and all who have seen him will agree with me, that *bluer* men there may be, but *blacker* men, never. Ye gods! what a battle! The result may be imagined; it certainly need not be described. J. M. McKim, of Philadelphia, describing that same conflict, said: "Ward looked like a statue of black marble of the old Egyptian sort, out of which our white civilization was hewn. He was a cloud to behold; but intellect lighted behind that cloud; and as he annihilated his opponent, he looked as rich in his blackness as the velvet pall upon the bier of an Emperor."

Garnet,† as an orator, is more polished than Ward, as well as more elaborate. He has more application as a student—is more consecutive in his thoughts, and employs more method in their arrangement. He would, consequently, be more pleasing to a select audience; while a promiscuous one would be more easily swayed by Ward. His personal appearance is fine. He is about five feet and two inches tall, erect of figure, and somewhat slender in build. He is as black as Ward, but of smoother texture of skin; has a fine eye, and prominent brow. He dresses in the best broadcloth, and with most scrupulous exactness; carries a cane, and altogether his presence impresses you with the fact, that, though somewhat aristocratic, he is, nevertheless, not only a well-bred man, but a most accomplished gentleman. He is a cousin of Ward, and is, as Ward is, a Southerner. Hot blood runs in his veins; and he would throttle the life out of a slave-holder with as little compunction of conscience as he would tread the life out of a snake. The following is taken from a written address delivered by this orator a few years since in Troy.

---

*Samuel Ringgold Ward (1817–c. 1866) was an abolitionist lecturer and the editor of the *Impartial Citizen* and *Provincial Freeman.*

†Henry Highland Garnet (1815–1882).

The silence that reigns in the region where the pale nations of the earth slumber is solemn and awful. But what think ye, when ye are told that every rood of this Union is the grave of a murdered man, and their epitaphs are written upon the monuments of the nation's wealth. Ye destroyers of my people draw near, and read the mournful inscription; aye, read it, until it is daguerreottyped on your souls. You have slain us all the day long. You have had no mercy! Legions of haggard ghosts stalk through the land, Behold, see, they come!—Oh, what myriads! Hark, hear their broken bones as they clatter together. With deep, unearthly voices, they cry, "We come, we come, for vengeance we come!" Tremble, guilty nation, for the God of Justice lives and reigns. The screaming of the eagle, as he darts through lightning and storm, is unheard because of these voices. The tocsin of the Sabbath, and the solemn organ are mocked by them. They drown the preacher's voice, and produce discord in the sacred choirs. Sworn Senators and perjured demagogues, as they officiate around the altar of Moloch in the national capitol—hear the wailings of the victims of base-bore democracy, and they are ill at ease in their unexampled hypocrisy. The father of waters may roar in his progress to the ocean—the Niagara may thunder, but these voices from the living and the dead will rise above them all.

This is eloquence. You being the judges, tell me does the history of English oratory contain aught more awfully grand in conception, or beautiful in expression?

In versatility of oratorical power, I know of no one who can begin to approach the celebrated Frederick Douglass. He, in very deed, sways a magic wand. In the ability to imitate, he stands almost alone and unapproachable; and there is no actor living, whether he be tragedian or comedian, who would not give the world for such a face as his. His slaveholder's sermon is a masterpiece in its line. When he rises to speak, there is a slight hesitancy in his manner, which disappears as he warms up to his subject. He works with the power of a mighty intellect, and in the vast audiences which he never fails to assemble, touches chords in the inner chambers thereof which vibrate music now sweet, now sad, now lightsome, now solemn, now startling, now grand, now majestic, now sublime. He has a voice of terrific power, of great compass, and under most admirable control. Douglass is not only great in oratory, tongue-wise, but, considering his circumstances of early life, still more marvelous in composition penwise.—He has no fear of man; is no abstractionist; has a first-rate philosophy of reform; believes the boy would never have learned to swim if he had not gone into the water; and is, consequently, particularly obnoxious to tavern-keepers and steamboat captains, and those in general who mix up character and color, man and his skin—and to all, in short, who have little hearts and muddy heads.—He is the pride of the colored man and the terror of slaveholders and their abettors.—Long may he live—an honor to his age, his race, his country, and the world.

Gladly would I devote a few lines to the eloquent Remond,* but I must not draw too largely on your patience. This orator has remarkable fluency, and on his favorite theme—prejudice against color—wields a sarcasm which bites the heart to its very core.

But what say you—shall we not hear Garrison, of Smith, of Phillips? Gladly also would I speak of those; but who, in one evening, can do justice to either Garrison, or Smith, or Phillips? Those are emphatically a nation's glory—earth's noblest spirits.—Great in oratory, they are greater still in the majesty of a character built upon, and interlocked by, the law of Eternal Rectitude. Garrison is the best misunderstood man in America. Regarded as rabid, fanatical, and almost inhuman, no man living presents a more consistent embodiment of whatsoever in Christianity is lovely and of good report. The charge that stands good against him is, that he is death to time-servers and those who make a mockery of the principles of Christianity and Reform. His oratory is peculiarly expressive of his character—remarkable for his serenity, and for that calmness which indicates great inward strength and power. Wendell Phillips is well known as emphatically *the* orator of New England. He has a vigorous declamation, which is well set off by a matchless beauty of diction. Indeed, no orator in America better unites in his style what are usually regarded as opposites—strength and polish. He is particularly felicitous in anecdote, and his speeches generally are as brilliant the day. It is a positive luxury to meet him in the street, so benignantly does he tip his hat to the humblest of his acquaintances. Gerrit Smith is one of the most remarkable men that ever lived in this age, or in any age: remarkable for his intellect, remarkable for his purity of heart, remarkable for his child-like simplicity, and for that majesty of soul which accepts to the full that sublime doctrine of Christian faith.—"Do unto others as ye would that others should do unto you." It is hardly a figure of speech to say that his character throughout is as luminous as the sunbeams. Where he treads, no angel of sorrow follows. His oratory is grandly impressive. He moves with slow steps, but steady purpose, and never misses his aim. His forte lies in argument, and illustration by the simplest figures. He has but little fancy, and never rants. His choice of words and structure of sentences are absolute perfection. He has a voice of great depth, and being as melodious as deep, it gives him enviable power over the hearts and sympathies of men. In personal appearance, he has no superior in America. His face is written all over with benevolence and every Christian grace.

I come now to the last division of this lecture. There are three specific fields for oratorical effort. These are, the bar, the pulpit, and the hall of legislation. To develop the speaking faculties, *more specifically* as such, the bar is unquestionably superior to the pulpit or the legislative hall. The opposing counsel, who sits with a dogged determination to controvert every position; twelve men gazing with all their might and main, and whom, for the time being, one can not help regarding as holding the scales of fate; the judge or judges eyeing one with the coolness and suspicion which contribute but little

---

*Charles Lenox Remond (1810–1873).

to one's comfort; all these have inevitably the tendency to force the advocate into a concentration of thought, and an energy of feeling, which all admit are the surest guarantee of effective and powerful delivery. For the development of the *highest* powers of the orator, the pulpit is probably superior to the bar. For the development of *perceptive* in oratory, the bar is superior to the pulpit; while the development of the *reflective*, the pulpit is superior to the bar. The lawyer deals with the concrete, the preacher with the abstract. The lawyer thinks, but he must do it rapidly, and consequently less profoundly; or if not less profoundly, certainly less comprehensively. The preacher thinks, but not compelled to do it rapidly, he may do it more profoundly. Legislative eloquence necessarily differs materially from that of either the pulpit or the bar. The preacher talks of heaven—why should he not be glowing? The lawyer of the wrongs of misfortunes of his client—why should he be dry and prosy? The legislator, as a *legislator*, discourses for the most part of abstract principles, measures of public policy, and of law, either national or municipal, and can hardly be expected to be more than dignified and convincing. There is yet another field for oratorical effort—and that is the public platform. Here "popular" eloquence produces its mighty effects. An analysis of this eloquence may be the theme for another lecture.

For oratorical purposes, the English language is not surpassed by any living tongue. It is not so compact, so abstruse, so subtle, as the language of the ancient Grecian, but it is much more simple in its construction, and, certainly, fully as impressive and commanding. It is a language of great wealth, being made up of contributions from almost every language under the sun. Its basis is Saxon and Celtic. It is of noble sound, but not so rich in melody as either the ancient Greek, or the modern Spanish and Italian. Charles V, speaking merrily, says, "We would speak Spanish with the Gods, Italian with our mistress, French with our friend, German with soldiers, *English with geese*, Hungarian with horses, and Bohemian with the devil."—The continuous hissing sound, so peculiar with the English, no doubt, induced the funny monarch to institute such a comparison. Language is but an expression of national mind and character. The Greek language is subtle and philosophical, because the Greeks were subtle and philosophical. The Latin is stiff, and right about face, because the Latins were stiff and right about face. The English is flexible and energetic, because those who speak it are in character flexible and energetic. It is not only true that as a nation's mind is, so will a nation's language be, but it is also true that as a language is, so will those who speak it be. Foreigners to a language, therefore, will assimilate in character, while *even in their own land*, to the people whose language they may speak. The Norman Conquest was greatly facilitated by teaching those who fled from Britain to Normandy, during the period of the Danish sway in Britain, to read and speak the Norman language. I have introduced this short dissertation on language, because I thought it not inappropriate in a lecture on oratory.

And, now, members of the Dialexian Society, having thus spoken of oratory—its origins, its purposes, its effects, and having illustrated the subject, as well as I was able, by a reference to some of its brightest lights, I now address to you a word, which, I trust, you will receive, as, indeed, I know you will, in kindness and in friendship. You live in a great country. So far as energy, intellect, and activity constitute greatness, the sun has never seen its equal. You not only live in a great country, but a country most remarkable for its spirit of compromise—for calling that which is bitter, sweet, and that which is bad, good. You live in a country where the combat deepens, and still deepens, between the spirit of freedom and the spirit of the pit.— Now, which side will ye choose? Need I put the question again? I trust not. May I not say, I *know* where you are?

Then, members of this society, as ye cultivate the oratorical, do it diligently, and with purpose; remembering that it is by the exercise of this weapon, perhaps more than any other, that America is to be made a free land, not in name only, but in deed and in truth. Remember, also, that as with individuals, so with nations; both can become effectual teachers of the democratic idea, only by exemplifying in their lives the principles they profess. Oh, America, that I could take thee to my bosom as *indeed* the land of the free.

> Thy hills and thy valleys are sacred all to me,
> No matter what in lands of others I may see.

And, lastly, let me take my seat in saying to you, *that he that would be a great orator, must have a great heart.*■

46 WHAT, TO THE SLAVE, IS THE FOURTH OF JULY?

Frederick Douglass

Frederick Douglass (1818–1895), the best-known black leader in nineteenth-century America, was born of an enslaved mother and a white father in Tuckahoe, Maryland. He never knew his mother well, but lived with his grandparents until the age of eight, when he was raised by an "Aunt Katy," who was in charge of rearing slave children on the plantation of Colonel Edward Lloyd. Sent to Baltimore after a year to live with the Auld family, he began to study reading with Mrs. Auld. When Mr. Auld forbade any further instruction, Douglass managed, by various devices, to learn anyway. To compel him to sub-

mit more readily to slavery, he was sent to Edward Covey, a "slave breaker" who specialized in cracking the spirit of slaves too difficult to handle. Beaten daily with stick and whip for the slightest infraction of impossibly strict rules, he finally decided to fight back, and, in a hand-to-hand struggle that lasted two hours, forced Covey to give up his plan to beat him. Thus, at the age of seventeen, Douglass discovered that he was not afraid to die and that the only way to halt a tyrant was to fight back.

Returned to Hugh Auld in Baltimore, he was apprenticed to a ship-yard to learn the trade of caulker. He not only learned the trade but also, by tracing the letters on the prows of ships, learned to write. On September 3, 1838, armed with seaman's papers supplied him by a free black, Douglass got on a train in Baltimore and escaped from slavery, via the Underground Railroad, to New Bedford, Massachusetts. Five months later he first came in contact with William Lloyd Garrison's antislavery weekly, the Liberator, *and in 1841 delivered his first speech at a convention of the Massachusetts Anti-Slavery Society. He was immediately employed as an agent of the society and rapidly became the most famous of the black abolitionists as well as one of the greatest orators of his day.*

At first Douglass confined his talks to accounts of his experiences as a slave, but soon he was denouncing slavery and calling for its immediate abolition. The more polished his speech became, the fewer people believed that he had ever been a slave. To dispel all doubts, he published his Narrative of the Life of Frederick Douglass *in 1845—in spite of the danger of reenslavement. Douglass resolved to go abroad, to England, and for two years he spoke against slavery in Ireland, Scotland, and England. In 1847, his legal freedom purchased by his British friends for 150 pounds, he left London to take up the battle against slavery again in this country. He moved to Rochester, New York, to start his newspaper, the* North Star, *later called* Frederick Douglass' Paper. *Soon he became famous as an antislavery editor as well as an orator.*

In 1852 Frederick Douglass was invited to address the citizens of Rochester at the Fourth of July celebration. The speech, delivered on July 5, is one of the most famous of his orations. Reprinted as a pamphlet, it reached a wide audience. Douglass reconstructs the speaking occasion. Dismissing the oratorical conventions that marked most Independence Day gatherings, Douglass aligns the American revolutionaries with the abolitionists and proclaims July Fourth to be the bitterest reminder of America's failed promise.

Douglass's discussion of the Fourth of July was a logical development from a speech he had delivered on May 11, 1847, to a meeting of the American Anti-Slavery Society, following his return from England.* In introducing Douglass, Garrison sought to mollify some of his critics who

---

*In the second speech, however, Douglass no longer regarded the Constitution as a proslavery document.

had accused him of treason because of his attack on the United States
while in England. Garrison assured the audience that Douglass really
loved his native land. Douglass, in the course of his speech, replied di-
rectly to Garrison as follows (quoting from the National Anti-Slavery
Standard, May 20, 1847):

I CANNOT AGREE with my friend Mr. Garrison, in relation to my love and attachment to this land. I have no love for America, as such; I have no patriotism; I have no country. What country have I? The institutions of this country do not know me, do not recognize me as a man. I am not thought of, spoken of, in any direction, out of the antislavery ranks as a man. I am not thought of, or spoken of, except as a piece of property belonging to some *Christian* slaveholder, and all the religious and political institutions of this country, alike pronounce me a slave and a chattel. Now, in such a country as this, I cannot have patriotism. The only thing that links me to this land is my family, and the painful consciousness that here there are three millions of my fellow creatures, groaning beneath the iron rod of the worst despotism that could be devised, even in Pandemonium; that here are men and brethren, who are identified with me by their complexion, identified with me by their hatred of slavery, identified with me by their love and aspirations for liberty, identified with me by the stripes upon their backs, their inhuman wrongs and cruel sufferings. This, and this only, attaches me to this land and brings me here to plead with you, and with this country at large, for the disenthrallment of my oppressed countrymen, and to overthrow this system of slavery which is crushing them to the earth. How can I love a country that dooms three millions of my brethren, some of them my own kindred, my own brothers, my own sisters, who are now clanking the chains of slavery upon the plains of the South, whose warm blood is now making fat the soil of Maryland and of Alabama, and over whose crushed spirits rolls the dark shadow of oppression, shutting out and extinguishing forever the cheering rays of that bright sun of Liberty lighted in the souls of all God's children by the Omnipotent hand of Deity itself? How can I, I say, love a country thus cursed, thus bedewed with the blood of my brethren? A country, the church of which, and the government of which, and the Constitution of which, is in favor of supporting and perpetuating this monstrous system of injustice and blood? I have not, I cannot have, any love for this country, as such, or for its Constitution. I desire to see it overthrown as speedily as possible, and its Constitution shivered in a thousand fragments, rather than this foul curse should continue to remain as now.

Here is the full text of Douglass's great speech, "What, to the Slave,
is the Fourth of July?" as quoted in the pamphlet Oration Delivered in

Corinthian Hall, *Rochester, by Frederick Douglass, July 5, 1852* (Rochester, 1852).

M r. President, friends and fellow citizens: He who could address this audience without a quailing sensation, has stronger nerves than I have. I do not remember ever to have appeared as a speaker before any assembly more shrinkingly, nor with greater distrust of my ability, than I do this day. A feeling has crept over me quite unfavorable to the exercise of my limited powers of speech. The task before me is one which requires much previous thought and study for its proper performance. I know that apologies of this sort are generally considered flat and unmeaning. I trust, however, that mine will not be so considered. Should I seem at ease, my appearance would much misrepresent me. The little experience I have had in addressing public meetings, in country school houses, avails me nothing on the present occasion.

The papers and placards say that I am to deliver a Fourth [of] July oration. This certainly sounds large, and out of the common way, for me. It is true that I have often had the privilege to speak in this beautiful Hall, and to address many who now honor me with their presence. But neither their familiar faces, nor the perfect gauge I think I have of Corinthian Hall seems to free me from embarrassment.

The fact is, ladies and gentlemen, the distance between this platform and the slave plantation, from which I escaped, is considerable—and the difficulties to be overcome in getting from the latter to the former are by no means slight. That I am here today is, to me, a matter of astonishment as well as of gratitude. You will not, therefore, be surprised, if in what I have to say I evince no elaborate preparation, nor grace my speech with any high-sounding exordium. With little experience and with less learning, I have been able to throw my thoughts hastily and imperfectly together; and trusting to your patient and generous indulgence, I will proceed to lay them before you.

This, for the purpose of this celebration, is the Fourth of July. It is the birthday of your National Independence, and of your political freedom. This, to you, is what the Passover was to the emancipated people of God. It carries your minds back to the day, and to the act of your great deliverance; and to the signs and to the wonders associated with that act and that day. This celebration also marks the beginning of another year of your national life; and reminds you that the Republic of America is now seventy-six years old. I am glad, fellow citizens, that your nation is so young. Seventy-six years, though a good old age for a man, is but a mere speck in the life of a nation. Three score years and ten is the allotted time for individual men; but nations number their years by thousands. According to this fact, you are, even now, only in the beginning of your national career, still lingering in the period of childhood. I repeat, I am glad this is so. There is hope in the thought, and hope is much needed, under the dark clouds which lower above the horizon. The eye of the reformer is met with angry flashes, portending disastrous times;

but his heart may well beat lighter at the thought that America is young, and that she is still in the impressible stage of her existence. May he not hope that high lessons of wisdom, of justice and of truth, will yet give direction to her destiny? Were the nation older, the patriot's heart might be sadder and the reformer's brow heavier. Its future might be shrouded in gloom and the hope of its prophets go out in sorrow. There is consolation in the thought that America is young. Great streams are not easily turned from channels worn deep in the course of ages. They may sometimes rise in quiet and stately majesty, and inundate the land, refreshing and fertilizing the earth with their mysterious properties. They may also rise in wrath and fury, and bear away on their angry waves the accumulated wealth of years of toil and hardship. They, however, gradually flow back to the same old channel and flow on as serenely as ever. But, while the river may not be turned aside, it may dry up and leave nothing behind but the withered branch and the unsightly rock, to howl in the abyss-sweeping wind, the sad tale of departed glory. As with rivers, so with nations.

Fellow citizens, I shall not presume to dwell at length on the associations that cluster about this day. The simple story of it is, that seventy-six years ago the people of this country were British subjects. The style and title of your "sovereign people" (in which you now glory) was not then born. You were under the British Crown. Your fathers esteemed the English government as the home government, and England as the fatherland. This home government, you know, although a considerable distance from your home, did, in the exercise of its parental prerogatives, impose upon its colonial children such restraints, burdens and limitations as, in its mature judgment, it deemed wise, right and proper.

But your fathers, who had not adopted the fashionable idea of this day, of the infallibility of government and the absolute character of its acts, presumed to differ from the home government in respect to the wisdom and the justice of some of those burdens and restraints. They went so far in their excitement as to pronounce the measures of government unjust, unreasonable and oppressive, and altogether such as ought not to be quietly submitted to. I scarcely need say, fellow citizens, that my opinion of those measures fully accords with that of your fathers. Such a declaration of agreement on my part would not be worth much to anybody. It would certainly prove nothing as to what part I might have taken had I lived during the great controversy of 1776. To say now that America was right and England wrong is exceedingly easy. Everybody can say it; the dastard, not less than the noble brave, can flippantly discant on the tyranny of England toward the American colonies. It is fashionable to do so; but there was a time when to pronounce against England and in favor of the cause of the colonies tried men's souls. They who did so were accounted in their day plotters of mischief, agitators and rebels, dangerous men. To side with the right against the wrong, with the weak against the strong, and with the oppressed against the oppressor— here lies the merit, and the one which, of all others, seems unfashionable in our day. The cause of liberty may be stabbed by the men who glory in the deeds of your fathers. But, to proceed.

Feeling themselves harshly and unjustly treated by the home government, your fathers, like men of honesty and men of spirit, earnestly sought redress. They petitioned and remonstrated; they did so in a decorous, respectful and loyal manner. Their conduct was wholly unexceptionable. This, however, did not answer the purpose. They saw themselves treated with sovereign indifference, coldness and scorn. Yet they persevered. They were not the men to look back.

As the sheet anchor takes a firmer hold when the ship is tossed by the storm, so did the cause of your fathers grow stronger as it breasted the chilling blasts of kingly displeasure. The greatest and best of British statesmen admitted its justice, and the loftiest eloquence of the British Senate came to its support. But, with that blindness which seems to be the unvarying characteristic of tyrants, since Pharaoh and his hosts were drowned in the Red Sea, the British government persisted in the exactions complained of.

The madness of this course, we believe, is admitted now, even by England; but we fear the lesson is wholly lost on our present rulers.

Oppression makes a wise man mad. Your fathers were wise men, and if they did not go mad, they became restive under this treatment. They felt themselves the victims of grievous wrongs, wholly incurable in their colonial capacity. With brave men there is always a remedy for oppression. Just here, the idea of a total separation of the colonies from the Crown was born! It was a startling idea, much more so than we at this distance of time regard it. The timid and the prudent (as has been intimated) of that day were, of course, shocked and alarmed by it.

Such people lived then, had lived before and will, probably, ever have a place on this planet; and their course, in respect to any great change (no matter how great the good to be attained, or the wrong to be redressed by it), may be calculated with as much precision as can be the course of the stars. They hate all changes, but silver, gold and copper change! Of this sort of change they are always strongly in favor.

These people were called tories in the days of your fathers; and the appellation probably conveyed the same idea that is meant by a more modern, though a somewhat less euphonious term, which we often find in our papers, applied to some of our old politicians.

Their opposition to the then dangerous thought was earnest and powerful; but, amid all their terror and affrighted vociferations against it, the alarming and revolutionary idea moved on, and the country with it.

On the second of July, 1776, the old Continental Congress, to the dismay of the lovers of ease, and the worshipers of property, clothed that dreadful idea with all the authority of national sanction. They did so in the form of a resolution; and as we seldom hit upon resolutions drawn up in our day whose transparency is all equal to this, it may refresh your minds and help my story if I read it.

[We] solemnly publish and declare, That these United Colonies are, and of Right, ought to be Free and Independent States; that they are Absolved from all Allegiance to the British Crown, and that all political connection between them and the State of Great Britain is and ought to be [totally] dissolved.

Citizens, your fathers made good that resolution. They succeeded; and today you reap the fruits of their success. The freedom gained is yours; and you, therefore, may properly celebrate this anniversary. The Fourth of July is the first great fact in your nation's history—the very ringbolt in the chain of your yet undeveloped destiny.

Pride and patriotism, not less than gratitude, prompt you to celebrate and to hold it in perpetual remembrance. I have said that the Declaration of Independence is the ringbolt to the chain of your nation's destiny; so, indeed, I regard it. The principles contained in that instrument are saving principles. Stand by those principles, be true to them on all occasions, in all places, against all foes, and at whatever cost.

From the round top of your ship of state, dark and threatening clouds may be seen. Heavy billows, like mountains in the distance, disclose to the leeward huge forms of flinty rocks! That bolt drawn, that chain broken, and all is lost. Cling to this day—cling to it, and to its principles, with the grasp of a storm-tossed mariner to a spar at midnight.

The coming into being of a nation, in any circumstances, is an interesting event. But, besides general considerations, there were peculiar circumstances which make the advent of this republic an event of special attractiveness.

The whole scene, as I look back to it, was simple, dignified and sublime. The population of the country, at the time, stood at the insignificant number of three millions. The country was poor in the munitions of war. The population was weak and scattered, and the country a wilderness unsubdued. There were then no means of concert and combination, such as exist now. Neither stream nor lightning had then been reduced to order and discipline. From the Potomac to the Delaware was a journey of many days. Under these and innumerable other disadvantages, your fathers declared for liberty and independence and triumphed.

Fellow citizens, I am not wanting in respect for the fathers of this republic. The signers of the Declaration of Independence were brave men. They were great men, too—great enough to give frame to great age. It does not often happen to a nation to raise, at one time, such a number of truly great men. The point from which I am compelled to view them is not, certainly, the most favorable; and yet I cannot contemplate their great deeds with less than admiration. They were statesmen, patriots and heroes, and for the good they did, and the principles they contended for, I will unite with you to honor their memory.

They loved their country better than their own private interests; and, though this is not the highest form of human excellence, all will concede that it is a rare virtue, and that when it is exhibited it ought to command respect. He who will intelligently lay down his life for his country is a man whom it is not in human nature to despise. Your fathers staked their lives, their fortunes and their sacred honor on the cause of their country. In their admiration of liberty, they lost sight of all other interests.

They were peace men; but they preferred revolution to peaceful submission to bondage. They were quiet men; but they did not shrink from agitating against oppression. They showed forbearance, but that they knew its limits. They believed in order, but not in the order of tyranny. With them, nothing was "settled" that was not right. With them, justice, liberty and humanity were "final," not slavery and oppression. You may well cherish the memory of such men. They were great in their day and generation. Their solid manhood stands out the more as we contrast it with these degenerate times.

How circumspect, exact and proportionate were all their movements! How unlike the politicians of an hour! Their statesmanship looked beyond the passing moment, and stretched away in strength into the distant future. They seized upon eternal principles and set a glorious example in their defense. Mark them!

Fully appreciating the hardships to be encountered, firmly believing in the right of their cause, honorably inviting the scrutiny of an on-looking world, reverently appealing to heaven to attest their sincerity, soundly comprehending the solemn responsibility they were about to assume, wisely measuring the terrible odds against them, your fathers, the fathers of this republic, did most deliberately, under the inspiration of a glorious patriotism and with a sublime faith in the great principles of justice and freedom, lay deep the cornerstone of the national superstructure, which has risen and still rises in grandeur around you.

Of this fundamental work, this day is the anniversary. Our eyes are met with demonstrations of joyous enthusiasm. Banners and pennants wave exultingly on the breeze. The din of business too is hushed. Even Mammon seems to have quitted his grasp on this day. The ear-piercing fife and the stirring drum unite their accents with the ascending peal of a thousand church bells. Prayers are made, hymns are sung and sermons are preached in honor of this day; while the quick martial tramp of a great and multitudinous nation, echoes back by all the hills, valleys and mountains of a vast continent, bespeak the occasion one of thrilling and universal interest—a nation's jubilee.

Friends and citizens, I need not enter further into the causes which led to this anniversary. Many of you understand them better than I do. You could instruct me in regard to them. That is a branch of knowledge in which you feel, perhaps, a much deeper interest than your speaker. The causes which led to the separation of the colonies from the British Crown have never lacked for a tongue. They have all been taught in your common schools, narrated at your firesides, unfolded from your pulpits, and thundered from your legislative halls, and are as familiar to you as household words. They form the staple of your national poetry and eloquence.

I remember also that as a people Americans are remarkably familiar with all facts which make in their own favor. This is esteemed by some as a national trait—perhaps a national weakness. It is a fact that whatever makes for the wealth or for the reputation of Americans and can be had cheap will be found by Americans. I shall not be charged with slandering Americans if I say I think the American side of any question may be safely left in American hands.

I leave, therefore, the great deeds of your fathers to other gentlemen whose claim to have been regularly descended will be less likely to be disputed than mine!

My business, if I have any here today, is with the present. The accepted time with God and His cause is the ever-living now.

> Trust no future, however pleasant,
>   Let the dead past bury its dead;
> Act, act in the living present,
>   Heart within, and God overhead.*

We have to do with the past only as we can make it useful to the present and to the future. To all inspiring motives, to noble deeds which can be gained from the past, we are welcome. But now is the time, the important time. Your fathers have lived, died, and have done their work, and have done much of it well. You live and must die, and you must do your work. You have no right to enjoy a child's share in the labor of your fathers, unless your children are to be blest by your labors. You have no right to wear out and waste the hard-earned fame of your fathers to cover your indolence. Sydney Smith[†] tells us that men seldom eulogize the wisdom and virtues of their fathers, but to excuse some folly or wickedness of their own. This truth is not a doubtful one. There are illustrations of it near and remote, ancient and modern. It was fashionable, hundreds of years ago, for the children of Jacob to boast, we have "Abraham to our father," when they had long lost Abraham's faith and spirit. That people contented themselves under the shadow of Abraham's great name, while they repudiated the deeds which made his name great. Need I remind you that a similar thing is being done all over this country today? Need I tell you that the Jews are not the only people who built the tombs of the prophets, and garnished the sepulchers of the righteous? Washington could not die till he had broken the chains of his slaves. Yet his monument is built up by the price of human blood, and the traders in the bodies and souls of men shout—"We have Washington to *our father.*"—Alas! that it should be so; yet so it is.

*From Henry Wadsworth Longfellow's "A Psalm of Life."
†Smith (1771–1845) was a Whig satirist and essayist.

The evil that men do, lives after them,
*The good is oft interred with their bones.**

Fellow citizens, pardon me, allow me to ask, why am I called upon to speak here today? What have I, or those I represent, to do with your national independence? Are the great principles of political freedom and of natural justice, embodied in that Declaration of Independence, extended to us? and am I, therefore, called upon to bring our humble offering to the national altar and to confess the benefits and express devout gratitude for the blessings resulting from your independence to us?

Would to God, both for your sakes and ours, that an affirmative answer could be truthfully returned to these questions! Then would my task be light and my burden easy and delightful. For *who* is there so cold that a nation's sympathy could not warm him? Who so obdurate and dead to the claims of gratitude that would not thankfully acknowledge such priceless benefits? Who so stolid and selfish that would not give his voice to swell the hallelujahs of a nation's jubilee, when the chains of servitude had been torn from his limbs? I am not that man. In a case like that, the dumb might eloquently speak, and the "lame man leap as an hart."

But such is not the state of the case. I say it with a sad sense of the disparity between us. I am not included within the pale of this glorious anniversary! Your high independence only reveals the immeasurable distance between us. The blessings in which you, this day, rejoice, are not enjoyed in common. The rich inheritance of justice, liberty, prosperity and independence, bequeathed by your fathers, is shared by you, not by me. The sunlight that brought light and healing to you, has brought stripes and death to me. This Fourth of July is *yours,* not *mine. You* may rejoice, *I* must mourn. To drag a man in fetters into the grand illuminated temple of liberty and call upon him to join you in joyous anthems were inhuman mockery and sacrilegious irony. Do you mean, citizens, to mock me, by asking me to speak today? If so, there is a parallel to your conduct. And let me warn you that it is dangerous to copy the example of a nation whose crimes, towering up to heaven, were thrown down by the breath of the Almighty, burying that nation in irrevocable ruin! I can today take up the plaintive lament of a peeled and woe-smitten people!

"By the rivers of Babylon, there we sat down. Yea! we wept when we remembered Zion. We hanged our harps upon the willows in the midst thereof. For there they that carried us away captive required of us a song; and they that wasted us required of us mirth, saying, Sing us one of the songs of Zion. How shall we sing the Lord's song in a strange land? If I forget thee, O Jerusalem, let my right hand forget for cunning. If I do not remember thee, let my tongue cleave to the roof of my mouth."†

Fellow citizens, above your national, tumultuous joy I hear the mournful

---

Julius Caesar, act III, scene 2.
†Psalm 137.

wail of millions! whose chains, heavy and grievous yesterday, are today rendered more intolerable by the jubilee shouts that reach them. If I do forget, if I do not faithfully remember those bleeding children of sorrow this day, "may my right hand forget her cunning, and may my tongue cleave to the roof of my mouth!" To forget them, to pass lightly over their wrongs and to chime in with the popular theme would be treason most scandalous and shocking and would make me a reproach before God and the world. My subject, then, fellow citizens, is American slavery. I shall see this day and its popular characteristics from the slave's point of view. Standing there identified with the American bondman, making his wrongs mine, I do not hesitate to declare, with all my soul, that the character and conduct of this nation never looked blacker to me than on this Fourth of July. Whether we turn to the declarations of the past or to the professions of the present, the conduct of the nation seems equally hideous and revolting. America is false to the past, false to the present, and solemnly binds herself to be false to the future. Standing with God and the crushed and bleeding slave on this occasion, I will, in the name of humanity which is outraged, in the name of liberty which is fettered, in the name of the Constitution and the Bible which are disregarded and trampled upon, dare to call in question and to denounce, with all the emphasis I can command, everything that serves to perpetuate slavery—the great sin and shame of America! "I will not equivocate; I will not excuse";* I will use the severest language I can command; and yet not one word shall escape me that any man, whose judgement is not blinded by prejudice, or who is not at heart a slaveholder, shall not confess to be right and just.

But I fancy I hear some one of my audience say, "It is just in this circumstance that you and your brother abolitionists fail to make a favorable impression on the public mind. Would you argue more and denounce less, would you persuade more and rebuke less, your cause would be much more likely to succeed." But, I submit, where all is plain there is nothing to be argued. What point in the antislavery creed would you have me argue? On what branch of the subject do the people of this country need light? Must I undertake to prove that the slave is a man? That point is conceded already. Nobody doubts it. The slaveholders themselves acknowledge it in the enactments of laws for their government. They acknowledge it when they punish disobedience on the part of the slave. There are seventy-two crimes in the state of Virginia which, if committed by a black man (no matter how ignorant he be), subject him to the punishment of death; while only two of the same crimes will subject a white man to the like punishment. What is this but the acknowledgment that the slave is a moral, intellectual and responsible being? The manhood of the slave is conceded. It is admitted in the fact that Southern statute books are covered with enactments forbidding, under severe fines and penalties, the teaching of the slave to read or to write. When

*These words were used by William Lloyd Garrison in the first issue of the *Liberator*, January 1, 1831.

you can point to any such laws in reference to the beasts of the field, then I may consent to argue the manhood of the slave. When the dogs in your streets, when the fowls of the air, when the cattle on your hills, when the fish of the sea and the reptiles that crawl shall be unable to distinguish the slave from a brute, *then* will I argue with you that the slave is a man!

For the present, it is enough to affirm the equal manhood of the Negro race. Is it not astonishing that, while we are plowing, planting and reaping, using all kinds of mechanical tools, erecting houses, constructing bridges, building ships, working in metals of brass, iron, copper, silver and gold; that, while we are reading, writing and ciphering, acting as clerks, merchants and secretaries, having among us lawyers, doctors, ministers, poets, authors, editors, orators and teachers; that, while we are engaged in all manner of enterprises common to other men, digging gold in California, capturing the whale in the Pacific, feeding sheep and cattle on the hillside, living, moving, acting, thinking, planning, living in families as husbands, wives and children, and, above all, confessing and worshiping the Christian's God and looking hopefully for life and immortality beyond the grave, we are called upon to prove that we are men!

Would you have me argue that man is entitled to liberty? that he is the rightful owner of his own body? You have already declared it. Must I argue the wrongfulness of slavery? Is that a question for republicans? Is it to be settled by the rules of logic and argumentation, as a matter beset with great difficulty, involving a doubtful application of the principle of justice, hard to be understood? How should I look today, in the presence of Americans, dividing and subdividing a discourse, to show that men have a natural right to freedom, speaking of it relatively and positively, negatively and affirmatively? To do so would be to make myself ridiculous and to offer an insult to your understanding. There is not a man beneath the canopy of heaven that does not know that slavery is wrong *for him.*

What, am I to argue that it is wrong to make men brutes, to rob them of their liberty, to work them without wages, to keep them ignorant of their relations to their fellow men, to beat them with sticks, to flay their flesh with the lash, to load their limbs with irons, to hunt them with dogs, to sell them at auction, to sunder their families, to knock out their teeth, to burn their flesh, to starve them into obedience and submission to their masters? Must I argue that a system thus marked with blood and stained with pollution is *wrong?* No! I will not. I have better employment for my time and strength than such arguments would imply.

What, then, remains to be argued? Is it that slavery is not divine; that God did not establish it; that our doctors of divinity are mistaken? There is blasphemy in the thought. That which is inhuman, cannot be divine! *Who* can reason on such a proposition? They that can, may; I cannot. The time for such argument is passed.

At a time like this, scorching irony, not convincing argument, is needed. O! had I the ability, and could reach the nation's ear, I would, today, pour out a fiery stream of biting ridicule, blasting reproach, withering sarcasm and stern rebuke. For it is not light that is needed, but fire; it is not the gentle shower, but thunder. We need the storm, the whirlwind, and the earthquake. The feeling of the nation must be quickened; the conscience of the nation must be roused; the propriety of the nation must be startled; the hypocrisy of the nation must be exposed; and its crimes against God and man must be proclaimed and denounced.

What, to the American slave, is your Fourth of July? I answer: a day that reveals to him, more than all other days in the year, the gross injustice and cruelty to which he is the constant victim. To him, your celebration is a sham; your boasted liberty an unholy license; your national greatness swelling vanity; your sounds of rejoicing are empty and heartless; your denunciation of tyrants brass-fronted impudence; your shouts of liberty and equality hollow mockery; your prayers and hymns, your sermons and thanksgivings, with all your religious parade and solemnity, are to Him mere bombast, fraud, deception, impiety and hypocrisy—a thin veil to cover up crimes which would disgrace a nation of savages. There is not a nation on the earth guilty of practices more shocking and bloody than are the people of the United States at this very hour.

Go where you may, search where you will, roam through all the monarchies and despotisms of the Old World, travel through South America, search out every abuse, and when you have found the last, lay your facts by the side of the everyday practices of this nation, and you will say with me, that, for revolting barbarity and shameless hypocrisy, America reigns without a rival.

Take the American slave trade, which, we are told by the papers, is especially prosperous just now. Ex-Senator Benton* tells us that the price of men was never higher than now. He mentions the fact to show that slavery is in no danger. This trade is one of the peculiarities of American institutions. It is carried on in all the large towns and cities in one half of this confederacy; and millions are pocketed every year by dealers in this horrid traffic. In several states this trade is a chief source of wealth. It is called (in contradistinction to the foreign slave trade) *the internal slave trade.* It is probably called so, too, in order to divert from it the horror with which the foreign slave trade is contemplated. That trade has long since been denounced by this government as piracy. It has been denounced with burning words from the high places of the nation as an execrable traffic. To arrest it, to put an end to it, this nation keeps a squadron, at immense cost, on the coast of Africa. Everywhere in this country it is safe to speak of this foreign slave trade as a most inhuman traffic, opposed alike to the laws of God and of man. The duty to extirpate and destroy it is admitted even by our doctors of divinity. In order to put an end to it, some of these last have consented that their colored brethren (nominally free) should leave this country, and establish themselves on the western coast of Africa! It is, however, a notable fact that, while so much execration is poured out by Americans upon all

*Thomas Hart Benton (1782–1858).

those engaged in the foreign slave trade, the men engaged in the slave trade between the states pass without condemnation, and their business is deemed honorable.

Behold the practical operation of this internal slave trade, the American slave trade, sustained by American politics and American religion. Here you will see men and women reared like swine for the market. You know what is a swine-drover? I will show you a man-drover. They inhabit all our Southern states. They perambulate the country and crowd the highways of the nation with droves of human stock. You will see one of these human flesh jobbers, armed with pistol, whip and bowie knife, driving a company of a hundred men, women and children, from the Potomac to the slave market at New Orleans. These wretched people are to be sold singly or in lots, to suit purchasers. They are food for the cotton field and the deadly sugar mill. Mark the sad procession, as it moves wearily along, and the inhuman wretch who drives them. Hear his savage yells and his bloodcurdling oaths, as he hurries on his affrighted captives! There, see the old man with locks thinned and gray. Cast one glance, if you please, upon that young mother, whose shoulders are bare to the scorching sun, her briny tears falling on the brow of the babe in her arms. See, too, that girl of thirteen, weeping—*yes*, weeping—as she thinks of the mother from whom she has been torn! The drove moves tardily. Heat and sorrow have nearly consumed their strength; suddenly you hear a quick snap, like the discharge of a rifle; the fetters clank, and the chain rattles simultaneously; your ears are saluted with a scream, that seems to have torn its way to the center of your soul! The crack you heard was the sound of the slave whip; the scream you heard was from the woman you saw with the babe. Her speed had faltered under the weight of her child and her chains! That gash on her shoulder tells her to move on. Follow this drove to New Orleans. Attend the auction; see men examined like horses; see the forms of women rudely and brutally exposed to the shocking gaze of American slave buyers. See this drove sold and separated forever; and never forget the deep, sad sobs that arose from that scattered multitude. Tell me, citizens, where, under the sun, you can witness a spectacle more fiendish and shocking. Yet this is but a glance at the American slave trade, as it exists, at this moment, in the ruling part of the United States.

I was born amid such sights and scenes. To me the American slave trade is a terrible reality. When a child, my soul was often pierced with a sense of its horrors. I lived on Philpot Street, Fell's Point, Baltimore, and have watched from the wharves the slave ships in the Basin, anchored from the shore, with their cargoes of human flesh, waiting for favorable winds to waft them down the Chesapeake. There was at that time a grand slave mart kept at the head of Pratt Street by Austin Woldfolk. His agents were sent into every town and county in Maryland, announcing their arrival, through the papers, and on flaming *handbills* headed "Cash for Negroes." These men were generally well-dressed men, and very captivating in their manners; ever ready to drink, to treat and to gamble. The fate of many a slave has depended upon the turn of a single card; and many a child has been snatched from the arms of its mother by bargains arranged in a state of brutal drunkenness.

The flesh mongers gather up their victims by dozens, and drive them, chained, to the general depot at Baltimore. When a sufficient number has been collected here, a ship is chartered for the purpose of conveying the forlorn crew to Mobile, or to New Orleans. From the slave prison to the ship, they are usually driven in the darkness of night; for since the antislavery agitation a certain caution is observed.

In the deep, still darkness of midnight I have been often aroused by the dead, heavy footsteps and the piteous cries of the chained gangs that passed our door. The anguish of my boyish heart was intense; and I was often consoled, when speaking to my mistress in the morning, to hear her say that the custom was very wicked; that she hated to hear the rattle of the chains and the heart-rending cries. I was glad to find one who sympathized with me in my horror.

Fellow citizens, this murderous traffic is today in active operation in this boasted republic. In the solitude of my spirit I see clouds of dust raised on the highways of the South; I see the bleeding footsteps; I hear the doleful wail of fettered humanity on the way to the slave markets, where the victims are to be sold like *horses, sheep* and *swine,* knocked off to the highest bidder. There I see the tenderest ties ruthlessly broken, to gratify the lust, caprice and rapacity of the buyers and sellers of men. My soul sickens at the sight.

> Is this the land your Fathers loved,
>   The freedom which they toiled to win?
> Is this the earth whereon they moved?
>   Are these the graves they slumber in?*

But a still more inhuman, disgraceful and scandalous state of things remains to be presented. By an act of the American congress, not yet two years old, slavery has been nationalized in its most horrible and revolting form. By that act, Mason and Dixon's line has been obliterated; New York has become as Virginia; and the power to hold, hunt and sell men, women and children as slaves remains no longer a mere state institution, but is now an institution of the whole United States. The power is coextensive with the star-spangled banner and American Christianity. Where these go, may also go the merciless slave hunter. Where these are, man is not sacred. He is a bird for the sportsman's gun. By that most foul and fiendish of all human decrees, the liberty and person of every man are put in peril. Your broad republican domain is hunting ground for *men. Not* for thieves and robbers, enemies of society, merely, but for men guilty of no crime. Your lawmakers have commanded all good citizens to engage in this hellish sport. Your President, your Secretary of State, your *lords, nobles* and ecclesiastics enforce, as a duty

*From John Greenleaf Whittier, "Stanzas for the Times."

you owe to your free and glorious country, and to your God, that you do this accursed thing. Not fewer than forty Americans have, within the past two years, been hunted down and, without a moment's warning, hurried away in chains and consigned to slavery and excruciating torture. Some of these have had wives and children, dependent on them for bread; but of this, no account was made. The right of the hunter to his prey stands superior to the right of marriage and to *all* rights in this republic, the rights of God included! For black men there is neither law nor justice, humanity nor religion. The Fugitive Slave *Law* makes mercy to them a crime; and bribes the judge who tries them. An American judge gets ten dollars for every victim he consigns to slavery, and five, when he fails to do so.* The oath of any two villains is sufficient, under this hell-black enactment, to send the most pious and exemplary black man into the remorseless jaws of slavery! His own testimony is nothing. He can bring no witnesses for himself. The minister of American justice is bound by the law to hear but *one* side; and *that* side is the side of the oppressor. Let this damning fact he perpetually told. Let it be thundered around the world that in tyrant-killing, king-hating, people-loving, democratic, Christian America the seats of justice are filled with judges who hold their offices under an open and palpable *bribe,* and are bound, in deciding the case of a man's liberty, *to hear only his accusers!*

In glaring violation of justice, in shameless disregard of the forms of administering law, in cunning arrangement to entrap the defenseless, and in diabolical intent, this Fugitive Slave Law stands alone in the annals of tyrannical legislation. I doubt if there be another nation on the globe having the brass and the baseness to put such a law on the statute book. If any man in this assembly thinks differently from me in this matter and feels able to disprove my statements, I will gladly confront him at any suitable time and place he may select.

I take this law to be one of the grossest infringements of Christian liberty, and if the churches and ministers of our country were not stupidly blind or most wickedly indifferent, they too would so regard it.

At the very moment that they are thanking God for the enjoyment of civil and religious liberty, and for the right to worship God according to the dictates of their own consciences, they are utterly silent in respect to a law which robs religion of its chief significance and makes it utterly worthless to a world lying in wickedness. Did this law concern the *"mint, anise and cummin,"* abridge the right to sing psalms, to partake of the sacrament or to engage in any of the ceremonies of religion, it would be smitten by the thunder of a thousand pulpits. A general shout would go up from the church demanding *repeal, repeal, instant repeal!* And it would go hard with that politician who presumed to solicit the votes of the people without inscribing this motto on his banner. Further, if this demand were not complied with,

---

*Under the Fugitive Slave Act of 1850 the federal commissioner was awarded ten dollars if he directed the escaped slave's return but only five dollars if he ordered the runaway's release.

another Scotland would be added to the history of religious liberty, and the stern old covenanters would be thrown into the shade. A John Knox would be seen at every church door and heard from every pulpit, and Fillmore would have no more quarter than was shown by Knox to the beautiful, but treacherous, Queen Mary of Scotland.* The fact that the church of our country (with fractional exceptions) does not esteem "the Fugitive Slave Law" as a declaration of war against religious liberty, implies that that church regards religion simply as a form of worship, an empty ceremony, and *not* a vital principle, requiring active benevolence, justice, love and good will towards man. It esteems sacrifice above mercy, psalm singing above right doing, solemn meetings above practical righteousness. A worship that can be conducted by persons who refuse to give shelter to the houseless, to give bread to the hungry, clothing to the naked, and who enjoin obedience to a law forbidding these acts of mercy is a curse, not a blessing to mankind. The Bible addresses all such persons as "scribes, pharisees, hypocrites, who pay tithe of *mint, anise* and *cummin,* and have omitted the weightier matters of the law, judgment, mercy and faith."[†]

But the church of this country is not only indifferent to the wrongs of the slave, it actually takes sides with the oppressors. It has made itself the bulwark of American slavery and the shield of American slave hunters. Many of its most eloquent divines, who stand as the very lights of the church, have shamelessly given the sanction of religion and the Bible to the whole slave system. They have taught that man may, properly, be a slave; that the relation of master and slave is ordained of God; that to send back an escaped bondman to his master is clearly the duty of all the followers of the Lord Jesus Christ; and this horrible blasphemy is palmed off upon the world for Christianity.

For my part, I would say, Welcome infidelity! welcome atheism! welcome anything—in preference to the gospel, *as preached by those divines.* They convert the very name of religion into an engine of tyranny and barbarous cruelty, and serve to confirm more infidels, in this age, than all the infidel writings of Thomas Paine, Voltaire and Bolingbroke put together have done! These ministers make religion a cold and flinty-hearted thing, having neither principles of right action nor bowels of compassion. They strip the love of God of its beauty and leave the throne of religion a huge, horrible, repulsive form. It is a religion for oppressors, tyrants, man stealers, and *thugs.* It is not that *"pure and undefiled religion"* which is from above, and which is *"first pure, then peaceable, easy to be entreated,* full of mercy and good fruits, *without partiality and without hypocrisy,"*[‡] but a religion which favors the rich against the poor; which exalts the proud above the humble; which divides mankind into two classes, tyrants and slaves; which says to the man in chains, *stay there,* and to the oppressor, *oppress on;* it is a reli-

---

*As president, Millard Fillmore (1800–1874) had signed the Fugitive Slave Act of 1850.
[†]Matthew, 23:23.
[‡]James 1:27, 3:17.

gion which may be professed and enjoyed by all the robbers and enslavers of mankind; it makes God a respecter of persons, denies his fatherhood of the race, and tramples in the dust the great truth of the brotherhood of man. All this we affirm to be true of the popular church, and the popular worship of our land and nation—a religion, a church, and a worship which, on the authority of inspired wisdom, we pronounce to be an abomination in the sight of God. In the language of Isaiah, the American church might be well addressed, "Bring no more vain oblations; incense is an abomination unto me: the new moons and Sabbaths, the calling of assemblies, I cannot away with; it is iniquity, even the solemn meeting. Your new moons, and your appointed feasts my soul hateth. They are a trouble to me; I am weary to bear them; and when ye spread forth your hands I will hide mine eyes from you. Yea! when ye make many prayers, I will not hear. *Your hands are full of blood*; cease to do evil, learn to do well; seek judgment; relieve the oppressed; judge for the fatherless; plead for the widow."*

The American church is guilty, when viewed in connection with what it is doing to uphold slavery; but it is superlatively guilty when viewed in its connection with its ability to abolish slavery.

The sin of which it is guilty is one of omission as well as of commission. Albert Barnes but uttered what the common sense of every man at all observant of the actual state of the case will receive as truth, when he declared that "there is no power out of the church that could sustain slavery an hour, if it were not sustained in it."[†]

Let the religious press, the pulpit, the Sunday school, the conference meeting, the great ecclesiastical, missionary, Bible and tract associations of the land array their immense powers against slavery and slaveholding; and the whole system of crime and blood would be scattered to the winds, and that they do not do this involves them in the most awful responsibility of which the mind can conceive.

In prosecuting the antislavery enterprise, we have been asked to spare the church, to spare the ministry; but *how*, we ask, could such a thing be done? We are met on the threshold of our efforts for the redemption of the slave, by the church and ministry of the country, in battle arrayed against us; and we are compelled to fight or flee. From *what* quarter, I beg to know, has proceeded a fire so deadly upon our ranks, during the last two years, as from the Northern pulpit? As the champions of oppressors, the chosen men of American theology have appeared—men honored for their so-called piety, and their real learning. The Lords of Buffalo, the Springs of New York, the Lathrops of Auburn, the Coxes and Spencers of Brooklyn, the Gannets and Sharps of Boston, the Deweys of Washington, and other great religious lights of the land have, in utter denial of the authority of *Him* by whom they professed to be called to the ministry, deliberately taught us, against the exam-

*Isaiah 1.
[†]Albert Barnes (1798–1870), *An Inquiry into the Scriptural Views of Slavery* (Philadelphia, 1846), 383.

ple of the Hebrews and against the remonstrance of the Apostles, *that we ought to obey man's law before the law of God.*[*]

My spirit wearies of such blasphemy; and how such men can be supported as the "standing types and representatives of Jesus Christ" is a mystery which I leave others to penetrate. In speaking of the American church, however, let it be distinctly understood that I mean the *great mass* of the religious organizations of our land. There are exceptions, and I thank God that there are. Noble men may be found, scattered all over these Northern states, of whom Henry Ward Beecher, of Brooklyn; Samuel J. May, of Syracuse; and my esteemed friend [Rev. R. R. Raymond] on the platform, are shining examples; and let me say further, that upon these men lies the duty to inspire our ranks with high religious faith and zeal, and to cheer us on in the great mission of the slave's redemption from his chains.

One is struck with the difference between the attitude of the American church toward the antislavery movement and that occupied by the churches in England toward a similar movement in that country. There, the church, true to its mission of ameliorating, elevating and improving the condition of mankind, came forward promptly, bound up the wounds of the West Indian slave, and restored him to his liberty. There, the question of emancipation was a high religious question. It was demanded in the name of humanity and according to the law of the living God. The Sharps, the Clarksons, the Wilberforces, the Buxtons, the Burchells, and the Knibbs were alike famous for their piety and for their philanthropy.[†] The antislavery movement *there* was not an antichurch movement, for the reason that the church took its full share in prosecuting that movement: and the antislavery movement in this country will cease to be an antichurch movement when the church of this country shall assume a favorable instead of a hostile position towards that movement.

Americans! your republican politics, not less than your republican religion, are flagrantly inconsistent. You boast of your love of liberty, your superior civilization and your pure Christianity, while the whole political power of the nation (as embodied in the two great political parties) is solemnly pledged to support and perpetuate the enslavement of three millions of your countrymen. You hurl your anathemas at the crowned-headed tyrants of Russia and Austria and pride yourselves on your democratic institutions, while you yourselves consent to be the mere *tools* and *bodyguards* of the tyrants of Virginia and Carolina. You invite to your shores fugitives of oppression from abroad, honor them with banquets, greet them with ovations, cheer them, toast them, salute them, protect them, and pour out your money

---

[*]At the request of the Union Safety Committee of New York City, formed by conservative merchants, the clergymen of New York agreed to set aside December 12, 1850, as a day on which sermons would be delivered upholding the Compromise of 1850, especially the Fugitive Slave Act. Practically all the sermons advised acquiescence to the law and denounced the "higher law" doctrine.

[†]Granville Sharp, Thomas Clarkson, William Wilberforce, Thomas Buxton, Thomas Burchell, and William Knibb.

to them like water; but the fugitives from your own land you advertise, hunt, arrest, shoot and kill. You glory in your refinement and your universal education; yet you maintain a system as barbarous and dreadful as ever stained the character of a nation—a system begun in avarice, supported in pride, and perpetuated in cruelty. You shed tears over fallen Hungary, and make the sad story of her wrongs the theme of your poets, statesmen and orators, till your gallant sons are ready to fly to arms to vindicate her cause against the oppressor;* but, in regard to the ten thousand wrongs of the American slave, you would enforce the strictest silence and would hail him as an enemy of the nation who dares to make those wrongs the subject of public discourse! You are all on fire at the mention of liberty for France or for Ireland, but are as cold as an iceberg at the thought of liberty for the enslaved of America. You discourse eloquently on the dignity of labor; yet, you sustain a system which, in its very essence, casts a stigma upon labor. You can bare your bosom to the storm of British artillery to throw off a three-penny tax on tea, and yet wring the last hard-earned farthing from the grasp of the black laborers of your country. You profess to believe "that of one blood God made all nations of men to dwell on the face of all the earth"† and hath commanded all men, everywhere, to love one another; yet you notoriously hate (and glory in your hatred) all men whose skins are not colored like your own. You declare before the world, and are understood by the world to declare, that you *"hold these truths to be self-evident, that all men are created equal; and are endowed by their Creator with certain unalienable rights; and that among these are, life, liberty and the pursuit of happiness"*; and yet, you hold securely, in a bondage which, according to your own Thomas Jefferson, *"is worse than ages of that which your fathers rose in rebellion to oppose," a seventh part* of the inhabitants of your country.

Fellow citizens, I will not enlarge further on your national inconsistencies. The existence of slavery in this country brands your republicanism as a sham, your humanity as a base pretense, and your Christianity as a lie. It destroys your moral power abroad; it corrupts your politicians at home. It saps the foundation of religion; it makes your name a hissing and a byword to a mocking earth. It is the antagonistic force in your government, the only thing that seriously disturbs and endangers your union. It fetters your progress; it is the enemy of improvement; the deadly foe of education; it fosters pride; it breeds insolence; it promotes vice; it shelters crime; it is a curse to the earth that supports it; and yet you cling to it as if it were the sheet anchor of all your hopes. Oh, be warned! Be warned! A horrible reptile is coiled up in your nation's bosom; the venomous creature is nursing at the tender breast of your youthful republic; *for the love of God, tear away* and fling from you the hideous monster, and *let the weight of twenty millions crush and destroy it forever!*

But it is answered in reply to all this, that precisely what I have now

---

*The fledgling Hungarian republic was invaded by Austria and Russia in 1849.
†Acts 17:26.

denounced is, in fact, guaranteed and sanctioned by the Constitution of the United States, that the right to hold and to hunt slaves is a part of that Constitution framed by the illustrious Fathers of this Republic.

Then, I dare to affirm, notwithstanding all I have said before, your fathers stooped, basely stooped

> *To palter with us in a double sense:*
> *And keep the word of promise to the ear,*
> *But break it to the heart.**

And instead of being the honest men I have before declared them to be, they were the veriest impostors that ever practiced on mankind. This is the inevitable conclusion, and from it there is no escape; but I differ from those who charge this baseness on the framers of the Constitution of the United States. It is a slander upon their memory, at least, so I believe. There is not time now to argue the Constitutional question at length; nor have I the ability to discuss it as it ought to be discussed. The subject has been handled with masterly power by Lysander Spooner, Esq., by William Goodell, by Samuel E. Sewall, Esq., and last, though not least, by Gerrit Smith, Esq. These gentlemen have, as I think, fully and clearly vindicated the Constitution from any design to support slavery for an hour.

Fellow citizens, there is no matter in respect to which the people of the North have allowed themselves to be so ruinously imposed upon as that of the proslavery character of the constitution. In that instrument, I hold, there is neither warrant, license nor sanction of the hateful thing; but, interpreted as it ought to be interpreted, the Constitution is a glorious liberty document. Read its preamble, consider its purposes. Is slavery among them? Is it at the gateway? Or is it in the temple? It is neither. While I do not intend to argue this question on the present occasion, let me ask, if it be not somewhat singular that, if the Constitution were intended to be, by its framers and adopters, a slaveholding instrument, why neither *slavery, slaveholding* nor *slave* can anywhere be found in it. What would be thought of an instrument, drawn up, legally drawn up, for the purpose of entitling the city of Rochester to a tract of land, in which no mention of land was made? Now, there are certain rules of interpretation for the proper understanding of all legal instruments. These rules are well established. They are plain, common-sense rules, such as you and I and all of us can understand and apply, without having passed years in the study of law. I scout the idea that the question of the constitutionality, or unconstitutionality of slavery, is not a question for the people. I hold that every American citizen has a right to form an opinion of the Constitution, and to propagate that opinion, and to use all honorable means to make his opinion the prevailing one. Without this right, the liberty of an American citizen would be as insecure as that of a Frenchman. Ex-

*Based on *Macbeth*, act V, scene 8, 20–22.

Vice-President Dallas tells us that the Constitution is an object to which no American mind can be too attentive, and no American heart too devoted. He further says, the Constitution, in its words, is plain and intelligible, and is meant for the home-bred, unsophisticated understanding of our fellow citizens. Senator Berrien tells us that the Constitution is the fundamental law, that which controls all others.* The charter of our liberties, which every citizen has a personal interest in understanding thoroughly. The testimony of Senator [Sidney] Breese, Lewis Cass, and many others that might be named, who are everywhere esteemed as sound lawyers, so regard the Constitution. I take it, therefore, that it is not presumption in a private citizen to form an opinion of that instrument.

Now, take the Constitution according to its plain reading, and I defy the presentation of a single proslavery clause in it. On the other hand, it will be found to contain principles and purposes, entirely hostile to the existence of slavery.

I have detained my audience entirely too long already. At some future period I will gladly avail myself of an opportunity to give this subject a full and fair discussion.

Allow me to say, in conclusion, notwithstanding the dark picture I have this day presented, of the state of the nation, I do not despair of this country. There are forces in operation which must inevitably work the downfall of slavery. "The arm of the Lord is not shortened,"[†] and the doom of slavery is certain. I, therefore, leave off where I began, with hope. While drawing encouragement from "the Declaration of Independence," the great principles it contains and the genius of American institutions, my spirit is also cheered by the obvious tendencies of the age. Nations do not now stand in the same relation to each other that they did ages ago. No nation can now shut itself up from the surrounding world and trot round in the same old path of its fathers without interference. The time was when such could be done. Long-established customs of hurtful character could formerly fence themselves in and do their evil work with social impunity. Knowledge was then confined and enjoyed by the privileged few, and the multitude walked on in mental darkness. But a change has now come over the affairs of mankind. Walled cities and empires have become unfashionable. The arm of commerce has borne away the gates of the strong city. Intelligence is penetrating the darkest corners of the globe. It makes its pathway over and under the sea, as well as on the earth. Wind, steam and lightning are its chartered agents. Oceans no longer divide, but link nations together. From Boston to London is now a holiday excursion. Space is comparatively annihilated. Thoughts expressed on one side of the Atlantic are distinctly heard on the other.

The far-off and almost fabulous Pacific rolls in grandeur at our feet. The Celestial Empire, the mystery of ages, is being solved. The fiat of the Al-

*Both George Dallas of Pennsylvania and John M. Berrien of Georgia supported the Compromise of 1850 and enforcement of the Fugitive Slave Law.
†Isaiah 59:1.

mighty, "Let there be Light," has not yet spent its force. No abuse, no out-rage, whether in taste, sport or avarice, can now hide itself from the all-per-vading light. The iron shoe and crippled foot of China must be seen in con-trast with nature. Africa must rise and put on her yet unwoven garment. "Ethiopia shall stretch out her hand unto God." In the fervent aspirations of William Lloyd Garrison, I say, and let every heart join in saying it,

> God speed the year of jubilee
>   The wide world o'er!
> When from their galling chains set free,
> Th' oppress'd shall vilely bend the knee,
> And wear the yoke of tyranny
>   Like brutes no more.
> That year will come, and freedom's reign,
> To man his plundered rights again
>   Restore.
>
> God speed the day when human blood
>   Shall cease to flow!
> In every clime be understood,
> The claims of human brotherhood,
> And each return for evil, good,
>   Not blow for blow;
> That day will come all feuds to end,
> And change into a faithful friend
>   Each foe.
>
> God speed the hour, the glorious hour,
>   When none on earth
> Shall exercise a lordly power,
> Nor in a tyrant's presence cower;
> But to all manhood's stature tower,
>   By equal birth!
> That hour will come, to each, to all,
> And from his prison-house, the thrall
>   Go forth.
>
> Until that year, day, hour, arrive
> With head, and heart, and hand I'll strive,
> To break the rod, and rend the gyve,
> The spoiler of his prey deprive—
>   So witness Heaven!
> And never from my chosen post,
> Whate'er the peril or the cost,
>   Be driven.*■

---

*William Lloyd Garrison, "The Triumph of Freedom," *Liberator*, January 10, 1845.

47 SNAKES AND GEESE

Sojourner Truth

The fourth National Woman's Rights Convention, held in New York City in September 1853, provided an "overt exhibition of that public sentiment woman was then combating," according to Stanton's History of Woman Suffrage (547). Young men bent on disrupting the proceedings paid for admission to the hall, then heaped abuse upon the women speakers. But no speaker at the "Mob Convention" received more demeaning and abusive treatment than Sojourner Truth, who by virtue of being both black and female combined "the two most hated elements of humanity" (567). Moreover, no speaker proved more capable of turning the hecklers' insults against them.

When Truth rose to speak in the afternoon session on September 7, the convention's second day, she was greeted with "a perfect storm of applause, hisses, groans and undignified ejaculations," according to the reporter for the New York Times.

> One lad, with red hair, whose education had evidently been grievously neglected, insinuated that the colored lady was not then acting in her accustomed sphere, by calling for "an oyster stew with plenty of crackers." Another scape-grace called vociferously for a "sixpenny plate of clam soup."

Undeterred, Truth "came forward to the desk, rolled up her eyeballs in scorn, and raised her hand and voice in wrath." Her remarks compare the taunts and hisses of the hecklers to the calls of snakes and geese and make clear that the movement for women's rights will not be delayed by such disruptions: "You may hiss as much as you like, like any other lot of geese, but you can't stop it; it's bound to come." Truth likens her audience to the biblical King Haman, persecutor of Jews, who was himself hanged on the gallows he had prepared for his victims.

Dressed in a blue gown and black pinafore, with a white cotton kerchief on her head, Truth spoke with anger and force at a volume sufficient to be heard over the interjections of her tormenters. According to the astonished Times reporter:

> Ye who have not heard the roar of the cataract can form but a meagre idea of the volume of sound that gushed forth upon the devoted audience. Imagine Trinity Church organ . . . with its low bass and trumpet stops pulled out, all the keys down, and two men and a boy working for dear life at the bellows, and you have a gentle specimen of the angry voice of Sojourner Truth.

Below is the text of Truth's speech, as published in the New York Times *of September 8, 1853, complete with the reporter's transcription of some of the audience comments—for and against Truth—shouted out during her speech. For further information, see Erlene Stetson and Linda David,* Glorying in Tribulation: The Lifework of Sojourner Truth *(East Lansing: Michigan State University Press, 1994); and Nell Irvin Painter, "Sojourner Truth in Life and Memory: Writing the Biography of an American Exotic,"* Gender and History *(1990), 3–16.*

It is good for me to come forth for to see what kind of spirit you are made of.* I see some of you have got the spirit of a goose, and a good many of you have got the spirit of snakes. [Great applause and cries of "Go on"— "That's the style"—"Show your pluck"—"Give it to them;" during which that young scrape-grace in the gallery called for a "small fry."] I feel at home here. [A venerable old gentleman occupying a front seat, said, "So you ought."] I was born in this State. I've been a slave in this State, and now I'm a good citizen of this State. [Vociferous demonstrations of applause.] I was born here, and I can tell you I feel to home here. [Queer man under the gallery: That's right. Make yourself at home, you're welcome; take a chair.] I've been looking round and watching things, and I know a little might 'bout Woman's Rights, too. [Applause, and cries of "Go it lively; you'll have a fair show."] I know it feels funny, kinder funny and tickling to see a colored woman get up and tell you about things and woman's rights, when we've all been trampled down so't nobody thought we'd ever git up again. But we have come up, and I'm here. There was a king in old times in the Scripiters that said he'd give away half of his kingdom, and hang some body as Haman. Now, he was more liberaler than the present King of the United State, 'cause he wouldn't do that for the women. [Roars of laughter, on the conclusion of which, a middle-aged gentleman, with a florid countenance, short hair and old fashioned shirt collar, ventured to correct the lady as to the title of our present Chief Magistrate, but the lady would not change the name, and continued.] But we don't want him to kill the men, nor we don't want half of his kingdom; we only want half of our rights, and we don't get them neither. But we'll have them, see'f we don't and you can't stop us, neither; see'f you can! [Applause, and some hissing.] Oh, you may hiss as much as you please, like any other lot of geese, but you can't stop it; it's bound to come. [That young rascal, with the dirty shirt and face—"Hurry up that stew; its bilin'."] You see the women don't get half as much rights as they ought to get. We want more, and will have it [Loud laughter.] Then you see the Bible says,

---

*In the version of the speech published in Elizabeth Cady Stanton, Susan B. Anthony, and Frances Gage, *History of Woman Suffrage,* vol. 1 (Rochester, N.Y.: Fowler and Wells, 1881), 567–68, the opening line is: "Is it not good for me to come and draw forth a spirit?" Carla Peterson has argued that this beginning reflects central African ceremonial practice; see *Doers of the Word* (New York: Oxford University Press, 1995), 54.

sons and daughters ought to behave themselves before their mothers; but they don't; I'm watching, and I can see them a snickering, and pinting and laughing at their mothers up here on the stage. [That young scape-grace again—"My mother ain't up there, an' I don't believe anybody's mother is." Applause.] They ought to be ashamed. They ought to know better, an' if they'd been brought up proper they would. [Queer man under the gallery— "They ought to be spanked." Roars of laughter.] Woman's sphere ought to rise—rise as high as hanged Haman, and spread out all over. [Great applause, and that queer man under the gallery insinuated that that might be done by the least possible extension of their bustles.] I'm round watching things, and I wanted to come up and say these few things to you, and I'm much obliged for your listening. I wanted to tell you a little might about Woman's Rights, and so I come out and said so. I'll be around agin sometime. I'm watching things, and I'll git up agin, an' tell you what time o'night it is. [Great applause.] And, with another request from the young rascals to "hurry up them stews and things," the lady took a seat on the steps, which lead to the platform.■

48 I SET OUT TO ESCAPE FROM SLAVERY

Stephen Pembroke

Stephen Pembroke and his two teenaged sons escaped from slavery in Maryland on May 21, 1854. Pursued to New York, they were captured and returned to Baltimore. Slaveholder Jacob Grove then wrote to Pembroke's brother, the Rev. James W. C. Pennington, offering to sell Stephen. On May 30, Pembroke was allowed to dictate a letter to his brother, encouraging him to pay Grove's price. "Act promptly, as I will have to be sold to the South," he told his brother. "My two sons were sold to the drivers" and "I am confined to my rooms with irons on." Pennington paid Groves, and Pembroke joined him in New York City.

Pennington (1807–1870) had himself escaped from slavery in 1827. He became a prominent antislavery lecturer in the 1830s and was pastor of the First Presbyterian Church. In 1841, he published A Textbook of the Origin and History of the Colored People, *one of the earliest works of African American history.*

On July 18, 1854, Pembroke and Pennington addressed a small audience in New York's Tabernacle. After Pembroke had spoken, Pennington informed the audience that although his brother was now legally manu-mitted, he "was still laboring under fear of slavery," afraid to walk the streets lest he be seized and returned. The speech is reprinted from John Blassingame, ed., Slave Testimony: Two Centuries of Letters, Speeches, In-terviews, and Autobiographies *(Baton Rouge: Louisiana State University Press, 1977), 167–68.*

I set out to escape from slavery on the 1st May last, with my two sons. We walked all night, and went fifty odd miles without stopping. We got as far as New-York City, where we were violently arrested, secured, and taken back to the South. I was treated in a bad manner here. I had no counsel, and did not know what the law was. I remained fifteen days in the South under chains, locked up by night. I ate and slept chained. I was kept so till my arms swelled and my appetite gone. I was so until bought through the benevolence of the public and the exertions of my brother, whom I had not seen for 30 years. Some suppose slavery not to be what it is said to be, but I am right down upon it. I was fifty years in it, and it has many degrees. I have been in three of them. In thirty years I was sold three times. I served one man for twenty years. He was a rigid and wicked man. I have seen men tied up, whipped, shot, and starved. Then there was a moderate degree; and then I got into that, which I left, after being twenty years in it. It has left life in me, that is all. I served a man twenty years for 400 dollars, and then he wanted 1000 dollars for me, after starving me and depriving me of all the comforts of life and worship of God.

The slave never knows when he is to be seized and scourged. My father was sold five times. The last time he was knocked down and seized by three men. I have seen men working all day, day in and day out, with iron collars on their necks, and so locked up at night, getting a pound of corn bread and half a pound of meat. I would rather die the death of the righteous than to be a slave, always under dread and never getting a good word. I used to say to my master, 'I am getting old, and ought to have some rest;' but he would answer, 'No sir, if you speak about freedom, I will sell you further South.'

For the last twenty years I had a free wife, and but for her labor I believe without the mercy of God, I would be this night in my grave. My pursuers were, I believe, in the same train by which I arrived here at 5 in the evening, and I was arrested at 7-¾ o'clock next morning. My pursuer told me there was a watch round the house all night. I had no counsel and did not know the law, nor what I should say, so I thought it better to let the law have its course. My first wife was a slave; so my five children are slaves too. Since my sons were arrested here, they were twice sold before my face. I saw them with their arms chained together, and my arms were chained, and my mas-ter's son lay in the room where I lay with a brace of pistols under his head; and when I turned over he would start up and lay his hand on me.

I know one man who gave his slave one hundred and fifty lashes in two days, and on the third he died. He crept into the field; and his master supposing he was sleeping, went up and cowhided him, but he was cowhiding a corpse, thinking he was asleep! Such is the condition of Slavery: it is a hard substance; you cannot break it or pull it apart, and the only way is to escape from it. I think it is the North that keeps up Slavery. Such is my opinion. I am thankful to the community that has been so kind and charitable to help me out of the scrape, and now I would like to have my sons out. (Applause)■

49 THERE IS NO FULL ENJOYMENT OF FREEDOM FOR ANYONE IN THIS COUNTRY

John Mercer Langston

 One of the foremost American orators, educators, and politicians of the nineteenth century, John Mercer Langston (1829–1897) was born in Virginia. After the death of his parents, Langston moved to Ohio, where he was educated by George Vachon, the first black graduate of Oberlin College. Langston entered Oberlin himself in 1844 and completed both his undergraduate degree (with high honors) and his M.A. there. Langston sought to enter law school in New York but was denied admission because of his color. The president of the law school offered to admit Langston if he pretended to be a Spaniard, but he refused. After reading law under the supervision of Judge Philemon Bliss, in whose home Langston lived, he was at last admitted to the Ohio bar in 1854.

In 1855, Langston was elected town clerk of Brownhelm Township, Ohio, and thus became perhaps the first African American voted to public office in the United States. In the April 20, 1855, edition of Frederick Douglass's Paper, *an elated Langston described the election of "the only colored man who lives in this township" "by a very handsome majority indeed:"*

> *It argues the steady march of the Anti-Slavery sentiment, and augurs the inevitable destruction and annihilation of American prejudice against colored men. What we so much need at this junction, and all along the future, is political influence; the bridle by which we can check and guide to our advantage the selfishness of American demagogues.*

*Langston's illustrious career was just beginning. He was later to serve as
a recruiter for the Massachusetts 54th Colored Infantry, inspector-general
of the Freedmen's Bureau, dean of the Howard University Law School,
acting president of Howard University, and U.S. minister to Haiti. He
was the first African American elected to the U.S. House of Representatives from Virginia. Although Langston made many famous speeches,
this little known early address, delivered on May 9, 1855, at the annual
meeting of the American Anti-Slavery Society, is among his finest. In
it he explores the ways in which slavery oppresses the ostensibly "free"
and insists that slavery is a national issue rather than a sectional one.
Langston endeavors to broaden the appeal of the antislavery movement
by explaining why those not enslaved have a direct personal stake in
abolition.*

    The text is taken from the Annual Report Presented to the American
Anti-Slavery Society By the Executive Committee At the Annual Meeting
*(New York: American Anti-Slavery Society, 1855), 181–86. For further in-
formation on the early years of Langston's life and career, see William
Cheek and Aimee Lee Cheek,* John Mercer Langston and the Fight for
Black Freedom, 1829–1865 *(Urbana: University of Illinois, 1989); and
Mary Frances Berry and John W. Blassingame,* Long Memory: The Black
Experience in America *(New York: Oxford University Press, 1982), 46–49.*

MR PRESIDENT, AND LADIES AND GENTLEMAN: Some great
man has remarked that a nation may lose its Liberty in a day, and be
a century in finding it out. There is not, within the length and breadth of
this entire Country, from Maine to Georgia, from the Atlantic to the Pacific
Ocean, a solitary man or woman, who is in the full possession of his or her
share of civil, religious, and political Liberty. This is a startling announcement, perhaps, in the heart and centre of a Country loud in its boasts of its
free institutions, its democratic organizations, its equality, its justice, and
its liberality. We have been in the habit of boasting of our Declaration of
Independence, of our Federal Constitution, of the Ordinance of 1787, and
various enactments in favor of popular Liberty, for so long, that we verily
believe that we are a Free people; and yet I am forced to declare, looking the
truth directly in the face, and seeing the power of American Slavery, that
there is not, within the bosom of this entire Country, a solitary man or
woman who can say, I have my full share of Liberty. Let the President of this
Society arm himself with the panoply of the Constitution of the United
States, the Declaration of Independence, and the Word of God, and stand up
in the presence of the people of South Carolina, and say, I believe in the sentiments contained in the Constitution of my Country, in the Declaration of
Independence, and in the Word of God, respecting the rights of man, and
where will be his legal protection? Massachusetts will sit quietly by and see
him outraged; the President of the United States will not dare to interfere
for his protection; he will be at the mercy of the tyrant Slaveholders. Why?

Because Slavery is the great lord of this Country, and there is no power in this Nation, to-day, strong enough to withstand it.

It would afford me great pleasure, Mr. President, to dwell upon the achievements already gained by the Anti-Slavery Movement. I know that they have been great and glorious; I know that this Movement has taught the American people who the Slave is, and what his rights are—that he is a man, and entitled to all the rights of a man; I know that the attention of the public has been called to the consideration of the colored people, and the attention of the colored people, themselves, has been awakened to their own condition, so that, with longing expectations, they begin to say, in the language of the poet:—

> "Oh tell me not that I am blessed,
>   Nor bid me glory in my lot,
> While plebian freemen are oppressed
>   With wants and woes that I have not.
> So let a cage, with grates of gold,
> And pearly roof, the eagle bold;
> Let dainty viands be his fare,
> And give the captive tend'rest care;
> But say, in luxury's limits pent,
> Find you the king of birds content?
> No; oft he'll sound the startling shriek,
> And beat the grates with angry beak.
> Precarious Freedom's far more dear
> Than all the prison's pampering cheer;
> He longs to seek his Eyrie seat—
>   Some cliff on Ocean's lonely shore,
> Whose old bare top the tempests beat,
>   And on whose base the billows roar;
> When, dashed by gales, they yawn like graves,
> He longs for joy to skim those waves,
> Or rise through tempest shrouded air
>   All thick and dark with loud winds swelling,
> To brave the lightning's lurid glare,
>   And talk with thunders in their dwelling."

As the mountain eagle hates the cage and loathes confinement, and longs to be free, so the colored man hates chains, loathes confinement, and longs to shoulder the responsibilities of a man. (Applause.) He longs to stand in the Church a man; he longs to stand up a man upon the great theatre of life, everywhere a man; for verily, he is a man, and may well adopt the sentiment of the Roman, Terence, when he said, *Homo sum, et nihil humani a me alienum puto.* I am a man, and there is nothing of humanity, as I think, estranged to me. Yes, the Anti-Slavery Movement has done this; and it has done more. It has revolutionized, to a great degree, the theology and religion of this Country; it has taught the American people that the Bible is not on the side of American Slavery. No, it cannot be. It was written in characters of light across the gateway of the old Mosaic system, "He that stealeth a man and selleth him, or if he be found in his hand, he shall surely be put to death." That is the only place in the Scriptures where the matter of chattel Slavery is mentioned, and the declaration of the Almighty, through Moses, is: "He that stealeth a man and selleth him, or if he be found in his hand, he shall surely be put to death." (Applause.) Theodore D. Weld was right when he said, "The Spirit of Slavery never takes refuge in the Bible *of its own accord.* The horns of the altar are its last resort. It seizes them, if at all, only in desperation—rushing from the terror of the avenger's arm. Like other unclean spirits, it hateth the light, neither cometh to the light, lest its deeds should be reproved. Goaded to madness in its conflicts with common sense and natural justice, denied all quarter, and hunted from every covert, it breaks, at last, into the sacred enclosure, and courses up and down the Bible, seeking rest and finding none. THE LAW OF LOVE, streaming from every page, flashes around it an omni-present anguish and despair. It shrinks from the hated light, and howls under the consuming touch, as the demoniacs recoiled from the Son of God and shrieked, 'Torment us not.' At last it slinks among the shadows of the Mosaic system, and thinks to burrow out of sight among its types and symbols. Vain hope! Its asylum is its sepulchre; its city of refuge, the city of destruction. It rushes from light into the sun; from heat into devouring fire; and, from the voice of God, into the thickest of His thunders."

Yes, the Anti-Slavery Movement has taught the American people this, and more than this. It has taught them that no political party, established on the basis of ignoring the question of Slavery, can live and breathe in the North. (Applause.) Where is the Whig party?

> "*Gone glimmering through the dream of things that were;*
> *A schoolboy's tale, the wonder of an hour.*"

The Anti-Slavery Movement has dug its grave deep; it has buried it, and is writing for its epitaph, "It was, but is no more." (Applause.) WITH DANIEL WEBSTER, the Whig Party breathed its last breath.

And where is the Democratic Party? It is in power, but all over it is written, *Mene, mene, tekel upharsin.** (Applause.)

I would like to dwell on these results of the Anti-Slavery Movement, but I want to make good, before this audience, my proposition, that there is not, within the length and breadth of this land, a solitary Freeman. The American People may be divided into four classes: the Slaves, the Slaveholders, the Non-Slaveholding Whites, and the Free People of color.

I need not undertake to show to this audience, that the American Slave is deprived of his rights. He has none. He has a body, but it is not his own;

---

*The words that according to Daniel 5:25 appeared on the wall during Belshazzar's feast.

he has an intellect, but he cannot think for himself; he has sensibility, but he must not feel for another. He can own nothing; all belongs to his master.

Then, as to the Slaveholder, we have all got to think that he has all rights. But a Slaveholder cannot sit on the bench or stand at the bar, in the forum or in the pulpit, and utter a solitary sentiment that could be construed as tending to create insubordination among the *Free* People of color, and insurrection among the Slaves. Look at the Press in the Southern States; it is muzzled, and dare not speak out a sentiment in favor of Freedom. Let but a sentiment tending towards abolition escape, and what is the consequence? Look at the *Parkville Luminary,** broken to atoms, and the people of that portion of Missouri avowing that that paper never uttered their sentiments or represented their views, and giving thanks to God Almighty that they have had the Mob spirit strong enough to destroy that Press. Is not this evidence sufficient to show that even Slaveholders, themselves, are not in possession of their full share of civil, religious, and political Liberty?

As to the great mass of the White People, at the North, have they their rights? I recollect, when the Anti-Slavery People held a Convention at Cleveland, in 1850, the question came up whether they should hold their next National Convention in the City of Washington. The strong political Anti-Slavery men of the Country were there. There were CHASE and LEWIS, of Ohio; CASSIUS M. CLAY, of Kentucky; LEWIS TAPPAN, of New York, and also many other strong men of the Party; and yet, when this question came up, how was it decided? That they would not hold the next National Convention at Washington. And what was the reason given? Because the people of that City may use violence towards us! Had the people their full share of Liberty, would they have been afraid to go to the Capital of the Country, and there utter their sentiments on the subject of Slavery, or any other topic?

But to make the fact more apparent, some two years afterwards, the great National Woman's Rights Convention was held in the same City; and there the very same question came up, whether they should hold their next Meeting at Washington or Pittsburg. How was it decided? As the question was about being put, LUCY STONE[†] came forward, and said, "I am opposed to going to the City of Washington. They buy and sell women there, and they might outrage us." So the Convention voted to hold the next Meeting at Pittsburg. Were they in the possession of their full share of Liberty? Think of it; our mothers, our wives, and our sisters, of the North, dare not go to the Capital of the Country, to hold a meeting to discuss the question of the rights of their own sex. And yet the Constitution declares that the "citizens of each State shall be entitled to all the rights and immunities of citizens in the several States."

I now wish to speak of another class, and more at length—of that class

*The print and presses of the *Industrial Luminary* (Parkville, Missouri) were destroyed by a mob after the paper editorialized in opposition to the efforts of many Missourians to establish residence in Kansas in order to vote for proslavery candidates in the March 1855 election of the territorial legislature.

[†]Lucy Stone (1818–1893) was a leading abolitionist and woman's rights speaker. She was a cofounder of the annual National Woman's Rights Conferences.

which I have the honor to represent—the Free People of color. What is our condition in respect to civil, religious, and political Liberty? In the State in which I live, (Ohio,) they do not enjoy the elective franchise, and why? It is owing to the indirect influence of American Slavery. Slavery in Kentucky, the adjoining State, says to the people of Ohio, you must not allow colored people to vote and be elected to office, because our Slaves will hear of it and become restless, and directly we shall have an insurrection, and our throats will be cut. And so the people of Ohio say to the colored people, that they cannot allow them the privilege of voting, notwithstanding the colored people pay taxes like others, and in the face of the acknowledged principle that taxation and representation should always go together. And I understand that in the State of New York, the colored man is only allowed the elective franchise through a property qualification, which amounts to nothing short of an insult; for it is not the colored man that votes, but the two hundred and fifty dollars that he may possess. It is not his manhood, but his money, that is represented. But that is the Yankee idea—the dollar and the cent. (Laughter.) In the State of Ohio, the colored man has not the privilege of sending his child to the white schools. Nor is he placed even in the penitentiary on a fair footing. (Laughter.) If a colored man knocks a white man down—perhaps in defence of his rights—he is sent to the penitentiary; and when he gets there, there is no discrimination made between him and the worst white criminal; but when he marches out to take his meal, he is made to march behind the white criminal, and you may see the prisoners marching—horse-thieves in front—colored people beyond. (Laughter.)

All the prejudice against color that you see in the United States is the fruit of Slavery, and is a most effectual barrier to the rights of the colored man. In the State of Illinois, they have a law something like this: that if any man comes there with the intent to make it his residence, he shall be taken up and fined ten dollars for the first offence; and if he is unable to pay it, he is put up and sold, and the proceeds of the sale are to go, first, towards paying the costs that may accrue in the case, and the residue towards the support and maintenance of a charity fund for the benefit of the *poor whites* of that State. (Laughter.) That is a part of the legislation of the State that STEPHEN A. DOUGLAS has the honor to represent. (Renewed laughter.) The public sentiment that is growing up in this Country, however, will soon, I hope, be the death of DOUGLAS, and of that sort of legislation.* (Applause.)

In the light, therefore, of all the facts, can there be any question that there is no full enjoyment of Freedom to any one in this Country. Could JOHN QUINCY ADAMS come forth from his mausoleum, shrouded in his grave clothes, and, in the name of the sovereignty of Massachusetts, stand up in Charleston, and protest against the imprisonment of the citizens of Massachusetts, as a violation of their constitutional rights, do you think the people of South Carolina would submit to it? Do you think the reverence due to his

*Douglas (1813–1861), Democratic senator from Illinois, introduced the Kansas-Nebraska bill in 1854 and supported the doctrine of "popular sovereignty" through which territories could decide for themselves whether to retain slavery when admitted as states.

name and character, or even the habiliments of the grave about him, would protect him from insult and outrage? And so far are the people of this Country lost to all sense of shame, that many would laugh at such an outrage.

American Slavery has corrupted the whole mass of American society. Its influence has pervaded every crevice and cranny of society. But, Mr. President, I am glad to know that a great change is coming on, and that the American people are beginning to feel that the question of Slavery is not one which affects the colored people alone. I am glad to know that they are beginning to feel that it is a National question, in which every man and woman is more or less interested. And when the people of the North shall rise and put on their strength, powerful though Slavery is and well nigh omnipotent, it shall die. It is only for the people to will it, and it is done. But while the Church and the political parties continue to sustain it; while the people bow down at its bloody feet to worship it, it will live and breathe. Now, the question comes home to us, and it is a practical question, in the language of MR. PHILLIPS,* "Shall Liberty die in this country? Has God Almighty scooped out the Mississippi Valley for its grave? Has he lifted up the Rocky Mountains for its monument? Has he set Niagara to hymn its requiem?" Sir, I hope not. I hope that the Mississippi Valley is to be its cradle; that the Rocky Mountains are to be the strong tablets upon which are to be written its glorious triumphs; and that Niagara has been set to hymn its triumphant song. (Applause.) But, my friends, the question is with us, Shall the Declaration of American Independence stand? Shall the Constitution of the United States, if it is Anti-Slavery, stand? Shall our free institutions triumph, and our Country become the asylum of the oppressed of all climes? Shall our Government become, in the language of ex-Senator ALLEN, "a democracy which asks nothing but what it concedes, and concedes nothing but what it demands, destructive to despotism, the conservator of liberty, life, and property?" May God help the right. (Applause.)■

50 THE TRIUMPH OF EQUAL SCHOOL RIGHTS IN BOSTON

William C. Nell

 During the 1820s and 1830s the public school system was established for white children, with blacks explicitly excluded. Separate schools for African Americans were often provided at private expense, if at all, and those with public funding were usually inferior to those provided for whites. African Americans and their allies began a

*Abolitionist lecturer Wendell Phillips (1811–1884).

campaign during the 1840s and 1850s throughout the North to supplant separate schools with integrated schools. Agitation to this end was pressed most vigorously through convention appeals, petitions, refusal to pay taxes, and litigation, but usually without success. But in Boston, where the most notable desegregation campaign took place, the battle for equal school rights was successful, and in large measure this was due to the untiring efforts and labors of the black abolitionist William Cooper Nell.

Connected with Garrison's Liberator *for many years, Nell won fame as an orator and also as one of the first African American historians. He began collecting historical data and produced in 1852 the study* Services of Colored Americans in the Wars of 1776 and 1812, *followed four years later by* Colored Patriots of the American Revolution. *But his leadership in the desegregation campaign in Boston's schools won Nell his greatest fame. Under his direction, African Americans in Boston deluged the Massachusetts legislature with petitions demanding the abolition of separate schools. Many withdrew their children from segregated schools and had them taught privately until in 1855 a law was enacted requiring public schools in the state to admit students without regard to color. Despite predictions of violence, school integration in Boston took place without serious incident and the victory in Boston inspired integrationist efforts in other parts of the country.*

On December 17, 1855, African Americans in Boston sponsored a meeting in the Southac Street Church for the purpose of presenting a testimonial to Nell "for his disinterested and untiring exertions procuring the opening of the public schools of the city to all children and youth within its limits, irrespective of complexional differences." After the presentation, Nell delivered an address, which follows; the text is taken from Triumph of Equal School Rights in Boston: Proceedings of the Presentation Meeting Held in Boston, December 17, 1855 *(Boston, 1856), 5–11. For further information, see Dorothy Porter Wesley, "Integration Versus Separatism: William Cooper Nell's Role in the Struggle for Equality," in Donald M. Jacobs, ed.,* Courage and Conscience: Black and White Abolitionists in Boston *(Bloomington: Indiana University Press, 1993), 207–24.*

MR. PRESIDENT, LADIES AND GENTLEMEN: The struggle for Equal School Rights, which for so long a series of years has taxed our hearts, our heads and our hands, having, through the aid of many friends, at length been triumphantly successful, it was but natural that the gratitude of parents and children should desire to make some record of the emotions awakened by such a signal and public good. With partial kindness, you have been pleased to make me the recipient of these honours, in recognition of the humble services it was my privilege to render the cause we all have loved so well.

Any attempt to express the feelings which swell my heart at this, the proudest moment of my life, it is no affectation to say, would be wholly unavailing. Your own hearts can best interpret mine. To be surrounded by such a constellation of friends from various walks of life, comprising those who have known me from early boyhood, and those of but recent acquaintance—realizing the fact that this is their united testimonial, approving my course in so glorious a reform—to be elaborate on such a theme calls for abilities far transcending any that I possess. I should be doing injustice, however, to my own sense of right were I to allow the occasion to pass without referring to others whose words and deeds, in promotion of the movement, should engrave their names indelibly upon the tablets of our memory.

To secure accuracy of names and dates, I have committed them to paper; but, anticipating the mental feast in reserve for us from the distinguished friends who have graced our meeting with their presence, I will be as brief as the circumstances will admit.

IN THE YEAR 1829, while a pupil in the basement story of the Belknap Street church, the Honorable Harrison Gray Otis, then mayor of the city, accompanied the Honorable Samuel T. Armstrong to an examination of the colored school. It chanced that Charles A. Battiste, Nancy Woodson and myself were pronounced entitled to the highest reward of merit. In lieu of Franklin Medals, legitimately our due, Mr. Armstrong gave each an order on Deacon James Loring's bookstore for the *Life of Benjamin Franklin.* This is the copy I received! The white medal scholars were invited guests to the Faneuil Hall dinner. Having a boy's curiosity to be spectator at the "feast of reason and the flow of soul," I made good my court with one of the waiters, who allowed me to seem to serve others as the fee for serving myself, the physical being then with me subordinate. Mr. Armstrong improved a prudent moment in whispering to me, "*You* ought to be here with the other *boys.*" Of course, the same idea had more than once been mine, but his remark, while witnessing the honors awarded to white scholars, only augmented my sensitiveness all the more, by the intuitive inquiry which I eagerly desired to express: "If you think so, why have you not taken steps to bring it about?"

The impression made on my mind, by this day's experience, deepened into a solemn vow that, God helping me, I would do my best to hasten the day when the color of the skin would be no barrier to equal school rights. . . . While I would not in the smallest degree detract from the credit justly due the *men* for their conspicuous exertions in this reform, truth enjoins upon me the pleasing duty of acknowledging that to the *women,* and the *children* also, is the cause especially indebted for success.

In the dark hours of our struggle, when betrayed by traitors within and beset by foes without, while some men would become lukewarm and indifferent, despairing of victory, then did the women keep the fame alive; and as their hopes would weave bright visions for the future, their husbands and brothers would rally for a new attack upon the fortress of Colorphobia. Yes, sir, it was the *mothers* (God bless them!) of these little bright-eyed boys and girls, who, through every step of our progress, were executive and vigilant, even to that memorable Monday morning (September 3, 1855), the trial hour, when the colored children of Boston went up to occupy the long-promised land. It was these mothers who accompanied me to the various schoolhouses, to residences of teachers and committeemen, to see the laws of the old Bay State applied in good faith.

An omniconsciousness of my own experience when a schoolboy—and how my heart would have leaped in the enjoyment then of equal school rights—has proved a strong incentive to my interest for your boys and girls; for, having none of my own, I took the liberty of adopting them all as my children. And the smiles of approbation with which so many of them have greeted me in their homes and the highways and byways of life have imparted to me a wealth of inspiration and encouragement not obtainable from any other source. He that makes glad the heart of a child receives in return whole volumes of benedictions and is richer far than if upon his brow were entwined a monarch's diadem.

These mothers have also labored at home to instill into the minds of their children the necessity of striving to obtain, as also to appreciate, those rights—emulating that New England mother who was said to mingle instruction in her children's bread and milk and put good morals into their apple pies! With commendable zeal, the boys and girls have endeavored to profit by these counsels.

On the morning preceding their advent to the public schools, I saw from my window a boy passing the exclusive Smith School,* where he had been a pupil, and raising his hands, he exultingly exclaimed to his companions, *"Goodbye forever, colored school! Tomorrow we are like other Boston boys."*

In my daily walks, I behold the companionship, in studies and healthful glee, of boys and girls of all colors and races in these temples of learning, so justly a theme of pride to every citizen—sights and sounds indeed to me chief among ten thousand, and altogether lovely.

And since the third of September to the present time, the sun, moon and stars are regular in their courses! No orb has proved so eccentric as to shoot madly from its sphere in consequence, and the State House on Beacon Hill, and old Faneuil Hall, remain as firm on their bases as ever. This union of mothers and children with husbands and fathers has contributed vastly to the great result. They have been the allied forces, which conquered our Sebastopol.

To the colored boys and girls of Boston it may now in truth be said, "The lines have fallen to you in pleasant places." Behold, you have a goodly heritage! May it stimulate you to heed the voice of Wisdom, as she sweetly offers the choicest treasures of her gathered stores:

With eager hand the glowing page to turn,

---

*The Smith School was founded in 1835. An all-white teaching staff taught an all-black student body until charges of racism and brutality produced a boycott in the 1840s. A black headmaster, Thomas Paul, Jr., was appointed in 1849, but the boycott continued. The Smith School closed in 1855, shortly after the passage of the school desegregation law.

To scan the earth and cleave the distant sky,
And find the force that holds the planets in their spheres.

Do not waste your spring of youth in idle dalliance, but plant rich seeds to blossom in your manhood and bear fruit when you are old. The public schools of Boston are the gateways to the pursuits of honor and usefulness, and if rightly improved by you, the imagination almost wearies as future prospects dawn upon its vision; for

Hills peep o'er hills, and Alps on Alps rise.

In response to your floral tribute, so pleasing and acceptable, allow me to say that I need it not as an evidence of your satisfaction with the rights obtained, or my participancy therein, for the pleasure of the service has abundantly rewarded me. Endeavor to retain the impressions made upon your memories by this meeting, for, after all, you children are the parties benefited. Your parents have labored to achieve this good for you, and to them you must ever render due honor. The three children of an Eastern lady were invited to furnish her with an expression of their love before she went on a long journey. One brought a marble tablet, with the inscription of her name; another presented her with a garland of flowers; the third entered her presence, and thus accosted her: "Mother, I have neither marble tablet nor fragrant nosegay, but I have a *heart. Here* your name is engraved; *here* your name is precious; and this *heart,* full of affection, will follow you wherever you travel, and remain with you wherever you repose." I know of no more appropriate advice to boys and girls than to commend their imitation of that child's example; and when a few short years shall have rolled away and all proscription shall have done its work in the land, may

You love at times to pause, and strew the way
With the wild flowers that luxuriant pend
From spring's gay branches, that whene'er you send
Your Memory to retrace your pilgrimage,
She by those flowers her winding course may bend,
Back through each twilight and each weary stage,
And with those early flowers wreathe the white brow of age.

I could cull from my chapter of experience and observation many an unkind and insulting remark uttered against the rights of colored children in Boston, by school-committee men, editors and others occupying responsible positions; but, as they can be reserved for future use to "point a moral" if *not* to "adorn a tale," let us, in this hour of victory, be magnanimous enough to cover with the charity of our silence the names of *all* who have opposed us.

Madam, in accepting this elegant token from your hands, I am not vain enough to monopolize the honor and gratitude so eminently due to those I have mentioned and others who have promoted this great work. Let it be regarded as a joint offering to them all, to be held in trust by me only so long as I am faithful to the elevation of those with whom I am identified by complexion and condition—the cause of humanity. May we all *Watch* each other, that our *hands* may be diligent—our *hours* consecrated, each *minute,* indeed every *second,* in that movement upon our *dial-plate* indicating a *chain* of Human Brotherhood. The associations of this evening will be *main-spring* henceforward—its recollections more fragrant than *choice flowers*— ever-enduring as *time.* Friends, go on!

> *"Oft as the memory of this hour returns,*
> *May friendship's flame within your bosoms burn,*
> *And, hand in hand, improvement's course pursue,*
> *Till scenes of earth have faded from your view;*
> *Then your glad spirits, freed from bonds of clay,*
> *Shall soar triumphant to the home of day—*
> *Where softer dews than Hermon's give perfume*
> *To flowers sweeter than in Sharon bloom,*
> *Entrancing music breathe in airs divine,*
> *And toil no more the spirit's flight confine;*
> *But ever onwards through its bright abode,*
> *Bask in the presence of its Maker, God."*■

51 WHAT, TO THE TOILING MILLIONS THERE, IS THIS BOASTED LIBERTY?

Sara G. Stanley

In 1856, five states permitted African American males to vote. Ohio was not among them. On January 16–18, 1856, forty dele-gates to the State Convention of Colored Men gathered in Columbus, Ohio, to issue an address to the state legislature petitioning for their franchise. Among other arguments, the convention delegates pointed to the belief of many in the legislature that "there is an irradicable differ-ence" between blacks and whites, arguing that "that very difference unfits them to represent us."*

*"Address to the Senate and the House of Representatives of the State of Ohio"

During the convention, the delegates heard an address by Sara G. Stanley, who represented the all-black Ladies' Anti-Slavery Society of Delaware, Ohio. Stanley's militant call for action, undertaken in "a radical, utilitarian spirit," registered a ringing denunciation of the gap between America's professed ideals and the "shadowy and indistinct" reality of those "boasted liberties," which remain "impalpable to our sense or touch." Stanley was unable to address the male convention herself, and so her remarks were read by delegate William Harris.

Stanley (1836–1918) was just twenty years old at the time of the Ohio convention and had left Oberlin College during her third year to teach school in the town of Delaware. From 1864 to 1870, Stanley taught freed men and women for the American Missionary Association in Norfolk, St. Louis, and Mobile. Her writings were published in the Weekly African-American *and other papers. For further information, see Ellen N. Lawson,* The Three Sarahs: Documents of Antebellum College Women *(New York: Edwin Mellen, 1984).*

The text of her address is taken from Philip S. Foner and George E. Walker, ed., Proceedings of the Black State Conventions, 1840–1865, *vol. 1 (Philadelphia: Temple University Press, 1979).*

*T*o the Convention of Disfranchised Citizens of Ohio:
    Gentlemen:—Convened as you are in the Capital City of our State—A State great in wealth, power, and political influence, an avowed devotee of Freedom, and a constituent part of a Christian Democratic Confederacy—to concoct measures for obtaining those rights and immunities of which unjust legislation has deprived you, we offer this testimonial of our sympathy and interest in the cause in which you are engaged—a cause fraught with infinite importance—and also express our earnest hope that such determination and invincible courage may be evinced by you in assembly as are requisite to meet the exigencies of the times.

    Truth, Justice and Mercy, marshaling their forces, sound the tocsin which summons the warrior in his burnished armor to the conflict against Error and Oppression. On earth's broad arenas—through Time's revolving cycles—this warfare has been continuous; and now here, in this most brilliant star in the galaxy of nations, where Christianity and civilization, with their inestimable accompaniments and proclivities, have taken their abode and add their benign light to her stellate brightness—bands of her offspring, in very truth her own, despised, persecuted and crushed, assemble in scattered fragments to take the oath of fealty to Freedom, and swear eternal enmity to Oppression; to enter into a bond sacred and inviolable, ever to wage interminable intellectual and moral war against the demon, and to demand the restoration of their birthright, *Liberty*—kindred of Deity. Nor is the path

(1856), in Philip S. Foner and George E. Walker, ed., *Proceedings of the Black State Conventions, 1840–1865,* vol. 1 (Philadelphia: Temple University Press, 1979), 311.

to victory strewn with flowers; obstacles formidable, and apparently insurmountable, arise ominously before even the most hopeful and ardent.

As the Alpine avalanche sweeps tumultuously adown the mountain, overwhelming the peasant and his habitation, so the conglomeration of hatred and prejudice against our race, brought together by perceptible accumulation, augmented and fostered by religion and science united, sweeps with seeming irresistible power toward us, menacing complete annihilation. But, should these things exercise a retarding influence upon our progressive efforts? Let American religion teach adoration to the demon Slavery, whom it denominates God: at the end, the book of record will show its falsity or truth. Let scientific research produce elaborate expositions of the inferiority and mental idiosyncrasy of the colored race; one truth, the only essential truth, is incontrovertible:—The Omnipotent, Omniscient God's glorious autograph—the seal of angels—is written on our brows, that immortal characteristic of Divinity—the rational, mysterious and inexplicable soul, animates our frames.

Then press on! Manhood's prerogatives are yours by Almighty fiat. These prerogatives American Republicanism, disregarding equity, humanity, and the fundamental principles of her national superstructure, has rendered a nonentity, while on her flag's transparencies and triumphal arches, stood beautifully those great, noble words: Liberty and Independence—Free Government—Church and State! And still they stand exponents of American character—her escutcheon wafts them on its star-spangled surface, to every clime—each ship load of emigrants from monarchical Europe, shout the words synonymous with Americans, their first paean in "the land of the free." Briery mountain, sparkling river, glassy lake, give back the echoes, soft and clear as if the melody was borrowed from the harps of angels. But strange incongruity! As the song of Freedom verberates and reverberates through the northern hills, and the lingering symphony quivers on the still air and then sinks away into silence, a low deep wail, heavy with anguish and despair, rises from the southern plains, and the clank of chains on human limbs mingles with the mournful cadence.

What to the toiling millions there, is this boasted liberty? What to us is this organic body—this ideal reduced to reality—this institution of the land?—A phantom, shadowy and indistinct—a disembodied form, impalpable to our sense or touch. In the broad area of this Republic there is no spot, however small or isolated, where the colored man can exercise his God-given rights. Genius of America! How art thou fallen, oh Lucifer, son of the morning how art thou fallen!

In view of these things, it is self-evident, and above demonstration that we, as a people, have every incentive to labor for the redress of wrongs. On our native soil, consecrated to freedom, civil liberties are denied us, and we are by compulsion subject to an atrocious and criminal system of political tutelage deleterious to the interest of the entire colored race, and antagonistical to the political axioms of this Republic.

Intuitively, then, we search for the panacea for the manifold ills which we suffer. One, and only one, exists; and when each individual among us realizes the absolute impossibility for him to perform any work of supererogation in the common cause, the appliances will prove its own efficacy; it is embodied in one potent word—ACTION. Let unanimity of action characterize us; let us reject the absurd phantasy of non-intervention; let us leave conservatism behind, and substitute a radical, utilitarian spirit, let us cultivate our moral and mental faculties, and labor to effect a general diffusion of knowledge, remembering that "ascendancy naturally and properly belongs to intellectual superiority."

Let "Excelsior" be our watchword; it is the inspiration of all great deeds, and by the universal adoption of this policy we will soon stand triumphantly above that ignorance and weakness of which slavery is the inevitable concomitant—will soon reach that apex of civilization and consequent power to which every earnest, impassioned soul aspires.

Continued and strenuous effort is the basis of all greatness, moral, intellectual, and civil. "Work, man," says Carlyle, "Work! work! thou hast all eternity to rest in."

To you, gentlemen, as representatives of the oppressed thousands of Ohio, we look hopefully. This convening is far from being nugatory or unimportant. "Agitation of thought is the beginning of truth," and furthermore, by pursuing such a line of policy as you in your wisdom may deem expedient, *tending toward that paramount object*, the results may transcend those attending similar assemblies which have preceded it. Sure, you are numerically small; but the race is not always gained by the swift, nor the battle by the strong, and it has become a truism that greatness is the legitimate result of labor, diligence, and perseverance.

It was a Spartan mother's farewell to her son, "Bring home your shield or be brought upon it." To you we would say, be true, be courageous, be steadfast in the discharge of your duty. The citadel of Error must yield to the unshrinking phalanx of truth. In our fireside circles, in the seclusion of our closets, we kneel in tearful supplication in your behalf. As Christian wives, mothers and daughters, we invoke the blessing of the King, Eternal and Immortal, "who sitteth upon the circle of the earth, who made the heavens with all their host," to rest upon you, and we pledge ourselves to exert our influence unceasingly in the cause of Liberty and Humanity.

Again we say, be courageous; be steadfast; unfurl your banner to the breeze—let its folds float proudly over you, bearing the glorious inscription, broad and brilliant as the material universe: *"God and Liberty!"* ■

52 THE NEGRO RACE, SELF-GOVERNMENT, AND THE HAITIAN REVOLUTION

James T. Holly

Throughout the pre–Civil War years, the Haitian Revolution was a topic of great interest to African Americans and served as a theme for many speeches.* But no one discoursed as effectively on the events in Haiti before, during, and after the first black republic in the Americas was established as did James T. Holly, a former shoemaker, in the following speech. Holly (1829–1911) was a frequent visitor to Haiti. On his return from the island in the Fall of 1855, he delivered this lecture on the history of Haiti as a vindication of the ability of black people to establish self-government and achieve progress. During the summer of 1856 he repeated the lecture, excerpts of which are presented here, in Ohio, Michigan, and Canada. As the foremost advocate of emigration to Haiti in the decade before the Civil War, Holly closed his lecture with a fervent appeal for African Americans to leave the United States and move to Haiti rather than to Africa. He himself finally settled in Haiti.

In 1857 the lecture was published† by the African-American Printing Company of New Haven, Connecticut, an organization formed to publish African American literature, especially writings and speeches favoring emigration. The pamphlet was dedicated by Holly to the Reverend William C. Munroe, Rector of St. Matthew's Church, Detroit, who had served as a missionary in Haiti.

THE TASK that I propose to myself in the present lecture is an earnest attempt to defend the inherent capabilities of the Negro race for self-government and civilized progress. For this purpose I will examine the events of Haitian history from the commencement of their revolution down to the present period, so far as the same may contribute to illustrate the points I propose to prove and defend. Permit me, however, to add, in extenuation of this last comprehensive proposition, that I must necessarily review these events hastily, in order to crowd them within the compass of an ordinary lecture.

---

*See, for example, James McCune Smith, *A Lecture on the Haytian Revolution: with a Sketch of the Character of Toussaint L'Ouverture (Delivered at the Stuyvesant Institute, for the benefit of the Colored Orphan Asylum, February 26, 1841)* (New York, 1841).

†James T. Holly, *A Vindication of the Capacity of the Negro Race for Self-Government and Civilized Progress as Demonstrated by Historical Events of the Haytian Revolution* (New Haven, 1857).

REASONS FOR ASSUMING SUCH A TASK

Notwithstanding the remarkable progress of philanthropic ideas and humanitarian feelings during the last half century, among almost every nation and people throughout the habitable globe, yet the great mass of the Caucasian race will deem the Negro as entirely destitute of those qualities on which they selfishly predicate their own superiority.

And we may add to this overwhelming class that cherish such self-complacent ideas of themselves—to the great prejudice of the Negro—a large quota also of that small portion of the white race, who profess to believe the truths "that God is no respecter of persons," and that "He has made of one blood all the nations that dwell upon the face of the earth." Yes, I say, we may add a large number of the noisy agitators of the present day, who would persuade themselves and the world that they are really Christian philanthropists, to that overwhelming crowd who openly traduce the Negro; because too many of those pseudo humanitarians have lurking in their heart of hearts a secret infidelity in regard to the real equality of the black man, which is ever ready to manifest its concealed sting, when the full and unequivocal recognition of the Negro in all respects is pressed home upon their hearts.

Hence, between this downright prejudice against this long-abused race, which is flauntingly maintained by myriads of their oppressors, on the one hand, and this woeful distrust of his natural equality among those who claim to be his friends, on the other, no earnest and fearless efforts are put forth to vindicate their character by even the few who may really acknowledge this equality of the races. They are overawed by the overpowering influence of the contrary sentiment. This sentiment unnerves their hands and palsies their tongue; and no pen is wielded or voice heard among that race of men which fearlessly and boldly places the Negro side by side with the white man as his equal in all respects. But to the contrary, everything is done by the enemies of the Negro race to vilify and debase them. And the result is that many of the race themselves are almost persuaded that they are a brood of inferior beings.

It is, then, to attempt a fearless but truthful vindication of this race with which I am identified—however feeble and immature that effort may be—that I now proceed to set forth the following address:

I wish, by the undoubted facts of history, to cast back the vile aspersions and foul calumnies that have been heaped upon my race for the last four centuries by our unprincipled oppressors, whose base interest, at the expense of our blood and our bones, have made them reiterate from generation to generation during the long march of ages everything that would prop up the impious dogma of our natural and inherent inferiority.

AN ADDITIONAL REASON FOR THE PRESENT TASK

But this is not all. I wish hereby to contribute my influence—however small that influence—to effect a grander and dearer object to our race than even this truthful vindication of them before the world. I wish to do all in my power to inflame the latent embers of self-respect that the cruelty and injustice of our oppressors have nearly extinguished in our bosoms during the midnight chill of centuries that we have clanked the galling chains of slavery. To this end, I wish to remind my oppressed brethren, that dark and dismal as this horrid night has been and sorrowful as the general reflections are, in regard to our race, yet, notwithstanding these discouraging considerations, there are still some proud historic recollections, linked indissolubly with the most important events of the past and present century, which break the general monotony and remove some of the gloom that hangs over the dark historic period of African slavery and the accursed traffic in which it was cradled.

THE REVOLUTIONARY HISTORY OF HAITI
THE BASIS OF THIS ARGUMENT

These recollections are to be found in the history of the heroic events of the Revolution of Haiti.

This revolution is one of the noblest, grandest, and most justifiable outbursts against tyrannical oppression that are recorded on the pages of the world's history.

A race of almost dehumanized men—made so by an oppressive slavery of three centuries—arose from their slumber of ages and redressed their own unparalleled wrongs with a terrible hand in the name of God and humanity.

In this terrible struggle for liberty, the Lord of Hosts directed their arms to be the instruments of His judgment on their oppressors, as the recompense of His violated law of love between man and his fellow, which these tyrants of the new world had been guilty of in the centuries of blood, wrong and oppression, which they had perpetrated on the Negro race in that isle of the Caribbean Sea.

But aside from this great providential and religious view of this great movement that we are always bound to seek for in all human affairs, to see how they square with the mind of God, more especially if they relate to the destinies of nations and people, the Haitian Revolution is also the grandest political event of this or any other age. In weighty causes and wondrous and momentous features, it surpasses the American Revolution, in an incomparable degree. The revolution of this country was only the revolt of a people already comparatively free, independent, and highly enlightened. Their greatest grievance was the imposition of three pence per pound tax on tea, by the mother country, without their consent. But the Haitian Revolution was a revolt of an uneducated and menial class of slaves against their tyrannical oppressors, who not only imposed an absolute tax on their unrequited labor, but also usurped their very bodies, and who would have been prompted by the brazen infidelity of the age then rampant to dispute with the Almighty the possession of the souls of these poor creatures, could such brazen effrontery have been of any avail, to have wrung more ill-gotten gain out of their victims to add to their worldly goods.

These oppressors, against whom the Negro insurgents of Haiti had to contend, were not only the government of a far-distant mother country, as in the case of the American Revolution; but unlike and more fearful than this revolt, the colonial government of Haiti was also thrown in the balance against the Negro revolters. The American revolters had their colonial government in their own hands, as well as their individual liberty at the commencement of the revolution. The black insurgents of Haiti had yet to grasp both their personal liberty and the control of their colonial government, by the might of their own right hands, when their heroic struggle began.

The obstacles to surmount and the difficulties to contend against in the American Revolution, when compared to those of the Haitian, were (to use a homely but classic phrase) but a "tempest in a teapot" compared to the dark and lurid thunderstorm of the dissolving heavens.

Never before, in all the annals of the world's history, did a nation of abject and chattel slaves arise in the terrific might of their resuscitated manhood and regenerate, redeem and disenthrall themselves by taking their station at one gigantic bound as an independent action among the sovereignties of the world.

It is, therefore, the unparalleled incidents that led to this wonderful event that I now intend to review rapidly, in order to demonstrate thereby the capacity of the Negro race for self-government and civilized progress, to the fullest extent and in the highest sense of these terms. . . .

THE SELF-POSSESSION OF THE BLACKS AN EVIDENCE OF THEIR CAPACITY FOR SELF-GOVERNMENT

The exceptional part which the blacks played in the moving drama that was then being enacted in Santo Domingo, by their stern self-possession amid the furious excitement of the whites, is one of the strongest proofs that can be adduced to substantiate the capabilities of the Negro race for self-government.

The *careless reserve* of the seemingly dehumanized black slave, who continued to toil and delve on in the monotonous round of plantation labor, under a cruel task master, in a manner so entirely heedless of the furious hurrahs for freedom and independence, the planting of Liberty poles surmounted by the cap of Liberty, and the erection of statues to the goddess of Liberty, which was going on around him—this apparent indifference and carelessness to the surging waves of freedom that were then awakening the despotisms of earth from their slumber of ages, showed that the slave understood and appreciated the difficulties of his position. He felt that the hour of destiny, appointed by the Almighty, had not yet tolled its summons for him to arise and avenge the wrong of ages.

He therefore remained heedless of the effervescence of liberty that bubbled over in the bosom of the white man, and continued at his sullen labors, biding his time for deliverance. And in this judicious reserve on the part of the blacks we have one of the strongest traits of self-government.

When we look upon this characteristic of cool self-possession, we cannot but regard it as almost a miracle under the circumstances. We cannot see what magic power could keep such a warm-blooded race of men in such an icebound spell of cold indifference, when every other class of men in that colony was flush with the excitement of *liberty* and the whole island was rocked to its center with the deafening surges of "Equality" that echoed from ten thousand throats.

One would have supposed, that at the very first sound of freedom, the 500,000 bondmen in that island, whose ancestry for three centuries had worn the yoke of slavery, would have raised up at once in their overwhelming numerical power and physical stalwartness and cried out "Liberty!" with a voice so powerful as to have cleft asunder the bowels of the earth and buried slavery and every Negro hater and oppressor who might dare oppose their just rights, in one common grave.

But, as I have said, they did no such thing; they had a conscious faith in the ultimate designs of God; and they silently waited, trusting to the workings of His overruling Providence to bring about the final day of their deliverance. In doing so, I claim they have given an evidence of their ability to govern themselves that ought to silence all proslavery calumniators of my race at once, and forever, by its powerful and undying refutation of their slanders. And let no one dare to rob them of this glorious trait of character, either by alleging that they remained thus indifferent, because they were too ignorant to appreciate the blessings of liberty or by saying that if they understood the import of these clamors for the Rights of Man, they were thus quiet, because they were too cowardly to strike for their disenthrallment.

The charge that they were thus ignorant of the priceless boon of freedom, is *refuted* by the antecedent history of the servile insurrections, which never ceased to rack that island from 1522 down to the era of Negro independence. The Negro insurgents, Polydore, Macandel* and Padrejan, who had at various times led on their enslaved brethren to daring deeds in order to regain their God-given liberty, brand that assertion as a libel on the Negro character, that says he was too cowardly to strike for the inheritance of its precious boon.

And the desperate resolution to be free that the Maroon Negroes[†] of the

---

*After he had run away in 1740, François Macandal (or Macandel) waged a relentless war against the landowners of Saint Domingue and poisoned a number of white settlers, overseers, and even some slaves who refused to turn against their slaveholders. In 1758, Macandal and his associates among the slaves made elaborate plans for an insurrection that would drive the whites off the island. But the plot, betrayed by a young black, was suppressed. Macandal was captured, was condemned to death, and was burned alive at Cap Français.

[†]Maroons were runaway slaves who established their own communities, in mountains, swamps, and forests. They were numerous in the Caribbean and Brazil but also ex-

island maintained for eighty-five years, by their valorous struggles in their wild mountain fastnesses against the concentrated and combined operations of the French and Spanish authorities then in that colony, and which finally compelled these authorities to conclude a treaty with the intrepid Maroon chief, Santiago, and thereby acknowledge their freedom forever thereafter— this fact, I say, proves him to be a base calumniator who shall dare to say that a keen appreciation of liberty existed not in the bosom of the Negroes of Santo Domingo.

But again, as to the plea of cowardice, in order to account for the fact of their cool self-possession amidst the first convulsive throes of revolutionary liberty, permit me to add in refutation of this fallacy that, if the daring incidents of antecedent insurrections do not sufficiently refute this correlative charge also, then the daring deeds of dreadless heroism performed by a Toussaint, a Dessalines, a Rigaud, and a Christophe, in the subsequent terrible but necessary revolution of the Negroes in which black troops gathered from the plantations of slavery met the best-appointed armies of France, and at various times those of England and Spain also, and proved their equal valor and prowess with these best-disciplined armies of Europe—this dreadless heroism evinced by the blacks, I say, is sufficient to nail the infamous imputation of cowardice to the wall at once and forever.

Hence, nothing shall rob them of the immaculate glory of exhibiting a stern self-possession in that feverish hour of excitement, when everybody around them was crying out "Liberty." And in this judicious self-control at this critical juncture, when their destiny hung on the decision of the hour, we have a brilliant illustration of the capacity of the race for self-government. . . .

The opportunity for the [free] men of color presented itself when the General Colonial Assembly of St. Marc's (already referred to) sent deputies to France, to present the result of its deliberations to the National Assembly, and to ask that august body to confer on the colony the right of self-government.

At this time, therefore, when the affairs of the colony were about to undergo examination in the supreme legislature of the mother country, the free men of color seized upon the occasion to send deputies to France also, men of their own caste, to represent their grievances and make their wishes known to the National Assembly. This discreet discernment of such an opportune moment to make such a movement divested of every other consideration shows a people who understand themselves, what they want, and how to seek it.

But when we proceed to consider the most approved manner in which

isted in the United States. Prior to the great Revolution of 1791 which led to the establishment of the black Republic of Haiti, Saint Domingue had a whole century of Maroon activity with bands of blacks establishing hideouts in the woods and the more inaccessible plantations, maintaining themselves by night raids on neighboring plantations for food and weapons.

the representations were made to the National Assembly by the colored delegates in behalf of their caste in the colony of Santo Domingo, and the influences they brought to bear upon that body as exhibited hereafter, we shall perceive thereby that they showed such an intimate acquaintance with the secret springs of governmental machinery as demonstrated at once their capacity to govern themselves.

This deputation first drew up a statement in behalf of their caste in the colony, of such a stirring nature as would be certain to command the national sympathy in their cause, when presented to the National Assembly. But previously to presenting it to that assembly, they took the wise precaution to wait upon the honorable president of that august body, in order to enlist and commit him in their favor, as the first steppingstone to secure the success of their object before the supreme legislature.

They prevailed in their mission to the president of the Assembly and succeeded in obtaining this very emphatic assurance from him: "No part of the nation shall vainly reclaim their rights before the assembly of the representatives of the French people."

Having accomplished this important step, the colored deputies next began to operate through the Abolition Society of Paris, called *"Les Amis des Noirs,"* upon such of the members of the Assembly as were affiliated with this society and thus already indirectly pledged to favor such a project as theirs, asking simple justice for their race. They were again successful, and Charles De Lameth, one of the zealous patrons of that society and an active member of the National Assembly, was engaged to argue their cause before the supreme legislature of the nation—although, strange to say, he was himself a colonial slaveholder at that time.

And at the appointed moment in the National Assembly, this remarkable man felt prompted to utter these astounding words in behalf of this oppressed and disfranchised class of the colony: "I am one of the greatest proprietors of Santo Domingo; yet I declare to you that, sooner than lose sight of principles so sacred to justice and humanity, I would prefer to lose all that I possess. I declare myself in favor of admitting the men of color to the rights of citizenship, and in favor of the freedom of the blacks."

Now let us for a moment stop and reflect on the measures resorted to by the colored deputies of Santo Domingo, in Paris, who, by their wise stratagems, had brought their cause step by step to such an eventful and auspicious crisis as this.

Could there have been surer measures concocted for the success of their plans than thus committing the president of the Assembly to their cause in the first place, and afterwards pressing a liberty-loving slaveholder into their service, to thunder their measures through the National Assembly by such a bold declaration?

Who among the old fogies of Tammany Hall*—that junta of scheming

*Tammany Hall was the leading Democratic club in New York City.

politicians who govern this country by pulling the wires of party and thereby making every official of the nation, from the President of the United States down to the Commissioners for Street Sweeping in the City of New York, dance as so many puppets at their bidding—I repeat it—who among these all powerful but venal politicians of old Tammany could have surpassed these tactics of those much-abused men of color who thus swayed the secret springs of the National Assembly of France? And who, after this convincing proof to the contrary, shall dare to say that the Negro race is not capable of self-government?

But to return to the thread of our narrative. When the secret springs had been thus secured in their behalf, they had nothing to fear from the popular heart of the nation, already keenly alive to the sentiments of Liberty, Equality and Fraternity, because the simple justice of their demands would commend them to the people as soon as they were publicly made known in France.

In order to make the very best impression on the popular heart of the nation, their petition demanding simple justice to their caste was accompanied with a statement very carefully drawn up.

In this statement they showed that their caste in the colony of Santo Domingo possessed one third of the real estate, and one fourth of the personal effects of the island. They also set forth the advantages of their position in the political and social affairs of Santo Domingo, as a balance of power in the hand of the imperial government of France, against the high pretensions of the haughty planters on the one hand and the seditious spirit of the poor whites on the other. And, as an additional consideration, by way of capping the climax, they offered, in the name and in behalf of the free men of color in the colony, six millions of francs as a loyal contribution to the wants and financial exigencies of the national treasury, to be employed in liquidating the debt of their common country.

Thus, if neither their wire-working maneuvers, the justice of their cause nor the conservative influence which their position gave them in the colony had been enough to secure the end which they sought, then the tempting glitter of so much cash could not be resisted when its ponderous weight was also thrown in the scale of justice. They succeeded, as a matter of course, in accomplishing their purpose; and the National Assembly of France promulgated a decree on the eighth of March, 1790, securing equal political rights to the men of color.

The very success of this movement and the means by which its success was effected, the opportune moment when it was commenced and the immense odds that were against those that sought its accomplishment—all these things must hereafter be emblazoned on the historic page as an everlasting tribute to the genius of the Negro race and remain an ineffaceable evidence of their capacity for self-government, that may be triumphantly adduced and proudly pointed at in this and every succeeding generation of the world, until the latest syllable of recorded time. . . .

THE AUSPICIOUS DAWN OF NEGRO RULE

Toussaint, by his acute genius and daring prowess, made himself the most efficient instrument in accomplishing these important results, contemplated by the three French commissioners, who brought the last decrees of the National Assembly of France, proclaiming liberty throughout the island to all the inhabitants thereof, and thus, like another Washington, proved himself the regenerator and savior of his country.

On this account, therefore, he was solemnly invested with the executive authority of the colony; and their labors having been thus brought to such a satisfactory and auspicious result, two of the commissioners returned home to France.

No man was more competent to sway the civil destinies of these enfranchised bondmen than he who had preserved such an unbounded control over them as their military chieftain and led them on to glorious deeds amid the fortunes of warfare recently waged in that island. And no one else could hold that responsible position of an official mediator between them and the government of France with so great a surety and pledge of their continued freedom as Toussaint L'Ouverture. And there was no other man, in fine, that these rightfully jealous freemen would have permitted to carry out such stringent measures in the island, so nearly verging to serfdom, which were so necessary at that time in order to restore industry, but one of their own caste whose unreserved devotion to the cause of their freedom placed him beyond the suspicion of any treacherous design to reenslave them.

Hence, by these eminent characteristics possessed by Toussaint in a superexcellent degree, he was the very man for the hour, and the only one fitted for the governorship of the colony calculated to preserve the interests of all concerned.

The leading commissioners of France then in the island duly recognized this fact and did not dispute with him the claim to this responsible position. Thus had the genius of Toussaint developed itself to meet an emergency that no other man in the world was so peculiarly prepared to fulfill; and thereby he has added another inextinguishable proof of the capacity of the negro for self-government.

But if the combination of causes which thus pointed him out as the only man that could safely undertake the fulfillment of the gubernatorial duties are such manifest proofs of Negro capacity, then the manner in which we shall see that he afterward discharged the duties of that official station goes still further to magnify the self-evident fact of Negro capability.

The means that he adopted to heal the internecine dissensions that threatened civil turmoil, and the manner in which he successfully counteracted the machinations of the ambitious General Hedouville, a French commissioner that remained in the colony, who desired to overthrow Toussaint, showed that the Negro chieftain was no tyro in the secret of government.

He also established commercial relations between that island and foreign nations; and he is said to be the first statesman of modern times who promulgated the doctrine of free trade and reduced it to practice. He also desired to secure a constitutional government to Santo Domingo, and for this purpose he assembled around him a select council of the most eminent men in the colony, who drew up a form of constitution under his supervision and approval, and which he transmitted with a commendatory letter to Napoleon Bonaparte, then First Consul of France, in order to obtain the sanction of the imperial government.

But that great bad man did not even acknowledge its receipt to Toussaint; but in his mad ambition he silently meditated when he should safely dislodge the Negro chief from his responsible position, as the necessary prelude to the reenslavement of his sable brethren, whose freedom was secure against his nefarious designs so long as Toussaint stood at the helm of affairs in the colony.

But decidedly the crowning act of Toussaint L'Ouverture's statesmanship was the enactment of the Rural Code, by the operation of which he was successful in restoring industrial prosperity to the island, which had been sadly ruined by the late events of sanguinary warfare. He effectually solved the problem of immediate emancipation and unimpaired industry, by having the emancipated slaves produce thereafter as much of the usual staple productions of the country as was produced under the horrible regime of slavery; nevertheless, the lash was entirely abolished, and a system of wages adopted, instead of the uncompensated toil of the lacerated and delving bondman.

In fact, the island reached the highest degree of prosperity that it ever attained, under the Negro governorship of Toussaint.

The Rural Code, by which so much was accomplished, instead of being the horrible nightmare of despotism—worse than slavery, that some of the proslavery calumniators of Negro freedom and rule would have us believe—was, in fact, nothing more than a prudent government regulation of labor, a regulation which made labor the first necessity of a people in a state of freedom, a regulation which struck a death blow at idleness, the parent of poverty and all the vices, a regulation, in fine, which might be adopted with advantage in every civilized country in the world, and thereby extinguish two thirds of the pauperisms, vagrancy and crime that curse these nations of the earth, and thus lessen the need for poorhouses, police officers, and prisons, that are now sustained at such an enormous expense for the relief of the poor and the correction of felons.

This Haitian Code compelled every vagabond or loafer about the towns and cities, who had no visible means of an honest livelihood, to find an employer and work to do in the rural districts. And if no private employer could be found, then the government employed such on its rural estates, until they had found a private employer. The hours and days of labor were prescribed by this code, and the terms of agreement and compensation between employer and employed were also determined by its provisions. Thus, there could be no private imposition on the laborers; and, as a further security against such a spirit, the government maintained rural magistrates and a rural police, whose duty it was to see to the faithful execution of the law on both sides.

By the arrangement of this excellent and celebrated code, everybody in the commonwealth was sure of work and compensation for the same, either from private employers or from the government. Nobody need fear being starved for want of work to support themselves, as is often the case among the laborers of Europe, and is fast coming to pass in the densely populated communities of this country, where labor is left to take care of itself under the private exploitation of mercenary capitalists. Under this code nobody need fear being exploited by such unprincipled and usurious men, who willingly take advantage of the poor to pay them starvation prices for their labor, because, against such, the law of Toussaint secured to each laborer a living compensation.

By the operation of this code, towns and cities were cleared of all those idle persons who calculate to live by their wits and who commit nine tenths of all the crimes that afflict civilized society. All such were compelled to be engaged at active industrial labors, and thus rendered a help to themselves and a blessing to the community at large.

By this industrial regulation, everything flourished in the island in an unprecedented degree; and the Negro genius of Toussaint, by a bold and straightforward provision for the regulation and protection of his emancipated brethren, effected that high degree of prosperity in Haiti, which all the wisdom of the British nation has not been able to accomplish in her emancipated West India colonies, in consequence of her miserable shuffling in establishing coolie and Chinese apprenticeship—that semisystem of slavery—in order to gratify the prejudices of her proslavery colonial planters, and because of the baneful influence of absentee landlordism, which seems to be an inseparable incident of the British system of property.

Thus did the Negro government of Santo Domingo show more paternal solicitude for the well-being of her free citizens than they ever could have enjoyed under the capricious despotism of individual masters who might pretend to care for them; and thus did it more truly subserve the purposes of a government than any or all of the similar organizations of civilization, whose only care and object seem to be the protection of the feudal rights of property in the hands of the wealthy few, leaving the honest labor of the many unprotected, and the poor laborer left to starve or to become a criminal, to be punished either by incarceration in the jails, prisons and dungeons provided for common felons, or executed on the gallows as the greatest of malefactors.

The genius of Toussaint by towering so far above the common ideas of this age in relation to the true purposes of government and by carrying out his bold problem with such eminent success, has thereby emblazoned on the historic page of the world's statesmanship a fame more enduring than Pitt,* who laid the foundation of a perpetual fund to liquidate the national debt of England.

*William Pitt the younger (1759–1806).

I say Toussaint has carved for himself a more enduring fame, because his scheme was more useful to mankind. The Negro statesman devised a plan that comprehended in its scope the well-being of the masses of humanity. But Pitt only laid a scheme whereby the few hereditary paupers pensioned on a whole nation, with the absurd right to govern it, might still continue to plunge their country deeper and deeper into debt, to subserve their own extravagant purposes, and then provide for the payment of the same out of the blood and sweat and bones of the delving operatives and colliers of Great Britain. Thus, then Toussaint by the evident superiority of his statesmanship has left on the pages of the world's statute book an enduring and irrefutable testimony of the capacity of the Negro for self-government and the loftiest achievements in national statesmanship.

And Toussaint showed that he had not mistaken his position by proving himself equal to that trying emergency when that demigod of the historian Abbott, Napoleon Bonaparte, First Consul of France, conceived the infernal design of reenslaving the heroic blacks of Santo Domingo, and who for the execution of this nefarious purpose sent the flower of the French Army and a naval fleet of fifty-six vessels under command of General Leclerc, the husband of Pauline, the voluptuous and abandoned sister of Napoleon.

When this formidable expedition arrived on the coast of Santo Domingo, the commander found Toussaint and his heroic compeers ready to defend their God-given liberty against even the terrors of the godless First Consul of France. Wheresoever these minions of slavery and despotism made their sacrilegious advances, devastation and death reigned under the exasperated genius of Toussaint.

He made that bold resolution and unalterable determination, which, in ancient times, would have entitled him to be deified among the gods; that resolution was to reduce the fair Edenlike Isle of Hispaniola to a desolate waste like Sahara and suffer every black to be immolated in a manly defense of his liberty, rather than the infernal and accursed system of Negro slavery should again be established on that soil. He considered it far better that his sable countrymen should be dead freemen than living slaves.

The French veterans grew pale at the terrible manner that the blacks set to work to execute this resolution. Leclerc found it impossible to execute his design by force; and he was only able to win the reconciliation of the exasperated blacks to the government of France by abandoning his hostilities and pledging himself to respect their freedom thereafter. It was then that the brave Negro generals of Toussaint went over in the service of Leclerc; and it was then that the negro chieftain himself resigned his post to the Governor General appointed by Napoleon, and went into the shades of domestic retirement at his home in Ennery.

Thus did Toussaint, by his firm resolution to execute his purpose, by his devotion to liberty and the cause of his race, so consistently maintained under all circumstances, more than deify himself; he proved himself more than a patriot; he showed himself to be the unswerving friend and servant of God and humanity.

Now, with the illustrious traits of character of this brilliant Negro before us, who will dare to say that the race who can thus produce such a noble specimen of a hero and statesman is incapable of self-government? Let such a vile slanderer, if there any longer remains such, hide his diminutive head in the presence of his illustrious Negro superior!

I know it may be said that, after all, Toussaint was found wanting in the necessary qualities to meet and triumph in the last emergency, when he was finally beguiled and sent to perish in the dungeons of France, a victim of the perfidious machinations of the heartless Napoleon.

On this point I will frankly own that Toussaint was deficient in those qualities by which his antagonist finally succeeded in getting him in his power.

So long as manly skill and shrewdness, so long as bold and open tactics and honorable stratagems were resorted to, the black had proved himself, in every respect, the equal of the white man. But the Negro's heart had not yet descended to that infamous depth of subtle depravity that could justify him in solemnly and publicly taking an oath, with the concealed, jesuitical purpose of thereby gaining an opportunity to deliberately violate the same. He had no conception, therefore, that the white man from whom he had learned all that he knew of true religion—I repeat it, he had no conception that the white man, bad as he was, slaveholder as he was—that *even* he was really so debased, vile and depraved as to be capable of such a double-dyed act of villainy as breaking an oath solemnly sealed by invoking the name of the Eternal God of Ages.

Hence, when the Captain General Leclerc said to Toussaint, in presence of the French and black generals, uplifting his hand and jeweled sword to heaven, "I swear before the face of the Supreme Being to respect the liberty of the people of Santo Domingo," Toussaint believed in the sincerity of this solemn oath of the white man. He threw down his arms and went to end the remainder of his days in the bosom of his family. This was, indeed, a sad mistake for him, to place so much confidence in the word of the white man. As the result of this first error, he easily fell into another equally treacherous. He was invited by General Brunet, another minion of Napoleon in Santo Domingo, to partake of the social hospitalities of his home; but, Toussaint, instead of finding the domestic civilities that he expected, was bound in chains, sent on board the *Hero*, a vessel already held in readiness for the consummation of the vile deed, in which he was carried a prisoner to France.

The magnanimous man bitterly repented at his leisure his too-great confidence in the word of the white man, in the cold dark dungeons of the castle of Joux. And the depth of his repentance was intensified by a compulsory fast ordered by that would-be great and magnanimous man, Napoleon Bonaparte, who denied him food and starved him to death.

Great God! how the blood runs chill, in contemplating the ignoble end of the illustrious Negro chieftain and statesman, by such base and perfidious means! . . .

Having now arrived at the epoch when the banners of Negro independence waved triumphantly over the Queen of the Antilles, if we look back at the trials and tribulations through which they came up to this point of national regeneration, we have presented to us, in the hardy endurance and perseverance manifested by them, in the steady pursuit of liberty and independence, the overwhelming evidence of their ability to govern themselves. For fourteen long and soul-trying years—twice the period of the revolutionary struggle of this country—they battled manfully for freedom. It was on the eighth of March, 1790, as we have seen, that the immortal man of color, Vincent Oje, obtained a decree from the National Assembly guaranteeing equal political privileges to the free men of color in the island. And, after a continued sanguinary struggle dating from that time, the never-to-be-forgotten self-emancipated black slave, Jean Jacques Dessalines, on the first of January, 1804, proclaimed Negro freedom and independence throughout the island of Santo Domingo.

That freedom and independence are written in the world's history in the ineffaceable characters of blood; and its crimsoned letters will ever testify of the determination of the ability of the Negro to be free, throughout the everlasting succession of ages. . . .

There have been but eight rulers in Haiti since 1804, counting separately, Christophe and Petion, who ruled contemporaneously. This is a period of fifty-three years down to the present time. And in the United States, since 1809, there have been ten different chief magistrates—a period of forty-eight years. Thus, this country has had two more rulers than Haiti, within a period five years less than the Haitian sovereignty.

The fact is, there is no nation in North America, but the United States, nor any in South America, except Brazil, that can pretend to compare with Haiti, in respect to general stability of government. The Spanish republics of America will have as many different rulers in eight years as Haiti has had in a half century.

And the colonial dependencies of European nations change governors at least three times as often as that Negro nation has done. This political stability, therefore, on the part of the Haitians indicates a vast remove from barbarism. It is far ahead of the anarchy of some so-called civilized nations. And it therefore indicates a high degree of civilization and progress. . . .

The overthrow of the government of Dessalines* by the spontaneous uprising of the people in their majesty, when it had become a merciless and tyrannical despotism, may also be noted here as another evidence of progress in political freedom of thought that made the race scorn to be tyrannized over by an oppressive master, whether that master was a cruel white tyrant or a merciless Negro despot. . . .

The Haitian people when governed by the crowned and imperial Dessalines testified their love of liberty by destroying the tyrant when he violated the constitution and overstepped the laws of his country.

---

*Dessalines proclaimed himself emperor on October 8, 1794, and was assassinated ten years later in the midst of a popular revolt against his rule.

The American people under a republican form of government manifest their want of a love of true liberty when they permit a vagabond set of politicians, whose character for rowdyism disgraces the nation, to enact such an odious law as the Fugitive Slave bill, violating the writ of habeas corpus and other sacred guarantees of the Constitution, and then tamely submit to this high-handed outrage because such unprincipled scoundrels voted in their insane revelry that it must be the supreme law of the land.

If there was one half of the real love of liberty among even the people of the professedly free Northern states as there is among the Negroes of Haiti, every one of their national representatives who voted for that infamous bill, or who would not vote instantaneously for its repeal, would be tried for his life, condemned and publicly executed as accessory to man stealing. Thus would a free people determined to preserve their liberties, rid themselves of a brood of petty tyrants who seek to impose their unhallowed partisan caprices upon the country, as the supreme law of the land, overriding even the Higher Law of God. And thus, in time would they exhibit an equally jealous regard for their rights as the Haitians did when they rid themselves of the tyrant Dessalines.

If such was the real love of liberty among the Northern people of this vainglorious Republic, we should soon annihilate that morally spineless class of politicians who need decision of character, when they get to Washington, to legislate for freedom. All such as were thus morally destitute of spinal vertebrae to resist the aggressions of the slave power in the national halls of legislation would also soon be physically deficient in their cervical vertebrae, when they returned home, to meet the extreme penalty of an outraged and indignant constituency.

But such a determined spirit of liberty does not exist here, and honest men must submit, therefore, with lamblike patience to this republican despotism of irresponsible political partisans who violate every just principle of law, because these unrighteous decrees are perpetrated in the name of the sovereign people.

Hence there is far more security for personal liberty and the general welfare of the governed among the monarchical Negroes of Haiti, where the rulers are held individually responsible for their public acts, than exists in this bastard democracy.

The single-necked despot is soon reached by the keen avenging ax of liberty, for any acts of despotism among the Haitian blacks; but here its dull and blunted edge lies useless, for it might be hurled in vain and fall powerless among a nameless crowd of millions.

CONCLUSION

But our historical investigations are at an end, and we must hasten to bring our reflections to a conclusion. I have now fulfilled my design in vindicating the capacity of the Negro race for self-government and civilized progress against the unjust aspersions of our unprincipled oppressors, by boldly examining the facts of Haitian history and deducing legitimate conclusions therefrom. I have summoned the sable heroes and statesmen of that independent isle of the Caribbean Sea and tried them by the high standard of modern civilization, fearlessly comparing them with the most illustrious men of the most enlightened nations of the earth; and in this examination and comparison the Negro race has not fallen one whit behind their contemporaries. And in this investigation I have made no allowance for the Negroes just emerging from a barbarous condition and out of the brutish ignorance of West Indian slavery. I have been careful not to make such an allowance, for fear that instead of proving Negro equality only, I should prove Negro superiority. I shun the point of making this allowance to the Negro, as it might reverse the case of the question entirely that I have been combating and, instead of disproving his alleged inferiority only, would on the other hand, go farther, and establish his superiority. Therefore as it is my design to banish the words "superiority" and "inferiority" from the vocabulary of the world, when applied to the natural capacity of races of men, I claim no allowance for them on the score of their condition and circumstances.

Having now presented the preceding array of facts and arguments to establish, before the world, the Negro's equality with the white man in carrying forward the great principles of self-government and civilized progress, I would now have these facts exert their legitimate influence over the minds of my race in this country, in producing that most desirable object of arousing them to a full consciousness of their own inherent dignity and thereby increasing among them that self-respect which shall urge them on to the performance of those great deeds which the age and the race now demand at their hands.

Our brethren of Haiti, who stand in the vanguard of the race, have already made a name and a fame for us that is as imperishable as the world's history. They exercise sovereign authority over an island that in natural advantages is the Eden of America and the garden spot of the world. Her rich resources invite the capacity of ten million human beings to adequately use them. It becomes, then, an important question for the Negro race in America to well consider the weighty responsibility that the present exigency devolves upon them, to contribute to the continued advancement of this Negro nationality of the New World until its glory and renown shall overspread and cover the whole earth and redeem and regenerate by its influence in the future the benighted fatherland of the race in Africa.

Here in this black nationality of the New World, erected under such glorious auspices, is the standpoint that must be occupied, and the lever that must be exerted, to regenerate and disenthrall the oppression and ignorance of the race throughout the world. We must not overlook this practical vantage ground which Providence has raised up for us out of the depths of the sea, for any man-made and utopian scheme that is prematurely forced upon us, to send us across the ocean, to rummage the graves of our ancestors, in fruitless and ill-directed efforts at the wrong end of human progress. Civilization and Christianity are passing from the East to the West; and their pristine splendor will only be rekindled in the ancient nations of the Old World after they have belted the globe in its westward course and revisited the Orient again. The Serpentine trial of civilization and Christianity, like the ancient philosophic symbol of eternity, must coil backward to its fountainhead. God, therefore, in permitting the accursed slave traffic to transplant so many millions of the race to the New World and educing therefrom such a Negro nationality as Haiti, indicates thereby that we have a work now to do here in the Western world, which in his own good times shall shed its Orient beams upon the fatherland of the race. Let us see to it that we meet the exigency now imposed upon us as nobly on our part at this time as the Haitians met theirs at the opening of the present century. And in seeking to perform this duty, it may well be a question with us whether it is not our duty to go and identify our destiny with our heroic brethren in that independent isle of the Caribbean Sea, carrying with us such of the arts, sciences and genius of modern civilization as we may gain from this hardy and enterprising Anglo-American race, in order to add to Haitian advancements, rather than to indolently remain here, asking for political rights which, if granted a social proscription stronger than conventional legislation, will ever render nugatory and of no avail the manly elevation and general well-being of the race. If one powerful and civilized Negro sovereignty can be developed to the summit of national grandeur in the West Indies, where the keys to the commerce of both hemispheres can be held, this fact will solve all questions respecting the Negro, whether they be those of slavery, prejudice or proscription, and wheresoever on the face of the globe such questions shall present themselves for a satisfactory solution.

A concentration and combination of the Negro race of the Western Hemisphere in Haiti, can produce just such a national development. The duty to do so is therefore incumbent on them. And the responsibility of leading off in this gigantic enterprise Providence seems to have made our peculiar task by the eligibility of our situation in this country as a point for gaining an easy access to that island. Then let us boldly enlist in this high pathway of duty, while the watchwords that shall cheer and inspire us in our noble and glorious undertaking shall be the soul-stirring anthem of God and Humanity.■

53 LIBERTY FOR SLAVES

Frances Ellen Watkins

Born of free parents in Baltimore, Frances Ellen Watkins (1825–1911) was a highly acclaimed poet, novelist, organizer, and lecturer. After teaching in New York and Pennsylvania, Watkins became a professional abolitionist lecturer employed by the Maine Anti-Slavery Society to speak throughout the Northeast. "Because she was so articulate and engaging as a public speaker," Hazel Carby writes, "some audiences thought Harper [Watkins's later married name] must be a man, while others thought she couldn't possibly be black and had to be painted." Few abolitionist writers or speakers could match Watkins's ability to express the horrors and oppressiveness of slavery or the yearning of African Americans for undiminished liberty. In her 1858 poem, "Bury Me in a Free land," Watkins explained that she wanted no slaves around her grave, because

> *I could not rest if I heard the tread*
> *Of a coffee-gang to the shambles led,*
> *And the mother's shriek of wild despair*
> *Rise like a curse on the trembling air.*

> *I could not rest if I heard the lash*
> *Drinking her blood at each fearful gash,*
> *And I saw her babes torn from her breast,*
> *Like trembling doves from their parent nest.*

> *I'd shudder and start, if I heard the bay*
> *Of the blood-hounds seizing their human prey:*
> *If I heard the captive plead in vain,*
> *As they tightened afresh his galling chain.*

Watkins married Fenton Harper in 1860 and returned to the lecture circuit upon his death in 1864. An avid promoter of temperance and women's rights, she served the national Women's Christian Temperance Union as head of the Department for Work Among Negroes and was among the organizers of the National Association of Colored Women in 1896. For more information, see Hazel Carby, Reconstructing Womanhood *(New York: Oxford University Press, 1987), 62–94; Dorothy Sterling,* We Are Your Sisters: Black Women in the Nineteenth Century *(New York: W. W. Norton, 1984), 159–64; Frances Smith Foster, ed.,* A Brighter Coming Day: A Frances Ellen Watkins Harper Reader *(New York: Feminist Press, 1990).*

The following speech is one of the few surviving examples of

*Watkins's antislavery oratory. It was delivered on the fourth anniversary
meeting of the New York Anti-Slavery Society on May 13, 1857. The text
is reprinted from the* National Anti-Slavery Standard, *May 23, 1857, p. 3.*

Could we trace the record of every human heart, the aspirations of every
immortal soul, perhaps we would find no man so imbruted and degraded that we could not trace the word liberty either written in living characters upon the soul or hidden away in some nook or corner of the heart.
The law of liberty is the law of God, and is antecedent to all human legislation. It existed in the mind of Deity when He hung the first world upon its
orbit and gave it liberty to gather light from the central sun.

Some people say, set the slaves free. Did you ever think, if the slaves
were free, they would steal everything they could lay their hands on from
now till the day of their death—that they would steal more than two thousand millions of dollars? (applause) Ask Maryland, with her tens of thousands of slaves, if she is not prepared for freedom, and hear her answer:
"I help supply the coffee-gangs of the South." Ask Virginia, with her hundreds of thousands of slaves, if she is not weary with her merchandise of
blood and anxious to shake the gory traffic from her hands, and hear her
reply: "Though fertility has covered my soil, through a genial sky bends over
my hills and vales, though I hold in my hand a wealth of water-power enough
to turn the spindles to clothe the world, yet, with all these advantages, one
of my chief staples has been the sons and daughters I send to the human
market and human shambles." (applause) Ask the farther South, and all the
cotton-growing States chime in, "We have need of fresh supplies to fill the
ranks of those whose lives have gone out in unrequited toil on our distant
plantations."

A hundred thousand new-born babes are annually added to the victims
of slavery; twenty thousand lives are annually sacrificed on the plantations
of the South. Such a sight should send a thrill of horror through the nerves
of civilization and impel the heart of humanity to lofty deeds. So it might,
if men had not found out a fearful alchemy by which this blood can be transformed into gold. Instead of listening to the cry of agony, they listen to the
ring of dollars and stoop down to pick up the coin. (applause)

But a few months since a man escaped from bondage and found a temporary shelter almost beneath the shadow of Bunker Hill. Had that man
stood upon the deck of an Austrian ship, beneath the shadow of the house
of the Hapsburgs, he would have found protection. Had he been wrecked
upon an island or colony of Great Britain, the waves of the tempest-lashed
ocean would have washed him deliverance. Had he landed upon the territory
of vine-encircled France and a Frenchman had reduced him to a thing and
brought him here beneath the protection of our institutions and our laws,
for such a nefarious deed that Frenchman would have lost his citizenship in
France. Beneath the feebler light which glimmers from the Koran, the Bey of

Tunis would have granted him freedom in his own dominions. Beside the ancient pyramids of Egypt he would have found liberty, for the soil laved by the glorious Nile is now consecrated to freedom. But from Boston harbour, made memorable by the infusion of three-penny taxed tea, Boston in its proximity to the plains of Lexington and Concord, Boston almost beneath the shadow of Bunker Hill and almost in sight of Plymouth Rock, he is thrust back from liberty and manhood and reconverted into a chattel. You have heard that, down South, they keep bloodhounds to hunt slaves. Ye blood-hounds, go back to your kennels; when you fail to catch the flying fugitive, when his stealthy tread is heard in the place where the bones of the revolutionary sires repose, the ready North is base enough to do your shameful service. (applause)

Slavery is mean, because it tramples on the feeble and weak. A man comes with his affidavits from the South and hurries me before a commissioner; upon that evidence *ex parte* and alone he hitches me to the car of slavery and trails my womanhood in the dust. I stand at the threshold of the Supreme Court and ask for justice, simple justice. Upon my tortured heart is thrown the mocking words, "You are a negro; you have no rights which white men are bound to respect"!* (loud and long-continued applause) Had it been my lot to have lived beneath the Crescent instead of the Cross, had injustice and violence been heaped upon my head as a Mohammedan woman, as a member of a common faith, I might have demanded justice and been listened to by the Pasha, the Bey or the Vizier; but when I come here to ask for justice, men tell me, "We have no higher law than the Constitution." (applause)

But I will not dwell on the dark side of the picture. God is on the side of freedom; and any cause that has God on its side, I care not how much it may be trampled upon, how much it may be trailed in the dust, is sure to triumph. The message of Jesus Christ is on the side of freedom, "I come to preach deliverance to the captives, the opening of the prison doors to them that are bound." The truest and noblest hearts in the land are on the side of freedom. They may be hissed at by slavery's minions, their names cast out as evil, their characters branded with fanaticism, but O, *"To side with Truth is noble when we share her humble crust Ere the cause bring fame and profit and it's prosperous to be just."*

May I not, in conclusion, ask every honest, noble heart, every seeker after truth and justice, if they will not also be on the side of freedom. Will you not resolve that you will abate neither heart nor hope till you hear the death-knell of human bondage sounded, and over the black ocean of slavery shall be heard a song, more exulting than the song of Miriam when it floated o'er Egypt's dark sea, the requiem of Egypt's ruined hosts and the anthem of the deliverance of Israel's captive people? (great applause)■

---

*Watkins paraphrases Chief Justice Roger Taney's majority opinion in the *Dred Scott* decision, issued two months before her speech.

54 IF THERE IS NO STRUGGLE THERE IS NO PROGRESS

Frederick Douglass

In 1833, after years of pressure by antislavery crusaders, the British government passed a bill for the abolition of slavery in the British West Indies, to go into effect on August 1, 1834. Although a system of apprenticeship continued until the end of 1838, limiting for several years the effectiveness of the law, the emancipation of the slaves in the West Indies stimulated the struggle against the institution in this country and was annually celebrated by the abolitionists. On August 3, 1857, the twenty-third anniversary, Frederick Douglass delivered a "West India Emancipation" speech at Canandaigua, New York. Most of the address was devoted to the significance of the British legislation, but the closing portions are of great importance as a presentation of Douglass's philosophy of militant abolitionism.

At first, Douglass, an avid disciple of William Lloyd Garrison, was guided by the concept that "moral suasion" was the chief weapon in the battle to end slavery. But new associations and his studies and thinking caused him to abandon faith in moral suasion and advance the doctrine that African Americans would never get their freedom unless they fought for it even at the cost of their lives. The African American, moreover, had to play a leading role in the fight against slavery rather than serve as a subordinate to white abolitionists. Although the Garrisonians bitterly attacked Douglass for breaking with their doctrines, accusing him of selfishly placing his own interests above those of the antislavery cause, he persisted in presenting his own antislavery philosophy and never more firmly and eloquently than in the concluding section of this 1857 "West India Emancipation" speech. This section, presented below, is taken from the pamphlet Two Speeches by Frederick Douglass, One on West India Emancipation . . . and the Other on the Dred Scott Decision . . . *(Rochester, 1857).*

THE GENERAL SENTIMENT of mankind is that a man who will not fight for himself, when he has the means of doing so, is not worth being fought for by others, and this sentiment is just. For a man who does not value freedom for himself will never value it for others, or put himself to any inconvenience to gain it for others. Such a man, the world says, may lie down until he has sense enough to stand up. It is useless and cruel to put a man on his legs, if the next moment his head is to be brought against a curbstone.

A man of that type will never lay the world under any obligation to him, but will be a moral pauper, a drag on the wheels of society, and if he too be identified with a peculiar variety of the race he will entail disgrace upon his race as well as upon himself. The world in which we live is very accommodating to all sorts of people. It will cooperate with them in any measure which they propose; it will help those who earnestly help themselves, and will hinder those who hinder themselves. It is very polite, and never offers its services unasked. Its favors to individuals are measured by an unerring principle in this—viz., respect those who respect themselves, and despise those who despise themselves. It is not within the power of unaided human nature to persevere in pitying a people who are insensible to their own wrongs and indifferent to the attainment of their own rights. The poet was as true to common sense as to poetry when he said,

Who would be free, themselves must strike the blow.[*]

When O'Connell, with all Ireland at his back, was supposed to be contending for the just rights and liberties of Ireland, the sympathies of mankind were with him, and even his enemies were compelled to respect his patriotism. Kossuth, fighting for Hungary with his pen long after she had fallen by the sword, commanded the sympathy and support of the liberal world till his own hopes died out. The Turks, while they fought bravely for themselves and scourged and drove back the invading legions of Russia, shared the admiration of mankind. They were standing up for their own rights against an arrogant and powerful enemy; but as soon as they let out their fighting to the Allies, admiration gave way to contempt. These are not the maxims and teachings of a coldhearted world. Christianity itself teaches that a man shall provide for his own house. This covers the whole ground of nations as well as individuals. Nations no more than individuals can innocently be improvident. They should provide for all wants—mental, moral and religious—and against all evils to which they are liable as nations. In the great struggle now progressing for the freedom and elevation of our people, we should be found at work with all our might, resolved that no man or set of men shall be more abundant in labors, according to the measure of our ability, than ourselves.

I know, my friends, that in some quarters the efforts of colored people meet with very little encouragement. We may fight, but we must fight like the Sepoys of India, under white officers. This class of Abolitionists don't like colored celebrations, they don't like colored conventions, they don't like colored antislavery fairs for the support of colored newspapers. They don't like any demonstrations whatever in which colored men take a leading part. They talk of the proud Anglo-Saxon blood as flippantly as those who profess to believe in the natural inferiority of races. Your humble speaker has been branded as an ingrate, because he has ventured to stand up on his own right and to plead our common cause as a colored man, rather than as a Garrisonian. I hold it to be no part of gratitude to allow our white friends to do

[*]Lord Byron, *Childe Harold's Pilgrimage* (1812), canto 2.

all the work, while we merely hold their coats. Opposition of the sort now referred to is partisan position, and we need not mind it. The white people at large will not largely be influenced by it. They will see and appreciate all honest efforts on our part to improve our condition as a people.

Let me give you a word of the philosophy of reform. The whole history of the progress of human liberty shows that all concessions yet made to her august claims have been born of earnest struggle. The conflict has been exciting, agitating, all-absorbing, and for the time being, putting all other tumults to silence. It must do this or it does nothing. If there is no struggle there is no progress. Those who profess to favor freedom and yet deprecate agitation are men who want crops without plowing up the ground; they want rain without thunder and lightning. They want the ocean without the awful roar of its many waters.

This struggle may be a moral one, or it may be a physical one, and it may be both moral and physical, but it must be a struggle. Power concedes nothing without a demand. It never did and it never will. Find out just what any people will quietly submit to and you have found out the exact measure of injustice and wrong which will be imposed upon them, and these will continue till they are resisted with either words or blows, or with both. The limits of tyrants are prescribed by the endurance of those whom they oppress. In the light of these ideas, Negroes will be hunted at the North and held and flogged at the South so long as they submit to those devilish outrages and make no resistance, either moral or physical. Men may not get all they pay for in this world, but they must certainly pay for all they get. If we ever get free from the oppressions and wrongs heaped upon us, we must pay for their removal. We must do this by labor, by suffering, by sacrifice, and if needs be, by our lives and the lives of others.

Hence, my friends, every mother who, like Margaret Garner, plunges a knife into the bosom of her infant to save it from the hell of our Christian slavery,* should be held and honored as a benefactress. Every fugitive from slavery who, like the noble William Thomas at Wilkes Barre, prefers to perish in a river made red by his own blood to submission to the hell hounds who were hunting and shooting him should be esteemed as a glorious martyr, worthy to be held in grateful memory by our people. The fugitive Horace, at Mechanicsburgh, Ohio, the other day, who taught the slave catchers from Kentucky that it was safer to arrest white men than to arrest him, did a most excellent service to our cause. Parker and his noble band of fifteen at Christiana, who defended themselves from the kidnapers with prayers and pistols, are entitled to the honor of making the first successful resistance to

---

*In January 1856, the Garner family, enslaved by Archibald K. Gaines of Kentucky, escaped and found refuge in Cincinnati. They were pursued and attacked. Before the group was captured, Margaret Garner killed one of her children and severely wounded two others "to save them all from slavery by death." She was tried on a murder charge in Cincinnati and found guilty but because of jurisdictional difficulties was returned to slavery in Kentucky.

the Fugitive Slave Bill.* But for that resistance, and the rescue of Jerry and Shadrack,† the man hunters would have hunted our hills and valleys here with the same freedom with which they now hunt their own dismal swamps.

There was an important lesson in the conduct of that noble Krooman in New York the other day, who, supposing that the American Christians were about to enslave him, betook himself to the masthead and with knife in hand said he would cut his throat before he would be made a slave. Joseph Cinque, on the deck of the *Amistad,* did that which should make his name dear to us. He bore nature's burning protest against slavery. Madison Washington who struck down his oppressor on the deck of the *Creole,* is more worthy to be remembered than the colored man who shot Pitcairn at Bunker Hill.‡

My friends, you will observe that I have taken a wide range, and you think it is about time that I should answer the special objection to this celebration. I think so too. This, then, is the truth concerning the inauguration of freedom in the British West Indies. Abolition was the act of the British government. The motive which led the government to act no doubt was mainly a philanthropic one, entitled to our highest admiration and gratitude. The national religion, the justice and humanity cried out in thunderous indignation against the foul abomination, and the government yielded to the storm. Nevertheless a share of the credit of the result falls justly to the slaves themselves. "Though slaves, they were rebellious slaves." They bore themselves well. They did not hug their chains, but according to their opportunities, swelled the general protest against oppression. What Wilberforce was endeavoring to win from the British senate by his magic eloquence the slaves themselves were endeavoring to gain by outbreaks and violence. The com-

---

*In the early dawn of September 11, 1851, an attack was made on the home of William Parker, of Christiana, Pennsylvania, to arrest some fugitive slaves said to be hidden there. Blacks in the neighborhood came to their defense, and a battle took place. Edward Gorsuch, a Maryland slaveholder, was killed by Parker, and Gorsuch's son was wounded. Parker escaped to Canada, assisted from Rochester by Frederick Douglass. Thirty-eight of the men involved in the battle, thirty-six blacks and two whites, were indicted for treason against the United States and were brought to trial in Lancaster County Courthouse. Castner Hanway, a Quaker who had refused to assist in capturing the fugitives, was the first to be tried. The jury found Hanway not guilty, and the others were released.

†The Jerry Rescue occurred at Syracuse, New York, on October 1, 1851. Gerrit Smith and other abolitionists forcibly rescued the fugitive slave Jerry McHenry, who had been seized and imprisoned by a deputy U.S. marshal, and helped him to escape to Canada and freedom.

In February 1851, Shadrack, a black waiter in Boston, was arrested and charged with having escaped from the South. Before the case was decided, a body of African Americans led by Lewis Hayden broke into the prison, seized Shadrack, and dispatched him to Canada.

‡British Major Pitcairn was killed, it is generally assumed, by a volley from the musket of Peter Salem, one of the African Americans who fought in the Battle of Bunker Hill.

bined action of one and the other wrought out the final result. While one showed that slavery was wrong, the other showed that it was dangerous as well as wrong. Mr. Wilberforce,* peace man though he was, and a model of piety, availed himself of this element to strengthen his case before the British Parliament, and warned the British government of the danger of continuing slavery in the West Indies. There is no doubt that the fear of the consequences, acting with a sense of the moral evil of slavery, led to its abolition. The spirit of freedom was abroad in the Islands. Insurrection for freedom kept the planters in a constant state of alarm and trepidation. A standing army was necessary to keep the slaves in their chains. This state of facts could not be without weight in deciding the question of freedom in these countries.

I am aware that the rebellious disposition of the slaves was said to arise out of the discussions which the Abolitionists were carrying on at home, and it is not necessary to refute this alleged explanation. All that I contend for is this: that the slaves of the West Indies did fight for their freedom, and that the fact of their discontent was known in England, and that it assisted in bringing about that state of public opinion which finally resulted in their emancipation. And if this be true, the objection is answered.

Again, I am aware that the insurrectionary movements of the slaves were held by many to be prejudicial to their cause. This is said now of such movements at the South. The answer is that abolition followed close on the heels of insurrection in the West Indies, and Virginia was never nearer emancipation than when General Turner kindled the fires of insurrection at Southampton.†

Sir, I have now more than filled up the measure of my time. I thank you for the patient attention given to what I have had to say. I have aimed, as I said at the beginning, to express a few thoughts having some relation to the great interests of freedom both in this country and in the British West Indies, and I have said all that I meant to say, and the time will not permit me to say more.■

---

*Wilberforce was active in the battle against the slave system in the British West Indies, but the struggle was actually led by Thomas Fowell Buxton. As Eric Williams has emphasized, however, it was the activities of the slaves themselves in repeated uprisings that played a decisive role in West Indies emancipation. See Eric Williams, *Capitalism and Slavery* (New York, 1961), 197.

†Nathaniel Turner led a slave rebellion in Virginia in 1831, sending shock waves throughout the region.

55 I WILL SINK OR SWIM WITH MY RACE

John S. Rock

Schoolteacher, dentist, physician, lawyer, graduate of the American Medical College in Philadelphia, member of the Massachusetts bar, proficient in Greek and Latin, Dr. John S. Rock was one of the leaders of the movement for equal rights for black Americans in the North. Dr. Rock used the lecture platform effectively to challenge the racist concept that blacks were inferior to whites. A good example is the following speech he delivered at Boston, March 5, 1858, at Boston's Fanueil Hall on the first annual Crispus Attucks Day, an observance organized by Boston's black abolitionists in response to the Dred Scott *decision. Revolutionary War relics were arrayed before the lectern, including paintings and memorabilia honoring black contributions to the American Revolution. Attucks Day was observed in Boston each year until 1870, when the Fifteenth Amendment was passed.*

Rock joined William Lloyd Garrison, Wendell Phillips, and Theodore Parker on the platform and delivered the most militant speech. Three years before the outbreak of the Civil War, Dr. Rock was predicting that African Americans were destined to play an important role in the impending military conflict over slavery. This speech is also notable for Rock's concluding statements on the beauty and power of black people.

John S. Rock was born in Salem, New Jersey, in 1825. He was a teacher in the public schools during 1844–1848, and in the following year he finished studying dentistry under Dr. Harbert Hubbard. In 1850 he began practicing dentistry in Philadelphia, and in 1851 he received a silver medal for the creation of artificial teeth and another silver medal for a prize essay on temperance. In 1852 he graduated from the American Medical College in Philadelphia, and the following year began the practice of medicine and dentistry in Boston. He was admitted to practice law in Massachusetts in 1861 and on September 21 of that year received a commission from the governor as justice of peace for seven years for the city of Boston and the County of Suffolk. In February 1865, having been supported in his candidacy by Charles Sumner, Rock was sworn in by Chief Justice Salmon P. Chase and became the first African American lawyer permitted to argue before the U.S. Supreme Court. He died in Boston on December 3, 1866.

Rock's speech was published in the Liberator, *March 12, 1858. For further information on the Crispus Attucks Day observances, see Benjamin Quarles,* Black Abolitionists *(New York: Oxford University Press, 1969), 232–35. On Rock, see James Oliver Horton and Lois E. Horton,* Black Bostonians: Family Life and Community Struggle in the Antebellum North *(New York: Holmes and Meier, 1979).*

L adies and Gentlemen: You will not expect a lengthened speech from me to-night. My health is too poor to allow me to indulge much in speech-making. But I have not been able to resist the temptation to unite with you in this demonstration of respect for some of my noble but misguided ancestors.

White Americans have taken great pains to try to prove that we are cowards. We are often insulted with the assertion, that if we had had the courage of the Indians or the white man, we would never have submitted to be slaves. I ask if Indians and white men have never been slaves? The white man tested the Indian's courage here when he had his organized armies, his battle-grounds, his places of retreat, with everything to hope for and everything to lose. The position of the African slave has been very different. Seized a prisoner of war, unarmed, bound hand and foot, and conveyed to a distant country among what to him were worse than cannibals; brutally beaten, half-starved, closely watched by armed men, with no means of knowing their own strength or the strength of their enemies, with no weapons, and without a probability of success. But if the white man will take the trouble to fight the black man in Africa or in Hayti, and fight him as fair as the black man will fight him there—if the black man does not come off victor, I am deceived in his prowess. But, take a man, armed or unarmed, from his home, his country, or his friends, and place him among savages, and who is he that would not make good his retreat? "Discretion is the better part of valor," but for a man to resist where he knows it will destroy him, shows more fool-hardiness than courage. There have been many Anglo-Saxons and Anglo-Americans enslaved in Africa, but I have never heard that they successfully resisted any government. They always resort to running indispensables.

The courage of the Anglo-Saxon is best illustrated in his treatment of the negro. A score or two of them can pounce upon a poor negro, tie and beat him, and then call him a coward because he submits. Many of their most brilliant victories have been achieved in the same manner. But the greatest battles which they have fought have been upon paper. We can easily account for this; their trumpeter is dead. He died when they used to be exposed for sale in the Roman market, about the time that Cicero cautioned his friend Atticus not to buy them, on account of their stupidity. A little more than half a century ago, this race, in connection with their Celtic neighbors, who have long been considered (by themselves, of course,) as the bravest soldiers in the world, so far forgot themselves as to attack a few cowardly, stupid negro slaves, who, according to their accounts, had not sense enough to go to bed. And what was the result? Why, sir, the negroes drove them out from the island like so many sheep, and they have never dared to show their faces, except with hat in hand.

Our true and tried friend, Rev. Theodore Parker* said, in his speech at the State House, a few weeks since, that "the stroke of the axe would have settled the question long ago, but the black man would not strike." Mr. Parker makes a very low estimate of the courage of his race, if he means that one, two or three millions of those ignorant and cowardly black slaves could, without means, have brought to their knees five, ten, or twenty millions of intelligent brave white men, backed up by a rich oligarchy. But I know of no one who is more familiar with the true character of the Anglo-Saxon race than Mr. Parker. I will not dispute this point with him, but I will thank him or any one else to tell us how it could have been done. His remark calls to my mind the day which is to come, when one shall chase a thousand, and two put ten thousand to flight. But when he says that "the black man *would not* strike," I am prepared to say that he does us great injustice. The black man is not a coward. The history of the bloody struggles for freedom in Hayti, in which the blacks whipped the French and the English, and gained their independence, in spite of the perfidy of that villainous First Consul, will be a lasting refutation of the malicious aspersions of our enemies. The history of the struggles for the liberty of the U.S. ought to silence every American calumniator. I have learned that even so late as the Texan war, a number of black men were found silly enough to offer themselves as living sacrifices for our country's shame. A gentleman who delivered a lecture before the New York Legislature, a few years since, whose name I do not now remember, but whose language I give with some precision, said, "In the Revolution, colored soldiers fought side by side with you in your struggles for liberty, and there is not a battle-field from Maine to Georgia that has not been crimsoned with their blood, and whitened with their bones." In 1814, a bill passed the Legislature of New York, accepting the services of 2000 colored volunteers. Many black men served under Com. McDonough when he conquered on lake Champlain. Many were in the battles of Plattsburgh and Sackett's Harbor, and General Jackson called out colored troops from Louisiana and Alabama, and in a solemn proclamation attested to their fidelity and courage.

The white man contradicts himself who says, that if he were in our situation, he would throw off the yoke. Thirty millions of white men of this proud Caucasian race are at this moment held as slaves, and bought and sold with horses and cattle. The iron heel of oppression grinds the masses of all the European races to the dust. They suffer every kind of oppression, and no one dares to open his mouth to protest against it. Even in the Southern portion of this boasted land of liberty, no white man dares advocate so much of the Declaration of Independence as declares that "all men are created free and equal, and have an inalienable right to life, liberty," &c.

White men have no room to taunt us with tamely submitting. If they

---

*Theodore Parker (1810–1860), a Unitarian clergyman and a leader in the antislavery movement, also addressed the Boston meeting.

were black men they would work wonders; but, as white men, they can do nothing. "O, Consistency, thou art a jewel!"

Now, it would not be surprising if the brutal treatment which we have received for the past two centuries should have crushed our spirits. But this is not the case. Nothing but a superior force keeps us down. And when I see the slaves rising up by hundreds annually, in the majesty of human nature, bidding defiance to every slave code and its penalties, making the issue Canada or death, and that too while they are closely watched by paid men armed with pistols, clubs and bowie-knives, with the army and navy of this great Model Republic arrayed against them, I am disposed to ask if the charge of cowardice does not come with an ill-grace.

But some men are so steeped in folly and imbecility; so lost to all feelings of their own littleness; so destitute of principle, and so regardless of humanity, that they dare attempt to destroy everything which exists in opposition to their interests or opinions which their narrow comprehensions cannot grasp.

We ought not to come here simply to honor those brave men who shed their blood for freedom, or to protest against the Dred Scott decision,* but to take counsel of each other, and to enter into new vows of duty. Our fathers fought nobly for freedom, but they were not victorious. They fought for liberty, but they got slavery. The white man was benefitted, but the black man was injured. I do not envy the white American the little liberty which he enjoys. It is his right, and he ought to have it. I wish him success, though I do not think he deserves it. But I would have all men free. We have had much sad experience in this country, and it would be strange indeed if we do not profit by some of the lessons which we have so dearly paid for. Sooner or later, the clashing of arms will be heard in this country, and the black man's services will be needed: 150,000 freemen capable of bearing arms, and not all cowards and fools, and three quarters of a million of slaves, wild with the enthusiasm caused by the dawn of the glorious opportunity of being able to strike a genuine blow for freedom, will be a power which white men will be "bound to respect." Will the blacks fight? Of course they will. The black man will never be neutral. He could not if he would, and he would not if he could. Will he fight for this country, right or wrong? This the common sense of every one answers; and when the time comes, and come it will, the black man will give an intelligent answer. Judge Taney may outlaw us; Caleb

*The reference is to the *Dred Scott* decision rendered by the Supreme Court on March 6, 1857. Dred Scott, a slave, had been brought into the Louisiana Territory north of the line above which slavery was prohibited by law. After he was returned to the slave state of Missouri, he sued for his freedom. Chief Justice Roger B. Taney, writing the majority opinion, held that Dred Scott could never be a citizen within the meaning of the Constitution and therefore had no right to sue in a federal court. Taney also went on to declare that the Missouri Compromise was unconstitutional when it forbade slavery above 36° 30′ north latitude.

Cushing* may show the depravity of his heart by abusing us; and this wicked government may oppress us; but the black man will live when Judge Taney, Caleb Cushing and this wicked government are no more. White men may despise, ridicule, slander and abuse us; they may seek as they always have done to divide us, and make us feel degraded; but no man shall cause me to turn my back upon my race. With it I will sink or swim.

The prejudice which some white men have, or affect to have, against my color gives me no pain. If any man does not fancy my color, that is his business, and I shall not meddle with it. I shall give myself no trouble because he lacks good taste. If he judges my intellectual capacity by my color, he certainly cannot expect much profundity, for it is only skin deep, and is really of no very great importance to any one but myself. I will not deny that I admire the talents and noble characters of many white men. But I cannot say that I am particularly pleased with their physical appearance. If old mother nature had held out as well as she commenced, we should, probably, have had fewer varieties in the races. When I contrast the fine tough muscular system, the beautiful, rich color, the full broad features, and the gracefully frizzled hair of the negro, with the delicate physical organization, wan color, sharp features and lank hair of the Caucasian, I am inclined to believe that when the white man was created, nature was pretty well exhausted—but determined to keep up appearances, she pinched up his features, and did the best she could under the circumstances. (Great laughter.)

I would have you understand, that I not only love my race, but am pleased with my color; and while many colored persons may feel degraded by being called negroes, and wish to be classed among other races more favored, I shall feel it my duty, my pleasure and my pride, to concentrate my feeble efforts in elevating to a fair position a race to which I am especially identified by feelings and by blood.

My friends, we can never become elevated until we are true to ourselves. We can come here and make brilliant speeches, but our field of duty is elsewhere. Let us go to work—each man in his place, determined to do what he can for himself and his race. Let us try to carry out some of the resolutions which we have made, and are so fond of making. If we do this, friends will spring up in every quarter, and where we least expect them. But we must not rely on them. They cannot elevate us. Whenever the colored man is elevated, it will be by his own exertions. Our friends can do what many of them are nobly doing, assist us to remove the obstacles which prevent our elevation, and stimulate the worthy to persevere. The colored man who, by dint of perseverance and industry, educates and elevates himself, prepares the way for others, gives character to the race, and hastens the day of general emancipation. While the negro who hangs around the corners of the streets, or lives in the grog-shops or by gambling, or who has no higher ambition

*Caleb Cushing (1800–1879), a leading Massachusetts Democrat, was a member of Congress from 1835 to 1843 and attorney general of the United States from 1853 to 1857.

than to serve, is by his vocation forging fetters for the slave, and is "to all intents and purposes" a curse to his race. It is true, considering the circumstances under which we have been placed by our white neighbors, we have a right to ask them not only to cease to oppress us, but to give us that encouragement which our talents and industry may merit. When this is done, they will see our minds expand, and our pockets filled with rocks. How very few colored men are encouraged in their trades or business! Our young men see this, and become disheartened. In this country, where money is the great sympathetic nerve which ramifies society, and has a ganglia in every man's pocket, a man is respected in proportion to his success in business. When the avenues to wealth are opened to us, we will then become educated and wealthy, and then the roughest looking colored man that you ever saw, or ever will see, will be pleasanter than the harmonics of Orpheus, and black will be a very pretty color. It will make our jargon, wit—our words, oracles; flattery will then take the place of slander, and you will find no prejudice in the Yankee whatever. We do not expect to occupy a much better position than we now do, until we shall have our educated and wealthy men, who can wield a power that cannot be misunderstood. Then, and not till then, will the tongue of slander be silenced, and the lip of prejudice sealed. Then, and not till then, will we be able to enjoy true equality, which can exist only among peers.

[A hymn entitled "Freedom's Battle," written for the occasion by Miss Frances E. Watkins, was then sung by a company of colored vocalists, Miss Adelaide V. Putnam presiding at the piano.]■

56 BREAK EVERY YOKE AND LET THE OPPRESSED GO FREE

Mary Ann Shadd

Mary Ann Shadd (1823–1893) was born into an affluent free black family in Wilmington, Delaware. She founded and taught in several schools for black children, always emphasizing what biographer Jason Silverman has identified as "her perennial themes: black independence and self-respect" ("Mary Ann Shadd," 88).

After the passage of the Fugitive Slave Act in 1850, Shadd joined thousands of other African Americans in emigrating to Canada. Unlike

*many other prominent emigrationists, Shadd believed that integration
into the mainstream of white society was the only way in which blacks
could gain their rights. To promote her views and to denounce separa-
tists, Shadd published the first issue of the* Provincial Freeman *in 1853,
thus becoming the first black woman newspaper editor in North America. The paper's motto (and Shadd's) was: "Self-reliance Is the Fine Road
to Independence."*

*After the Civil War, Shadd moved to Washington, D.C., where, at the
age of forty-six, she became the first woman to enroll in the law school
of Howard University. She received her degree in 1883. She was an active
campaigner for women's suffrage and founded the Colored Women's Progressive Franchise Association. Shadd had believed in and lectured about
the connectedness of women's rights and the antislavery cause since the
early 1850s. This relationship is apparent in her sermon on the evening of
Sunday, April 6, 1858, to an audience in Chatham, Canada. The text is
reprinted with the permission of the Archives of Toronto, Ontario, and
was previously published in volume 2 of C. Peter Ripley, ed.,* The Black
Abolitionist Papers *(Chapel Hill: University of North Carolina Press,
1991). For more information, see Jason H. Silverman, "Mary Ann Shadd
and the Search for Equality," in Leon Litwack and August Meier, eds.,*
Black Leaders of the Nineteenth Century *(Urbana: University of Illinois
Press, 1988), 87–102.*

1st business of life[,] to love the Lord our God with heart and soul, and
our neighbor as our self.

We must then manifest love to God by obedience to his will—we must
be cheerful workers, in his cause at all times—on the Sabbath and other days.
The more readiness we Evince the more we manifest our love, and as our
field is directly among those of his creatures made in his own image in acting as themself who is no respecter of persons we must have failed in our
duty until we become decided to waive all prejudices of Education birth nation or training and make the test of our obedience God's Equal command
to love the neighbor as ourselves.

These two great commandments, and upon which rest all the Law and
the prophets, cannot be narrowed down to suit us but we must go up and
conform to them. They proscribe neither nation nor sex—our neighbor may
be Either the oriental heathen the degraded Europe and or the Eslaved colored
American. Neither must we prefer sex the Slave mother as well as the Slave-
father. The oppress, or nominally free woman of every nation or clime in
whose Soul is as Evident by the image of God as in her more fortunate contemporary of the male sex has a claim upon us by virtue of that irrevocable
command Equally as urgent. We cannot successfully Evade duty because the
Suffering fellow woman ~~be~~ is only a *woman!* She too is a neighbor. The good
Samaritan of this generation must not take for their Exemplars the priest

and the Levite when a fellow wom[an] is among thieves—neither will they find their Excuse in the *custom* as barbarous and anti-christian as any promulgated by pious Brahmin that [word crossed out] they may be only females. The spirit of true philanthropy knows *no sex.* The true christian will not seek to Exhume from the grave of the past [word crossed out] its half developed customs and insist upon them as a substitute for the plain teachings of Jesus Christ, and the Evident deductions of a more Enlightened humanity.

There is too a fitness of time for any work for the benefit of God's human creatures. We are told to keep Holy the Sabbath day. In what manner? Not by following simply the injunctions of those who bind heavy burdens, to say nothing about the same but as a man is better than a sheep but combining with God's worship the most active vigilance for the resurector from degradation violence and sin his creatures. In these cases particularly was the Sabbath made for man and *woman* if you please as there may be those who will not accept the term man in a generic sense. Christ has told us as it is lawful to lift a sheep out of the ditch on the Sabbath day, i[f] a man is much better than a sheep.

Those with whom I am identified, namely the colored people of this country—and the women of the land are in the pit figurat[ively] ~~speaking~~ are cast out. These were Gods requirements during the Prophecy of Isaiah and they are in full force today. God is the same yesterday today and forever. And upon this nation and to this people they come with all their significance within your grasp are three or four millions in chains in your southern territory and among and around about you are half a million allied to them by blood and to you by blood as were the Hebrew servants who realize the intensity of your *hatred and oppression. You are the government what it does to [th] you Enslaves the poor whites The free colored people The Example of slave holders to access all.*

What we aim to do is to put away this Evil from among you and thereby pay a debt you now owe to humanity and to God and so turn from their chanel the bitter waters of a moral servitude that is about overwhelming yourselves.

I speak plainly because of a common origin and because were it not for the monster slavery we would have a common destiny here—in the land of our birth. And because the policy of the American government so singularly set aside allows to all free speech and free thought: As the law of God must be to us the higher law in spite of powers principalities selfish priests or selfish people to whom the minister it is important the [that?] we assert boldly that no where does God look upon this the chief crimes with the least degree of allowance nor are we justified in asserting that he will tolerate those who in any wise support or sustain it.

Slavery American slavery will not bear moral tests. It is ~~in~~ Exists by striking down all the moral safeguards to society by—it is not then a moral institution. You are called upon as a man to deny and disobey the most noble impulses of manhood to aid a brother in distress—to refuse to strike from the limbs of those not bound for any crime the fetters by which his Escape is obstructed. The milk of human kindness must be transformed into the bitter waters of hatred—you must return to his master he that hath Escaped, no matter how Every principle of manly independence revolts at the same. This feeling Extends to Every one allied by blood to the slave. And while we have in the North those who stand as guards to the institution the[y] must also volunteer as [s]hippers away of the nominally free. You must drive fr[om] his home by a hartless [os]tracism to the heathen shores when they fasted, bowed themselves, and spread sack cloth and ashes under them. Made long prayers [&c.] that they might be seen of men, but Isaiah told them God would not accept them. They must repent of their sins—put away iniquity from among them and then should their light shine forth.

But we are or may be told that slavery is only an Evil not a sin, and that too by those who say it was allowed among the Jews and therefore ought to be Endured. Isaiah sets that matter to rest he shows that it is a sin handling it less delicately than many prophets in this generation. These are the sins that we are to spare not the sin of Enslaving men—of keeping back the hire of the laborer. You are to loose the bands of wickedness, to undo the heavy burdens to break *Every* yoke and to let the oppressed go free. To deal out bread to the hungry and to bring the poo[r] [word missing] speaking. Their cry has long been ascending to the Lord who then will assume the responsibility of prescribing times and seasons ~~and~~ [word crossed out] for the pleading of their cause—of and righteous cause—and who shall overrule the voice of woman? Emphatically the greatest sufferer from chattel slavery or political proscription on this God's footstool? Nay we have Christs Example who heald the sexes indiscriminately thereby implying an Equal inheritance—who rebuf[f]ed the worldling Martha and approved innovator Mary. [The Him] who respected not persons [two words crossed out] but who imposes Christian duties alike upon all sexes, and who in his wise providence metes out his retribution alike upon all.

No friends we suffer the oppressors of the age to lead us astray; instead of going to the source of truth for guidance we let the adversary guide us as to what is our duty and Gods word. The Jews thought to that they were doing [H]is requirements when they did only that which was but a small sacrifice.■

57 SHOULD COLORED MEN BE SUBJECT TO THE PENALTIES OF THE FUGITIVE SLAVE LAW?

Charles H. Langston

Charles H. Langston (1817–1892), a black leader in Ohio, was especially active in resisting the Fugitive Slave Act. In September 1858 he joined with students of Oberlin College and citizens of the town in rescuing John Price, a recaptured fugitive slave, who was being held in the neighboring town of Wellington. Price was removed from custody and transported to Canada and freedom. Langston was the second to be tried for violating the law in the famous case, and he delivered a brilliant and moving speech in answer to the question of the judge as to why the sentence should not be pronounced. His speech struck the court so favorably that even though he was sentenced to twenty days' imprisonment and fined $100 and costs amounting to $872.72, it was a much lighter sentence than that given to his white predecessor, whose actions were judged equally "criminal." One aspect of Langston's defense that is especially interesting is his plea that he was not tried before an unprejudiced jury of peers. But Langston's defense rests primarily on his denunciation of the unjust law under which he was convicted.

John Mercer Langston, Charles Langston's famous brother, later professor of law at Howard University and congressman from Virginia, wrote an account of the "Oberlin-Wellington Rescue" in the Anglo-African Magazine *of June 1859 (pages 209–16), printing his brother's speech to the court. He described Charles Langston as follows: "He is widely known as a devoted and laborious advocate of the claims of the Negro to liberty and its attendant blessings. Discreet and farseeing, uncompromising and able, he has labored most efficiently in behalf of the slave and the disfranchised American." The speech was reprinted in pamphlet form and in leading newspapers throughout the North.*

I AM for the first time in my life before a court of justice, charged with the violation of law, and am now about to be sentenced. But before receiving that sentence, I propose to say one or two words in regard to the mitigation of that sentence, if it may be so construed. I cannot, of course, and do not expect that which I may say will in any way change your predetermined line of action. I ask no such favor at your hands.

I know that the courts of this country, that the laws of this country, that the governmental machinery of this country, are so constituted as to oppress and outrage colored men, men of my complexion. I cannot then, of course, expect, judging from the past history of the country, any mercy from the laws, from the Constitution, or from the courts of the country.

Some days prior to the thirteenth day of September, 1858, happening to be in Oberlin on a visit, I found the country round about there and the village itself filled with alarming rumors as to the fact that slave catchers, kidnapers, Negro stealers were lying hidden and skulking about, waiting some opportunity to get their bloody hands on some helpless creature to drag him back—or for the first time—into helpless and lifelong bondage. These reports becoming current all over that neighborhood, old men and innocent women and children became exceedingly alarmed for their safety. It was not uncommon to hear mothers say that they dare not send their children to school, for fear they would be caught and carried off by the way. Some of these people had become free by long and patient toil at night, after working the long, long day for cruel masters, and thus at length getting money enough to buy their liberty. Others had become free by means of the good will of their masters. And there were others who had become free by the intensest exercise of their God-given powers—by escaping from the plantations of their masters, eluding the bloodthirsty patrols and sentinels so thickly scattered all along their path, outrunning bloodhounds and horses, swimming rivers and fording swamps, and reaching at last, through incredible difficulties, what they, in their delusion, supposed to be free soil. These three classes were in Oberlin, trembling alike for their safety, because they well knew their fate should those men-hunters get their hands on them.

In the midst of such excitement the thirteenth day of September was ushered in—a day ever to be remembered in the history of that place, and I presume no less in the history of this court—on which those men, by lying devices, decoyed into a place where they could get their hands on him—I will not say a slave, for I do not know that, but a *man,* a *brother*—who had a right to his liberty under the laws of God, under the laws of nature and under the Declaration of American Independence.

In the midst of all this excitement, the news came to us like a flash of lightning that an actual seizure under and by means of fraudulent pretenses had been made!

Being identified with that man by color, by race, by manhood, by sympathies, such as God had implanted in us all, I felt it my duty to go and do what I could toward liberating him. I had been taught by my Revolutionary father—and I say this with all due respect to him—and by his honored associates that the fundamental doctrine of this government was that *all* men have a right, to life and liberty, and coming from the Old Dominion I brought into Ohio these sentiments, deeply impressed upon my heart; I went to Wellington, and hearing from the parties themselves by what authority the boy was held in custody, I conceived from what little knowledge I had of law that they had no right to hold him. And as your Honor has repeatedly laid down the law in this court, a man is free until he is proven to be legally restrained of his liberty, and I believed that upon the principle of law those men were bound to take their prisoner before the very first magistrate they found and there establish the facts set forth in their warrant, and that until they did this, every man should presume that their claim was unfounded, and to institute such proceedings for the purpose of securing an investigation as they might find warranted by the laws of this state. Now, sir, if that is not the plain, common sense and correct view of the law, then I have been misled by your Honor and by the prevalent received opinion.

It is said that they had a warrant. Why then should they not establish its validity before the proper officers? And I stand here today, sir, to say that with an exception of which I shall soon speak, *to procure such a lawful investigation of the authority under which they claimed to act was the part I took in that day's proceedings, and the only part.* I supposed it to be my duty as a citizen of Ohio—excuse me for saying that, sir—as an *outlaw of the United States,* to do what I could to secure at least this form of justice to my brother whose liberty was in peril. *Whatever more than that has been sworn to on this trial as an act of mine is false, ridiculously false.* When I found these men refusing to go, according to the law, as I apprehended it, and subject their claim to an official inspection, and that nothing short of a habeas corpus would oblige such an inspection, I was willing to go even thus far, supposing in that county a sheriff, might, perhaps, be found with nerve enough to serve it. In this I again failed. Nothing then was left me, nothing to the boy in custody, but the confirmation of my first belief that the pretended authority was worthless, and the employment of those means of liberation which belong to us. With regard to the part I took in the forcible rescue which followed, I have nothing to say further than I have already said. The evidence is before you. It is alleged that I said, "We will have him anyhow." *This I never said.* I did say to Mr. Lowe, what I honestly believed to be the truth, that the crowd were very much excited, many of them averse to longer delay, and bent upon a rescue at all hazards; and that, he being an old acquaintance and friend of mine, I was anxious to extricate him from the dangerous position he occupied and therefore advised that he urge Jennings to give the boy up. Further than this I did not say, either to him or any one else.

The law under which I am arraigned is an unjust one, one made to crush the colored man, and one that outrages every feeling of humanity, as well as every rule of right. I have nothing to do with its constitutionality; about that I care but little. I have often heard it said by learned and good men that it was unconstitutional; I remember the excitement that prevailed throughout all the free states when it was passed; and I remember how often it has been said by individuals, conventions, legislatures, and even *judges,* * that it never

* At this point in his report of the speech, John Mercer Langston appended the following footnote:

"The following resolutions were reported to and adopted by an indignation meeting held in Cleveland shortly after the passage of the Fugitive Slave Law, Judge Hiram V. Wilson being on the Committee on Resolutions:

"1. *Resolved,* That the passage of the Fugitive Slave Law was an act unauthorized by could be, never should be, and never was meant to be enforced. I had always believed, until contrary appeared in the actual institution of proceedings, that the provisions of this odious statute would never be enforced within the bounds of this state.

But I have another reason to offer why I should not be sentenced, and one that I think pertinent to the case. I have not had a trial before a jury of my peers. The common law of England—and you will excuse me for referring to that, since I am but a private citizen—was that every man should be tried before a jury of men occupying the same position in the social scale with himself. That lords should be tried before a jury of lords; that peers of the realm should be tried before peers of the realm; vassals before vassals, and *aliens before aliens*; and they must not come from the district where the crime was committed, lest the prejudices of either personal friends or foes should affect the accused. The Constitution of the United States guarantees, not merely to its citizens, but *to all persons*, a trial before an *impartial* jury. I have had no such trial.

The colored man is oppressed by certain universal and deeply fixed *prejudices.* Those jurors are well known to have shared largely in these prejudices, and I therefore consider that they were neither impartial, nor were they a jury of my peers. And the prejudices which white people have against colored men grow out of the facts that we have as a people *consented* for two hundred years to be *slaves* of the whites. We have been scourged, crushed and cruelly oppressed, and have submitted to it all tamely, meekly, peaceably—I mean as a people, and with rare individual exceptions—and today you see us thus, meekly submitting to the penalties of an infamous law. Now the Americans have this feeling, and it is an honorable one, that they will respect those who will rebel at oppression but despise those who tamely submit to outrage and wrong; and while our people, as people, submit, they will as a people be despised. Why, they will hardly meet on terms of equality with us in a whisky shop, in a car, at a table, or even at the altar of God—so

the Constitution, hostile to every principle of justice and humanity, and if persevered in, fatal to Human Freedom.

"2. *Resolved,* That the law strikes down some of the dearest principles upon which our fathers predicated their right to assert and maintain their independence, and is characterized by the most tyrannical exercise of power; and that it cannot be sustained without repudiating the doctrines of the Declaration of Independence and the principles upon which all free governments rest.

"3. *Resolved,* That tyranny consists in the willfully violating, by those in power, of man's natural right to his personal security, personal liberty and private property; and it matters not whether the act is exercised by one man or a million men, it is equally unjust, unrighteous, and destructive of the ends of all just governments.

"4. *Resolved,* That regarding some portions of the Fugitive Law as unconstitutional, and the whole of it as oppressive, unjust and unrighteous, we deem it the duty of every good citizen to *denounce, oppose and resist,* by all proper means, the execution of said law, and that we demand its immediate and unconditional repeal, and will not cease to agitate the question, and use all our powers to secure that object, until it is accomplished."

thorough and hearty a contempt have they for those who will meekly *lie still* under the heel of the oppressor. The jury came into the box with that feeling. They know they had that feeling, and so the court knows now and knew then. The gentleman who prosecuted me, the court itself, and even the counsel who defended me, have that feeling.

I was tried by a jury who were prejudiced, before a court that was prejudiced, prosecuted by an officer who was prejudiced, and defended, though ably, by counsel that was prejudiced. And therefore, it is, your Honor, that I urge by all that is good and great in manhood that I should not be subjected to the pains and penalties of this oppressive law, when I have *not* been tried, either by a jury of my peers or by a jury that were impartial.

One more word, sir, and I have done. I went to Wellington, knowing that colored men have no rights in the United States which white men are bound to respect; that the courts had so decided; that Congress had so enacted; that the people had so decreed.

There is not a spot in this wide country, not even by the altars of God nor in the shadow of the shafts that tell the imperishable fame and glory of the heroes of the Revolution; no, nor in the old Philadelphia Hall, where any colored man may dare to ask a mercy of a white man. Let me stand in that Hall and tell a United States marshal that my father was a Revolutionary soldier, that he served under Lafayette and fought through the whole war, and that he fought for *my* freedom as much as for his own, and he would sneer at me and clutch me with his bloody fingers and say he has a *right* to make me a slave! And when I appeal to Congress, they say he has a right to make me a slave; when I appeal to your Honor, *your Honor* says he has a right to make me a slave, and if any man, white or black, seeks an investigation of that claim, they make themselves amenable to the pains and penalties of the Fugitive Slave Act, for *black men have no rights which white men are bound to respect.** I, going to Wellington with the full knowledge of all this, knew that if that man was taken to Columbus, he was hopelessly gone, no matter whether he had ever been in slavery before or not. I knew that I was in the same situation myself, and that by the decision of your Honor, if any man whatever were to claim me as his slave and seize me, and my brother, being a lawyer, should seek to get out a writ of habeas corpus to expose the falsity of the claim, he would be thrust into prison under one provision of the Fugitive Slave Law, for interfering with the man claiming to be in pursuit of a fugitive, and I, by the perjury of a solitary wretch, would by another of its provisions be helplessly doomed to lifelong bondage, without the possibility of escape.

Some may say that there is no danger of free persons being seized and carried off as slaves. No one need labor under such a delusion. Sir, *four* of

---

*Langston paraphrases Chief Justice Roger Taney's opinion in the *Dred Scott* decision of 1857.

the eight persons who were first carried back under the act of 1850 were afterwards proved to be *free men.* They were free persons, but wholly at the mercy of the oath of one man. And but last Sabbath afternoon, a letter came to me from a gentleman in St. Louis, informing me that a young lady who was formerly under my instructions at Columbus, a free person, is now lying in the jail at that place, claimed as the slave of some wretch who never saw her before and waiting for testimony from relatives at Columbus to establish her freedom. I could stand here by the hour and relate such instances. In the very nature of the case they must be constantly occurring. A letter was not long since found upon the person of a counterfeiter when arrested, addressed to him by some Southern gentleman, in which the writer says:

"Go among the niggers: find out their marks and scars; make good descriptions and send to me, and I'll find masters for 'em."

That is the way men are carried "back" to slavery.

But in view of all the facts, I say that if ever again a man is seized near me and is about to be carried southward as a slave, before any legal investigation has been had, I shall hold it to be my duty, as I held it that day, to secure for him, if possible, a legal inquiry into the character of the claim by which he is held. And I go further: I say that if it is adjudged illegal to procure even such an investigation, then we are thrown back upon those last defenses of our rights which cannot be taken from us, and which God gave us that we need not be slaves. I ask your Honor, while I say this, to place yourself in my situation, and you will say with me that if your brother, if your friend, if your wife, if your child, had been seized by men who claimed them as fugitives, and the law of the land forbade you to ask any investigation and precluded the possibility of any legal protection or redress, then you will say with me that you would not only demand the protection of the law, but you would call in your neighbors and your friends and would ask them to say with you that these, your friends, *could not* be taken into slavery.

And now I thank you for this leniency, this indulgence, in giving a man unjustly condemned by a tribunal before which he is declared to have no rights, the privilege of speaking in his own behalf. I know that it will do nothing toward mitigating your sentence, but it is a privilege to be allowed to speak, and I thank you for it. I shall submit to the penalty, be it what it may. But I stand here to say, that if, for doing what I did on that day at Wellington, I am to go in jail six months and pay a fine of a thousand dollars, according to the Fugitive Slave Law—and such is the protection the laws of this country afford me—I must take upon myself the responsibility of self-protection; when I come to be claimed by some perjured wretch as his slave, I shall never be taken into slavery. And as in that trying hour I would have others do to me, as I would call upon my friends to help me, as I would call upon you, your Honor, to help me, as I would call upon you [to the District Attorney] to help me, and upon you [to Judge Bliss], and upon you [to his counsel], *so help me* God I stand here to say that I will do all I can for any man thus seized and held, though the inevitable penalty of six months' imprisonment and one thousand dollars fine for each offense hangs over me! We have all a common humanity, and you all would do that; your manhood would require it, and no matter what the laws might be, you would honor yourself for doing it, while your friends and your children to all generations would honor you for doing it, and every good and honest man would say you had done *right!*■

58 WHY SLAVERY IS STILL RAMPANT

Sarah Parker Remond

Until the rise of Frederick Douglass, Charles Lenox Remond was the best-known black abolitionist, and he continued to be impor- tant in the movement until the Civil War. Less well known is Remond's sister Sarah Parker Remond. She was born about 1815 in Salem, Massa- chusetts, of John and Nancy Remond. Her father, a native of the island of Curaçao, came to America at an early age. He later became a hair- dresser in Salem, and his daughter and son were well educated. Sarah Remond joined the antislavery movement and by 1857 was speaking with her brother at meetings in upstate New York. She also shared the platform with Susan B. Anthony at antislavery conventions. She gained fame as an antislavery speaker during the course of a lecture tour of Ire- land and England in 1859. As one of the few black women antislavery orators from the United States to address audiences in these countries, her presence was widely reported in the British press.

On September 17, 1859, the Manchester Times *carried an account of Remond's speech at the Athenaeum in Manchester, England. Introduced by the mayor of Manchester, Remond began by informing the audience that she appeared as the agent of no society and was speaking simply on her own responsibility, but that in feeling and in principle she was identified "with the ultra-Abolitionists of America." She continued:*

ALTHOUGH the anti-slavery enterprise was begun some thirty years ago, the evil is still rampant in the land. As there are some young people present—and I am glad to see them here, for it is important that they should understand this subject—I shall briefly explain that there are thirty- two states, sixteen of which are free and sixteen slave states. The free states are in the north. The political feelings in the north and south are essentially different, so is the social life. In the north, democracy, not what the Americans call democracy, but the true principle of equal rights, prevails—I speak of the white population, mind—wealth is abundant; the country, in every material sense, flourishes. In the south, aristocratic feelings prevail, labor is dishonorable, and five millions of poor whites live in the most degrading ignorance and destitution. I might dwell long on the miserable condition of these poor whites, the indirect victims of slavery; but I must go on to speak of the four millions of slaves. The slaves are essentially *things*, with no rights, political, social, domestic, or religious; the absolute victims of all but irresponsible power. For the slave there is no home, no love, no hope, no help; and what is life without hope? No writer can describe the slave's life; it cannot be told; the fullest description ever given to the world does not skim over the surface of this subject.

You may infer something of the state of society in the southern states when I tell you there are eight hundred thousand mulattoes, nine-tenths of whom are the children of white fathers, and these are constantly sold by their parents, for the slave follows the condition of the mother. Hence we see every shade of complexion amongst the slaves, from the blackest African hue to that of women and men in whose cheeks the lily and the rose vie for predominance. To describe to you the miserable poor whites of the South, I need only quote the words of Mr. Helper, a Southerner, in his important work on slavery,* and the testimony also of a Virginian gentleman of my acquaintance. The five millions poor whites are most of them in as gross a state of ignorance as Mrs. Stowe's "Topsey," in *Uncle Tom's Cabin.*

The free colored people of the northern states are, for no crime but merely the fact of complexion, deprived of all political and social rights. Whatever wealth or eminence in intellect and refinement they may attain to, they are treated as outcasts; and white men and women who identify themselves with them are sure to be insulted in the grossest manner.

I do not ask your political interference in any way. This is a moral question. Even in America the Abolitionists generally disclaim every other ground but the moral and religious one on which this matter is based. You send missionaries to the heathen; I tell you of professing Christians practicing what is worse than any heathenism on record. How is it that we have come to this state of things, you ask. I reply, the whole power of the country is in the hands of the slaveholders. For more than thirty years we have had a slaveholding President, and the Slave Power has been dominant. The consequence has been a series of encroachments, until now at last the slave trade is reopened and all but legitimised in America. It was a sad backward step when England last year fell into the trap laid by America and surrendered the right of search. Now slavers ply on the seas which were previously guarded by your ships. We have, besides, an internal slave trade. We have states where,

---

*The reference is to *The Impending Crisis*, published in 1857 by Hinton Rowe Helper, a North Carolina "poor white," in which he attacked slavery as detrimental to the prosperity of the South and the hopes of the poor whites of the region.

I am ashamed to say, men and women are reared, like cattle, for the market. When I walk through the streets of Manchester and meet load after load of cotton, I think of those eighty thousand cotton plantations on which was grown the one hundred and twenty-five millions of dollars' worth of cotton which supply your market, and I remember that not one cent of that money ever reached the hands of the laborers.

Here is an incident of slave life for you—an incident of common occurrence in the South. In March, 1859, a slave auction took place in the city of Savannah. Three hundred and forty-three slaves, the property of Pierce Butler—the husband of your own Fanny Kemble—were sold, regardless of every tie of flesh and blood; old men and maidens, young men, and babes of fifteen months—there was but one question about them, and that was decided at the auction-block. Pierce Butler, the owner, resides in Philadelphia, and is a highly-respected citizen and a member of a Church. He was reputed a kind master, who rarely separated the families of his slaves. The financial crisis took place, and I have given you the result to his human property. But Mr. Butler has in no wise lost caste amongst his friends; he still moves in the most respectable society, and his influence in his Church is so great that, with other members, he has procured the removal from the pulpit of Rev. Dudley Tyng, who had uttered a testimony against slavery; and in that pulpit, the man who now preaches, Mr. Prentice by name, is the owner of a hundred slaves. Such is the state of public opinion in America, and you find the poison running through everything. With the exception of the Abolitionists, you will find people of all classes thus contaminated. The whole army and navy of the United States are pledged to pursue and shoot down the poor fugitives, who, panting for liberty, fly to Canada, to seek the security of the British flag. All denominations of professing Christians are guilty of sustaining or defending slavery. Even the Quakers must be included in this rule.

Now I ask for your sympathy and your influence, and whoever asked English men and women in vain? Give us the power of your public opinion, it has great weight in America. Words spoken here are read there as no words written in America are read. Lord Brougham's testimony on the first of August resounded through America;* your Clarkson and your Wilberforce are names of strength to us. I ask you, raise the moral public opinion until its voice reaches the American shores. Aid us thus until the shackles of the American slave melt like dew before the morning sun. I ask for especial help from the women of England. Women are the worst victims of the Slave Power. I am met on every hand by the cry "Cotton!" "Cotton!" I cannot stop to speak of cotton while men and women are being brutalized. But there is an answer for the cotton cry too, and the argument is an unanswerable one.

Before concluding I shall give you a few passages from the laws of the slave states. By some of these laws, free coloured people may be arrested in

*On August 1, 1859, Lord Brougham addressed a London gathering, including Sarah Parker Remond, in observance of the anniversary of West Indian emancipation.

the discharge of their lawful business; and, if no papers attesting their freedom can be found on them, they are committed to jail; and, if not claimed within a limited time, they may be sold to pay the jail fees. By another law, any person who speaks at the bar, bench, on the stage, or in private, to the slaves, so as to excite insurrection, or brings any paper or pamphlet of such nature into the state, shall be imprisoned for not less than three nor more than twenty-one years; or shall suffer death as the judge decides. I could read such laws for hours, but I shall only add that in Maryland there is at present a gentleman in prison, condemned for ten years, because a copy of Uncle Tom's Cabin was found in his possession.* The laws are equally severe against teaching a slave to read—against teaching even the name of the good God.■

59 THE AMERICAN GOVERNMENT AND THE NEGRO

Robert Purvis

Robert Purvis was born on November 4, 1810, in Charleston, South Carolina, the son of William Purvis, an English merchant, and a Jewish-Moorish mother, Harriet Judah. In 1819 William Purvis sent the entire family to Philadelphia, where his three sons could be educated. He died in 1825, leaving an inheritance of $125,000. Robert Purvis was educated in private schools in Philadelphia and spent some time at Pittsfield Academy and at Amherst College. But he left college to devote himself to the antislavery movement and at the age of seventeen made his first public speech against slavery. Purvis, who lived in a fine home in a suburb of Philadelphia, was one of a group of black Americans who gave Garrison money to help him launch the Liberator *in 1831. Two years later Purvis became a charter member of the American Anti-Slavery Society and was also a founder of the Pennsylvania Anti-Slavery Society, unofficial "president" of the Pennsylvania Underground Railroad, and a vigorous fighter against discrimination until his death in 1898.*

*In 1857 Samuel Green, a free black in Maryland, was sentenced to ten years in the Baltimore penitentiary by the Maryland court because he was found in possession of a copy of *Uncle Tom's Cabin.* He spent five years in prison, winning his freedom in the summer of 1862.

At the twenty-seventh anniversary of the American Anti-Slavery Society in New York City, May 8, 1860, Purvis, a leading figure on the antislavery lecture platform, delivered a stirring denunciation of the American government for its treatment of the black Americans. On the eve of the Civil War, Purvis recounts the record of African American military service on behalf of the country. In contrast he offers bitter testimony of the failure of the government to secure the rights of its black citizens.

Purvis's speech is taken from the Liberator, *May 18, 1860.*

M R. PRESIDENT—As one of your speakers to-day, I feel myself embarrassed by two opposite and conflicting feelings: one is a painful and distressing sense of my incapacity for the duty which you have imposed upon me, and the other is an irrepressible desire to do or say something effective for a cause which is dearer to me than my heart's blood. Sir, I need not say here that I belong to that class who, at the South, are bought, sold, leased, mortgaged, and in all respects treated as absolute property; I belong to the class who, here at the North, are declared, by the highest tribunal known to your government, to possess "no *rights* that a *white* man is bound to respect."*

I say *your* government—it is not mine. Thank God, I have no willing share in a government that deliberately, before the world, and without a blush, declares one part of its people, and that for no crime or pretext of crime, disfranchised and outlawed. For such a government, I, as a man, can have no feeling but of *contempt, loathing,* and *unutterable abhorrence!* And, sir, I venture to affirm that there is no man in this audience, who has a spark of manhood in him, who has a tittle of genuine self-respect in his bosom, that will not justify me in these feelings.

What are the facts in the case? What is the attitude of your boasting, braggart republic toward the 600,000 free people of color who swell its population and add to its wealth? I have already alluded to the dictum of Judge Taney in the notorious Dred Scott decision. That dictum reveals the animus of the whole government; it is a fair example of the cowardly and malignant spirit that pervades the entire policy of the country. The end of that policy is, undoubtedly, to destroy the colored man, as a man, to prevent him from having any existence in the land except as a "chattel personal to all intents, constructions and purposes whatsoever." With this view, it says a colored man shall not sue and recover his lawful property; he shall not bear arms and train in the militia; he shall not be a commander of a vessel, not even of the meanest craft that creeps along the creeks and bays of your Southern coast; he shall not carry a mail-bag, or serve as a porter in a post-office; and he shall not even put his face in a United States court-room for any purpose, except by the sufferance of the white man. I had occasion, a few days since, to go to the United States court-room in the city of Philadelphia. My errand was a proper one; it was to go bail for one of the noble band of colored men

---

*A reference to the *Dred Scott* decision.

who had so bravely risked their lives for the rescue of a brother man on his way to eternal bondage. As I was about entering the door, I was stopped, and ordered back. I demanded the reason. "I have my order," was the reply. What order? "To keep out all colored people." Now, sir, who was the man that offered me this indignity? It was Deputy-Marshal Jenkins, the notorious slave-catcher. And why did he do it? Because he had his orders from pious, praying, Christian Democrats, who hold and teach the damnable doctrine that the "black man has no rights that the white man is bound to respect." It is true that Marshal Yost, to whom I indignantly appealed, reversed this man's orders, and apologized to me, assuring me that I could go in and out at my pleasure. But, sir, the apology made the matter worse; for, mark you, it was not me personally that was objected to, *but the race* with which I stand identified. Great God! who can think of such outrages, such meanness, such dastardly, cowardly cruelty, without burning with indignation, and choking for want of words with which to denounce it? And in the case of the noble little band referred to, the men who generously, heroically risked their lives to rescue the man who was about being carried back to slavery; look at their conduct; you know the circumstances. We recently had a slave trial in Philadelphia—no new thing in the city of *"Brotherly Love."* A victim of Virginia tyranny, a fugitive from Southern injustice, had made good his escape from the land of whips and chains to Pennsylvania, and had taken up his abode near the capital of the State. The place of his retreat was discovered; the bloodhounds of the law scented him out, and caught him; they put him in chains and brought him before Judge Cadwallader—a man whose pro-slavery antecedents made him a fitting instrument for the execution of the accursed Fugitive Slave law. The sequel can easily be imagined. Brewster, a leading Democrat—the man who, like your O'Conor* of this city, has the unblushing hardihood to defend the enslavement of the black man upon principle—advocated his return. The man was sent into life-long bondage. While the trial was going on, slaveholders, Southern students and pro-slavery Market-street salesmen were freely admitted; but the colored people, the class most interested, were carefully excluded. Prohibited from entering, they thronged around the door of the courthouse. At last the prisoner was brought out, handcuffed and guarded by his captors; he was put into a carriage which started off in the direction of the South. Some ten or twelve brave black men made a rush for the carriage, in hopes of effecting a rescue; they were overpowered, beaten, put under arrest and carried to prison, there to await their trial, before this same Judge Cadwallader, for violating the Fugitive Slave law! Mark you, they may go into the court-room as *prisoners,* but not as *spectators!* They may not have an opportunity of hearing the law expounded, but they may be punished if they make themselves chargeable with violating it!

Sir, people talk of the bloody code of Draco, but I venture to assert, with-

*Charles O'Conor, a Democratic Party lawyer in New York, was an open supporter of slavery and the slaveholders.

out fear of intelligent contradiction, that, all things considered, that code was mild, that code was a law of love, compared with the hellish laws and precedents that disgrace the statue-books of this modern Democratic, Christian Republic! I said that a man of color might not be a commander of the humblest craft that sails in your American waters. There was a man in Philadelphia, the other day, who stated that he owned and sailed a schooner between that city and different ports in the State of Maryland—that his vessel had been seized in the town of Easton, (I believe it was,) or some other town on the Eastern Shore, on the allegation that, contrary to law, there was no white man on board. The vessel constituted his entire property and sole means of supporting his family. He was advised to sue for its recovery, which he did, and, after a long and expensive litigation, the case was decided in his favor. But by this time the vessel had rotted and gone to wreck, and the man found himself reduced to beggary. His business in Philadelphia was to raise $50 with which to take himself and family out of this cursed land, to a country where liberty is not a mockery, and freedom a mere idle name!

Sir, look for a moment at the detestable meanness of this country! What was the cause of your war of the Revolution? The tyrannical doctrine of taxation without representation! Who was the first martyr in your revolutionary war? Crispus Attucks, a negro. It was a black man's blood that was the first to flow in behalf of American independence. In the war of 1812, what class of your inhabitants showed themselves more unselfishly loyal and patriotic than the free people of color? None, sir. In Philadelphia the colored people organized themselves into companies, and vied with their more favored fellow-citizens in the zeal of their efforts to guard and protect the city. In Louisiana their bravery and soldier-like behavior was such as to elicit the warmest encomiums from General Jackson, the commander-in-chief of the Southern army. Listen to the language of General Jackson on that memorable occasion:—

"HEADQUARTERS, SEVENTH MILITARY DISTRICT,
Mobile, September 21, 1814.

To the Free Colored Inhabitants of Louisiana:
    Through a mistaken policy, you have heretofore been deprived of a participation in the glorious struggle for national rights in which our country is engaged. This no longer shall exist.
    As sons of freedom, you are now called upon to defend our most inestimable blessings. As Americans, your country looks with confidence to her adopted children for a valorous support, as a faithful return for the advantages enjoyed under her mild and equitable government. As fathers, husbands and brothers, you are summoned to rally around the standard of the Eagle, to defend all which is dear in existence. Your country, although calling for your exertions, does not wish you to engage in her cause without remunerating you for the

services rendered. Your intelligent minds are not to be led away by false representations. Your love of honor would cause you to despise the man who should attempt to deceive you. With the sincerity of a soldier, and in the language of truth, I address you.

To every noble-hearted free man of color, volunteering to serve during the present contest with Great Britain, and no longer, there will be paid the same bounty, in money and lands, now received by the white soldiers of the United States—namely, one hundred and twenty-four dollars in money and one hundred and sixty acres of land. The non-commissioned officers will be appointed from among yourselves.

Due regard will be paid to the feelings of freemen and soldiers. You will not, by being associated with white men, in the same corps, be exposed to improper comparisons, or unjust sarcasm. As a distinct, independent battalion or regiment, pursuing the path of glory, you will, undivided, receive the applause and gratitude of your countrymen. To assure you of the sincerity of my intentions, and my anxiety to engage your invaluable services to our country, I have communicated my wishes to the Governor of Louisiana, who is fully informed as to the manner of enrollments, and will give you every necessary information on the subject of this address.

ANDREW JACKSON
Major-General Commanding."

This was the language of General Jackson at the opening of the campaign. Now hear him at its close:

"Soldier—When, on the banks of the Mobile, I called you to take up arms, inviting you to partake the perils and glory of your white fellow-citizens, I expected much from you; for I was not ignorant that you possessed qualities most formidable to an invading enemy; I knew with what fortitude you could endure hunger and thirst, and all the fatigues of a campaign; I knew well how you loved your native country, and that you, as well as ourselves, had to defend what man holds most dear—his parents, wife, children and property—you have done more than I expected. In addition to the previous qualities I before knew you to possess, I found among you a noble enthusiasm, which leads to the performance of great things. Soldiers! the President of the United States shall hear how praiseworthy was your conduct in the hour of danger, and the representatives of the American people will give you the praise your exploits entitle you to. Your General anticipates them in applauding your noble ardor.

The enemy approaches, his vessels cover our lakes; our brave citizens are united; all contention has ceased among them; their only dispute is who shall win the prize of valor, or who the most glory, its noblest reward. By order,

THOS. BUTLER, Aid-de-Camp."

Sir, much as this country is indebted to the colored people for their aid in times of war, they are under still greater obligations for their services in time of peace. They have tilled your soil; their labor, South and North, has been a mine of wealth to you. Belie them as you will, a more honest, industrious, orderly or useful class, take them as a whole, is not to be found in the country. What is the testimony of your Baltimore Slaveholders' Convention—a convention called for the very purpose of denouncing the free blacks of Maryland as a nuisance that ought to be abated, either by their expulsion from the state or their reduction to slavery? What was the testimony of that convention of the enemies of the black man? Why, that they were not a nuisance, but a useful class of the population, adding much to the wealth and prosperity of the State, and that their expulsion would be both impolite and inhuman! The same testimony, in effect, is borne by Judge Catron, of Tennessee, and by the Governor of Missouri. I hold in my hand an extract from the New Orleans *Picayune,* of like testimony, which I will read:— "Our free colored population form a distinct class from those elsewhere in the United States. Far from being antipathetic to the whites, they have followed in their footsteps, and progressed with them, with a commendable spirit of emulation, in the various branches of industry most adapted to their sphere. Some of our best mechanics and artisans are to be found among the free colored men. They form the great majority of carpenters, tailors, shoemakers, &c., whose sudden emigration from this community would certainly be attended with some degree of annoyance; while we count them, in no small numbers, excellent musicians, jewelers, goldsmiths, tradesmen and merchants. As a general rule, the free colored people of Louisiana, and especially of New Orleans, the "creole colored people," as they style themselves, are a sober, industrious and moral class, far advanced in education and civilization. From that class came the battalion of colored men who fought for the country under General Jackson in 1814–15, and whose remnants, veterans whom age has withered, are taken by the hand, on the anniversary of the glorious eighth of January, by their white brethren, and who proudly march with them under the same flag."

Sir, what class of your population are more peaceable and orderly than the free people of color? Who makes your mobs on your canal lines, and in the construction of your railroads? Who swell your mobs in your beer gardens, and in your Sunday excursions? Who make your Native and Anti-Native American mobs? Your Forrest and Macready mobs, which the military have to be called out to be put down? I am sure, not the colored people! Not the native-born Americans who have tilled your soil in times of war, and whose reward has been disfranchisement and threatened annihilation, but your foreign-born European immigrants of yesterday—men who can't speak your language, and don't respect your laws. These are the people who are invested with all the franchises of the country, including that of trampling on the black men. These are the people who are, at the same time, the most turbulent and most insolent class of the whole American population. I am not what is called a Native American—I don't believe in measuring a man's rights either by the place of his birth or the color of his skin. I believe in the equal natural rights of all men; and hence it is that I protest against the anti-republican and unjust distinctions in favor of a stranger and foreigner against a native-born American, against whom no charge can be made except that of the complexion which the Almighty God has given him.

But, sir, narrow and proscriptive as, in my apprehension, is the spirit of what is called Native Americanism,* there is another thing I regard as tenfold more base and contemptible, and that is your American Democracy—your piebald and rotten Democracy, that talks loudly about equal rights, and at the same time tramples one-sixth of the population of the country in the dust, and declares that they have "no rights which a white man is bound to respect." And, sir, while I repudiate your Native Americanism and your bogus Democracy, allow me to add, at the same time, that I am not a Republican. I could not be a member of the Republican party if I were so disposed; I am disfranchised; I have no vote; I am put out of the pale of political society. The time was in Pennsylvania, under the old Constitution, when I could go to the polls as other men do, but your modern Democracy have taken away from me that right.† Your Reform Convention, your Pierce Butlers—the man who, a year ago, put up nearly four hundred human beings on the block in Georgia, and sold them to the highest bidder—your Pierce Butlers disfranchised me, and I am without any political rights whatever. I am taxed to support a government which takes my money and tramples on me. But, sir, I would not be a member of the Republican party if it were in my power. How could I, a colored man, join a party that styles itself emphatically the "white man's party"? How could I, an Abolitionist, belong to a party that is and must of necessity be a pro-slavery party? The Republicans may be, and doubtless are, opposed to the extension of slavery, but they are sworn to support, and they *will* support, slavery where it already exists. Sir, elect Wm. Seward,‡ that noblest Roman of them all, to the Presidency to-morrow, and the slaveholders of the South will have in that fact a guarantee of safety in

---

*The native American movement opposed foreign immigration, especially of Irish Catholics. Its strength was reflected in the rise of the Know-Nothing Party in the 1850s.

†In 1838 the legislature of Pennsylvania passed legislation disfranchising the free people of color in the state. Robert Purvis chaired a protest meeting of Pennsylvania African Americans opposing the legislation and one of the authors of an "Appeal of Forty Thousand Citizens Threatened with Disfranchisement to the People of Pennsylvania."

‡William H. Seward, U.S. senator from New York, was a leading antislavery spokesperson. In 1858, he argued that the dispute over slavery was an "irrepressible conflict." He became Lincoln's secretary of state.

the possession of their human property such as the election of no other man can give them. Sir, Mr. Seward believes in an "irrepressible conflict between enduring and antagonistic forces." But what intelligent slaveholder of the South does not believe the same thing? Sir, don't let us be carried away by fine-sounding abstractions; let us have something practical; give us a weaker man; give us another James Buchanan, or Franklin Pierce, and we will have an irrepressible conflict that all men can see and understand—a conflict like that which took place between the anti-slavery missionaries and pro-slavery planters of Jamaica—a conflict which precipitated the act of emancipation by the British Government, which set free in a day 800,000 human beings!

No, sir, I am not a Republican. I can never join a party, the leaders of which conspire to expel us from the country. This is what your Bateses and Wades, Blairs, Doolittles and Greeleys are now doing. It is true they talk of doing it with our 'own consent.' But what of that? Let it once be settled in the public mind that we ought to leave the country, and it will not be long till measures are taken to compel us to leave. It is the old spirit of African Colonization revived under a new name; it is the old snake with a new skin—nothing more, nothing less. Sir, what right have Republican leaders to be plotters for the removal of a class of people who have expressed no desire to leave, but who, on the contrary, have expressed a strong purpose not to leave. Forty-three years ago, when the infamous scheme of African Colonization was first proposed, a public meeting of the colored people of Philadelphia was called to express their sentiments in regard to the measure. My honored father-in-law, the late James Forten, presided at the meeting, and the following is an extract from their proceedings:—"Whereas our ancestors (not of choice) were the first successful cultivators of the wilds of America, we, their descendants, feel ourselves entitled to participate in the blessings of her luxuriant soil, which their blood and sweat enriched; and that any measure, or system of measures, having a tendency to banish us from her bosom would not only be cruel, but in direct violation of those principles which have been the boast of this republic."

Now, sir, in connection with this, let me read an extract from the New York *Tribune*. Mr. [Horace] Greeley was replying to an article in the Detroit *Free Press*. Hear what he says:—"Now, we cannot presume to give advice in the premises, because we make no pretensions to special interest in or liking for the African race. We love liberty, equality, justice, humanity—we will maintain the right of every man to himself and his own limbs and muscles; for in so doing we maintain and secure our own rights; but we do not like negroes, and heartily wish no individual of that race had ever been brought to America. We hope the day will come when the whole negro race in this country, being fully at liberty, will gradually, peacefully, freely draw off and form a community by themselves, somewhere toward the Equator, or join their brethren in lineage in Africa or the West Indies."

Mr. Greeley may, as he says, love liberty, &c., but I say that any man who can thus gratuitously express his dislike for an oppressed race, and thus wantonly disregard their feelings, however much of a political reformer he may be, is lacking in the nobler sentiments of a man and the instincts of a true gentleman. Mr. Greeley and other Republican leaders in the party seem disposed to put this Colonization project into their creed, or make it a plank in their platform. Let them do so, and they will sink their party so deep in the abyss of perdition that the trump of the angel Gabriel would not bring it to a resurrection. Sir, have these men, who talk thus flippantly about not liking the negro race, no feeling, or do they suppose we have none? Are we not men? "Have we not eyes, hands, organs, dimensions, senses, affections, passions? fed with the same food, hurt with the same weapons, subject to the same diseases, healed by the same means, warmed and cooled by the same winter and summer? If you prick us, do we not bleed? if you tickle us, do we not laugh? if you poison us, do we not die? and if you wrong us, shall we not revenge?" Sir, in contrast with the feelings manifested by Greeley and other Republican leaders toward the colored man,* look at that noble martyr and saint, the immortal hero of Harper's Ferry! John Brown† believed that he professed, and practised what he believed:

> 'He nobly acted what he nobly thought,
> And sealed by death the lessons which he taught.'

He believed that the black man was a man, and he laid down his life to secure for him the rights of man. Who can look at the noble hero, and see him stoop on his way to the scaffold to kiss the negro child, and not be struck with admiration at his fidelity and sublime consistency? Sir, the Anti-Slavery cause is onward; its doctrines are destined to triumph in the country; and no party can succeed that refuses to acknowledge it. Slavery will be abolished in this land, and with it, that twin relic of barbarism, prejudice against color. (Loud applause.)■

---

*In 1860 the Democrats charged that the Republicans, if they should win the presidential election, would abolish slavery and extend civil rights to blacks. Republican spokesmen, answering this charge, openly proclaimed the party a "white man's party." Horace Greeley, editor of the *New York Tribune* and an influential Republican spokesperson, declared publicly that the Republican Party sought no more than to restrict slavery to the existing states and did not aim to abolish slavery or to extend equal rights to free blacks.

†Leading a group of nineteen men that included five African Americans and his own sons, John Brown (1800–1859) attacked the Federal arsenal at Harper's Ferry, Virginia, October 16, 1859, with the aim of fomenting a slave revolt and eventually establishing a black republic in the mountains of Virginia. Brown and his men captured the arsenal, but the next day a company of U.S. Marines under Colonel Robert E. Lee assaulted the group, killed ten, and took Brown prisoner. After a hurried trial, the wounded Brown was sentenced to be hanged. Brown's bravery and dignity during the trial and on the scaffold moved millions of people to regard him as a hero.

60 I DO NOT BELIEVE IN THE ANTISLAVERY OF ABRAHAM LINCOLN

H. Ford Douglas

Although few African Americans could vote in the presidential campaign of 1860, all were confronted with the question of whom to support. There were four candidates for the presidential office, and many African Americans preferred Abraham Lincoln, the Republican nominee, though few were enthusiastic about him. Some, however, regarded Lincoln as no better than the other candidates, an advocate of white supremacy and an opponent of equality for blacks. The most outspoken black critic of Lincoln was H. Ford Douglas, of Illinois.

A fugitive slave from Virginia, Douglas (1831–1865) established himself as an orator at midwestern black state conventions of the early 1850s. An ardent emigrationist, Douglas debated John Mercer Langston on the subject before the 1854 National Emigration Convention. In 1856, he became part owner of the Provincial Freeman and supported emigration efforts in Canada West and Central America.

Sponsored by abolitionist Parker Pillsbury and the Massachusetts Anti-Slavery Society, Douglas came east during the 1860 campaign and delivered a series of speeches attacking the Republican candidate. On July 4, he spoke at Framingham, Massachusetts, at a mass meeting sponsored by the Massachusetts Anti-Slavery Society, held, in the words of the call, "to consider the solemn and pregnant issues of the hour—how best to preserve the principles of the Revolution and carry them forward to a speedy and enduring triumph." Before a crowd of more than two thousand, Douglas not only catalogued the reasons why no friend of the slave could support Lincoln but also challenged the advocates of racial inferiority, among whom he listed the Republican presidential candidate. Douglas's speech outraged some in the audience, including U.S. senator Henry Wilson of Massachusetts, who rose after Douglas to defend his party, its nominee, and himself. Douglas's speech is especially interesting in view of the continuing controversy over the man long hailed as the "Great Emancipator." It also contains a forceful denunciation of the speaking occasion, July 4, which Douglas "would rather curse than bless."

For further information on Douglas, see Robert L. Harris, Jr., "H. Ford Douglas: Afro-American Antislavery Emigrationist," Journal of Negro History 62 (July 1917), 217–34; and Orville A. Hitchcock and Ota T. Reynolds, "Ford Douglas' Fourth of July Oration, 1860," in J. Jeffrey Auer, ed., Antislavery and Disunion, 1858–1863 (Gloucester, Mass.: Peter

Smith, 1964), 133–51. The text of Douglas's speech comes from the Liberator, July 13, 1860.

M R. PRESIDENT, LADIES AND GENTLEMEN: I hope that my friends will not do me the injustice to suppose for a single moment that I have any connection either by blood or politically, with Stephen Arnold Douglas,* of Chicago. I am somewhat proud of the name of Douglas. It was once, in the history of dear old Scotia, a tower of strength on the side of free principles;† and so firmly did they oppose the usurpations of royal power, that, on one of the kings of Scotland coming to the throne, he issued an edict, expelling from his realm every man who bore that hated name; and I cannot account for the signal departure from the ancient and hereditary principles by one who bears that name, upon any other theory than that of bastard blood.

There are a great many people in this country who seem to be in love with Stephen A. Douglas, and to regard him as a great statesman. It seems to me that there are certain elements necessary to true statesmanship. In the first place, a statesman must have a heart—that is one of the essential elements of statesmanship. Now, who supposes that Stephen A. Douglas has a heart? I cannot account for the existence of so mean a man as Douglas on any other theory than that of the transmigration of souls. It was held by one of the old philosophers of Greece that when a man died, somebody was born, and that the soul of the dead entered the body of the newborn; but when Douglas was born, nobody happened to die!

But, ladies and gentlemen, I had no intention of making these remarks. We are here for the purpose of celebrating the Fourth of July. Eighty-four years ago today, this nation had its birth. We stand, to-day, a governmental prodigy, surpassing, in our extraordinary growth, any of the states of ancient or modern times. But nations who seek success amid the possibilities of the future are not measured by the accumulation of wealth or by the breadth of territorial domain; for down beneath the glittering splendor which the jeweled hand of Croesus has lifted up to intoxicate the gaze of the unthinking multitude, there will be found a silent and resistless influence working its way beneath the surface of society and shaping the destiny of men.

*Stephen Arnold Douglas (1831–1861) was the Democratic senator from Illinois. He infuriated all antislavery groups when he introduced the Kansas-Nebraska bill in 1854, with its provision permitting the existence of slavery in territories above the line delimiting it in the Missouri Compromise. Antislavery people also disliked Douglas's advocacy of the doctrine of popular sovereignty under which the people of a territory have the right to decide for themselves whether they wish the territory to be admitted to the Union as a slave or a free state.

†The Scottish hero Douglass was celebrated in Sir Walter Scott's poem "Lady of the Lake." Frederick Douglass, after he escaped from slavery, derived his name from Scott's hero.

When John Adams wrote that this would always be a day of bonfires and rejoicing, he did not foresee the evils which half a century would bring, when his own son, standing in his place amid the legislators of the Republic, would shame posterity into a brave indifference to its empty ceremonies. John Quincy Adams said, twenty years ago, that "the preservation, propagation and perpetuation of slavery is the vital animating spirit of the national government,"* and this truth is not less apparent today. Every department of our national life—the President's chair, the Senate of the United States, the Supreme Court, and the American pulpit—is occupied and controlled by the dark spirit of American slavery. We have four parties in this country that have marshaled themselves on the highway of American politics, asking for the votes of the American people to place them in possession of the government. We have what is called the Union party, led by Mr. Bell of Tennessee;† we have what is called the Democratic party, led by Stephen A. Douglas, of Illinois; we have the party called the Seceders, or the Slave-Code Democrats, led by John C. Breckinridge, of Kentucky‡ and then we have the Republican party, led by Abraham Lincoln, of Illinois.§ All of these parties ask for your support, because they profess to represent some principle. So far as the principles of freedom and the hopes of the black man are concerned, all these parties are barren and unfruitful; neither of them seeks to lift the Negro out of his fetters and rescue this day from odium and disgrace.

Take Abraham Lincoln. I want to know if any man can tell me the difference between the antislavery of Abraham Lincoln and the antislavery of the old Whig party or the antislavery of Henry Clay? Why, there is no difference between them. Abraham Lincoln is simply a Henry Clay Whig, and he believes just as Henry Clay believed in regard to this question. And Henry Clay was just as odious to the antislavery cause and antislavery men as ever

*After serving as President of the United States from 1825 to 1829, John Quincy Adams (1767–1848) served as a member of the House of Representatives, played a leading role in opposition to the extension of slavery, and championed the right of petition for antislavery men and women. He made this statement during the congressional debate over excluding abolition petitions. For the background of the statement, see Russel B. Nye, *Fettered Freedom: A Discussion of Civil Liberties and the Slavery Controversy in the United States, 1830 to 1860* (East Lansing, Mich.: Michigan State University Press, 1949), 35–49.

†John Bell (1797–1869), U.S. senator from Tennessee, was the leader of the conservative elements in the South that supported both slavery and the Union. He was nominated for the presidency in 1860 by the Constitutional Union Party.

‡In April 1860, the Democratic national convention met at Charleston but split over the question of federal protection of slavery in the territories. When this proposal by the delegates from the eight southern states was rejected, they withdrew and the convention adjourned. On June 18 the Democrats reconvened at Baltimore, but this time when the southern delegates again left, the convention nominated Stephen A. Douglas on a popular sovereignty platform. On June 28, the southern delegates who had bolted the convention met in Baltimore and chose John C. Breckinridge (1821–1875) of Kentucky for president on a platform advocating federal protection of slavery in the territories.

§The Republican Party, meeting in Chicago, nominated Abraham Lincoln as their presidential candidate on May 18, 1860.

was John C. Calhoun.* In fact, he did as much to perpetuate Negro slavery in this country as any other man who has ever lived. Henry Clay once said "That is property which the law declares to be property," and that "two hundred years of legislation have sanctioned and sanctified property in slaves."[†] Wherever Henry Clay is today in the universe of God, that atheistic lie is with him, with all its tormenting memories.

I know Abraham Lincoln, and I know something about his antislavery. I know the Republicans do not like this kind of talk, because, while they are willing to steal our thunder, they are unwilling to submit to the conditions imposed upon that party that assumes to be antislavery. They say that they cannot go as fast as you antislavery men go in this matter; that they cannot afford to be uncompromisingly honest, or so radical as you Garrisonians; that they want to take time; that they want to do the work gradually. They say, "We must not be in too great a hurry to overthrow slavery; at least, we must take half a loaf, we cannot get the whole." Now, my friends, I believe that the very best way to overthrow slavery in this country is to occupy the highest possible antislavery ground. Washington Irving tells a story of a Dutchman who wanted to jump over a ditch, and he went back three miles in order to get a good start, and when he got up to the ditch he had to sit down on the wrong side to get his breath. So it is with these political parties; they are compelled, they say, when they get up to the ditch of slavery, to stop and take breath.

I do not believe in the antislavery of Abraham Lincoln, because he is on the side of this slave power of which I am speaking, that has possession of the federal government. What does he propose to do? Simply to let the people and the territories regulate their domestic institutions in their own way. In the great debate between Lincoln and Douglas in Illinois, when he was interrogated as to whether he was in favor of the admission of more slave states in the Union, he said, that so long as we owned the territories, he did not see any other way of doing than to admit those states when they made application, *with or without slavery*.[‡] Now, that is Douglas' doctrine; it is stealing the thunder of Stephen A. Douglas.

In regard to the repeal of the Fugitive Slave Law, Abraham Lincoln oc-

---

*John C. Calhoun (1782–1850) was the outstanding champion of slavery in the U.S. Senate between 1832 and 1850.

[†]Clay made these remarks on the floor of the U.S. Senate on February 7, 1839. *Congressional Globe*, 25th Congress, 3d session, 357–58.

[‡]In the election for senator from Illinois in 1858, Lincoln, the Republican candidate, and Douglas, the Democratic candidate, conducted a series of seven debates throughout the state. It is not clear what source H. Ford Douglas used to describe Lincoln's position during the debates on the question of slavery in the territories, since Lincoln made it clear that while neither he nor the Republican Party wished to interfere with slavery where it already existed, both flatly opposed the further extension of slavery. Moreover, Lincoln was nominated for the presidency in 1860 on a platform that denied "the authority of Congress, of a territorial legislature, or of any individuals to give legal existence to slavery in any territory of the United States."

cupies the same position that the old Whig party occupied in 1852. They asserted then, in their platform, that they were not in favor of the repeal of that law, and that they would do nothing to lessen its efficiency. What did he say at Freeport?* Why, that the South was entitled to a Fugitive Slave Law; and although he thought the law could be modified a little, yet, he said, if he was in Congress, he would have it done in such a way as *not to lessen its efficiency!* Here, then, is Abraham Lincoln in favor of carrying out that infamous Fugitive Slave Law, that not only strikes down the liberty of every black man in the United States, but virtually the liberty of every white man as well; for, under that law, there is not a man in this presence who might not be arrested today upon the simple testimony of one man, and, after an *ex parte* trial, hurried off to slavery and to chains. Habeas corpus, trial by jury—those great bulwarks of freedom, reared by the blood and unspeakable woe of your English ancestors, amidst the conflicts of a thousand years—are struck down by this law; and the man whose name is inscribed upon the Presidential banner of the Republican party is in favor of keeping it upon the statute book!

Not only would I arraign Mr. Lincoln in regard to that law, for his proslavery character and principles, but when he was a member of the House of Representatives, in 1849, on the tenth day of January, he went through the District of Columbia and consulted the prominent proslavery men and slave-holders of the District, and then went into the House of Representatives and introduced, on his own responsibility, a fugitive-slave law for the District of Columbia. It is well known that the law of 1793 did not apply to the District, and it was necessary, in order that slaveholders might catch their slaves who sought safety under the shadow of the Capitol, that a special law should be passed for the District of Columbia; and so Mr. Lincoln went down deeper into the proslavery pool than ever Mr. Mason of Virginia did in the Fugitive Slave Law of 1850. Here, then, is the man who asks for your votes and for the votes of the antislavery people of New England; who, on his own responsibility, without any temptation whatever, introduced into the District of Columbia a fugitive-slave law!† That is a fact for the consideration of antislavery men.

Then, there is another item which I want to bring out in this connection. I am a colored man; I am an American citizen, and I think that I am entitled to exercise the elective franchise. I am about twenty-eight years old, and I would like to vote very much. I think I am old enough to vote, and I think that, if I had a vote to give, I should know enough to place it on the side of freedom.‡ No party, it seems to me, is entitled to the sympathy of antislavery

*The second in the series of Lincoln-Douglas debates took place on August 27, 1858, at Freeport, Illinois.

†Douglas does not mention the fact that when Lincoln served in Congress in the years 1847–1849, he voted against the Mexican War and, on January 10, 1849, introduced a resolution proposing the abolition of slavery in the District of Columbia.

‡After H. Ford Douglas had completed his speech, Frank B. Sanborn, an antislavery leader in New England and former associate of John Brown, declared: "When I reflect . . .

men, unless that party is willing to extend to the black man all the rights of a citizen. I care nothing about that antislavery which wants to make the territories free, while it is unwilling to extend to me, as a man, in the free states, all the rights of a man. In the state of Illinois, where I live—my adopted state—I have been laboring to make it a place fit for a decent man to live in. In that state, we have a code of black laws that would disgrace any Barbary State, or any uncivilized people in the far-off islands of the sea. Men of my complexion are not allowed to testify in a court of justice where a white man is a party. If a white man happens to owe me anything, unless I can prove it by the testimony of a white man, I cannot collect the debt. Now, two years ago, I went through the state of Illinois for the purpose of getting signers to a petition asking the legislature to repeal the "Testimony Law," so as to permit colored men to testify against white men. I went to prominent Republicans, and among others, to Abraham Lincoln and Lyman Trumbull,* and neither of them dared to sign that petition, to give me the right to testify in a court of justice! In the state of Illinois, they tax the colored people for every conceivable purpose. They tax the Negro's property to support schools for the education of the white man's children, but the colored people are not permitted to enjoy any of the benefits resulting from that taxation. We are compelled to impose upon ourselves additional taxes in order to educate our children. The state lays its iron hand upon the Negro, holds him down, and puts the other hand into his pocket and steals his hard earnings, to educate the children of white men; and if we sent our children to school, Abraham Lincoln would kick them out, in the name of Republicanism and antislavery!

I have, then, something to say against the antislavery character of the Republican party. Not only are the Republicans of Illinois on the side of slavery, and against the rights of the Negro but even some of the prominent Republicans of Massachusetts are not acceptable to antislavery men in that regard. In the Senate of the United States, some of your Senators from the New England states take special pains to make concessions to the slave power, by saying that they are not in favor of bringing about Negro equality; just as Abraham Lincoln did down in Ohio two years ago. When he went there to stump that state, the colored people were agitating the question of suffrage in that state. The *Ohio Statesman*, a paper published in Columbus, asserted, on the morning of the day that Mr. Lincoln made his speech, that he was in favor of Negro equality; and Mr. Lincoln took pains at that time to deny the

that Mr. Douglas, with every power, with every talent, which, had he been of our own race, would have secured him a prominent position, not only among the citizens, but among the rulers of this country, and remember that instead of this, in his adopted state—a state which he earned by his heroic escape from slavery—he has not a single political right—when I reflect on this, it seems to me that our whole nation, our whole system of society, is not worth a straw" (*Liberator*, July 13, 1860).

*Lyman Trumbull (1813–1896) was U.S. senator from Illinois between 1855 and 1873. A leader of the Republican Party, he supported Lincoln in 1860.

allegation, by saying that he was not in favor of bringing about the equality of the Negro race; that he did not believe in making them voters, in placing them in the jury box, or in ever bringing about the political equality of the races. He said that so long as they lived here, there must be an inferior and superior position, and that he was, as much as anybody else, in favor of assigning to white men the superior position.*

There is a good deal of talk in this country about the superiority of the white race. We often hear, from this very platform, praise of the Saxon race. Now, I want to put this question to those who deny the equal manhood of the Negro: What peculiar trait of character do the white men of this country possess, as a mark of superiority, either morally or mentally, that is not also manifested by the black man, under similar circumstances? You may take down the white and black part of the social and political structure, stone by stone, and in all the relations of life, where the exercise of his moral and intellectual functions is not restricted by positive law, or by the arbitrary restraints of society, you will find the Negro the equal of the white man in all the elements of head and heart. Of course, no one pretends that all men are mentally equal, or morally equal, any more than we do that all men are of the same weight, or equal in physical endowments. Here in this country, under the most favorable circumstances, we have idiots and fools, some in the lunatic asylum, and others, in the high places of government, who essay to be statesmen, who ought to be there. You say to the German, the Hungarian, the Irishman, as soon as he lands here, "Go out on the highway of the world's progress, and compete with me, if you can, in the race for empire and dominion." You throw no fetters upon that ever-restless sea of energies that chafes our shores, saying, "Thus far shalt thou go, but no further." No, with all that magnanimity which must be ever-present in the true soul, you say to the foreigner, whose liberty has been cloven down upon some disastrous European battlefield, whose fortune has been wrecked and lost amid the storms of adversity abroad, "Come here and better your condition, if you can!" I remember that a few years ago, when a Hungarian refugee—not an American citizen; he had only declared his intention to become one—was arrested in the harbor of Smyrna, for an offense against the Austrian government, Captain Ingraham, of the American warship *St. Louis*, demanded, in the name of the federal government, his instant release, and under the cover of her guns, the shackles of Austrian bondage melted from his limbs, and Martin Kozta walked the deck of that vessel a free man, as proud of his adopted country as we were of the gallant deed. That poor Hungarian, in the hour of his misfortune, could look at the American flag as it gleamed in the sunlight of the Austrian sky, and as he looked at its stars, that symbolized

---

*During Lincoln's early career in the Illinois legislature he voted in favor of a bill that, while eliminating real estate ownership as a prerequisite to the right to vote, restricted the vote to whites only. During the Lincoln-Douglas debates, Lincoln came out against slavery but also made it clear that he did not believe in the equality of the races and that the white race should be in a superior position.

a constellation of republican states, he could feel all the poetic inspiration of Halleck when he sang,

> *Flag of the seas! on Ocean's wave*
> *Thy stars shall glitter o'er the brave!*
> *When death, careering on the gale,*
> *Sweeps darkly 'round the bellied sail,*
> *And frighted waves rush wildly back*
> *Before the broadside's reeling rack,*
> *The dying wanderer of the sea,*
> *Shall look at once to heaven and thee,*
> *And smile to see thy splendors fly,*
> *In triumph o'er his closing eye.*

But no colored man can feel any of this inspiration. We are denied all participation in the government; we remember that the flag only covers us as slaves, and that our liberties are only respected and our rights only secured to us, when, escaping from the beak of the American eagle, we can nestle in the shaggy mane of the British lion; and feeling this, we can feel no inspiration when we look at the American flag.

But I was speaking in reference to the gratuitous concessions of some of our Republican leaders. Some three or four months ago a bill was under consideration in the Senate of the United States for the purpose of establishing a school for the education of free colored children in the District of Columbia. The matter created some discussion in the Senate, and, under the lash of Senator Mason, and other slave-drivers of the South, your own Senator, Mr. Wilson* caved in on this question and admitted, in the presence of the Senate, and with all Massachusetts to read his words, that the Negro was inferior. Now, I do not believe that the Negro is inferior. Man's ability wholly depends upon surrounding circumstances. You may take all of those races that have risen from the lowest estate of degradation to the highest eminence of intellectual and moral splendor, and you will discover that no race has ever yet been able, by any internal power and will of its own, to lift itself into respectability, without contact with other civilized tribes. Rome served as the scaffolding for the erection of the tribes of Western Europe into that huge political constellation whose drumbeats follow the sun round the world. When Julius Caesar landed in Britain, he found the ancestors of this boasted English race a miserable set of barbarians, bowing down to stocks and stones, and painting their bodies in fantastic colors. They were carried to Rome by the soldiers of Caesar and sold in the streets for five dollars; and so thoroughly brutalized were they that Cicero, the great Roman orator, said

---

*Henry Wilson (1812–1875) was U.S. senator from Massachusetts between 1855 and 1873. A leading opponent of slavery, he was one of the founders of the Republican Party. In 1872 he was elected vice president of the United States on the Republican ticket with Grant as president.

that the meanest slaves in Rome came from Great Britain; and, writing to his friend Atticus, he advised him not to buy the worthless wretches. Emerson says that it took many generations to trim and comb and perfume the first boatload of Norse pirates into royal highnesses and most noble knights of the garter; and yet, every spark and ornament of regal splendor dates back to the twenty thousand thieves that landed at Hastings. You will find, after that, I think, that there is no truth in the assertion that the Negro is inferior.

The men who justify slavery upon the assumed inferiority of the Negro race, are very slow to admit these facts. They are just as tardy in admitting that the remains of ancient grandeur, which have been exhumed from beneath the accumulated dust of forty centuries, were wrought by the ingenuity and skill of the Negro race, ere the Saxon was known in history. We are informed that the scepter of the world passed from the colored to the white race at the fall of Babylon. I know ethnological writers tell us we do not look like the Egyptian. They dig up an Egyptian mummy that has been dead and buried three thousand years, that once tripped "the light fantastic toe" amid the gilded halls of the Pharaohs, over whose grave the storms of thirty or forty centuries have swept, and because it doesn't look just like a Mississippi Negro of today, set it down that there is a difference in species between them! I admit that centuries of oppression, under a vertical sun, may have worked marvelous changes not only in the physical, but in the intellectual characteristics of the race—I know it has. All other races are permitted to travel over the wild field of history and pluck the flowers that blossom there, to glean up the heroes, philosophers, sages and poets, and put them into a galaxy of brilliant genius and claim all the credit to themselves; but if a black man attempts to do so, he is met at the threshold by the objection, "You have no ancestry behind you."

Now, friends, I am proud of the Negro race, and I thank God today that there does not course in my veins a single drop of Saxon blood.* The blood that I boast was immortalized in Scotland's song and story at a time when the Saxon was wearing an iron collar, with the name of his Norman master written thereon. (Applause.) There was never such a subjugated race in the world as were the Saxons in the days of William the Conqueror. So thoroughly humbled and degraded were they, that Macaulay says it was considered as disgraceful for a Norman to marry a Saxon as it is now for a white person to marry a negro. I am proud of the Negro race. I think that *Negro* looks just as well on paper and sounds just as sweetly to the ear as *Saxon;* and I believe that by education, by wealth, by religion, the Negro may make that name as honorable as ever was that of *Saxon,* while the Saxon, by the practice of the opposite vices, may drag himself down as low as the Negro. I believe that man, like certain productions of the vegetable kingdom, will

---

*Years later, W. E. B. Du Bois used almost the same language in his autobiography: "I was born . . . with a flood of Negro blood, a strain of French, a bit of Dutch, but, thank God, no Anglo-Saxon" (*Darkwater: Voices from Within the Veil* [New York: Harcourt, Brace and Howe, 1920], 9).

grow better in some soils than in others. God has given us a goodly land in which to build up an empire of thought; it ought also to be an empire of freedom. The anti-slavery men of the country intend to make this truly 'the land of the free and the home of the brave,' by coming to such meetings as these on gala days. When Boston conservatism goes down to the Music Hall to air itself in Everett's lying eulogy,* we mean to come here and criticise the various political parties, in order to rescue this day from priestly cant and from political mockery.

Oh, no, friends; we colored men may well feel proud of our ancestors. Why, we were held in very high esteem by the ancient Greeks. There is a Grecian fable that we descended from the gods. Virgil says that Jupiter, in his aerial chariot, sailing through the skies, went so near the sun that it burnt his face black; and on that hypothesis they account for the existence of the colored race! The father of Grecian poetry, standing away back in the gray dawn of history, has struck some noble lines from his lyre, in praise of our ancestors of the sunny clime.[†]

> *The sire of Gods, and all the ethereal train*
> *On the warm limits of the farthest main,*
> *Now mix with mortals, nor disdain to grace*
> *The feast of Ethiopia's blameless race.*

Friends, I have no idea that those men who talk about the inferiority of the Negro race really believe it. They think it is absolutely necessary, for the success of their party, to cater to the dark spirit of slavery. But, after all, I say that the Negro is a man, and has all the elements of manhood, like other men; and by the way, I think that, in this country, he has the *highest* element of manhood. Certainly he has developed here its highest element. I do not believe that the highest element of manhood is the ability to fight. If he is the noblest man who can do the most fighting, then you ought to elect John C. Heenan, the 'Benecia Boy,' as President of the United States. If muscle is evidence of the highest manhood, you will find any of the 'short boys' of New York, any of the 'plug-uglies' and ugly plugs (laughter) of Tammany Hall, better qualified to be President of the United States than Abraham Lincoln. The negro is emphatically a Christian man; patient under long suffering, as ready to forgive an injury as the Saxon is to inflict one; he would rather 'bear the ills he has, than fly to others that he knows not of.' (Applause.) You may dwarf his manhood by the iron of bondage, you may dry up the fountain of his intellectual life, but you can never destroy his faith in God, and the ultimate triumph of His almighty purpose. Over a sea of blood and tears, he catches, in every lull of the midnight storm that breaks around him, the [indecipherable] small voice that bids him 'Hope on, hope

---

*On the same day that Douglas spoke, Edward Everett delivered an oration entitled "Vindication of American Institutions," commissioned by the city authorities of Boston.

[†]Homer repeatedly praised the Ethiopians in his epic poems.

ever!' He constitutes the very oxygen of civilization, potent in that arterial action that imparts life and health to the permanent and successful achievements of the human race. Therefore, I do not like these gratuitous admissions on the part of men who go to Congress from New England with an anti-slavery purpose in their hearts.

But, my friends, I must bring my remarks to a close; and I say, that in view of the fact that the influence of slavery is dominant in every department of the government, I would rather curse than bless the hour that marked the fatal epoch in American history, when we threw off the yoke of a decent despotism, to become, in turn, the slaves of a mean and arrogant democracy.

Mark Antony said over the dead body of the old Roman, "I come to bury Caesar, not to praise him." (Applause.) Four million of my countrymen in chains today, ground between these two huge lies—like the upper and nether millstone—the Constitution of the United States and the Fourth of July, send me to the platform to bury the memory of that hour that witnessed the separation of these colonies from the mother country; for had we remained lined to her by political and social ties, we should inevitably have marched to freedom and equality, as she has done. England stands to-day with the trophies of a thousand years clustering around her head, as young and as vigorous in all the elements that promise future physical and intellectual development, as when, upon the fields of Cressy and Agincourt, her sons shattered, as with an iron mace, the embattled legions of France. She stands today, and has stood for a quarter of a century, upon the side of freedom; while here in republican America we have, for the last eighty-three years, been constantly tending toward a despotism baser and blacker than anything that history has yet recorded. I say, then, I would rather curse than bless the day that marked the separation. Hunkerism,* every where, as I said before, will go out to-day to be glorified in the sunlight of lying eulogy poured upon the dead fathers, whose faithlessness to every principle of freedom will yet cause their names to become a hissing and a byword to the ages yet to come. "Proclaim liberty throughout all the land, to all the inhabitants thereof" is the inscription upon the bell that hangs in "Independence Hall," in Philadelphia; but the old bell, more modest than the people, cracked the first time it was rung, because it had not *brass* enough to tell the lie again!

Hypocrisy is not a growth peculiar to American soil, but it has reached the most hateful development here. American slavery, the worst form of despotism ever imposed upon any people, is endorsed by Church and state as a great missionary institution. Eighty-four years ago today, your fathers, true to the impulses that brought them from the father land, spoke this nation into existence, breathed into it the breath of life, by asserting the selfhood of every human being. They had descended from men who, for two hundred years, had battled for freedom of conscience against the despotism of the bloody Stuarts; and when, in 1765, the British government passed the Stamp Act, and attempted to enforce it by British bayonets, against the will and

* A slang expression for those opposed to progress, derived from the popular nickname of the conservative faction of the Democratic Party in mid-nineteenth-century New York.

wishes of the American people, the Roundhead and the Cavalier went up to Bunker Hill, and entered their bleeding protest against George the Third, 'by the Grace of God.' In this, I say, they were true to their manly impulses. They declared that "all men are created equal"; and brave men from beyond the Rhine, and from the Rhine, and from the vine-clad hills of France, viewing from a distance that sublime struggle for the establishment of a free government, threw themselves at once into the conflict, and by their noble devotion to our cause, gave their names to history as a part of the glories of the Republic. But what did the fathers do to justify the expectations of these gallant strangers? Let four millions of slaves in our land answer the question! The liberty that Lafayette fought for, our fathers, in an hour of compromise, forgot, and went into a convention and sold the liberty of the black man, in order to form this guilty "covenant with death and agreement with hell";* and I say, that so long as that compromise exists, we are bound to stand outside the government and to commit ourselves to the dark spirit of slavery and to the political expediency of the hour.

The Constitution of the United States is the Janus of the American Capitol, looking both ways, assuming any color, according as we turn the political kaleidoscope. This is the one redeeming feature in it—that we cannot understand its carefully concealed purpose without the aid of contemporary history. Goethe says that no work is complete, unless it involves some mystery. I believe that the Constitution, in that respect, may be tortured into a virtuous instrument. It does involve a great mystery. But, as anti-slavery men, seeking the overthrow of slavery in the shortest possible way, we have to deal with the facts of the government as the fathers made it and construed it, while they lived. I am willing, for one, to accept the unbroken testimony of three-quarters of a century against the anti-slavery character of the American Constitution, and not dodge behind its equivocal phrases for the purpose of cheating the slaveholder, and saving the memory of our dishonest and time-serving fathers from the gibbet of impartial history. Achilles, the hero of the Illiad, is introduced by Homer as saying these memorable words: "I detest, as the very gates of hell, the wretch who has the baseness to say one thing, and mean another." I do not believe that the fathers wrote that Constitution, intending it to serve the purposes of freedom, and then turned round and construed it on the side of despotism and slavery. If they did, then were they a mean set of contemptible hypocrites, and deserving of the scathing denunciation of every friend of humanity. I do not believe it.

My friends, you may think this is a little radical, and you may, on this account, be unwilling to receive some of the other truths that I have been trying to impress upon you. There is some danger of anti-slavery men saying too much. I remember an anecdote that illustrates this very well. In a little

---

*The quotation is from William Lloyd Garrison, who described the Constitution, which guaranteed slavery, as "a covenant with death and an agreement with hell" and publicly burned copies of the document. See "In Compromise with Slavery," in *Selections from the Writings and Speeches of William Lloyd Garrison* (Boston: R. F. Wallcut, 1852), 140.

town in the State of New York, there lived a very pious family,—a father and mother, and two children, a son and daughter. They all belonged to the village church, except the son. He was rather a wild young man; but during a revival of religion in the village, he was induced by his parents to make application to the church for admission to membership. The deacon was somewhat of an old fogy, and did not believe in receiving him without first putting him through the catechism, to find out what his opinions were in regard to religion. So the first question he thought he would put to him was this: 'Do you believe that Jonah was swallowed by the whale, and that he was three days and three nights in the whales's belly?' 'Does father believe that?' asked the young man. 'Yes,' said the deacon. 'And mother, too?' 'Yes.' 'And the church, too?' 'Yes.' 'Well,' says he, 'I believe it.' 'Well, sir, do you believe that Daniel was thrown into the lion's den, and that those ferocious lions refused to eat Daniel, but as soon as his accusers were thrown in, they devoured them?' 'Does father believe it?' 'Yes,' 'And mother?' 'Yes.' 'And the church?' 'Yes.' 'Well, I believe it, then.' 'Well,' says the deacon, 'do you believe that Shadrach, Meshech and Abednego were thrown into a fiery furnace, heated seven times hotter than was necessary, and that those Hebrew children passed through the flames, and came out without so much as the smell of fire upon their garments?' 'Does the church believe it?' 'Yes.' 'And father, too?' 'Yes.' 'And mother?' 'Yes.' 'Well,' says he, 'I'll be d——d if I believe it, *nor the fish story either!*' (Loud laughter.) You see, friends, there is danger of saying too much!

But what shall I say, in closing my imperfect remarks? I know very well how imperfectly I have said my say. What can I say, then, as a black man, other than to thank the men and the women of New England who have so nobly stood by the rights and liberties of my unfortunate race during these long years of suffering and sorrow, feeling, as their only compensation, that every wrong and every outrage which we suffer

> 'In the hot conflict of the right, shall be
> A token and a pledge of victory'?

I know that, as anti-slavery men, occupying the high vantage ground of right, entering our earnest protest against government and church, there are many difficulties yet to be overcome before men shall fully realize the grandeur of our position. As our dear good friend, GERRIT SMITH,* has said, 'The cause is too sublime, in its all-embracing purpose, for the hypocrisy and cowardice of the age.' But the martyr spirit that inaugurated this movement to free a deeply wronged and injured people is not dead. As Romeo says,—

> 'Beauty's ensign yet
> Is crimson in thy lips, and in thy cheeks,
> And Death's pale flag is not advanced there.'

---

*Smith (1797–1874) was a wealthy philanthropist and political abolitionist who helped plan and finance John Brown's raid on Harper's Ferry.

What an army of brave men the moral and political necessities of twenty-five years ago pushed upon this platform to defend, with more than Spartan valor, this last Thermopylae of the New world! Then it was that our friend MR. GARRISON* could, with inspiration not of earth, brave a Boston mob, in defence of his convictions of right, in words of consuming fire from the dastardly, mean and craven cowards that thirsted for his blood. THEODORE D. WELD,† then in the freshness of youth, full of hope in ultimate success, his lips touched with a live coal from the altar of God, such as inspired the Hebrew prophet, plead like an angel, trumpet-tongued, against the deep damnation of human slavery. Then it was that the noble BERIAH GREEN,‡ with a logic as strong as the concatenations of an almighty purpose, was preaching himself out of every pulpit in New England. Then it was that ELIJAH P. LOVEJOY,§ whose mantle now covers a noble brother, (applause,) gave to the cause the printed sheet and the spoken word within the very sight of the fortress of the evil doer. These were brave men. Then, too, it was that that other good friend, WENDELL PHILLIPS, brought to the Anti-Slavery platform the rare gifts of scholarly culture and a magnificent rhetoric, to meet the rounded periods of New England's hunkerism in Faneuil Hall. Then it was that such men as QUINCY and HOVEY and ELLIS GRAY LORING placed themselves upon the Anti-Slavery platform, as offering upon the altar of Freedom.‖ Oh, it costs men something to take such a stand! The men who go out into the desert of old institutions, and attempt to tear down the rotten customs of society clothed in purple and fine linen, will find the 'property and standing' and gilded respectability of the age passing them by on the other side. As James Russell Lowell has sung—

> *'Then to side with Truth is noble, when we share her wretched crust,*
> *Ere her cause bring fame and profit, and 'tis prosperous to be just;*
> *Then it is the brave man chooses, while the coward stands aside,*
> *Doubting in his abject spirit till his Lord is crucified,*
> *And the multitude make virtue of the faith they had denied.'*

At that time, colored men had not demonstrated to the American people any of that ability which has since cropped out and developed itself, as a living testimony against the argument of the natural inferiority of the colored race. Many who have since added fresh trophies to American oratory were then in their chains. HENRY HIGHLAND GARNETT had scarcely begun to give an earnest of that splendid ability which has since manifested itself in the orator and the gentleman; the trumpet-notes of my namesake, FREDERICK DOUGLASS, had not yet stirred the intellectual sea of two

*William Lloyd Garrison, editor of the *Liberator.*

†Abolitionist author of *American Slavery As It Is* (1839).

‡Green (1797–1874) was president of the Interracial Oneida Institute and among the founders of the American Anti-Slavery Society.

§Antislavery journalist Elijah Lovejoy was killed by a mob in Illinois in 1837.

‖Abolitionists Edmund Quincy, Charles Fox Hovey (1807–1859), and Boston attorney Ellis Gray Loring.

continents to the enormities of this country; neither had there flashed over the Bay state the fiery and impetuous eloquence of CHARLES LENOX REMOND. Great changes have been wrought in the character of this anti-slavery work in thirty years. ALVAN STEWART is dead; JAMES G. BIRNEY is dead; ELIJAH P. LOVEJOY sleeps in a martyr's grave on the banks of the father of waters; ELLIS GRAY LORING is dead; THEODORE PARKER is dead. All these, and many other noble workers, have gone; as Whittier says—

> 'They died—their brave hearts breaking slow,—
>   But, self-forgetful to the last,
> In words of cheer and bugle-glow,
>   Their breath upon the darkness passed.'

But, friends, while the busy fingers of our memories are gathering flowers to bestrew the graves of the sainted dead, let us not forget one other name— one other of those 'immortal names, that are not born to die.' We are standing to-day by the fresh-made grave of JOHN BROWN.* (Applause.) He has been gathered to his Father's bosom from a Virginia scaffold. Lamartine, the great French orator, said once that Wilberforce went up to Heaven with a million of broken fetters in his hand, as evidence of a life well spent. JOHN BROWN has gone to join the glorious company of 'the just made perfect' in the eternal adoration of the living God, bearing in his right hand the history of an earnest effort to break four millions of fetters, and 'proclaim liberty throughout all the land, to all the inhabitants thereof.' (Loud and prolonged applause.)■

61 A PLEA FOR FREE SPEECH

Frederick Douglass

At a meeting in Boston's Tremont Temple on December 3, 1860, to commemorate the anniversary of John Brown's execution, ruffians hired by merchants engaged in the southern trade invaded the hall, disrupted the proceedings, and singled out Frederick Douglass, one of the speakers, for attack. Fighting "like a trained pugilist," the great aboli-

---

*Brown was executed in December 1859 after his capture during the assault on the Federal arsenal at Harper's Ferry, Virginia.

tionist was thrown "down the staircase to the floor of the hall" according to the correspondent for the Liberator.

The meeting was adjourned to a church on Joy Street. As the audience poured into the street, many African Americans were seized, knocked down, trampled upon, and a number seriously injured. "The mob was howling with rage," Douglass recalled years later.

A few days later, on December 10, Douglass spoke in Boston's Music Hall. After delivering a prepared lecture, "Self-Made Men," Douglass requested that he "be allowed to make some remarks" regarding the December 3 incident. He then presented one of the most stirring pleas for free speech in American history. He describes at length the attack on the meeting by both "respectable gentlemen" and rowdies. The right of free speech, he emphasizes, is basic to all other rights. Douglass also finds in the attempted suppression of his speech confirmation of the power of oratory to produce social change.

The speech is taken from the Liberator, *December 14, 1860.*

BOSTON is a great city and Music Hall has a fame almost as extensive as Boston. Nowhere more than here have the principles of human freedom been expounded. But for the circumstances already mentioned, it would seem almost presumptuous for me to say anything here about these principles. And yet, even here, in Boston, the moral atmosphere is dark and heavy. The principles of human liberty, even if correctly apprehended, find but limited support in this hour of trial. The world moves slowly, and Boston is much like the world. We thought the principle of free speech was an accomplished fact. Here, if nowhere else, we thought, the right of the people to assemble and to express their opinion was secure. Dr. Channing had defended the right,* Mr. Garrison had practically asserted the right, and Theodore Parker had maintained it with steadiness and fidelity to the last.[†]

But here we are today contending for what we thought was gained years ago. The mortifying and disgraceful fact stares us in the face, that though Faneuil Hall and Bunker Hill monument stand, freedom of speech is struck down. No lengthy detail of facts is needed. They are already notorious; far more so than will be wished ten years hence.

The world knows that last Monday a meeting assembled to discuss the question, "How Shall Slavery Be Abolished?" The world also knows that that meeting was invaded, insulted, captured by a mob of gentlemen, and thereafter broken up and dispersed by the order of the mayor, who refused to protect it, though called upon to do so. If this had been a mere outbreak of

*William Ellery Channing (1810–1884), a Unitarian clergyman, was an ardent foe of slavery and a noted social reformer in the decades before the Civil War.

[†]Theodore Parker (1810–1860) was a Unitarian clergyman, active in opposition to the Fugitive Slave Act and in support of John Brown's raid on Harper's Ferry.

passion and prejudice among the baser sort, maddened by rum and hounded on by some wily politician to serve some immediate purpose—a mere exceptional affair—it might be allowed to rest with what has already been said. But the leaders of the mob were gentlemen. They were men who pride themselves upon their respect for law and order.

These gentlemen brought their respect for the law with them and proclaimed it loudly while in the very act of breaking the law. Theirs was the law of slavery. The law of free speech and the law for the protection of public meetings they trampled underfoot, while they greatly magnified the law of slavery.

The scene was an instructive one. Men seldom see such a blending of the gentlemen with the rowdy, as was shown on that occasion. It proved that human nature is very much the same, whether in tarpaulin or broadcloth. Nevertheless, when gentlemen approach us in the character of lawless and abandoned loafers—assuming for the moment their manners and tempers— they have themselves to blame if they are estimated below their quality. No right was deemed by the fathers of the government more sacred than the right of speech. It was, in their eyes, as in the eyes of all thoughtful men, the great moral renovator of society and government. Daniel Webster called it a home-bred right, a fireside privilege. Liberty was meaningless where the right to utter one's thoughts and opinions had ceased to exist. That, of all rights, is the dread of tyrants. It is the right which they first of all strike down. They know its power. Thrones, dominions, principalities, and powers, founded in injustice and wrong, are sure to tremble, if men are allowed to reason of righteousness, temperance, and of a judgment to come in their presence. Slavery cannot tolerate free speech. Five years of its exercise would banish the auction block and break every chain in the South. They will have none of it there, for they have the power. But shall it be so here?

*'Shall tongues be mute,' &c.**

Even here in Boston, and among the friends of freedom, we hear two voices: one denouncing the mob that broke up our meeting on Monday as a base and cowardly outrage; and another deprecating and regretting the holding of such a meeting, by such men, at such a time. We are told that the meeting was ill-timed, and the parties to it unwise.

Why, what is the matter with us? Are we going to palliate and excuse a palpable and flagrant outrage on the right of free speech, by implying that only a particular description of persons should exercise that right? Are we, at such a time, when a great principle has been struck down, to quench the moral indignation which the deed excites, by casting reflections upon those on whose persons the outrage has been committed? After all the arguments for liberty to which Boston has listened for more than a quarter of a century,

*Douglass quotes from the beginning of John Greenleaf Whittier's "Voice of New England."

has she yet to learn that the time to assert a right is the time when the right itself is called in question, and that the men of all others to assert it are the men to whom the right has been denied?

It would be no indication of the right of speech to prove that certain gentlemen of great distinction, eminent for their learning and ability, are allowed to freely express their opinions on all subjects, including the subject of slavery. Such a vindication would need, itself, to be vindicated. It would add insult to injury. Not even an old-fashioned Abolition meeting could vindicate that right in Boston just now. There can be no right of speech where any man, however lifted up, or however humble, however young, or however old, is overawed by force and compelled to suppress their honest sentiments.

Equally clear is the right to hear. To suppress free speech is a double wrong. It violates the right of the hearer as well as those of the speaker. It is just as criminal to rob a man of his right to speak and hear as it would be to rob him of his money. I have no doubt that Boston will vindicate this right. But in order to do so, there must be no concessions to the enemy. When a man is allowed to speak because he is rich and powerful, it aggravates the crime of denying the right to the poor and humble.

The principle must rest upon its own proper basis. And until the right is accorded to the humblest as freely as to the most exalted citizen, the government of Boston is but an empty name and its freedom a mockery. A man's right to speak does not depend upon where he was born or upon his color. The simple quality of manhood is the solid basis of the right—and there let it rest forever.■

62 LET US TAKE UP THE SWORD

Alfred M. Green

As the Civil War erupted, many of those who had most strongly denounced the government and urged emigration (including Ford Douglas and Martin Delaney) worked most diligently to promote black enlistment in the Union army and to transform the mission of the war to abolition.

Although black soldiers had fought in the American Revolution and in the War of 1812, a federal law barred them from serving in state militias, and there were no African Americans in the regular United States Army. Despite this, in the first weeks after the outbreak of the Civil War, Northern blacks offered their services to the government to help suppress the rebellion. In the following speech delivered by Alfred M. Green, a Philadelphia schoolteacher, at a meeting of Philadelphia African Americans on April 20, 1861, barely a week after Fort Sumter, blacks are called upon to join the ranks of the Union army and fight to destroy slavery. Although these and other offers were spurned by the federal and state governments, which responded that "this is a white man's war," Green continued to urge African Americans to fight for the right to serve in the Union army. In a letter to the Anglo-African *of October 12, 1861, he wrote: "No nation has ever or ever will be emancipated from slavery . . . but by the sword, wielded too by their own strong arms. It is a foolish idea for us to still be nursing our past grievances to our own detriment, when we should as one man grasp the sword."*

Green's speech, presented here, is taken from Alfred M. Green, Letters and Discussions on the Formation of Colored Regiments *(Philadelphia, 1862), 3–4.*

T HE TIME HAS ARRIVED in the history of the great Republic when we may again give evidence to the world of the bravery and patriotism of a race in whose hearts burns the love of country, of freedom, and of civil and religious toleration. It is these grand principles that enable men, however proscribed, when possessed of true patriotism, to say, "My country, right or wrong, I love thee still!"

It is true, the brave deeds of our fathers, sworn and subscribed to by the immortal Washington of the Revolution of 1776, and by Jackson and others in the War of 1812, have failed to bring us into recognition as citizens, enjoying those rights so dearly bought by those noble and patriotic sires.

It is true that our injuries in many respects are great; fugitive-slave laws, Dred Scott decisions, indictments for treason, and long and dreary months of imprisonment. The result of the most unfair rules of judicial investigation has been the pay we have received for our solicitude, sympathy and aid in the dangers and difficulties of those "days that tried men's souls."

Our duty, brethren, is not to cavil over past grievances. Let us not be derelict to duty in the time of need. While we remember the past and regret that our present position in the country is not such as to create within us that burning zeal and enthusiasm for the field of battle which inspires other men in the full enjoyment of every civil and religious emolument, yet let us endeavor to hope for the future and improve the present auspicious moment for creating anew our claims upon the justice and honor of the Republic; and, above all, let not the honor and glory achieved by our fathers be blasted or sullied by a want of true heroism among their sons.

Let us, then, take up the sword, trusting in God, who will defend the right, remembering that these are other days than those of yore; that the world today is on the side of freedom and universal political equality; that the war cry of the howling leaders of Secession and treason is: "Let us drive back the advance guard of civil and religious freedom; let us have more slave territory; let us build stronger the tyrant system of slavery in the great American Republic. Remember, too, that your very presence among the troops of the North would inspire your oppressed brethren of the South with zeal for the overthrow of the tyrant system, and confidence in the armies of the living God—the God of truth, justice and equality to all men.■

63 WHAT IF THE SLAVES ARE EMANCIPATED?

John S. Rock

When the Civil War began, in April 1861, the sole Northern aim was restoration of the Union. But as the war continued, it became increasingly clear that to adhere to this position was to guarantee victory for the Confederacy. Thousands of slaves were doing the physical labor of the Confederate army—permitting the soldiers to conserve their strength for fighting, while millions of slaves were producing the sinews of war. Hence, black and white abolitionists argued soon after the outbreak of the war that the struggle could not be won nor could the Union be restored without the abolition of slavery. Repeatedly, however, they were forced to answer the question, What should we do with the slaves when they are emancipated? In a speech delivered on January 23, 1862, before the Massachusetts Anti-Slavery Society, John S. Rock, a prominent Boston dentist, attorney, and orator, came to grips with this question. Rock not only dealt with the emancipation of the slaves as a military necessity to guarantee a Union victory over the Confederacy, but also discussed the future of the free black in a white society. Before his predominantly white audience, Rock explored the roots and myths of race prejudice.

Rock's speech is presented here as published in the Liberator, *February 4, 1862.*

LADIES AND GENTLEMEN: I am here not so much to make a speech as to add a little more *color* to this occasion. (Laughter)

I do not know that it is right that I should speak, at this time, for it is said that we have talked too much already; and it is being continually thundered in our ears that the time for speech-making has ended, and the time for action has arrived. Perhaps this is so. This may be the theory of the people, but we all know that the active idea has found but little sympathy with either of our great military commanders, or the national Executive; for they have told us, again and again, that "patience is a cure for all sores," and that we must wait for the "good time," which, to us, has been long a-coming.

It is not my desire, neither is it the time for me to criticize the government, even if I had the disposition so to do. The situation of the black man in this country is far from being an enviable one. Today our heads are in the lion's mouth, and we must get them out the best way we can. To contend against the government is as difficult as it is to sit in Rome and fight with the Pope. It is probable that, if we had the malice of the Anglo-Saxon, we would watch our chances and seize the first opportunity to take our revenge. If we attempted this, the odds would be against us, and the first thing we should know would be—nothing! The most of us are capable of perceiving that the man who spits against the wind, spits in his own face! (Laughter)

While Mr. Lincoln has been more conservative than I had hoped to find him,* I recognize in him an honest man, striving to redeem the country from the degradation and shame into which Mr. Buchanan and his predecessors have plunged it.[†]

This nation is mad. In its devoted attachment to the Negro, it has run crazy after him and now, having caught him, hangs on with a deadly grasp, and says to him, with more earnestness and pathos than Ruth expressed to Naomi, "Where thou goest, I will go; where thou lodgest, I will lodge; thy people shall be my people, and thy God my God."

Why this wonderful attachment? My brother (Mr. Remond)[‡] spoke ably and eloquently to you this afternoon, and told you of the cruel and inhuman prejudices of the white people of this country. He was right. But has he not failed to look on the other side of this question? Has he not observed the deep and abiding affection that they have for the negro, which "neither height, nor depth, nor principalities, nor powers, nor things present nor to come, can separate from this love," which reaches to their very souls? (Renewed laughter and applause.)

I do not deny that there is a deep and cruel prejudice lurking in the bosoms of the white people of this country. It is much more abundant in the North than in the South. Here, it is to be found chiefly among the higher and lower classes; and there is no scarcity of it among the poor whites at the South. The cause of this prejudice may be seen at a glance.

The educated and wealthy class despise the Negro, because they have

---

*Most African Americans were more critical of Lincoln, condemning the president for failing to make emancipation the key issue of the war. This criticism mounted after September 11, 1861, when Lincoln modified General John C. Fremont's proclamation freeing the slaves of every rebel in the state of Missouri.

[†]James Buchanan (1791–1868), who was president when the secession movement took place, declared that secession was unconstitutional but insisted that Congress had no power under the Constitution to prevent it.

[‡]Black abolitionist Charles Lenox Remond (1810–1873).

robbed him of his hard earnings, or, at least, have got rich off the fruits of his labor; and they believe if he gets his freedom, their fountain will be dried up and they will be obliged to seek business in a new channel. Their "occupation will be gone." The lowest class hate him because he is poor, as they are, and he is a competitor with them for the same labor. The poor ignorant white man, who does not understand that the interest of the laboring classes is mutual, argues in this wise: "Here is so much labor to be performed. That Negro does it. If he was gone, I should have his place." The rich and the poor are both prejudiced from interest, and not because they entertain vague notions of justice and humanity. While uttering my solemn protest against this American vice, which has done more than any other thing to degrade the American people in the eyes of the civilized world, I am happy to state that there are many who have never known this sin, and many others who have been converted to the truth by the "foolishness of antislavery preaching," and are deeply interested in the welfare of the race and never hesitate to use their means and their influence to help break off the yoke that has been so long crushing us. I thank them all, and hope the number may be multiplied, until we shall have a people who will know no man save by his virtues and his merits.

Now, it seems to me that a blind man can see that the present war is an effort to nationalize, perpetuate and extend slavery in this country. In short, slavery is the cause of the war: I might say, is *the* war itself. Had it not been for slavery, we should have had no war! Through two hundred and forty years of indescribable tortures, slavery has wrung out of the blood, bones and muscles of the Negro hundreds of millions of dollars and helped much to make this nation rich. At the same time, it has developed a volcano which has burst forth, and, in a less number of days than years, has dissipated this wealth and rendered the government bankrupt! And, strange as it may appear, you still cling to this monstrous iniquity, notwithstanding it is daily sinking the country lower and lower! Some of our ablest and best men have been sacrificed to appease the wrath of this American god. There was Fremont*—God bless him (loud applause)—who, under pretense of frauds in his contracts, to the amount of several thousand dollars, was set aside for a Hunker kidnapper. If Fremont made a mistake of a few thousand dollars,— which no one claims was intentional, on his part,—what do you think of the terrible delay which has cost, and is costing, us two millions a day? Who is responsible for this great sacrifice of treasure? (Hear, hear.) Then, there was Mr. Cameron,† the hem of whose garment was not soiled with Anti-Slavery, except what he got from his official position, as it was forced upon his convictions. But, standing where he did, he saw the real enemy of the

---

*John C. Fremont was the Republican Party's first presidential nominee. He lost to Buchanan in 1856.

†Simon Cameron (1799–1889), Lincoln's secretary of war, opposed Lincoln by advocating the freeing and arming of slaves. In January 1862, Cameron was sent to Moscow as minister to Russia.

country; and because he favored striking at its vitals, his head was cut off, and that of a Hunker's* substituted!

There is a storm in that cloud which, today, though no larger than a man's hand, is destined to sweep over this country and wake up this guilty nation. Then we shall know where the fault is, and if these dry bones can live! The government wishes us to bring back the country to what it was before. This is possible; but what is to be gained by it? If we are fools enough to retain the cancer that is eating out our vitals when we can safely extirpate it, who will pity us if we see our mistake when we are past recovery? The Abolitionists saw this day of tribulation and reign of terror long ago and warned you of it; *but you would not hear!* You now say that it is their agitation, which has brought about this terrible civil war! That is to say, your friend sees a slow match set near a keg of gunpowder in your house and timely warns you of the danger which he sees is inevitable; you despise his warning and, after the explosion, say if he had not told you of it it would not have happened!

Now, when some leading men who hold with the policy of the President and yet pretend to be liberal argue that while they are willing to admit that the slave has an undoubted right to his liberty, the master has an equal right to his property; that to liberate the slave would be to injure the master, and a greater good would be accomplished to the country in these times by the loyal master's retaining his property than by giving to the slave his liberty—I do not understand it so. Slavery is treason against God, man and the nation. The master has no right to be a partner in a conspiracy which has shaken the very foundation of the government. Even to apologize for it, while in open rebellion, is to aid and abet in treason. The master's right to his property in human flesh cannot be equal to the slave's right to his liberty. The former right is acquified, either by kidnapping or unlawful purchase from kidnappers, or inheritance from kidnappers. The very claim invalidates itself. On the other hand, liberty is the inalienable right of every human being; and liberty can make no compromise with slavery. The goodness of slavery to the master can bear no relative comparison to the goodness of liberty to the slave. Liberty and slavery are contraries, and separated from each other as good from evil, light from darkness, heaven from hell. (Applause.) We trace effects to their cause. The evils brought upon the slave and the free colored man are traced to slavery. If slavery is better than freedom, its effects must also be better; for the better effect is from the better cause, and the better results from the better principle; and conversely, of better effects and results, the causes and principles are better. The greater good is that which we would most desire to be the cause to ourselves and our friends, and the greater evil is that which would give us the deeper affliction to have involved upon them or ourselves. Now, there is no sane man who would not rather have his liberty, and be stripped of every other earthly comfort, and see his

---

*Slang for the conservative wing of the New York Democratic Party, applied more generally to opponents of progress.

friends in a like situation, than be doomed to slavery with its indescribable category of cruelty and wrongs—

"Sometimes loaded with heavy chains,
and flogged till the keen lash stains."

It may be an easy matter to apologize for slavery but after applying the great test,—the Golden Rule—of "doing unto others as we would have them do unto us," we must admit that no apology can be made for slavery. And of all the miserable miscreants who have attempted to apologize for, and extol, the happy condition of the slave, I have never seen one of them willing to take the place of one of these so-called "happy creatures." (Loud applause.)

Today, when it is a military necessity and when the safety of the country is dependent upon emancipation, our humane political philosophers are puzzled to know what would become of the slaves if they were emancipated! The idea seems to prevail that the poor things would suffer if robbed of the glorious privileges they now enjoy! If they could not be flogged, half-starved, and work to support in ease and luxury those who have never waived an opportunity to outrage and wrong them, they would pine away and die! Do you imagine that the Negro can live outside of slavery? Of course, now they can take care of themselves and their masters too; but if you give them their liberty, must they not suffer? Have you never been able to see through all this? Have you not observed that the location of this organ of sympathy is in the pocket of the slaveholder and the man who shares in the profits of slave labor? Of course you have; and pity those men who have lived upon their ill-gotten wealth. You know, if they do not have somebody to work for them, they must leave their gilded *salons* and take off their coats and roll up their sleeves and take their chances among the *live* men of the world. This, you are aware, these respectable gentlemen will not do, for they have been so long accustomed to live by robbing and cheating the Negro that they are sworn never to work while they can live by plunder.

Can the slaves take care of themselves? What do you suppose becomes of the thousands who fly ragged and penniless from the South every year, and scatter themselves throughout the free states of the North? Do they take care of themselves? I am neither ashamed nor afraid to meet this question. Assertions like this, long uncontradicted, seem to be admitted as established facts. I ask your attention for one moment to the fact that colored men at the North are shut out of almost every avenue to wealth, and yet, strange to say, the proportion of paupers is much less among us than among you! Are the beggars in the streets of Boston colored men? In Philadelphia, where there is a larger free colored population than is to be found in any other city in the free states, and where we are denied every social privilege and are not even permitted to send our children to the schools that we are taxed to support or to ride in the city horsecars, yet even there we pay taxes enough to support our own poor, and have a balance of a few thousand in our favor, which goes to support those "poor whites" who "can't take care of themselves."

Many of those who advocate emancipation as a military necessity seem puzzled to know what is best to be done with the slave, if he is set at liberty. Colonization in Africa, Haiti, Florida and South America are favorite theories with many well-informed persons. This is really interesting! No wonder Europe does not sympathize with you. You are the only people, claiming to be civilized, who take away the rights of those whose color differs from your own. If you find that you cannot rob the Negro of his labor and of himself, you will banish him! What a sublime idea! You are certainly a great people! What is your plea? Why, that the slaveholders will not permit us to live among them as freemen, and that the air of Northern latitudes is not good for us! Let me tell you, my friends, *the slaveholders are not the men we dread!* They do not desire to have us removed. The Northern proslavery men have done the free people of color tenfold more injury than the Southern slaveholders. In the South, it is simply a question of dollars and cents. The slaveholder cares no more for you than he does for me. They enslave their own children and sell them, and they would as soon enslave white men as black men. The secret of the slaveholder's attachment to slavery is to be found in the dollar, and *that* he is determined to get without working for it. There is no prejudice against color among the slaveholders. Their social system and one million of mulattoes are facts which no arguments can demolish. If the slaves were emancipated, they would remain where they are. Black labor in the South is at a premium. The free man of color has always had the preference over the white laborer. Many of you are aware that Southerners will do a favor for a free colored man, when they will not do it for a white man in the same condition in life. They believe in their institution because it supports them.

Those who say that the air of Northern latitudes is not good for us, that we cannot withstand the cold, and that white men cannot bear the heat, evince their ignorance of the physical capacity of both races. To say that black men cannot bear the cold, or white men the heat, is to assert that which is at variance with the truth. I do not deny that black men from hot countries suffer much from the cold when they come here. But a black man who comes from Cuba suffers no more from the cold than a white man from that country. A colored man born in Boston bears the cold quite as well as a white man who is born here. There has not been a greater proportion of deaths among the white men who have gone from the Northern States to the West Indies than with the colored men who have gone there from the same states. There has been a terrible mortality among the colored people from the North who have recently gone to Hayti. The people from all tropical countries suffer when they come here. Even those white men who come from higher European latitudes suffer from our unequal temperature. It is said that white men cannot bear the heat of the tropics. My answer to this is that they do bear it. I do not deny that God may have made the negro out of a little better material than he made the white man. (Laughter.) Perhaps he is physically his superior. I think you must admit that he has more fortitude. One thing we do know, and that is, white men don't like to work and earn their own bread, and will not, if the blacks will earn it for them. (Laughter.) In the Gulf States the average life of a field slave is from seven to eight years. Do you imagine that white men, if obliged to work, would die off faster than that? (Hear, hear.) You have been used to hearing but one side of this question. The lions have had no painters. (Hear.) When black men write and speak, you must expect to see both sides and the edges. (Laughter.) My experience is, that white men can bear the heat of the South, and we know that in the North they are firemen in our steamers, and in our factories and foundries, where they undergo a heat to be found no where in the tropics— subject also to the sudden alternations from heat to cold—a variation at this season of the year of from seventy-five to a hundred degrees; and yet they bear it, and no one thinks for a moment that the life of a white fireman on a steamer or in a factory is less than that of a colored man in the same situation. (Applause.)

I have no word to say against Liberia or Hayti. The people of those countries will compare favorably with those of other countries in a similar situation. The tropics are not favorable to activity and enterprise. The labor of the tropics has been chiefly forced labor. Those who have not been forced to labor have remained idle. Indeed, idleness is the child of the tropics. Black men in the South are without doubt almost as lazy as the white men there, and you would probably witness their aversion to labor as you do that of the whites, was it not that their labor is forced from them at the end of the cat-o-nine-tails and the muzzle of the musket. All men are lazy. No class of men would labor was it not for the necessity, and the reward that sweetens labor. But few men can withstand a torrid sun—all shrink from it; and in a hot day a man, whether black or white, goes as instinctively to the shade as a rat to the best cheese. (Laughter and applause.)

Other countries have been held out as homes for us. Why is this? Why is it that the people from all other countries are invited to come here and we are asked to go away? Is it to make room for the refuse population of Europe? Or why is it that the white people of this country desire to get rid of us? Does anyone pretend to deny that this is our country? Or that much of the wealth and prosperity found here is the result of the labor of our hands? Or that our blood and bones have crimsoned and whitened every battlefield from Maine to Louisiana? Why this desire to get rid of us? Can it be possible that because the nation has robbed us for nearly two and a half centuries and, finding that she can no longer and preserve her character among nations, now, out of hatred, wishes to banish because she cannot continue to rob us? Or why is it? Be patient and I will tell you! The free people of color have succeeded, in spite of every effort to crush them, and we are today a living refutation of that shameless assertion that we "can't take care of ourselves," in a state of freedom. Abject as our condition has been, our whole lives prove us superior to the influences that have been brought upon us to crush us. This could not have been said of your race when it was oppressed and enslaved! Another reason is, this nation has wronged us and for this reason many hate us. The Spanish proverb is—"since I have wronged you, I have never liked you." This is true not only of Spaniards and Americans, but of every other class of people. When a man wrongs another, he not only hates him, but tries to make others dislike him. Strange as this may appear, it is nevertheless painfully true. You may help a man during his life-time, and you are a capital fellow; but your first refusal brings down his ire, and shows you his ingratitude. When he has got all he can from you, he has no further use for you. When the orange is squeezed, we throw it aside. The black man is a good fellow while he is a slave and toils for nothing; but the moment he claims his own flesh and blood and bones he is a most obnoxious creature, and there is a proposition to get rid of him! He is happy while he remains a poor, degraded, ignorant slave, without even the right to his own offspring. While in this condition, the master can ride in the same carriage, sleep in the same bed, and nurse from the same bosom. But give this same slave the right to use his own legs, his hands, his body and his mind, and this happy and desirable creature is instantly transformed into a miserable loathsome wretch, fit only to be colonized somewhere near the mountains of the moon, or eternally banished from the presence of all civilized beings. You must not lose sight of the fact that it is the emancipated slave and the free colored man whom it is proposed to remove—not the slave; this country and climate are perfectly adapted to Negro slavery; it is the free black that the air is not good for! What an idea! A country good for slavery, and not good for freedom! This idea is monstrous and unworthy of even the Fejee islanders. All the Emigration and Colonization Societies that have been formed, have been auxiliaries of the Slave Power, and established for this purpose, and the great desire to make money out of our necessities. (Loud applause.)

It is true, a great many simple minded people have been induced to go to Liberia and to Hayti, but, be assured, the more intelligent portion of the colored people will remain here; not because we prefer being oppressed here to being free men in other countries, but we will remain because we believe our future prospects are better here than elsewhere, and because our experience has proved that the greater proportion of those who have left this country during the last thirty years have made their condition worse, and would have gladly returned if they could have done so. You may rest assured that we shall remain here—here, where we have withstood almost everything. Now, when our prospects begin to brighten, we are the more encouraged to stay, pay off the old score and have a reconstruction of things. There are those of us who believe that we have seen the star of our redemption rising in the east, and moving southward. (Applause.)

The government is now trying to untie the knot which must be cut. Here you perceive it is mistaken. The North is in error. She has suffered the South, like a wayward child, to do as she would, and now, when she would restrain her, she finds trouble. If you wish to prevent a pending evil, destroy the source at once. If the first sparks were quenched, there would be no flame, for how can he kill who dares not be angry? or how can he be perjured who fears an oath? All public outrages of a destroying tendency and oppression are but childish sports let alone till they are ungovernable. The choking of the fountain is the surest way to cut off the source of the river. The Government has not had the courage to do this. Having sown the wind, they are now reaping the whirlwind: but in the end I think it will be conceded by all, that we shall have gathered in a glorious harvest. (Loud applause.)

I do not regard this trying hour as a darkness. The war that has been waged on us for more than two centuries has opened our eyes and caused us to form alliances, so that instead of acting on the defensive we are now prepared to attack the enemy. This is simply a change of tactics. I think I see the finger of God in all this. Yes, *there* is the handwriting on the wall: *I come not to bring peace, but the sword. Break every yoke, and let the oppressed go free. I have heard the groans of my people and am come down to deliver them!* (Loud and long-continued applause.)

At present, it looks as though we were drafting into a foreign war; and if we do have one, slavery must go down with it. It is not the time now for me to discuss the relation of the black man to such a war. Perhaps no one cares what we think or how we feel on this subject. You think yourselves strong now. The wisest man and the strongest man is generally the most ignorant and the most feeble. Be not deceived. No man is so feeble that he cannot do you an injury! (Hear, hear.) If you should get into a difficulty of this kind, it would be to your interest that we should be your friends. You remember the lion had need of the mouse. (Applause.) You have spurned our offers, and disregarded our feelings, and on this account we have manifested but little interest in, and have been apparently indifferent observers of this contest; but appearances are deceitful—every man who snores is not asleep. (Applause.)

I believe the conduct of both the bond and the free has been exceedingly judicious. It is times like these that try men. It is storms and tempests that give reputation to pilots. If we have a foreign war, the black man's services will be needed. Seventy-five thousand freemen capable of bearing arms, and three-quarters of a million of slaves wild with the enthusiasm caused by the dawn of the glorious opportunity of being able to strike a genuine blow for freedom, will be a power that "white men will be bound to respect." (Applause.) Let the people of the United States do their duty, and treat us as the people of all other nations treat us—as men; if they will do this, our last drop of blood is ready to be sacrificed in defence of the liberty of this country. (Loud applause.) But if you continue to deny us our rights, and spurn our offers except as menials, colored men will be worse than fools to take up arms at all. (Hear, hear.) We will stand by you, however, and wish you that success which you will not deserve. (Applause.)

This rebellion for slavery means something! Out of it emancipation must spring. I do not agree with those men who see no hope in this war. There is nothing in it but hope. Our cause is onward. As it is with the sun, the clouds often obstruct his vision, but in the end we find there has been no standing still. It is true the government is but little more antislavery now than it was at the commencement of the war; but while fighting for its own existence, it has been obliged to take slavery by the throat, and sooner or later *must* choke her to death. (Loud applause.) Jeff Davis is to the slaveholders what Pharaoh was to the Egyptians, and Abraham Lincoln and his successor, John C. Fremont, (applause,) will be to us what Moses was to the Israelites. (Continued applause.) I may be mistaken, but I think the sequel will prove that I am correct. I have faith in God and gun-powder and lead, (loud applause,) and believe we ought not to be discouraged. (Applause.) We have withstood the sixth trial, and in the seventh our courage must not falter. I thank God I have lived to see this great day, when the nation is to be weighed in the balances, and I hope not found wanting. (Applause.) This State and the National Government have treated us most shamefully, but as this is not the first time, I suppose we shall live through it. In the hour of danger, we have not been found wanting. As the Government has not had the courage to receive the help that has been standing ready and waiting to assist her, we will now stand still, and see the salvation of our people. (Applause.)■

64 WE ASK FOR OUR RIGHTS

John S. Rock

During the spring and summer of 1862, President Lincoln and the U.S. Congress began to move toward emancipation. On March 6, Lincoln recommended federal compensation to any state adopting gradual emancipation. Congress prohibited slavery in all U.S. territories and, in April, approved the abolition of slavery in Washington, D.C. On July 17, Congress declared all slaves escaped from Confederate slaveholders to be "forever free" once they crossed Union lines. On July 22, President Lincoln secretly submitted the first draft of the Emancipation Proclamation to his cabinet. It was to be announced publicly on September 22, following the Union victory in the Battle of Antietam.

Addressing the West Indies Emancipation Day celebration, August 1, 1862, at Abington, Massachusetts, John S. Rock advanced what was probably the first demand for distribution of land to slaves emancipated during the Civil War. At the same time, he pointed out that the end of slavery was not the only issue confronting the nation, for the African American in the free states was also oppressed and racial prejudice was *as prevalent in the Union as in the Confederacy. To emancipate the slaves and at the same time continue to deprive black people of their full rights would be a hollow victory. Rock concludes his address with a demand that black regiments be accepted into the Union forces. Dr. Rock's speech is taken from the* Liberator, *August 15, 1862.*

Mr. President, Ladies and Gentlemen,—The day that we have assembled here to celebrate has been made sacred in the world's calendar. Twenty-four years ago, the friends of freedom in Great Britain and in her Colonies held grand jubilees, and thanked God and their rulers that 800,000 human chattels were that day transformed into men, and that the slave could never again clank his chains on British soil.

The British Government has, by this act, set us an example which I think hundreds within the sound of my voice would rejoice to see imitated by the United States. (Applause.) What our President means to do in *this* direction, God only knows. I do not pretend to be able to discern the probable results of this war better than he can, but I think I can see as far into the millstone as the man who picks it; and if I do not know all about the white man, I have learned something of the black,—enough at least to say that you have made a mistake by spurning valuable friends, who have stood ready to help you. I have never doubted but that the President was on the side of freedom and humanity, but I confess I do not understand how it is, that when the national life has been assailed, he has not availed himself of all the powers given him; and, more especially, why he has not broken every yoke, and let the oppressed go free.* There may be many reasons why he should do as he has done; but I am puzzled to know why he, as a constitutional man and a patriot, has delayed enforcing laws recently enacted for the overthrow of rebellion. We all know that emancipation, if early proclaimed, would not only have saved many precious lives, but the nation itself. Why then delay, when delays are dangerous, and may prove fatal?

I believe the only salvation to be obtained for this country must be through the hearty cooperation of the oppressed, bond and free.

It is indeed humiliating to the civilization and Christianity of the nineteenth century that to-day, in one of the most, if not the most enlightened nation on the globe, there exists a "peculiar" and popular "institution," which robs men not only of their earnings, but of themselves and their families; abolishes the marriage relation, ignores chastity, and makes woman the hapless victim of the most depraved wretches, and inflicts upon all who resist its progress tortures which the most barbarous savages of the most barbarous age would have scorned to have inflicted upon their bitterest enemies.

*On May 19, Lincoln revoked the order of General David Hunter proclaiming martial law and immediate emancipation of all slaves in Georgia, Florida, and South Carolina, fearing the reaction of the border states. Lincoln was denounced by Frederick Douglass and other abolitionists.

Our enemies argue that West India Emancipation has failed. So have the despots of Europe always said that democratical institutions are a failure. (Hear.) We know that Democracy is now undergoing a terrible trial; but who is there who has lost confidence in the people, and is willing to yield to the "divine right of kings"? If this Government fails now, it will not be because we have reposed too much confidence in the people, but because we have relied too much on the few, who will have proved themselves unworthy of our confidence. (Applause.)

What are the facts about British Emancipation? Did the freed men become idle, disorderly, or bad citizens, after they were emancipated? Not at all. They have been good citizens, and industrious to a remarkable degree, considering the climate and its resources, and the low wages paid for labor. It is true that many of the poor planters were left to suffer. Poor things, they had taken no thought for the morrow, but depended solely upon having their pockets filled by gold wrung from the sweat and life-blood of the unpaid laborer. There was no chance for them to steal: they were too proud to beg, and too lazy to work. (Applause.) How could they help suffering? Many who were wealthy were ruined. I will tell you how this was done. They attempted to crush freed men by refusing to employ them. Many of those who did employ them, gave them so little that they were unable to provide for their necessities. This aroused the freed men, and many of those who had saved up something during the four years' apprenticeship immediately preceding emancipation, bought small parcels of land, and, instead of working for the planters, they became small proprietors and worked for themselves. This effort on the part of the planters to crush out free laborers was not without its good effects. It taught the blacks the necessity of self-reliance, and the planter that the laborer was worthy of his hire. The exports, as a matter of course, were less, because, instead of cultivating cotton and sugar, the freed men were obliged to turn their attention to cultivating the necessaries of life. This enabled them to throw away the coarse and unhealthy food that they were formerly obliged to eat, and live on better diet. Their new relation created new wants. Many things which had been denied them in slavery they were able to get when free, and the surplus of their gardens or fields, instead of being exported, were exchanged in many instances for the luxuries of a higher state, and by their means their labor was turned into a new channel. The reason why it was impossible for Jamaica to export so much as formerly was because the planters failed to encourage labor, and the people consumed more than before of that which was produced. You will please bear in mind that a larger proportion of the exports from the British West Indies is now produced upon the estates of men once held as slaves. (Applause.)

The English Government, instead of setting the planters to work to compensate the slaves for what they had plundered from them, paid the planters with British gold, the price of their blood to which they had not the shadow of a right, neither by the laws of God nor of nature. (Applause.) Robbed of everything but their liberty, and without any assistance, the new creatures sprang into a new life, and have nobly vindicated their capacity to enjoy and appreciate their freedom. Why talk about compensating masters? Compensate them for what? What do you owe them? What does [sic] the slaves owe them? What does society owe them? Compensate the master? No, never. (Applause.) It is the slave who ought to be compensated. The property of the South is by right the property of the slave. You talk of compensating the master who has stolen enough to sink ten generations, and yet you do not propose to restore even a part of that which has been plundered. This is rewarding the thief. Have you forgotten that the wealth of the South is the property of the slave? Will you keep back the price of his blood, which is upon you and upon your children? Restore to him the wealth of the South, and he will engage to continue to take care of the master well, as he has always been obliged to do, and make a good speculation by the transaction. (Applause.) This you owe to the slave; and if you do your duty, posterity will give to you the honor of being the first nation that dared to deal justly by the oppressed.

Freedom in the West Indies is a success. It is a success everywhere whether gained peaceably or by the sword. (Applause.) We learn by the last census that there is in the Island of Jamaica one hundred and eighty-two churches, exclusive of the Church of England, and that the average attendance on the day schools is 33,521; that crime has diminished, and that the moral character of the whole people is greatly improved. Jamaica has at present some colored men that any country could well afford to be proud of; comprising artists, mechanics, manufacturers, merchants, physicians, professors, advocates, judges and legislators, each honorably filling his station, and proving that the colored man is capable of the highest refinement and culture. Many of these men, you remember, were once slaves. What has been done in Jamaica may be done in the United States. (Applause.)

Our Government has recognized the Governments of Liberia and Hayti. What sort of logic is it that regards the blacks in America as creatures having no rights, but the moment they emigrate to Hayti or Liberia, they are entitled to consideration? Why are we now standing still? Why is it that emancipation is not declared? Can it be possible that we fear Jeff. Davis will "bang us" all, (laughter) and wish to trim our conduct so that we can say to him, "Have we not been good and faithful servants? Are we not entitled to your favors?" Why such pandering to the pro-slavery, or rather secession, element in our midst? Why this Northern servility? I have been told that it is the natural repugnance of the races; that the whites will always have their prejudices, and on this account it would not do to emancipate the blacks, for it would be impossible for the two races to exist together as equals. You may believe this, but I do not believe it. That there are many ignorant white people who believe all they have heard against us, I do not pretend to deny; but I do deny that the masses of the intelligent whites are prejudiced against us. The most bitter pro-slavery man in this State, who would send me to the mountains of the moon tomorrow, would insult any daughter, if I had one, the moment my back was turned. This is the character of the negro-haters of this country. (Laughter.) I never saw a pro-slavery man or a colonizationist who was not, when he had a chance, an amalgamationist. (Laughter and applause.) Though often men in high position, they are generally men with low moral ideas, who seek by words to conceal their real motives. They are opposed to emancipation because that will carry certain legal rights with it, and will elevate the moral standard. The design is to keep the race ignorant and degraded, and without legal or moral rights, that it may be at the mercy of the depraved. I do not think the whites have much prejudice, when I see them preferring the society of the most degraded blacks to that of cultivated whites (hear, hear); and in this I am confirmed by the fact that there is no prejudice against black men or black women, so long as they remain slaves. This prejudice is not natural. The white child cries after the black wet-nurse, and refuses to be comforted by its mother (laughter and applause); and the mulatto child is dandled on the knee of its white father until he gets "hard up," then he sells it. (Applause.)

Emancipation will entirely revolutionize society. This system of free love must be abolished. This will be no child's play. (Laughter.) When the government has been brought to the saving knowledge of emancipation, then the anti-slavery work will have but fairly commenced. I hope our friends will not stop now, and think their work is done. The slaves have toiled for you for more than two centuries. It is but right that you should do something for them. (Applause.) They have a heavy claim against you—a long catalogue of outrage and oppression. You must not forsake them now. The slaves are to be educated for a higher civilization, they need your friendship, and we ask you to cooperate with us, and help clear the way. All I ask for the black man is an unobstructed road and a fair chance. (Applause.)

The present position of the colored man is a trying one; trying because the whole nation seems to have entered into a conspiracy to crush him. But few seem to comprehend our position in the free States. The masses seem to think that we are oppressed only in the South. This is a mistake; we are oppressed everywhere in this slavery-cursed land. Massachusetts has a great name, and deserves much credit for what she has done, but the position of the colored people in Massachusetts is far from being an enviable one. While colored men have many rights, they have but few privileges here. To be sure, we are seldom insulted by the vulgar passers by, we have the right of suffrage, the free schools and colleges are opened to our children, and from them have come forth young men capable of filling any post of profit or honor. But there is no field for these young men. Their education aggravates their suffering. The more highly educated the colored man is, the more keenly he suffers. The educated colored man meets, on the one hand, the embittered prejudices of the whites, and on the other the jealousies of his own race. The colored man who educates his son, educates him to suffer. The more ignorant the colored man, the more happy he must be. If we are never to derive the benefits of an education, it would be a misfortune for us to see inside of a school house. You can hardly imagine the humiliation and contempt a colored lad must feel in graduating the first in his class, and then being rejected everywhere else because of his color. To the credit of the nineteenth century, be it said, the United States is the only civilized country mean enough to make this invidious distinction. No where in the United States is the colored man of talent appreciated. Even in Boston, which has a great reputation for being anti-slavery, he has no field for his talent. Some persons think that, because we have the right of suffrage, and enjoy the privilege of riding in the cars, there is less prejudice here than there is farther South. In some respects this is true, and in others it is not true. We are colonized in Boston. It is five times as difficult to get a house in a good location in Boston as it is in Philadelphia, and it is ten times more difficult for a colored mechanic to get employment than in Charleston. Colored men in business in Massachusetts receive more respect, and less patronage, than in any place that I know of. In Boston we are proscribed in some of the eating-houses, many of the hotels, and all the theatres but one. Boston, though anti-slavery and progressive, supports, in addition to these places, two places of amusement, the sole object of which is to caricature us, and to perpetuate the existing prejudices against us. I now ask you, is Boston anti-slavery? Are not the very places that proscribe us sustained by anti-slavery patronage? Do not our liberal anti-slavery politicians dine at the Revere House, sup at the Parker House, and take their cream and jellies at Copeland's?

The friends of slavery are everywhere withdrawing their patronage from us, and trying to starve us out by refusing to employ us even as menials. When our laboring men go to them for work, as heretofore, they reply, "Go to the Abolitionists and republicans, who have turned the country upside down"! The laboring men who could once be found all along the wharves of Boston, can now be found only about Central wharf, with scarcely encouragement enough to keep soul and body together. You know that the colored man is proscribed in some of the churches, and that this proscription is carried even to the grave-yards. This is Boston—by far the best, or at least the most liberal large city in the United States.

Now, while our enemies are endeavoring to crush us, and are closing the avenues from which we have wrung out our humble subsistence, is there anything higher opened to us? Who is taking our boys into their stores at a low salary, and giving them a chance to rise? Who is admitting them into their workshops, or into their counting-room? Or who is encouraging those who are engaged in trade or business! With the exception of a handful of Abolitionists and Republicans, there are none. This is the kind of friendship that we need. It is not unpopular now to be anti-slavery, and there are many who speak kindly of us when their hearts are far from us. True friends are few, or, as Shakespeare has it,

> "Words are easy as the wind,
> Faithful friends are hard to find."

This, I think, is the experience of most men. Many of us have learned to appreciate the Spanish proverb—"He's my friend who grinds at my mill." In New England, colored mechanics get but little patronage. Indeed, a trade is of but little use to any of us, unless we can, like the tailor of Campillo, afford to work for nothing, and find thread.

Friends, I ask you to look into this matter. You can assist the colored man, but you cannot elevate him; this must be done by his own exertions. Every colored man who succeeds is an unanswerable argument in favor of emancipation. The encouragement of one colored man stimulates others. Now, we have nothing to stimulate our youth. They see many of us struggling against fearful odds, without friends or even kind words, and they become discouraged. The success of such a man as Frederick Douglass is worth more to the race than a pile of resolutions and speeches high as Bunker Hill monument. Had it not been for the Abolitionists, the brilliant genius of Mr. Douglass would probably have died with him. All honor to those noble men and women, who had the courage to do what they did! His success is our success, is the success of a great cause. (Applause.)

It is in this way that we ask our friends to help open to us these thoroughfares, through which all others are encouraged to pass, and in this manner breathe into the anti-slavery movement the breath of life. Then we will become educated and wealthy; and then the roughest looking colored man that you ever saw, or ever will see, will be pleasanter than the harmonies of Orpheus; and black will be a very pretty color. (Laughter and applause.) It will make our jargon, wit; our words, oracles; flattery will then take the place of slander, and you will find no prejudice in the Yankee whatever. (Laughter.)

We desire to take part in this contest, and when our Government shall see the necessity of using the loyal blacks of the free States, I hope it will have the courage to recognize their manhood. It certainly will not be mean enough to force us to fight for your liberty, (after having spurned our offers)—and then leave us when we go home to our respective States to be told that we cannot ride in the cars, that our children cannot go to the public schools, that we cannot vote; and if we don't like that state of things, there is an appropriation to colonize us. We ask for our rights. Hardships and dangers are household words with us. We are not afraid to dig or to fight. A few black acclimated regiments would shake the Old Dominion. When will there be light enough in the Cabinet to see this? (Applause.)■

65 LINCOLN'S COLONIZATION PROPOSAL IS ANTI-CHRISTIAN

Isaiah C. Wears

On August 14, 1862, President Lincoln met with five African American men from the District of Columbia to enlist their support for his plan for colonizing the black population of the United States in Central America and other countries. He told the five that racial differences between black and white made it impossible for them to live as equals and promised them governmental assistance if they would recruit colored families to settle in Central America. Complete separation of the races was the only solution, he said. "But for your race among us," he emphasized, "there could not be war, although many men engaged on either side do not care for you one way or the other. Nevertheless, I repeat, without the institution of slavery, and the colored race as a basis, the war could not have an existence. It is better for us both, therefore, to be separated."

Accounts of this interview were widely publicized in the Northern press and infuriated many African Americans. The Statistical Association of the Colored People of Philadelphia met on August 15, and in a speech, Isaiah C. Wears (1822–1900), association president, voiced black opposition to Lincoln's plan. The speech by Wears, a barber and Republican politician, was then sent to the committee of African Americans who had visited President Lincoln to assist them in framing their reply to the chief executive. "No previous time, in our humble judgment," the letter declared, "has ever presented itself for a committee of colored men by a bold, judicious, manly and righteous decision to make an impression on the enlightened and civilized mind of the world as in this instance." The correspondence was signed by Wears and William Still, corresponding secretary of the association. Both Wears and Still were prominent Philadelphia leaders, and both were active in the city's Vigilance Committee to aid fugitive slaves.

Wears's answer to President Lincoln's proposal is excerpted from the Christian Recorder *(Philadelphia), August 23, 1862.*

TO BE ASKED, after so many years of oppression and wrong have been inflicted in a land and by a people who have been so largely enriched by the black man's toil, to pull up stakes in a civilized and Christian nation and to go to an uncivilized and barbarous nation, simply to gratify an unnatural wicked prejudice emanating from slavery, is unreasonable and anti-Christian in the extreme.

How unaccountably strange it seems, that wise men familiar with the history of this country, with the history of slavery, with the rebellion and its merciless outrages, yet are apparently totally ignorant of the true cause of the war—or, if not ignorant, afraid or ashamed to charge the guilt where it belongs.

Men profess to believe in God and the Bible, justice and humanity, but notwithstanding numerous examples in every age's history vividly showing how cruel has been the oppressor's rule and how invariably his heinous practices have brought on wars and destruction, with God's sore displeasure and heavy judgments—it is easy, nevertheless, to find excuses to ignore truth, to defy God's vengeance and trample on his creatures.

Says the President: The colored race are the cause of the war. So were the children of Israel the cause of the troubles of Egypt. So was Christ the cause of great commotions in Judea, in this same sense; and those identified with Him were considered of the baser sort, and really unfit for citizenship.

But surely the President did not mean to say that our race was the cause of the war, but the occasion thereof.

If black men are here in the way of white men, they did not come here of their own accord. Their presence is traceable to the white man's lust for power, love of oppression and disregard of the plain teachings of the Lord Jesus Christ, whose rule enjoins upon all men to "do unto others as they would be done by." Although a man may have had the misfortune to fall among thieves and become wounded and distressed by the wayside, the great Exemplar would not recognize the right of either the Levite or priest to shield themselves behind their prejudices or selfishness and thus leave him to suffer.

But it is not the Negro that is the cause of the war; it is the unwillingness on the part of the American people to do the race simple justice. It is not social equality to be made the equal of the white man, to have kind masters to provide for him, or to find for him congenial homes in Africa or Central America that he needs, but he desires not to be robbed of his labor—to be deprived of his God-given rights.

The effect of this scheme of colonization, we fear, will be to arouse prejudice and to increase enmity against us, without bringing with it the remedy proposed or designed.

Repentance is more needed on the part of our oppressors than anything else. Could a policy that would lead to this wholesome course be adopted, some bright hope might be seen for the triumph of freedom and justice.

If the African race are not of a color most pleasing to their fairer-skinned brother, let the fault be charged upon the Creator, as the same hand that made the white man made the black man also. God has revealed no distinction in His word, touching the color of a man's skin.

But we are to leave this country on the score of selfishness to make room for our selfish white neighbor to sail smoothly, it was intimated.

True, enactments of terrible severity may be passed calculated to ostracize us—it will be strange if the President's suggestions do not directly invite persecutions of an aggravating character. But in our sober reflections, let us remember that Great Britain has got possessions adapted to our people, both of Southern and Northern birth in the Canada, and the West Indies, that are free for all colors—governed by laws that recognize no difference of a complexional character—admit all as equal citizens who will support the government. The humblest fugitive slave as well as those of noblest blood alike find protection on British soil.

The panting bondmen have always found a sure refuge in Canada, and yearly our labor has been sought by Englishmen for the West Indies. The doors, therefore, are wide open in these civilized lands, thank God. Under the laws of Great Britain, colored men are neither debarred from citizenship nor soldier's rights and duties when their services are required.

That it is hard for those who have all their lives been submitting to the wrongs heaped upon the black man, or identified with parties oppressing him, now in this fearful crisis to make the marvelous change that justice demands, none can question.

A very appropriate paragraph occurs in a letter from a friend, which came to hand months back, which I will here quote:

"Has slavery so paralyzed the arm of the nation, that there is no strength to grapple with it? Is there not a story told of a man who fell asleep in an arbor, to whose entrance came a snake so surcharged with venom that the man died poisoned by its breath? Does not the state of our country suggest a parallel case, poisoned to its heart's deep core by its guilty contact with slavery?"

In these remarks, though coming from one of the race considered to be inferior, lies in a nutshell the grand secret of all the nation's trouble. And it seems reasonable to infer that the nation shall not again have peace and prosperity until prejudice, selfishness and slavery are sorely punished in the nation.■

66 THE NEGROES IN THE UNITED STATES OF AMERICA

Sarah Parker Remond

 During the Civil War, Sarah Remond's public lectures in Britain encouraged her audiences to avert possible diplomatic recognition of the Confederacy. Union blockades of Confederate ports had effectively diminished Southern cotton exports, thus threatening some British textile mills. Remond and others sought to cultivate popular sympathy

with the struggle for emancipation, laboring as what historian Benjamin Quarles has called black "ministers without portfolios."* Quarles credits visiting black lecturers with the development of a resurgent British abolitionism that influenced the outcome of the Civil War.

In her 1862 address before the International Congress of Charities, Correction, and Philanthropy, Remond summarized her rhetorical obstacles as she urged her audience, "Let no diplomacy of statesmen, no intimidation of slaveholders, no scarcity of cotton, no fear of slave insurrections, prevent the people of Great Britain from maintaining their position as the friend of the oppressed Negro, which they deservedly occupied previous to the disastrous civil war."

Upon her return to the United States after the war, Remond and Charles Lenox Remond, her brother, campaigned for the American Equal Rights Association, combining their advocacy of women's suffrage and full citizenship rights for African Americans. Later, she began a new life and career as she moved to Florence, Italy, and in 1871 received her degree as doctor of medicine. For further information, see Ruth Bogin, "Sarah Parker Remond: Black Abolitionist From Salem," Essex Institute Historical Collections *110 (April 1971), 120–49; and Quarles,* Black Abolitionists *(New York: Oxford University Press, 1969).*

The text of the speech, delivered in London in late 1862, is reprinted from the Journal of Negro History *27 (April 1942), 216–18.*

Amid the din of civil war, and the various and antagonistic interests arising from the internal dissensions now going on in the United States of North America, the negroes and their descendants, whether enslaved or free, desire and need the moral support of Great Britain, in this most important but hopeful hour of their history. They, of all others, have the most at stake; not only material prosperity, but "life, liberty, and the pursuit of happiness." Almost simultaneously with the landing of the Pilgrim Fathers in 1620, a slave-ship, a Dutch vessel, with twenty negroes stolen from Africa, entered Chesapeake Bay, and sailed on to Jamestown. Here the twenty negroes were landed, and chattel slavery established in the New World; a sad, sad hour for the African race. These twenty human souls were landed most opportunely. The infant colony was then in a perilous condition; many of the colonists had died from exposure and hardships; many others from incompetency to grapple with their fate. Those who survived had become almost disheartened, when the arrival of the negroes gave new vitality to the enfeebled colony at Virginia, and revived the sinking colonists. The negroes were received as a farmer receives a useful and profitable animal; although, at that time, their services were invaluable. In return for their services, they and their posterity have been doomed to a life of slavery. Then took root chattel slavery,

*"Ministers Without Portfolios," *Journal of Negro History* 39 (January 1954), 27–42.

which has produced such physical, mental, and moral degradation upon an unprotected and unoffending race. It has always been exceedingly difficult to ascertain the exact number of slaves in the Southern states; the usual estimate is about four and a half millions. These human chattels are but property in the estimation of slave-holders, and receive by public opinion, established custom, and law, only the protection which is generally given to animals. From the son of a southern slaveholder, Mr. H. R. Helper of North Carolina, we have the number of slaves in the Southern states:—These human chattels, the property of three hundred and forty-seven thousand slave-owners, constitute the basis of the working class of the entire south; in fact, they are the bone and sinew of all that makes the south prosperous, the producers of a large proportion of the material wealth, and of some of the most important articles of consumption produced by any working class in the world. The New Orleans *Delta* gives the following:—"The cotton plantations in the south are about eighty thousand, and the aggregate value of their annual product, at the present prices of cotton (before the civil war). is fully one hundred and twenty-five millions of dollars. There are over fifteen thousand tobacco plantations, and their annual products may be valued at fourteen millions of dollars. There are two thousand six hundred sugar plantations, the products of which average annually more than twelve millions of dollars." Add to this the domestic labour of the slaves as household servants &c., and you have some conception of the material wealth produced by the men and women termed chattels. The bulk of this money goes to the support of the slaveholders and their families; therefore the dependence of slaveholders upon their chattels is complete. Slave labour was first applied to the cultivation of tobacco, and afterwards to that of rice; but rice is produced only in a very limited locality; cotton is the great staple and source of prosperity

Negroes in the United States of America

Alabama	342,844	Brought up	1,321,767
Arkansas	47,100	Louisiana	244,809
Delaware	2,290	Maryland	90,368
Florida	39,310	Mississippi	309,878
Georgia	381,622	Missouri	87,422
Kentucky	210,981	N. Carolina	288,548
Tennessee	239,459	S. Carolina	384,984
Texas	58,161	Virginia	472,528
Carried up	1,321,767	Total	3,200,304

Free Coloured Population, South	228,138
Free Coloured Population, North	196,116
	424,254

These figures are taken from Hinton Rowan Helper, *The Impending Crisis of the South: How to Meet It* (New York: Burdick Brothers, 1857), 144, and were derived originally from the 1850 census. For further information see Hugh C. Bailey, *Hinton Rowan Helper: Abolitionist-Racist* (University: University of Alabama Press, 1965).

and wealth, the nucleus around which gathers immense interests. Thousands among the commercial, manufacturing, and working classes, on both sides of the Atlantic, are dependent upon cotton for all material prosperity; but the slaves who have produced two-thirds of the cotton do not own themselves; their nominal wives and their children may at any moment be sold. I call them nominal *wives,* because there is no such thing as legal marriage permitted either by custom or law. The free operatives of Britain are, in reality, brought into almost personal relations with slaves during their daily toil. They manufacture the material which the slaves have produced, and although three thousand miles of ocean roll between the producer and the manufacturer and the operatives, they should call to mind the fact, that the cause of all the present internal struggle, now going on between the northern states and the south, the civil war and its attendant evils, have resulted from the attempt to perpetuate negro slavery. In a country like England, where the manufacturer pays in wages alone £11,000,000, and the return from the cotton trade is about £80,000,000 annually—where four millions of the population are almost directly interested—where starvation threatens thousands—it is well that the only remedy which can produce desirable and lasting prosperity should receive the moral support of every class—*emancipation.*

Let no diplomacy of statesmen, no intimidation of slaveholders, no scarcity of cotton, no fear of slave insurrections, prevent the people of Great Britain from maintaining their position as the friend of the oppressed negro, which they deservedly occupied previous to the disastrous civil war. The negro, and the nominally free coloured men and women, north and south, of the States, in every hour of their adversity, have ever relied upon the hope that the moral support of Britain would always be with the oppressed. The friends of the negro should recognize the fact, that the process of degradation upon this deeply injured race has been slow and constant, but effective. The real capacities of the negro race have never been thoroughly tested; and until they are placed in a position to be influenced by the civilizing influences which surround freemen, it is really unjust to apply to them the same test, or to expect them to attain the same standard of excellence, as if a fair opportunity had been given to develop their faculties. With all the demoralizing influences by which they are surrounded, they still retain far more of that which is humanizing than their masters. No such acts of cruelty have ever emanated from the victims of slavery in the Southern states as have been again and again practised by their masters.■

67 FREEDOM'S JOYFUL DAY

Reverend Jonathan C. Gibbs

Throughout the North, African Americans held meetings and church services on January 1, 1863, to commemorate and celebrate the issuance of the Emancipation Proclamation. Unfortunately, most of the speeches delivered by African American leaders at these celebrations were either not reported in the press or have disappeared. One that has been preserved was delivered by Jonathan C. Gibbs (c. 1827–1874), pastor of the First African Presbyterian Church of Philadelphia. Gibbs studied at Dartmouth and Princeton Theological Seminary before assuming his pastorate and was active in the Underground Railroad and black convention movement in the 1850s. After the war, he served as a missionary to freedmen and women in North Carolina and Florida and as Florida's secretary of state, acting governor, and superintendent of public instruction.

In the speech that follows, Reverend Gibbs does not confine himself to celebrating the Proclamation, but calls for meaningful freedom for African Americans, including full participation in the war effort. The Proclamation, he cautions, is but a "half-measure," when full commitment to equality is needed.

Excerpts from the speech are presented here, taken from the Christian Recorder, *January 17, 1863.*

THE MORNING DAWNS! The long night of sorrow and gloom is past, rosy-fingered Aurora, early born of day, shows the first faint flush of her coming glory, low down on the distant horizon of Freedom's joyful day. O day, thrice blessed, that brings liberty to four million native-born Americans. O Liberty! O sacred rights of every human soul! O source of knowledge, of justice, of civilization, of Christianity, of strength, of power, bless us with the inspiration of thy presence. Today, standing on the broad platform of the common brotherhood of men, we solemnly appeal to the God of justice, our common Father, to aid us to meet manfully the new duties, the new obligations that this memorable day will surely impose.

The Proclamation has gone forth, and God is saying to this nation by its legitimate constitute head, Man must be free.

Scout, deride, malign this intimation, as the enemies of God and man will and may, the American people must yield to His inscrutable fiat, or the legacy of their fathers will be squandered 'midst poverty, ignorance, blood and shame. . . . The people must support this Proclamation, heartily, earnestly, strengthening the hands of our government by all the energies and resources they possess, or in a short time the question will not be whether black men are to be slaves, but whether white men are to be free! You had better a thousand times let us into the full light of liberty with yourselves, than that yourselves come into a condition equal to that of the slave at the South. We pray you this day, be just to yourselves, and then to us you *must* be true.

The black people of this country are thoroughly loyal. We are above disloyalty to the government. You may suspect a Garrisonian Abolitionist, but you cannot possibly suspect us. All our hopes and interests lie in the success of our government. We clearly discern that this is a contest between civilization and barbarism, two antagonistic systems of government, two fundamental principles that oppose each other. The black man is only a sort of accident connected with this struggle. The man who stoops to malign or abuse us as the cause of this war is, in point of intelligence, away down along the apes; he must be given up as a hopeless blockhead. If the same state of things existed in any country in the world, that exists in this, and all parties were white, or were black, just such a contest must come between these two antagonistic systems as we witness this day in our country, and one or the other of these systems must prevail. Which shall it be?

O, God, we appeal to *Thee*. Let this strife be so decided that justice, truth, honor may not be put to shame. You, my country, entered into a solemn covenant with God in 1776 and declared before highest Heaven that your first and only purpose was to foster and cherish the equality and fraternity of man. How have you kept this covenant? Let Dred Scott decisions, fugitive-slave laws, the judicial murders of Denmark Vesey, Nat Turner, John Brown, Gabriel* and numerous others testify. . . .

Feeble-minded men are constantly asking what is to be done with the black, and the only alternative that presents itself to them is to send the bondman to the Torrid Zone where a civilization exists, if any at all, that is so nearly allied to barbarism that he may rationally expect that his posterity will relapse into the darkness of heathenism. And with such a solution they rest satisfied in one direction, but are highly dissatisfied in another, wondering, they say, at our singular obstinacy in refusing to leave our native land and go to Africa or some other hot country. It is our patriotism that prevents us, our strong love for America, our native land. . . .

Give unto us the same guarantee of life, liberty and protection in the pursuit of happiness that you so cheerfully award to others, and make the very same demands of us to support the government you make of others. In a word, enfranchise and arm the blacks North and South, and put them under the intelligent direction of a strong central government at New Orleans, or Charleston, South Carolina. Enfranchise and arm the black man. Let there

---

*In 1800, in Henrico Country, Virginia, Gabriel Prosser led a slave insurrection, which was frustrated by informers. Scores of slaves were arrested, thirty-five were executed, and Prosser, captured after having escaped, was executed.

be no half measures; half measures are dangerous measures in times like these. . . .

Many persons are asking, Will black men fight? That is not what they mean. The question they are asking is simply this: Have white men of the North the same moral courage, the pluck, the grit, to lay down their foolish prejudice against the colored man and place him in a position where he can bear his full share of the toils and dangers of this war? That is the question that all such persons are asking, and no other. . . . We, the colored men of the North, put the laboring oar in your hands; it is for white men to show that they are equal to the demands of these times, by putting away their stupid prejudices. We are not children, but men, and are in earnest about the matter. There is not a battlefield throughout the country, from the days of '76 until now, but what our bones lie bleaching with yours. I *know* whereof I affirm, and I challenge contradiction. In the very first resistance that was made to British aggression in the Revolution of '76 was a black man, Crispus Attucks, who led the attack and was some of the first slain.

Did not a regiment of Rhode Island's freed blacks on the river Delaware at Red Bank, withstand three successive bayonet charges of British soldiers and finally wipe out the minions of British thralldom? What is the testimony of Andrew Jackson on this subject (a man who knew how to deal with traitors)? What has made the name of Haiti a terror to tyrants and slaveholders throughout the world, but the terrible fourteen years' fight of black men against some of the best troops of Napoleon—and the black men wiped them out. There are some fights that the world will never forget, and among them is the fight of black men for liberty on the Island of Haiti. . . .

Your destiny as white men and ours as black men are one and the same; we are all marching on to the same goal. If you rise, we will rise in the scale of being. If you fall, we will fall; but you will have the worst of it. . . .

Finally, let us offer the homage of grateful hearts to the friends of liberty and human progress the world over, for the hopes and prospects now before us, confidently predicting that the future will show that no efforts made in behalf of the bondman in this country were in vain. The sum of human happiness in this country will be increased, and God honored by the utter destruction of the hideous system of American slavery. . . . ■

68 ADDRESS TO THE YOUTH

Sarah J. Woodson

Sarah Jane Woodson was an influential black nationalist, educator, and national leader of the temperance movement. Born in 1825 in Chillicothe, Ohio, she was the youngest of Thomas and Jemimma Riddle Woodson's eleven children. Shortly after their arrival in Ohio in 1820, her parents helped form the first black Methodist church west of the Alleghenies after experiencing racial discrimination within the established congregations. When Woodson was five, her family joined several others in the establishment of a separate and self-sufficient black farming community in Berlin Crossroads, Ohio. By 1840, the community had grown to twenty-three families and had established its own schools, stores, and churches. Woodson's father and two brothers (including her brother Lewis Woodson, an early black nationalist) were ministers in the A.M.E. church, and she became an active member following her conversion in 1839.

Sarah Woodson completed the collegiate program at Oberlin in 1856, becoming one of the first African American women to graduate from college. After graduation, she taught in black community schools in Ohio for several years. In 1863, she delivered a speech entitled "Address to Youth" to the members of the Ohio Colored Teachers' Association, an organization that had been formed in 1860. In her speech, which she gave in the midst of the Civil War and in the wake of the Emancipation Proclamation, Woodson urges African American youth to join in the political and social revolutions that have been produced by the conflict. She pleads with her young audience to take advantage of new educational opportunities, for "the obstacles which have so long barred you from the portals of knowledge, are fast being removed." In particular, she encourages students to pursue education and careers in the sciences, "from which you have hitherto been ousted with tenacious jealousy." Throughout the speech, Woodson appeals to an emerging sense of black nationalism.

In 1866, Woodson was appointed "Preceptress of English and Latin and Lady Principal and Matron" at Wilberforce University in Xenia, Ohio, where her brother Lewis was a trustee. She thus became the first African American woman member of a college faculty.

In 1868, Woodson married Jordan Winston Early, a minister in the A.M.E. church, and until his death in 1903 taught in and administered black schools in the Tennessee communities where his churches were located. In 1888, she succeeded Frances E. W. Harper as national Superintendent of the Colored Division of the Women's Christian Temperance Union. In the four years she held this position, she delivered over one

hundred lectures in five states, speaking of the need for blacks to organ-
ize for self-improvement. Although she sometimes worked with white re-
formers, she lived and worked primarily within black-led communities
and was a powerful advocate of self-help. She died in 1907.

For further information about Woodson, see Ellen N. Lawson, "Sarah
Woodson Early: Nineteenth Century Black Nationalist 'Sister,' " Umoja:
A Scholarly Journal of Black Studies *5 (Summer 1981), 15–26. The speech*
text appears in Daniel A. Payne, ed., The Semi-Centenary and the Retro-
spection of the African Methodist Episcopal Church *(Baltimore: Sher-*
wood, 1866) 134–39.

That we are beings who occupy a place among intelligent existences, and
are endowed with minds capable of endless duration, and unlimited
improvement, is a fact which should engage the attention, and enlist the energies of every individual.

The faculties of the mind, though scarcely perceptible in the first stages
of human existence, may, by means of proper culture, become so expended
and developed as to form one of the noblest structures of God's creation.

The cultivation of the mind, then, is the first object to which the youthful attention should be directed. By cultivation is implied the education and
training of each faculty, so as not only to be able to acquire a mere physical
subsistence, but to apply the means which will invigorate, and strengthen;
to enlighten and refine each part, that it may perform its function in such
a manner as to elevate the being to that degree of perfection, which will
enable him to occupy a position among the higher orders of creation, which
the Great Author designed him to enjoy.

It is a fact worthy of notice, that things which are most valuable are
placed the farthest from the reach of common agencies. The Creator, in wisdom, has seen fit to place the bright gems, and richest treasures of earth, the
deepest beneath the soil; so, in like manner, has he concealed the richest
treasures that the mind possess beneath the grosser senses, to be drawn forth
only by the most patient, and persevering energy. It is natural that human
beings should acquire possessions; and that they should desire those especially which are the most eminent among mortals; yet few of real value ever
came into our hands by means of accident.

No man was ever a skilled architect, or physician, or mechanic by
chance. The excellencies of the mental powers are not the gifts of genius, or
the intuitions of nature; but the precious boon is obtained, or, the shining
goal reached, only by those whose care has been the most unceasing, and
whose zeal has been the most untiring.

Wealth and honor are not the offspring of ease and luxury, but they are
the legitimate reward of constant toil and perseverance. Neither is mental
opulence, or intellectual competency enjoyed by the imbecile and indolent.

No one ever slaked his thirst for knowledge from a fountain which gushed spontaneously; but he who would taste the delicious stream must dig deep and toil hard, ere he can enjoy a draught of the pellucid waters.

The knowledge of arts and sciences, which are the most profound and intricate in themselves, and which most deeply concern us, is not granted on easier terms than these. Not even the lowest organs of the body, not a muscle or a sinew can perform its action without having undergone a lengthened and elaborate process of instruction. The hand, the ear, the eye, must each be trained and taught. And though we may be unconscious of the education, it has as really been received, as that was by which we learned to read and write.

If, then, the most corporeal sense demands an appropriate education, without which they would prove rather incumbrances than messengers with which we keep up our communications with the external world, shall we suppose that the noblest capacities of man's spirit are alone independent of all training and culture? That the baser senses only are capable of refinement and expansion? That in the whole territory of human nature, this is the only field that promises to reward the tillage with no fruit?

But this question more deeply concerns the youth of the present than of any other age. An age in which intellectual acquirements are more widely diffused than any other preceding it. Let not, then, the youth of the present age, who are the subjects of oppression and outrage, suppose that they are not called upon to solve the questions which so much interest every individual. What are our relations to God and to the universe? What is required of us in the present age? and what are we doing to facilitate the prospects of our people in the future? It is true, that we experience daily many discouragements, and the path of intellectual prosperity seems obstructed with innumerable difficulties, yet the fact is none the less obvious, that we are called upon to act as great a part as any other people, in the great work of human refinement and moral elevation. Yes, we, as a people, have severe conflicts, both with regard to our individual and national rights. We inherit from our fathers nought but subjugation and dishonor. No history records the deeds of our great and good, no tongue ever heralded the praise of our brave and noble. No banner was ever inscribed with the insignia of our national existence; yet our history, humiliating as it may be, is not without a precedent.

Others have endured trials similar to ours, in their struggles for national existence. Yet, by a succession of events, they passed unscathed to the highest point of national glory. God's chosen people were overwhelmed in Egyptian darkness, only that the light of Jehovah's truth might be revealed amid the thunderings of Sinai.

If you take a retrospect of the past, you perceive that in the darkest periods, when truth and virtue appeared to sleep, when science had dropped her telescope and philosophy its torch, when the world would have seemed to be standing still, the inscrutable wisdom of Divine Providence was preparing new agents, and evolving new principles, to aid in the work of individual and social improvement.

It would appear as if the world, like the year, had its seasons; and that the seed disseminated in spring time, must first die before it can vegetate and produce the rich harvests of autumn. The developments of one period seem obscured for a season, by the unfolding of the great mysterious curtain, by which to disclose the glories of the next.

History has marked to us such periods, and we are disheartened by the necessary and successive seasons of darkness, because the revolution is so great, or, our own position so humble, that we cannot look beyond the shade that surrounds us, and behold the distant but gradual approach of a better day. Though for a season darkness has covered the land, and gross darkness the people, and the energies of our people have been stultified by the accumulated prejudices of generations, which have been heaped upon us, yet there is reason to be encouraged, for

> "From the darkest night of sorrow,
> From the deadliest field of strife
> Dawns a clearer, brighter morrow,
> Springs a truer, nobler life."

Yes, the sombre clouds of ignorance and superstition which so long enshrouded us and seemed ready to close upon us, as the funeral pall of our national existence, is being dispersed before the light of eternal truth. The sign of promise, the great precursor of a brighter day, has already enlightened the long night of our oppression, and the broad sun of our liberty begins to illuminate our political horizon. The mighty empire of despotism and oppression is trembling to its foundation, it must soon crumble and fall; but will we submit to sink and be buried beneath its ruins? Will we alone be quiescent and passive, while all around us is agitation and progress?

Do the revolutions which surround us awaken in our souls no desire to partake of the onward movement? The world moves right on, and he who moves not with it, must be crushed beneath its revolving wheels. You stand on the eve of a brighter day than has ever enlightened your pathway. The obstacles which have so long barred you from the portals of knowledge, are fast being removed, and the temple of science from which you have hitherto been ousted with tenacious jealousy, will soon disclose to you the glory of his inner sanctuary. Wisdom, with a friendly hand, beckons you to enter and revel in her courts. Suffer not the evanescent pleasures of sensual gratifications to allure you from the pursuit of the great object which lies before you. Will you not arouse from the long slumber of inactivity which pervades you, and prepare for the events which the revolutions of the affairs of men are fast bringing upon you? Who shall answer for you, when you are called upon to take your position among the nations of the earth, if you are found wanting in mental capacity and intellectual energy?

If the high privileges you now enjoy pass by you unimproved, and you are found incapable to fill positions of trust and honor in coming life, great will be your condemnation.

Apply your minds, then, early and vigorously to those studies which will not only endow you with the power and privilege to walk abroad, interested spectators of all that is magnificent and beautiful, above and around you, but to commune with that which is illustrious in the records of the past, and noble and divine in the development of the future.

Would you be eminent among your fellow-mortals, and have your name inscribed on the pages of history, as a living representative of truth, morality and virtue? Would you, by deeds of heroism and noble achievements, vie with the proud sons of honor, and share with them the immortal wreath which the hand of time has placed upon their brow? Would you ascend the hill of science, and there contend with their votaries for the laurels plucked from its fair summit? Would you penetrate the secret labyrinths of the universe, and gather from their hoarded mysteries that knowledge which will bless generations to come? Then apply your minds to study, profound, intricate study. Let your time, your money, your interest all be spent in the pursuit of this one great object, the improvement of your mind. It is only from the deepest furrows that the richest harvests are gathered. The breathings of genius are not produced "ad libitum." The lyres of the soul bring no sound to the touch of unpracticed hands. So the creative powers of the mind are never developed till drawn forth by the deep, harrowing process of education. Oh, there are wells of inspiration in every human heart, from which angels might draw, and leave them unexhausted. Fathom the depths of your nature, draw from its profound resources those principles which will ennoble and strengthen your intellectual powers. Educate the youth of the present, and our nation will produce a constellation of glowing minds, whose light will brighten the path of generations to come. Hitherto there has scarcely been a mind among us, which has sent forth a spark into the vast region of science. The arts have received but little attention, and literature has found no place among us. Yet, by the efforts which may be put forth by the present generation, the arts, science and literature may be as widely diffused among us, and we may become as eminent, in point of intellectual attainments, as any people who have had an existence.

We call upon you to accept the means which God has placed in your power. The great and the good, and the noble, who have preceded you, and have bequeathed to you the hoarded treasures of their richly cultivated minds, call upon you. The voice of millions, who are perishing without a ray of intellectual light, call upon you. Everything above and around you combine to stimulate you to the work of removing darkness and error, and establishing truth and virtue. And may God speed the work, till science, philosophy and religion, the great elevators of fallen humanity, shall have completed the work of moral refinement, and we in the enjoyment of all our rights, both political and civil, will stand at the summit of national glory.■

69 THE MORAL AND SOCIAL ASPECT OF AFRICA

Martin Robinson Delany

In 1859 Martin R. Delany traveled in Africa for about a year, seeking places to which black Americans might emigrate. He signed treaties with eight kings of Abeokuta for grants of land to establish colonies in the Yoruba area. From Africa, Delany went on to London and was invited to attend the International Statistical Congress in July 1860. The entire diplomatic corps of the United States, including the American ambassador, George Mifflin Dallas, a former vice president of the United States, was present when Lord Brougham, the eighty-two-year-old British legal reformer and antislavery advocate, said to the American ambassador: "I hope our friend Mr. Dallas will forgive me reminding him that there is a Negro present, a member of the Congress." Since the others had responded to Lord Brougham's introduction, Delany decided to say a few words: "I pray your Royal Highness will allow me to thank his lordship, who is always a most unflinching friend of the Negro, and I assure your Royal Highness and his lordship that I am a man" (London Times, *July 25, 1860). This one-sentence speech provoked an international incident. With the exception of one delegate from Boston, who represented his state only, the entire American delegation walked out of the Congress in protest. For several days, the British and American press was filled with editorials and letters discussing the incident.*

Before he left London, Delany, unperturbed by the controversy over his brief speech, read a paper on his researches in Africa before the Royal Geographical Society. He continued to lecture on Africa in England and Scotland for almost seven months and returned to the United States in 1861, six weeks after the Civil War had broken out. Although interest in emigration among blacks had subsided, Delany lectured on Africa in various northern cities during the next few years. None of these lectures were reported in the press except one, delivered in Chicago in the spring of 1863, and this was a detailed summary of Delany's remarks coupled with direct quotations from the lecture. However, because it is one of the few speeches of this black nationalist reported in detail and because it helped create a different image of Africa among Americans than was available at the time in books and magazines, it is important to include in this collection.

The summary of Delany's lecture is reprinted from the Liberator *of May 1, 1863, which, in turn, reprinted it from the* Chicago Tribune.

A LECTURE BY a gentleman of color is a sort of a "rare bird on the earth," and is very like a "black swan." Rare as the thing may be, however, it is not an impossibility, as Dr. Delaney [*sic*] and a few other men of his blood and race, have occasionally proved, although at wide intervals of time and space. We ought not, perhaps, to be surprised at any unusual manifestation of talent in a negro. Toussaint L'Ouverture has redeemed the whole race of blacks by the magnificence of his talents and career. We do not mean to say that Mr. Delaney is a Toussaint L'Ouverture, but we do say that he is a better specimen of his race that any we, for our part, have seen before, and that he is by no means a bad lecturer.

He was not ashamed, he said, to be called a negro. If curly hair and a black face helped to make a negro, then he was a negro, and a full-blooded one at that. He had no need to be ashamed of his type or origin. He has a good head and intelligent face—just the kind of a head which a phrenologist would tell you a man ought to have who makes natural observations and accumulates scientific facts.

The dress which the Doctor wore on the platform was a long dark-colored robe, with curious scrolls upon the neck as a collar. He said it was the wedding dress of a Chief, and that the embroidery was insignia, and had a specific meaning well understood in African high circles. He wore it because he thought it becoming, and fitting the occasion.

He wanted to say what he knew of the negro race, not on the coast of Africa, but of the interior Africans, of whom so little is known—the Africans of the Niger Valley. The audience would be surprised to hear that even the Liberians had never until lately been ten miles beyond their territory; and so nothing could be expected from them. He was sorry to say, too, that American school-books inculcated, notwithstanding recent discoveries, very erroneous notions of the country, describing it as sandy and barren, the soil unproductive, the air full of pestilence, the vegetation poisonous, the very animals unusually ferocious. All this is more or less false, so far as the interior of Africa is concerned. He had travelled three thousand miles in the country, and had seen it in all its phases of social and moral life. The language of a people is a good sign of its civility; and the African language is derived from fixed roots; it is not a jargon, but abounds in vowels, and is very melodious, and capable of expressing a wide range of feeling and sentiment. The people speak clearly and well, without hesitation. They are very polite, and make numerous salutations on all occasions, at out-going and in-coming, at bed-time, and in the morning at meals, and generally everywhere. The stranger must not reply to each salutation, but when he takes his leave, he makes a long salaam by bowing his head and body, and by a peculiar intonation of the voice.

The Doctor produced a grammar of the language, and made quotations from it. It was written by a native African, who had also composed numerous school-books, and made translations from the Bible.

As specimens of the moral culture of the people, he read some of the African proverbs, which though doubtless original, have a peculiar Christian flavor. One of them ran very much after the style of the Gold Rule, thus: "He who injures another, injures himself." Another reads thus: "The sword does not know the hand of the blacksmith" (who made it).

One of the poets, whilst singing the occupations of the people, has these descriptions of them: "The day dawns; the trader takes his goods; the spinner her distaff; the soldier his shield; the hunter his bow and quiver." After giving us these and other specimens of the writing talent of the Africans, the Doctor suddenly came down on Robert Bonner, his weekly *Ledger*, who said in it, awhile ago, or allowed somebody else to say it, that the African, having no poetic faculty, is incapable of civilization. He reminded his audience of the simple and beautiful extemporaneous song which the negro woman sang over poor Mungo Park, the traveller, when he sat sorrowing by her tent door, and whom she supplied, in her womanly kindness, with milk. The truth was, that the African was naturally poetic, and expressed his feelings at all times of passion and emotion in musical and rhythmical words. He read some pretty verses composed by African children, which were translated by one of our missionaries on the spot. They were certainly very simple, and at the same time very hopeful products, describing the pleasure they felt at seeing the beauty and color of certain African birds, no description of which, the Doctor said, has appeared in any book on ornithology.

Alluding to the morals of the people, he said there was a mistake about it very current in these parts and elsewhere. It was thought that because polygamy was tolerated amongst them, there must be immorality also. Polygamy was an old and venerable institution, and had a genuine Oriental origin. Solomon was the arch-polygamist of the world, and the Africans who followed his example were no worse than he. It was the rich only, however, who had many wives; the poor could not afford to keep them. But women were universally respected in Africa, and the men paid them chivalrous attention. They were not allowed to do any physical labor whatever, except draw water; and this they insisted upon as their peculiar right and privilege. This also was an Oriental custom of immemorial usage; and was frequently alluded to in the Scriptures. He had seen seven hundred women coming out of the gates of a city in the evening, carrying water-pots on their heads, as they did in the days of Jacob. Chastity was a sacred thing amongst them, and any one violating or insulting a woman was decapitated. These bigamists had one who was mistress of the household, and had her maids of honor, who attended her, and ministered to the wants of the guests. They loved these wives better than most civilized people often do theirs. A chief who had lost his wife was asked why he did not marry again. "Because," he said, "I shall never find a woman who will love me as she did." There was no savagery in this reply, and it might readily enough have been uttered by a white man.

The betrothal of young people is made at a very early age, and when it is consummated, the maiden wears a bracelet on her arm, which is made of some inscrutable metallic substance, of which the Doctor could give no account.

An African house, belonging to a bigwig negro, was described as an immense building, the windows and doors of which opened on the inside, looking upon the court-yards. These houses often contained hundreds of women, who were called wives by courtesy, but were not so in reality; as the custom of the country required every rich man to support as many females as he could. These were daily occupied in spinning, basket making, weaving, cotton fabric, &c. which they sold in the markets. They often went far into the country in groups selling provisions along with their wares, and the Doctor never heard of any of them being molested.

From what the lecturer said, the houses of the rich were a sort of factory, where the surplus women were taught to work, and where they were protected. They supported themselves. One of these houses put our own hotels, which are, nevertheless, "some pumpkins," into a complete shadow. It is owned by a chief, and covers 1200 square feet, and built of unhewn brick. Another contains a thousand females, and is about the rival of Solomon's immense court of concubines.

Women are always admitted to council meetings. He was present at one, when the wife of a chief leaned her head on his shoulder, and made many suggestions. He thought the hint might be taken in countries a long way from Africa.

Another feature of manners was given which we thought very interesting. It was the respect which youth always had to age, no matter whether the person were rich or poor.

In these interior and remote regions, the people were ruled by a king, whom they elected themselves. Kings, and their sons and families, were all amenable to the law. Litigation begins always in the morning, and defendant's counsel has always the last speech.

Numerous examples of the industry of the Africans were given. They cultivated the lands, and made them as productive as gardens. All the staple cereals of a tropical clime were grown in abundance, and every species of fruit. They were workers in iron and other metals, and made excellent leather and glass. They were a religious people naturally; and he never met a Pagan in all his travels.

At the close of the lecture, various specimens of native manufacture were shown to the audience.■

70 THE GOOD TIME IS AT HAND

Robert Purvis

The thirtieth annual meeting of the American Anti-Slavery Society, held at Cooper Institute in New York City on May 12, 1863, was a joyous occasion. The Emancipation Proclamation had been issued four months earlier, and the war for the preservation of the Union had clearly become one for the total abolition of slavery. African Americans were being recruited in ever increasing numbers in the Union army and were being granted rights long denied them. Overjoyed at the change of heart of the Lincoln administration, some were willing to forgive its earlier hesitations and delays. In his speech to the American Anti-Slavery Society, Robert Purvis expressed the joy most African Americans felt at the turn the war had taken.

Born in South Carolina, Purvis (1810–1898) was among the organizers of the American Anti-Slavery Society and the Pennsylvania Anti-Slavery Society. He and his family sheltered fugitive slaves in their home and he was an outspoken opponent of the Fugitive Slave Law and those that upheld it, vowing in 1859 "to kill every oppressor" that threatened the fugitive's freedom.

The text of the speech is from the Liberator, May 22, 1863.

Mr. CHAIRMAN, LADIES AND GENTLEMEN—It is bad taste, I know, in a speaker, to begin with an apology, and to talk about himself; but I must ask to be excused if I offend in both these particulars. I cannot speak to order, as some people, more happily constituted can, I cannot, in cold blood, arrange a speech beforehand, and yet I dare not trust the impulse of the moment. It is the misfortune of natures born near the sun that their blood will not obey the helm of their judgment. I don't know why it is, therefore, that my friends on the Committee of Arrangements so persistently urge me to speak. No, sir—I will correct myself—I *do* know why; it is because I am identified with the confessedly oppressed race in this country; and you will allow me to say, sir, that by reason of that identification, waiving all objection, I consent to speak.

Mr. Chairman, this is a proud day for the "colored" man. For the first time since this Society was organized, I stand before you a recognized citizen of the United States. (Applause.) And, let me add, for the first time since your government was a government, it is an honor to be a citizen of the United States! Sir, old things are passing away, all things are becoming new. Now a black man has rights, under this government, which every white man, here and everywhere, is bound to respect. (Applause.) The damnable doctrine of the detestable Taney is no longer the doctrine of the country.[*] The Slave Power no longer rules at Washington. The slaveholders and their miserable allies are biting the dust, and Copperhead Democracy has come to grief. The black man is a citizen—all honor to Secretary Bates, who has so pronounced him![†] The black man can take out a passport, and travel to

---

[*]Purvis refers to Justice Taney's decision in the *Dred Scott* decision of 1857, which ruled that African Americans could not be U.S. citizens.

[†]U.S. Attorney General Edward Bates, in response to an inquiry from Treasury Secretary Salmon P. Chase, ruled that every free person born in the United States was "*prima facie* a citizen."

the uttermost parts of the earth, protected by the broad aegis of the government—all honor to Secretary Seward, who was the first to recognize this right! The black man is a citizen soldier, standing on an equality in the rank and file with the white soldier—all honor to Secretary Stanton and the rest of the Administration! Sir, I know very well that this government is not yet all that it ought to be. I know that Mr. Bates is not considered a progressive man, and that Mr. Seward has incurred the severe displeasure of loyal anti-slavery people. But, sir, these gentlemen have in a signal manner recognized my rights, and the rights of my oppressed country men. They have officially invested us with the prerogatives of which we have been basely robbed, and I would be false to my nature, false to my convictions, false to my best feelings, did I not thus publicly testify my sense of respect and heartfelt gratitude. Say what you please of Mr. Seward, condemn as you may his shortcomings and his failures—I make no apology for either; but it must always be owned, to his immortal honor, that he has from the beginning been the fast friend of the "man of color." From the time when, as Governor of this Empire State, he refused to deliver up to the Governor of Virginia certain black refugees, to the day when, as a lawyer, he defended the idiotic black culprit Freeman, and from that day till the present time, Mr. Seward has been the unprejudiced respecter of the black man's equal rights, and, as such, I feel bound here and everywhere to honor him.* I have said that I consider it an honor to be a citizen of this republic, and I repeat it. I am proud to be an American citizen. You know, Mr. Chairman, how bitterly I used to denounce the United States as the basest despotism the sun ever shone upon; and I take nothing back that ever I said. When this government was, as it used to be, a slave-holding oligarchy; when such imbecile and heartless cravens as our Buchanan and your Pierce were its nominal rulers; when its powers were used and abused by slaveholding, slave-breeding traitors, such as Jefferson Davis, and Howell Cobb and Thief Floyd, and Isaac Toucey; and when the old Jesuit Taney was unshorn of his power as Chief President in its Temple of Justice; then, sir, I hated it with a wrath which words could not express, and I denounced it with all the bitterness of my indignant soul. (Applause.) My friends would urge me to moderate my tone, but it was impossible; out of the bitterness of the heart, the mouth would speak. I was a victim, stricken, degraded, injured, insulted in my person, in my family, in my friends, in my estate; I returned bitterness for bitterness, and scorn for scorn. I am the same man still, and I must be allowed, as some would say, though I do not, to err on the other extreme. I forget the past; joy fills my soul at the prospect of the future. I leave to others the needful duty of censure. But, I hear some of my hearers saying, "It is too soon to begin to rejoice; don't halloo till you are out of the woods; don't be too sure of the future—wait and see." No, sir, I will not wait—I cannot be mistaken. My instincts, in this matter at least, are unerring. The good time which has so long been coming is at hand. I feel it, I see it in the air, I read it in the signs of the

---

*William H. Seward (1801–1872) served as Lincoln's secretary of state.

times; I see it in the acts of Congress, in the abolition of slavery in the District of Columbia, in its exclusion from the Territories, in solemn treaties for the effectual suppression of the infernal foreign slave trade, in the acknowledgement of the black republics of Hayti and Liberia. I see it in the new spirit that is in the army; I see it in the black regiment of South Carolina—(applause;) I see it in the 54th Regiment of Massachusetts; I see it in the order of Adjutant-General Thomas, forming a black brigade at Memphis; I see it, above all, and more than all, in THE GLORIOUS AND IMMORTAL PROCLAMATION OF ABRAHAM LINCOLN ON THE FIRST OF JANUARY, 1863. (Cheers.) By that imperishable instrument, the three million of slaves in the rebel States are legally and irrevocably free! (the opinion of Mr. Greeley of the *Tribune* to the contrary notwithstanding.) By that immortal document, all the remaining slaves of the country are in effect promised their freedom. In *spirit* and in *purpose,* thanks to *Almighty God!* this is no longer a slaveholding republic. The fiat has gone forth which, when this rebellion is crushed—and it will be crushed as sure as there is a God in heaven—the fiat has gone forth which, in the simple but beautiful language of the President, "will take all burdens from off all backs, and make every man a freeman."

Sir, this is a glorious contest. It is not simply and solely a fight about the black man. It is not merely a war between the North and the South. It is a war between freedom and despotism the world over. If this government had only the South to contend with, their work would be soon done. But it is with the South backed up by pro-slavery Europe and pro-slavery England, that this government has to contend. It is pro-slavery England that furnishes to the rebels the arms, ammunition, ships, encouragement and money with which to carry out the base slaveholding, slave-breeding conspiracy. I say pro-slavery England, for, Mr. Chairman, I need not tell you that there are two Englands—anti-slavery England that manumitted her 800,000 slaves, and the England that opposed, as long as there was any hope of success, that glorious act; the England that now speaks in our favor in the voice of John Bright and William E. Forester, and that noble man and unequalled orator, George Thompson, and the England which holds the reins of power in its hands, and uses that power, as far as it *dares*, to break down this government. Sir, the former England I honor and adore; the latter, the England which now uses and abuses the great power of that great country, I abhor and repudiate. When I was in England, many years ago, it was my good fortune to be introduced to Ireland's great Liberator, Daniel O'Connell. Before extending his hand to me, he said that "he would never take the hand of an American, unless he knew him to be an anti-slavery man." Thanking him for his noble resolution, and declaring myself at the same time to be an Abolitionist, he grasped me warmly by the hand, and shook it heartily. It was a great striking circumstance, and left a deep impression upon my mind. Mr. Chairman, I am now prepared to practice the lesson I then learned. O'Connell has gone, and, alas! his spirit has gone with him. The foulest and bitterest enemies of freedom and the black man are countrymen of the great Liberator. If, hereafter, any one coming from Great Britain, be he Saxon or Celt, should seek an introduction to one so humble as myself, I think, before extending my hand, I would feel bound to say, What sort of an Englishman or Irishman are you? Are you of the herd that support the slaveholding rebels, and that build Alabama corsairs and Florida pirates to prey on the commerce of Freedom? If you are, I will have nothing to do with you; I regard you as an enemy of God and of the human race. But if your sympathies are with struggling Freedom, and your hatred towards its enemies, then give me your hand.

Mr. Chairman, I had intended to say something about the Copperhead Democrats,* but these dastards don't trouble me now. They are as malignant, as venomous, as traitorous as ever, and perhaps more so, but their power is gone, and their days are numbered. They are

> *"Their country's curse, their children's shame,*
> *Outcasts of virtue, peace, and fame."*

They may, in their baseness and pusillanimity, denounce the black man as inferior, as do you Vallandighams†—I trust he has got his deserts at last—(applause)—Morses and Coxes, down to your ex-Congressman Biddle, or they may hound on an Irish mob, as do your Fernando Woods and Bobby Brookses in your streets; but I repeat it, sir, their power is gone.

Mr. Chairman, I end as I began: This is a proud day for the "colored man," and a day of glorious promise for the country. Our work as Abolitionists is not finished. Much remains to be done. But we have thousands upon thousands of helpers. Anti-slavery societies and anti-slavery agents are now numerous and powerful. The United States Senate and House of Representatives, the State Legislatures, the "Union Leagues" are anti-slavery societies; the Cabinet at Washington is a great Executive Committee, and thousands of its civil and military officers are its agents. Our country is not yet free, but thank God for those signs of the times that unmistakably indicate that it soon will be! With a future so glorious before us, may we not, in the eloquent language of Curran, say "to the stranger and the sojourner" who sets his foot on the soil of America, "he treads on ground that is holy, and consecrated by the genius of universal emancipation. No matter in what language his doom may have been pronounced; no matter what complexion, incompatible with freedom, an Indian or an African sun may have burned upon him; no matter in what disastrous battle his liberty may have been cloven down; no matter with what solemnities he may have been devoted upon the altar of slavery; the first moment he touches the sacred soil of [America,] the altar and the god sink together in the dust, his soul walks abroad in her own majesty, his body swells beyond the measure of his chains, that burst from around him, and he stands redeemed, regenerated and disen-

---

*The Copperheads supported peaceful reconciliation with the South.
†Clement L. Vallandigham (1820–1871) of Ohio, the leading Copperhead opponent of Lincoln's war policies, was arrested and banished to the Confederacy in 1864.

thralled by the irresistible Genius of *Universal Emancipation."* [Enthusiastic applause.]

[The choir then sang Mrs. Howe's "Battle Hymn of the Republic," the congregation joining in the chorus at each verse.]■

71 THE POSITION AND DUTIES OF THE COLORED PEOPLE

J. W. C. Pennington

On July 11, 1863, the provost marshal's office opened for conscription in New York City. That same day wild mobs began to riot, and for five infamous days they stormed through the streets of New York City, unleashing their hatred against the National Conscription Act and committing unspeakable atrocities against the black community, murdering or maiming any African American whom they came upon. The riots went unchecked until eleven Union regiments were released by the secretary of war to quell the rioters.

The Draft Riots resulted from a combination of factors. New York City's poorer white classes, supporters of the Democratic Party, were not, in the main, sympathetic to the war's purposes and feared the emancipation of the slaves would be followed by an influx of black workers who would compete for their jobs. There was a huge criminal class in the city, and the riots gave an opportunity for looting. The Conscription Act passed by the government aroused indignation because it allowed richer members of the community to buy their way out of the draft.

After the riots had been crushed, many African Americans in the North met to discuss its significance for their future. The most important speech arising out of these meetings was delivered by James W. C. Pennington in Poughkeepsie, New York, on August 24, 1863. Pennington (1809–1870) had been born in slavery on the Eastern Shore of Maryland and was trained as a blacksmith, a trade he followed until he was about twenty-one, when he decided to run away. Pennington was befriended by a Pennsylvania Quaker, stayed with him for six months, and began what was to be an extensive education under his direction. After attending evening school in Long Island, he taught in black schools and, at the same time, studied theology. Pennington became a pastor in the African Congregational Church, held pastorates in Hartford, Connecticut, and repre-

*sented that state at the World's Anti-Slavery Convention in London in
1843. He was also a delegate to the World's Peace Society meeting in London that same year. He bought his freedom in 1851 for $150. Pennington
was the author of* A Text Book of the Origin and History, &c., &c., of the
Colored People, *published in 1841, and* The Fugitive Blacksmith, *the
story of his early life, published in London in 1849. In 1855, together
with Dr. James McCune Smith and the Reverend Henry Highland
Garnet, the Reverend Pennington organized the Legal Rights Association
for the purpose of establishing the rights of African Americans to the public conveyances in the city.*

Pennington's speech as presented here is taken from the Principia
*(New York), January 7, 14, 1864. In it, he urges armed self-defense and
stresses the importance of recording first person accounts of the riots by
African Americans so that their history will be preserved. Pennington dis-
putes the white rioters' claims that abolition is the purpose of the war
and urges black leadership in the postwar efforts to aid the freed persons.
For more information, see Iver Bernstein,* New York City Draft Riots
(New York: Oxford University Press, 1990).

T he mob against the colored people of New York in July 1863, was not
the first of its kind, and it may not be the last.

THE MOB OF 1740.

In the year 1740, when New York was a British, and a slaveholding city,
it was the scene of one of the most curious and malignant attacks upon the
colored people to be found on record. At that time the white population of
the city was 10,000; and the colored population was 2,000. By a wicked trick
of some evil minded persons, combined with the fears of the timid, a report
was gotten up that the negroes of the city, along with a few whites, had entered into a conspiracy to burn the city, and murder all the white inhabitants, except a few of the females. It was charged, that this scheme embraced
Long Island—then called "Nassau;"—and extended even to South Carolina.
The result was a legalised mob or public persecution which lasted for more
than a year, during which time the entire colored population were subject to
the most cruel and unheard of insults, abuses and injuries. There were 160
trials on charge of conspiracy with intent to commit arson and murder. Sev-
enty-one were condemned to banishment, or to be sold to the West Indies,
18 were branded; and 13 were burned at the stake. The remaining 58 being
the slaves of influential owners were acquitted. The volume containing the
account of this affair covers nearly 400 pages. It was compiled by the Supreme Court where the trials were held, and is falsely styled, "The Negro
Plot."

Shame has blushed the book out of print. But the records of the old Provincial Supreme Court in the archieves [sic] in the City Hall, contain all the

facts, consisting of the indictment,* against Caesar, Quack, Cuffeo, &c., &c. Proclamations of the Governor, charges to juries, addresses to the prisoners, when sentenced, altogether forming a cabinet of curiosities. Time corrected the tongue of slander. It fully transpired, that instead of its being a plot of the negroes against the lives and property of the whites, it was a plot of the whites against the lives and liberties of the negroes.

THE MOB OF 1863.

And, now, after the lapse of more than a hundred and twenty years, we are called to witness a similar, but far more diabolical conspiracy and riotous outrage against the lives and liberties of the descendants of the same people, in the same city.

What shall we call the mob of July 1863? Although I am not now assuming the responsible task of giving it a full designation; yet, I may remark in passing, that intelligent colored men of studious minds, owe it to themselves to record this mob in history by its right name. We should let no mere considerations of present relief deter us from bringing out all the facts, that will fasten the weight of responsibility where it belongs.

If it is an Irish Catholic mob prompted by American Protestant demagogues and negro haters, let it be hereafter known as such in history. If it was a desperate effort to resurrect the old rabid and hateful spirit of colonization, so let it be known to be. If it was an attempt of the southern rebels to plant the black flag of the slavery propagandist on the banks of the Hudson, let future generations so read it. Ye living historians, record the truth, the whole truth and nothing but the truth.

ITS ANTECEDENTS.

The elements of this mob have been centering and gathering strength in New York, for more than two years. And, as soon as the rebellion broke out, prominent colored men in passing the streets, were often hailed as "Old Abe," or "Jeff. Davis," evidently to feel their loyal pulse, and as it become evident that our sympathies were with the Federal government, we became objects of more marked abuse and insult. From many of the grocery corners,

---

*The forms of these indictments is, "the King against Caesar" &c. The allegations embrace the charge of an intention to overthrow His Majesty's government, in the Province, and siege upon the whole country. At that early date, the colored men of New York had a society called the Geneva Club, which was supposed, by the whites, to be substantially a Masonic body. This gave offence to the white men of that fraternity; and the blacks were ordered to disband the society, and to abstain from meetings of any kind, either at night, on holiday, or Sundays. The magistrates throughout the city and province were strictly charged with the duty of breaking up all such gatherings. To add to the excitement, it was alleged that some colored enthusiast, had prophecied that Long Island, and York Island were to be sunk, about the time, so the people suffered, in part, for opinions' sake. [Pennington's note.]

stones, potatoes, and pieces of coal, would often be hurled, by idle young loafers, standing about, with the consent of the keepers of those places, and very often by persons in their employ. The language addressed to colored men, not seemly to record on paper, became the common language of the street, and even of some of the fashionable avenues. The streets were made to ring with words, and sayings, the most filthy, and yet no effort was made by magistrates, the press, or authorities, to suppress these ebulitions of barbarism. In no other country in the world would the streets of refined cities be allowed to be polluted, as those of New York have been, with foul and indecent language, without a word of the rebuke from the press, the pulpit, or the authorities. Every loafer, from the little rebel, who could but just tussle over the curb stone, up to the lusty mutton fisted scamp who could throw a stone of half a pound's weight, across the street at a colored man's head, might anywhere about the city, on any day, and at any hour, salute colored persons with indecent language, using words surcharged with filth, malice, and brutal insult. And what has been the result? Why, just what we might have expected,—the engendering of a public feeling unfriendly toward colored people. This feeling, once created, might at any moment be intensified into an outbreak against its unoffending objects. We have, in this way, been made the victims of certain antagonisms.

OPPOSITION TO THE DRAFT.

I. The opposition to the draft comes largely from that class of men of foreign birth who have declared their intention to become citizens, but who have not done so. They have been duly notified that they could leave the country within sixty days, or submit to the draft. As soon as the President's proclamation containing this notice was made public, men of foreign birth, of this class, began to speak openly against the draft. And for obvious cause. They do not wish to leave the country, and they do not wish to fight. They came to make money, and so far as the war interferes with their schemes, they oppose it.

Now, dishonest politicians aim to make these men believe that the war has been undertaken to abolish slavery; and so far as they believe so, their feelings are against colored people, of course.

From this class, there has been a very considerable mob element. Many of them are a little too shame-faced to be seen with a stone or brick-bat in their hands in the streets; but they have, in large numbers encouraged the mobbing of the colored people. It is known that they have allowed loafers to congregate in their places of business and concoct their plans. Yea, not a few of these men are among your grocerymen, and others that you deal with, and are extremely malignant in their feelings. They are fair to your face, and will take your money, but behind your back, *it is "nigger."* These men know perfectly well, that in the countries from which they come, conscription laws, of a far more strict, and severe character exist, and they also know that they would not dare to resist those laws, if they were there; and hence their opposition to the draft is ungrateful and revolutionary. Many of this class of men are not so ignorant as to believe that the war is carried on by the President to abolish slavery. They have other objects in view. They fall in with the cry against the negro, only for effect.

CATHOLICISM AND PROTESTANTISM.

II. The next point of antagonism which has developed itself in the recent attack upon us, is that between CATHOLICISM, and PROTESTANTISM.

Why have *Irish Catholics* lead the way in the late murderous attack upon the *colored protestants?* It is not known that a single colored catholic family or individual suffered during the late riots, at the hands of the Irish, except by mistake. If the colored people, as a body, were Roman Catholics, there would be no attacks made upon them by Irish Catholics. During the Sabbaths of the riots, while colored protestant churches were closed; and colored protestant ministers had to take shelter out of the city of New York, colored members of Catholic churches were quietly worshipping in Catholic churches without insult, or molestation.

As to the color of the skin. Everybody knows, that Catholics consist of all colors in the known world. In other countries, black priests, officials, and members, are as common as the sun that shines.

As to the labor question. If colored mechanics, and laborers; and all our women and youth who earn wages, were Catholics, we should hear no objection from the Irish Catholics about their employment, because the wages would be good Catholic money, and would go to extend that church.

The Irish objection to us is then, not as colored laborers; but as *colored protestant* laborers.

The American people may take a lesson from this, and judge what may come next.

THE LABOR QUESTION.

Let us look at the labor question a little more closely, and see what must be the greed of those who would have us believe that there is not room and labor enough in this country for the citizens of foreign birth, and the colored people of native growth. The legitimate territory of these United States, is about 3,306,863 acres. That is ten times larger than Great Britain and France together. Three times larger than Britain, France, Austria, Prussia, Spain, Portugal and Denmark; and only one-sixth less, in extent, than the fifty-nine, or sixty republics and empires of Europe put together. And yet there are those who would teach the British and other foreigners the selfish and greedy idea that there is not room enough in this country for them and the colored man. Such a notion is ridiculous.

LESSONS OF DUTY.

The foregoing state of fact suggests some lessons of duty.

1st. We must study the use of arms, for *self-defense.* There is no principle of civil, or religious obligation, that requires us to live on, in hazard, and leave our persons, property, and our wives and children at the mercy of barbarians. Self-defense is the first law of nature.

2nd. We must enter into a solemn free colored *protestant industrial or labor league.*

Let the greedy foreigner know that a part of this country BELONGS TO US; and that we assert the right to live and labor here: That in New York and other cities, we claim the right to buy, hire, occupy and use houses and tenements, for legal considerations; to pass and repass on the streets, lanes, avenues, and all public ways. Our fathers have fought for this country, and helped to free it from the British yoke. We are now fighting to help to free it from the combined conspiracy of Jeff. Davis and Co.; we are doing so with the distinct understanding, that WE ARE TO HAVE ALL OUR RIGHTS AS MEN AND AS CITIZENS, and that there are to be no side issues, no RESERVATIONS, either political, civil, or religious. In this struggle we know nothing but God, Manhood, and American Nationality, full and unimpaired.

The right to labor, earn wages, and dispose of our earnings for the support of our families, the education of our children, and to support religious institutions of our free choice, is inherent. No party, or power, in politics, or religion, can alienate this right.

No part of our influence has been used to prevent foreigners from coming to this country and enjoying its benefits. We have done them no wrong. What we ask in return is, NONINTERVENTION. LET US ALONE.

3rd. Let us place our daughters, and younger sons in industrial positions, however humble; and secure openings where they may be usefully employed. Every father, and every mother may be of service, not only to their own children, but also to those of others. You will have many applications for "colored help." Be useful to applicants. Prepare your sons and daughters for usefulness, in all the branches of domestic labor and service.

4th. Let our able bodied men go into the United States service. There is no better place for them. If I had a dozen sons, I would rather have them in the United States army and navy, than to have them among our loose population. The army of the United States must, hereafter, be the great bulwark of our life, as a nation. The rebellion has rendered it necessary that we should have a powerful standing army. Colored men should enter the army in force, for the sake of the strength it will give them, the education they will obtain, the pay they will get; and the good service they will do for God, the country, and the race.

COLONIZATION INFLUENCES.—EDUCATION.

5th. We should reconstruct our Union against the insidious influences of colonization. It is a fact, that the time our present troubles began, colored men were very much divided, on the question of our continuance in the country. Hardly any two of our leading men were agreed about the matter. Some had squarely gone over to colonization, adopting the views of those who hold that a black man can never be a man, in this country. Many angry discussions had taken place. Old friendships were broken up, and a bitter spirit had been engendered among us. All this is to be traced to the insidious influences of colonizationists. It is a fact that, for several years past, any prominent colored man in the city of New York who would not cave in, on *"the colored car"* system, and go for some modified scheme of colonization, was sure to be marked; and special effort made to break him down. This influence has been most deadly. Years will not redeem us from its effects. At this moment, while the great and glorious southern field of usefulness is spreading and widening before us, there is no adequate plan, or movement on foot among us, for raising up proper agents to occupy the field. Why is this the case? What are we, ministers and teachers, doing? Why is there not some great movement going on, to bring forward young men and women of color for the southern field? These questions are to the point, and call for action, on the part of our ministers and teachers, who are in positions of influence.

We have no right to leave it to the government entirely, nor to any one denomination of whites, to supply this vast field, which is opening before us. Evil always grows out of monopoly. With the exception of what the Zion A. M. E., and the A. M. E. churches have done in the way of supplying ministers and teachers for the South, the colored churches North, are doing nothing. Some years ago it was found that eighty, or one hundred thousand of the southern slaves were held as Presbyterian property. Doubtless the great mass of those are now on the freedman's list; but what are the northern Presbyterians doing for their freed brethren? Is there a single colored Congregational or Presbyterian Church in New England, New York, New Jersey, or Pennsylvania, that has a young man in course of training for a teacher, or minister, with reference to the southern field? And echo answers, is there one? Thirty years hard and self-denying labors among the Congregational and Presbyterian churches of color, entitles me to speak, at least to them, upon this subject of religious and educational commissions to the South. These two wealthy bodies have a few semi-mission churches scattered about, in the North—for really not one of them is self-sustaining—but they have no plan for supplying the race with a sufficient number of instructors in this country. Would not some of our influential colored men do well to use an influence with a view to advance this cause *or, will they continue to let the colonization influence neutralize their zeal for the advancement of home interests?* It is painful to notice, that among the most indifferent to the cause of education, are some, who in former years, have, themselves been the recipients of liberal aid, when they were seeking education; and who now, since they have got into position, seem to be actuated by a jealousy, lest they should encourage too much competition.

I have recently heard of the case of a young man who applied to a colored Presbyterian clergyman for counsel and aid to enable him to obtain an education for the ministry, and was advised to go and join a body where it would require less education to be a minister. The young man was a member of that minister's church, and that church is under the care of one of the wealthiest Presbyteries in the city of New York. Now, it is known that that colored minister is strongly under the influence of prominent men of the colonization school. Hence the tree is known by its fruit. It has been part of the deep laid plan to divide the councils of colored men, and beset the government to unite colonization with emancipation. But God be thanked, that while emancipation is going on well, the unseemly colonization scheme which the President was induced to hitch on to his plan, has proved a failure. This fact should open the eyes of colored men who have been deluded by colonization emissaries.

About a year and a half ago, an official of the colonization society in New York remarked to me, with an appearance of satisfaction, that there was no doubt that the government would appropriate a large amount of money for colonization purposes. But as I said, thank God, it has failed. It is now evident that the country has no colored men to spare to people foreign countries; and no money to spare for expatriating them. The old colonization scheme has been buried so deep, that a century will not give it a resurrection.

SPIRIT OF PATRIOTISM.—FAITH IN GOD.

Lastly, We should remember that emancipation was resorted to, as a purely military necessity imposed upon this Government in the Providence of an alwise God. The President has no alternative but to fall into the powerful current of events which God had put in motion.

This view of the subject is essential to the cultivation of a true and lofty spirit of patriotism. A true patriot must always feel that he owns and contends for property which God gave him, whether it be life, or liberty, or the pursuit of happiness. His greatest strength will be in the firm conviction that God is transacting his business, so to speak; even though he be called to pass through bitter waters of adversity, he feels that God has not undertaken for him in vain.

When the hand of God is with us, we are strong, and when he shows us his will, in regard to our duties, we should be in earnest to do it.

A TERRIBLE CONTINGENCY.

An intelligent view of the history of God's providential dealings with slavery, leave no room to doubt that its doom is sealed in this country; but let us not forget that there is yet a terrible contingency before us. We may have to face, in the field, an army of our own colored brethren of the South! Already it is known that the southern commanders have made use of slaves in battle. And already it is rumored that the Confederate Government thinks seriously of arming the slaves as a retaliative military necessity. It is admitted, that from 1,750,000 to 2,000,000 out of the 4,000,000 of the slaves are yet in the possession of the rebels; of this number they can spare for arms at least 300,000 able bodied men. These men armed and so used, certainly cannot be expected to exercise any more liberty of choice than the poor white union men. So that if those men remain beyond our reach, and are armed and commanded by the Confederates to fight us, they will be obliged to do so. If we take them prisoners, I suppose they will have to be exchanged as others. If they desert and come to us, the case will be different. It is presumed they will do so, when the opportunity presents itself—but, how much mischief they may be compelled to do, in the meantime, it is impossible to foresee.

In my opinion, nothing is more likely to take place, under French influence, than this arming of the slaves by the rebels with the promise of freedom. It would be but a reproduction of the French plan in St. Domingo in 1794, to be followed by the same treachery by the Confederates, should they use the slaves successfully.

I have no doubt that Louis Napoleon is advising Jeff. Davis to this plan. Every week's delay in crushing out this rebellion increases the danger that the slaves may be brought into the field against us. I confess I am not of the number of those who covet such an event, with the expectation that the slaves would come to us *en masse.* It is not to be expected that, in the event of the rebels arming the slaves they would neglect also to present them with every possible allurement to fight hard; and at the same time, to surround them with every imaginable obstacle to their desertion. On our side, the only wise and safe course is to press rapidly into the heart of the slave country, and work out the problem of the Proclamation of freedom. We must prove to the slaves that we have both the will and the power to give effect to the proclamation, and that it is not a mere sound, reaching their ears, upon the wings of the wind. Here is where our danger lies. The President is right. The proclamation is the word of God's holy Providence, so to speak; but the great North is slow to repent of slavery. There is yet a great deal of wicked, angry, and unrighteous feeling in the heart of the Northern people. It may be that God intends to use the sword as a lance to bleed the whole nation, until she begins to faint, for very loss of blood, and then to swathe up the opened vein, and apply restoratives.

Let us, then, not flatter ourselves that we shall escape. Let us not be deceived by those who would persuade us that there is any destiny for us, as an integral part of this American nation, separate from the nation, as a whole. If the slaves are brought into the field by the Confederates, it will be a sad and awful day for us.

CONCLUSION.

We conclude, then, that those who, in the late riots undertook to expel by murder, fire, and persecution, the colored people for the accomplishment, either of sham democratic, or Roman Catholic propagandism, have undertaken a heavy and dangerous task, a task in which all the plans and purposes of a just God are against them. And it now remains to be seen whether intelligent colored men among us who have suffered in the late riots will allow the history of that outrageous scheme to pass unrecorded. Shall a few thousand dollars of relief money, and a few words of good counsel, and consolation, be a sufficient inducement to neglect our own history? Remember, that one of the great tests of civilization, is that a people should be able to record their own annals, by the pens of their own historians.

How does the matter sum up? It sums up thus; for more than a year, the riot spirit had been culminating, before it burst forth. The police authorities were frequently applied to, by respectable colored persons, without being able to obtain any redress when assaulted and abused in the streets. We have sometimes pointed to the aggressors but no arrests have been made. We have appealed to them for protection and apprised them of the fact that we had good reason to believe that a general attack was about to be made upon us, under false pretenses. We have pointed to the street corners, and to the rowdies who stand at them, and in open day light assaulted colored persons, in passing. We have presented proof sufficient to indict houses where rioters assembled. We have named men who hired idle boys to throw stones at colored men, and offered to prove it. The hand of the ruffian has done its work, in sending to the bar of God, a number of swift witnesses against the perpetrators of the deeds of July, 1863. The better class of people of New York city would doubtless feel relief, could these departed spirits be called back to their earthly homes, and their testimony, now recorded on the book of God against the bloody city, be erased. But as now, no power can restore those valuable members of society, so the full history of the riot must stand in all its painful bearings.

The loss of life and property make only a small part of the damage. The breaking up of families; and business relations just beginning to prosper: the blasting of hopes just dawning; the loss of precious harvest time which will never again return; the feeling of insecurity engendered; the confidence destroyed; the reaction; and lastly, the gross insult offered to our character as a people, sum up a weight of injury which can only be realized by the most enlightened and sensitive minds among us.

The injury extends to our churches, schools, societies for mutual aid and improvement, as well as to the various branches of industry. And amidst the most honest, trustworthy, useful laborious, pious, and respected, none have suffered more than the sisters of the laundry. These excellent women are the support of our churches, ministers, and the encouragement of our school teachers. In these worthy women, New York landlords have found their best tenants. Many of them are the only support of orphan children. Many of them, the wives of absent seamen, and some of coasting men, and others who are absent during the week, but spend their Sabbaths in the city. The nature of the business of these women is such, that they are entrusted by their customers with large quantities of valuable clothing, from Monday morning until Saturday evening, when they are expected to return them, to a piece, in perfect order. The attack made upon the houses of the colored people has had the effect to render it extra hazardous to have valuable articles in their houses in trust, as anything found in their houses by rioters would be looked upon as common plunder.

The pretense, therefore, that there was no intention, on the part of the rioters, to injure our women is false. The severest blow was aimed at them.

There was not only an attempt to murder, *en masse,* their only male protectors, but it was the design of the rioters also to render their homes dangerous and insecure, both for life and business.

For all the purposes, therefore, of social, civil, and religious enjoyment, and right, we hold New York solemnly bound to insure us, as citizens, permanent security in our homes. Relief, and damage money, is well enough. But it cannot atone, fully, for evils done by riots. It cannot bring back our murdered dead. It cannot remove the insults we feel; and finally, it gives no proof that the people have really changed their minds for the better, towards us.

During the late riots, my wife, and other lone females in the same tenement house, were repeatedly annoyed and threatened with mob law and violence. When there was not a man about the house, by night or by day, the rioters prowled about, watching for the return of absent marked victims. Failing to secure those, the defenceless women were repeatedly ordered, or mobishly advised to leave the house, and told that they *"must not be seen to carry a parcel away in their hands!"* Such was the treatment which our females received at the hands of the New York mobites, in the absence of their male protectors, which leaves no manner of doubt that a part of the hellish scheme was to mob and otherwise maltreat our women. Read this, and judge of its design:

"The mob will come to this house, soon. You nigger wenches must leave here, and you must not carry away a bundle, or anything, with you."

Such is a copy of a paper stuck under the door.■

72 A TRIBUTE TO A FALLEN BLACK SOLDIER

J. Stanley

As the need for manpower for the war increased, Washington permitted southern black troops to be recruited. But until December 1862, a national call for black volunteers had not been issued. The final Emancipation Proclamation, however, announced that freed slaves *would be received into the armed forces of the United States "to garri-son forts, positions, stations, and other places, and to man vessels of all sorts in said service." Early in 1863, a bill was passed in the House authorizing the president "to enroll, arm, equip and receive into the land and naval service of the United States such number of volunteers as he may deem useful to suppress the present rebellion." The Senate re-turned the bill to the House, deeming it unnecessary legislation, since the president had such power under previous acts of Congress such as the Confiscation Act and the Militia Act, both passed on July 17, 1862. Acting on this interpretation, Governor John A. Andrew of Massachu-setts asked permission of the War Department to raise two regiments of African American troops to serve for three years. Having received per-mission, Governor Andrew announced the formation of the Fifty-fourth Massachusetts Regiment, the first black regiment to be recruited in the North. Since Massachusetts's black population was too small to fill up a regiment, recruiting was done from all over the North.*

Governor Andrew had said that his reputation would stand or fall with the success or failure of the Fifty-fourth Massachusetts. In the battle of Fort Wagner, July 18, 1863, the regiment covered itself with glory. "It made Fort Wagner such a name to the colored race as Bunker Hill has been for ninety years to the white Yankees," declared the New York Tribune.

On September 8, 1863, the Young Men's Literary Association together with the citizens of Chicago gathered at Bethel Church to pay respect to a former member, Sergeant Joseph Wilson, of the Fifty-fourth Massachu-setts Regiment of Colored Volunteers, who had lost his life in the charge on Fort Wagner, "manfully fighting 'to uphold his country's banner.'" J. Stanley delivered a tribute to Sergeant Wilson. The following excerpts from that tribute are taken from the Christian Recorder, *September 23, 1863.*

THREE YEARS AGO, Joseph Wilson came among us an entire stranger, an obscure young man. At the formation of the Y.M.L. Association he became one of its first members. We found him modest and unpresuming. Wherever he was called upon to serve the Association, either as an officer or committeeman, he cheerfully assented. Feeling the want of early advantages, he ever manifested a strong desire for all useful information and instruction. The deceased, prior to the breaking-out of the rebellion, interested him-self in a corps of citizen soldiery. Here the genius of the man developed it-self; he excelled his companions in the healthy exercise of drilling; on this subject his mind was clear and comprehensive; in a word, he was a natural soldier.

When the Commonwealth of Massachusetts sent her agents to Illinois to recruit men for her colored regiments, Joseph Wilson was the first to en-roll his name for the gallant Fifty-fourth. Need I tell you, fellow citizens, that the Fifty-fourth have won for themselves and their race imperishable honor? Need I tell you they have forever settled the question that colored men can and will fight? Yes, through God they have proved their fighting qualities, and have hurled into the teeth of their enemies the base and foul calumny that we are incapable of defending ourselves and the government which has so long oppressed us. If you ask for proof of this assertion, I shall with pride refer you to the victories achieved by colored troops in Kansas, at New Orleans, Milliken's Bend,* on the coast of Florida, Port Hudson,† and last, but not least, in South Carolina, where the brave and gallant Wilson fell in front of Fort Wagner. Imagine you see the commanding general placing to the right and advance of the column a regiment of colored men that has never seen service nor stood in front of an enemy? Why was such an honor conferred upon black men? And why were they selected from among the thousands of their white companions in arms, who had fought on many a field of battle? What motive prompted General Gilmore to place Colonel Shaw's command where death and destruction awaited them? . . . ‡

He believed in the efficiency of the colored men whom he placed in front of his advancing columns; he knew well the danger to be met, the great labor to be performed; and it required men fearless of all consequences, whose souls were deeply imbued with the wrongs heaped upon them, to undertake this gigantic work. What has been the result?

We are told that upon that colored regiment was concentrated the fire of ten thousand rebels, from a battery impregnable—yet those men composing the Fifty-fourth Regiment, and in the face of a most deadly fire, attempted to storm the fort. The order was given to advance. On they went through a hail storm of shot and shell, trampling over the dead bodies of their comrades, until they reached the rebel parapets.

Their numbers being small, compared to their enemies, they were compelled to fall back; again and again they advanced to their work of death. Three successive times they mounted the parapet and called for reinforcements, but none came. Their only alternative was to give up the position won, which had cost so much labor, blood and sacrifice of life. Over six hundred of their number fell, to rise no more. Among them was the gallant Sergeant Wilson. But he met his fate like a hero and soldier. Singlehanded, he contended with four powerful cavalrymen until three of that number were made to bite the dust, and at his feet lay cold in death. But with strength exhausted, and no friend near to lend a helping hand, the fourth, demonlike, rushed upon him and took his life. Let the memory of Joseph Wilson be en-

---

*On July 7, 1863, two regiments of newly recruited freedmen repulsed a Confederate attack on Milliken's Bend, a Union outpost on the Mississippi River, above Vicksburg.

†On May 27, 1863, two regiments of New Orleans free blacks and Louisiana ex-slaves participated in an assault on Port Hudson, a Confederate stronghold on the lower Mississippi. The attack failed, but the African Americans fought heroically, advancing over open ground in the face of deadly artillery fire.

‡Colonel Robert Shaw, the youthful white colonel of the Massachusetts Fifty-fourth Regiment, was killed in the assault on Fort Wagner.

graved on the heart of every colored man who has felt the strong arm of oppression.

Behold what a spectacle is presented to the world by the colored race of this country. It ought to excite the sympathy and compel the admiration of men and angels. Doomed through long centuries of barbarism to all the degradations of slavery, we find many of our people, with singular unanimity, forgetting their unnumbered wrongs and the powerful provocations to revenge, coming heartily to the support of the Union cause; and, by their fidelity, their courage and their Christian forgiveness of all they have suffered, trying to win some higher and better place, some recognition, however faint, in the estimation of those by whom they have been oppressed.

They ask only a chance to prove their manhood. Ignorant and debased as we are by what we have endured and suffered, we still entreat them by all that is patriotic in government and sacred in religion to be the witnesses of what we will and can do, to establish our claims to be recognized as men worthy of a chance in the wide world to earn our bread, worthy of the enjoyment of the commonest right, the right to own ourselves.

On many a bloody field, at the head of many a desperate charge, in many a hazardous venture, their regiments have done deeds that white men, with all their boasting, might envy. Their true heroism is as much in their mercy and forgiveness of centuries of intolerable outrage and injury as in their readiness to encounter a new and more infernal slavery, the torture of the whip and faggot, and a lingering and cruel death in defense of the right.■

73 THE MISSION OF THE WAR

Frederick Douglass

In Lincoln at Gettysburg: The Words That Remade America *(New York: Simon and Schuster, 1992), Garry Wills describes the efforts of both North and South "to win the battle for* interpreting *Gettysburg as soon as the physical battle had ended." "Lincoln is after even larger game," he writes. "He means to 'win' the whole Civil War in ideological terms as well as military ones. And he will succeed: the Civil War* is *to most Americans, what Lincoln wanted it to* mean. *Words had to complete the work of the guns" (37–38).*

But Lincoln was certainly not fighting single-handed in this larger battle, as the following speech should make clear. Indeed, as Douglass bluntly notes in his 1876 "Oration in Memory of Abraham Lincoln," Lin-

coln was late and reluctant to join the ideological fray. Douglass and other black abolitionists had argued since the onset of hostilities that the "rebellion will be broken" only "when our government shall bravely avow this to be an Abolition war" (Douglass's speech, quoted here, appears elsewhere in this volume).

Chief among the issues that confronted the nation during the war, in Douglass's opinion, was the pressing problem of the African American's status as a free person. In his speech "The Mission of the War," which he repeated week after week in different communities late in 1863 and early in 1864, he warned abolitionists that "there never was a time when antislavery work was more needed than now" and impressed upon the nation the necessity of securing full freedom for African Americans. This speech contains Douglass's vision of a reunified and reconstituted nation—not the "broken constitution and dead Union" that existed before the war, but "a unity of which the great principles of liberty and equality . . . are the cornerstone." On January 13, 1864, he was invited to deliver the speech at a meeting sponsored by the Women's Loyal League at Cooper Institute in New York City. This was probably Douglass's most important speech during the Civil War. It is taken from the text that appeared in the New-York Tribune, *January 14, 1864.*

L ADIES AND GENTLEMEN: By the mission of the war I mean nothing occult, arbitrary or difficult to be understood, but simply those great moral changes in the fundamental condition of the people, demanded by the situation of the country plainly involved in the nature of the war, and which, if the war is conducted in accordance with its true character, it is naturally and logically fitted to accomplish.

Speaking in the name of Providence, some men tell me that slavery is already dead, that it expired with the first shot at Sumter. This may be so, but I do not share the confidence with which it is asserted. In a grand crisis like this, we should all prefer to look facts sternly in the face and to accept their verdict whether it bless or blast us. I look for no miraculous destruction of slavery. The war looms before me simply as a great national opportunity, which may be improved to national salvation, or neglected to national ruin. I hope much from the bravery of our soldiers, but in vain is the might of armies if our rulers fail to profit by experience and refuse to listen to the suggestions of wisdom and justice. The most hopeful fact of the hour is that we are now in a salutary school—the school of affliction. If sharp and signal retribution, long protracted, wide-sweeping and overwhelming, can teach a great nation respect for the long-despised claims of justice, surely we shall be taught now and for all time to come. But if, on the other hand, this potent teacher, whose lessons are written in characters of blood and thundered to us from a hundred battlefields shall fail, we shall go down as we shall deserve to go down, as a warning to all other nations which shall come after us. It is not pleasant to contemplate the hour as one of doubt and danger.

We naturally prefer the bright side, but when there is a dark side it is folly to shut our eyes to it or deny its existence.

I know that the acorn involves the oak, but I know also that the commonest accident may destroy its potential character and defeat its natural destiny. One wave brings its treasure from the briny deep, but another often sweeps it back to its primal depths. The saying that revolutions never go backward must be taken with limitations. The Revolution of 1848 was one of the grandest that ever dazzled a gazing world. It overturned the French throne, sent Louis Philippe into exile, shook every throne in Europe, and inaugurated a glorious Republic. Looking from a distance, the friends of democratic liberty saw in the convulsion the death of kingcraft in Europe and throughout the world. Great was their disappointment. Almost in the twinkling of an eye, the latent forces of despotism rallied. The Republic disappeared. Her noblest defenders were sent into exile, and the hopes of democratic liberty were blasted in the moment of their bloom. Politics and perfidy proved too strong for the principles of liberty and justice in that contest. I wish I could say that no such liabilities darken the horizon around us. But the same elements are plainly involved here as there. Though the portents are that we shall flourish, it is too much to say that we cannot fail and fall. Our destiny is to be taken out of our own hands. It is cowardly to shuffle our responsibilities upon the shoulders of Providence. I do not intend to argue but to state facts.

We are now wading into the third year of conflict with a fierce and sanguinary rebellion, one which, at the beginning of it, we were hopefully assured by one of our most sagacious and trusted political prophets would be ended in less than ninety days; a rebellion which, in its worst features, stands alone among rebellions a solitary and ghastly horror, without a parallel in the history of any nation, ancient or modern; a rebellion inspired by no love of liberty and by no hatred of oppression, as most other rebellions have been, and therefore utterly indefensible upon any moral or social grounds; a rebellion which openly and shamelessly sets at defiance the world's judgment of right and wrong, appeals from light to darkness, from intelligence to ignorance, from the ever-increasing prospects and blessings of a high and glorious civilization to the cold and withering blasts of a naked barbarism; a rebellion which even at this unfinished stage of it counts the number of its slain not by thousands nor by tens of thousands, but by hundreds of thousands; a rebellion which in the destruction of human life and property has rivaled the earthquake, the whirlwind and the pestilence that walketh in darkness and wasteth at noonday. It has planted agony at a million hearthstones, thronged our streets with the weeds of mourning, filled our land with mere stumps of men, ridged our soil with two hundred thousand rudely formed graves and mantled it all over with the shadow of death. A rebellion which, while it has arrested the wheels of peaceful industry and checked the flow of commerce, has piled up a debt heavier than a mountain of gold to weigh down the necks of our children's children. There is no end to the mischief wrought. It has brought ruin at home, contempt abroad, has cooled our friends, heated our enemies and endangered our existence as nation.

Now, for what is all this desolation, ruin, shame suffering and sorrow? Can anybody want the answer? Can anybody be ignorant of the answer? It has been given a thousand times from this and other platforms. We all know it is slavery. Less than a half a million of Southern slaveholders—holding in bondage four million slaves—finding themselves outvoted in the effort to get possession of the United States government, in order to serve the interests of slavery, have madly resorted to the sword—have undertaken to accomplish by bullets what they failed to accomplish by ballots. That is the answer.

It is worthy of remark that secession was an afterthought with the rebels. Their aim was higher; secession was only their second choice. Who was going to fight for slavery in the Union? It was not separation, but subversion. It was not Richmond, but Washington. It was not the Confederate rag, but the glorious Star-Spangled Banner.

Whence came the guilty ambition equal to this atrocious crime. A peculiar education was necessary to this bold wickedness. Here all is plain again. Slavery—the peculiar institution—is aptly fitted to produce just such patriots, who first plunder and then seek to destroy their country. A system which rewards labor with stripes and chains, which robs the slave of his manhood and the master of all just consideration for the rights of his fellow man—has prepared the characters, male and female, that figure in this rebellion—and for all its cold-blooded and hellish atrocities. In all the most horrid details of torture, starvation and murder in the treatment of our prisoners, I behold the features of the monster in whose presence I was born, and that is slavery. From no sources less foul and wicked could such a rebellion come. I need not dwell here. The country knows the story by heart. But I am one of those who think this rebellion—inaugurated and carried on for a cause so unspeakably guilty and distinguished by barbarities which would extort a cry of shame from the painted savage—is quite enough for the whole lifetime of any one nation, though the lifetime should cover the space of a thousand years. We ought not to want a repetition of it. Looking at the matter from no higher ground than patriotism—setting aside the high considerations of justice, liberty, progress and civilization—the American people should resolve that this shall be the last slaveholding rebellion that shall ever curse this continent. Let the War cost more or cost little, let it be long or short, the work now begun should suffer no pause, no abatement, until it is done and done forever.

I know that many are appalled and disappointed by the apparently interminable character of this war. I am neither appalled nor disappointed without pretending to any higher wisdom than other men. I knew well enough and often said it: once let the North and South confront each other on the battlefield, and slavery and freedom be the inspiring motives of the respective sections, the contest will be fierce, long and sanguinary. Governor Seymour* charges us with prolonging the war, and I say the longer the better if it must be so—in order to put an end to the hell-black cause out of which the rebellion has risen.

Say not that I am indifferent to the horrors and hardships of the war. I am not indifferent. In common with the American people generally, I feel the prolongation of the war a heavy calamity, private as well as public. There are vacant spaces at my hearthstone which I shall rejoice to see filled again by the boys who once occupied them, but which cannot be thus filled while the war lasts, for they have enlisted "during the war."[†]

But even from the length of this struggle, we who mourn over it may well enough draw some consolation when we reflect upon the vastness and grandeur of its mission. The world has witnessed many wars—and history records and perpetuates their memory—but the world has not seen a nobler and grander war than that which the loyal people of this country are now waging against the slaveholding rebels. The blow we strike is not merely to free a country or continent, but the whole world, from slavery; for when slavery fails here, it will fall everywhere. We have no business to mourn over our mission. We are writing the statutes of eternal justice and liberty in the blood of the worst of tyrants as a warning to all aftercomers. We should rejoice that there was normal life and health enough in us to stand in our appointed place, and do this great service for mankind.

It is true that the war seems long. But this very slow progress is an essential element of its effectiveness. Like the slow convalescence of some patients the fault is less chargeable to the medicine than to the deep-seated character of the disease. We were in a very low condition before the remedy was applied. The whole head was sick and the whole heart faint. Dr. Buchanan and his Democratic friends had given us up and were preparing to celebrate the nation's funeral. We had been drugged nearly to death by proslavery compromises. A radical change was needed in our whole system. Nothing is better calculated to effect the desired change than the slow, steady and certain progress of the war.

I know that this view of the case is not very consoling to the peace Democracy. I was not sent and am not come to console this breach of our political church. They regard this grand moral revolution in the mind and heart of the nation as the most distressing attribute of the war, and howl over it like certain characters of whom we read—who thought themselves tormented before their time.

---

*Horatio Seymour (1810–1886), Democratic governor of New York and leader of the "Peace Democracts," opposed the Emancipation Proclamation, urged an early end to the war, and was labeled a Copperhead by Horace Greeley. Seymour denounced the arrest of Clement L. Vallandigham, leader of the Copperheads—those in the North who favored the South.

†Both of Douglass's sons, Charles and Lewis, enlisted in the Fifty-fourth Massachusetts Regiment.

Upon the whole, I like their mode of characterizing the war. They charge that it is no longer conducted upon constitutional principles. The same was said by Breckinridge and Vallandigham. They charge that it is not waged to establish the Union as it was. The same idea has occurred to Jefferson Davis. They charge that this is a war for the subjugation of the South. In a word, that it is an Abolition war.

For one, I am not careful to deny this charge. But it is instructive to observe how this charge is brought and how it is met. Both warn us of danger. Why is this war fiercely denounced as an Abolition war? I answer, because the nation has long and bitterly hated Abolition and the enemies of the war confidently rely upon this hatred to serve the ends of treason. Why do the loyal people deny the charge? I answer, because they know that Abolition, though now a vast power, is still odious. Both the charge and the denial tell how the people hate and despise the only measure that can save the country.

An Abolition war! Well, let us thank the Democracy for teaching us this word. The charge in a comprehensive sense is most true, and it is a pity that it is true, but it would be a vast pity if it were not true. Would that it were more true than it is. When our government and people shall bravely avow this to be an Abolition war, then the country will be safe. Then our work will be fairly mapped out. Then the uplifted arm of the nation will swing unfettered to its work, and the spirit and power of the rebellion will be broken. Had slavery been abolished in the Border States at the very beginning of the war, as it ought to have been—had it been abolished in Missouri, as it would have been but for Presidential interference—there would now be no rebellion in the Southern states, for, instead of having to watch these Border States, as they have done, our armies would have marched in overpowering numbers directly upon the rebels and overwhelmed them. I now hold that a sacred regard for truth, as well as sound policy, makes it our duty to own and avow before heaven and earth that this war is, and of right ought to be, an Abolition war.

The abolition of slavery is the comprehensive and logical object of the war, for it includes everything else which the struggle involves. It is a war for the Union, a war for the Constitution, I admit; but it is logically such a war only in the sense that the greater includes the lesser. Slavery has proved itself the strong man of our national house. In every rebel state it proved itself stronger than the Union, stronger than the Constitution, and stronger than the Republican institutions. It overrode majorities, made no account of the ballot box, and had everything its own way. It is plain that this strong man must be bound and cast out of our house before Union, Constitution and Republican institutions can become possible. An Abolition war, therefore, includes Union, Constitution, Republican institutions, and all else that goes to make up the greatness and glory of our common country. On the other hand, exclude Abolition, and you exclude all else for which you are fighting.

The position of the Democratic party in relation to the war ought to surprise nobody. It is consistent with the history of the party for thirty years. Slavery, and only slavery, has been its recognized master during all that time. It early won for itself the title of being the natural ally of the South and of slavery. It has always been for peace or against peace, for war and against war, precisely as dictated by slavery. Ask why it was for the Florida War, and it answers, slavery. Ask why it was for the Mexican War, and it answers, slavery. Ask why it was for the annexation of Texas, and it answers, slavery. Ask why it was opposed to the habeas corpus when a Negro was the applicant, and it answers slavery. Ask why it is now in favor of the habeas corpus, when rebels and traitors are the applicants for its benefits, and it answers, slavery. Ask why it was for mobbing down freedom of speech a few years ago, when that freedom was claimed by the Abolitionists, and it answers, slavery. Ask why it now asserts freedom of speech, when sympathizers with traitors claim that freedom, and again slavery is the answer. Ask why it denied the right of a state to protect itself against possible abuses of the Fugitive Slave Bill, and you have the same old answer. Ask why it now asserts the sovereignty of the states separately as against the states united, and again slavery is the answer. Ask why it was opposed to giving persons claimed as fugitive slaves a jury trial before returning them to slavery; ask why it is now in favor of giving jury trial to traitors before sending them to the forts for safekeeping; ask why it was for war at the beginning of the Rebellion; ask why it has attempted to embarrass and hinder the loyal government at every step of its progress, and you have but one answer, slavery.

The fact is, the party in question—I say nothing of individual men who were once members of it—has had but one vital and animating principle for thirty years, and that has been the same old horrible and hell-born principle of Negro slavery.

It has now assumed a saintly character. Its members would receive the benediction due to peacemakers. At one time they would stop bloodshed at the South by inaugurating bloody revolution at the North. The livery of peace is a beautiful livery, but in this case it is a stolen livery and sits badly on the wearer. These new apostles of peace call themselves Peace Democrats, and boast that they belong to the only party which can restore the country to peace. I neither dispute their title nor the pretensions founded upon it. The best that can be said of the peacemaking ability of this class of men is their bitterest condemnation. It consists in their known treachery to the loyal government. They have but to cross the rebel lines to be hailed by the traitors as countrymen, clansmen, kinsmen, and brothers beloved in a common conspiracy. But, fellow-citizens, I have far less solicitude about the position and the influence of this party than I have about that of the great loyal party of the country. We have much less to fear from the bold and shameless wickedness of the one than from the timid and short-sighted policy of the other.

I know we have recently gained a great political victory; but it remains to be seen whether we shall wisely avail ourselves of its manifest advantages. There is danger that, like some of our Generals in the field, who, after soundly whipping the foe, generously allow him time to retreat in order, reorganize his forces, and intrench himself in a new and stronger position, where it will require more power and skill to dislodge him than was required to vanquish him in the first instance. The game is now in our hands. We can put an end to this disloyal party by putting an end to Slavery. While the Democratic party is in existence as an organization, we are in danger of a slaveholding peace, and of Rebel rule. There is but one way to avert this calamity, and that is destroy Slavery and enfranchise the black man while we have the power. While there is a vestige of Slavery remaining, it will unite the South with itself, and carry with it the Democracy of the North. The South united and the North divided, we shall be hereafter as heretofore, firmly held under the heels of Slavery.

Here is a part of the platform of principles upon which it seems to me every loyal man should take his stand at this hour:

First: That this war, which we are compelled to wage against slaveholding rebels and traitors, at untold cost of blood and treasure, shall be, and of right ought to be, an Abolition war.

Secondly: That we, the loyal people of the North and of the whole country, while determined to make this a short and final war, will offer no peace, accept no peace, consent to no peace, which shall not be to all intents and purposes an Abolition peace.

Thirdly: That we regard the whole colored population of the country, in the loyal as well as in the disloyal states, as our countrymen—valuable in peace as laborers, valuable in war as soldiers—entitled to all the rights, protection, and opportunities for achieving distinction enjoyed by any other class of our countrymen.

Fourthly: Believing that the white race has nothing to fear from fair competition with the black race, and that the freedom and elevation of one race are not to be purchased or in any manner rightfully subserved by the disfranchisement of another, we shall favor immediate and unconditional emancipation in all the states, invest the black man everywhere with the right to vote and to be voted for, and remove all discriminations against his rights on account of his color, whether as a citizen or as a soldier.

Ladies and gentlemen, there was a time when I hoped that events unaided by discussions would couple this rebellion and slavery in a common grave. But, as I have before intimated, the facts do still fall short of our hopes. The question as to what shall be done with slavery—and especially what shall be done with the Negro—threaten to remain open questions for some time yet.

It is true we have the Proclamation of January 1863. It was a vast and glorious step in the right direction. But unhappily, excellent as that paper is—and much as it has accomplished temporarily—it settles nothing. It is still open to decision by courts, canons and Congresses. I have applauded that paper and do now applaud it, as a wise measure—while I detest the motive and principle upon which it is based. By it the holding and flogging of Negroes is the exclusive luxury of loyal men.[*]

Our chief danger lies in the absence of all moral feeling in the utterances of our rulers. In his letter to Mr. Greeley the President told the country virtually that the abolition or non-abolition of slavery was a matter of indifference to him.[†] He would save the Union with slavery or without slavery. In his last Message he shows the same moral indifference, by saying as he does say that he had hoped that the rebellion could be put down without the abolition of slavery.[‡]

When the late Stephen A. Douglas uttered the sentiment that he did not care whether slavery were voted up or voted down in the territories, we thought him lost to all genuine feeling on the subject, and no man more than Mr. Lincoln denounced that sentiment as unworthy of the lips of any American statesman. But today, after nearly three years of a slaveholding rebellion, we find Mr. Lincoln uttering substantially the same heartless sentiments. Douglas wanted popular sovereignty; Mr. Lincoln wants the Union. Now did a warm heart and a high moral feeling control the utterance of the President, he would welcome, with joy unspeakable and full of glory, the opportunity afforded by the rebellion to free the country from the matchless crime and infamy. But policy, policy, everlasting policy, has robbed our statesmanship of all soul-moving utterances.

The great misfortune is and has been during all the progress of this war, that the government and loyal people have not understood and accepted its true mission. Hence we have been floundering in the depths of dead issues. Endeavoring to impose old and worn-out conditions upon new relations— putting new wines into old bottles, new cloth into old garments and thus making the rent worse then before.

Had we been wise we should have recognized the war at the outset as at once the signal and the necessity for a new order of social and political re-

---

[*]The Emancipation Proclamation pertained only to slaves in states "in rebellion against the United States," permitting slavery to continue in the loyalist states and in the Union-occupied areas of Louisiana and Virginia.

[†]On August 19, 1862, Horace Greeley published in the *New York Tribune* an appeal to Lincoln entitled "The Prayer of Twenty Millions." Greeley demanded that Lincoln make emancipation one of the aims of the war. Although Lincoln had already determined to issue an emancipation proclamation, he did not reveal it in his public letter to Greeley. He wrote in part: "My paramount object in this struggle is to save the Union, and is not either to save or to destroy slavery. If I could save the Union without freeing any slave, I would do it; and if I could save it by freeing some and leaving others alone, I would also do that." See Roy P. Basler, ed., *The Collected Works of Abraham Lincoln*, vol. 5 (New Brunswick, N.J.: Rutgers University Press, 1953), 388–89.

[‡]Douglass is referring to the following sentence in Lincoln's annual message to Congress, December 8, 1863: "According to our political system, as a matter of civil administration, the general government had no lawful power to effect emancipation in any state, and for a long time it had been hoped that the rebellion could be suppressed without resorting to it as a military measure." See John Nicolay and John Hay, eds., *Complete Works of Abraham Lincoln*, vol. 9 (New York: Tandy, 1894/1905), 246.

lations among the whole people. We could, like the ancients, discern the face of the sky, but not the signs of the times. Hence we have been talking of the importance of carrying on the war within the limits of a Constitution broken down by the very people in whose behalf the Constitution is pleaded! Hence we have from the first been deluding ourselves with the miserable dream that the old Union can be revived in the states where it has been abolished.

Now, we of the North have seen many strange things and may see many more; but that old Union, whose canonized bones we saw hearsed in death and inurned under the frowning battlements of Sumter, we shall never see again while the world standeth. The issue before us is a living issue. We are not fighting for the dead past, but for the living present and the glorious future. We are not fighting for the old Union, nor for anything like it, but for that which is ten thousand times more important; and that thing, crisply rendered, is national unity. Both sections have tried Union. It has failed.

The lesson for the statesmen at this hour is to discover and apply some principle of government which shall produce unity of sentiment, unity of idea, unity of object. Union without unity is, as we have seen, body without soul, marriage without love, a barrel without hoops, which falls at the first touch.

The statesmen of the South understood this matter earlier and better than the statesmen of the North. The dissolution of the Union on the old bases of compromise was plainly foreseen and predicted thirty years ago. Mr. Calhoun, and not Mr. Seward, is the original author of the doctrine of the irrepressible conflict. The South is logical and consistent. Under the teachings of their great leader they admit into their form of government no disturbing force. They have based their Confederacy squarely on their cornerstone. Their two great and all-commanding ideas are, first, that slavery is right, and second, that the slaveholders are a superior order or class. Around these two ideas their manners, morals, politics, religion and laws revolve. Slavery being right, all that is inconsistent with its entire security is necessarily wrong, and of course ought to be put down. There is no flaw in their logic.

They first endeavored to make the federal government stand upon their accursed cornerstone; and we but barely escaped, as you well know, that calamity. Fugitive-slave laws, slavery-extension laws, and Dred Scott decisions were among the steps to get the nation squarely upon the cornerstone now chosen by the Confederate states. The loyal North is less definite in regard to the necessity of principles of national unity. Yet, unconsciously to ourselves, and against our own protestations, we are in reality, like the South, fighting for national unity—a unity of which the great principles of liberty and equality, and not slavery and class superiority, are the cornerstone.

Long before this rude and terrible war came to tell us of a broken Constitution and a dead Union, the better portion of the loyal people had outlived and outgrown what they had been taught to believe were the requirements of the old Union. We had come to detest the principle by which slavery had a strong representation in Congress. We had come to abhor the idea of being called upon to suppress slave insurrections. We had come to be ashamed of slave hunting, and being made the watchdogs of slaveholders, who were too proud to scent out and hunt down their slaves for themselves. We had so far outlived the old Union four years ago that we thought the little finger of the hero of Harpers Ferry of more value to the world struggling for liberty than all the first families of old Virginia put together.

What business, then, have we to be pouring out our treasure and shedding our best blood like water for that old worn-out, dead and buried Union, which had already become a calamity and a curse? The fact is, we are not fighting for any such thing, and we ought to come out under our own true colors, and let the South and the whole world know that we don't want and will not have anything analogous to the old Union.

What we now want is a country—a free country—a country not saddened by the footprints of a single slave—and nowhere cursed by the presence of a slaveholder. We want a country which shall not brand the Declaration of Independence as a lie. We want a country whose fundamental institutions we can proudly defend before the highest intelligence and civilization of the age. Hitherto we have opposed European scorn of our slavery with a blush of shame as our best defense. We now want a country in which the obligations of patriotism shall not conflict with fidelity to justice and liberty. We want a country, and are fighting for a country, which shall be free from sectional political parties—free from sectional religious denominations—free from sectional benevolent associations—free from every kind and description of sect, party, and combination of a sectional character. We want a country where men may assemble from any part of it, without prejudice to their interests or peril to their persons. We are in fact, and from absolute necessity, transplanting the whole South with the higher civilization of the North. The New England schoolhouse is bound to take the place of the Southern whipping post. Not because we love the Negro, but the nation; not because we prefer to do this, because we must or give up the contest and give up the country. We want a country, and are fighting for a country, where social intercourse and commercial relations shall neither be embarrassed nor embittered by the imperious exactions of an insolent slaveholding oligarchy, which required Northern merchants to sell their souls as a condition precedent to selling their goods. We want a country, and are fighting for a country, through the length and breadth of which the literature and learning of any section of it may float to its extremities unimpaired, and thus become the common property of all the people—a country in which no man shall be fined for reading a book, or imprisoned for selling a book—a country where no may man be imprisoned or flogged or sold for learning to read, or teaching a fellow mortal how to read. We want a country, and are fighting for a country, in any part of which to be called an American citizen shall mean as much as it did to be called a Roman citizen in the palmiest days of the Roman Empire.

We have heard much in other days of manifest destiny.* I don't go all the lengths to which such theories are pressed, but I do believe that it is the manifest destiny of this war to unify and reorganize the institutions of the country, and that herein is the secret of the strength, the fortitude, the persistent energy—in a word, the sacred significance—of this war. Strike out the high ends and aims thus indicated, and the war would appear to the impartial eye of an onlooking world like little better than a gigantic enterprise for shedding human blood.

A most interesting and gratifying confirmation of this theory of its mission is furnished in the varying fortunes of the struggle itself. Just in proportion to the progress made in taking upon itself the character I have ascribed to it has the war prospered and the rebellion lost ground.

Justice and humanity are often overpowered, but they are persistent and eternal forces, and fearful to contend against. Let but our rulers place the government fully within these trade winds of omnipotence, and the hand of death is upon the Confederate rebels. A war waged as ours seemed to be at first, merely for power and empire, repels sympathy though supported by legitimacy. If Ireland should strike for independence tomorrow, the sympathy of this country would be with her, and I doubt if American statesmen would be more discreet in the expression of their opinions of the merits of the contest than British statesmen have been concerning the merits of ours. When we were merely fighting for the old Union the world looked coldly upon our government. But now the world begins to see something more than legitimacy, something more than national pride. It sees national wisdom aiming at national unity, and national justice breaking the chains of a long-enslaved people. It is this new complexion of our cause which warms our hearts and strengthens our hands at home, disarms our enemies and increases our friends abroad. It is this more than all else which has carried consternation into the bloodstained halls of the South. It has sealed the fiery and scornful lips of the Roebucks and Lindsays of England, and caused even the eloquent Mr. Gladstone to restrain the expression of his admiration for Jeff Davis and his rebel nation. It has placed the broad arrow of British suspicion on the prows of the rebel rams in the Mersey and performed a like service in France. It has driven Mason, the shameless man hunter, from London, where he never should have been allowed to stay for an hour, except as a bloodhound is tolerated in Regent Park for exhibition.†

---

*"Manifest destiny," a phrase associated with expansionism, was based on the idea that God had set aside the American continents and their neighboring islands for the expansion of the system of government of the American people. In the late 1840s and 1850s, the concept of manifest destiny was used to justify the expansion of slavery into new lands such as Mexico and Cuba.

†James Murray Mason (1798–1871) was the Confederate diplomatic commissioner to England, when he and John Slidell were seized on board the *Trent* by Captain Wilkes of the U.S. Navy. Although he was well received when he arrived in England in 1862, the British government refused to receive him officially, and he was unable to achieve British recognition of the Confederacy or intervention in its behalf.

We have had, from the first, warm friends in England. We owe a debt of respect and gratitude to William Edward Forster, John Bright, Richard Cobden, and other British Statesmen, in that they outran us in comprehending the high character of our struggle. They saw that this must be a war for human nature, and walked by faith to its defense while all was darkness about us—while we were yet conducting it in profound reverence for slavery.

I know we are not to be praised for this changed character of the war. We did our very best to prevent it. We had but one object at the beginning, and that was, as I have said, the restoration of the old Union; and for the first two years the war was kept to that object strictly, and you know full well and bitterly with what results. I will not stop here to blame and denounce the past; but I will say that the most of the blunders and disasters of the earlier part of the war might have been avoided had our armies and generals not repelled the only true friends the Union cause had in the rebel states. The Army of the Potomac took up an anti-Negro position from the first and has not entirely renounced it yet. The colored people told me a few days ago in Washington that they were the victims of the most brutal treatment by these Northern soldiers when they first came there. But let that pass. Few men, however great their wisdom, are permitted to see the end from the beginning. Events are mightier than our rulers, and these divine forces, with overpowering logic, have fixed upon this war, against the wishes of our government, the comprehensive character and mission I have ascribed to it. The collecting of revenue in the rebel ports, the repossession of a few forts and arsenals and other public property stolen by the rebels, have almost disappeared from the recollection of the people. The war has been a growing war in every sense of the word. It began weak and has risen strong. It began low and has risen high. It began narrow and has become broad. It began with few and now, behold, the country is full of armed men, ready, with courage and fortitude, to make the wisest and best idea of American statesmanship the law of the land.

Let, then, the war proceed in its strong, high and broad course till the rebellion is put down and our country is saved beyond the necessity of being saved again!

I have already hinted at our danger. Let me be a little more direct and pronounced.

The Democratic party, though defeated in the elections last fall, is still a power. It is the ready organized nucleus of a powerful proslavery and pro-rebel reaction. Though it has lost in members, it retains all the elements of its former power and malevolence.

That party has five very strong points in its favor, and its public men and journals know well how to take advantage of them.

First: There is the absence of any deep moral feeling among the loyal people against slavery itself, their feeling against it being on account of its rebellion against the government, and not because it is a stupendous crime against human nature.

Secondly: The vast expense of the war and the heavy taxes in money as well as men which the war requires for its prosecution. Loyalty has a strong back, but taxation has often broken it.

Thirdly: The earnest desire for peace which is shared by all classes except government contractors who are making money out of the war; a feeling which may be kindled to a flame by any serious reverses to our arms. It is silent in victory but vehement and dangerous in defeat.

Fourthly: And superior to all others, is the national prejudice and hatred toward all colored people of the country, a feeling which has done more to encourage the hopes of the rebels than all other powers beside.

Fifthly: An Abolitionist is an object of popular dislike. The guilty rebel who with broad blades and bloody hands seeks the life of the nation, is at this hour more acceptable to the Northern Democracy than an Abolitionist guilty of no crime. Whatever may be a man's abilities, virtue or service, the fact that he is an Abolitionist makes him an object of popular hate.

Upon these five strings the Democrats still have hopes of playing themselves into power, and not without reason. While our government has the meanness to ask Northern colored men to give up the comfort of home, endure untold hardships, peril health, limbs and life itself, in its defense, and then degrades them in the eyes of other soldiers, by offering them the paltry sum of seven dollars per month, and refuses to reward their valor with even the hope of promotion—the Democratic party may well enough presume upon the strength of popular prejudice for support.

While our Republican government at Washington makes color and not character the criterion of promotion in the Army and degrades colored commissioned officers at New Orleans below the rank to which even the rebel government had elevated them, I think we are in danger of a compromise with slavery.

Our hopeful Republican friends tell me this is impossible—that the day of compromise with slavery is past. This may do for some men, but will not do for me.

The Northern people have always been remarkably confident of their own virtue. They are hopeful to the last. Twenty years ago we hoped that Texas could not be annexed; but if that could not be prevented we hoped that she would come in a free state. Thirteen years ago we were quite sure that no such abomination as the Fugitive Slave Bill could get itself on our national statute book; but when it got there we were equally sure that it never could be enforced. Four years ago we were sure that the slave states would not rebel, but if they did we were sure it would be a very short rebellion. I know that times have changed very rapidly, and that we have changed with them. Nevertheless, I know also we are the same old American people, and that what we have done once we may possibly do again. The leaven of compromise is among us. I repeat, while we have a Democratic party at the North trimming its sails to catch the Southern breeze in the next Presidential election, we are in danger of compromise. Tell me not of amnesties and oaths of allegiance. They are valueless in the presence of twenty hundred millions invested in human flesh. Let but the little finger of slavery get back into this Union, and in one year you shall see its whole body again upon our backs.

While a respectable colored man or woman can be kicked out of the commonest streetcar in New York where any white ruffian may ride unquestioned, we are in danger of a compromise with slavery. While the North is full of such papers as the New York *World, Express* and *Herald,* firing the nation's heart with hatred to Negroes and Abolitionists, we are in danger of a slaveholding peace. While the major part of antislavery profession is based upon devotion to the Union rather than hostility to slavery, there is danger of a slaveholding peace. Until we shall see the election of November next, and that it has resulted in the election of a sound antislavery man as President, we shall be in danger of a slaveholding compromise. Indeed, as long as slavery has any life in it anywhere in the country, we are in danger of such a compromise.

Then there is the danger arising from the impatience of the people on account of the prolongation of the war. I know the American people. They are an impulsive people, impatient of delay, clamorous for change, and often look for results out of all proportion to the means employed in attaining them.

You and I know that the mission of this war is national regeneration. We know and consider that a nation is not born in a day. We know that large bodies move slowly—and often seem to move thus when, could we perceive their actual velocity, we should be astonished at its greatness. A great battle lost or won is easily described, understood and appreciated, but the moral growth of a great nation requires reflection, as well as observation, to appreciate it. There are vast numbers of voters, who make no account of the moral growth of a great nation and who only look at the war as a calamity to be endured only so long as they have no power to arrest it. Now, this is just the sort of people whose votes may turn the scale against us in the last event.

Thoughts of this kind tell me that there never was a time when antislavery work was more needed than now. The day that shall see the rebels at our feet, their weapons flung away, will be the day of trial. We have need to prepare for that trial. We have long been saved a proslavery peace by the stubborn, unbending persistence of the rebels. Let them bend as they will bend, there will come the test of our sternest virtues.

I have now given, very briefly, some of the grounds of danger. A word as to the ground of hope. The best that can be offered is that we have made progress—vast and striking progress—within the last two years.

President Lincoln introduced his administration to the country as one which would faithfully catch, hold and return runaway slaves to their masters. He avowed his determination to protect and defend the slaveholder's right to plunder the black laborer of his hard earnings. Europe was assured by Mr. Seward that no slave should gain his freedom by this war. Both the President and the Secretary of State have made progress since then.

Our generals, at the beginning of the war, were horribly proslavery. They took to slave catching and slave killing like ducks to water. They are now very generally and very earnestly in favor of putting an end to slavery. Some of them, like Hunter and Butler, because they hate slavery on its own account, and others, because slavery is in arms against the government.

The rebellion has been a rapid educator. Congress was the first to respond to the instinctive judgment of the people, and fixed the broad brand of its reprobation upon slave hunting in shoulder straps. Then came very temperate talk about confiscation, which soon came to be pretty radical talk. Then came propositions for Border State, gradual, compensated, colonized emancipation. Then came the threat of a proclamation, and then came the Proclamation. Meanwhile the Negro had passed along from a loyal spade and pickax to a Springfield rifle.

Haiti and Liberia are recognized. Slavery is humbled in Maryland, threatened in Tennessee, stunned nearly to death in western Kentucky, and gradually melting away before our arms in the rebellious states.

The hour is one of hope as well as danger. But whatever may come to pass, one thing is clear: The principles involved in the contest, the necessities of both sections of the country, the obvious requirements of the age, and every suggestion of enlightened policy demand the utter extirpation of slavery from every foot of American soil, and the enfranchisement of the entire colored population of the country. Elsewhere we may find peace, but it will be a hollow and deceitful peace. Elsewhere we may find prosperity, but it will be a transient prosperity. Elsewhere we may find greatness and renown, but if these are based upon anything less substantial than justice they will vanish, for righteousness alone can permanently exalt a nation.

I end where I began—no war but an Abolition war; no peace but an Abolition peace; liberty for all, chains for none; the black man a soldier in war, a laborer in peace; a voter at the South as well as at the North; America his permanent home, and all Americans his fellow countrymen. Such, fellow citizens, is my idea of the mission of the war. If accomplished, our glory as a nation will be complete, our peace will flow like a river, and our foundation will be the everlasting rocks.■

74 GIVE US EQUAL PAY AND WE WILL GO TO WAR

Reverend J. P. Campbell

Although most of the outstanding African American leaders in the North served as recruiting agents urging blacks to join the Union army, the response from black men was less enthusiastic than they had anticipated. In part, the reason was that for the first time, owing to the booming war economy, African Americans enjoyed full employment. But the main reason was the fact that black soldiers did not enjoy equal rights with white soldiers and experienced discrimination in such matters as pay, opportunities to become officers, and provisions and equipment. African Americans were paid $10 per month, $3 of which were deducted for clothing, while white privates received $13 per month plus a clothing allowance of $3.50. When Maryland, which had recently abolished slavery, was called upon to fill its quota for the Union army, a meeting of African American men was held in Baltimore, on February 29, 1864, at the Methodist Episcopal Sharp Street Church, for the purpose of hearing addresses to encourage black volunteers. ("This was the first meeting of the kind ever held in the city of Baltimore or in the State of Maryland," a reporter wrote.) The leading address was delivered by the Reverend J. P. Campbell, of Trenton, New Jersey, a high official of the African Methodist Episcopal Church. The Reverend Mr. Campbell used the opportunity to mobilize pressure upon Congress to achieve passage of a bill equalizing the pay of black soldiers. On June 15, 1864, Congress finally provided equal pay for African American soldiers. His speech, presented here in part, is taken from the Christian Recorder, *March 19, 1864.*

IF WE ARE ASKED the question why it is that black men have not more readily enlisted in the volunteer service of the United States government since the door has been opened to them, we answer, the door has not been fairly and sufficiently widely opened. It has been opened only in part, not the whole of the way. That it is not sufficiently and fairly opened will appear from the action of the present Congress upon the subject of the pay of colored soldiers. It shows a strong disposition not to equalize the pay of soldiers without distinction on account of color.

When the news of the first gun fired upon the flag of the Union at old Sumter reached the North, the friends of the Union were called upon to defend that flag. The heart of the black man at that hour responded to the call. He came forward at once and offered his services to the government, and failed to act immediately, because he was denied the opportunity of so doing.

He was met with the cold, stern and chilling rebuke, that this was not the Negro's war, not a war upon slavery, and that in it the services of the Negro were not wanted; that slavery had nothing to do with the war, or the war with slavery; that it was purely a war for the safety of the Union and its preservation, without reference to the slavery question.

But the time came when it was thought that under very great restrictions, as by giving him unequal pay and restraining him from being an officer in the Army, the Negro might be allowed to bear arms. Afterward, the black man, saying nothing about officeholding for the time being, asked the government to acknowledge the justice of his claim to equal pay with the white soldier and to recommend the same to the then ensuing Congress, to be made law. The government pledged itself to this recommendation, and many colored men enlisted upon the faith which they had in the government and the future good legislation of Congress upon the subject of giving to black soldiers equal pay and equal bounties with white soldiers, and that all other necessary and needed provisions would be to both the same. Congress met, and the good President Lincoln, with the excellent Secretary of War, Mr. Stanton, proved faithful to their promise. They laid the matter before Congress in their Annual Message and Report. But, alas, that honorable body hesitates to act, and that, too, while the country and its liberties are in danger and calamity by armed rebellion against the government.

Now, we say to our honorable Senators and Representatives in Congress, gentlemen, don't be afraid to do the black man justice. He will not abuse your confidence in his fidelity to the Constitution and the Union. He will never prove himself a traitor by his acts. He will never prove himself to be unworthy of receiving at your hands the rights and privileges which justice and equity demand.

Give to the black man those simple demands set forth in this bill of particulars, and he will rush to the defense of his country by thousands. His heart within him pants for the opportunity to show himself a man, capable of discharging all the duties of a common manhood, in whatever sphere that manhood may be called to act. Here we are, by thousands and ten thousands, standing ready to move at the nod of your august and mighty fiat. The state of Maryland wants to fill up her last quota of men demanded by the call of the President. This, with a little more time allowed, may be done, if she will do justice to the black citizens of her own soil. They are strong men, and true to the country which gave them birth. They will be ready, at the first sound of the bugle, to fill up the balance of Maryland's apportionment.

The law requires that black men shall pay as much commutation money as white men pay.* We ask, then, that the same pay, bounty, pensions, rights and privileges be given to black men that are given to white men, and they will go to the war, without paying the commutation money.

We want an equal chance to show our equal manhood and love for the

*Under this law a man drafted in the Union army could pay for a substitute who would replace him.

Constitution and the Union. Under the above-named circumstances, we are standing ready to respond to the call of the government and go to defend our common country against the encroachment of an armed rebellion.

In conclusion, we ask the question, Will you have us? Will you accept of us upon equal terms with white men in the service of our country? We await, with deep solicitude and anxiety, the action of a government and people whom, with all their faults, we love, and whom we are willing to defend with our lives, liberty and sacred honor in common with white men. Will you have us so to do? That is the question. We ask for equal pay and bounty, not because we set a greater value upon money than we do upon human liberty, compared with which money is mere trash; but we contend for equal pay and bounty upon the principle that if we receive equal pay and bounty when we go into the war, we hope to receive equal rights and privileges when we come out of the war. If we go in equal in pay, we hope to come out equal in enfranchisement.

Is that an unreasonable hope or an unjust claim? It takes as much to clothe and feed the black man's wife as it does the white man's wife. It takes as much money to go to market for the black man's little boys and girls as it does for the white man's little boys and girls. We have yet to learn why it is that the black soldier should not receive the same compensation for labor in the service of his country that the white soldier receives. There is no financial embarrassment, as in the case of Mr. Jefferson Davis' government at Richmond. Our great and good financier, Mr. Salmon P. Chase, Secretary of the Treasury, has money enough to carry on the war, and some millions of gold and silver to sell. Give us equal pay, and we will go to the war—not pay on mercenary principles, but pay upon the principles of justice and equity.■

75 EVERY MAN SHOULD STAND EQUAL BEFORE THE LAW

Arnold Bertonneau

The question of reconstruction of the southern states arose during the war, and one of the first states where the issue developed was Louisiana. African Americans in New Orleans called for the right of black men free before the war to vote in the reconstructed state, but President Lincoln, in announcing his reconstruction policy on December

8, 1863, restricted the right to vote in Louisiana to whites. New Orleans blacks refused to accept this exclusion from the ballot box, and on January 5, 1864, they drew up a petition to extend the franchise to "all the citizens of Louisiana of African descent, born free before the rebellion" and addressed it to both President Lincoln and the Congress. The petition bore the signatures of more than one thousand men, and two of the signers, Jean Baptiste Roudanez and E. Arnold Bertonneau (who had originally fought for the Confederacy), were selected to take the petition to Washington.

Once in Washington, Roudanez and Bertonneau were persuaded by Charles Sumner and other Republicans to modify their petition to Congress into an appeal for universal suffrage, extending the franchise to freedpersons. This was a groundbreaking and controversial step and was widely debated by black leaders in the year that followed. They presented it to Lincoln on March 12, and it was introduced in the Senate by Charles Sumner on March 15.

Before they returned to New Orleans, Roudanez and Bertonneau were invited by Republican leaders in Massachusetts to a dinner in their honor in Boston on April 12, 1864. After an introduction by Governor John A. Andrew, Arnold Bertonneau delivered the following speech to the diners. It is taken from the Liberator, *April 15, 1864. For further information on the New Orleans petition, see David C. Rankin, "The Origins of Negro Leadership in New Orleans During Reconstruction," in Howard N. Rabinowitz, ed.,* Southern Black Leaders of the Reconstruction Era *(Urbana: University of Illinois Press, 1982), 155–90.*

BEFORE THE OUTBREAK of the rebellion, Louisiana contained about forty thousand free colored people, and three hundred twelve thousand persons held in slavery. In the city of New Orleans, there were upwards of twenty thousand free persons of color. Nearly all the free persons of color read and write. The free people have always been on the side of law and good order, always peaceful and self-sustaining, always loyal. Taxed on an assessment of more than fifteen million dollars—among many other things, for the support of public-school education—debarred from the right of sending their children to the common schools which they have been and are compelled to aid in supporting, taxed on their property, and compelled to contribute toward the general expense of sustaining the state, they have always been and now are prohibited from exercising the elective franchise.

When the first fratricidal shot was fired at Sumter, and Louisiana had joined her fortunes with the other seceding states, surrounded by enemies educated in the belief that "Africans and their descendants had no rights that white men were bound to respect,"* without arms and ammunition, or any means of self-defense, the condition and position of our people were ex-

---

*Bertonneau refers to the *Dred Scott* decision of 1857.

tremely perilous. When summoned to volunteer in the defense of the state and city against Northern invasion, situated as we were, could we do otherwise than heed the warning and volunteer in the defense of New Orleans? Could we have adopted a better policy? In the city of New Orleans, under the Confederate government, we raised one regiment of a thousand men, the line officers of which were colored.

When General Butler captured New Orleans,* and drove the rebel soldiers from the state, the colored people were the most truly loyal citizens to welcome his coming. Indeed, from the time that General Jackson, when Louisiana was threatened during the last war with Great Britain by an overwhelming British force, issued his famous appeal to the "noble-hearted, generous free men of color"—for so he called them in his proclamation, censuring the "mistaken policy" before pursued, of exempting them from military service, calling upon them as "Americans" and "sons of freedom" for aid and support—our fathers rallied to arms, and drove the red coats from the soil. I say, from that time to the present, the free colored people of Louisiana have always been loyal and ready and willing to defend the "Stars and Stripes." General Butler understood this. He knew instinctively who were loyal and who were not, on whom he could implicitly rely, in whose fidelity he could safely trust; and adopting the policy of that noble, brave and clear-sighted general who dared to take the responsibility, he received into the ranks of the Union army, the colored volunteer soldiers of New Orleans.

Under General Butler, we had a foretaste of freedom. The colored people of Louisiana venerate his name; with us it is a household word. We bless his memory and shall always hold it in grateful remembrance. We felt that we were men and citizens, and were to be treated as such; we were animated by new hopes and new desires; we felt that there was a new life opened before us; so we gave our imagination full scope and play. The tyrant who was cruel to his slave was summoned before that general, and received proper punishment. The sympathizers with the rebellion, who wantonly insulted Union troops, were reminded that they could not do so with safety. Gentlemen and ladies of color were allowed to ride in public conveyances and were respectfully treated. Soon, however, the scene changed. General Butler was removed, and again a portentous cloud darkened the bright horizon of our future prospects. Our hope gave place to our fears; and with all true and loyal citizens of our state and city, we regretted the removal of a general who was determined to bring Louisiana back into the Union, free as in the state of Massachusetts.

While General Banks was at the seize of Port Hudson, again the city of

---

*Benjamin F. Butler (1818–1893) commanded the land forces in the capture of New Orleans by the Union army in 1862 and was military commander of the city until removed and transferred to the Department of East Virginia. While in New Orleans, Butler earned the hatred of southern whites because he used black troops and because he generally treated blacks as being entitled to equal rights.

New Orleans was threatened by the enemy, and fears were entertained that the rebel troops would take the city. At the call of General Shepley, the colored people again rallied under the banner of the Union, and in forty-eight hours raised the first regiment and were ready for duty. They were promised the same pay and rations as other soldiers. At the expiration of forty days service, we were discharged; and when the time for payment arrived, each man being charged for his uniform, and his wages cut down to seven dollars per month, it was ascertained that each soldier was indebted to the government six dollars and ninety-seven cents. The soldiers composing this regiment are men of business and culture, mostly engaged in commercial and industrial pursuits, while some are artisans; and notwithstanding they closed their places of business, quit their various occupations, and joined in the defense of New Orleans, this sum stands charged against these soldiers in the books of the general government this day.

Some months ago, General Shepley, the military governor of Louisiana, issued an order, directing all Union male citizens over twenty-one years to register their names, that it might be ascertained who had a right to vote in the reorganization of civil government in the state of Louisiana. The free colored citizens applied for leave to register their names, but were refused the right to do so. They applied to the Military Governor and to General Banks, without success. An election took place, and no colored citizens were permitted to vote. In our struggle to gain the right to vote, we were aided and assisted by many of our most influential and truly loyal Union citizens. Their noble efforts in our behalf we shall never forget. To influence the action and to obtain the elective franchise for our people, we, as delegates of the free colored population of Louisiana, visited Washington to lay the matter before President Lincoln and the Congress of the country.* We ask that, in the reconstruction of the state government there, the right to vote shall not depend on the color of the citizen; that the colored citizen shall have and enjoy every civil, political and religious right that white citizens enjoy; in a word, that every man shall stand equal before the law. To secure these rights, which belong to every free citizen, we ask the aid and influence of every true loyal man all over the country. Slavery, the curse of our country, cannot exist in Louisiana again.

In order to make our state blossom and bloom as the rose, the character of the whole people must be changed. As slavery is abolished, with it must vanish every vestige of oppression. The right to vote must be secured; the doors of our public schools must be opened, that our children, side by side, may study from the same books, and imbibe the same principles and pre-

---

*Lincoln was moved by the petition to write a private note to Governor Michael Hahn in Louisiana suggesting that in the forthcoming constitutional convention "some of the colored people" might be granted the suffrage, "as, for instance, the very intelligent, and especially those who have fought gallantly in our ranks." But even this modest suggestion was rejected.

cepts from the Book of Books, learn the great truth that God "created of one blood all nations of men to dwell on all the face of the earth"; so will caste, founded on prejudice against color, disappear.

Massachusetts has always been foremost in every good work. She, first of all the states, by positive law, struck the shackles from the limbs of every bondman within her limits. It was Massachusetts who first acknowledged the colored man as a citizen and gave him political equality. And today, by your enlightened legislation, no prescriptive laws remain on your statute book. In your state, color is no legal disqualification for any office of trust or power.

Mr. President, when we return to New Orleans, we shall tell our friends that in Massachusetts we could ride in every public vehicle; that the colored children not only were allowed to attend public schools with white children, but they were compelled by law to attend such schools; that we visited your courts of justice and saw colored lawyers defending their clients; and we shall tell them, too, of this most generous welcome extended to us by you. It will prove most grateful to their feeling, animate them with new hope and desires, and will prove a grand stimulus to renewed efforts for the acquisition of every right that can be guaranteed to them by law.■

76 LET THE MONSTER PERISH

Henry Highland Garnet

The Emancipation Proclamation had freed slaves only where the Federal troops were not in control to enforce the order—that is, those slaves living in areas still in rebellion against the government of the United States. It had specifically ruled out of the terms of emancipation all slave areas where Federal troops were present, in Louisiana, Virginia, and the border states. Slavery was legally ended by the Thirteenth Amendment to the Constitution. In April 1864 and January 1865, the Senate and House, respectively, voted for the adoption of an amendment to the Constitution providing that neither slavery nor involuntary servitude, except as punishment for crime for which the party had been convicted, should exist within the United States or any place under its jurisdiction. The amendment was then sent to the states for ratification, which occurred in December 1865.

On February 12, 1865, in the hall of the House of Representatives, the Reverend Henry Highland Garnet preached a sermon commemorat-

ing the passage of the Thirteenth Amendment by Congress. At the time, Garnet was pastor of the Fifteenth Street Presbyterian Church in Washington, D.C. Born in slavery, Garnet (1815–1882) was a leading abolitionist and supporter of African emigration. During the Civil War, he recruited black troops for the Union army. His sermon in the House of Representatives made him the first African American to speak in the halls of Congress. In addition to praising the action of Congress, Garnet included an eloquent appeal for equal rights. The drive for equal rights was also advanced in early 1865 by the formation of the National Equal Rights League, through which African American citizens in several states met in the waning days of the war to formulate and press their demands.

  Garnet's sermon, reprinted here, is taken from A Memorial Discourse by Rev. Henry Highland Garnet, Delivered in the Hall of the House of Representatives, Washington, D.C. on Sabbath, February 12, 1865, With an Introduction by James McCune Smith *(Philadelphia, 1865). For further information on Garnet, see Earl Ofari,* Let Your Motto Be Resistance: The Life and Thought of Henry Highland Garnet *(Boston: Beacon, 1972); and Joel Schor,* Henry Highland Garnet *(Westport, Conn.: Greenwood, 1977).*

For they bind heavy burdens and grievous to be borne, and lay them on men's shoulders, but they themselves will not move them with one of their fingers.—Matthew 23:4.

IN THIS CHAPTER, of which my text is a sentence, the Lord Jesus addressed his disciples, and the multitude that hung spellbound upon the words that fell from his lips. He admonished them to beware of the religion of the Scribes and Pharisees, which was distinguished for great professions, while it succeeded in urging them to do but a little, or nothing that accorded with the law of righteousness.

In theory they were right; but their practices were inconsistent and wrong. They were learned in the law of Moses and in the traditions of their fathers, but the principles of righteousness failed to affect their hearts. They knew their duty but did it not. The demands which they made upon others proved that they themselves knew what things men ought to do. In condemning others they pronounced themselves guilty. They demanded that others should be just, merciful, pure, peaceable and righteous. But they were unjust, impure, unmerciful—they hated and wronged a portion of their fellowmen, and waged a continual war against the government of God.

Such was their conduct in the Church and in the state. We have modern Scribes and Pharisees, who are faithful to their prototypes of ancient times.

With sincere respect and reverence for the instruction, and the warning given by our Lord, and in humble dependence upon him for his assistance, I shall speak this morning of the Scribes and Pharisees of our times who rule the state. In discharging this duty, I shall keep my eyes upon the picture which is painted so faithfully and lifelike by the hand of the Saviour.

Allow me to describe them. They are intelligent and well-informed, and can never say, either before an earthly tribunal or at the bar of God, "We knew not of ourselves what was right." They are acquainted with the principles of the law of nations. They are proficient in the knowledge of Constitutional law. They are teachers of common law, and frame and execute statute law. They acknowledge that there is a just and impartial God, and are not altogether unacquainted with the law of Christian love and kindness. They claim for themselves the broadest freedom. Boastfully they tell us that they have received from the court of heaven the Magna Charta of human rights that was handed down through the clouds and amid the lightnings of Sinai, and given again by the Son of God on the Mount of Beatitudes while the glory of the Father shone around him. They tell us that from the Declaration of Independence and the Constitution they have obtained a guaranty of their political freedom, and from the Bible they derive their claim to all the blessings of religious liberty. With just pride they tell us that they are descended from the Pilgrims, who threw themselves upon the bosom of the treacherous sea and braved storms and tempests that they might find in a strange land and among savages free homes where they might build their altars that should blaze with acceptable sacrifice unto God. Yes! they boast that their fathers heroically turned away from the precious light of Eastern civilization and, taking their lamps with oil in their vessels, joyfully went forth to illuminate this land, that then dwelt in the darkness of the valley of the shadow of death. With hearts strengthened by faith they spread out their standard to the winds of heaven, near Plymouth Rock; and whether it was stiffened in the sleet and frosts of winter, or floated on the breeze of summer, it ever bore the motto, "Freedom to worship God."

But others, their fellow men, equal before the Almighty and made by Him of the same blood, and glowing with immortality, they doom to lifelong servitude and chains. Yes, they stand in the most sacred places on earth, and beneath the gaze of the piercing eye of Jehovah, the universal Father of all men, and declare that "the best possible condition of the Negro is slavery."

In the name of the Triune God I denounce the sentiment as unrighteous beyond measure, and the holy and the just of the whole earth say in regard to it, Anathema maranatha.

What is slavery? Too well do I know what it is. I will present to you a bird's eye view of it; and it shall be no fancy picture, but one that is sketched by painful experience. I was born among the cherished institutions of slavery. My earliest recollections of parents, friends, and the home of my childhood are clouded with its wrongs. The first sight that met my eyes was a Christian mother enslaved by professed Christians, but, thank God, now a saint in heaven.* The first sounds that startled my ear and sent a shudder through my soul were the cracking of the whip and the clanking of chains. These sad memories mar the beauties of my native shores and darken all the

---

*Garnet's mother was Henrietta Garnet. He was born a slave, at New Market, Kent County, Maryland, in 1815.

slaveland, which, but for the reign of despotism, had been a paradise. But those shores are fairer now. The mists have left my native valleys, and the clouds have rolled away from the hills, and Maryland, the unhonored grave of my fathers, is now the free home of their liberated and happier children.

Let us view this demon, which the people have worshipped as a God. Come forth, thou grim monster, that thou mayest be critically examined! There he stands. Behold him, one and all. Its work is to chattelize man; to hold property in human beings. Great God! I would as soon attempt to enslave Gabriel or Michael as to enslave a man made in the image of God, and for whom Christ died. Slavery is snatching man from the high place to which he was lifted by the hand of God, and dragging him down to the level of the brute creation, where he is made to be the companion of the horse and the fellow of the ox.

It tears the crown of glory from his head and as far as possible obliterates the image of God that is in him. Slavery preys upon man, and man only. A brute cannot be made a slave. Why? Because a brute has not reason, faith, nor an undying spirit, nor conscience. It does not look forward to the future with joy or fear, nor reflect upon the past with satisfaction or regret. But who in this vast assembly, who in all this broad land, will say that the poorest and most unhappy brother in chains and servitude has not every one of these high endowments? Who denies it? Is there one? If so, let him speak. There is not one; no, not one.

But slavery attempts to make a man a brute. It treats him as a beast. Its terrible work is not finished until the ruined victim of its lusts and pride and avarice and hatred is reduced so low that with tearful eyes and feeble voice he faintly cries, "I am happy and contented. I love this condition."

> *Proud Nimrod first the bloody chase began,*
> *A mighty hunter he; his prey was man.*

The caged lion may cease to roar, and try no longer the strength of the bars of his prison, and lie with his head between his mighty paws and snuff the polluted air as though he heeded not. But is he contented? Does he not instinctively long for the freedom of the forest and the plain? Yes, he is a lion still. Our poor and forlorn brother whom thou hast labeled "slave," is also a man. He may be unfortunate, weak, helpless and despised and hated; nevertheless he is a man. His God and thine has stamped on his forehead his title to his inalienable rights in characters that can be read by every intelligent being. Pitiless storms of outrage may have beaten upon his defenseless head, and he may have descended through ages of oppression; yet he is a man. God made him such, and his brother cannot unmake him. Woe, woe to him who attempts to commit the accursed crime.

Slavery commenced its dreadful work in kidnaping unoffending men in a foreign and distant land, and in piracy on the seas. The plunderers were not the followers of Mahomet, nor the devotees of Hinduism, nor benighted pagans, nor idolaters, but people called Christians, and thus the ruthless traders in the souls and bodies of men fastened upon Christianity a crime and stain at the sight of which it shudders and shrieks.

It is guilty of the most heinous iniquities ever perpetrated upon helpless women and innocent children. Go to the shores of the land of my forefathers, poor bleeding Africa, which, although she has been bereaved and robbed for centuries, is nevertheless beloved by all her worthy descendants wherever dispersed. Behold a single scene that there meets your eyes. Turn not away either from shame, pity or indifference, but look and see the beginning of this cherished and petted institution. Behold a hundred youthful mothers seated on the ground, dropping their tears upon the hot sands, and filling the air with their lamentations.

Why do they weep? Ah, Lord God, thou knowest! Their babes have been torn from their bosoms and cast upon the plains to die of hunger, or to be devoured by hyenas or jackals. The little innocents would die on the "middle passage,"* or suffocate between the decks of the floating slave pen, freighted and packed with unparalleled human woe, and the slavers in mercy have cast them out to perish on their native shores. Such is the beginning, and no less wicked is the end of that system which Scribes and Pharisees in the Church and the state pronounce to be just, humane, benevolent and Christian. If such are the deeds of mercy wrought by angels, then tell me what works of iniquity there remain for devils to do?

This commerce in human beings has been carried on until three hundred thousand have been dragged from their native land in a single year. While this foreign trade has been pursued, who can calculate the enormities and extent of the domestic traffic which has flourished in every slave State, while the whole country has been open to the hunters of men.

It is the highly concentrated essence of all conceivable wickedness. Theft, robbery, pollution, unbridled passion, incest, cruelty, cold-blooded murder, blasphemy, and defiance of the laws of God. It teaches children to disregard parental authority. It tears down the marriage altar and tramples its sacred ashes under its feet. It creates and nourishes polygamy. It feeds and pampers its hateful handmaid, prejudice.

It has divided our national councils. It has engendered deadly strife between brethren. It has wasted the treasure of the Commonwealth and the lives of thousands of brave men, and driven troops of helpless women and children into yawning tombs. It has caused the bloodiest civil war recorded in the book of time. It has shorn this nation of its locks of strength that was rising as a young lion in the Western world. It has offered us as a sacrifice to the jealousy and cupidity of tyrants, despots, and adventurers of foreign countries. It has opened a door through which a usurper, a perjured but powerful prince, might stealthily enter and build an empire on the golden borders of our south-western frontier, and which is but a steppingstone to fur-

---

*During the African slave trade the voyage from Africa to the Americas was popularly referred to as the "middle passage." Overcrowding caused widespread deaths among the slaves.

ther and unlimited conquests on this continent. It has desolated the fairest portions of our land, "until the wolf long since driven back by the march of civilization returns after the lapse of a hundred years and howls amidst its ruins."

It seals up the Bible and mutilates its sacred truths, and flies into the face of the Almighty, and impiously asks, "Who art thou that I should obey thee?" Such are the outlines of their fearful national sin; and yet the condition to which it reduces man, it is affirmed, is the best that can possibly be devised for him.

When inconsistencies similar in character, and no more glaring, passed beneath the eye of the Son of God, no wonder he broke forth in language of vehement denunciation. Ye Scribes, Pharisees, and hypocrites! Ye blind guides! Ye compass sea and land to make one proselyte, and when he is made ye make him twofold more the child of hell than yourselves. Ye are like unto whited sepulchers, which indeed appear beautiful without, but within are full of dead men's bones and all uncleanness!

Let us here take up the golden rule, and adopt the self-application mode of reasoning to those who hold these erroneous views. Come, gird up thy loins and answer like a man, if thou canst. Is slavery, as it is seen in its origin, continuance and end, the best possible condition for thee? Oh, no! Wilt thou bear that burden on thy shoulders, which thou wouldst lay upon thy fellow man? No. Wilt thou bear a part of it, or remove a little of its weight with one of thy fingers? The sharp and indignant answer is no, no! Then how, and when, and where, shall we apply to thee the golden rule, which says, "Therefore all things that ye would that others should do to you, do ye even so unto them, for this is the law of the prophets."

Let us have the testimony of the wise and great of ancient and modern times:

> Sages who wrote and warriors who bled.

Plato declared that "Slavery is a system of complete injustice."
Socrates wrote that "Slavery is a system of outrage and robbery."
Cyrus said, "To fight in order not to be a slave is noble."

If Cyrus had lived in our land a few years ago he would have been arrested for using incendiary language, and for inciting servile insurrection, and the royal fanatic would have been hanged on a gallows higher than Haman. But every man is fanatical when his soul is warmed by the generous fires of liberty. Is it then truly noble to fight in order not to be a slave? The Chief Magistrate of the nation, and our rulers, and all truly patriotic men think so; and so think legions of black men, who for a season were scorned and rejected, but who came quickly and cheerfully when they were at last invited, bearing a heavy burden of proscriptions upon their shoulders, and having faith in God, and in their generous fellow-countrymen, they went forth to fight a double battle. The foes of their country were before them, while the enemies of freedom and of their race surrounded them.

Augustine, Constantine, Ignatius, Polycarp, Maximus, and the most illustrious lights of the ancient church denounced the sin of slave-holding.

Thomas Jefferson said at a period of his life, when his judgment was matured, and his experience was ripe, "There is preparing, I hope, under the auspices of heaven, a way for a total emancipation."

The sainted Washington said, near the close of his mortal career, and when the light of eternity was beaming upon him, "It is among my first wishes to see some plan adopted by which slavery in this country shall be abolished by law. I know of but one way by which this can be done, and that is by legislative action, and so far as my vote can go, it shall not be wanting."

The other day, when the light of Liberty streamed through this marble pile, and the hearts of the noble band of patriotic statesmen leaped for joy, and this our national capital shook from foundation to dome with the shouts of a ransomed people, then methinks the spirits of Washington, Jefferson, the Jays, the Adamses, and Franklin, and Lafayette, and Giddings, and Lovejoy, and those of all the mighty, and glorious dead, remembered by history, because they were faithful to truth, justice, and liberty, were hovering over the august assembly. Though unseen by mortal eyes, doubtless they joined the angelic choir, and said, Amen.

Pope Leo X testifies, "That not only does the Christian religion, but nature herself, cry out against a state of slavery."

Patrick Henry said, "We should transmit to posterity our abhorrence of slavery." So also thought the Thirty-eighth Congress.

Lafayette proclaimed these words: "Slavery is a dark spot on the face of the nation." God be praised, that stain will soon be wiped out.

Jonathan Edwards declared "that to hold a man in slavery is to be every day guilty of robbery, or of man stealing."

Rev. Dr. William Ellery Channing, in a *Letter on the Annexation of Texas* in 1837, writes as follows:

"The evil of slavery speaks for itself. To state is to condemn the institution. The choice which every freeman makes of death for his child and for every thing he loves in preference to slavery, shows what it is. The single consideration that by slavery one human being is placed powerless and defenceless in the hands of another to be driven to whatever labor that other may impose, to suffer whatever punishment he may inflict, to live as his tool, the instrument of his pleasure, this is all that is needed to satisfy such as know the human heart and its unfitness for irresponsible power, that of all conditions slavery is the most hostile to the dignity, self-respect, improvement, rights, and happiness of human beings. . . . Every principle of our government and religion condemns slavery. The spirit of our age condemns it. . . . Is there an age in which a free and Christian people shall deliberately resolve to extend and perpetuate the evil? In so doing we cut ourselves off from the communion of nations; we sink below the civilization of our age; we invite the scorn, indignation, and abhorrence of the world."

Moses, the greatest of all lawgivers and legislators, said, while his face was yet radiant with the light of Sinai: "Whoso stealeth a man, and selleth him, or if he be found in his hand, he shall surely be put to death." The destroying angel has gone forth through his land to execute the fearful penalties of God's broken law.

The Representatives of the nation have bowed with reverence to the Divine edict, and laid the axe at the root of the tree, and thus saved succeeding generations from the guilt of oppression, and from the wrath of God.

Statesmen, Jurists, and Philosophers, most renowned for learning, and most profound in every department of science and literature, have testified against slavery. While oratory has brought its costliest, golden treasures, and laid them on the altar of God and of freedom, it has aimed its fiercest lightning and loudest thunder at the strongholds of tyranny, injustice, and despotism.

From the days of Balak to those of Isaiah and Jeremiah, up to the times of Paul, and through every age of the Christian Church, the sons of thunder have denounced the abominable thing. The heroes who stood in the shining ranks of the hosts of the friends of human progress, from Cicero to Chatham, and Burke, Sharp, Wilberforce, and Thomas Clarkson, and Curran, assaulted the citadel of despotism. The orators and statesmen of our own land, whether they belonged to the past, or to the present age, will live and shine in the annals of history, in proportion as they have dedicated their genius and talents to the defence of Justice and man's God-given rights.

All the poets who live in sacred and profane history have charmed the world with their most enchanting strains, when they have tuned their lyres to the praise of Liberty. When the Muses can no longer decorate her altars with their garlands, then they hang their harps upon the willows and weep.

From Moses to Terrence and Homer, from thence to Milton and Cowper, Thomson and Thomas Campbell, and on to the days of our own bards, our Bryants, Longfellows, Whittiers, Morrises, and Bokers, all have presented their best gifts to the interests and rights of man.

Every good principle and every great and noble power have been made the subject of the inspired verse and the songs of poets. But who of them has attempted to immortalize slavery? You will search in vain the annals of the world to find an instance. Should any attempt the sacrilegious work, his genius would fall to the earth as if smitten by the lightning of heaven. Should he lift his hand to write a line in its praise, or defense, the ink would freeze on the point of his pen.

Could we array in one line, representative of all the families of men, beginning with those lowest in the scale of being, and should we put to them the question, Is it right and desirable that you should be reduced to the condition of slaves, to be registered with chattels, to have your persons and your lives and the products of your labor subjected to the will and the interests of others? Is it right and just that the persons of your wives and children should be at the disposal of others and be yielded to them for the purpose of pampering their lusts and greed of gain? Is it right to lay heavy burdens on other men's shoulders which you would not remove with one of your fingers? From the rude savage and barbarian the negative response would come, increasing in power and significance as it rolled up the line. And when those should reply, whose minds and hearts are illuminated with the highest civilization and with the spirit of Christianity, the answer deep-toned and prolonged would thunder forth, no, no!

With all the moral attributes of God on our side, cheered as we are by the voices of universal human nature—in view of the best interests of the present and future generations—animated with the noble desire to furnish the nations of the earth with a worthy example, let the verdict of death which has been brought in against slavery by the Thirty-eighth Congress be affirmed and executed by the people. Let the gigantic monster perish. Yes, perish now and perish forever!

> Down let the shrine of Moloch sink,
>   And leave no traces where it stood;
> No longer let its idol drink,
>   His daily cup of human blood.
> But rear another altar there,
>   To truth, and love, and mercy given,
> And freedom's gift and freedom's prayer,
>   Shall call an answer down from heaven.

It is often asked when and where will the demands of the reformers of this and coming ages end? It is a fair question, and I will answer.

When all unjust and heavy burdens shall be removed from every man in the land. When all invidious and proscriptive distinctions shall be blotted out from our laws, whether they be constitutional, statute or municipal laws. When emancipation shall be followed by enfranchisement, and all men holding allegiance to the government shall enjoy every right of American citizenship. When our brave and gallant soldiers shall have justice done unto them. When the men who endure the sufferings and perils of the battlefield in the defense of their country, and in order to keep our rulers in their places, shall enjoy the well-earned privilege of voting for them. When in the army and navy, and in every legitimate and honorable occupation, promotion shall smile upon merit without the slightest regard to the complexion of a man's face. When there shall be no more class legislation and no more trouble concerning the black man and his rights than there is in regard to other American citizens. When, in every respect, he shall be equal before the law, and shall be left to make his own way in the social walks of life.

We ask, and only ask, that when our poor, frail barks are launched on life's ocean,

> Bound on a voyage of awful length
>   And dangers little known,

that, in common with others, we may be furnished with rudder, helm and sails and charts and compass. Give us good pilots to conduct us to the open seas; lift no false lights along the dangerous coasts, and if it shall please God to send us propitious winds or fearful gales, we shall survive or perish as our energies or neglect shall determine. We ask no special favors, but we plead for justice. While we scorn unmanly dependence; in the name of God, the universal Father, we demand the right to live and labor and enjoy the fruits of our toil. The good work which God has assigned for the ages to come will be finished when our national literature shall be so purified as to reflect a faithful and a just light upon the character and social habits of our race, and the brush and pencil and chisel and lyre of art shall refuse to lend their aid to scoff at the afflictions of the poor or to caricature or ridicule a long-suffering people. When caste and prejudice in Christian churches shall be utterly destroyed and shall be regarded as totally unworthy of Christians, and at variance with the principles of the Gospel. When the blessings of the Christian religion and of sound religious education shall be freely offered to all, then, and not till then, shall the effectual labors of God's people and God's instruments cease.

If slavery has been destroyed merely from *necessity*,* let every class be enfranchised at the dictation of *justice.* Then we shall have a Constitution that shall be reverenced by all, rulers who shall be honored and revered, and a Union that shall be sincerely loved by a brave and patriotic people, and which can never be severed.

Great sacrifices have been made by the people; yet, greater still are demanded ere atonement can be made for our national sins. Eternal justice holds heavy mortgages against us and will require the payment of the last farthing. We have involved ourselves in the sin of unrighteous gain, stimulated by luxury and pride and the love of power and oppression; and prosperity and peace can be purchased only by blood and with tears of repentance. We have paid some of the fearful installments, but there are other heavy obligations to be met.

The great day of the nation's judgment has come, and who shall be able to stand? Even we, whose ancestors have suffered the afflictions which are inseparable from a condition of slavery, for the period of two centuries and a half, now pity our land and weep with those who weep.

Upon the total and complete destruction of this accursed sin depends the safety and perpetuity of our Republic and its excellent institutions.

Let slavery die. It has had a long and fair trial. God himself has pleaded against it. The enlightened nations of the earth have condemned it. Its death warrant is signed by God and man. Do not commute its sentence. Give it no respite, but let it be ignominiously executed.

Honorable Senators and Representatives, illustrious rulers of this great nation, I cannot refrain this day from invoking upon you, in God's name,

---

*In issuing the Emancipation Proclamation, on January 1, 1863, President Lincoln described it "as a fit and necessary war measure for suppressing said rebellion." See John Nicolay and John Hay, eds., *Complete Works of Abraham Lincoln,* vol. 8 (New York: Tandy, 1894/1905), 162–63.

the blessings of millions who were ready to perish, but to whom a new and better life has been opened by your humanity, justice and patriotism. You have said, "Let the Constitution of the country be so amended that slavery and involuntary servitude shall no longer exist in the United States, except in punishment for crime." Surely, an act so sublime could not escape divine notice; and doubtless the deed has been recorded in the archives of heaven. Volumes may be appropriated to your praise and renown in the history of the world. Genius and art may perpetuate the glorious act on canvas and in marble, but certain and more lasting monuments in commemoration of your decision are already erected in the hearts and memories of a grateful people.

The nation has begun its exodus from worse than Egyptian bondage; and I beseech you that you say to the people that they go forward. With the assurance of God's favor in all things done in obedience to his righteous will, and guided by day and by night by the pillars of cloud and fire, let us not pause until we have reached the other and safe side of the stormy and crimson sea. Let freemen and patriots mete out complete and equal justice to all men and thus prove to mankind the superiority of our democratic, republican government.

Favored men, and honored of God as his instruments, speedily finish the work which he has given you to do. Emancipate, enfranchise, educate, and give the blessings of the gospel to every American citizen.

> Hear ye not how, from all high points of Time,—
>   From peak to peak adown the mighty chain
> That links the ages—echoing sublime
>   A Voice Almighty—leaps one grand refrain.
> Wakening the generations with a shout,
> And trumpet—call of thunder—Come ye out!
>
> Out from old forms and dead idolatries;
>   From fading myths and superstitious dreams:
> From Pharisaic rituals and lies,
>   And all the bondage of the life that seems!
> Out—on the pilgrim path, of heroes trod,
> Over earth's wastes, to reach forth after God!
>
> The Lord hath bowed his heaven, and come down!
>   Now, in this latter century of time,
> Once more his tent is pitched on Sinai's crown!
>   Once more in clouds must Faith to meet him climb!
> Once more his thunder crashes on our doubt
> And fear and sin—"My people! come ye out!"
>
> From false ambitions and base luxuries;
>   From puny aims and indolent self-ends;
> From cant of faith, and shams of liberties,
>   And mist of ill that Truth's pure day-beam bends:

Out, from all darkness of the Egypt-land,
Into my sun-blaze on the desert sand!

*   *   *

Show us our Aaron, with his rod in flower!
* Our Miriam, with her timbrel-soul in tune!*
And call some Joshua, in the Spirit's power,
* To poise our sun of strength at point of noon!*
*   God of our fathers! over sand and sea,*
*   Still keep our struggling footsteps close to thee!**

Then before us a path of prosperity will open, and upon us will descend the mercies and favors of God. Then shall the people of other countries, who are standing tiptoe on the shores of every ocean, earnestly looking to see the end of this amazing conflict, behold a Republic that is sufficiently strong to outlive the ruin and desolations of civil war, having the magnanimity to do justice to the poorest and weakest of her citizens. Thus shall we give to the world the form of a model Republic, founded on the principles of justice and humanity and Christianity, in which the burdens of war and the blessings of peace are equally borne and enjoyed by all.■

77 COLORED MEN STANDING IN THE WAY OF THEIR OWN RACE

James Lynch

 At the May 1865 meeting of the Young Men's Literary and Debating Society of Philadelphia, James Lynch delivered the following brief but significant speech. Lynch was born in Baltimore on January 8, 1839, and was educated there. In 1858 he joined the Presbyterian Church of New York but soon thereafter was accepted by the African Methodist Episcopal Conference in Indiana. In 1863 he went to South Carolina as one of the first A.M.E. missionaries to the freedmen and women. From 1866 to June 15, 1867, Lynch was editor of the Christian Recorder *in Philadelphia but resigned his editorship in 1867 to organize for the Republicans in Mississippi. He "was widely regarded as the greatest orator" of the Reconstruction stump speakers, according to Eric Foner, "and his eloquence held gatherings of 3,000 freedmen or more*

*Atlantic Monthly (1862).

*spellbound for hours at a time" (*Reconstruction, *286). Later he was
with the Freedmen's Bureau in Mississippi and in 1871 was elected secretary of state. He died on December 18, 1872.*

Lynch's speech as presented here is taken from the Christian Recorder, *May 13, 1865. In it, he confronts lingering questions of color
prejudice within the African American community and argues that racial unity is the key to progress in the postwar era. For more information
on Lynch, see Eric Foner,* Reconstruction: America's Unfinished Revolution *(New York: Harper and Row, 1988).*

It is strange, but true, that we have such men among us. First on the list
stand those who set no value on the ability of their race and adopt the
opinions respecting them that prejudiced white men hold. Among these we
find those who prefer white men as religious instructors, as teachers, physicians and lawyers, because they are white. They are studious in disparaging
their own color, and paying homage to a supposed native superiority of the
whites.

Then comes another class, who are always in the market for the white
man's purchase. If they are flattered, feted or pecuniarily rewarded, they will
kiss the hand of the oppressor and ally themselves with the enemies or dis-
paragers of their race.

Another class is found in those who pride themselves on the color of
their skins, feeling that a light complexion imparts superiority. It is questionable whether there is in existence a more contemptible feeling than this,
for while it assumes superiority over the darker skin, it confesses inferiority
to the lighter, or white, person. Certainly if A is superior and B is his inferior, then a white man, who has nothing else but white blood in his veins
must be superior to A, and A is the inferior.*

Those colored persons who hold this idea are holding to that which has
been, and to some degree still is, the infamy of the nation, on which God is
writing, with the iron pen of providence, in letters of blood, a death sentence.
They are opposing themselves to God and the defenders of humanity.

Still another class are those who succumb to the prejudices of white
men, and while they are loudmouthed for their right to ride in railroad cars
and visit public places of instruction or amusement, they will not shave colored men in their barber shops nor accommodate them with a meal in their
restaurants. The plea is that they will "lose customers." Well, white men
can urge with equal force the same plea; and there is no reason why white

*Lynch's discussion is reminiscent of Lincoln's attack on slavery in 1854, in which
he said: "If A can prove, however conclusively, that he may of right enslave B, why may
not B snatch the same argument and prove equally that he may enslave A? You say A is
white and B is black. It is color, then; the lighter having the right to enslave the darker?
Take care. By this rule you are to be slave to the first man you meet with a fairer skin
than your own." See "Fragment on Slavery," in Abraham Lincoln, *Speeches and Writings,
1832–1858,* ed. Don Fehrenbach (New York: Library of America, 1985), 303.

men shall be expected to sacrifice more for colored men than colored men will for themselves.

It is cheering to think that the number of colored men who stand in the way of their race are in the minority by great odds. Still their existence is to be deplored, and if they be dragged forth into burning sunlight of public opinion their baleful and miasmatic influence will soon be dried up by its heat. We echo Stanford's thrilling word, in reference to our people, "Action!" We want a healthy public sentiment among us, enlightened and energetic, that like an ever-flowing current, will sweep away the Tories and the Judases from their footings.■

78 ADVICE TO EX-SLAVES

Martin Robinson Delany

Martin Robinson Delany (1812–1885) was born in Charles Town, Virginia (now West Virginia), the grandson of slaves and the son of free blacks. Delany received his first instruction in reading from ped- dlers of books, continued his studies under the Reverend Lewis Wood- son in Pittsburgh, and went on to become a doctor, despite being forced to leave Harvard Medical School after one semester because of the pro- tests of white students. His book, The Condition, Elevation, Emigration, and Destiny of the Colored People of the United States, Politically Con- sidered, *published in Philadelphia in 1852 at his own expense, is a re- markable source of information about the free black population in the antebellum North and contains important suggestions for improvement of their conditions. One sentence in the appendix of his book is the most quoted in the work: "We are a nation within a nation, as the Poles in Russia, the Hungarians in Austria, the Welsh, Irish and Scotch in the British dominions." Therefore Delany advocated founding a new nation on the eastern coast of Africa "for the settlement of colored adventurers from the United States and elsewhere." In 1859 Delany traveled in Af- rica, seeking places to which African Americans might emigrate. He re- turned to the United States in 1861, six weeks after the Civil War had broken out. He was one of seventy-five black officers in the Union army.*

In February 1865, Martin R. Delany was commissioned as major of infantry and ordered to recruit an "armée d'Afrique" in South Carolina. But the end of the war cut short the project. Delany, however, continued to work in the South, serving for three years in the Freedmen's Bureau.

*In this capacity, he delivered a speech to a meeting of freedmen and
women at St. Helena Island, South Carolina, in July 1865. No report of
the speech appeared in the contemporary press, but an account is in the
files of the Freedmen's Bureau in the National Archives. Evidently the bureau heads feared Delany's militancy and sent a lieutenant in the Union
army to report back what he had told the freedmen and women in his address. As the comments of the lieutenant reveal, Delany's advice to the
ex-slaves to stand up for full freedom and resist reenslavement by arms
if necessary, frightened the whites who were present and, indeed, the
officer himself. Delany seeks to instill in the freedmen and women a
sense of their own worth and prospects, to caution against peonage and
deceitful white "benefactors," and to build support for the educational
and agricultural programs of the Freedmen's Bureau.*

*Delany's speech is published below as it was reported in the letter of
Lieutenant Edward M. Stoeber. The entire letter is included to give the
reader a picture of the setting and the reactions to the speech. We are indebted to William Loren Katz for calling this document to our attention.*

*For more information, see Nell Irvin Painter, "Martin R. Delany:
Elitism and Black Nationalism," in Leon Litwack and August Meier,
eds.,* Black Leaders of the Nineteenth Century *(Urbana: University of Illinois Press, 1988); and Dorothy Sterling,* The Making of an Afro-American: Martin Robinson Delany *(Garden City, N.Y.: Doubleday, 1971).*

Headquarters, Assistant Commissioner
Bureau Refugees, Freedmen and Abandoned Lands
South Carolina, Georgia and Florida.
Beaufort, S.C., July 24th, 1865.

Br[eve]t Maj. S. M. Taylor
Asst. Adj't Gen'l.

Major:
   In obedience to your request, I proceeded to St. Helena Island, yesterday morning for the purpose of listening to the public delivery of a
lecture by Major Delany 104th Ne[gro] S.C. Troops.
   I was accompanied by Lieut. A. Whyte jr 128th Ne[gro] S.C. Troops,
Com[an]d'g Post.
   The meeting was held near "Brick Church," the congregation numbering from 500 to 600.
   As introduction Maj. Delany made them acquainted with the fact,
that slavery is absolutely abolished, throwing thunders of damnations
and maledictions on all the former slaveowners and people of the
South, and almost condemned their souls to hell. He says "It was
only a War policy of the Government, to declare the slaves of the

South free, knowing that the whole power of the South, laid in the possession of the Slaves. But I want you to understand, that we would not have become free, had we not armed ourselves and fought out our independence" (this he repeated twice). He further says, "If I had been a slave, I would have been most troublesome and not to be conquered by any threat or punishment. I would not have worked, and no one would have dared to come near me, I would have struggled for life or death, and would have thrown fire and sword between them.

"I know *you* have been good, only too good. I was told by a friend of mine that when owned by a man and put to work on the field, he laid quietly down, and just looked out for the overseer to come along, when he pretended to work very hard. But he confessed to me, that he never had done a fair day's work for his master. And so he was right, so I would have done the same, and all of you ought to have done the same.

"People say that you are too lazy to work, that you have no intelligence to get on for yourselves, without being guided and driven to the work by overseers. I say it is a lie, and a blasphemous lie, and I will prove it to be so.

"I am going to tell you now, *what* you are worth. As you know Christopher Columbus landed here in 1492. They came here only for the purpose to dig gold, gather precious pearls, diamonds and all sorts of jewels, only for the proud Aristocracy of White Spaniards and Portuguese, to adorn their persons, to have brooches for their breasts, earrings for their ears, Bracelets for their ankles and rings for their limbs and fingers. They found here (red men) Indians whom they obliged to dig and work and slave for them—but they found out that they died away too fast and cannot stand the work. In course of time they had taken some blacks (Africans) along with them and put *them* to work— they could not stand it—and yet the Whites say they are superior to our race, though they could not stand it. (At the present day in some of the Eastern parts of Spain, the Spaniard there (having been once conquered by the black race) have black eyes, black hair, black complexion. They have Negro blood in them!!) The work was so profitable which those poor blacks did, that in the year 1502 Charles the V. gave permission to import into America yearly 4,000 blacks. The profit of these sales was so immense, that afterwards even the Virgin Queen of England and James the II. took part in the Slave trade and were accumulating great wealth for the Treasury of the Government. And so you *always* have been the means of riches.

"I tell you I have been all over Africa (I was born there)* and I tell you (as I told to the Geographical Faculty of London) that those

---

*Delany was born in northern Virginia in 1812. He may have referred to his parents, who traced their ancestry to African chieftains.

people there, are a well-driving class of cultivators, and I never saw or heard of one of our brethren there to travel without taking seeds with him as much as he can carry and to sow it wherever he goes to, or to exchange it with his brethren.

"So you ought further to know, that all the spices, cotton, rice, and coffee has only been brought over by *you*, from the land of our brethren.

"Your masters who lived in opulence, kept you to hard work by some contemptible being called overseer—who chastised and beat you whenever he pleased—while your master lived in some Northern town or in Europe to squander away the wealth only you acquired for him. He never earned a single Dollar in his life. You men and women, every one of you around me, made thousands and thousands of dollars for your master. Only you were the means for your masters to lead the ideal and inglorious life, and to give his children the education, which he denied to you, for fear you may awake to conscience.* If I look around me, I tell you all the houses of this Island and in Beaufort, they are all familiar to my eye, they are the same structures which I have met with in Africa. They have all been made by the Negroes, you can see it by such exteriors.

"I tell you they (white man) cannot teach you anything, and they could not make them because they have not the brain to do it. (after a pause) At least I mean the Southern people; Oh the Yankees they are smart. Now tell me from all you have heard from me, are you not worth anything? Are you those men whom they think, God only created as a curse and for a slave? Whom they do not consider their equals? As I said before the Yankees are smart; there are good ones and bad ones. The good ones, if they are good they are very good, if they are bad, they are very bad. But the worst and most contemptible, and even worse than even your masters were, are those Yankees, who hired themselves as *overseers.*

"Believe not in these School teachers, Emissaries, Ministers, and agents, because they never tell you the truth, and I particularly warn you against those Cotton Agents, who come honey mouthed unto you, their only intent being to make profit by your inexperience.

"If there is a man who comes to you, who will meddle with your affairs, send him to one of your more enlightened brothers, who shall ask him who he is, what business he seeks with you, etc.

Believe none but those Agents who are sent out by Government, to enlighten and guide you. I am an officer in the service of the U.S. Government, and ordered to aid Gen'l Saxton, who has been only lately appointed Asst Comr from South Carolina. So is Gen'l Wild Asst Comr for Georgia.

---

*The word was probably "consciousness."

"When Chief Justice Chase* was down here to speak to you, some of those malicious and abominable New York papers derived from it that he only seeks to be elected by you as President. I have no such ambition, I let them have for a President a white or a black one. I don't care who it be—it may be who has a mind to. I shall not be intimidated whether by threats or imprisonment, and no power will keep me from telling you the truth. So I expressed myself even at Charleston, the hotbed of those scoundrels, your old masters, without fear or reluctance.

"So I will come to the main purpose for which I have come to see you. As before the whole South depended upon you, now the *whole country* will depend upon you. I give you an advice how to get along. Get up a community and get all the lands you can—if you cannot get any singly.

"Grow as much vegetables, etc, as you want for your families; on the other part of the land you cultivate Rice and Cotton. Now for instance 1. Acre will grow a crop of Cotton of $90—now a land with 10 Acres will bring $900 every year: if you cannot get the land all yourself,—the community can, and so you can divide the profit. There is Tobacco for instance (Virginia is the great place for Tobacco). There are whole squares at Dublin and Liverpool named after some place of Tobacco notoriety, so you see of what enormous value your labor was to the benefits of your masters. Now you understand that I want you to be the producers of this country. It is the wish of the Government for you to be so. We will send friends to you, who will further instruct you how to come to the end of our wishes. You see that by so adhering to our views, you will become a wealthy and powerful population.

"Now I look around me and notice a man, barefooted, covered with rags and dirt. Now I ask, what is that man doing, for whom is he working. I hear that he works for that and that farmer for 30 cents a day. I tell you that must not be. That would be cursed slavery over again. I will not have it, the Government will not have it, and the Government shall hear about it. I will tell the Government. I tell you slavery is over, and shall never return again. We have now 200,000 of our men well drilled in arms and used to War fare and I tell you it is with you and them that slavery shall not come back again, if you are determined it will not return again.

"Now go to work, and in a short time I will see you again, and other friends will come to show you how to begin.—Have your fields

---

*Chief Justice of the Supreme Court Salmon Portland Chase (1808–1873) began an extended southern tour in May 1865 to investigate conditions in the states lately in rebellion. At Charleston, South Carolina, and elsewhere he addressed audiences of blacks, advocating black suffrage.

in good order and well tilled and planted, and when I pass the fields and see a land well planted and well cared for, then I may be sure from the look of it, that it belongs to a free Negro, and when I see a field thinly planted and little cared for, then I may think it belongs to some man who works it with slaves. The Government decided that you shall [keep] one third of the produce of the crops, from your employer, so if he makes $3—you will have to get $1.—out of it for your labor.

The other day some plantation owners in Virginia and Maryland offered $5.—a month for your labor, but it was indignantly rejected by Gen'l Howard, the Commissioner for the Government."*

These are expressions, as far as I can remember, without having made notes at the time.

The excitement with the congregation was immense, groups were formed talking over what they have heard, and ever and anon cheers were given to some particular sentence of the speech.

I afterwards mingled with several groups, to hear their opinions. Some used violent language, "saying they would get rid of the Yankee employer."—"That is the only man who ever told them the truth." "That now those men have to work themselves or starve or leave the country, we will not work for them any more."

Some Whites were present, and listened with horror depicted in their faces to the whole performance. Some said, "What shall become of us now?" And if such a speech should be again given to those men, there will be open rebellion.

Major Delany was afterwards corrected by Mr. Town the Superintendent at that place, to the effect, that the pay of labourers on this Island is not 30 cents a day, but 30 cents a task, and that a man can easily make from 75 to 90 cents a day. Major Delany then corrected himself accordingly, saying that he must be misinformed.

My opinion of the whole affair is that Major Delany is a thorough hater of the white race and excites the colored people unnecessarily. He even tries to injure the magnanimous conduct of the Government towards them, either intentionally or through want of knowledge.

He tells them to remember "that they would not have become *free,* had they not *armed themselves* and *fought for their independence.* This is a falsehood and a misrepresentation.—Our President Abraham Lincoln declared the colored race free, before there was even an idea of arming colored men.[†] This is decidedly calculated to create bad feeling against the Government.

---

*Oliver Otis Howard (1830–1909), brigadier general in the Union army, was appointed on May 12, 1865, by President Johnson to be commissioner of the newly established Bureau of Refugees, Freedmen, and Abandoned Lands (Freedmen's Bureau), for which position he had been selected by Lincoln.

†This statement, of course, is inaccurate. Blacks sought to enlist in the Union army as soon as the war started but were rejected. The enlistment of African American troops

By giving them some historical facts and telling them that neither Indians nor Whites could stand the work, in this country, he wants to impress them (the colored men) with the idea that he in fact is not only a superior, in a physical view, but also in intelligence.—He says, "believe none of those ministers, schoolteachers, Emissaries, because they never tell you the truth." It is only to bring distrust against all, and gives them to understand that they shall believe men of their own race. He openly acts and speaks contrary to the policy of the Government, advising them not to work for any man, but for themselves.

The intention of our Government, that all the men should be employed by their former masters, as far as possible, and contracts made between as superintended by some Officer empowered by the Government.

He says it would be old slavery over again, if a man should work for an employer, and *that* it must not be. Does he not give a hint of what they should do by his utterings "that if he had been a slave etc?; or by giving narrative of the slave who did not work for his master?—further as he says: "that a field should show by its appearance by whom and for whom it is worked?"

The mention of having two hundred thousand men well drilled in arms:—does he not hint to them what to do?; if they should be compelled to work for employers?

In my opinion of this discourse he was trying to encourage them to break the peace of society and force their way by insurrection to a position he is ambitious they should attain to.

I am Major,
Very Respectfully,
Your obedient servant,
(Sgd) Edward M. Stoeber
1st Lieut 1014th U.S.C.T.

A true Copy
(Sgd) Edward M. Stoeber
1st Lieut 104th U.S.C.T.■

in the Union army began in late 1862 before Lincoln issued the Emancipation Proclamation.

79 AN APPEAL FOR AID TO THE FREEDMEN

J. Sella Martin

The Reverend J. Sella Martin (1832–1876) has long been recognized as "one of the most eloquent and able platform orators of the antebellum period" (John E. Bruce). Martin was born into slavery in Charlotte, North Carolina, and sold eight times while still a child. After his escape in 1856, he entered the ministry. He became pastor of Boston's First Independent Baptist Church on Joy Street, such a regular site of antislavery and black community meetings that it became known as the "Abolition Church." Martin was a nationally renowned antislavery speaker who advocated both slave insurrections and, until the Civil War, emigration to Africa in response to intractable American racism. Breaking with the strict Garrisonian line, Martin was active in politics. In January 1870, he became editor of New Era, a Washington-based weekly journal "for Colored America," soon purchased by Frederick Douglass. Martin committed suicide in 1876.

The following speech text, partly in summary form, of an address delivered in Aberdeen, Scotland, appeared in the New Orleans Tribune (the first black daily newspaper in the United States) of November 12, 1865. After the Civil War, Martin, acting as an agent for the American Missionary Association, made two trips to Britain, where he gained several thousand dollars in contributions to support the freedpeople. In this speech, Martin seeks to impress upon his Scottish audience that they, having supported abolition, have a duty to support the freedpeople and to prove doubting Americans wrong.

ABOUT THE time your Chairman was in the United States I was a slave. Ten years ago I was a slave in the Southern States, with very little hopes of gaining my freedom, and with no hope at all of seeing within so short a period as ten years my whole race redeemed and disenthralled from bondage. I had no hope of it; and it is now almost too glorious for me to credit it when I set to reflecting upon it. I was here four years ago during the American war, and had I then come to Aberdeen I must have spoken to you of the almost unparalleled tyranny of the slave-holders and the altogether unparalleled sufferings of the slaves. I come to-night to tell you a different tale from what I had to tell then—to speak in a different strain from that. I cannot but be grateful for the sympathy we have before obtained from Scotland and Scotchmen in the cause of the slave, but I do not come now to ask you to exercise your moral sympathy; I come to ask you to recognize the answer to your own prayers—the legitimate result of the moral sympathy which you have been exercising on the side of the slave. Hitherto you have been speaking to the American people and with a sincerity they could not understand sometimes, and with a severity that made them wince—now we ask you to show proof by some practical demonstration that your speaking was not cant and that your addresses to the United States carried along with them the recognition of duty—that you were ready to help them out of the difficulties that might attend the doing of their duty on the part of the people of the United States.

I ask your sympathy then. I ask your money now, to enable the American people to meet those difficulties that are the legitimate outgrowth of the system. Mr. Martin then went on to say that there are those out of whom slavery has crushed all vitality. The average of life on the cotton plantations has never been more than nine years, seldom more than seven. Disease, neglect, and want of food, make the percentage unable to work, very large. Add to this the fact, that slavery is not an educator for any good thing—it does not foster a physical frame, still less give good intellectual, moral, or spiritual training.

Under it falsehood, dishonesty, lack of purity, and of religious feeling are fostered; and all these things stand in the way and form serious difficulties. With all this before you, I am ready (said the speaker), to answer the question—why do not the American people meet their own responsibilities—the effects of their own sin? The Americans are like every other people. There are many good people, some active people, and a great many indifferent people among them. And then it must not be forgotten that, in addition to the freed negroes, there are four millions of white men, more degraded, more brutal than even they, who, when the war began, were thrown upon the charge of the Northern people. In their aid the people have been laboring, and it is marvellous the exertions that have been made for these two classes, considering the responsibilities of the war and the ill-feeling that was engendered by it. Mr. Martin then entered at some length into the various objections urged both in this country and in America (for they all go the same around) such as that the negro is an inferior being, that he is lazy, and content with his lot as a slave, &c. As to his inferiority, he had never heard of a monkey that could speak or a negro who could not—when that had been seen, he would give in on that point. (Applause.)

But even granting that we were inferior, that is no reason why he should be neglected, but indeed an argument to the contrary. If an inferior race are to be enslaved, it means—carrying the argument to its legitimate issues,—that the superior in every class and clime would enslave the inferior till we might have all the archangels slaveholders. Then as to his being lazy and contented with his lot, the negro certainly did not show that when he left the surety of the plantation for the hard work and risks of the army. But it was the old slaveholding argument—to say at one moment that the slave if free would not work, and in the next breath declare that if free he would take the bread out of the poor Irishman's mouth. (Laughter.) Well, if able to take bread out of anybody's mouth, it was likely he would be able to put it into his own. Mr. Martin, in conclusion, forcibly urged the necessity of aid being given immediately. The South is exhausted, and will take time to recover, and the pressure of winter is coming on, so that if we are to discuss general questions affecting the negro in place of supplying his want of food and clothing, in face of the severe weather, this discussion will have to go on over his starved corpse.■

80 DELIVER US FROM SUCH A MOSES

Lewis Hayden

On October 24, 1864, Andrew Johnson, addressing the black population of Nashville, denounced slavery and the "damnable aristocracy" that had profited from human bondage, and expressed the belief that only local men, white and black, should have a voice in the reconstruction of the seceded states. He ventured the hope that, "as in the days of old," a Moses might arise "to lead them safely to their Promised Land of freedom and happiness." The audience thereupon cried, "You are our Moses!" Johnson responded: "Humble and unworthy as I am, if no better shall be found, I will indeed be your Moses, and lead you through the Red Sea of war and bondage to a fairer future of liberty and peace." But when Lewis Hayden visited the South to encourage freedmen to join the Masonic Order, he found the man who had promised to become a new "Moses" was instrumental in assisting the former slaveholders to return the freedpersons to a status resembling slavery. In a bitter attack on President Johnson before the Prince Hall Grand Lodge of Free and Accepted Masons in Boston, of which he was Grand Master, on December 27, 1865, Hayden called for deliverance of his people from the policies of Andrew Johnson.

Born in slavery, Lewis Hayden watched as the members of his family were separated and sold and his mother driven to madness. Sold twice at auction himself, Hayden was thirty-three years old and married by the time he managed to escape from slavery. He had taught himself to read by painfully struggling through discarded newspapers and the Bible. In a dramatic flight in a hack with his wife and son, he fled from Kentucky to Canada; later he moved to Detroit, where he built a church and school. Finally he moved to Boston, where he became a leading figure in the black community and established a clothing store. When he died, he left an estate of five thousand dollars, which went to establish a scholar-

ship fund for black medical students at Harvard Medical School. During his life, Hayden put much of the profit from his clothing store into the abolition movement and also helped raise funds for John Brown's attack at Harper's Ferry.

The text below is from a lengthy speech by Hayden published as a pamphlet under the title "Address before Prince Hall Grand Lodge of Free and Accepted Masons of the State of Massachusetts, at the Festival of St. John the Evangelist, December 27, 1865, by Lewis Hayden, Grand Master" *(Boston, 1866), 8–10.*

IN EACH OF THE PLACES I visited, there is evidently a deep and unalterable purpose in the hearts of the old oppressors to blast, or at least to crush out, the rising hopes and dawning prospects of their late bondmen. I rejoice, on the other hand, to be able to say that there is among our people that unwavering trust in God, and that abiding faith in the justice of their cause, which enable them to look to the future, not only with hope and confidence, but with exultation, feeling that

> *Truth, crushed to earth, shall rise again;*
> *The eternal years of God are hers;*
> *But Error wounded, writhes in pain,*
> *And dies among his worshipers.*

This, let me be understood, is the feeling of our people in the cities. With the dwellers in the country, it is different. Away from the cities and the seaboard, the condition of the colored man is deplorable enough today. Lacking the intelligence and opportunities of the freemen in the city—never having enjoyed the same advantages—he is still almost completely at the mercy of his old master. If the latter treats him kindly, it is well; but if ill-used and oppressed, in nine cases out of ten he has no remedy. There is no power under heaven to which he can appeal for redress. The United States Army can do nothing for him, for it has gone. If an agent of the Freedmen's Bureau happens along, no complaint can reach his ear till it has been forestalled by the story of the master and his interested attentions. The power of organized and concentrated effort, which may be available in the city, is denied to him. What, then, can he do? On what possible loop can he hang one solitary hope? God help him! For Andrew Johnson will not—although he was to be our Moses to lead us to liberty and equality; instead of which, I fear he will prove to be the Pharaoh of our day. In this we ought not to be deceived; for it is plain that he who undertakes to be the friend of the black man in this land of Negro haters, will not have the Negro haters all over the country singing praises to him, as you see they are now doing to our said Moses; so much so, that the astonished people stand off amazed, and know not what to do or to say. First they look at him; then at Gettysburg; then at Pittsburgh Landing; then at Milliken's Bend; then at Andersonville; and then at a murdered

President. With all these things before them, and ere they have had time for reflection, they are startled by the perpetration of some new act of high-handed infidelity, which well serves his purpose to hide some former wrong. As an evidence of some of his new acts of infidelity, they beheld him, within three days after the murder of our ever-to-be-lamented President, Abraham Lincoln, standing before God and, in the presence of an outraged nation, solemnly declaring that he would make treason a crime, and punish the traitor. Has he done either? No. Then, what has he done? you ask. My answer is that he has done much to make treason a virtue, by elevating traitors to offices of honor and trust, to be paid for their services in such offices by the taxing of the widows and orphans, whose fathers and husbands their own hands have slain. By these acts he has honored and given new license to traitors to perpetuate outrages and crimes. Humanity revolts and refuses to believe that man, made in the image of God, could so debase and belie his nature as to be guilty of such wrong against his fellow man. But did they not murder their slaves with impunity while they had a moneyed interest in them? If so, will they not slaughter the freedmen in whom they have no such interest, with such an one at the head of the nation fostering and honoring traitors? Were it not that we are forbidden to speak against those in authority, I should say, the Lord rebuke thee and deliver us from such a Moses.■

81 WE ARE ALL BOUND UP TOGETHER

Frances Ellen Watkins Harper

By the time of the Civil War, Frances Ellen Watkins (1825–1911) had achieved recognition as a leading poet and lecturer of the period. Watkins married Fenton Harper in 1860 and lived with him on a farm in Ohio. After his death in 1864, the Harper farm was sold to pay off debts, and she was left no assets by which to support her daughter, Mary, and her husband's three children from a previous marriage. She returned to the lecture circuit and supplemented her income through teaching and book sales.

Following the war, Harper embarked upon a major lecture tour of the South, in which she spoke to both white and black audiences of the importance of national reconciliation and attention to the desperate needs of freedpeople. Her tour was fraught with danger, as Harper "braved the suspicion of southern blacks who were wary of fast-talking Yankees of

*any hue and of Southern whites whose methods of dealing with outside
agitators were not softened if that agitator happened to be a woman," according to biographer Frances Smith Foster (*A Brighter Coming Day, *19).*

*Harper was active in support of various social movements, particu-
larly temperance, women's suffrage, and equal rights. Despite the racism
that infected white-dominated women's rights organizations of the period, Harper worked closely with such white leaders as Elizabeth Cady
Stanton, Susan B. Anthony, and Frances E. Willard. She attended major
women's rights conventions (sometimes as the only African American
present or permitted to speak) and appealed both to the pursuit of mutual interests and to the recognition of the sometimes divergent needs
and priorities of African American women.*

*In May 1866, Harper delivered the following address to the Eleventh
National Women's Rights Convention in New York, joining Stanton,
Anthony, and Lucretia Mott, who were among the featured speakers. As
biographer Foster notes, "This speech marked the beginning of Harper's
prominence in national feminist organizations" (*A Brighter Coming Day,
*216). Harper begins by describing the economic hardships she had re-
cently faced after the death of her husband—hardships, she notes, that
would have been substantially less if she had enjoyed the legal status
and protections accorded to men. But after drawing common purpose
with her predominantly white audience on the need for removal of legal
discrimination suffered on account of sex, Harper makes clear that black
and white American women face vastly different degrees of subjugation:
"You white women speak here of rights," she reminds them. "I speak of
wrongs." In addition to the injustices faced by members of her white
audience as women, Harper observes, she must face a daily barrage of insult and discrimination, much of it imposed by white women. "I do not
believe that white women are dew-drops just exhaled from the skies,"
she says.*

*At the 1869 convention of the Equal Rights Association (ERA), the
strained alliance between black and white feminists was shattered.
Harper sided with Frederick Douglass in supporting the Fifteenth Amendment's provision for black male suffrage. Anthony and Stanton left the
ERA to form the National Woman Suffrage Association and sought affiliation with southern segregationists in pursuit of women's suffrage. "The
white women all go for sex," Harper observed, "letting race occupy a minor position."*

The text of Harper's speech was published in We Are All Bound Up
Together: Proceedings of the Eleventh Women's Rights Convention *(May
1866), 45–48, and was reprinted in Frances Smith Foster, ed.,* A Brighter
Coming Day: A Frances Ellen Watkins Harper Reader *(New York: Feminist Press, 1990), 217–19. For a discussion of the relationship between
white and black feminists in the nineteenth century, see Shirley Yee,*
Black Women Abolitionists: A Study in Activism, 1828–1860 *(Knoxville:*

University of Tennessee Press, 1992), 136–54; and Paula Giddings, When and Where I Enter: The Impact of Black Women on Race and Sex in America *(New York: Bantam Books, 1984).*

I feel I am something of a novice upon this platform. Born of a race whose inheritance has been outrage and wrong, most of my life had been spent in battling against those wrongs. But I did not feel as keenly as others, that I had these rights, in common with other women, which are now demanded. About two years ago, I stood within the shadows of my home. A great sorrow had fallen upon my life. My husband had died suddenly, leaving me a widow, with four children, one my own, and the others stepchildren. I tried to keep my children together. But my husband died in debt; and before he had been in his grave three months, the administrator had swept the very milk-crocks and wash tubs from my hands. I was a farmer's wife and made butter for the Columbus market; but what could I do, when they had swept all away? They left me one thing—and that was a looking glass! Had I died instead of my husband, how different would have been the result! By this time he would have had another wife, it is likely; and no administrator would have gone into his house, broken up his home, and sold his bed, and taken away his means of support.

I took my children in my arms, and went out to seek my living. While I was gone; a neighbor to whom I had once lent five dollars, went before a magistrate and swore that he believed I was a non-resident, and laid an attachment on my very bed. And I went back to Ohio with my orphan children in my arms, without a single feather bed in this wide world, that was not in the custody of the law. I say, then, that justice is not fulfilled so long as woman is unequal before the law.

We are all bound up together in one great bundle of humanity, and society cannot trample on the weakest and feeblest of its members without receiving the curse in its own soul. You tried that in the case of the negro. You pressed him down for two centuries; and in so doing you crippled the moral strength and paralyzed the spiritual energies of the white men of the country. When the hands of the black were fettered, white men were deprived of the liberty of speech and the freedom of the press. Society cannot afford to neglect the enlightenment of any class of its members. At the South, the legislation of the country was in behalf of the rich slaveholders, while the poor white man was neglected. What is the consequence to-day? From that very class of neglected poor white men, comes the man who stands to-day, with his hand upon the helm of the nation. He fails to catch the watchword of the hour, and throws himself, the incarnation of meanness, across the pathway of the nation. My objection to Andrew Johnson is not that he has been a poor white man; my objection is that he keeps "poor whits" all the way through. (Applause.) That is the trouble with him.

This grand and glorious revolution which has commenced, will fail to reach its climax of success, until throughout the length and brea[d]th of the

American Republic, the nation shall be so color-blind, as to know no man by the color of his skin or the curl of his hair. It will then have no privileged class, trampling upon and outraging the unprivileged classes, but will be then one great privileged nation, whose privilege will be to produce the loftiest manhood and womanhood that humanity can attain.

I do not believe that giving the woman the ballot is immediately going to cure all the ills of life. I do not believe that white women are dew-drops just exhaled from the skies. I think that like men they may be divided into three classes, the good, the bad, and the indifferent. The good would vote according to their convictions and principles; the bad, as dictated by preju[d]ice or malice; and the indifferent will vote on the strongest side of the question, with the winning party.

You white women speak here of rights. I speak of wrongs. I, as a colored woman, have had in this country an education which has made me feel as if I were in the situation of Ishmael, my hand against every man, and every man's hand against me. Let me go to-morrow morning and take my seat in one of your street cars—I do not know that they will do it in New York, but they will in Philadelphia—and the conductor will put up his hand and stop the car rather than let me ride.

A Lady—They will not do that here.

Mrs. Harper—They do in Philadelphia. Going from Washington to Baltimore this Spring, they put me in the smoking car. (Loud Voices—"Shame.") Aye, in the capital of the nation, where the black man consecrated himself to the nation's defence, faithful when the white man was faithless, they put me in the smoking car! They did it once; but the next time they tried it, they failed; for I would not go in. I felt the fight in me; but I don't want to have to fight all the time. To-day I am puzzled where to make my home. I would like to make it in Philadelphia, near my own friends and relations. But if I want to ride in the streets of Philadelphia, they send me to ride on the platform with the driver. (Cries of "Shame.") Have women nothing to do with this? Not long since, a colored woman took her seat in an Eleventh Street car in Philadelphia, and the conductor stopped the car, and told the rest of the passengers to get out, and left the car with her in it alone, when they took it back to the station. One day I took my seat in a car, and the conductor came to me and told me to take another seat. I just screamed "murder." The man said if I was black I ought to behave myself. I knew that if he was white he was not behaving himself. Are there not wrongs to be righted?

In advocating the cause of the colored man, since the Dred Scott decision, I have sometimes said I thought the nation had touched bottom. But let me tell you there is a depth of infamy lower than that. It is when the nation, standing upon the threshold of a great peril, reached out its hands to a feebler race, and asked that race to help it, and when the peril was over, said, You are good enough for soldiers, but not good enough for citizens. When Judge Taney said that the men of my race had no rights which the white man was bound to respect, he had not seen the bones of the black man bleaching outside of Richmond. He had not seen the thinned ranks and the

thickened graves of the Louisiana Second, a regiment which went into battle
nine hundred strong, and came out with three hundred. He had not stood at
Olustee and seen defeat and disaster crushing down the pride of our banner,
until word was brought to Col. Hallowell, "The day is lost; go in and save
it;" and black men stood in the gap, beat back the enemy, and saved your
army.* (Applause.)

We have a woman in our country who has received the name of
"Moses,"[†] not by lying about it, but by acting it out (applause)—a woman
who has gone down into the Egypt of slavery and brought out hundreds of
our people into liberty. The last time I saw that woman, her hands were
swollen. That woman who had led one of Montgomery's most successful ex-
peditions, who was brave enough and secretive enough to act as a scout for
the American army, had her hands all swollen from a conflict with a brutal
conductor, who undertook to eject her from her place. That woman, whose
courage and bravery won a recognition from our army and from every black
man in the land, is excluded from every thoroughfare of travel. Talk of giving
women the ballot-box? Go on. It is a normal school, and the white women
of this country need it. While there exists this brutal element in society
which tramples upon the feeble and treads down the weak, I tell you that if
there is any class of people who need to be lifted out of their airy nothings
and selfishness, it is the white women of America. (Applause.)■

82 THESE ARE REVOLUTIONARY TIMES

Reverend E. J. Adams

*On March 2, 1867, Congress overrode President Johnson's vetoes
and passed a series of Reconstruction acts. New governments were
to be established in the South by delegates to conventions elected by
universal manhood suffrage, and these governments were to guarantee
black voting and officeholding rights and to ratify the Fourteenth
Amendment, which conferred state and national citizenship on "all persons born or naturalized in the United States" and prohibited the denial to any person of the equal protection of the law.*

Although many freedpeople were sorely disappointed that the legisla-

*At the battle of Olustee in Florida on February 20, 1864, the Fifty-fourth Massachu-
setts Regiment halted the Confederates' rout of Union forces.
[†]Harriet Tubman.

tion did not provide for the distribution of land, they hailed the action of Congress in a series of meetings. On March 19, 1867, a great mass meeting was held at Charleston, South Carolina, to voice approval of the congressional legislation and to act upon the report of a committee of thirteen appointed to draft a platform for the organization of the Union Republican Party. The meeting was called without regard to race or color, but as might be expected, the gathering was mainly composed of African Americans. At the conclusion of the reading of the resolutions, the Reverend E. J. Adams, a leader of the black community in Charleston, called for the adoption of the report and delivered the address below.

The Reverend Mr. Adams correctly related events occurring in the United States to revolutionary changes taking place elsewhere in the world. Much of his address was directed toward defending the principle of universal suffrage. Many of the arguments he advanced were put forth by other speakers, but he was one of the few to justify the enfranchisement of the former slaves on the ground that it was a reparation "for the long years of slavery and disfranchisement of the now colored citizens of the United States." He closed his address amid "great cheering" with a keen sally at the bogey of social equality.

The text of the speech presented here is taken from the Charleston Courier, *March 22, 1867.*

FELLOW CITIZENS: These are revolutionary times. For many years a contest, terrible in its nature, has been waged between despotism and republican principles, between freedom and slavery, until finally we behold the genius of republican liberty bearing its escutcheon upon the threshold of the capitol of every nation, waving its banner in triumph over every continent, sea and ocean. The sacred fire pent up in the bosom of the Italian nation, like the fires of Vesuvius, hath recently burst forth in all its sublimity, scattering its enemies and unshackling itself from that despotism which trampled it under its feet for nearly two centuries. Russia hath given freedom to over thirty millions of serfs,* and Germany hath recently extricated itself from the despotism of Europe. We find today Canada struggling for liberty, and Ireland too is endeavoring to grasp the flag of liberty. So, too, with regard to our nation. The little leaven that was planted in this country when the government was founded has succeeded in permeating itself through every fiber of this great body politic, and now the flag that once floated over four millions of slaves, today waves in triumph over more than thirty millions of freemen. The bloody crimson stripes of that banner, once emblematic of the bloody furrows ploughed upon the quivering flesh of four million of slaves, today is emblematic of the bloody sacrifice offered upon the altars of American liberty.

We owe a debt of everlasting gratitude—first, to Almighty God; second,

*Serfdom was abolished in Russia by the act of emancipation of February 19, 1861.

to the Congress of the United States—for the boon of freedom which both the white man and the black man today enjoy. We thank God because He has overruled the desires, the intentions and the will of men. When our war first broke out, it was the idea even of the Republican party, and even of the most radical of that party, that slavery should be confined to where it then existed; that it should have no further advancement, or be introduced into any of the territories shortly to become states. But the overruling hand of Providence, whose ways are in the whirlwind, brought good out of the wind, and today we can say, as Joseph said to his brethren, "As for you, ye meant evil unto me, but God meant it unto good to bring to pass that which has this day saved much people alive."

These resolutions vindicate universal suffrage, for which, thank God, we are in the enjoyment of today. I vindicate universal suffrage, first, because of a man's volition. I am in favor of universal suffrage, upon the ground that every man is endowed with a certain degree of volition, having the right to choose or refuse that which is good or evil; that he has the right to choose the God whom he will serve, and if a man may choose the God he wishes to serve, has he not an equal right to choose the ruler that shall rule over him?

Some are opposed to universal suffrage on the ground that a black man is not capable of exercising that right with judgment. But let me tell you that all men may be led instinctively to do that which is right, or choose the wrong. Those men who are led instinctively to support the liberty of the country in the time of war by placing the ballot box in their hands, will also be led to support the right in the time and hour of peace. Universal suffrage is the only reward that can be given for the long years of slavery and disfranchisement of the now colored citizens of the United States.

Universal suffrage is compatible with the genius of our Republic. This could not be a republic in every sense of the word unless universal suffrage is accorded to all men alike. The meaning of republicanism is that all men alike have the right to enjoy the privilege of the ballot box.

Again, a perfect Union, justice, domestic tranquillity, the common defense, the general welfare, and the blessings of liberty cannot be secured without universal suffrage. It is the only means of defense for the illiterate and the poor. The educated, the rich and the wealthy have advantages over the poor, who must necessarily have some means by which their liberties and the blessings of republican institutions may be enjoyed.

Again, universal suffrage, universal education, an equal chance to acquire wealth, will fit the colored man for any position, social or political. I do not, however, wish to be understood that I advocate or wish for social equality. God forbid that. For some of my mean white drunken enemies may sneak into my house and marry my daughter.■

83 EQUAL RIGHTS FOR ALL: THREE SPEECHES

Sojourner Truth

Although she was already over eighty years of age, Sojourner Truth, the great warrior for human freedom, was still actively engaged in the cause. A pioneer in the struggle for women's rights as well as freedom from slavery, Sojourner Truth made the rights of women a topic for many of her talks in the years following emancipation. She took strong exception to the understanding by Reverend Adams and others that "universal suffrage" meant the vote for men only.

On May 9 and 10, 1867, she spoke three times at the first annual meeting of the American Equal Rights Association held in New York City. Founded by Elizabeth Cady Stanton, Wendell Phillips, and Theodore Tilton, the Equal Rights Association was intended to be an umbrella organization uniting the efforts of the American Anti-Slavery Society toward equal rights for African Americans with those of the new National Woman Suffrage Association. The call for the first convention of the Equal Rights Association explained:

> The object of this Association is to "secure Equal Rights to all American citizens, especially the Right of Suffrage, irrespective of race, color, or sex." American Democracy has interpreted the Declaration of Independence in the interest of slavery, restricting suffrage and citizenship to a white male minority. . . . Let Democracy be defined anew, as the government of the people, *AND THE WHOLE PEOPLE.*
>
> Let the gathering, then, at this anniversary be, in numbers and character, worthy, in some degree, the demands of the hour. The black man, even the black soldier, is yet but half emancipated, nor will be, until full suffrage and citizenship are secured to him in the Federal Constitution. Still more deplorable is the condition of the black woman; and legally, that of the white woman is no better! Shall the sun of the nineteenth century go down on wrongs like these, in this nation, consecrated in its infancy to justice and freedom? Rather let our meeting be pledge as well as prophecy to the world of mankind, that the redemption of at least one great nation is near at hand."

This coalition was soon to disintegrate, as prominent women suffragists such as Susan B. Anthony refused to support the ratification of the Fifteenth Amendment ("I would sooner cut off my right hand," she remarked, "than ask the ballot for the black man and not for woman"). But Anthony was present at the first meeting of the Equal Rights Associa-

*tion, and she and Lucretia Mott, the society's president, took turns intro-
ducing the speeches by Sojourner Truth.*

*The three speech texts are taken from volume 2 of Elizabeth Cady
Stanton, Susan B. Anthony, and Matilda J. Gage, eds.,* History of Woman
Suffrage *(Rochester, N.Y.: Susan B. Anthony, 1889), 193–94, 222, 224–25.
For further information, see Nell Irvin Painter,* Sojourner Truth: A Life, a
Symbol *(New York: W. W. Norton, 1996).*

M *ay 9.* My friends, I am rejoiced that you are glad, but I don't know
how you will feel when I get through. I come from another field—the
country of the slave. They have got their liberty—so much good luck to have
slavery partly destroyed; not entirely. I want it root and branch destroyed.
Then we will all be free indeed. I feel that if I have to answer for the deeds
done in my body just as much as a man, I have a right to have just as much
as a man. There is a great stir about colored men getting their rights, but not
a word about the colored women; and if colored men get their rights, and not
colored women theirs, you see the colored men will be masters over the
women, and it will be just as bad as it was before. So I am for keeping the
thing going while things are stirring; because if we wait till it is still, it
will take a great while to get it going again. White women are a great deal
smarter, and know more than colored women, while colored women do not
know scarcely anything. They go out washing, which is about as high as a
colored woman gets, and their men go about idle, strutting up and down; and
when the women come home, they ask for their money and take it all, and
then scold because there is no food. I want you to consider on that, chil'n. I
call you chil'n; you are somebody's chil'n, and I am old enough to be mother
of all that is here. I want women to have their rights.* In the courts women
have no right, no voice; nobody speaks for them. I wish woman to have her
voice there among the pettifoggers. If it is not a fit place for women, it is
unfit for men to be there.

I am above eighty years old; it is about time for me to be going. I have
been forty years a slave and forty years free, and would be here forty years
more to have equal rights for all. I suppose I am kept here because something
remains for me to do; I suppose I am yet to help to break the chain. I have
done a great deal of work; as much as a man, but did not get so much pay.

---

*The transcript of the speech in the *New York World* of May 10, 1867, offers a different account of this passage: "I want the colored women to understand that if she earns
anything it is her own. But if a colored wife goes out to do a little washing—that is about
as high as black folks get—(laughter), when she comes back with a little money the husband comes in, Where have you been? To work. Well, you got paid? Yes. Then let me have
it. But I want to buy so and so for the children. Well, I don't want words about it. So hand
it over. (Laughter.) So he takes it and walks away, nobody knows where. . . . The man
claims her money, body, and everything for himself. (Laughter and applause.) It's not right.
Now's the time to make strong appeal for women's rights."

I used to work in the field and bind grain, keeping up with the cradler; but men doing no more, got twice as much pay; so with the German women. They work in the field and do as much work, but do not get the pay. We do as much, we eat as much, we want as much. I suppose I am about the only colored woman that goes about to speak for the rights of the colored women. I want to keep the thing stirring, now that the ice is cracked. What we want is a little money. You men know that you get as much again as women when you write, or for what you do. When we get our rights we shall not have to come to you for money, for then we shall have money enough in our own pockets; and may be you will ask us for money. But help us now until we get it. It is a good consolation to know that when we have got this battle once fought we shall not be coming to you any more. You have been having our rights so long, that you think, like a slave-holder, that you own us. I know that it is hard for one who has held the reins for so long to give up; it cuts like a knife. It will feel all the better when it closes up again. I have been in Washington about three years, seeing about these colored people. Now colored men have the right to vote. There ought to be equal rights now more than ever, since colored people have got their freedom. I am going to talk several times while I am here; so now I will do a little singing. I have not heard any singing since I came here.

(Accordingly, suiting the action to the word, Sojourner sang, "We are going home." "There, children," said she, "in heaven we shall rest from all our labors; first do all we have to do here. There I am determined to go, not to stop short of that beautiful place, and I do not mean to stop till I get there, and meet you there, too.")

May 10. SOJOURNER TRUTH was called for and said: I am glad to see that men are getting their rights, but I want women to get theirs, and while the water is stirring I will step into the pool. Now that there is a great stir about colored men's getting their rights is the time for women to step in and have theirs. I am sometimes told that "Women aint fit to vote. Why, don't you know that a woman had seven devils in her: and do you suppose a woman is fit to rule the nation?" Seven devils aint no account; a man had a legion in him. [Great laughter.] The devils didn't know where to go; and so they asked that they might go into the swine. They thought that was as good a place as they came out from. [Renewed laughter.] They didn't ask to go into sheep—no, into the hog; that was the selfishest beast; and man is so selfish that he has got women's rights and his own too, and yet he won't give women their rights. He keeps them all to himself. If a woman did have seven devils, see how lively she was when they were cast out, how much she loved Jesus, how she followed Him. When the devils were gone out of the man, he wanted to follow Jesus, too, but Jesus told him to go home, and didn't seem to want to have him round. And when the men went to look for Jesus at the sepulchre they didn't stop long enough to find out whether he was there or not; but Mary stood there and waited, and said to Him, thinking it was the gardener,

"Tell me where they have laid Him and I will carry Him away." See what a spirit there is. Just so let women be true to this object, and the truth will reign triumphant.

Evening, May 10. Miss ANTHONY announced that they would have another opportunity to hear Sojourner Truth, and, for the information of those who did not know, she would say that Sojourner was for forty years a slave in this State. She is not a product of the barbarism of South Carolina, but of the barbarism of New York, and one of her fingers was chopped off by her cruel master in a moment of anger.

SOJOURNER TRUTH said: I have lived on through all that has taken place these forty years in the anti-slavery cause, and I have plead with all the force I had that the day might come the colored people might own their soul and body. Well, the day has come, although it came through blood. It makes no difference how it came—it did come. [Applause.] I am sorry it came in that way. We are now trying for liberty that requires no blood—that women shall have their rights—not rights from you. Give them what belongs to them; they ask it kindly too. [Laughter.] I ask it kindly. Now I want it done very quick. It can be done in a few years. How good it would be. I would like to go up to the polls myself. [Laughter.] I own a little house in Battle Creek, Michigan. Well, every year I got a tax to pay. Taxes, you see, be taxes. Well, a road tax sounds large. Road tax, school tax, and all these things. Well, there was women there that had a house as well as I. They taxed them to build a road, and they went on the road and worked. It took 'em a good while to get a stump up. [Laughter.] Now, that shows that women can work. If they can dig up stumps they can vote. [Laughter.] It is easier to vote than dig stumps. [Laughter.] It doesn't seem hard work to vote, though I have seen some men that had a hard time of it. [Laughter.] But I believe that when women can vote there won't be so many men that have a rough time gettin' to the polls. [Great laughter.] There is danger of their life sometimes. I guess many have seen it in this city. I lived fourteen years in this city. I don't want to take up time, but I calculate to live. Now, if you want me to get out of the world, you had better get the women votin' soon. [Laughter.] I shan't go till I can do that.■

84 TO MY WHITE FELLOW CITIZENS

B. K. Sampson

During and after the Civil War, the black population of Ohio increased more than that of any other state, due to migration from the South. Yet in the fall of 1867, a statewide referendum for black suffrage was resoundingly defeated and the Democrats won control of both houses in the legislative elections. Weeks later, on Thanksgiving Day, 1867, the white citizens of Fairfield, Ohio, invited B. K. Sampson, a young black orator in the community, to be the speaker at the festivities that had been planned. The invitation aroused considerable comment in Ohio and other parts of the country, since Fairfield had a reputation of having been exceedingly hostile to the presence of black people. But the white citizens came "from far and near," and Sampson delivered a speech, the major portion of which appears below, as taken from the Christian Recorder, *January 13, 1868.*

Sampson begins by directly confronting the history of prejudice in the community and audience before him; he attempts to find common ground in the Union cause of the Civil War and to extend this common purpose to the postwar era. He concludes in sermonic fashion, calling upon his sinful "congregation" to renounce racial prejudice.

MY WHITE FELLOW CITIZENS: Whatever may have been your motives for elevating me with this profound honor, I know not; but as a black man, fully appreciating the tokens of this public regard, I make you my audience. With all veneration we come to return thanks to Almighty God for the munificent blessings which He has vouchsafed to the American people. I understand that you have been an austere people; that you have hated with a perfect hatred every likeness of the Negro, and that to the Southern lords you have long bowed. No proposition or measure concerning justice to the black man ever met your approval. Your reckless persistency in wrong has gained for you much publicity. No man of somber complexion could tarry in your midst and call his life his own. Even a dark-skinned white man would find himself unsafe among you. You lapsed from the doctrines of our fathers to a perverted idea of democracy, and through your apostasy your children deemed it right to be called democratic. They become indoctrinated in the faith, and slavery became the stone of the corner on which was founded the Democratic party.

The American government has long been looked upon as the purest and best under the sun; but the great obstruction in her path to national glory, was the blasting system of human slavery. To sanctify and make it right was arrayed the learning and genius of some of our ablest men. Our popular institutions had gained the envy of the world. None dared defend the poor; none pleaded their cause. Thus, for over three fourths of a century, we have lived, little expecting the terrible calamity which has come upon us, though Henry had exclaimed, "Give me liberty, or give me death!" and Jefferson had forewarned his countrymen, that "God's justice would not sleep forever." The voice of sublimest wisdom had long admonished us of the impending dangers; still the nation, with its blind infatuation, moved on to almost inevitable disaster.

Again and again our national sky was lighted up by the fierce flames of war, and in every contest in which our country was involved, the colored man bounded forth to defend his imperiled land. Still he was denied the sacred boon of liberty and the blessings of political freedom, until the final overthrow of the bloody conspiracy which threatened to destroy the government. Then the blacks took up arms for the defense of the national cause . . . and in a short time thousands of thousands of colored volunteers were in the field. O, glorious hour for those who prayed for deliverance from captivity! Their prayers were heard in heaven. The old system of slavery was broken. Brilliant victory followed victory in rapid succession; the doomed are redeemed; the nation is free, and slavery is dead.

Let us solemnize this day with thanksgiving and gratulation. Republican liberty is no longer an experiment. It has been permanently established on these shores of the Western world, and here it shall flourish forever. . . . Most perfidious, then, is he who cannot unite with the beating hearts of the millions in general gratitude for national unity and freedom. Not only to you, then, but to every friend of civil liberty throughout the world, I remark, that the offerings we make will avail nothing, unless we pledge ourselves to make this liberty the liberty of all men; unless we renounce our former predilections, abandon every feeling of malignancy and repugnance to every species of humanity, and swear hostility to every kind of injustice. . . .

Mr. Chairman, my heart swells with the most ardent hopes for the future which awaits the rising generation. Sir, I am aware that even at this time our colored brethren are bowed down under the most depressing influences in the Southern states. They have been put to torture and to death by the fiendish traitors who plotted treason against the government. Still the dark mantle of oppression wraps itself about us. We have long been discarded as the ailing child in the great American family. But no longer must this be. We are the allies of the government against all foes, whether at home or abroad. We are the lawful heirs of the government and cannot be disinherited. We are a part and parcel of the government; we are with the government to all intents and purposes. Why, then, withhold the right of suffrage from the colored man? Why refuse to invest him with the power of protection and equality before the law? Is it that he is too ignorant to appreciate the intrinsic value of the power he wields through the ballot box? One fourth of the white population of this country know nothing about the Constitution and laws under which they vote, and among the more illiterate class votes have been used for speculation and gain. So far, the history of the black man has shown that he has sacredly guarded and preserved every personal and political right accorded him by the government. Far be it from me to make any right more or less than a natural right. When President Andrew Johnson told Major Stevens that the right of suffrage is a mere political and not a natural right, he said what a majority of the intelligent people of the country do not believe. I know that it is a natural right. It is the common heritage of all mankind, wherever protection and allegiance are implied. It is as ancient as the first-born of humanity, and no written document or constitution can justly withhold it. To do this would give to the monarchist undisputed sway; then would representative democracies lose their brightest gems. But truth is our strong ally. It is the same now as when it spoke through the thunders and smoke of Sinai, and though the whole world of political tricksters move against us with their false arguments, *magna est veritas, et praevalebit. . . .*

Do you desire then, my friends, to see the righteousness of God prevail? Commit yourselves, I exhort you, in His great name to His cause. Do you want to see the blacks elevated to the position of freemen? Then subdue all these passions of prejudice and injustice. Create within your midst a sentiment of purest philanthropy; a sentiment so radical in its nature that the hearts of the people shall become influenced with the spirit of equality and right. Then will the government of God and all men of all races become one grand mutuality of intellectual and moral design.

85 BREAK UP THE PLANTATION SYSTEM

Francis L. Cardozo

The constitutional conventions elected under the Reconstruction Acts of Congress were the first state assemblies in which African Americans participated as elected representatives of the people. In the South Carolina convention of 1868 there were forty-eight white delegates and seventy-six black, fully two-thirds of whom had once been enslaved. One of the most frequently discussed issues at the South Carolina convention was the land question and the cry for partition of the large estates and distribution among the poorer black and white population. An extended debate raged around a proposed stay law designed to prevent the sale of large plantations for debt. Francis L. Cardozo, a leading African American in the Reconstruction era, who was later South Carolina's secretary of state and state treasurer, delivered an important speech opposing the stay law on the grounds that nine-tenths of the debts on the plantations were contracted for the sale of slaves. By taking this opportunity to throw the plantations upon the market, he insisted, they would be striking at the plantation system, "one of the greatest bulwarks of slavery," by breaking up the estates and selling them in small lots to the freedmen and women. Unfortunately, the convention did not take a stand in favor of breaking up the large plantations and distributing the land among the freedpeople and poor whites—a failure generally recognized today to have been the most serious weakness of Radical Reconstruction.

Francis Louis Cardozo (1837–1903) was a freeborn son of a Jewish economist in Charleston and an African American woman. After his elementary schooling, he became a journeyman carpenter. His savings, gained through summer employment and a thousand-dollar scholarship, enabled him to go to the University of Glasgow and then for two years to attend a theological school in London. At the outbreak of the Civil War he was a Presbyterian minister in New Haven, but when the conflict ended he went as principal to Avery Institute in Charleston and entered politics. Throughout his political career, he remained an active scholar and teacher. He was professor of Latin at Howard University from 1868 to 1872 and was named principal of the Colored High School of Washington, D.C., in 1884.

In this speech, Cardozo begins by differentiating his appeal from those of other black delegates who have preceded him. Although Cardozo identifies slavery as the root cause of the plantation owners' financial woes, he argues against the stay laws primarily on the basis of class and attempts to forge an alliance between the freed people and the poor whites who would benefit from land reform.

Cardozo's speech of January 14, presented here, is taken from the Proceedings of the Constitutional Convention of South Carolina, 1868, *vol. 1 (Charleston, 1868), 115–18. He is profiled in Rev. William J. Simmons,* Men of Mark: Eminent, Progressive and Rising *(1887), 428–31.*

IN DISCUSSING this measure, I would say to the gentleman who preceded me, and those who will follow, that they will accomplish their object much sooner and with much more satisfaction by not impugning the motives of those with whom they differ. The gentleman who spoke last, made gratuitous assumptions and ascribed mercenary motives that, were it not for personal friendship, might be retorted upon him with perhaps worse effect than he made them. He asserted that the gentlemen who opposed him opposed his race. I intend to show that his race is not at all connected with the matter. In giving my view of the measure, I shall not resort to mere declamations or appeals to passion or prejudice. In the first place, I doubt its legality. It is true, it is said the Convention does not propose to legislate, but I contend that a request from this body carries a certain moral influence. It shows what it would do if it had the power. It is virtually legislation. I regard any stay law as unjust and unconstitutional. It is unjust to the creditors. Let every man who contracts a debt, pay it. If he is an honest man he will pay his debts at any sacrifice. In our country it is unfortunate, as Americans, that we have a character by no means enviable as repudiators. Look at the attempt to repudiate the national debt. As an American, I protest against any further repudiation whatever, either in the form of a stay law or illegal legislation. I deem it inappropriate for us to touch the matter at all. We are sent here to form a Constitution. To travel outside of our proper province, will probably be to incur odium, displeasure and dissatisfaction. I wish to confine the action of this Convention to its proper sphere. The first question that arises is, what claim have these debtors on our sympathies more than creditors? Are the debtors greater in number than creditors? If we legislate in favor of any, will it be doing the greatest good to the greatest number? I maintain it will not. It is a class measure. This will be but the beginning. We will be burdened with applications, and the burden will be upon those who introduced this measure, not upon those who refused to legislate for other special favorite classes. I ask not only what are the claims of the debtors, but also what are the nature of these sales? Was it the transfer of real estate? I think everyone here will say no. Nine tenths of the debts were contracted for the sale of slaves. I do not wish we should go one inch out of the way to legislate either for the buyer or seller. They dealt in that kind of property, they knew its precarious tenure, and therefore let them suffer. When the war commenced every rebel sold his property to give money to a common cause. And their slaves were sold for the same object, to maintain a war waged for the purpose of perpetually enslaving a people. That was the object. The ladies of the South stripped themselves of their jewels, and the men sold their lands and their slaves for that object. Now, let them suffer for it. As the gentleman from Charleston very ably said, "they have cast the die, let them take the chances."

There is also another reason, and one of the strongest, why the Convention should not take any action on the subject, but postpone it indefinitely. One of the greatest bulwarks of slavery was the infernal plantation system, one man owning his thousand, another is twenty, and another fifty thousand acres of land. This is the only way by which we will break up that system, and I maintain that our freedom will be of no effect if we allow it to continue. What is the main cause of the prosperity of the North? It is because every man has his own farm and is free and independent. Let the lands of the South be similarly divided. I would not say for one moment they should be confiscated, but if sold to maintain the war, now that slavery is destroyed, let the plantation system go with it. We will never have true freedom until we abolish the system of agriculture which existed in the Southern states. It is useless to have any schools while we maintain this stronghold of slavery as the agricultural system of the country. The gentleman has said that if these plantations were sold now, they would pass into the hands of a few mercenary speculators. I deny it and challenge a single proof to sustain the assertion. On the contrary I challenge proof to show that if the plantations are not sold, the old plantation masters will part with them. If they are sold, though a few mercenary speculators may purchase some, the chances are that the colored man and the poor man would be the purchasers. I will prove this, not by mere assertion, but by facts. About one hundred poor colored men of Charleston met together and formed themselves into a Charleston Land Company. They subscribed for a number of shares at $10 per share, one dollar payable monthly. They have been meeting for a year. Yesterday they purchased six hundred acres of land for $6,600 that would have sold for $25,000 or $50,000 in better times. They would not have been able to buy it had not the owner through necessity been compelled to sell. This is only one instance of thousands of others that have occurred in this city and state. I look upon it, therefore, as the natural result of the war that this system of large plantations, of no service to the owner or anybody else, should be abolished.

I think Providence has not only smiled upon every effort for abolishing this hideous form of slavery, but that since the war it has given unmistakable signs of disapprobation wherever continued, by blasting the cotton crops in that part of the country. Men are now beginning not to plant cotton but grain for food, and in doing so they are establishing a system of small farms, by which not only my race, but the poor whites and ninety-nine hundredths of the other thousands will be benefited. The real benefit from this legislation would inhere to not more than thirty thousand landholders against the seven hundred thousand poor people of the State. If we are to legislate in favor of a class at all, any honest man, any man who has the interest of the people at heart will legislate in favor of the greater number. In speaking against the landholders, and in taking this position I do not cherish one feeling of enmity against them as a class or individuals. But this question takes a larger range and is one in which the whole country is involved. I can never sacrifice the interests of nine or ten millions to the interests of three hundred thousand, more especially when the three hundred thousand initiated the war and were the very ones who established an infernal Negro code and want to keep their lands until better times. They do not want that a nigger or a Yankee shall ever own a foot of their land. Now is the time to take the advantage. Give them an opportunity, breathing time, and they will reorganize the same old system they had before the war. I say, then, just as General Grant said when he had Lee hemmed in around Petersburg, now is the time to strike, and in doing so we will strike for our people and posterity, and the truest interest of our country.■

86 JUSTICE SHOULD RECOGNIZE NO COLOR

William H. Grey

The Arkansas Constitutional Convention met in January and February 1868 to frame a new constitution under the provisions of the congressional Reconstruction Acts. During the debate over a new constitution, a white delegate spoke against black suffrage. He was effectively answered by William H. Grey (Gray), a black delegate from Phillips County, in the following speech, which is taken from The American Annual Cyclopedia, *vol. 8 (1869), 33–35.*

Grey challenges the assumption of his white opponents that whites exercise the franchise responsibly, whereas blacks would not. Grey notes that every objection raised against African American suffrage applies in greater measure to white voters and makes clear the importance of the right to vote in the protection of other rights.

Before the war, Grey had served as a free servant of Virginia governor Henry A. Wise and accompanied him to sessions of Congress. Grey was a leader of the First Convention of Colored Citizens held in Little Rock in late 1865, where he proclaimed those gathered to be "Americans in America, One and Indivisible."

IT APPEARS to me the gentleman has read the history of his country to little purpose. When the Constitution was framed, in every state but South Carolina free Negroes were allowed to vote. Under British rule this class was free, and he interpreted that "we the people" in the preamble of the Constitution meant all the people of every color. The mistake of that period was that these free Negroes were not represented in *propria persona* in that constitutional convention, but by the Anglo-Saxon. Congress is now correcting that mistake. The right of franchise is due the Negroes bought by the blood of forty thousand of their race shed in three wars. The troubles now on the country are the result of the bad exercise of the elective franchise by unintelligent whites, the "poor whites" of the South. I could duplicate every Negro who cannot read and write, whose name is on the list of registered voters, with a white man equally ignorant. The gentleman can claim to be a friend of the Negro, but I do not desire to be looked upon in the light of a client. The government has made a solemn covenant with the Negro to vest him with the right of franchise if he would throw his weight in the balance in favor of the Union and bare his breast to the storm of bullets; and I am convinced that it would not go back on itself. There are thirty-two million whites to four million blacks in the country, and there need be no fear of Negro domination. The state laws do not protect the Negro in his rights, as they forbade their entrance into the State. I am not willing to trust the rights of my people with the white men, as they have not preserved those of their own race, in neglecting to provide them with the means of education. The Declaration of Independence declared all men born free and equal, and I demand the enforcement of that guarantee made to my forefathers, to every one of each race, who had fought for it. The constitution which this ordinance would reenact is not satisfactory, as it is blurred all over with the word *white.* Under it one hundred and eleven thousand beings who live in the state have no rights which white men are bound to respect.* My people might be ignorant, but I believe with Jefferson that ignorance is no measure of a man's rights. Slavery has been abolished, but it left my people in a condition of peonage or caste worse than slavery, which had its humane masters. White people should look to their own ancestry; they should recollect that women were disposed of on the James River, in the early settlement of the country, as wives, at the price of two hundred pounds of tobacco. When we have had eight hundred years as the whites to enlighten ourselves, it will be time enough to pronounce them incapable of civilization and enlightenment. The last election showed that they were intelligent enough to vote in a solid mass with the party that would give them their rights, and that too in face of the influence of the intelligence and wealth of the State, and in face of threats to take the bread from their very mouths. I have no antipathy toward the whites; I would drop the curtain of oblivion on the sod which contains the bones of my oppressed and wronged ancestors for two hundred and fifty years. Give us the franchise, and if we do not exercise it properly, you have the numbers to take it away from us. It would be impossible for the Negro to get justice in a State whereof he was not a full citizen. The prejudices of the entire court would be against him. I do not expect the Negro to take possession of the government; I want the franchise given him as an incentive to work to educate his children. I do not desire to discuss the question of inferiority of races. Unpleasant truths must then be told; history tells us of your white ancestors who lived on the acorns which dropped from the oaks of Didona, and then worshiped the tree as a God. I call upon all men who would see justice done, to meet this question fairly, and fear not to record their votes.

[In the session of January 29th, he said:] Negroes vote in Ohio and Massachusetts, and in the latter State are elected to high office by rich men. He had found more prejudice against his race among the Yankees; and if they did him a kind act, they did not seem to do it with the generous spirit of Southern men. He could get nearer the latter; he had been raised with them. He was the sorrier on this account that they had refused him the rights which would make him a man, as the former were willing to do. He wanted this a white man's government, and wanted them to do the legislating as

*A reference to the *Dred Scott* decision of 1857.

they had the intelligence and wealth; but he wanted the power to protect himself against unfriendly legislation. Justice should be like the Egyptian statue, "blind and recognizing no color." ■

87 I CLAIM THE RIGHTS OF A MAN

Reverend Henry McNeal Turner

As each of the ten former Confederate states fulfilled the require-ments set by the Reconstruction Acts of Congress, it was restored to the union. On July 21, 1868, Georgia was restored. But white Demo-crats, the majority of the legislature, voted to unseat the two Republican state senators and twenty-five Republican state representatives on the grounds that they were black. On September 3, 1868, Henry McNeal Turner, one of the expelled members, stood before the assembled repre-sentatives and delivered a magnificent attack on the men who had re-fused to seat the African American senators and representatives.

Turner (1834–1915) was born in Columbia, South Carolina, of free black parents, and in 1855 moved to Macon, where he joined the African Methodist Episcopal Church and became a preacher. "His eloquence," a church paper noted later, "attracted the attention of the white citizens, who considered him to be 'too smart a nigger' to remain in the South, and he was obliged to leave." Turner went to Baltimore and finally to Washington as pastor of Israel Bethel Church. Here he rapidly became a leader of the black community and an outstanding and militant fighter for racial justice in the capital. In 1863 he was appointed by President Lincoln as chaplain to the first U.S. black troops. After the war Turner moved to Georgia, where he continued preaching and played a prominent part in Reconstruction politics. "I was, on one occasion," he wrote in the Christian Recorder *of March 24, 1866, "lecturing to the young men on the political prospects of the colored people, when it was announced they were preparing outdoors to shoot me through the window. I cried out to let them shoot, and commenced speaking on as I had been. . . . In a few moments the church was picketed by brave young men, and everything went on smoothly. This is the second time my life has been aimed at through the window. But I am still alive." This fearlessness is reflected in his lengthy but militant speech in defense of the rights of African Americans in Georgia to sit in the legislature, excerpts from which follow.*

Before he was declared ineligible for membership in the Georgia House, Turner had introduced two bills of a progressive nature, neither of which passed. One called for an eight-hour day for laborers, and the other sought to prevent common carriers "from distinguishing between white and colored persons in the quality of accommodations furnished." His experiences in Georgia during Reconstruction convinced Turner that whites would never allow African Americans to "rise above a state of serfdom," and he became a supporter of emigration to Africa. In 1880 Turner was ordained bishop in the African Methodist Episcopal Church. He died in Windsor, Canada, in 1915.

Turner's speech has been preserved in Ethel Maude Christler's "Participation of Negroes in the Government of Georgia, 1867–1870" (master's thesis, Atlanta University, June 1932), 82–96. Christler copied the speech from a pamphlet in which it was published that she obtained from Bishop J. S. Flipper of Atlanta.

MR SPEAKER: Before proceeding to argue this question upon its intrinsic merits, I wish the members of this House to understand the position that I take. I hold that I am a member of this body. Therefore, sir, I shall neither fawn nor cringe before any party, nor stoop to beg them for my rights. Some of my colored fellow members, in the course of their remarks, took occasion to appeal to the sympathies of members on the opposite side, and to eulogize their character for magnanimity. It reminds me very much, sir, of slaves begging under the lash. I am here to demand my rights and to hurl thunderbolts at the men who would dare to cross the threshold of my manhood. There is an old aphorism which says, "fight the devil with fire," and if I should observe the rule in this instance, I wish gentlemen to understand that it is but fighting them with their own weapon.

The scene presented in this House, today, is one unparalleled in the history of the world. From this day, back to the day when God breathed the breath of life into Adam, no analogy for it can be found. Never, in the history of the world, has a man been arraigned before a body clothed with legislative, judicial or executive functions, charged with the offense of being a darker hue than his fellow men. I know that questions have been before the courts of this country, and of other countries, involving topics not altogether dissimilar to that which is being discussed here today. But, sir, never in the history of the great nations of this world—never before—has a man been arraigned, charged with an offense committed by the God of Heaven Himself. Cases may be found where men have been deprived of their rights for crimes and misdemeanors; but it has remained for the state of Georgia, in the very heart of the nineteenth century, to call a man before the bar, and there charge him with an act for which he is no more responsible than for the head which he carries upon his shoulders. The Anglo-Saxon race, sir, is a most surprising one. No man has ever been more deceived in that race than I have been for the last three weeks. I was not aware that there was in the character of that race so much cowardice or so much pusillanimity. The treachery which has been exhibited in it by gentlemen belonging to that race has shaken my confidence in it more than anything that has come under my observation from the day of my birth.

What is the question at issue? Why, sir, this Assembly, today, is discussing and deliberating on a judgment; there is not a Cherub that sits around God's eternal throne today that would not tremble—even were an order issued by the Supreme God Himself—to come down here and sit in judgment on my manhood. Gentlemen may look at this question in whatever light they choose, and with just as much indifference as they may think proper to assume, but I tell you, sir, that this is a question which will not die today. This event shall be remembered by posterity for ages yet to come, and while the sun shall continue to climb the hills of heaven.

Whose legislature is this? Is it a white man's legislature, or is it a black man's legislature? Who voted for a constitutional convention, in obedience to the mandate of the Congress of the United States? Who first rallied around the standard of Reconstruction? Who set the ball of loyalty rolling in the state of Georgia? And whose voice was heard on the hills and in the valleys of this state? It was the voice of the brawny-armed Negro, with the few humanitarian-hearted white men who came to our assistance. I claim the honor, sir, of having been the instrument of convincing hundreds—yea, thousands—of white men, that to reconstruct under the measures of the United States Congress was the safest and the best course for the interest of the state.

Let us look at some facts in connection with this matter. Did half the white men of Georgia vote for this legislature? Did not the great bulk of them fight, with all their strength, the Constitution under which we are acting? And did they not fight against the organization of this legislature? And further, sir, did they not vote against it? Yes, sir! And there are persons in this legislature today who are ready to spit their poison in my face, while they themselves opposed, with all their power, the ratification of this Constitution. They question my right to a seat in this body, to represent the people whose legal votes elected me. This objection, sir, is an unheard-of monopoly of power. No analogy can be found for it, except it be the case of a man who should go into my house, take possession of my wife and children, and then tell me to walk out. I stand very much in the position of a criminal before your bar, because I dare to be the exponent of the views of those who sent me here. Or, in other words, we are told that if black men want to speak, they must speak through white trumpets; if black men want their sentiments expressed, they must be adulterated and sent through white messengers, who will quibble and equivocate and evade as rapidly as the pendulum of a clock. If this be not done, then the black men have committed an outrage, and their representatives must be denied the right to represent their constituents.

The great question, sir, is this: Am I a man? If I am such, I claim the rights of a man. Am I not a man because I happen to be of a darker hue than honorable gentlemen around me? Let me see whether I am or not. I want to convince the House today that I am entitled to my seat here. A certain gentleman has argued that the Negro was a mere development similar to the orangoutang or chimpanzee, but it so happens that, when a Negro is examined, physiologically, phrenologically and anatomically, and I may say, physiognomically, he is found to be the same as persons of different color. I would like to ask any gentleman on this floor, where is the analogy? Do you find me a quadruped, or do you find me a man? Do you find three bones less in my back than in that of the white man? Do you find fewer organs in the brain? If you know nothing of this, I do; for I have helped to dissect fifty men, black and white, and I assert that by the time you take off the mucous pigment—the color of the skin—you cannot, to save your life, distinguish between the black man and the white. Am I a man? Have I a soul to save, as you have? Am I susceptible of eternal development, as you are? Can I learn all the arts and sciences that you can? Has it ever been demonstrated in the history of the world? Have black men ever exhibited bravery as white men have done? Have they ever been in the professions? Have they not as good articulative organs as you? Some people argue that there is a very close similarity between the larynx of the Negro and that of the orangoutang. Why, sir, there is not so much similarity between them as there is between the larynx of the man and that of the dog, and this fact I dare any member of this House to dispute. God saw fit to vary everything in nature. There are no two men alike—no two voices alike—no two trees alike. God has weaved and tissued variety and versatility throughout the boundless space of His creation. Because God saw fit to make some red, and some white, and some black, and some brown, are we to sit here in judgment upon what God has seen fit to do? As well might one play with the thunderbolts of heaven as with that creature that bears God's image—God's photograph.

The question is asked, "What is it that the Negro race has done?" Well, Mr. Speaker, all I have to say upon the subject is this: If we are the class of people that we are generally represented to be, I hold that we are a very great people. It is generally considered that we are the children of Canaan, and the curse of a father rests upon our heads, and has rested, all through history. Sir, I deny that the curse of Noah had anything to do with the Negro.* We are not the Children of Canaan; and if we are, sir, where should we stand? Let us look a little into history. Melchizedek was a Canaanite; all the Phoenicians—all those inventors of the arts and sciences—were the posterity of Canaan; but, sir, the Negro is not. We are the children of Cush, and

---

*The "Curse of Ham" (Genesis 9:25–27) was used from the beginning of the African slave trade in the fifteenth century to prove that the Bible justified black enslavement. Ham's descendants—supposedly the black race—were to be slaves because he had seen Noah in his nakedness: "Cursed be Canaan; a servant of servants shall he be unto his brethren." For a detailed analysis of the role of the "curse of Ham" myth in antebellum proslavery thought, see Thomas V. Peterson, *Ham and Japheth: The Mythic World of Whites in the Antebellum South* (Metuchen, N.J.: Scarecrow Press, 1978).

Canaan's curse has nothing whatever to do with the Negro. If we belong to that race, Ham belonged to it, under whose instructions Napoleon Bonaparte studied military tactics. If we belong to that race, Saint Augustine belonged to it. Who was it that laid the foundation of the great Reformation? Martin Luther, who lit the light of gospel truth—a light that will never go out until the sun shall rise to set no more; and, long ere then, Democratic principles will have found their level in the regions of Pluto and of Prosperpine. . . .

The honorable gentleman from Whitfield (Mr. Shumate), when arguing this question, a day or two ago, put forth the proposition that to be a representative was not to be an officer—"it was a privilege that citizens had a right to enjoy." These are his words. It was not an office; it was a "privilege." Every gentleman here knows that he denied that to be a representative was to be an officer. Now, he is recognized as a leader of the Democratic party in this House, and generally cooks victuals for them to eat; makes that remarkable declaration, and how are you, gentlemen on the other side of the House, because I am an officer, when one of your great lights says that I am *not* an officer? If you deny my right—the right of my constituents to have representation here—because it is a "privilege," then, sir, I will show you that I have as many privileges as the whitest man on this floor. If I am not permitted to occupy a seat here, for the purpose of representing my constituents, I want to know how white men can be permitted to do so. How can a white man represent a colored constituency, if a colored man cannot do it? The great argument is: "Oh, we have inherited" this, that and the other. Now, I want gentlemen to come down to cool, common sense. Is the created greater than the Creator? Is man greater than God? It is very strange, if a white man can occupy on this floor *a seat created by colored votes*, and a black man cannot do it. Why, gentlemen, it is the most shortsighted reasoning in the world. A man can see better than that with half an eye; and even if he had no eye at all, he could forge one, as the Cyclops did, or punch one with his finger, which would enable him to see through that.

It is said that Congress never gave us the right to hold office. I want to know, sir, if the Reconstruction measures did not base their action on the ground that no distinction should be made on account of race, color or previous condition? Was not that the grand fulcrum on which they rested? And did not every reconstructed state have to reconstruct on the idea that no discrimination, in any sense of the term, should be made? There is not a man here who will dare say No. If Congress has simply given me a merely sufficient civil and political rights to make me a mere political slave for Democrats, or anybody else—giving them the opportunity of jumping on my back in order to leap into political power—I do not thank Congress for it. Never, so help me God, shall I be a political slave. I am not now speaking for those colored men who sit with me in this House, nor do I say that they endorse my sentiments [cries from the colored members, "We Do!"], but assisting Mr. Lincoln to take me out of servile slavery did not intend to put me and my race into *political* slavery. If they did, let them take away my ballot—I do not want it, and shall not have it. [Several colored members: "Nor we!"] I don't want to be a mere tool of that sort. I have been a slave long enough already.

I tell you what I would be willing to do: I am willing that the question should be submitted to Congress for an explanation as to what was meant in the passage of their Reconstruction measures, and of the Constitutional Amendment. Let the Democratic party in this House pass a resolution giving this subject that direction, and I shall be content. I dare you, gentlemen, to do it. Come up to the question openly, whether it meant that the Negro might hold office, or whether it meant that he should merely have the right to vote. If you are honest men, you will do it. If, however, you will not do that, I would make another proposition: Call together, again, the convention that framed the constitution under which we are acting; let them take a vote upon the subject, and I am willing to abide by their decision. . . .

These colored men, who are unable to express themselves with all the clearness and dignity and force of rhetorical eloquence, are laughed at in derision by the Democracy of the country. It reminds me very much of the man who looked at himself in a mirror and, imagining that he was addressing another person, exclaimed: My God, how ugly you are!" These gentlemen do not consider for a moment the dreadful hardships which these people have endured, and especially those who in any way endeavored to acquire an education. For myself, sir, I was raised in the cotton field of South Carolina, and in order to prepare myself for usefulness, as well to myself as to my race, I determined to devote my spare hours to study. When the overseer retired at night to his comfortable couch, I sat and read and thought and studied, until I heard him blow his horn in the morning. He frequently told me, with an oath, that if he discovered me attempting to learn, that he would whip me to death, and I have no doubt he would have done so, if he had found an opportunity. I prayed to Almighty God to assist me, and He did, and I thank Him with my whole heart and soul. . . .

So far as I am personally concerned, no man in Georgia has been more conservative than I. "Anything to please the white folks" has been my motto; and so closely have I adhered to that course, that many among my own party have classed me as a Democrat. One of the leaders of the Republican party in Georgia has not been at all favorable to me for some time back, because he believed that I was too "conservative" for a Republican. I can assure you, however, Mr. Speaker, that I have had quite enough, and to spare, of such "conservatism" . . .

But, Mr. Speaker, I do not regard this movement as a thrust at me. It is a thrust at the Bible—a thrust at the God of the Universe, for making a man and not finishing him; it is simply calling the Great Jehovah a fool. Why, sir, though we are not white, we have accomplished much. We have pioneered civilization here; we have built up your country; we have worked in your fields and garnered your harvests for two hundred and fifty years! And what do we ask of you in return? Do we ask you for compensation for the sweat our fathers bore for you—for the tears you have caused, and the hearts you have broken, and the lives you have curtailed, and the blood you have spilled? Do we ask retaliation? We ask it not. We are willing to let the dead past bury its dead; but we ask you, now for our *rights.* You have all the elements of superiority upon your side; you have our money and your own; you have our education and your own; and you have our land and your own too. We, who number hundreds of thousands in Georgia, including our wives and families, with not a foot of land to call our own—strangers in the land of our birth; without money, without education, without aid, without a roof to cover us while we live, nor sufficient clay to cover us when we die! It is extraordinary that a race such as yours, professing gallantry and chivalry and education and superiority, living in a land where ringing chimes call child and sire to the church of God—a land where Bibles are read and Gospel truths are spoken, and where courts of justice are presumed to exist; it is extraordinary that, with all these advantages on your side, you can make war upon the poor defenseless black man. You know we have no money, no railroads, no telegraphs, no advantages of any sort, and yet all manner of injustice is placed upon us. You know that the black people of this country acknowledge you as their superiors, by virtue of your education and advantages. . . .

You may expel us, gentlemen, but I firmly believe that you will some day repent it. The black man cannot protect a country, if the country doesn't protect him; and if, tomorrow, a war should arise, I would not raise a musket to defend a country where my manhood is denied. The fashionable way in Georgia, when hard work is to be done, is for the white man to sit at his ease while the black man does the work; but, sir, I will say this much to the colored men of Georgia, as, if I should be killed in this campaign, I may have no opportunity of telling them at any other time: Never lift a finger nor raise a hand in defense of Georgia, until Georgia acknowledges that you are men and invests you with the rights pertaining to manhood. Pay your taxes, however, obey all orders from your employers, take good counsel from friends, work faithfully, earn an honest living, and show, by your conduct, that you can be good citizens.

Go on with your oppressions. Babylon fell. Where is Greece? Where is Nineveh? And where is Rome, the Mistress Empire of the world? Why is it that she stands, today, in broken fragments throughout Europe? Because oppression killed her. Every act that we commit is like a bounding ball. If you curse a man, that curse rebounds upon you; and when you bless a man, the blessing returns to you; and when you oppress a man, the oppression also will rebound. Where have you ever heard of four millions of freemen being governed by laws, and yet have no hand in their making? Search the records of the world, and you will find no example. "Governments derive their just powers from the consent of the governed." How dare you to make laws by which to try me and my wife and children, and deny me a voice in the making of these laws? I know you can establish a monarchy, an autocracy, an oligarchy, or any other kind of *ocracy* that you please; and that you can declare whom you please to be sovereign; but tell me, sir, how you can clothe me with more power than another, where all are sovereigns alike? How can you say you have a republican form of government, when you make such distinction and enact such proscriptive laws?

Gentlemen talk a good deal about the Negroes "building no monuments." I can tell the gentlemen one thing: that is, that we could have built monuments of fire while the war was in progress. We could have fired your woods, your barns and fences, and called you home. Did we do it? No, sir! And God grant that the Negro may never do it, or do anything else that would destroy the good opinion of his friends. No epithet is sufficiently opprobrious for us now. I saw, sir, that we have built a monument of docility, of obedience, of respect, and of self-control, that will endure longer than the Pyramids of Egypt.

We are a persecuted people. Luther was persecuted; Galileo was persecuted; good men in all nations have been persecuted; but the persecutors have been handed down to posterity with shame and ignominy. If you pass this bill, you will never get Congress to pardon or enfranchise another rebel in your lives. You are going to fix an everlasting disfranchisement upon Mr. Toombs* and the other leading men of Georgia. You may think you are doing yourselves honor by expelling us from this House; but when we go, we will do as Wickliffe† and as Latimer did. We will light a torch of truth that will never be extinguished—the impression that will run through the country, as people picture in their mind's eye these poor black men, in all parts of this Southern country, pleading for their rights. When you expel us, you make us forever your political foes, and you will never find a black man to vote a Democratic ticket again; for, so help me God, I will go through all the length and breadth of the land, where a man of my race is to be found, and advise him to beware of the Democratic party. Justice is the great doctrine taught in the Bible. God's Eternal Justice is founded upon Truth, and the man who steps from Justice steps from Truth, and cannot make his principles to prevail.

I have now, Mr. Speaker, said all that my physical condition will allow me to say. Weak and ill, though I am, I could not sit passively here and see the sacred rights of my race destroyed at one blow. We are in a position somewhat similar to that of the famous "Light Brigade," of which Tennyson says, they had

Cannon to right of them,
Cannon to left of them,
Cannon in front of them,
Volleyed and thundered.

*Robert A. Toombs (1810–1885) had been secretary of state in the Confederacy and as one of the Confederate leaders was disfranchised and barred from holding public office under the Radical Republican plan of Reconstruction.

†John Wycliffe (c. 1328–1384) was the English religious leader who stood up against the abuses of the Church, championed the cause of the poor, opposing serfdom, and laid the foundations of Lollard thought and practice in England. His influence spread to Bohemia and formed the basis of the Hussite movement.

I hope our poor, downtrodden race may act well and wisely through this period of trial, and that they will exercise patience and discretion under all circumstances.

You may expel us, gentlemen, by your votes, today; but, while you do it, remember that there is a just God in Heaven, whose All-Seeing Eye beholds alike the acts of the oppressor and the oppressed, and who, despite the machinations of the wicked, never fails to vindicate the cause of Justice, and the sanctity of His own handiwork.*■

88 FINISH THE GOOD WORK OF UNITING COLORED AND WHITE WORKINGMEN

Isaac Myers

Virtually all the labor unions of the 1860s barred African Americans from membership. But at the third national convention of the National Labor Union, held in Philadelphia, August 1869, 9 of the 142 delegates were African Americans. One of these delegates was Isaac Myers, representing the Colored Caulkers' Trades Union Society of Baltimore and the first important black labor leader in the United States. During the convention, Myers was commissioned by the black delegates to voice their thanks for the "unanimous recognition" of the African American worker's right to representation in the gathering. The speech he delivered on August 18, 1869, is a historic appeal for unity of black and white workers and probably the first published labor speech of a black union leader. The reporter for the New York Times of August 19, 1869, where the speech appeared, wrote: "The whole Convention listened . . . with the most profound attention . . . and at its close many delegates advanced and warmly congratulated him" (1).

Myers was born in Baltimore in 1835 and at the age of sixteen was apprenticed to a prominent local African American to learn the ship-caulking trade. Four years later he was in charge of the caulking of large

---

*After finishing his speech, Turner led the black delegates out of the hall. At the doorway, Turner turned to face the white legislators and scraped the mud off his shoes. At the insistence of Congress, which refused to admit Georgia to the Union until it seated the black legislators, the expelled members of the Georgia legislature were readmitted in 1869 with pay for lost time.

clipper ships. In 1865 a strike of white workers to protest the presence of black mechanics and longshoremen resulted in the dismissal of over a hundred African Americans from their jobs in the Baltimore shipyards. As a result of this crisis, Myers helped organize a union of black workers in the shipyards and established the Chesapeake Marine Railway and Dry Dock Company, a cooperative venture, owned entirely by African Americans.

M*r. President and Members of the National Labor Convention:*
GENTLEMEN: It would be an act of great injustice to your Godlike charity should I allow the deliberations of this convention to close without returning you the thanks of four millions of our race for your unanimous recognition of their right to representation in this Convention. We sympathize with you in the loss of your great leader and champion, the immortal WILLIAM H. SYLVIS.* God in his wisdom has called him to "that bourne whence no traveler returns," and our prayers shall ever be that his immortal spirit shall ever hover around the Throne, and bathe its wings in the morning dews of Heaven. He labored incessantly for you and your posterity. No distance was too far for him to travel. No hours of labor were too long for him to work while he advocated eight hours for you—eight hours for rest, eight hours for study, and eight hours for work. He gave all of his hours in laboring to bring about that glorious result. His heart, soul, mind and strength were absorbed in his labor of love, and to-day, by one stroke of the unerring pen of President U. S. GRANT, you are enjoying the first fruits of victory. Write his faults in the sand, and his virtues in the granite.

GENTLEMEN, silent but powerful and far-reaching is the revolution inaugurated by your act of taking the colored laborer by the hand and telling him that his interest is common with yours, and that he should have an equal chance in the race for life. These declarations of yours are ominous, and will not only be felt throughout the length and breadth of this great Republic, but will become another great problem in American politics for the kings and dynasties of Europe to solve. It is America and it is only Americans that can work up and work out such great revolutions in a day. God grant that it may be as lasting as the eternal hills. I speak today for the colored men of the whole country, from the Lakes to the Gulf—from the Atlantic to the Pacific—from every hilltop, valley and plain throughout our vast domain, when I tell you that all they ask for themselves is a fair chance;

---

*William H. Sylvis (1828–1869) was a labor leader and reformer. He served as treasurer of the Iron-Moulders International Union and helped rebuild it after the Civil War. He was an organizer of the first meeting of the National Labor Union (NLU), a cross-trades assembly, in Baltimore in 1866. In 1868, he was elected president of the NLU, the leader of 600,000 organized workers. He supported the eight-hour day, greater security for "the sewing-women and daughters of toil in this land," and affiliation of labor with the First International. He died at the age of forty-one on July 27, 1869.

that you and they may make one steady and strong pull until the laboring man of this country shall receive such pay for time made as will secure them a comfortable living for their families, educate their children and leave a dollar for a rainy day and old age. Slavery, or slave labor, the main cause of the degradation of white labor, is no more. And it is the proud boast of my life that the slave himself had a large share in the work of striking off the fetters that bound him by the ankle, while the other end bound you by the neck.

The white laboring men of the country have nothing to fear from the colored laboring man. We desire to see labor elevated and made respectable; we desire to have the highest rate of wages that our labor is worth; we desire to have the hours of labor regulated, as well to the interest of the laborer and the capitalist. And you, gentlemen, may rely on the support of the colored laborers of this country in bringing about this result. If they have not strictly observed these principles in the past, it was because the doors of the workshops of the North, East and West were firmly bolted against them, and it was written over the doors: "No Negro admitted here." Thus barred out, thus warned off, his only hope was to put his labor in the market to be controlled by selfish and unscrupulous speculators who will dare do any deed to advance their own ends.

Mr. President and gentlemen, American citizenship with the black man is a complete failure if he is proscribed from the workshops of this country, if any man cannot employ him who chooses, and if he cannot work for any man whom he will. If citizenship means anything at all, it means the freedom of labor, as broad and as universal as the freedom of the ballot. I cannot tell how far your action in admitting colored delegates on this floor is going to influence the minor organizations throughout the country. Shall they still proscribe the colored labor, or will they feel bound to follow your noble example of Monday? The question being today asked by the colored men of this country is only to be answered by the white men of the country. We mean in all sincerity a hearty cooperation. You cannot doubt us. Where we have had the chance, we have always demonstrated it. We carry no prejudices. We are willing to forget the wrongs of yesterday and let the dead past bury its dead. An instance of this may be found in my own native Maryland. After we had been driven from shipyard to shipyard, until at last we were kicked completely out and cast upon the cold charity of the world, we formed a cooperative union, got it incorporated, raised $40,000, bought a shipyard,* gave employment to all of our men and now pay them, outside of

---

*The Chesapeake Marine Railway and Dry Dock Company in Baltimore was organized by Isaac Myers in 1865. Within four months he raised ten thousand dollars cash in shares sold to African Americans at five dollars each and purchased a yard and railway worth forty thousand dollars. The company secured a number of government contracts, employed white mechanics as well as black, and paid off its debt within five years. It remained in existence until 1876, when the shift to steel ships forced it to close down. But its very existence forced the white caulkers' union to admit African Americans.

their wages, fifty percent on their investment. And is that all? No. We give employment to a large number of the men of your race, without regard to their political creed, and to the very men who once sought to do us injury. So you see, gentlemen, we have no prejudice. We have issued a call for a National Labor Convention, to meet in the City of Washington the first Monday in December next.* Delegates will be admitted without regard to color, and I hope you will be well represented in that convention. Questions of the mightiest importance to the labor interest of the United States will be disposed of. We will be very glad to have your cooperation there, as you have ours now. The resolutions of this convention will have an important bearing on that convention. The more you do here, the less we will have to do there.

The colored men of this nation are entirely opposed to the repudiation of the national debt.† They go in for every honest dollar borrowed to be honestly paid back, and on the terms stipulated in the original agreement. Any other course is more ruinous to the laborer than to the capitalist. The permanence, not of this administration nor of any other, but of the government itself, depends on the honest paying of its debts. A dishonest government, like a dishonest individual, will be arrested, tried, convicted, and punished.

The money borrowed was from individual pockets. The slaveholders of the South and their sympathizers in the North forced us to borrow that money. It was borrowed to put down the rebellion, not to put down slavery, for that was not in the contract. Liberty to the slave was a bird hatched by the eggs of the rebellion. And of all men in the United States, the laboring men of the North, East and West are most benefited by the money borrowed. You know that had you not whipped slavery, slavery would have whipped you. If the rebellion had succeeded, slavery would have soon spread over the entire country, and you white laboring men of the country would have been forced to work for what a man chose to give you, and that very often under the lash, as was the case in South Carolina. What has stopped this? The money that our government borrowed in good faith. Has the government paid too much for its use? We think you will find it is no fault of the government, but of those who rebelled against it. These are questions that require your weightiest consideration. The workingmen of this country are a vast power, can take care of themselves, and will not be hoodwinked by any political demagogue in or out of power. What we want is low prices for the necessaries of life, and honest administration of the government, reasonable hours of labor, and such a compensation for the time made as will afford us an inde-

---

*In 1869 a call for a National Colored Labor Convention to meet in Washington was issued by the Maryland State Convention of Negro Workers. The convention met on December 5 and organized the National Colored Labor Union with Isaac Myers as president.

†During the Civil War, the government had issued greenbacks. The greenbacks had depreciated, but the bankers had used these greenbacks to buy government bonds, which were redeemable in gold and paid interest in gold. Many trade unions favored repudiating these public debts to force bankers who invested in U.S. bonds to put their capital into industrial, commercial and manufacturing enterprises.

pendent living. We want no land monopolies, any more than money monopolies or labor monopolies. We want the same chance for the poor as is accorded to the rich—not to make the rich man poorer, but the poor man richer. We do not propose to wage a war on capital, and we do not intend to let capital wage a war on us. Capital and labor must work in harmony; reforms, to be made successful, must be founded on the soundest principles of political economy. We feel that in the person of President Grant the workingmen have a strong friend. After the quibbling of the Attorney General, and others in authority, whether Congress meant you should have a day's wages for eight hours' labor,* President Grant ordered, and it was declared, that eight hours was a day's labor, for which there should be no reduction of pay. His is a type of Americanism as handed down by the Fathers. He cannot be an aristocrat, he cannot feel himself above the common people, and any measure looking to the elevation of the workingmen of this country, we believe, is sure to have his support. The colored men of the country, we believe, are sure to have his support. The colored men of the country thoroughly indorse him.[†]

Gentlemen, again thanking you for what you have done, and hoping you may finish the good work of uniting the colored and white workingmen of the country by some positive declaration of this convention,[‡] I wish you a complete success.■

---

*On June 25, 1868, Congress passed a bill providing for an eight-hour day for laborers, mechanics, and all other workers in federal employ. Wages were cut by government officials, however, when the eight-hour law became effective. In 1869, responding to protests from organized labor, President Grant issued an executive order that "no reduction should be made in the wages by the day to such laborers . . . on account of such reduction in the hours of labor." See David Montgomery, *Beyond Equality: Labor and the Radical Republicans, 1862–1872* (New York: Knopf, 1967), 320.

[†]There was a strong movement in the National Labor Union to organize a labor reform party, and it was hoped that African Americans would support labor's drive for independent political action. But as Myers indicated, African Americans in the vast majority supported the Republican Party as the party of Lincoln and the one that had pushed through a radical program of Reconstruction. Hence his warm endorsement of President Grant.

[‡]The convention of the National Labor Union did pass a resolution that read: "The National Labor Union knows no North, no South, no East, no West, neither color nor sex on the question of the rights of labor, and urges our colored fellow members to form organizations in all legitimate ways, and send their delegates from every state in the Union to the next congress." In addition, a special committee was appointed to "organize the colored men of Pennsylvania into labor unions." Unfortunately, few trade unions were willing to listen to this appeal, and when the committee reported on its work to the next convention, it stated that many unions would not accept black mechanics, and proposed that blacks be organized into separate Jim Crow locals.

89 COMPOSITE NATION

Frederick Douglass

This largely forgotten and previously unpublished speech offers perhaps the fullest expression of Douglass's views on the peculiar nature and possible futures of his country. In the aftermath of the Civil War, Douglass saw the United States "at the beginning of our ascent" toward a position of global "power, responsibility and duty." Douglass argued that its destiny could only be achieved if America adopted the principle of absolute equality and overcame the historical conflict between the composite character of its population and the "compromising spirit which controlled the ruling power of the country." "Every nation," he insisted, "owing to its peculiar character and composition, has a definite mission in the world." In Douglass's view, the unique mission of the United States is to provide "the most perfect illustration of the unity and dignity of the human family, that the world has ever seen."

Douglass was especially forceful in arguing in support of equal rights for Chinese immigrants. Almost 300,000 Chinese arrived in the United States between 1849 (the year after gold was discovered in California) and 1882. Chinese laborers played a vital role in the development of many vital industries in the West. Upon the completion of the transcontinental railroad in 1869, thousands of Chinese workers (who comprised 86 percent of the project's workforce) were laid off and migrated to various parts of the country in search of employment. The "Chinese problem" was treated as a national crisis. An editorialist for the New York Times *warned on September 3, 1865, that if, in addition to the "four millions of degraded negroes in the South,"*

> *there were to be a flood-tide of Chinese population—a population befouled with all the social vices, with no knowledge or appreciation of free institutions or constitutional liberty, with heathenish souls and heathenish propensities, whose character, and habits and modes of thought are firmly fixed by the consolidating influences of ages upon ages—we should be prepared to bid farewell to republicanism.*

Hundreds of Chinese and Chinese-Americans were murdered, most by mob violence, in the 1870s, a period in which a nationwide campaign of lynching and other forms of violence and terrorism was also launched against African Americans. In 1882, the Chinese Exclusion Act was passed by Congress, not to be repealed until the Second World War.

In this speech, Douglass urges that the United States welcome Chinese immigration and put aside its racist fears of "Yellow Peril." He endorses essentialist notions of racially based difference but argues that a composite of all races is superior to any in isolation. Douglass's speech was presented in Boston as part of the Parker Fraternity Course on December 7, 1869. Founded in 1858 by the abolitionist minister Theodore Parker and other members of the Twenty-eighth Congregational Society, the course was a series of lectures in which, as Parker wrote in his journal, "men and women were invited to speak who had something to say upon all the great humane subjects of the day, to which the ordinary lyceums in cities seldom tolerate any direct allusion."

The speech text as printed here has been assembled from partial texts in the Library of Congress collection of Douglass's papers and at the Douglass Memorial Home in Anacostia, Virginia. For further information, see Roger Daniels, Asian America: Chinese and Japanese in the United States Since 1850 *(Seattle: University of Washington Press, 1988), 29–66; and Shih-Shan Henry Tsai,* The Chinese Experience in America *(Bloomington: Indiana University Press, 1986).*

As nations are among the largest and the most complete divisions into which society is formed, the grandest aggregations of organized human power; as they raise to observation and distinction the world's greatest men, and call into requisition the highest order of talent and ability for their guidance, preservation and success, they are ever among the most attractive, instructive and useful subjects of thought, to those just entering upon the duties and activities of life.

The simple organization of a people into a National body, composite or otherwise, is of itself an impressive fact. As an original proceeding, it marks the point of departure of a people, from the darkness and chaos of unbridled barbarism, to the wholesome restraints of public law and society. It implies a willing surrender and subjection of individual aims and ends, often narrow and selfish, to the broader and better ones that arise out of society as a whole. It is both a sign and a result of civilization.

A knowledge of the character, resources and proceedings of other nations, affords us the means of comparison and criticism, without which progress would be feeble, tardy, and perhaps, impossible. It is by comparing one nation with another, and one learning from another, each competing with all, and all competing with each, that hurtful errors are exposed, great social truths discovered, and the wheels of civilization whirled onward.

I am especially to speak to you of the character and mission of the United States, with special reference to the question whether we are the better or the worse for being composed of different races of men. I propose to consider first, what we are, second, what we are likely to be, and, thirdly, what we ought to be.

Without undue vanity or unjust depreciation of others, we may claim to be, in many respects, the most fortunate of nations. We stand in relation to all others, as youth to age. Other nations have had their day of greatness and glory; we are yet to have our day, and that day is coming. The dawn is already upon us. It is bright and full of promise. Other nations have reached their culminating point. We are at the beginning of our ascent. They have apparently exhausted the conditions essential to their further growth and extension, while we are abundant in all the material essential to further national growth and greatness.

The resources of European statesmanship are now sorely taxed to maintain their nationalities at their ancient height of greatness and power.

American statesmanship, worthy of the name, is now taxing its energies to frame measures to meet the demands of constantly increasing expansion of power, responsibility and duty.

Without fault or merit on either side, theirs or ours, the balance is largely in our favor. Like the grand old forests, renewed and enriched from decaying trunks once full of life and beauty, but now moss-covered, oozy and crumbling, we are destined to grow and flourish while they decline and fade.

This is one view of American position and destiny. It is proper to notice that it is not the only view. Different opinions and conflicting judgments meet us here, as elsewhere.

It is thought by many, and said by some, that this Republic has already seen its best days; that the historian may now write the story of its decline and fall.

Two classes of men are just now especially afflicted with such forebodings. The first are those who are croakers by nature—the men who have a taste for funerals, and especially National funerals. They never see the bright side of anything and probably never will. Like the raven in the lines of Edgar A. Poe they have learned two words, and these are "never more." They usually begin by telling us what we never shall see. Their little speeches are about as follows: You will *never* see such Statesmen in the councils of the nation as Clay, Calhoun and Webster. You will *never* see the South morally reconstructed and our once happy people again united. You will *never* see the Government harmonious and successful while in the hands of different races. You will *never* make the negro work without a master, or make him an intelligent voter, or a good and useful citizen. This last *never* is generally the parent of all the other little nevers that follow.

During the late contest for the Union, the air was full of nevers, every one of which was contradicted and put to shame by the result, and I doubt not that most of those we now hear in our troubled air, will meet the same fate.

It is probably well for us that some of our gloomy prophets are limited in their powers, to prediction. Could they command the destructive bolt, as readily as they command the destructive word, it is hard to say what might happen to the country. They might fulfill their own gloomy prophesies. Of course it is easy to see why certain other classes of men speak hopelessly concerning us.

A Government founded upon justice, and recognizing the equal rights of all men; claiming higher authority for existence, or sanction for its laws, than *nature*, reason, and the regularly ascertained will of the people; steadily refusing to put its sword and purse in the service of any religious creed or family is a standing offense to most of the Governments of the world, and to some narrow and bigoted people among ourselves.

To those who doubt and deny the preponderance of good over evil in human nature; who think the few are made to rule, and the many to *serve*; who put rank above brotherhood, and race above humanity; who attach more importance to ancient forms than to the living realities of the present; who worship power in whatever hands it may be lodged and by whatever means it may have been obtained; our Government is a mountain of sin, and, what is worse, its [*sic*] seems confirmed in its transgressions.

One of the latest and most potent European prophets, one who has felt himself called upon for a special deliverance concerning us and our destiny as a nation, was the late Thomas Carlyle.* He described us as rushing to ruin, not only with determined purpose, but with desperate velocity.

How long we have been on this high road to ruin, and when we may expect to reach the terrible end our gloomy prophet, enveloped in the fogs of London, has not been pleased to tell us.

Warnings and advice are not to be despised, from any quarter, and especially not from one so eminent as Mr. Carlyle; and yet Americans will find it hard to heed even men like him, if there be any in the world like him, while the animus is so apparent, be[i]tter and perverse.

A man to whom despotism is Savior and Liberty the destroyer of society,—who, during the last twenty years of his life, in every contest between liberty and oppression, uniformly and promptly took sides with the oppressor; who regarded every extension of the right of suffrage, even to white men in his own country, as shooting Niagara; who gloats over deeds of cruelty, and talked of applying to the backs of men the beneficent whip, to the great delight of many, the slave drivers of America in particular, could have little sympathy with our Emancipated and progressive Republic, or with the triumphs of liberty anywhere.

But the American people can easily stand the utterances of such a man. They however have a right to be impatient and indignant at those among ourselves who turn the most hopeful portents into omens of disaster, and make themselves the ministers of despair when they should be those of hope, and help cheer on the country in the new and grand career of justice upon which it has now so nobly and bravely entered.

Of errors and defects we certainly have not less than our full share, enough to keep the reformer awake, the statesman busy, and the country in a pretty lively state of agitation for some time to come. Perfection is an object to be aimed at by all, but it is not an attribute of any form of Government. Neutrality is the law for all. Something different, something better, or something worse may come, but so far as respects our present system and

---

*Carlyle (1795–1881) was a Scottish essayist and social historian.

form of Government, and the altitude we occupy, we need not shrink from comparison with any nation of our times. We are to-day the best fed, the best clothed, the best sheltered and the best instructed people in the world.

There was a time when even brave men might look fearfully at the destiny of the Republic. When our country was involved in a tangled network of contradictions; when vast and irreconcilable social forces fiercely disputed for ascendancy and control; when a heavy curse rested upon our very soil, defying alike the wisdom and the virtue of the people to remove it; when our professions were loudly mocked by our practice and our name was a reproach and a by word to a mocking earth; when our good ship of state, freighted with the best hopes of the oppressed of all nations, was furiously hurled against the hard and flinty rocks of derision, and every cord, bolt, beam and bend in her body quivered beneath the shock, there was some apology for doubt and despair. But that day has happily passed away. The storm has been weathered, and portents are nearly all in our favor.

There are clouds, wind, smoke and dust and noise, over head and around, and there always will be; but no genuine thunder, with destructive bolt, menaces from any quarter of the sky.

The real trouble with us was never our system or form of Government, or the principles under lying it; but the peculiar composition of our people; the relations existing between them and the compromising spirit which controlled the ruling power of the country.

We have for a long time hesitated to adopt and may yet refuse to adopt, and carry out, the only principle which can solve that difficulty and give peace, strength and security to the Republic, *and that is* the principle of absolute *equality*.

We are a country of all extremes—, ends and opposites; the most conspicuous example of composite nationality in the world. Our people defy all the ethnological and logical classifications. In races we range all the way from black to white, with intermediate shades which, as in the apocalyptic vision, no man can name a number.

In regard to creeds and faiths, the condition is no better, and no worse. Differences both as to race and to religion are evidently more likely to increase than to diminish.

We stand between the populous shores of two great oceans. Our land is capable of supporting one fifth of all the globe. Here, labor is abundant and here labor is better remunerated than any where else. All moral, social and geographical causes, conspire to bring to us the peoples of all other over populated countries.

Europe and Africa are already here, and the Indian was here before either. He stands to-day between the two extremes of black and white, too proud to claim fraternity with either, and yet too weak to with stand the power of either. Heretofore the policy of our government has been governed by race pride, rather than by wisdom. Until recently, neither the Indian nor the negro has been treated as a part of the body politic. No attempt has been made to inspire either with a sentiment of patriotism, but the hearts of both races have been diligently sown with the dangerous seeds of discontent and hatred.

The policy of keeping the Indians to themselves, has kept the tomahawk and scalping knife busy upon our borders, and has cost us largely in blood and treasure. Our treatment of the negro has slacked humanity, and filled the country with agitation and ill-feeling and brought the nation to the verge of ruin.

Before the relations of these two races are satisfactorily settled, and in spite of all opposition, a new race is making its appearance within our borders, and claiming attention. It is estimated that not less than one-hundred thousand Chinamen, are now within the limits of the United States. Several years ago every vessel, large or small, of steam or sail, bound to our Pacific coast and hailing from the Flowery kingdom, added to the number and strength of this new element of our population.

Men differ widely as to the magnitude of this potential Chinese immigration. The fact that by the late treaty with China, we bind ourselves to receive immigrants from that country only as the subjects of the Emperor, and by the construction, at least, are bound not to [naturalize] them, and the further fact that Chinamen themselves have a superstitious devotion to their country and an aversion to permanent location in any other, contracting even to have their bones carried back, should they die abroad, and from the fact that many have returned to China, and the still more stubborn [fact] that resistance to their coming has increased rather than diminished, it is inferred that we shall never have a large Chinese population in America. This however is not my opinion.

It may be admitted that these reasons, and others, may check and moderate the tide of immigration; but it is absurd to think that they will do more than this. Counting their number now, by the thousands, the time is not remote when they will count them by the millions. The Emperor's hold upon the Chinamen may be strong, but the Chinaman's hold upon himself is stronger.

Treaties against naturalization, like all other treaties, are limited by circumstances. As to the superstitious attachment of the Chinese to China, that, like all other superstitions, will dissolve in the light and heat of truth and experience. The Chinaman may be a bigot, but it does not follow that he will continue to be one, to-morrow. He is a man, and will be very likely to act like a man. He will not be long in finding out that a country which is good enough to live in, is good enough to die in; and that a soil that was good enough to hold his body while alive, will be good enough to hold his bones when he is dead.

Those who doubt a large immigration, should remember that the past furnishes no criterion as a basis of calculation. We live under new and improved conditions of migration, and these conditions are constantly improving. America is no longer an obscure and inaccessible country. Our ships are in every sea, our commerce in every port, our language is heard all around the globe, steam and lightning have revolutionized the whole domain of human thought. Changed all geographical relations, make a day of the present seem equal to a thousand years of the past, and the continent that Columbus only conjectured four centuries ago is now the centre of the world.

I believe that Chinese immigration on a large scale will yet be our irrepressible fact. The spirit of race pride will not always prevail. The reasons for this opinion are obvious; China is a vastly overcrowded country. Her people press against each other like cattle in a rail car. Many live upon the water, and have laid out streets upon the waves. Men, like bees, want elbow room. When the hive is overcrowded, the bees will swarm, and will be likely to take up their abode where they find the best prospect for honey. In matters of this sort, men are very much like bees. Hunger will not be quietly endured, even in the celestial empire, when it is once generally known that there is bread enough and to spare in America. What Satan said of Job is true of the Chinaman, as well as of other men, "All that a man hath will he give for his life." They will come here to live where they know the means of living are in abundance.

The same mighty forces which have swept to our shores the overflowing populations of Europe; which have reduced the people of Ireland three millions below its normal standard; will operate in a similar manner upon the hungry population of China and other parts of Asia. Home has its charms, and native land has its charms, but hunger, oppression, and destitution, will desolve these charms and send men in search of new countries and new homes.

Not only is there a Chinese motive behind this probable immigration, but there is also an American motive which will play its part, one which will be all the more active and energetic because there is in it an element of pride, of bitterness, and revenge.

Southern gentlemen who led in the late rebellion, have not parted with their convictions at this point, any more than at others. They want to be independent of the negro. They believed in slavery and they believe in it still. They believed in an aristocratic class and they believe in it still, and though they have lost slavery, one element essential to such a class, they still have two important conditions to the reconstruction of that class. They have intelligence and they have land. Of these, the land is the more important. They cling to it with all the tenacity of a cherished superstition. They will neither sell to the negro, nor let the carpet baggers have it in peace, but are determined to hold it for themselves and their children forever. They have not yet learned that when a principle is gone, the incident must go also; that what was wise and proper under slavery, is foolish and mischievous in a state of general liberty; that the old bottles are worthless when the new wine has come; but they have found that land is a doubtful benefit where there are no hands to till it.

Hence these gentlemen have turned their attention to the Celestial Empire. They would rather have laborers who will work for nothing; but as they cannot get the negroes on these terms, they want Chinamen who, they hope, will work for next to nothing.

Companies and associations may be formed to promote this Mongolian invasion. The loss of the negro is to gain them, the Chinese; and if the thing works well, abolition, in their opinion, will have proved itself to be another blessing in disguise. To the statesman it will mean Southern independence. To the pulpit it will be the hand of Providence, and bring about the time of the universal dominion of the Christian religion. To all but the Chinaman and the negro, it will mean wealth, ease and luxury.

But alas, for all the selfish inventions and dreams of men! The Chinaman will not long be willing to wear the cast off shoes of the negro, and if he refuses, there will be trouble again. The negro worked and took his pay in religion and the lash. The Chinaman is a different article and will want the cash. He may, like the negro, accept Christianity, but unlike the negro he will not care to pay for it in labor under the lash. He had the golden rule in substance, five hundred years before the coming of Christ, and has notions of justice that are not to be confused or bewildered by any of our *"Cursed be Canaan"* religion. *

Nevertheless, the experiment will be tried. So far as getting the Chinese into our country is concerned, it will yet be a success. This elephant will be drawn by our Southern brethren, though they will hardly know in the end what to do with him.

Appreciation of the value of Chinamen as laborers will, I apprehend, become general in this country. The North was never indifferent to Southern influence and example, and it will not be so in this instance.

The Chinese in themselves have first rate recommendations. They are industrious, docile, cleanly, frugal; they are dexterious of hand, patient of toil, marvelously gifted in the power of imitation, and have but few wants. Those who have carefully observed their habits in California, say they can subsist upon what would be almost starvation to others.

The conclusion of the whole will be that they will want to come to us, and as we become more liberal, we shall want them to come, and what we want will normally be done.

They will no longer halt upon the shores of California. They will borrow no longer in her exhausted and deserted gold mines where they have gathered wealth from bareness, taking what others left. They will turn their backs not only upon the Celestial Empire, but upon the golden shores of the Pacific, and the wide waste of waters whose majestic waves spoke to them of home and country. They will withdraw their eyes from the glowing west and fix them upon the rising sun. They will cross the mountains, cross the plains, descend our rivers, penetrate to the heart of the country and fix their homes with us forever.

---

*Douglass refers to the passage from Genesis 9:25–27 ("Cursed be Canaan; a servant of servants shall he be unto his brethren") long used to suggest that the Bible justified slavery.

Assuming then that this immigration already has a foothold and will continue for many years to come, we have a new element in our national composition which is likely to exercise a large influence upon the thought and the action of the whole nation.

The old question as to what shall be done with [the] negro will have to give place to the greater question, "what shall be done with the mongolian" and perhaps we shall see raised one even still greater question, namely, what will the mongolian do with both the negro and the whites?

Already has the matter taken this shape in California and on the Pacific Coast generally.* Already has California assumed a bitterly unfriendly attitude toward the Chinamen. Already has she driven them from her altars of justice.† Already has she stamped them as outcasts and handed them over to popular contempt and vulgar jest. Already are they the constant victims of cruel harshness and brutal violence. Already have our Celtic brothers, never slow to execute the behests of popular prejudice against the weak and defenseless, recognized in the heads of these people, fit targets for their shilalahs. Already, too, are their associations formed in avowed hostility to the Chinese.

In all this there is, of course, nothing strange. Repugnance to the presence and influence of foreigners is an ancient feeling among men. It is peculiar to no particular race or nation. It is met with not only in the conduct of one nation toward another, but in the conduct of the inhabitants of different parts of the same country, some times of the same city, and even of the same village. "Lands intersected by a narrow frith, abhor each other. Mountains interposed, make enemies of nations." To the Hindoo, every man not twice born, is Mleeka. To the Greek, every man not speaking Greek, is a barbarian. To the Jew, every one not circumcised, is a gentile. To the Mahometan, every man not believing in the prophet, is a kaffe. I need not repeat here the multitude of reproachful epithets expressive of the same sentiment among ourselves. All who are not to the manor born, have been made to feel the lash and sting of these reproachful names.

For this feeling there are many apologies, for there was never yet an error, however flagrant and hurtful, for which some plausible defense could not be framed. Chattel slavery, king craft, priest craft, pious frauds, intolerance, persecution, suicide, assassination, repudiation, and a thousand other errors and crimes, have all had their defenses and apologies.

Prejudice of race and color has been equally upheld. The two best arguments in its defense are, first, the worthlessness of the class against which it is directed; and, second; that the feeling itself is entirely natural.

---

*California had adopted a number of anti-Chinese measures since 1850, including taxes on Chinese entry, school segregation, restrictions on hospital access, and taxes designed to drive Chinese workers out of mining and other industries. The California Workingman's Society was organized in 1869–70 to ensure that "all those of Mongolian origin should be prohibited from entering California."

†In 1854, the California Supreme Court ruled that Chinese and Chinese Americans could not testify in court against whites.

The way to overcome the first argument is, to work for the elevation of those deemed worthless, and thus make them worthy of regard and they will soon become worthy and not worthless. As to the natural argument it may be said, that nature has many sides. Many things are in a certain sense natural, which are neither wise nor best. It is natural to walk, but shall men therefore refuse to ride? It is natural to ride on horseback, shall men therefore refuse steam and rail? Civilization is itself a constant war upon some forces in nature; shall we therefore abandon civilization and go back to savage life?

Nature has two voices, the one is high, the other low; one is in sweet accord with reason and justice, and the other apparently at war with both. The more men really know of the essential nature of things, and of the true relation of mankind, the freer they are from prejudices of every kind. The child is afraid of the giant form of his own shadow. This is natural, but he will part with his fears when he is older and wiser. So ignorance is full of prejudice, but it will disappear with enlightenment. But I pass on.

I have said that the Chinese will come, and have given some reasons why we may expect them in very large numbers in no very distant future. Do you ask, if I favor such immigration, I answer *I would.* Would you have them naturalized, and have them invested with all the rights of American citizenship? *I would.* Would you allow them to vote? *I would.* Would you allow them to hold office? *I would.*

But are there not reasons against all this? Is there not such a law or principle as that of self preservation? Does not every race owe something to itself? Should it not attend to the dictates of common sense? Should not a superior race protect itself from contact with inferior ones? Are not the white people the owners of this continent? Have they not the right to say, what kind of people shall be allowed to come here and settle? Is there not such a thing as being more generous than wise? In the effort to promote civilization may we not corrupt and destroy what we have? Is it best to take on board more passengers than the ship will carry?

To all this and more I have one among many answers, altogether satisfactory to me, though I cannot promise that it will be so to you.

I submit that this question of Chinese immigration should be settled upon higher principles than those of a cold and selfish expediency.

There are such things in the world as human rights. They rest upon no conventional foundation, but are eternal, universal, and indestructible. Among these, is the right of locomotion; the right of migration; the right which belongs to no particular race, but belongs alike to all and to all alike. It is the right you assert by staying here, and your fathers asserted by coming here. It is this great right that I assert for the Chinese and the Japanese, and for all other varieties of men equally with yourselves, now and forever. I know of no rights of race superior to the rights of humanity, and when there is a supposed conflict between human and national rights, it is safe to go to the side of humanity. I have great respect for the blue eyed and light haired races of America. They are a mighty people. In any struggle for the good things of this world they need have no fear. They have no need to doubt that they will get their full share.

But I reject the arrogant and scornful theory by which they would limit migratory rights, or any other essential human rights to themselves, and which would make them the owners of this great continent to the exclusion of all other races of men.

I want a home here not only for the negro, the mulatto, and the Latin races; but I want the Asiatic to find a home here in the United States, and feel at home here, both for his sake and for ours. Right wrongs no man. If respect is had to majorities, the fact that only one fifth of the population of the globe is white, the other four fifths are colored, ought to have some weight and influence in disposing of this and similar questions. It would be a sad reflection upon the laws of nature and upon the idea of justice, to say nothing of a common Creator, if four fifths of mankind were deprived of the rights of migration to make room for the one fifth. If the white race may exclude all other races from this continent, it may rightfully do the same in respect to all other lands, islands, capes and continents, and thus have all the world to itself. Thus what would seem to belong to the whole, would become the property only of a part. So much for what is right, now let us see what is wise.

And here I hold that a liberal and brotherly welcome to all who are likely to come to the United states, is the only wise policy which this nation can adopt.

It has been thoughtfully observed, that every nation, owing to its peculiar character and composition, has a definite mission in the world. What that mission is, and what policy is best adapted to assist in its fulfillment, is the business of its people and its statesmen to know, and knowing, to make a noble use of said knowledge.

I need not stop here to name or describe the missions of other and more ancient nationalities. Ours seems plain and unmistakable. Our geographical position, our relation to the outside world, our fundamental principles of Government, world embracing in their scope and character, our vast resources, requiring all manner of labor to develop them, and our already existing composite population, all conspire to one grand end, and that is to make us the most perfect national illustration of the unity and dignity of the human family, that the world has ever seen.

In whatever else other nations may have been great and grand, our greatness and grandeur will be found in the faithful application of the principle of perfect civil equality to the people of all races and of all creeds, and to men of no creeds. We are not only bound to this position by our organic structure and by our revolutionary antecedents, but by the genius of our people. Gathered here, from all quarters of the globe by a common aspiration for rational liberty as against caste, divine right Governments and privileged classes, it would be unwise to be found fighting against ourselves and among ourselves; it would be madness to set up any one race above another, or one religion above another, or proscribe any on account of race color or creed.

The apprehension that we shall be swamped or swallowed up by mongolian civilization; that the Caucasian race may not be able to hold their own against that vast incoming population, does not seem entitled to much respect. Though they come as the waves come, we shall be all the stronger if we receive them as friends and give them a reason for loving our country and our institutions. They will find here a deeply rooted, indigenous, growing civilization, augmented by an ever increasing stream of immigration from Europe; and possession is nine points of the law in this case, as well as in others. They will come as strangers, we are at home. They will come to us, not we to them. They will come in their weakness, we shall meet them in our strength. They will come as individuals, we will meet them in multitudes, and with all the advantages of organization. Chinese children are in American schools in San Francisco, none of our children are in Chinese schools, and probably never will be, though in some things they might well teach us valuable lessons. Contact with these yellow children of the Celestial Empire would convince us that the points of human difference, great as they, upon first sight, seem, are as nothing compared with the points of human agreement. Such contact would remove mountains of prejudice.

It is said that it is not good for man to be alone. This is true not only in the sense in which our woman's rights friends so zealously and wisely teach, but it is true as to nations.

The voice of civilization speaks an unmistakable language against the isolation of families, nations and races, and pleads for composite nationality as essential to her triumphs.

Those races of men which have maintained the most separate and distinct existence for the longest periods of time; which have had the least intercourse with other races of men, are a standing confirmation of the folly of isolation. The very soil of the national mind becomes, in such cases, barren, and can only be resuscitated by assistance from without.

Look at England, whose mighty power is now felt, and for centuries has been felt, all around the world. It is worthy of special remark, that precisely those parts of that proud Island which have received the largest and most diverse populations, are to-day, the parts most distinguished for industry, enterprise, invention and general enlightenment. In Wales, and in the Highlands of Scotland, the boast is made of their pure blood and that they were never conquered, but no man can contemplate them without wishing they had been conquered.

They are far in the rear of every other part of the English realm in all the comforts and conveniences of life, as well as in mental and physical development. Neither law nor learning descends to us from the mountains of Wales or from the Highlands of Scotland. The ancient Briton whom Julius Caesar would not have as a slave, is not to be compared with the round, burly, a[m]plitudinous Englishman in many of the qualities of desirable manhood.

The theory that each race of men has some special faculty, some peculiar gift or quality of mind or heart, needed to the perfection and happiness of the whole is a broad and beneficent theory, and, besides its beneficence, has in its support, the voice of experience. Nobody doubts this theory when applied to animals and plants, and no one can show that it is not equally true when applied to races.

All great qualities are never found in any one man or in any one race. The whole of humanity, like the whole of everything else, is ever greater than a part. Men only know themselves by knowing others, and contact is essential to this knowledge. In one race we perceive the predominance of imagination; in another, like the Chinese, we remark its total absence. In one people, we have the reasoning faculty, in another, for music; in another, exists courage; in another, great physical vigor; and so on through the whole list of human qualities. All are needed to temper, modify, round and complete.

Not the least among the arguments whose consideration should dispose to welcome among us the peoples of all countries, nationalities and color, is the fact that all races and varieties of men are improvable. This is the grand distinguishing attribute of humanity and separates man from all other animals. If it could be shown that any particular race of men are literally incapable of improvement, we might hesitate to welcome them here. But no such men are anywhere to be found, and if there were, it is not likely that they would ever trouble us with their presence.

The fact that the Chinese and other nations desire to come and do come, is a proof of their capacity for improvement and of their fitness to come.

We should take council of both nature and art in the consideration of this question. When the architect intends a grand structure, he makes the foundation broad and strong. We should imitate this prudence in laying the foundation of the future Republic. There is a law of harmony in all departments of nature. The oak is in the acorn. The career and destiny of individual men are enfolded in the elements of which they are composed. The same is true of a nation. It will be something or it will be nothing. It will be great, or it will be small, according to its own essential qualities. As these are rich and varied, or poor and simple, slender and feeble, broad and strong, so will be the life and destiny of the nation itself.

The stream cannot rise higher than its source. The ship cannot sail faster than the wind. The flight of the arrow depends upon the strength and elasticity of the bow; and as with these, so with a nation.

If we would reach a degree of civilization higher and grander than any yet attained, we should welcome to our ample continent all nations, kindreds [sic] tongues and peoples; and as fast as they learn our language and comprehend the duties of citizenship, we should incorporate them into the American body politic. The outspread wings of the American eagle are broad enough to shelter all who are likely to come.

As a matter of selfish policy, leaving right and humanity out of the question, we cannot wisely pursue any other course. Other Governments mainly depend for security upon the sword; ours depends mainly upon the friendship of its people. In all matters,—in time of peace, in time of war, and at all times,—it makes its appeal to all the people, and to all classes of the people. Its strength lies in their friendship and cheerful support in every time of need, and that policy is a mad one which would reduce the number of its friends by excluding those who would come, or by alienating those who are already here.

Our Republic is itself a strong argument in favor of composite nationality. It is no disparagement to Americans of English descent, to affirm that much of the wealth, leisure, culture, refinement and civilization of the country are due to the arm of the negro and the muscle of the Irishman. Without these and the wealth created by their sturdy toil, English civilization had still lingered this side of the Alleghanies [sic], and the wolf still be howling on their summits.

To no class of our population are we more indebted to valuable qualities of head, heart and hand than the German. Say what we will of their lager, their smoke and their metaphysics they have brought to us a fresh, vigorous and child-like nature; a boundless facility in the acquisition of knowledge; a subtle and farreaching intellect, and a fearless love of truth. Though remarkable for patient and laborious thought the true German is a joyous child of freedom, fond of manly sports, a lover of music, and a happy man generally. Though he never forgets that he is a German, he never fails to remember that he is an American.

A Frenchman comes here to make money, and that is about all that need be said of him. He is only a Frenchman. He neither learns our language nor loves our country. His hand is on our pocket and his eye on Paris. He gets what he wants and like a sensible Frenchman, returns to France to spend it.

Now let me answer briefly some objections to the general scope of my arguments. I am told that science is against me; that races are not all of one origin, and that the unity theory of human origin has been exploded. I admit that this is a question that has two sides. It is impossible to trace the threads of human history sufficiently near their starting point to know much about the origin of races.

In disposing of this question whether we shall welcome or repel immigration from China, Japan, or elsewhere, we may leave the differences among the theological doctors to be settled by themselves.

Whether man originated at one time and one or another place; whether there was one Adam or five, or five hundred, does not affect the question.

The grand right of migration and the great wisdom of incorporating foreign elements into our body politic, are founded not upon any genealogical or archeological theory, however learned, but upon the broad fact of a common human nature.

Man is man, the world over. This fact is affirmed and admitted in any effort to deny it.

The sentiments we exhibit, whether love or hate, confidence or fear, respect or contempt, will always imply a like humanity.

A smile or a tear has no nationality; joy and sorrow speak alike to all nations, and they, above all the confusion of tongues, proclaim the brotherhood of man.

It is objected to the Chinaman that he is secretive and treacherous, and will not tell the truth when he thinks it for his interest to tell a lie.

There may be truth in all this; it sounds very much like the account of man's heart given in the creeds. If he will not tell the truth except when it is for his interest to do so, let us make it for his interest to tell the truth. We can do it by applying to him the same principle of justice that we apply to ourselves.

But I doubt if the Chinese are more untruthful than other people. At this point I have one certain test,—mankind are not held together by lies. Trust is the foundation of society. Where there is no truth, there can be no trust, and where there is no trust there can be no society. Where there is society, there is trust, and where there is trust, there is something upon which it is supported. Now a people who have confided in each other for five thousand years; who have extended their empire in all direction till it embraces one fifth of the population of the globe; who hold important commercial relations with all nations; who are now entering into treaty stipulations with ourselves, and with all the great European powers, cannot be a nation of cheats and liars, but must have some respect for veracity. The very existence of China for so long a period, and her progress in civilization, are proofs of her truthfulness. But it is said that the Chinese is a heathen, and that he will introduce his heathen rights and superstitions here. This is the last objection which should come from those who profess the all conquering power of the Christian religion. If that religion cannot stand contact with the Chinese, religion or no religion, so much the worse for those who have adopted it. It is the Chinaman, not the Christian, who should be alarmed for his faith. He exposes that faith to great dangers by exposing it to the freer air of America. But shall we send missionaries to the heathen and yet deny the heathen the right to come to us? I think that a few honest believers in the teachings of Confucius would be well employed in expounding his doctrines among us.

The next objection to the Chinese is that he cannot be induced to swear by the Bible. This is to me one of his best recommendations. The American people will swear by anything in the heavens above or in the earth beneath. We are a nation of swearers. We swear by a book whose most authoritative command is to swear not at all.

It is not of so much importance what a man swears by, as what he swears to, and if the Chinaman is so true to his convictions that he cannot be tempted or even coerced into so popular a custom as swearing by the Bible, he gives good evidence of his integrity and his veracity.

Let the Chinaman come; he will help to augment the national wealth. He will help to develop our boundless resources; he will help to pay off our national debt. He will help to lighten the burden of national taxation. He will give us the benefit of his skill as a manufacturer and tiller of the soil, in which he is unsurpassed.

Even the matter of religious liberty, which has cost the world more tears, more blood and more agony, than any other interest, will be helped by his presence. I know of no church, however tolerant; of no priesthood, however enlightened, which could be safely trusted with the tremendous power which universal conformity would confer. We should welcome all men of every shade of religious opinion, as among the best means of checking the arrogance and intolerance which are the almost inevitable concomitants of general conformity. Religious liberty always flourishes best amid the clash and competition of rival religious creeds.

To the minds of superficial men, the fusion of different races has already brought disaster and ruin upon the country. The poor negro has been charged with all our woes. In the haste of these men they forgot that our trouble was not ethnographical, but moral; that it was not a difference of complexion, but a difference of conviction. It was not the Ethiopian as a man, but the Ethiopian as a slave and a covetted article of merchandise, that gave us trouble.

I close these remarks as I began. If our action shall be in accordance with the principles of justice, liberty, and perfect human equality, no eloquence can adequately portray the greatness and grandeur of the future of the Republic.

We shall spread the network of our science and civilization over all who seek their shelter whether from Asia, Africa, or the Isles of the sea. We shall mold them all, each after his kind, into Americans; Indian and Celt; negro and Saxon; Latin and Teuton; Mongolian and Caucasian; Jew and Gentile; all shall here bow to the same law, speak the same language, support the same Government, enjoy the same liberty, vibrate with the same national enthusiasm, and seek the same national ends.■

90 THEN I BEGAN TO LIVE

Sojourner Truth

 *On January 1, 1871, a "large gathering and eloquent speeches" in Boston's Tremont Temple commemorated the eighth anniversary of emancipation. The event was sponsored by the National Association for the Spread of Temperance and Night Schools Among the Freed People of the South. The evening's speakers emphasized the unfinished work of emancipation, particularly the need for land reform through which the freedpersons could become self-sufficient. At the age of eighty-three, So-*

journer Truth addressed the assembly and, at the conclusion of her re-marks, urged its members to sign the following petition:

TO THE SENATE AND HOUSE OF REPRESENTATIVES, in Congress Assembled:—
   Whereas, From the faithful and earnest representations of Sojourner Truth (who has personally investigated the matter), we believe that the freed colored people in and about Washington, dependent upon government for support, would be greatly benefited and might be-come useful citizens by being placed in a position to support them-selves: We, the undersigned, therefore earnestly request your honor-able body to set apart for them a portion of the public land in the West, and erect buildings thereon for the aged and infirm, and other-wise legislate so as to secure the desired results.

The speech through which Sojourner Truth sought to persuade her audience to endorse this proposal is highly autobiographical and relates her own sense of dignity and self-sufficiency to that which she believed might be encouraged among freed persons through land grants. "The search for land, the need to hold on to land," writes Vincent Harding, was "central to the black hope for a new life in America" (There Is a River, 315).
   The speech text is taken (without dialect) from Olive Gilbert's Narra-tive of Sojourner Truth *(1850; reprint, New York: Oxford University Press, 1991), 213–16, based on a contemporary report in the* Boston Post. *See also Vincent Harding,* There Is a River *(New York: Harcourt Brace Jovanovich, 1981).*

Well, children, I'm glad to see so many together. If I am eighty-three years old, I only count my age from the time that I was emancipated. Then I began to live. God is a-fulfilling, and my lost time that I lost being a slave was made up. When I was a slave I hated the white people. My mother said to me when I was to be sold from her, "I want to tell you these things that you will always know that I have told you, for there will be a great many things told you after I start out of this life into the world to come." And I say this to you all, for here is a great many people, that when I step out of this existence, that you will know what you heard old Sojourner Truth tell you.
   I was bound a slave in the State of New York, Ulster County, among the low Dutch. When I was ten years old, I couldn't speak a word of English, and have no education at all. There's wonder what they have done for me. As I told you, when I was sold, my master died, and we was going to have a auc-tion. We was all brought up to be sold. My mother, my father was very old, my brother younger than myself, and my mother took my hand. There opened a canopy of heaven, and she sat down and I and my brother sat down

by her, and she says, "Look up to the moon and stars that shine upon your father and upon your mother when you're sold far away, and upon your brothers and sisters, that is sold away," for there was a great number of us, and was all sold away before my remembrance. I asked her who had made the moon and the stars, and she says, "God," and says I, "Where is God" "Oh!" says she, "child, he sits in the sky, and he hears you when you ask him when you are away from us to make your master and mistress good, and he will do it."

When we were sold, I did what my mother told me; I said, O God, my mother told me if I asked you to make my master and mistress good, you'd do it, and they didn't get good. [Laughter.] Why, says I, God, maybe you can't do it. Kill them. [Laughter and applause.] I didn't think he could make them good. That was the idea I had. After I made such wishes my conscience burned me. Then I would say, O God, don't be mad. My master makes me wicked; and I often thought how people can do such abominable wicked things and their conscience not burn them. Now I only made wishes. I used to tell God this—I would say, "Now, God, if I was you, and you was me [laughter], and you wanted any help I'd help you;—why don't you help me? [Laughter and applause.] Well, you see I was in want, and I felt that there was no help. I know what it is to be taken in the barn and tied up and the blood drawn out of your bare back, and I tell you it would make you think about God. Yes, and then I felt, O God, if I was you and you felt like I do, and asked me for help I would help you—now why won't you help me?

Truly I don't know but God has helped me. But I got no good master until the last time I was sold, and then I found one and his name was Jesus. Oh, I tell you, didn't I find a good master when I used to feel so bad, when I used to say, O God, how can I live? I'm sorely oppressed both within and without. When God gave me that master he healed all the wounds up. My soul rejoiced. I used to hate the white people so, and I tell you when the love came in me I had so much love I didn't know what to love. Then the white people came, and I thought that love was too good for them. Then I said, Yea, God, I'll love everybody and the white people too. Ever since that, that love has continued and kept me among the white people. Well, emancipation came; we all know; can't stop to go through the whole. I go for agitating. But I believe there are works belong with agitating, too. Only think of it! Ain't it wonderful that God give love enough to the Ethiopians to love you?

Now, here is the question that I am here to-night to say. I've been to Washington, and I find out this, that the colored people that are in Washington living on the government[,] that the United States ought to give them land and move them on it. They are living on the government, and there's people taking care of them costing you so much, and it don't benefit them at all. It degrades them worse and worse. Therefore I say that these people, take and put them in the West where you can enrich them. I know the good people in the South can't take care of the negroes as they ought to, 'cause the rebels won't let them. How much better will it be for to take those colored people and give them land? We've ain't land enough for a home, and it

would be a benefit for you all and God would bless the whole of you for doing it. They say, let them take care of themselves. Why, you've taken that
all away from them. Ain't got nothing left. Get these colored people out of
Washington off of the government, and get the old people out and build them
homes in the West, where they can feed themselves, and they would soon be
able to be a people among you. That is my commission. Now agitate those
people and put them there; learn them to read one part of the time and learn
them to work the other part of the time.

(At this moment a member in the audience arose and left, greatly to the
disturbance of the lady, who could with difficulty make herself heard.)

I'll hold on a while. Whoever is agoin' let him go. When you tell about
work here, then you don't have to scud. [Laughter and applause.] I tell you I
can't read a book, but I can read the people. [Applause.] I speak these things
so that when you have a paper [her petition] come for you to sign, you can
sign it.■

91 ABOLISH SEPARATE SCHOOLS

Hiram R. Revels

*From 1869 to 1901, from the Forty-first Congress through the Fifty-
sixth, twenty-two black Americans, all with the backing of the Republican Party, were elected to Congress from the southern states—
twenty to the House of Representatives and two to the Senate. The first
African American seated in Congress was Hiram Rhodes Revels (1827–
1901), who served as senator from Mississippi from February 25, 1870,
to March 13, 1871. He was born in Fayetteville, North Carolina, attended seminaries in Indiana and Ohio, graduated from Knox College
in Bloomington, Illinois, and was ordained a minister in the African
Methodist Episcopal Church at Baltimore in 1845. At the outbreak of
the Civil War, Revels assisted in organizing the first two black regiments in Maryland, and he himself served as chaplain of a black regiment at Vicksburg, Mississippi, in 1864. He settled in Natchez after the
Civil War, was elected alderman of the city in 1868, and became a member of the state senate in 1870. Upon the readmission of Mississippi to
representation in the Union he was elected to the U.S. Senate and survived white efforts to refuse to seat him.*

*On February 8, 1871, the Senate Committee on the District of Co-
lumbia brought in a report on the District's schools which contained the*

clause "And no distinction on account of race, color, or previous condi-
tion of servitude shall be made in the admission of pupils to any of the
schools under the control of the Board of Education, or in the mode of
education or treatment of pupils in such schools."* Immediately a move
arose in the Senate to strike out the antisegregation clause, and an
amendment was offered leaving the choice of segregation or desegregation
to the Board of Education in the District. Against this amendment Revels
delivered a powerful plea that dealt with discrimination not only in edu-
cation but in travel and in all aspects of life. Revels argued that the de-
portment of black people was in no way responsible for prejudice; that it
was the duty of the federal government actively to resist the spread of seg-
regation, and that people learned prejudice against color by living under
Jim Crow restrictions. Revels felt compelled to reassure his white fellow
senators that "mixed schools are very far from bringing about social
equality" and will not lead to greater social interchange. Neither Revels's
plea nor those of Senator Charles Sumner and others prevailed, and
school segregation remained legal in the District of Columbia until the
Supreme Court decision of May 17, 1954.

Senator Revels's speech is taken from the Congressional Globe. *For*
additional information on Revels and other African American repre-
sentatives of the Reconstruction era, see William L. Clay, Just Permanent
Interests: Black Americans In Congress, 1870–1991 *(New York: Amistad,*
1992).

M R. PRESIDENT, I rise to express a few thoughts on this subject. It is
not often that I ask the attention of the Senate on any subject, but
this is one on which I feel it is my duty to make a few brief remarks.

In regard to the wishes of the colored people of this city, I will simply
say that the trustees of colored schools and some of the most intelligent colored men of this place have said to me that they would have before asked for
a bill abolishing the separate colored schools and putting all children on an
equality in the common schools if they had thought they could obtain it.
They feared they could not; and this is the only reason why they did not ask
for it before.

I find that the prejudice in this country to color is very great, and I sometimes fear that it is on the increase. For example, let me remark that it matters not how colored people act, it matters not how they behave themselves,
how well they deport themselves, how intelligent they may be, how refined
they may be—for there are some colored persons who are persons of refinement; this must be admitted—the prejudice against them is equally as great
as it is against the most low and degraded colored man you can find in the
streets of this city or in any other place.

This, Mr. President, I do seriously regret. And is this prejudice right?

*Congressional Globe, 41st Congress, 3d session, part 2, p. 1054.

Have the colored people done anything to justify the prejudice against them that does exist in the hearts of so many white persons, and generally of one great political party in this country? Have they done anything to justify it? No, sir. Can any reason be given why this prejudice should be fostered in so many hearts against them simply because they are not white? I make these remarks in all kindness, and from no bitterness of feeling at all.

Mr. President, if this prejudice has no cause to justify it, then we must admit that it is wicked, we must admit that it is wrong; we must admit that it has not the approval of Heaven. Therefore I hold it to be the duty of this nation to discourage it, simply because it is wicked, because it is wrong, because it is not approved of by Heaven. If the nation should take a step for the encouragement of this prejudice against the colored race, can they have any ground upon which to predicate a hope that Heaven will smile upon them and prosper them? It is evident that it is the belief of Christian people in this country and in all other enlightened portions of the world that as a nation we have passed through a severe ordeal, that severe judgments have been poured upon us on account of the manner in which a poor, oppressed race was treated in this country.

Sir, this prejudice should be resisted. Steps should be taken by which to discourage it. Shall we do so by taking a step in this direction, if the amendment now proposed to the bill before us is adopted? Not at all. That step will rather encourage, will rather increase this prejudice; and this is one reason why I am opposed to the adoption of the amendment.

Mr. President, let me here remark that if this amendment is rejected, so that the schools will be left open for all children to be entered into them, irrespective of race, color, previous condition, I do not believe the colored people will act imprudently. I know that in one or two of the late insurrectionary states the legislatures passed laws establishing mixed schools,* and the colored people did not hurriedly shove their children into those schools; they were very slow about it. In some localities where there was but little prejudice or opposition to it they entered them immediately; in others they did not do so. I do not believe that it is in the colored people to act rashly and unwisely in a manner of this kind.

But, sir, let me say that it is the wish of the colored people of this District, and of the colored people over this land, that this Congress shall not do anything which will increase that prejudice which is now fearfully great against them. If this amendment be adopted you will encourage that preju-

---

*The two states were South Carolina and Louisiana. The South Carolina General Assembly of 1868 provided that all schools "supported in whole or in part by public funds shall be free and open to all the children and youths of the state without regard to race or color." Louisiana provided: "There shall be no separate schools or institutions of learning established exclusively for any race in the state of Louisiana." See Joel Williamson, *After Slavery: The Negro in South Carolina During Reconstruction, 1861–1877* (Chapel Hill: University of North Carolina Press, 1965), 219; Roger A. Fischer, *The Segregation Struggle in Louisiana, 1862–1877* (Urbana: University of Illinois Press, 1974), 51.

dice; you will increase that prejudice; and, perhaps, after the encouragement thus given, the next step may be to ask Congress to prevent them from riding in the streetcars, or something like that. I repeat, let no encouragement be given to a prejudice against those who have done nothing to justify it, who are poor and perfectly innocent, as innocent as infants. Let nothing be done to encourage that prejudice. I say the adoption of this amendment will do so.

Mr. President, I desire to say here that the white race has no better friend than I. The Southern people know this. It is known over the length and breadth of this land. I am true to my own race. I wish to see all done that can be done for their encouragement, to assist them in acquiring property, in becoming intelligent, enlightened, useful, valuable citizens. I wish to see this much done for them, and I believe God makes it the duty of this nation to do this much for them; but at the same time, I would not have anything done which would harm the white race.

Sir, during the canvass in the state of Mississippi I traveled into different parts of that state, and this is the doctrine that I everywhere uttered: That while I was in favor of building up the colored race I was not in favor of tearing down the white race. Sir, the white race need not be harmed in order to build up the colored race. The colored race can be built up and assisted, as I before remarked, in acquiring property, in becoming intelligent, valuable, useful citizens, without one hair upon the head of any white man being harmed.

Let me ask, will establishing such schools as I am now advocating in this District harm our white friends? Let us consider this question for a few minutes. By some it is contended that if we establish mixed schools here a great insult will be given to the white citizens, and that the white schools will be seriously damaged. All that I ask those who assume this position to do is to go with me to Massachusetts, to go with me to some other New England states where they have mixed schools,* and there they will find schools in as prosperous and flourishing a condition as any to be found in any part of the world. They will find such schools there; and they will find between the white and colored citizens friendship, peace and harmony.

When I was on a lecturing tour in the state of Ohio, I went to a town,

---

*By the 1840s integrated schools existed in many Massachusetts communities, but Boston's schools were still segregated. In 1849 Benjamin Roberts, an African American, sued the Primary School Committee of Boston for excluding his daughter from the school in her neighborhood. Roberts, who was represented by Charles Sumner and black lawyer Robert Morris, lost in the courts. In his argument to the court, Sumner insisted that a separate school could never be equal, but the state supreme court upheld the legality of separate schools. Led by William C. Nell, however, hundreds of blacks and whites petitioned the Massachusetts legislature for a law abolishing separate schools, and blacks of Boston also took their children out of separate schools and had them taught privately until the legislature gave in. In 1855 the Massachusetts legislature enacted a law requiring public schools to admit students without regard to color.

the name of which I forget. The question whether it would be proper or not to establish mixed schools had been raised there. One of the leading gentlemen connected with the schools in that town came to see me and conversed with me on the subject. He asked me, "Have you been to New England, where they have mixed schools?" I replied, "I have sir." "Well," said he, "please tell me this: does not social equality result from mixed schools?" "No, sir; very far from it," I responded. "Why," said he, "how can it be otherwise?" I replied, "I will tell you how it can be otherwise, and how it is otherwise. Go to the schools and you see there white children and colored children seated side by side, studying their lessons, standing side by side and reciting their lessons, and perhaps in walking to school they may walk together; but that is the last of it. The white children go to their homes; the colored children go to theirs; and on the Lord's day you will see those colored children in colored churches, and the white children in white churches; and if an entertainment is given by a white family, you will see the white children there, and the colored children at entertainments given by persons of their color." I aver, sir, that mixed schools are very far from bringing about social equality.

Then, Mr. President, I hold that establishing mixed schools will not harm the white race. I am their friend. I said in Mississippi, and I say here, and I say everywhere, that I would abandon the Republican party if it went into any measures of legislation really damaging to any portion of the white race; but it is not in the Republican party to do that.

In the next place, I desire to say that school boards and school trustees and railroad companies and steamboat companies are to blame for the prejudice that exists against the colored race, or to their disadvantage in those respects. Go to the depot here, now, and what will you see? A well-dressed colored lady with her little children by her side, whom she has brought up intelligently and with refinement, as much so as white children, comes to the cars; and where is she shown to? Into the smoking car, where men are cursing, swearing, spitting on the floor; where she is miserable, and where her little children have to listen to language not fitting for children who are brought up as she has endeavored to bring them up to listen to.

Now, sir, let me ask, why is this? It is because the white passengers in a decent, respectable car are unwilling for her to be seated there? No, sir; not as a general thing. It is a rule that the company has established, that she shall not go there.

Let me give you a proof of this. Some years ago I was in the state of Kansas and wanted to go on a train of cars that ran from the town where I lived to St. Louis, and this rule prevailed there, that colored people should go into the smoking car. I had my wife and children with me and was trying to bring up my children properly, and I did not wish to take them into the smoking car. So I went to see the superintendent who lived in that town, and I addressed him thus: "Sir, I propose to start for St. Louis tomorrow on your road, and wish to take my family along; and I do not desire to go into the smoking car. It is all that I can do to stand it myself, and I do not wish my wife and children to go there and listen to such language as is uttered there by men talking, smoking, spitting, and rendering the car very foul; and I want to ask you now if I cannot obtain permission to take my family into a first-class car, as I have a first-class ticket?" Said he: "Sir, you can do so; I will see the conductor and instruct him to admit you." And he did admit me, and not a white passenger objected to it, not a white passenger gave any evidence of being displeased because I and my family were there.

Let me give you another instance. In New Orleans, and also in Baltimore, cities that I love and whose citizens I love, some trouble was raised some time ago because colored people were not allowed to ride in the streetcars. The question was taken to the courts; and what was the decision? That the companies should make provision for colored passengers to go inside of the cars. At first they had a car with a certain mark, signifying that colored people should enter. I think the words were, in Baltimore, "Colored people admitted into this car"; and in New Orleans they had a star upon the car. They commenced running. There would be a number of white ladies and white gentlemen who wanted to go in the direction that this car was going, and did not want to wait for another; and notwithstanding there was a number of colored persons in the car, they went in and seated themselves just as if there had not been a colored person there. The other day in Baltimore, I saw one of these cars passing along with the words, "Colored persons admitted into this car." The car stopped, and I saw a number of white ladies and gentlemen getting in, and not one colored person there. It was the same way in New Orleans. Let me tell you how it worked in New Orleans. The company finally came to the conclusion that if white persons were willing to ride with them without a word of complaint, they could not consistently complain of colored persons going into cars that were intended for white persons; and so they replaced their rule and opened the cars for all to enter. And ever since that time all have been riding together in New Orleans,* and there has not been a word of complaint. So it will be I believe in regard to the school. Let lawmakers cease to make the difference, let school trustees and school boards cease to make the difference, and the people will soon forget it.

Mr. President, I have nothing more to say. What I have said I have said in kindness; and I hope it will be received in that spirit.■

---

*Streetcar segregation was practiced as company policy from the time the cars were placed in service in New Orleans in the 1820s. A few of the omnibus lines excluded blacks altogether, but others operated special cars for colored passengers, identified by large stars painted on the front, rear, and both sides. This practice continued until immediately following the Civil War. In May 1867, a massive demonstration led to the desegregation of streetcars. The evidence of segregated transportation in Baltimore, mentioned by Senator Revels, is not clear. The first Jim Crow laws in Maryland were not passed until 1904, when the General Assembly enacted two laws imposing segregation of the races on all railroads and steamships in the state.

92 THE KU KLUX OF THE NORTH

Isaiah C. Wears

In 1838, Pennsylvania removed the right of African Americans to vote, and it was not until ratification of the Fifteenth Amendment that they regained that right. Several thousand African Americans appeared at the Philadelphia polls in the fall of 1870. In one ward all white men were allowed to vote first, and black men, formed into a separate waiting line, voted afterward. When it was reported that the waiting African Americans were not being allowed to vote, General E. M. Gregory, U.S. marshal for the eastern district of Pennsylvania, sent in a company of marines to keep order and protect black voters. In the fall election of 1871, no federal troops were used in Philadelphia, and violence ensued. Race hatred, stirred up before and during the election campaign, culminated in the murder of three African Americans and the injury of many others. Among those killed was Octavius V. Catto, who had been commissioned a major in the infantry during the Civil War and who after the war had become a high school principal and firm advocate of equal rights in Philadelphia. A large meeting of black citizens was held, "the object of which was to give expression of sorrow at the untimely death of Professor O. V. Catto, Messrs. Chase, Gordon, Boiden, and others." Isaiah C. Wears, a leading Philadelphia African American, delivered the main address.

Catto received a hero's funeral and was buried with full military honors. No one was ever brought to justice for his death.

The address presented here comes from the Christian Recorder, *November 18, 1871.*

MR. CHAIRMAN, . . . To us these scenes are nothing new. Their horrible and community-disgracing record dates back a whole generation. At last we have gained the public ear; at last, through the success of Republican principles, we are able to hold up to public execration the authors of our woes. The party that stands guilty of the crimes of today is the same class of merciless persecutors that have followed and dogged us as no other people in this country have been followed, and this, too, under the blazing sunlight of a Christian civilization. Whenever and wherever we have made any effort to lift ourselves, mobs were sent to burn our dwellings, our schoolhouses, our churches, and our orphan asylums, hanging us to lampposts and clubbing us to death on the highways. Indeed, this persecuting spirit has been so intense, the ostracism inflicted upon us so murderous, its appetite for such immeasurable cruelties so insatiate, that even death itself the common leveler of us all, could not intervene or withstand its potential sway. No; they followed us to the graveyard and barred there the gates of the cities of the dead against us. The men who aided in these things are the authors and instigators of these murders.

It is a disagreeable duty to speak about the unpleasant truths that stand out disgustingly conspicuous in this terrible affair, yet 'tis a duty nevertheless. . . . Proclamations offering thousands for the arrest of murderers may be seen everywhere. If you would find the murderers, come with me to the laudable places of amusement, to the situations of instruction and, in some cases, of devotion, and see there the prescription inflicted upon us. Arrest this blighting—this withering ostracism. Convict it before the country and the world, then these murders will cease, and the reward will be justly earned. As it is, let the most intelligent and respectable among us attempt to avail himself of the accommodations of even a third- or fourth-rate hotel, he will be driven away like a dog. There are men claiming position in the higher walks of life who have nothing but their color to recommend them, hence they fight for it in this way; they labor to keep alive public sentiment, the logical consequence of which is the murder of our people. Whenever you hear a man threaten or suggest a probable "war of races," be satisfied that you have before you a murderer, and though his instrument or agent may not be present he is willing to wait until some turbulent state of public feeling offers an opportune moment to hiss his kennel of savage hounds upon us. Low men often exhibit the instincts of brutes. We know that the commonest and most cowardly cur upon a door mat joins readily in chase of the pursued. We are inhumanly dealt with by the meanest and shabbiest of men only when they find grades of society above them banded against us. Let us then turn our attention to the real authors of these murders.

The Ku Klux of the South are not by any means the lower classes of society.* The same may be said of the Ku Klux of the North. Both are industriously engaged in trying to break us down into beggary and crime.

And even now the sad events that call us here tonight come at this juncture to give practical life to the very sentiment that they were intended to destroy—"they meant it for evil God meant it for good." Let us so accept it. Let no man think that we ask for people's pity or commiseration. What we do ask is fairness and equal opportunities in the battle of life. We are friends of our country; treat us as well as you do its enemies; we have fought to defend her, let us have the same chances as those who have fought against her; then if we gravitate to the bottom there is just where we belong.

---

*During Reconstruction the advocates of white supremacy banded together in the South in secret organizations, of which the most important was the Ku Klux Klan. Disguised by hoods, the Klan roamed the countryside, shooting, flogging and terrorizing African Americans and their supporters, burning homes and public buildings, and perpetrating all sorts of acts of violence. Recent studies have confirmed Wears's statement that "respectable" white Southerners were influential in these terrorist organizations. See Eric Foner, *Reconstruction: America's Unfinished Revolution* (New York: Harper and Row, 1988), 425–44.

We're men and fear no rivals now;
  Freed from the shackles of the rod,
We only ask with lifted brow,
  Justice from man and strength from God.■

93 THE RIGHT OF WOMEN TO VOTE

Mary Ann Shadd Cary

Before the Civil War, Mary Ann Shadd Cary established a formidable reputation as a reporter, editor (she was the first black woman newspaper editor in North America), orator, and debater in support of abolitionism and emigration. After the war, Cary moved to Washington, D.C., where she served as principal of several public high schools and wrote regularly for Frederick Douglass's New National Era *and other papers. In 1869, at the age of forty-six, Cary became the first woman student in the Howard University Law School. She received her degree in 1883.*

Cary was an ardent champion of women's suffrage and, in particular, of the importance of the franchise for African American women. Cary joined the Universal Franchise Association (founded in 1867) soon after her arrival in Washington and spoke as its representative at the Colored National Labor Union convention in December 1869. After the suffrage movement split at the 1869 equal rights convention over the question of whether to support the Fifteenth Amendment granting black men, but not women, the vote, Cary aligned with Elizabeth Cady Stanton, Susan B. Anthony, and the new National Woman's Suffrage Association. In December 1870 and January 1872, Cary attended the women's suffrage conventions in Washington, D.C. Following each of these conventions, a delegation of the suffragists met with members of the Judiciary Committee of the U.S. House of Representatives to present petitions (including Victoria Woodhull's famed memorial) and deliver speeches. Cary probably drafted the following speech for the second of these meetings.

Cary addresses the committee "as a colored woman, a resident of this District, a tax-payer of the same." As a "citizen" according to the Fourteenth and Fifteenth Amendments, she argues, she is entitled to full citizenship rights. Where Stanton and Anthony chose to denigrate black men in their quest to win the ballot for women, Cary instead praises the extension of the franchise to African American men and uses the princi-

ples avowed in the passage of the Fifteenth Amendment to argue for the extension of the franchise to black women. African American women, she argues, share with black men "the responsibilities of freedom from chattel slavery," just as they shared the denial of suffrage and other civil rights for more than two hundred years. Because the contributions of black men to the Union victory figured prominently in the public advocacy of the Fifteenth Amendment, Cary highlights the actions of black women in the Union cause.

In an act of civil disobedience in March 1874, Cary joined sixty-three other women in attempting to register to vote in the District of Columbia. When they were turned away, they obtained notarized statements that they had been denied the right to register. As a writer and lecturer, Cary remained active in the battle for women's suffrage in both the United States and Canada. She addressed the National Woman Suffrage Association convention in 1878 and founded the Colored Women's Progressive Franchise Association.

The text of Cary's speech is taken from a manuscript in her own hand in the Moorland-Spingarn Research Center at Howard University and is reprinted with the center's permission. The text has been reproduced here complete with Cary's revisions. The date of its composition is not entirely clear, nor is it certain whether Cary ever actually presented the speech.

For further information on Cary and her suffrage work, see Jason H. Silverman, "Mary Ann Shadd and the Search for Equality," in Leon Litwack and August Meier, eds., Black Leaders of the Nineteenth Century *(Urbana: University of Illinois Press, 1988); Paula Giddings,* When and Where I Enter: The Impact of Black Women on Race and Sex in America *(New York: William Morrow, 1984); and Rosalyn Terborg-Penn,* Afro-Americans in the Struggle for Woman Suffrage *(Ph.D. diss., Howard University, 1977).*

M r. Chairman, and gentlemen of the Judiciary Committee:—In respectfully appearing before you, to solicit in concert with *these* ladies, your good offices, in securing to the women of the United States, and *particularly,* to the women of the District of Columbia, the right *to vote,*—a right exerc[ized] by a portion of American women, at one period, in the hi[story]—of this country,—I am not vain enough to suppose, for (———) moment, that words of mine could add one iota of weight to the arguments from these learned and earnest women, nor that I could bring out material facts not heretofore used by them in one state or another of this advocacy. But, as a colored woman, a resident of this District, a tax-payer of the same;—as one of a *class* equal in point of *numbers* to the male colored voters herein; claiming affiliation with two and a half millions of the same sex, in the country at large,—included in the provisions of recent constitutional amendments,—and not least, by virtue of a decision of the Supreme Court of this District a *citizen*,—my presence, at this time, and on an errand so important, may not I trust be without slight significance.

The crowning glory of American citizenship is that it may be shared equally by people of every nationality, complexion and sex, should they of foreign birth so *desire*; and ~~that~~ in the inscrutable rulings of an All-wise providence, millions of citizens of every complexion, and embracing *both sexes*, are born upon the soil and claim the honor. I would be particularly clear upon this point. By the provisions of the 14th & 15th amendments to the Constitution of the United States,—a logical sequence of which is the representation by colored men of time-honored commonwealths in both houses of Congress,—millions of colored *women*, to-day, share with colored men the responsibilities of freedom from chattel slavery. From the introduction of ~~freedom~~ African slavery to its extinction, a period of more than two hundred years, *they* ~~shared~~ *equally* with fathers, brothers, denied the right to vote. This fact of their investiture with the privileges of free women of the same time and by the same amendments which disentralled their kinsmen and conferred upon the latter the right of franchise, without so endowing themselves is one of the anomalies of a measure of legislation otherwise grand in conception and consequences beyond comparison. The colored women of this country though heretofore silent, in great measure upon this question of the right to vote by the women of the [copy missing], so long and ardently the cry of the noblest of the land, have neither been indifferent to their own just claims under the amendments, in common with colored men, nor to the demand for political recognition so justly made every where ~~within its borders~~ throughout the land.

The strength and glory of a free nation, is *not so much* in the size and equipments of its armies, as in the *loyal hearts* and willing hands of its *men* and *women*; And this fact has been illustrated in an eminent degree by well-known events in the history of the United States. To the ~~white~~ women of the nation conjointly with the men, it is indebted for arduous and dangerous personal service, and generous expenditure of time, wealth and counsel, so indispensable to success in its hour of danger. The colored *women* though humble in sphere, and unendowed with worldly goods, yet, led as by inspiration,—not only fed, and sheltered, and guided in *safety* the prisoner soldiers of the Union when escaping from the enemy, or the soldier who was compelled to risk life *itself* in the struggle to break the back-bone of rebellion, but gave their *sons* and brothers to the armies of the nation and their prayers to high Heaven for the success of the Right.

The surges of fratricidal war have passed we hope never to return; the premonitions of the future, are peace and good will; these blessings, so greatly to be desired, can only be made permanent, in responsible governments,—based as you affirm upon the consent of the governed,—by giving to both sexes practically the equal powers conferred in the provisions of the Constitution as amended. In the District of Columbia ~~over which Congress has exclusive jurisdiction~~ the women in common with the women of the states and territories, feel keenly the discrimination against them in the retention of the word *male* in the organic act for the same, and as by reason of its retention, all the evils incident to partial legislation are endured by them, they sincerely, hope that the word *male* may be stricken out by Congress on your recommendation without delay. Taxed, and governed in other respects, without their consent, they respectfully demand, that the principles of the *founders* of the government may *not* be disregarded in their case: but, as there are *laws* by which they are tried, with penalties attached thereto, that they may be invested with the right to vote as do men, that thus as in all Republics *indeed*, they may in future, be governed by their own consent.■

94 A PLEA IN BEHALF OF THE CUBAN REVOLUTION

Henry Highland Garnet

The Cuban revolution to gain independence from Spain began on October 10, 1868. It lasted for ten years and ended in a shaky victory for Spain. During these ten years, many Americans repeatedly voiced support for the Cuban revolutionary cause and urged the government of the United States to recognize the Cuban rebels so that they could purchase arms in this country. African Americans were some of the most vocal supporters of the Cuban revolution, especially after the constitutional convention of Cuban revolutionists, which met at Guaimaro on April 10, 1869, and adopted the first Constitution of Free Cuba, whose twenty-fourth article declared that "all the inhabitants of the Republic are absolutely free." The success of the Cuban revolution would mean the end of slavery on the island. Another reason for black Americans' support of the revolution was that blacks in Cuba under the leadership of the great Cuban guerrilla fighter Antonio Maceo had played an important role in the struggle against Spain. Unfortunately, public pressure for recognition of Cuban belligerency did not sway the U.S. government. In August 1869, President Grant favored extending recognition to the Cuban revolutionists and actually ordered a proclamation written that would accord them recognition. But Hamilton Fish, secretary of state, succeeded first in delaying the proclamation and then in completely suppressing it. Thereafter, Grant consistently avoided recognizing the revolutionaries.

In December 1872, black citizens in New York City called for a meet-

*ing to be held at Cooper Institute in behalf of the Cuban rebels to take
proper action "to advance the cause of freedom." The key speech at the
meeting, held on December 13, 1872, was delivered by the Reverend
Henry Highland Garnet, secretary of the Cuban Anti-Slavery Committee.
It is presented here as it appeared in* Slavery in Cuba: A Report of the Proceedings of the Meeting Held at Cooper Institute, New York City, December 13, 1872 *(New York, 1872), 15–18 (copy in Columbia University Library).*

M R. CHAIRMAN, in the invitation that I received to attend this meeting and take part in the proceedings, I recognize the call of liberty and the groans of five hundred thousand of our enslaved fellow men. We
who have passed through the terrible ordeal of the struggle for freedom and
equal rights which in 1861 brought the two divisions of our country into
deadly conflict and culminated in the complete overthrow of despotism in
the United States, are in hearty sympathy with the patriots of Cuba, and we
pray God that he will give strength to the arms of the defenders of freedom
and cause the propitious winds to sweep over the fruitful island, that shall
bear aloft in the skies the flag of the free. In the annals of poetry, in which
glow the promises of the better days that are to dawn upon the earth and the
prophecies that foretell the final reign of universal liberty, there is none that
gives greater assurance to the struggling but invincible sons of freedom
throughout the whole world than is found in this stanza:

> *Freedom's battle once begun,*
> *Bequeathed from bleeding sire to son,*
> *Though baffled oft is ever won.*

I see before me tonight many native Cubans, who, driven by the fierce
fire of Spanish oppression, have sought and found shelter in our free land.
Permit me to assure you, my exiled friends, that I know that I am justified
in saying to you that this meeting, and millions of American citizens, bid
you Godspeed in your noble cause; and in their behalf I extend to you my
hand, pledging ourselves to stand united with you in your efforts for the promotion of the interests of liberty and the universal brotherhood of man. My
sympathies were drawn to your cause when I saw the article in the constitution of the patriots: *"All the people of Cuba are absolutely free."* But not
now, for the strong hand of tyranny is clutching the throat of liberty, and
the government of the island is not yours. But Cuba must be free. God has
decreed it, and the spirit of the age approves it. Slavery shall be blotted out
from every island in the Western Sea, as it has been banished from the Western Continent. The shores of our Republic shall not be washed by the waves
made bloody by Cuban slavery. When the new and free flag of Cuba shall be
triumphantly unfurled to the breeze of heaven, bearing for its motto, "Impartial Liberty and Equality," then shall the spirit of that article of your con-

stitution, to which I have referred, be carried out. We regret that we cannot give you that material aid we would wish to afford you, but we can do one thing—we can create a public sentiment in this land that will urge our government to acknowledge the belligerent rights of the patriots of Cuba. The sympathies of the government of the United States are strongly in favor of Cuban liberty, and when the time shall come when, in conformity with international law they can render Cuba the aid she needs, I believe it will not be withheld.* Aside from humanitarian considerations, I think I may safely say that all the civilized nations that once maintained human slavery in the Western world, and have abolished it, are utterly opposed to giving Spain the monopoly of that diabolical system. Let slavery and involuntary servitude perish at once and forever from every inch of soil in the continent, and in Cuba and Porto Rico. I have twice visited Cuba and have witnessed the horrors of slavery as it exists here, and allow me to state that the slavery recently abolished in our country was mild when compared with the crime that Spain today upholds in Cuba. I have seen slave ships enter the port of Havana, and cargoes of miserable men and women, some dying and some of them dead, dragged and hurried from the decks of slavers and thrown upon the shores. You cannot forget, Cubans, the immortal mulatto poet of your country, the brave and heroic Plácido.† Like yourselves, you know that he loved liberty and freely offered himself on her sacred altar. He was accused of being concerned in an attempted insurrection, and was condemned to die the death of a traitor. When he was led forth to death, he cried:

> O Liberty! I hear thy voice calling me
> Deep in the frozen regions of the North, afar,
> With voice like God's, and vision like a star.

God grant that liberty from her home in "the frozen regions of the North" may continue to call in trumpet tones until she shall arouse every patriotic son of Cuba to unconquerable resistance to slavery. As I have al-

---

*Garnet's faith in the Grant administration was not shared by most of those at the meeting. The black citizens present unanimously declared that the government had been remiss in not recognizing the belligerency of the Cuban revolutionists and resolved that "we, therefore, after four years' patient waiting, deem it our duty, and do hereby petition our government at Washington, the President and Congress of the United States, to accord to the Cuban patriots that favorable recognition that four years' gallant struggle for freedom justly entitled them to." See *Slavery in Cuba: A Report of the Proceedings of the Meeting Held at Cooper Institute, New York City, December 13, 1872* (New York, 1872).

†Gabriel de la Concepción Valdés, known as "Plácido," was a free Cuban black who became famous for his poems written to celebrate anniversaries and birthdays. On the surface there was nothing revolutionary in these verses, but underneath there was always an affirmation of his hatred of tyrants and love for freedom. So great was the fear of slave rebellions in Cuba that his verses could no longer be tolerated. In 1844 "Plácido" was arrested on the trumped-up charge of being an agent for a British abolitionist and of having been selected as president of the republic to be set up by a group of slave conspirators. Though the evidence against him was obtained by torture, he was executed.

ready said, we cannot give you the material aid we would wish to, for the reason that our government holds diplomatic relations with Spain. I wish that we had none. . . . If our relations with Spain retard the progress of liberty in Cuba and Porto Rico, I had almost said that I am sorry that we have any. Haiti has disenthralled herself, and with her own strong arm has broken the tyrant's power. All the nations on the American continent have done likewise, and when Cuba shall have succeeded the last foul blot of slavery will be removed from our portion of the globe.* Let us pray and work, and success will at last crown our efforts.■

95 THE CIVIL RIGHTS BILL

Robert Browne Elliott

The speeches of the first African American congressional representatives dealt with a wide variety of legislation, but many were appeals for the passage of a civil rights bill introduced by Senator Charles Sumner in Congress in the fall of 1871. Sumner's bill proposed to secure equality of civil rights to African Americans all over the country and prohibited discrimination in railroads, theaters, hotels, schools, cemeteries, and churches and on juries. In February 1875, after Sumner's death, a diluted version of his bill, omitting discrimination in schools and cemeteries, became a law. In 1883 the U.S. Supreme Court declared unconstitutional the Civil Rights Act of 1875.

All seven African American members of the Forty-third Congress spoke in support of the bill during the floor debates. Most recounted personal experiences of discrimination in transportation, accommodation, and dining. Black spectators crowded the gallery to witness the debates.

Robert Browne Elliott (1842–1884), a representative from South Carolina, delivered a speech in favor of the civil rights bill in Congress on January 6, 1874. In this speech, reprinted below, Elliott refutes the states' rights doctrine expounded by white southern representatives and grounds his defense of federal actions in the equal protection clause of the Fourteenth Amendment. His address received national attention.

Elliott was born free in Boston, of West Indian descent. He was educated abroad, first in Jamaica and then in England. He graduated from Eton with honors in 1859. While in England he also studied law and was

---

*Slavery was not abolished in Cuba until October 7, 1886.

Robert Browne Elliott

*admitted to the bar and practiced in Columbia, South Carolina. After
serving as a member of the South Carolina House of Representatives
from July 6, 1868, to October 23, 1870, and as assistant adjutant general
of South Carolina, 1869–1871, he was elected as a Republican to the
Forty-second Congress from the Third District of South Carolina. He was
reelected but resigned on November 1, 1874, and returned to the South
Carolina House of Representatives, where he became speaker. Elliott
spoke French, German, Spanish, and Latin and had the largest private library in the state of South Carolina. He was among the most renowned
orators of the period.*

The speech presented below is taken from the pamphlet Civil
Rights—Speech of Hon. Robert B. Elliott of South Carolina, in the House
of Representatives, January 6, 1874 *(Washington, D.C.: Beardsley and
Snodgrass, n.d.). For further information, see Peggy Lamson,* The Glorious
Failure: Black Congressman Robert Browne Elliott and the Reconstruc-
tion in South Carolina *(New York: Norton, 1973).*

MR. SPEAKER: While I am sincerely grateful for this high mark of
courtesy that has been accorded to me by this House, it is a matter
of regret to me that it is necessary at this day that I should rise in the presence of an American Congress to advocate a bill which simply asserts equal
rights and equal public privileges for all classes of American citizens. I regret, sir, that the dark hue of my skin may lend a color to the imputation
that I am controlled by motives personal to myself in my advocacy of this
great measure of national justice. Sir, the motive that impels me is restricted
by no such narrow boundary, but is as broad as your Constitution. I advocate
it, sir, because it is right. The bill, however, not only appeals to your justice,
but it demands a response from your gratitude.

In the events that led to the achievement of American independence the
Negro was not an inactive or unconcerned spectator.* He bore his part
bravely upon many battlefields, although uncheered by that certain hope of
political elevation which victory would secure to the white man. The tall
granite shaft, which a grateful State has reared above its sons who fell in defending Fort Griswold against the attack of Benedict Arnold, bears the name
of Jordan Freeman, and other brave men of the African race, who there cemented with their blood the cornerstone of the Republic.† In the state which
I have the honor in part to represent (South Carolina) the rifle of the black
man rang out against the troops of the British Crown in the darkest days of
the American Revolution. Said General Greene, who has been justly termed

---

*Some five thousand African Americans fought in the revolutionary army, of whom
many were slaves.
†When the British, led by Benedict Arnold, stormed Fort Griswold on September 6,
1781, and massacred the defenders, those killed included Jordan Freeman and Lambert
Latham, two African Americans. Before dying, Freeman managed to kill a British major
named Montgomery. Latham had more than thirty wounds in his body.

the "Washington of the North," in a letter written by him to Alexander Hamilton, on the tenth of January, 1781, from the vicinity of Camden, South Carolina: "There is no such thing as national character or national sentiment. The inhabitants are numerous, but they would be rather formidable abroad than at home. There is a great spirit of enterprise among the black people, and those that come out as volunteers are not a little formidable to the enemy."*

At the battle of New Orleans under the immortal Jackson, a colored regiment held the extreme right of the American line unflinchingly and drove back the British column that pressed upon them at the point of the bayonet. So marked was their valor on that occasion that it evoked from their great commander the warmest encomiums, as will be seen from his dispatch announcing the brilliant victory.

As the gentleman from Kentucky (Mr. Beck), who seems to be the leading exponent on this floor of the party that is arrayed against the principle of this bill, has been pleased, in season and out of season, to cast odium upon the Negro and to vaunt the chivalry of his state, I may be pardoned for calling attention to another portion of the same dispatch. Referring to the various regiments under his command, and their conduct on that field which terminated the second war of American Independence, General Jackson says, "At the very moment when the entire discomfiture of the enemy was looked for with a confidence amounting to certainty, the Kentucky reinforcements, in whom so much reliance had been placed, ingloriously fled."

In quoting this indisputable piece of history, I do so only by way of admonition and not to question the well attested gallantry of the true Kentuckian, and to the gentleman that it would be well that he should not flaunt his heraldry so proudly while he bears this bar sinister on the military escutcheon of his state—a state which answered the call of the Republic in 1861, when treason thundered at the very gates of the capital, by coldly declaring her neutrality in the impending struggle.† The Negro, true to that patriotism and love of country that have ever marked and characterized his history on this continent, came to the aid of the government in its efforts to maintain the Constitution. To that government he now appeals; that constitution he now invokes for protection against outrage and unjust prejudices founded upon caste.

But, sir, we are told by the distinguished gentleman from Georgia (Mr. Stephens)‡ that Congress has no power under the Constitution to pass such

---

*Both General Nathaniel Greene and Alexander Hamilton made strenuous efforts to persuade South Carolina and Georgia to permit the enrollment of blacks as soldiers. Their effort, as well as one by Congress, failed.

†Kentucky maintained neutrality until September 1861, when the legislature voted to remain loyal to the Union.

‡Alexander Hamilton Stephens (1812–1883), member of Congress from Georgia from 1843 to 1859, became vice president of the Confederate States of America. He was imprisoned at the end of the war, then was paroled and was elected U.S. senator during President Andrew Johnson's Reconstruction but was refused his seat by Congress. From 1873 to 1882 he was a member of the House of Representatives.

a law, and that the passage of such an act is in direct contravention of the rights of the states. I cannot assent to any such proposition. The Constitution of a free government ought always to be construed in favor of human rights. Indeed, the thirteenth, fourteenth, and fifteenth amendments, in positive words, invest Congress with the power to protect the citizen in his civil and political rights. Now, sir, what are civil rights? Rights natural, modified by civil society. Mr. Lieber* says: "By civil liberty is meant, not only the absence of individual restraint, but liberty within the social system and political organism—a combination of principles and laws which acknowledge, protect and favor the dignity of man . . . civil liberty is the result of man's twofold character as an individual and social being, so soon as both are equally respected."

Alexander Hamilton, the right-hand man of Washington in the perilous days of the then infant Republic; the great interpreter and expounder of the Constitution, says: "Natural liberty is the gift of a beneficent Creator to the whole human race; civil liberty is founded on it, civil liberty is only natural liberty modified and secured by civil society."

In the French constitution on June, 1793, we find this grand and noble declaration:

"Government is instituted to insure to man the free use of his natural and inalienable rights. These rights are equality, liberty, security, property. All men are equal by nature and before the law. * * * Law is the same for all, be it protective or penal. Freedom is the power by which man can do what does not interfere with the rights of another; its basis is nature, its standard is justice, its protection is law, its moral boundary is the maxim: 'Do not unto others what you do not wish they should do unto you'."

Are we then, sir, with the amendments to our Constitution staring us in the face; with these grand truths of history before our eyes; with innumerable wrongs daily inflicted upon five million citizens demanding redress, to commit this question to the diversity of legislation? In the words of Hamilton, "Is it the interest of the government to sacrifice individual rights to the preservation of the rights of an artificial being called the states? There can be no truer principle than this, that every individual of the community at large has an equal right to the protection of government. Can this be a free government if partial distinctions are tolerated or maintained?"

The rights contended for in this bill are among "the sacred rights of mankind, which are not to be rummaged for among old parchments or musty records; they are written as with a sunbeam in the whole volume of

*Francis Lieber (1800–1872), educator and political philosopher, was born in Germany and came to the United States in 1827. He was professor of history and political economy at Columbia University from 1857 to 1865 and at Columbia Law School from 1865 to 1872. He wrote many books on political science, including *On Civil Liberty and Self-Government* (2 volumes, 1853).

human nature, by the hand of the divinity itself, and can never be erased or obscured by mortal power."

But the Slaughterhouse cases!—The Slaughterhouse cases!*

The honorable gentleman from Kentucky,[†] always swift to sustain the failing and dishonored cause of proscription, rushes forward and flaunts in our faces the decision of the Supreme Court of the United States in the Slaughterhouse cases, and in that act he has been willingly aided by the gentleman from Georgia.[‡] Hitherto, in the contests which have marked the progress of the cause of equal civil rights, our opponents have appealed sometimes to custom, sometimes to prejudice, more often to pride of race, but they have never sought to shield themselves behind the Supreme Court. But now, for the first time, we are told that we are barred by a decision of that court, from which there is no appeal. If this be true we must stay our hands. The cause of equal civil rights must pause at the command of a power whose edicts must be obeyed till the fundamental law of our country is changed.

Has the honorable gentleman from Kentucky considered well the claim he now advances? If it were not disrespectful I would ask, has he ever read the decision which he now tells us is an insuperable barrier to the adoption of this great measure of justice?

In the consideration of this subject, has not the judgment of the gentleman from Georgia been warped by the ghost of the dead doctrines of states' rights? Has he been altogether free from prejudices engendered by long training in that school of politics that well-nigh destroyed this government?

Mr. Speaker, I venture to say here in the presence of the gentleman from Kentucky and the gentleman from Georgia, and in the presence of the whole country, that there is not a line or word, not a thought or dictum even, in the decision of the Supreme Court in the great Slaughterhouse cases, which casts a shadow of doubt on the right of Congress to pass the pending bill, or to adopt such other legislation as it may judge proper and necessary to secure perfect equality before the law to every citizen of the Republic. Sir, I protest against the dishonor now cast upon our Supreme Court by both the gentleman from Kentucky and the gentleman from Georgia. In other days, when the whole country was bowing beneath the yoke of slavery, when press, pulpit, platform, Congress and courts felt the fatal power of the slave oligarchy,

*The Slaughterhouse Cases of 1873 did not directly involve rights of African Americans, but the Court frequently referred to these cases in later interpretations of those rights. The legislature of Louisiana had passed a statute that granted one corporation a monopoly of the slaughterhouse business within certain parishes of New Orleans and thus deprived more than a thousand persons of the right to engage in business. In the majority opinion, the Supreme Court said that the Thirteenth, Fourteenth, and Fifteenth Amendments had no purpose except the protection of the freedom of African Americans. The business of slaughtering cattle in New Orleans, which the legislature had converted into a monopoly, could proceed in such manner as the state might dictate, without infringement of any right, privilege, or immunity conferred upon citizens of the United States by the Fourteenth Amendment.

[†]James F. Beck, Democrat from Kentucky.

[‡]Representative Alexander H. Stephens, former vice president of the Confederacy, delivered the major speech in opposition to the civil rights bill.

I remember a decision of that court which no American now reads without shame and humiliation. But those days are past; the Supreme Court of today is a tribunal as true to freedom as any department of this government, and I am honored with the opportunity of repelling a deep disgrace which the gentleman from Kentucky, backed and sustained as he is by the gentleman from Georgia, seeks to put upon it.

What were these Slaughterhouse cases? The gentleman should be aware that a decision of any court should be examined in the light of the exact question which is brought before it for decision. That is all that gives authority to any decision.

The State of Louisiana, by act of her Legislature, had conferred on certain persons the exclusive right to maintain stock-landings and slaughterhouses within the city of New Orleans, or the parishes of Orleans, Jefferson, and Saint Bernard, in that State. The corporation which was thereby chartered were invested with the sole and exclusive privilege of conducting and carrying on the live-stock, landing, and slaughter-house business within the limits designated.

The supreme court of Louisiana sustained the validity of the act conferring these exclusive privileges, and the plaintiffs in error brought the case before the Supreme Court of the United States for review. The plaintiffs in error contended that the act in question was void, because, first, it established a monopoly which was in derogation of common right and in contravention of the common law; and, second, that the grant of such exclusive privileges was in violation of the thirteenth and fourteenth amendments of the constitution of the United States.

It thus appears from a simple statement of the case that the question which was before the court was not whether a State law which denied to a particular portion of her citizens the rights conferred on her citizens generally, on account of race, color, or previous condition of servitude, was unconstitutional because in conflict with the recent amendments, but whether an act which conferred on certain citizens exclusive privileges for police purposes was in conflict therewith, because imposing an involuntary servitude forbidden by the thirteenth amendment, or abridging the rights and immunities of citizens of the United States, or denying the equal protection of the laws, prohibited by the fourteenth amendment.

On the part of the defendants in error it was maintained that the act was the exercise of the ordinary and unquestionable power of the State to make regulation for the health and comfort of society—the exercise of the police power of the State, defined by Chancellor Kent to be "the right to interdict unwholesome trades, slaughter-houses, operations offensive to the senses, the deposit of powder, the application of steam-power to propel cars, the building with combustible materials, and the burial of the dead in the midst of dense masses of population, on the general and rational principle that every person ought so to use his own property as not to injure his neighbors, and that private interests must be made subservient to the general interests of the community."

The decision of the Supreme Court is to be found in the 16th volume of

Wallace's Reports, and was delivered by Associate Justice Miller. The court hold, first, that the act in question is a legitimate and warrantable exercise of the police power of the State in regulating the business of stock-landing and slaughtering in the city of New Orleans and the territory immediately contiguous. Having held this, the court proceeds to discuss the question whether the conferring of exclusive privileges, such as those conferred by the act in question, is the imposing of an involuntary servitude, the abridging of the rights and immunities of citizens of the United States, or the denial to any person within the jurisdiction of the State of the equal protection of the laws.

That the act is not the imposition of an involuntary servitude the court hold to be clear, and they next proceed to examine the remaining questions arising under the fourteenth amendment. Upon this question the court hold that the leading and comprehensive purpose of the thirteenth, fourteenth, and fifteenth amendments was to secure the complete freedom of the race, which, by the events of the war, had been wrested from the unwilling grasp of their owners. I know no finer or more just picture, albeit painted in the neutral tints of true judicial impartiality, of the motives and events which led to these amendments. Has the gentleman from Kentucky read these passages which I now quote? Or has the gentleman from Georgia considered well the force of the language therein used? Says the court on page 70:

> The process of restoring to their proper relations with the Federal Government and with the other States those which had sided with the rebellion, undertaken under the proclamation of President Johnson in 1865, and before the assembling of Congress, developed the fact that, notwithstanding the formal recognition by those States of the abolition of slavery, the condition of the slave race would, without further protection of the Federal Government, be almost as bad as it was before. Among the first acts of legislation adopted by several of the States in the legislative bodies which claimed to be in their normal relations with the Federal Government, were laws which imposed upon the colored race onerous disabilities and burdens, and curtailed their rights in the pursuit of life, liberty, and property to such an extent that their freedom was of little value, while they had lost the protection which they had received from their former owners from motives both of interest and humanity.

They were in some States forbidden to appear in the towns in any other character than menial servants. They were required to reside on and cultivate the soil, without the right to purchase or own it. They were excluded from any occupations of gain, and were not permitted to give testimony in the courts in any case where a white man was a party. It was said that their lives were at the mercy of bad men, either because the laws for their protection were insufficient or were not enforced.

These circumstances, whatever of falsehood or misconception may have been mingled with their presentation, forced upon the statesmen who had conducted the Federal Government in safety through the crisis of the rebellion, and who supposed that by the thirteenth article of amendment they had secured the result of their labors, the conviction that something more was necessary in the way of constitutional protection to the unfortunate race who had suffered so much. They accordingly passed through Congress the proposition for the fourteenth amendment, and they declined to treat as restored to their full participation in the Government of the Union the States which had been in insurrection until they ratified that article by a formal vote of their legislative bodies.

Before we proceed to examine more critically the provisions of this amendment, on which the plaintiffs in error rely, let us complete and discuss the history of the recent amendments, as that history related to the general purpose which pervades them all. A few years' experience satisfied the thoughtful men who had been the authors of the other two amendments that, notwithstanding the restraints of those articles on the States and the laws passed under the additional powers granted to Congress, these were inadequate for the protection of life, liberty, and property, without which freedom to the slave was no boon. They were in all those States denied the right of suffrage. The laws were administered by the white man alone. It was urged that a race of men distinctively marked as was the negro, living in the midst of another and dominant race, could never be fully secured in their person and their property without the right of suffrage.

Hence the fifteenth amendment, which declares that "the right of a citizen of the United States to vote shall not be denied or abridged by any State on account of race, color, or previous condition of servitude." The negro having, by the fourteenth amendment, been declared to be a citizen of the United States, is thus made a voter in every State of the Union.

We repeat, then, in the light of this recapitulation of events almost too recent to be called history, but which are familiar to us all, and on the most casual examination of the language of these amendments, no one can fail to be impressed with the one pervading purpose found in them all, lying at the foundation of each, and without which none of them would have been even suggested: we mean, the freedom of the slave race, the security and firm establishment of that freedom, and the protection of the newly-made freeman and citizen from the oppressions of those who had formerly exercised unlimited dominion over him. It is true that only the fifteenth amendment in terms mentions the negro by speaking of his color and his slavery. But it is just as true that each of the other articles was addressed to the grievances of that race, and designed to remedy them, as the fifteenth.

These amendments, one and all, are thus declared to have as their all-pervading design and ends the security of the recently enslaved race, not only their nominal freedom, but their complete protection from those who had formerly exercised unlimited dominion over them. It is in this broad light that all these amendments must be read, the purpose to secure the perfect equality before the law of all citizens of the United States. What you give to one class you must give to all, what you deny to one class you shall deny to all, unless in the exercise of the common and universal police power of the state, you find it needful to confer exclusive privileges on certain citizens, to be held and exercised still for the common good of all.

Such are the doctrines of the Slaughterhouse cases—doctrines worthy of the Republic, worthy of the age, worthy of the great tribunal which thus loftily and impressively enunciates them. Do they—I put it to any man, be he lawyer or not; I put it to the gentleman from Georgia—do they give color even to the claim that this Congress may not now legislate against a plain discrimination made by state laws or state customs against that very race for whose complete freedom and protection these great amendments were elaborated and adopted? Is it pretended, I ask the honorable gentleman from Kentucky or the honorable gentleman from Georgia—is it pretended anywhere that the evils of which we complain, our exclusion from the public inn, from the saloon and table of the steamboat, from the sleeping coach on the railway, from the right of sepulture in the public burial ground, are an exercise of the police power of the state? Is such oppression and injustice nothing but the exercise by the state of the right to make regulations for the health, comfort and security of all her citizens? Is it merely enacting that one man shall so use his own as not to injure another's? Is the colored race to be assimilated to an unwholesome trade or to combustible materials, to be interdicted, to be shut up within prescribed limits? Let the gentleman from Kentucky or the gentleman from Georgia answer. Let the country know to what extent even the audacious prejudice of the gentleman from Kentucky will drive him, and how far even the gentleman from Georgia will permit himself to be led captive by the unrighteous teachings of a false political faith.

If we are to be likened in legal view to "unwholesome trades," to "large and offensive collections of animals," to "noxious slaughterhouses," to "the offal and stench which attend on certain manufactures," let it be avowed. If that is still the doctrine of the political party, to which the gentlemen belong, let it be put upon record. If state laws which deny us the common rights and privileges of other citizens, upon no possible or conceivable ground save one of prejudice, or of "taste" as the gentleman from Texas termed it, and as I suppose the gentlemen will prefer to call it, are to be placed under the protection of a decision which affirms the right of a state to regulate the police power of her great cities, then the decision is in conflict with the bill before us. No man will dare maintain such a doctrine. It is as shocking to the legal mind as it is offensive to the heart and conscience of all who love justice or respect manhood. I am astonished that the gentleman from Kentucky or the gentleman from Georgia should have been so grossly misled as to rise here and assert that the decision of the Supreme Court in these cases was a denial to Congress of the power to legislate against discriminations on account of race, color or previous conditions of servitude because that Court has decided that exclusive privileges conferred for the common protection of the lives and health of the whole community are not in violation of the recent amendments. The only ground upon which the grant of exclusive privileges to a portion of the community is ever defended is that the substantial good of all is promoted; that in truth it is for the welfare of the whole community that certain persons should alone pursue certain occupations. It is not the special benefit conferred on the few that moves the legislature, but the ultimate and real benefit of all, even of those who are denied the right to pursue those specified occupations. Does the gentleman from Kentucky say that my good is promoted when I am excluded from the public inn? Is the health or safety of the community promoted? Doubtless his prejudice is gratified. Doubtless his democratic instincts are pleased; but will he or his able coadjutor say that such exclusion is a lawful exercise of the police power of the state, or that it is not a denial to me of the equal protection of the laws? They will not so say.

But each of these gentlemen quote at some length from the decision of the court to show that the court recognizes a difference between citizenship of the United States and citizenship of the states. That is true and no man here who supports this bill questions or overlooks the difference. There are privileges and immunities which belong to me as a citizen of the United States, and there are other privileges and immunities which belong to me as a citizen of my state. The former are under the protection of the Constitution and laws of the United States, and the latter are under the protection of the constitution and laws of my state. But what of that? Are the rights which I now claim—the right to enjoy the common public conveniences of travel on public highways, of rest and refreshment at public inns, of education in public schools, of burial in public cemeteries—rights which I hold as a citizen of the United States or of my state? Or, to state the question more exactly, is not the denial of such privileges to me a denial to me of the equal protection of the laws? For it is under this clause of the Fourteenth Amendment that we place the present bill, no state shall "deny to any person within its jurisdiction the equal protection of the laws." No matter, therefore, whether his rights are held under the United States or under his particular state, he is equally protected by this amendment. He is always and everywhere entitled to the equal protection of the laws. All discrimination is forbidden; and while the rights of citizens of a state as such are not defined or conferred by the Constitution of the United States, yet all discrimination, all denial of equality before the law, all denial of equal protection of the laws whether state or national laws, is forbidden.

The distinction between the two kinds of citizenship is clear, and the Supreme Court has clearly pointed out this distinction, but it has nowhere written a word or line which denies to Congress the power to prevent a denial of equality of rights whether those rights exist by virtue of citizenship of the United States or of a state. Let honorable members mark well this distinction. There are rights which are conferred on us by the United States. There are other rights conferred on us by the states of which we are individually the citizens. The Fourteenth Amendment does not forbid a state to deny to all its citizens any of those rights which the state itself has conferred with certain exceptions which are pointed out in the decision which we are examining. What it does forbid is inequality, is discrimination or, to use the words of the amendment itself, is the denial "to any person within its jurisdiction, the equal protection of the laws." If a state denies to me rights which are common to all her other citizens, she violates this amendment, unless she can show, as was shown in the Slaughterhouse cases, that she does it in the legitimate exercise of her police power. If she abridges the rights of all her citizens equally, unless those rights are specifically guarded by the Constitution of the United States, she does not violate this amendment. This is not to put the rights which I hold by virtue of my citizenship of South Carolina under the protection of the national government; it is not to blot out or overlook in the slightest particular the distinction between rights held under the United States and rights held under the states; but it seeks to secure equality to prevent discrimination, to confer as complete and ample protection on the humblest as on the highest.

The gentleman from Kentucky, in the course of the speech to which I am now replying, made a reference to the state of Massachusetts which betrays again the confusion which exists in his mind on this precise point. He tells us that Massachusetts excludes from the ballot box all who cannot read and write, and points to that fact as the exercise of a right which this bill would abridge or impair. The honorable gentleman from Massachusetts (Mr. Dawes) answered him truly and well, but I submit that he did not make the best reply, why did he not ask the gentleman from Kentucky if Massachusetts had ever discriminated against any of her citizens on account of color or race or previous condition of servitude? When did Massachusetts sully her proud record by placing on her statute book any law which admitted to the ballot the white man and shut out the black man? She has never done it; she will not do it; she cannot do it so long as we have a Supreme Court which reads the constitution of our country with the eyes of justice; nor can Massachusetts or Kentucky deny to any man on account of his race, color or previous condition of servitude, that perfect equality of protection under the laws so long as Congress shall exercise the power to enforce by appropriate legislation the great and unquestionable securities embodied in the Fourteenth Amendment to the Constitution.

But, sir, a few words more as to the suffrage regulation of Massachusetts.

It is true that Massachusetts in 1857, finding that her illiterate population was being constantly augmented by the continual influx of ignorant emigrants, placed in her constitution the least possible limitation consistent with manhood suffrage to stay this tide of foreign ignorance. Its benefit has been fully demonstrated in the intelligent character of the voters of that honored Commonwealth, reflected so conspicuously in the able Representatives she has to-day upon this floor. But neither is the inference of the gentleman from Kentucky legitimate, nor do the statistics of the census of 1870, drawn from his own State, sustain his astounding assumption. According to the statistics we find the whole white population of that State is 1,098,692; the whole colored population 222,210. Of the whole white population who cannot write we find 201,077; of the whole colored population who cannot write, 126,048; giving us, as will be seen, 96,162 colored persons who can write to 897,615 white persons who can write. Now, the ratio of the colored population to the white is as 1 to 5, and the ratio of the illiterate colored population to the whole colored population is as 1 to 2; the ratio of the illiterate white population is to the whole white population as 1 is to 5. Reducing this, we have only a preponderance of three-tenths in favor of the whites as to literacy, notwithstanding the advantages which they have always enjoyed* and do now enjoy of free-school privileges, and this, too, taking solely into account the single item of being unable to write; for with regard to the inability to read, there is no discrimination in the statistics between the white and colored population. There is, moreover, a peculiar felicity in these statistics with regard to the State of Kentucky, quoted so opportunely for me by the honorable gentleman; for I find that the population of that State, both with regard to its white and colored populations, bears the same relative rank in regard to the white and colored populations of the United States; and, therefore, while one negro would be defranchised were the limitation of Massachusetts put in force, nearly three white men would at the same time be deprived of the right of suffrage—a consummation which I think would be far more acceptable to the colored people of that State than to the whites.

Now, sir, having spoken as to the intention of the prohibition imposed by Massachusetts, I may be pardoned for a slight inquiry as to the effect of this prohibition. First, it did not in any way abridge or curtail the exercise of the suffrage by any person who enjoyed such right. Nor did it discriminate against the illiterate native and the illiterate foreigner. Being enacted for the good of the entire commonwealth, like all just laws, its obligations fell equally and impartially on all its citizens. And as a justification for such a measure, it is a fact too well known almost for mention here that Massachusetts had, from the beginning of her history, recognized the inestimable value of an educated ballot, by not only maintaining a system of free schools, but also enforcing an attendance thereupon, as one of the safeguards for the preservation of a real republican form of government. Recurring then, sir, to the possible contingency alluded to by the gentleman from Kentucky, should the state of Kentucky, having first established a system of common schools whose doors shall swing open freely to all, as contemplated by the provisions of this bill, adopt a provision similar to that of Massachusetts, no one would have cause justly to complain. And if in the coming years the result of such legislation should produce a constituency rivaling that of the old Bay State, no one would be more highly gratified than I. Mr. Speaker, I have neither the time nor the inclination to notice the many illogical and

---

*Before the Civil War, the teaching of reading and writing to slaves was illegal in every southern state except Tennessee.

forced conclusions, the numerous transfers of terms, or the vulgar insinuations which further encumber the argument of the gentleman from Kentucky. Reason and argument are worse than wasted upon those who meet every demand for political and civil liberty by such ribaldry as this—extracted from the speech of the gentleman from Kentucky: "I suppose there are gentlemen on this floor who would arrest, imprison, and fine a young woman in any state of the South if she were to refuse to marry a Negro man on account of color, race or previous condition of servitude, in the event of his making her a proposal of marriage and her refusing on that ground. That would be depriving him of a right he had under the amendment, and Congress would be asked to take it up and say, 'This insolent white woman must be taught to know that it is a misdemeanor to deny a man marriage because of race, color or previous condition of servitude,' and Congress will be urged to say after a while that that sort of thing must be put a stop to, and your conventions of colored men will come here asking you to enforce that right."

Now, sir, recurring to the venerable and distinguished gentleman from Georgia (Mr. Stephens) who has added his remonstrance against the passage of this bill, permit me to say that I share in the feeling of high personal regard for that gentleman which pervades this House. His years, his ability, and his long experience in public affairs entitle him to the measure of consideration which has been accorded to him on this floor. But in this discussion I cannot and will not forget that the welfare and rights of my whole race in this country are involved. When, therefore, the honorable gentleman from Georgia lends his voice and influence to defeat this measure, I do not shrink from saying that it is not from him that the American House of Representatives should take lessons in matters touching human rights or the joint relations of the state and national governments. While the honorable gentleman contented himself with harmless speculations in his study, or in the columns of a newspaper, we might well smile at the impotence of his efforts to turn back the advancing tide of opinion and progress, but, when he comes again upon this national arena, and throws himself with all his power and influence across the path which leads to the full enfranchisement of my race, I meet him only as an adversary; nor shall age or any other consideration restrain me from saying that he now offers this government, which he has done his utmost to destroy, a very poor return for its magnanimous treatment, to come here and seek to continue, by the assertion of doctrines obnoxious to the true principles of our government, the burdens and oppressions which rest upon five millions of his countrymen who never failed to lift their earnest prayers for the success of this government when the gentleman was seeking to break up the union of these states and to blot the American Republic from the galaxy of nations. [Loud applause.]

Sir, it is scarcely twelve years since that gentleman shocked the civilized world by announcing the birth of a government which rested on human slavery as its cornerstone.* The progress of events has swept away that pseudo

*Alexander Stephens, vice president of the Confederacy, said of the Confederate

government which rested on greed, pride and tyranny; and the race whom he then ruthlessly spurned and trampled on is here to meet him in debate, and to demand that the rights which are enjoyed by its former oppressors— who vainly sought to overthrow a government which they could not prostitute to the base uses of slavery—shall be accorded to those who even in the darkness of slavery kept their allegiance true to freedom and the Union. Sir, the gentleman from Georgia has learned much since 1861; but he is still a laggard. Let him put away entirely the false and fatal theories which have so greatly marred an otherwise enviable record. Let him accept, in its fullness and beneficence, the great doctrine that American citizenship carries with it every civil and political right which manhood can confer. Let him lend his influence with all his masterly ability, to complete the proud structure of legislation which makes this nation worthy of the great declaration which heralded its birth, and he will have done that which will most nearly redeem his reputation in the eyes of the world and best vindicate the wisdom of that policy which has permitted him to regain his seat upon this floor.

To the diatribe of the gentleman from Virginia (Mr. Harris) who spoke on yesterday, and who so far transcended the limits of decency and propriety as to announce upon this floor that his remarks were addressed to white men alone, I shall have no word of reply. Let him feel that a Negro was not only too magnanimous to smite him in his weakness, but was even charitable enough to grant him the mercy of his silence. I shall, sir, leave to others less charitable the unenviable and fatiguing task of sifting out of that mass of chaff the few grains of sense that may, perchance deserve notice. Assuring the gentleman that the Negro in this country aims at a higher degree of intellect than that exhibited by him in this debate, I cheerfully commend him to the commiseration of all intelligent men the world over—black men as well as white men.

Sir, equality before the law is now the broad, universal, glorious rule and mandate of the Republic. No state can violate that. Kentucky and Georgia may crowd their statute books with retrograde and barbarous legislation; they may rejoice in the odious eminence of their consistent hostility to all the great steps of human progress which have marked our national history since slavery tore down the Stars and Stripes on Fort Sumter; but, if Congress shall do its duty, if Congress shall enforce the great guarantees which the Supreme Court has declared to be the one pervading purpose of all the recent amendments, then their unwise and unenlightened conduct will fall with the same weight upon the gentlemen from those states who now lend their influence to defeat this bill, as upon the poorest slave who once had no rights which the honorable gentlemen were bound to respect.

But, sir, not only does the decision in the Slaughterhouse cases contain

States of America in a March 21, 1861, speech in Savannah, Georgia: "its foundations are laid, its cornerstone rests upon the great truth that the Negro is not equal to the white man. That slavery-subordination to the superior race is his natural and normal condition." See Frank Moore, ed., *The Rebellion Record*, vol. 1 (New York: G. P. Putnam, 1862), 45.

nothing which suggests a doubt of the power of Congress to pass the pending bill, but it contains an express recognition and affirmance of such power. I quote from page 81 of the volume:

> "Nor shall any State deny to any person within its jurisdiction the equal protection of the laws:"
>
> In the light of the history of these amendments and the pervading purpose of them which we have already discussed, it is not difficult to give a meaning to this clause. The existence of laws in the states where the newly emancipated Negroes resided, which discriminated with gross injustice and hardship against them as a class, was the evil to be remedied by this clause, and by it such laws are forbidden.
>
> If, however, the states did not conform their views to its requirements, then, by the fifth section of the article of amendment, Congress was authorized to enforce it by suitable legislation. We doubt very much whether any action of a state not directed by way of discrimination against the Negroes as a class, or on account of their race, will ever be held to come within the purview of this provision. It is so clearly a provision for that race and that emergency, that a strong case would be necessary for its application to any other. But as it is a state that is to be dealt with, and not alone the validity of its laws, we may safely leave that matter until Congress shall have exercised its power, or some case of state oppression, by denial of equal justice in its courts, shall have claimed a decision at our hands.

No language could convey a more complete assertion of the power of Congress over the subject embraced in the present bill than is here expressed. If the states do not conform to the requirements of this clause, if they continue to deny to any person within their jurisdiction the equal protection of the laws or, as the Supreme Court had said, "deny equal justice in its Courts" then Congress is here said to have power to enforce the Constitutional guarantee by appropriate legislation. That is the power which this bill now seeks to put in exercise. It proposes to enforce the Constitutional guarantee against inequality and discrimination by appropriate legislation. It does not seek to confer new rights, nor to place rights conferred by state citizenship under the protection of the United States, but simply to prevent and forbid inequality and discrimination on account of race, color or previous condition of servitude. Never was there a bill more completely within the constitutional power of Congress. Never was there a bill which appealed for support more strongly to that sense of justice and fair play which has been said, and in the main with justice, to be a characteristic of the Anglo-Saxon race. The Constitution warrants it; the Supreme Court sanctions it; justice demands it.

Sir, I have replied to the extent of my ability to the arguments which have been presented by the opponents of this measure. I have replied also to some of the legal propositions advanced by gentlemen on the other side; and now that I am about to conclude, I am deeply sensible of the imperfect manner in which I have performed the task. Technically, this bill is to decide upon the civil status of the colored American citizen; a point disputed at the very formation of our present form of government, when by a short-sighted policy repugnant to true republican government, one Negro counted as three fifths of a man. The logical result of this mistake of the framers of the Constitution strengthened the cancer of slavery, which finally spread its poisonous tentacles over the Southern portion of the body politic. To arrest its growth and save the nation we have passed through the harrowing operation of intestine war, dreaded at all times, resorted to at the last extremity, like the surgeon's knife, but absolutely necessary to extirpate the disease which threatened with the life of the nation the overthrow of civil and political liberty on this continent. In that dire extremity the members of the race which I have the honor in part to represent—the race which pleads for justice at your hands to-day—forgetful of their inhuman and brutalizing servitude at the South, their degradation and ostracism at the North, flew willingly and gallantly to the support of the national government. Their sufferings, assistance, privations and trials in the swamps and in the rice fields, their valor on the land and on the sea, form a part of the ever-glorious record which makes up the history of a nation preserved, and might, should I urge the claim, incline you to respect and guarantee their rights and privileges as citizens of our common Republic. But I remember that valor, devotion and loyalty are not always rewarded according to their just deserts, and that after the battle some who have borne the brunt of the fray may, through neglect or contempt, be assigned to a subordinate place, while the enemies in war may be preferred to the sufferers.

The results of the war, as seen in reconstruction, have settled forever the political status of my race. The passage of this bill will determine the civil status, not only of the Negro, but of any other class of citizens who may feel themselves discriminated against. It will form the capstone of that temple of liberty, begun on this continent under discouraging circumstances, carried on in spite of the sneers of monarchists and the cavils of pretended friends of freedom, until at last it stands, in all its beautiful symmetry and proportions, a building the grandest which the world has ever seen, realizing the most sanguine expectations and the highest hopes of those who, in the name of equal, impartial and universal liberty, laid the foundation stone.

The Holy Scriptures tell us of an humble handmaiden who long, faithfully and patiently gleaned in the rich fields of her wealthy kinsman, and we are told further that at last, in spite of her humble antecedents she found favor in his sight. For over two centuries our race has "reaped down your fields," the cries and woes which we have uttered have "entered into the ears of the Lord of Sabaoth" and we are at last politically free. The last vestiture only is needed—civil rights. Having gained this, we may, with hearts overflowing with gratitude and thankful that our prayer has been answered, repeat the prayer of Ruth: "Entreat me not to leave thee, or to return from following after thee; for whither thou goest, I will go; and where thou lodgest, I will lodge; thy people shall be my people, and thy God my God; where thou diest I will die, and there will I be buried; the Lord do so to me, and more also, if ought but death part thee and me." [Great applause.]■

96 EQUALITY BEFORE THE LAW

John Mercer Langston

The battle for an effective and meaningful civil rights law was waged by African Americans outside Congress as well as in the halls of the legislative body. On May 17, 1874, in a speech at Oberlin College, of which he was a graduate, John Mercer Langston (1829–1897) brilliantly depicted the prevailing prejudices against black Americans and analyzed the reasons for the enactment of the bill proposed by Senator Sumner, partly based on the evolution of the American concept of citizenship. At the end of his address, he urged African Americans to rally in support of the Cuban people then engaged in the long and bitter war for independence from Spain.

Born in slavery in Virginia, Langston was emancipated after the death of his father and slaveholder and was sent to Ohio, where he attended school. He graduated from the literary department of Oberlin College in 1849 and from the theological department in 1852. He studied law and was admitted to the bar in 1854. In 1855 he became the first African American elected to public office in the United States when he won the post of township clerk in Brownhelm, Ohio. During the Civil War he was a recruiter for the famed Colored Regiments of the Fifty-fourth and Fifty-fifth of Massachusetts and the Fifth Ohio. He was dean of the law department of Howard University from 1869 to 1876 and served in Congress from September 23, 1890, to March 3, 1891, representing the Fourth District of Virginia.

On May 17, 1874, Langston returned to Oberlin to celebrate the anniversary of the adoption of the Fifteenth Amendment. He presented the following address and, according to the Oberlin Weekly News, *"held the unbroken attention of his audience to the close," whereupon "the expressions of approval were loud and protracted."*

The speech text appears in John M. Langston, Freedom and Citizen-

ship: Selected Lectures and Addresses of John M. Langston, with an introductory sketch by Rev. J. E. Rankin *(Washington, D.C., 1883), 141–61.*

M R. PRESIDENT AND FRIENDS: I thank you for the invitation
which brings me before you at this time, to address you upon this
most interesting occasion. I am not unmindful of the fact that I stand in the
presence of instructors, eminently distinguished for the work which they
have done in the cause of truth and humanity. Oberlin was a pioneer in the
labor of abolition.* It is foremost in the work of bringing about equality of
the Negro before the law. Thirty years ago on the first day of last March, it
was my good fortune, a boy seeking an education, to see Oberlin for the first
time. Here I discovered at once that I breathed a new atmosphere. Though
poor, and a colored boy, I found no distinction made against me in your hotel, in your institution of learning, in your family circle. I come here today
with a heart full of gratitude, to say to you in this public way that I not only
thank you for what you did for me individually, but for what you did for the
cause whose success makes this day the colored American a citizen sustained in all the rights, privileges and immunities of American citizenship
by law.

As our country advances in civilization, prosperity and happiness, cultivating things which appertain to literature, science and law, may your
Oberlin, as in the past, so in all the future, go forward, cultivating a noble,
patriotic, Christian leadership. In the name of the Negro, so largely blest and
benefited by your institution, I bid you a hearty Godspeed.

Mr. President, within less than a quarter of a century, within the last
fifteen years, the colored American has been raised from the condition of
four footed beasts and creeping things to the level of enfranchised manhood.
Within this period the slave oligarchy of the land has been overthrown, and
the nation itself emancipated from its barbarous rule. The compromise
measures of 1850, including the Fugitive Slave law, together with the whole
body of law enacted in the interest of slavery, then accepted as finalities, and
the power of leading political parties pledged to their maintenance have, with
those parties, been utterly nullified and destroyed. In their stead we have a
purified Constitution and legislation no longer construed and enforced to
sanction and support inhumanity and crime, but to sustain and perpetuate
the freedom and the rights of us all.

Indeed, two nations have been born in a day. For in the death of slavery,
and through the change indicated, the colored American has been spoken
into the new life of liberty and law; while new, other and better purposes,

---

*Oberlin College was a center of abolitionism before the Civil War and was a sta-
tion on the Underground Railroad. Oberlin students and professors were involved in the
Oberlin-Wellington Rescue of 1858, in which Langston's brother, Charles, played a leading
role in defying the Fugitive Slave Act of 1850.

aspirations and feelings have possessed and moved the soul of his fellow countrymen. The moral atmosphere of the land is no longer that of slavery and hate; as far as the late slave, even, is concerned, it is largely that of freedom and fraternal appreciation.

Not forgetting the struggle and sacrifice of the people, the matchless courage and endurance of our soldiery, necessary to the salvation of the Government and Union, our freedom and that reconstruction of sentiment and law essential to their support, it is eminently proper that we all leave our ordinary callings this day, to join in cordial commemoration of our emancipation, the triumph of a movement whose comprehensive results profit and bless without discrimination as to color or race.

Hon. Benjamin F. Butler, on the 4th day of July last, in addressing his fellow-citizens of Massachusetts, at Framingham, used the following language, as I conceive, with propriety and truth:

> "But another and, it may not be too much to say, greater event has arisen within this generation. The rebellion sought to undo all that '76 had done, and to dissolve the nation then born, and to set aside the Declaration that all men are created equal, with certain inalienable rights, among which are life, liberty and the pursuit of happiness. The war that ensued in suppressing this treasonable design, demanded so much greater effort, so much more terrible sacrifice, and has imprinted itself upon the people with so much more sharpness and freshness, that we of the present, and still more they of the coming generation, almost forgetting '76, will remember '61 and '65, and the wrongs inflicted upon our fathers by King George and his ministers will be obliterated by the remembrance of the Proclamation of Emancipation, the assassination of the President, the restoration of the Union, and the reconstruction of the country in one united, and as we fondly trust, never to be dissevered nation."

The laws of a nation are no more the indices of its public sentiment and its civilization, than of its promise of progress toward the permanent establishment of freedom and equal rights. The histories of the empires of the past, no less than the nations of the present, bear testimony to the truthfulness of this statement. Because this is so, her laws, no less than her literature and science, constitute the glory of a nation, and render her influence lasting. This is particularly illustrated in the case of Rome, immortalized, certainly, not less by her laws than her letters or her arms. Hence, the sages, the jurists, and the statesmen of all ages, since Justinian, have dwelt with delight and admiration upon the excellences and beauties of Roman jurisprudence. Of the civil law Chancellor Kent eloquently says: "It was created and matured on the banks of the Tiber, by the successive wisdom of Roman statesmen, magistrates and sages; and after governing the greatest people in the ancient world for the space of thirteen or fourteen centuries, and undergoing extraordinary vicissitudes after the fall of the Western Empire, it was revived, admired and studied in northern Europe, on account of the variety and excellence of its general principles. It is now taught and obeyed not only in France, Spain, Germany, Holland, and Scotland, but in the islands of the Indian Ocean and on the banks of the Mississippi and the St. Lawrence. So true, it seems, are the words of d'Augesseau, that "the grand destinies of Rome are not yet accomplished; she reigns throughout the world by her reason, after having ceased to reign by her authority." And the reason through which she here reigns, is the reason of the law.

It is no more interesting to the patriot than to the philanthropist to trace the changes which have been made during the last decade in our legislation and law. Nor is there anything in these changes to cause regret or fear to the wise and sagacious lawyer or statesman. This is particularly true since, in the changes made, we essay no novel experiments in legislation and law, but such as are justified by principles drawn from the fountains of our jurisprudence, the Roman civil and the common law. It has been truthfully stated that the common law has made no distinction on account of race or color. None is now made in England or in any other Christian country of Europe. Nor is there any such distinction made, to my knowledge in the whole body of the Roman civil law.

Among the changes that have been wrought in the law of our country, in the order of importance and dignity, I would mention, first, that slavery abolished, not by State but national enactment, can never again in the history of our country be justified or defended on the ground that it is a municipal institution, the creature of State law. Henceforth, as our emancipation has been decreed by national declaration, our freedom is shielded and protected by the strong arm of national law. Go where we may, now, like the atmosphere about us, law protects us in our locomotion, our utterance, and our pursuit of happiness. And to this leading and fundamental fact of the law the people and the various States of the Union are adjusting themselves with grace and wisdom. It would be difficult to find a sane man in our country who would seriously advocate the abrogation of the 13th amendment to the Constitution.

In our emancipation it is fixed by law that the place where we are born is *ipso facto* our country; and this gives us a domicile, a home. As in slavery we had no self ownership, nor interest in anything external to ourselves, so we were without country and legal settlement. While slavery existed, even the free colored American was in no better condition; and hence exhortations, prompted in many instances by considerations of philanthropy and good-will, were not infrequently made to him to leave his native land, to seek residence and home elsewhere, in distant and inhospitable regions. These exhortations did not always pass unheeded; for eventually a national organization was formed, having for its sole purpose the transportation to Africa of such colored men as might desire to leave the land of their birth to find settlement in that country. And through the influence of the African

Colonization Society not a few, even, of our most energetic, enterprising, industrious and able colored men, not to mention thousands of the humbler class, have been carried abroad.

It may be that, in the providence of God, these persons, self-expatriated, may have been instrumental in building up a respectable and promising government in Liberia, and that those who have supported the Colonization Society have been philanthropically disposed, both as regards the class transported and the native African. It is still true, however, that the emancipated American has hitherto been driven or compelled to consent to expatriation because denied legal home and settlement in the land of his nativity. Expatriation is no longer thus compelled; for it is now settled in the law, with respect to the colored, as well as all other native-born Americans, that the country of his birth, even this beautiful and goodly land, is his country. Nothing, therefore, appertaining to it, its rich and inexhaustible resources, its industry and commerce, its education and religion, its law and Government, the glory and perpetuity of its free institutions and Union, can be without lively and permanent interest to him, as to all others who, either by birth or adoption, legitimately claim it as their country.

With emancipation, then, comes also that which is dearer to the true patriot than life itself: country and home. And this doctrine of the law, in the broad and comprehensive application explained, is now accepted without serious objection by leading jurists and statesmen.

The law has also forever determined, and to our advantage, that nativity, without any regard to nationality or complexion, settles, absolutely, the question of citizenship. One can hardly understand how citizenship, predicated upon birth, could have ever found place among the vexed questions of the law; certainly American law. We have only to read, however, the official opinions given by leading and representative American lawyers, in slaveholding times, to gain full knowledge to the existence of this fact. According to these opinions our color, race and degradation, all or either, rendered the colored American incapable of being or becoming a citizen of the United States. As early as November 7th, 1821, during the official term of President Monroe, the Hon. William Wirt, of Virginia, then acting as Attorney-General of the United States, in answer to the question propounded by the Secretary of the Treasury, "whether free persons of color are, in Virginia, citizens of the United States within the intent and meaning of the acts regulating foreign and coasting trade, so as to be qualified to command vessels," replied, saying among other things: "Free Negroes and mulattoes can satisfy the requisitions of age and residence as well as the white man; and if nativity, residence and allegiance combined (without the rights and privileges of a white man) are sufficient to make him a citizen of the United States, in the sense of the Constitution, then free Negroes and mulattoes are eligible to those high offices," (of President, Senator or Representative,) "and may command the purse and sword of the nation." After able and elaborate argument to show that nativity in the case of the colored American does not give citizenship, according to the meaning of the Constitution of the United States, Mr. Wirt concludes his opinion in these words: "Upon the whole, I am of the opinion that free persons of color, in Virginia, are not citizens of the United States, within the intent and meaning of the acts regulating foreign and coasting trade, so as to be qualified to command vessels."

This subject was further discussed in 1843, when the Hon. John C. Spencer, then Secretary of the Treasury, submitted to Hon. H. S. Legare, Attorney-General of the United States, in behalf of the Commissioner of the General Land Office, with request that his opinion be given thereon, "whether a free man of color, in the case presented, can be admitted to the privileges of a pre-emptioner under the act of September 4, 1841." In answering this question, Mr. Legare held: "It is not necessary, in my view of the matter, to discuss the question how far a free man of color may be a citizen in the highest sense of that word that is, one who enjoys in the fullest manner all the *jura civitatis* under the Constitution of the United States. It is the plain meaning of the act to give the right of pre-emption to all denizens; any foreigner who had filed his declaration of intention to become a citizen is rendered at once capable of holding land." Continuing, he says: "Now, free people of color are not aliens, they enjoy universally (while there has been no express statutory provision to the contrary) the rights of denizens."

This opinion of the learned Attorney-General, while it admits the free man of color to the privileges of a pre-emptioner under the act mentioned, places him legally in a nondescript condition, erroneously assuming, as we clearly undertake to say, that there are degrees and grades of American citizenship. These opinions accord well with the *dicta* of the Dred-Scott decision, of which we have lively remembrance.

But a change was wrought in the feeling and conviction of our country, as indicated in the election of Abraham Lincoln President of the United States. On the 22nd day of September, 1862, he issued his preliminary Emancipation Proclamation. On the 29th day of the following November Salmon P. Chase, then Secretary of the Treasury, propounded to Edward Bates, then Attorney-General, the same question in substance which had been put in 1821 to William Wirt, viz.: "Are colored men citizens of the United States, and therefore competent to command American vessels?" The reasoning and the conclusion reached by Edward Bates were entirely different from that of his predecessor, William Wirt. Nor does Edward Bates leave the colored American in the anomalous condition of a "denizen." In his masterly and exhaustive opinion, creditable alike to his ability and learning, his patriotism and philanthropy, he maintains that "free men of color, if born in the United States, are citizens of the United States; and, if otherwise qualified, are competent, according to the acts of Congress, to be masters of vessels engaged in the coasting trade. In the course of his argument he says:

1. "In every civilized country the individual is born to duties and rights, the duty of allegiance and the right to protection, and these are correlative obligations, the one the price of the other, and they

constitute the all-sufficient bond of union between the individual and his country, and the country he is born in is *prima facie* his country.

2. "And our Constitution, in speaking of natural-born citizens, uses no affirmative language to make them such, but only recognizes and reaffirms the universal principle, common to all nations and as old as political society, that the people born in the country do constitute the nation, and, as individuals, are natural members of the body politic.

3. "In the United States it is too late to deny the political rights and obligations conferred and imposed by nativity; for our laws do not pretend to create or enact them, but do assume and recognize them as things known to all men, because pre-existent and natural, and, therefore, things of which the laws must take cognizance.

4. "It is strenuously insisted by some that 'persons of color,' though born in the country, are not capable of being citizens of the United States. As far as the Constitution is concerned, this is a naked assumption, for the Constitution contains not one word upon the subject.

5. "There are some who, abandoning the untenable objection of color, still contend that no person descended from Negroes of the African race can be a citizen of the United States. Here the objection is not color but race only. * * * * The Constitution certainly does not forbid it, but is silent about race as it is about color.

6. "But it is said that African Negroes are a degraded race, and that all who are tainted with that degradation are forever disqualified for the functions of citizenship. I can hardly comprehend the thought of the absolute incompatibility of degradation and citizenship; I thought that they often went together.

7. "Our nationality was created and our political government exists by written law, and inasmuch as that law does not exclude persons of that descent, and as its terms are manifestly broad enough to include them, it follows, inevitably, that such persons born in the country must be citizens unless the fact of African descent be so incompatible with the fact of citizenship that the two cannot exist together."

When it is recollected that these broad propositions with regard to citizenship predicated upon nativity, and in the case of free colored men, were enunciated prior to the first day of January, 1863, before emancipation, before even the 13th amendment of the Constitution was adopted; when the law stood precisely as it was, when Wirt and Legare gave their opinions, it must be conceded that Bates was not only thoroughly read in the law, but bold and sagacious. For these propositions have all passed, through the 14th amendment, into the Constitution of the United States, and are sustained by a wise and well-defined public judgment.

With freedom decreed by law, citizenship sanctioned and sustained thereby, the duty of allegiance on the one part, and the right of protection on the other recognized and enforced, even if considerations of political necessity had not intervened, the gift of the ballot to the colored American could not have long been delayed. The 15th amendment is the logical and legal consequences of the 13th and 14th amendments of the Constitution. Considerations of political necessity, as indicated, no doubt hastened the adoption of this amendment. But in the progress of legal development in our country, consequent upon the triumph of the abolition movement, its coming was inevitable. And, therefore, as its legal necessity, as well as political, is recognized and admitted, opposition to it has well-nigh disappeared. Indeed, so far from there being anything like general and organized opposition to the exercise of political powers by the enfranchised American, the people accept it as a fit and natural fact.

Great as the change has been with regard to the legal status of the colored American, in his freedom, his enfranchisement, and the exercise of political powers, he is not yet given the full exercise and enjoyment of all the rights which appertain by law to American citizenship. Such as are still denied him are withheld on the plea that their recognition would result in social equality, and his demand for them is met by considerations derived from individual and domestic opposition. Such reasoning is no more destitute of logic than law. While I hold that opinion sound which does not accept mere prejudice and caprice instead of the promptings of nature, guided by cultivated taste and wise judgment as the true basis of social recognition; and believing, too, that in a Christian community, social recognition may justly be pronounced a duty, I would not deal in this discussion with matters of society. I would justify the claim of the colored American to complete equality of rights and privileges upon well considered and accepted principles of law.

As showing the condition and treatment of the colored citizens of this country, anterior to the introduction of the Civil Rights Bill, so called, into the United States Senate, by the late Hon. Charles Sumner,* I ask your attention to the following words from a letter written by him:

"I wish a bill carefully drawn, supplementary to the existing Civil Rights Law, by which all citizens shall be protected in equal rights:—

"1. On railroads, steamboats and public conveyances, being public carriers.
"2. At all houses in the nature of 'inns.'
"3. All licensed houses of public amusement.
"4. At all common schools.

"Can you do this? I would follow as much as possible the language of the existing Civil Rights Law, and make the new bill supplementary."

---

*Sumner died on March 11, 1874. As he lay on his deathbed, too sick to recognize visitors, he kept entreating: "You must take care of the civil-rights bill—my bill, the civil-rights bill—don't let it fail." See David Herbert Donald, *Charles Sumner and the Rights of Man* (New York: Knopf, 1948), 586.

It will be seen from this very clear and definite statement of the Senator, that in his judgment, in spite of and contrary to common law rules applied in the case, certainly of all others, and recognized as fully settled, the colored citizen was denied those accommodations, facilities, advantages and privileges, furnished ordinarily by common carriers, inn-keepers, at public places of amusement and common schools; and which are so indispensable to rational and useful enjoyment of life, that without them citizenship itself loses much of its value, and liberty seems little more than a name.

The judicial axiom, *"omnes homines oequales sunt,"* is said to have been given the world by the jurisconsults of the Antonine era. From the Roman, the French people inherited this legal sentiment; and, through the learning, the wisdom and patriotism of Thomas Jefferson and his Revolutionary compatriots, it was made the chief corner-stone of jurisprudence and politics. In considering the injustice done the colored American in denying him common school advantages, on general and equal terms with all others, impartial treatment in the conveyances of common carriers, by sea and land, and the enjoyment of the usual accommodations afforded travelers at public inns, and in vindicating his claim to the same, it is well to bear in mind this fundamental and immutable principle upon which the fathers built, and in the light of which our law ought to be construed and enforced. This observation has especial significance as regards the obligations and liabilities of common carriers and inn-keepers; for from the civil law we have borrowed those principles largely which have controlling force in respect to these subjects. It is manifest, in view of this statement, that the law with regard to these topics is neither novel nor unsettled; and when the colored American asks its due enforcement in his behalf, he makes no unnatural and strange demand.

Denied, generally, equal school advantages, the colored citizen demands them in the name of that equality of rights and privileges which is the vital element of American law. Equal in freedom, sustained by law; equal in citizenship, defined and supported by the law; equal in the exercise of political powers, regulated and sanctioned by law; by what refinement of reasoning, or tenet of law, can the denial of common school and other educational advantages be justified? To answer, that so readeth the statute, is only to drive us back of the letter to the reasonableness, the soul of the law, in the name of which we would, as we do, demand the repeal of that enactment which is not only not law, but contrary to its simplest requirements. It may be true that that which ought to be law is not always so written; but, in this matter, that only ought to remain upon the statute book, to be enforced as to citizens and voters, which is law in the truest and best sense.

Without dwelling upon the advantages of a thorough common school education, I will content myself by offering several considerations against the proscriptive, and in favor of the common school. A common school should be one to which all citizens may send their children, not by favor, but by right. It is established and supported by the Government; its criterion is a public foundation; and one citizen has as rightful claim upon its privileges and advantages as any other. The money set apart to its organization and support, whatever the sources whence it is drawn, whether from taxation or appropriation, having been dedicated to the public use, belongs as much to one as to another citizen; and no principle of law can be adduced to justify any arbitrary classification which excludes the child of any citizen or class of citizens from equal enjoyment of the advantages purchased by such fund, it being the common property of every citizen equally, by reason of its public dedication.

Schools which tend to separate the children of the country in their feelings, aspirations and purposes, which foster and perpetuate sentiments of caste, hatred, and ill-will, which breed a sense of degradation on the one part and of superiority on the other, which beget clannish notions rather than teach and impress an omnipresent and living principle and faith that we are all Americans, in no wise realize our ideal of common schools, while they are contrary to the spirit of our laws and institutions.

Two separate school systems, tolerating discriminations in favor of one class against another, inflating on the one part, degrading on the other; two separate school systems, I say, tolerating such state of feeling and sentiment on the part of the classes instructed respectively in accordance therewith, cannot educate these classes to live harmoniously together, meeting the responsibilities and discharging the duties imposed by a common government in the interest of a common country.

The object of the common school is two-fold. In the first place it should bring to every child, especially the poor child, a reasonable degree of elementary education. In the second place it should furnish a common education, one similar and equal to all pupils attending it. Thus furnished, our sons enter upon business or professional walks with an equal start in life. Such education the Government owes to all classes of the people.

The obligations and liabilities of the common carrier of passengers can, in no sense, be made dependent upon the nationality or color of those with whom he deals. He may not, according to law, answer his engagements to one class and justify non-performance or neglect as to another by considerations drawn from race. His contract is originally and fundamentally with the entire community, and with all its members he is held to equal and impartial obligation. On this subject the rules of law are definite, clear, and satisfactory. These rules may be stated concisely as follows: It is the duty of the common carrier of passengers to receive all persons applying and who do not refuse to obey any reasonable regulations imposed, who are not guilty of gross and vulgar habits of conduct, whose characters are not doubtful, dissolute or suspicious or unequivocally bad, and whose object in seeking conveyance is not to interfere with the interests or patronage of the carrier so as to make his business less lucrative.

And, in the second place, common carriers may not impose upon passengers oppressive and grossly unreasonable orders and regulations. Were there doubt in regard to the obligation of common carriers as indicated, the authorities are abundant and might be quoted at large. Here, however, I need not make quotations. The only question which can arise as between myself and any intelligent lawyer, is as to whether the regulation made by common carriers of passengers generally in this country, by which passengers and colored ones are separated on steamboats, railroad cars, and stage coaches, greatly to the disadvantage, inconvenience, and dissatisfaction of the latter class, is reasonable. As to this question, I leave such lawyer to the books and his own conscience. We have advanced so far on this subject, in thought, feeling, and purpose, that the day cannot be distant when there will be found among us no one to justify such regulations by common carriers, and when they will be made to adjust themselves, in their orders and regulations with regard thereto to the rules of the common law. The grievance of the citizen in this particular is neither imaginary nor sentimental. His experience of sadness and pain attests its reality, and the awakening sense of the people generally, as discovered in their expressions, the decisions of several of our courts, and the recent legislation of a few States, shows that this particular discrimination, inequitable as it is illegal, cannot long be tolerated in any section of our country.

The law with regard to inn-keepers is not less explicit and rigid. They are not allowed to accommodate or refuse to accommodate wayfaring persons according to their own foolish prejudices or the senseless and cruel hatred of their guests.

Their duties are defined in the following language, the very words of the law:

> "Inns were allowed for the benefit of travelers, who have certain privileges whilst they are in their journeys, and are in a more peculiar manner protected by law.
>
> "If one who keeps a common inn refuses to receive a traveler as a guest into his house, or to find him victuals or lodging upon his tendering a reasonable price for the same, the inn-keeper is liable to render damages in an action at the suit of the party grieved, and may also be indicted and fined at the suit of the King.
>
> "An inn-keeper is not, if he has suitable room, at liberty to refuse to receive a guest who is ready and able to pay him a suitable compensation. On the contrary, he is bound to receive him, and if, upon false pretences, he refuses, he is liable to an action."

These are doctrines as old as the common law itself; indeed, older, for they come down to us from Gaius and Papinian. All discriminations made, therefore, by the keepers of public houses in the nature of inns, to the disadvantage of the colored citizen, and contrary to the usual treatment accorded travelers, is not only wrong morally, but utterly illegal. To this judgment the public mind must soon come.

Had I the time, and were it not too great a trespass upon your patience, I should be glad to speak of the injustice and illegality, as well as inhumanity, of our exclusion, in some localities, from jury, public places of learning and amusement, the church and the cemetery. I will only say, however, (and in this statement I claim the instincts, not less than the well-formed judgment of mankind, in our behalf,) that such exclusion at least seems remarkable, and is difficult of defense upon any considerations of humanity, law, or Christianity. Such exclusion is the more remarkable and indefensible since we are fellow-citizens, wielding like political powers, eligible to the same high official positions, responsible to the same degree and in the same manner for the discharge of the duties they impose; interested in the progress and civilization of a common country, and anxious, like all others, that its destiny be glorious and matchless. It is strange, indeed, that the colored American may find place in the Senate, but it is denied access and welcome to the public place of learning, the theatre, the church and the graveyard, upon terms accorded to all others.

But, Mr. President and friends, it ill becomes us to complain; we may not tarry to find fault. The change in public sentiment, the reform in our national legislation and jurisprudence, which we this day commemorate, transcendent and admirable, augurs and guarantees to all American citizens complete equality before the law, in the protection and enjoyment of all those rights and privileges which pertain to manhood, enfranchised and dignified. To us the 13th amendment of our Constitution, abolishing slavery and perpetuating freedom; the 14th amendment establishing citizenship and prohibiting the enactment of any law which shall abridge the privileges or immunities of citizens of the United States, or which shall deny the equal protection of the laws to all American citizens; and the 15th amendment, which declares that the RIGHT of citizens of the United States to vote shall not be denied or abridged by the United States or by any State, on account of race, color, or previous condition of servitude, are national utterances which not only recognize, but sustain and perpetuate our freedom and rights.

To the colored American, more than to all others, the language of these amendments is not vain. To use the language of the late Hon. Charles Sumner, "within the sphere of their influence no person can be *created*, no person can be *born*, with civil or political privileges not enjoyed equally by all his fellow-citizens; nor can any institution be established recognizing distinction of birth. Here is the great charter of every human being, drawing vital breath upon this soil, whatever may be his condition and whoever may be his parents. He may be poor, weak, humble or black; he may be of Caucasian, Jewish, Indian or Ethiopian race; he may be of French, German, English or Irish extraction; but before the Constitution all these distinctions disappear. He is not poor, weak, humble or black; nor is he Caucasian, Jew, Indian or Ethiopian; nor is he French, German, English or Irish—he is a *man*, the equal of all his fellow-men. He is one of the children of the State, which like an impartial parent, regards all its offspring with an equal care. To some it may justly allot higher duties according to higher capacities; but it welcomes all to its equal hospitable board. The State, imitating the Divine Justice, is no respecter of persons."

With freedom established in our own country, and equality before the law promised in early Federal, if not State legislation, we may well consider our duty with regard to the abolition of slavery, the establishment of freedom and free institutions upon the American continent, especially in the island of the seas, where slavery is maintained by despotic Spanish rule, and where the people declaring slavery abolished,* and appealing to the civilized world for sympathy and justification of their course, have staked all upon "the dread arbitrament of war." There can be no peace on our continent, there can be no harmony among its people till slavery is everywhere abolished and freedom established and protected by law; the people themselves, making for themselves, and supporting their own government. Every nation, whether its home be an island or upon a continent, if oppressed, ought to have, like our own, a "new birth of freedom," and its "government of the people, by the people, and for the people," shall prove at once its strength and support.

Our sympathies especially go out towards the struggling patriots of Cuba. We would see the "Queen of the Antilles" free from Spanish rule; her slaves all freemen, and herself advancing in her freedom, across the way of national greatness and renown. Or if her million and a half inhabitants, with their thousands of rich and fertile fields, are unable to support national in-dependence and unity, let her not look for protection from, or annexation to, a country and government despotic and oppressive in its policy. By its prox-imity to our shores, by the ties of blood which connect its population and ours; by the examples presented in our Revolutionary conflict, when France furnished succor and aid to our struggling but heroic fathers; by the lessons and examples of international law and history; by all the pledges made by our nation in favor of freedom and equal rights, the oppressed and suffering people of Cuba may justly expect, demand our sympathies and support in their struggle for freedom and independence. Especially let the colored American realize that where battle is made against despotism and oppres-sion, wherever humanity struggles for national existence and recogni-tion, there his sympathies should be felt, his word and succor inspiriting, encouraging and supporting. To-day let us send our word of sympathy to the struggling thousands of Cuba, among whom, as well as among the people of Porto Rico, we hope soon to see slavery, indeed, abolished,† free institutions firmly established, and good order, prosperity and happiness secured. This accomplished, our continent is dedicated to freedom and free institutions; and the nations which compose its population will enjoy sure promise of na-tional greatness and glory. Freedom and free institutions should be as broad as our continent. Among no nation here should there be found any enslaved or oppressed. "Compromises between right and wrong, under pretence of ex-

---

*At the constitutional convention at Guaimaro, April 10, 1869, six months after the Ten Years' War for independence started, the Cuban revolutionists adopted the first con-stitution of free Cuba. The twenty-fourth article declared that "all the inhabitants of the Republic are absolutely free."

†Spain emerged victorious from the Ten Years' War, and slavery was not abolished in Cuba until October 7, 1886.

pediency," should disappear forever; our house should be no longer divided against itself; a new corner-stone should be built into the edifice of our national, continental liberty, and those who "guard and support the structure," should accept, in all its comprehensiveness, the sentiment that all men are created equal, and that governments are established among men to defend and protect their inalienable rights to life, liberty, and the pursuit of happiness.■

97 THE CIVIL RIGHTS BILL

James T. Rapier

One of the most effective speeches in Congress in support of the civil rights bill was delivered on February 4, 1875, by James T. Rapier, representative from Alabama. No one better described how a black man felt as an alien in his own native land or more brilliantly posed the question of why African Americans who had given so much to save the nation were still denied their basic rights. Like Langston, Rapier explores the bitter fact that a black person could be admitted to the U.S. Senate yet denied access to schools, restaurants, inns, and railroad cars. Rapier begins with a reflexive analysis of his complex, humiliating, and treacherous rhetorical situation, in which he must come "hat in hand" before his white "colleagues" to plead for equal treatment, yet avoid any suggestion of "social equality." Rapier's speech eloquently tells what it means to be a man who is "half free and half slave."

Rapier was born in Florence, Alabama, in 1839, of a white father and black mother. He studied at Montreal College in Canada and the University of Glasgow in Scotland. Returning to Alabama after the Civil War, Rapier was successively a delegate to the Reconstruction constitutional convention, a newspaper editor, a labor organizer, and the secretary of the Alabama Equal Rights League. In 1872 he was elected to Congress from the Second Congressional District of Alabama. He served one term, during which he fought repeatedly for civil rights. Rapier died in 1883.

Rapier's text is taken from the Congressional Record, *43d Congress, 1st session, volume 2, part 1, 565–67. For more information on Rapier, see William L. Clay,* Just Permanent Interests: Black Americans in Congress, 1870–1991 *(New York: Amistad, 1992); and Eric Foner,* Freedom's

Lawmakers: A Directory of Black Officeholders During Reconstruction
(New York: Oxford University Press, 1993).

M r. Speaker, I had hoped there would be no protracted discussion on the civil-rights bill. It has been debated all over the country for the last seven years; twice it has done duty in our national political campaigns; and in every minor election during that time it has been pressed into service for the purpose of intimidating the weak white men who are inclined to support the republican ticket. I was certain until now that most persons were acquainted with its provisions, that they understood its meaning; therefore it was no longer to them the monster it had been depicted, that was to break down all social barriers, and compel one man to recognize another socially, whether agreeable to him or not.

I MUST CONFESS it is somewhat embarrassing for a colored man to urge the passage of this bill, because if he exhibits an earnestness in the matter and expresses a desire for its immediate passage, straightway he is charged with a desire for social equality, as explained by the demagogue and understood by the ignorant white man. But then it is just as embarrassing for him not to do so, for, if he remains silent while the struggle is being carried on around, and for him, he is liable to be charged with a want of interest in a matter that concerns him more than any one else, which is enough to make his friends desert his cause. So in steering away from Scylla I may run upon Charybdis. But the anomalous and, I may add, the supremely ridiculous position of the Negro at this time, in this country, compels me to say something. Here his condition is without comparison, parallel alone to itself. Just that the law recognizes my right upon this floor as a lawmaker, but that there is no law to secure to me any accommodations whatever while traveling here to discharge my duties as a Representative of a large and wealthy constituency. Here I am the peer of the proudest, but on a steamboat or car I am not equal to the most degraded. Is not this most anomalous and ridiculous?

What little I shall say will be more in the way of stating the case than otherwise, for I am certain I can add nothing to the arguments already made in behalf of the bill. If in the course of my remarks I should use language that may be considered inelegant, I have only to say that it shall be as elegant as that used by the opposition in discussing this measure; if undignified, it shall not be more so than my subject; if ridiculous, I enter the plea that the example has been set by the democratic side of the House, which claims the right to set examples.

I wish to say in justice to myself that no one regrets more than I do the necessity that compels one to the manor born to come in these halls with hat in hand (so to speak) to ask at the hands of his political peers the same public rights they enjoy. And I shall feel ashamed for my country if there be any foreigners present who have been lured to our shores by the popular but untruthful declaration that this land is the asylum of the oppressed, to hear a member of the highest legislative body in the world declare from his place, upon his responsibility as a Representative, that, notwithstanding his political position, he has no civil rights that another class is bound to respect.

Here a foreigner can learn what he cannot learn in any other country, that it is possible for a man to be half free and half slave, or, in other words, he will see that it is possible for a man to enjoy political rights while he is denied civil ones; here he will see a man legislating for a free people, while his own chains of slavery hang about him and are far more galling than any the foreigner left behind him; here he will see and what is not to be seen elsewhere, that position is no mantle of protection in our "land of the free and home of the brave"; for I am subjected to far more outrages and indignities in coming to and going from this capital in discharge of my public duties than any criminal in the country provided he be white. Instead of my position shielding me for insult, it too often invites it.

Let me cite a case. Not many months ago Mr. Cardozo,* treasurer of the state of South Carolina, was on his way home from the West. His route lay through Atlanta. There he made request for a sleeping berth. Not only was he refused this, but he was denied a seat in a first-class carriage, and the parties went so far as to threaten to take his life because he insisted upon his rights as a traveler. He was compelled, a most elegant and accomplished gentleman, to take a seat in the dirty smoking car, along with the travelling rabble, or else be left, to the detriment of his public duties.

I affirm, without the fear of contradiction, that any white ex-convict (I care not what may have been his crime, nor whether the hair on the shaven side of his head has had time to grow out or not) may start with me today to Montgomery, that all the way down he will be treated as a gentleman, while I will be treated as the convict. He will be allowed a berth in a sleeping car with all its comforts, while I will be forced into a dirty, rough box with the drunkards, apple sellers, railroad hands, and next to any dead that be in transit, regardless of how far decomposition may have progressed. Sentinels are placed at the doors of the better coaches, with positive instructions to keep persons of color out; and I must do them the justice to say that they guard these sacred portals with a vigilance that would have done credit to the flaming swords at the gates of Eden. Tender, pure, intelligent young ladies are forced to travel in this way if they are guilty of the crime of color, the only unpardonable sin known in our Christian and Bible lands, where sinning against the Holy Ghost (whatever that may be) sinks into significance when compared with the sin of color. If from any cause we are compelled to lay over, the best bed in the hotel is his if he can pay for it, while I am invariably turned away, hungry and cold, to stand around the railroad station until the departure of the next train, it matters not how long, thereby endangering my health, while my life and property are at the mercy of any highwayman who may wish to murder and rob me.

*Francis Louis Cardozo, South Carolina's first African American secretary of state and treasurer.

And I state without the fear of being gainsaid, the statement of the gentleman from Tennessee to the contrary notwithstanding, that there is not an inn between Washington and Montgomery, a distance of more than a thousand miles, that will accommodate me to bed or meal. Now, then, is there a man upon this floor who is so heartless, whose breast is so void of the better feelings, as to say that this brutal custom needs no regulation? I hold that it does and that Congress is the body to regulate it. Authority for its action is found not only in the Fourteenth Amendment to the Constitution, but by virtue of that amendment (which makes all persons born here citizens) authority is found in Article 4, Section 2, of the federal Constitution, which declares in positive language that "the citizens of each state shall have the same rights as the citizens of the several states." Let me read Mr. Brightly's comment upon this clause; he is considered good authority, I believe. In describing the several rights he says they may all be comprehended under the following general heads: "Protection by the government; the enjoyment of life and liberty, with the right to acquire and possess property of every kind, and to pursue and obtain happiness and safety; the right of a citizen of one state to pass through or to reside in any other state for purposes of trade, agriculture, professional pursuits, or otherwise."

It is very clear that the right of locomotion without hindrance and everything pertaining thereto is embraced in this clause; and every lawyer knows if any white man in antebellum times had been refused first-class passage in a steamboat or car, who was free from any contagious disease, and was compelled to go on deck of a boat or into a baggage car, and any accident had happened to him while he occupied that place, a lawsuit would have followed and damages would have been given by any jury to the plaintiff; and whether any accident had happened or not in the case I have referred to, a suit would have been brought for a denial of rights, and no one doubts what would have been the verdict. White men had rights then that common carriers were compelled to respect, and I demand the same for the colored men now.

Mr. Speaker, whether this deduction from the clause of the Constitution just read was applicable to the Negro prior to the adoption of the several late amendments to our organic law is now a question, but that it does apply to him in his new relations no intelligent man will dispute. Therefore I come to the national, instead of going to the local legislatures for relief, as has been suggested, because the grievance is national and not local; because Congress is the lawmaking power of the general government, whose duty it is to see that there be no unjust and odious discriminations made between citizens. I look to the government in the place of the several states, because it claims my first allegiance, exacts at my hands strict obedience to its laws, and because it promises in the implied contract between every citizen and the government to protect my life and property. I have fulfilled my part of the contract to the extent I have been called upon, and I demand that the government, through Congress, do likewise. Every day my life and property are exposed, are left to the mercy of others, and will be so as long as every hotelkeeper, railroad conductor and steamboat captain can refuse me with impunity the accommodations common to other travelers. I hold further, if the government cannot secure the citizen his guaranteed rights it ought not to call upon him to perform the same duties that are performed by another class of citizen who are in the free enjoyment of every civil and political right.

Sir, I submit that I am degraded as long as I am denied the public privileges common to other men, and that the members of this House are correspondingly degraded by recognizing my political equality while I occupy such humiliating position. What a singular attitude for lawmakers of this great nation to assume, rather come down to me than allow me to go up to them. Sir, did you ever reflect that this is the only Christian country where poor, finite man is held responsible for the crimes of the infinite God whom you profess to worship? But it is; I am held to answer for the crime of color, when I was not consulted in the matter. Had I been consulted, and my future fully described, I think I should have objected to being born in this Gospel land. The excuse offered for all this inhuman treatment is that they consider the Negro inferior to the white man, intellectually and morally. This reason might have been offered and probably accepted as truth some years ago, but not one now believes him incapable of a high order of culture, except someone who is himself below the average of mankind in natural endowments. This is not the reason, as I shall show before I have done.

Sir, there is a cowardly propensity in the human heart that delights in oppressing somebody else, and in the gratification of this base desire we always select a victim that can be outraged with safety. As a general thing, the Jew has been the subject in most parts of the world; but here the Negro is the most available for this purpose; for this reason in part he was seized upon, and not because he is naturally inferior to anyone else. Instead of his enemies believing him to be incapable of a high order of mental culture, they have shown that they believe the reverse to be true, by taking the most elaborate pains to prevent his development. And the smaller the caliber of the white man the more frantically has he fought to prevent the intellectual and moral progress of the Negro, for a simple but good reason that he has most to fear from such a result. He does not wish to see the Negro approach the high moral standard of a man and gentleman.

Let me call your attention to a case in point. Some time since, a well-dressed colored man was traveling from Augusta to Montgomery. The train on which he was stopped at a dinner house. The crowd around the depot, seeing him well dressed, fine-looking, and polite, concluded he must be a gentleman (which was more than their righteous souls could stand), and straightway they commenced to abuse him. And, sir, he had to go into the baggage car, open his trunks, show his cards, faro bank, dice, et cetera, before they would give him any peace; or, in other words, he was forced to give satisfactory evidence that he was not a man who was working to elevate the moral and intellectual standards of the Negro before they would respect him. I have always found more prejudice existing in the breast of men who have feeble minds and are conscious of it, than in the breast of those who have towering intellects and are aware of it. Henry Ward Beecher reflected the feelings of the latter class when on a certain occasion he said: "Turn the Negro loose; I am not afraid to run the race of life with him." He could afford to say this, all white men cannot; but what does the other class say? "Build a Chinese wall between the Negro and the school house, discourage in him pride of character and honest ambition, cut him off from every avenue that leads to the higher grounds of intelligence and usefulness, and then challenge him to a contest upon the highway of life to decide the question of superiority of race." By their acts, not by their words, the civilized world can and will judge how honest my opponents are in their declarations that I am naturally inferior to them. No one is surprised that this class opposes the passage of the civil-rights bill, for if the Negro were allowed the same opportunities, the same rights of locomotion, the same rights to comfort in travel, how could they prove themselves better than the Negro?

Mr. Speaker, it was said, I believe by the gentleman from Kentucky, [MR. BECK,] that the people of the South, particularly his State, were willing to accord the colored man all the rights they believe him guaranteed by the Constitution. No one doubts this assertion. But the difficulty is they do not acknowledge that I am entitled to any rights under the organic law. I am forced to this conclusion by reading the platforms of the democratic party in the several States. Which one declares that that party believes in the constitutionality of the Reconstruction Acts or the several amendments? But upon the other hand, they question the constitutionality of every measure that is advanced to ameliorate the condition of the colored man; and so skeptical have the Democracy become respecting the Constitution, brought about by their unsuccessful efforts to find constitutional objections to every step that is taken to elevate the negro, that now they begin to doubt the constitutionality of the Constitution itself. The most they have agreed to do, is to obey present laws bearing on manhood suffrage until they are repealed by Congress or decided to be unconstitutional by the Supreme Court.

Let me read what the platform of the democratic party in Alabama has to say on this point:

> The democratic and conservative party of the State of Alabama, in entering upon the contest for the redemption of the state government from the radical usurpers who now control it, adopt and declare as their platform—
> 1. That we stand ready to obey the Constitution of the United States and the laws passed in pursuance thereof; and the constitution and law of the State of Alabama, so long as they remain in force and unrepealed.

I will, however, take the gentleman at his word; but must be allowed to ask if so why was it, even after the several amendments had been officially announced to be part of the Federal Constitution, that his State and others refused to allow the negro to testify in their courts against a white man? If they believed he should be educated (and surely this is a right) why was it that his school-houses were burned down, and the teachers who had gone down on errands of mercy to carry light into dark places driven off, and in some places killed? If they believe the negro should vote, (another right, as I understand the Constitution,) why was it that Ku-Klux Klans were organized to prevent him from exercising the right of an American citizen, namely, casting the ballot—the very thing they said he had a right to do?

The professed belief and practice are sadly at variance, and must be intelligently harmonized before I can be made to believe that they are willing to acknowledge that I have any rights under the Constitution or elsewhere. He boasts of the magnanimity of Kentucky in allowing the negro to vote without qualification, while to enjoy the same privilege in Massachusetts he is required to read the constitution of that State. He was very unhappy in this comparison. Why, sir, his State does not allow the negro to vote at all. When was the constitution of Kentucky amended so as to grant him the elective franchise? They vote there by virtue of the fifteenth amendment alone, independent of the laws and constitution of that Commonwealth; and they would to-day disfranchise him if it could be done without affecting her white population. The Old Bay State waited for no "act of Congress" to force her to justice to all of her citizens, but in *ante bellum* days provided in her constitution that all male persons who could read and write should be entitled to suffrage. That was a case of equality before the law, and who had a right to complain? There is nothing now in the amended Federal Constitution to prevent Kentucky from adopting the same kind of clause in her constitution, when the convention meets to revise the organic law of that State, I venture the assertion that you will never hear a word about it; but it will not be out of any regard for her colored citizens, but the respect for that army of fifty-thousand ignorant white men she has within her borders, many of whom I see every time I pass through that State, standing around the several depots continually harping on the stereotyped phrase, "The damned negro won't work."

I would not be surprised though if she should do better in the future. I remember when a foreigner was just as unpopular in Kentucky as the negro is now; when the majority of the people of that State were opposed to according the foreigner the same rights they claimed for themselves; when that class of people were mobbed in the streets of her principal cities on account of their political faith, just as they have done the negro of the last seven years. But what do you see to-day? One of that then proscribed class is Kentucky's chief Representative upon this floor. Is not this an evidence of a returning sense of justice? If so, would it not be reasonable to predict that she will in the near future send one of her now proscribed class to aid him in representing her interests upon this floor?

Mr. Speaker, there is another member of this body who has opposed the passage of this bill very earnestly, whose position in the country and peculiar relations to the Government compel me to refer to him before I conclude. I allude to the gentleman from Georgia, [MR. STEPHENS].* He returns to this House after an absence of many years with the same old ideas respecting State-rights that he carried away with him. He has not advanced a step; but unfortunately for him the American people have, and no longer consider him a fit expounder of our organic law. Following to its legitimate conclusion the doctrine of State-rights, (which of itself is secession,) he deserted the flag of his country, followed his State out of the Union, and a long and bloody war followed. With its results most men are acquainted and recognize; but he, Bourbon-like, comes back saying the very same things he used to say and swearing by the same gods he swore by in other days. He seems not to know that the ideas which he so ably advanced for so many years were by the war swept away, along with that system of slavery which he intended should be the chief corner-stone, precious and elect, of the transitory kingdom over which he was second ruler.

Sir, the most of us have seen the play of Rip Van Winkle, who was said to have slept twenty years in the Katskill Mountains. On his return he found that the small trees had grown up to be large ones; the village of Falling Waters had improved beyond his recollection; the little children that used to play around his knees and ride into the village upon his back had grown up to be men and women and assumed the responsibilities of life; most of his friends, including Nick Vedder, had gone to that bourn whence no traveler returns; but, saddest of all, his child, "Mene," could not remember him. No one can see him in his efforts to recall the scenes of other days without being moved almost to tears. This, however, is fiction. The life and actions of the gentleman from Georgia most happily illustrate this character. This is a case where truth is stranger than fiction; and when he comes into these Halls advocating the same old ideas after an absence of so many years, during which time we have had a conflict of arms such as the world never saw, that revolutionized the entire body-politic, he stamps himself as a living "Rip Van Winkle."

I reiterate, that the principles of "State-rights," for the recognition of which, he now contends, are the ones that were in controversy during our late civil strife. The arguments *pro* and *con* were heard in the roar of battle, amid the shrieks of the wounded, and the groans of the dying; and the decision was rendered amid shouts of victory by the Union soldiers. With it all appear to be familiar except him, and for his information I will state that upon this question an appeal was taken from the forum to the sword, the highest tribunal known to man, that it was then and there decided that National rights are paramount to State-rights, and that liberty and equality before the law should be coextensive with the jurisdiction of the Stars and Stripes. And I will further inform him that the bill now pending is simply to give practical effect to that decision.

I sympathize with him in his inability to understand this great change. When he left here the negro was a chattel, exposed for sale in the market

---

*Alexander H. Stephens served as vice president of the Confederacy.

places within a stone's throw of the Capitol; so near that the shadow of the Goddess of Liberty reflected by rising sun would fall within the slave-pen as a forcible reminder that there was no hopeful day, nothing bright in the future, for the poor slave. Then no negro was allowed to enter these Halls and hear discussions on subjects that most interested him. The words of lofty cheer that fell from the lips of Wade, Giddings, Julian, and others were not allowed to fall upon his ear. Then, not more than three negroes were allowed to assemble at any place in the capital of the nation without special permission from the city authorities. But on his return he finds that the slave-pens have been torn down, and upon their ruins temples of learning have been erected; he finds that the Goddess of Liberty is no longer compelled to cover her radiant face while she weeps for our national shame, but looks with pride and satisfaction upon a free and regenerated land; he finds that the laws and regulations respecting the assembling of negroes are no longer in force, but on the contrary he can see on any public holiday the Butler Zouaves, a fine-looking company of colored men, on parade.

Imagine, if you can, what would have been the effect of such a sight in this city twelve years ago. Then one negro soldier would have caused utter consternation. Congress would have adjourned; the Cabinet would have sought protection elsewhere; the President would have declared martial law; troops and marines would have been ordered out; and I cannot tell all that would have happened; but now such a sight does not excite a ripple on the current of affairs; but over all, and worse to him than all, he finds the negro here, not only a listener but a participant in debate. While I sympathize with him in his inability to comprehend his marvelous change, I must say in all earnestness that one who cannot understand and adjust himself to the new order of things is poorly qualified to teach this nation the meaning of our amended Constitution. The tenacity with which he sticks to his purpose through all the vicissitudes of life is commendable, though his views be objectionable.

While the chief of the late confederacy is away in Europe fleeing the wrath to come in the shape of Joe Johnston's history of the war,[*] his lieutenant, with a boldness that must challenge the admiration of the most impudent, comes into these Halls and seeks to commit the nation through Congress to the doctrine of State-rights, and thus save it from the general work that followed the collapse of the rebellion. He had no other business here. Read his speech on the pending bill; his argument was cunning, far more ingenious than ingenuous. He does not deny the need or justness of the measure, but claims that the several States have exclusive jurisdiction of the same. I am not so willing as some others to believe in the sincerity of his assertions concerning the rights of the colored man. If he were honest in this matter, why is it he never recommended such a measure to the Georgia Legislature? If the several States had secured to all classes within

[*]Joseph E. Johnston, *Narrative of Military Operations Directed During the Late War Between the States* (New York: Appleton, 1874).

their borders the rights contemplated in this bill, we would have had no need to come here; but they having failed to do their duty, after having had ample opportunity, the General Government is called upon to exercise its right in the matter.

Mr. Speaker, time will not allow me to review the history of the American Negro, but I must pause here long enough to say that he has not been properly treated by this nation; he has purchased and paid for all, and for more than, he has yet received. Whatever liberty he enjoys has been paid for over and over again by more than two hundred years of forced toil; and for such citizenship as is allowed him he paid the full measure of his blood, the dearest price required at the hands of any citizen. In every contest, from the beginning of the Revolutionary struggle down to the War Between the States, has he been prominent. But we all remember in our late war when the government was so hard pressed for troops to sustain the cause of the Union, when it was so difficult to fill up the ranks that had been so fearfully decimated by disease and the bullet; when every train that carried to the front a number of fresh soldiers brought back a corresponding number of wounded and sick ones; when grave doubts as to the success of the Union arms had seized upon the minds of some of the most sanguine friends of the government; when strong men took counsel of their fears; when those who had all their lives received the fostering care of the nation were hesitating as to their duty in that trying hour, and others questioning if it were not better to allow the star of this Republic to go down and thus be blotted out from the great map of nations than to continue the bloodshed; when gloom and despair were widespread; when the last ray of hope had nearly sunk below our political horizon, how the Negro then came forward and offered himself as a sacrifice in the place of the nation, made bare his breast to the steel, and in it received the thrusts of the bayonet that were aimed at the life of the nation by the soldiers of that government in which the gentleman from Georgia figured as second officer.

Sir, the valor of the colored soldier was tested on many a battlefield, and today his bones lie bleaching beside every hill and in every valley from the Potomac to the Gulf; whose mute eloquence in behalf of equal rights for all before the law, is and ought to be far more persuasive than any poor language I can command.

Mr. Speaker, nothing short of a complete acknowledgment of my manhood will satisfy me. I have no compromises to make, and shall unwillingly accept any. If I were to say that I would be content with less than any other member upon this floor I would forfeit whatever respect any one here might entertain for me, and would thereby furnish the best possible evidence that I do not and cannot appreciate the rights of a freeman—just what I am charged with by my political enemies. I cannot willingly accept anything less than my full measure of rights as a man, because I am unwilling to present myself as a candidate for the brand of inferiority, which will be as plain and lasting as the mark of Cain. If I am to be thus branded, the country must do it against my solemn protest.

Sir, in order that I might know something of the feelings of a freeman, a privilege denied me in the land of my birth, I left home last year and traveled six months in foreign lands, and the moment I put my foot upon the deck of a ship that unfurled a foreign flag from its masthead, distinctions on account of my color ceased. I am not aware that my presence on board the steamer put her off her course. I believe we made the trip in the usual time. It was in other countries than my own that I was not a stranger, that I could approach a hotel without the fear that the door would be slammed in my face. Sir, I feel this humiliation very keenly; it dwarfs my manhood, and certainly it impairs my usefulness as a citizen.

The other day when the centennial bill was under discussion I would have been glad to say a word in its favor, but how could I? How would I appear at the centennial celebration of our national freedom, with my own galling chains of slavery hanging about me? I could no more rejoice on that occasion in my present condition than the Jews could sing in their wonted style as they sat as captives beside the Babylonish streams; but I look forward to the day when I shall be in the full enjoyment of the rights of a freeman, with the same hope they indulged, that they would again return to their native land. I can no more forget my manhood, than they could forget Jerusalem.

After all, this question resolves itself to this: either I am a man or I am not a man. If one, I am entitled to all the rights, privileges and immunities common to any other class in this country; if not a man, I have no right to vote, no right to a seat here; if no right to vote, then 20 percent of the members on this floor have no right here, but, on the contrary, hold their seats in violation of the law. If the Negro has no right to vote, then one eighth of your Senate consists of members who have no shadow of a claim to the places they occupy; and if no right to vote, a half-dozen governors in the South figure as usurpers.

This is the legitimate conclusion of the argument, that the Negro is not a man and is not entitled to all the public rights common to other men, and you cannot escape it. But when I press my claims I am asked, "Is it good policy?" My answer is, "Policy is out of the question; it has nothing to do with it; that you can have no policy in dealing with your citizens; that there must be one law for all; that in this case justice is the only standard to be used, and you can no more divide justice than you can divide Deity." On the other hand, I am told that I must respect the prejudices of others. Now, sir, no one respects reasonable and intelligent prejudice more than I. I respect religious prejudices, for example, these I can comprehend. But how can I have respect for the prejudices that prompt a man to turn up his nose at the males of a certain race, while at the same time he has a fondness for the females of the same race to the extent of cohabitation? Out of four poor unfortunate colored women, who from poverty were forced to go to the lying-in branch of the Freedman's Hospital here in the District last year, three gave birth to children whose fathers were white men, and I venture to say that if they were members of this body, would vote against the civil-rights bill. Do you, can you wonder at my want of respect for this kind of prejudice? To make me feel uncomfortable appears to be the highest ambition of many white men. It is to them a positive luxury, which they seek to indulge at every opportunity.

I have never sought to compel any one, white or black, to associate with me, and never shall; nor do I wish to be compelled to associate with any one. If a man does not wish to ride with me in the streetcar, I shall not object to his hiring a private conveyance; if he does not wish to ride with me from here to Baltimore, who shall complain if he charter a special train? For a man to carry out his prejudices in this way would be manly and would leave no cause for complaint, but to crowd me out of the usual conveyance into an uncomfortable place with persons for whose manners I have a dislike, whose language is not fit for ears polite, is decidedly unmanly and cannot be submitted to tamely by anyone who has a particle of self-respect.

Sir, this whole thing grows out of a desire to establish a system of "caste," an anti-republican principle, in our free country. In Europe they have princes, dukes, lords, &c., in contradistinction to the middle classes and peasants. Further East they have the brahmans or priests, who rank above the sudras or laborers. In those countries distinctions are based upon blood and position. Every one there understands the custom and no one complains. They, poor innocent creatures, pity our condition, look down upon us with a kind of royal compassion, because they think we have no tangible lines of distinction, and therefore speak of our society as being vulgar. But let not our friends beyond the seas lay the flattering unction to their souls that we are without distinctive lines; that we have no nobility; for we are blessed with both. Our distinction is color, (which would necessarily exclude the brahmans,) and our lines are much broader than anything they know of. Here a drunken white man is not only equal to a drunken negro, (as would be the case anywhere else,) but superior to the most sober and orderly one; here an ignorant white man is not only the equal of an unlettered negro, but is superior to the most cultivated; here our nobility cohabit with our female peasants, and they throw up their hands in holy horror when a male of the same class enters a restaurant to get a meal, and if he insist upon being accommodated our scion of royalty will leave and go to the arms of his colored mistress and there pour out his soul's complaint, tell her of the impudence of the "damned nigger" in coming to a table where a white man was sitting.

What poor, simple-minded creatures these foreigners are. They labor under the decision that they monopolize the knowledge of the courtesies due from one gentleman to another. How I rejoice to know that it is a delusion. Sir, I wish some of them could have been present to hear the representative of the F.F.V.'s* upon this floor (and I am told that that is the highest degree that society has yet reached in this country) address one of his peers, who dared asked him a question, in this style; "I am talking to white men." Suppose Mr. Gladstone—who knows no man but by merit—who in violation of our custom entertained the colored jubilee singers at his home last summer, or the Duke of Broglie, had been present and heard this eloquent remark drop

---

*"First Families of Virginia" is a satirical reference to the claims of aristocratic lineage by many families.

from the lips of this classical and knightly member, would they not have hung their heads in shame at their ignorance of politeness, and would they not have returned home, repaired to their libraries, and betaken themselves to the study of Chesterfield on manners? With all these absurdities staring them in the face, who can wonder that foreigners laugh at our ideas of distinction?

Mr. Speaker, though there is not a line in this bill the Democracy approve of, yet they made the most noise about the school clause. Dispatches are freely sent over the wires as to what will be done with the common-school system in the several Southern states in the event this bill becomes a law. I am not surprised at this, but, on the other hand, I looked for it. Now what is the force of that school clause? It simply provides that all the children in every state where there is a school system supported in whole or in part by general taxation shall have equal advantages of school privileges. So that if perfect and ample accommodations are not made convenient for all the children, then any child has the right to go to any school where they do exist. And that is all there is in this school clause. I want some one to tell me of any measure that was intended to benefit the Negro that they have approved of. Of which one did they fail to predict evil? They declared if the Negroes were emancipated that the country would be laid waste, and that in the end he would starve, because he could not take care of himself. But this was a mistake. When the Reconstruction acts were passed and the colored men in my state were called upon to express through the ballot whether Alabama should return to the Union or not, white men threw up their hands in holy horror and declared if the Negro voted that never again would they deposit another ballot. But how does the matter stand now? Some of those very men are in the Republicans ranks, and I have known them to grow hoarse in shouting for our platforms and candidates. They hurrah for our principles with all the enthusiasm of a newborn soul, and, sir, so zealous have they become that in looking at them I am amazed and am often led to doubt my faith and feel ashamed for my lukewarmness. And those who have not joined our party are doing their utmost to have the Negro vote with them. I have met them in the cabins night and day where they were imploring him, for the sake of old times, to come up and vote with them.

I submit, Mr. Speaker, that political prejudices prompt the Democracy to oppose this bill as much as anything else. In the campaign of 1868 Joe Williams, an uncouth and rather notorious colored man, was employed as a general Democratic canvasser in the South. He was invited to Montgomery to enlighten us, and while there he stopped at one of the best hotels in the city, one that would not dare entertain me. He was introduced at the meeting by the chairman of the Democratic executive committee as a learned and elegant, as well as eloquent, gentleman. In North Alabama he was invited to speak at the Seymour and Blair barbecue,* and did address one of the larg-

---

*In the presidential campaign of 1868, Horatio Seymour and Francis P. Blair were the presidential and vice presidential candidates of the Democratic Party. Ulysses S. Grant, the Republican presidential candidate, was elected.

est audiences, composed largely of ladies, that ever assembled in that part of the state. This I can prove by my simon-pure Democratic colleague, Mr. Sloss, for he was chairman of the committee of arrangements on that occasion, and I never saw so radiant with good humor in all my life as when he had the honor of introducing "his friend," Mr. Williams. In that case they were extending their courtesies to a coarse, vulgar stranger, because he was a Democrat, while at the same time they were hunting me down as a partridge on the mount, night and day, with their Ku Klux Klan, simply because I was a Republican and refused to bow at the foot of their Baal. I might enumerate many instances of this kind, but I forbear. But to come down to a later period, the Greeley campaign.* The colored men who were employed to canvass North Carolina in the interest of the Democratic party were received at all the hotels as other men and treated, I am informed, with marked distinction. And in the state of Louisiana a very prominent colored gentleman saw proper to espouse the Greeley cause, and when the fight was over and the McEnery government saw fit to send on a committee to Washington to present their case to the President, this colored gentleman was selected as one of that committee. On arriving in the city of New Orleans prior to his departure he was taken to the St. Charles, the most aristocratic hotel in the South. When they started he occupied a berth in the sleeping car; at every eating house he was treated like the rest of them, no distinction whatever. And when they arrived in Montgomery, I was at the depot, just starting for New York. Not only did the conductor refuse to allow me a berth in the sleeping car, but I was also denied a seat in the first-class carriage. Now, what was the difference between us? Nothing but our political faith. To prove this I have only to say that just a few months before this happened, he, along with Frederick Douglass and others, was denied the same privileges he enjoyed in coming here. And now that he has returned to the right party again I can tell him that never more will he ride in another sleeping car in the South unless this bill becomes law. There never was a truer saying than that circumstances alter cases.

Mr. Speaker, to call this land the asylum of the oppressed is a misnomer, for upon all sides I am treated as a pariah. I hold that the solution of this whole matter is to enact such laws and prescribe such penalties for their violation as will prevent any person from discriminating against another in public places on account of color. No one asks, no one seeks the passage of law that will interfere with any one's private affairs. But I do ask the enactment of a law to secure me in the enjoyment of public privileges. But when I ask this I am told that I must wait for public opinion; that it is a matter that cannot be forced by law. While I admit that public opinion is a power, and in many cases is a law of itself, yet I cannot lose sight of the fact that both statute law and the law of necessity manufacture public opinion. I re-

*In the presidential election of 1872, Horace Greeley was the candidate of the Liberal Republican Party and of the Democratic Party. Grant, the Republican candidate, was reelected.

member it was unpopular to enlist Negro soldiers in our late war, and after they enlisted it was equally unpopular to have them fight in the same battles; but when it became a necessity in both cases, public opinion soon came around to that point. No white father objected to the Negro's becoming food for powder if thereby his son could be saved. No white woman objected to the Negro marching in the same ranks and fighting in the same battles if by that her husband could escape burial in our savannas and return to her and her little ones.

Suppose there had been no Reconstruction Acts nor amendments to the Constitution, when would public opinion in the South have suggested the propriety of giving me the ballot? Unaided by law when would public opinion have prompted the administration to appoint members of my race to represent this government at foreign courts? It is said by some well-meaning men that the colored man has now every right under the common law; in reply I wish to say that that kind of law commands very little respect when applied to the rights of colored men in my portion of the country; the only law that we have any regard for is uncommon law of the most positive character. And I repeat, if you will place upon your statute books laws that will protect me in my rights, that public opinion will speedily follow.

Mr. Speaker, I trust this bill will become law, because it is a necessity, and because it will put an end to all legislation on this subject. It does not and cannot contemplate any such ideas as social equality; nor is there any man upon this floor so silly as to believe that there can be any law enacted or enforced that would compel one man to recognize another as his equal socially; if there be, he ought not to be here, and I have only to say that they have sent him to the wrong public building. I would oppose such a bill as earnestly as the gentleman from North Carolina, whose associations and cultivations have been of such a nature as to lead him to select the crow as his standard of grandeur and excellence in the place of the eagle, the hero of all birds and our national emblem of pride and power. I will tell him that I have seen many of his race to whose level I should object to being dragged.

Sir, it matters not how much men may differ upon the question of state and national rights; here is one class of rights, however, that we all agree upon, namely, individual rights, which include the right of every man to select associates for himself and family, and to say who shall and who shall not visit at his house. This right is God-given and custom-sanctioned, and there is, and there can be, no power overruling your decision in this matter. Let this bill become law, and not only will it do much toward giving rest to this weary country on this subject, completing the manhood of my race and perfecting his citizenship, but it will take him from the political arena as a topic of discussion where he has done duty for the last fifty years, and thus freed from anxiety respecting his political standing, hundreds of us will abandon the political fields who are there from necessity, and not from choice, and seek other and more pleasant ones; and thus relieved, it will be the aim of the colored man as well as his duty and interest, to become a good citizen, and to do all in his power to advance the interests of a common country.∎

98 THE GREAT PROBLEM TO BE SOLVED

Frances Ellen Watkins Harper

Frances Ellen Watkins Harper (1825–1911), distinguished poet, novelist, and antislavery lecturer and agent, was born in Baltimore of free parents. She was educated at her uncle's school for black children, moved to Ohio in 1850, and taught domestic science at Union Seminary, at Columbia. In 1853 she went to Little York, Pennsylvania, to work with the Underground Railroad. She was engaged as a full-time lecturer in 1854 by the Anti-Slavery Society of Maine. Her first book, Poems on Various Subjects, *was published the same year. Her books of antislavery and religious verse sold widely, and her novel,* Iola Leroy; or, The Shadows Uplifted, *is among the most important American literary works of the Reconstruction era. After the Civil War, Harper worked as a representative of the Women's Christian Temperance Union, specializing in work among African Americans.*

On April 14, 1875, Harper delivered an address at the Centennial Anniversary of the Pennsylvania Society for Promoting the Abolition of Slavery, held in Philadelphia. She spoke at a time when blacks in the South were being massacred and otherwise intimidated by illegal organizations like the Ku Klux Klan and the White Leagues. Harper argues that African Americans must organize to complete the work of Reconstruction rather than relying on political parties or organizations and that black women should play an important role in these efforts.

The speech was originally published in Centennial Anniversary of the Pennsylvania Society for Promoting the Abolition of Slavery *(Philadelphia: Grant, Faires and Rodgers, 1876), 29–32, and was reprinted in Alice Moore Dunbar, ed.,* Masterpieces of Negro Eloquence *(New York: Bookery, 1914), 101–6. For further information, see Frances Smith Foster, ed.,* A Brighter Coming Day: A Frances Ellen Watkins Harper Reader *(New York: Feminist Press, 1990).*

LADIES AND GENTLEMEN: The great problem to be solved by the American people, if I understand it, is this: Whether or not there is strength enough in democracy, virtue enough in our civilization, and power enough in our religion to have mercy and deal justly with four millions of people but lately translated from the old oligarchy of slavery to the new commonwealth of freedom; and upon the right solution of this question depends in a large measure the future strength, progress and durability of our nation. The most important question before us colored people is not simply what the Democratic party may do against us or the Republican party do for us; but what are we going to do for ourselves? What shall we do toward developing our character, adding our quota to the civilization and strength of the country, diversifying our industry, and practicing those lordly virtues that conquer success and turn the world's dread laugh into admiring recognition? The white race has yet work to do in making practical the political axiom of equal rights and the Christian idea of human brotherhood; but while I lift mine eyes to the future I would not ungratefully ignore the past. One hundred years ago and Africa was the privileged hunting ground to Europe and America, and the flag of different nations hung a sign of death on the coasts of Congo and Guinea, and for years unbroken silence had hung around the horrors of the African slave trade. Since then Great Britain and other nations have wiped the bloody traffic from their hands and shaken the gory merchandise from their fingers, and the brand of piracy has been placed upon the African slave trade. Less than fifty years ago mob violence belched out its wrath against the men who dared to arraign the slave holder before the bar of conscience and Christendom. Instead of golden showers upon his head, he who garrisoned the front had a halter around his neck.* Since, if I may borrow the idea, the nation has caught the old inspiration from his lips and written it in the new organic world. Less than twenty-five years ago slavery clasped hands with King Cotton, and said slavery fights and cotton conquers for American slavery. Since then slavery is dead, the colored man has exchanged the fetters on his wrist for the ballot in his hand. Freedom is king, and Cotton a subject.

It may not seem to be a gracious thing to mingle complaint in a season of general rejoicing. It may appear like the ancient Egyptians seating a corpse at their festal board to avenge the Americans for their shortcomings when so much has been accomplished. And yet, with all the victories and triumphs which freedom and justice have won in this country, I do not believe there is another civilized nation under heaven where there are half as many people who have been brutally and shamefully murdered, with or without impunity, as in this Republic within the last ten years. And who cares? Where is the public opinion that has scorched with red-hot indignation the cowardly murderers of Vicksburg and Louisiana?† Sheridan lifts up the veil from Southern society, and behind it is the smell of blood and our bones scattered at the grave's mouth; murdered people; a White League with its "covenant of death and agreement with hell." And who cares? What city pauses one hour to drop a pitying tear over these mangled corpses, or has forged against the perpetrator one thunderbolt of furious protest? But let there be a supposed or real invasion of Southern rights by our soldiers, and our great commercial emporium will rally its forces from the old man in his classic shades, to clasp hands with "dead rabbits" and "plug-uglies" in protesting

---

*In 1835, William Lloyd Garrison was dragged by an antiabolitionist mob through the streets of Boston with a rope around his neck. In order to prevent a lynching, the authorities placed him in the local prison.
†The reference is to terrorist campaigns by the White Leagues in Mississippi and Louisiana, which resulted in the slaying of many African Americans.

against military interference. What we need today in the onward march of humanity is a public sentiment in favor of common justice and simple mercy. We have a civilization which has produced grand and magnificent results, diffused knowledge, overthrown slavery, made constant conquests over nature, and built up a wonderful material property. But two things are wanting in American civilization—a keener and deeper, broader and tenderer sense of justice; a sense of humanity, which shall crystallize into the life of the nation the sentiment that justice, simple justice, is the right, not simply of the strong and powerful, but of the weakest and feeblest of all God's children; a deeper and broader humanity, which will teach men to look upon their feeble brethren not as vermin to be crushed out, or beasts of burden to be bridled and bitten, but as the children of the living God; of that God who we may earnestly hope is in perfect wisdom and in perfect love working for the best good of all. Ethnologists may differ about the origin of the human race. Huxley may search for it in protoplasm, and Darwin send for the missing links,* but there is one thing of which we may rest assured—that we all come from the living God and that He is the common Father. The nation that has no reverence for man is also lacking in reverence for God and needs to be instructed.

As fellow citizens, leaving out all humanitarian views—as a mere matter of political economy—it is better to have the colored race a living force animated and strengthened by self-reliance and self-respect, than a stagnant mass, degraded and self-condemned. Instead of the North relaxing its efforts to defuse education in the South, it behooves us for our national life to throw into the South all the healthful reconstructing influences we can command. Our work in this country is grandly constructive. Some races have come into this world and overthrown and destroyed. But if it is glory to destroy, it is happiness to save; and oh, what a noble work there is before our nation! Where is there a young man who would consent to lead an aimless life when there are such glorious opportunities before him? Before our young men is another battle—not a battle of flashing swords and clashing steel, but a moral warfare, a battle against ignorance, poverty and low social condition. In physical warfare the keenest swords may be blunted and the loudest batteries hushed; but in the great conflict of moral and spiritual progress your weapons shall be brighter for their service and better for their use. In fighting truly and nobly for others you win the victory for yourselves.

Give power and significance to your life, and in the great work of up-building there is room for woman's work and woman's heart. Oh, that our hearts were alive and our vision quickened, to see the grandeur of the work that lies before. We have some culture among us, but I think our culture lacks enthusiasm. We need a deep earnestness and a lofty unselfishness to round out our lives. It is the inner life that develops the outer, and if we are in earnest the precious things lie all around our feet, and we need not

*Thomas Henry Huxley was the author of *Man's Place in Nature* (1863), and Charles Darwin published his famous *Origin of Species by Means of Natural Selection* in 1859.

waste our strength in striving after the dim and unattainable. Women, in your golden youth; mother, binding around your heart all the precious ties of life,—let no magnificence of culture, or amplitude of fortune, or refinement of sensibilities, repel you from helping the weaker and less favored. If you have ampler gifts, hold them as larger opportunities with which you can benefit others. Oh, it is better to feel that the weaker and feebler our race the closer we will cling to them, than it is to isolate ourselves from them in selfish, or careless unconcern, saying there is a lion without. Inviting you to this work I do not promise you fair sailing and unclouded skies. You may meet with coolness where you expect sympathy; disappointment where you feel sure of success; isolation and loneliness instead of heart support and cooperation. But if your lives are based and built upon these divine certitudes, which are the only enduring strength of humanity, then whatever defeat and discomfiture may overshadow your plans or frustrate your schemes, for a life that is in harmony with God and sympathy for man there is no such word as *fail*. And in conclusion, permit me to say, let no misfortunes crush you, no hostility of enemies or failure of friends discourage you. Apparent failure may hold in its rough shell the germs of a success that will blossom in time, and bear fruit throughout eternity. What seemed to be a failure around the Cross of Calvary and in the garden has been the grandest recorded success.■

99 ORATION IN MEMORY OF ABRAHAM LINCOLN

Frederick Douglass

 On April 14, 1876, the anniversary of Lincoln's assassination and of the emancipation of the slaves in the District of Columbia, the Freedmen's Memorial Monument to Abraham Lincoln was unveiled in Lincoln Park, Washington, D.C. The idea of the monument originated with Charlotte Scott, a former slave, on the day following Lincoln's assassination, and African Americans contributed $16,242 toward its completion. By a joint resolution, Congress declared the day a holiday. President Ulysses S. Grant and his cabinet, Supreme Court justices, and many senators and congressional representatives were present. Frederick Douglass delivered the main address on the occasion.

Disregarding the speaking conventions normally associated with

*such dedication ceremonies, Douglass gave a speech remarkably frank in
its assessment of Lincoln. Douglass had been an outspoken critic of Lincoln in the early years of the war, citing his colonization proposals, his
professed willingness to maintain slavery to preserve the Union, and his
overruling of abolition orders by regional commanders as proof that Lincoln was more foe than friend to African Americans. While mainly lauda-
tory of Lincoln on this occasion, Douglass also notes that he "was pre-
eminently the white man's President, entirely devoted to the welfare of
the white man." Noting that "truth is proper and beautiful at all times
and in all places," Douglass offers one of the most balanced interpretations of Lincoln's attitude toward slavery and the African American. It is
taken from* Inaugural Ceremonies of the Freedmen's Memorial Monument
to Abraham Lincoln, Washington City, April 14, 1876 *(St. Louis, 1876),
16–26.*

Friends and Fellow-citizens: I warmly congratulate you upon the highly
interesting object which has caused you to assemble in such numbers
and spirit as you have today. This occasion is in some respect remarkable.
Wise and thoughtful men of our race, who shall come after us, and study the
lesson of our history of the United States; who shall survey the long and
dreary spaces over which we have traveled; who shall count the links in the
great chain of events by which we have reached our present position, will
make a note of this occasion; they will think of it and speak of it with a
sense of manly pride and complacency.

I congratulate you, also, upon the very favorable circumstances in which
we meet today. They are high, inspiring, and uncommon. They lend grace,
glory, and significance to the object for which we have met. Nowhere else in
this great country, with its uncounted towns and cities, unlimited wealth,
and immeasurable territory extending from sea to sea, could conditions be
found more favorable to the success of this occasion than here.

We stand today at the national center to perform something like a national act—an act which is to go into history; and we are here where every
pulsation of the national heart can be heard, felt, and reciprocated. A thousand wires, fed with thought and winged with lightning, put us in instanta-
neous communication with the loyal and true men all over this country.

Few facts could better illustrate the vast and wonderful change which
has taken place in our condition as a people than the fact of our assembling
here for the purpose we have today. Harmless, beautiful, proper, and praiseworthy as this demonstration is, I cannot forget that no such demonstration
would have been tolerated here twenty years ago. The spirit of slavery and
barbarism, which still lingers to blight and destroy in some dark and distant
parts of our country, would have made our assembling here the signal and
excuse for opening upon us all the flood-gates of wrath and violence. That
we are here in peace today is a compliment and a credit to American civilization, and a prophecy of still greater national enlightenment and progress

in the future. I refer to the past not in malice, for this is no day for malice; but simply to place more distinctly in front the gratifying and glorious change which has come both to our white fellow-citizens and ourselves, and to congratulate all upon the contrast between now and then; the new dispensation of freedom with its thousand blessings to both races, and the old dispensation of slavery with its ten thousand evils to both races—white and black. In view, then, of the past, the present, and the future, with the long and dark history of our bondage behind us, and with liberty, progress, and enlightenment before us, I again congratulate you upon this auspicious day and hour.

Friends and fellow-citizens, the story of our presence here is soon and easily told. We are here in the District of Columbia, here in the city of Washington, the most luminous point of American territory; a city recently transformed and made beautiful in its body and in its spirit; we are here in the place where the ablest and best men of the country are sent to devise the policy, enact the laws, and shape the destiny of the Republic; we are here, with the stately pillars and majestic dome of the Capitol of the nation looking down upon us; we are here, with the broad earth freshly adorned with the foliage and flowers of spring for our church, and all races, colors, and conditions of men for our congregation—in a word, we are here to express, as best we may, by appropriate forms and ceremonies, our grateful sense of the vast, high, and preeminent services rendered to ourselves, to our race, to our country, and to the whole world by Abraham Lincoln.

The sentiment that brings us here to-day is one of the noblest that can stir and thrill the human heart. It has crowned and made glorious the high places of all civilized nations with the grandest and most enduring works of art, designed to illustrate the characters and perpetuate the memories of great public men. It is the sentiment which from year to year adorns with fragrant and beautiful flowers the graves of our loyal, brave, and patriotic soldiers who fell in defence of the Union and liberty. It is the sentiment of gratitude and appreciation, which often, in the presence of many who hear me, has filled yonder heights of Arlington with the eloquence of eulogy and the sublime enthusiasm of poetry and song; a sentiment which can never die while the Republic lives.

For the first time in the history of our people, and in the history of the whole American people, we join in this high worship, and march conspicuously in the line of this time-honored custom. First things are always interesting, and this is one of our first things. It is the first time that, in this form and manner, we have sought to do honor to an American great man, however deserving and illustrious. I commended the fact to notice; let it be told in every part of the Republic; let men of all parties and opinions hear it; let those who despise us, not less than those who respect us, know that now and here, in the spirit of liberty, loyalty, and gratitude, let it be known everywhere, and by everybody who takes an interest in human progress and in the amelioration of the condition of mankind, that, in the presence and with the approval of the members of the American House of Representatives, reflecting the general sentiment of the country; that in the presence of that august body, the American Senate, representing the highest intelligence and the calmest judgment of the country; in the presence of the Supreme Court and Chief-Justice of the United States, to whose decisions we all patriotically bow; in the presence and under the steady eye of the honored and trusted President of the United States, with the members of his wise and patriotic Cabinet, we, the colored people, newly emancipated and rejoicing in our blood-bought freedom, near the close of the first century in the life of this Republic, have now and here unveiled, set apart, and dedicated a monument of enduring granite and bronze, in every line, feature, and figure of which the men of this generation may read, and those of after-coming generations may read, something of the exalted character and great works of Abraham Lincoln, the first martyr President of the United States.

Fellow-citizens, in what we have said and done today, and in what we may say and do hereafter, we disclaim everything like arrogance and assumption. We claim for ourselves no superior devotion to the character, history, and memory of the illustrious name whose monument we have here dedicated today. We fully comprehend the relation of Abraham Lincoln both to ourselves and to the white people of the United States. Truth is proper and beautiful at all times and in all places, and it is never more proper and beautiful in any case than when speaking of a great public man whose example is likely to be commended for honor and imitation long after his departure to the solemn shades, the silent continents of eternity. It must be admitted, truth compels me to admit, even here in the presence of the monument we have erected to his memory, Abraham Lincoln was not, in the fullest sense of the word, either our man or our model. In his interests, in his associations, in his habits of thought, and in his prejudices, he was a white man.

He was preeminently the white man's President, entirely devoted to the welfare of white men. He was ready and willing at any time during the first years of his administration to deny, postpone, and sacrifice the rights of humanity in the colored people to promote the welfare of the white people in this country. In all his education and feeling he was an American of the Americans. He came into the Presidential chair upon one principle alone, namely, opposition to the extension of slavery. His arguments in furtherance of this policy had their motive and mainspring in his patriotic devotion to the interests of his own race. To protect, defend, and perpetuate slavery in the states where it existed Abraham Lincoln was not less ready than any other President to draw the sword of the nation. He was ready to execute all the supposed guarantees of the United States Constitution in favor of the slave system anywhere inside the slave states. He was willing to pursue, recapture, and send back the fugitive slave to his master, and to suppress a slave rising for liberty, though his guilty master were already in arms against the Government. The race to which we belong were not the special objects of his consideration. Knowing this, I concede to you, my white fellow-citizens, a preeminence in this worship at once full and supreme. First, midst, and last, you and yours were the objects of his deepest affection and his most earnest solicitude. You are the children of Abraham Lincoln. We are at best only his step-children; children by adoption, children by forces of circumstances and necessity. To you it especially belongs to sound his praises, to preserve and perpetuate his memory, to multiply his statues, to hang his pictures high upon your walls, and commend his example, for to you he was a great and glorious friend and benefactor. Instead of supplanting you at his altar, we would exhort you to build high his monuments; let them be of the most costly material, of the most cunning workmanship; let their forms be symmetrical, beautiful, and perfect; let their bases be upon solid rocks, and their summits lean against the unchanging blue, overhanging sky, and let them endure forever! But while in the abundance of your wealth, and in the fullness of your just and patriotic devotion, you do all this, we entreat you to despise not the humble offering we this day unveil to view; for while Abraham Lincoln saved for you a country, he delivered us from a bondage, according to Jefferson, one hour of which was worse than ages of the oppression your fathers rose in rebellion to oppose.

Fellow-citizens, ours is no new-born zeal and devotion—merely a thing of this moment. The name of Abraham Lincoln was near and dear to our hearts in the darkest and most perilous hours of the Republic. We were no more ashamed of him when shrouded in clouds of darkness, of doubt, and defeat than when we saw him crowned with victory, honor, and glory. Our faith in him was often taxed and strained to the uttermost, but never failed. When he tarried long in the mountain; when he strangely told us that we were the cause of the war; when he still more strangely told us that we were to leave the land in which we were born;[*] when he refused to employ our arms in defence of the Union; when, after accepting our services as colored soldiers, he refused to retaliate our murder and torture as colored prisoners; when he told us he would save the Union if he could with slavery; when he revoked the Proclamation of Emancipation of General Fremont;[†] when he refused to remove the popular commander of the Army of the Potomac,[‡] in the days of its inaction and defeat, who was more zealous in his efforts to protect slavery than to suppress rebellion; when we saw all this, and more, we were at times grieved, stunned, and greatly bewildered; but our hearts believed while they ached and bled. Nor was this, even at that time, a blind and unreasoning superstition. Despite the mist and haze that surrounded him; despite the tumult, the hurry, and confusion of the hour, we were able to take a comprehensive view of Abraham Lincoln, and to make reasonable allowance for the circumstances of his position. We saw him, measured him, and estimated him; not by stray utterances to injudicious and tedious delegations, who often tried his patience; not by isolated facts torn from their

---

[*]In a meeting with five African American men on August 14, 1862, Lincoln outlined a plan to colonize the American free black population in Africa and Central America. "But for your race among us," Lincoln told them, "there could not be war."

[†]On August 30, 1861, Fremont issued a proclamation of martial law in Missouri, freeing all slaves in the state. On September 11, Lincoln overturned Fremont's order.

[‡]George McClellan.

connection; not by any partial and imperfect glimpses, caught at inopportune moments; but by a broad survey, in the light of the stern logic of great events, and in view of that divinity which shapes our ends, rough hew them how we will, we came to the conclusion that the hour and the man of our redemption had somehow met in the person of Abraham Lincoln. It mattered little to us what language he might employ on special occasions; it mattered little to us, when we fully knew him, whether he was swift or slow in his movements; it was enough for us that Abraham Lincoln was at the head of a great movement, and was in living and earnest sympathy with that movement, which, in the nature of things, must go on until slavery should be utterly and forever abolished in the United States.

When, therefore, it shall be asked what we have to do with the memory of Abraham Lincoln, or what Abraham Lincoln had to do with us, the answer is ready, full, and complete. Though he loved Caesar less than Rome, though the Union was more to him than our freedom or our future, under his wise and beneficent rule we saw ourselves gradually lifted from the depths of slavery to the heights of liberty and manhood; under his wise and beneficent rule, and by measures approved and vigorously pressed by him, we saw that the handwriting of ages, in the form of prejudice and proscription, was rapidly fading away from the face of our whole country; under his rule, and in due time, about as soon after all as the country could tolerate the strange spectacle, we saw our brave sons and brothers laying off the rags of bondage, and being clothed all over in the blue uniforms of the soldiers of the United States; under his rule we saw two hundred thousand of our dark and dusky people responding to the call of Abraham Lincoln, and with muskets on their shoulders, and eagles on their buttons, timing their high footsteps to liberty and union under the national flag; under his rule we saw the independence of the black republic of Haiti, the special object of slaveholding aversion and horror, fully recognized, and her minister, a colored gentleman, duly received here in the city of Washington;* under his rule we saw the internal slave-trade, which so long disgraced the nation, abolished, and slavery abolished in the District of Columbia;† under his rule we saw for the first time the law enforced against the foreign slave trade, and the first slave-trader hanged like any other pirate or murderer;‡ under his rule, assisted by the greatest captain of our age, and his inspiration, we saw the Confederate States, based upon the idea that our race must be slaves, and slaves forever, battered to pieces and scattered to the four winds; under his rule, and in the fullness of time, we saw Abraham Lincoln, after giving the slave holders three months' grace in which to save their hateful slave system, penning the immortal paper, which, though special in its language, was general in its

---

*The U.S. government extended diplomatic recognition to Haiti and Liberia in 1862.
†Slavery was abolished in the District of Columbia by the act of Congress in April, 1962.
‡Nathaniel P. Gordon was captured with his ship *Erie*, with 893 slaves aboard, off the African coast by a U.S. war vessel. He was hanged on February 7, 1862.

principles and effect, making slavery forever impossible in the United States. Though we waited long, we saw all this and more.

Can any colored man, or any white man friendly to the freedom of all men, ever forget the night which followed the first day of January, 1863, when the world was to see if Abraham Lincoln would prove to be as good as his word? I shall never forget that memorable night, when in a distant city I waited and watched at a public meeting, with three thousand others not less anxious than myself, for the word of deliverance which we have heard read today. Nor shall I ever forget the outburst of joy and thanksgiving that rent the air when the lightning brought to us the emancipation proclamation. In that happy hour we forgot all delay, and forgot all tardiness, forgot that the President had bribed the rebels to lay down their arms by a promise to withhold the bolt which would smite the slave-system with destruction; and we were henceforward willing to allow the President all the latitude of time, phraseology, and every honorable device that statesmanship might require for the achievement of a great and beneficent measure of liberty and progress.

Fellow-citizens, there is little necessity on this occasion to speak at length and critically of this great and good man, and of his high mission in the world. That ground has been fully occupied and completely covered both here and elsewhere. The whole field of fact and fancy has been gleaned and garnered. Any man can say things that are true of Abraham Lincoln, but no man can say anything that is new of Abraham Lincoln. His personal traits and public acts are better known to the American people than are those of any other man of his age. He was a mystery to no man who saw him and heard him. Though high in position, the humblest could approach him and feel at home in his presence. Though deep, he was transparent; though strong, he was gentle; though decided and pronounced in his convictions, he was tolerant towards those who differed from him, and patient under reproaches. Even those who only knew him through his public utterance obtained a tolerably clear idea of his character and personality. The image of the man went out with his words, and those who read them knew him.

I have said that President Lincoln was a white man, and shared the prejudices common to his countrymen towards the colored race. Looking back to his times and to the condition of his country, we are compelled to admit that this unfriendly feeling on his part may be safely set down as one element of his wonderful success in organizing the loyal American people for the tremendous conflict before them, and bringing them safely through that conflict. His great mission was to accomplish two things; first, to save his country from dismemberment and ruin; and, second, to free his country from the great crime of slavery. To do one or the other, or both, he must have the earnest sympathy and the powerful cooperation of his loyal fellow-countrymen. Without this primary and essential condition to success his efforts must have been vain and utterly fruitless. Had he put the abolition of slavery before the salvation of the Union, he would have inevitably driven from him a powerful class of the American people and rendered resistance to rebellion impossible. Viewed from the genuine abolition ground, Mr. Lincoln seemed tardy, cold, dull, and indifferent; but measuring him by the sentiment of his country, a sentiment he was bound as a statesman to consult, he was swift, zealous, radical, and determined.

Though Mr. Lincoln shared the prejudices of his white fellow-countrymen against the Negro, it is hardly necessary to say that in his heart of hearts he loathed and hated slavery. . . . * The man who could say, "Fondly do we hope, fervently do we pray, that this mighty scourge of war shall soon pass away, yet if God wills it continue till all the wealth piled by the two hundred years of bondage shall have been wasted, and each drop of blood drawn by the lash shall have been paid for by one drawn by the sword, the judgments of the Lord and true and righteous altogether," gives all needed proof of his feeling on the subject of slavery. He was willing, while the South was loyal, that it should have its pound of flesh, because he thought that it was so nominated in the bond; but farther than this no earthly power could make him go.

Fellow-citizens, whatever else in this world may be partial, unjust, and uncertain, time, time! is impartial, just, and certain in its action. In the realm of mind, as well as in the realm of matter, it is a great worker, and often works wonders. The honest and comprehensive statesman, clearly discerning the needs of his country, and earnestly endeavoring to do his whole duty, though covered and blistered with reproaches, may safely leave his course to the silent judgment of time. Few great public men have ever been the victims of fiercer denunciation than Abraham Lincoln was during his administration. He was often wounded in the house of his friends. Reproaches came thick and fast upon him from within and from without, and from opposite quarters. He was assailed by Abolitionists; he was assailed by slaveholders; he was assailed by the men who were for peace at any price; he was assailed by those who were for a more vigorous prosecution of the war; he was assailed for not making the war an abolition war; and he was bitterly assailed for making the war an abolition war.

But now behold the change: the judgment of the present hour is, that taking him for all in all, measuring the tremendous magnitude of the work before him, considering the necessary means to ends, and surveying the end from the beginning, infinite wisdom has seldom sent any man into the world better fitted for his mission than Abraham Lincoln. His birth, his training, and his natural endowments, both mental and physical, were strongly in his favor. Born and reared among the lowly, a stranger to wealth and luxury, compelled to grapple single-handed with the flintiest hardships of life, from tender youth to sturdy manhood, he grew strong in the manly and heroic qualities demanded by the great mission to which he was called by the votes

* "I am naturally anti-slavery. If slavery is not wrong, nothing is wrong. I cannot remember when I did not so think and feel" (Lincoln to Albert G. Hodges of Kentucky, April 4, 1864). See Roy P. Basler, ed., *Collected Works of Abraham Lincoln*, vol. 7 (New Brunswick, N.J.: Rutgers University Press, 1953), 281–82.

of his countrymen. The hard condition of his early life, which would have depressed and broken down weaker men, only gave greater life, vigor, and buoyancy to the heroic spirit of Abraham Lincoln. He was ready for any kind and any quality of work. What other young men dreaded in the shape of toil, he took hold of with the utmost cheerfulness.

> *"A spade, a rake, a hoe,*
> *A pick-axe, or a bill;*
> *A hook to reap, a scythe to mow,*
> *A flail, or what you will."*

All day long he could split heavy rails in the woods, and half the night long he could study his English Grammar by the uncertain flare and glare of the light made by a pine-knot. He was at home on the land with his axe, with his maul, with gluts, and his wedges; and he was equally at home on water, with his oars, with his poles, with his planks, and with his boat-hooks. And whether in his flat-boat on the Mississippi River, or at the fireside of his frontier cabin, he was a man of work. A son of toil himself, he was linked in brotherly sympathy with the sons of toil in every loyal part of the Republic. This very fact gave him tremendous power with the American people, and materially contributed not only to selecting him to the Presidency, but in sustaining his administration of the Government.

Upon his inauguration as President of the United States, an office, even when assumed under the most favorable conditions, fitted to tax and strain the largest abilities, Abraham Lincoln was met by a tremendous crisis. He was called upon not merely to administer the Government, but to decide, in the face of terrible odds, the fate of the Republic.

A formidable rebellion rose in his path before him; the Union was already practically dissolved; his country was torn and rent asunder at the center. Hostile armies were already organized against the Republic, armed with the munitions of war which the Republic had provided for its own defence. The tremendous question for him to decide was whether his country should survive the crisis and flourish, or be dismembered and perish. His predecessor in office had already decided the question in favor of national dismemberment, by denying to it the right of self-defence and self-preservation—a right which belongs to the meanest insect.

Happily for the country, happily for you and for me, the judgment of James Buchanan, the patrician, was not the judgment of Abraham Lincoln, the plebeian. He brought his strong common sense, sharpened in the school of adversity, to bear upon the question. He did not hesitate, he did not doubt, he did not falter; but at once resolved that at whatever peril, at whatever cost, the union of the States should be preserved. A patriot himself, his faith was strong and unwavering in the patriotism of his countrymen. Timid men said before Mr. Lincoln's inauguration, that we had seen the last President of the United States. A voice in influential quarters said, "Let the Union slide." Some said that a Union maintained by the sword was worthless. Others said a rebellion of 8,000,000 cannot be suppressed; but in the midst of all this tumult and timidity, and against all this, Abraham Lincoln was clear in his duty, and had an oath in heaven. He calmly and bravely heard the voice of doubt and fear all around him; but he had an oath in heaven, and there was not power enough on earth to make this honest boatman, back-woodsman, and broad-handed splitter of rails evade or violate that sacred oath. He had not been schooled in the ethics of slavery; his plain life had favored his love of truth. He had not been taught that treason and perjury were the proof of honor and honesty. His moral training was against his saying one thing when he meant another. The trust that Abraham Lincoln had in himself and in the people was surprising and grand, but it was also enlightened and well founded. He knew the American people better than they knew themselves, and his truth was based upon this knowledge.

Fellow-citizens, the fourteenth day of April, 1865, of which this is the eleventh anniversary, is now and will ever remain a memorable day in the annals of this Republic. It was on the evening of this day, while a fierce and sanguinary rebellion was in the last stages of its desolating power; while its armies were broken and scattered before the invincible armies of Grant and Sherman; while a great nation, torn and rent by war, was already beginning to raise to the skies loud anthems of joy at the dawn of peace, it was startled, amazed, and overwhelmed by the crowning crime of slavery—the assassination of Abraham Lincoln. It was a new crime, a pure act of malice. No purpose of the rebellion was to be served by it. It was simple gratification of a hell-black spirit of revenge. But it has done good after all. It has filled the country with a deeper abhorrence of slavery and a deeper love for the great liberator.

Had Abraham Lincoln died from any of the numerous ills to which flesh is heir; had he reached that good old age of which his vigorous constitution and his temperate habits gave promise; had he been permitted to see the end of his great work; had the solemn curtain of death come down but gradually—we should still have been smitten with a heavy grief, and treasured his name lovingly. But dying as he did die, by the red hand of violence, killed, assassinated, taken off without warning, not because of personal hate—for no man who knew Abraham Lincoln could hate him—but because of his fidelity to union and liberty, he is doubly dear to us, and his memory will be precious forever.

Fellow-citizens, I end, as I began, with congratulations. We have done a good work for our race today. In doing honor to the memory of our friend and liberator, we have been doing highest honors to ourselves and those who come after us; we have been fastening ourselves to a name and fame imperishable and immortal; we have also been defending ourselves from a blighting scandal. When now it shall be said that the colored man is soulless, that he has no appreciation of benefits or benefactors; when the foul reproach of ingratitude is hurled at us, and it is attempted to scourge us beyond the range of human brotherhood, we may calmly point to the monument we have this day erected to the memory of Abraham Lincoln.■

100 THE SIOUX'S REVENGE

B. T. Tanner

On June 25, 1876, Colonel George A. Custer and his army were annihilated in the Battle of Little Big Horn. Custer's "last stand" against Crazy Horse and Sitting Bull made him a hero to most white Americans, but most black Americans did not mourn his death. At the Sabbath service at Bethel Church in Philadelphia, July 13, 1876, two African American speakers discussed the fatal outcome of Custer's war against the Lakota Indians in Dakota, invading lands that had been ceded to the Lakota by treaty in 1868. One was Dr. Henry McNeal Turner, who, in the course of his remarks about the retributive justice of God, said: "I am sorry for the General,* as I would be for any other man, but I could not forget that the General has been an apologist, and a defender of those who have been murdering Republicans in the South, and that hundreds of black men greater than General Custer ever was are sleeping in bloody graves, with the sanction and approval of this same picayune General. . . . Thousands of our race have been murdered for nothing except to gratify the ungodly spleen of such men as Custer, and no tears were shed for them." Dr. Turner's speech was followed by the Reverend B. T. Tanner's remarks, the text of which also appeared in the Christian Recorder, *July 20, 1876.*

Benjamin Tucker Tanner was born of free parents in Pittsburgh in 1835. He worked his way through Pennsylvania's Avery College as a barber, then attended Western Theological Seminary. During and after the Civil War, Tanner organized schools and Sabbath schools for freed people, while establishing a national reputation as an orator and author of works including Apology for African Methodism *and* The Negro, African and American. *In 1868, he was appointed editor of the* Christian Recorder, *the influential newspaper of the A.M.E. Church.*

I CAN ALMOST SEE the grim visage of the terrible Sioux light up with joy at the idea of having at last got revenge of the "long-haired chief"; almost hear the unearthly laughter, if a Sioux ever laughs, as around his campfire he tells of the slaughter of the fatal June twenty-fifth. Say what you will, the Sioux has a human soul within him—a soul that is conscious of wrongs perpetrated upon his tribe, until it has become as an outcast in its own land. And, taught by a Christian government that the proper thing to do in the case of wrongs perpetrated is to seek revenge, he has acted upon

---

*Custer had been a major general during the Civil War, but he had lost his title when the volunteer army was disbanded following Appomattox.

it, to the grief of the whole nation. But why should the nation grieve other than it is human to grieve for friends stricken down. Surely it cannot expect other than that they may perish by the sword, who take the sword. Of all our military captains, Custer was the one who took pleasure in the sword. He was the *beau sabreur* of our Army and with joy did he unsheathe it to strike down the "red nagurs" of the Far West—the "red nagurs," as the men of his command felt free to call the Indians in his presence. Custer hated the Indians, as he hated any man of color. Upon the morning of his fatal departure from the main body of his troops, his insisting upon having his command "homogenous" occasioned the absence of comrades that might possibly have saved him and his brave Seventh. But alas, the offer was rejected.*

Of course, we gathered here today do not feel as the nation feels, nor can we—nor can any Negro. Does one say he does? He is either a fool or hypocrite. Our blood has flowed and is flowing too freely for us to go into any hysterics of grief for the loss of this commander and his command; however gallant he, however patriotic they were. Have we tears to shed—and we have—we shed them for the scores and hundreds of our people who die violently every day in the South. Have we a heart to bleed, it is rather for our brothers cowardly assaulted and more cowardly riddled with Southern bullets. It cannot be that all the blood shedding is to be on one side.

Far be it from me to have had one so eagle-like as George A. Custer slain by warlike savages. Neither would I have had him fighting them. By the sacred obligations of treaty, no white man had any right or business to the Black Hill country. It belongs to the Sioux, and is guaranteed him by the nation. As well might the President allow men to come and put me out of my own house, as allow settlers to possess themselves of that region. If, therefore, the Sioux make war for his rights he does no more than the common law sanctions and the thing to do is not to fight him, but to secure him his right.■

---

*Black soldiers had volunteered to assist Custer's army but had been rejected. Isaiah Dorman, however, who had served as a courier for the War Department in the Dakota territory, and may have been part Sioux, was assigned to Custer's command at the colonel's request for an interpreter and was the only black man in the expedition. Dorman was among the 264 men who fought and died with Custer. For reasons never made clear, the Sioux did not scalp and mutilate Dorman as they did the white soldiers.

101

HOW LONG? HOW LONG, O HEAVEN?

Reverend Henry McNeal Turner

The wave of brutal assaults on African Americans in the South by the Ku Klux Klan and other extralegal organizations reached its climax on July 9, 1876, in Hamburg, South Carolina. The black militia members of the city were attacked by three hundred armed whites and ordered to give up their arms. When they refused, the whites opened fire on the building in which the militia were assembled. A piece of artillery was used to attack the building, and after twenty-five of the black militia were captured, five were marked out, one by one, and shot to death in the presence of a large body of their captors. The white mob then attacked and looted the homes and shops of the black community. Governor D. H. Chamberlain of South Carolina wrote that the Hamburg massacre "presents a darker picture of human cruelty than the slaughter of Custer and his soldiers, for they were shot in open battle. The victims at Hamburg were murdered in cold blood after they had surrendered and were utterly defenseless." Seven men were tried for the murders; all were acquitted.

Bitterly denouncing the merciless attacks upon African Americans in the South, Henry McNeal Turner (1834–1915) delivered a stinging sermon at Union Church in Philadelphia on August 5, 1876. It is interesting that Turner's suggestion that black Americans appeal to European nations for assistance in their struggle for survival anticipated such appeals to the Paris Peace Conference at Versailles and to the United Nations.

The following excerpts of Turner's remarks appeared in the Christian Recorder, *August 10, 1876.*

I n 1833 the authorities of South Carolina hanged twenty-eight colored men because they were suspicioned of conspiring to assert and take their freedom—six at one time, twenty-two at another—and yet the blood of a mouse was not shed, throughout the whole so-called conspiracy.* Nevertheless, upon this trumped-up charge, they hanged several colored men, who, for Christian integrity and loyalty to law and order, were as far ahead of the

---

*In Charleston, South Carolina, in 1822, a huge slave plot was uncovered. Its leader was Denmark Vesey, a free black carpenter who had bought his own liberty when he won a fifteen-hundred-dollar raffle. The conspiracy had been planned for four years, and the slaves involved had hidden away weapons and ammunition. The authorities, alerted by two house slaves, arrested 131 suspects. Federal troops stood by to protect the city as the twenty-eight blacks found guilty and sentenced to death were led to the gallows.

Calhouns, Rhetts, Brookses, Adamses, et cetera, as Gabriel is ahead of the devil. Yet, when a disloyal white general and his diabolical crew, incarnate fiends, brutally murder and maim for life nearly or quite a dozen of the colored defenders of that state and of the nation, scores of newspapers loom up with wicked apologies, and thousands of pretended church members openly endorse the act. Still we talk about this being a Christian country. Did you ever read the history of the Dark Ages? I have, and I have read of nothing being perpetrated during that long night of dissipation and cruelty, which surpassed the deeds of horror that have been committed in Louisiana, Georgia, Mississippi, South Carolina, and other states, where not only do men pretend to be civilized, but Christianized.

The acts of blood and carnage which have disgraced this nation for the last half-dozen years and are justified by a whole party that even essays to make a President are so revolting to the very instincts of a savage that I should not be surprised to see Hottentots coming as missionaries to this country. The cold-blooded murders that have been perpetrated in this country with impunity and silent approval could not have gone on in any European country without causing a war and arousing the whole continent.

And if we colored people were not so blind and stupid, we would hold a convention somewhere and send a delegation to England, Germany, France, or to all the civilized countries in the Old World, and ask them to interfere in our behalf and save us from mad frenzy of infuriated mobs, before whom the national government, with its immense army and navy, quails and sinks in the dust. I had rather live under a monarch, autocrat, despot, or under any impartial authority than pretend to live under a mobocracy, with no power in the state or nation to quell and bid them stop. How long? How long, O Heaven, before this condition of things will change? When will thy justice, O God, avenge our wrongs?■

102 SOCIALISM: THE REMEDY FOR THE EVILS OF SOCIETY

Peter H. Clark

Peter H. Clark, principal of the Colored High School in Cincinnati, Ohio, was probably the first African American Socialist. Born in Cincinnati in 1829, Clark was the grandson of the southern white explorer William Clark, of the 1804 Lewis and Clark expedition.

Peter Clark worked as a schoolteacher and was active in the black convention movement of the 1850s. He founded his own newspaper, the Herald of Freedom, *and was a correspondent for* Frederick Douglass' Paper. *He was a Republican until 1877, when, disillusioned with the Republican Party's indifference to the problems of black Americans in the South and concerned about the growing power of industrial capitalists, he joined the socialist movement, becoming a member of the Workingmen's Party of the United States (founded in Philadelphia in 1876), and publicly proclaimed himself in favor of socialism.*

Below is the speech Clark delivered at Cincinnati on July 22, 1877, to a huge crowd of striking railroad workers. The great railroad strike of 1877 began in July when the principal railroads instituted the third 10 percent wage cut since the beginning of the depression in 1873. At Martinsburg, West Virginia, a strike broke out, and spontaneously, without united leadership, it spread to a dozen railroad centers, including Cincinnati. Scores were killed during the strike, millions of dollars' worth of property was burned, and hundreds of factories were closed by strikers. President Rutherford B. Hayes used federal troops against strikers; it was the second time the U.S. Army had been sent in to break a strike.* This was the setting for Clark's speech.

The Cincinnati Commercial *(July 23, 1877), which published the speech in full,† commented: "The intelligent colored teacher and speaker was introduced . . . as the first speaker, and was well received. His calm face had a soothing effect upon the excited multitude." In one of the earliest known speeches of an African American Socialist, Clark casts the railroad strike in terms of a broader class struggle and sees a fundamental reformation of the American economic system as the solution to the poverty and strife of the 1870s.*

G ENTLEMEN: If I had the choosing of a motto for this meeting, I should select the words of the patriotic and humane Abraham Lincoln, "With malice toward none, with charity for all, with firmness in the right as God gives us to see the right." These words, so full of that charity which we should exercise toward each other, are especially suited to this day and time, when wrongs long condemned have at last been resisted and men are bleeding and dying in the busy centers of our population, and all over the land other men, with heated passions, are assembling to denounce the needless slaughter of innocent men who, driven by want, have appealed to force for that justice which was otherwise refused to them. . . .

---

*For further information, see Philip S. Foner, *The Great Labor Uprising of 1877* (New York: Monad Press, 1977).

†Extracts from this speech can be found in Herbert G. Gutman, "Peter H. Clark: Pioneer Negro Socialist, 1877," *Journal of Negro Education* 34 (Fall 1965), 413–18. See also Philip S. Foner, "Peter H. Clark: Pioneer Black Socialist," *Journal of Ethnic Studies* 5 (Fall 1977), 17–35.

I sympathize in this struggle with the strikers, and I feel sure that in this I have the cooperation of nine tenths of my fellow citizens. The poor man's lot is at best a hard one. His hand-to-hand struggle with the wolf of poverty leaves him no leisure for any of the amenities of life, his utmost rewards are a scanty supply for food, scanty clothing, scanty shelter, and if perchance he escapes a pauper's grave [he] is fortunate. Such a man deserves the aid and sympathy of all good people, especially when, in the struggle for life, he is pitted against a powerful organization such as the Baltimore and Ohio Railroad or Pennsylvania Central. The Baltimore and Ohio Railroad was taken possession of by the government during the war, and was rebuilt in a manner, from end to end. Such a firm roadway, such tunnels and bridges, are rarely seen as are possessed by that road, and at the end the road was turned over to its owners in a better condition than it had ever been, so that much of the outlay which other roads are compelled to make was saved to this. They were paid for the use of the road many millions of dollars and the managers have lately declared a dividend of ten percent, and if their stock was watered, as I have no doubt it is, this ten percent is equivalent to fifteen or twenty percent upon the capital actually invested in it. Yet this road, so built, so subsidized, so prosperous, if we may judge from its dividend, declares itself compelled to put the wages of its employees down to starvation rates. Either they were not honestly able to declare that dividend or they are able to pay living wages to the men whom they employ. The blood of those men murdered at Baltimore cries from the ground against these men who by their greed have forced their men to the desperate measure of a strike, and then invoked the strong arm of the government to slaughter them in their misery.

The too-ready consent of the state and national governments to lend themselves to the demand of these wealthy corporations cannot be too severely condemned. Has it come to this, that the President of a private corporation can, by the click of a telegraphic instrument, bring state and national troops into the field to shoot down American citizens guilty of no act of violence? For you observe that neither at Grafton, Baltimore or Pittsburgh was there violence offered to persons or property until the troops were deployed upon the scene. At Grafton it is noticeable that women, wives and mothers, were the chief forces employed by the strikers to keep others from taking their places.

The sight of the soldiery fired the hot blood of the wronged men, and they met force with force. Whether they are put down or not, we are thankful that the American citizen, as represented by these men, was not slave enough to surrender without resistance the right to appeal for a redress of grievances. When that day comes that a mere display of force is sufficient to awe a throng of Americans into submission, the people will have sunk too low to be entrusted with self-government.

Those men will be avenged—nobly avenged. Capital has been challenged to the contest; and in the arena of debate, to which in a few days the question will be remanded, the American people will sit as judges, and just as surely as we stand here, their decision will be against monopolists and in favor of the workingmen. In twenty years from today there will not be a railroad in the land belonging to a private corporation; all will be owned by the government and worked in the interests of the people. Machinery and land will, in time, take the same course, and cooperation instead of competition will be the law of society. The miserable condition into which society has fallen has but one remedy, and that is to be found in Socialism.

Observe how all civilized communities pass from a condition of what is called prosperity to one of depression and distress. Observe how continually these fluctuations occur; how the intervals between them grow shorter; how each one is more violent than the last, the distress produced more widespread. Observe, too, that after each the number of capitalists decrease, while those who remain grow more wealthy and more powerful, while those who have failed join the great army of workers who hang forever on the ragged edge of pauperism.

The so-called periods of prosperity are more properly periods of unrestrained speculation. Money accumulates in the hands of the capitalists, [through (?)] some governmental device as a tariff or the issue of greenbacks. This abundance tempts men to embark in business enterprises which seem to promise rich returns. For a time all goes well, shops are crowded with busy men, and all [are] ready to say, "Behold how prosperous we are!" But there comes a check to all this. The manufacturers begin to talk about a glutted market. There has been overproduction. There comes the period of sharp competition. Prices are reduced, goods are sold at cost—below cost— then comes the crash, bosses fail, shops are closed, men are idle, and the miserable workmen stand forth, underbidding each other in the labor market. If the competition be too sharp, they resort to strikes as in the present instance. Then comes violence, lawlessness, bloodshed and death.

People who talk of the anarchy of socialism surely cannot have considered these facts. If they had, they would have discovered not a little of anarchy on their side of the question.

It is folly to say that a condition of poverty is a favorable one, and to point to men who have risen to affluence from that condition. For one man who is strong through the hindrances of poverty, there are ten thousand who fail. If you take ten thousand men and weigh them with lead and cast them into the midst of Lake Erie, a few may swim out but the majority will be drowned.

This condition of poverty is not a favorable one either for the individual or for the nation. Especially is it an unfavorable condition for a nation whose government lies in the hands of all its citizens. A monarchy or an aristocracy can afford to have the mass of its citizens steeped in poverty and ignorance. Not so in a republic. Here every man should be the owner of wealth enough to render him independent of the threats or bribes of the demagogue. He should be the owner of wealth enough to give leisure for that study which will qualify him to study and understand the deep questions of public policy which are continually demanding solution. The more men there are who have this independence, this leisure, the safer we are as a nation; reduce the number, and the fewer there are, the more dangerous the situation. So alarming has been the spread of ignorance and poverty in the past generation, that whole cities in our land—whose states, indeed—are at the mercy of an ignorant rabble who have no political principle except to vote for the men who pay the most on election days and who promise to make the biggest dividend of public stealing. This is sadly true, nor is the Negro, scarcely ten years from slavery, the chief sinner in this respect.

That this evil of poverty is partially curable, at least, I am justified in thinking, because I find each of the great political parties offering remedies for the hard times and the consequent poverty. Many wise men, learned in political economy, assure us that their doctrines, faithfully followed, will result in a greater production of wealth and a more equal division of the same. But as I have said before, there is but one efficacious remedy proposed, and that is found in Socialism.

The present industrial organization of society has been faithfully tried and has proven a failure. We get rid of the king, we get rid of the aristocracy, but the capitalist comes in their place, and in the industrial organization and guidance of society his little finger is heavier than their loins. Whatever Socialism may bring about, it can present nothing more anarchical than is found in Grafton, Baltimore and Pittsburgh today. . . .

To increase the volume of the currency, which is the remedy proposed by some, means simply that money shall be made so abundant that the capitalist, in despair of any legitimate returns in the way of interest, shall embark in any and all enterprises which promise returns for the idle cash in his coffers. It means a stimulation of production in a community already suffering from excess of production; it means speculation, competition, finally a reduction of values, bankruptcy, ruin. The American people have traveled that path so frequently in the past fifty years that it requires no prophetic powers to map out the certain course which will be pursued. Already our capitalists rush to invest their money at four and a half percent in markets which a short time since gave readily two percent a month. Increase your volume—let it be either greenbacks or silver—and we enter on the career I have described with a certainty that the gulf at the end is deeper and more hopeless than the one in which we now wallow.

Trades-unions, Grangers, Sovereigns of Industry, cooperative stores and factories are alike futile.* They are simply combinations of laborers who

---

*During the depression years many radicals grew to believe that trade unions and strikes were useless in solving the problems of workers under capitalism. Grangers, or Patrons of Husbandry, were farmers' organizations formed in the Midwest after the Civil War. Although they concerned themselves with educational and social activities, their principal objective was the furtherance of state legislation designed to protect farmers against the economic abuses of railroads, storage warehouses, and grain elevators. The Order of the Sovereigns of Industry grew out of the Grangers and was mainly concerned with establishing consumers' cooperatives for the distribution of necessaries of life among wage earners. The Sovereigns cooperated in several cases with the Patrons of Husbandry and

seek to assume toward their own unfortunate fellows who are not members the attitude that the capitalist assumes toward them. They incorporate into their constitutions all the evil principles which afflict society. Competition, overproduction mark their stores and factories as much as do those of individual enterprises, and when the periodic crash comes, they succumb as readily as any.

All these plans merely poultice the ulcer in the body politic which needs Constitutional treatment. The momentary improvement they produce is always succeeded by a corresponding depression. The old fable of Sisyphus is realized, and the heavy stone rolled to the top of the mountain with infinite labor rolls back again.

The government must control capital with a strong hand. It is merely the accumulated results of industry, and there would be no justice should a few score bees in the hive take possession of the store of honey and dole it out to the workers in return for services which added to their superabundant store. Yet such is the custom of society.

Future accumulations of capital should be held sacredly for the benefit of the whole community. Past accumulations may be permitted to remain in private hands until, from their very uselessness, they will become a burden which their owners will gladly surrender.

Machinery too, which ought to be a blessing but is proving to be a curse to the people should be taken in hand by the government and its advantages distributed to all. Captain Cutter wrote in his song of steam:

> *Soon I intend ye may go and play,*
> *While I manage this world myself.*

Had he written, ye may go and starve, it would have been nearer the truth. Machinery controlled in the interests of labor would afford that leisure for thought, for self-culture, for giving and receiving refining influences, which are so essential to the full development of character. "The ministry of wealth" would not be confined to a few, but would be a benefit to all.

Every railroad in the land should be owned or controlled by the government. The title of private owners should be extinguished, and the ownership vested in the people. All a road will need to meet will be a running expense and enough to replace waste. The people can then enjoy the benefit of travel, and where one man travels now, a thousand will travel then. There will be no strikes, for the men who operate the road will be the recipient of its profits.

Finally, we want governmental organization of labor so that ruinous competition and ruinous overproduction shall equally be avoided, and these

---

even united with the Grangers to maintain a cooperative store. The total membership of the Sovereigns of Industry in 1875–1876 was said to be 40,000, of whom 75 percent were in New England and 43 percent in Massachusetts. The organization's decline started in 1875, and by 1878 it was passing out of existence.

commercial panics which sweep over and engulf the world will be forever prevented.

It will be objected that this is making our government a machine for doing for the citizen everything which can be more conveniently done by combined than by individual effort. Society has already made strides in the direction of Socialism. Every drop of water we draw from hydrants, the gas that illumines our streets at night, the paved streets upon which we walk, our parks, our schools, our libraries, are all outgrowths of the Socialistic principle. In that direction lies safety.

Choose ye this day which course ye shall pursue.

Let us, finally, not forget that we are American citizens, that the right of free speech and of a free press is enjoyed by us. We are exercising today the right to assemble and complain of our grievances. The courts of the land are open to us, and we hold in our hands the all-compelling ballot.

There is no need for violent counsels or violent deeds. If we are patient and wise, the future is ours.■

103 REASONS WHY THE COLORED AMERICAN SHOULD GO TO AFRICA

John E. Bruce

With the outbreak of the Civil War, the emigration movement to Africa among black Americans took second place to the struggle to achieve emancipation and political and civil rights. But as the promise of Reconstruction turned into a nightmare for African Americans, the back-to-Africa movement once again emerged. Agents of the American Colonization Society claimed in 1877 to have enrolled thousands of southern blacks ready to emigrate, and in April 1878, two hundred black South Carolinians embarked by steamship for Liberia.

In October 1877, journalist John E. Bruce delivered a speech in Philadelphia urging a return to Africa as the only real solution for African Americans. Bruce (1856–1924), born in slavery in Maryland, wrote for many leading newspapers and magazines and was a popular speaker. He was later active in the Afro-American League and was among the founders of the Negro Society for Historical Research. After the First World

War, he became an enthusiastic supporter of Marcus Garvey's Universal Negro Improvement Association.

In his 1877 address, Bruce anticipates Garvey as he outlines a series of reasons why African Americans should return to the homeland, emphasizing especially the fact that even after the constitutional amendments adopted since the Civil War, they were only "nominally free." The major portion of Bruce's speech, as excerpted from the Christian Recorder, *November 1, 1877, appears below. For further information, see Ralph L. Crowder, "John Edward Bruce: Pioneer Black Nationalist,"* Afro-Americans in New York Life and History *2 (July 1978), 47–66.*

I SHALL ENDEAVOR to show tonight why the colored American should emigrate to Africa—*first,* because Africa is his fatherland; *secondly,* because, before the war, in the South he was a slave, and in the North, a victim of prejudice and ostracism; and *thirdly,* because, since the close of the war, although he has been freed by emancipation and invested with enfranchisement, he is only nominally free; and lastly, because he is still a victim of prejudice, and practically proscribed socially, religiously, politically, educationally, and in the various industrial pursuits.

First, then, he should emigrate to Africa because it is his fatherland. Africa is a country rich in its productions, offering untold treasures to the adventurer who may go there. It has a peculiar claim upon the colored American in this country, and that claim is as just and as equitable as any could be. One hundred and fifty millions of our people are on the other side of the broad Atlantic, groveling in darkness and superstition; five millions are on this side surrounded by all the advantages that could be desired in the march toward civilization. It is our duty to carry to those benighted, darkened minds a light to guide them in the march toward civilization. For centuries the colored race has not been highly educated. This has not always been the fact, and history, which shows what has been done, proves what may yet be. The Africans held possession of southern Egypt when Isaiah wrote, "Ethiopia shall soon stretch out her hands unto God." When the Queen of Sheba brought added wealth to the treasures of Solomon, and when a princely and learned Ethiopian became a herald of Christ before Paul the Hebrew, Cornelius, or the European soldiers were converted. The race to whom had been given the wonderful continent of Africa, can be educated and elevated to wealth, power and station among the nations of the earth.

Secondly, why the colored American should emigrate to Africa is because, before the war, in the South he was a slave and in the North a victim of prejudice and ostracism. During the cruel days of slavery the colored American had no right which the white American was bound to respect; he was a nonentity before the law—an automaton with an immortal soul. "Old Massa" had full power and control over him and his posterity. His relatives, his children and friends who were dear to him were snatched up any time by "Old Massa" and sold into slavery, driven into misery everlasting, woe and discontentment. So much for slavery.

Thirdly, why the colored American should emigrate to Africa is because, since the war, although he has been freed by emancipation and invested with enfranchisement, he is only nominally free. His rights are abridged; he is an American only in name. The doors of the public schools are closed against his children, notwithstanding the fact that he is taxed to support them. The common carriers, hotels and places of amusement, refuse to recognize him as a free man; no matter what his rank or station may be, he cannot enjoy the privileges which the Constitution (the supreme law of the land) guarantees to the humblest citizen. The atrocious massacre of unoffending colored men during the past five years in the states of Mississippi, South Carolina and Louisiana have blackened the page of American history and cast a gloom over the whole civilized world. Innocent men and women were butchered in cold blood by the inhuman wretches who glory in the name "American citizen." These brutal murders were committed in defiance of all law and justice. Men can never forget them. The blood of thousands of our race cries aloud unto the God of justice, and the day of retribution is not far distant.

And lastly, why the colored American should emigrate to Africa is because he is still a victim of prejudice, and practically proscribed socially, religiously and politically. He cannot enter a hotel and obtain accommodations without paying a double price, should he be successful in entering at all. If he go to the church of God in this Christian land, he is thrust into the gallery. If he wants to go South, he is packed in the car nearest the engine so that he will be the first killed in case of a collision. Politically he is a failure and cannot begin to compete with his white brother. He is used by him in all dirty jobs to advance his interests—to fill his pockets with ill-gotten gains; he is virtually a tool and a scapegoat in this respect, and he is regarded as an indispensable auxiliary in time of elections by these unscrupulous and unprincipled demagogues, who are a disgrace and a curse to such a republic as this claims to be.

And now Mr. President, I think I have shown why the colored American should emigrate to Africa. It is to his interest and his gain to do so. He is surrounded on every hand by prejudice and opposition, and it remains for him to carve out for himself a destiny among the nations of the earth.■

104

THE DESTINED SUPERIORITY OF THE NEGRO

Alexander Crummell

Born in New York in 1819, eminent scholar Alexander Crummell attended the African Free School and graduated from Beriah Green's integrated Oneida Institute in 1839. Crummell was ordained as a priest in the Protestant Episcopal Church and was active in antislavery efforts and the convention movement. Crummell lived abroad for a quarter of a century. Living in England from 1848 to 1853, he graduated from Queen's College, Cambridge. He then journeyed as an Episcopal missionary to Liberia and became a citizen of that country and a member of the faculty at Monrovia's Liberia College. Dismissed from his teaching post and fearful for his life, Crummell left Liberia in 1872.

"The 1870s," according to biographer Wilson Moses, "marked a dramatic shift in Crummell's political ideology" (Alexander Crummell, 207). Crummell refashioned sermons originally written to extol Liberian nationalism and "recast them as American loyalist manifestos," abandoning appeals for African American efforts to establish a separate black nation. Nevertheless, Crummell's American sermons retain powerful elements of Pan-Africanism.

In "The Destined Superiority of the Negro," Crummell's Thanksgiving sermon of 1877, he searches the history of Africans and African Americans for clues to God's plans for them. "Is this a race doomed for destruction?" Crummell asks. Instead, Crummell argues, the centuries of slavery and abuse endured by African Americans should be regarded as "disciplinary and preparative" for a destined moral role in worldly affairs. Such trials, he insists, show that God "is graciously interested in such a people." Crummell embraces certain characteristics sometimes used in derogatory stereotyping of blacks, such as adaptability and imitation, and claims them as qualities that demonstrate greater capacity for survival, education and cultural growth than is possessed by Caucasians. Let us "march on in the pathway of progress," he instructs his listeners, "to that superiority and eminence which is our rightful heritage, and which is evidently the promise of our God!"

The speech was delivered in the same fateful year when President Hayes withdrew most federal troops from the South, initiating a period of racist violence and persecution. Crummell argues for a kind of social Darwinism in which the sterner the test, the greater the people who survive it.

The speech text is taken from Alexander Crummell, The Greatness of Christ and Other Sermons (New York: Thomas Whittaker, 1882), 332–52. We are grateful to Professor Wilson Jeremiah Moses, author of

Alexander Crummell: A Study of Civilization and Discontent *(New York: Oxford University Press, 1989), for providing us with this text. See also Detine L. Bowers, "Alexander Crummell," in Richard Leeman, ed.,* African-American Orators: A Bio-Critical Sourcebook *(Westport, Conn.: Greenwood, 1996), 51–59.*

Isaiah LXI, 7. *For your shame ye shall have double, and for confusion they shall rejoice in their portion.*

The promise contained in the text is a variation from the ordinary rule of the divine government. In that government, as declared in the Holy Scriptures, shame signifies the hopeless confusion and the utter destruction of the wicked. But in this passage we see an extraordinary display of God's forbearance and mercy. Shame, here, is less intense than in other places. In this case it stands, indeed, for trial and punishment, but for punishment and trial which may correct and purify character.

The allusion is supposed to refer to the Jews after their restoration, and the passage is regarded as teaching that, for all their long-continued servitude and suffering, God, in the end, would make them abundant recompenses. Great shame and reproach He had given them, through long centuries; but when discipline and trial had corrected and purified them, He promises them double honor and reward.

As thus explained, the text opens before us some interesting features of God's dealing with nations; by the light of which we may, perchance, somewhat determine the destiny of the race with which we are connected. My purpose is to attempt, this morning, an investigation of God's disciplinary and retributive economy in races and nations; with the hope of arriving at some clear conclusions concerning the destiny of the Negro race.

1. Some peoples God does not merely correct; He destroys them. He visits them with deep and abiding shame. He brings upon them utter confusion. This is a painful but a certain fact of Providence. The history of the world is, in one view, a history of national destructions. The wrecks of nations lie everywhere upon the shores of time. Real aboriginal life is rarely found. People after people, in rapid succession, have come into constructive being, and as rapidly gone down; lost forever from sight beneath the waves of a relentless destiny. We read in our histories of the great empires of the old world; but when the traveller goes abroad, and looks for Nineveh and Babylon, for Pompeii and Herculaneum, he finds nought but the outstretched graveyards which occupy the sites of departed nations. On the American continent, tribe after tribe have passed from existence; yea, there are Bibles in Indian tongues which no living man is now able to read. Their peoples have all perished!

When I am called upon to account for all this loss of national and tribal life, I say that God destroyed them. And the declaration is made on the strength of a principle attested by numerous facts in sacred and profane history; that when the sins of a people reach a state of hateful maturity, then God sends upon them sudden destruction.

Depravity prepares some races of men for destruction. Every element of good has gone out of them. Even the most primitive virtues seem to have departed. A putrescent virus has entered into and vitiated their whole nature. They stand up columnar ruins! Such a people is doomed. It cannot live. Like the tree "whose root is rottenness," it stands awaiting the inevitable fall. That fall is its property. No fierce thunder-bolt is needed, no complicated apparatus of ethereal artillery. Let the angry breath of an Archangel but feebly strike it, and, tottering, it sinks into death and oblivion!

Such was the condition of the American Indian at the time of the discovery of America by Columbus. The historical fact abides, that when the white man first reached the shores of this continent he met the tradition of a decaying population.

The New Zealand population of our own day presents a parallel care. By a universal disregard of the social and sanitary conditions which pertain to health and longevity, their physical constitution has fallen into absolute decay; and ere long it also must become extinct.

Indeed, the gross paganism of these two peoples was both moral and physical stagnation; was domestic and family ruin; and has resulted in national suicide! It came to them as the effect, the direct consequence of great penal laws established by the Almighty, in which are wrapped the punishment of sin. Hence, if you reject the idea of direct interference in the affairs of peoples, and take up the idea of law and penalty, or that of cause and effect, it amounts to the same thing. Whether through God's fixed law, or directly, by His personal, direful visitation, the admission is the same. The punishment and the ruin come from the throne of God!

The most striking instances of the working of this principle of ruin are set before us in the word of God. The case of Egypt is a signal one. For centuries this nation was addicted to the vilest sins and the grossest corruption. There was no lack of genius among them, no imbecility of intellect. It was a case of wanton, high-headed moral rebellion. As generations followed each other, they heaped up abominations upon the impurities of their ancestors, until they well-nigh reached the heavens. Then the heavens became darkened with direful wrath! The earth quaked and trembled with God's fearful anger; and judgment upon judgment swept, like lava, over the doomed people, assuring them of the awful destruction which always waits upon sin. And the death of the first-born at the Passover, and the catastrophe of the Red Sea, showed that the crisis of their fate had come.

In precisely the same manner God dealt with the wicked people of Assyria, Babylon, Tyre, and Persia. Read the prophecies concerning these nations, and it seems as though you could see an august judge sitting upon the judgment-seat, and, of a sudden, putting on his black cap, and, with solemn gesture and a choked utterance, pronouncing the sentence of death upon the doomed criminals before him!

2. Turn now to the more gracious aspects of God's economy. As there

are people whom He destroys, so on the other hand there are those whom, while indeed He chastises, yet at the same time He preserves. He gives them shame, but not perpetual shame. He disciplines; but when discipline has worked out its remedial benefits, he recompenses them for their former ignominy, and gives them honor and prosperity.

The merciful aspect of God's economy shines out in human history as clearly as His justice and judgment. The Almighty seizes upon superior nations and, by mingled chastisement and blessings, gradually leads them on to greatness. That this discipline of nations is carried on in the world is evident. Probation, that is, as designed to teach self-restraint, and to carry on improvement, is imposed upon them, as well as upon individuals. It is part of the history of all nations and all races; only some will not take it; seem to have no moral discernment to use it; and they, just like wilful men, are broken to pieces. Some, again, fit themselves to it, and gain all its advantages. What was the servile sojourn of the children of Israel, four hundred years, in Egypt, but a process of painful preparation for a coming national and ecclesiastical responsibility? What, at a later period, the Babylonish captivity, but a corrective ordeal, to eliminate from them every element of idolatry? What was the feudality of Europe, but a system of training for a high and grand civilization?

Now it seems to me that these several experiments were not simply judicial and retributive. For vengeance crushes and annihilates; but chastisement, however severe, saves, and at the same time corrects and restores. We may infer, therefore, that these several providences were a mode of divine schooling, carried on by the Almighty for great ends which He wished to show in human history.

But how! in what way does God carry on His system of restorative discipline? The universal principle which regulates this feature of the Divine system is set forth very clearly in the Eighteenth Psalm: "With the merciful thou wilt shew thyself merciful; with an upright man thou wilt shew thyself upright; with the pure thou wilt shew thyself pure; and with the froward thou wilt shew thyself froward." These words show the principles by which God carries on His government. And they apply as well to organic society as to single persons.

We have already seen that with the froward God showed Himself froward; that is, those who resist Him, God resists, to their utter shame and confusion. Their miseries were not corrective or disciplinary. They were the blows of avenging justice; the thunder-bolts of final and retributive wrath! In their case, moreover, there was a constitutional fitness to destruction, brought upon them by their own immoral perverseness. So, too, on the other hand, we may see qualities which God favors, albeit He does put the peoples manifesting them to trial and endurance. He sees in them cultivated elements of character, which, when brought out and trained, are capable of raising them to superiority. He does not see merit; and it is not because of desert that He bestows His blessings. But when the Almighty sees in a nation or people latent germs of virtues, he seizes upon and schools them by trial and discipline; so that by the processes of divers correctives, these virtues may bud and blossom into beautiful and healthful maturity.

Now, when the Psalmist speaks of the merciful, the upright, and the pure, he does not use these terms in an absolute sense, for in that sense no such persons exist. He speaks of men comparatively pure, upright, and merciful. Some of the nations, as I have already pointed out, were at the lowest grade of moral turpitude. On the other hand, there are and ever have been heathen peoples less gross and barbarous than others; peoples with great hardihood of soul; peoples retaining the high principle of right and justice; peoples with rude but strong virtues, clinging to the simple ideas of truth and honor; peoples who guarded jealously the purity of their wives and the chastity of their daughters; peoples who, even with a false worship, showed reluctance to part with the gleams which came, though but dimly, from the face of the one true God of heaven!

Now the providence of God intervenes for the training and preservation of such peoples. Thus we read in Genesis that, because of man's universal wickedness, "it repented the Lord that he had made man"; but immediately it says that He approved "just Noah, and entered into covenant with him." So, after the deluge, God saw, amid universal degeneracy, the conspicuous piety of one man; for obedience and faith were, without doubt, original though simple elements of Abraham's character. To these germinal roots God brought the discipline of trial; and by them, through this one man, educated up a people who, despite their faults, shed forth the clearest religion light of all antiquity, and to whom were committed the oracles of God.

The ancient Greeks and Romans were rude and sanguinary Pagans; and so, too, the Germans and the Scandinavian tribes. Yet they had great, sterling virtues. The Greeks were a people severely just; the Spartans, especially, rigidly simple and religious. The Romans were unequalled for reverence for law and subjection to legitimate authority. Tacitus, himself a heathen, extols the noble and beneficent traits of German character, and celebrates their hospitality and politeness. The Saxons, even in a state of rudeness, were brave, though fierce; truthful; with strong family virtues, and great love of liberty.

Added to these peculiarities we find the following characteristics common to each and all these people—common, indeed, to all strong races; wanting in the low and degraded. The masterful nations are all, more or less, distinguished for vitality, plasticity, receptivity, imitation, family feeling, veracity, and the sentiment of devotion. These qualities may have been crude and unbalanced. They existed perchance right beside most decided and repulsive vices; but they were deeply imbedded in the constitution of these people; and served as a basis on which could be built up a character fitted to great ends.

Archbishop Trench, in his comment upon the words of the "Parable of the Sower,"—that is, that "They on the good ground are they who, in an honest and good heart, having heard the word, keep it"—says, "that no heart can be said to be absolutely good; but there are conditions of heart in which the truth finds readier entrance than in others." So we maintain that there are conditions of character and of society, to which the divine purposes of grace and civilization are more especially fitted, and adapt themselves. Such, it is evident, is the explanation of the providential spread of early civilization. It passed by the more inane peoples, and fastened itself to the strong and masculine. Such, too, was the spontaneous flow of early Christianity from Jerusalem. It sought, as by a law of affinity, the strong colonies of Asia Minor, and the powerful states along the Mediterranean; and so spread abroad through the then civilized Europe.

Does God then despise the weak? Nay, but the weak and miserable peoples of the earth have misused their prerogatives, and so unfitted themselves to feel after God.

And because they have thus perverted the gifts of God, and brought imbecility upon their being, they perish. The iniquity of the Amorites in Joshua's day was full—as you may see in Leviticus xviii—full of lust and incest and cruelty and other unspeakable abominations; and they were swept from the face of the earth! They perished by the sword; but the sword is not an absolute necessity to the annihilation of any corrupt and ruined people. Their sins, of themselves, eat out their life. With a touch they go. It was because of the deep and utter demoralization of Bois Gilbert that he fell before the feeble lance of Ivanhoe; for, in the world of morals, weakness and death are ofttimes correlative of baseness and infamy.

On the other hand the simplest seeds of goodness are pleasing to the Almighty, and He sends down the sunshine of His favor and the dews of His conserving care into the darkest rubbish, to nourish and vivify such seeds, and to "give them body as it pleaseth Him; and to every seed his own body." And the greatness of the grand nations has always sprung from the seeds of simple virtues which God has graciously preserved in them; which virtues have been cultured by gracious providences or expanded by Divine grace, into true holiness.

3. Let us not apply the train of thought thus presented to the history and condition of the Negro; to ascertain, if possible, whether we can draw therefrom expectation of a future for this race.

At once the question arises: Is this a race doomed to destruction? or is it one possessed of those qualities, and so morally disciplined by trial, as to augur a vital destiny, and high moral uses, in the future?

To the first of these questions I reply that there is not a fact, pertinent to this subject, that does not give a most decisive negative. The Negro race, nowhere on the globe, is a doomed race!

It is now five hundred years since the breath of the civilized world touched, powerfully, for the first time, the mighty masses of the Pagan world in America, Africa, and the isles of the sea. And we see, almost everywhere, that the weak, heathen tribes of the earth have gone down before the civilized European. Nation after nation has departed before his presence, tribe after tribe! In America the catalogue of these disastrous eclipses overruns, not only dozens, but even scores of cases. Gone, never again to take rank among the tribes of men, are the Iroquois and the Mohegans, the Pequods and the Manhattans, the Algonquins and the brave Mohawks, the gentle Caribs, and the once refined Aztecs!

In the Pacific seas, islands are scattered abroad like stars in the heavens; but the sad fact remains that from many of them their population has departed, like the morning mist. In other cases, as in the Sandwich Islands, they have long since begun their "funeral marches to the grave!" Just the reverse with the Negro! Wave after wave of a destructive tempest has swept over his head, without impairing in the least his peculiar vitality. Indeed, the Negro, in certain localities, is a superior man, to-day, to what he was three hundred years ago. With an elasticity rarely paralleled, he has risen superior to the dread inflictions of a prolonged servitude, and stands, to-day, in all the lands of his thraldom, taller, more erect, more intelligent, and more aspiring than any of his ancestors for more than two thousand years of a previous era. And while in other lands, as in cultivated India, the native has been subjected to a foreign yoke, the negro races of Africa still retain, for the most part, their original birthright. Their soil has not passed into the possession of foreign people. Many of the native kingdoms stand this day, upon the same basis of power which they held long centuries ago. The adventurous traveler, as he passes farther and farther into the interior, sends us reports of populous cities, superior people, and vast kingdoms; given to enterprise, and engaged in manufactures, agriculture, and commerce.

Even this falls short of the full reality. For civilization, at numerous places, as well in the interior as on the coast, has displaced ancestral heathenism; and the standard of the Cross, uplifted on the banks of its great rivers, at large and important cities, and in the great seats of commercial activity, shows that the Heralds of the Cross have begun the conquest of the continent for their glorious King. Vital power, then, is a property of the Negro family.

But has this race any of those other qualities, and such a number of them, as warrants the expectation of superiority? Are plasticity, receptivity, and assimilation among his constitutional elements of character?

So far as the first of these is concerned there can be no doubt. The flexibility of the negro character is not only universally admitted; it is often formulated into a slur. The race is possessed of a nature more easily moulded than any other class of men. Unlike the stolid Indian, the Negro yields to circumstances, and flows with the current of events. Hence the most terrible afflictions have failed to crush him. His facile nature wards off, or else, through the inspiration of hope, neutralizes their influences. Hence, likewise, the pliancy with which, and without losing his distinctiveness, he runs into the character of other people; and thus bends adverse circumstances to his own convenience; thus, also, in a measurable degree, linking the fortunes of his superiors to his own fate and destiny.

These peculiarities imply another prime quality, anticipating future superiority; I mean imitation. This is also universally conceded, with, however, a contemptuous fling, as though it were an evidence of inferiority. But Burke tells us that "imitation is the second passion belonging to society; and this passion," he says, "arises from much the same cause as sympathy." This forms our manners, our opinions, our lives. It is one of the strongest links of society. Indeed, all civilization is carried down from generation to generation, or handed over from the superior to the inferior, by the means of this principle. A people devoid of imitation are incapable of improvement, and must go down; for stagnation of necessity brings with it decay and ruin.

On the other hand, the Negro, with a mobile and plastic nature, with a strong receptive faculty, seizes upon and makes over to himself, by imitation, the better qualities of others. First of all, observe that, by a strong assimilative tendency, he reduplicates himself, by attaining both the likeness of and an affinity to the race with which he dwells; and then, while retaining his characteristic peculiarities, he glides more or less into the traits of his neighbor. Among Frenchmen, he becomes, somewhat, the lively Frenchmen; among Americans, the keen, enterprising American; among Spaniards, the stately, solemn Spaniard; among Englishmen, the solid, phlegmatic Englishman.

This peculiarity of the Negro is often sneered at. It is decried as the simulation of a well-known and grotesque animal. But the traducers of the Negro forget that "the entire Grecian civilization is stratified with the elements of imitation; and that Roman culture is but a copy of a foreign and alien civilization." These great nations laid the whole world under contribution to gain superiority. They seized upon all the spoils of time. They became cosmopolitan thieves. They stole from every quarter. They pounced, with eagle eye, upon excellence wherever discovered, and seized upon it with rapacity. In the Negro character resides, though crudely, precisely the same eclectic quality which characterized those two great, classic nations; and he is thus found in the very best company. The ridicule which visits him goes back directly to them. The advantage, however, is his own. Give him time and opportunity, and in all imitative art he will rival them both.

This quality of imitation has been the grand preservative of the Negro in all the lands of his thraldom. Its bearing upon his future distinction in Art is not germain to this discussion; but one can clearly see that this quality of imitation, allied to the receptivity of the race, gives promise of great fitness for Christian training, and for the higher processes of civilization.

But observe, again, that the imitative disposition of the negro race leads to aspiration. Its tendency runs to the higher and the nobler qualities presented to observation. Placed in juxtaposition with both the Indian and the Caucasian, as in Brazil and in this land, the race turns away from the downward, unprogressive Indian, and reaches forth for all the acquisitions of the Caucasian or the Spaniard. And hence wherever the Negro family has been in a servile position, however severe may have been their condition, without one single exception their native capacity has always "glinted forth / Amid the storm;" preserving the captive exiles of Africa from utter annihilation; stimulating them to enterprise and aspiration; and, in every case, producing men who have shown respectable talent as mechanics and artisans; as soldiers, in armies; as citizens of great commonwealths; not unfrequently as artists; not seldom as scholars; frequently as ministers of the Gospel; and at times as scientific men, and men of letters.

I referred, at the beginning, and as one of the conditions of a Divine and merciful preservation of a people—for future uses, to the probation of discipline and trial, for the cultivation of definite moral qualities. Is there any such large fact in the history of this race? What else, I ask, can be the significance of the African slave-trade? What is the meaning of our deep thraldom since 1620? Terrible as it has been, it has not been the deadly hurricane portending death. During its long periods, although great cruelty and widespread death have been large features in the history of the Negro, nevertheless they have been overshadowed by the merciful facts of great natural increase, much intellectual progress, the gravitation of an unexampled and world-wide philanthropy to the race, singular religious susceptibility and progress, and generous, wholesale emancipations, inclusive of millions of men, women, and children.

This history, then, does not signify retribution; does not forecast extinction. It is most plainly disciplinary and preparative. It is the education which comes from trial and endurance; for with it has been allied, more or less, the grand moral training of the religious tendencies of the race.

Here, then are the several conditions, the characteristic marks which, in all history, have served to indicate the permanency and the progress of races. In all other cases they have been taken as forecasting greatness. Is there any reason for rejecting their teachings, and refusing their encouragements and inspirations, when discovered in the Negro?

I feel fortified, moreover, in the principles I have today set forth, by the opinions of great, scrutinizing thinkers. In his treatise on Emancipation, written in 1840, Dr. Channing says: "The Negro is one of the best races of the human family. He is among the mildest and gentlest of men. He is singularly susceptible of improvement."[*]

Alexander Kinmont, in his "Lectures on Man," declares that "the sweet graces of the Christian religion appear almost too tropical and tender plants to grow in the soil of the Caucasian mind; they require a character of human nature of which you can see the rude lineaments in the Ethiopian, to be implanted in, and grow naturally and beautifully withal."[†] Adamson, the traveller who visited Senegal, in 1754, said: "The Negroes are sociable, humane, obliging, and hospitable; and they have generally preserved an estimable simplicity of domestic manners. They are distinguished by their tenderness for their parents, and great respect for the aged—a patriarchal virtue which, in our day, is too little known." Dr. Raleigh, also, at a recent meeting in London, said: "There is in these people a hitherto undiscovered mine of love, the development of which will be for the amazing welfare of the world. . . . Greece gave us beauty; Rome gave us power; the Anglo-Saxon race united

[*]William Ellery Channing (1780–1842), *Emancipation* (Boston: E. P. Peabody, 1840).
[†]Alexander Kinmont (1799–1838), *Twelve Lectures on the Natural History of Man and the Rise and Progress of Philosophy* (Cincinnati: U. P. James, 1839).

and mingles these; but in the African people there is the great, gushing wealth of love which will develop wonders for the world."

1. We have seen, today, the great truth, that when God does not destroy a people, but, on the contrary, trains and disciplines it, it is an indication that He intends to make something of them, and to do something for them. It signifies that He is graciously interested in such a people. In a sense, not equal, indeed, to the case of the Jews, but parallel, in a lower degree, such a people are a "chosen people" of the Lord. There is, so to speak, a *covenant* relation which God has established between Himself and them; dim and partial, at first, in its manifestations; but which is sure to come to the sight of men and angels, clear, distinct, and luminous. You may take it as a sure and undoubted fact that God presides, with sovereign care, over such people; and will surely preserve, educate, and build them up.

2. The discussion of this morning teaches us that the Negro race, of which we are a part, and which, as yet, in great simplicity and with vast difficulties, is struggling for place and position in this land, discovers, most exactly, in its history, the principle I have stated. And we have in this fact the assurance that the Almighty is interested in all the great problems of civilization and of grace carrying on among us. All this is God's work. He has brought this race through a wilderness of disasters; and at last put them in the large, open place of liberty; but not, you may be assured, for eventual decline and final ruin. You need not entertain the shadow of a doubt that the work which God has begun and is now carrying on, is for the elevation and success of the Negro. This is the significance and the worth of all effort and all achievement, of every signal providence, in this cause; or, otherwise, all the labors of men and all the mightiness of God is vanity! Nothing, believe me, on earth; nothing brought from perdition, can keep back this destined advance of the Negro race. No conspiracies of men nor of devils! The slave trade could not crush them out. Slavery, dread, direful, and malignant, could only stay it for a time. But now it is coming, coming, I grant, through dark and trying events, but surely coming. The Negro—black, curly-headed, despised, repulsed, sneered at—is, nevertheless, a vital being, and irrepressible. Everywhere on earth has been given him, by the Almighty, assurance, self-assertion, and influence. The rise of two Negro States within a century, feeble though they be, has a bearing upon this subject. The numerous emancipations, which now leave not more than a chain or two to be unfastened, have, likewise, a deep, moral significance. Thus, too, the rise in the world of illustrious Negroes, as Touissant [Toussaint] L'Ouverture, Henry Christophe, Benjamin Banneker, Eustace the Philanthropist, Stephen Allan Benson, and Bishop Crowther.

With all these providential indications in our favor, let us bless God and take courage. Casting aside everything trifling and frivolous, let us lay hold of every element of power, in the brain; in literature, art, and science; in industrial pursuits; in the soil; in cooperative association; in mechanical ingenuity; and above all, in the religion of our God; and so march on in the pathway of progress to that superiority and eminence which is our rightful heritage, and which is evidently the promise of our God!■

105
MIGRATION IS THE ONLY REMEDY FOR OUR WRONGS

Robert J. Harlan

In 1877 Republican president Rutherford B. Hayes withdrew the last federal troops from the South and announced that local government would be left to "the honorable and influential Southern whites." The hopes of African Americans raised by enfranchisement during Radical Reconstruction were soon relentlessly dashed by varying kinds of disfranchisement. Although it was not until the 1890s that legal disfranchisement got under way, techniques ranging from outright violence and intimidation to the more subtle devices of a poll tax and highly complex ballot procedures originated in some southern states as early as the withdrawal of federal troops. Conditions for African Americans, now mostly second-class citizens, rapidly became intolerable. Peonage, inadequate educational opportunities, mob law and violence, and loss of political rights made life in the South increasingly unattractive to many blacks. The first major exodus occurred in January and February 1879 and centered in, but was not confined to, southern Louisiana. A bad crop, a devastating yellow fever epidemic, an unsuccessful effort on the part of black tenants to force a reduction in rent, prompted approximately fifty thousand African Americans to move from the South. Many of them headed for Kansas.* Most, however, were unprepared for the bitter cold of Missouri and Kansas and had hardly enough funds to keep them alive when they reached the Kansas plains. Gradually, the emigration fever subsided.

There was sharp difference among African American leaders as to the wisdom of the "great exodus." Frederick Douglass opposed the exodus, since "it leaves the whole question of equal rights on the soil of the South open and still to be settled." Continued migration, Douglass argued, "would make freedom and free institutions depend upon migration rather than protection."[†]

Douglass's position was challenged by Robert James Harlan, Richard T. Greener, and other leaders. Harlan (1816–1897) was the son of Judge James Harlan and an African American woman, and was the half brother of U.S. Supreme Court justice John Marshall Harlan, who issued a stinging dissent in the 1896 Plessy v. Ferguson *civil rights case. In 1849, Robert Harlan struck it rich in the California goldfields, then invested*

---

*See Nell Irvin Painter, *Exodusters: Black Migration to Kansas After Reconstruction* (New York: Knopf, 1977).

[†]"The Negro Exodus from the Gulf States: Address Before the Convention of the American Social Science Association, Saratoga Springs, September 12, 1879," in Philip S. Foner, ed. *The Life and Writings of Frederick Douglass*, vol. 4 (New York: International Publishers, 1955), 336.

in real estate and a stable of race horses in Cincinnati. He married Josephine Floyd, daughter of the governor of Virginia, who had been a major general in the Confederate Army. Fleeing American prejudice, Harlan and his children spent nearly a decade in Europe. Harlan returned to the United States after losing his fortune during the Civil War, then devoted the remainder of his life to political activism. In 1875, he raised a battalion of four hundred African American men (the forerunner of the Ninth Ohio Battalion that served in World War I) and was commissioned a colonel by President Hayes.

In 1879, Harlan and others responded to the call for a "national conference of colored men of the United States," held in the state capitol of Nashville, Tennessee, that would "meet and present to the country some of the reasons that agitated the public mind in regard to the colored people." The mass migration from the South, although not on the original agenda for the conference, had assumed such proportions by the time the meeting was held that much of the deliberations were devoted to the question of whether it was an appropriate course of action. In his speech to the conference on May 8, 1879, Harlan defended migration not only as a way to escape oppression but also as a means of protest and resistance that would inflict economic hardship on the South and gain the attention of the North.

The speech text is taken from the Proceedings of the National Conference of Colored Men of the United States *(Washington, D.C.: Rufus H. Darby, 1879), 30–32.*

Mr. President, as to the present migration movement of the colored people, let it be understood that we have the lawful right to stay or to go wherever we please. The southern country is ours. Our ancestors settled it, and from the wilderness formed the cultivated plantation, and they and we have cleared, improved, and beautified the land.

Whatever there is of wealth, of plenty, of greatness, and of glory in the South, the colored man has been, and is, the most important factor. The sweat of his brow, his laborer's toil, his patient endurance under the heat of the semi-tropical sun and the chilling blasts of winter, never deterred the laborer from his work.

The blood of the colored man has fertilized the land and has cemented the Union. Aware of these facts, we should be baser than the willing slaves did we consent to the dictation of any men or body of men as to where we may go, when we shall go, or how long we shall stay.

The Republic owes to every citizen protection for his home and security for his rights. Let this security be given, and until that be done, let us cry aloud against those who refuse it, whether in the North or in the South. Let us remember all such in our prayers to the God of Liberty and of Justice, that He may punish them as they deserve. Let us remember them at the ballot-box, and fail not to inflict the retribution which they so justly deserve, and if we be obstructed in casting our votes, we can go where there will be no hindrance, and where we can vote as we please.

He who submits in silence to an injury may be avenged by a righteous heaven, but has little hope from man. Let us, therefore, keep the wrongs under which we labor before the public until an awakened sense of right and justice on both sides of Mason and Dixon's line shall work out a remedy. They need not tell us that there is no way to right our wrongs. The trouble is not in the want of a way; it is the want of a will. Let us exert the will and the way will be found. But this may take time, and while time runs many of us may perish. If the Government shall fail to give protection to our people, it can do no less than aid those who wish to change their habitations to safer and better homes.

With these views before us, and believing in an all-wise Providence, we would be recreant to our principles, to our creed, to our race, and to our God should we neglect to use all the means in our power to bring about the desired results.

Such a measure would have a double effect; it would arouse the attention and self-interest of the North that the laws should be sternly enforced that regulate the purity of the ballot and security for the persons of the colored race, and it would strongly appeal to the interest and humanity of the Southern people to see that they should not lose an industrious and worthy population by reason of lawlessness and inhumanity. Let us, therefore, insist on some such measure as an alternative right.

Let us demand that the principles we assert be declared essential, in resolutions of legislatures and conventions, and made a part of our party platform.

Let us agitate, even as other classes agitate when their rights and wishes are disregarded.

We are Americans, and let us act as Americans have ever done when denied their rights. Cry aloud and spare not until our injuries are known and our wrongs are redressed and our demands are granted.

Let us frame an address and make an appeal to Congress for relief. Although the Democrats are in a majority, no matter. Some Democrats have a sense of justice, and others assume the virtue if they have it not; let us put them to the test. Let our motto be "Protection to our homes or homes elsewhere," and until the Government can be brought to aid migration, let private kindliness and enterprise be brought into action. Let us appeal to the people of the North, to corporations and to common carriers for aid, so that all who are oppressed in the land of their birth may find freedom in the land of their adoption. If the leading men of the South will make another Egypt of these bright and sunny valleys, then must the oppressed go forth into the promised land of liberty, into the Western States and Territories, where the people are at peace and the soil is free, and where every man can secure a home for himself and family with none to molest him or make him afraid.

Already many have seen the beacon light of hope and are making their way toward it, and if the oppression is continued more and more will burst their chains and take the road to liberty.

There are some signs of objection to this on the part of the land-owners. They want the colored man to stay and till the soil. Very well; then let them treat him justly and fairly and protect him from criminal lawlessness. If they cannot or will not do this, they have no more right to ask him to stay, as they have no legal right to forbid him to go, and any attempt to restrain this movement will be vain and futile.

It is not a flight of fugitive slaves, but a voluntary movement of freemen, seeking liberty and security. It is the exercise of the right of any American to better his condition by going from one part of the country to another, just as interest or fancy may lead him. If we cannot do this, we are not free, no more than are the serfs of Russia, who, until lately, were a part of the estate and sold as such, but, if *we* are to be re-enslaved we may as well die on the road to liberty as at the feet of tyrants. We may as well expire contending for liberty, aye, and far better, than in base submission to degrading slavery.

At present there seems to be no alternative.

The reaction has robbed Southern Republicans, both white and colored, of their votes and of their voices, and this has thrown the nation into the hands of our opponents, who are determined to strip us of the last measure of protection.

Our political rights in these States are wholly suspended or abrogated. We have nothing but the mockery of legal proceedings, and Attorney-General Devens,* the constitutional adviser of the President, informs us that there is no prospect of justice from Southern tribunals for the colored man. Possibly he did not intend to convey that impression, but if not, what does he mean? You may study his long and carefully prepared paragraphs without coming to any other conclusion than this, that at present there is no hope for justice to the colored man from Southern courts.

If, then, all stay, all must submit. If some go they will be free, and possibly, by their going, they will awake the ruling minds of the South to a sense of the necessity of what is right.

For these reasons, therefore, I am an advocate for migration as the only present practicable remedy for our wrongs, and I am for the exercise of that remedy in a large measure and at all hazards.∎

---

*Charles Devens (1820–1891) of Massachusetts was appointed U.S. attorney general by President Hayes.

106 RACE UNITY

Ferdinand L. Barnett

On May 6–9, 1879, a national conference of African American men met in Nashville, Tennessee. Most of those present came from all sections of the South, but five Midwestern states and Oregon, the District of Columbia and Pennsylvania also sent delegates. Most of the discussion dealt with the problems of poverty and insecurity of the black people of the South, but one delegate from Chicago discussed the general problem of race unity. He was Ferdinand L. Barnett, and his speech carried the full title "Race Unity—Its Importance and Necessity—Causes Which Retard Its Development—How It May Be Secured—Our Plain Duty." Barnett calls upon African Americans to unite both politically and economically; to set aside jealousy and in-fighting, to assist those less fortunate, to support black-owned businesses and hire black workers; to ensure that black students have black teachers.

Ferdinand Lee Barnett, graduate of Chicago's College of Law, was founder and editor of the Chicago Conservator, *which began publication in 1878. Later, he was the first African American assistant state's attorney of Illinois, and in 1906 he was defeated by 304 votes for Judge of the Municipal Court. In 1895 Barnett married the journalist Ida B. Wells, a militant fighter against lynching.*

Barnett's speech of May 9 is taken from the Proceedings of the National Conference of Colored Men of the United States, Held in the State Capitol at Nashville, Tennessee, May 6, 7, 8, and 9, 1879 *(Washington, D.C., 1879), 83–86.*

Mr. Chairman and Gentlemen of the Conference: The subject assigned me is one of great importance. The axioms which teach us of the strength in unity and the certain destruction following close upon the heels of strife and dissension, need not be here repeated. Race elevation can be attained only through race unity. Pious precepts, business integrity, and moral stamina of the most exalted stamp, may win the admiration for a noble few, but unless the moral code, by the grandeur of its teachings, actuates every individual and incites us as a race to nobler aspirations and quickens us to the realization of our moral shortcomings, the distinction accorded to the few will avail us nothing. The wealth of the Indies may crown the efforts of fortune's few favored ones. They may receive all the homage wealth invariably brings, but unless we as a race check the spirit of pomp and display, and by patiently practicing the most rigid economy, secure homes for ourselves and children, the preferment won by a few wealthy ones will prove short-lived and unsatisfactory. We may have our educational lights here and

there, and by the brilliancy of their achievements they may be living witnesses to the falsity of the doctrine of our inherited inferiority, but this alone
will not suffice. It is a general enlightenment of the race which must engage
our noblest powers. One vicious, ignorant Negro is readily conceded to be a
type of all the rest, but a Negro educated and refined is said to be an exception. We must labor to reverse this rule; education and moral excellence
must become general and characteristic, with ignorance and depravity for the
exception.

Seeing, then, the necessity of united action and universal worth rather
than individual brilliancy, we sorrowfully admit that race unity with us is
a blessing not yet enjoyed, but to be possessed. We are united only in the
conditions which degrade, and actions which paralyze the efforts of the worthy, who labor for the benefit of the multitude. We are a race of leaders, everyone presuming that his neighbor and not himself was decreed to be a fol-
lower. To-day, if any one of you should go home and announce yourself
candidate for a certain position, the following day would find a dozen men
in the field, each well prepared to prove that he alone is capable of obtaining
and filling the position. Failing to convince the people, he would drop out
[of] the race entirely or do all in his power to jeopardize the interest of a
more successful brother.

Why this non-fraternal feeling? Why such a spirit of dissension? We attribute it, first, to lessons taught in by-gone days by those whose security
rested in our disunion. If the same spirit of race unity had actuated the Negro which has always characterized the Indian, this Government would have
trembled under the blow of that immortal hero, John Brown, and the first
drop of fratricidal blood would have been shed, not at Fort Sumter, but at
Harper's Ferry. Another cause may be found in our partial enlightenment.
The ignorant man is always narrow-minded in politics, business or religion.
Unfold to him a plan, and if he cannot see some interest resulting to self,
however great the resulting good to the multitude, it meets only his partial
approbation and fails entirely to secure his active co-operation. A third reason applies, not to the unlearned, but to the learned. Too many of our learned
men are afflicted with a mental and moral aberration, termed in common
parlance "big-headed." Having reached a commendable degree of eminence,
they seem to stand and say, "Lord, we thank Thee we are not as other men
are." They view with perfect unconcern the struggles of a worthy brother;
they proffer him no aid, but deem it presumption in him to expect it. They
may see a needed step but fail to take it. Others may see the necessity, take
steps to meet it, and call them to aid. But, no; they did not lead; they will
not follow, and half of their influence for good is sacrificed by an insane jealousy that is a consuming fire in every bosom wherein it finds lodgment.

A few of the prominent causes which retard race unity having been noticed, let us look for the remedy. First, our natural jealousy must be overcome. The task is no easy one. We must look for fruits of our labor in the
next generation. With us our faults are confirmed. An old slave once lay dying, friends and relatives were gathered around. The minister sat at the bed-

side endeavoring to prepare the soul for the great change. The old man was willing to forgive every one except a certain particularly obstreperous African who had caused him much injury. But being over-persuaded he yielded and said: "Well, if I dies I forgives him, but if I lives—dat darkey better take care." It is much the same with us; when we die our natures will change, but while we live our neighbors must take care. Upon the young generation our instruction may be effective. They must be taught that in helping one another they help themselves; and that in the race of life, when a favored one excels and leads the rest, their powers must be employed, not in retarding his progress, but in urging him on and inciting others to emulate his example.

We must dissipate the gloom of ignorance which hangs like a pall over us. In former days we were trained in ignorance, and many of my distinguished hearers will remember when they dare not be caught cultivating an intimate acquaintance with the spelling-book. But the time is passed when the seeker-after-knowledge is reviled and persecuted. Throughout the country the public school system largely obtains; books without number and papers without price lend their enlightenment; while high schools, colleges and universities all over our broad domain throw open their inviting doors and say, "Whosoever will may come."

We must not fail to notice any dereliction of our educated people. They must learn that their duty is to elevate their less favored brethren, and this cannot be done while pride and conceit prevent them from entering heartily into the work. A spirit of missionary zeal must actuate them to go down among the lowly, and by word and action say: "Come with me and I will do you good."

We must help one another. Our industries must be patronized, and our laborers encouraged. There seems to be a natural disinclination on our part to patronize our own workmen. We are easily pleased with the labor of the white hands, but when the same is known to be the product of our own skill and energy, we become extremely exacting and hard to please. From colored men we expect better work, we pay them less, and usually take our own good time for payment. We will patronize a colored merchant as long as he will credit us, but when, on the verge of bankruptcy he is obliged to stop the credit system, we pass by him and pay our money to the white rival. For these reasons our industries are rarely remunerative. We must lay aside these "besetting sins" and become united in our appreciation and practical encouragement of our own laborers.

Our societies should wield their influence to secure colored apprentices and mechanics. By a judicious disposition of their custom, they might place colored apprentices in vocations at present entirely unpracticed by us. Our labor is generally menial. We have hitherto had a monopoly of America's menial occupations, but thanks to a progressive Caucasian element, we no longer *suffer* from that monopoly. The white man enters the vocations hitherto exclusively ours, and we must enter and become proficient in professions hitherto exclusively practiced by him.

Our communities must be united. By concerted action great results can be accomplished. We must not only act upon the defensive, but when necessary we should take the offensive. We should jealously guard our every interest, public and private. Let us here speak of our schools. They furnish the surest and swiftest means in our power of obtaining knowledge, confidence and respect. There is no satisfactory reason why all children who seek instruction should not have full and equal privileges, but law has been so perverted in many places, North and South, that sanction is given to separate schools; a pernicious system of discrimination which invariably operates to the disadvantage of the colored race. If we are separate, let it be from "turret to foundation stone." It is unjust to draw the color line in schools, and our communities should resent the added insult of forcing the colored pupils to receive instructions from the refuse material of white educational institutions. White teachers take colored schools from necessity, not from choice. We except of course those who act from a missionary spirit.

White teachers in colored schools are nearly always mentally, morally, or financially bankrupts, and no colored community should tolerate the imposition. High schools and colleges are sending learned colored teachers in the field constantly, and it is manifestly unjust to make them stand idle and see their people taught by those whose only interest lies in securing their monthly compensation in dollars and cents. Again, colored schools thrive better under colored teachers. The St. Louis schools furnish an excellent example. According to the report of Superintendent Harris, during the past two years the schools have increased under colored teachers more than fifty per cent, and similar results always follow the introduction of colored teachers. In case of mixed schools our teachers should be eligible to positions. They invariably prove equal to their requirements. In Detroit and Chicago they have been admitted and proved themselves unquestionably capable. In Chicago their white pupils outnumber the colored ten to one, and yet they have met with decided success. Such gratifying results must be won by energetic, united action on the part of the interested communities. White people grant us few privileges voluntarily. We must wage continued warfare for our rights, or they will be disregarded and abridged.

Mr. President, we might begin to enumerate the rich results of race unity at sunrise and continue to sunset and half would not be told. In behalf of the people we are here to represent, we ask for some intelligent action of this Conference; some organized movement whereby concerted action may be had by our race all over the land. Let us decide upon some intelligent, united system of operation, and go home and engage the time and talent of our constituents in prosperous labor. We are laboring for race elevation, and race unity is the all-important factor in the work. It must be secured at whatever cost. Individual action, however insignificant, becomes powerful when united and exerted in a common channel. Many thousand years ago, a tiny coral began a reef upon the ocean's bed. Years passed and others came. Their fortunes were united and the structure grew. Generations came and went, and corals by the million came, lived, and died, each adding his mite to the work, till at last the waters of the grand old ocean broke in ripples around their tireless heads, and now, as the traveler gazes upon the reef, hundreds of miles in extent, he can faintly realize what great results will follow united action. So we must labor, with the full assurance that we will reap our reward in due season. Though deeply submerged by the wave of popular opinion, which deems natural inferiority inseparably associated with a black skin, though weighted down by an accursed prejudice that seeks every opportunity to crush us, still we must labor and despair not—patiently, ceaselessly, and unitedly. The time will come when our heads will rise above the troubled waters. Though generations come and go, the result of our labors will yet be manifest, and an impartial world will accord us that rank among other races which all may aspire to, but only the worthy can win.■

107   REDEEM THE INDIAN

Blanche K. Bruce

The traditional Indian policy of the United States government, as pursued by the army and the Interior Department, was one of extermination. As a result, by 1880 there were hardly two hundred thousand native Americans remaining in the United States. In 1871, Congress had broken its treaty agreements dealing with Indian peoples as independent nations, enabling the railroads to cross the Great Plains and opening more Indian lands to white farmers and ranchers. While some, as expressed in Alexander Crummell's 1877 address on "The Destined Superiority of the Negro," saw the Indian as doomed for extinction, others sought to "redeem" the Indians by removing them from their own culture and religion and introducing them to fixed-site agriculture and Christianity. Bills that were introduced in Congress proposed breaking up tribal autonomy even on the reservation, to divide up reservation land and give each family head 160 acres to cultivate, and, after a probation period of twenty-five years, full rights of ownership and full citizenship in the United States.

In support of such a bill, Blanche Kelso Bruce (1841–1898), the first African American to serve a full term as a U.S. senator, spoke in the Senate on April 17, 1880. Bruce was born in slavery in Virginia on March 1, 1841. He escaped from slavery during the Civil War, taught school in Missouri, attended Oberlin College, Ohio, and moved to Mississippi during Reconstruction. There he became a successful planter, was elected sena-

tor from Mississippi in 1874, and served from March 4, 1875, to March 3, 1881.

The speech reproduced below was delivered on April 17, 1880. In it Bruce denounced the policy "that has kept the Indian a fugitive and a vagabond, that has bred discontent, suspicion, and hatred in the mind of the red man." The proposals Bruce favored were finally enacted in 1887 in the Dawes Act, although the United States did not grant full citizenship to all American Indians until 1924. The program Bruce advocated, however, did the Indians more harm than good, although he was not aware at the time that it did so. When the land was divided under the Dawes Act, the poorest territory was usually given to the Indians, and the best was sold to white settlers. Even where they gained good land, inexperience with ownership and with legal matters left individual Indians vulnerable to the same kind of deceitful practice that had marked the making of tribal treaties. Moreover, "the plastic hand of Christian civilization" when it was applied as Bruce and others recommended replaced a program of physical extermination with one of cultural genocide.

The speech is taken from the Congressional Record, *46th Congress, 2d session, part 3, 2195–96. For further information on Bruce, see William Harris, "Blanche K. Bruce of Mississippi: Conservative Assimilationist," in Howard Rabinowitz, ed.,* Southern Black Leaders of the Reconstruction *(Urbana: University of Illinois Press, 1982).*

M R. PRESIDENT, I shall support the pending bill, and without attempting a discussion of the specific features of the measure, I desire to submit a few remarks upon the general subject suggested by it.

Our Indian policy and administration seem to me to have been inspired and controlled by a stern selfishness, with a few honorable exceptions. Indian treaties have generally been made as the condition and instrument of acquiring the valuable territory occupied by the several Indian nations and have been changed and revised from time to time as it became desirable that the steadily growing, irrepressible white races should secure more room for their growth and more lands for their occupancy; and wars, bounties and beads have been used as auxiliaries for the purpose of temporary peace and security for the whites, and as the preliminary to further aggressions upon the red man's land, with the ultimate view of his expulsion and extinction from the continent.

No set purpose has been evinced in adequate, sufficient measure to build him up, to civilize him, and to make him part of the great community of states. Whatever of occasional and spasmodic effort has been made for his redemption from savagery and his perpetuity as a race, has been only sufficient to supply that class of exceptions to the rule necessary to prove the selfishness of the policy that we allege to have practiced toward him.

The political or governmental idea underlying the Indian policy is to maintain the paramount authority of the United States over the Indian Territory and over the Indian tribes, yet recognizing tribal independence and autonomy and a local government, un-American in structure and having no reference to the Constitution or laws of the United States, so far as the tribal governments affect the persons, lives and rights of the members of the tribe alone. Currently with the maintenance of a policy thus based, under treaty obligations, the government of the United States contributes to the support, equipments and comforts of these Indians, not only by making appropriations for food and raiment but by sustaining blacksmiths, mechanics, farmers, millers and schools in the midst of the Indian reservations. This government also, in its treaties and its enforcement thereof, encourages and facilitates the missionary enterprises of the different churches which look to the Christianization and education of the Indians distributed throughout the public domain. The effort, under these circumstances, to preserve peace among the Indian tribes in their relations to each other and in their relations to the citizens of the United States becomes a very onerous and difficult endeavor, and has not heretofore produced results that have either satisfied the expectations and public sentiment of the country, vindicated the wisdom of the policy practiced toward their people, or honored the Christian institutions and civilizations of our great country.

We have in the effort to realize a somewhat intangible ideal—to wit, the preservation of Indian liberty and the administration and exercise of national authority—complicated an essentially difficult problem by surrounding it with needless and equivocal adjuncts; we have rendered a questionable policy more difficult of successful execution by basing it upon a political theory which is un-American in character, and which, in its very structure, breeds and perpetuates the difficulties sought to be avoided and overcome.*

Our system of government is complex in that it recognizes a general and local jurisdiction, and seeks to subserve and protect the rights of the individual and of the different political communities and the great aggregates of society making up the nation, by a division of authority distributed among general and local agencies, which are required like "the wheels within wheels" of Ezekiel's vision, to so move in their several appropriate spheres as shall not only prevent attrition and collision, but as shall secure unity in the system, in its fullest integrity, currently with the enjoyment of the largest liberty by the citizen.

Our system, I repeat, is complex, but it is nevertheless homogeneous. It is not incongruous; the general and local organisms belong to the same great class; they are both American, and they are moved by and respond to the same great impulse—the popular will of the American people.

Now, the political system that underlies our Indian policy is not only complex but it is incongruous, and one of the governments embraced in the system, ostensibly to secure the largest license and independence to the red

---

*For many Radical Republicans, the concept of Indian autonomy conflicted with their efforts to establish federal authority over the states. States' rights had been the primary argument of opponents to the 1875 civil rights bill.

race affected by the subject of this nondescript policy, is foreign in its character; the individuals and the system of laws are neither American. All the contradictions, the absurdities, and impossibilities developed and cropping out on the surface of our administration of Indian affairs are referable to this singular philosophy upon which, as a political theory, the Indian policy of the United States rests.

Now, sir, there must be a change in the Indian policy if beneficent practical results are expected, and any change that gives promise of solving this red-race problem must be a change based upon an idea of harmony, and not at war, with our free institutions. If the Indian is expected and required to respond to federal authority; if this people are expected to grow up into organized and well-ordered society; if they are to be civilized, in that the best elements of their natures are to be developed in the exercise of their best functions, so as to produce individual character and social groups characteristic of enlightened people; if this is to be done under our system, its ultimate realization requires an adoption of a political philosophy that shall make the Indians, as an individual and as a tribe, subjects of American law and beneficiaries of American institutions, by making them first American citizens, and clothing them, as rapidly as their advancement and location will permit, with the protective and ennobling prerogatives of such citizenship.

I favor the measure pending, because it is a step in the direction that I have indicated. You propose to give the Indian not temporary but permanent residence as a tribe, and not tribal location, but by a division of lands in severalty you secure to him the individual property rights which, utilized, will sustain life for himself and family better than his nomadic career. By this location you lay the foundation of that love of country essential to the patriotism and growth of a people, and by the distribution of lands to the individual, in severalty, you appeal to and develop that essential constitutional quality of humanity, the disposition to accumulate, upon which, when healthily and justly developed, depends the wealth, the growth, the power, the comfort, the refinement and the glory of the nations of the earth.

The measure also, with less directness, but as a necessary sequence to the provisions that I have just characterized, proposes, as preliminary to bringing the red race under the operation of our laws, to present the best phases of civilized life. Having given the red man a habitat, having identified the individual as well as the tribe with his new home, by securing his individual interests and rights therein, having placed these people where law can reach them, govern them and protect them, you purpose a system of administration that shall bring them in contact not with the adventurer of the border, not a speculative Indian agent, not an armed blue-coated soldier, but with the American people, in the guise and fashion in which trade, commerce, arts—useful and attractive—in the panoply that loving peace supplies, and with the plenty and comforts that follow in the footsteps of peace, and for the first time in the Indian's history, he will see the industrial, commercial, comfortable side of the character of the American people, will find his contact and form his associations with the citizens of the great Republic, and not simply and exclusively its armed men—its instruments of justice and destruction. So much this measure, if it should be a type of the new policy, will do for the Indian; and the Indian problem—heretofore rendered difficult of solution because of the false philosophy underlying it and the unjust administration too frequently based upon it, a polity that has kept the Indian a fugitive and a vagabond, that has bred discontent, suspicion and hatred in the mind of the red man—will be settled, not immediately, in a day or a year, but it will be put in course of settlement, and the question will be placed where a successful issue will be secured beyond a peradventure.

Mr. President, the red race are not a numerous people in our land, not equaling probably a half million souls, but they are the remnants of a great and multitudinous nation, and their hapless fortunes heretofore not only appeal to sympathy and to justice in any measures that we may take affecting them, but the vigor, energy, bravery and integrity of this remnant entitle them to consideration on the merits of the question.

Our age has been signalized by the grand scientific and mechanical discoveries and inventions which have multiplied the productive forces of the world. The power of nature has been harnessed to do the work of man, and every hour some new discovery contributes to swell the volume of the physical energies and its utilization, human ingenuity and thought have already been directed to the conservation, to the economy against the waste, of the physical forces. The man is considered a public benefactor who can utilize waste fuel, who can convert to some practical end some physical energy still lost, to a percent at least, through the imperfection of the machinery employed.

Now sir, the Indian is a physical force; a half million vigorous, physical, intellectual agents ready for the plastic hand of Christian civilization, living in a country possessing empires of untilled and uninhabited lands. The Indian tribes, viewed from this utilitarian standpoint, are worth preservation, conservation, utilization and civilization, and I believe that we have reached a period when the public sentiment of the country demands such a modification in the Indian policy, in its purposes and in its methods, as shall save and not destroy these people.

There is nothing in the matter of obstructions, as suggested by the opponents of this measure, to convince me that the new policy is either impracticable or visionary. As a people, our history is full of surmounted obstacles; we have been solving difficult problems for more than a hundred years; we have been settling material, moral and great political questions that, before our era, had been unsolved, and the possible questions that, before our era, had been unsolved, and the possible solution of which, even among the timid in our midst, was questioned.

The Indian is human, and no matter what his traditions or his habits, if you will locate him and put him in contact, and hold him in contact, with the forces of our civilization, his fresh, rugged nature will respond, and the fruit of his endeavor, in his civilization and development, will be the more permanent and enduring because his nature is so strong and obdurate. When you have no longer made it necessary for him to be a vagabond and fugitive; when you have allowed him to see the lovable and attractive side of our civilization as well as the stern military phase; when you have made the law apply to him as it does to others, so that the ministers of the law shall not only be the executors of its penalties but the administrators of its saving, shielding, protecting provisions, he will become trustful and reliable; and when he is placed in position in which not only to become an industrial force—to multiply his comforts and those of his people—but the honest, full sharer of the things he produces, savage life will lose its attractions, and the hunter will become the herdsman, the herdsman in his turn the farmer, and the farmer the mechanic, and out of the industries and growth of the Indian homes will spring up commercial interests and men competent to foster and handle them.

The American people are beginning to reach the conscientious conviction that redemption and civilization are due to the Indian tribes of the United States, and the present popular purpose is not to exterminate them but to perpetuate them on this continent.

The Indian policy has never attracted so much attention as at the present time,* and the public sentiment demands that the new departure on this question shall ultimate in measures, toward the wild tribes of America, that shall be Christian and righteous in their character. The destruction of this vigorous race, rather than their preservation and development, is coming to be considered not only an outrage against Christian civilization, but an economic wrong to the people of the United States; and the people of America demand that the measures and administration of government relative to these people shall proceed upon the wise and equitable principles that regulate the conduct of public affairs relative to every other race in the Republic, and when rightful conceptions obtain in the treatment of the red race, the Indian question, with its cost, anxieties and wars, will disappear.■

---

*During the 1870s, wars between the Indian and the U.S. Army occurred frequently as Indians reacted in anger to encroachments on their reservations. In 1876, four years before Bruce delivered his speech, the Lakota annihilated Colonel Custer in the Battle of Little Bighorn. A year after Bruce spoke, in 1881, great attention was drawn to the Indian question by the publication of Helen Hunt Jackson's *A Century of Dishonor*, a scorching indictment of traditional governmental policy toward the Indians.

108 THESE EVILS CALL LOUDLY FOR REDRESS

John P. Green

In May 1884, seventy-five delegates from twelve states, nearly all located in the North, convened in Pittsburgh to examine the problems of African Americans and apply pressure on the Republican Party to deal with them. The leading address was delivered by John P. Green, a member of the Ohio state legislature. Green was born in North Carolina in 1845 and moved to Cleveland at the age of twelve. After graduation from high school he studied law, spent a few years in South Carolina during Reconstruction, and upon his return to Cleveland was elected justice of the peace for three successive terms. In 1881, he was elected to the lower house of the state legislature. Green was the first African American to serve in the state senate, where he championed civil rights and introduced the state Labor Day bill, which became law in 1890 and made him known as the "Daddy of Labor Day." He served in the Post Office Department in Washington under Presidents William McKinley and Theodore Roosevelt.

Green's speech to the Pittsburgh convention combines an indictment of the treatment of black people in American society and a plea to the Republican Party to live up to its platforms. Green's speech offers a grim catalog of racial violence and pervasive discrimination in the post-Reconstruction era. He dismisses hopes that prejudice will be lessened by black social or moral improvement; no "laudable ambition, profound learning, suavity of manner, or correctness of deportment can open for him the doors which caste has closed against him," Green warns. Instead, he argues, African American advancement depends upon political unity and the willingness to abandon political parties unwilling to promote social justice.

The speech appeared in the New York Globe, *May 3, 1884.*

MR. CHAIRMAN AND GENTLEMEN: The Negro-hating class of the United States, not satisfied that they robbed us of our liberties and for two hundred and fifty years subjected us to bondage worse than death, which prostituted our manhood and denied us all the essentials to the pursuit of happiness, have today, like their Attic prototype, prepared for us a Procrustean bed, to which we must conform or lie in torture on it. If too short, they would stretch us to its dimensions, and if we overreach, curtail our fair proportions. Such an emergency as this, my friends, we are here to ponder over, and how we best may meet it.

It is a sad reflection for the young colored men of this day and generation that, although they are nominally free, they are as a matter of fact so proscribed and hampered by class legislation, unjust decisions and caste distinctions, as almost to produce in their mind the conviction that the term *citizen* is a delusion and a snare, meaning one thing in the North and another in the South, everywhere varying in its signification, according to the color of the person to whom it is applied. Turn where he may, he is confronted with a discouraging paradox. In Ohio, Indiana, and other states of the North, for instance, the colored man is a citizen and by implication the equal of every other citizen; yet if he has in his veins "a distinct and visible admixture of African blood," he is not, according to law, the equal of the white citizen. In South Carolina, Georgia, and all Southern states, he has the right of suffrage, nominally, but he finds that custom has made "a scarecrow of the law" and he has neither a "free ballot nor a fair count." At every point, although to the manor born, at home, and in the midst of friends (?) he is none the less an alien and an outcast—hated, shunned and despised.

An incredulous and thoughtless public, though meaning well enough, will perhaps question the truthfulness of the foregoing statements of so direct and grave a nature, and challenge us to the proof—a task to which I now cheerfully address myself. The situation is, for many reasons, particularly painful to colored people in the Northern States, though not so grave as in the South.

A quaint maxim, though full of meaning, is that which says, "Blessed is he that expecteth nothing, for he shall not be disappointed." The colored people of the Northern States have not reached this beatific condition of mind; on the contrary they are full of expectation, and failing to receive, they are grievously disappointed. Many of us have come to this cold climate, risking life itself, and leaving behind us the blandishments of a tropical clime, where

> "Gentle gales,
> Fanning their ediferous wings, dispense
> Native perfumes."

Animated by the same spirit of liberty which prompted the Pilgrim fathers to moor their frail barks beside old Plymouth Rock, in the midst of a fierce New England Winter. We sighed for liberty, and were willing to brave the bleak North winds and blighting frosts, to woo the fair goddess, if haply we might claim her for our own. Some of us, more favored than the rest, have attained to a degree of culture which renders even a silver weight of oppression as odious and painful to bear as the galling chains of bondage. Now, to people actuated by such motives and governed by such desires, what can be more hateful than a law like the following, found upon the pages of the revised statutes of Ohio, and to the same effect in other Northern states: "A person of pure white blood who intermarries, or has illicit carnal intercourse with any Negro, or person having a distinct and visible admixture of African blood; or any Negro, or person having a distinct and visible admixture of African blood, who intermarries, or has illicit carnal intercourse with any person of pure white blood, shall be fined not less than one hundred dollars, or imprisoned not more than three months, or both" (R. S. 6987). Here, then, is a statute that prescribes and limits our social status, and makes criminal in us an act which is permitted to every other race under the sun, and today, unless he has been pardoned, a colored man languishes in prison in the city of Toledo, Ohio, for marrying a white woman, an act which is not denied to any man in the state of Ohio, except to those of African descent. Far be it from me—or any other colored man, so far as my knowledge goes—to entertain a desire to trespass on the society of any person, or force our company on one who does not desire it, be she white or colored; for our social domain is sufficiently broad and varied to satisfy the most exacting, embracing, as it does, ladies of all shades of color to be found on the habitable globe. But to sit still, in this progressive age, with an obnoxious law, which discriminates against us on account of our racial affinity, staring us in the face, and menacing our future welfare, would be not only unwise, but criminal.

Again, in the revised statutes of Ohio (4008), we find the following: "When in the judgment of the Board [of Education] it will be for the advantage of the district to do so, it may organize separate schools for colored children." You will note the fact that the organization of these separate schools for colored children depends, not on what may be considered for the best good of the children, but upon what the Board may judge "for the advantage of the district." And so, with poor schoolhouses and in many instances ignorant teachers, we are, for the greater part, compelled to be contented; and our delicate little children trudge their weary way through mud and slush, and rain and snow, for miles and miles; even though a well-appointed schoolhouse may be situated within a rod of their father's house. If this be justice, then away with it! Give us one law for all, as equal in its application as it is universal in its operation, and which will not give to one famishing child bread, while it cast to another a stone. If the foregoing statements surprise and humiliate well-meaning American citizens, what shall be said of the ineffable crimes which stain the records of Southern events during the past decade, while the perpetrators of them stalk through the land unmolested? By the lurid glare of the incendiary torch, and the cruel hiss of the Ku Klux lash, liberty has been led captive and trembles in chains. Upon the escutcheons of three proud states the names Hamburg, Danville* and Copiah are written in deep-dyed characters.

> *Here's the smell of blood still, (that)*
> *All the perfumes of Arabia will not sweeten.*

---

*A massacre of African Americans occurred on July 8, 1876, in Hamburg, South Carolina. On November 4, 1883, a major race riot broke out in Danville, Virginia. It began after an African American accidently jostled a white man in the streets, and it ended with the killing of four blacks and one white.

Laws passed ostensibly for the punishment and suppression of crime, but in reality to entrap and enslave the ignorant and too-confining freedmen, are seized upon as a sure and never-failing source for the supply of labor for the coal mines of Alabama, and the construction of public works in most of the Southern states.* Speaking of this system, a committee of the Mississippi legislature says: "Crimes have been committed under the guise of law, more cruel and offensive than in the Fleet and Marshalsea under the English system." And in regard to the subletting system the report says: "It is so horrible that the committee deems it improper to make public its horrors." Some one may say, "These laws are of a general nature, and hence bear equally upon persons of both races." There might be some ground on which to base such a statement, were it not for the glaring facts that in those states where these systems are in vogue, the laboring and lower classes are composed almost exclusively of colored people, and the juries, judges and witnesses are nearly all white men who believe that the natural estate of the Negro is to labor for them and for the additional reason that the convicts so sentenced and ill-treated are almost exclusively colored. We are told that under this infamous system it is considered the proper thing to sentence a man twenty years for a simple larceny, twenty years for hog stealing, twelve months for stealing five dollars worth of gunny sacks; and that the annual death rate among those employed in railroad construction in the State of North Carolina was 178 in an average number of 776, during the years 1879 and 1880; also that not a word is given to account for the deaths of 158 of these men, except that eleven were shot down in trying to escape from this heartless butchery—(see Geo W. Cable in *Century Magazine*, Feby, 1884). To stigmatize the foregoing as contemptible, and a travesty on common decency (to say nothing of justice) but faintly expresses my feelings with reference to the matter. "A free ballot and a fair count" is a platitude that exists in the fertile imagination and speech of the orator, but is never experienced as a practical reality.

By shotgun practice, tissue ballot frauds, the "eight-box item," and a most cowardly "dark-lantern" policy, persisted in by the dominant class in the late rebellious States, a passive majority have been practically disfranchised and remanded to a condition of serfdom.

These evils call loudly for redress, and woe betide us if we heed not the cry! But listen, my friends, and I will speak to you of another monster of evil, whose gargantuan proportions, restricted to no particular section of this

---

*The reference is to the convict-lease system, under which African Americans, in the main, were arrested for petty offenses and were leased out by the state to private corporations and contractors, with the payment going to the state. Basically, it was a system for the recruitment of cheap labor for the benefit of corporations and individuals and a source of revenue for the state. In January 1888, for example, the Tennessee Coal, Iron and Railroad Company in Birmingham, Alabama, was given an exclusive contract for ten years to use all state convicts as laborers in its coal mines. The company promised to compensate the state at a rate ranging from nine dollars to eighteen dollars a month, depending on the classification of the convict.

country, cast a baleful shadow, to dwarf and blight the energies of every colored American. I refer to caste prejudice; an influence as widespread as it is obnoxious to its victims; which defies all statutory enactments, yields to no physical pressure and will, I fear, succumb only to the stern logic of events. It is so thoroughly woven in the texture of our social fabric that it confronts a colored man wheresoever he may turn. Is there a youth of African descent born in this land of liberty, in the full blaze of our boasted civilization, whose hopes beat high and whose aspirations would lead him up the mount of fame? Then let him not imagine that any laudable ambition, profound learning, suavity of manner, or correctness of deportment can open for him the doors which caste has closed against him, or make for him a place at the fireside of the dominant race. If he would keep alive the precious germ and make it bear perennial fruit, let him stop this bane as he would the deadly simoon and seek for strength and encouragement from that source from which all blessings flow.

However, the worst phase of this iniquity does not consist in the fact that the colored American is, at home, a social pariah, whose very touch is shunned; it lies deeper than this, and becomes oppressive, when met in the commercial world, obstructing our progress and keeping us poor. The road to clerical positions is nearly blocked by it; the doors of schoolhouses are closed against us asking positions as teachers, unless it be in schools for colored children exclusively, and our ministers are remanded to the pulpits of colored organizations. The doors to lodges and benevolent associations refuse to open to us knocking, while barbershops, restaurants, hotels and common carriers either refuse flatly to accommodate us, or else make us feel that we are of the despised race by insulting us. Recognizing the fact that matters of a strictly social nature will regulate themselves, and that every man has a right to select his own company, no gentleman or lady of color demands or expects any legislation in this behalf, for to do so would be superlative nonsense. But while the foregoing is true, it is none the less a fact that, where this prejudice intervenes to rob us of the means necessary to the enjoyment of our civil rights, we do complain, and look to the government to protect and shield us by direct legal enactment. And here again we are confronted by another paradox, as enunciated by our model Supreme Court;* that is to say, the Constitution has created us citizens, but, except in the territories, has conferred upon us no rights which Congress can protect us in. True, the same article of the constitution which says we are citizens, says: "The Congress shall have power to enforce by appropriate legislation the provisions of this article." Yet, if the Supreme Court is correct, it is of no more effect than a sounding brass and a tinkling cymbal.

If this be true, then we are poor indeed. I challenge the correctness of that decision! Call it presumption, call it impertinence, if you please, I still question its correctness and fail to find any tenable argument, resting in

---

*Green is referring to the decision of the Supreme Court in 1883 declaring unconstitutional most of the provisions of the Civil Rights Act of 1875.

good morals, fair dealings, or even elementary principles of law, to sustain it. Hence we complain that even the fountain of law has been poisoned against us by the odious prejudice of which we speak. There has never, since the formation of this government, been a decision which so [unintelligible] our sensibilities, and lowered in our estimation the dignity of our Supreme Court, as the so-called "Civil Rights Decision." [unintelligible] contradictory of what seemed to be the express will of the people, technical and strained in favor of proscription, narrow in its grasp of the present status of the American people, it seemed to lack in every essential of justice, or even dignity; and gained conspicuousness only for the reasons that the subject matter was grave, and the result so disappointing to many, as to stamp it as the meanest decision extant in the United States of America. When the Dred Scott decision was rendered, by this same court, a thrill of horror ran through the length and breadth of this land, such as had never been known before, and the eyes of our oldest inhabitants flash yet, at the very mention of it. But when we consider the relative difference between the status of the colored Americans then and now, the Dred Scott decision is a thing of joy and beauty, compared with the Civil Rights decision. When the former was rendered the colored people of the country, with the exception of the veriest fragment in the North, were slaves. The tendency was to tighten the bonds, tear away all barriers which impeded the growth and spread of the institution of slavery, and save the Union at any cost. We expected little and got less, in fact were regarded by many, as simply the innocent bone of contention between the respective sections, the North and the South. Not so now; we have borne arms, and placed our bodies between the flag and harm, as the dismembered forms of our veteran soldiers fully attest. We organized and preserved a form of government in the late rebellious States, where no one else could be trusted to perform the duty. Our condition has been changed by three different amendments to the constitution, so that now there is no doubt as to our civil status and [we] are citizens in the strict sense of the term, and demand and expect those rights which that wicked decision denies to us. Well has that eminent jurist and statesman, Mr. Justice Harlan, observed in his dissenting opinion,* "To-day it is the colored race which is denied by corporations and individuals wielding public authority the rights fundamental in their freedom and citizenship. At some future time it may be some other race that will fall under the ban. If the constitutional amendments be forced according to the intent with which I conceive they were adopted, there cannot be in this Republic any class of human beings in practical subjection to another class, with power in the latter to dole out just such privileges as they may choose to grant. The supreme law of the land has decreed that no authority shall be exercised in this country, in respect of civil rights, against freemen and citizens because of their race, color, or previous condition of servitude." It is a strange fact, that constitutional

---

*John Marshall Harlan of Kentucky was the only dissenter in the Court's decision.

authority has been found for every act deemed essential to the preservation of the Union, or our commercial integrity, even to the supplemental issue of paper currency by the government; but when the protection of the colored citizen in his rights and privileges has been considered, no constitutional authority could be found to lean upon. Why is this true may I ask? Is it because we are numerically weak? No; for the last census proves that we constitute about the one-eighth part of all the people in this country. Is it because we have shown ourselves unfriendly to the best interests of the land? No; for in every time of need, from the Revolutionary War down to the present time when called upon we have answered with alacrity; and during our Civil War, we even begged for arms to fight for the Union, before they were given to us, and when permitted, bore them gallantly on many a bloody field of battle. Is it because we are lazy, and belong to a non-producing class of citizens? No; for the last census shows that in 1880 there were produced in those States South where the colored element constitutes the bone and sinew in agricultural pursuits, *5,435,845 Bales of Cotton.* And the returns of 1880 show that in addition to a large crop of cotton, there were produced in these same states, of tobacco 350,264,853 pounds; and of rice 110,130,573 pounds. Now, the South being almost exclusively an agricultural section, it is easy to be seen that if it were possible to eliminate the colored element, the remainder would be little else than "chivalry," ballot-box stuffers, ku-klux and rioters. In view of the premises, upon what hypothesis can we account for our treatment, unless it be that there is a disposition on the part of many to keep us down, and prevent us from gaining that wealth, intelligence and influence which our natural talents and energy entitle us to? However, let us not waste previous time in grieving over the past and present. Life is short, and what we do must be done quickly.

> *"To mourn a mischief that is past and gone*
> *Is the next way to draw new mischief on.*
> *What cannot be preserved when fortune takes,*
> *Patience her injury a mockery makes.*
> *The robbed that smiles steals something from the*
>   *thief;*
> *He robs himself that spends a bootless grief."*

It is truthfully said "that every cloud has a silver lining," and "the night is long that never finds a day;" therefore, since we have for so long a time dwelt in the darkness bordering on despair, let us take courage, and like men, organize for an earnest, persistent effort in behalf of our rights, in this our country and native land. For resources, we enter this contest armed with ambition, numbers, physical and intellectual energy, the ballot and the right; not much of wealth, but with a spirit so broken and tempered by our past sufferings, that we can labor and wait for its fruition.

"Sweet are the uses of adversity,
Which like the toad, ugly and venomous,
Wears yet a precious jewel in his head."

Our race pride ought to be such as to inspire a feeling of union in our ranks. "In union there is strength," is a maxim that loses none of its force by age; it is just as true now as it ever was; and happy the people who, guided by wisdom, will act in accordance with its spirit. To illustrate the truth of this maxim, and the necessity of united action on our part, is not a difficult matter, since examples are to be found on every hand. Imagine an army without a recognized leader unsustained by a systematic organization of the forces under his command. What could he do without his legions, cohorts, maniples and centuries? or to use a more modern phrase, divisions, brigades, regiments and companies; all actuated by the same motives, and sustained by the same laudable ambition to be and to do something, in the cause of freedom? Here is union in the strictest sense, even to the texture, style and color of the uniforms, the tap of the drum, the step and the glance of the eye. The result is that when they are hurled against undisciplined and disorganized forces, they conquer; all victory perches on their banners, and honor awaits their return from the field of carnage. Take a well regulated business house as another illustration, and you will see the effect of united action in a marked degree. Every person in the huge establishment, from the proprietor down to the janitor, has his duty assigned to him, and is made to feel that he is just as much a part of that commercial entity as a cog is a part of a wheel or a wheel a part of the complex machinery which constitutes the mighty engine, and so he is; for should the least person fail to perform his duty in its proper time and manner, there would be a jar and break, which might seriously impair the success of the whole undertaking, until harmony could be restored. But working together with a perfect system and unison, the institution rises to affluence, success and fame. What I have said of armies and commercial enterprises can be as truthfully said of corporations, churches and races of people, which have been governed by this principle. Take the East India Company of England, the Standard Oil Company of the United States, the great religious denominations, and those races that have made their nationality and consanguinity their bond of union, just as the English, French and Jews have, and you will find that they have gone on from one degree of strength to another, until they are monumental testimonials of the strength of union. Being so organized and equipped, we must declare openly and without reserve against wrongs of all kinds that oppress and hinder us. If our brethren in the South are oppressed, inhumanly murdered, we must cry aloud for redress, being not intimidated by the jeers and taunts of the thoughtless and heartless time-servers, who in terms of derision cry out "bloody shirt," hoping thereby to shut our mouths. Redress may not speedily come, but there are in this broad land a goodly number who have "not yet bowed the knee to Baal," and in the end they will join us in our efforts in behalf of humanity, and lead us on to success. Are our liberties bartered away under the guise of law, by political tricksters, and those who labor to serve the present day? Let us not sit in silence and passively submit; but on the contrary, let us sound aloud the tocsin of war, and resent the injury, as being an insult offered to freemen, who, knowing their rights, dare maintain them. However, it is not always the best policy to undertake by violent means what may be accomplished by a gentle mode of proceeding. To "beard the lion in his den," is an expression abounding in poetry, but not always discreet or satisfactory in application. Rome lost several great armies, containing some of her best blood and most valorous youths, in her vain attempts to conquer the veteran troops of that African military prodigy, Hannibal, on open fields of valor; and it was only after the great Fabius Maximus adopted his so-called "fabian" policy, which consisted of a series of evasions and stratagems that success attended her efforts to drive the invader from her soil and preserve her autonomy. Now, in going forth to conquer prejudice, and win for ourselves respectful treatment, we have to contend with a more wily and powerful opponent than ever Rome did. Our opponents are well supplied with the sinews of war—with numbers, bravery and skill; and we had just as well attempt to annihilate the rock of Gibraltar by rushing headlong against it, as to undertake to conquer them by force. Fortunately for us, however, there are other means at our disposal, which will just as surely win for us as if the fates had already decreed it. I do not refer to any policy of deceit, to any stratagems or methods subversive of what is honorable and just. I would rather lead you to take advantage of those noble impulses of the Anglo-Saxon race—those properties of mind which lead them to admire and respect corresponding traits of character when discovered in others; and to those weaknesses of character, if you please, which lead them to sacrifice everything but life for the sake of power and gain. It has for many years been a favorite theory with me that the colored American is ostracised and shunned, not because of his complexion, but because of his recent status as a slave in this country, and the additional fact that, he is left by reason thereof, comparatively poor and illiterate. It would require a very great degree of charity on the part of any people, taking human nature as it is, to lay aside all prejudice, and take to their association and confidence any class of people who could bring nothing in the way of wealth or refinement, or influence in return. Therefore ought we not to study the Anglo-Saxon race in their country, with a view to ascertaining their characteristics, to the end that we may by meeting them gain their respect and consideration. We are told by Tupper in his proverbial philosophy that "Equity demandeth recompense," which is to say, what is worth having is worth striving for. If we find that knowledge is dear to the dominant race, then let us "search for her as for hid treasure;" do they worship money? then let us supply the golden calf for them; or is it power of a political nature that they would have, then see to it that the precious boon, the right of suffrage which we possess, is used to the best advantage for the upbuilding of our cause. The Americans have been not ineptly termed a community of merchants, for in all mercantile and speculative ventures, we have but few equals, and certainly no superiors. Far be it from my intention to suggest in the remotest degree, that we should offer our votes as legitimate matter of merchandise, for this would be contemptible beyond all measure; but I do say, with all the emphasis I can command, that in the future no party or political faction in the United States should be trusted with them, until they have first by pledges and guarantees of a reasonable nature, satisfied us that they will guide and protect us all our rights and privileges as American citizens. History has recorded the fact that we as a class are deeply imbued with the spirit of gratitude. Nor are we unmindful or neglectful of those who in the past have befriended us. But it is none the less a fact that we cannot live on the remembrance of things past; for we are taught to pray, "Give us this day our daily bread."

It will hardly be disputed that in the past, when we were bowed down in grief and sorrow, that grand organization known as the Republican party, like a white-winged angel of mercy, came to our rescue and pulled us out of the slough of despond, placed our feet upon the rock of liberty, threw about our shoulders the mantle of citizenship and, placing in our hands improved arms and the ballot as our shield of defense, if properly used, bade us advance and protect ourselves in the rights of life, liberty and the pursuit of happiness. For all this we are grateful, and say "God bless the Grand Old Party!" But this is not sufficient; it must do more ere its noble mission will be fulfilled. In its platforms, and by the utterances of some of its most conspicuous standard-bearers, it has declared in favor of the equality of all men before the law. Nay, more; we have been taught to believe by the platforms and declarations of that party in the past, that it stood for just such a centralized form of government as could and would protect the humblest citizen in all the fundamental rights implied in the term, and would merit and gain the dignified term *nation.* Will it longer stand by in silence, while good men and true are denied their citizenship in sections of this country, and murdered while quietly attempting to maintain them? Is it ready now to admit that this government has not the power under the law to protect the humblest citizen in the enjoyment of his civil liberties? That its only power is to tax and draft for war, giving nothing in return? Or will it stand by the doctrine that this government is of the people and for the people, having in its organism those essential inherent qualities which will perpetuate its own existence, and gain the respect and love of the citizen? If the former, we would none of it; but if the latter, then we are willing to once again rally to its support and contribute of our votes and influence, and of our blood if need be, as we have done many other times in the past, to the end that it may maintain its position of proud eminence. There is one danger, however, incident to this age of magic that we must guard against. I refer to the danger of being too easily discouraged. Our progress during the past two decades has been of such a phenomenal nature that we are apt to become discouraged if we do not see the results of our labor speedily appear. This should not be; for though the picture disclosed to our view is a sad one in many respects, when compared with that which confronted us twenty years ago it is full of encouragement. From every section of this glorious land come encouraging reports as to the progress of the colored Americans. In the South, where his name is legion, he only needs protection and a little encouragement, to enable him to become a strong tower of defense. Thoroughly American in all his feeling and sympathies, with a willing heart and strong arm, the United States may well be proud of him as a reliable source of strength in time of need. He is accumulating wealth and heaping up stores of knowledge, and his influence is destined to be felt for good for all time to come. Scorning not earning his living by the sweat of his brow, he would encourage that sentiment which seeks to dignify honest labor, not enslave it, and the future will prove the wisdom of his course.

> "Let us then be up and doing,
>   With a heart for any fate;
> Still achieving, still pursuing,
>   Learn to labor and to wait." *■

109 NEGRO EDUCATION—ITS HELPS AND HINDRANCES

William H. Crogman

William Henry Crogman (1841–1931) was born on the island of St. Martin. Orphaned as a boy, he spent eleven years at sea and voyaged around the world. After the U.S. Civil War, Crogman entered Pierce Academy in Massachusetts. He was a brilliant scholar and in 1868 was named to the English faculty of Claflin College in South Carolina. Two years later, he entered the classical course at Atlanta University and graduated first in his class in 1876. Crogman became professor of classics at Atlanta's Clark University and was named its president in 1903.

Crogman was a nationally renowned lecturer. He was described by William Simmons in Men of Mark *(1887) as the "master of a clear, elegant style" and as possessing a "vein of natural humor running through his whole discourse" that "gives him power to hold the close attention of his audience to his thoughtful and well balanced addresses" (695–96).*

In his address on July 16, 1884, to the predominantly white National Educational Association convention in Madison, Wisconsin, Crogman be-

*From Henry Wadsworth Longfellow, *A Psalm of Life* (1839).

gins by detailing the educational progress of African Americans since the
end of the Civil War. While mindful of the contributions of some whites,
Crogman makes clear that most of the credit for the establishment of
black educational institutions and for the success of black students belongs to African Americans themselves. These accomplishments are all
the more impressive, as Crogman argues in the second half of his speech,
because of the extraordinary obstacles they have faced in achieving them,
including forced migration, racist terrorism, lack of facilities and debili-
tating poverty. Crogman's address offers a stirring account of the postwar
efforts to expand educational and social opportunities for freedpersons
and other African Americans.

But whatever the formal education of the African American, Crogman
argues in the concluding section of his address, it will be insufficient for
social progress so long as there exists "this counter-education which is
continually going on in society." Racial prejudice instructs the black pupil, he laments, that no amount of education or refinement will earn a
room in a first-class car or hotel. Crogman himself refused to ride on the
segregated streetcars of Atlanta, choosing instead to walk more than
three miles to his office.

Crogman believed that teachers have a special opportunity and responsibility to encourage social justice. In the forward to Talks for the
Times, a collection of Crogman's addresses, Rev. E. W. Lee of the A.M.E.
Church of Rome, Georgia, attests that Crogman's "earnestness and faithfulness in the class-room, where he is so much at home, produces an eloquence more effective than a thousand orators upon the stage." At the
end of his address, Crogman charges his fellow teachers to preach equality in the classroom, so that "twenty years hence, when some Negro addresses the National Educational Association of the United States, he
will have the exquisite pleasure, denied me to-night, of thanking you for
the helps, without reminding you of the hindrances."

The text of the speech is taken from W. H. Crogman, Talks for the
Times (South Atlanta, Ga.: Franklin, 1896), 45–69.

I appreciate most heartily the invitation extended to me to speak before
you to-night with regard to the educational interests of my people in the
South. Nor can I well suppress within me the feeling that this act of courtesy
on your part was prompted by a generous consideration for a race long obscured, but now hopefully struggling into light under the benign influences
of Christian liberty. Surely, too, it will be a little encouraging to that race
to think that, notwithstanding all the discouragements of the past, notwithstanding all the embarrassments, not withstanding all the misgivings and
speculations with regard to its intellectual and moral capacity, it has, nevertheless, within twenty short years of freedom, been found worthy of recognition by you, and given to-day several representatives among the educators

of this great nation. Verily the world has been moving, and we have been moving in it.

But whatever may have been the advancement of the race within these years, whatever its progress, it would ill become me, I suppose, to speak of it at all in a boastful manner; for that advancement, that progress, is due as much, I suspect, to your generous assistance, as to our earnest endeavors. As a race, we have been greatly helped in our struggles up toward a higher and better life; helped from many and from various directions; helped by the Nation, the State, and the Church; helped by individuals, and helped by organizations; helped in money and helped in prayers. In a word, the history of the nineteenth century does not present a page more luminous, a page more creditable to our civilization, than that on which are recorded the benevolences of the American people to their "brother in black." As a representative of the race, I take very great pleasure in making before you to-night this grateful acknowledgement.

Nor would we, on the other hand, have you ignore the fact that we have also helped ourselves. Freedom was a great educator to the Negro, as it usually has been to other people. Indeed, it must ever be the base of all true education, whether of a race or of an individual. To build upon anything narrower would be useless; for when you begin to educate a human being it is hard to tell to what altitude he may rise. Let him feel that the earth is beneath him, God above him, and nothing in the intermediate space to check his growth or chill his aspirations, and then you may begin to teach him the alphabet.

Many things, doubtless, have come to the Negro in this country in the inverted order, but his freedom and his education in the natural. Under the inspiration of the former, and the light reflected from the latter, he has been enabled, within the last two decades, to learn quite a number of things about himself and other people, and has been led to the discovery of this simple but solemn truth, namely, that whatever may be the number of his friends, and however unbounded their generosity, a true and manly independence can only be reached by self-exertion.

How this discovery has affected his character and influenced his actions is apparent, I think, to any candid and observant mind. It may be seen in his desire to acquire landed property—to own some spot of ground upon which he may stand up erect, and which, unencumbered, he may transmit to posterity; it may be seen in his efforts for more and better education. Never was there a time in the history of this country when there were so many colored children in school as there are to-day. Never was there a time where the colored people, independent of State aid, supported so many private schools for the education of their children as they are supporting to-day. Indeed, it is not uncommon now to find, even in the rural districts of the South, here and there, a settlement where the three-months summer school provided by the State is supplemented by a three-months winter school sustained by the parents. One of the very best graded schools in the city of Atlanta—a school that would reflect no discredit on the city of Madison—one of the very best graded schools, with kindergarten attached, taught by a proficient corps of white lady teachers from the North, enrolling nearly five hundred pupils annually, and annually sending away from its doors, because of lack of room, scores of applicants for admission, this school, I say, has for the last six years been supported by the colored people of Atlanta as a private school; partly because the educational facilities afforded by the city have not been quite adequate to the demand made upon it for instruction, and partly because of the excellence of the work ever done in that school. From one who has a right to know I learn that, within the last six years, the colored people have paid into that school, for the education of their children not less than $20,000. Certainly this looks a little like effort on the part of the Negro to help himself to an education. I am informed that similar schools exist in other large cities of the South. I know that such do exist in the cities of Charleston and Savannah.

Last year, in the four institutions of higher learning, established in Atlanta by Northern benevolence, there were, in round numbers, twelve hundred students. Of these, Atlanta University enrolled 310; Clark University, 222; the Baptist Seminary for males, about 140; and the Baptist Seminary for females, 500. But Atlanta is only one of the great centers of education in the South. There is Nashville, literally girdled by institutions; there is New Orleans. In fact, you will find to-day in every Southern State, one or more institutions for the higher training of Negro youth, and the very fact that all these institutions are more or less crowded yearly, and the very fact that frequent appeal goes out from them to Christian philanthropy for more buildings, for increased accommodations, are proof conclusive, I think, that the Negro not only appreciates the advantages held out to him, but is also exerting himself to enjoy them.

Dr. Ruffner, for many years superintendent of public instruction for the State of Virginia, in one of his reports, a few years ago, bore this testimony to the credit of the Negro: "He wants to do right, and is the most amiable of races. The Negro craves education, and I believe his desire has increased; it certainly has not diminished. He makes fully as great sacrifices to send his children to school as the laboring classes of the whites. The civilization of the race is progressing and even faster than his thoughtful friends anticipated."

I turn for a moment from the school to the Church, where evidences of self-help are as striking, if not more so. To be brief, and to speak from accurate knowledge, I will confine myself to the work of the denomination with which I am connected. Immediately after the war, the Methodist Episcopal Church entered the South, and began its work among the colored people. To-day it has among them a membership of 200,000 superintended by the same bishops who preside over the work here in the North. At the beginning, twenty years ago, and for some years after, all the Churches among the colored people were supported, either in whole or in part, by funds from the Missionary Society. To-day, it is safe to say nearly one half of them are self-supporting. In the Savannah Conference, included within the State of Georgia, we have 15,000 members, and about a hundred churches. Of the latter, fifty-six are entirely self-supporting.

I have dwelt on these particulars because, unfortunately, there are still some persons who, reading Negro history with their prejudices rather than with their eyes, deny us even the credit for what little we have achieved for ourselves, and persist in holding us up to the public as that abnormal baby which never grows, which cannot grow, and which the American people must nurse for all time.

In the *North American Review* for this very month, Senator Morgan of Alabama, in a discussion of the "Future of the Negro,"* has this remarkable passage: "For fifteen years, every means that Congress could devise has been supplied to the Negro race to enable them to attain a condition which will protect them in all their rights, liberties, and privileges that are enjoyed by the whites. To the personal and political power of the ballot have been added the guardianship of the Freedmen's Bureau, the Freedmen's Bank and its branches, the civil rights statutes, and all the power of tyrannical courts to enforce their alleged civil rights; and still they are no stronger as a race, and probably no better as individuals than they were at the beginning of these efforts." I say this is a remarkable passage; remarkable because coming from a United States Senator, who ought to be better informed with regard to a race in whose midst he lives. He cannot see that we are stronger as a race, or better as individuals, than we were fifteen years ago, and that, too, in the face of the following array of facts, which were collected, not by black,† but by white, men, and widely circulated a short time ago through the medium of the press: "The colored people have already nearly 1,000,000 children in school; publish over 80 newspapers; furnish nearly 16,000 school-teachers; about 15,000 students in the high schools and colleges; about 2,000,000 members in the Methodist and Baptist Churches; own 680,000 acres of land in Georgia alone, and over 5,000,000 in the whole South; the increase in the production of cotton since emancipation has been 1,000,000 bales per year, or one-third more than that raised while working under the lash; and had deposited in the fraudulent Freedmen's Bank $56,000,000; besides, colored men have engineered and nearly completed a railroad in North Carolina, and they are assessed $91,000,000 of taxable property." The editor of the paper from which this bit of information was clipped, asks the question, "How do these facts impress you, when you consider that this race did not own itself twenty-two years ago?" I repeat the question, "How do these facts impress you," gentlemen? Have they at all any significance? Are they at all indicative of industry, of thrift, of economy, of growth, intellectual and moral? If they are, then verily the Negro, outside of the help he has received from friendly

---

*Senator John T. Morgan's comment, along with the contrasting views of Frederick Douglass, Richard T. Greener, and others, appeared in the *North American Review* 139:332 (July 1884), 78–99.

†I learned since that these statistics were collected by Dr. Alexander Crummell of Washington, D.C., the Nestor of Negro Scholars. [Speaker's footnote.]

sources, has helped himself creditably in all those things which pertain to the building up of an intelligent and virtuous people. I am aware, of course, that all our achievements, taken in the aggregate, are but small, compared with the vast responsibilities which still lie before us; but they, nevertheless, constitute a beginning and that beginning is very auspicious.

The unfairness of our critics lies, usually, in the fact that they see but one side of the question; for, while they recognize very readily our weakness and our vices, and while, for the purpose of bringing out into bold relief those weaknesses, they invariably marshal to the front our helps; somehow, and in some way, the other fact seems to escape them, namely, that we have also had some hindrances. Let us consider some of these in a dispassionate way.

At the close of the war, the Negro found himself in the condition of a man who wakes up out of sleep in the midst of a dream in which all things seemed strange and confused. It took him some time to adjust himself to the new state of affairs. He was restless; he could hardly realize that he was free. As the impotent man, sitting at the gate of the temple, when healed by Peter, not only praised God, but walked and leaped to satisfy himself of the genuineness of his cure, so the Negro, to test his freedom, began to move about. His movements, at first, were individual, then general, as leaders sprang into existence; and it is really remarkable how many are the leaders when the members are ignorant. For the first ten or twelve years after the war nothing was more common in the South than leaders. Every little politician, every crank, constituted himself a Moses to lead the Negro somewhere; and various were their cries. One cried, "On to Arkansas!" and another "On to Texas!" and another "On to Africa!" and each one had a following more or less. One man told me that he had succeeded in leading away from South Carolina and Georgia to Arkansas and Texas 35,000 persons. That was in 1874. In December, 1879, the following appeared in the *Southwestern Christian Advocate* published at New Orleans:

"The departure of Negroes from Texas to Kansas and the North has assumed large proportions the past few weeks. On an average, from 1,000 to 1,200 have gone every week. As a rule, they are of the better class, and have money to pay their fares, or to go on teams, and have something left to buy homes with. While the larger numbers go by railroad, many are going with teams. In one camp, one of our ministers counted two hundred going thus, leisurely and comfortably. On the International Railroad over two hundred tickets were sold at a small station in one day. The company had been several days gathering at that point. We went into one car and counted *ninety*, men, women, and children. They all had first-class tickets—the railroad will sell no others to them—and the fare of that company, in that one car, amounted to over $1,000. Just now the tide flows from Waller and Grimes counties. Private meetings are being held in many other counties, and every indication is that there will be a much greater movement in the spring than even the one going on now."

Besides these spontaneous and voluntary movements there were also forced movements—movements caused by tyrannical and unjust treatment—such as the memorable exodus some few years ago, when thousands fled from the levees of Mississippi to perish in the snows of Kansas. Now, whatever good may have resulted from any of these movements, and I am not prepared to say that individuals were not benefited by some of them, it has ever been my opinion that, by keeping the people in an unsettled state; and by frequently disturbing the growth of the home, they hindered much the cause of popular education.

Again, no one, I suppose, will question the truth of the assertion that the South, at the close of the war, was not in a condition to undertake the education of the masses. Crippled in her resources, and without a common school system she was left to confront the most awful responsibilities ever thrust upon a people. That she succeeded as soon as she did in establishing a common school system is creditable to her common sense and good judgment.

But if the South was not in a condition at the close of the war to enter upon the education of the masses, neither was she in any mood to rush enthusiastically into the work of Negro education. To prove that she was would be to prove that human nature has undergone a radical change. But Mrs. Partington says that she finds that there is a good deal of the old "human natur" in folks to-day. The South grew gradually up to the idea of Negro education, some States, to their credit, leading off in advance of others. I don't know which was first. I do know that Georgia was not last; for, as late as July, 1879, Mrs. Harriet Beecher Stowe, writing in one of the leading magazines of the country on the "Education of the Freedmen," says: "With this enlightened policy of other States, it surprises us to find that in Kentucky the colored race have no share of the common school fund, and are opposed by peculiar laws. A colored school-house is not allowed within a mile of a white school, nor in towns within six hundred feet." It is easy to see, then, that the present state of affairs in the South, as they relate to education in general, and to Negro education in particular, did not fly into existence at the stroke of a magician's wand, nor sprang they forth as the fabled goddess, full-armed from the head of Jupiter. They are the result of gradual and steady growth. But, as the old adage has it, "While the grass is growing the horse is starving"; so, while things were taking years to settle down, while opinions were conflicting one with another, while Southern mind was seeking a stable equilibrium, while public sentiment was crystallizing around the idea of popular education, the black child, and the white child, too, had to wait impatiently for their intellectual pabulum; and, had it not been for the timely efforts of the Christian Church, during those years of uncertainty and delay; had it not been for the philanthropic heart of the North, that sent down to us, without stint, both money and men, it is hard to say what would have been the fate of the black child, at least, and of the country in which he lives. The South, then, to be judged fairly to-day, must be judged not simply by what she has done, but also by what she has prepared to do; nor must the advancement of the Negro be judged merely by the

length of time he has been free, as if that period had been one of uninter-
rupted progress, but also by the time it took to give him a start. I understand
that in horse-racing and boat-racing a great deal of importance is attached
to the start. Everything must be ready, the preparations complete, the oars-
men trained. To-day the Negro has a better start than he had twenty years
ago. For this reason I shall expect more from him in the next twenty than
in the last. He has now, as you have seen, several thousand trained teachers
of his own race. Besides the continued aid of the Church, he has the benefit,
little or much, of the common school fund throughout the South, and, more
than this, he is receiving gradually the recognition, sympathy, and influence
of some of the best white men of the South. Prominent among these, and
pre-eminently worthy of recognition, is Dr. Atticus G. Haygood, of Georgia,
the morning star of a better day, the Christian knight whose white plume,
seen in the thickest of the fray, is rallying many stout hearts and strong
hands to the cause of humanity.* His church, or, rather, the branch of the
Christian Church to which he belongs, has established a school for colored
youth in the city of Augusta, GA—Payne Institute—at the head of which is
Dr. Callaway, assisted by Prof. Walker, of South Carolina, and others, all
Southern men. That school to-day is the lone star of Southern Methodism;
but it shines with an auspicious light. It will be the brightest star in a constellation of similar schools by and by. The world is moving, and its movements are ever in the direction of humanity. Gethsemane and Calvary shall
yet conquer.

Some time ago I read an article written by an Ohio man who seemed to
know all about us. He had spent a couple of years in the South teaching
Negroes. From the tone of his article it was evident that he had been disappointed in more ways than one. At any rate, in that article, he poured out
without stint his vials of wrath upon the Negroes' heads. He told all about
them, what they could do and what they couldn't; and that article was made
up of more couldn'ts than coulds. Among other defects of the race, he made
the marvelous discovery that Negro children down South couldn't learn as
fast as white children up in Ohio. Well! When I read that I said to myself,
If black children down on Southern plantations and white children up in
Ohio are expected to-day to move *pari passu* along the lines of education, it
is high time for our Anglo-Saxon friends to begin a thorough revision of their
philosophy. To leave out of consideration an inheritance of two thousand
years of trained intellect, the white child's cradle was rocked by an intelligent hand; his early footsteps directed by an intelligent mind. It was his good
fortune to be born in an intelligent home. From the time when his eyes and
his ears opened, he has been receiving instruction. There are pictures on the
wall for him to gaze upon; there are carpets on the floor for him to walk
upon. There is neatness, there is comfort, there is order in that home—that
home more potent in its influence than school or college. The white child
hears intelligent conversation daily; daily he imbibes new ideas. He is in a
magnificent school. How many are his helps, how few his hindrances!

---

*Haygood was a prominent Methodist bishop and an outspoken opponent of lynching.

Come with me to the cabin of the South—I will not call it a home. Look into it. Perhaps it is one room, in which live father, mother, and several children. In this they cook and eat and sleep. Father and mother are not models of intelligence; O, no! Poor creatures!

> *"Knowledge to their eyes her ample page,*
> *Rich with the spoils of time, did ne'er unroll."*

Here are no art decorations; here nothing to instruct the eye, to elevate the soul. Here the ear drinks in more often the "loud laugh that speaks the vacant mind." Yet, here, too, is a school; and the black child is pupil here. Alas! how few are his helps; how many his hindrances!

Recognizing this fact, namely, that the education of the colored people must be greatly hindered so long as the home militates against the school, the various Christian denominations laboring in the South have begun, in connection with their institutions of learning, the establishment of "model homes," or "school of domestic economy," where our girls are taught to do all manner of housework, and are instructed in all the properties pertaining to a well-regulated Christian home.

To meet the question now which might be rising in your minds, and which has been asked me at different times by white friends, "Why do not our people, as they are now accumulating means, move out of those cabins and build them good homes." I reply, that many have done so, and are doing, all over the South. In the city of Atlanta, the colored people have secured many comfortable and some few elegant homes. I find, however, that the majority of those who have done so are the younger people and their parents who have been reached by the schools, the former directly, the latter indirectly. The large number of the older people are inclined to cling to their former mode of living. In this they are not peculiar. They only illustrate the lack of taste and the power of association. To have men surround themselves with beautiful things there must be first created within them a taste for the beautiful. In these cabins, too, the older people have experienced their joys and their sorrows. Their little ones were born here. Their aged ones died here. If, therefore, it be true that "home is where the heart is," these cabins are their homes, notwithstanding they are a hindrance to the education of the people.

But I must hasten to a close, for I wish to tell you in a few brief sentences what I regard above all and above every other, the greatest and most aggravating hindrance to the education of the Negro in this country, and I shall speak very plain, for he who has convictions and not the courage to express them, is unworthy to stand where I am standing to-night. I say that most aggravating hindrance to the education of the Negro to-day, is the counter-education which is continually going on in society.

In the school-room the Negro is taught one thing; in society another. In the school-room he is instructed in the same Bible which you study. He is taught that God made him, that Christ redeemed him, that the Holy Spirit sanctifies him. In society he is taught, that, although God made him and

Christ died for him, yet there is a vast difference between a white man and a black, a wall of partition between a Jew and a Samaritan, between a Brahmin and a Pariah. In the school-room he is taught the dignity of manhood after the American idea—taught that

> *"The rank is but the guinea's stamp*
> *The man's the gowd for a' that"*

In society he is taught that rank or no rank, although a man, he is a black man; hence not a man "for a' that." In the school-room he is taught that character is only shibboleth demanded in civilized society, that learning, that culture and refinement, are the only passports needed. In society he is taught that whatever may be his character, his culture, or his refinement, he must not attempt to enter any and every hotel in this country, and that he must sometimes, after paying first-class fare, ride with his family in a second-class smoking-car among drunkards and blasphemers. It was only two weeks ago I read in the *Christian Advocate,* the leading paper of the Methodist Episcopal Church, published in New York City, the following:

"Prof. R. T. Greener has recently made an extended tour through the Southern States. His opinions of the progress of his race—as reported by the daily press—are worthy of great respect. Few men are better qualified to form a correct judgment. He finds more pride of race, more independence of character, greater neatness of dress, a stronger desire to enter business, and increasing thirst for education. He expresses high admiration for the work of the missionary teachers. He found the Negro not only in the cotton field and tobacco factory, but acting as carpenter, wheelwright, hackman (often owning the stable), blacksmith, brakeman, and in other avocations. He returns very greatly encouraged as to the future of his race. It is a burning disgrace that this cultured gentleman was four times ordered out of 'first-class' cars, and it is to his credit that in each case he refused to go."

Now, who is this Prof. Greener?* He is nothing less than a graduate from old Harvard. I know him well, and knew his mother before him. But what does society care about a Harvard graduate, if his complexion is tinged with the hated color? Prof. Greener's is very little tinged. He is nearer your color than mine. Now, ladies and gentlemen, I submit, here are two lines of education running counter to each other. Here are two forces acting upon the Negro, one in a straight line along the plane of manhood, the other urging him downward. Consequently, if you would find his true position in society, you must seek it along the resultant of these two forces, and whenever found it will be a position beneath the American idea of manhood—beneath God's.

---

*Richard Theodore Greener (1844–1922) was the first African American graduate of Harvard (1870). He served as professor of metaphysics and logic at the University of South Carolina and professor and dean of the Howard University School of Law before being appointed the first U.S. consul to Vladivostok (1898–1905). See Allison Blakely, "Richard T. Greener and the 'Talented Tenth's' Dilemma," *Journal of Negro History* 59 (October 1974), 305–21.

What is to be the outcome of this? It must certainly be clear to you that the more you educate a man, the more sensitive you make him to bad treatment. What is to be the outcome? There are men who are devising makeshifts, men who, in the language of Dr. Callaway, of Georgia, are inquiring, "What shall we do with the Negro?" instead of "What shall we do for him?" You can't do anything with him. He is in God's hands. You can do much for him. You can do simple justice to him. In the *Popular Science Monthly* for February, 1883, Prof. E. W. Gilliam advises colonization as the only "remedy." Colonize whom? Colonize men with the ballot in their hands, and with half the white people protesting against their departure? For Anglo-Saxons will fight over ideas, and to many of them the Negro in this country represents an idea. Colonization will not solve the problem. The thousands that go will be as a "drop in the bucket" to the millions that remain.

Another author, in a pamphlet more remarkable for its bitterness than its logic, thinks we ought to be helped to go to the newly founded States of the Congo, where we may display our capacity for self-government in the land of our fathers. Now, that is worth a good deal as rhetoric; but surely the author is un-happy in his reference to the land of our "fathers," for he has ignored the serious fact, that, of the six and a half million of us in this country, fully a million and a half would have considerable difficulty in finding the land of our "fathers." Undoubtedly we should find in Africa the land of our mothers, but the land of our fathers we should certainly have to seek somewhere else. Perhaps along the shores of the North Sea and the borders of the Scandinavian peninsula.

The only remedy, then, for these social troubles, the only one which God can approve, is even-handed justice meted out to every man. Why, when the Almighty sent Columbus to discover this country, he did so because he was tired looking down upon the tyranny of the old world and the oppression of his people, and desired to establish here a home for mankind. It is said that Columbus, on landing, took possession of the new world in the name of the Castilian sovereigns. If that intrepid mariner had had the light of the nineteenth century, he would have taken possession of it in the name of God and destiny. I repeat, the solution of this race problem, so-called, must be simple. Justice meted out to your brother man. Go, preach this in your pulpits. Go, teach this in your school-rooms. Go, educate the people up to where they stood in the days of George the Third, when they declared, and staked their lives and their fortunes on the declaration, "that all men are created equal; that they are endowed by their Creator with certain inalienable rights; that among these are life, liberty, and the pursuit of happiness." Go, teach this I say, in the spirit and in the letter, in the school-room and by the fireside; and twenty years hence, when some Negro addresses the National Education Association of the United States, he will have the exquisite pleasure, denied me to-night, of thanking you for the helps, without reminding you of the hindrances.■

110

THE STONE CUT OUT OF THE MOUNTAIN

John Jasper

John Jasper (1812–1901), one of the most popular preachers of the late nineteenth century, was born in slavery in Fluvanna County, Virginia. After his conversion in 1837, he gained fame as a preacher, especially of funeral sermons. During the Civil War, he preached to wounded soldiers in Confederate hospitals. Gaining his freedom at the end of the war with seventy-three cents in his pocket and forty-two dollars in debt, Jasper established his own congregation in Richmond.

Jasper received national notoriety for his sermon "The Sun Do Move," first preached around 1880 and delivered as many as 250 times. Disbelieving scientific pronouncements to the contrary, Jasper in earnest faith declared that the sun revolved around the earth. Jasper's sermons attracted large audiences of both blacks and whites. He drew upon a stock of unwritten sermons, repeated and extemporaneously altered to suit the occasion. "I don't get my sermons out of grammars and rhetorics," he told his listeners, "but the spirit of the Lord puts them in my mind and makes them burn in my soul." His sermons were generally short by the standards of the day, rarely exceeding fifty minutes, although "on extraordinary occasions he took no note of time," according to biographer William Hatcher.

The following sermon was delivered on Sunday afternoon, July 20, 1884. An observer later described the scene, as Jasper "mounted the pulpit with the dash of an athlete and tripped around the platform during the preliminaries with the air of a racer. A sense of triumph imparted to his face the triumphant glow." Taking Daniel 2:45 as his text, Jasper spins a story of the mighty but unrighteous who will be laid low by the great "stone cut out of the mountain" that has been rolling and growing from Nebuchadnezzar's times to the present. Jasper's sermon is often self-referential. Towards its conclusion, he responds to critics who denounced his sermons such as "The Sun Do Move" as the work of an "old fogey."

The text of the sermon appears in dialect (removed here), as transcribed by William E. Hatcher, in John Jasper: The Unmatched Negro Philosopher and Preacher *(New York: Fleming H. Revell, 1908), 108–20.*

I stand before you today on legs of iron and none can stay me from preaching the Gospel of the Lord God. I know well enough that the old devil is mad as a tempest about my being here; he knows that my call to preach comes from God, and that's what makes him so mad when he sees Jasper ascend the pulpit, for he knows that the people is going to hear a message straight from heaven. I don't get my sermons out of grammars and rhetorics, but the Spirit of the Lord puts them in my mind and makes them burn in my soul.

It has always been one of the ways of God to set up men as rulers of the people. You know that God ordains kings and rulers and—what kind of bothers some of us—He don't always make it a point to put up good men. You know that our Lord gives Judas a place among the twelve, and he turned out to be one of the grandest rascals under the sun.

Just so Nebuchadnezzar was appointed of the Lord to be the king of Babylon—that same robber that took the vessels out of the temple at Jerusalem and lugged them away to his own country. That man had one of the powerfullest kingdoms ever known on this flat earth. He ruled over many countries and many smaller kingdoms, and even had under his hands the servants on the plantation and the beasts of the field. He was one of these unlimited monarchs. He asked nobody no odds, and did just what he wanted to do, and I cannot stop to tell you with what a strong hand and outstretched arm he ruled the people with an iron rod. It came to pass that one time this king that did not fear God (though God had set him up) had a dream. Dreams is awfully curious things. They used to frighten folks out of their senses and I tell you they sometimes frighten folks now. I've had many dreams in my day that got mighty close to me. They graveled into the very cords of my soul, and made me feel like the ground under my feet was liable to give way any time, and I don't doubt that hundreds of you that hear me now have been frightened and could not eat nor sleep nor work with any peace because you done have strange dreams. You better watch them dreams. In the ancient days the Lord spoke to folks in dreams. He warned them, and I don't doubt that he does that way sometimes now.

Nebuchadnezzar's dream stirred him powerful. He rolled all night and did not sleep a wink. So he sent out and got magicians and the astrologers and the sorcerers and the Chaldeans, and they were brought unto him. He tell them that he had dreamed a dream that had troubled his spirit. And the Chaldeans asked him what that dream was. The king say that the dream done gone clear out of him, and he can't catch the straight of it to save his soul. He tell them, moreover, that they got to dig up the dream and work up the meaning too, and if they don't that he's going to have them cut all to pieces and turn their houses into a dunghill, and then he tells them that if they will get the dream back for him and give the explanation he going to give them nice gifts and put great honors on them. It was too much for the Chaldeans. They couldn't dream the king's dream for him and they come square out and tell Nebuchadnezzar there's no man on earth could show such a matter to the king, and that in their opinion there is no king on the earth that would ask for such a thing from prophet or magician.

Then Nebuchadnezzar got high. He went on a tear and you know when a king gets mad you better get out of his way. He has got the power; and so he up and sent out a decree through all the regions of the kingdom that all the wise men everywhere should be slain. Just see what a made man will do when he get furious mad. They got no more sense than a mad tiger or a roaring lion. Just before the slaughter of the wise men come on, Daniel hear about it, and he asked the king's captain what it was all about and why the king was so hasty and the captain told Daniel all about it. Daniel brushed himself up quick and struck out to see the king and ask him to hold up the execution of his bloody prophecy, and he'd promise to explain his dream to him. Then Daniel goes off and gets all his Godly friends together and asks them to pray to the God of heaven that he and his friends should not perish in the slaughter of the tricksters of that country. One thing the Lord can't do—He can't refuse to answer the cries of His people; and when all that praying was going on God appeared to Daniel in the night and revealed to him the secret of the king—and what do you reckon? When the Lord give Daniel that dream and the interpretation thereof, Daniel raised a great shout and give thanks to God for what the Lord had done for him. But he didn't shout long, for he had important business to attend to; and very soon he went to the king and carried with him the secret that the king had demanded at the hands of the astrologers and magicians. He told the king right to his face the thing that he had dreamed, and what God meant by it. Truly Daniel did behave hisself before the king in a very pretty and becoming manner. He tell the king that he does not have no more sense than other people, and that he was not prepared to do things that other men could do, but that it was by the power of God that all this matter had been made known to him. He told the king that what he saw was a great image; that the image was bright and splendid and the form of it was terrible; that the head of it was of fine gold, his breast and arms of silver, his belly and thighs of brass, and his legs of iron and his feet part of iron and part of clay. And he tell the king further that he saw a stone that was cut without hands out'n the mountain and that the stone smote the image upon his feet and broke them in pieces and that the stone that broke the image became a great mountain and filled all the world. Then Daniel—that brave and fearless brother, that never quailed before the mightiest ruler of the earth—faced the king and tell him an awful and a warning truth. He say to him, "You is a great king now. You have a mighty country and all power, and the glory covers the ground. Man and beast and fowl obey you. You is the head of gold—but after you will come another kingdom that shall not be like your'n, but still it shall be big and there shall come another kingdom and there shall be a fourth kingdom strong as iron, and this kingdom shall bruise and smash all the other kingdoms.

And then Daniel gets to the big point. He tells the king that the Lord is going to set up a kingdom and that in the times to come that kingdom shall crush and consume all the other kingdoms. That shall be the kingdom of God on the earth and that kingdom shall stand forever and ever. You knows how you saw that stone that was cut out'n the mountain and how that broke in pieces the iron, the brass, the clay, the silver, and the gold, and my God have made known to you, O king, what shall take place in the great hereafter, and this is the dream and the interpretation thereof.

That was a mighty sermon that Daniel preached to Nebuchadnezzar. It ought to have saved him, but it look like it made him worse. The devil got him for that time and he turn right against the Lord God and sought out not his statutes and counted his ways unholy.

You know about that image. It was made of gold, and was threescore cubits high and six cubits wide, and it was set up in the plain of Durer, not far from Babylon. You know a cubit is about eighteen inches, and if you multiply that by threescore cubits you get 1080 inches, which means that image was ninety foot high and nine feet broad. So you see Nebuchadnezzar got to be a God-maker, and when he got this great image built he sent out to get all the princes and governors and all the rest of the swell folks to come and bow down and worship that great image that he had set up. Now this was the great folly and shame of the king. By that deed he defied the Lord God and the wrath of the Lord was stirred against him.

And now, my brethren, you remember Daniel told the king that the image that he saw in his dream was himself ruling over all the other kingdoms. He told him also that the stone that was cut out of the mountain and come rolling down the craggy sides and broke in pieces the iron, the brass and the clay, that that was the kingdom of the Lord Jesus Christ. And he tell him, furthermore, that the coming of the stone to be a great mountain means the growth of the kingdom of our Lord 'til it shall fill this world and shall triumph over the other kingdoms. Daniel tell the king that his kingdom was going to be taken from him, because he had not feared the God of heaven, and in his folly and crimes he turned away from that God that rules in the heaven and holds the nations of the earth in the palms of his hands. He told him that the kingdom of Satan, that arch enemy of God, was going to tumble flat, because that stone cut out of the mountain would roll over Satan's dominions and crush it in to flinders.

Glory to God in the highest; that stone cut out of the mountain is a mighty roller. Nothing can stay its terrible progress! They that fight against Jehovah had better look out—that stone is still rolling and the first thing they know it will crush down upon them and they will sink to rise no more. Our God is a consuming fire, and he will overturn and overturn 'til the foundations of sin is broken upon. You just wait a little. The time is fast rolling on. Even now I hear my Saviour saying to His Father, "Father, I can stay here no longer; I must get up this morning, I am going out to call My people from the field; they have been abused and laughed at and been made a scoffing long enough for My name's sake. I can stay no longer. My soul cries for my children. Gabriel, get down your trumpet this morning; I want you to do some blowing. Blow gently and easy at first, but let My people hear your golden notes. They will come when I call."

Ah, my brethren, you and I will be there when that trumpet sounds. I don't think I shall be alarmed, because I know it is my King marshalling His people home. It won't frighten you, my sisters; it will have the sweetness of Jesus' voice to you; and, oh, how it will ring out that happy morning when our king shall come to gather the ransomed of the Lord to Himself. Then you shall have a new and holy body, and with it your glorified spirit shall be united, and on that day we shall go to see the Father and He shall smile and say: "These is my children; they have washed their robes and made them white in the blood of the Lamb; they have come out of great tribulation and they shall be with Me forever and ever." I expect to be there.

"Well, Jasper," you say, "Why do you expect to be there? How you know? You read the fourteenth chapter of John, will you? "I go to prepare a place for you," and that word is the rule; and so you will see old John Jasper right there and King Jesus shall come out to meet us and take us in and show us the mansions that he have prepared for us.

O Lucifer how thou have fallen! You proud ones will find then that your days is over, and ye that have despised the children of my God will sink down into hell, just as low as it is possible to get. You needn't tell Him that you have preached in His name, and in His name done many wonderful works. You can't fool Him! He'll frown down on you and say "I don't know you, and I don't want to know you, and I don't want to see you. Get out of my sight forever, and go to your place, among the lost."

Ah, truly, it is a mighty stone, been rolling all these centuries, rolling today. May it roll through the kingdom of darkness and crush the enemies of God. That stone done got so big that it is higher than heaven, broader than the earth, and deeper than hell itself. But don't be deceived. Don't think I don't let you off. I got something more for you yet.

You remember Daniel and Shadrach, Meshach and Abednego. They all stubbornly refused to bow down to Nebuchadnezzar's golden image. They stood straight up. They wouldn't bend a knee nor crook a toe, and them Chaldeans was watching them. That's the way it always is, the devil's folks is always a watching us trying to get something on us and to get us into trouble and with too many of us they succeed. They saw that Daniel and his friends would not get down like they done, and up they jumped and away they cut and come to the king.

"Oh, king, live forever," they say. "You know, O king, what you said—that decree that you made that at the sound of the cornet, the flute, the harp, the sackbut, the saltry and the dulcimer and all kinds of music, that every-body should fall down and worship the golden image, and that those that does not fall down and worship should be put in the furnace; and now, O king, they say that a lot of those men done refuse. They don't regard you. They hate your gods and despise that image that you set up.

Of course the old king got mad again and in his fury brought these three before him. He asked them if what he had heard about them was so—about their not worshipping the golden image. "Maybe you made a mistake," the king say, "but we're going to have it over again, and if when the band strikes up next time you will get up and worship it'll go easy with you, and if you don't the fires in the furnace will be started quick as lightning and into it every one of you shall go."

These was young men, but, ah, I tell you, they was of loyal stock. They was just as calm as sunrise in the morning. They said: "Oh, king, we ain't careful to answer about this matter. If you like to cast us into the furnace, our God that we serve is able to get us out. We ain't going to bow, and we never will bow to your God, and you just as well understand."

Right then the men went to heat up the furnace. They was told to heat it up seven times hotter than was the general rule and they had some giants to tie Shadrach, Meshach and Abednego, and they took the young men away into the furnace. The heat was so terrible that the flames shot out and set fire to the men that had put the Hebrew children in and the poor wretches was burned up, but not a hair of the three was singed, and they come out a smiling and not a blister on them from head to foot. They did not even have a smell of fire about their persons, and they look just like they just come out of dressing rooms.

Nebuchadnezzar was there, and he say: "Look in that furnace there. We didn't put but three persons in there, did we?" And they told him that was so. Then he sure turn pale, and look scared like he going to die and he say:

"Look there; I see four men inside and walking through the fire, and the form of the fourth is like the Son of God," and it look like the king got converted that day, for he lift up his voice and the praise of the God of Shadrach, Meshach and Abednego.

Ah, great is this story; they that trust in God shall never be put to confusion. The righteous always comes out conquerers and more than conquerers. Kings may hate you, friends despise you, and cowards backbite you, but God is your deliverer.

But I done forget. This old time religion is not good enough for some folks in these last days. Some call this kind of talk foolishness, but if that be true then the Bible, and heaven, and these Christians' hearts, is full of that kind of foolishness. If this be old fogey religion, then I want my church crowded with old fogeys.

What did John see over there in Patmos? He say he saw the four and twenty elders seated round the throne of God and casting their glittering crowns of gold at the feet of King Jesus, and he say that out of the throne come lightning and thunders and voices and the seven lamps burning before the throne of God. And there before the throne was the sea of glass, and round about the throne was the four living creatures full of eyes before and behind, and they never cease crying: "Holy, Holy, Holy is the Lord God almighty that died to take away the sins of the world."

You call that old fogey. Just look away over yonder in the future. Do you see that sea of glass and the saints of God that was all bruised and mangled by the fiery darts of the wicked? I hear the singing! What is their song? Oh, how it rolls! And the chorus is: "Redeemed, redeemed, washed in the blood of the Lamb." Call them old fogeys, do you? Well, you may, for they that has been that way from the time that Abel, the first man, a saved soul told the news of salvation to the angels.

"Well, Jasper, have you got any religion to give away?"

I'se free to say that I ain't got as much as I want. For forty-five years I been begging for more and I ask for more in this trying hour. But, bless God,

I'se got religion to give away. The Lord has filled my hands with the Gospel, and I stand here to offer free salvation to any that will come. If in this big crowd there is one lost sinner that has not felt the cleansing touch of my Saviour's blood, I ask him to come today and he shall never die.■

111 REASONS FOR A NEW POLITICAL PARTY

Reverend Henry McNeal Turner

The abandonment of Radical Reconstruction by the Republican Party caused a number of black Americans to question the wisdom of supporting the party of Abraham Lincoln, but it was not until the Supreme Court decision of 1883 nullifying the Civil Rights Act of 1875 that disenchantment with the Republican Party made considerable headway among African Americans. Henry McNeal Turner broke with the Republican Party soon after the decision, and publicly advised others to do likewise. In a speech in Atlanta, Georgia, February 12, 1886, Turner argued that there was no significant difference between the parties so far as African Americans were concerned and that black voters should withhold their support from both.

Turner spoke out in favor of a new political party to fulfill the promise of the Civil War and Reconstruction. As a strict temperance man, he favored unity of all nondrinking Americans regardless of color to achieve this goal. The dramatic resurgence of the temperance movement in the 1870s (including the 1874 establishment of the Women's Christian Temperance Union, which was the nation's largest women's group by the time Turner spoke) led Turner to believe it could be the basis for a moral reform coalition. Here is a major extract from this speech, taken from the text published in the Christian Recorder, *April 1, 1886.*

I HAVE NOT DESERTED the Republican party, the Republican party has deserted me and seven millions of my race—under circumstances, too, of the most dastardly character known in human events. . . . We know what the Republican party has done. But, unfortunately, we know too much. We know that after it freed the Negro and pretended to clothe him with the aegis of citizenship, by making him a voter, officeholder, juror, et cetera, that it was a hard task to get an enactment through Congress that contemplated anything like civil rights; and that after the Negro held conventions, wrote petitions, whined and howled in ghastly refrains all over the land from year to year, until a feeble civil rights act was passed, that a Republican Supreme Court (really a conclave of human donkeys) there in Washington City declared the whole thing null and void, thus leaving the Negro, both those freed and who were free before, in a condition compared with which the serfs of Russia are lords. Never was a people left in such a degraded situation since time began, under a status of pretended citizenship, yet the Republican party gives that infamous decision a virtual acquiescence by such a dead silence that cannot be interpreted other than as an approval of it. . . .

The sequence of that decision and the reticence of the Republican party, amounting to a virtual approval, has entailed upon the Negro of the South a species of degradation almost indescribable. Our ladies are robbed daily and insulted upon the public highways by railroad roughs brought here from the ends of the earth, even down to Swedes who can scarcely utter the language of their insults. We are put in front of baggage cars in many instances, so that, if an accident should happen, the trunks and other baggage would fare better than the Negro in the smashup. We must either starve along the highways or travel or go to the kitchen and buy scraps, not being allowed even to enter the dining room to eat at a separate table, when in many instances the boardinghouse itself does not compare with my kitchen. Right here at our depot in Atlanta, I cannot enter the lunch stand and drink a cup of tea at the counter much less at a table. If I get the tea at all, it must be sent outdoors. These and a hundred other reasons which I cannot enumerate prompt a desire in me for a new party.

A great moral temperance party, a party that will take up the work of reform and equity where the Republican party laid it down, and carry it to successful completion. Between the Democratic party and the Republican party there is no difference at present, so far as it affects the Negro; one holds and the other throttles, one robs and the other looks with a smile, one steals and the other conceals, one lampoons and the other says well done. Therefore, as a man, a free man, a free-born man though a Negro, I cannot support either one of these parties as such. I mean upon their respective merits, nor will I ever do so while both ignore my civil rights. Thus my reasons for clamoring for a third party or a new party, a great moral-reform party, a party that good men of all parties, shades and complexions can join and finish the work of humanity.

A civilization that does not comprehend humanity is rotten, corrupt and evanescent. Our country cannot stand with seven millions of enemies in it, and every Negro who has any of the nobler instincts in his nature will loathe this country as long as his humanity is proscribed, insulted and outraged. These are only a few of my reasons for wanting a third party. Let us have a great party made up of sober men, no liquor-drinking men, men of high moral sentiments, a party whose policy will be right and not anything for success, and my word for it, millions of sober Republicans and sober Democrats and nonpartisans and ministers of the gospel and philanthropists and humanitarians North and South will rally to its support. . . . ■

112

THE PRESENT RELATIONS OF LABOR AND CAPITAL

T. Thomas Fortune

The year 1886 was one of intense struggle between labor and capital in the United States. In cities and towns the armies of labor organized and gave expression to the pent-up bitterness of years of exploitation in a series of strikes that shook the nation to its foundation. On May 1, 1886, about 350,000 workers in 11,562 establishments in the country at large went on strike for an eight-hour day.

This was the setting for the speech delivered on April 20, 1886, by T. Thomas Fortune (1856–1928) before the Brooklyn (New York) Literary Union. Born in slavery in Florida, Fortune saw the Ku Klux Klan in action as a boy. With little formal education, but with practical knowledge of the printer's trade, Fortune came to New York in 1879 and rose to become one of the leading journalists of his day. He became part owner and editor of his own newspaper, the Globe, *which later became the* Freeman, *and finally the* New York Age.

Fortune was influenced by Karl Marx and Henry George, as demonstrated in his remarkable book Black and White: Land, Labor and Politics in the South, *published in New York in 1884. In this speech, he identifies a basic human right to the necessities of life and, aligning the plight of poor black laborers with that of subservient classes around the world, predicts a coming revolution of labor in the reallocation of wealth. One of the most militant and influential black leaders of the late nineteenth century, Fortune was also, paradoxically, a close friend, defender, adviser, and ghostwriter for Booker T. Washington. In the 1890s, Fortune was among the founders of the National Afro-American League and the National Afro-American Council, forerunners of modern national civil rights organizations.*

The speech text is taken from the New York Freeman, *May 1, 1886.*

I DO NOT EXAGGERATE the gravity of the subject when I say that it is now the very first in importance not only in the United States but in every country in Europe. Indeed the wall of industrial discontent encircles the civilized globe.

The iniquity of privileged class and concentrated wealth has become so glaring and grievous to be borne that a thorough agitation and an early readjustment of the relation which they sustain to labor can no longer be delayed with safety to society.

It does not admit of argument that every man born into the world is justly entitled to so much of the produce of nature as will satisfy his physical necessities; it does not admit of argument that every man, by reason of his being, is justly entitled to the air he must breathe, the water he must drink, the food he must eat and the covering he must have to shield him from the inclemency of the weather. These are self-evident propositions, not disputed by the most orthodox advocate of excessive wealth on the one hand and excessive poverty on the other. That nature intended these as the necessary correlations of physical being is abundantly proved in the primitive history of mankind and in the freedom and commonality of possession which now obtain everywhere among savage people. The moment you deny to a man the unrestricted enjoyment of all the elements upon which the breath he draws is dependent, that moment you deny to him the inheritance to which he was born.

I maintain that organized society, as it obtains today, based as it is upon feudal conditions, is an outrageous engine of torture and an odious tyranny; that it places in the hands of a few the prime elements of human existence, regardless of the great mass of mankind; that the whole aim and necessity of the extensive and costly machinery of the law we are compelled to maintain grows out of the fact that this fortunate or favored minority would otherwise be powerless to practice upon the masses of society the gross injustice which everywhere prevails.

For centuries the aim and scope of all law have been to more securely hedge about the capitalist and the landowner and to repress labor within a condition wherein bare subsistence was the point aimed at.

From the institution of feudalism to the present time the inspiration of all conflict has been that of capitalist, landowner and hereditary aristocracy against the larger masses of society—the untitled, the disinherited proletariat of the world.

This species of oppression received its most memorable check in the great French Revolution, wherein a new doctrine became firmly rooted in the philosophy of civil government—that is, that the toiling masses of society possessed certain inherent rights which kingcraft, hereditary aristocracy, landlordism and usury mongers must respect. As a result of the doctrine studiously inculcated by the philosophers of the French Revolution we had the revolt of the blacks of Haiti, under the heroic Toussaint L'Ouverture, the bloody Dessalines and the suave, diplomatic and courtly Christophe, by which the blacks secured forever their freedom as free men and their independence as a people; and our own great Revolution, wherein the leading complaint was taxation by the British government of the American colonies without conceding them proportionate representation. At bottom in each case, bread and butter was the main issue. So it has always been. So it will continue to be, until the scales of justice are made to strike a true balance between labor on the one hand and the interest on capital invested and the wages of superintendence on the other. Heretofore the interest on capital and the wages of superintendence have absorbed so much of the wealth produced as to leave barely nothing to the share of labor.

It should be borne in mind that of this trinity labor is the supreme potentiality. Capital, in the first instance, is the product of labor. If there had never been any labor there would not now be any capital to invest. Again, if a bonfire were made of all the so-called wealth of the world it would only require a few years for labor to reproduce it; but destroy the brawn and muscle of the world and it could not be reproduced by all the gold ever delved from the mines of California and Australia and the fabulous gems from the diamond fields of Africa. In short, labor has been and is the producing agency, while capital has been and is the absorbing or parasitical agency.

Should we, therefore, be surprised that with the constantly growing intelligence and democratization of mankind labor should have grown discontented at the systematic robbery practiced upon it for centuries, and should now clamor for a more equitable basis of adjustment of the wealth it produces?

I could name you a dozen men who have in the last forty or fifty years amassed among them a billion dollars, so that a millionaire has become as common a thing almost as a pauper. How came they by their millions? Is it possible for a man in his lifetime, under the most favorable circumstances, to amass a million dollars? Not at all! The constitution of our laws must be such that they favor one as against the other to permit of such a glaring disparity.

I have outlined for you the past and present relations of capital and labor. The widespread discontent of the labor classes in our own country and in Europe gives emphasis to the position here taken.

I abhor injustice and oppression wherever they are to be found, and my best sympathies go out freely to the struggling poor and the tyranny-ridden of all races and lands. I believe in the divine right of man, not of caste or class, and I believe that any law made to perpetuate or to give immunity to these as against the masses of mankind is an infamous and not-to-be-borne infringement of the just laws of the Creator, who sends each of us into the world as naked as a newly fledged jay bird and crumbles us back into the elements of Mother Earth by the same processes of mutation and final dissolution.

The social and material differences which obtain in the relations of mankind are the creations of man, not of God. God never made such a spook as a king or a duke; he never made such an economic monstrosity as a millionaire; he never gave John Jones the right to own a thousand or a hundred thousand acres of land, with their complement of air and water. These are the conditions of man, who has sold his birthright to the Shylocks of the world and received not even a mess of pottage for his inheritance. The thing would really be laughable, if countless millions from the rice swamps of the Carolinas to the delvers in the mines of Russian Siberia, were not ground to powder to make a holiday for some selfish idler.

Everywhere labor and capital are in deadly conflict. The battle has been raging for centuries, but the opposing forces are just now in a position for that death struggle which it was inevitable must come before the end was. Nor is it within the scope of finite intelligence to forecast the lines upon which the settlement will be made. Capital is entrenched behind ten centuries of law and conservatism, and controlled withal by the wisest and coolest heads in the world. The inequality of the forces joined will appear very obvious. Yet the potentiality of labor will be able to force concessions from time to time, even as the commoners of England have through centuries been able to force from royalty relinquishment of prerogative after prerogative, until, from having been among the most despotic of governments under Elizabeth, the England of today under Queen Victoria is but a royal shadow. So the time may come when the forces of labor will stand upon absolute equality with those of capital, and that harmony between them obtain which has been sought for by wise men and fools for a thousand years.■

113

HOW SHALL WE MAKE THE WOMEN OF OUR RACE STRONGER?

Olivia A. Davidson

A co-founder of Tuskegee Institute and a leading advocate and practitioner of educational reform, Olivia Davidson was born in 1854 and was raised in Ohio. She studied at the Albany Enterprise Academy and at the age of sixteen began her teaching career. After four years' work in the Memphis, Tennessee, school system, Davidson entered the senior class at Hampton Institute, from which she graduated in 1879. Booker T. Washington, a Hampton graduate, was the commencement speaker.

Two years later, Davidson moved to Tuskegee, where she not only taught but, as assistant principal, helped devise the curriculum and raise needed funds. Washington later observed that the early success of the school owed "more to Miss Davidson than to anyone else."* Following the death of Washington's first wife, he and Davidson married on August 11, 1886, a few months after she delivered an important speech to the members of the Alabama State Teachers' Association in Selma on April 21.

In her speech, Davidson depicts the true reformer as one who works

---

*Booker T. Washington, *The Story of My Life and Work* (Toronto: J. L. Nichols, 1900), 85.

to counter the lingering effects of slavery "in the form of physical, mental and moral deformity" that "has left its impress upon us" for "generations to come." In particular, she argues that uplift of the African American people must concentrate on the education and improvement of women and girls, for "it is with our women that the purity and safety of our families rest, and what our families are the race will be."

Davidson addresses three realms of female nature—physical, moral, and intellectual—insisting that all three are interrelated and must be developed. "Three-fourths of the colored women," she observes, "are overworked and under-fed." She links their physical exhaustion partly to lack of training in food preparation and comments that "any school that succeeds in arousing in one of our young women an ambition to become a good cook does God and humanity a noble service."

Davidson identifies the school room as a site of "intellectual emancipation" but also urges familiarity with pupils' home environments and circumstances in order to best assist them. Women teachers, she maintains, should demonstrate interest in girl pupils and provide role models "that would still further arouse their ambition to become good women." Davidson imagines the prospective roles of African American women in both the private sphere of domestic provision for the family and in the public realm of service, then merges the two realms in the conclusion to her remarks.

Always in precarious health herself, Davidson died of tuberculosis in 1889. Her tombstone reads: "She lived to the truth."

The speech text was originally published in the proceedings of the Fifth Annual Session of the Alabama State Teachers' Association Held at Selma, Alabama, April 21–24, 1886 (Tuskegee, 1887), 3–8, and is reprinted in volume 2 of Louis R. Harlan, ed., The Booker T. Washington Papers (Urbana: University of Illinois Press, 1972), 298–305. For further information on Davidson, see Carolyn Dorsey, "The Pre-Hampton Years of Olivia A. Davidson," Hampton Review 1 (Fall 1988), 44–52; and "Despite Poor Health: Olivia Davidson Washington's Story," Sage: A Scholarly Journal on Black Women 2 (Fall 1985), 69–72.

I feel the honor as well as the responsibility of this opportunity of appearing before this audience to-day. Public speaking is not to my taste. For years past my life has been full of work, but generally in a different direction—at least by different methods, and if I consulted my inclinations I would not be before you to-day, but in view of the vast amount that may be said and done in the direction of the subject, I have chosen, to a convention of teachers who are inquiring for ideas from any source, I may be able to say something at least suggestive.

How shall we make the women of our race stronger physically, morally and intellectually? Many of the ideas that I shall bring before you in my endeavor to find a few answers to this question are not really new, but as far as their application to every day life among our people goes, they are new, in the main. Several years of work in positions that have brought me in close contact with many of the women and girls of the race have brought a deep conviction of the need for them of physical, mental and moral development.

It is true there is no people or class of people whose development in all these directions is perfectly symmetrical, or what it should be in any one of them, but among all people except uncivilized ones, more prominence is given all these phases of development than we are giving them.

First, let us consider how the physical development of one woman can be accomplished: James Freeman Clarke, in his inimitable essay on the training and care of the body,* says, "Good health is the basis of all physical, intellectual and moral development. We glorify God with our bodies by keeping them in good health." Mainly because I believe this is true, I have put this part of my subject first.

I think most people would be surprised at the result if a test were in some way given with a view to finding a few perfectly healthy women in any of our communities. Diogenes' search after an honest man was more fruitful of results than this one would be. Why is this? Why are there so many of us miserable invalids either utterly incapable of rendering service in any station or to whom life is a burden, because of the effort of will necessary to be put forth constantly if any thing is accomplished? Nervous and organic diseases have laid tyrannous hands upon us and are leading us helpless captives away from the highest avenues of usefulness into the darker ways of suffering and too often of selfish narrowness, for though a strong, earnest spirit may rise above, and inspire a weak body, generally the weakness of the body will crop the wings and keep the soul from soaring.† To answer specifically why this is true is, of course, impossible, but when great and universal evils exist there are usually general causes that can be formulated. First in the list of causes of our physical weakness, I would put the use of stimulants and of tobacco. A large part of the suffering from diseases of various kinds among us comes directly from the use of alcoholic drinks, and all our united influence should be given to deliver ourselves and our afflicted sisters from this frightful wellspring of suffering. The evils that come to us from the use of these drinks are of two kinds—those inherited from intemperate parents and those brought upon ourselves by our own intemperance.

I do not mean to speak in general of the evils of intemperance, but only of its evil results upon our bodies.

First let us speak of inherited evils. That the sins of the fathers are visited upon the children is no more true anywhere than it is here. The drunken parent destroys or weakens not alone the body God gave him for the temple of his own soul, but transmits to the child a heritage of suffering, perhaps observable in general organic weakness or in fearful deformities or painful

---

*Self-Culture: Physical, Intellectual, Moral and Spiritual (Boston, 1880).
†When Davidson sought to volunteer as a nurse during the 1878 yellow fever epidemic in Memphis, she was turned down because of her poor health.

diseases. Perhaps the commonest form the inherited evils take is the first—inherited weakness. This is especially true of women whose more delicate organizations are more easily affected. As the child grows to womanhood the weaknesses are developed into diseases by the hardships and exposures incident to such a life as is an outgrowth of the intemperance of the father or the mother.

Teachers, especially you who are in the country, can do much towards mitigating this evil by exerting a strong and aggressive influence against the use of whiskey. By precept and example help the people to the conviction that its use is sapping away their own and their children's strength. Take no part in, and frown upon, the tendency to enter into shameful excesses at the holidays when the farmers have "settled" their accounts, which is often but another way of saying they have gone more deeply in debt for a jug of whiskey.

I have put the use of whiskey first in my list of causes, but now that I begin to think and write of another fruitful source of suffering, I am almost persuaded that it should come first. I refer to the use of tobacco. How sad that any one, least of all, a woman, should defile the beautiful temple, all clean and pure and undefiled when received from God's hands by making it reek with the foul fumes of tobacco! "My Father's house is a house of prayer, but ye have made it a den of thieves." Your soul's house is the rightful temple of God, but ye have made it a den of filth. I can not speak too strongly against one of the commonest forms of the use of tobacco among Southern colored women, and indeed among all classes of Southern women—the use of snuff. Aside from the fact that the habit is a disgusting one, its influence upon the health is most pernicious. No human body can be vigorous and healthy when part of its daily food is tobacco.

Another source of suffering less serious only because less universal, is the use of morphine and similar drugs. This is a surer destroyer of every power of body, mind and soul than any mentioned, and though its victims are now fewer, it is to be feared their number is on the increase. One way of working against this evil is by resisting the administration of morphine in any form by physicians except in cases of extremist suffering, for more harm than good is done the entire system, especially the nervous system, by giving it. The taste formed this way often becomes a confirmed habit impossible to be gotten rid of.

Aside from these particulars, the general manner of living in the homes where most of the colored girls' and women's lives are spent is productive of disease. Go into the miserable shanties and hovels in town or country in which the majority of them live and you have all about you germinators of disease. Insufficiency, if not actual want, is plainly written every where on fire, food and raiment, while the cracks in floor and walls tell their own tale of suffering and exposure. Here mothers and daughters toil from Monday morning till Sunday morning over the wash tub or ironing table or at the sewing machine, as often as necessary benumbing the brain and straining the back by carrying huge baskets of clothes on their heads longer or shorter distances. Added to all this is their general carelessness in the care of themselves arising from their complete ignorance of the laws of health. Some one has said, "Cleanliness is next to Godliness," but I would say that cleanliness is godliness. No soul can be a godly one that willingly inhabits an unclean body or submits to unclean outer surroundings. We can help here by using every opportunity for inspiring in those with whom we come in contact, an ambition to have better homes, and by teaching them in every way possible how to care for their bodies. Here, my sister teachers, is a wide and special field for you. By your own example in dress and daily habits as well as by precepts show them how to clothe and care for themselves according to hygienic laws. In the schoolroom teach physiology and hygiene by general lessons if you don't have the regular text-book work in them.

It is safe to say that three-fourths of the colored women are overworked and under-fed, and are suffering to a greater or less degree from sheer physical exhaustion. The overworking is generally a result of underfeeding, and this is a result of their ignorance of the art of cooking. If ever in their possession, good cooking is a lost art now among the colored women in general of the South. The rations of sodden, unappetizing food that are served three times a day in most families are so many outrages upon those faithful but much abused servants, the digestive organs.

Any school that succeeds in arousing in one of our young women an ambition to become a good cook does God and humanity a noble service.

Seeds of disease and suffering are sown in infancy, childhood and girlhood by mothers, at first, through ignorance of proper methods of caring for their little ones from the time of their birth, and later through carelessness and ignorance in allowing them to go blindly on, ignorant of the laws of life, leaving them to come unshielded by any word of advice or caution to the possession of knowledge, whose possession is vicious in its influence upon health and character only, because its acquirement is made a thing of chance, or which the child feels she must obtain surreptitiously.

I beg the women of this convention to be earnest in their endeavors to shield the young girls in their districts from the fearful sins of ignorance in this direction. Try to make the mothers feel the serious responsibility that rests upon them. Show them in every way you can how to shield their girls from wrong and suffering brought on by pernicious habits.

Let us now turn to the consideration of that part of the question which asks how can we make the women of our race stronger intellectually. I would not have you think, especially you my brother teachers, that we are seeking to find out how we can produce more "strong minded" women as that term is used in its most objectionable sense. Indeed, it would require stronger evolutionary force than even Prof. Huxley* would dare to advocate to evolve strong-minded women out of [the] mass of intellectually deformed beings who compose the female portion of our race.

*English biologist Thomas Henry Huxley (1825–1895), author of *Man's Place in Nature* (1865), was a noted defender of Darwinism.

Slavery with its offsprings of misery in the form of physical, mental and moral deformity has left its impress upon us, and its influence will be seen in us, for generations to come. It must be [the] work of the earnest reformers among us in each generation to make this influence weaker and to hasten the day when slavery with all its entail will be a thing of the past indeed.

The school room must mainly be the place in which, and the teacher's hand the one by which, the intellectual emancipation of the women of our race is accomplished. It is our privilege to have in hand a large part of the mental development of the colored women of the generations to come directly after us.

Let us see to it that nothing on our part is left undone toward bringing them back to the estate of mental vigor in which God placed them.

We cannot indeed expect them to spring Minerva-like into his estate, from the very grasp of the monster, slavery, but by careful and patient training, they can be brought to it.

In the school room the teacher should aim to make the work such as will best train the girls' mental powers in their fourfold nature. In order to do this, he must himself know what these powers are, and be able to inquire wisely in his study of his pupil what they are capable of, in each individual. In case his previous preparation for his work has not given him this knowledge his first endeavor should be, to fit himself for it by study. John Locke, Froebel, Pestalozzi and many others have in their writings made the way so plain that no earnest seeker can greatly err in finding it.

And here, though it is not exactly within the province of my paper, I want to urge upon the younger teachers in this association the importance of fitting themselves by constant study and reading for their work.

We now come to the part of the subject that is of most vital importance to us as a race or as individuals.

We glorify God with our bodies, by keeping them in good health. We glorify Him in a higher degree by so training and strengthening our mental powers that they will be capable of clear and protracted thought and the direction of wise actions; but above all this we can glorify God by permitting our moral natures to attain their full growth. This is true of all humanity, and it is equally true that all humanity fail to reach full moral growth, but it is especially true of our race, and most especially true of the women among us.

Two hundred years of such training as was given in the school of slavery, was calculated to dwarf the moral nature of its pupils. The disregard of family relations, of personal rights, of the property of others, and hundreds of other outrages upon human rights, from which the slaves were sufferers, or in which they were participants, or of which they were daily witnesses, were not without their influence upon character, and that influence is still strong upon us. This influence is seen in the looseness with which our family relations are regarded to-day, in the weak cry, if any, of the outraged virtue and purity that goes up from among us, when immorality in the form of sins against social or moral laws is found in our midst, in the number of our women who are daily brought before the police courts in our large cities, and [in the] low moral tone that is almost a second nature in the majority of us and gives color to the commonest transactions of our every day life.

Much that has been suggested in this paper as a means to bring about physical and mental health will also obtain here. You cannot succeed in getting a woman to see that she is injuring her health by the use of tobacco or whiskey, or by keeping herself and surroundings in filth, and to be willing to reform in these matters without raising the tone of that women's moral nature. There are action and reaction here that are equal; and in the case of many doubtless the desire for physical good is the only motive of action you can appeal to successfully. Though something can be done by us by patient and wise effort for the moral uplifting of the more mature women, the young women and girls are the hope of the race, and fortunately it is over them that with wise and Christian effort we can gain our strongest influence. The forces we have to work against are inherent tendencies, home influences, evil associations and in some cases the tendency to devour low literature. Here again their lives are against them. Take the life of the average country girls, in their homes they huddle at night in sleeping rooms with fathers, brothers and often the hired hands; day by day they work beside men in the fields, often untidily and often indecently dressed. All this through the week. Saturday, they come streaming into town to stand about on the streets or in stores and saloons, dip snuff, beg for treats, gossip and listen to, and pass jokes that ought to be insults to any girl or woman in whom there is a spark of womanly modesty. Over all this is thrown an atmosphere of looseness in thought, language and action. Little here to cultivate moral sentiment, but much to blunt it. That we should make any thing but comparatively rapid progress against all this is not to be expected under any circumstances, and if we go into a community and be mere school teachers in the narrowest use of that term, we shall not make any headway against it. It is in this respect—the routine work of the schoolroom forms so small a part of the work of the earnest teacher—that the colored school teachers' lives are peculiar.

We must work outside the school-room, we must see the girls in their homes, make friends with them, be interested in them if we would help them. I have in mind a teacher who went into one of the worst communities. The very atmosphere of the place was immoral. The result of two years' earnest, patient work there on her part was, that in every home in the community, the spirit of improvement was noticeable; and she did it mainly through the girls. She made friends of them, she visited their homes, she organized them into self and home improvement clubs, got them to give up taking snuff, to lay aside the old white cotton wraps and arrange their hair neatly, to wear collars, cuffs and aprons to school, encourage them to plant flowers in their yards, gave them pictures and papers (supplied by friends whom she had interested in them) for their walls, and so appealed to their pride, and modesty, and self-respect that there was no longer the Saturday Hegira to town, and in [the] majority of the families, separate sleeping apartments were provided. Among the more thoughtful and intelligent she formed a reading club, and read to them or told them about the lives of noble women and other things that would still further arouse their ambition to become good women. What this teacher did we can do and perhaps some of us are doing.

We cannot too seriously consider this question of the moral uplifting of our women for it is of national importance to us. It is with our women that the purity and safety of our families rest, and what our families are the race will be.■

114 INTRODUCTION OF MASTER WORKMAN POWDERLY

Frank J. Ferrell

Read in isolation, the introduction that the African American labor leader Frank Ferrell gave Master Workman Terence V. Powderly at the Richmond convention of the Knights of Labor would seem remarkable only for its brevity. But as a response to recent racial incidents involving black conventioneers while in Richmond, Ferrell's act in speaking held enormous symbolic importance for the African American Knights and others who supported social equality. At the same time, Ferrell's brief speech and other acts of color-line defiance spurred outrage in the racist white press.

By 1886, there were more than 60,000 African American members of the Noble Order of the Knights of Labor. Black workers who had long been excluded from most labor unions found greater acceptance among the Knights, although not without painful exceptions and limitations. Some Knights saw the organization not simply as a union for labor nego-tiation but as a vehicle for broad social change, particularly with regard to racial equality. These views were far from universally held among the Knights, however. When General Master Workman Powderly toured the South in 1885, the year before the Richmond convention, he addressed white and black members in separate appearances arranged by the white Southern coordinators of his tour. There were many black Knights in the South (more than 5,000 in Virginia alone), yet they remained barred from general union with white members.

When the delegates of New York's District 49 learned that their Afri-

can American members would not be permitted to stay in the same hotel as whites attending the Richmond convention, the Forty-niners protested by bringing tents and camping together. They also met with Powderly, demanding that he support the protest by permitting one of their members, Frank Ferrell, socialist and chief engineer of the New York Post Office, to appear onstage during the convention and to introduce Governor Fitzhugh Lee. Powderly expressed support for the Forty-niners' stand but worried about community reaction, suggesting instead that he would be honored to have himself introduced to the convention by Ferrell.

Prior to Ferrell's convention speech, he and the Forty-niners created a sensation by attending a performance at the Academy of Music, as Ferrell became the first African American to occupy an orchestra seat in a Richmond theater. At the close of the convention, several thousand black residents of Richmond attended the convention picnic, thus creating the largest integrated social gathering in the city's history. Ferrell's actions and speech were seen by many as triggers for these events. The Richmond State editorialized that while African Americans should receive equal citizenship rights, the social equality and intermingling encouraged by Ferrell were unthinkable; "Now and then, however, some imprudent fellow is found who is eager to have at least the appearance of enjoying a social equality that never can be and never should be his."

The New York Times of October 7, 1886, reported that there were widespread mutterings of discontent on Monday when it became known that General Master Workman Powderly was introduced to the tenth annual convention of the Knights of Labor by a colored man Frank Ferrell of New York, and that Ferrell's introductory remarks immediately followed the address of welcome delivered by Gov. Fitzhugh Lee. The latter had no idea that such a programme had been determined upon, and Powderly had been harshly criticized for taking advantage of Gov. Lee, on the ground that he should have understood the situation. It is thoroughly understood here that in the North there would have been nothing deserving of unusual comments in the fact that white and colored man occupied the same stage at a public meeting; but it is claimed that Northern men are well aware that the social relations existing between whites and blacks in the South are as opposite as the poles.

Stunned by the volume and vehemence of criticism he received following the convention, including a petition of protest from white Southern Knights, Powderly quickly disavowed any support for social equality between the races. Nevertheless, black workers joined the Knights of Labor in increasing numbers and represented the bulk of new members after 1886.

The text of Ferrell's speech of October 3, 1886, was originally published in the Proceedings, General Assembly, Knights of Labor (1886), 7–8,

and reprinted in Philip S. Foner and Ronald L. Lewis, eds., The Black
Worker During the Era of the Knights of Labor, *volume 3 of* The Black
Worker: A Documentary History from Colonial Times to the Present
*(Philadelphia: Temple University Press, 1978), 106, which also reprints
many press accounts of the convention. See also Claudia Miner, "The
1886 Convention of the Knights of Labor,"* Phylon *44 (1983), 147–59.*

Governor Lee [of Virginia] and Gentlemen of the Convention: It is with
much pleasure and gratification that I introduce to you Mr. T. V.
Powderly, of the State of Pennsylvania, who will reply to the address of welcome of Governor Lee, of this State, which is one of the oldest states in the
avenue of political influence of our country. He is one of the thoughtful men
of the nation, who recognizes the importance of this gathering of the toiling
masses in this our growing Republic. As Virginia has led in the aspirations
of our country in the past, I look with much confidence to the future, in the
hope that she will lead in the future to the realization of the objects of noble
Order. It is with extreme pleasure that we, the representatives from every
section of our country, receive the welcome of congratulation for our efforts
to improve the condition of humanity. One of the objects of our Order is the
abolition of these distinctions which are maintained by creed or color. I believe I present to you a man above the superstitions which are involved in
these distinctions.* My experience with the noble Order of the Knights of
Labor and my training in my district, have taught me that we have worked
so far successfully toward the extinction of these regrettable distinctions. As
we recognize and repose confidence in all men for their worth in society, so
can we repose confidence in one of the noblest sons of labor—T. V. Powderly—
whom I now take the pleasure of presenting to you.■

---

*Terence Powderly's own recollection of Ferrell's speech, as recorded in his diary,
differs slightly here, adding a clear statement of equality as exhibited on the speaking platform. "As Virginia has led in the aspiration of our country in the past, I look with much
confidence that she will lead in the future with the realization of the objects of this noble
Order which include the abolition of those distinctions which are maintained by class, by
creed, by color, and by nationality. I believe that I present you with a man whose mind is
above the superstitions which are involved in these distinctions. *Here we stand as brethren and equal*" (quoted in Miner, "The 1886 Convention," 151; emphasis added).

115 I AM AN ANARCHIST

Lucy E. Parsons

Lucy E. Parsons (1853–1942) was quite literally a revolutionary woman. She was a leading figure of American anarchism and the radical labor movement whose personal motto and advice to "tramps, the unemployed, disinherited and miserable" was simple: "learn the use of explosives." She was also an electrifying speaker whose orations have been unpublished and largely forgotten.

Born (perhaps in slavery) in Waco, Texas, she married Albert R. Parsons, a white journalist who was shot in the effort to register black voters. With Klan activity on the rise in Waco and the threatened enforcement of antimiscegenation law, Albert and Lucy left for Chicago, arriving in 1873. Chicago in the mid-1870s was a hotbed of radical organizing in response to unemployment and destitution on a vast scale during the prolonged recession. Lucy and Albert Parsons became actively involved in the Knights of Labor and the Socialist Revolutionary Clubs, editing a radical paper, the Alarm, *and participating in numerous demonstrations. By the early 1880s, they were disillusioned with electoral politics and instead supported "military organization and the study of revolutionary tactics."*

On May 1, 1886, Lucy and Albert Parsons helped organize a general strike in support of the eight-hour working day. Two days later, strikers at the McCormick Harvester factory were gunned down by police. On May 4, Albert was among the featured speakers at a rally held in Chicago's Haymarket Square to protest the killings. As the rally was dispersing, a bomb was thrown by an unidentified assailant, killing a police officer. Albert Parsons and eight others were arrested. For speaking in such a way as to inspire the bomber to violence, Parsons was convicted in October 1886 and was sentenced to die on December 3. After the sentence was pronounced, Lucy Parsons took her husband's hand and said: "I now go forth to take your place." Within hours of the sentencing, Lucy Parsons was aboard a train to Cincinnati, the first stop on a seven-week speaking tour designed to raise the more than twelve thousand dollars needed to appeal the case to the Illinois Supreme Court. She created a furor almost wherever she went, attracting venomous press coverage and provoking police harassment and occasional arrest. Her audiences ranged from a few dozen in cases where the authorities succeeded in discouraging attendance to more than five thousand at New York's Cooper Union.

Lucy Parsons's initial speaking tour succeeded in gaining attention and badly needed funds for her husband's appeal. On November 27, a

*stay of execution was granted and after a brief period in Chicago she re-
sumed her grueling tour. Despite being seriously ill through much of the
fall, by February Parsons delivered over forty speeches in seventeen
states. She entered Kansas City on the afternoon of December 19, 1886,
the day before her scheduled lecture and slipped unnoticed into a meeting of local socialists. As the principal speaker was saying "When there
are no kings there shall be no war; when there's no poverty there shall be
no crime," Parsons entered the auditorium unannounced and said: "They
call us anarchists for preaching that doctrine." According to the* Kansas
City Times *account (whose headline read: "Loud-Mouthed Treason"),
"the 250 men and women cheered and stamped the floor until the building almost shook, shouting 'Parsons! Parsons! Parsons!' " Parsons spoke
briefly, inviting the crowd to attend her major address at Kump's Hall the
following evening.*

*In her Kump's Hall address, delivered on December 20, Parsons
grounds her promotion of anarchism (to which the defense of her husband is clearly subordinate) in the failure of government and capitalism
to cope with mass misery. "Do you wonder why there are anarchists in
this country, in this great land of liberty, as you love to call it?" she
asks; "Go to New York," whose East Side slums in the 1880s, nicknamed
"The Typhus Ward," were among the most densely populated and disease-
ridden in the world. Speaking in Kansas City shortly after the dedication
of the Statue of Liberty, Parsons saw in Bartholdi's New York Harbor
sculpture the height of hypocrisy. In Omaha two days later, she returned
to the subject, noting, "Within the shadder of that statue, hundreds of
families have been dumped upon the street because they could not pay
the rent of their miserable tenements. The cheek of a brass monkey is
nothing compared to the brazen cheek of that statue." Political liberties
are of little value to starving people, she argues: "Bread is freedom." Although the light-skinned Parsons is said to have "passed for white," perhaps to avoid arrest for intermarriage or the prejudice of white leftists,
the press coverage of this and many of her speeches identifies her as
black, and she speaks directly in this speech of racial equality.*

*Despite the success of Parsons's speaking tour in raising funds (an es-
timated $750 per week) and public awareness, Albert Parsons was exe-
cuted in November 1887. At least partly because of Lucy Parsons's efforts, Albert and the others executed attained a lasting status among the
national and international left as martyrs. Lucy Parsons remained an
activist until her accidental death in 1942. She was the only woman to
address the founding convention of the Industrial Workers of the World
(Wobblies) in 1905, edited several radical newspapers, and continued
to speak and go to jail in demonstrations for the homeless and unemployed.*

The text of Parsons's speech comes from the Kansas City Journal *of
December 21, 1886, and appears in the Albert R. Parsons Papers at the*

State Historical Society of Wisconsin. See also Carolyn Ashbaugh, Lucy Parsons: American Revolutionary *(Chicago: Charles H. Kerr, 1976).*

I am an anarchist. I suppose you came here, the most of you, to see what a real, live anarchist looked like. I suppose some of you expected to see me with a bomb in one hand and a flaming torch in the other, but are disappointed in seeing neither. If such has been your ideas regarding an anarchist, you deserved to be disappointed. Anarchists are peaceable, law abiding people. What do anarchists mean when they speak of anarchy? Webster gives the term two definitions—chaos and the state of being without political rule. We cling to the latter definition. Our enemies hold that we believe only in the former.

Do you wonder why there are anarchists in this country, in this great land of liberty, as you love to call it? Go to New York. Go through the by-ways and alleys of that great city. Count the myriads starving; count the multiplied thousands who are homeless; number those who work harder than slaves and live on less and have fewer comforts than the meanest slaves. You will be dumbfounded by your discoveries, you who have paid no attention to these poor, save as objects of charity and commiseration. They are not objects of charity, they are the victims of the rank injustice that permeates the system of government, and of political economy that holds sway from the Atlantic to the Pacific. Its oppression, the misery it causes, the wretchedness it gives birth to, are found to a greater extent in New York than elsewhere. In New York, where not many days ago two governments united in unveiling a statue of liberty, where a hundred bands played that hymn of liberty, 'The Marseillaise.' But almost its equal is found among the miners of the West, who dwell in squalor and wear rags, that the capitalists, who control the earth that should be free to all, may add still further to their millions! Oh, there are plenty of reasons for the existence of anarchists.

But in Chicago they do not think anarchists have any right to exist at all. They want to hang them there, lawfully or unlawfully. You have heard of a certain Haymarket meeting.* You have heard of a bomb. You have heard of arrests and of succeeding arrests effected by detectives. Those detectives! There is a set of men—nay, beasts—for you! Pinkerton detectives! They would do anything. I feel sure capitalists wanted a man to throw that bomb at the Haymarket meeting and have the anarchists blamed for it. Pinkerton could have accomplished it for him. You have heard a great deal about bombs. You have heard that the anarchists said lots about dynamite. You have been told that Lingg made bombs. He violated no law. Dynamite bombs can kill, can murder, so can Gatling guns. Suppose that bomb had been thrown by an anarchist. The constitution says there are certain inalienable

*For a thorough account of the bombing and its aftermath, see Paul Avrich, *The Haymarket Tragedy* (Princeton: Princeton University Press, 1984).

rights, among which are a free press, free speech and free assemblage. The citizens of this great land are given by the constitution the right to repel the unlawful invasion of those rights. The meeting at Haymarket square was a peaceable meeting. Suppose, when an anarchist saw the police arrive on the scene, with murder in their eyes, determined to break up that meeting, suppose he had thrown that bomb; he would have violated no law. That will be the verdict of your children. Had I been there, had I seen those murderous police approach, had I heard that insolent command to disperse, had I heard Fielden say, 'Captain, this is a peaceable meeting,' had I seen the liberties of my countrymen trodden under foot, I would have flung the bomb myself. I would have violated no law, but would have upheld the constitution.

If the anarchists had planned to destroy the city of Chicago and to massacre the police, why was it they had only two or three bombs in hand? Such was not their intention. It was a peaceable meeting. Carter Harrison, the mayor of Chicago, was there. He said it was a quiet meeting. He told Bonfield* to send the police to their different beats. I do not stand here to gloat over the murder of those policemen. I despise murder. But when a ball from the revolver of a policeman kills it is as much murder as when death results from a bomb.

The police rushed upon that meeting as it was about to disperse. Mr. Simonson talked to Bonfield about the meeting.† Bonfield said he wanted to do the anarchists up. Parsons went to the meeting. He took his wife, two ladies and his two children along. Toward the close of the meeting, he said, 'I believe it is going to rain. Let us adjourn to Zeph's hall.' Fielden said he was about through with his speech and would close it at once. The people were beginning to scatter about, a thousand of the more enthusiastic still lingered in spite of the rain. Parsons, and those who accompanied him started for home. They had gone as far as the Desplaine's street police station when they saw the police start at a double quick. Parsons stopped to see what was the trouble. Those 200 policemen rushed on to do the anarchists up. Then we went on. I was in Zeph's hall when I heard that terrible detonation. It was heard around the world. Tyrants trembled and felt there was something wrong.

The discovery of dynamite and its use by anarchists is a repetition of history. When gun-powder was discovered, the feudal system was at the height of its power. Its discovery and use made the middle classes. Its first discharge sounded the death knell of the feudal system. The bomb at Chicago sounded the downfall of the wage system of the nineteenth century. Why? Because I know no intelligent people will submit to despotism. The first means the diffusion of power. I tell no man to use it. But it was the

---

*Captain John Bonfield was the commander of the Desplaines Police Station who ordered the police assault on the Haymarket gathering.

†Barton Simonson testified that Bonfield complained to him shortly before the meeting that the anarchists always have "their women and children with them at meetings so the police could not get at them." See Avrich, *The Haymarket Tragedy*, 212.

achievement of science, not of anarchy, and would do for the masses. I suppose the press will say I belched forth treason. If I have violated any law, arrest me, give me a trial, and the proper punishment, but let the next anarchist that comes along ventilate his views without hindrance.

Well, the bomb exploded, the arrests were made and then came that great judicial farce, beginning on June 21. The jury was impaneled. Is there a Knight of Labor here? Then know that a Knight of Labor was not considered competent enough to serve on that jury. 'Are you a Knight of Labor?' 'Have you any sympathy with labor organizations?' were the questions asked each talisman. If an affirmative answer was given, the talisman was bounced. It was not are you a Mason, a Knight Templar? O, no! [Great applause.] I see you read the signs of the times by that expression. Hangman Gary, miscalled judge, ruled that if a man was prejudiced against the defendants, it did not incapacitate him for serving on the jury. For such a man, said Hangman Gary, would pay closer attention to the law and evidence and would be more apt to render a verdict for the defense. Is there a lawyer here? If there is he knows such a ruling is without precedent and contrary to all law, reason or common sense.

In the heat of patriotism the American citizen sometimes drops a tear for the nihilist of Russia. They say the nihilist can't get justice, that he is condemned without trial. How much more should he weep for his next door neighbor, the anarchist, who is given the form of trial under such a ruling.

There were 'squealers' introduced as witnesses for the prosecution. There were three of them. Each and every one was compelled to admit they had been purchased and intimidated by the prosecution. Yet Hangman Gary held their evidence as competent. It came out in the trial that the Haymarket meeting was the result of no plot, but was caused in this wise. The day before the wage slaves in McCormick's factory had struck for eight hours labor, McCormick, from his luxurious office, with one stroke of the pen by his idle, be-ringed fingers, turned 4,000 men out of employment. Some gathered and stoned the factory. Therefore they were anarchists, said the press. But anarchists are not fools; only fools stone buildings. The police were sent out and they killed six wage slaves. You didn't know that. The capitalistic press kept it quiet, but it made a great fuss over the killing of some policemen. Then these crazy anarchists, as they are called, thought a meeting ought to be held to consider the killing of six brethren and to discuss the eight hour movement. The meeting was held. It was peaceable. When Bonfield ordered the police to charge those peaceable anarchists, he hauled down the American flag and should have been shot on the spot.

While this judicial farce was going on the red and black flags were brought into court, to prove that the anarchists threw the bomb. They were placed on the walls and hung there, awful specters before the jury. What does the black flag mean? When a cable gram says it was carried through the streets of a European city it means that the people are suffering—that the men are out of work, the women starving, the children barefooted. But, you say, that is in Europe. How about America? The Chicago *Tribune* said there were 30,000 men in that city with nothing to do. Another authority said there were 10,000 barefooted children in mid-winter. The police said hundreds had no place to sleep or warm. Then President Cleveland issued his Thanksgiving proclamation and the anarchists formed in procession and carried the black flag to show that these thousands had nothing for which to return thanks. When the Board of Trade, that gambling den, was dedicated by means of a banquet, $30 a plate, again the black flag was carried, to signify that there were thousands who couldn't enjoy a 2 cent meal.

But the red flag, the horrible red flag, what does that mean? Not that the streets should run with gore, but that the same red blood courses through the veins of the whole human race.* It meant the brotherhood of man. When the red flag floats over the world the idle shall be called to work. There will be an end of prostitution for women, of slavery for man, of hunger for children.

Liberty has been named anarchy. If this verdict is carried out it will be the death knell of America's liberty. You and your children will be slaves. You will have liberty if you can pay for it. If this verdict is carried out, place the flag of our country at half mast and write on every fold 'shame.' Let our flag be trailed in the dust. Let the children of workingmen place laurels to the brow of these modern heroes, for they committed no crime. Break the two fold yoke. Bread is freedom and freedom is bread.■

116 MOB VIOLENCE

Samuel Allen McElwee

Born in slavery in 1858, Samuel Allen McElwee taught himself to read after the end of the Civil War. Attending school for the three months a year that his farm life would allow, McElwee thirsted for education. He entered Oberlin but was unable to meet the expenses. For years he struggled to gather the funds necessary to return to college, through teaching jobs and door-to-door sales of patent medicines. McElwee finally entered Fisk University in Nashville, graduated in 1882, and completed a law degree at Central Tennessee College in 1885.

*The account of Parsons's speech in the *Kansas City Times* (December 21, 1886) transcribes her as saying the red flag symbolizes "a common humanity, the same red blood whether that of the African or Caucasian."

McElwee was elected to the Tennessee state legislature in 1882, while he was still a student at Fisk, and was reelected in 1884 against a popular white opponent. He gained a reputation as a formidable orator and debater on the floor of the legislature and sponsored several successful bills. During his second term, he was nominated to be Speaker of the House. Although he did not win the Speaker's chair, McElwee was reelected in 1886. He was the last African American to serve in the Tennessee state legislature until 1965.

On February 23, 1887, McElwee took the floor of the Tennessee state legislature to speak on behalf of a proposed antilynching bill. His address failed to win passage of the bill but provided a powerful indictment of mob violence and of the complicity of the press through their inattention to the "new race war." "Great God," McElwee asks, "when will this nation treat the Negro as an American citizen!"

Excerpts from the speech were published in the Union, *a Nashville newspaper, and were reprinted in Reverend William J. Simmons,* Men of Mark: Eminent, Progressive and Rising *(1887).*

I t is remarkable to note the sameness with which all these reports read. It seems as if some man in this country had the patent by which these reports are written. Statistics do not show the number of Negroes who have in the past few years been sentenced in Judge Lynch's court, but judging from the number coming under our observation we are convinced that the number is most astounding. So prevalent and constant are the reports flashed over the country in regard to lynching of Negroes that we are forced to seek shelter with the poets and cry, "O for a lodge in some vast wilderness, some boundless contiguity of shade, where rumor of oppression and deceit, of successful or unsuccessful mobs might never reach me more." My ear is pained, my soul is sick with every day's report of wrong and outrage perpetrated upon the Negroes by mob violence. I am not here, Mr. Speaker, asking any special legislation in the interest of the Negroes, but in behalf of a race of outraged human beings. I stand here to-day and enter my most solemn protest against mob violence in Tennessee. Hundreds of Negroes, yes thousands, from all parts of this Southland, are to-day numbered with the silent majority, gone to eternity without a tomb to mark their last resting place, as the result of mob violence for crimes which they never committed. As we to-day legislate on this question, the spirits of the Negroes made perfect in the paradisiacal region of God, in convention assembled, with united voices, are asking the question, "Great God, when will this Nation treat the Negro as an American citizen, whether he be in Maine, among her tall pines, or in the South, where the magnolia blossoms grow?" Mr. Speaker, Tennessee should place the seal of eternal condemnation upon mob violence. "Your sins will find you out." The spirit of God will not always strive with man. For years, American slavery was the great sin of the Nation. In the course of time God made clear his disapproval of this National sin by a National calamity. Four years of destructive and bloody war rent our country in twain and left our Southland devastated. The war came as the result of sin; let us sin no more lest a greater calamity befall us. We have had several cases of mob violence in Tennessee within the past six months. The saying that "light itself is a great corrective," is as true as trite. What is the position of the public press on mob violence?

I stand here to-day, Mr. Speaker, as a member of this body and a lover of my people, and indict the public press of the State for condoning, by its silence, the wrongs and outrages perpetrated upon the Negroes of the State by mob violence. Who doubts for a moment but that the public press of the State could burn out mob violence in Tennessee as effectually as the mirrors of Archimedes burned the Roman ships in the harbor of Syracuse? Read the dailies and the majority of the weeklies, and you will find them on the mobs at Jackson, Dyersburg and McKenzie as dumb as an oyster. The mob at Dyersburg took place in broad day-light, and as the result of that mob hundreds of Negroes refused to attend the second annual exhibition of the West Tennessee Colored Fair Association, which was held at Dyersburg in October, 1886. The mob at Jackson is without a parallel in the annals of our State. Go with me, Mr. Speaker and gentlemen, to Jackson and look at that poor woman, with that weakness and tenderness common to women, as she is taken from the jail and followed by that motly crowd to the courtyard. The bell is rung, they enter the jail and strip her of every garment, and order her to march—buffeting, kicking, and spearing her with sharp sticks on the march. "She was led as a sheep to the slaughter; and like a lamb dumb before her shearer, so opened she not her mouth." She was swung up, her body riddled with bullets and orders issued not to interfere with her until after nine o'clock the next morning, in order that she might be seen. Men who spoke against it and said it was an outrage, had to leave town. Others who thought of giving vent to their feelings *en masse* by series of resolutions, were told that they had not better attempt it. Mr. Speaker, society prepares crime and the criminal is only the instrument by which it is accomplished.

I therefore again indict the public press and citizens of Madison county for the foul play upon the person of Eliza Wood, and hold them to a strict account before the bar of eternal justice for the wrong done. The mobs of Jackson, McKenzie and Dyersburg are mentioned because they are the most recent, not because they are exceptional or that we lack other examples. Grant, for the sake of argument, that these parties were guilty, does that make it right and accord with our principles of justice. When the citizens of Madison, Dyer and Carroll go to judgment with the blood of Eliza Wood, Matt Washington and Charles Dinwiddie on their garments, it will be more tolerable for Sodom and Gomorrah in that day than it will be for Jackson, Dyersburg and McKenzie. For two hundred and fifty years, Mr. Speaker, we were regarded as chattel. More than twenty years ago we were made citizens, and as such we ask at your hands that protection which is common to American citizens. The sainted Garfield told us to go home and make friends with our neighbors. We are here to-day knocking at your door and ask that you "entreat us not to leave you or return from following after you; for whither you go we will go, and where you lodge we will lodge; your people shall be our people, and your God our God; where you die will we die, and there will be buried; the Lord do so unto us, and more also, if aught but death part you and us." If this mob violence continues, its influence upon society will be worse than the malign influence which Cataline wielded over the reckless and abandoned youth of Rome. Mob violence is sowing in America a seed that will ripen in a conspiracy that will eclipse in gigantic proportions the great conspiracy of Cataline to lay Rome in ashes and deluge its streets in blood, for the purpose of enriching those who were to apply the torch and wield the dagger. Mr. Speaker, the time has passed in the history of this Nation for race wars. We cannot afford it. There are at present questions of very great importance demanding the attention of both races. They call for the united effort on the part of both. The labor question, tariff and public service are all important, the interest of the white man is the interest of the black man, that which hurts one will hurt the other; therefore, as a humble representative of the Negro race, and as a member of this body, I stand here to-day and wave the flag of truce between the races and demand a reformation in Southern society by the passage of this bill.■

117 WOMAN'S PLACE IN THE WORK OF THE DENOMINATION

Mary V. Cook

In the last two decades of the nineteenth century, black Baptist women worked to reshape the organizational structure of church society (resulting in the formation of the Women's Convention in 1900) and to fashion and promote a feminist theology. "Within this female-centered context," writes Evelyn Brooks Higginbotham, "they accentuated the theme of woman as saving force, rather than woman as victim; they thereby encouraged an aggressive womanhood that felt a personal responsibility to labor, no less than men, for the salvation of the world."*

Beginning in the 1880s, Virginia Broughton, Lucy Wilmot Smith, and

---

*Evelyn Brooks Higginbotham, "The Feminist Theology of the Black Baptist Church, 1880–1900," in Amy Swerdlow and Hannah Lessinger, eds., *Class, Race, and Sex: The Dynamics of Control* (Boston: G. K. Hall, 1983), 31.

Mary V. Cook used the forum of the male-dominated annual meetings of the American National Baptist Convention to make speeches on behalf of women's greater participation in the ministerial and social work of the church. They also strove to reshape theological understanding and depiction of women, through reinterpretation of biblical language and scholarly analysis of the lives and works of women.

Mary V. Cook of Kentucky was among the most erudite and militant of the black feminist theologians. She attended the State University in Louisville, graduating from the Normal Department in 1883. Upon her graduation as valedictorian of her class, she was made permanent professor of Latin and principal of the Normal Department, the largest in the university, while continuing her studies in classics. She graduated from the classical program in May 1887, three months before delivering the following address to the American National Baptist Convention in Mobile, Alabama, on August 26.

Like Maria Stewart more than half a century before, Cook in this address explicitly challenges St. Paul's injunction against the speaking of women. "All good causes owe their success to the push of woman," she reminds her listeners. She embraces both domestic and public spheres of women's works and expresses the call felt by many women "to lead into the paths of peace and righteousness. Should women be silent in this busy, restless world of missions and vast church enterprises? No! A long, loud No! Give place for her, brethren. Be ready to accept her praying heart, her nimble fingers, her willing hands, her swift feet, her quick eye, her charming voice, and the powers of her consecrated intellect. The pulpit, the pew, the choir, the superintendent's chair, the Sunday School teacher's place, the Bible student, the prayer circle, the sick bed, the house of mourning, the foreign mission field, all these are her place." Cook praises the Baptist church as the denomination most open to women's participation and most willing to give women access to its "platforms and deliberations." But this praise is also a goad to further action.

In the decade following this speech, Cook undertook extensive and well-received lecture tours, particularly in the Northeast, where her four-month tour in 1889 was sponsored by the American Baptist Woman's Home Mission Society of Boston. Writing in 1892, biographer L. A. Scruggs described Cook as "favorably known by almost all the leading men and women of the race in the country, and is more widely known, possibly, in the New England States than any other colored woman" (128).

The text of Cook's speech is taken from the Journal and Lectures of the Second Anniversary of the American National Baptist Convention *(1887), 45–56. A biographical sketch of Cook appears in L. A. Scruggs,* Women of Distinction: Remarkable in Works and Invincible in Character *(Raleigh, N.C.: L. A. Scruggs, 1892), 120–28. On the black Baptist women's movement, see Evelyn Brooks Higginbotham,* Righteous Discon-

tent: The Women's Movement in the Black Baptist Church, 1880–1920
(Cambridge, Mass.: Harvard University Press, 1993).

How pleasant it is to wander over, and enjoy this beautiful world God has made. Its green meadows, its beautiful fields, its dense forests with wild flowers and rippling streams, its wide expanse of water and lofty mountains all delight us. But while charmed with its beauty, our joy is greater if we can comprehend that it "was without form and void" and contrast its present beauty with the roughness of its former state. So in viewing the wonders of divine grace, we need to note its results in connection with what might have been, and before attempting to describe woman's work in the denomination and the great blessings God has bestowed upon her, we will first consider her condition when His gospel found her, that we may better appreciate the grace which wrought the change. Among all nations woman was degraded. Besides being bartered or sold as a thing of merchandise, there were barbarous laws and customs among the Phoenicians, Armenians, Carthaginians, Medes and Persians, and all too revolting and indecent to be mentioned. Greece, whose land abounded in scholars, heroes, and sages where the sun of intellect illumined the world, looked upon her as an object "without a soul." Gibbon says; "the Romans married without love, or loved without delicacy or respect."*

In China, Japan and Africa the condition is the same except where christianity has emancipated her. And wherever the religion of the true Messiah has spread its snowy white pinions and lighted up the deep dark recesses of man's heart, woman has been loved adored respected. I will not affirm that all virtue and joy were unknown: There are some fertile spots in the most arid deserts; there is light in the darkest places amid all this wickedness and infidelity. God has preserved the spark of faith, purity, and love. Though we live in the Nineteenth century, and have it in its beauty and strength, our own beloved America is not free from the curse. Modern Athens is not totally unlike ancient Athens.

The leaven of infidelity is infesting this land. Immoralities, indecencies and crimes as revolting as ever withered and blighted a nation are of usual occurrence. They fearlessly maintain their hold and flaunt their wicked banners in the face of the government which is either too corrupt to care, or to timid to oppose. Who is to wipe these iniquities from our land if it be not christian women? A reform in these things can not be effected by the ballot, by political station, or by mere supremacy of civil law. It must come by woman's unswerving devotion to a pure and undefiled christianity, for to that alone, woman owes her influence, her power and all she is. To establish this truth we will recount history as its light comes to us from the pages of

---

*Cook quotes Edward Gibbon (1737–1794), *The Decline and Fall of the Roman Empire* (1776).

the Bible. Fortunately the records of the past, present an array of heroic and saintly women whose virtues have made the world more tolerable; and chief among these are the wives, mothers and daughters of the Holy Scriptures.

In the formation of the world when the beasts of the field, the fowls of the air, the fish of the sea and the beautiful garden of Paradise were made for the happiness of man, and when man himself was made in the image of his Creator, God plucked Eve from the side of Adam "without childhood or growth" to be "a helpmeet for him." When Adam first looked upon her he was enraptured with the perfectness of her form, the splendor of her beauty, the purity of her countenance and in this excess of joy he exclaimed: "bone of my bone, flesh of my flesh; therefore shall a man leave his father and mother and shall cleave unto his wife." They knew naught but divine happiness. Their hearts were filled with pure love unsullied by sin, but alas! in a short time the scene was changed—Eve was tempted—partook of the forbidden fruit and gave to Adam and he did eat. In this fallen state they were driven from the garden, yet she proved still a helpmeet for her husband, sharing his sorrow as she had shared his joy. Many have been the reproaches uttered against her—few have been her defenders. Dr. Pendleton says: "Eve acting under a mistake and a delusion was by no means excusable, but Adam was far more inexcusable than she for he acted intelligently as well as voluntarily. He knew what he was doing." There is much to admire in the character of Sarah, wife of Abraham, her reverence for her husband; her devotion to her son; her faithfulness to duty; her willingness in its performance. She was beautiful, chaste, modest and industrious—all these she sacrificed for the good and welfare of those around her. It was in this family God preserved the seed of righteousness. Also we find Miriam cheering on the hosts of Israel with her timbrel in her hands as she uttered the songs of praise "Sing, sing ye to the Lord, for he has triumphed gloriously, the horse and his rider hath he thrown into the sea."God's thought and appreciation of woman's work appears when he appoints Deborah to be a warrior, judge and prophet. Her work was distinct from her husband's who, it seems took no part whatever in the work of God while Deborah was inspired by the Eternal expressly to do His will and to testify to her countrymen that He recognizes in His followers neither male nor female, heeding neither the "weakness" of one, nor the strength of the other, but strictly calling those who are perfect at heart and willing to do his bidding. She was a woman of much meekness and humility, but of great force of character. Her song of praise, when Israel overcame the enemy, has only been excelled by the Psalms of David: "and Israel had rest forty years." Mention might also be made of Huldah, wife of Shallum, who dwelt in Jerusalem in a college, to whom went Hilkiah, the priest, and Ahikam, and Achbor and Shapham and Asaiah to enquire concerning the words of the book that was found in the house of the Lord. It was a woman whom God had chosen as a medium between Him and His people who would faithfully report all that he desired. Huldah's dwelling in college shows that she was anxious to become familiar with the law—to better prepare herself for the work of Him Who had called her. Woman's faith and devotion are beautifully illustrated by the touching scene between Ruth and Naomi, when Naomi besought Ruth to return to the home of her birth, thinking that the pleasure of childhood days had endeared it to her, and when Ruth with that pathos of devotion, and fairness said: "Entreat me not to leave thee, or to return from following after thee: For whither thou goest, I will go; and where thou lodgest, I will lodge; thy people shall be my people and thy God my God; where thou diest I will die, and there will I be buried; the Lord do so to me and more too if aught but death part thee and me." We cannot forget the maternal tenderness of Hagar, the well kept promise of Hannah, the filial devotion of Jephthah's daughter, nor the queenly patriotism of Esther. But no woman bore such recognition as Mary the mother of Jesus, who was chosen to bear a prominent part in human regeneration. After the fall of our first parents, God promised that a virgin should bear a son who should be the Redeemer of the human race. The memory of this promise was preserved through all nations, and each was desirous of the honor. The story of the birth of Romulus and Remus coincides with the miraculous birth of Jesus Christ. Silvia became their mother by the God Mars, even as Christ was the son of the Holy Ghost. An effort was made to take the life of these boys by throwing the cradle which contained them into the river Arnio, whence it was carried into the Tiber. The cradle was stranded at the foot of Palatine and the infants were carried by a she-wolf into her den where they were tenderly cared for. This escape is likened to the flight into Egypt, and while this story has become a myth, the birth of Christ becomes more and more a reality. There are others who claim this mysterious birth. The most revered goddess of the Chinese sprung from the contact of a flower. Buddha was claimed to have been borne by a virgin named Maha-Mahai, but none realized the power of the words spoken by the angel, *"Hail full of grace, the Lord is with thee! Blessed are thou among women,* save Mary." History and tradition tell us she excelled all her young companions in her intelligence and skill. Denis, the Areopagite says: "She was a dazzling beauty." St. Epiphanius, writing in the fourth century, from traditions and manuscripts says: ["]In stature she was above the medium, her hair was blonde; her face oval; her eyes bright and slightly olive in color; her eyebrows perfectly arched, her nose equaline and of irreproachable perfection and her lips were ruby red. The ardent sun of her country had slightly bronzed her complexion; her hands were long, her fingers were slender" as a virgin she honored one of the most beautiful virtues of woman; as a mother she nourished a Redeemer. She gave the world an example of non-excelled maternal devotion; of the most magnificent grief which history affords. The life of Christ furnishes many examples of woman's work, love and devotion. They took part in the Savior's work, followed Him on His journeys, believed on Him and loved Him. They were "last at the cross and first at the grave." Christ did certainly atone for the sins of man, but His mission to woman was a great deal more; for He has not only saved her soul, but actually brought out and cultivated her intellect for the good of His cause. He was her friend, her counselor and her Savior. She bathed His feet with her tears and wiped them with the hairs of her head. He found comfort in the home of Mary and Martha when burdened, or tired from a day's journey. At the well of Samaria He converses with a woman which was unlawful for a man of respect to do, but He not only talked with her but permitted her to do good for mankind and the advancement of His cause. Filled with enthusiasm she leaves her water pot and hastens to proclaim her loyalty to One Who had won her heart and spoken to her of "living water." She testified that she had seen the true Messiah and invites others to see Him for themselves. To Mary Magdalene was the commission given to bear the joyful intelligence that Jesus had risen. It was the women more than men whose faith ventured to show Jesus those personal kindnesses which our Lord ever appreciated. In the lives and acts of the Apostles women are discovered praying, prophesying and spreading the gospel. Prominent for good works and alms deeds which she did was Dorcas. Like the Savior she went about doing good, but in the midst of this usefulness she died and so great was the grief of the widows unto whom she had ministered that the Lord again restored her to them. Paul placed much value on the work of Phebe and commends her to the churches as "our sister." Phebe was a deaconess of the church of Cenchrea and was, no doubt a great helper of Paul's "in the gospel." In the letter she carries to Rome, mention is made of quite a number of women who had been co-workers with the apostle. One of the first on the list was Priscilla, the wife of Aquilla who had with her husband laid down her neck for him. She possessed high qualities and did active work in the cause which she espoused. Lydia was the first European convert—after she received the word into her heart; at once opens her house and offers a home to the apostle who had been instrumental in her conversion. At Thessalonica we find "the chief women not a few" among the workers of the church. The church today wants more Priscillas, Phebes, Chloes, Elizabeths, Marys, Annas, Tryphenas, Tryphosas, Julias and Joannas to labor in the gospel; to give of their substance; to follow Jesus; to be willing to sacrifice their substance; to follow Jesus; to be willing to sacrifice their lives for the love they bear their Lord. It is not christianity which disparages the intellect of woman and scorns her ability for doing good, for its records are filled with her marvelous successes. Emancipate woman from the chains that now restrain her and who can estimate the part she will play in the work of denomination? In the Baptist denomination women have more freedom than in any other denomination on the face of the earth. I am not unmindful of the kindness you noble brethren have exhibited in not barring us from your platforms and deliberations. All honor I say to such men. Every woman in the world ought to be a Baptist, for in this blessed denomination men are even freer than elsewhere. Free men cannot conscientiously shut the doors against those whom custom has limited in privileges and benefits. As the vitalizing principles of the Baptists expand and permeate the religious principles of the world women will become free. As the Bible is an iconoclastic weapon—it is bound to break down images of error that have been raised. As no one studies it so closely as the Baptists their women shall take the lead. History gives a host of women who have achieved and now enjoy distinction as writers, linguists, poets, physicians, lecturers, editors, teachers and missionaries. Visit the temples of the living God and there you will find them kneeling at His shrine as ready now as in centuries past, to attest their faith by their suffering and if need be by the sacrifice of life. As they by their numbers, who followed Christ up Calvary's rugged road, caused the cowardice of man to blush, so in the crowds of worshippers who do Him honor to-day put to shame the indifference and the coldness of man's allegiance to God. But to the limited subject,

WHAT IS DENOMINATIONAL WORK?

I deem it to be the most honorable, the most exalted and the most enviable. It strengthens the link between the church militant and the church triumphant—between man and his Creator. All Woman who are truly christians are candidates in this broad field of labor. It calls for valiant hearted women who will enlist for life. None whose soul is not overflowing with love for Christ and whose chief aim is not to save souls need apply. Success need not necessarily depend on learning, genius, taste, style, elegant language, nor a rapid use of the tongue, but it is the earnestness of the soul, the simplicity of the Word accompanied by the Spirit of the living God. The Maker of all has wisely distributed these talents and whatever characterizes the individual He has commanded to "to occupy till I come" and to use well the talent entrusted to your care. It often happens that some humble woman bent on her staff full of fervor yet unlettered, does more by her upright living, her words of counsel, her ardent prayers "that go up to God as a sweet smelling savor" than many who pick their words and try to appear learned. This denominational work demands active labor in and for the churches. It does not demand that every woman shall be a Deborah, a Huldah, a Dorcas, or a Peebe [Phoebe?]—It simply asks that every woman be a woman—a christian woman who is willing to consecrate all for the cause of Christ. A story is told of a woman who when she was unable to express intelligently and satisfactorily what the Lord had done for her and when the anxious crowd was about to turn away disappointed she exclaimed: "I cannot talk for Him, but I can die for Him." "Whosoever will lose his life for my sake, the same shall save it." To serve the church we must die daily to selfishness, pride, vanity, a lying tongue, a deceitful heart and walk worthy of the calling in Christ Jesus. We are to pray without ceasing—to be fervent in season and out of season—"to present our bodies a living sacrifice, holy and acceptable before God which is our reasonable service." We are to speak as the spirit shall give utterance, that He may work in us to will and to do His good pleasure. I know Paul said "Let the woman keep silence in the churches" but because he addressed this to a few Grecian and Asiatic woman who were wholly given up to idolatry and the fashion of the day is no reason why it should be quoted to the pious women of the present. A woman may suffer martyrdom, she may lift her voice in song, she may sacrifice modesty to collect money from the church, for her work in this particular is considered essential and it matters not how prominent a place she occupies in fairs, festivals, sociables, tea parties, concerts and tableaux, but to take part in the business meeting of the church is wholly out of place because Paul said so. We are apt to quote Paul and shut our eyes and ears to the recognition and privilege Christ, his Master, gave, us, and not only did the Apostle appreciate the labors of women, and show towards them the greatest care and tenderest affection, but we find him in some places greatly dependent upon them, for co-operation in the foundation of the churches. But a change is coming; it has already commenced, and God is shaking up the church—He is going to bring it up to something better and that, too, greatly through the work of the women. Already the harvest is great. Can ye not discern the signs of the time? Do you not see how wickedness and crime are flooding our country—how tares are growing up in the midst of the wheat? See the foothold the Catholics are getting in our christian land. They are taking our children putting clothes on their backs, food in their mouths and educating them that they must swell their number and represent their claim. See how nations, every where, are opening to the reception of the gospel. Listen to the cry of Africa's heathen sons—note the rush of other denominations to offer their faith, their belief, to satisfy the hunger of their souls and quench the thirst of their spirits. Can ye not discern the signs? It is quite time christian soldiers were taking the field for Christ. The doctrines of our denomination must be so thoroughly diffused that a man though he be a fool need not err. A good pastor should have a good wife. He should find in her rest from care; comfort when distressed; his depressed spirits must be lifted by her consoling words; she must be his wisdom; his courage; his strength; his hope; his endurance. She is to beautify his home and make it a place of peace and cheerfulness—she is to be an example worthy of pattern for the neighborhood in which she lives—she is to take the lead in all worthy causes. Women are to look after the spiritual interest of the church as well as the men. Let them be punctual at services and make the prayer meeting interesting. Woman's power of song, her heartfelt prayer, her ability to go into the highways and hedges and compel singers to come in, have marked her as proficient in revivals. A praying mother exerts more influence over the minds of the youth than all else. The recollections of such seasons when the tender plants were garnered in can never be effaced. The voice of that sainted mother still lingers upon them, and memory can never relinquish the priceless treasure she holds. Some of our best men owe their conversion and all that they are to the influence of a sainted mother, a devoted sister or some dear female friend. For money raising woman has no equals.

Our churches are largely supported by her financial efforts, but she should discountenance many of the plans to which she and her daughters are subjected—they are gates of vice that lead to destruction—this begging money from any and every body only invites and encourages insults and it must be stopped. Our churches must have some system in money raising and thereby save the girls. Many a girl with good intent got her start downward by this very act of soliciting money. A woman's place is to assist the pastor, work in the Sabbath school, visit the sick, to care for the sick and lift up the fallen. She has a conspicuous place in

THE NEWSPAPER WORK OF THE DENOMINATION,

which is a powerful weapon for breaking down vice, establishing virtue, spreading the gospel and disseminating a general knowledge of the work of the denomination. Here she can command the attention of thousands. She can thunder from the editor's chair and make the people hear. It has a wider circulation and as has been said "penetrates the most remote corners of the country." In this field we need strong intellectual women. We need women of courage, who dare defend the faith and make the truth felt. As an editor a woman can better reach the mothers, daughters and sisters. Let her be a regular correspondent. Let the articles be strong and vigorous, let them show thought, learning and an earnestness for the cause represented. If she cannot be a regular correspondent she should write occasionally such articles as will give the people something to think and talk about. She should make them so plain and attractive that children will read them with eagerness and let some be especially to them; make them feel that some one else is interested in them besides mother and father and endeavor to impress them with upright living. Assist the editor in getting subscribers and see that a Baptist paper is in every home. See that the Baptist family reads your denominational paper.

The field of juvenile literature is open. I said recently before the National Press Convention, held in Louisville Ky. there are now published 24 secular papers and magazines in the United States for the children with a circulation of 775,934. The largest of which is the "Youth's Companion" with a circulation of 385,251. Of the religious journals there are 47 with 678,346 circulation. Sunday School Journal (Methodist) claim 81,090: "The Sunday School Times" 77,5000 [sic] and "Our Young People" 47,000. Of this number, 71 secular and religious papers, there is not one so far as I know, edited especially for colored children. There is a little paper whose name does not appear on the list that is written for the colored youth, being edited and controlled by Miss J. P. Moore of Louisiana. It is known as "Hope" and though of humble pretentions, in its silent way it is sowing seed from which shall spring an abundant harvest.

The educational work of the denomination belongs principally to woman. Three centuries ago women were almost universally uneducated and a half century ago found American women shut out from all places of learning. Ignorance seemed a bliss while wisdom a foolish idea. A young girl in Italy and a young widow in France almost simultaneously conceived the idea of educating young girls. It was the beginning of an institution that was destined to reform the world and this they comprehended, for they said "This regeneration of this corrupt world must be accomplished by children, for children will reform the families, families will reform the provinces and the provinces will reform the world." Mademoiselle de Sainte-Beuve, foundress of the "Ursilines" of France, purchased a house at the Faubourg St. Jacques where she had two hundred pupils. It was her delight to watch them in their sport and as she looked upon them with maternal gaze she charmingly said "They sprung not from her loins, but from her heart." At her death her portrait represented her before a window, her eyes fixed with intent devotion upon a garden full of beehives, with the legend "Mother of Bees." Mary Lyons, in our own century, opened the way, and established Mount Holly Seminary, the first institution established for girls.* This is what woman has done, and may not our women do ever more for the denomination with the surrounding advantages? May they not found more "Spelman" and "Hartshorn" seminaries, more "Vassars?"† The women have been promoted from mere kitchen drudgery, household duties, and gossiping from house to house—they can teach not as subordinates merely, but as principals, as professors. Woman has not only the art of inspiring the affections in her pupils, but also in keeping them interested in the tasks to be performed. I think the duty of our women is to impressibly teach the Scriptures and the doctrines of our denomination to the young under their care. I think we talk and preach baptism, "The Lord's Supper," and the "Final Perseverance of the Saints," too little. Not one-half of the members of our churches can give a doctrinal reason why they are Baptists. We are too fearful of feelings, when we have the Bible that makes the Baptist churches on our side. They should instill in the child's mind love toward God, his Creator, his Benefactor, his Saviour, and respect for all mankind.

As an author, woman has shown rare talents. The profession of mind affords the strongest evidence that God created her for society. As the fragrance which is in the bud will, when the bud expands, escape from its confinement and diffuse itself through the surrounding atmosphere, so if forms of beauty and sublimity are in the mind, they will exhibit themselves, and operate on other minds. The genius of woman was long hidden. Greece had a Sappho and a Carina; Israel had a Miriam. Antiquity turned a deaf ear to the cultivation of woman's talent. The home of Cicero and Virgil neglected her intellect, but the revolution of ages and the progress of the present century have wrought a new change of affairs, and now woman has the pen, and participates in the discussion of the times. It was when Christianity and infidelity were wrestling in Europe, that Hannah More‡ came from retirement to take part in the contest. It was when slavery was at its highest, that Phillis Wheatly, Francis Ellen Harper, and Harriet Beecher Stowe, gave vent to their fullness of their souls in beautiful lines of poetry and prose. The human voice is fast receding; the written voice predominates. Since this is true, let

---

*Mary Lyon founded Mount Holyoke Seminary in 1837.

†Vassar College for women was founded in 1865; Spelman, a pioneer college for black women, was founded as a seminary in 1881.

‡Hannah More (d. 1833) anonymously published *Thoughts on the Importance of the Manners of the Great* in 1788, sparking much debate about which great male thinker of the day had written the work. Her authorship was later revealed, and she became a popular novelist.

the women see that the best and purest literature comes from them. Let them feel that they are called upon to consecrate all to truth and piety. Lecturers address the people through the sense of hearing; writing through the sense of sight. Many persons will pay goodly sums to hear a good talk on some subject, rather than spend the time investigating books. As public lecturers women have been successful, and have secured good audiences. Rev. Mr. Higginson* says: "Among the Spanish Arabs women were public lecturers and secretaries of kings, while Christian Europe was sunk in darkness. In Italy, from the fifteenth to the nineteenth century, it was not esteemed unfeminine for women to give lectures in public to crowded and admiring audiences. They were freely admitted members of learned societies, and were consulted by men of prominent scientific attainments as their equals in scholarship."

All good causes owe their success to the push of woman. The temperance cause had its origin in her, and to-day finds noble advocates in the persons of Frances E. Harper and Frances E. Willard.[†] Indeed, the place of woman is broad, and of the vocations of life none are so grand, so inspiring, as that of being a missionary. Long before the organization of any general missionary society of our denomination in this country, Christian women were actively engaged in prosecuting the work of home missions. Little bands of women organized in the churches to help the pastors in the poor churches, by sending clothing and other supplies needed. When the Foreign Mission Enterprise was begun, it found in these women ready and powerful allies— they sent up contributions annually for both Home and Foreign work. The first missionary society ever organized in the country was by the women in 1800. It was composed of fourteen women. From this many branches sprang. The women of to-day are realizing that in the homes among the degraded there is a great work to be done. It belongs to woman's tender nature, sympathy, and love, to uplift the fallen. A home can not be raised above the mother, nor the race above the type of womanhood, and no women are more ready to respond to the call than the women of the Baptist Church. They feel the necessity of meeting the responsibility with organized forces in the field. Many have been effected, and great has been the result.

This work is not exclusively confined to the churches, but to orphans, asylums, hospitals, prisons, alms-houses, on the street, in the home, up the alley, and in all places where human souls are found, have woman, with her love for Christ and fallen humanity, found her way, amid the jeers and scorn of those who were too foolish to care for any other save self and household.

Woman sways a mighty influence. It began with Eve in the Garden of Eden, and is felt even now. It has not been exaggerated nor exhausted. She

*Thomas Wentworth Higginson (1823–1911) was an outspoken abolitionist and advocate of women's suffrage.
†Willard (1839–1898) was president of the Woman's Christian Temperance Union (WCTU); poet, novelist, suffragist, and former antislavery lecturer Frances E. W. Harper (1825–1911) was president of the WCTU's Colored Division.

exalts man to the skies, or casts him beneath the brutes. She makes him strong or she makes him weak. Under her influence nations rise or fall. In the dark days of Rome, when woman received her most cruel treatment from the hand of her lord, Cato said: "Even then the Romans governed the world, but the women governed the Romans."

Bad women sometimes have great power with men. It was Phryne who inspired the chisel of Praxiteles. Cotytto had her altars at Athens and Corinth under the title of "Popular Venus." Aspasia decided peace or war, directing the counsel of Pericles. Demosthenes, the great orator, cast himself at the feet of Lais, and history gives scores of instances where women governed the passions of men for good or evil. It was Delilah who, by her words, persuaded Sampson to tell wherein his strength lay, and which Milton has so beautifully portrayed in these words:

> "Of what I suffer, she was not the prime cause, but I myself,
> Who vanquished with a peal of words (Oh, weakness)!
> Gave up my forte of silence to a woman."

It came to pass when Solomon was old, that his wives turned away his heart after other gods, and his heart was not perfect with the Lord his God, as was the heart of his father, David. There was none like unto Ahab, who did sell himself to work wickedness in the sight of God, whom Jezebel, his wife, stirred up. There are good women like Volumna, the mother of Coriolanus, who saved Rome by her influence over her son. The women of this country inspired the fathers and sons on to battle, and in all the affairs of life woman has encouraged or discouraged men; he is moved by her faintest smile, her lightest whisper. The Duke of Halifax says: "She has more strength in her looks than we have in our laws, and more power by hers than we have in our arguments." Though woman is a mixture of good and evil, be it said to her credit, that history has never recorded a single instance where she denied her Saviour. Her influence is entwined with every religion, and diffuses itself through every circle where there is mind to act upon. It gives tone to religion and morals and forms the character of man. Every woman is the center around which others move. She may send forth healthy, purifying streams, which will enlighten the heart and nourish the seeds of virtue; or cast a dim shadow, which will enshroud those upon whom it falls in moral darkness. Woman should consecrate her beauty, her wit, her learning, and her all, to the cause of Christ. She should put aside selfishness, for a selfish person is not only hideous, but fiendish, and destructive. She should not rest at ease, heedless of the perishing souls who need her prayers, her songs of praise, her words of counsel, her interpretations of the Scriptures for their salvation. Many a conversion has been attributed to some soul-stirring song; indeed, there is no music so penetrating, so effective as that produced by the human voice. Much good has been accomplished by a well written tract commending some word of God, which has certainly not returned unto Him void, but has prospered in the thing whereunto God sent it. Often a short article, setting forth some digestible truth, is like seed sown in good ground, which will bring forth a hundred fold, or like bread cast upon the water, that may be seen and gathered after many days hence.

Perhaps the most important place of woman in the denomination is to teach the children at home, and wherever she can reach them, to love God, to reverence His holy name, and to love the Baptist Church. The moral training of the youth is the highest kind, and it is of vast importance that the first opportunity be seized for installing into the minds of children the sentiment of morality and religion, and the principles of the Baptist doctrine. The future of the denomination depends on the rising generation, and too much care can not be taken in the development of their characters. It requires constant, anxious watching to realize the embryo. Though the seed be long buried in dust, it shall not deceive your hopes—"the precious gain shall never be lost, for grace insures the crop."

The only foundation for all Christian graces is humility. Practice, as far as possible, Christ's meekness, his benevolence, his forgiveness of injuries, and his zeal for doing good. Woman is the hope of the Church, the hope of the world. God is slowly but surely working out the great problem of woman's place and position in life. Virtue will never reign supreme, and vice will never be wiped from the land, until woman's work of head, heart, and hand is recognized and accepted. No great institution has flourished without her support, neither has man succeeded without her, but the two must be unified. The work is not confined within the narrow limits of the church walls, not to the prayers sent forth or the songs sung. It extends far beyond this. Her work is in every cause, place, and institution where Christianity is required. The platform is broad, and upon it she must stand. Although the responsibilities to be met are great, the position is to be maintained. China, with her degraded million, India, with her ignorance and idolatry, dark and benighted Africa, yea, the world, with its sin and wickedness, all have just and imperative claims on woman, such as she can and must meet.

Dear women, the cry comes to us from afar to bring the light of love, and to lead into the paths of peace and righteousness. From your ranks, as mother, wife, daughter, sister, friend, little as you have hitherto thought of it, are to come the women of all professions, from the humble Christian to the expounder of His word; from the obedient citizen to the ruler of the land. This may be objectionable to many, but no profession should be recognized that fails to recognize Christ, and all the Christians have a legal right where He is, for "with Him there is neither Jew nor Greek, there is neither bond nor free, there is neither male nor female, for ye are all one in Christ Jesus." There is no necessity for a woman to step over the bounds of propriety, or to lay aside modesty, to further the work, and she will not, if God be her guide. If, indeed, the King of all the Universe chooses a woman to kill a man who had opposed Israel for twenty years, it is all right, and who dare question God's right, if he raise up a woman who shall become a judge, and a leader of his people? God, at one time, used a dumb brute to do His service, and that alone is sufficient to convince any one that He can use whom He will, and glorify himself by whatever means he pleases to employ. Should woman be silent in this busy, restless world of missions and vast church enterprises? No! A long, loud No! Give place for her, brethren. Be ready to accept her praying heart, her nimble fingers, her willing hands, her swift feet, her quick eye, her charming voice, the superintendent's chair, the Sunday School teacher's place, the Bible student, the prayer circle, the sick bed, the house of mourning, the foreign mission field, all these are her place.

Dear brethren, point them out, direct my sisters, and help them to work for Christ. My dear sisters, wherever you are, and wherever this paper may be mentioned, remember that there is no department of your life that you can not bend your influence to the benefit of our blessed denomination. Let us take sharpness out of our tongues and put in our pens; take the beauty from our face and put it into our lives; let us love ourselves less and God more; work less for self-aggrandizement, and more for the Church of Christ.

> "Do not then stand idly waiting,
>   For some greater work to do,
> Fortune is a lazy goddess—
>   She will never come to you.
>
> "Go, and toil in any vineyard,
>   Do not fear to do and dare;
> If you want a field of labor,
>   You can find it anywhere." ■

118 HOW SHALL WE GET OUR RIGHTS?

Reverend M. Edward Bryant

On December 4, 1887, the African American citizens of Selma, Alabama, celebrated the anniversary of the Emancipation Proclamation and the Thirteenth Amendment. The Reverend M. Edward Bryant, an editor and minister of that city, delivered an address that militantly advocated uniting all African Americans in favor of complete freedom. His speech is noteworthy for its emphasis on the need for unity of oppressed people, regardless of color, against their exploiters, for its support of labor unions, and for its call for resistance to violence and for the building of black economic and political power. Bryant identifies

the industrialist "robber barons" of the late nineteenth century as the
modern descendants of the slaveholders and "the colored and poor
whites" as trapped in "a system worse than slavery." Yet, he advises,
"the Negro has great latent power," and Bryant advocates a plan of
specific actions by which "to use this power wisely."

The address presented here in part has been taken from the text that
appeared in the Christian Recorder, *January 19, 1888.*

IT BELONGS to us and to our children with strong propriety to celebrate this day. We see around us thousands of blessings which force emotions inexpressible in words and actions, which call upon us in the still small voice of gratitude and in the thunder tones of race pride and race appreciation to celebrate the day with songs, music, marches, acclamations, prayers and sermons. . . . But when we revisit the old plantation and the "nigger quarters" and in imagination hear the baying of the "nigger hounds," the low, brutal cursings of the overseer, and see the "nigger lash"; when we again pass through and by the swamps where we used to hide as "runaway niggers"; when we behold the fields fertilized with, and since cursed, by our spilled blood and that of our fathers and mothers—these things call upon us to do more than rejoice. They call upon us to bring our children to the altar, as Hamilcar did his son Hannibal, and make them swear never to rest contented night nor day until the tyrannical spirit of oppression which yet lingers in this land and the sprouts of the deadly upas tree of slavery shall be plucked up by root and branch, and a man and a woman shall be known, by the way they conduct themselves, without regard to color.

Let the world know that we prefer death by assassination, by drowning, by fire, by wild beasts, as the martyrs in the Middle Ages, as the Haitians under Toussaint, as the Americans under the British, to such liberty as we have today. The white fathers died that their children might be free. Does the Negro love *his* children?

Against that honest class of whites who are in favor of giving us our rights I have nothing to say but praise. Neither do I plead for war or resort to force, but a fixed, unyielding, unalterable determination to defend ourselves when attacked and to petition, persuade and demand our rights whatever may be the consequences. They would die before they would endure what we are enduring. History proves this. . . .

This is a day of great rejoicing and thanksgiving with us, and rightly so. But the Negro is yet to create his own national thanksgiving and celebration day by some mighty achievements of his own. He is yet to march his own army across the Red Sea and erect his own monuments, and his own poets are yet to compose and sing his own triumphal songs. . . .

What kind of government is this under which we live today? . . . The fathers of this country who wrote and laid down their lives for the grand, godlike proposition, "All men are created equal," were martyrs to the freedom of the earth. Today we honor them. But descendants of these almost-inspired men have disgraced their fathers and have followed in the track of the ancient doctrines that "might makes right," until they plunged this country into the cursed system of slavery which has brought the curse of almighty God upon this land—plunged it into civil internecine war and nearly destroyed the government of the fathers. Not yet satisfied, these descendants are still trying to perpetuate a system worse than slavery upon the colored and poor whites of this country which threatens the curse of God again upon this land. The laborers of this country are oppressed and downtrodden. In the North, the Goulds,* Vanderbilts,† are the oppressors and tyrants. In the South, the legislatures, social system, landowners, advance houses and in fact two thirds of the whites are the usurpers, tyrants, oppressors. . . .

The Negro is so treated today in regard to his civil, political and social rights in many parts that any condition would be preferable to his present condition. That in this country and under this government all men are created equal, is especially in the South a lie. It is a lie in our courts, it is a lie on railroads and steamboats; it is a lie in hotels; it is a lie in the streets, woods; it is a lie as it flaunts to the breezes on sea and in foreign parts; it is a lie in church; it is a lie at the sacrament table; it is a lie at the dying bed; a lie with the dead; a lie in the graveyard; it is a lie everywhere.

We are robbed, swindled, cheated, assassinated, falsely imprisoned, lynched, told to stand back and every indignity heaped upon us. The future will tell a sad story if this is continued. . . .

The dominant race up to this very moment insist upon describing the limits, prescribing the prerogatives of colored Americans. They say, you can't enter this car, you can't vote here, you can't work here, you shall not publish newspapers to stir up niggers concerning their rights, you can't hold office. Your wives and children and property shall not have the same protection we have. I do not advocate force. The logic of peace should be exhausted before any appeal is made to force. But we should have an intelligent understanding of what are our rights, and then we should have the courage to maintain and defend those rights. We should contend for our rights on every ground and protect them against outrage. The man or the party who attempts to abridge our rights, crush our manhood and womanhood because of our color, must be looked upon as robbers, villains, usurpers, tyrants.

A lot of fools have advanced the theory that "if we give the Negro his civil and political rights this will bring about social equality." What are civil rights? "All such as affect the whole people are regulated by them in their collective capacity as a government." "Social rights" are regulated wholly by individual tastes and inclinations. Social equality can never arise except by the consent of the parties themselves. We want civil and political rights. We

*Jay Gould (1836–1892) was a wealthy railroad financier well known for his unscrupulous practices.

†Cornelius Vanderbilt (1794–1877) was a steamship and railroad baron, owner of the New York Central Railroad.

helped to develop this country and are doing so now. We pay taxes and it is one of your laws that taxation without representation is tyranny. What should the Negro be advised to do under the circumstances?

1. Join the Knights of Labor and every other organization which promises to struggle to bring about a revolution and reformation in our affairs.

2. Organize leagues to raise money to prosecute railroads, steamboats, stores, hotels, and every one who tries to abridge our rights.

3. Organize leagues, not to create confusion, but to defend ourselves when attacked, just as the whites have always done.

4. Trade with your own business houses and those white men only who treat us right.

5. Never work any man's land who in any way abridges or helps to abridge our rights.

6. Support your own newspapers and never those who seek every opportunity to throw mud at us. No one can tell what and how much good our newspapers are doing to uplift the race.

7. Build schools everywhere, controlled and taught by yourselves, where true manhood and womanhood are taught. You need never expect a Negro child to be properly taught in a school which Southern white people control. His education and training and avarice disqualify him for the work.

Do you say you are afraid to try these things? Every true man despises a coward. His own children learn to hate him. His wife ought to leave him. "Eternal vigilance is the price of liberty." . . . We want honest, intelligent, temperance, levelheaded, common-sense leaders who cannot be bought, and these leaders want followers who cannot be bought.

The colored people are waking up. A new race is coming on the stage. These persons are realizing that they must, through actual acquirements, succeed to their places in the affairs of this nation. We must take our cause in our hands very largely. We must press it in the social, civil, literary, artistic and business circles. Yes, we must press it everywhere. Congress, United States Commissioners, Supreme Court, President, have virtually said they cannot enforce the laws in the states. The Negro must stop whining and crying because the powers will not protect him. Wipe away tears, hush crying, be a man, protect himself, then go to law.

Has the Negro the power to carry out the above measures? The Negro has great latent power. He only needs to learn how to use this power wisely. The Negro is the laborer, the producer of this country. All professions, and business enterprises depend to a large extent upon agriculture. Let the Negro own his own homes, stock, control all products which are made by the race. . . . Then let race unite into one solid compact, and then ally itself with other suffering peoples as opportunities offer, and join the parties needing and bidding for his votes. Let him do away with political demagogues and select his best men as leaders and there will be a mighty revolution in this land. . . . The result will be that the great business houses which directly and indirectly are supported by us will go down and their owners must go to work or go somewhere else. In either case they will grow weaker and we stronger and stronger. . . . We can and must undermine our oppressors by controlling our own moneys until "All men are created equal" becomes a truth in this land.

Let me state here that some white people may think my remarks are severe. But let me state: all such must remember that I am a southerner by birth and education and have inherited from my ancestors as much of the chivalric blood as they have. Secondly, I have read their histories and learned how to act and what to advise from them themselves. If they want to understand me let them take their wife and children and put them in the place of mine and let them take my place. . . .

Colored men of America, we have made great advances, but we have not reached Canaan. We must still contend against the Amalekites, Hittites, Hivites and Philistines. May the God who presides over the destinies of nations help us to work out our destiny. Physical slavery has fallen. Let us unite to break the chains of prejudice, ostracism, deprivation of civil, political and social rights, and the sins that are worse than physical slavery.■

119   IMPORTANCE OF RACE PRIDE

Edward Everett Brown

Edward Everett Brown, a distinguished African American lawyer, delivered an address on the importance of race pride before the Colored National League of Boston, March 5, 1888. The Colored National League was formed in 1876 in reaction to the Republican Party's failure to uphold the Fourteenth and Fifteenth Amendments. It was dissolved in 1900.

In this speech, Brown identifies race pride, the will to "at all times . . . love better than all things colored men and things of our own race," as the key to black advancement and the lessening of white prejudice. Brown exemplifies this approach by reciting the accomplishments of prominent black attorneys of Boston who achieved great success and grudging respect from the white legal establishment.

Brown was born in New Hampshire in 1858. He studied law in the office of Judge John White of the New Hampshire probate court, attended Boston University Law School, and was admitted to the Boston bar in 1884. In 1886, he formed the first black law firm in the state of Massachusetts along with fellow attorneys James Harris Wolff and Edward Gar-

rison Walker. The text of the address comes from the New York Age, *March 24, 1888.*

The subject of race pride is to my mind one of the most important and worthy to be considered at this time. It is a question which includes true manhood, courage and patriotism. We are living in a remarkable age when every race is struggling and fighting to make progress. Among the many, and the one I am most interested in, and to which I am proud to belong, is the Negro race. A man ought not to be ashamed of the race with which he is identified, since such a thing tends to degrade true manhood. One of the greatest stumbling blocks to-day that impedes the progress of the race in this mighty republic is because too many colored men have not the pride of race at heart; do not give their sympathy nor support to forward any great movement that is started to protect our interests, to secure us the equal privileges that all other citizens enjoy. We lack that patriotism which is a love for one's own race whose existence is recognized in the hearts of the people in every clime and every nation. The most sterile regions of the earth and the most uncompromising circumstances cannot quench in the hearts of men a love of the land which gave them birth. It is at once their happiness and their pride. It incites them to heroic action. It gives them a consciousness of secure repose. It fills them with aspirations for their country's highest welfare. It sends them out to achieve that welfare at the cost of all earthly possessions. It makes them forget all things for the land they love the best, and leads them with a self-sacrificing devotion that inspires admiration to willingly give up life itself and all that makes life worth the living if their country demands its sacrifice. However poor, or weak, or insignificant one's country may be, still that love does not die out.

The German's eyes are strangely moistened when he thinks of the fatherland, dear still though its oppression drove him forth. The bosom of the Hungarian swells with honest pride when he remembers the glory of his country's history, or weeps over her sad fate as she lies bleeding beneath the tyrant's foot. He is proud when he thinks of the Hungarian heros and martyrs, who animated by the love of freedom and fatherland, went forth calmly to battle for liberty and right, singing their national hymns, rushing with Spartan bravery into the jaws of death and destruction. And as they fell dying on the field of blood and carnage, their bodies riddled with shot and shell, and with their last expiring breath shouting for their native country. The Irishman whose beautiful land has been cursed for ages by cruel oppression on the one hand and fierce and bloody vindictiveness on the other, which God has made so bright but selfish man has so cruelly darkened over by his sin, never forgets the old country to which his hopes return and in which his memories are buried, where are the graves of his fathers and where he hopes himself to die. The Irishman's heart swells with honest pride when he thinks of the noble men of his own race like Daniel O'Connell, Grattan, Curran, and the immortal hero, Robert Emmet, whose young life was so cruelly taken by tyrannical England, because he was fighting for liberty and freedom, determined on delivering his country from the yoke of a foreign and unrelenting tyranny, and from the galling yoke of a domestic faction. And although to-day Ireland is ground, suffering and bleeding under the iron heel of British oppression, and he is driven from the land of his birth to seek a home in a foreign land, he is proud of Ireland and his race. And in the naughty contest that is going on to-day between England and Ireland in its fight for home rule, we see Irishmen all over the civilized world standing together manfully, shoulder to shoulder, united in heart, in sympathy in determination and purpose, laying aside self, willing to sacrifice life itself, happiness, that the land they love the best may take its place among the nations of the earth, free from the cruel chains of a tyranny worse than death, and that the sons and daughters of the Emerald Isle may return to their native land and around their firesides have a grand reunion.

Why should any man of African descent be ashamed of his race? Why should he consider himself inferior to a man of Anglo-Saxon descent? Why should he play the part of a coward and bow down and cringe and tamely submit to every indignity and outrageous insult that are constantly being heaped upon him? We have much to be proud of, as we calmly stop and consider what has been accomplished. It has been said that it is impossible to civilize us. Is it impossible to civilize man in one part of the earth more than in another? Turn back the pages of history and see if Rome, Greece, France, Germany or England was the cradle of civilization. The answer is no. For as far back as the lamp of tradition reaches, Africa was the cradle of science while Rome and Greece were clothed in darkness. As far back as the first rudiments of improvement can be traced they came from the very headwaters of the Nile, far in the interior of Africa, and it is an undisputed fact that there have been found in shapeless ruins, the monuments of this primeval civilization. While the northern and western parts of Europe were yet barbarous, the Mediterranean coast of Africa was filled with cities, museums, and churches. Every colored man who is interested in the progress of his race, ought to be proud of the glorious achievements of the race, especially when he thinks of the courage, the bravery displayed by black men when the black clouds of war burst upon this great nation from the time of the Revolution when that noble, heroic, immortal black patriot—Crispus Attucks—fired with the love of liberty and freedom, fell dead in King street, Boston, fighting with that noble band against British tyranny and oppression. And in every great contest that has taken place in this country black men were always in the front ranks, notwithstanding the fact that they were not recognized as men. They always fought with Spartan bravery and heroism to defend the institutions of America from the ruthless hand of the invader.

Since the ancient temples of slavery, rendered venerable alone by their antiquity, have crumbled into dust, the Negro has made rapid strides in this country, in spite of all the obstacles he has had to contend with. His influence to-day is being felt as never before in this great republic. In every department of industry, in its higher scientific branches, the Negro is proving to the world beyond any question that he is the equal and in many cases the superior of his Anglo-Saxon brother, if an equal opportunity be given him. The time has come now when the Negro asks no favors because he is colored, but he is willing to stand or fall upon his merits in the great battle of life, and prove by his brains, his ambition, his pluck, his perseverance, his integrity, his patriotism, that he is a man created in the image of God with all the attributes of true manhood. In education the advancement of the Negro has been marvelous, when we consider that he was ground down so many years under that damnable accursed system of slave oligarchy that will always stain the fair fame of this great republic. Schools and colleges have sprung up as if by magic, which are sending forth an army of competent, well trained, young colored men and women full of ambition, pride, enthusiasm, pluck, push and determination, bound to climb up the dizzy heights of the Alps, and then cross over, understanding that beyond the Alps lies Italy, which means that their honest efforts have been crowned with success. In politics to-day the Negro is a very important factor. This is acknowledged by distinguished statesmen and politicians, for he is fast learning to think and act for himself. He has made up his mind that he will no longer bow down and be the slave of any party, that he will no longer support any man for public office who is an enemy of the race. It is a source of congratulation that in Boston and all over this country colored men see the necessity of banding themselves together in solid organization, firmly resolved to wage never ceasing warfare against American prejudice to secure equal rights and equal privileges.

What we need is more confidence in each other. Laying aside petty jealousy, making a contribution of our best powers of mind and soul to benefit our race. A great many movements that have been started honestly and in good faith by noble, unselfish, courageous, intelligent colored men to promote and advance the interests of the race, have been killed by the mean, contemptible, designing treachery of other colored men, who false to themselves and to their race, prove traitors and stab the movement in the back with their cruel daggers, as the Roman conspirators did Caesar in the senate chamber. There is a mighty work to be done in this country to elevate the race and we need men of courage and principle who will contend for equal rights and never rest until those rights are guaranteed us. It is outrageous to know at this late day there is so much mean contemptible prejudice and discrimination shown toward our race in this country in restaurants, schools, railroads and public places of amusements. It is a disgrace to American civilization that in Washington, the capital of the nation, where the colored population is so extensive, that black children are prohibited from attending the same schools with the whites. And it is more disgraceful still that the colored people themselves are in part responsible for this state of affairs; because they fear that colored principals and school teachers would lose their situations, they submit to this galling state of serfdom, degrade their manhood and stifle conscience. If they had a few men like our distinguished fellow-citizen whom we all respect and admire for his fearless independence,

his unswerving fidelity to principle and truth—Hon. James M. Trotter*—
who gave up a good situation in the Boston Post Office sooner than degrade
his manhood and sell out his principle, they might accomplish something.
Or if they had more men like Hon. Edwin G. Walker, our honored president,
who like his distinguished father has always been a true and tried friend to
the Negro race under all circumstances, fighting manfully and courageously
to defend the rights of black men, giving his time, his money, his influence,
his ability, his magic eloquence to elevate them to a higher plan, a man that
loves gold as well as any man, but never loved it well enough to turn traitor
and play Benedict Arnold with his race, and whose name will live in the
heart of a grateful people when the names of some other men will sleep in
forgotten graves. We often have exhibitions of the degrading influences that
have come down to us as a result of the terrible system of slavery that the
race has been under until within a very short time. So terrible has been its
effects upon some of our people, that even now there are those who are even
recognized by a large number of colored people, who have the effrontery to
stand up and say that the Negro has no capacity for any position in which
he can display qualifications like those exhibited by white men.

Not long since a member of this league made sweeping charges that the
professional men of Boston are incompetent. He is very anxious to know
what the colored lawyers know about constitutional law, commercial law,
chancery, medical jurisprudence, and criminal law. Knowing nothing himself about law, he claims that the colored lawyers are incompetent, possess
no influence, no standing, and have accomplished nothing in their profession. If he had been competent to criticise and honestly judge, he could have
made an examination and found out what was the standing of the colored
lawyers and what success they had met with. Our honored president, Hon.
Edwin G. Walker,[†] who has been a member of the Massachusetts bar almost
twenty-five years, has achieved remarkable success in spite of all the obstacles and prejudice he has had to contend with. He has had during all these
years a large and extensive practice in the highest courts of this commonwealth and other courts of New England. He has tried with great success
many important civil cases against great corporations, municipalities, cases
intricate and complicated which demonstrated his profound knowledge of
the law. He has tried with great skill many real estate and will cases, and
others in contract which proved beyond question his thorough knowledge of
commercial law. He has also made his mark in the trial of equity and chancery cases. He has had a large practice in the United States courts. During
his professional career he has been appointed a number of times by judges
of our State courts, a member of a commission to examine applicants as to

*Trotter (1842–1892) resigned his position with the Boston Post Office in 1882 when
a white man with less experience was promoted instead of him. Because of the incident,
Trotter switched to the Democratic Party. He was appointed recorder of deeds in Washington, D.C., by President Grover Cleveland in 1887.

†Walker (1831–1901) was a prominent Boston attorney. Active in politics, he was
nominated for president of the United States in 1896 on the Negro Party ticket.

their qualifications to become members of the Massachusetts bar. His great ability has been recognized by the Supreme Court in other ways, notably by selecting him over a dozen times to defend murder cases, which he did with most consummate skill and eloquence, winning his cases and proving that he was a master of the criminal law. Reverently do I pass by those two distinguished New England jurists, Robert Morris* and the late Judge George L. Ruffin,[†] whose work at the bar, on the rostrum, or wherever the manhood of the Negro was challenged, was always such as to convince the unwilling or the doubting that he, whoever he might be that crossed swords with either of them, would meet a foe worthy of his steel.

Mr. James H. Wolff,[‡] a college trained gentleman who has been a member of the Suffolk bar for thirteen years, and seven years admitted to practice in the United States courts, has established an excellent reputation among the fraternity for being a sound, practical, well read, common sense lawyer, thoroughly conversant with the abstruse problems of commercial law. He has tried successfully many important civil and criminal cases in the highest courts of this State and other States. One notable case was that of Henry Taylor, a graduate of Boston University Law School who was a member of the Massachusetts bar, but removed to the city of Baltimore, there making an application for admission to practice in the courts of Maryland, which application was denied by a prejudiced court on account of his color. Mr. Wolff was in Baltimore at the time and appeared as counsel for Mr. Taylor, argued his case at great length before the full bench of the Court of Appeals for the State of Maryland. The brief presented was an elaborate and exhaustive one, raising the constitutionality of the statute of Maryland prohibiting colored men from admission to the bar in that State. The brief was replete with learning and deep reasoning, all the decisions being quoted bearing upon the rights of citizens from the foundation of the government. The Chief Justice was so impressed with the scholarly argument of Mr. Wolff, although a man full of bitter prejudice against color; yet he had the manhood to state in open court that the brief showed great ability and careful preparation, and was worthy of the most serious consideration. Is not this positive evidence that we do have colored lawyers who have a profound knowledge of constitutional law, bearing in mind that Mr. Wolff is comparatively speaking a young man. He has also argued cases of importance before the Supreme Court of Massachusetts with skill and ability. He was for a number of years retained counsel for a national bank in the city of Boston and drew up the

*Robert Morris, Sr. (1823–1882), was among the first African American lawyers and was the first black member of the American judiciary.

†George Ruffin (1834–1886) was the first African American to graduate from a university law school (Harvard, 1869), served in the Massachusetts state legislature, and was the first northern African American to be appointed a municipal judge (1883).

‡James Harris Wolff, Brown's law partner, was admitted to the Massachusetts bar in 1875, then moved to Maryland, where he became the first African American lawyer admitted to practice in the U.S. Circuit Court. He later returned to Boston, where he twice served as judge advocate in the Massachusetts Grand Army of the Republic.

original papers of incorporation of the bank, and is counsel now for a number of business houses in Boston.

The younger men of the bar fresh from the university, notably Mr. Ruffin, Mr. Wilson, and Mr. Plummer, are also worthy to be mentioned. Mr. Ruffin is a quiet and unassuming gentleman, possessing a liberal education. He has a good legal mind, fine reasoning powers, and is thoroughly conversant in every department of the law. He has tried with great skill and ability a number of very important civil cases in the highest courts of the commonwealth and met with good success. Mr. Wilson, a graduate of Boston University Law School, is a well read lawyer of good sound judgment, intelligence and common sense. In the few years that he has been a member of the Boston bar he has acquitted himself nobly and well. He has tried successfully a number of good cases showing skill and ability of superior order, and gives promise of an honorable career in the future, and is destined to take high rank in the profession in spite of all the obstacles he has to contend with. Mr. Plummer is one of the best examples of energy, push and determination to succeed, that we have among us, whether as a lawyer or a colored man. Viewed strictly as a lawyer he is perhaps entitled to more credit than any young colored man to-day at the bar. Starting out under the most adverse circumstances, working through a cloud dense and heavy with all that has beset any of his race in the battle of life, he finally succeeded by the aid of the evening high school; from there to the office of an attorney, where he remained until he stepped up into the Boston University Law School, emerging from that famous institution well equipped to enter upon the life of a lawyer. And in the few years that he has been a member of the Suffolk bar he has won the respect of the judges and the attorneys and has proved beyond all question his capacity to try cases upon the law and evidence, in a way that is creditable to himself and gives promise of a brilliant career in the future. Every colored man and woman who loves the race ought to point out such men with pride and satisfaction, because it is a well known fact that these men have to fight their way against heavy odds every day of their lives.*

Every colored man in Boston ought to feel proud, happy, and encouraged when he thinks of the success that has crowned the efforts of the colored merchants in Boston. Walking up Washington street with strangers, I have often stopped to admire and praise the magnificent tailoring establishment owned by a colored man who came to this city a number of years ago a poor boy, and has worked his way up from the lowest round of the ladder to the highest, gaining a reputation in the mercantile community of Boston as a first-class tailor and business man, second to none in his line—Mr. J. H. Lewis. Besides Mr. Lewis we have Mr. T. A. Ridley, Mr. George Glover, Mr. Wardell and Mr. Benjamin Washington carrying on business successfully with credit to themselves and the race.

---

*For further information on the history and accomplishments of African Americans in the legal professions, see J. Clay Smith, Jr., *Emancipation: The Making of the Black Lawyer, 1844–1944* (Philadelphia: University of Pennsylvania Press, 1993).

The hour is come when a courageous stand must be taken against the ruthless oppressors of our race. We owe it to the thousands who are wearing out a miserable existence under the galling yoke of prejudice and oppression. We owe it to ourselves if we would be true men and not the menials of tyrants. Let us have more self-respect, to be proud of our color and boast of our nationality, at all times to love better than all things colored men and things of our own race. Let us learn to trust those who are honest and capable of leading better than those of other races. Let us use every effort to hurl men, whether they be black or white, from place and power when they fail to subserve our interests and see that we get fair play and equal chance in all the walks of life. I believe that the race is destined to attain a high standing on this continent when colored men learn to stand together, shoulder to shoulder, marching forward proudly to battle for equal rights. Even now the forces are at work beneath the still surface that promise fair in the near future to burst forth like the bright sun, proud monarch of the Heavens at early dawn, dissipating the clouds of darkness, rising higher and higher in his progress in his fiery chariot, sending forth his dazzling rays upon the fields of waving grain, beautiful flowers, the lofty mountain peaks, upon valley, hill and dale, illuminating all nature, making it bright, beautiful and grand, the acknowledged king of day. So this principle of race pride is destined to throw light upon the race and accomplish grand and glorious results. Under its vivifying influence many darkened homes are destined to be made happier, under its magnetic touch the scalding bitter tears of Southern mothers will be dried up. No more will the colored man be looked upon as a thing. No longer will he be spit upon and abused by mean, contemptible and designing men. No more will he be an object of ridicule, scorn and contempt. No more will he be shot down in cold blood for exercising his right of franchise, for the black cloud of prejudice will pass away, for the strong arm of justice, mercy and right will defend and protect him.■

120 WOMAN SUFFRAGE

Frederick Douglass

Next to abolition and the battle for equal rights for African Americans, the cause closest to the heart of Frederick Douglass was woman's rights. The masthead of his paper, the North Star, *featured the slogan, "Right is of no sex." Douglass was one of the few men present at the pioneer woman's rights convention held at Seneca Falls, New York, in July 1848, and it was he who persuaded Elizabeth Cady*

*Stanton to press for suffrage and who seconded the resolution proposed
by Stanton that it was "the duty of the women of this country to secure
to themselves their sacred right to the elective franchise."* But Douglass
parted company with Stanton and Anthony in 1869 in the controversy
over the Fifteenth Amendment, arguing that prejudice and violence
against black men made their need for the franchise more pressing.
Stanton and Anthony left the Equal Rights Association, split the suffrage movement, and sometimes employed racist rhetoric in their efforts
to secure the vote for women. In 1895, Anthony insisted that Douglass
not attend the Atlanta convention of the National American Woman Suffrage Association for fear that his presence might antagonize white
southern members.*

*Yet Douglass remained a constant champion of the right of women to
vote. In April 1888, in a speech before the International Council of
Women, in Washington, D.C., Douglass recalls his role at the Seneca
Falls convention and once again comes out strongly for woman suffrage.
Douglass also, however, provides a keen rhetorical analysis of suffrage advocacy, past and present. The early speaker for woman's rights, he argues, faced even greater obstacles than the antislavery orator, by having
to convince unwilling listeners that a problem existed. As for the present, Douglass insists that it is women, not men, who should be the primary spokespersons for the movement. The text of Douglass's address appeared in the* Woman's Journal, *April 14, 1888.*

M rs. President, Ladies and Gentlemen:—I come to this platform with
unusual diffidence. Although I have long been identified with the
Woman's Suffrage movement, and have often spoken in its favor, I am somewhat at a loss to know what to say on this really great and uncommon occasion, where so much has been said.

When I look around on this assembly, and see the many able and eloquent women, full of the subject, ready to speak, and who only need the
opportunity to impress this audience with their views and thrill them with
"thoughts that breathe and words that burn," I do not feel like taking up
more than a very small space of your time and attention, and shall not. I
would not, even now, presume to speak, but for the circumstance of my early
connection with the cause, and of having been called upon to do so by one
whose voice in this Council we all gladly obey. Men have very little business
here as speakers, anyhow; and if they come here at all they should take back
benches and wrap themselves in silence. For this is an International Council,
not of men, but of women, and woman should have all the say in it. This is
her day in court.

I do not mean to exalt the intellect of woman above man's; but I have
heard many men speak on this subject, some of them the most eloquent

---

*William McFeely, *Frederick Douglass* (New York: W. W. Norton, 1991), 156.

to be found anywhere in the country; and I believe no man, however gifted with thought and speech, can voice the wrongs and present the demands of women with the skill and effect, with the power and authority of woman herself. The man struck is the man to cry out. Woman knows and feels her wrongs as man cannot know and feel them, and she also knows as well as he can know, what measures are needed to redress them. I grant all the claims at this point. She is her own best representative. We can neither speak for her, nor vote for her, nor act for her, nor be responsible for her; and the thing for men to do in the premises is just to get out of her way and give her the fullest opportunity to exercise all the powers inherent in her individual personality, and allow her to do it as she herself shall elect to exercise them. Her right to be and to do is as full, complete and perfect as the right of any man on earth. I say of her, as I say of the colored people, "Give her fair play, and hands off."

There was a time when, perhaps, we men could help a little. It was when this woman suffrage cause was in its cradle, when it was not big enough to go alone, when it had to be taken in the arms of its mother from Seneca Falls, N.Y., to Rochester, N.Y., for baptism. I then went along with it and offered my services to help it, for then it needed help; but now it can afford to dispense with me and all of my sex. Then its friends were few—now its friends are many. Then it was wrapped in obscurity—now it is lifted in sight of the whole civilized world, and people of all lands and languages give it their hearty support. Truly the change is vast and wonderful.

I thought my eye of faith was tolerably clear when I attended those meetings in Seneca Falls and Rochester, but it was far too dim to see at the end of forty years a result so imposing as this International Council, and to see yourself and Miss Anthony alive and active in its proceedings. Of course, I expected to be alive myself, and am not surprised to find myself so; for such is, perhaps, the presumption and arrogance common to my sex. Nevertheless, I am very glad to see you here to-day, and to see this great assembly of women. I am glad that you are its president. No manufactured "boom," or political contrivance, such as make presidents elsewhere, has made you president of this assembly of women in this Capital of the Nation. You hold your place by reason of eminent fitness, and I give you joy that your life and labors in the cause of woman are thus crowned with honor and glory. This I say in spite of the warning given us by Miss Anthony's friend against mutual admiration.

There may be some well-meaning people in this audience who have never attended a woman suffrage convention, never heard a woman suffrage speech, never read a woman suffrage newspaper, and they may be surprised that those who speak here do not argue the question. It may be kind to tell them that our cause has passed beyond the period of arguing. The demand of the hour is not argument, but assertion, firm and inflexible assertion, assertion which has more than the force of an argument. If there is any argument to be made, it must be made by the opponents, not by the friends of woman suffrage. Let those who want argument examine the ground upon which they base their claim to the right to vote. They will find that there is not one reason, not one consideration, which they can urge in support of man's claim to vote, which does not equally support the right of woman to vote.

There is to-day, however, a special reason for omitting argument. This is the end of the fourth decade of the woman suffrage movement, a kind of jubilee which naturally turns our minds to the past.

Ever since this Council has been in session, my thoughts have been reverting to the past. I have been thinking more or less, of the scene presented forty years ago in the little Methodist Church at Seneca Falls, the manger in which this organized suffrage movement was born. It was a very small thing then. It was not then big enough to be abused, or loud enough to make itself heard outside, and only a few of those who saw it had any notion that the little thing would live. I have been thinking, too, of the strong conviction, the noble courage, the sublime faith in God and man it required at that time to set this suffrage ball in motion. The history of the world has given to us many sublime undertakings, but none more sublime than this. It was a great thing for the friends of peace to organize in opposition to war; it was a great thing for the friends of temperance to organize against intemperance; it was a great thing for humane people to organize in opposition to slavery; but it was a much greater thing, in view of all the circumstances, for woman to organize herself in opposition to her exclusion from participation in government. The reason is obvious. War, intemperance and slavery are open, undisguised, palpable evils. The best feelings of human nature revolt at them. We could easily make men see the misery, the debasement, the terrible suffering caused by intemperance; we could easily make men see the desolation wrought by war and the hell-black horrors of chattel slavery; but the case was different in the movement for woman suffrage. Men took for granted all that could be said against intemperance, war and slavery. But no such advantage was found in the beginning of the cause of suffrage for women. On the contrary, everything in her condition was supposed to be lovely, just as it should be. She had no rights denied, no wrongs to redress. She herself had no suspicion but that all was going well with her. She floated along on the tide of life as her mother and grandmother had done before her, as in a dream of Paradise. Her wrongs, if she had any, were too occult to be seen, and too light to be felt. It required a daring voice and a determined hand to awake her from this delightful dream and call the nation to account for the rights and opportunities of which it was depriving her. It was well understood at the beginning that woman would not thank us for disturbing her by this call to duty, and it was known that man would denounce and scorn us for such a daring innovation upon the established order of things. But this did not appall or delay the word and work.

At this distance of time from that convention at Rochester, and in view of the present position of the question, it is hard to realize the moral courage it required to launch this unwelcome movement. Any man can be brave when the danger is over, go to the front when there is no resistance, rejoice when the battle is fought and the victory is won; but it is not so easy to venture upon a field untried with one-half the whole world against you, as these women did.

Then who were we, for I count myself in, who did this thing? We were few in numbers, moderate in resources, and very little known in the world. The most that we had to commend us was a firm conviction that we were in the right, and a firm faith that the right must ultimately prevail. But the case was well considered. Let no man imagine that the step was taken recklessly and thoughtlessly. Mrs. Stanton had dwelt upon it at least six years before she declared it in the Rochester convention. Walking with her from the house of Joseph and Thankful Southwick, two of the noblest people I ever knew, Mrs. Stanton, with an earnestness that I shall never forget, unfolded her views on this woman question precisely as she had in this Council. This was six and forty years ago, and it was not until six years after, that she ventured to make her formal, pronounced and startling demand for the ballot. She had, as I have said, considered well, and knew something of what would be the cost of the reform she was inaugurating. She knew the ridicule, the rivalry, the criticism and the bitter aspersions which she and her co-laborers would have to meet and to endure. But she saw more clearly than most of us that the vital point to be made prominent, and the one that included all others, was the ballot, and she bravely said the word. It was not only necessary to break the silence of woman and make her voice heard, but she must have a clear, palpable and comprehensive measure set before her, one worthy of her highest ambition and her best exertions, and hence the ballot was brought to the front.

There are few facts in my humble history to which I look back with more satisfaction than to the fact, recorded in the history of the woman-suffrage movement, that I was sufficiently enlightened at that early day, and when only a few years from slavery, to support your resolution for woman suffrage. I have done very little in this world in which to glory except this one act—and I certainly glory in that. When I ran away from slavery, it was for myself; when I advocated emancipation, it was for my people; but when I stood up for the rights of woman, self was out of the question, and I found a little nobility in the act.

In estimating the forces with which this suffrage cause has had to contend during these forty years, the fact should be remembered that relations of long standing beget a character in the parties to them in favor of their continuance. Time itself is a conservative power—a very conservative power. One shake of his hoary locks will sometimes paralyze the hand and palsy the tongue of the reformer. The relation of man to woman has the advantage of all the ages behind it. Those who oppose a readjustment of this relation tell us that what is always was and always will be, world without end. But we have heard this old argument before, and if we live very long we shall hear it again. When any aged error shall be assailed, and any old abuse is to be removed, we shall meet this same old argument. Man has been so long the king and woman the subject—man has been so long accustomed to com-

mand and woman to obey—that both parties to the relation have been hardened into their respective places, and thus has been piled up a mountain of
iron against woman's enfranchisement.

The same thing confronted us in our conflicts with slavery. Long years
ago Henry Clay said, on the floor of the American Senate, "I know there is
a visionary dogma that man cannot hold property in man," and, with a brow
of defiance, he said, "That is property which the law makes property. Two
hundred years of legislation has sanctioned and sanctified Negro slaves as
property." But neither the power of time nor the might of legislation has been
able to keep life in that stupendous barbarism.

The universality of man's rule over woman is another factor in the resistance to the woman-suffrage movement. We are pointed to the fact that
men have not only always ruled over women, but that they do so rule everywhere, and they easily think that a thing that is done everywhere must be
right. Though the fallacy of this reasoning is too transparent to need refutation, it still exerts a powerful influence. Even our good Brother Jasper yet
believes, with the ancient Church, that the sun "do move," notwithstanding
all the astronomers of the world are against him.* One year ago I stood on
the Pincio in Rome and witnessed the unveiling of the statue of Galileo. It
was an imposing sight. At no time before had Rome been free enough to
permit such a statue to be placed within her walls. It is now there, not with
the approval of the Vatican. No priest took part in the ceremonies. It was all
the work of laymen. One or two priests passed the statue with averted eyes,
but the great truths of the solar system were not angry at the sight, and the
same will be true when woman shall be clothed, as she will yet be, with all
the rights of American citizenship.

All good causes are mutually helpful. The benefits accruing from this
movement for the equal rights of woman are not confined or limited to
woman only. They will be shared by every effort to promote the progress
and welfare of mankind every where and in all ages. It was an example and
a prophecy of what can be accomplished against strongly opposing forces,
against time-hallowed abuses, against deeply entrenched error, against world-
wide usage, and against the settled judgment of mankind, by a few earnest
women, clad only in the panoply of truth, and determined to live and die in
what they considered a righteous cause.

I do not forget the thoughtful remark of our president in the opening
address to this International Council, reminding us of the incompleteness
of our work. The remark was wise and timely. Nevertheless, no man can
compare the present with the past, the obstacles that then opposed us, and
the influences that now favor us, the meeting in the little Methodist chapel
forty years ago, and the Council in this vast theater today, without admitting
that woman's cause is already a brilliant success. But, however this may be
and whatever the future may have in store for us, one thing is certain—this

---

*Douglass refers to the popular black preacher John Jasper, whose sermon, "The Sun
Do Move," achieved great notoriety for its insistence that the sun revolves around the
Earth.

new revolution in human thought will never go backward. When a great truth once gets abroad in the world, no power on earth can imprison it, or prescribe its limits, or suppress it. It is bound to go on till it becomes the thought of the world. Such a truth is woman's right to equal liberty with man. She was born with it. It was hers before she comprehended it. It is inscribed upon all the powers and faculties of her soul, and no custom, law or usage can ever destroy it. Now that it has got fairly fixed in the minds of the few, it is bound to become fixed in the minds of the many, and be supported at last by a great cloud of witnesses, which no man can number and no power can withstand.

The women who have thus far carried on this agitation have already embodied and illustrated Theodore Parker's* three grades of human greatness. The first is greatness in executive and administrative ability; second, greatness in the ability to organize; and, thirdly, in the ability to discover truth. Wherever these three elements of power are combined in any movement, there is a reasonable ground to believe in its final success; and these elements of power have been manifest in the women who have had the movement in hand from the beginning. They are seen in the order which has characterized the proceedings of this Council. They are seen in the depth and comprehensiveness of the discussions had upon them in this Council. They are seen in the fervid eloquence and downright earnestness with which women advocate their cause. They are seen in the profound attention with which woman is heard in her own behalf. They are seen in the steady growth and onward march of the movement, and they will be seen in the final triumph of woman's cause, not only in this country, but throughout the world.■

121

I DENOUNCE THE SO-CALLED EMANCIPATION AS A STUPENDOUS FRAUD

Frederick Douglass

In the winter of 1888 Frederick Douglass visited South Carolina and Georgia to obtain a firsthand picture of the conditions of black people in the South during the post-Reconstruction era. He was deeply shocked by what he discovered. On April 10, soon after his re-

---

*Parker (1810–1860) was an abolitionist theologian and minister who supported John Brown's raid on Harper's Ferry.

turn, he wrote to one of the leaders of a movement encouraging the emigration of southern blacks to the Northwest: "I had hope that the relations subsisting between the former slaves and the old master class would gradually improve; but while I believed this, and still have some such weak faith, I have of late seen enough, heard enough and learned enough of the condition of these people in South Carolina and Georgia to make me welcome any movement which will take them out of the wretched condition in which I now know them to be. While I shall continue to labor for increased justice to those who stay in the South, I give you my hearty 'Godspeed' your emigration scheme. I believe you are doing a good work."

A few days later, on April 16, 1888, he spoke in Washington at the celebration of the twenty-sixth anniversary of emancipation in the District of Columbia. His address, one of the most effective he ever delivered, revealed how deeply he had been moved by his southern tour. His voice quivered with rage as he described how the African American was "nominally free" but actually a slave. In earnest tones, he told the nation: "I here and now denounce his so-called emancipation as a stupendous fraud—a fraud upon him, a fraud upon the world." He drew a terrifying picture of the exploitation of southern blacks, and he denounced the national government for having abandoned the African American, ignored his rights as an American citizen, and left "him" "a deserted, a defrauded, a swindled, and an outcast man—in law, free; in fact, a slave."

Douglass's speech created a sensation. Senator George B. Edmonds called it "the greatest political speech that I have read or heard in perhaps twenty years" and urged that it "be printed broadcast throughout our land." Below is Douglass's great and searing indictment of the treatment of African Americans in the years following the overthrow of Reconstruction. The text is reprinted from the Washington National Republican, *April 17, 1888.*

FRIENDS AND FELLOW CITIZENS: it has been my privilege to assist in several anniversary celebrations of the abolition of slavery in the District of Columbia, but I remember no occasion of this kind when I felt a deeper solicitude for the future welfare of our emancipated people than now.

The chief cause of anxiety is not in the condition of the colored people of the District of Columbia, though there is much that is wrong and unsatisfactory here, but the deplorable condition of the Negro in the Southern states. At no time since the abolition of slavery has there been more cause for alarm on this account than at this juncture in our history.

I have recently been in two of the Southern states—South Carolina and Georgia—and my impression from what I saw, heard and learned there is not favorable to my hopes for the race. I know this is a sad message to bring you

*Philip S. Foner, *Voice of Black America,* vol. 1 (New York: Capricorn, 1972), 551.

on this twenty-sixth anniversary of freedom in the District of Columbia, but I know too, that I have a duty to perform and that duty is to tell the truth, and nothing but the truth, and I should be unworthy to stand here, unworthy of the confidence of the colored people of this country, if I should from any considerations of policy withhold any fact or feature of the condition of the freedmen which the people of this country ought to know.

The temptation on anniversary occasions like this is to prophesy smooth things, to be joyful and glad, to indulge in the illusions of hope—to bring glad tidings on our tongues, and words of peace reveal. But while I know it is always easier to be the bearer of glad tidings than sad ones, while I know that hope is a powerful motive to exertion and high endeavor, while I know that people generally would rather look upon the bright side of their condition than to know the worst; there comes a time when it is best that the worst should be made known, and in my judgment that time, in respect to the condition of the colored people of the South, is now. There are times when neither hope nor fear should be allowed to control our speech. Cry aloud and spare not, is the word of wisdom as well of Scripture. "Ye shall know the truth, and the truth shall make you free," applies to the body not less than the soul, to this world not less than the world to come. Outside the truth there is no solid foundation for any of us, and I assume that you who have invited me to speak, and you who have come to hear me speak, expect me to speak the truth as I understand the truth.

The truth at which we should get on this occasion respects the precise relation subsisting between the white and colored people of the South, or, in other words, between the colored people and the old master class of the South. We have need to know this and to take it to heart.

It is well said that "a people may lose its liberty in a day and not miss it in half a century," and that "the price of liberty is eternal vigilance." In my judgment, with my knowledge of what has already taken place in the South, these wise and wide-awake sentiments were never more apt and timely than now.

I have assisted in fighting one battle for the abolition of slavery, and the American people have shed their blood in defense of the Union and the Constitution, and neither I nor they should wish to fight this battle over again; and in order that we may not, we should look the facts in the face today and, if possible, nip the evil in the bud.

I have no taste for the role of an alarmist. If my wishes could be allowed to dictate my speech I would tell you something quite the reverse of what I now intend. I would tell you that everything is lovely with the Negro in the South; I would tell you that the rights of the Negro are respected, and that he has no wrongs to redress; I would tell you that he is honestly paid for his labor; that he is secure in his liberty; that he is no longer subject to lynch law; that he has freedom of speech; that the gates of knowledge are open to him; that he goes to the ballot box unmolested; that his vote is duly counted and given its proper weight in determining result; I would tell you that he is making splendid progress in the acquisition of knowledge, wealth and influence; I would tell you that his bitterest enemies have become his warmest friends; that the desire to make him a slave no longer exists anywhere in the South; that the Democratic party is a better friend to him than the Republican party, and that each party is competing with the other to see which can do the most to make his liberty a blessing to himself and to the country and the world. But in telling you all this I should be telling you what is absolutely false, and what you know to be false, and the only thing which would save such a story from being a lie would be its utter inability to deceive.

What is the condition of the Negro at the South at this moment? Let us look at it both in the light of facts and in the light of reason. To understand it we must consult nature as well as circumstances, the past as well as the present. No fact is more obvious than the fact that there is a perpetual tendency of power to encroach upon weakness, and of the crafty to take advantage of the simple. This is as natural as for smoke to ascend or water to run down. The love of power is one of the strongest traits in the Anglo-Saxon race. This love of power common to the white race has been nursed and strengthened at the South by slavery; accustomed during two hundred years to the unlimited possession and exercise of irresponsible power, the love of it has become stronger by habit. To assume that this feeling of pride and power had died out and disappeared from the South is to assume a miracle. Any man who tells you that it has died out or has ceased to be exercised and made effective, tells you that which is untrue and in the nature of things could not be true. Not only is the love of power there, but a talent for its exercise has been fully developed. This talent makes the old master class of the South not only the masters of the Negro, but the masters of Congress and, if not checked, will make them the masters of the nation.

It was something more than an empty boast in the old times, when it was said that one slave master was equal to three Northern men. Though this did not turn out to be true on the battlefield, it does seem to be true in the councils of the nation. In sight of all the nation these ambitious men of the South have dared to take possession of the government which they, with broad blades and bloody hands, sought to destroy; in sight of all the nation they have disregarded and trampled upon the Constitution, and organized parties on sectional lines. From the ramparts of the Solid South, with their 153 electoral votes in the Electoral College, they have dared to defy the nation to put a Republican in the Presidential chair for the next four years, as they once threatened the nation with civil war if it elected Abraham Lincoln. With this grip on the Presidential chair, with the House of Representatives in their hands, with the Supreme Court deciding every question in favor of the states, as against the powers of the federal government, denying to the government the right to protect the elective franchise of its own citizens, they may well feel themselves masters, not only of their former slaves, but of the whole situation. With these facts before us, tell me not that the Negro is safe in the possession of his liberty. Tell me not that power will not assert itself. Tell me not that they who despise the Constitution they have sworn to support will respect the rights of the Negro, whom they already despise.

Tell me not that men who thus break faith with God will be scrupulous in keeping faith with the poor Negro laborer of the South. Tell me not that a people who have lived by the sweat of other men's faces, and thought themselves Christian gentlemen while doing it, will feel themselves bound by principles of justice to their former victims in their weakness. Such a pretense in face of facts is shameful, shocking and sickening. Yet there are men at the North who believe all this.

Well may it be said that Americans have no memories. We look over the House of Representatives and see the Solid South enthroned there. We listen with calmness to eulogies of the South and of the traitors, and forget Andersonville.* We look over the Senate and see the Senator from South Carolina, and we forget Hamburg.† We see Robert Smalls cheated out of his seat in Congress,‡ and forget the *Planter*, and the service rendered by the colored troops in the late war for the Union.

Well, the nation may forget; it may shut its eyes to the past and frown upon any who may do otherwise, but the colored people of this country are bound to keep fresh a memory of the past till justice shall be done them in the present. When this shall be done we shall as readily as any other part of our respected citizens plead for an act of oblivion.

We are often confronted of late in the press and on the platform with the discouraging statement that the problem of the Negro as a free man and a citizen is not yet solved; that since his emancipation he has disappointed the best hopes of his friends and fulfilled the worst predictions of his enemies, and that he has shown himself unfit for the position assigned him by the mistaken statesmanship of the nation. It is said that physically, morally, socially and religiously he is in a condition vastly more deplorable than was his condition as a slave; that he has not proved himself so good a master to himself as his old master was to him; that he is gradually, but surely, sinking below the point of industry, good manners and civilization to which he attained in a state of slavery; that his industry is fitful; that his economy is wasteful; that his honesty is deceitful; that his morals are impure; that his domestic life is beastly; that his religion is fetichism, and his worship is simply emotional; and that, in a word, he is falling into a state of barbarism.

Such is the distressing description of the emancipated Negro as drawn by his enemies and as it is found reported in the journals of the South. Unhappily, however, it is a description not confined to the South. It has gone

*Andersonville was the notorious Confederate prison in southwestern Georgia for Union prisoners, who were packed together with little food and hardly any medicine. From June to September 1864, some 8,589 prisoners died in Andersonville.

†On July 9, 1876, in Hamburg, South Carolina, three hundred armed whites attacked and murdered members of the town's black militia. Five of the militia members were shot after surrendering.

‡In 1886, Robert Smalls was not seated in Congress as representative from South Carolina, even though he spoke for his right to his seat. In 1862, while Smalls was in the Confederate Navy, he made a daring escape with the ship *Planter*, into the northern lines and was subsequently commissioned as a captain in the Union navy.

forth to the North. It has crossed the ocean; I met with it in Europe. And it has gone as far as the wings of the press and the power of speech can carry it. There is no measuring the injury inflicted upon the Negro by it. It cools our friends, heats our enemies, and turns away from us much of the sympathy and aid which we need and deserve to receive at the hands of our fellow men.

But now comes the question, Is this description of the emancipated Negro true? In answer to this question I must say, Yes and no. It is not true in all its lines and specifications and to the full extent of the ground it covers, but it certainly is true in many of its important features, and there is no race under heaven of which the same would not be equally true with the same antecedents and the same treatment which the Negro is receiving at the hands of this nation and the old master class, to which the Negro is still a subject.

I admit that the Negro, and especially the plantation Negro, the tiller of the soil, has made little progress from barbarism to civilization, and that he is in a deplorable condition since his emancipation. That he is worse off, in many respects, than when he was a slave, I am compelled to admit, but I contend that the fault is not his, but that of his heartless accusers. He is the victim of a cunningly devised swindle, one which paralyzes his energies, suppresses his ambition, and blasts all his hopes; and though he is nominally free he is actually a slave. I here and now denounce his so-called emancipation as a stupendous fraud—a fraud upon him, a fraud upon the world. It was not so meant by Abraham Lincoln; it was not so meant by the Republican party; but whether so meant or not, it is partially a lie, keeping the word of promise to the ear and breaking it to the heart.

Do you ask me why the Negro of the plantation has made so little progress, why his cupboard is empty, why he flutters in rags, why his children run naked, and why his wife hides herself behind the hut when a stranger is passing? I will tell you. It is because he is systematically and universally cheated out of his hard earnings. The same class that once extorted his labor under the lash now gets his labor by a mean, sneaking, and fraudulent device. That device is a trucking system which never permits him to see or to save a dollar of his hard earnings. He struggles and struggles, but, like a man in a morass, the more he struggles the deeper he sinks. The highest wages paid him is eight dollars a month, and this he receives only in orders on the store, which, in many cases, is owned by his employer. The scrip has purchasing power on that one store, and that one only. A blind man can see that the laborer is by this arrangement bound hand and foot, and is completely in the power of his employer. He can charge the poor fellow what he pleases and give what kind of goods he pleases, and he does both. His victim cannot go to another store and buy, and this the storekeeper knows. The only security the wretched Negro has under this arrangement is the conscience of the storekeeper—a conscience educated in the school of slavery, where the idea prevailed in theory and practice that the Negro had no rights which white men were bound to respect, an arrangement in which everything in the way of food or clothing, whether tainted meat or damaged cloth, is deemed good enough for the Negro. For these he is often made to pay a double price.

But this is not all, or the worst result of the system. It puts it out of the power of the Negro to save anything of what he earns. If a man gets an honest dollar for his day's work, he has a motive for laying it by and saving it for future emergency. It will be as good for use in the future and perhaps better a year hence than now, but this miserable scrip has in no sense the quality of a dollar. It is only good at one store and for a limited period. Thus the man who has it is tempted to get rid of it as soon as possible. It may be out of date before he knows it, or the storekeeper may move away and it may be left worthless on his hands.

But this is not the only evil involved in this satanic arrangement. It promotes dishonesty. The Negro sees himself paid but limited wages—far too limited to support himself and family, and that in worthless scrip—and he is tempted to fight the devil with fire. Finding himself systematically robbed he goes to stealing and as a result finds his liberty—such as it is—taken from him, and himself put to work for a master in a chain gang, and he comes out, if he ever gets out, a ruined man.

Every Northern man who visits the old master class, the landowners and landlords of the South, is told by the old slaveholders with a great show of virtue that they are glad that they are rid of slavery and would not have the slave system back if they could; that they are better off than they were before, and much more of the same tenor. Thus Northern men come home duped and go on a mission of duping others by telling the same pleasing story.

There are very good reasons why these people would not have slavery back if they could—reasons far more creditable to their cunning than to their conscience. With slavery they had some care and responsibility for the physical well-being of their slaves. Now they have as firm a grip on the freedman's labor as when he was a slave and without any burden of caring for his children or himself. The whole arrangement is stamped with fraud and is supported by hyprocrisy, and I here and now, on this Emancipation Day: denounce it as a villainous swindle, and invoke the press, the pulpit and the lawmaker to assist in exposing it and blotting it out forever.

We denounce the imposition upon the working classes of England, and we do well, but in England this trucking system is abolished by law. It is a penal offense there, and it should be made so here. It should be made a crime to pay any man for his honest labor in any other than honest money. Until this is done in the Southern states the laborer of the South will be ground to the earth, and progress with him will be impossible. It is the duty of the Negro press to take up the subject. The Negro, where he may have a vote, should vote for no man who is not in favor of making this scrip and truck system unlawful.

I come now to another feature of Southern policy which bears hard and heavily on the Negro laborer and land renter. It is found in the landlord-and-tenant laws. I will read and extract to you from these laws that you may see how completely and rigidly the rights of the landlord are guarded and how entirely the tenant is in the clutches of the landlord:

REVISED CODE OF MISSISSIPPI

SEC. 1301. Every lessor of land shall have a lien on all the agricultural products of the leased premises, however and by whomsoever produced, to secure the payment of the rent and the market value of all advances made by him to his tenant for supplies for the tenant and others for whom he may contract.

SEC. 1304. When any landlord or lessor shall have just cause to suspect and shall verily believe that his tenant will remove his effects from the leased premises to any other place within or without the county before the rent or claims for supplies will fall due, so that no distress can be made, such landlord or lessor on making oath thereof, and of the amount the tenant is to pay, and at what time the same will fall due, and giving a bond as required in the preceding section, may, in like manner obtain an attachment against the goods and chattels of such tenant, and the officers making the distress shall give notice thereof and advertise the property distrained for sale, in the manner directed in the last preceding section, and if such tenant shall not, before the time appointed for such sale, give bond with sufficient security in double the amount of the rent, or other demand payable to the plaintiff, conditioned for the payment of said rent or other thing at the time it shall be due, with all cost, the goods distrained, or so much thereof as shall be necessary, shall be sold by the said officer at public sale to the highest bidder for cash, and out of the proceeds of the sale he shall pay to the plaintiff the amount due him, deducting interest for the time until the same shall become payable.

SEC. 1361. Said lien shall exist by virtue of the relation of the parties as employer and employee, and without any writing or recording.

SEC. 1362. Provides that any person who aids or assists in removing anything subject to these liens; without the consent of the landlord, shall, upon conviction, be punished by a fine of not more than $500, and be imprisoned in the county jail not more than six months, or be either such fine and imprisonment.

VOORHEE'S REVISED LAWS OF LA. 2D

SEC. 2165. Article 287 shall be so amended that a lessor may obtain a writ of provisional seizure even before the rent is due, and it shall be sufficient to entitle the lessor of the writ to swear to the amount which he claims, whether due or not due, and that he has good reasons to believe that the lessee will remove the furniture or property upon which he has a lien or privilege out of the premises, and that he may be, therefore, deprived of his lien.

LAWS OF FLORIDA-M'CLELLAN'S DIGEST

SEC. I, chapter 137. All claims for rent shall be a lien on agricultural products raised on the land rented, and shall be superior to all other liens and claims, though of older date, and also a superior lien on all other property of the lessee of his sublessee, or assigns usually kept on the premises, over any lien acquired subsequently to such property having been bought on the premises leased.

CODE OF ALABAMA

SEC. 3055, chapter 6. Lien continues and attaches to crop of succeeding years. When the tenant fails to pay any part of such rent or advances, and continues his tenancy under the same landlord for the next succeeding year for which the original lien for advances, if any remain unpaid, shall continue on the articles advanced or property purchased with money advanced or obtained by barter in exchange for articles advanced, and for which a lien shall also attach to the crop of such succeeding year.

You have thus seen a specimen, and a fair specimen, of the landlord-and-tenant laws of several of the old slave states; you have thus seen how scrupulously and rigidly the rights of the landlords are guarded and protected by these laws; you have thus seen how completely the tenant is put at the mercy of the landlord; you have thus seen the bias, the motive, and intention of the legislators by whom these laws have been enacted, and by whom they have been administered; and now you are only to remember the sentiment in regard to the Negro, peculiar to the people of the South, and the character of the people against whom these laws are to be enforced, and the fact that no people are better than their laws, to have a perfectly just view of the whole situation.

To my mind these landlord-and-tenant laws are a disgrace and a scandal to American civilization. A more skillfully contrived device than these laws to crush out all aspiration, all hope of progress in the landless Negro could not well be devised. They sound to me like the grating hinges of a slave prison. They read like the inhuman bond of Shylock, stipulating for his pound of flesh. They environ the helpless Negro like the devil-fish of Victor Hugo, and draw the blood from every pore. He may writhe and twist, and strain every muscle, but he is held and firmly bound in a strong, remorseless and deadly grasp, from which only death can free him. Floods may rise, droughts may scorch, the elements may destroy his crops, famine may come, but whatever else may happen, the greedy landlord must have from his tenant the uttermost farthing. Like the den of the lion, all toes in its path turn inward.

The case is aggravated when you think of the illiteracy and ignorance of the people who sign land leases. They are ignorant of the terms of the contract, ignorant of the requirements of the law, and are thus absolutely in the power of the landholder.

You have heard much, read much, and thought much of the flagrant injustice, the monstrous cruelty and oppression inflicted on the tenant class in Ireland. I have no disposition to underrate the hardships of that class. On the contrary, I deplore them. But knowing them as I do* and deploring them as I do, I declare to you that the condition of the Irish tenant is merciful, tender and just, as compared with the American freedman. There are thousands in Ireland today who fix the price of their own rent, and thousands more for whom the government itself measures the amount of rent to be paid, not by the greed of the landlord, but by the actual value of the land and its productions, and by the ability of the tenant to pay.

But how is it with us? The tenant is left in the clutches of the landlord. No third party intervenes between the greed and power of one and the helplessness of the other. The landholder imposes his price, exacts his conditions, and the landless Negro must comply or starve. It is impossible to conceive of conditions more unfavorable to the welfare and prosperity of the laborer. It is often said that the law is merciful, but there is no mercy in this law.

Now let us sum up some of the points in the situation of the freedman. You will have seen how he is paid for his labor, how a full-grown man gets only eight dollars a month for his labor, out of which he has to feed, clothe and educate his children. You have seen how even this sum is reduced by the infamous truck system of payment. You have seen how easily he may be charged with one third more than the value of the goods that he buys. You have seen how easily he may be compelled to receive the poorest commodities at the highest prices. You have seen how he is never allowed to see or handle a dollar. You have seen how impossible it is for him to accumulate money or property. You have seen how completely he is chained to the locality in which he lives. You have seen, therefore, that having no money, he cannot travel or go anywhere to better his condition. You have seen by these laws that even on the premises which he rents he can own nothing, possess nothing. You have seen that he cannot sell a sheep, or a pig, or even a chicken without the consent of the landlord, whose claim to all he has is superior and paramount to all other claims whatsoever. You have seen all this and more, and I ask, in view of it all, How, in the name of human reason, could the Negro be expected to rise higher in the scale of morals, manner, religion and civilization than he has done during the twenty years of his freedom. Shame, eternal shame, on those writers and speakers who taunt, denounce and disparage the Negro because he is today found in poverty, rags and wretchedness.

But again, let us see what are the relations subsisting between the Negro and the state and national governments—what support, what assistance he has received from either of them. Take his relation to the national government and we shall find him a deserted, a defrauded, a swindled, and an out-

---

*During his trip abroad in 1845–46, Douglass toured all of Ireland and delivered more than fifty lectures there.

cast man—in law free, in fact a slave; in law a citizen, in fact an alien; in law a voter, in fact a disfranchised man. In law, his color is no crime; in fact his color exposes him to be treated as a criminal. Toward him every attribute of a just government is contradicted. For him, it is not a government of the people, by the people, and for the people. Toward him it abandons the beneficent character of a government, and all that gives a government the right to exist. The true object for which governments are ordained among men is to protect the weak against the encroachments of the strong, to hold its strong arm of justice over all the civil relations of its citizens and to see that all have an equal chance in the race of life. Now, in the case of the Negro citizen, our national government does precisely the reverse of all this. Instead of protecting the weak against the encroachments of the strong, it tacitly protects the strong in its encroachments upon the weak. When the colored citizens of the South point to the fourteenth and fifteenth amendments of the Constitution for the protection of their civil and political rights, the Supreme Court of the United States turns them out of court and tells them they must look for justice at the hands of the states, well knowing that those states are, in effect, the very parties that deny them justice. Thus is the Negro citizen swindled. The government professes to give him citizenship and silently permits him to be divested of every attribute of citizenship. It demands allegiance, but denies protection. It taxes him as a citizen in peace, and compels him to bear arms and meet bullets in war. It imposes upon him all the burdens of citizenship and withholds from him all its benefits.

I know it is said that the general government is a government of limited powers. It was also once said that the national government could not coerce a state and it is generally said that this and that public measure is unconstitutional. But whenever an administration has had the will to do anything, it has generally found Constitutional power to do it. If the general government had the power to make black men citizens, it has the power to protect them in that citizenship. If it had the right to make them voters it has the right to protect them in the exercise of the elective franchise. If it has this right, and refuses to exercise it, it is a traitor to the citizen. If it has not this right, it is destitute of the fundamental quality of a government and ought to be hissed and hurried out of the sisterhood of government, a usurper, a sham, a delusion and a snare.

On the other hand, if the fault is not in the structure of the government, but in the treachery and indifference of those who administer it, the American people owe it to themselves, owe it to the world, and the Negro, to sweep from place and power those who are thus derelict in the discharge of their place in the government who will not enforce the Constitutional right of every class of American citizen.

I am a Republican. I believe in the Republican party. My political hopes for the future of the colored people are enforced in the character and composition, in the wisdom and justice, in the courage and fidelity of the Republican party. I am unable to see how any honest and intelligent colored man can be a Democrat or play fast and loose between the two parties. But while

I am Republican and believe in the party, I dare to tell that party the truth. In my judgment it can no longer repose on the history of its grand and magnificent achievements. It must not only stand abreast with the times, but must create the times. Its power and greatness consisted in this at the beginning. It was in advance of the times and made the times when it abolished the slave trade between the states, when it emancipated the slaves of the District of Columbia, when it stemmed the bloody tide of disunion, when it abolished slavery in all the states, when it made the Negro a soldier and a citizen, when it conceded to him the elective franchise; and now, in my judgment, the strength, success and glory of the Republican party will be found in its holding that advanced position. It must not stand still or take any step backward. Its mission is to lead, not to follow; to make circumstances, not to be made by them. It is held and firmly bound by every sentiment of justice and honor to make a living fact out of the dead letter of the Constitutional amendments. It must make the path of the black citizen to the ballot box as safe and smooth as that of the white citizen. It must make it impossible for a man like James Russell Lowell* to say he sees no difference between the Democratic party and the Republican party. If it fails to do all this, I for one shall welcome the bolt which shall scatter it into a thousand fragments.

The supreme movement in the life of the Republican party is at hand. The question, to be or not to be, will be decided at Chicago, and I reverently trust in God that it my be decided rightly. If the platform it shall adopt shall be in accordance with its earlier antecedents; if the party shall have the courage in its maturity which it possessed and displayed in its infancy; if it shall express its determination to vindicate the honor and integrity of the Republican by stamping out the fraud, injustice and violence which make elections in the South a disgrace and scandal to the Republic, and place a man on the platform with a clear head, a clean hand and a heroic heart, the country will triumphantly elect him. If it, however, should fail to elect him, we shall have done our duty and shall still have under us a grand party of the future, certain of success.

I do not forget that there are other great interests beside the Negro to be thought of. The civil service is a great interest, protection to American industry is a great interest, the proper management of our finances so as to promote the business and prosperity of the country is a great interest; but the national honor—the redemption of our national pledge to the freedmen, the supremacy of the Constitution in the fullness of its spirit and in the completeness of its letter over all the states of the Union alike—is an incomparably greater interest than all others. It touches the soul of the nation, which against all things else should be preserved. Should all be lost but this, the nation would be like Chicago after the fire—more prosperous and beau-

*James Russell Lowell (1819–1891), poet, essayist, editor, and diplomat, frequently wrote against slavery in his poetry. In his *Bigelow Papers* (1848) he had opposed the Mexican War.

tiful than ever. But what I ask of the Republican party requires no sacrifice or postponement of the material interest of the country. I simply say to the Republican party: Those things ye ought to have done and not to have left the others undone, and the present is the time to enforce this lesson.

The time has come for a new departure as to the kind of man who is to be the standard-bearer of the Republican party. Events are our instructors. We have had enough of names, we now want things. We have had enough of good feeling, enough of shaking hands over the bloody chasm, enough of conciliation, enough of laudation of the bravery of our Southern brethren. We tried all that with President Hayes, of the purity of whose motives I have no shadow of doubt. His mistake was that he confided in the honor of the Confederates, who were without honor. He supposed that if left to themselves and thrown upon their honor they would obey the Constitution they had sworn to support and treat the colored citizens with justice and fairness at the ballot box.* Time has proved the reverse to all this, and this fact should cure the Republican party of adopting in its platform any such soft policy or any such candidate. Let us have a candidate this time of pronounced opinions and, above all, a backbone. . . .

There has been no show of federal power in the borders of the South for a dozen years. Its people have been left to themselves. Northern men have even refrained from going among them in election times to discuss the claims of public men, or the wisdom of public measures. They have had the field all to themselves, and we all know just what has come of it, and the eyes of the leaders of the Republican party are, I trust, wide open. Mr. James G. Blaine, after, as well as before, he failed of his election,† pointed out the evil which now besets us as a party and a nation. Senator John Sherman‡ knows full well that the Solid South must be broken, that the colored citizen must not be cheated out of his vote any longer and that the Constitution must be obeyed in all parts of the country alike; that individual states are great, but that the United States are greater. He has said the right word, and said it calmly but firmly, in the face of the South itself, and I thank him and honor him for it. I am naming no candidate for the presidency. Any one of the dozen statesmen whose names are in the air, and many whose names are

---

*When Rutherford B. Hayes removed the troops from Louisiana and South Carolina, he wrote in his diary that the governors and legislatures of these two states had pledged to observe the Thirteenth, Fourteenth, and Fifteenth Amendments. He concluded: "I am confident this is a good work. Time will tell." Eighteen months later he was deeply shocked that Louisiana and South Carolina were not keeping their promises. Gravely, he wrote: "By State legislation, by frauds, by intimidation and by violence of the most atrocious character, colored citizens have been deprived of the right of suffrage—a right guaranteed by the Constitution, and to the protection of which the people of those States have been solemnly pledged." T. Harry Williams, ed., *Hayes: The Diary of a President, 1875–1881* (New York: D. McKay, 1964), 122, 196.

†James Gillespie Blaine (1830–1893) was the Republican candidate for president in 1884 against Grover Cleveland, the victorious Democratic candidate.

‡John Sherman (1823–1900), author of the Sherman Anti-Trust Act of 1890, was a leading Republican senator and U.S. secretary of state (1897–1898).

not, would suit me and gain my best word and vote. There is one who has
not been named and not likely to be named, who would suit me and who
would fulfill the supreme demand of the hour; and that man is a Southern
man. I refer to the Honorable John M. Harlan, Justice of the Supreme Court
of the United States, who, true to his convictions, stood by the plain intention of the Fourteenth Amendment of the Constitution of the United States
in opposition to all his brothers on the bench.* The man who could do that
in the circumstances in which he was placed, if made President of the United
States, could be depended upon in any emergency to do the right thing.

But, as I have said, I am not naming candidates. The candidate of the
Republican party will, in all the likelihoods of the case, be my candidate. I
am no partisan. I have no ambition to be the first to name any man or make
any man obliged to me for naming him for the high office of President. Other
men may do this, and I have no disposition to find fault with them for doing
it. If, however, John A. Logan were living I might name him.† I am sure he
would not allow himself to be trifled with, or allow the Constitution to be
defied or trampled in the dust. I have faith also, in Roscoe Conkling,‡ whose
dangerous illness we all deplore and whose recovery we profoundly and anxiously desire. With such a man in the Presidential chair, the red shirt and
rifle, horseback and tissue-ballot plan of South Carolina and the Mississippi
bulldozing plan would receive no encouragement.§

I am, however, not here to name men. My mission now, as all along during nearly fifty years, is to plead the cause of the dumb millions of our countrymen against injustice, oppression, meanness and cruelty, and to hasten
the day when the principles of liberty and humanity expressed in the Declaration of Independence and the Constitution of the United States shall be
the law and the practice of every section, and of all the people of this great
country without regard to race, sex, color or religion.■

---

*John Marshall Harlan (1833–1911), born in Kentucky, served on the U.S. Supreme
Court from 1877 to 1911, during which time he consistently supported rights of black
Americans. He dissented in the *Civil Rights Cases* of 1883 and the *Plessy v. Ferguson*
decision of 1896, in both cases denouncing the deprivation of the constitutional rights of
African Americans under the Fourteenth Amendment.

†John A. Logan (1826–1886), a Union general and frequent supporter of African American rights, was U.S. senator from Illinois (1871–1877; 1879–1886).

‡Roscoe Conkling (1829–1888), leader of the Republican Party in New York and senator from that state between 1867 and 1881, was a staunch opponent of reconciliation with
the South. He headed the so-called Stalwart faction in the Republican Party, which stood
for upholding the rights of African Americans under the Constitutional amendments
adopted during Reconstruction.

§In states where African Americans were a majority or nearly so, virtual disfranchisement of blacks was accomplished without legal action, after the overthrow of Reconstruction, by such devices as the Mississippi Plan, which used violence to force African Americans to desist from political action. "Red Shirts" were armed vigilantes on horseback in
South Carolina.

122 ORGANIZED RESISTANCE IS OUR BEST REMEDY

John E. Bruce

Among the many proposals made during the post-Reconstruction period as to how best to meet the violence experienced daily by African Americans was one advanced by John E. Bruce, a leading journalist, calling for "a resort to force under wise and discreet leaders." Basing his advice on the ancient principle of self-defense, Bruce called upon African Americans to meet force with force. His speech was delivered on October 5, 1889, but the occasion and place where it was made are not indicated in the manuscript in Bruce's papers.

John E. Bruce, better known to the public as "Bruce Grit," was born in Piscataway, Maryland, February 22, 1856. In the Colored American *of February 16, 1901, he was described as "the prince of Negro newspaper correspondents, having for the past twenty-six years represented papers in the West Indies, Africa and various sections of America." Bruce was the author of many pamphlets dealing with problems of black people, including* The Blood Record, *a review of lynchings in the United States "by civilized white men." His papers are available in the Schomburg Library in New York City. The text of the address presented here is in manuscript, dated October 5, 1889, Folder No. 7, John E. Bruce Collection, Schomburg Collection, New York Public Library.**

I FULLY REALIZE the delicacy of the position I occupy in this discussion and know too well that those who are to follow me will largely benefit by what I shall have to say in respect to the application of force as one of the means to the solution of the problem known as the Negro problem. I am not unmindful of that fact that there are those living who have faith in the efficacy of submission, who are impregnated with the slavish fear which had its origin in oppression and the peculiar environments of the slave period. Those who are thus minded will advise a pacific policy in order, as they believe, to effect a settlement of this question, with which the statesmanship of a century has grappled without any particularly gratifying results. Agitation is a good thing, organization is a better thing. The million Negro voters of Georgia, and the undiscovered millions in other Southern states—undiscovered so far as our knowledge of their number exists—could with proper organization and intelligent leadership meet force with force with most beneficial results. The issue upon us cannot be misunderstood by those who

*For further information see Peter Gilbert, ed., The Selected Writings of John E. Bruce: Militant Black Journalist (New York: Arno Press, 1971).

are watching current events. . . . The man who will not fight for the protection of his wife and children is a *coward* and deserves to be ill treated. The man who takes his life in his hand and stands up for what he knows to be right will always command the respect of his enemy.

Submission to the *dicta* of the Southern bulldozers is the basest cowardice, and there is no just reason why manly men of any race should allow themselves to be continually outraged and oppressed by their equals before the law . . .

Under the present conditions of affairs the only hope, the only salvation for the Negro is to be found in a resort to force under wise and discreet leaders. He must sooner or later come to this in order to set at rest for all time to come the charge that he is a moral coward. . . .

The Negro must not be rash and indiscreet either in action or in words but he must be very determined and terribly in earnest, and of one mind to bring order out of chaos and to convince Southern rowdies and cutthroats that more than two can play at the game with which they have amused their fellow conspirators in crime for nearly a quarter of a century. Under the Mosaic dispensation it was the custom to require an eye for an eye and a tooth for a tooth under no less barbarous civilization than that which existed at that period of the world's history; let the Negro require at the hands of every white murderer in the South or elsewhere a life for a life. If they burn our houses, burn theirs, if they kill our wives and children, kill theirs, pursue them relentlessly, meet force with force everywhere it is offered. If they demand blood, exchange it with them, until they are satiated. By a vigorous adherence to this course the shedding of human blood by white men will soon become a thing of the past. Wherever and whenever the Negro shows himself to be a man he can always command the respect even of a cutthroat. Organized resistance to organized resistance is the best remedy for the solution of the vexed problem of the century, which to me seems practical and feasible, and I submit this view of the question, ladies and gentleman, for your careful consideration.■

123 NATIONAL PERILS

William Bishop Johnson

As African Americans sought greater organizational strength with which to combat the rising tide of racist violence and discrimination, they turned not only to the creation of new secular associations but to the black Church. Washington minister William Bishop Johnson was a leader in the politicization of the Baptist Church, the largest single denomination of African Americans.

Johnson was born on December 11, 1858, in Toronto. After attending school in Buffalo, New York, he graduated as valedictorian and class orator from Wayland Seminary in Richmond, Virginia, in 1879. He was a professor of mathematics and political science at Wayland for twelve years, serving simultaneously as pastor of the Second Baptist Church in Washington, D.C. Johnson was active in the formation and development of the American Baptist National Convention, an independent organization of black churches formed after long-standing difficulties with white Baptists. In 1895, it would become the National Baptist Convention, "the largest Afro-American organization in the nation," according to Ralph Luker; " 'the church with the soul of a nation,' cradling the aspirations of black Americans for national recognition into the twentieth century" (The Social Gospel in Black and White, 55). *Johnson organized the National Baptist Educational convention, which coordinated all schools run by black Baptists. Beginning in 1893, he served as managing editor of the National Baptist Convention's* National Baptist Magazine.

The American Baptist National Convention declared Sunday, October 20, 1889, a day set apart "for prayer that Southern outrages might cease" (The Scourging of a Race, 133). *Johnson delivered the following sermon that day at Washington's Second Baptist Church. In it, Johnson catalogs various threats facing the nation, including illiteracy, intemperance, and the "red-handed and heartless socialist," anarchist, and nihilist who is "thirsty for blood." Although there are many threats facing the American republic, Johnson makes clear, African Americans are not among them and have done nothing to provoke the violence directed against them. He predicts that newfound black organizational strength will triumph and "what we call the patient, humble Negro will have gone and a countless army of strong men, who know their rights and will contend for them, will have taken their place." While not encouraging violence, Johnson does urge his congregation to arm themselves in self-defense. They should buy land, he tells them, "and then prepare to stay on that land if every inch must be converted into a fort with Winchester and Gatling guns to keep off the wildcats and crows."*

The text of Johnson's militant sermon appears in his collection, The Scourging of a Race, and Other Sermons and Addresses *(Washington, D.C.: Murray Brothers, 1904), which includes a brief biographical sketch written by E. M. Brawley. See also Ralph Luker,* The Social Gospel in Black and White: American Racial Reform, 1885–1912 *(Chapel Hill: University of North Carolina Press, 1991).*

"Righteousness exalteth a nation, but sin is a reproach to any people."— *Proverbs xiv, 34.*

Human life is full of perils. No matter from what standpoint it is viewed, it is perilous. We are launched upon the great ocean of time, ignorant of what the future has in store for us. In vain we try to divine what the developments of to-morrow may be, and are confronted in each step of our history with a demonstration of the truth. "What a day may bring forth is uncertain." Four things are inseparably connected—time and eternity, life and death. An army more numerous than that of Goths or Vandals invades this globe. Fourteen hundred millions of human beings tread our earth. Each fearfully and wonderfully made; each making for himself a history which must give permanence to his future state, when time shall cease its revolutions; each touching the other with his influence, either for good or evil; each struggling for existence; now wrestling with adversity; now with prosperity; now under the cloud; now basking in the sunshine; and whether awake or asleep, whether active or inactive, all on a ceaseless march to the city of the mute-tongued dead.

Now, what is true of individuals is no less true in national life. Nations make records, exert influence, enjoy prosperity, suffer adversity, contend in the school of human experience for an existence, live and die, the same as individuals. The same law which governs the individual regulates the actions of nations, so that all are bound with the common bonds of brotherhood, and none can say to his brother, "I have no need of thee."

In the march of progress, it is well to stop and see what obstacles have been overcome; for there can be no progress, without obstacles; they are the measuring rods by which the individual sees how far he has come, and gets in position to grasp the great problems the future shall present. There is no life without shadows and clouds; no day without the night, even though, the night be Egyptian darkness, for He who holdeth the waters in the hollow of His hand and maketh the winds, His chariot marks out the course of the king of day, saying

> "Roll on, thou imperial majesty of the day!
> Step forth and guild the sky and earth
> And let no ruthless hand of time, no age, with its disease and death,
> Attempt to thwart the will of Him who called thee into birth."

So we call you to-day to consider briefly some national perils, and see the relation the Negro sustains to them.

The greatest nation on earth is America; great in its wide and varied natural resources; its sweeping rivers creeping majestically and silently to their outlet; in its broad lakes, bearing upon their restless bosoms the white-winged messengers of commerce; in its towering mountains, whose rugged peaks bathe their hoary heads in the clouds; its fertile valleys, in whose productive soil wave the golden wheat; the white-capped cotton, or the nutritious rice; great in its extensive plains, inviting the pasture of rich-blooded stock and extending its freedom to the prancing and fiery steed; in its multitudinous grades of mineral, whose veins traverse circuitous routes in subterranean chambers. Great in intellectual giants; producing scholars, scientists, artists, philosophers—who in their ramblings have discovered the secrets of the most distant stars, vanquished time and space, taught the vapors to toil, the lightning to speak, and the wind to worship; stolen the witchery of earth and sky, and gathered them into her enchanted chambers, and by books have echoed the crash of revolutions and the silent thunders of thought. But with all her greatness she must pause, and from the mountain top of opportunity note the perils that surround her and threaten to forever bedim her glory and relegate her to the shades of oblivion.

Several forces are working silently to undermine our prosperity. There stands the red-handed and heartless socialist—with lighted torch and dynamite bomb, ready to apply it to church and school, to state house and private dwelling. He is thirsty for blood; he is an enemy to those rights which give the privilege of private property; he hisses at and insults the American flag; he makes incendiary speeches, inflaming the passions of his fellows, and seeks with sleepless vigilance to destroy the order of good government. He cries, "Away with the state, away with all authority, away with the family, away with religion."

The socialist is indeed the product of ignorance, for as men are enlightened, they see at once the divine mission and arrangement of the church, the home, and the state. "Order is heaven's first law," for where confusion reigns there is sin and every evil work.

The socialist, the anarchist, the nihilist, are all children of the same parent—the devil. They are the factors in our national system that are a standing menace to the nation's future prosperity. A great deal is said of the Negro as a citizen and a part of our social system, but the Negro never has nor can be so antagonistic to the well being of the American people as this foreign element that sweeps in on us like a modern Pharaoh's plague, and threatens to tear down all the civilization that our fathers have produced in the centuries of our existence.

Another evil is the illiteracy of the masses. With all the increasing labors of our public school system in the various states, our colleges and universities, our seminaries and private schools; with the expenditure annually of public moneys for the education of the people, yet the greater portion of the population grows up in ignorance. Much is said of Negro illiteracy, but the colored people are thirsty for knowledge. They are a reading people; old men with gray hairs and large families are seeking light and knowledge until to-day it is a rare thing to find a colored man without intelligent ideas. There are some, it is true, but in comparison with the whites and their centuries of superior advantages, the colored man makes an excellent showing.

Ignorance obstructs virtue, imperils piety, hinders industry and prosperity, and destroys everything good it touches. Now the best policy any government can adapt is that which can stem the tide of ignorance and place in the hands of every man the torch of knowledge, so that he can better know his duty to both God and man.

The great arch-fiend, the inveterate and unrelenting enemy of our time, is intemperance. It is the parent of vice and immorality, the thief of virtue and honor, the destroyer of intellect, the murderer of everything good in man, and the curse which not only affects the age in which it lives, but extends its influence to future ages and touches with its withering, blighting finger generations yet unborn. Intemperance, for these reasons, is a great peril to the nation; it increases the army of paupers and tramps; is a continuous draft on the public fund, fills the poor houses, jails, insane asylums and other institutions supported by the State, with inmates. Reliable statistics show that over four billion dollars are annually spent for liquor in the United States; that 737,296,554 gallons of liquor were made last year; 150,000 human beings sent to drunkards' graves. What an army to be ushered before God! How vast the evil! Of this number, some may have been mighty in the councils of the church and state; many may have made a glorious history for themselves among men, but they are gone forever and forgotten.

So we stand as a nation, enjoying almost unconfined prosperity; the wonder of the age in progress, the observed of observers, and yet carrying with and in us the very forces which will destroy us forever, unless properly controlled.

But what about the Negro? He is not a dangerous element; he is industrious, good-natured, honest—for his honesty has been tested both as a slave and freeman—when he stayed at home while his master went forth to fight to keep him a slave, he watched with a sleepless eye, and protected with a strong arm his wife and daughters. As a freeman, he has no representatives in Canada, and a very few in jails and penitentiaries in comparison with others. He is grateful to the party that assisted in giving him freedom, and feels that it is his unfailing friend, and believes it best not to give up the old friend for the new. There are perils surrounding us. But does the Negro make them? Is he responsible for them? He is improving intellectually; he has acquired over $2,000,000 in property; built costly and magnificent churches in every city of the Union; organized all kinds of secret societies, but has never made them the means of overthrowing law and order; of intimidating citizens in the exercise of their constitutional rights; of insulting the American flag or banding the race in an agreement with death and covenant with hell, to murder and lynch, regardless of the majesty of the law, and defy detection. When he organizes, it is either for moral, material, religious, or intellectual purposes. Now, I am not prepared to think this will always be so. He is learning how organizations can be made to help in securing his rights. He has gotten some important lessons from the socialist and the Irishman; and he is not a silent watcher for naught; he is taking notes, and what will be the result, the future alone must reveal; but the Negro of the next twenty years will be a different individual from the Negro of to-day. What we call the patient, humble Negro will have gone and a countless army of strong men, who know their rights and will contend for them, will have taken their place. The prejudice of ignorant southern white people will have weakened before the strong arm of resistance which will be stretched forth every time a right is infringed upon; our people must, in the mean time, get property, buy land, own houses and lots in the south and west and then prepare themselves to stay on that land if every inch must be converted into a fort with Winchester and Gatling guns to keep off the wildcats and crows. Israel remained in Egypt and mourned, and God told them to come forth, but they passed through many bloody struggles before they reached Canaan. War is an evil, but of "two evils we are to choose the lesser." All war does not mean bloodshed; the Reformation under Luther was a bloodless battle, but it threw off the yoke of bondage. All war does not mean reeking battlefields and clashing arms, but a struggle for right against wrong, and truth against error. Let our people in those localities where there is no hope of building up themselves leave and locate where they can get property and educate their children for the coming crisis, get education and money. Knowledge is power; so is money. Wealth is the king whose scepter sways over all classes—the rich and poor, young and old, white and black—all. We must look out for ourselves; we have been taking care of the white people for over 270 years; it is now time for us to build for ourselves and the future. We are 7,000,000 strong, interwoven into the being of this republic; we are in their blood, their homes, their schools, their courts; with them, waking or sleeping, in their downsitting and uprising; we are irrepressible—almost omnipresent—they cannot kill us out, for the more they hang the more numerous the army becomes. Extermination won't do; lynching won't do; intimidation won't do. Nothing but giving him what is justly his as a citizen, if he is a foreigner—and he is not. Assimilate him; make him a part; don't try to throw him off. There is no enmity strong enough, for he is in the blood and bone of the nation, and if left undisturbed, will do no harm; but if stirred may grasp the pillars, like Samson of old, of our temple's liberties and leave a shapeless mass of confusion at our feet.

Righteousness exalteth a nation. It is only when men recognize God that they rise; only when they walk the paths that Jehovah points out that they live and die in peace. It is the Gospel that saves men, and it is the Gospel of righteousness that brings that happy period when men shall learn war no more, but beat their swords into plowshares and their spears into pruning hooks.■

124   IT IS TIME TO CALL A HALT

T. Thomas Fortune

The first major black protest organization after the Reconstruction period was the National Afro-American League. The League was initiated by T. Thomas Fortune, the editor of the New York Age. *Born in slavery in 1856 in Florida and with little formal education, Fortune*

*came to New York in 1879 and rose to become one of the most promi-
nent journalists of his day and part owner and editor of his own newspaper, the* Globe.

*In 1887 Fortune called upon African Americans to form an organiza-
tion to fight for the rights denied them. At the founding convention of the
League held in Chicago in January 1890, 141 delegates from twenty-three
states assembled to form a permanent organization, independent of established political parties. As temporary chair of the convention, Fortune delivered a long, stirring address. Fortune offers a historical defense of agitation and resistance; like thunderstorms, he argues, "revolutions clarify
the social and civil atmosphere." He calls upon his fellow league members to "stand shoulder to shoulder" to protest and organize resistance.
The convention, led by Fortune, adopted proposals for an Afro-American
bank, industrial education and black self-determination in political, economic, and cultural affairs. By 1893, however, the league had disbanded.
It was succeeded in 1898 (also with Fortune's leadership) by the Afro-
American Council. These groups were forerunners of the major twentieth-
century civil rights organizations.*

The text is from the New York Age, *January 25, 1890. For further in-
formatin on Fortune and the Afro-American League, see August Meier,*
Negro Thought in America, 1880–1915 *(Ann Arbor: University of Michigan Press, 1963).*

L ADIES AND GENTLEMEN OF THE AFRO-AMERICAN LEAGUES:
— We are met here to day, representatives of 8,000,000 freemen, who
know our rights and have the courage to defend them. We are met here to
day to emphasize the fact that the past condition of dependence and helplessness upon men who have used us for selfish and unholy purposes, who
have murdered and robbed and outraged us, must be reversed.

It is meet and proper that we have met for such high purpose upon the
free soil of Illinois. It was here that Elijah Lovejoy, the first martyr to freedom's sacred cause, died that we might be free.* It was here that Abraham
Lincoln lived, and in this soil he sleeps, having died 'that the Nation shall,
under God, have a new birth of freedom, and that the government of the
people, by the people and for the people shall not perish from earth.' It was
here that John Alexander Logan,[†] like Saul of Tarsus, was convicted of his
error in persecuting the people of the Lord, and buckled on his sword and
went forth to lead the volunteer hosts in freedom's fight, pausing not until
struck down at his post of duty by the angel of death; he, too, sleeps in the
imperial soil 'where law and order reign,' 'where government is supreme.'

---

*Abolitionist newspaper editor Elijah Lovejoy was murdered by a mob in Alton, Illi-
nois, in 1837.

[†]John Alexander Logan (1826–1886), Republican senator from Illinois, recruited for
and served with the Thirty-first Illinois Regiment in the Civil War.

And we do not forget the living sons of this soil who fought in freedom's ranks when we mention here the names of Gen. Walter Q. Gresham, or Private Fifer, the Chief Executive of this Commonwealth, and of his generous opponent, Gen. John M. Palmer.

Upon such historic ground, surrounded by the spirits of such famous dead, and cheered by the presence of such living friends of the black soldiers who followed where they led—:

> 'Into the jaws of death,
> Into the mouth of hell'—

borne down in the wild charge, baptized with fire and shot and shell, contending like heroes for freedom's priceless smile, shall we not take fresh courage? Shall we not bravely buckle on the armor and march with unhesitating step, with unfaltering hearts to the convention before us for absolute justice under the constitution? By the name of Elijah Lovejoy, embalmed in song and story, by the name of Abraham Lincoln, which shall illustrate and illuminate the pages of history brightest in the annals of our glory; by the names of the black heroes who died at Battery Wagner, Fort Pillow and the awful crater at Petersburg—by the names of these honored dead I conjure the spirit of universal emancipation to be with us here, and to enthuse us with the devotion to high principle which Wm. Lloyd Garrison emphasized when he exclaimed, 'I am in earnest; I will not equivocate, I will not retreat a single inch—and I will be heard.'

Fellow-members of the League, I congratulate you upon your presence here. I congratulate you upon the high resolve, the manly inspiration, which impelled you to this spot. I congratulate you that you have aroused from the lethargy of the past, and that you now stand face to face, brave men and true, with the awful fact that 'who would be free themselves must strike the blow.' I congratulate you that you now recognize the fact that a great work remains for you to do, and that you are determined, with the countenance of Jehovah, to do it. And, finally, I congratulate myself that I have been chosen as the humble spokesman to voice at this time and in this manner the high resolves which move you as one man to perfect an organization which shall secure to ourselves and to our children the blessings of citizenship so generally denied us.

The spirit of agitation which has brought us together here comprehends in its vast sweep the entire range of human history. The world has been rocked in the cradle of agitation from Moses to Gladstone. The normal condition of mankind is one of perpetual change, unrest and aspiration—a contention of the virtues against the vices of mankind. The great moving and compelling influence in the history of the world is agitation, and the greatest of agitators was He, the despised Nazarene, whose doctrines have revolutionized the thought of the ages.

The progress of mankind has been greatest in eras of most unrest and innovation. Iconoclasm has always been the watchword of progress.

It was an idle dream of the poet that a time would ever come in the history of the race

> *"When the war drum beats no longer,*
>   *When the battle flag is furled,*
> *In the parliament of nations,*
>   *The federation of the world.*

Equally fatuous was Longfellow's lament that

> *Were half the power that fills the world with terror,*
> *Were half the wealth bestowed on camps and courts*
> *Given to redeem the human mind from error,*
> *There were no need of arsenals and forts.*

Apathy leads to stagnation. The arsenal, the fort, the warrior are as necessary as the school, the church, the newspapers and the public forum of debate. It is a narrow and perverted philosophy which condemns as a nuisance agitators. It is this sort of people who consider nothing to be sacred which stands in the pathway of the progress of the world. Like John crying in the wilderness, they are the forerunners of change in rooted abuses which revolutionize society.

Demosthenes, thundering against the designs of Philip of Macedon upon the liberties of Greece; Cicero, holding up to scorn and ridicule the schemes of Cataline against the freedom of Rome; Oliver Cromwell, baring his sturdy breast to the arrows of royalty and nobility to preserve to Englishmen the rights contained in Magna Charta; Patrick Henry, fulminating against the arrogant and insolent encroachments of Great Britain upon the rights of the American colonies; Nat Turner, rising from the dust of slavery and defying the slave oligarchy of Virginia, and John Brown, resisting the power of the United States in a heroic effort to break the chains of the bondsman—these are some of the agitators who have voiced the discontent of their times at the peril of life and limb and property, Who shall cast the stone of reproach at these children of the race? Who shall say they were not heroes born to live forever in the annals of song and story?

Revolutions are of many sorts. They are either silent and unobservable, noiseless as the movement of the earth on its axis, or loud and destructive, shaking the earth from centre to circumference, making huge gaps in the map of earth, changing the face of empires, subverting dynasties and breaking fetters asunder or riveting them anew.

Jesus Christ may be regarded as the chief spirit of agitation and innovation. He himself declared, 'I come not to bring peace, but a sword.'

St. Paul, standing upon Mars Hill, read the death sentence of Grecian and Roman mythology in the simple sentence, 'Whom ye ignorantly worship Him I declare unto you.'

A portion of mankind remains always conservative, while the other portion is moved by the spirit of radicalism; and no man can predict where the conflict may lead when once the old idea and the new one conflict, and must needs appeal to the logic of revolution to arbitrate between them. Few Romes are large enough to hold a Caesar and a Brutus. The old idea and the new idea, the spirit of freedom and the spirit of tyranny and oppression cannot live together without friction. The agitator must never be in advance of his times. The people must be prepared to receive the message that he brings them. The harvest must be ripe for the sickle when the reaper enters the field.

As it was in ancient Greece and Rome, so it is in modern Europe and America. The just cause does not always prevail. The John Browns and Nat Turners do not always find the people ready to receive the tidings of great joy they bring them.

Martin Luther, opposing the vice and corruption and superstition of the religion of his times, putting in motion influences which aroused all Christendom, needed only to have failed in his self-imposed reformation to have died by the tortures of the thumbscrew and the rack of the Inquisition.

Nothing succeeds like success, nothing is more severely condemned than failure.

Napoleon Bonaparte, at the head of a million soldiers, firmly seated upon the throne of the Bourbons of France, is courted and flattered and feared by the whole of Europe. Whipped at Waterloo, his vast armies scattered and demoralized, exiled to a rock in the Atlantic Ocean, chained as Prometheus, all pronounce him a Corsican adventurer, a base upstart, a human monster.

It does not pay to fail.

Napoleon Bonaparte was the avenging Nemesis of the medieval conditions of government and society. He heralded the reaction against abuses in civil and ecclesiastical administration which had been the slowly developed fungi of centuries. It was terrific, but it was necessary. It is always the most drastic medicine that kills the deep-seated disease—or the patient. We yet live in the swim of that tremendous revolution. To it we may trace the dominating impulses that lead to the independence of the United States, the independence of Hayti and San Domingo, the independence of the South American Republics, the abolition of slavery in the British West Indies, the liberation of the Russian serfs, the abolition of slavery in this country, the recent manumission of Brazilian slaves, and that agitation for larger individual freedom, battling against the incubus of conservation,—whether in the garb of tyranny in the state, oppressions of the nobility, superstitious and unjust assumptions of priestly inquisitors, as in Europe, or of arrogant and insolent intolerance, as in the United States.

Agitations are inevitable. They are as necessary to social organism as blood is to animal organism. Revolutions follow as a matter of course. Each link in the long chain of human progress is indelibly marked as the result of a revolution. The thunder storm clarifies the atmosphere and infuses into the veins of all animal life new vigor and new hopes. Revolutions clarify the social and civil atmosphere. They sober the nation; they sharpen the wits of the people; they make rights and privileges which have been the bone of contention all the more precious, because of the severe labor which consecrated them anew to ourselves and to our posterity. The benefits that come to us as the rewards of our genius, untiring industry, and frugality are more highly and justly prized than benefits that come to us by indirection and without our seeking. The spendthrifts of our society are those who reap where others have sown, who spend what others have toiled to amass.

The aspirations of the human soul, like the climbing vine, are forever in the line of greater freedom, fuller knowledge, ampler possessions. These aspirations find always opposing aspirations. It is true of nations seeking after greater reforms. To accomplish these agitation is necessary.

The imperial eagle, the emblem of our National prowess and unconquerable aspiration, builds his nest in the loftiest peaks of the highest mountains. He knows his supreme power and he exercises it. His eaglets, when they burst from the chrysalis which had nurtured their infancy, gaze first into the face of the lordly sun. The first law of the eagle's nature is aggressiveness. Resistance remains the most pronounced characteristic of his existence.

Wherein does the eagle differ from the strong nations of the world?

The revolutionary intuitions of mankind are fundamental and sleepless. It is because of this fact that agitators like the Roman Gracchi, the German Luther, the British Cromwell, the American John Brown and William Lloyd Garrison, for examples, cut such a considerable figure in the history of every nation and every epoch. It is the discontent, the restlessness, the sleepless aspiration of humanity, voiced by some braver, some more far-seeing member of society, some man ready to be a martyr to his faith or wear the crown of victory, which keep the world in a ferment of excitation and expectancy, and which force the adoption of those reforms which keep society from retrograding to the conditions of savage life, from which it has slowly and painfully moved forward. There can be no middle ground in social life. There must be positive advancement or positive decline.

Social growth is the slowest of all growths.

Fellow-members of the League, it is matter of history that the abolition of slavery was the fruit of the fiercest and most protracted agitation in the history of social reforms. Begun practically in 1816 by Benjamin Lundy,* having been the chief bone of contention at the very birth of the republic, the agitation for the emancipation of the slave did not cease until Abraham Lincoln issued the Emancipation Proclamation in 1863. When emancipation was an established fact, when the slave had been made a freeman and the freeman had been made a citizen, the Nation reached the conclusion that its duty was fully discharged. A reaction set in after the second election of Gen. Grant to the presidency in 1872, and terminated after the election of Mr. Hayes in 1876, when the Afro-American citizen was turned over to the tender mercies of his late masters—deserted by the Nation, deserted by the party he had served in peace and in war, left poor and defenseless to fight a

---

*Lundy was editor of the abolitionist newspaper *Genius of Universal Emancipation.*

foe who had baffled the entire Nation through four years of bloody and destructive war.

Patient as a slave, heroic as a soldier, faithful to every trust as a citizen, and faithful above all to the country his valor aided to consecrate anew to the great destiny treason had attempted to destroy, and to the great party God had used to consummate His gracious purposes, even when that party had deserted him, had offered him as a sacrifice upon the altar of expediency and selfish advantage, the Afro-American in every situation has proved himself true to the duty imposed upon him—true to his country, true to his friends, rising always and at all times to the sublime principles which are at the bed-rock of the Federal union. In sunshine and in storm, in the prosperity of peace, and in the convulsion and devastation of war, he has shown that he is a man and a brother.

His sublime faith in the Government, his implicit obedience to the law, his undeviating devotion to the party which led him as Moses led the children of Israel out of the house of bondage—all this, the noblest conduct of which men are capable, has been used against him as a crime instead of a virtue, as a badge of servility rather than as an ensign of the greatest nobility, hitching upon him the sobriquets of cowardice and ignorance. Is it cowardice in a society governed by law to wait upon the eternal justice of the law to vindicate its outraged majesty? In the Afro-American it has been so charged. Is it a crime, a badge of ignorance, to be loyal to friends and consistent in hatred of tireless foes? In the Afro-American it has been so charged.

Ladies and gentlemen, we have been robbed of the honest wages of our toil; we have been robbed of the substance of our citizenship by murder and intimidation; we have been outraged by enemies and deserted by friends; and because in a society governed by law, we have been true to the law, true to treacherous friends, and as true in distrust of our enemies, it has been charged upon us that we are not made of the stern stuff which makes the Anglo-Saxon race the most consummate masters of hypocrisy, of roguery, of insolence, of arrogance, and of cowardice, in the history of races.

Was ever race more unjustly maligned than ours? Was ever race more shamelessly robbed than ours? Was ever race used to advance the political and pecuniary fortunes of others as ours? Was ever race so patient, so law abiding, so uncomplaining as ours?

Ladies and gentlemen, it is time to call a halt. It is time to begin to fight fire with fire. It is time to stand shoulder to shoulder as men. It is time to rebuke the treachery of friends in the only way that treachery should be rebuked. It is time to face the enemy and fight him inch by inch for every right he denies us.

We have been patient so long that many believe that we are incapable of resenting insult, outrage and wrong; we have so long accepted uncomplainingly all that injustice and cowardice and insolence heaped upon us, that many imagine that we are compelled to submit and have not the manhood necessary to resent such conduct. When matters assume this complexion, when oppressors presume too far upon the forbearance and the helplessness of the oppressed, the condition of the people affected is critical indeed. Such is our condition today. Because it is true; because we feel that something must be done to change the condition; because we are tired of being kicked and cuffed by individuals, made the scapegoats of the law, used by one party as an issue and by another as a stepping stone to place and power, and elbowed at pleasure by insolent corporations and their minions, corporations which derive their valuable franchises in part by consent of these very people they insult and outrage—it is because of the existence of these things that we are assembled here to day—determined to perfect an organization whose one mission shall be to labor by every reasonable and legal means to right the wrongs complained of, until not one right justly ours under the Constitution is denied us.

Ladies and gentlemen, I stand here today and assert in all soberness that we shall no longer accept in silence a condition which degrades our manhood and makes a mockery of our citizenship. I believe I voice the sentiments of each member of the League here assembled when I assert that from now and hence we shall labor as one man, inspired with one holy purpose, to wage relentless opposition to all men who would degrade our manhood and who would defraud us of the benefits of citizenship, guaranteed alike to all born upon this soil or naturalized by the Constitution which has been cemented and made indestructible by our blood in every war, foreign or domestic, waged by this grand Republic. And it is our proud boast that never in the history of this government has an Afro-American raised the hand of treason against the star spangled banner. Loyal in every condition to the flag of the Union—as slave, as contraband of war, as soldier and as citizen—we feel that we have a right to demand of the government we have served so faithfully the measure of protection guaranteed to us and freely granted to the vilest traitor who followed Robert E. Lee. There are Afro-American veterans in every State in the Union, of whom it may be said:

> If you ask from whence they came,
>   Our answer it shall be,
> They came from Appomattox
>   And its famous apple tree.

In the name of these veterans, who like their white comrades went back to their homes after the toils of war and mingled in the pursuits of peace, aiding by their industry to pay the enormous debt contracted to vindicate the right of every man born on this soil to be free indeed—in the name of these veterans who wore the blue, we appeal here to-day to the loyal people of the Nation, to frown upon the manifold wrongs practiced upon us, and to give their sympathy and their support to the movement we have met to inaugurate to combat these wrongs. It is a reproach to this Nation that one man entitled to the protection of the laws should be outraged in his person or in his property, and be unable to get redress. It is a shame and disgrace to the entire people that the arm of the government, which is long enough to reach the naturalized Irishman in British dungeons, to ward off the conscriptions of the German government when it would lay unholy hands upon a naturalized German—I say it is a shame and a disgrace that the government has the power to protect the humblest of its citizens in foreign lands and has not the power to protect its citizens at home—if we have a black face. Venerable prelates of the church have been insulted and outraged by corporations; refined and delicate women have been submitted to the grossest indignity on the public highway; men and women are lynched and flogged every day; and a million voters are practically disfranchised, have no representation in Federal or State legislature; and we are told by the supreme court of the land that the government which made the citizen and conferred co-equal rights upon him has no power to protect him in the vital matters here recited. If this be true, if it be true that the power which can create has no power to protect the creature, then it is high time that it secure to itself the necessary power. We appeal to the Nation, which fears a righteous God and loves justice, to judge if our contention here is unreasonable, and we here demand of the party now in power, which has promised so much and which enjoyed our best confidence and our support in the past, that it make good the promises made, that it pay us for our confidence and support in the past, or abide the consequences. We are weary of the empty promises of politicians and the platitudes of national conventions, and we demand a fulfillment of the stipulations in the bond as a condition of our further confidence and support. We do not mince our words here. For the constitutional opponents of our rights we have no faith, no confidence, and no support, and of professed friends we here demand that they perform their part of the contract, which alone can justify the sacrifices we have been called upon to make. If it cannot do this, then it has ceased to be the party of Lincoln, of Sumner, of Wilson, and of Logan, and deserves to die, and will die, that another party may rise to finish the uncompleted work, even as the Whig party died that the Republican party might triumph in the Nation.

I am no hero worshipper. Parties are not things [unintelligible] [But are brought] into existence by men to serve certain ends. They are the creatures and not the creators of men. When they have fulfilled the objects for which they were created or when they prove false to the great purpose of their creation, what further use are they? None certainly to us if they do not give us in return for our support the measure of justice and consideration in party management and benefits commensurate with the service we render. I do not speak here as a partisan; I speak as an Afro-American, first, last, and all the time, ready to stab to death any party which robs me of my confidence and vote and straightway asks me 'what are you going to do about it?' I have served the Republican party, the Prohibition party, and the Democratic party, and I speak with the wisdom of experience when I declare that none of them cares a fig for the Afro-American further than it can use him. In seeking to rebuke false friends we often make false alliances. If we shall serve the party and the men, as Afro-Americans, who serve us best, in the present posture of our citizenship, we shall follow the dictates of the highest wisdom and the most approved philosophy. It will be sound policy on the part of the Leagues here assembled to leave the local Leagues free to pursue such political course in its immediate community as the best interests of the race will seem to dictate. In National affairs it does not seem wise to me for the League to commit itself officially to any party. Let parties commit themselves to the best interests of Afro-American citizens, and it will then be time enough for us to commit ourselves to them. We have served parties long enough without benefit to the race. It is now time for parties to serve us some, if they desire our support.

I am now and I have always been a race man and not a party man. Let this League be a race league. To make it anything else is to sow the seed of discord, disunion, and disaster at the very beginning of our important work. We stand for the race, and not for this party or that party, and we should know a friend from a foe when we see him.

And now, ladies and gentlemen, it is time that I confine myself to the special matters which have moved us to congregate in this proud city of the West.

There come periods in the history of every people when the necessity of their affairs makes it imperative that they take such steps as will show to the world that they are worthy to be free, and therefore entitled to the sympathy of all mankind and to the cooperation of all lovers of justice and fair play. To do this they must unequivocally show that while they may solicit the sympathy and cooperation of mankind, they have the intelligence and courage to know what are their rights and manfully to contend for them, even though that sympathy and cooperation be ungenerously denied them.

I am in no sense unmindful of the vastness of the undertaking; but this instead of being a drawback, is rather an incentive to prosecute the matter with more earnestness and persistence.

I now give in consecutive order the reasons which in my opinion justify the organization of the National Afro-American League, to wit:

1. The almost universal suppression of our ballot in the South, and consequent 'taxation without representation,' since in the cities, counties and States where we have undisputed preponderating majorities of the voting population we have, in the main, no representation, and therefore no voice in the making and enforcing the laws under which we live.

2. The universal and lamentable reign of lynch and mob law, of which we are made the victims, especially in the South, all the more aggravating because all the machinery of the law making and enforcing power is in the hands of those who resort to such outrageous, heinous and murderous violations of the law.

3. The unequal distribution of school funds, collected from all taxpayers alike, and to the equal and undivided benefits of which all are alike entitled.

4. The odious and demoralizing penitentiary system of the South, with its chain gangs, convict leases and indiscriminate mixing of males and females.

5. The almost universal tyranny of common carrier corporations in the South—railroad, steamboat and other—in which the common rights of men and women are outraged and denied by the minions of these corporations, acting under implicit order in most cases, as well as by common passengers, who take the matter in their own hands as often as they please, and are in no instances pursued and punished by the lawful authorities.

6. The discrimination practiced by those who conduct places of public accommodation, and are granted a license for this purpose, such as keepers of inns, hotels and conductors of theatres and kindred places of amusement, where one man's money, all things being equal, should usually be as good as another's.

7. The serious question of wages, caused in the main by the vicious industrial system in the South, by the general contempt employers feel for employees, and by the overcrowded nature of the labor market.

These matters reach down into the very life of our people; they are fundamentally the things which in all times have moved men to associate themselves together in civil society for mutual benefit and protection, to restrain the rapacious and unscrupulous and to protect the weak, the timid and the virtuous; and whenever and wherever a condition of affairs obtains when these principles are disregarded and outraged, it becomes the imperative duty of the aggrieved to take such steps for their correction as the condition of affairs seems to warrant.

I know, ladies and gentlemen of the league, that those who are looking to this organization, people in every section of the country, for some sensible action which shall assist in solving the great problems which confront us, as well as the croaking, skeptical few, who do not expect that we shall be able to advance or to accomplish anything which shall survive the hour of our adjournment, have their eyes upon us. I have confidence in the great race of which I am proud to be a member. I have confidence in its wisdom and its patriotism [unintelligible] self-sacrifice for the common good. I have faith in the God who rules in the affairs of men, and who will not leave us alone to our own devices if we shall make an honest effort to assist ourselves. Thus fortified in my faith, what have I to propose as remedies for some if not all of the evils against which we have to contend? It shall not be said that I have called you here to a barren feast; it shall not be said by friend or foe that I am an impracticable visionary, a man chasing shadows—a man who denounces the fearful structure in which we abide and would tear it down without offering at least a substitute to replace it.

I have pondered long and seriously on the evils which beset us, and I have sought, as light was given me, for an antidote to them if such there be. I lay them before you, and you are here to adopt or reject them. I propose, then,

1. The adoption by this league of an Afro-American Bank, with central offices in some one of the great commercial centres of the republic and branches all over the country. We need to concentrate our earnings, and a

bank is the proper place to concentrate them. And I shall submit a bank scheme which I have devised in the hope to meet the requirements of the situation.

I propose (2) the establishment of a bureau of emigration. We need to scatter ourselves more generally throughout the republic.

I propose (3) the establishment of a committee on legislation. We need to have a sharp eye upon the measures annually proposed in the Federal and State legislatures affecting us and our interests, and there are laws everywhere in the republic the repeal of which must engage our best thought and effort.

I propose (4) the establishment of a bureau of technical industrial education. We need trained artisans, educated farmers and laborers more than we need educated lawyers, doctors, and loafers on the street corners. The learned professions are overcrowded. There is not near so much room at the top as there was in the days of Daniel Webster.

And I propose (5) lastly the establishment of a bureau of cooperative industry. We need to buy the necessaries of life cheaper than we can command them in many States. We need to stimulate the business instinct, the commercial predisposition of the race. We not only want a market for the products of our industry, but we want and must have a fair, and a living return for them.

To my mind the solution of the problems which make this league a necessity is to be found in the five propositions here stated. Their successful execution will require the very highest order of executive ability and the collection and disbursement of a vast sum of money. Have we brains and the necessary capital to put these vast enterprises into successful motion? I think we have. There are 8,000,000 of us in this country. Some of us are rich and some of us are poor. Some of us are wise and some are foolish. Let us all—the rich and the poor, the wise and the foolish—resolve to unite and pull together, and the results will speak for themselves. Let us destroy the dead weight of poverty and ignorance which pulls us down and smothers us with the charity, the pity and the contempt of mankind, and all other things will be added unto us.

I think this League should have its stronghold in the Southern States. It is in those States that the grievances we complain of have most glaring and oppressive existence; it is in those States that the bulk of our people reside. The League in the North and West will serve to create public opinion in those sections and to coerce politicians into taking a broader view of our grievances and to compel them to pay more respect to our representations and requests than they have ever done before. This will follow fast upon organization and capable management; because we have learned by experience that intelligent sympathy can only be created by intelligent agitation, and that the respect of politicians can only be secured by compulsion, such alone as thorough organization can bring to bear. In the North and West we are not restrained in the free exercise of the ballot, but aside from this, what benefit accrues to us? Elections come and pass, parties are successful or defeated, but the influence of the race remains simply worthless, the victor and the vanquished alike treating us with indifference or contempt after the election. Every year the indifference and contempt are shown in more pronounced and different ways. It is only by proper organization and discipline that anything to our advantage can be accomplished. In the South like results will follow, save in larger measures, and perhaps at greater cost to individual members of the League, since free speech and action are things which must be fought for there. It cannot be denied that in the South free speech and free action are not tolerated. The white men of that section, in defiance of all constitution and law, have taken affairs into their own hands, and crush out, or attempt to do it, all opinions not in accord with theirs. And this is not only true in matters of a political nature, but of an economical nature.

It is stated by those who ought to know that the colored laboring masses of the South are fast falling into a condition not unlike in its terrible features the chattel slavery abolished by constitutional enactment.

We have it in the newspapers and we have it from the lips of our own men fresh from all sections of the South that the condition of the Afro-American laborers of their section is simply atrocious and appalling, that the employers of such labor, backed up by ample legislation are by all the machinery of the law, and tyrannical in the conduct of their affairs, in so far that colored laborers have no 'appeal from Caesar drunk to Caesar sober.'

The people suffer in silence. This should not be. They should have a voice. The grievances they are forced to suffer should be known of all the world and they must be. An organization national in its ramifications, such as we propose, would be such a voice, so loud that it would compel men to hear it; for if it were silenced in the South, it would be all the louder in the North and the West.

Whenever colored men talk of forming anything in which they are to be the prime movers and their grievances are to be the subjects to be agitated, a vast array of men, mostly politicians, and newspaper editors, more or less partisan, and therefore interested in keeping colored voters in a helpless state as far as disorganization and absence of responsible leadership can effect this, cry aloud that 'colored men should be the last persons to draw the color line.' So they should be; so they have been; and they would never have drawn any such line, or proposed that any such line be drawn, if white men had not first drawn it, and continue to draw it now in religion, in politics, in educational matters, in all moral movements, like that of temperance for instance. We have not drawn the color line. The A.M.E. Church, did its founders establish it because they did not care to worship with their co-religionists? Not a bit of it. They established that magnificent religious organization as a rebuke and a protest against the peanut gallery accommodations offered by white Christians, so-called, to colored Christians. The same spirit actuated the founders of the Zion A.M.E. Church and the Colored M.E. Church.

It was not the colored Christians, but the white Christians, who, to their eternal shame and damnation, drew the color line, and continue to draw it, even unto this hour. Turn to the Masonic, the Odd Fellows and the Knights of Pythias orders—did colored men draw the line in these? Did they set up colored lodges all over the country because they did not wish to fraternize with the white orders? The answer can be inferred when it is stated that white Masons, white Odd Fellows and white Knights of Pythias even at this hour refuse to fraternize with or to recognize the legality or regularity of the orders their actions caused Afro-Americans to establish. Do Afro-Americans desire separate Grand Lodges in the Temperance Order? Did they ask for such? No! But the British and American Good Templars have re-united, and the only condition on which the American order would consent to reunion was that the British order would acknowledge that its action of thirteen years ago in seceding from the order on the color question was not odious and unsound in principle.

Ladies and gentlemen, let us stand up like men in our own organizations where color will not be a brand of odium. The eternal compromises of our manhood and self-respect, true of the past, must cease. Right is right, and we should at no time, or under any circumstances compromise upon anything but absolute right. If the white man cannot rescue our drunkards and evangelize our sinners except by insulting us, let him keep away from us. His contamination under such conditions does us more harm than good. It is not we who have drawn the color line. That is pure nonsense.

Take our public schools—take the schools and colleges throughout the land; who draw the color line in these? Is there an Afro-American school of any sort in the South where a white applicant would be refused admission on account of his color? Not one! Is there a white school in the South where a colored applicant would not be refused admission on account of his color? Not one! The thing is plain. The white man draws the color line in everything he has anything to do with. He is saturated with the black mud of prejudice and intolerance.

Leadership must have a following, otherwise it will run to seed and wither up, be of no benefit to the race or to the persons possessing the superior capacity. An army without a general is a mob, at the mercy of any disciplined force that is hurled against it; and a disorganized leaderless race is nothing more than a helpless, restless mob.

All those men who have profited by our disorganization and fattened on our labor by class and corporate legislation, will oppose this Afro-American League movement. In the intensity of their opposition they may resort to the coward argument of violence; but are we to remain forever inactive, the victims of extortion and duplicity on this account? No, sir. We propose to accomplish our purposes by the peaceful methods of agitation, through the ballot and the courts, but if others use the weapons of violence to combat our peaceful arguments, it is not for us to run away from violence. A man's a man, and what is worth having is worth fighting for. It is proudly claimed that 'the blood of the martyrs is the seed of the Church.' Certainly the blood of antislavery champions was the seed of Garrison's doctrine of 'the genius of universal emancipation.'* Certainly the blood of Irish patriots has been the seed of Irish persistence and success; certainly the blood of Negro patriots was the seed of the independence of Hayti and San Domingo; and in the great revolution of our own country the cornerstones of American freedom were cemented with the blood of black patriots who were not afraid to die; and the refrain which celebrates the heroism and martyrdom of the first men who died that the American colonies might be free will reverberate down the ages.

> 'Long as in freedom's cause the wise contend
> Dear to your country shall your fame extend;
> While to the world the lettered stone shall tell
> Where Caldwell, Attucks, Grey and Mavarick fell.'

Attucks, the black patriot—he was no coward! Toussaint L'Ouverture—he was no coward! Nat Turner—he was no coward! And the two hundred thousand black soldiers of the last war—they were no cowards! If we have a work to do, let us do it. And if there come violence, let those who oppose our just cause 'throw the first stone.' We have wealth, we have intelligence, we have courage; and we have a great work to do. We should therefore take hold of it like men, not counting our time and means and lives of any consequence further than they contribute to the grand purposes which call us to the work.

And now, ladies and gentlemen, in concluding the pleasant task set before me here by your kindness, I would reduce the whole matter, so far as this league is concerned to the following proposition: A large portion of our fellow citizens have determined that the material, civil and political rights conferred upon Afro-Americans by the 13th, 14th and 15th amendments to the Federal Constitution shall not be enjoyed by the beneficiaries of them. To all practical intents and purposes these rights have been denied and are withheld, and especially so in the Southern States. That the majority shall not rule; that the laborer shall be robbed of his wages without redress at law; that the citizen shall enjoy no common and civil rights a brute would not scorn; that the principle[s] of taxation and representation are inseparably correlated is without force is fact, as regards Afro-Americans—here is the work before us.

As the agitation which culminated in the abolition of African slavery in this country covered a period of fifty years, so may we expect that before the rights conferred upon us by the war amendments are fully conceded, a full century will have passed away. We have undertaken no child's play. We have undertaken a serious work which will tax and exhaust the best intelligence and energy of the race for the next century.

Are we equal to the task imposed upon us?

*Abolitionist William Lloyd Garrison (1805–1879) was editor of the *Liberator* and a founder of the American Anti-Slavery Society.

If we are true to ourselves, if we are true to our posterity, if we are true to our country, which has never been true to us, if we are true to the sublime truths of Christianity, we shall succeed—we cannot fail.

We shall fight under the banner of truth. We shall fight under the banner of justice. We shall fight under the banner of the Federal Constitution. And we shall fight under the banner of honest manhood. Planting ourselves firmly upon these truths, immutable and as fixed in the frame-work of social and political progress as the stars in the heavens, we shall eventually fight down opposition, drive caste intolerance to the wall, crush out mob and lynch law, throttle individual insolence and arrogance, vindicate the right of our women to the decent respect of lawless rowdies, and achieve at last the victory which crowns the labors of the patient, resourceful, and the uncompromising warrior.

And may the God of Nations bestow upon us and our labors His approving smile and lead us out of the house of bondage into the freedom of absolute justice under the Constitution.

[Rev. G. W. Clinton of Pennsylvania introduced a resolution proposing that the address of Mr. Fortune be voted the sentiments of the League. Carried.]■

125 HARVARD CLASS DAY ORATION

Clement Garnett Morgan

The selection of Clement Garnett Morgan (1859–1929) as Harvard's 1890 Class Day speaker attracted national attention, much of it hostile. As the first African American student elected to this honor (and one of only six black students who had yet graduated from Harvard), Morgan was praised by black newspapers and some others as proof of the ability of African Americans to take advantage of expanded educational opportunities. Many whites, however, such as the editorialist for the Jackson, Mississippi, Clarion-Ledger, *reacted to Morgan's achievement with undiminished racism: "If every Negro in Mississippi was a graduate of Harvard and had been elected class president," the paper claimed, "he would not be as well fitted to exercise the rights of suffrage as the Anglo-Saxon farm laborer."*

Morgan's oration calls upon his classmates to serve the interests of those denied their privileges, "him who has not like advantages with you, the man struggling against odds, who in the depths of ignorance,

*rudeness and wretchedness, it may be, in longing and striving, in his im-
perfect human way, for something higher, better, nobler, truer." Morgan
knew of such struggles. He was born into slavery. After the Civil War,
his family moved from northern Virginia to Washington, D.C., where he
completed high school but lacked the funds necessary to attend college.
After working for several years, he entered Boston Latin School and was
admitted to Harvard, along with his more famous classmate W. E. B.
Du Bois. In 1893, Morgan graduated from Harvard Law School and developed a law practice in Boston. He was active in local politics, particularly in issues of school funding and school segregation. In 1905, he joined
Du Bois in the Niagara Movement and in vocal opposition to what he perceived to be the accommodationist politics of Booker T. Washington.*

*Morgan's speech is reprinted from the program of the 1890 Class Day
exercises by permission of the Harvard University Archives. Further information may be found in Jonathan Cedarbaum, "Clement Garnett
Morgan,"* Harvard Magazine *(May-June 1992), 36. We are grateful to
Hilmar Jensen for bringing the speech to our attention.*

LADIES AND GENTLEMEN:—CLASSMATES:—"Help them who cannot help again."

Keen joy or grief we must often bear alone, whether we will or not. So,
on this our Class Day, we, knowing joys which others may not share, come
yet with sorrows which they can scarcely be expected to feel or even understand. Still we can spend but a moment sighing, since Alma Mater knows,
as every mother will tell you, that the strength or tenderness of filial affection is measured, not by sighs and tears at parting, but by strictness in keeping precepts. So, in these days we live in thought of those teachings which
have for us been the same as for all Harvard men, whether expressed in "piety, morality and learning," in "knowledge and godliness," in "Truth for
Christ and the Church," or in simple Truth, embracing all: for it is by truth,
which, as an active living principle, becomes our "ought," our "must," that
we answer the questions which each of us puts to himself to-day, "What is
my relation to the world about me?" and "Where can I help?" Every son of
Harvard imbued with this principle, going forth "with freedom to think,"
"with patience to bear," and "for right ever bravely to live," has been aptly
described in the words of Browning:

> *"One who never turned his back, but marched breast forward,
> Never doubted clouds would break,
> Never dreamed though right were worsted, wrong would triumph,
> Held, we fall to rise, are baffled to fight better,
> Sleep to wake."*

And is not the example of every one of them acting upon us, as it has acted upon no class before? Let two instances at the beginning of our university life assure us that it is:

You remember that to us entering college there was entrusted the keeping of that which is ever held dearest here—of worship. It was because the strength of character of those preceding us warranted the belief that voluntary devotion, "a thing unique in university training in the world," would not suffer at our hands; that there might be written over our chapel doors, "not compulsion, but invitation." How glad we were last fall to hear that the departure had more than met expectations! And yet, let us not forget, its continued success rests largely on you and on me,—the first ripe fruits of it; for our new system is after all an old one. We saw its complete foreshadowing in the thought out of the "Upanishads" which to-day in the midst of our questioning seems to say, "Worship and despair not; if not on a high plane, give lower service, seek to reach men; if thou canst not worship meaningly, toil; in work is the blessing of man."

The second instance:—We had had about a month to set up our ideals, when the day of our quarter millennial celebration came. What an impressive sight was the line of procession past the buildings, through the yard, here into the theatre! And then the meaning of it all! You will recall how, in the evening, we, with an enthusiasm which modesty could not check, did not forbear boasting that "these two hundred fifty years are for Ninety." You doubtless see the transparency now. A jest do you say? I am sure it was, but that jest to-day becomes our earnest. Those years were for us, and bringing with them great privileges, put upon us like obligations and responsibilities.

There occurs to me a case from history where a memorable victory was won under the influence of the spell of mere antiquity. When Napoleon, on the plains of Egypt, pointing to those monuments of human endeavor and of human achievement, said to his soldiers: "Remember that from the top of those pyramids forty centuries look down upon you," those few simple words carried with them the inspiration which won the "Battle of the Pyramids." In the years which we claimed, and which now in their turn claim us, there is no such charm, but holding you and me there is a greater power,—the spirit of plain, zealous, single-minded men, who, preferring the hardships of the wilderness to beds of ease under tyranny, among their first acts set up in this place on the basis of sound hearing, civil and religious liberty; of men, who in the hour of their country's need, leaving home, friends, social position, worldly honor, all that could make life worth living, gave themselves a willing sacrifice, if only they might make way for liberty, for truth and for humanity. This is the power holding you and me, making those two hundred fifty years ours.

The example of these men shows clearly that the true road to success, to any excellence, is that of plain, genuine simplicity, sincerity and unselfishness; for this, and this alone, leads to the culture, the character and the civilization which stand the test of time.

Their example shows, too, that the man for any great work in any age must be earnest, faithful, patient,—the man who can wait, if need be;—not, bear in mind, he who stands idly waiting, but he who, while waiting, works, with the earnestness of life, with the faithfulness of industry, and with the patience of heroism, of farsightedness, and of unshaken confidence in that "Force always at work to make the best better, the worst good." To him, biding his time, the bitterest tear becomes as sweet spring water.

Their example shows also, in the words of him who once chid us for indifference here, that "power, ability, influence, character and virtue are only trusts with which to serve our time." The purposes of an education are but two: (1) adding, by diligence, discovery and invention, to the thought and to the material development of the world; and (2) informing, moving, directing, uplifting men. Both of these have one end, the well-being of mankind. Then he serves his time best who serves humanity best; and who does so serves best his country and his Alma Mater.

From the oration of the two hundred and fiftieth anniversary you will, I am sure, remember this thought; "The only way in which our civilization can be maintained, even at the level it has reached,—the only way in which that level can be made more general and be raised higher, is by bringing the influence of the more cultivated to bear with more energy and directness on the less cultivated, and by opening more inlets to those indirect influences which make for refinement of mind and body. Democracy must show its capacity for producing, not a higher average man, but the highest possible types of manhood in all its manifold varieties, or it is a failure." It is not, I think, assuming too much to say that in seeking to bring "the influence of the more cultivated to bear with energy and directness on the less cultivated," to make it impossible for democracy to be a failure, is your duty and mine,— a duty from which the only escape is performance.

Public speakers say that they make it a point to hit in their audience the man farthest off, assured that if he hear, all others must. Do you then in your relation with the world, in your service to humanity, make it your business to reach the lowest man? I use the word in no vulgar sense; for we here scarcely need the aid of any philosopher to know that the great thing in the world is Man. I know, like travelers up a mountain side, looking back, our heads may grow giddy with the heights we have reached, but looking beyond and seeing the summit so far off it seems we have not begun to climb and our foolish pride goes. I mean him who has not like advantages with you, the man struggling against odds, who in the depths of ignorance, rudeness and wretchedness, it may be, is longing and striving, in his imperfect human way, for something higher, better, nobler, truer,—reach him, for to him making a fight in the face of difficulties, there are two spurs: one, opposition, developing strength; the other a cheering word from those who in nobleness of heart do, by their sympathy, make the fight with him. Of the first he will always have enough; alas, if you withhold from him the second! No evil is greater or farther reaching in its consequences than that of disregard for the dictates and demands of humanity. Then make him feel the possibilities within him and help him to develop those possibilities.

There are ways to that above and beyond Sir Launfal's,—giving from a sense of duty, but insulting to the dignity of human nature,—ways, too, which never descend to patronage, hurting alike to helper and to helped. These will suggest themselves in obedience to will. A striking case, lately brought to our notice by the newspapers, is that of the college settlement in New York, where a few heroic women, with brave hearts and a purpose, carry on successfully a plan for helping others in a real human way. As we read of them we could scarcely help thinking that Brook Farms may fail but Rivington Settlements must persist. You will remember that here a few years ago we were told by the Scotch scholar visiting us of a similar plan in operation among university men in his country. The same thing you will find, too, among students in London. We know of something of the kind here in a modest way. What an advance since the days of Horace Greeley if men are to be saved by the college graduate and not from him!

There is no intention of making missionaries of you except in that larger sense in which every man is a missionary, but prominent in our college conference this year has been this thought: "What the world needs is what Margaret Fuller calls the spiritual man of the world."* Now we do not think the world scandalous, skeptical, or epicurean, nor do we believe nothing remains but hunger and cant, still it is in some respects a queer world, for with it you are at once "the fast set" and expected leaders of a great moral movement. However, you must fill the bill. There is abundant need for giving the world the assurance which Goethe gave Carlyle: "It is still possible that man be a man." Indeed, from one act here, small in and of itself, the world expects, nay, demands of us that assurance. When, conscious of a possible taunt of writhing under defeat, we took a stand against professionalism in college athletics, we put ourselves on record, virtually saying that the winning or losing of a game, a match, or a race, is one matter, but the means of gain or loss is a far different thing; the principles underlying sports, as those governing conduct, reconcile means with ends only when both are honorable. The protest, though ill-received, was nevertheless right, and will, I believe, lead to fairer and better athletics; at any rate, having taken high ground, we have no retreat which is not disgraceful.

Looking from our college world to the great world outside University gate, we cannot fail to see a great moral movement going on; it leads a Russian count from the court to a bench with the cobblers, it dismisses in Germany a "man of iron will" and teaches him that there volutionary [sic] minority which he feared must not stand in the way of the greatest good to the greatest number and of right and fair play for all; it acts on the brain of an unpretentious man, and sets agoing the thought of the whole country. You may not agree with Tolstoi in some of his theories,—though take him for all in all, he is one of the grand examples of our time; for from the day on which the first rude savage freely gave his life for the advancement of his tribe, down to the day of John Brown of Ossawattomie at Harper's Ferry, men have

---

*Margaret Fuller (1810–1850) was a prominent transcendentalist, journalist, and author of *Woman in the Nineteenth Century* (1845).

seen that the noblest thing on earth, that which most surely touches the heart, is vicarious suffering, human self-sacrifice;—you may question the outcome of the efforts of William of Germany and of the Berlin Conference; you may find fault with the methods of the nationalists; but you cannot deny that the purpose of all of these is not only to help men to a comfortable living, but to add to their intellectual and moral welfare.

This movement, not yet developed into widespread enthusiasm for humanity, waits "men of thought and men of action to clear the way," and looks with anxious eyes on you. Believing with Emerson that the test of civilization is not in the census, nor in the size of cities, nor in the crops, but in the kind of man the country turns out, see to it that our civilization stand the test by taking the Calibans of our soil and making Prosperos of them, by making the peasant brain wise. Intelligence is virtue's own handmaid, labor's helpmeet; if the one have not her aid, nor the other her companionship, vice and misery result. You have in the truth the strongest argument for developing and stimulating the intellectual faculties of every human being. Here in America, where the humblest man counts one, and where however much some may look down, their neighbor will not be found looking up, it is especially imperative that every man be a thinker.

Classmates of Ninety, looking over our number here I find we touch by actual residence, extreme points, East and West, North and South, in our country; we cannot go away rightly impressed with the deepest meanings of this place without feeling impelled to add somewhat to its greatness. To do that, what you and I must take account of is, not success, but that which alone deserves it, endeavor. "The measure of a nation's true success," says Mr. Lowell, "is the amount it has contributed to the thought, the moral energy, the spiritual hope and consolation of mankind."* So then it must be our endeavor to open to every man, woman and child in this land every door leading to intelligence and virtue. The time has come when honorable men disdain to be guilty of accusing their fellows of ignorance and vice while they either deliberately dam up the "inlets to the influences which make for refinement of mind and body," or else in their indifference turn not a hand to give free passage to them. The case before us requires not so much words, as work with might and main. Let each of us do his duty and in that find our relation to the world about us; there, see where we may help. So, and only so, were those two hundred fifty years, ours, and we in our turn theirs.■

*James Russell Lowell (1819–1891) was a poet, essayist, and antislavery activist.

126 EDUCATION AND THE PROBLEM

Joseph C. Price

▦ *Virtually forgotten today, Joseph C. Price was once internationally celebrated as an orator, organizational leader, and educator. In* The Negro in American History *(1914), John Cromwell ventured that "it is doubtful if the nineteenth century produced a superior or more popular orator of the type that enlists the sympathies, entertains and compels conviction."* * *W. E. B. Du Bois, who as a college student heard Price lecture in Boston's Tremont Temple, pronounced him "the acknowledged orator of his day" and wrote in the* Crisis *in 1922: "I like to think of Joseph C. Price, tall, of superb physique, and of Unmixed African Blood, as the epitome of his country's nationalistic characteristic."* † *After Price's untimely death at the age of thirty-nine, Frederick Douglass lamented that "the race has lost its ablest advocate."* ‡

Price was born in Elizabeth City, North Carolina, on February 10, 1854. Although his father was enslaved, his mother was free, and he followed her status. After teaching himself to read and write, Price entered school at the age of twelve. He briefly attended Shaw University in Raleigh in 1873, then, after religious conversion, entered Lincoln University to prepare for the ministry. He captured every major oratorical prize at Lincoln, graduated as valedictorian in 1879, and completed the classical program two years later.

Price rose to regional prominence as an eloquent delegate to the General Conference of the A.M.E. Zion Church in 1880 and in the North Carolina prohibition campaign the following year. In 1881, as a delegate to the World's Ecumenical Conference of Methodism, held in London, he delivered an unscheduled speech from the floor that created a sensation. Dubbed "The World's Orator" by the British press, he embarked upon a speaking tour of Britain in the weeks following the London conference and raised the eleven thousand dollars necessary to found Zion Wesley College (later Livingstone) in Salisbury, North Carolina. He served as Livingstone's president until his death of Bright's disease in 1893.

Price successfully appealed to both white and black, southern and northern, conservative and more militant audiences. In January 1890, Price was elected national president of the Afro-American League at its founding convention in Chicago. One month later, at the convention of the rival Equal Rights League in Washington, he was elected chairman

---

*John W. Cromwell, *The Negro in American History* (Washington, D.C.: American Negro Academy, 1914), 171.

†W. E. B. Du Bois, "An Estimate of Joseph C. Price," *Crisis* 23 (March 1922), 225.

‡"Progressive Review," *A.M.E. Zion Quarterly Review* 4 (1894), 184.

by acclamation. Price was selected as the principal African American speaker at the World's Congress of Races at the Chicago Exposition of 1893 (replaced, because of his fatal illness, by Frederick Douglass), and some have argued that, had he lived, it would probably have been he rather than Booker T. Washington who would have addressed Atlanta's Cotton States Exposition in 1895.

One of Price's greatest speaking triumphs occurred at the annual meeting of the National Education Association (NEA), held in Minneapolis, July 10–12, 1890. The NEA convention was riven with controversy over the proposal of southern white delegates that African Americans be excluded from membership and the threat of a separate, segregated Southern Education Association. Price spoke after Judge A. A. Gunby, who warned of "the menace of Negro rule" and pleaded for northern support of the southern proposals. Price was the primary opposing speaker. During Gunby's speech, a note was passed to Price by a lawyer friend, saying: "Price, eight million human beings are hanging on your lips today." At the end of Price's speech, Walls reports, the audience members "were calling out vociferous approval to his sentiments and showering him with waving handkerchiefs and fans. They literally mobbed him with hearty manifestations of approval . . . and even Judge Gunby moved up to take his hand as Price retired from the stand and the audience was rushing involuntarily toward him. The judge said proudly, 'You are a Southerner too!' " (Joseph Charles Price, 354–55).

The text of Price's speech, along with those of Judge Gunby and other participants, was published in National Education Association, Journal of Proceedings and Addresses (Topeka: Kansas Publishing, 1890), 267–76. For further information on Price, see William Jacob Walls, Joseph Charles Price: Educator and Race Leader (Boston: Christopher, 1943); and August Meier, Negro Thought in America, 1880–1915 (Ann Arbor: University of Michigan Press, 1963).

If I had a thousand tongues and each tongue were a thousand thunderbolts and each thunderbolt had a thousand voices, I would use them all today to help you understand a loyal and misrepresented and misjudged people.*

The real question implied in this subject, as I understand it, is, Will education solve the race problem? With such an idea in view, it is but proper that we have some conception of what the problem is, in order that we may select the best means for its solution; for it is evident that all remedies, whether for the removal of disorders in the body, or in the social state—

---

*This opening paragraph does not appear in the NEA's *Proceedings* transcript but was reported by Dr. Edward Moore, an instructor at Livingstone who attended the speech (in Walls, *Joseph Charles Price*, 355).

whether in physianthropy or sociology—must be in proportion to their affected parts or abnormal conditions.

It is further observable that the length of time a malady is allowed to grow, or an evil condition is permitted to exist and develop baneful results, has much to do with the nature of the forces that will neutralize the growth or destroy the evil. It is not infrequently the case that the age of a complaint or an undesirable state of affairs has to determine, to a very large degree, the means of resistance, or the remedies which will effect the cure. More is true. As it is admitted that time is a large element in the stubbornness of a condition or evil, so it is also true that time, coupled with the highest wisdom of administration, becomes an indispensable element in producing the healthier and more desirable conditions. It is further patent to every thoughtful mind that there are complex irregularities in the human system, as well as in the body politic, that no single remedy or manner of procedure can regulate. In such cases we have to proceed step by step, and take only one phase of the complaint at a time; and the remedies that are efficient in one stage are totally inadequate to the other. Each stage has its peculiar prescription—some requiring milder, and others severer antidotes; and whenever these antidotes are used substitutionally, we are thwarted in our desired end, and our purposes often miscarry.

The negro problem is different from the Indian or Chinese question. In the negro, we find a commendable absence of all the stubborn and discordant characteristics which are peculiar to the Indian or the Chinaman; and yet, the negro problem, together with its solution, is the all-absorbing topic of the country, and the negro, in the opinion of some, is the only destructive element, and least acceptable member of the body politic of America.

The race problem, as now understood, had its beginning in 1620, when the negroes were forced to accept this country as their home. So, in one form or another, the negro question has been before the country for two hundred and seventy years, and this question, with its constant and incident dangers, has been a source of anxiety and vexation, and rock of offense, during all those years.

Now if the difficulties involved in the problem inhere in the negro as a race, it is but natural that we should seek to change, not his color, but his character, under reasonable and fair encouragements to do so; and if they are the results of preconceived opinions, or even conscientious convictions, produced by unfavorable and misleading environments, these opinions and convictions must change—all other things being equal—with a change of the environments.

The "peculiar institution" continued to grow, with all its attendant evils, until it threatened the very life of the republic; so much so, until it was declared by one of the wisest men the country ever produced, that the nation could not live half free and half slave.* Every means possible was

*Abraham Lincoln, Speech at the Republican State Convention, Springfield, Illinois, June 16, 1858.

called into requisition to solve this phase of the negro question in America, and it was only solved permanently and effectively by the bloody arbitrament of arms. Slavery is no more, and can never exist again in this country, simply because it was settled right. But this does not argue that every phase of this question must be settled in the same manner, or by the same means.

WHAT DO WE MEAN BY THE SOLUTION OF THE PROBLEM?

The solution of the race problem means the satisfactory and harmonious adjustment of the racial relation in the South and in the country as well, on the principles of humanity and justice. In other words, it is the concession to the negro of all the inalienable rights that belong to him as a man and as a member of that family of which God is the common Father; and the granting to him all the civil immunities and political privileges guaranteed to every other citizen by the authority and power of the Constitution of the American Government. To do this solves the problem; not to do it is to leave it unsolved; and to leave it unsolved, in the face of the growing numbers and increasing intelligence of the negro, is to intensify the bitterness between the races, and to involve both in a conflict more destructive and widespread than the country has hitherto witnessed.

SLAVERY AT THE BOTTOM OF IT ALL.

Slavery, as a system, degraded the negro to the level of the brute, because it denied him the untrammeled exercise of all the instincts of a higher and better manhood. It recognized no moral sensibility in man or woman, regarded no sacred and inviolable relation between husband and wife, sundered at will or caprice the tenderest ties that the human heart is capable of forming or the mind is able to conceive. Such a system had the support of the highest tribunal of men, and even the representatives of the church of God came to its rescue and defense, with all the weight of its divine authority and power. From the maternal knee, the table, the family altar, the forum, and the pulpit was the lesson taught that the person of sable hue and curly hair was a doomed, and therefore an inferior, race—not entitled to a place in the brotherhood of men. This impression, made on childhood's plastic nature, grew with his growth, and strengthened with the power of increasing years. To deepen the blot, and intensify the damning heresy, the law of the land wrote him down as a chattel, that is, cattle, and forbade the training of the mind and the culture of the heart, by making learning on his part, and teaching on the part of others, a crime. It is not surprising, then, that men brought up in the face of such a system for two hundred and fifty years should be skeptical as to the real manhood of the negro, and hesitate to give him a place in the one-blood family.

The feeling against the negro, which helps to make our race problem, is called prejudice, and is not without some grounds. For two hundred and fifty years the white man of the South saw only the animal, or mechanical, side of the negro. Wherever he looked, there was degradation, ignorance, superstition, darkness there, and nothing more, as he thought. The man was overshadowed and concealed by the debasing appetites and destructive and avaricious passions of the animal; therefore the race problem of to-day is not an anomaly—it is the natural and logical product of an environment of centuries. I am no pessimist. I do not believe we are approaching a race war in the South. I entertain an impression, which is rapidly deepening into a conviction, that the problem can and will be solved peaceably; but this can only be done by changing the character of the environment which has produced it. It is an unfavorable condition which has given the country a race problem, and it will never be solved until we put at work the forces that will give us a changed condition. This does not argue nor imply the removal of the environment, as is suggested by colonization, deportation, or amalgamation; but it does mean a transformation of the same environment.

THE REAL ELEMENT OF POWER IN THE RACE PROBLEM.

What is the great element of power in the race problem? It is opposition to the claims of manhood and constitutional rights as made by the negro or his friends, because it is thought that he is not in all things a man like other men. It is an avowed determination to resist the full exercise of his inalienable and God-given rights. It is a premeditated purpose not to give him justice. In some portions of the country this spirit is more violent than in others; but it manifests itself, in one form or another, the land over. Sometimes it denies to the man of the negro race the exercise of his elective franchise; refuses to accord him first-class accommodations in public highways of travel, on land or sea, when he pays for the same; denies him, however competent and qualified, an opportunity to earn an honest living, simply because he belongs to a different race; and seeks to organize a Southern Educational Association, because it is said that the National Educational Association "has some ways that do not at all accord with the conditions of Southern society," or "for obvious reasons"; and, as one has said, "to be out of smelling distance of the sable brother." When it is asked, Why this opposition, this determination, and this premeditated purpose against the human and constitutional rights of a man and citizen? we are told, directly and indirectly, that while there are rare and commendable exceptions, the race, as such, is ignorant, poverty-stricken, and degraded. Now if ignorance, poverty, and moral degradation are the grounds of objection against the negro, it is not difficult to discover that the knotty elements of the race problem are the intellectual, moral, and material conditions of the negro race. It is reasonable, therefore, to suppose that if we can find the means that will change these conditions, we have found a key to the problem, and gone a great distance toward its satisfactory solution. Of course none of us would argue that intelligence, or even education, is a panacea for all the ills of mankind; for, even when educated, a Nero, a Robespierre, a Benedict Arnold, an absconding state treasurer, or a New York sneak-thief, would not necessarily be impossibilities. I do not argue that increased intelligence, or multiplied facilities for education, will, by some magic spell, transform the negro into the symmetry, grace, and beauty of a Grecian embodiment of excellence. It is certainly not my humble task to attempt to prove that education will, in a day, or a decade, or a century, rid the black man of all the physical peculiarities and deformities, moral perversions and intellectual distortions which are the debasing and logical heritage of more than two and a half centuries of enslavement. It is, nevertheless, reasonable to assume that, admitting the ordinary human capabilities of the race, which no sane and fair-minded man will deny, it can be readily and justly predicated that if the same forces applied to other races are applied to the negro, and these forces are governed by the same eternal and incontrovertible principles, they will produce corresponding results and make the negro as acceptable to the brotherhood of men as any other race laying claims to the instincts of our common humanity. I believe that education, in the full sense of the term, is the most efficient and comprehensive means to this end, because in its results an answer is to be found to all the leading objections against the negro which enter into the make-up of the so-called race problem.

Let us examine more minutely these elements of the problem, in order to justify the reasonableness of our position. The Southern problem shows its intense forms most in those sections and States where the negroes are in the majority. This is because the whites, as they say, fear negro supremacy. This supremacy is feared on account of the ignorance of the negro voter. It is concluded that the majority of voters being ignorant, they would put ignorant or illiterate men in charge of the affairs of the county, State, or section; and this would work to the bankruptcy or destruction of the county, State or section thus governed or controlled. Hence, it is claimed that opposition to the exercise of negro franchise, by whatever means, is a patriotic duty—a matter of self-preservation. Now it is evident that so far as this objection is concerned, education or increased intelligence among those representing the majority is the remedy. Ignorance being the ground of objection, if this cause is removed (and it can be by widespread intelligence), the objection must disappear as the darkness recedes at the approach of the light of the sun. None of us, even negroes, desire to be officered by ignorant or incompetent men. It is the patriotic duty of every man to bring about such reforms as will put only the duly qualified in positions of responsibility and power. But this ought only to be done by lawful means and by forces that are acknowledged to be in every way legitimate and in harmony with the humane spirit of our times. Dr. T. T. Eaton, writing on the Southern problem, in the Christian Union, June 5, says: "It does seem a great outrage to practically deprive American citizens of the right to vote; but it is a greater outrage to destroy all the ends of government by putting an inferior and semi-barbarous race in control of a superior race who own the property and have the intelligence." It not only seems but is a great outrage to deprive American citizens of the right to vote, except on the conditions sustained by law, and not by mobs and the caprices of men. Such mob violence is the more reprehensible, when it is taken for granted that these outrages are the only way of escape from the conditions confronting us.

WHAT OUGHT TO BE DONE?

If the voter is unprepared to exercise his franchise aright, then prepare him for its intelligent use, or deprive him of it by constitutional enactments. The latter cannot now be done, but the former can and ought to be done, and by doing so we will save the negro from unlawful oppression and outrage simply because he claims his rights, and save the nation from the disgrace and burning shame because it denies him these rights. Intelligence is universally admitted to be the prime requisite for good-citizenship. Whenever this condition of things obtains there will be no necessity or fear of "destroying all the ends of government by putting a semi-barbarous race in control of a superior race who own the property and have the intelligence." For it is true and unalterable as expressed by Dr. A. G. Haygood, of Georgia, in his "Pleas for Progress," when he says: "Good government implies intelligence, and universal suffrage demands universal education." It cannot now be said, as it was stated fifty years ago, that a negro cannot be educated. The history of education among the colored people for a quarter of a century does not confirm the statement. The noble men and women who went into the South as missionaries, and felt their way through the smoke of battle and stepped over crimson battle-fields and among the wounded and the dying to bring intelligence to the negroes, were taunted as going on a fool's errand. But the tens of thousands of young men and women in the schools of high grade established by Northern service and philanthropy—a million negro children in the public schools of the South—are an imperishable monument to the wisdom of their action. I again quote from Dr. Haygood, who is an authority on this subject:* "All told, fully fifty millions of dollars have gone into the work of their [negro] education since 1865. Of this fifty millions, more than half has been Southern money." The negroes have made more progress in elementary and other education during these twenty-three years than any other illiterate people in the world, and they have justified the philanthropy and public policy that made the expenditure.

WHITES MUST BE EDUCATED, AS WELL.

It must be remembered, however, that there is more to be done than the education of the blacks, as a solution to the race problem; for much of the

---

*Southern Methodist Bishop Atticus G. Haygood was president of Emory University and author of *Our Brother in Black* (1881).

stubbornness of the question is involved in the ignorant, lawless and vicious whites of the South, who need education worse than many of the blacks. To educate one race and neglect the other, is to leave the problem half solved, for there is a class of whites in the South, to some extent, more degraded and hopeless in their mental and moral condition than the negro. This is the class to which many of the actual outrages are more attributable than to any other class. Educate these, as well as the blacks, and our problem is shorn of its strength. When we call to mind the fact that seventy per cent of the colored vote in the South is illiterate, and thirty per cent of the white vote in the same condition, it is not difficult for one to discern that education of the blacks and whites, as well, is not only necessary for the solution of the race problem and for good government, but for the progress and prosperity of that section where such illiteracy obtains. For the safety of the republic, the perpetuity of its glory and the stability of its institutions are commensurate, with the intelligence and morality of its citizens, whether they be black men or white men.

THE POVERTY OF THE NEGRO.

The poverty of the negro is another stubborn element of the problem. It is urged that the wealth and intelligence of the South must not suffer a man, if he is poor and black, to exercise the prerogatives of American citizenship. Strange doctrine this, in a republic which is a refuge for the oppressed from all lands under the sun, and the so-called land of the free! But will education help to remove this objectionable element in the negro? It is the object of all education to aid man in becoming a producer as well as a consumer. To enable men and women to make their way in life and contribute to the material wealth of their community or country, to develop the resources of their land, is the mainspring in the work of all our schools and public or private systems of training. From a material point of view we find that one of the great differences—in fact, contrasts—between the North and the South, is a difference of widespread intelligence. Labor, skilled or intelligent, coupled with the impetus arising from capital, will touch the South as with a magnetic hand, and that region with marvelous resources and immeasurable capabilities will blossom as the rose. It is a matter of observation and history that a section or country that seeks to keep its labor-producing class ignorant, keeps itself poor; and the nation or state that fails to provide for the education of its whole people, especially its industrial forces, is considered woefully lacking in statesmanship and devoid of the essential elements in material progress and prosperity. To this general rule the negro is no exception. To educate him, then, makes him an industrial factor of the state, and argues his own changed condition from repulsive property to more acceptable conditions of wealth. Whatever strengthens the negro of the South adds to the strength and wealth of that section; and nothing militates against the negro but militates against the South as well. Even in his present condition of illiteracy, the negro is evidently the backbone of the labor element of the

South. He is, therefore, a wealth-producer now. Whether he reaps all the benefit of his labor or not, it is clear that he is the prime element in its growing and boasted prosperity. The late Henry W. Grady* said, just before his death, that the negroes in his State (Georgia) paid taxes on twenty million dollars' worth of property, and that the negroes in the South contribute a billion dollars' worth of products every year to the material prosperity of that section. The Atlanta *Constitution*, speaking of the negroes in Texas, said recently that they own a million acres of land and pay taxes on twenty million dollars' worth of property, have two thousand churches, two thousand benevolent associations, ten high schools, three thousand teachers, twenty-three doctors, fifteen lawyers, one hundred merchants, five hundred mechanics, fifteen newspapers, hundreds of farmers and stockmen, and several inventors. Now these two States are but samples of the wealth-producing results of twenty-five years of labor. If this has been their progress when it is admitted they have been under the hampering influence of ignorance, not to speak of other disadvantages, it is fair to assume that under the stimulus of intelligence they will do a hundred-fold more, and year by year and decade by decade change their poverty-stricken state, and thus remove another element in the problem, and thereby hasten its solution.

But it is not necessary for me to stand in this intelligent and representative presence and argue the advantages of education to alter the material condition of countries or races. Intelligence and industry have always demanded the respectful consideration of men, no matter how intense their opinions to the contrary; and it has been their universal opinion that these forces have been the leverage to lift their less-fortunate fellows to their proper place on the plane of political and civil equality. These industrial forces are the things that must enter as a key into the solution of the problem. It will be as impossible to deny to a people thus gifted with intelligence and exercising it in wise and consistent efforts in the accumulation of wealth, their inalienable and constitutional rights, as it is to keep back the sweep of the cyclone with a wave of the hand, or hinder the swell of the sea by stamping on its shore.

THE MORAL CONDITION OF THE RACE.

But it is further argued that the negro is not entitled to his rights in the human brotherhood, and under the constitution of his country, because his standard of morality is low. Now the question that at once presents itself, is this: Does education help to improve the moral condition of a people? If this be granted, it is not hard to conclude that such a means will be a long step toward the removal of this element of the problem. We will not assume, however, that education is a synonym for morality, for it is clear that many per-

---

*Henry W. Grady (1850–1889) was an editor and part owner of the *Atlanta Constitution* who gained fame as a public speaker on behalf of "The New South" and national reconciliation.

sons and some races claiming a superiority of intelligence are not always models of moral purity. But, while this is true, it is an unusual position for one to hold that intelligence is a hinderance to the development of virtuous tendencies. It is, rather, conceded that ignorance is a great source of immorality; and this is made emphatic when we take into consideration the fact that conscience, enlightened or unenlightened, determines to a large degree the moral acts of men. It cannot be denied that what may be termed an innate moral consciousness is subject to education in order to make it a safe guide in the realm of moral obligation. I think it is Dr. Buchner, who says in his "Treatise on Man": "It is a generally recognized fact, and moreover sufficiently proved by history, that the idea of morality in the general, as in the particular, becomes further and more strongly developed in proportion as culture, intelligence and knowledge of the necessary laws of the common weal increase." The negro's moral condition, against which objection is raised, is the result of his training in the peculiar institution. It taught him no moral obligations of the home, for it recognized no home in the civilized sense of the term; it rather encouraged him to violate the sacred bonds of husband and wife, because, in so doing, he was taught the advancement of the interest of his master in adding to the number and value of his human stock for the plantation or the market. He was prompted, under scanty provisions for physical sustenance, to appropriate his master's hog or chicken to his own strength and comfort, on the principle and argument that he was simply improving his master's property. When a woman was made to feel that her honor, which is the glory of every true woman, was not her right, but subject to the carnal caprice of a master, it is not strange that an impression thus deepened by centuries of outrage should make her rather lightly regard this honor just after escape from such a school and from under such a system of instruction. It is certainly apparent, in the light of what has already been done for the moral improvement of the negro, that education will undo much of that which slavery has done to him.

Hear what Dr. Haygood says: "No theory of universal education entertained by a rational people proposes knowledge as a substitute for virtue, or virtue as a substitute for knowledge. Both are necessary. Without virtue, knowledge is unreliable and dangerous; without knowledge, virtue is blind and impotent." . . . "I must say a word in defense," says this same authority, "of the negroes, particularly those living in the Southern States. Considering the antecedents of the race in Africa, in those States before the emancipation, and their condition to-day, the real surprise is that there is so much virtue and purity among them." . . . "Above all things," says Dr. Haygood, "let the white people set them better examples." Since progress has already been made in this direction, we are permitted to hope that education will continue its beneficent work in the moral reformation of the people. Education will certainly afford a better knowledge of the duties of the home, a keener appreciation of the obligations of the marriage state, a more consistent regard for the rights and the property of others, and a clearer conception of what virtue in womanhood signifies, and, therefore, a more determined purpose and means of defending that honor from the assaults of any man, even at the very risk of their lives.

THE GREAT WORK TO BE DONE.

The great work of education among negroes consists in leading them out of the errors which centuries of a debasing servitude fastened upon them; but even when this is done, the negro will not be an embodiment of every moral excellence, but he will at least stand on the same plane of morals with the other representatives of our common and fallen humanity, and whatever is the possibility and hope of one will be the possibility and hope of the other, so far as education is concerned; for under it, we believe that the negro can be and do what any other race can do, from the tickling of the soil with his hoe and plow, to make it burst forth into life-giving fruitage, to the lifting of world upon world upon the lever of his thought, that they may instruct and entertain him as they pass his vision in grandeur in the heavens.

But do we find in the negro exclusively all the immorality involved in the solution of the race problem? Not by any means. After the necessary evidence is given which entitles a man to the recognition of his rights, and these rights are still denied, then, the one denying them becomes the moral law-breaker; for morality, according to a scholarly authority (and he is not writing on the race problem in America), may be defined as a law of mutual respect for the general and private equal rights of man for the purpose of securing general human happiness. Everything that injures or undermines this happiness and this respect, is evil; everything that advances them, is good. "The greatest sinners, therefore," says this authority, "are egoists, or those who place their own I higher than the interests and the lives of the common weal, and endeavor to satisfy it at the cost and to the injury of those possessing equal rights."

CHRISTIAN EDUCATION.

We have said nothing of Christian education; but it is reasonable to conclude that white or black men, under the influence of Christian intelligence, are prepared to solve all the problems peculiar to our earthly state, for Christianity levels all the distinctions of race. It is this spirit that struck the conceit of the Jew and broke down the middle wall of cruel separation between him and the Gentile world. It taught the Greek that humanity was a term for the wide brotherhood of all races, which he did not realize before; for all other races were regarded and despised as barbarians by him until Paul, from Mars Hill, thundered in the eager eyes and anxious ears of the Athenian the new doctrine that God had made of one blood all nations of men to dwell on all the face of the earth. The Roman, according to Geike, considered all who did not belong to his own state, as hostes or enemies, and held that the only law between them and those who were not Romans was that of the strong to subjugate such races, if they could, plunder their possessions, and make the people slaves. "It was left to Christ," says this authority, "to proclaim the brotherhood of all nations by revealing God as their common Father in Heaven." If Christian education or a full knowledge of the principles of Christianity will not solve our relations with men, we are seriously at fault in our professed religion, and deplorable in our spiritual condition. For a people imbued with the spirit of the Christ idea cannot defraud a brother of a penny, nor rob him of his labor, nor deny him the rights which he has in common with other men; for by these principles we are taught to

> *"Evince your ardent love for God*
> *By the kind deeds ye do for men."*

Dr. Chapin well says: "The great doctrine of human brotherhood, of the worth of a man, that he is not to be trod upon as a footstool or dashed in pieces as a worthless vessel, and the doctrines of popular liberty, education, and reform—all these have become active and every-day truths under the influence of Christianity." If Christian education is not to produce these results, the country and the race have a dark and uninviting future, for one has truly said, "There are mysteries which, if not solved by the truths of Christianity, darken the universe."

But I do not despair of the solution of the problem under Christian intelligence, as it radiates from the indiscriminating Cross of Calvary. For the principles of this grand system, both in the hearts and in the dominion of men, are all-conquering, either sooner or later, in their onward sweep around the world. No error can forever withstand their power. It may be stubborn, and even violent for awhile, but it must eventually give way to truth, for it is unalterable, as declared by Dr. Chapin, that "before the love which is in God, all things are sure to come around to His standard, and the most gigantic iniquity of earth strikes its head at last against the beam of God's providence and goes down."■

127 LYNCH LAW IN ALL ITS PHASES

Ida B. Wells

As the "Red Record" of lynching reached epidemic proportions, with over one thousand African Americans murdered by mobs in a decade, many African American leaders sought to bring national attention to the issue, appeal for federal intervention, and deny the claims through which lynching was rationalized. The most outspoken and successful of these crusaders was Ida B. Wells.

The eldest of eight children born to enslaved parents in Holly Springs, Mississippi, Wells (1862–1931) was an influential journalist, editor, lecturer, and organizer. Fired from her job as a teacher in Tennessee because of her court battles against segregated public transportation, Wells turned to journalism. She became half owner of the Memphis Free Speech *newspaper in 1892 and promptly editorialized against the lynchings of three of her friends who had been falsely accused of rape. A mob destroyed the offices of the newspaper on May 27 while Wells was away in Philadelphia.*

Wells began organizing and speaking on behalf of an international campaign against lynching. She toured England in 1893 and 1894 and lectured in many American cities. In her speeches and writings, Wells employed graphic, detailed descriptions of specific lynchings and analyzed the media accounts through which her audiences were likely to have heard of them. Wells sought to forge an interracial antilynching alliance among churches, national organizations such as the YWCA and WCTU, and newly established clubs for women of color. In 1893, she married lawyer and civil rights activist Ferdinand Lee Barnett, the editor of the Chicago Conservator.

Wells was a great admirer of Frederick Douglass and shared his vision of the United States as an essentially "composite nation," a term she employs in this and other speeches. The admiration and influence were mutual. "Early in her life," Douglass biographer William McFeely has written, "Ida Wells may have been inspired by Frederick Douglass, but he, at the end of his, was driven back into the fray by Wells."* Wells enlisted his active support for the antilynching campaign, and he provided a preface to her 1895 pamphlet, A Red Record, *a statistical analysis of lynching and its causes.*

In her speech in Boston's Tremont Temple on February 13, 1893, Wells describes the path that brought her to activism and meditates upon the relationship of lynch law to American civil religion and self-image. In her use of "My Country! 'Tis of Thee" to conclude her speech, Wells anticipates Martin Luther King's "I Have a Dream" speech seventy years later. Both speakers look to the lyrics of that national hymn for promises and national aspirations yet to be fulfilled. Both look forward to the day when the United States is a "sweet land of liberty" where "freedom does ring" (in Wells's modification of the lyric) "from every mountainside," when the song can be sung by all Americans without irony or hypocrisy.

The text of Wells's speech was published in Our Day, *May 1893, 333–37, and was reprinted in Mildred Thompson's* Ida B. Wells-Barnett: An Exploratory Study of an American Black Woman, 1893–1930 *(New York: Carlson, 1990). See also Paula Giddings,* When and Where I Enter: The

---

*William McFeely, *Frederick Douglass* (New York: W. W. Norton, 1991), 377.

Impact of Black Women on Sex and Race in America *(New York: William Morrow, 1984).*

Iam before the American people to-day through no inclination of my own, but because of a deep-seated conviction that the country at large does not know the extent to which lynch law prevails in parts of the Republic nor the conditions which force into exile those who speak the truth. I cannot believe that the apathy and indifference which so largely obtains regarding mob rule is other than the result of ignorance of the true situation. And yet, the observing and thoughtful must know that in one section, at least, of our common country, a government of the people, by the people, and for the people, means a government by the mob; where the land of the free and home of the brave means a land of lawlessness, murder and outrage; and where liberty of speech means the license of might to destroy the business and drive from home those who exercise this privilege contrary to the will of the mob. Repeated attacks on the life, liberty and happiness of any citizen or class of citizens are attacks on distinctive American institutions; such attacks imperiling as they do the foundation of government, law and order, merit the thoughtful consideration of far-sighted Americans; not from a standpoint of sentiment, not even so much from a standpoint of justice to a weak race, as from a desire to preserve our institutions.

The race problem or negro question, as it has been called, has been omnipresent and all-pervading since long before the Afro-American was raised from the degradation of the slave to the dignity of the citizen. It has never been settled because the right methods have not been employed in the solution. It is the Banquo's ghost of politics, religion, and sociology which will not down at the bidding of those who are tormented with its ubiquitous appearance on every occasion. Times without number, since invested with citizenship, the race has been indicted for ignorance, immorality and general worthlessness—declared guilty and executed by its self-constituted judges. The operations of law do not dispose of negroes fast enough, and lynching bees have become the favorite pastime of the South. As excuse for the same, a new cry, as false as it is foul, is raised in an effort to blast race character, a cry which has proclaimed to the world that virtue and innocence are violated by Afro-Americans who must be killed like wild beasts to protect womanhood and childhood.

Born and reared in the South, I had never expected to live elsewhere. Until this past year I was one among those who believed the condition of the masses gave large excuse for the humiliations and proscriptions under which we labored; that when wealth, education and character became more general among us, the cause being removed the effect would cease, and justice be accorded to all alike. I shared the general belief that good newspapers entering regularly the homes of our people in every state could do more to bring about this result than any agency. Preaching the doctrine of self-help, thrift and economy every week, they would be the teachers to those who had been deprived of school advantages, yet were making history every day—and train to think for themselves our mental children of a larger growth. And so, three years ago last June, I became editor and part owner of the *Memphis Free Speech*. As editor, I had occasion to criticize the city School Board's employment of inefficient teachers and poor school-buildings for Afro-American children. I was in the employ of that board at the time, and at the close of that school-term one year ago, was not re-elected to a position I had held in the city schools for seven years. Accepting the decision of the Board of Education, I set out to make a race newspaper pay—a thing which older and wiser heads said could not be done. But there were enough of our people in Memphis and surrounding territory to support a paper, and I believed they would do so. With nine months hard work the circulation increased from 1,500 to 3,500; in twelve months it was on a good paying basis. Throughout the Mississippi Valley in Arkansas, Tennessee and Mississippi on plantations and in towns, the demand for and interest in the paper increased among the masses. The newsboys who would not sell it on the trains, voluntarily testified that they had never known colored people to demand a paper so eagerly.

To make the paper a paying business I became advertising agent, solicitor, as well as editor, and was continually on the go. Wherever I went among the people, I gave them in church, school, public gatherings, and home, the benefit of my honest conviction that maintenance of character, money getting and education would finally solve our problem and that it depended on us to say how soon this would be brought about. This sentiment bore good fruit in Memphis. We had nice homes, representatives in almost every branch of business and profession, and refined society. We had learned that helping each other helped all, and every well-conducted business by Afro-Americans prospered. With all our proscription in theatres, hotels and on railroads, we had never had a lynching and did not believe we could have one. There had been lynchings and brutal outrages of all sorts in our own state and those adjoining us, but we had confidence and pride in our city and the majesty of its laws. So far in advance of other Southern cities was ours, we were content to endure the evils we had, to labor and to wait.

But there was a rude awakening. On the morning of March 9, the bodies of three of our best young men were found in an old field horribly shot to pieces. These young men had owned and operated the "People's Grocery," situated at what was known as the Curve—a suburb made up almost entirely of colored people—about a mile from city limits. Thomas Moss, one of the oldest letter-carriers in the city, was president of the company, Calvin McDowell was manager and Will Stewart was a clerk. There were about ten other stockholders, all colored men. The young men were well known and popular and their business flourished, and that of Barrett, a white grocer who kept store there before the "People's Grocery" was established, went down. One day an officer came to the "People's Grocery" and inquired for a colored man who lived in the neighborhood, and for whom the officer had a warrant. Barrett was with him and when McDowell said he knew nothing as to the whereabouts of the man for whom they were searching, Barrett, not the officer, then accused McDowell of harboring the man, and McDowell gave the lie. Barrett drew his pistol and struck McDowell with it; thereupon McDowell, who was a tall, fine-looking six-footer, took Barrett's pistol from him, knocked him down and gave him a good thrashing, while Will Stewart, the clerk, kept the special officer at bay. Barrett went to town, swore out a warrant for their arrest on a charge of assault and battery. McDowell went before the Criminal Court, immediately gave bond and returned to his store. Barrett then threatened (to use his own words) that he was going to clean out the whole store. Knowing how anxious he was to destroy their business, these young men consulted a lawyer who told them they were justified in defending themselves if attacked, as they were a mile beyond city limits and police protection. They accordingly armed several of their friends—not to assail, but to resist the threatened Saturday night attack.

When they saw Barrett enter the front door and a half dozen men at the rear door at 11 o'clock that night, they supposed the attack was on and immediately fired into the crowd, wounding three men. These men, dressed in citizen's clothes, turned out to be deputies who claimed to be hunting another man for whom they had a warrant, and whom any one of them could have arrested without trouble. When these men found they had fired upon officers of the law, they threw away their firearms and submitted to arrest, confident they should establish their innocence of intent to fire upon officers of the law. The daily papers in flaming headlines roused the evil passions of the whites, denounced these poor boys in unmeasured terms, nor permitted them a word in their own defense.

The neighborhood of the Curve was searched next day, and about thirty persons were thrown into jail, charged with conspiracy. No communication was to be had with friends any of the three days these men were in jail; bail was refused and Thomas Moss was not allowed to eat the food his wife prepared for him. The judge is reported to have said, "Any one can see them after three days." They were seen after three days, but they were no longer able to respond to the greetings of friends. On Tuesday following the shooting at the grocery, the papers which had made much of the sufferings of the wounded deputies, and promised it would go hard with those who did the shooting, if they died, announced that the officers were all out of danger, and would recover. The friends of the prisoners breathed more easily and relaxed their vigilance. They felt that as the officers would not die, there was no danger that in the heat of passion the prisoners would meet violent death at the hands of the mob. Besides, we had such confidence in the law. But the law did not provide capital punishment for shooting which did not kill. So the mob did what the law could not be made to do, as a lesson to the Afro-American that he must not shoot a white man,—no matter what the provocation. The same night after the announcement was made in the papers that the officers would get well, the mob, in obedience to a plan known to every prominent white man in the city, went to the jail between two and three o'clock in the morning, dragged out these young men, hatless and shoeless, put them on the yard engine of the railroad which was in waiting just behind the jail, carried them a mile north of city limits and horribly shot them to death while the locomotive at a given signal let off steam and blew the whistle to deaden the sound of the firing.

"It was done by unknown men," said the jury, yet the *Appeal-Avalanche,* which goes to press at 3 a.m., had a two-column account of the lynching. The papers also told how McDowell got hold of the guns of the mob and as his grasp could not be loosened, his hand was shattered with a pistol ball and all the lower part of his face was torn away. There were four pools of blood found and only three bodies. It was whispered that he, McDowell, killed one of the lynchers with his gun, and it is well known that a policeman who was seen on the street a few days previous to the lynching, died very suddenly the next day after.

"It was done by unknown parties," said the jury, yet the papers told how Tom Moss begged for his life, for the sake of his wife, his little daughter and his unborn infant. They also told us that his last words were, "If you will kill us, turn our faces to the West."

All this we learn too late to save these men, even if the law had not been in the hands of their murderers. When the colored people realized that the flower of our young manhood had been stolen away at night and murdered, there was a rush for firearms to avenge the wrong, but no house would sell a colored man a gun; the armory of the Tennessee Rifles, our only colored military company, and of which McDowell was a member, was broken into by order of the Criminal Court judge, and its guns taken. One hundred men and irresponsible boys from fifteen years and up were armed by order of the authorities and rushed out to the Curve, where it was reported that the colored people were massing, and at point of the bayonet dispersed these men who could do nothing but talk. The cigars, wines, etc., of the grocery stock were freely used by the mob, who possessed the place on pretence of dispersing the conspiracy. The money drawer was broken into and contents taken. The trunk of Calvin McDowell, who had a room in the store, was broken open, and his clothing, which was not good enough to take away, was thrown out and trampled on the floor.

These men were murdered, their stock was attached by creditors and sold for less than one-eighth of its cost to that same man Barrett, who is to-day running his grocery in the same place. He had indeed kept his word, and by aid of the authorities destroyed the People's Grocery Company root and branch. The relatives of Will Stewart and Calvin McDowell are bereft of their protectors. The baby daughter of Tom Moss, too young to express how she misses her father, toddles to the wardrobe, seizes the legs of the trousers of his letter-carrier uniform, hugs and kisses them with evident delight and stretches up her little hands to be taken up into the arms which will nevermore clasp his daughter's form. His wife holds Thomas Moss, Jr., in her arms, upon whose unconscious baby face the tears fall thick and fast when she is thinking of the sad fate of the father he will never see, and of the two helpless children who cling to her for the support she cannot give.

Although these men were peaceable, law-abiding citizens of this country, we are told there can be no punishment for their murderers nor indemnity for their relatives.

I have no power to describe the feeling of horror that possessed every member of the race in Memphis when the truth dawned upon us that the protection of the law which we had so long enjoyed was no longer ours; all this had been destroyed in a night, and the barriers of the law had been thrown down, and the guardians of the public peace and confidence scoffed away into the shadows, and all authority given into the hands of the mob, and innocent men cut down as if they were brutes—the first feeling was one of utter dismay, then intense indignation. Vengeance was whispered from ear to ear, but sober reflection brought the conviction that it would be extreme folly to seek vengeance when such action meant certain death for the men, and horrible slaughter for the women and children, as one of the evening papers took care to remind us. The power of the State, country and city, the civil authorities and the strong arm of the military power were all on the side of the mob and of lawlessness. Few of our men possessed firearms, our only company's guns were confiscated, and the only white man who would sell a colored man a gun, was himself jailed, and his store closed. We were helpless in our great strength. It was our first object lesson in the doctrine of white supremacy; an illustration of the South's cardinal principle that no matter what the attainments, character or standing of an Afro-American, the laws of the South will not protect him against a white man.

There was only one thing we could do, and a great determination seized upon the people to follow the advice of the martyred Moss, and "turn our faces to the West," whose laws protect all alike. The *Free Speech* supported by our ministers and leading business men advised the people to leave a community whose laws did not protect them. Hundreds left on foot to walk four hundred miles between Memphis and Oklahoma. A Baptist minister went to the territory, built a church, and took his entire congregation out in less than a month. Another minister sold his church and took his flock to California, and still another has settled in Kansas. In two months, six thousand persons had left the city and every branch of business began to feel this silent resentment of the outrage, and failure of the authorities to punish the lynchers. There were a number of business failures and blocks of houses were for rent. The superintendent and treasurer of the street railway company called at the office of the *Free Speech*, to have us urge the colored people to ride again on the street cars. A real estate dealer said to a colored man who returned some property he had been buying on the installment plan: "I don't see what you 'niggers' are cutting up about. You got off light. We first intended to kill every one of those thirty-one niggers' in jail, but concluded to let all go but the 'leaders.' " They did let all go to the penitentiary. These so-called rioters have since been tried in the Criminal Court for the conspiracy of defending their property, and are now serving terms of three, eight, and fifteen years each in the Tennessee State prison.

To restore the equilibrium and put a stop to the great financial loss, the next move was to get rid of the *Free Speech,*—the disturbing element which kept the waters troubled; which would not let the people forget, and in obedience to whose advice nearly six thousand persons had left the city. In casting about for an excuse, the mob found it in the following editorial which appeared in the Memphis *Free Speech,*—May 21, 1892: "Eight negroes lynched at Little Rock, Ark., where the citizens broke into the penitentiary and got their man; three near Anniston, Ala., and one in New Orleans, all on the same charge, the new alarm of assaulting white women—and three near Clarksville, Ga., for killing a white man. The same program of hanging—then shooting bullets into the lifeless bodies was carried out to the letter. Nobody in this section of the country believes the old threadbare lie that negro men rape white women. If Southern white men are not careful they will overreach themselves, and public sentiment will have a reaction. A conclusion will then be reached which will be very damaging to the moral reputation of their women." Commenting on this, *The Daily Commercial* of Wednesday following said: "Those negroes who are attempting to make lynching of individuals of their race a means for arousing the worst passions of their kind, are playing with a dangerous sentiment. The negroes may as well understand that there is no mercy for the negro rapist, and little patience with his defenders. A negro organ printed in this city in a recent issue published the following atrocious paragraph: 'Nobody in this section believes the old threadbare lie that negro men rape white women. If Southern white men are not careful they will overreach themselves and public sentiment will have a reaction. A conclusion will be reached which will be very damaging to the moral reputation of their women.' The fact that a black scoundrel is allowed to live and utter such loathsome and repulsive calumnies is a volume of evidence as to the wonderful patience of Southern whites. There are some things the Southern white man will not tolerate, and the obscene intimidation of the foregoing has brought the writer to the very uttermost limit of public patience. We hope we have said enough."

The Evening *Scimitar* of the same day copied this leading editorial and added this comment: "Patience under such circumstances is not a virtue. If the negroes themselves do not apply the remedy without delay, it will be the duty of those he has attacked, to tie the wretch who utters these calumnies to a stake at the intersection of Main and Madison streets, brand him in the forehead with a hot iron and—"

Such open suggestions by the leading daily papers of the progressive city of Memphis were acted upon by the leading citizens and a meeting was held at the Cotton Exchange that evening. *The Commercial* two days later had the following account of it:

ATROCIOUS BLACKGUARDISM.
There will be no Lynching and no Repetition of the Offense.
   In its issue of Wednesday *The Commercial* reproduced and commented upon an editorial which appeared a day or two before in a ne-

gro organ known as the *Free Speech.* The article was so insufferably and indecently slanderous that the whole city awoke to a feeling of intense resentment which came within an ace of culminating in one of those occurrences whose details are so eagerly seized and so prominently published by Northern newspapers. Conservative counsels, however, prevailed, and no extreme measures were resorted to. On Wednesday afternoon a meeting of citizens was held. It was not an assemblage of hoodlums or irresponsible fire-eaters, but solid, substantial business men who knew exactly what they were doing and who were far more indignant at the villainous insult to the women of the South than they would have been at any injury done themselves. This meeting appointed a committee to seek the author of the infamous editorial and warn him quietly that upon repetition of the offense he would find some other part of the country a good deal safer and pleasanter place of residence than this. The committee called a negro preacher named Nightingale, but he disclaimed responsibility and convinced the gentlemen that he had really sold out his paper to a woman named Wells. This woman is not in Memphis at present. It was finally learned that one Fleming, a negro who was driven out of Crittenden Co. during the trouble there a few years ago, wrote the paragraph. He had, however, heard of the meeting, and fled from a fate which he feared was in store for him, and which he knew he deserved. His whereabouts could not be ascertained, and the committee so reported. Later on, a communication from Fleming to a prominent Republican politician, and that politician's reply were shown to one or two gentlemen. The former was an inquiry as to whether the writer might safely return to Memphis, the latter was an emphatic answer in the negative, and Fleming is still in hiding. Nothing further will be done in the matter. There will be no lynching, and it is very certain there will be no repetition of the outrage. If there should be—Friday, May 25.

The only reason there was no lynching of Mr. Fleming who was business manager and half owner of the *Free Speech,* and who did not write the editorial, was because this same white Republican told him the committee was coming, and warned him not to trust them, but get out of the way. The committee scoured the city hunting him, and had to be content with Mr. Nightingale who was dragged to the meeting, shamefully abused (although it was known he had sold out his interest in the paper six months before). He was struck in the face and forced at the pistol's point to sign a letter which was written by them, in which he denied all knowledge of the editorial, denounced and condemned it as slander on white women. I do not censure Mr. Nightingale for his action because, having never been at the pistol's point myself, I do not feel that I am competent to sit in judgment on him, or say what I would do under such circumstances.

I had written that editorial with other matter for the week's paper before leaving home the Friday previous for the General Conference of the A.M.E. Church in Philadelphia. The conference adjourned Tuesday, and Thursday, May 25, at 3 p.m., I landed in New York City for a few days' stay before returning home, and there learned from the papers that my business manager had been driven away and the paper suspended. Telegraphing for news, I received telegrams and letters in return informing me that the trains were being watched, that I was to be dumped into the river and beaten, if not killed; it had been learned that I wrote the editorial and I was to be hanged in front of the court-house and my face bled if I returned, and I was implored by my friends to remain away. The creditors attached the office in the meantime and the outfit was sold without more ado, thus destroying effectually that which it had taken years to build. One prominent insurance agent publicly declares he will make it his business to shoot me down on sight if I return to Memphis in twenty years, while a leading white lady had remarked that she was opposed to the lynching of those three men in March, but she did wish there was some way by which I could be gotten back and lynched.

I have been censured for writing that editorial, but when I think of the five men who were lynched that week for assault on white women and that not a week passes but some poor soul is violently ushered into eternity on this trumped-up charge, knowing the many things I do, and part of which I tried to tell in the *New York Age* of June 25, (and in the pamphlets I have with me) seeing that the whole race in the South was injured in the estimation of the world because of these false reports, I could no longer hold my peace, and I feel, yes, I am sure, that if it had to be done over again (provided no one else was the loser save myself) I would do and say the very same again.

The lawlessness here described is not confined to one locality. In the past ten years over a thousand colored men, women and children have been butchered, murdered and burnt in all parts of the South. The details of these horrible outrages seldom reach beyond the narrow world where they occur. Those who commit the murders write the reports, and hence these lasting blots upon the honor of a nation cause but a faint ripple on the outside world. They arouse no great indignation and call forth no adequate demand for justice. The victims were black, and the reports are so written as to make it appear that the helpless creatures deserved the fate which overtook them.

Not so with the Italian lynching of 1891. They were not black men, and three of them were not citizens of the Republic, but subjects of the King of Italy. The chief of police of New Orleans was shot and eleven Italians were arrested charged with the murder; they were tried and the jury disagreed; the good, law-abiding citizens of New Orleans thereupon took them from the jail and lynched them at high noon. A feeling of horror ran through the nation at this outrage. All Europe was amazed. The Italian government demanded thorough investigation and redress, and the Federal Government promised to give the matter the consideration which was its due. The diplomatic relations between the two countries became very much strained and for a while war talk was freely indulged. Here was a case where the power of the Federal Government to protect its own citizens and redeem its pledges to a friendly power was put to the test. When our State Department called upon the authorities of Louisiana for investigation of the crime and punishment of the criminals, the United States government was told that the crime was strictly within the authority of the State of Louisiana, and Louisiana would attend to it. After a farcical investigation, the usual verdict in such cases was rendered: "Death at the hand of parties unknown to the jury," the same verdict which has been pronounced over the bodies of over 1,000 colored persons! Our general government has thus admitted that it has no jurisdiction over the crimes committed at New Orleans upon citizens of the country, nor upon those citizens of a friendly power to whom the general government and not the State government has pledged protection. Not only has our general government made the confession that one of the states is greater than the Union, but the general government has paid $25,000 of the people's money to the King of Italy for the lynching of those three subjects, the evil-doing of one State, over which it has no control, but for whose lawlessness the whole country must pay. The principle involved in the treaty power of the government has not yet been settled to the satisfaction of foreign powers; but the principle involved in the right of State jurisdiction in such matters, was settled long ago by the decision of the United States Supreme Court.

I beg your patience while we look at another phase of the lynching mania. We have turned heretofore to the pages of ancient and medieval history, to roman tyranny, the Jesuitical Inquisition of Spain for the spectacle of a human being burnt to death. In the past ten years three instances, at least, have been furnished where men have literally been roasted to death to appease the fury of Southern mobs. The Texarkana instance of last year and the Paris, Texas, case of this month are the most recent as they are the most shocking and repulsive. Both were charged with crimes from which the laws provide adequate punishment. The Texarkana man, Ed Coy, was charged with assaulting a white woman. A mob pronounced him guilty, strapped him to a tree, chipped the flesh from his body, poured coal oil over him and the woman in the case set fire to him. The country looked on and in many cases applauded, because it was published that this man had violated the honor of the white woman, although he protested his innocence to the last. Judge Tourjee in the Chicago *Inter-Ocean* of recent date says investigation has shown that Ed Coy had supported this woman, (who was known to be of bad character,) and her drunken husband for over a year previous to the burning.

The Paris, Texas, burning of Henry Smith, February lst, has exceeded all the others in its horrible details. The man was drawn through the streets on a float, as the Roman generals used to parade their trophies of war, while the scaffold ten feet high, was being built, and irons were heated in the fire. He was bound on it, and red-hot irons began at his feet and slowly branded his body, while the mob howled with delight at his shrieks. Red hot irons were run down his throat and cooked his tongue; his eyes were burned out, and when he was at last unconscious, cotton seed hulls were placed under him, coal oil poured all over him, and a torch applied to the mass. When the flames burned away the ropes which bound Smith and scorched his flesh, he was brought back to sensibility—and burned and maimed and sightless as he was, he rolled off the platform and away from the fire. His half-cooked body was seized and trampled and thrown back into the flames while a mob of twenty thousand persons who came from all over the country howled with delight, and gathered up some buttons and ashes after all was over to preserve for relics. The man was charged with outraging and murdering a four-year-old white child, covering her body with brush, sleeping beside her through the night, then making his escape. If true, it was the deed of a madman, and should have been clearly proven so. The fact that no time for verification of the newspaper reports was given, is suspicious, especially when I remember that a negro was lynched in Indianola, Sharkey Co., Miss., last summer. The dispatches said it was because he had assaulted the sheriff's eight-year-old daughter. The girl was more than eighteen years old and was found by her father in this man's room, who was a servant on the place.

These incidents have been made the basis of this terrible story because they overshadow all others of a like nature in cruelty and represent the legal phases of the whole question. They could be multiplied without number—and each outrival the other in the fiendish cruelty exercised, and the frequent awful lawlessness exhibited. The following table shows the number of black men lynched from January 1, 1882, to January 1, 1892: In 1882, 52; 1883, 39; 1884, 53; 1885, 77; 1886, 73; 1887, 70; 1888, 72; 1889, 95; 1890, 100; 1891, 169. Of these 728 black men who were murdered, 269 were charged with rape, 253 with murder, 44 with robbery, 37 with incendiarism, 32 with reasons unstated (it was not necessary to have a reason), 27 with race prejudice, 13 with quarreling with white men, 10 with making threats, 7 with rioting, 5 with miscegenation, 4 with burglary. One of the men lynched in 1891 was Will Lewis, who was lynched because "he was drunk and saucy to white folks." A woman who was one of the 73 victims in 1886, was hung in Jackson, Tenn., because the white woman for whom she cooked, died suddenly of poisoning. An examination showed arsenical poisoning. A search in the cook's room found rat poison. She was thrown into jail, and when the mob had worked itself up to the lynching pitch, she was dragged out, every stitch of clothing torn from her body, and was hung in the public court house square in sight of everybody. That white woman's husband has since died, in the insane asylum, a raving maniac, and his ravings have led to the conclusion that he and not the cook, was the poisoner of his wife. A fifteen-year-old colored girl was lynched last spring, at Rayville, La., on the same charge of poisoning. A woman was also lynched at Hollendale, Miss., last spring, charged with being an accomplice in the murder of her white paramour who had abused her. These were only two of the 159 persons lynched in the South from January 1, 1892, to January 1, 1893. Over a dozen black men have been lynched already since this new year set in, and the year is not yet two months old.

It will thus be seen that neither age, sex nor decency are spared. Although the impression has gone abroad that most of the lynchings take place because of assaults on white women only one-third of the number lynched in the past ten years have been charged with that offense, to say nothing of those who were not guilty of the charge. And according to law none of them were guilty until proven so. But the unsupported word of any white person for any cause is sufficient to cause a lynching. So bold have the lynchers become, masks are laid aside, the temples of justice and strongholds of law are invaded in broad daylight and prisoners taken out and lynched, while governors of states and officers of law stand by and see the work well done.

And yet this Christian nation, the flower of the nineteenth century civilization, says it can do nothing to stop this inhuman slaughter. The general government is willingly powerless to send troops to protect the lives of its black citizens, but the state governments are free to use state troops to shoot them down like cattle, when in desperation the black men attempt to defend themselves, and then tell the world that it was necessary to put down a "race war."

Persons unfamiliar with the condition of affairs in the Southern States do not credit the truth when it is told them. They cannot conceive how such a condition of affairs prevails so near them with steam power, telegraph wires and printing presses in daily and hourly touch with the localities where such disorder reigns. In a former generation the ancestors of these same people refused to believe that slavery was the "league with death and the covenant with hell." Wm. Lloyd Garrison* declared it to be, until he was thrown into a dungeon in Baltimore, until the signal lights of Nat Turner† lit the dull skies of Northampton County, and until sturdy old John Brown made his attack on Harper's Ferry. When freedom of speech was martyred in the person of Elijah Lovejoy‡ at Alton, when the liberty of free-discussion in Senate of the Nation's Congress was struck down in the person of the fearless Charles Sumner,§ the Nation was at last convinced that slavery was not only a monster by a tyrant. That same tyrant is at work under a new name and guise. The lawlessness which has been here described is like unto that which prevailed under slavery. *The very same forces are at work now as then.* The attempt is being made to subject to a condition of civil and industrial dependence, those whom the Constitution declares to be free men. The events which have led up to the present wide-spread lawlessness in the South can be traced to the very first year Lee's conquered veterans marched from Appomattox to their homes in the Southland. They were conquered in war, but not in spirit. They believed as firmly as ever that it was their right to rule black men and dictate to the National Government. The Knights of White

---

*Garrison (1805–1879) was the abolitionist editor of the *Liberator* and cofounder of the American Anti-Slavery Society.

†Turner led the bloodiest slave rebellion in U.S. history in 1831.

‡Abolitionist editor Lovejoy was killed by a mob in Alton, Illinois, in 1837.

§In 1856, Senator Sumner of Massachusetts was severely beaten in the Senate by Congressman Brook of South Carolina.

Liners, and the Ku Klux Klans were composed of veterans of the Confederate army who were determined to destroy the effect of all the slave had gained by the war. They finally accomplished their purpose in 1876. The right of the Afro-American to vote and hold office remains in the Federal Constitution, but is destroyed in the constitution of the Southern states. Having destroyed the citizenship of the man, they are now trying to destroy the manhood of the citizen. All their laws are shaped to this end,—school laws, railroad car regulations, those governing labor liens on crops,—every device is adopted to make slaves of free men and rob them of their wages. Whenever a malicious law is violated in any of its parts, any farmer, any railroad conductor, or merchant can call together a posse of his neighbors and punish even with death the black man who resists and the legal authorities sanction what is done by failing to prosecute and punish the murders. The Repeal of the Civil Rights Law removed their last barrier and the black man's last bulwark and refuge.* The rule of the mob is absolute.

Those who know this recital to be true, say there is nothing they can do—they cannot interfere and vainly hope by further concession to placate the imperious and dominating part of our country in which this lawlessness prevails. Because this country has been almost rent in twain by internal dissension, the other sections seem virtually to have agreed that the best way to heal the breach is to permit the taking away of civil, political, and even human rights, to stand by in silence and utter indifference while the South continues to wreak fiendish vengeance on the irresponsible cause. They pretend to believe that with all the machinery of law and government in its hands; with the jails and penitentiaries and convict farms filled with pretty race criminals; with the well-known fact that no negro has ever been known to escape conviction and punishment for any crime in the South—still there are those who try to justify and condone the lynching of over a thousand black men in less than ten years—an average of one hundred a year. The public sentiment of the country, by its silence in press, pulpit and in public meetings has encouraged this state of affairs, and public sentiment is stronger than law. With all the country's disposition to condone and temporize with the South and its methods; with its many instances of sacrificing principle to prejudice for the sake of making friends and healing the breach made by the late war; of going into the lawless country with capital to build up its waste places and remaining silent in the presence of outrage and wrong—the South is as vindictive and bitter as ever. She is willing to make friends as long as she is permitted to pursue unmolested and uncensured, her course of proscription, injustice, outrage and vituperation. The malignant misrepresentation of General Butler,† the uniformly indecent and abusive assault

*In 1883, the U.S. Supreme Court ruled that the 1875 Civil Rights Act was unconstitutional.
†In 1861, Union General Benjamin F. Butler declared the slaves of Confederates to be "contraband of war" and authorized their liberation by Union troops.

of this dead man whose only crime was a defence of his country, is a recent proof that the South has lost none of its bitterness. The *Nashville American,* one of the leading papers of one of the leading southern cities, gleefully announced editorially that " 'The Beast is dead.' Early yesterday morning, acting under the devil's orders, the angel of Death took Ben Butler and landed him in the lowest depths of hell, and we pity even the devil the possession he has secured." The men who wrote these editorials are without exception young men who know nothing of slavery and scarcely anything of the war. The bitterness and hatred have been instilled in and taught them by their parents, and they are men who make and reflect the sentiment of their section. The South spares nobody else's feelings, and it seems a queer logic that when it comes to a question of right, involving lives of citizens and the honor of the government, the South's feelings must be respected and spared.

Do you ask the remedy? A public sentiment strong against lawlessness must be aroused. Every individual can contribute to this awakening. When a sentiment against lynch law as strong, deep and mighty as that roused against slavery prevails, I have no fear of the result. It should be already established as a fact and not as a theory, that every human being must have a fair trail for his life and liberty, no matter what the charge against him. When a demand goes up from fearless and persistent reformers from press and pulpit, from industrial and moral associations that this shall be so from Maine to Texas and from ocean to ocean, a way will be found to make it so.

In deference to the few words of condemnation uttered at the M.E. General Conference last year, and by other organizations, Governors Hogg of Texas, Northern of Georgia, and Tillman of South Carolina, have issued proclamations offering rewards for the apprehension of lynchers. These rewards have never been claimed, and these governors knew they would not be when offered. In many cases they knew the ringleaders of the mobs. The prosecuting attorney of Shelby County, Tenn., wrote Governor Buchanan to offer a reward for the arrest of the lynchers of three young men murdered in Memphis. Everybody in that city and state knew well that the letter was written for the sake of effect and the governor did not even offer the reward. But the country at large deluded itself with the belief that the officials of the South and the leading citizens condemned lynching. The lynchings go on in spite of offered rewards, and in face of Governor Hogg's vigorous talk, the second man was burnt alive in his state with the utmost deliberation and publicity. Since he sent a message to the legislature the mob found and hung Henry Smith's stepson, because he refused to tell where Smith was when they were hunting for him. Public sentiment which shall denounce these crimes in season and out; public sentiment which turns capital and immigration from a section given over to lawlessness; public sentiment which insists on the punishment of criminals and lynchers by law must be aroused.

It is no wonder in my mind that the party which stood for their years as the champion of human liberty and human rights, the part of great moral ideas, should suffer overwhelming defeat when it has proven recreant to its professions and abandoned a position it created; when although its followers were being outraged in every sense, it was afraid to stand for the right, and appeal to the American people to sustain them in it. It put aside the question of a free ballot and fair count of every citizen and give its voice and influence for the protection of the coat instead of the man who wore it, for the product of labor instead of the laborer; for the seal of citizenship rather than the citizen, and insisted upon the evils of free trade instead of the sacredness of free speech. I am no politician but I believe if the Republican party had met the issues squarely for human rights instead of the tariff it would have occupied a different position to-day. The voice of the people is the voice of God, and I long with all the intensity of my soul for the Garrison, Douglass, Sumner, Whittier, and Phillips who shall rouse this nation to a demand that from Greenland's icy mountains to the coral reefs of the Southern seas, mob rule shall be put down and equal and exact justice be accorded to every citizen of whatever race, who finds a home within the borders of the land of the free and the home of the brave.

Then no longer will our national hymn be sounding brass and a tinkling cymbal, but every member of this great composite nation will be a living, harmonious illustration of the words, and all can honestly and gladly join in singing:

> My country! 'tis of thee,
> Sweet land of liberty
> Of thee I sing.
> Land where our fathers died,
> Land of the Pilgrim's pride,
> From every mountain side
> Freedom does ring.*■

---

*For further information on the uses of the song "America" by African American orators and performers, see Robert Branham, " 'Of Thee I Sing': Contesting 'America,' " *American Quarterly* 48 (December 1996), 623–52.

128

THE INTELLECTUAL PROGRESS OF THE COLORED WOMEN OF THE UNITED STATES SINCE THE EMANCIPATION PROCLAMATION

Fannie Barrier Williams

From 1893 to the beginning of the Great Depression, Fannie Barrier Williams (1855–1944) was among the best known African American lecturers and a leader of the women's club movement and various philanthropic causes. Born and raised in Brockport, New York, she graduated from the State Normal School at Brockport in 1870 and studied at the New England Conservatory of Music and Washington's School of Fine Arts. Williams helped found the National League of Colored Women in 1893. In Chicago, she was active in the creation of equal employment opportunities, helping to found Provident Hospital with an integrated medical staff and lobbying local employers to hire African American women as secretaries and clerical staff. After 1900, she and her husband, the lawyer S. Laing Williams, became strong supporters of Booker T. Washington's self-help programs.

Williams was one of six African American women selected to speak before the World's Congress of Representative Women in May 1893 (Frances Watkins Harper, Anna Julia Cooper, Fannie Jackson Coppin, Sarah J. Woodson Early, and Hallie Quinn Brown also spoke). The congress was part of Chicago's Columbian Exposition, whose American exhibition, housed in the appropriately named "White City," systematically excluded Americans of color. Frederick Douglass and Ida B. Wells were in the Haitian pavilion, where Wells handed out copies of her pamphlet The Reason Why The Colored American is not in the World's Columbian Exposition.

Williams urges the white women in her audience to learn more about black women and the special disabilities they face from racial discrimination. "They are the only women in the country," she reminds her listeners, "for whom real ability, virtue, and special talents count for nothing when they become applicants for respectable employment." Although a few African American women, all of whom had been active in the development of the women's club movement, were permitted to address the World's Congress, considerable tension developed when they sought inclusion in national temperance and women's suffrage campaigns. Thus, as Hazel Carby has written in Reconstructing Womanhood *(New York: Oxford University Press, 1987), "to appear as a black woman on the platform of the Congress of Representative Women was to be placed in a highly contradictory position, at once part of and excluded from the dominant discourse of white women's politics" (6).*

In her address, Williams insists that despite great adversity, "our women have the same character and mettle that characterize the best of American women," and as a result must be "a part of the social forces that must help to determine the questions that so concern women generally."

The text of her speech is from May Wright Sewall, ed., The World's Congress of Representative Women *(New York: Rand, McNally, 1894), 696–711.*

Less than thirty years ago the term progress as applied to colored women of African descent in the United States would have been an anomaly. The recognition of that term to-day as appropriate is a fact full of interesting significance. That the discussion of progressive womanhood in this great assemblage of the representative women of the world is considered incomplete without some account of the colored women's status is a most noteworthy evidence that we have not failed to impress ourselves on the higher side of American life.

Less is known of our women than of any other class of Americans.

No organization of far-reaching influence for their special advancement, no conventions of women to take note of their progress, and no special literature reciting the incidents, the events, and all things interesting and instructive concerning them are to be found among the agencies directing their career. There has been no special interest in their peculiar condition as native-born American women. Their power to affect the social life of America, either for good or for ill, has excited not even a speculative interest.

Though there is much that is sorrowful, much that is wonderfully heroic, and much that is romantic in a peculiar way in their history, none of it has as yet been told as evidence of what is possible for these women. How few of the happy, prosperous, and eager living Americans can appreciate what it all means to be suddenly changed from irresponsible bondage to the responsibility of freedom and citizenship!

The distress of it all can never be told, and the pain of it all can never be felt except by the victims, and by those saintly women of the white race who for thirty years have been consecrated to the uplifting of a whole race of women from a long-enforced degradation.

The American people have always been impatient of ignorance and poverty. They believe with Emerson that "America is another word for opportunity," and for that reason success is a virtue and poverty and ignorance are inexcusable. This may account for the fact that our women have excited no general sympathy in the struggle to emancipate themselves from the demoralization of slavery. This new life of freedom, with its far-reaching responsibilities, had to be learned by these children of darkness mostly without a guide, a teacher, or a friend. In the mean vocabulary of slavery there was no definition of any of the virtues of life. The meaning of such precious terms as marriage, wife, family, and home could not be learned in a school-house. The blue-back speller, the arithmetic, and the copy-book contain no magical cures for inherited inaptitudes for the moralities. Yet it must even be counted as one of the most wonderful things in human history how promptly and eagerly these suddenly liberated women tried to lay hold upon all that there is in human excellence. There is a touching pathos in the eagerness of these millions of new home-makers to taste the blessedness of intelligent womanhood. The path of progress in the picture is enlarged so as to bring to view these trustful and zealous students of freedom and civilization striving to overtake and keep pace with women whose emancipation has been a slow and painful process for a thousand years. The longing to be something better than they were when freedom found them has been the most notable characteristic in the development of these women. This constant striving for equality has given an upward direction to all the activities of colored women.

Freedom at once widened their vision beyond the mean cabin life of their bondage. Their native gentleness, good cheer, and hopefulness made them susceptible to those teachings that make for intelligence and righteousness. Sullenness of disposition, hatefulness, and revenge against the master class because of two centuries of ill-treatment are not in the nature of our women.

But a better view of what our women are doing and what their present status is may be had by noticing some lines of progress that are easily verifiable.

First it should be noticed that separate facts and figures relative to colored women are not easily obtainable. Among the white women of the country independence, progressive intelligence, and definite interests have done so much that nearly every fact and item illustrative of their progress and status is classified and easily accessible. Our women, on the contrary, have had no advantage of interests peculiar and distinct and separable from those of men that have yet excited public attention and kindly recognition.

In their religious life, however, our women show a progressiveness parallel in every important particular to that of white women in all Christian churches. It has always been a circumstance of the highest satisfaction to the missionary efforts of the Christian church that the colored people are so susceptible to a religion that marks the highest point of blessedness in human history.

Instead of finding witchcraft, sensual fetishes, and the coarse superstitions of savagery possessing our women, Christianity found them with hearts singularly tender, sympathetic, and fit for the reception of its doctrines. Their superstitions were not deeply ingrained, but were of the same sort and nature that characterize the devotees of the Christian faith everywhere.

While there has been but little progress toward the growing rationalism in the Christian creeds, there has been a marked advance toward a greater refinement of conception, good taste, and the proprieties. It is our young women coming out of the schools and academies that have been insisting upon a more godly and cultivated ministry. It is the young women of a new generation and new inspirations that are making tramps of the ministers who once dominated the colored church, and whose intelligence and piety were mostly in their lungs. In this new and growing religious life the colored people have laid hold of those sweeter influences of the King's Daughters, of the Christian Endeavor and Helping Hand societies, which are doing much to elevate the tone of worship and to magnify all that there is blessed in religion.

Another evidence of growing intelligence is a sense of religious discrimination among our women. Like the nineteenth century women generally, our women find congeniality in all the creeds, from the Catholic creed to the no-creed of Emerson. There is a constant increase of this interesting variety in the religious life of our women.

Closely allied to this religious development is their progress in the work of education in schools and colleges. For thirty years education has been the magic word among the colored people of this country. That their greatest need was education in its broadest sense was understood by these people more strongly than it could be taught to them. It is the unvarying testimony of every teacher in the South that the mental development of the colored women as well as men has been little less than phenomenal. In twenty-five years, and under conditions discouraging in the extreme, thousands of our women have been educated as teachers. They have adapted themselves to the work of mentally lifting a whole race of people so eagerly and readily that they afford an apt illustration of the power of self-help. Not only have these women become good teachers in less than twenty-five years, but many of them are the prize teachers in the mixed schools of nearly every Northern city.

These women have also so fired the hearts of the race for education that colleges, normal schools, industrial schools, and universities have been reared by a generous public to meet the requirements of these eager students of intelligent citizenship. As American women generally are fighting against the nineteenth century narrowness that still keeps women out of the higher institutions of learning, so our women are eagerly demanding the best of education open to their race. They continually verify what President Rankin of Howard University recently said, "Any theory of educating the Afro-American that does not throw open the golden gates of the highest culture will fail on the ethical and spiritual side."

It is thus seen that our women have the same spirit and mettle that characterize the best of American women. Everywhere they are following in the tracks of those women who are swiftest in the race for higher knowledge.

To-day they feel strong enough to ask for but one thing, and that is the same opportunity for the acquisition of all kinds of knowledge that may be accorded to other women. This granted, in the next generation these progressive women will be found successfully occupying every field where the highest intelligence alone is admissible. In less than another generation American literature, American art, and American music will be enriched by productions having new and peculiar features of interest and excellence.

The exceptional career of our women will yet stamp itself indelibly upon the thought of this country.

American literature needs for its greater variety and its deeper soundings that which will be written into it out of the hearts of these self-emancipating women.

The great problems of social reform that are now so engaging the highest intelligence of American women will soon need for their solution the reinforcement of that new intelligence which our women are developing. In short, our women are ambitious to be contributors to all the great moral and intellectual forces that make for the greater wealth of our common country.

If this hope seems too extravagant to those of you who know these women only in their humbler capacities, I would remind you that all that we hope for and will certainly achieve in authorship and practical intelligence is more than prophesied by what has already been done, and more that can be done, by hundreds of Afro-American women whose talents are now being expended in the struggle against race resistance.

The power of organized womanhood is one of the most interesting studies of modern sociology. Formerly women knew so little of each other mentally, their common interests were so sentimental and gossipy, and their knowledge of all the larger affairs of human society was so meager that organization among them, in the modern sense, was impossible. Now their liberal intelligence, their contact in all the great interests of education, and their increasing influence for good in all the great reformatory movements of the age has created in them a greater respect for each other, and furnished the elements of organization for large and splendid purposes. The highest ascendancy of woman's development has been reached when they have become mentally strong enough to find bonds of association interwoven with sympathy, loyalty, and mutual trustfulness. To-day union is the watchword of woman's onward march.

If it be a fact that this spirit of organization among women generally is the distinguishing mark of the nineteenth century woman, dare we ask if the colored women of the United States have made any progress in this respect?

For peculiar and painful reasons the great lessons of fraternity and altruism are hard for the colored women to learn. Emancipation found the colored Americans of the South with no sentiments of association. It will be admitted that race misfortune could scarcely go further when the terms fraternity, friendship, and unity had no meaning for its men and women.

If within thirty years they have begun to recognize the blessed significance of these vital terms of human society, confidence in their social development should be strengthened. In this important work of bringing the race together to know itself and to unite in work for a common destiny, the women have taken a leading part.

Benevolence is the essence of most of the colored women's organizations. The humane side of their natures has been cultivated to recognize the duties they owe to the sick, the indigent and ill-fortuned. No church, school,

or charitable institution for the special use of colored people has been allowed to languish or fail when the associated efforts of the women could
save it.

It is highly significant and interesting to note that these women, whose
hearts have been wrung by all kinds of sorrows, are abundantly manifesting
those gracious qualities of heart that characterize women of the best type.
These kinder sentiments arising from mutual interests that are lifting our
women into purer and tenderer relationship to each other, and are making
the meager joys and larger griefs of our conditions known to each other, have
been a large part of their education.

The hearts of Afro-American women are too warm and too large for race
hatred. Long suffering has so chastened them that they are developing a special sense of sympathy for all who suffer and fail of justice. All the associated interests of church, temperance, and social reform in which American
women are winning distinction can be wonderfully advanced when our
women shall be welcomed as co-workers, and estimated solely by what they
are worth to the moral elevation of all the people.

I regret the necessity of speaking to the question of the moral progress
of our women, because the morality of our home life has been commented
upon so disparagingly and meanly that we are placed in the unfortunate position of being defenders of our name.

It is proper to state, with as much emphasis as possible, that all questions relative to the moral progress of the colored women of America are
impertinent and unjustly suggestive when they relate to the thousands of
colored women in the North who were free from the vicious influences of
slavery. They are also meanly suggestive as regards thousands of our women
in the South whose force of character enabled them to escape the slavery
taints of immorality. The question of the moral progress of colored women
in the United States has force and meaning in this discussion only so far as
it tells the story of how the once-enslaved women have been struggling for
twenty-five years to emancipate themselves from the demoralization of their
enslavement.

While I duly appreciate the offensiveness of all references to American
slavery, it is unavoidable to charge to that system every moral imperfection
that mars the character of the colored American. The whole life and power
of slavery depended upon an enforced degradation of everything human in
the slaves. The slave code recognized only animal distinctions between the
sexes, and ruthlessly ignored those ordinary separations that belong to the
social state.

It is a great wonder that two centuries of such demoralization did not
work a complete extinction of all the moral instincts. But the recuperative
power of these women to regain their moral instincts and to establish a respectable relationship to American womanhood is among the earlier evidences of their moral ability to rise above their conditions. In spite of a
cursed heredity that bound them to the lowest social level, in spite of everything that is unfortunate and unfavorable, these women have continually

shown an increasing degree of teachableness as to the meaning of women's relationship to man.

Out of this social purification and moral uplift have come a chivalric sentiment and regard from the young men of the race that give to the young women a new sense of protection. I do not wish to disturb the serenity of this conference by suggesting why this protection is needed and the kind of men against whom it is needed.

It is sufficient for us to know that the daughters of women who thirty years ago were not allowed to be modest, not allowed to follow the instincts of moral rectitude, who could cry for protection to no living man, have so elevated the moral tone of their social life that new and purer standards of personal worth have been created, and new ideals of womanhood, instinct with grace and delicacy, are everywhere recognized and emulated.

This moral regeneration of a whole race of women is no idle sentiment— it is a serious business; and everywhere there is witnessed a feverish anxiety to be free from the mean suspicions that have so long underestimated the character strength of our women.

These women are not satisfied with the unmistakable fact that moral progress has been made, but they are fervently impatient and stirred by a sense of outrage under the vile imputations of a diseased public opinion.

Loves that are free from the dross of coarseness, affections that are un-sullied, and a proper sense of all the sanctities of human intercourse felt by thousands of these women all over the land plead for the recognition of their fitness to be judged, not by the standards of slavery, but by the higher stand-ards of freedom and of twenty-five years of education culture, and moral con-tact.

The moral aptitudes of our women are just as strong and just as weak as those of any other American women with like advantages of intelligence and environment.

It may now perhaps be fittingly asked, What mean all these evidences of mental, social, and moral progress of a class of American women of whom you know so little? Certainly you can not be indifferent to the growing needs and importance of women who are demonstrating their intelligence and capacity for the highest privileges of freedom.

The most important thing to be noted is the fact that the colored people of America have reached a distinctly new era in their career so quickly that the American mind has scarcely had time to recognize the fact, and adjust itself to the new requirements of the people in all things that pertain to citi-zenship.

Thirty years ago public opinion recognized no differences in the colored race. To our great misfortune public opinion has changed but slightly. His-tory is full of examples of the great injustice resulting from the perversity of public opinion, and its tardiness in recognizing new conditions.

It seems to daze the understanding of the ordinary citizen that there are thousands of men and women everywhere among us who in twenty-five years have progressed as far away from the non-progressive peasants of the "black belt" of the South as the highest social life in New England is above the lowest levels of American civilization.

The general failure of the American people to know the new generation of colored people, and to recognize this important change in them, is the cause of more injustice to our women that can well be estimated. Further progress is everywhere seriously hindered by this ignoring of their improvement.

Our exclusion from the benefits of the fair play sentiment of the country is little less than a crime against the ambitions and aspirations of a whole race of women. The American people are but repeating the common folly of history in thus attempting to repress the yearnings of progressive humanity.

In the item of employment colored women bear a distressing burden of mean and unreasonable discrimination. A Southern teacher of thirty years' experience in the South writes that "one million possibilities of good through black womanhood all depend upon an opportunity to make a living."

It is almost literally true that, except teaching in colored schools and menial work, colored women can find no employment in this free America. They are the only women in the country for whom real ability, virtue, and special talents count for nothing when they become applicants for respectable employment. Taught everywhere in ethics and social economy that merit always wins, colored women carefully prepare themselves for all kinds of occupation only to meet with stern refusal, rebuff, and disappointment. One of countless instances will show how the best as well as the meanest of American society are responsible for the special injustice to our women.

Not long ago I presented the case of a bright young woman to a well-known bank president of Chicago, who was in need of a thoroughly competent stenographer and typewriter. The president was fully satisfied with the young woman as exceptionally qualified for the position, and manifested much pleasure in commending her to the directors for appointment, and at the same time disclaimed that there could be any opposition on account of the slight tinge of African blood that identified her as a colored woman. Yet, when the matter was brought before the directors for action, these mighty men of money and business, these men whose prominence in all the great interests of the city would seem to lift them above all narrowness and foolishness, scented the African taint, and at once bravely came to the rescue of the bank and of society by dashing the hopes of this capable yet helpless young woman. No other question but that of color determined the action of these men, many of whom are probably foremost members of the humane society and heavy contributors to foreign missions and church extension work.

This question of employment for the trained talents of our women is a most serious one. Refusal of such employment because of color belies every maxim of justice and fair play. Such refusal takes the blessed meaning out of all the teachings of our civilization, and sadly confuses our conceptions of what is just, humane, and moral.

Can the people of this country afford to single out the women of a whole race of people as objects of their special contempt? Do these women not belong to a race that has never faltered in its support of the country's flag in every war since Attucks fell in Boston's streets?

Are they not the daughters of men who have always been true as steel against treason to everything fundamental and splendid in the republic? In short, are these women not as thoroughly American in all the circumstances of citizenship as the best citizens of our country?

If it be so, are we not justified in a feeling of desperation against that peculiar form of Americanism that shows respect for our women as servants and contempt for them when they become women of culture? We have never been taught to understand why the unwritten law of chivalry, protection, and fair play that are everywhere the conservators of women's welfare must exclude every woman of a dark complexion.

We believe that the world always needs the influence of every good and capable woman, and this rule recognizes no exceptions based on complexion. In their complaint against hindrances to their employment colored women ask for no special favors.

They are even willing to bring to every position fifty per cent more of ability than is required of any other class of women. They plead for opportunities untrammeled by prejudice. They plead for the right of the individual to be judged, not by tradition and race estimate, but by the present evidences of individual worth. We believe this country is large enough and the opportunities for all kinds of success are great enough to afford our women a fair chance to earn a respectable living, and to win every prize within the reach of their capabilities.

Another, and perhaps more serious, hindrance to our women is that nightmare known as "social equality." The term equality is the most inspiring word in the vocabulary of citizenship. It expresses the leveling quality in all the splendid possibilities of American life. It is this idea of equality that has made room in this country for all kinds and conditions of men, and made personal merit the supreme requisite for all kinds of achievement.

When the colored people became citizens, and found it written deep in the organic law of the land that they too had the right to life, liberty, and the pursuit of happiness, they were at once suspected of wishing to interpret this maxim of equality as meaning social equality.

Everywhere the public mind has been filled with constant alarm lest in some way our women shall approach the social sphere of the dominant race in this country. Men and women, wise and perfectly sane in all things else, become instantly unwise and foolish at the remotest suggestion of social contact with colored men and women. At every turn in our lives we meet this fear, and are humiliated by its aggressiveness and meanness. If we seek the sanctities of religion, the enlightenment of the university, the honors of politics, and the natural recreations of our common country, the social equality alarm is instantly given, and our aspirations are insulted. "Beware of social equality with the colored American" is thus written on all places sacred or profane, in this blessed land of liberty. The most discouraging and demoralizing effect of this false sentiment concerning us is that it utterly ignores individual merit and discredits the sensibilities of intelligent womanhood. The sorrows and heartaches of a whole race of women seem to be matters of no concern to the people who so dread the social possibilities of these colored women.

On the other hand, our women have been wonderfully indifferent and unconcerned about the matter. The dread inspired by the growing intelligence of colored women has interested us almost to the point of amusement. It has given to colored women a new sense of importance to witness how easily their emancipation and steady advancement is disturbing all classes of American people. It may not be a discouraging circumstance that colored women can command some sort of attention, even though they be misunderstood. We believe in the law of reaction, and it is reasonably certain that the forces of intelligence and character being developed in our women will yet change mistrustfulness into confidence and contempt into sympathy and respect. It will soon appear to those who are not hopelessly monomaniacs on the subject that the colored people are in no way responsible for the social equality nonsense. We shall yet be credited with knowing better than our enemies that social equality can neither be enforced by law nor prevented by oppression. Though not philosophers, we long since learned that equality before the law, equality in the best sense of that term under our institutions, is totally different from social equality.

We know, without being exceptional students of history, that the social relationship of the two races will be adjusted equitably in spite of all fear and injustice, and that there is a social gravitation in human affairs that eventually overwhelms and crushes into nothingness all resistance based on prejudice and selfishness.

Our chief concern in this false social sentiment is that it attempts further progress toward the higher sphere of womanhood. On account of it, young colored women of ambition and means are compelled in many instances to leave the country for training and education in the salons and studios of Europe. On many of the railroads of this country women of refinement and culture are driven like cattle into human cattle-cars lest the occupying of an individual seat paid for in a first-class car may result in social equality. This social quarantine on all means of travel in certain parts of the country is guarded and enforced more rigidly against us than the quarantine regulations against cholera.

Without further particularizing as to how this social question opposes our advancement, it may be stated that the contentions of colored women are in kind like those of other American women for greater freedom of development. Liberty to be all that we can be, without artificial hindrances, is a thing no less precious to us than to women generally.

We come before this assemblage of women feeling confident that our progress has been along high levels and rooted deeply in the essentials of intelligent humanity. We are so essentially American in speech, in instincts, in sentiments and destiny that the things that interest you equally interest us.

We believe that social evils are dangerously contagious. The fixed policy of persecution and injustice against a class of women who are weak and defenseless will be necessarily hurtful to the cause of all women. Colored women are becoming more and more a part of the social forces that must help to determine the questions that so concern women generally. In this Congress we ask to be known and recognized for what we are worth. If it be the high purpose of these deliberations to lessen the resistance to women's progress, you can not fail to be interested in our struggles against the many oppositions that harass us.

Women who are tender enough in heart to be active in humane societies, to be foremost in all charitable activities, who are loving enough to unite Christian womanhood everywhere against the sin of intemperance, ought to be instantly concerned in the plea of colored women for justice and humane treatment. Women of the dominant race can not afford to be responsible for the wrongs we suffer, since those who do injustice can not escape a certain penalty.

But there is no wish to overstate the obstacles to colored women or to picture their status as hopeless. There is no disposition to take our place in this Congress as faultfinders or suppliants for mercy. As women of a common country with common interests, and a destiny that will certainly bring us closer to each other, we come to this altar with our contribution of hopefulness as well as with our complaints.

When you learn that womanhood everywhere among us is blossoming out into greater fullness of everything that is sweet, beautiful, and good in women; when you learn that the bitterness of our experience as citizen-women has not hardened our finer feelings of love and pity for our enemies; when you learn that fierce opposition to the spheres of our employment has not abated the aspirations of our women to enter successfully into all the professions and arts open only to intelligence, and that everywhere in the wake of enlightened womanhood our women are seen and felt for the good they diffuse, this Congress will at once see the fullness of our fellowship, and help us to avert the arrows of prejudice that pierce the soul because of the color of our bodies.

If the love of humanity more than the love of races and sex shall pulsate throughout all the grand results that shall issue to the world from this parliament of women, women of African descent in the United States will for the first time begin to feel the sweet release from the blighting thrall of prejudice.

The colored women as well as all women, will realize that the inalienable right to life, liberty, and the pursuit of happiness is a maxim that will become more blessed in its significance when the hand of woman shall take it from its sepulture in books and make it the gospel of every-day life and the unerring guide in the relations of all men, women, and children.■

129 WOMEN'S CAUSE IS ONE AND UNIVERSAL

Anna Julia Cooper

Following the main address of Fannie Barrier Williams to Chicago's World's Congress of Representative Women on May 18, 1893, Anna Julia Cooper offered a brief but powerful speech on the accomplishments and agenda of African American women. She emphasizes to her predominantly white audience that African American women were "doubly enslaved" before emancipation, denied education, financial resources, civil liberties, and recognition. "We were utterly destitute," she observes. Yet against all odds, she recounts, women of color since the Civil War have established a remarkable record of educational, organizational, and professional achievement.

Cooper was herself a brilliant exemplar of black women's achievement. She was born in slavery in 1858 and survived until 1964, the year after the March on Washington. During the course of her long and active life, she earned her B.A. and M.A. at Oberlin College and in 1925 completed her Ph.D. at the Sorbonne. She spent much of her teaching career as an instructor of Latin and mathematics at Washington's prestigious M Street High School (later Dunbar High School), where she also served as principal from 1902 to 1906.

Cooper traveled around the world to address conferences on issues of education and social justice and in the 1890s emerged as a leader of efforts to combat racist violence and to forge organizational links between African American women and the predominantly white women's rights groups, which often excluded or openly derided them. In the concluding section of her 1893 address to a "representative" congress that almost completely excluded women of color, Cooper appeals to solidarity of interests and commitment. "Women's wrongs are thus indissolubly linked with all undefended woe," she proclaims, and the white woman's cause will not be won until "the universal title of humanity to life, liberty and the pursuit of happiness is conceded to be inalienable to all."

Cooper's speech text appears in May Wright Sewall, ed., The World's Congress of Representative Women *(Chicago: Rand, McNally, 1894), 711–15. See also Anna Julia Cooper,* A Voice from the South: By a Black Woman from the South *(1892) (New York: Oxford University Press, 1988); and Drema Lipscomb, "Anna Julia Cooper," in Richard Leeman, ed.,* African-American Orators: A Bio-Critical Sourcebook *(Westport, Conn.: Greenwood, 1996), 41–50.*

The higher fruits of civilization can not be extemporized, neither can they be developed normally, in the brief space of thirty years. It requires the long and painful growth of generations. Yet all through the darkest period of the colored women's oppression in this country her yet unwritten history is full of heroic struggle, a struggle against fearful and overwhelming odds, that often ended in a horrible death, to maintain and protect that which woman holds dearer than life. The painful, patient, and silent toil of mothers to gain a free simple title to the bodies of their daughters, the despairing fight, as of an entrapped tigress, to keep hallowed their own persons, would furnish material for epics. That more went down under the flood than stemmed the current is not extraordinary. The majority of our women are not heroines—but I do not know that a majority of any race of women are heroines. It is enough for me to know that while in the eyes of the highest tribunal in America she was deemed no more than a chattel, an irresponsible thing, a dull block, to be drawn hither or thither at the volition of an owner, the Afro-American woman maintained ideals of womanhood unshamed by any ever conceived. Resting or fermenting in untutored minds, such ideals could not claim a hearing at the bar of the nation. The white woman could at least plead for her own emancipation; the black woman, doubly enslaved, could but suffer and struggle and be silent. I speak for the colored women of the South, because it is there that the millions of blacks in this country have watered the soil with blood and tears, and it is there too that the colored woman of America has made her characteristic history, and there her destiny is evolving. Since emancipation the movement has been at times confused and stormy, so that we could not always tell whether we were going forward or groping in a circle. We hardly knew what we ought to emphasize, whether education or wealth, or civil freedom and recognition. We were utterly destitute. Possessing no homes nor the knowledge of how to make them, no money nor the habit of acquiring it, no education, no political status, no influence, what could we do? But as Frederick Douglass had said in darker days than those, "One with God is a majority," and our ignorance had hedged us in from the fine-spun theories of agnostics. We had remaining at least a simple faith that a just God is on the throne of the universe, and that some how—we could not see, nor did we bother our heads to try to tell how—he would in his own good time make all right that seemed most wrong.

Schools were established, not merely public day-schools, but home training and industrial schools, at Hampton, at Fisk, Atlanta, Raleigh, and other central stations, and later, through the energy of the colored people themselves, such schools as the Wilberforce, the Livingstone, the Allen, and the Paul Quinn were opened. These schools were almost without exception coeducational. Funds were too limited to be divided on sex lines, even had it been ideally desirable; but our girls as well as our boys flocked in and battled for an education. Not even then was that patient, untrumpeted heroine, the slave-mother, released from self-sacrifice, and many an unbuttered crust was eaten in silent content that she might eke out enough from her poverty to send her young folks off to school. She "never had the chance," she would tell you, with tears on her withered cheek, so she wanted them to get all they could. The work in these schools, and in such as these, has been like the little leaven hid in the measure of meal, permeating life throughout the length and breadth of the Southland, lifting up ideals of home and of womanhood; diffusing a contagious longing for higher living and purer thinking, inspiring woman herself with a new sense of her dignity in the eternal purposes of nature. To-day there are twenty-five thousand five hundred and thirty colored schools in the United States with one million three hundred and fifty-three thousand three hundred and fifty-two pupils of both sexes. This is not quite the thirtieth year since their emancipation, and the colored people hold in landed property for churches and schools twenty-five million dollars. Two and one half million colored children have learned to read and write, and twenty-two thousand nine hundred and fifty-six colored men and women (mostly women) are teaching in these schools. According to Doctor Rankin, President of Howard University, there are two hundred and forty-seven colored students (a large percentage of whom are women) now preparing themselves in the universities of Europe. Of other colleges which give the B.A. course to women, and are broad enough not to erect barriers against colored applicants, Oberlin, the first to open its doors to both woman and the negro, has given classical degrees to six colored women, one of whom, the first and most eminent, Fannie Jackson Coppin,* we shall listen to tonight. Ann Arbor and Wellesley have each graduated three of our women; Cornell University one, who is now professor of sciences in a Washington high school. A former pupil of my own from the Washington High School, who was snubbed by Vassar, has since carried off honors in a competitive examination in Chicago University. The medical and law colleges of the country are likewise bombarded by colored women, and every year some sister of the darker race claims their professional award of "well done." Eminent in their profession are Doctor Dillon and Doctor James, and there sailed to Africa last month a demure little brown woman who had just outstripped a whole class of men in a medical college in Tennessee.

In organized efforts for self-help and benevolence also our women have been active. The Colored Women's League, of which I am at present corresponding secretary, has active, energetic branches in the South and West. The branch in Kansas City, with a membership of upward of one hundred and fifty, already has begun under their vigorous president, Mrs. Yates, the erection of a building for friendless girls. Mrs. Coppin will, I hope, herself tell you something of her own magnificent creation of an industrial society in Philadelphia. The women of the Washington branch of the league have subscribed to a fund of about five thousand dollars to erect a woman's building for educational and industrial work, which is also to serve as headquarters for gathering and disseminating general information relating to the efforts of our women. This is just a glimpse of what we are doing.

Now, I think if I could crystallize the sentiment of my constituency, and

---

*Coppin (1837–1913) was born in slavery in Washington, D.C. She graduated from Oberlin College in 1865, served for many years as principal of the Institute for Colored Youth in Philadelphia, and became national president of the Women's Home and Foreign Missionary Society of the A.M.E. Church.

deliver it as a message to this congress of women, it would be something like this: Let woman's claim be as broad in the concrete as in the abstract. We take our stand on the solidarity of humanity, the oneness of life, and the unnaturalness and injustice of all special favoritisms, whether of sex, race, country, or condition. If one link of the chain be broken, the chain is broken. A bridge is no stronger than its weakest part, and a cause is not worthier than its weakest element. Least of all can woman's cause afford to decry the weak. We want, then, as toilers for the universal triumph of justice and human rights, to go to our homes from this Congress, demanding an entrance not through a gateway for ourselves, our race, our sex, or our sect, but a grand highway for humanity. The colored woman feels that woman's cause is one and universal; and that not till the image of God, whether in parian or ebony, is sacred and inviolable; not till race, color, sex, and condition are seen as the accidents, and not the substance of life; not till the universal title of humanity to life, liberty, and the pursuit of happiness is conceded to be inalienable to all; not till then is woman's lesson taught and woman's cause won—not the white woman's, nor the black woman's, not the red woman's, but the cause of every man and of every woman who has writhed silently under a mighty wrong. Woman's wrongs are thus indissolubly linked with all undefended woe, and the acquirement of her "rights" will mean the final triumph of all right over might, the supremacy of the moral forces of reason, and justice, and love in the government of the nations of earth.■

130 JUSTICE OR EMIGRATION SHOULD BE OUR WATCHWORD

Bishop Henry McNeal Turner

In the years between Reconstruction and World War I, the chief advocate of emigration of black Americans to Africa was Bishop Henry McNeal Turner of the African Methodist Episcopal Church. Turner was convinced that there was no future for the African diaspora in the United States, dominated as it was by white racism, and his conviction was fully fixed in 1883, when the Supreme Court nullified the Civil Rights Act of 1875 in a decision declaring that the federal government could not prevent racial discrimination by private parties. During the next decade, Turner was further convinced of the necessity for emigration to Africa by the increasing tempo of lynching and racist vio-

lence. In 1893, Turner summoned a representative gathering of "the friends of African repatriation or Negro nationalism elsewhere" but not the "stay-at-home portion" of the race. Many black leaders agreed to attend, but most opposed mass emigration, and in the face of strong opposition, Turner shifted the emphasis of the meeting from emigration to general protest. To the National Council of Colored Men, which met in Cincinnati in November 1893, Turner delivered an eloquent opening address, outlining the terrible plight of African Americans and pleading for action to alleviate their condition. His speech is also significant for the fact that it is one of the earliest, carefully outlined plans for reparations for the unpaid labor of African Americans during the years of their enslavement.

Like Ida B. Wells, Turner draws upon the lyrics of the song "America" ("My Country 'Tis of Thee") in his speech. But whereas Wells uses the lyrics of the national hymn as a jeremiad, a prophecy of coming justice, Turner rejects the song as a cruel hoax and pledges never again to sing it.

The more than six hundred delegates voted against emigration but agreed to step up the fight for justice at home. They sent memorials to Congress, to the state governors, and to the American people; and they formed an Equal Rights Council with Turner as chancellor.

Turner's speech text appeared in the Voice of Missions, *Atlanta, December 1893. See also Edwin S. Redkey, ed.,* Respect Black: The Writings and Speeches of Henry McNeal Turner *(New York: Arno Press, 1971).*

GENTLEMEN OF THE NATIONAL COUNCIL: In pursuance of a call issued September 30th, by the solicitation and endorsement of over three hundred prominent and distinguished members of our race, from every section of the United States, we have assembled in a national convention today. The circumstances that bring us together are of the most grave, serious and solemn character that could command attention and sober consideration. Our anomalous condition as a race and the increasing evils under which we exist have impressed me for the last four years that a national convention or council of our people should assemble and speak to the country, at least, or sue in some other respects for better conditions.

You are here assembled to consider and pass upon our condition as a distinct and specific race, yet a part of the aggregated people of the United States of America. I use the term specific race because of the special or specific legislation which has been enacted by the states, and the judicial decisions which apply and affect our rights and privileges in contradistinction to every other portion of the American people, whether claiming citizenship or occupying a place here as temporary inhabitants. The scum of creation can come to this country and receive kinder and more just treatment than we who were born and reared here. Thus the black, yet patient, loyal and ever faithful children of the United States are individualized and made the vic-

tims of class legislation, and the subjects of close discrimination, class proscription and race prejudice in a manner and to an extent that the world at
present offers no parallel; and it is a question if history furnishes another
instance.

Let us, by way of premises itemize a few facts, connected with our career in this country, deserving more than a transient notice. We have been
inhabitants of this continent for 273 years, and a very limited part of the
time we were citizens—I mean from the ratification of the Fourteenth Amendment of the national Constitution, until the Supreme Court of the United
States, October 15, 1883, declared that provision of the Constitution null
and void, and decitizenized us. Now, what does history set forth relative to
our conduct and behavior during this our long residence?

While it is true that we were brought here as captive heathens, through
the greed and avarice of the white man, to serve him as a slave, I believe
that an over-ruling Providence suffered it to be because there was a great and
grand purpose to be subserved, and that infinite wisdom intended to evolve
ultimate good out of a temporary evil, and that in the ages to come, the glory
of God will be made manifest and that millions will thank heaven for the
limited toleration of American slavery. All of you may not accept my sentiments upon this point, but I believe there is a God, and that he takes cognizance of human events; for such a stupendous evil could not have existed
so long, affecting the destiny of the unborn, without a glorious purpose in
view.

However, since our forced introduction into this land, willingly or unwillingly, mankind will accord to us a fidelity to every interest that will
command the respect of the world forever.

As slaves, in the aggregate, we were obedient, faithful and industrious. We felled the forests, tilled the ground, pioneered civilization and were
harmless. As far back as 1704, long before the establishment of an independent nation was ever dreamed of, we find the colonies enacting laws for the
enlistment of black men to fight the Spanish and French invaders; and in
1708, a hundred years before the African slave trade was arrested by congressional enactments, we find black men being manumitted by colonial legislation for bravery and heroism in defending the territory of His Majesty, and
in some instances, when maimed, provided with a liberal pension. It was for
this heroic integrity and incorruptible trustworthiness that Negro slaves acquired their freedom so early in the history of the institution, and laws were
even enacted to protect them and their children in the enjoyment of the freedom thus conferred. History also informs us that during the early settlement of this country, the Negro would work for his master during the days
and watch the skulking and murderous Indians by night, who sought his master's life and the lives of his wife and children. The first blood that crimsoned
the soil for American independence was the blood of the Negro, Crispus Attucks, in the tea riot in the streets of Boston. Over five thousand Negro patriots fought in the revolutionary war for freedom from British domination
and American independence. Peter Salem, a Negro though he was, turned

the tide of victory in favor of the Americans at the battle of Bunker Hill by a shot from his gun which killed a British major. General Jackson issued an official proclamation complimenting the bravery and patriotism of black men in the war of 1812 at the battle of New Orleans. 185,000 Negro soldiers came to the defense of the stars and stripes in the late internecine war between the North and South, and 46,000 of them are now sleeping in bloody graves for the integral unity of a nation that cares nothing for them. On the other hand, respecting the powers that be, the Negro was as loyal to the Confederate flag as he was to the federal. For, while every available white man in the South was fighting for what would be regarded as his rights, the Negro, in the field and pursuing every form of industry, was the base of supply, and at the same time the virtual custodian of every white lady and child in the South, and nobody has proclaimed this fact louder and in more complimentary terms than the brave Confederate soldier. Singular and strange as it may appear to some present, a black man completed the Goddess of Liberty which ornaments the dome of our national capitol;* and it will stand there, heaven high, as a monument to his genius and industry for ages to come. Yet, this same Goddess of Liberty has been transformed into a lying strumpet so far as she symbolizes the civil liberties of the black man.

But why consume your valuable time in an attempt to particularize the characteristics and fidelity of the black man to every industry and patriotic emergency in the past as we are willing to be weighed in the balance with any other portion of humanity, under similar circumstances, who has ever lived.

I am willing to accord to the white man every meed of honor that ability, grit, backbone, sagacity, tact and invincibility entitle him to. For this Anglo-Saxon, I grant, is a powerful race; but put him in our stead, enslave him for 250 years, emancipate him and turn him loose upon the world, without education, without money, without horse or mule or a foot of land, when passion engendered by war was most intense, to eke out a subsistence from nothing beyond the charity of an indignant people on the one hand, and cold-shouldering and proscriptive people on the other; and I do not believe he would have equaled us in respect, obedience, fidelity and accomplished results and maintained the pacific equilibrium we have. Our nation freed the black man as a war measure, I grant, but that freedom entailed and left upon us a mendicancy that the unborn will ask the reason why. Even the usufruct claim, guaranteed to the serfs of Russia†—a nation at that time regarded as semicivilized—was denied the freedmen by this so-called enlightened and Christian nation.

The mule and forty acres of land, which has been so often ridiculed for

*The reference is to African American artisan Stephen Fortune.
†The Russian emancipation act was promulgated in 1861, but the Russian peasant was given some opportunity to acquire land, even though at an exorbitant price, and was left undisturbed as an independent tiller of the soil.

being expected by the black man, was a just and righteous expectation,* and had this nation been one-fiftieth part as loyal to the black man, as he has been to it, such a bestowment would have been made, and the cost would have been a mere bagatelle, compared with the infinite resources of this Republic, which has given countless millions to foreigners, to come into the country and destroy respect for the Sabbath, flood the land with every vice known to the ends of the earth, and form themselves into anarchial bands for the overthrow of its institutions and venerated customs.

Nevertheless, freedom had been so long held up before us as man's normal birthright, and as the bas-relief of every possibility belonging to the achievements of manhood, that we received it as heaven's greatest boon and nursed ourselves into satisfaction, believing that we had the stamina, nor only to wring existence out of our poverty, but also wealth, learning, honor, fame and immortality.

But through some satanic legerdemain, within the last three or four years, the most fearful crimes have been charged upon members of our race, known to the catalogue of villainy, and death and destruction have stalked abroad with an insatiable carnivoracity, that not only beggars description, but jeopardizes the life of every Negro in the land—as anyone could raise an alarm by crying rape, and some colored man must die, whether he is the right one or not, or whether it was the product of revenge or the mere cracking of a joke.

I stated in the call of Sept. 30th:

> That owing to the dreadful, horrible, anomalous and unprecedented condition of our people in the United States, it would seem that some common action, move or expression on our part, as a race, is demanded. The revolting, hideous, monstrous, unnatural, brutal and shocking crimes charged upon us daily, on the one hand, and the reign of mobs, lynchers, and fire-fiends, and midnight and midday assassins on the other, necessitated a national convention on our part, for the purpose of crystalizing our sentiments and unifying our endeavors for better conditions in this country, or a change of base for existence.

The terms employed, you will observe, are the most severe that can be found in the English language, as applied both to our condition and to the daily charges made by the public press against our civilization as a race and our morality and humanity, and if true, stamps us as the most degraded race that ever existed. Almost every day the very lightning of heaven is made to flash these horrible deeds from one end of the continent to the other; the

---

*"Forty acres and a mule" was the slogan popularized among freed persons during and after the Civil War. It expressed their hope that they would obtain land and a mule from the federal government so as not to be at the mercy of the white planters.

allegations being that we are outraging and raping white women to such an extent that an editor of the *Christian Advocate* proclaims to the world that "three hundred white women have been raped by Negroes within the proceeding three months." In other words, a high ecclesiastical representative charges that the members of our race are perpetrating a hundred rapes a month upon the white women of the country. Another public daily paper tells the civilized world that Negroes raped seven hundred white women from the first day of last January up to October 10th, which is undoubtedly the most revolting and blood-curdling charge ever presented against a people since time began. Without, however, attempting to number the white women that black men have been charged with outraging, it is known to all present that not a week, and at times scarcely a day, has passed in the last three or four years but what some colored man has been hung, shot or burned by mobs of lynchers, and justified or excused upon the plea that they had outraged some white married or single woman, or some little girl going to or from school. These crimes alleged against us, whether true or false, have been proclaimed by the newspapers of the country in such horrific terms that it would seem like an amazing grace that has held back the curse of God and the vengeance of man, to enable us to meet here today. For if the accusations are even half true, we must be allied to a race of such incarnate fiends that no hopeful prospect illumines our future.

Now, gentlemen, I shall not presume to affirm or deny the monstrous imputations,* but certainly as a specific and a race largely regarded as alien by the white people of the country, we owe it to ourselves and posterity to inquire into this subject and give it the most patient, thorough and impartial investigation that ever fell to the lot of man. If the charges are true, then God has no attribute that will side with us. Nature has no member, no potential factor, that will defend us, and while we may not all be guilty, nor one in ten thousand, it nevertheless shows, if true, that there is a libidinous taint, a wanton and lecherous corruption that is prophetic of a dreadful doom, as there must be a carnal blood poison in the precincts of our race that staggers the most acute imagination in determining its woeful results. Nor can we excuse it, palliate it or manifest indifference upon the postulation that it is a righteous retribution upon the white man for the way he treated our women for hundreds of years. For if the countercharge is true, we certainly did not visit swift vengeance upon the white man, as he is doing upon us by his lawless mobs. There is but one recourse left us that will command the respect of the civilized world and the approval of God, and that is to investigate the facts in the premises, and if guilty, acknowledge it, and let us organize against the wretches in our own ranks. Let us call upon the colored ministry to sound it from the pulpit, our newspapers to brand it with infamy daily, weekly, monthly and yearly. Let us put a thousand lecturers

---

*Other African Americans of the period, notably Ida B. Wells, vehemently denied and conclusively disproved these allegations.

in the field and canvass every section of the land, and denounce the heinous crime. Let us organize ourselves into societies, associations and reforming bands, and let them hold public meetings, print circulars and awaken among our young men a better sentiment. And if nothing else will prevail, and law-lessness is to be the order of the day, it would be a thousand times more to our credit, as a race, to organize all over the land against our own rapers, and have passwords, grips and signs, and if we can find out that the act is even contemplated, that we catch the individual and severely punish him, even if the punishment should consist of the infliction of a thousand lashes, and if we can detect any one in the act, catch him and treat him as God did Cain of old—put a mark upon him, cut off his right ear, brand the letter R on his cheek or forehead, symbolic of raper, that his infamous deed may dis-grace him through life and condemn his memory when dead.

And let us do everything within the bounds of human endeavor to arrest this flood tide of vice and redeem the good name which we have borne through all the ages, for the protection of female honor. For even among the heathen Africans, whatever else may be said about them, the world will have to admit that they are the purest people, outside of polygamy, in their con-nubial and virgin morals, upon the face of the globe. White women, to my personal knowledge, hundreds of miles interiorward in Africa, can remain in their midst and teach school for years without being insulted, which proves to a demonstration that where our natures have not been distorted and abnormalized, that we are the most honorable custodians of female vir-tue now under heaven. I have been told by white ladies in Africa, from Lou-isiana, South Carolina, New York, Nebraska, England and Ireland, that no white lady would be improperly approached in Africa in a lifetime, unless she made herself unusually forward. . . .

[In the West Indian Islands] records show that only one rape has been charged upon a black man since 1832, and that occurred 16 years ago, while 11 rapes have been charged upon white men, 9 of which were perpetrated upon black women and 2 upon white women. It may be, however, due to the fact that there the laws and institutions recognize the black man as a full-fledged citizen and a gentleman, and his pride of character and sense of dignity are not degraded and self-respect imparts a higher prompting and gentlemanly bearing to his manhood, and makes him a better citizen and inspires him with more gallantry and nobler principles. For like begets like. While in this country we are degraded by the public press, degraded by class legislation, degraded on the railroads after purchasing first-class tickets, de-graded at the hotels and barber shops, degraded in many states at the ballot box, degraded in most of the large cities by being compelled to rent houses in alleys and the most disreputable streets. Thus we are degraded in so many respects that all the starch of respectability is taken out of the manhood of millions of our people, and as degradation begets degradation, it is very pos-sible that in many instances we are guilty of doing a series of infamous things that we would not be guilty of, if our environments were different.

Think of it! The great World's Fair, or exposition, at Chicago, out of more than ten thousand employees, gave no recognition to the colored race beyond taking charge of the toilet rooms.

I would not have you understand that I am denying, condoning or excusing the crime of rape, as is being charged to a greater or less extent upon the members of our race; nor must we, in convention assembled, jump at a hasty and rash conclusion; but I fear much of it, if true, is due to our unnatural and immethodical environments and ignoble status, nor do I for one believe that we will ever stand out in the symmetrical majesty of higher manhood, half free and half slave—hence my African preferences, of which you have so often heard, or Negro nationalization elsewhere, where we can cultivate the higher properties or virtues of our manhood.

But gentlemen, we are here, and for all I know we are here to stay for an indefinite time, at all events, and we must adjust ourselves to our surroundings and put forth the utmost endeavor to improve our behavior and merit the favor of God and man. I appeal to this intelligent body of gentlemen, elected representatives of our people, from all parts of the country, while in Council assembled, to rigidly inquire into our condition and conduct, especially as it relates to the outraging of white ladies . . . Let no spleenishness, or counter-prejudice, or spirit of revenge, or even the conviction that some have been put to death innocently, bar us from doing our whole duty. Let us do right, though others do wrong. Let us be cool-headed, calculating, and show the world that we wish to be fair and just.

Let us not convert this convention into another mob, nor prematurely denounce the black rapers or white lynchers until we shall appoint a committee or committees and let them sit day and night until every man present goes before them and testifies to all he may know personally, and presents all the documents he may be in possession of, bearing upon the question; and if, after a patient investigation, we find that we have been malignly misrepresented, let us have the manhood, courage to dare to say so in no uncertain terms and thus vindicate our good name before the world; but should we find that a part of the accusations are true, while even much may be false, let us say so. For honesty will be the best policy in dealing with this question, as it is in dealing with every other. We are a free people, North and South, East and West, so far as our locomotion and individualities are concerned, and we will have our own destiny to work out, and nobody cares anything about us particularly, and we had just as well be honest and true to God and the right, as to be insincere, and cater to any whim, whether it is popular among the whites or among the blacks.

The United States Congress and Supreme Court both have dumped the Negro. Our supposed Constitutional rights have been nullified, and the President of the United States can do nothing but give us few secondhand positions, and those of us who are not dead are simply living by the grace of our respective communities, and we had as well realize our situation and pander to no sentimentality, but that which involves our honor and manhood. Therefore, I submit the matter to your wise and prudent judgement.

But gentlemen of the convention, there is another side to this question. Under the genius and theory of civilization throughout the world, no man is guilty of any crime, whatever, until he is arrested, tried by an impartial process of law and deliberately convicted. The Supreme Court of England, on one occasion, set aside the verdict of a lower court because a case had been tried too hastily to allow deliberation and sober thought to gain the ascendancy in the community. Lynching a man is an act of barbarism and cannot be justified by even what a distinguished bishop terms "emotional insanity." For even insanity has no authority to intrude its maddened vengeance upon the law and order of the public. Judge O'Neil, of South Carolina, many years ago, long before freedom was contemplated, sentenced two white men to the gallows for putting a slave Negro to death without legal process, and they were hung dead by the neck, and the militia of South Carolina turned out in regiments to see that the sentence was fully executed. This, too, was at a time when the theory prevailed that black men, especially slaves, had no rights that white men were bound to respect. But now, a quarter of a century after we are free, a mob can band themselves together and hang a Negro about perpetrating a rape upon some white woman, but rarely give the name of the individual, and when you visit the community and inquire as to who it was thus outraged, in many instances, nobody knows, and the mob is justified upon the plea that the Negro confessed it. Confessed it to whom? Confessed it to a set of bloody-handed murderers, just as though a set of men who were cruel enough to take the life of another were too moral to tell a lie. Strange, too, that the men who constitute these banditti can never be identified by the respective governors or the law officers, but the newspapers know all about them—can advance what they are going to do, how and when it was done, how the rope broke, how many balls entered the Negro's body, how loud he prayed, how piteously he begged, what he said, how long he was left hanging, how many composed the mob, the number that were masked, whether they were prominent citizens or not, how the fire was built that burnt the raper, how the Negro was tied, how he was thrown into the fire, and the whole transaction; but still the fiendish work was done by a set of "unknown men."

I fear that what I have been told in confidence by prominent white men, that a large number of associations are in existence, bound by solemn oaths and pledged to secrecy by the most binding covenants, to exterminate the Negro by utilizing every possible opportunity, has more truth in it than I was at first inclined to believe. For the white people all over the country have everything in their own hands, can do absolutely as they please in administering their own created laws to the Negro. They have all the judges, and all the juries, and virtually all the lawyers, all the jails, all the penitentiaries, all the ropes, all the powder, and all the guns; at least they manufacture them all, and why these hasty, illegal executions unless Negro extermination is the object desired? They evidently must fear a public trial, otherwise it is very singular that they should be so anxious to silence the tongue and close the lips of the only one who can speak in his own defense by putting him to death so hastily and without judge or jury. The white people of this country, almost without exception, claim to be constitutionally superior to the black man. Then why should a race so superior and so numerically, financially, and intellectually in advance of the colored man be so afraid of a raping wretch that they will not allow him a chance to open his inferior lips in his own defense? Gentlemen, it is a serious question, and this Council must consider and pass upon both of these grave issues—the black rapers on the one hand, and the exterminators of the blacks on the other.

I know it is held that if you give a Negro who is charged with outraging a white woman a fair trial, that the process of the law will be so long, tedious and so many technicalities are liable to be raised, that the time and expense would be worth more than the life of the victim. But rather than flood the land with blood, especially if it should be innocent blood, and the retributive vengeance of an angry God, we had far better ask for the old slave time trial before a justice of the peace, and abide by its consequences, for such as are accused of this revolting crime, or, vulgar and shocking as it would be, do the next-best thing, and the thing that will effectually cure this evil, if you should find that it actually exists. Let the raper be castrated and let him live and remain as a monument of his folly and madness. Certainly he will never repeat the crime, and it would be far better than shedding so much of what may be innocent blood. So far as I am individually concerned, if there is no way to rid the country of these lynching mobs, I had rather for this convention to make a national request of all the law officers in the land when they capture a raper, or a so-called raper, to castrate him and turn him loose. It would be far better for the country and for its future than to be taking so much of human life.

Let us ask Congress for a law to banish them from the country. Thousands of white criminals were banished from England over here, all through the seventeenth century, and many of the offspring of these banished criminals are the lynchers of today. If Rome, Scotland and England could banish their irredeemable white criminals, surely this country can banish its black criminals. But spare the lives of the wretches. For there is but one deed that God permits the taking of human life for, anyway, and that is for the crime of murder. Horrible as the crime of raping may be, it is a grave question whether it merits the death penalty or not. I do not believe it does when there are so many other ways he can be adequately punished, unless the perpetration of the satanic deed involves the death of the outraged. Left to me individually, I would enact a law to cut off his ear or a part of his nose, or brand raper upon his forehead or his cheek, or castrate him. The old adage, so familiar to the ancients, is as true today in taking life as it was then: Blow for blow, / Blood for blood. / Thou shalt reap / What thou has sown.

And unless this nation, north and south, east and west, awakes from its slumber and calls a halt to the reign of blood and carnage in this land, its dissolution and utter extermination is only a question of a short time. For Egypt went down; Greece went down; Babylon went down; Nineveh went down; Rome went down, and other nations numerically stronger than the United States, and the spirit of conquest, cruelty, injustice and domination was the death of them all and the United States will never celebrate another centennial of undivided states, without a change of program. A Negro is a very small item in the body politic of this country, but his groans, prayers and innocent blood will speak to God day and night, and the God of the poor and helpless will come to his relief sooner or later, and another fratricidal war will be the sequence, though it may grow out of an issue as far from the Negro as midday is from midnight. For this is either a nation or a travesty. If it is a nation, every man East and West, North and South, is bound to the protection of human life and the institutions of the country; but if it is a burlesque or a national sham, then the world ought to know it. The North is responsible for every outrage perpetrated in the South, and the South is responsible for every outrage perpetrated in the North, and so of the East and West, and it is no use to blame the South and excuse the North, or blame the North and excuse the South. For every species of injustice perpetrated upon the Negro, every man in every portion of this nation, if it is a nation, is responsible.

The truth is, the nation as such has no disposition to give us manhood protection anyway. Congress had the Constitutional power to pursue a run-away slave, by legislation, into any state and punish the man who would dare conceal him, and the Supreme Court of the United States sustained its legislation so long as slavery existed. Now the same Supreme Court has the power to declare, that the Negro has no civil rights under the general government that will protect his citizenship and authorizes the states to legislate upon and for us, as they may like; and they are passing special acts to degrade the Negro, by authority of the said high tribunal, and Congress proposes no remedy by legislation or by such a Constitutional amendment as will give us the status of citizenship in the nation that it is presumed we are to love and to sacrifice our lives, if need be, in defense of. Yet Congress can legislate for the protection of the fish in the sea and the seals that gambol in our waters, and obligate its men, its money, its navy, its army and its flag to protect, but the eight million or ten million of its black men and women, made in the image of God, possessing $265,000,000 worth of taxable property, with all their culture, refinement in many instances, and noble bearing, must be turned off to become the prey of violence, and when we appeal to the general government for recognition and protection, Justice, so called, drops her scales and says, Away with you.

I am abused as no other man in this nation, because I am an African Emigrationist, and while we are not here assembled to consider that question, nor do I mention it at the present time to impose it upon you, but if the present condition of things is to continue, I had, not only rather see my people in the heart of Africa, but in icebound, ice-covered, and ice-fettered Greenland.

"Give me liberty, or give me death!"

Other American Negroes may sing—

My country, 'tis of thee,
Sweet land of liberty,
Of thee we sing.

But here is one Negro, whose tongue grows palsied, whenever he is invited to put music to these lines.

Foreigners may come here from the ends of the earth, and corrupt the country with their vices and diseases, and there is no law or judicial decision to frown them down. John Chinaman, after feasting on opium, is of such exhalted consequences that the United States Congress declares by special enactment, that no Negro shall testify in the courts of the land about anything connected with his citizenship.

Even United States Senators literally gamble over us, if the reports of the Associated Press be true. For the senators of the Western states are represented as telling the Southern senators that we voted with you against the election bill, commonly known as the Force Bill, with the promise upon your part that you would vote with us on the silver question; and as an evidence that there might be some truth in the Associated Press dispatches, which were telegraphed over the country, we see that a large portion of the Southern senators really did stand by the Western senators and fought manfully.

As one, I feel grateful for many things that have been done for us within the last thirty years. I am thankful for Mr. Lincoln's manumitting Proclamation, for its ratification by Congress, for the thirteenth, fourteenth and fifteenth amendments to the Constitution, which were placed there by the American people for the benefit of our race, even if the United States Supreme Court has destroyed the Fourteenth Amendment by its revolting decision.

I am thankful to our generous-hearted friends of the North who have given voluntarily millions upon millions to aid in our education. I am thankful to the South for the school laws they have enacted and for the generous manner they have taxed themselves in building and sustaining schools for our enlightenment and intellectual and moral elevation. But, if this country is to be our home, the Negro must be a self-controlling, automatic factor of the body politic or collective life of the nation. In other words, we must be full-fledged men. Otherwise we will not be worth existence itself.

To passively remain here and occupy our present ignoble status, with the possibility of being shot, hung or burnt, not only when we perpetrate deeds of violence ourselves, but whenever some bad white man wishes to dark his face and outrage a female, as I am told is often done, is a matter of serious reflection. To do so would be to declare ourselves unfit to be free men or to assume the responsibilities which involve fatherhood and existence. For God hates the submission of cowardice. But on the other hand to talk about physical resistance is literal madness. Nobody but an idiot would

give it a moment's thought. The idea of eight or ten million ex-slaves contending with sixty million people of the most powerful race under heaven.
Think of two hundred and sixty-five millions of dollars battling with one
hundred billion of dollars! Why, we would not be a drop in the bucket. It is
folly to indulge such a thought for a moment.

Since I have called this convention, hundreds of letters have been written to me, but I will only refer to two, which were evidently written by men
of prominence. One from New York says: "The colored people are such cowards is the reason they have so many things to complain of and until they
fight and die a little it will continue to be the case." But another letter from
Philadelphia says: "You Negroes had better not provoke a conflict with the
white people at your convention in Cincinnati, for if you do the whites,
North and South, will join together and exterminate the last one of you from
the face of the land. Take warning now, for I know the sentiment of the
North, and the South justly hates you." Of the two letters referred to, the
latter, I fear, deserves more attention than the former; for it appears to be
the desire of some of the white people of the United States, to provoke some
kind of race war as in every instance when a race war, is spoken of, it comes
from some white quarter. The black man never thinks about it, much less
speaks about it, for where individual conflicts take place between white and
colored men, in a thousand cases to one they are provoked by the former. I
know the Negro as well as any man that breathes the breath of life, and I
affirm before earth and heaven today, that no such project has ever been contemplated, nor do I believe it ever will be. We have been reared in this country to revere, honor and love the whites, and we delight to do it when they
will give us half a chance.

I know that thousands of our people hope and expect better time for the
Negro in this country, but as one I see no signs of a reformation in our condition; to the contrary, we are being more and more degraded by legislative
enactments and judicial decisions. Not a thing has been said or done that
contemplates our elevation or the promotion of our manhood in twelve or
fifteen years, outside of promoting our education in erecting schools for our
general enlightenment; but a hundred things have been done to crush out
the last vestige of self-respect and avalanche us with contempt. My remedy,
without a change, is, as it would be folly to attempt resistance and our appeals for better conditions are being unheeded, for that portion of us, at least,
who feel we are self-reliant, to seek other quarters. There are many propositions before the colored people of this country. Some favor a partial African
emigration, and I am one of that number; others favor Mexican emigration,
Canadian emigration, Central and South American emigration, while the
Honorable John Temple Graves, one of the profoundest thinkers, most brilliant orators and broadest humanitarians in the country,* advocates the set-

---

*John Temple Graves (1856–1925) was a southern editor and political speaker in Flor-
ida and Georgia during the 1880s and a prominent lecturer in the early 1900s. Although
he supported the plan for a separate black state, he was also a white supremacist who

ting apart of a portion of the public domain as a separate and distinct state, where we can have our own governors, United States Senator, members of the lower house of Congress, and all the machinery of state, and thereby have a chance to speak for ourselves, where we can be heard, and give evidence of statesmanship to show to the world that we are capable of self-government, and where our educated sons and daughters can practicalize the benefits of their culture. The position of Mr. Graves may not commend itself to the favorable consideration of all present, any more than my African sentiments or the Mexican, Canadian, or Central American theories, but we must do something. We must agree upon some project. We must offer some plan of action to our people or admit that we are too ignorant and worthless to do anything. This nation justly, righteously and divinely owes us for work and services rendered, billions of dollars, and if we cannot be treated as American people, we should ask for five hundred million dollars, at least, to begin an emigration somewhere, if we cannot receive manhood recognition here at home, for it will cost sooner or later *far more than* that amount to keep the Negro down unless they reestablish slavery itself. Freedom and perpetual degradation are not in the economy of human events. It is against reason, against nature, against precedent and against God. A people who read, attend schools, receive the instruction of the pulpits, write for the public press, think and furnish famous orators, cannot be chained to degradation forever. They will be a menace to the land, and God himself, with all the laws of nature, will help them to fight the injustice, and no pomp or boast of heraldry can prevent it, yet it may involve horror to both races. Money to leave and build up a nation of our own, where we can respect ourselves at least, or *justice* at the hands of the American nation, should be the watchword of every Negro in the land.

I have been more or less all over the world, and have mingled among people of many tongues, but I have never found such a condition of things as there is here in the United States.

I was told in England by old, gray-haired, and baldheaded white men, that they had never known of a man being lynched or put to death without due process of law. Yet every nation upon the face of the globe was represented there, as British ships go everywhere and return with representatives of all people, while in this country, so many of us are killed, that dead bodies hanging to some tree limb and pierced with bullets are so common that they are regarded as current events. What would have horrorized our fathers and mothers is passed by in these degenerate days as a natural occurrence. The Negro may be exterminated, but in the accomplishment of the heaven-defying job, a crop of imbruted children will grow up, who will annihilate each other. "For whatsoever a man soweth, that shall he also reap," is the declaration of the word of God, and all history confirms its truth.

The Negro, at best, in this country, occupies a very low plane. Look at

fanned the flames of racial animosity in the South, particularly as editor of the *Atlanta News* and *Atlanta Georgian* during 1906–1907.

the Greek, Latin and mathematical scholars employed as Pullman-car porters and other college-bred young men, restricted by the sphere of a scullion, because color prejudice bars them from employment in harmony with their culture. Yet the Negro is the nearest competitor in aptitude, physical endurance, industrial application and punctuality to business, the white man has on the face of the globe; and because this fact is well known, the moment some ignorant white man gets into some legislature, he is offering a bill to increase the degradation of the Negro. For you never find such bills or resolutions emanating from first-class white gentlemen. All of these discriminating and proscribing laws that have been enacted against the colored people on these railroads have originated with what we used to call, in slave time, "poor white trash." True, some of them since freedom have climbed up a little and have got to be Congressmen and even governors of states, but it is the same old second-class roughs, who can find nothing else to think or talk about but the ghost of the Negro. Yet the first-class white men and the entire nation North and South are responsible, and the God of nations will so hold them. I refer to these facts merely to show you that degradation or extermination appears to hold a prominent place in the minds of the ruling powers of this country, and I cannot believe that our freedom which cost so much blood and treasure was intended for any such ultimatum.

But some of you may think that I am overgloomy, too despondent, that I have reached the plane of despair; and should any one present so presume, you will be not much at fault. For I confess that I have seen so much and know so much about American prejudice, that I have no hope in the future success of my race in our present situation.

But you will discover that in this address, I have largely spoken for myself. You will have time enough, and I know you have the ability to speak for yourselves. Should we differ, as we naturally will, let us defend our respective positions and sentiments with the best logical arguments we are able to advance. Slurs, philippics, witty utterances, light anecdotes, innuendoes, cutting remarks, sarcasm, tirades and bitter invectives should not be indulged in in this convention. Men of ability will not do it; they will have too many other things to say. Moreover, if we cannot now, surrounded as we are by mobs, lynchers, ropes, bullets, fire, proscription, color prejudice, decitizenship, blood, carnage, death and extermination, present a united front of action, although we may differ in opinions, then there is no unity of action in us and our destiny is a hopeless one.

You evidently see from the points I have endeavored to raise, and many more that I have not touched, that our condition in this country inferiorates us, and no amount of booklearning, divested of manhood respect and manhood promptings, will ever make us a great people, for, underlying all school culture, must exist the consciousness that I am somebody, that I am a man, that I am as much as anybody else, that I have rights, that I am the creature of law and order, that I am entitled to respect, and that every avenue to distinction is mine. For where this consciousness does not form the substratum of any people, inferioration, retrogression and ultimate degradation will be the result. And seeing that this is our status in the United States today, it devolves upon us to project a remedy for our condition, if such a remedy is obtainable, or demand of this nation, which owes us billions of dollars for work done and services rendered, five hundred million dollars to commence leaving it; or endorse the petition of the colored lawyers' convention, which was held in Chattanooga, Tennessee, asking Congress for a billion dollars for the same purpose. For I can prove, by mathematical calculation, that this nation owes us forty billion dollars for daily work performed.

The one great desideratum of the American Negro is manhood impetus. We may educate and acquire general intelligence, but our sons and daughters will come out of college with all their years of training and drift to the plane of the scullion, as long as they are restricted, limited and circumbounded by colorphobia. For abstract education elevates no man, nor will it elevate a race. What we call the heathen African will strut around in his native land, three fourths naked, and you can see by the way he stands, talks and acts, that he possesses more manhood than fifty of some of our people in this country, and any ten of our most distinguished colored men here; and until we are free from menace by lynchers, hotels, railroads, stores, factories, restaurants, barbershops, courthouses and other places, where merit and worth are respected, we are destined to be a dwarfed people. Our sons and daughters will grow up with it in their very flesh and bones.

Gentlemen of the National Council, I leave the grave, solemn and awful subject with you.■

131 THE ETHICS OF THE HAWAIIAN QUESTION

William Saunders Scarborough

William Saunders Scarborough was born near Macon, Georgia, February 16, 1852, the son of a free black father and an enslaved mother. He took his mother's status, as the law required. After the Civil War, he studied at schools established by the Freedmen's Bureau and was the first graduate of Atlanta University. He continued his studies at Oberlin College, from which he graduated in 1875, and, though only twenty-three, became professor of Latin and Greek at Wilberforce University in Ohio. To help his students, Scarborough wrote a textbook, First Lessons in Greek, which was widely used as a textbook in both

*black and white institutions, including Yale University. The book was
frequently cited to refute the myth that blacks were incapable of master-
ing the complications of Greek conjugation.* In 1882, a year after his
book was published, Scarborough was elected a member of the American Philological Association. In 1908 he was appointed president of Wilberforce and served until 1920 while continuing his scholarly activities
in the field of linguistics and writing and speaking on race relations.*

*In March 1894, Scarborough, then professor at Wilberforce Univer-
sity, delivered a scorching attack on the move to annex Hawaii in a
speech delivered to students, faculty, and guests at the university.[†] The
speech was notable for its exposure of the imperialist forces behind annexation and the role that racial issues played in the determination of
American businessmen in Hawaii to control the island in their own interests. Scarborough also indicted the missionaries for their role in the island.*

Scarborough's address presented here is taken from the Christian Recorder, *March 15, 1894.*

NOT LONG AGO there was a prize fight in Jacksonville, Florida, between two well-known pugilists, James Corbett and Charles Mitchell.
The contest was to decide which of the two should have the honor (?) of being
the champion of the world. The victor was to receive in addition, a purse of
twenty thousand dollars or more. Strenuous efforts are said to have been put
forth by the governor of the state to prevent the contest from taking place.

---

*U.S. vice president and proslavery senator from South Carolina John C. Calhoun
(1782–1850) is said to have claimed "that if he could find a Negro who knew the Greek
syntax, he would then believe that the Negro was a human being and should be treated
as a man." See Alexander Crummell, "The Attitude of the American Mind Toward the
Negro Intellect" (1897), which appears elsewhere in this volume.

[†]In 1890, 99 percent of Hawaiian exports consisted of sugar for the American main-
land. In that year Congress admitted other foreign sugars (as well as Hawaii's) duty-free;
but the Louisiana planters persuaded Congress to give United States growers a bounty of
two cents a pound. Hawaii's single-crop economy, controlled by white—mainly American-
descended—planters, who had displaced the native Hawaiians from their land, was severely wounded. At the same time, native Hawaiians were becoming more and more dissatisfied with a constitution they had been forced to accept, under which control of the
government was in the hands of white foreigners, while property qualifications disfranchised most native citizens. Hawaiian discontent spread after 1891, when Queen Liliuo-
kalani, a strong and resolute opponent of white rule, became head of the government. In
1893 the white businessmen, aided by John L. Stevens, the American minister of Hawaii,
who had secured for them the protection of American troops landed from a cruiser, rose
up in rebellion. Stevens immediately recognized the provisional government set up by the
rebels, who lost no time in dispatching a five-man commission to Washington to negotiate
a treaty of annexation. This treaty, sent to the Senate by the retiring President Benjamin
Harrison, who favored it, was held up by Democratic opposition and was still under discussion when Grover Cleveland became president. Cleveland rejected the treaty of annexation. Hawaii was annexed during the Spanish-American War in the wave of imperialist
expansion that featured the conflict.

Even state militia were assembled in considerable numbers to assist the governor in carrying out his purposes. "There shall be no fight in the state of Florida" was the edict that came forth from the executive mansion; and the Christian world gladly gave its approval of the governor's veto. There was a fight, however, as all well know, and large crowds assembled to witness the gladiatorial combat. The *"hoc habet" "hoc habet"* differed in no respect from that of similar gatherings of ancient Rome and even now of Spanish bullfights, where each party shouts for his especial favorite in the words quoted or something similar.

Prize fighting is objected to on the ground that it is not only brutal and demoralizing, but a curse to civilization and destructive of our moral and social interests, while it fosters gambling and a spirit of hatred and murder— exerting a bad influence generally. Taking up this strain, the pulpits throughout the land assailed and abused the participants, while they invoked the vengeance of God upon their heads. The clergy were unsparing in their denunciations of prize fighting and prize fighters. The religious press united with the pulpit and the best class of the secular newspapers did likewise. It was clear that public sentiment was against it, as it ought to have been, and that there was a determination to prevent it at all events.

While all must approve of the efforts put forth to check such inhuman contests and consign them to oblivion, it is our opinion that prize fighting is a very small thing as compared with the wrong inflicted upon a weak and defenseless people like the Hawaiians by a strong power like our own. The annexationists, so called, are at the bottom of the Hawaiian imbroglio, and the assistance rendered them by the United States minister in his official capacity, makes our government equally culpable and ought to cause the whole nation to bow its head in shame.

The sin of prize fighting is subjective rather than objective and affects those taking part directly or indirectly more than anyone else. The purloining of a kingdom, great or small, is infinitely more disastrous to all parties concerned than the Corbett-Mitchell contest could possibly be. The consequences are far more reaching than it is possible for those to be which attend a prize fight where two men meet by common consent and agree to bruise and batter one another up for their own amusement and the greatest purse offered the victor. If the former has an ethical phase, certainly the latter has also, and it is upon this I wish to offer some observations. In regard to the Hawaiian question, we find that almost the entire clergy favor the scheme of the annexationists and the *modus operandi* adopted by the supporters of the so-called Provisional Government to wrest a throne from the hands of those to whom it rightly belongs. The religious press as a whole has joined the *hoi polloi* and united its voice with the rest of annexation sympathizers in the *"hoc habet"* cry, not that Corbett has won or that Mitchell is the winner, but that the *Provisional Government is the head of the Hawaiian affairs and it should be let alone.*

The secular press as a whole is divided by party lines, with truth left out. There are some exceptions of course. The Democracy as a rule supports the administration, while the Republican press takes up the gauntlet for Mr. Harrison. Both the President and ex-President committed blunders from beginning to end, but the former's are much less serious than the latter's. The former's were rather in practice than in theory, while the latter's were both in practice and theory. Mr. Cleveland is to be commended for the courage of his convictions. The issues involved in the Hawaiian problem should be calmly considered and calmly discussed and weighed without reference to party or party lines. It is not a party question, but a question of rights and duties—the rights of the Hawaiians and the duty of the United States. The annexation scheme has fallen to the ground. "The stolen kingdom" presented by missionaries or missionaries' sons of the United States failed to carry, as it deserved to do. It has been denied that it is a "stolen kingdom" and we are challenged and called upon to prove it. Here is our proof. In the language of the objector* himself:

The missionaries' sons in Hawaii comprise, first, about four hundred persons from age to infancy, who are directly sprung from the sixty original missionaries and who still continue to reside. A majority live in America. Added to this number by marriage are perhaps a hundred others, perhaps, most American-born. Numbering probably five hundred more are a body of people closely connected with the former in business and church relations and who are in active sympathy with them. This thousand people of all ages constitute the nucleus of our strong and progressive American colony of over three thousand persons. There are also the leading and influential element shaping political and social opinions among the great majority of 22,000 whites of the country. Until last May railed at as missionaries, it is now the order of the day to term them missionaries; children and no credit to their parents.

This strong little community of one thousand souls has recently built and paid for a church costing a hundred and thirty thousand dollars and said to surpass any church edifice on the Pacific coast in beauty outside and within. They statedly contribute thirty thousand dollars per annum for church and missionary purposes, besides numberless local and irregular benefactions for schools and other causes. By force of character and culture they occupy a majority of the highest public positions. Two out of three of the supreme judges are sons of missionaries; three out of the four ministers of state are the same. Of the Hawaiian legation at Washington, Thurston was grandson and Alexander a son of missionaries, men who would have distinction in any community. Three sons of missionaries by most honorable exertions are among the wealthiest of sugar planters and men of great beneficence. For presumable good reasons this large and reputable body of white natives and old residents of Hawaii are practically

*Rev. Sereno Bishop in the New York *Independent.*—W. S. S.

unanimous for the overthrow of the monarchy and for annexation to the United States. In accord with them are the great majority of the right-living and intelligent class of the native Hawaiians. Now as to the charge of tendering the stolen kingdom, the only right Liliuo-kalani or Kaiualani can claim in the matter is that the welfare of the kingdom calls for their rule. It cannot be stolen from them. They may have some claim for support as being put out of place. No one will re-fuse them such support when they are ready to make terms for it.

This is a strained view to take of the question and lacks the elements of sincerity. In the first place, where did the foreigners get an island to tender to America? How did they get into power? What legal right can they lay to the possession they now claim? Certainly not by right of conquest nor by series of wars did they triumph, for, as they are in the minority, being hardly a handful they could make but slight resistance to the powers that be. The Hawaiian authorities certainly did not make them a present of the country, nor did they voluntarily relinquish their claims to it. No such irregular method of doing business as this is anywhere referred to. No, it was a sys-tematic scheme laid long and deep to cheat these people out of their own, and they have succeeded admirably. It was by the grace of the Hawaiians that our first missionaries were allowed to land upon their territory, and this is the reward the islanders are receiving in return. Of course, it is taken for granted that the sole purpose of these missionaries was to educate and Chris-tianize the natives and make them better men and women, or else foreigners would never have been allowed the freedom of the soil. Subsequent events however would indicate that these people had another object in view. The charges against the character of the queen amount to but little. Examples are not wanting at the present day of plenty other monarchs whose character could vie in this especial respect with that of the ex-queen. But these still hold their scepters with right unquestioned by other nations on this account.

The annexation movement was the consummation of one of the most gigantic schemes to steal from a poor helpless people what was as much theirs as America was the Indians' before the days of Columbus. What is the most peculiar about the matter is that the Christian world seems to sanction on a big scale what it condemns on a small one. If the United States fails to right the wrong it committed by its agents, it will deserve the condemnation of all Christendom. It cannot afford to pass over the matter lightly whatever be the attitude of the adherents to the Provisional Government. It is a ques-tion of ethics and upon ethical grounds it must be settled—if rightly settled at all—everything else to the contrary.

We have strong evidence of the fact that it is not so much an immoral and dissolute queen as it is a question of color and nationality. It is an eth-nological question as well. A proof of this is seen in the nature and character of the caricatures of the deposed ruler that have filled the daily papers. These journals have taken especial pains to enlarge the racial phases of the question that they regard decidedly objectionable in order that they might stir up the prejudices of the people to the extent that they would look over the ethical phase and prevent justice from being done. By way of illustration we note the following:

"I think," says a prominent Buffalo contractor and one who has spent some time on the island, "that President Cleveland has been misinformed about what the people on the Island really want. The temper of the white inhabitants is strongly in favor of the Provisional Government, although they are in the minority—being about one fifth of the entire population. It would be a vain injustice to the whites to force royalty upon them. They do not want to be ruled by a dissolute *negress any more than would the people of Alabama.* They have established such a government as they desire and now simply want to be let alone."

If the good people, whether missionaries or sons of missionaries, find the moral atmosphere out of harmony with their own, let them untie and attempt to cancel the evil of which they complain by raising the moral standard of these islanders, by raising their aspirations making them better citizens. The end sought will come in time, and the example set will be worth all the time spent in bringing about the change.

It is said on good authority that Queen Liliuokalani is no better or no worse than many other women of her race. "Her devotion to religion has induced her to do many praiseworthy acts. She has always been generous to the poor and an active worker in the hospitals and homes for the destitute or unfortunate. She is at times exceedingly fervent in her devotion, attending prayer meetings regularly and lifting her voice in loud and earnest supplications. Now and then she exhorts her followers to repentance."

Whatever may be said to the contrary, it seems to be a fact that at the time of the landing of the *Boston* with her men the queen's troops were the only organized armed forces and were in control of the city; that the United States Marine forces were stationed opposite the government building across the streets with Gatling guns ready for action at a moment's notice; that these troops were landed by request of the United States' minister and those who were the instigators of the riotous movement; that these troops were landed twenty-four hours before the Provisional Government was proclaimed and that the government *de facto* and *de jure* asked the protection of the United States' troops but was refused by order of the United States' Minister Stevens, who was in sympathy with the revolutionists and was their abettor and accomplice in overturning the queen's government.

Again, the evidence seems to be conclusive that the palace was not seized by a mob of thirty armed men until twenty-four hours after the landing of our Marine forces, and that the presence of the latter was designed to intermediate the rightful ruler, "a menace against her" if she attempted to resist the revolutionists. That it was a success goes without saying; that the United States through its minister was a party to the deal is equally true. We have further evidence that the queen was given to understand that she must vacate; that it was the desire of the United States' minister that she should surrender her authority at least until the authorities at Washington should pass upon the situation.

Liliuokalani would naturally infer from this, that she would be restored, if she should peacefully abdicate and leave the matter of the United States for arbitration. To emphasize this perfidious action we need only to add that the Provisional Government declared that its existence would be determined by annexation or union with the United States or whatever the latter should agree upon. The revolutionists could not have maintained their own a fraction of the day if the United States troops had not been employed as a menace and an intimidation, which is evidently in violation of our neutrality laws and places us in a very humiliating position before the world.

The adherents of the Provisional Government declare after they had become firmly established in power that it was their intention to disfranchise a large percentage of the natives and supporters of the royal government, that they might perpetuate their ill-gotten lease of power. Well may these men fear for their heads, after the conception and execution of such a scheme. Who would not? Minister Thurston has not only been outspoken, but defiant on more occasions than one, and the very government against which he has spoken in terms not the most complimentary, for not adopting the annexation scheme, receives him as the accredited minister from a government whose right to exist is more than questionable in the minds of many.

Right the wrong at whatever cost, and if there is to be a Provisional or any other form of government aside from a monarchy, let it come in the regular order and legitimately. Only this will satisfy the demands of justice.

The Christian Church, the religious and secular press, and every American citizen that has in any way sympathized with or given encouragement to a sort of men whose purpose has been all along to throttle justice and enthrone a sham government under the false name of a Provisional Government or a Republic to further their own selfish ends, should *blush with shame and veil their faces, sitting in sackcloth and ashes.*■

132 ADDRESS TO THE FIRST NATIONAL CONFERENCE OF COLORED WOMEN

Josephine St. Pierre Ruffin

In a widely published response to Ida B. Wells's antilynching campaign, John Jacks, president of the Missouri Press Association, denounced black women as "wholly devoid of morality" and as "prostitutes, thieves and liars" (Wesley, The History of the National Association of Colored Women's Clubs, *28). Influential black newspaper editor and clubwoman Josephine St. Pierre Ruffin circulated copies of Jacks's letter in her call for African American women "to stand before the world and declare ourselves and our principles." One hundred women from ten states met, forming the basis for the first national organization of black women.*

Ruffin (1842–1924) was born in Boston and schooled in Salem until the desegregation of Boston's schools in 1855. She and her husband, lawyer and judge George Lewis Ruffin, lived in England for several years, then returned to Boston. They were friends of Frederick Douglass and William Lloyd Garrison and active in many civil rights and charitable causes.

Josephine St. Pierre Ruffin was a member of the New England Women's Club, founded by Julia Ward Howe, and worked closely with Howe, Elizabeth Cady Stanton, and Susan B. Anthony in campaigns for women's suffrage. After the death of her husband in 1886, Ruffin became an editor for the Boston Courier, *an African American weekly journal. In 1894, she founded the Women's New Era Club, a charitable association of sixty prominent Bostonians of color, and edited its monthly publication, the* Woman's Era.

Ruffin bitterly resented the exclusion of women of color from most white-dominated national women's organizations. In 1900, when she attended the Milwaukee convention of the General Federation of Women's Clubs as the delegate for three groups, two predominantly white and one African American, southern white women prevented representation of the New Era Club. Ruffin refused to accept the offer that she attend as representative of the two white-dominated clubs and withdrew from the convention under protest.

Ruffin organized and convened the First National Conference of Colored Women at the Charles Street A.M.E. Church in Boston in 1895. Its primary business was the planning of a national organization that would unite the many African American women's clubs that had emerged in the previous decade. In her address to the conference participants on July

29, Ruffin argues that the clubs that had sprung up across the country served as a "general preparation for a large union," which would be "led and directed by women for the good of women and men, for the benefit of all humanity." She welcomes the "active interest" of men in the planned organization and makes clear that she and those gathered are "not drawing the color line" but need the opportunity to speak among themselves and to take leadership for their own welfare.

During the year that followed, the National Federation of Afro-American Women and the National League of Colored Women were founded and engaged in a brief rivalry for national leadership. They were united in 1896 to form the National Association of Colored Women, with Mary Church Terrell as president and Ruffin's journal, the Woman's Era, *as its official publication.*

The text of Ruffin's speech appeared in the Woman's Era *2 (August 1895), 13–15. See also Charles H. Wesley,* The History of the National Association of Colored Women's Clubs: A Legacy of Service *(Washington, D.C.: NACW., 1984).*

It is with especial joy and pride that I welcome you all to this, our first conference. It is only recently that women have waked up to the importance of meeting in council, and great as has been the advantage to women *generally*, and important as it is and has been that they should confer, the necessity has not been nearly so great, matters at stake not nearly so vital, as that *we*, bearing peculiar blunders, suffering under especial hardships, enduring peculiar privations, should meet for a "good talk" among ourselves. Although rather hastily called, you as well as I can testify how long and how earnestly a conference has been thought of and hoped for and even prepared for. These women's clubs, which have sprung up all over the country, built and run upon broad and strong lines, have all been a preparation, small conferences in themselves, and their spontaneous birth and enthusiastic support have been little less than inspirational on the part of our women and a general preparation for a large union such as it is hoped this conference will lead to. Five years ago we had no colored women's club outside of those formed for special work; to-day, with little over a month's notice, we are able to call representatives from more than twenty clubs. It is a good showing, it stands for much, it shows that we are truly American women, with all the adaptability, readiness to seize and possess our opportunities, willingness to do our part for good as other American women.

The reasons why we should confer are so apparent that it would seem hardly necessary to enumerate them, and yet there is none of them but demand our serious consideration. In the first place we need to feel the cheer and inspiration of meeting each other, we need to gain the courage and fresh life that comes from the mingling of congenial souls, of those working for the same ends. Next, we need to talk over not only those things which are of vital importance to us as women, but also the things that are of special interest to us as *colored* women, the training of our children, openings for our boys and girls, how they can be prepared for occupations and occupations may be found or opened for them, what *we* especially can do in the moral education of the race with which we are identified, our mental elevation and physical development, the home training it is necessary to give our children in order to prepare them to meet the peculiar conditions in which they shall find themselves, how to make the most of our own, to some extent, limited opportunities, these are some of our own peculiar questions to be discussed. Besides these are the general questions of the day, which we cannot afford to be indifferent to: temperance, morality, the higher education, hygiene and domestic questions. If these things need the serious consideration of women more advantageously placed by reason of all the aid to right thinking and living with which they are surrounded, surely we, with everything to pull us back, to hinder us in developing, need to take every opportunity and means for the thoughtful consideration which shall lead to wise action.

I have left the strongest reason for our conferring together until the last. All over America there is to be found a large and growing class of earnest, intelligent, progressive colored women, women who, if not leading full useful lives, are only waiting for the opportunity to do so, many of them warped and cramped for lack of opportunity, not only to do more but to *be* more; and yet, if an estimate of the colored women of America is called for, the inevitable reply, glibly given is: "For the most past ignorant and immoral, some exceptions, of course, but these don't count."

Now for the sake of the thousands of self-sacrificing young women teaching and preaching in lonely southern backwoods for the noble army of mothers who has given birth to these girls, mothers whose intelligence is only limited by their opportunity to get at books, for the sake of the fine cultured women who have carried off the honors in school here and often abroad, for the sake of our own dignity, the dignity of our race, and the future good name of our children, it is "mete, right and our bounden duty" to stand forth and declare ourselves and principles, to teach an ignorant and suspicious world that our aims and interests are identical with those of all good aspiring women. Too long have we been silent under unjust and unholy charges; we cannot expect to have them removed until we disprove them through *ourselves.* It is not enough to try to disprove unjust charges through individual effort, that never goes any further. Year after year southern women have protested against the admission of colored women into any national organization on the ground of the immorality of these women, and because all refutation has only been tried by individual work the charge has never been crushed, as it could and should have been at the first. Now with an army of organized women standing for purity and mental worth, we in ourselves deny the charge and open the eyes of the world to a state of affairs to which they have been blind, often willfully so, and the very fact that the charges, audaciously and flippantly made, as they often are, are of so humiliating and delicate a nature, serves to protect the accuser by driving the helpless accused into mortified silence. It is to break this silence, not by noisy protestations of what we are not, but by a dignified showing of what we are and hope to become that we are impelled to take this step, to make of this gathering an object lesson to the world. For many and apparent reasons it is especially fitting that the *women* of the race take the lead in this movement, but for all this we recognize the necessity of the sympathy of our husbands, brothers and fathers.

Our woman's movement is woman's movement in that it is led and directed by women for the good of women and men, for the benefit of *all* humanity, which is more than any one branch or section of it. We want, we ask the active interest of our men, and, too, we are not drawing the color line; we are women, American women, as intensely interested in all that pertains to us as such as all other American women: we are not alienating or withdrawing, we are only coming to the front, willing to join any others in the same work and cordially inviting and welcoming any others to join us.

If there is any one thing I would especially enjoin upon this conference it is union and earnestness. The questions that are to come before us are of too much import to be weakened by any trivialities or personalities. If any differences arise let them be quickly settled, with the feeling that we are all workers to the same end, to elevate and dignify colored American womanhood. This conference will not be what I expect if it does not show the wisdom, indeed the absolute necessity of a national organization of our women. Every year new questions coming up will prove it to us. This hurried, almost informal convention does not begin to meet our needs, it is only a beginning, made here in dear old Boston, where the scales of justice and generosity hang evenly balanced, and where the people "dare be true" to their best instincts and stand ready to lend aid and sympathy to worthy strugglers. It is hoped and believed that from this will spring an organization that will in truth bring in a new era to the colored women of America.■

133 ATLANTA EXPOSITION ADDRESS

Booker T. Washington

Few speeches in American history have had the lasting impact of Booker T. Washington's address at the Cotton States and International Exposition held in Atlanta, Georgia, on September 18, 1895. It was this speech that propelled Washington to national fame and estab-

lished him in the minds of many (particularly whites) as the *leader and spokesperson for African Americans.*

Booker T. Washington (1856–1915) was born into slavery on a plantation in Virginia. Soon after emancipation, the family moved near Charleston, West Virginia, where he mastered the alphabet from a Webster's spelling book, secured by his mother. He attended an elementary school for black children, working five hours before school in a salt furnace and mine. In 1872, at the age of seventeen, he set out for Hampton Institute, about five hundred miles away, with a few dollars. Earning his board and expenses as a janitor, he spent three years at Hampton and was greatly influenced by the ideas of industrial education for African Americans espoused by General Samuel C. Armstrong, the principal. In 1881 he was chosen by General Armstrong to head the normal school being started at Tuskegee, Alabama. Emphasizing industrial education and the acquisition of manual skills, Washington and others built Tuskegee from a dilapidated shanty with forty students into a world-famous institution, which at the time of his death had more than a hundred buildings, owned two thousand acres of local land, and boasted an endowment of nearly $290,000; its 197 faculty members taught 1,537 African American students. The male students learned farming, carpentry, blacksmithing, and similar vocations, and the girls learned sewing, flower gardening, and practical housekeeping. A good part of the funds for Tuskegee came from northern capitalists who responded favorably to Washington's emphasis on industrial education for African Americans and his assurance that, once employed in industry, they would prove to be faithful workers who avoided trade unions and strikes.

If Washington's speech at the Cotton States and International Exposition gained him stature as a national leader, this is a role constructed in part by Washington himself in the speech, as he purports to convey "the sentiment of the masses of my race." At different points in his speech, he pretends to subdivide his audience, first admonishing "those of my race" (while whites "overhear" his instructions) to abandon plans of emigration, then addressing whites as a self-nominated spokesperson for black Americans.

Washington spoke at a time when African Americans in the South were being denied the ballot in deliberate defiance of the Fourteenth and Fifteenth Amendments, subjected to lynching, and forced to live under a system of strict racial segregation. Washington proposed a "compromise" by which African Americans would not ask for social or political equality in return for a pledge that they would be provided with industrial training and the opportunity to take a place in the economic development of the New South. He stressed that black Americans must win dignity and respect by self-help and emphasized responsibilities rather than rights. For Washington, economic advancement was the key to eventual power and justice. His speech also served as a rebuttal to the resurgent interest among African Americans in emigration. "Cast down your bucket where you are," he told his black listeners, while encouraging whites in his audience to hire black labor without fear that it would lead to intermingling. "In all things purely social we can be as separate as the fingers," he reassured them, "yet one as the hand" in the pursuit of mutual progress.

Washington's proposal was welcomed with relief by many whites as evidence of black acceptance of the order of white supremacy and an indefinite deferral of full-citizenship rights. White southern women in the audience covered the stage with flowers, the governor of Georgia (a former slaveholder and Confederate officer) bounded across the stage to shake Washington's hand, and the editor of the Atlanta Constitution hailed the speech as "the beginning of a moral revolution in America" and Washington as "a wise counselor and safe leader." While some black leaders, such as his future foe W. E. B. Du Bois, initially praised the speech, others, as we shall see, condemned its accommodation of racism.

Some scholars have pointed out that Washington did not entirely neglect the struggle for equal rights and contributed secretly to protest activities.* His influence soon extended far beyond Tuskegee. Presidents of the United States asked his advice when appointing African Americans to federal offices, and he exercised powerful influence over black publications. He supported black business enterprises and in 1900 organized the National Negro Business League.

Here is the text of Washington's Atlanta Exposition Address, taken from his autobiography, Up from Slavery (New York: Doubleday, 1901). See also Philip S. Foner, ed., "Early Opposition to Washington's Ideas," Journal of Negro History 55 (October 1970), 343–47.

M R. PRESIDENT and gentlemen of the Board of Directors and citizens: One third of the population of the South is of the Negro race. No enterprise seeking the material, civil or moral welfare of this section can disregard this element of our population and reach the highest success. I but convey to you, Mr. President and Directors, the sentiment of the masses of my race when I say that in no way have the value and manhood of the American Negro been more fittingly and generously recognized than by the managers of this magnificent Exposition at every stage of its progress. It is a recognition that will do more to cement the friendship of the two races than any occurrence since the dawn of our freedom.

Not only this, but the opportunity here afforded will awaken among us a new era of industrial progress. Ignorant and inexperienced, it is not strange that in the first years of our new life we began at the top instead of at the bottom; that a seat in Congress or the state legislature was more sought than

---

*See Louis R. Harlan, "The Secret Life of Booker T. Washington," Journal of Southern History 37 (August 1971), 393–416.

real estate or industrial skill; that the political convention or stump speaking had more attractions than starting a dairy farm or truck garden.

A ship lost at sea for many days suddenly sighted a friendly vessel. From the mast of the unfortunate vessel was seen a signal, "Water, water; we die of thirst!" The answer from the friendly vessel at once came back, "Cast down your bucket where you are." A second time the signal, "Water, water; send us water!" ran up from the distressed vessel, and was answered, "Cast down your bucket where you are." And a third and fourth signal for water was answered, "Cast down your bucket where you are." The captain of the distressed vessel, at last heeding the injunction, cast down his bucket, and it came up full of fresh, sparkling water from the mouth of the Amazon River. To those of my race who depend on bettering their condition in a foreign land or who underestimate the importance of cultivating friendly relations with the Southern white man, who is their next-door neighbor, I would say, "Cast down your bucket where you are"—cast it down in making friends in every manly way of the people of all races by whom we are surrounded.

Cast it down in agriculture, mechanics, in commerce, in domestic service, and in the professions. And in this connection it is well to bear in mind that whatever other sins the South may be called to bear, when it comes to business, pure and simple, it is in the South that the Negro is given a man's chance in the commercial world, and in nothing is this Exposition more eloquent than in emphasizing this chance. Our greatest danger is that in the great leap from slavery to freedom we may overlook the fact that the masses of us are to live by the productions of our hands, and fail to keep in mind that we shall prosper in proportion as we learn to dignify and glorify common labor and put brains and skill into the common occupations of life; shall prosper in proportion as we learn to draw the line between the superficial and the substantial, the ornamental gewgaws of life and the useful. No race can prosper till it learns that there is as much dignity in tilling a field as in writing a poem. It is at the bottom of life we must begin, and not at the top. Nor should we permit our grievances to overshadow our opportunities.

To those of the white race who look to the incoming of those of foreign birth and strange tongue and habits for the prosperity of the South, were I permitted I would repeat what I say to my own race, "Cast down your bucket where you are." Cast it down among the eight millions of Negroes whose habits you know, whose fidelity and love you have tested in days when to have proved treacherous meant the ruin of your firesides. Cast down your bucket among these people who have, without strikes and labor wars, tilled your fields, cleared your forests, built your railroads and cities, and brought forth treasures from the bowels of the earth, and helped make possible this magnificent representation of the progress of the South. Casting down your bucket among my people, helping and encouraging them as you are doing on these grounds, and to education of head, hand and heart, you will find that they will buy your surplus land, make blossom the waste places in your fields, and run your factories. While doing this, you can be sure in the future, as in the past, that you and your families will be surrounded by the most patient, faithful, law-abiding and unresentful people that the world has seen. As we have proved our loyalty to you in the past, in nursing your children, watching by the sickbed of your mothers and fathers, and often following them with tear-dimmed eyes to their graves, so in the future, in our humble way, we shall stand by you with a devotion that no foreigner can approach, ready to lay down our lives, if need be, in defense of yours, interlacing our industrial, commercial, civil and religious life with yours in a way that shall make the interests of both races one. In all things that are purely social we can be as separate as the fingers, yet one as the hand in all things essential to mutual progress.

There is no defense or security for any of us except in the highest intelligence and development of all. If anywhere there are efforts tending to curtail the fullest growth of the Negro, let these efforts be turned into stimulating, encouraging, and making him the most useful and intelligent citizen. Effort or means so invested will pay a thousand per cent interest. These efforts will be twice blessed—"blessing him that gives and him that takes." There is no escape through law of man or God from the inevitable:—

> The laws of changeless justice bind
>   Oppressor with oppressed;
> And close as sin and suffering joined
>   We march to fate abreast.

Nearly sixteen millions of hands will aid you in pulling the load upward, or they will pull against you the load downward. We shall constitute one third and more of the ignorance and crime of the South, or one third its intelligence and progress; we shall contribute one third to the business and industrial prosperity of the South, or we shall prove a veritable body of death, stagnating, depressing, retarding every effort to advance the body politic.

Gentlemen of the exposition, as we present to you our humble effort at an exhibition of our progress, you must not expect overmuch. Starting thirty years ago with ownership here and there in a few quilts and pumpkins and chickens (gathered from miscellaneous sources), remember the path that has led from these to the inventions and production of agricultural implements, buggies, steam engines, newspapers, books, statuary, carving, paintings, the management of drugstores and banks, has not been trodden without contact with thorns and thistles. While we take pride in what we exhibit as a result of our independent efforts, we do not for a moment forget that our part in this exhibition would fall short of your expectations but for the constant help that has come to our educational life, not only from the Southern states, but especially from Northern philanthropists, who have made their gifts a constant stream of blessing and encouragement.

The wisest among my race understand that the agitation of questions of social quality is the extremist folly, and that progress in the enjoyment of all the privileges that will come to us must be the result of severe and constant struggle rather than of artificial forcing. No race that has anything to contribute to the markets of the world is long in any degree ostracized. It is important and right that all privileges of the law be ours, but it is vastly more important that we be prepared for the exercises of these privileges. The opportunity to earn a dollar in a factory just now is worth infinitely more than the opportunity to spend a dollar in an opera-house.

In conclusion, may I repeat that nothing in thirty years has given us more hope and encouragement, and drawn us so near to you of the white race, as this opportunity offered by the Exposition; and here bending, as it were, over the altar that represents the results of the struggles of your race and mine, both starting practically empty-handed three decades ago, I pledge that in your effort to work out the great and intricate problem which God has laid at the doors of the South, you shall have at all times the patient, sympathetic help of my race; only let this be constantly in mind, that, while from representations in these buildings of the product of the field, of forest, of mine, of factory, letter and art, much good will come, yet far above and beyond material benefits will be that higher good, that, let us pray God, will come in a blotting-out of sectional differences and racial animosities and suspicions, in a determination to administer absolute justice, in a willing obedience among all classes to the mandates of law. This, this coupled with our material prosperity, will bring into our beloved South a new heaven and a new earth.■

134

A PLEA AGAINST THE DISFRANCHISEMENT OF THE NEGRO

Thomas E. Miller

After the overthrow of Radical Reconstruction in South Carolina, the conservative white element continued to govern the state under the constitution of 1868 adopted by black and white delegates. In 1892, however, the extreme white supremacists, led by U.S. senator Benjamin R. "Pitchfork" Tillman, gained control of the legislature and by a small majority in 1894 carried the referendum for a new convention on the issue of restricting the black vote and delivering South Caro-

lina from the "shame" of being governed under the "Radical rag" of
1868.

Representation in the 1895 Constitutional Convention included 122
Tillmanite Democrats, 42 conservative Democrats, and 6 black Republicans. Dominated by the Tillmanites, the Committee on the Rights of
Suffrage reported a new amendment to the Constitution that provided suffrage for male citizens over twenty-one who could meet the qualifications of residence in the state for two years, in the county for one year,
and in the precinct for four months, and who had paid the poll tax at
least six months before the elections. These were calculated to eliminate
many African Americans because of their mobility and their inability to
pay their poll taxes in May, a time when ready cash was least available
to sharecroppers and farmers. But the chief proposal to disfranchise black
South Carolinians was the literacy requirement, a provision that regis-
trants must prove to the satisfaction of the board that they could read
and write any section of the Constitution; if they failed to meet this test
they might register only if they owned and paid taxes on property as-
sessed at three hundred dollars or more. The board, of course, would be
able to overlook any number of white illiterates and paupers.

Even though they knew it was futile, the black delegates to the convention fought the white supremacists and made appeals for the maintenance of unrestricted suffrage. The first and most eloquent of the six
speeches was made on October 26, 1895, by Thomas Ezekiel Miller. He re-
viewed the history of black people in America, citing the martyrdom of
Crispus Attucks and the favorable comments of Charles Pinckney and
Henry Laurens, South Carolina leaders during the American Revolution,
on the contributions of black soldiers in the War of Independence. He
made an appeal to those who feared the disfranchisement of poor whites,
pointing out that the three-hundred-dollar property qualifications would
not afford a sufficient alternative for those who were poor as well as illiterate. Miller openly challenged the upholders of the lost-cause tradition.

So effective was Miller's speech that Tillman was forced to reply. He
dragged out the issue of black domination and fraud during the era of Reconstruction as justification for disfranchising the black voters. Miller
then spoke again, fearlessly defending the record of the African American
during Reconstruction. Even the white supremacist Columbia Register
was impressed, and it commented on October 27, "Miller's speech Friday
was an eloquent appeal on behalf of the Negro. While listening to his
soaring flights, many of the delegates regretted that they felt an inexora-
ble determination not to accede to this plea, a determination born of
stern necessity." As predicted, the convention proceeded to disfranchise
the black citizens of South Carolina.

Miller's speeches were not published in the official journal of the convention. They appeared (along with briefer speeches of the other African
American delegates) in a pamphlet published at her own expense by

Mary J. Miller, who wrote in a preface: "That the country may read these speeches and learn to know these brave and true men, I have edited a few of their arguments and prepared this pamphlet. I regard them as gems of Negro eloquence."

Thomas E. Miller was born a free black in Ferebeeville, South Carolina, on June 17, 1849. He moved with his parents to Charleston in 1851 and attended the public schools in Charleston and in Hudson, New York. During this time he worked as a newsboy on a railroad. He graduated from Lincoln University, Pennsylvania, in 1872, and moved to Grahamville, South Carolina, where he served as a school commissioner of Beaufort County. In 1888 he was elected to Congress and served one term (September 24, 1889, to March 3, 1891) during which he spoke out vigorously against the lynching and exploitation of black people in the South. In 1894 he was returned to the state House of Representatives, and in 1896 he was elected president of the State Colored College in Orangeburg. He died in Charleston on April 8, 1938.

Here are significant excerpts from Miller's speeches in the Constitutional Convention of 1895. They are taken from Mary J. Miller, The Suffrage: Speeches by Negroes in the Constitutional Convention: The Part Taken by Colored Orators in Their Fight for a Fair and Impartial Ballot *(n.d.), 5–16.*

MR. PRESIDENT: As an American citizen, as one who yields to no man in respect for the laws of the United States and South Carolina, as one who loves the past history of our nation and the dear old state when that history has been for the good and benefit of mankind, as one who has never by word or vote committed an act that in any way tended to destroy the rights of any citizen white or black, as one who wishes to see every male citizen—and woman too—who is not disqualified on account of crime or mental condition the equal of every other citizen in the enjoyment of inalienable rights, the chief of which is to have a voice in the government, I approach the discussion of the proposed disfranchisements of the common people of South Carolina, white and black.

Mr. President, the conservative force in our state is the common people, the burden-bearing people, and, sir, when you say that three hundred dollars and the capacity to read and write are the requirements to be possessed by voters, you are striking at the root of the tree of universal government. I ask in the name of the brotherhood of man and equal citizenship of the American people that I should not be trammeled by rules making my say a short one. I ask forbearance and the necessary time to discuss this all-important question, and I do hope and believe that, although I am in a feeble minority, that all-powerful majority will hear me, because I approach the discussion with malice toward none, but with a loving hope for the final settlement of this very vexed question. May the spirits of the departed patriots, who have shed their blood for the rights of man on this soil bear witness of our condition and in some way hover over us and guide us to the right. . . .

Hand in hand with a united effort, the white man and the black reclaimed this country and made it the asylum of the oppressed from every clime. And here today, Mr. President, after a residence of more than 250 years, with love and affection for the government, after having borne our part in every struggle and answered to every call, after having proven to the world that we are conservative in thought and action, lovable in our natures, forebearing toward our oppressor, living under and by the laws at all times, we are confronted at this hour, the noonday of peace and unity in the nation, the noonday of prosperity and hope, the noonday of this magnificent existence of ours with this proposition to disfranchise the common people; to take from them the dearest right, the right to vote. Oh, Mr. President, why is this to be done? Is there anybody here who can or dare deny that the sole purpose for which this convention was called is for the disfranchisement of the common people, and the Negro more especially? If there is such a person I ask him to read the speeches of the leaders who forced this conversation upon us against the will of the people, and they will all be convinced that the only thing for which this convention was called is for the disfranchisement of that class of people, whose chief lot has been to toil, toil, toil. With no hopes but to toil! Then if the speeches leave any reasonable doubt I ask him to read this article of disfranchisement, the article that has been pronounced by Senator Irby as a political monstrosity, and he will be thoroughly convinced that the purpose for which this convention was called is to disfranchise the Negro in the rice fields and his poor, uneducated white brother, who plows the bobtail ox or mule on the sandhills. He will be convinced that this convention was called to disfranchise the Negro in every walk of life and the poor white boy who edits a newspaper in which he speaks fulsomely for the greatest of all misnomers and Southern bugbears—white supremacy. There is no hope for him, though he wields an eloquent pen, if he is poor. His forefathers may have come here, and, like the Negro, spilt his blood, shed his tear, and toiled to plant this magnificent tree of liberty, but if this monstrosity becomes the law, there is no hope for him but to toil and grovel in poverty, because for the want of three hundred dollars, though an educated Caucasian, he is no better off than his ignorant brother in black skin. Trickery is not legislation. These little innocent "ifs" and "ors" may in the hands of skilled manipulators of fraudulent registration enable the poor, illiterate white men to vote at one or two succeeding elections, but in less than six years, under the part of this law saying that a man cannot read and write a section of the Constitution, that a man cannot vote who does not own three hundred dollars' worth of property, a governor will be elected who will turn the machinery over to the wealthy, to the managers of corporate rights, to the goldbugs, to the whisky trust, and we will have a spectacle like this: The poor, ignorant white man, the poor, educated white man, the poor, ignorant Negro, and the poor, educated Negro will be nonentities in the government, with no voice to say who shall rule, with no representation in the legislative halls, with no representation in the courts; it will be turning back the wheel of progress, and revolution should never go backward. . . .

Why do they say that the Negro must be disfranchised? Is it because he is lawless? No! Is it because he is riotous in the discharge of the right suffrage? No! They answer, "Because his skin is black, he should not vote. Because his skin is black, he is inferior. Because he did not fight for the ballot, he should not have it. Because we are a conquered people and were conquered by the national government, in the name of the Negro, he shall not vote."

Mr. President, these are some of the reasons given by those who swear by the altar of liberty that we shall not be citizens. Why have they thus sworn? Mr. President, this country and its institutions are as much the common birthright and heritage of the American Negro as it is the possession of you and yours. We have fought in every Indian war, in every foreign war, in every domestic struggle by the side of the white soldiers from Boston Common and Lake Erie to the Mississippi Valley and the banks of the Rio Grande . . .

But, Mr. President, although we have pursued this land of our birth by our past deeds, you and yours say that we must not vote, because we are an alien race. Aliens, say you, because our skins are black. But oh! Mr. President,

> 'Tis neither birth, race, clime or clan,
> 'Tis brain, not skin, nor hair, that makes the man.

Call us aliens? We, *aliens*? The people who were the foundation of the American civilization, *aliens*? A people who, by their sweat, assisted in clothing the barren rocks of the Northeast in verdure, who drained the swamps of the South, and made them to mimic gold in the harvest time; who by their endurance, toil and suffering made it possible for our white neighbors to establish this government, the asylum of us all; who by their toil developed the canal and railroad systems of this country—call us *aliens*? Then to whom can the term *citizens* be applied? A residence of our foreparents of near three hundred years; birth and rearage here; our adaptation to the wants of the country; our labor and forbearance; our loyalty to the government—are all these elements indices of an alien race? If we are aliens, then who are the citizens? It is true that we did not come here of our own volition, nor is the epoch of our coming one to be remembered with delight. There was no Castle Garden open to us; no merchant princes with a philanthropic hand extended to us; no Christian mission inviting us to come; but against our will, in chains, we were dragged from our native land to assist in converting the wilds of America into homes of freemen; to assist in establishing this government, the best that has ever been given to man. Its foundations were laid by our toil and sufferings; its growth and development have been matured by our blood. Whether on the farms, in the workshops, the canals, the railroads, or in your homes—wherever work was to be done, obstacles overcome, and barren hills to be fertilized—there, at all times, the white man could rely upon the Negro, and he has never failed him. The Negro has borne the burden of toil, and for what? To plan a civilization from which he is to be forever excluded. No, no, no! We have purchased it with labor; we have purchased it with afflictions; we have purchased it with loyalty; we have purchased it with blood drawn at the point of the lash of the taskmaster; we have purchased it with blood spilt upon the field of battle; it is ours by all the laws of right and justice. Right, under the watchful care of God, makes might. It is ours; absolutely ours. We are no more aliens to this country or to its institutions than our brothers in white. We have instituted it; our forefathers paid dearly for it. The broken hearts of those who first landed here is the first price that was paid for the blessings for which we now contend. By the God of right, by the God of justice, by the God of love, we will stay here and enjoy it, share and share alike with those who call us aliens and invite us to go. Together we planted the tree of liberty and watered its roots with our tears and blood, and under its branches we will stay and be sheltered.

Mr. President, those of you who seek to deny us this boon of citizenship tell the North a tale of woe and say that good government and white supremacy are in danger, and to protect the sweets of domestic happiness that were bequeathed us by our fallen sires, white and black, it is necessary to disfranchise the Negro. Shades of those departed heroes, bear witness to what I here say: The Negro does not by his presence retard the wheels of progress. The Negro will never by his vote overthrow good government. The Negro will never by any act of his seek to destroy white supremacy. He is nonobstructive; he is the best element of conservative citizenship in the South. Into his hands is the keeping of peace and happiness of the Southern people. But the Honorable George D. Tillman says that the South is a conquered province. The majority of you blame the poor Negro for the humility inflicted upon you during that conflict, but he had nothing to do with it. It was your love of power and your supreme arrogance that brought it upon yourselves. You are too feeble to settle up with the government for that old grudge. This hatred has been centered upon the Negro; and he is the innocent sufferer of your spleen. But, sirs, we are here. We intend to obey every phase of law that you may legislate against us. We intend to continue to love and forgive you for what you are doing to us. We intend to remain here and cause the South to blossom anew by our toil and suffering. We intend to place our case in the hands of God and the American white people, and while we are waiting for the full enjoyment of the blessings about which Jefferson wrote, for which Washington fought, and Attucks died, let me remind you of the truism that the part is not greater than the whole, and we know that we are compelled to move along within our circumscribed limits until the majority of the white sons and daughters of the South, yea, the entire nation, shall cease to be fooled into the belief that by reason of the Negro's presence, white supremacy is in danger. This is a white man's country, it is claimed, and I will not discuss it, but let me recall to you the words of the sainted

Lincoln: "You can fool all of the people sometimes, you can fool some of the people all the time, but you can't fool all the people all the time."*

The flame of education in this nation is ablaze and sheds its rays from every hilltop and amid the dales, and through and by means of education the scales of prejudice and false impressions will drop from the eyes of every white man, high and low. And they, right here in the South, will in time accord us every right and shed blood by our sides to maintain it. But to say that we are not fitted to enjoy the rights of a voter at this time is false, absolutely false, for we are the conservative element of Southern citizenship.

Senator Tillman, in an interview a few days ago, said that the Southern white man is the true friend of the Negro, and he asked the North to keep out of this discussion and deliver the rights of the Negro citizenship to his proffered, tender mercy. I would not deny that the Southern white man is friendly to the Negro and will and does assist him as long as he does not attempt to don the habiliments of American citizenship, but if he attempts to clothe himself in the garb of citizenship and claim equal rights before the law and under the Stars and Stripes, the average man becomes cantankerous and he imagines things that are impossible, and if he chances to be a leader, he flaunts into the face of the American nation the false flag of the fear of Negro domination. The Negroes do not want to dominate. They do not want and would not have social equality, but they do want to cast a ballot for the men who make their laws and administer the laws. Is there anything new in this plaintive appeal to the nation, asking in the name of friendship for and to the Negro to be left with the Negro and his rights in their hands? Why, sirs, it is not, for it was the cry of the feudal lords when they were grinding the white slaves of Europe between the millstones of misery and poverty. It was the cry of the school of slavery when the chains of servitude were riveted around the necks of the slaves of this continent, and the thoughtful are always reminded that when the lords of the soil ask the common people to surrender to them their rights, whether their intention is so to do or not, they are building barriers between people who surrender to them their rights. . . .

In the image of God, made He man, all equal, in the possession of inalienable rights, but at all times it has been the property-owning class who have sought to grind down, impoverish and brutalize their own blood if that blood was in the body of the poor and the weak. It is against class legislation that I stand here and raise my voice, and in the name of the poor, struggling white man and the peaceful, toiling, loving Negro. I ask that this act of feudal barbarism against the poor and common people do not be engrafted into and become a part of the Magna Charta of free white and black South Carolinians.

Mr. President, it is the boast that no illiterate white man shall be dis-

---

*Attributed to Abraham Lincoln in Alexander McClure, *Lincoln's Yarns and Stories* (Chicago: J. C. Winston, 1904).

franchised. It is the boast that the illiterate and educated poor Negro shall be disfranchised. Pass the law and you disfranchise them both, unless trickery and fraud are to be enthroned at our election booths. Pass this law, and you disfranchise all the laboring people, white and black, unless you so administer this law, which is the avowed intention of your leaders, as to discriminate against the Negro. Such a discrimination, Mr. President will be nullification of the Fifteenth Amendment. In the thirties our stamens played at the game of nullification,* and ever thereafter they taught nullification until their teachings culminated in secession and secession led to war, and a brother's hand was imbued in a brother's blood in that fight which was the struggle of the common people against the slaveholding class; the common people won that fight, and hence, by reason of false teaching, and by South Carolina placing her interests in the hand of selfish and ambitious men in the past, we are in this deplorable condition. Right is right, because God is God. Let us, as sons of South Carolina, dare to do right to all our citizens, for it is the only safe course of our citizens or state to follow. Therefore, I do hope that the enacting words of the articles of disfranchisement will be stricken out. It is hard to kick against the pricks. The majority of the white people of this nation are the common laboring class, and they will not sit down idly and see South Carolina again nullify any law that secures to the common people rights that are sacred to every freeman. . . .

Oh! countrymen, there is no good to come of this state out of this proposed act. Let us kill it and return to the constitutional provisions that we now have relating to the subject. I would that you could see the future as I see it. I would that our statesmen would use their energies and their great brain development in a better cause. I would that they would formulate plans by which our waste places could be reclaimed. Labor to bring immigrants into the confines of the dear old state. Strive to induce capital to come into our midst. Strive to teach the masses the lessons to forbear and stand the ills we have and ask God to assist us in a united effort, with the one purpose, and that purpose to make South Carolina the home of free, loving, prosperous humanity. Labor, let us all, to banish from our state caste prejudice and hatred of one man toward another. Let us cease to legislate in favor or against any class of people. Let us tell our people that this is the common heritage of whites and blacks, and it is our duty as free men to live in peace and assist in the government of the state.

Let us labor to prove that we are all a part of this nation, that we love her and intend to make this part of our common country the most glorious and certain place for peace and happiness of any portion of our great domain.

---

*In his "South Carolina Exposition" (1828), John C. Calhoun of South Carolina preached states' rights and the right of a state to nullify an unjust federal law, the state being the judge of what constituted injustice. On November 24, 1832, the legislature of South Carolina passed the Ordinance of Nullification, making the tariff acts of 1828 and 1832, as passed by the Congress of the United States, illegal in South Carolina. President Andrew Jackson received congressional authority to carry out the revenue acts involved in the "Force Bill" of March 2, 1833, but a compromise tariff was finally adopted.

The gentleman from Edgefield (Mr. Tillman) has read from the "Book of Fraud" to prove that my race is not qualified to vote, and why so? Is he ignorant of the way in which the book was made up? If he from experience knew so much about it as I do, he would not quote from it so freely. It was prepared by a partisan committee, and it is greatly colored.

But, Mr. President, I will not discuss the thread-worn tale so eloquently rehearsed by the two gentlemen from Edgefield, (Messrs. Tillman and Sheppard), but I do remind them and this convention that the white people of South Carolina themselves are more responsible for the state of affairs which existed during what they call "the dark period of their struggle," than is the Negro or carpetbagger. Though they had been in rebellion, seeking to destroy the very foundation of the greatest government ever planned and maintained, Congress by humane and charitable acts made it possible for them and the Negroes as co-heirs to reconstruct their own state governments; but with a haughtiness that showed their contempt for favors bestowed, they stood aloof, refused to vote or assist in reconstructing what in mad folly they had destroyed. A new class of rulers called carpetbaggers came among the ignorant Negroes, some of them honest and with patriotic motives. The country had been desolated by five years of war. County jails and courthouses had been destroyed, bridges burned, ferries broken up and roads cut to pieces—all of which had to be reconstructed. Charitable and penal institutions had to be rebuilt and maintained, and city, village, and town governments reestablished, making this a period peculiarly adapted to peculation, jobbery and plunder. Is it to be wondered at that right on the heels of a great war, with so much to be done anew, there was jobbery and peculation? There were many avenues to be traversed, great and diversified work to be done, and it was therefore impossible to keep out of the administration of affairs men who came among us for plunder. Why continue to hold that picture up to prove the worthlessness of a race? Removed so far as we are from it why continue to say that by reason of such acts we should not be entrusted with the right to vote?

Strange as it may appear, I plead specially for the Negro; during the three years he was the major factor in making and sustaining the government of South Carolina, that is from 1873 to 1876, he displayed greater conservative force, appreciation for good laws, knowledge of the worth of honest financial legislation, regard for the rights of his fellow citizens in relation to property and aptitude for honest financial legislation, regard for the right of his fellow citizens in relation to property and aptitude for honest financial state legislation than has ever been shown by any other people. "Fresh from the auction block and the slave pen," in the words of Professor Bryce, "ten-year-old children were more fitted to exercise the right to franchise." They first elected whom they supposed to be their friends, but in the short period of less than five years we who participated in that government learned that though they were our friends, any act on their part predicated upon plunder meant universal destruction, and from 1873 to 1876, inclusive, the record made by Negro legislators and Negroes charged with fiduciary trusts in the management of the government for certain reforms, has never been surpassed in any of the conservative state of New England. It is but too true, "the evil one does lives after him—the good is oft interred with his bones." . . . *

We were eight years in power. We had built schoolhouses, established charitable institutions, built and maintained the penitentiary system, provided for the education of the deaf and dumb, rebuilt the jails and courthouses, rebuilt the bridges and reestablished the ferries. In short, we had reconstructed the state and placed it upon the road to prosperity and, at the same time, by our acts of financial reform transmitted to the Hampton government an indebtedness not greater by more than $2,500,000 than was the bonded debt of the state in 1868, before the Republican Negroes and their white allies came into power.†

I stand here pleading for justice to a people whose rights are about to be taken away with one fell swoop, and I don't stand here answering any personal allusions, but representing the interests of the most conservative element of the Southern citizenship.

What is the trouble? The trouble comes from this, Mr. President. One white faction in South Carolina has been arrayed against another, and to prevent us from standing up in a representative capacity in a minority as representatives of the majority, they have rehashed this stale tale that has been written and read by the North, East and West until judgment has been passed upon it.

Because there had been robbery and fraud and perjury during a part of the time of Negro domination as it is called, it must not be thought that all Negroes were dishonest, any more than that all white men in New York were dishonest because Tweed and his gang had been corrupt.‡ That did not signify that all of the men who put Tweed into the office was corrupt.

Because white Democrats voted solidly for, and by their votes elected, the most corrupt judge (Thomas J. Mackey) that has ever disgraced the judicial ermine in South Carolina, why should the white people of our state be pronounced as venal as that arch scoundrel?

Oh, Mr. President, peace! Peace! Peace is the thing that I ask. But can we hope for peace and good feeling between the two races when such exhibitions as that made here by the gentleman from Edgefield is repeated?

---

*William Shakespeare, *Julius Caesar*, act III, scene 2, line 79.

†In his evaluation of the benefits of Reconstruction, Miller was pointing out facts that were to be ignored by most historians until very recently. In the *American Historical Review* of July 1910, W. E. B. Du Bois published an article entitled "Reconstruction and Its Benefits" that supported in detail the thesis Miller had advanced fifteen years earlier. Du Bois's point of view, however, was dismissed by contemporary historians.

‡The Tweed Ring was a political organization in New York City from 1860 to 1871, ruled by "Boss" Tweed; it was notorious for graft and corruption. After the Ring was overthrown in 1871, it was discovered that the city debt had been increased from $20,000,000 to $101,000,000. Tweed was ultimately arrested, and he died in prison.

Peace! Peace! Peace, happiness and prosperity, and the hope for a brighter day seems withered!

What right would I have to recall the scenes of Hamburg and Ellenton, where the helpless Negroes were murdered in cold blood?* What right would I have to refer to the fact that a gentleman on this floor treasures as a parlor ornament a rifle which he claims he used at those riots?

Peace! Peace to all men! Judge these educated white people by what they are doing, and ask them if the poor ignorant Negro should be thus judged. . . .

I want a united people. Let us forever bury all the bad deeds of both races of the past. Let us try to bear and forbear. Let us strive to bind up the wounds, old wounds of long, long ago, with bandages of loving kindness toward the two races. God has placed your race and my race here on this continent; together it is our lot to dwell. Oh, countrymen, of this Southland, one and all, white and black, let us be just, one to another; let us at all times speak only the truth about our people and the old state; let us labor to unite our people for the good of the people in common; let us secure to our children prosperity and happiness founded upon the rock of justice and peace, justice and peace, justice and peace!■

135 THE AFRICAN IN AFRICA AND THE AFRICAN IN AMERICA

John H. Smyth

By the 1890s, many African Americans had again become disillusioned about the prospects for social change in the United States. The unraveling of Reconstruction, mounting disfranchisement, and dwindling numbers of black officeholders, combined with a terrifying resurgence of racist violence, social discrimination, and "scientific" racism, persuaded many African Americans to consider emigration to Africa. Emigrationists such as Bishop Henry McNeal Turner argued that whites would never grant social equality to blacks and urged that millions of African Americans relocate in the African "fatherland."

Chicago's segregated Columbian Exposition of 1893 had its counter-

---

*On July, 9, 1876, an armed white mob attacked the black militia of Hamburg, South Carolina, murdering several of the militia leaders after they had surrendered.

part in the week-long World Congress on Africa held in Chicago in August 1893, at which Turner, Alexander Crummell, Frederick Douglass, and more than four dozen other leaders debated the merits of emigration. Yet few blacks from the South, where perhaps the strongest support existed for emigration, attended the Chicago congress, and the foes of African migration held sway.

The second Congress on Africa was convened in Atlanta in conjunction with the city's Cotton States and International Exposition on December 13–15, 1895, at which Booker T. Washington delivered his most famous address. Washington's charge to African Americans to "cast down your bucket where you are—cast it down in making friends in every manly way of the people of all races by whom we are surrounded" was a direct response to the calls for emigration by Turner and others and should be understood in the context of a raging contemporary debate among African Americans over this issue.

The Atlanta Congress on Africa was conducted under the auspices of the Stewart Missionary Foundation of the Gammon Theological Seminary. The African missionary work of the Methodists, Baptists, Presbyterians, and Congregationalists provided a base of support for emigration by encouraging an additional rationale for moving (bringing Christianity, education and social assistance to Africans) and by maintaining a constant exposure of black Americans to guest speakers visiting from Africa.

Among the most noteworthy speeches given at the Congress was that delivered by John H. Smyth, editor of the Richmond Reformer, who had served for nine years as minister to Liberia. In this stirring, enduring statement of black nationalism, Smyth demands pride and knowledge of African accomplishment and cultural heritage. Smyth dismisses the popular notion that the forced removal of Africans to America has been a source of cultural refinement and uplift. "In making us Anglo-Saxons by environment," he argues, "we have lost not only in soul, but exteriorly."

Smyth responds directly to the assimilationist ideals pronounced at the conference by T. Thomas Fortune and at the Exposition by Washington. Those who remain in America and do not emigrate, he maintains, must recognize that "though we are a part of this great national whole, we are a distinct and separate part, an alien part racially, and destined to be so by the immutable law of race pride, which is possessed by our white fellow-citizens, if not by us." Disavowing the "melting pot," in which racial differences would disappear, Smyth endorses a "race allegiance" that "is compatible with patriotism, with love of the land that gave us birth." At the same time, Smyth makes clear that Africans are not one people but many different cultures.

The text of Smyth's speech was published in J. W. E. Bowen, ed., Africa and the American Negro . . . Addresses and Proceedings of the Congress on Africa (Atlanta: Gammon Theological Seminary, 1896), 69–83. Additional information on the Congress may be found in Ralph E. Luker, The Social Gospel in Black and White (Chapel Hill: University of North

Carolina Press, 1991), 48–52. On Smyth, see Walter Williams, "Nineteenth Century Pan-Africanist: John Henry Smyth," Journal of Negro History *63 (January 1978), 18–25, and William Simmons,* Men of Mark *(1887), 872–77.*

The fact will be readily admitted by those most familiar with the sentiment of a large and not unimportant portion of our American citizenship, who, by the fortunes and misfortunes of war, viewed from the standpoint of one or the other combatants of the sanguinary struggle of 1861–62–63–64, were made equal before the law with all other citizens, that as a class they are averse to the discussion of Africa, when their relationship with that ancient and mysterious land and its races is made the subject of discourse or reflection. The remoteness of Africa from America may be a reason for such feeling; the current opinions are derived, that the African is by nature an inferior man, may be a reason. The illiteracy, poverty, and degradation of the Negro, pure and simple, as known in Christian lands, may be a reason in connection with the partially true and partially false impression that the Negroes, or Africans, are pagan and heathen as a whole, and as a sequence hopelessly degraded beings. These may be some of the reasons that make the subject of Africa discordant and unmusical to our ears. It is amid such embarrassments that the lecturer, the orator, the missionary must present Africa to the Negro in Christian America.

In view of recent newspaper articles about migration of Negroes to Liberia, so much has been recently said by men of African descent of prominence, and by men of like prominence of uncertain descent, and by men of other races than the Negro, of Liberia and Africa generally, that I deem it a duty as an American citizen and a Negro, in vindication of the men and women of like descent with myself, citizens of the United States, to state some facts explanatory of and in rebuttal of much that has been said, ignorantly, unwisely and unsympathetically, to the detriment of the effort being made at self-government in Liberia, West Africa. The people who constitute the inhabitants and citizenship of Liberia (the largest portion of the latter class are American Negroes from the Southern part of the United States) are possessed of and imbued with the sentiment and the civilization peculiar to this section of our country. That these immigrant Negroes who migrated to West Africa, or began migration as far back as 1820, and who continue to go thither, have a better field there, with less embarrassing environment, to prove their capacity for self-government, for leadership in State-craft than their brethren in the northern, western and southern portions of the United States, will scarcely be seriously denied or questioned. This conceded, it seems to me that wisdom, self-respect, race loyalty, and American patriotism would show themselves richer to withhold judgment as to the success of the experiment being made in Africa for self-government until such time as this immigrant people and their descendants have lived in Liberia, Sierra Leone, the Gold Coast, the Camaroons and other parts of west Africa long enough to assimilate the sentiment of liberty and rule, the general heritage and possession of the native African, than it has shown itself in echoing the expression of opinion of white men, whatever their learning or literary capacity, who estimate the progress of the Negro by the standard of their own race with its superior opportunities, advantages and facilities.

Until we have demonstrated ability for organization, for government, and have shown effective cohesiveness and leadership here in the United States, it may be a little immodest to hastily and unadvisedly make up the record adverse to our immediate kith and kin, who less than sixty years ago made the first step on lines of independent form of government of themselves, and have successfully maintained themselves against the greed of Spain, the aggrandizement of France, and the envy and cupidity of the merchant class of England without active assistance or defense of our formidable North African squadron; without an army and without more than one gunboat, the property of the Republic.

Liberia is the only democratic republican form of government on the continent of Africa of which we have any knowledge. The civilization of the people constituting the majority of the citizenship of Liberia is American. It embraces that phase of our American system which has made the autonomy of the south distinct from that of all other parts of our common country. This is the resultant of the outgrowth of the laws and customs of the severalty as well as the jointness of that system of government which exists in the South. In so far as the civilization of the United States on analysis is differentiated as northern, southern, eastern, and western, and in the south as Virginian, Carolinian, Georgian, it may be said, that the people composing the nation have transferred such American phases of government to this part of Africa.

The pioneers of this colony, the descendants of them, and the immigrants that have gone from here at varying periods of time within sixty years, like those of us who have remained, have been the unhappy victims of the influences of an alien, racial oppression; are fragments of races and tribes, and lack much in capacity for maintaining a stable form of government without the aid which comes from the moral support of the United States. But notwithstanding the embarrassments and difficulties of this youthful nation, the elements of success are being gradually, surely and deeply laid in industrial and agricultural concerns. The masses of the people are directing their effort to agriculture, the development of the soil, and are leaving the matter of coast-commerce or barter to the few.

No epitome or summary of Liberia would be worthy of the name which failed to take note of the renaissance of education under the scholarly Blyden and Freeman, both of whom have been presidents of Liberia College. When the former scholar came to the presidency of the college, then was commenced the work of the adaptation of the training of the youth for the definitive and distinct purpose of advancing the nation on the line of race. This institution has sent forth strong Negro men, who are unperverted in their instincts, strong in their race loyalty, and unhampered by a civilization upon which the individuality of the race is not stamped. Such a civilization, un-modified, is unsuited to the African in Africa, or out of Africa and although it may develop him religiously, in manly, self-reliant feeling, it will make him a weakling and will be destructive of true manhood, self-respect and race integrity. In illustration of the method of training the mind of the Negro youth of Liberia, the following from the inaugural of the late president of the college, Dr. Edward Wilmot Blyden, on assuming the presidency, will make clear Liberian higher training. After alluding to the leading epochs in the history of civilization, the theocratic, the Greek age, the medieval age, the modern age and its subdivisions, the age since the French Revolution, the distinguished president said of the curriculum of the college: "We shall permit in our curriculum the unrestricted study of the first four epochs, but especially the second, third, and fourth epochs, from which the present civi-lization of Western Europe is mainly derived. There has been no period of history more full of suggestive energy, both physical and intellectual, than these epochs. Modern Europe boasts of its period of intellectual activity, but none can equal, for life and freshness, the Greek and Roman prime. No mod-ern writers will ever influence the destiny of the race to the same extent that the Greeks and the Romans have done. We can afford then to exclude them as subjects of study, at least in the earlier college years, the events of the fifth and sixth epochs, and the works which in large numbers have been written during these epochs. I know that during these periods some of the greatest works of human genius have been composed. I know that Shake-speare and Milton, Gibbon and Macaulay, Hallam and Lecky, Froude, Stubbs, and Green, belong to these periods. It is not in my power, even if I had the will, to disparage the works of these masters; but what I wish to say is, that these are not works on which the mind of the youthful African should be trained.

"It was during the sixth period that the transatlantic slave trade arose, and these theories—theological, social, and political—were invented for the degradation and proscription of the Negro. This epoch continues to this day, and has an abundant literature and a prolific authorship. It has produced that whole tribe of declamatory Negrophobists, whose views, in spite of their emptiness and impertinence, are having their effect upon the ephemeral lit-erature of the day, a literature which is shaping the life of the Negro in Christian lands. His whole theory of life, quite contrary to what his nature intends, is being influenced, consciously and unconsciously, by the general conceptions of his race entertained by the manufacturers of this literature, a great portion of which, made for to-day, will not survive the next genera-tion.

"I admit that in this period there have been able defenses of the race written, but they have all been in the patronizing or apologetic tone, in spirit of that good-natured man who assured the world that

> 'Fleecy locks and dark, complexion
> Cannot forfeit nature's claim.'

"Poor Phillis Wheatly, a native of Africa, educated in America, in her attempts at poetry, is made to say, in what her biographer calls 'spirited lines,' 'Remember Christian Negroes, black as Cain, may be refined, and join the angelic train.' The arguments of Wilberforce, the eloquence of Wendell Phillips, the pathos of Uncle Tom's Cabin, are all in the same strain, that Negroes have souls to save as white men have, and that the strength of nature's claim is not impaired by their complexion and hair.

"We surely cannot indulge with the same feelings of exultation that the Englishman or American experiences in the proud boast that we speak the language that Shakespeare spoke. The faith and morals which Milton held, for that "language" in some of its finest utterances patronizes and apologizes for us, and that "faith" has been hitherto powerless to save us from proscription and insult. It is true that culture is one, and the effects of true culture are the same; but the native capacities of mankind differ, and their work and destiny differ, so that the road by which one man may attain to the highest efficiency is not that which would conduce to the success of another. The special road that has led to the success and elevation of the Anglo-Saxon is not that which would lead to the success and elevation of the Negro, though we shall resort to the same means of general culture which enabled the Anglo-Saxon to find out for himself the way in which he ought to go."

But to return. It was not the privilege of ancient foreign civilization to know Africa except superficially, and with equal truth it may be asserted that the world of foreign races to Africa is ignorant of Africa now, and always has been as to her races, although millions of her sons and daughters, and their million descendants, have been placed in most intimate and unfortunate relation with many great and remarkable alien races.

This absence of knowledge concerning a continent so related as Africa has been to the past and present of European and American nations, may be accounted for in the selfishness of man's nature, the disposition to concern one's self, to the exclusion and the neglect of others, with racial characteristics which create an interest in those of a race for that race alone, which produces pride of race, a possession of every race, unless destroyed by oppression, which produces indifference to other races than one's own, save in so far as others may be made to conserve the interest of one's own race.

The continent of Africa is to-day the most interesting of the eastern hemisphere to the scientist, the political economist, the philanthropist and the religious propagandist, and the plunderers of weak and defenseless humanity. It will not be possible for me to speak of the races of the whole continent. My purpose is to speak of Africa in America and Africa in Africa, confining myself to a portion of the races of West and Central Africa, for the purpose of arousing an active spirit of inquiry as to a continent and a people, to which we are bound by the blood that courses our veins and by whatever of self-respect we possess.

We are taught by holy writ that God set bounds to the habitations of men. One race he established upon the continent of Africa, another upon the continent of Asia, another upon the continent of Europe, and a heterogeneity of races upon the continent of America, and fragmentary peoples inhabit the isles of the sea. In this various apportionment of races, wisdom and beneficence are shown. If we fail to see the former, we cannot doubt the latter, since "He does all things well."

In the light of these facts I fail to see a providence in bringing the Negro here, in making of him, at best, a moral and mental imitation of an original such as he can never be. Every step made by the Negro and his progeny, brought here a man and trained a slave, has continued him slave, though the institution as such has perished. The inherited taint of the institution has removed him further and further from the land of his fathers, from his tribal and racial traditions (valued heritages of a people), and has tended to make latent in him, if it has not wholly destroyed his best racial peculiarities and characteristics. In making us Anglo-Saxons by environment, we have lost not only in soul, but exteriorly, as objectified in the various types among us, nomenclatured colored people. However distasteful to the Caucasian the statement of the fact may be, the Negro who has grown to manhood under their alien Christian civilization, alien to the Negro and [in many respects] to Christ, is in his virtues and vices more Caucasian than African.

These considerations are serious to the Negro who feels any pride in being connected with races which aggregate, as known, more than 200,000,000 souls, who have an inalienable right to a continent as rich in its flora and fauna and mineral deposits (to say the least) as any other the sun warms with its heat and upon which the rains descend to make fruitful. Serious, indeed, must these considerations be to the Negro of the Americas and the Antilles, the descendants of those races whose moral elevation and mental ripeness in the morning of time manifested themselves in the conception and execution of those wonders of the ages, the pyramids, the sphynxes, and that musical colossus, Black Memnon, so fashioned that for two hundred years, on the rising of the god of day, as its rays shone upon it, it became musical with the concord of sweet sounds. Serious must these considerations be to the descendants of those races who erected these most beautiful temples and obelisks which have existed for centuries, the superscriptions within and upon which are yet to be interpreted by the descendants of Negro architects and builders; the ruins of which in their moral sublimity, stand as sentinels of time all along the delta and banks of the Nile, and are seen at Alexandria, Philae, Elephantine, Thebes and Karnac, representing their builders feeling after God in their desire for immortality.

These works of art and utility survive, in ruins, the perished civilizations of Asia, the cradle of the human race, and will survive the civilizations of Europe and this last, vigorous, Herculean civilization of America, which is but an evolution of Europe. These ruins have been the surprise and admiration of all other civilizations. These ruins have seen other civilizations in their dawn, their noontide, and will, notwithstanding the vandalism of the Caucasian, continue beyond his day. Those perished peoples of Africa furnished Europe with letters, sciences, and arts, although we, their lineal heirs, by the selfishness, greed, and ingratitude of the Caucasian, have been denied, until within the century, the title of human beings, and within three decades have only been regarded as equals before the law in a land of liberty and law. Two hundred and fifty years have removed us to a far greater distance from Africa than the geographical measurement that separates America from Africa, and to-day that continent is perhaps of less interest to the educated and refined Negro of America than to his thrifty, industrious, and adventurous white fellow-citizen.

There is error in a system of religion, a mistake in a system of education that so alienates brother from brother and sister from sister. Especially is this so when they trace their lineage from the same race stock.

It is lamentable that two hundred and fifty-years have removed us to a far greater distance from Africa than the geographical measurement which separates America from Africa, and to-day that continent is perhaps of less interest to the educated and refined Negro of America than to his thrifty, industrious, and adventurous white fellow-citizen.

Says an eminent English divine: "Neither Greek nor Roman culture had power to spread beyond themselves, and we have the testimony of the Emperor Julian to this. He considered the barbarous western nations incapable of culture. The fact was that Rome did not try to civilize in the right way. Instead of drawing forth the native energies of these nations, while it left them free to develop their own national peculiarities in their own way, it imposed on them from without the Roman education. It tried to turn them into Romans. Where this effort was unsuccessful, the men remained barbarous; where it was successful, the nation lost its distinctive elements in the Roman elements, at least until after some centuries the overwhelming influence of Rome had perished. Meantime they were not Britons nor Gauls, but spurious Romans. The natural growth of the people was arrested. Men living out of their native element became stunted and spiritless."

The peculiar character of a nation is not lost in Christianity, but, so far as it is good, develops and intensifies itself. People should be allowed to grow naturally into their distinctive type and place in the world.

The wrong done us here in America, the wrong done us in Turkey in Asia, and Turkey in Europe, and Constantinople, is being recognized at the center of Anglo-Saxon civilization, as is honestly indicated by utterances such as these: "It is too late to ask, 'Are we our brother's keeper?'" Three centuries ago the plea might have seemed specious, but since then Europe has made itself guilty towards Africa of the blackest series of crimes that stain the foul record of civilized history. The actual appalling state of things in Africa is the result of the policy of Europe towards the African races. European contact has brought in its train not merely the sacrifice, amid unspeakable horrors, of the lives and liberties of twenty million Negroes for the American market alone, but political disintegration, social anarchy, moral and physical debasement, the decay of the simple arts and industries which had been developed during centuries of undisturbed and uneventful existence. Christian Europe, it is true, no longer openly tolerates the slave trade, but Christian Europe furnishes the arms by means of which the slave trade is carried on. The European explorer paves the way for the Arab man-hunter; in his track follow not the blessings of civilization, but conflagration, rapine, and murder, and European trade, while extinguishing native handcrafts, places within the African's grasp the power of self-destruction by spirits and of mutual destruction by firearms.

"We are now consciously confronted by all these evils and responsibilities. They have been slowly forced upon our recognition as one traveler after another opened a chink into the darkness of the heart of Africa. That a debt of reparation is due from the white man to the black can no longer be denied. It *must* be paid somehow; it *may* be paid for weal and not for woe. A duty left undone is a Nemesis, pursuing to destruction; a duty to be done is simply a problem to be solved. What shall it be for us? The public voice has already spoken. The blunder and the crime of the abandonment of Khartum will not be repeated. Henceforth, at least ostensibly, the salvation of Africa is the policy of Europe.

"There remains, then, only the question as to the best means of carrying it into execution. And here, too, ignorance is giving place to better knowledge. Our conduct is, as it were, shaping itself, and for once commercial and national advantages are found combined with the highest interest of humanity."

I am aware that it will be insisted by some who have failed to give this matter the consideration which it merits, that we are a part of the greatest composite nationality, and therefore, any influence that would make the Negro less American and more African than he is, would be injurious to the best interest of our American nation. I would gladly impress upon persons entertaining such thoughts, that race allegiance is compatible with patriotism, with love of the land that gave us birth. This has been abundantly shown to be true with reference to the Jews. Whatever doubts may be entertained upon this point on account of their wide religious divergence from other religionists, must undergo a change in the presence of the admonition given in a missive sent to Israel by the prophet Jeremiah, and which has been faithfully conformed to by Israel and the descendants of Israel: "Serve the King of Babylon, and live. Build ye houses and dwell in them; and plant gardens and eat the fruits of them. And seek the welfare of the city whither I have caused you to be carried away captives, and pray unto the Lord for it; for in the peace thereof shall ye have peace."

Though we are a part of this great national whole, we are a distinct and separate part, an alien part racially, and destined to be so by the immutable law of race pride, which is possessed by our white fellow-citizens, if not by us. The sentiment, the something stronger than sentiment which makes an English American proud of his connection with Britain, a French American proud of his connection with La Belle France, and a German American fondly attached to the memories of the fatherland, and all European races of their Aryan descent, has something that partakes of the moral sublime. Truly "language and religion do not make a race."

The characteristics, peculiarities, idiosyncrasies and habits have been determined by what has been displayed and noted of Negroes under influences foreign to them and beyond their control. This has been the cause of inaccurate knowledge of the races of Africa on the part of the whites, and inaccurate knowledge on the part of the Negroes themselves.

The elements of character of American whites are to be learned in the light of their free, unhampered ancestry and brethren in Europe.*

The civilized Negro here has but recently emerged from slavery and been recognized a freeman; and though guaranteed in the possession of political rights, is still hampered by his inability to understand himself, by the conviction that on account of the political unity of the races here, his end must be reached by pursuit of the same line followed by the controlling races.

The condition of the race and present here makes the American Negro African, without the peculiarities of his race; an African only as to the hue of his skin and his blood. The black man here is Americanized, and as a sequence, sectionalized.

Now the difference between Africa in America, and Africa in Africa being recognized, let us look to Africa in Africa. The races of Africa have not been a subject of Caucasian study.

The Egyptian, Carthaginian, and Moorish people are imperfectly known, and the interior, eastern, western races, are still more imperfectly understood, and for very prudential reasons,—the uncompromising conditions of climate toward European peoples, and the almost insuperable difficulties of ingress to the country. Says Amelia B. Edwards, in her cleverly written book, "A Thousand Miles up the Nile," of African races: "As with these fragments of the old tongue, so with the races, subdued again and again by invading hordes; intermixed for centuries together with Phoenician, Persian, Greek, Roman, and Arab blood, it fuses these heterogeneous elements in one common mould, reverts persistently to the early type, and remains African to the last. So strange is the tyranny of natural forces. The sun and soil of Africa demand one special breed of men, and will tolerate no other. Foreign residents cannot rear children in the country. In the Isthmus of Suez, which is considered the healthiest part of Egypt, an alien population of twenty thousand persons failed in the course of ten years to rear one infant born upon the soil. Children of an alien father and an Egyptian mother will die off in the same way in early infancy, unless brought up in simple native fashion. And it is affirmed of the descendants of mixed marriages, that after the third generation the foreign blood seems to be eliminated, while the traits of the race are restored in their original purity."

Another reason, race pride, so natural to all races, will always be a good and sufficient reason to deter the Saxon from recognizing excellences in a race foreign and alien to his race. Now, if we would know the Negro in his

*Partitioning of Africa between European Nations and Races.—*Edinburgh Review,* October 1889.

African home, we are to seek that knowledge of his true character through him.

The testimony of Africans, distinguished for their knowledge of their countrymen, for their learning and character, should be looked to, and consulted as authorities in these matters. The Arku and Ebo races are not to be known through the flippant and inconsiderate statements of some ignorant European who finds to his surprise and annoyance that he cannot successfully take advantage of them in a business transaction, and as a consequence declares the former people a deceptive, ignorant class, and the latter an insolent, lazy set. You are to read the history of these races in the light of what the learned Dr. Africanus Horton has written in his "Africa and the Africans," and what his lordship Bishop Crowther experienced in his successful labor of love among his own and other races.

A comprehensive knowledge of the Christian, Mohammedan, and heathen Africans of Central and West Africa must be read in the light of the full and exhaustive information to be found in the writings of Edward W. Blyden, D.D., LL.D., late president of Liberia's college. Christianity in the third and fourth centuries among the Africans must be studied, in the Africans' fathers, and in Lloyd's North African Church and in Abyssinian traditions.

The missionary work in West Africa in the fifteenth century may be read in the voluminous Spanish and Portuguese and Italian state papers and travels. A few most valuable ones as to the Congo races are to be found in an English translation made during the reigns of Henry VIII and Elizabeth. Bishops Crowther and Coleson may be read on African character with profit. There are two classics, African, which should be read: A. H. L. Heeren, African Researches,* and a portion of Herodotus.

For quite fair treatment of African character, French and German explorations are interesting, and in English, Mungo Park, Livingstone, and Gordon Pasha.

Having directed attention to the means and some of the sources to be relied on for facts concerning native African character, I now point to some illustrations of error and wrong in dealing with the African in Africa.

It is not to our century alone that we are to look for active but mistaken effort to christianize Africa. There has existed no African mission, which in the same period of time, attained to such proportions as the Portuguese mission in the Congo region during the fifteenth century. A cathedral and churches adorned, beautified, and glorified that portion of West Africa, and a Congo gentleman, after pursuing the necessary course of study in Spain prescribed for the priesthood, was made a bishop, and returned to his country to carry on the work of christianizing his people through the religion of

---

*Arnold H. L. Heeren (1760–1842), *Historical Researches into the Politics, Intercourse, and Trade of the Carthaginians, Ethiopians, and Eqyptians* (London: H. G. Bonn, 1854–56).

Catholic Rome. All this work passed away. The ships which brought priests as outward passengers took the human product of the race back as homeward cargo. The theory and practice of the European being in opposition, the one to the other, the work perished. The fetich of the cross in the hands of the Portuguese, did not deter them from knavery and theft and murder, and the Congoes concluded that their fetishes were less harmful than the alien Portuguese.

Africans cannot be influenced by aliens, who, however Christian, seek to subvert their manhood. With the African at home, service to God and service to his fetich will not be yielded if manhood be the sacrifice.

He may be forced to accept a dogma or a religion, but will not receive either under such circumstances. Alien races can aid the progress of Christianity and civilization among Africans, but cannot control it with hope of ultimate success in Africa. Mr. Venn would have probably ranked, as the chief work of his official life, his careful and prolonged labors for the organization of native churches. All his measures converged to this point, the formation wherever the Gospel was proclaimed, of a native church, which should gradually be enfranchised from all supervision by a foreign body, and should become, in his phraseology, "self-supporting, self-governing, self-extending." He carefully discriminated between missionary work carried on by foreigners and Christianity acclimated and so become indigenous in a national church. The one was the means, the other the end; the one the scaffolding, the other the building it leaves behind when the scaffolding is removed; the one subject to constant changes and modifications, as fresh circumstances develop themselves, the other growing up to the measure of the stature of the perfect man, only changing by gradually putting away childish things and reliance on external help and control.

In the British colony of Sierra Leone opportunity is afforded to study native character, as at no other place with which I am acquainted. The representatives of not less than a hundred tribes may be seen here and of not a few races. Here one may see the stately and grave Mandingo, the diplomatic Soosoo, the frail but handsome Foulah, and the paragon of men, the magnificent Jollof, "his complexion free from any taint of Abyssinian blue or Nubian bronze, intensely, lustrously, magnificently black."

Of the foregoing races there has been no acceptance of anything of foreign civilization. These races represent a very high and unique type of Mohammedanism and Arabic training. They have adopted the religion of the Prophet and made it to conform to themselves. They have written their own commentaries on the sacred book. They are not controlled by the Arab, the Persian, or the Turk as to their conception of the Koran. Their women share in common with the men in the instructions of the masters. But there are two distinct races here, and some of each of them in Liberia, the Ebo and Arku races, among whom is displayed the highest type of English civilization, with their free, unhampered peculiarities and idiosyncrasies. These two races control and direct commercial interest in Sierra Leone, on the Gold coast and at Lagos, and have brought peace to war and order from confusion on the independent Negro nations of Abbeokuta.

Among these races, in religion are the Crowthers; in medical and surgical science, the Davises and Hortons; in jurisprudence, the Lewises and McCarthys; in pure scholarship, the Blydens, Coles, and Quakers; in the mercantile profession, the Boyles, Williams, Grants, and Sawyers. The time was when these two races were opposed to each other, but happily much of the tribal hatred has been destroyed by contact and education. These people are distinct in their bent of character. The Arku race is marked by a suavity of manner, a disposition to please, which borders on obsequiousness, and are industrious. They live upon a very little that they may save very much. They are never found to be improvident. The women make most affectionate wives, and have no peers in the world in their disposition to prove themselves helpmeets. It is said that the refusal by a husband to allow an Arku wife to help him, not infrequently causes marital difficulties. She prefers to trade than to remain indoors attending to her domestic affairs and babies. In complexion this race represents the average dark complexion of the American Negro.

The Ebo is a proud, daring race. They are always industrious, are fond of display, and in their hospitality are ostentatious. It may be asserted that there exists no evidence to show these people ever to have been pagan, in their home on the Niger or elsewhere. As a race they have never received either Christianity or Mohammedanism, but claim to believe sincerely in God. Those in the British colony have assimilated Christianity and some have attained to the highest culture and refinement. The first Negro graduate of Oxford was an Ebo. The most distinguished physician—Negro physician— living up to 1884 was Dr. Horton, an Ebo. The knowledge of reading and writing and ciphering in short, rudimentary training in this colony, has been very thorough. To Wilberforce and Venn be lasting honor and praise for their effective work in the British colonies of West Africa.

The entire coasts of this continent are surrounded by and permeated with a deadly malaria which makes Africa feared. In the future there will be cause for, and there will be much rejoicing that an Almighty wisdom has made the coasts generally alluvial, and has given a few broad and possibly navigable highways to the interior, the banks of which are charnel houses to aliens.

The aboriginal tribes and races subject to Liberia, excepting the American Liberians, are estimated at three-fourths of a million souls. The principal races here are Mandingos, Kru and Graybo and Bassa people, cognate races; Veys, Golas and Pesseys. My contact has been with these races in the civilized settlements, and in their own towns and villages. It would be a task to describe them with the accuracy their tribal and racial differences merit.

The Mandingos are a Mohammedan, proselytizing race, strictly sober, industrious, intellectual and sincere, serious men. Their women are handsome and models of chastity. The English explorer, Winwood Reed, in his

Savage Africa pays them this compliment reluctantly. Marriages rarely occur between women of this race and Christians or pagans. The Kru race, evidently a central African people, occupy that portion of country lying between grand Bassa and Cape Palmas, and are to be seen on every ship from Sierra Leone to Congo river. To west African commerce he is an indispensable factor, since European sailors cannot work the cargo of a ship south of nor in the port of Freetown. The race is divided into two classes, mariners and agriculturists, the latter being typical landsmen in ignorance of the sea. The sailor class, like their class among the Caucasians, are simple-hearted, improvident, and are devotedly attached to their families. Wherever found these men may be recognized, the identification being an India ink mark extending from the roots of the nose to the hair, and an arrow-shaped mark from the ear tending toward the center of the cheek. They have much cunning in their nature, are not wanting in courage, are marked for endurance and industry as laborers, but so far as training in books has been carried on among them, they have shown themselves possessed of ordinary intellectual ability.

To the Kru race the two Americas are chiefly indebted for the catching and embarking of Africans upon slave ships. It is currently reported and generally believed these people have never themselves been enslaved. The Spaniards, Portuguese, English, and American pirates, in the interest of the nefarious slave traffic, gave them immunity from capture and slavery for the invaluable service they rendered their bad cause. Strange as it may seem, they are said never to have held slaves, nor do they to-day hold slaves, and will not keep one as a slave in their household. A slave may be adopted in a Kru family, may intermarry with the race as a freeman, but not as a slave. Physically, they are a very superior race of men and women. The Greyboes resemble in appearance the Krues, with the exception of a lighter complexion, being a dark reddish brown, and are dissimilar in being more intellectual than the Krues. They have the scriptures, and other books of their history and traditions written in Roman characters in their own tongue. The guttural sound of the Dutch language is peculiar to both the Kru and Greybo languages. Intellectually, the Greyboes are a very remarkable people. The most eminent surgeon Liberia ever had was of this race; so also the first Hebrew scholar. They are a warrior race, powerful in stature, very brave, and marked for their courage, as the Americo-Liberian's experience attests. They have their own representatives in the Legislature. The Bassas are inferior to the Greyboes, and in some respects not the equals of the Krues. Notwithstanding this fact, they have produced soldiers of no mean order, and assimilate the Christian civilization about them as readily as the Americo-Liberian acquires their language.

In this matter I am reminded of the very great importance of the native languages as a valuable auxiliary in the spread and extension of civilization among African races. To use the terse language of his lordship, Bishop Crowther, "men think accurately in their own tongue."

The Golas as a race are courageous and intrepid, and kindly in their relation with the Americo-Liberian, preferring peace with them to war. The Pesseys, once a martial race, have by internal dissension and wars with other races, to an alarming extent lost their independence and many of that once noble race have been made captives to other peoples and slaves. As slaves they are highly valued, being indefatigable laborers, and therefore admired bondsmen by their masters. Their language has the softness and liquid sweetness of Italian, being a striking contrast to the harshness of the Kru and Greybo tongue.

Now I approach the consideration briefly of a people little known to the explorer of Central or Western Africa, though unquestionably a Central African people but destined to be, should they prove as numerous as supposed, one of the first races of the continent, the Veys. Complexionally, this race is black and brown, the women of which are distinguished for facial beauty and the symmetry of physical proportion, while the men are not wanting in elegance and strength of physique. They have grace in carriage, and in language there is a sweetness and harmony in utterance that reminds one of what music is. They have wonderful address, great tact, and the women possess the airs, graces and fineness which are attributed to the women of France.

The Veys do not display industry in manual labor to the extent of other races. They prefer those callings and employments which require the smallest amount of physical exertion. Notwithstanding this fact, there are blacksmiths, cloth weavers and skillful workmen in silver and gold, but the majority of them are mercantile in their tastes and pursuits, and are, therefore, traders.

This race is highly intellectual. As a semi-civilized people they claim the first importance among the West African and Negritian races. The acquired philological capability of the Veys is not traceable to any ulterior influences, but is from within. Domestic slavery exists among them, and their laws are not unlike those of ancient Rome and old Saxon enactments and customs. The children follow the condition of the mother. If the mother be a bondwoman, the issue is a slave. Marriage between slaves and free persons are prohibited, and where the prohibition is disregarded, the offender, the slave, is punished with death. Manumission is very rare among the slaves, and neither obedience or industry in peace nor heroism in war mitigates the condition of the slave. Once a slave, always a slave. The system in its operation is of a patriarchal character. A parallel; by reference to Stubb's Constitutional History of England, vol. I., page 44, we read of the ancient Saxons. Rudolph, the author of the Translation, Sancte Alexandri, writing about A.D. 1863, describes the Saxons of the early Frank Empire thus: —*—*—*— "Of the distinctions of race and nobility they are most tenaciously careful, they scarce ever (and here the writer quotes the Germania) allow themselves to be infected by any marriages with other or inferior races, and try to keep their nationality apart, sincere and unlike any other. Hence, the universal prevalence of one physical type. The race consists of four ranks of men, the noble, the free, the freedmen, and the servi. And it is by law established that no order shall; in contracting marriages, remove the landmarks of its own class, but noble must marry noble, freeman, freewoman; freedman, freed-woman; serf, handmaid: If any take a wife of different or higher rank than his own, he has to expiate the act with his life."

I should perhaps leave an impression which would be misleading as to Liberia and Africa unless I be more explicit. If you have observed, in any utterance of mine, anything about Africa which seems to possess in itself, or as to the races of that continent, a roseate hue, be pleased to remember that I have faintly, and with unartistic hand, shown you a part of this garden of the Lord and limned its inhabitants with the pencil and brush of an ama-teur; and I appeal to Mungo Park, the sainted Livingstone, Barth, Schwein-furth, Nachtigal, and I may risk Stanley in the rear of this galaxy of friends of Africa, for more accurate data and for larger and fuller experiences. But I may astound you when I say that Africa fears not the invasion of her shores by Europe and the rightful acquisition of her territory, and that no Negro who knows Africa regards the European's advent there as a menace to the progress and advancement of her races, except when they bring with them rum and fire-arms. I am pronouncedly, and have been since I first stepped upon the soil of my fatherland in 1878, an African colonizationist, but I am so in a strictly qualified sense, as is shown in the official statement made to my and your government—made from the United States Consulate-General, Monrovia under the date of February 21, 1883.

It may not be inopportune or out of place to say, in the interest of the prospective immigrant and in the interest of Liberia, that it is perhaps un-wise for persons to emigrate here simply for the purpose of being free and enjoying complete civil liberty and social equality. The State is young, and, though poor in developed resources, is vigorous in purpose and effort, and needy only of additional influences of civilization which are possessed by those who, at their homes, have displayed the ability of independent labor and proprietorship. That is to say, that the man needed as an immigrant here is one who, in his home, displays industry and fixedness of purpose suffi-cient to cause him to stick at work of some kind until he has earned and saved enough to purchase a comfortable home, is competent to control it and does control it, or a man who has entered upon a business and has self-denial enough to continue in it to the end of respectably supporting himself and family, or who has made himself a boost of some supporting trade—a man who is not directly dependent upon being a common servant, and who is not an ignorant laborer incapable of turning up something by his innate good sense and the God-given push within him.

Liberia possesses no large class of citizens who need or are able to em-ploy a servant class from a foreign country. Intelligent laborers are needed, not ignorant ones. The constitution of this Republic guarantees to each im-migrant so much cultivable land. The purpose of such grant is obvious; the improvement of it, the means of supporting one's self from the soil is the consideration for the gift, thereby winning from the forest and jungle valued lands capable of indefinite production, and winning from ignorance the native races by the pursuit of the arts of peace. Such results can be obtained alone through intelligent, persistent industry.

All agricultural labor, all coast labor, loading and unloading vessels, and fishing, all house service, are carried on, in general, by aborigines. Farm labor is worth from $2.50 to $4.00 per month, exclusive of housing and feeding. This is paid principally in goods, or one-half goods and the other half money. Where this labor is well fed, and treated well, it is honest and reliable—where these conditions are met there is no lack of it. The labor performed by the citizen class is farm proprietorship, trader, merchant, professional, and governmental. There is a minority of farm laborers of the civilized Liberian class.

A clear understanding of the conditions of labor here is important to that class of foreign Negroes who contemplate settlement here. The possession of a few hundred dollars, skill in labor, and executive ability, constitute a capital that cannot but secure a most comfortable living here with a probability of wealth.

Unless the Negro out of Africa goes to Africa seeking a home because he has none; goes of his own volition, with as correct a knowledge of Africa as may be obtained from the writings of trustworthy African travelers and explorers and missionaries, reinforced by race loyalty, and with greater confidence in himself and his race than in any alien self and alien race; goes from a sense of duty imposed by his Christian enlightenment, and not unprovided with ability and previous experience to organize and control labor, with as ample means as he would go with from the Atlantic coast of the United States to the Pacific slope for the purpose of engaging in business, he is wholly and entirely unsuited for Africa, and would impede by his presence not only the progress of Liberia (if he went thither), but any part of Africa by his unprofitable presence, and ought to be denied the right to expatriate himself.

If by anything that I have said you have been impressed with the fact that you are descendants of African races and as a consequence that you are a separate and distinct people from Caucasian races, and that the highest excellence to which an individual can attain must be to work according to the bent of his genius, and the other to work in harmony with God's design in his creation, on his race line; if I have impressed you at all with the wisdom or propriety of confiding in the highest Negro authorities and the best alien writings; for reliable data respecting our race in the fatherland, and thereby awakened in you an interest and sincere desire for the well being of Africa and her races, for our people, and for accurate information concerning that most ancient, and most mysterious of lands; then I feel conscious of having made a contribution of information not wholly valueless to my countrymen that may tend to modify and dissipate general ignorance of us and of our antecedents and their country; and I have done something toward awakening your dormant self-respect, and given you some conception of the dignity which attaches to Negro manhood, and created in you a preference for your race before all other races; and this sentiment, if produced, will place you *en rapport* with the Negroes in Africa, who have no conception of any land greater, more beautiful than their own; any men braver and manlier than themselves, any women better, lovelier, and handsomer than African women. Then you will retire from this place with a feeling of stimulus rather than of satiety, of unrest rather than of repose; then shall I retire from my effort to interest you in Africa in Africa, and Africa in America with satisfied pride in having performed something of duty as a Negro—clear in his conviction of the high destiny in reserve for Africa and its races, and of your duty to be loyal to the race, since true allegiance will make us sharers in that glory which the sacred writing declares shall come, when Ethiopia shall stretch forth her hand unto God.■

136 WE ARE STRUGGLING FOR EQUALITY

John Hope

Five months after Booker T. Washington had announced his policy of accommodation at the Atlanta Exposition, an important attack on this ideology by an African American was delivered by John Hope (1868–1936), one of the outstanding college presidents in American history. Hope delivered the blast at Washington in a speech before the black debating society of Nashville on George Washington's birthday, 1896.*

Hope was the son of James Hope, a Scot who came to America and established a cotton mill in Augusta, Georgia, in 1845. He moved to New York after selling his mill and became a wine importer. Here he met a former slave named Fannie, and after the Civil War, the couple returned to Augusta, where John Hope was born, the third of the couple's children. Until his father's death, John had a secure childhood, but when he was only eight years old, he witnessed the 1876 Hamburg, South Carolina, massacre, in which the black militiamen of that city were attacked and overwhelmed by an armed white mob, three hundred strong, who summarily executed a number of their captives. The massacre was followed by an armed reign of terror against the black community.

---

*For criticism of Washington's Atlanta Exposition speech by black Americans even before Hope expressed these views, *see* Philip S. Foner, ed., "Early Opposition to Washington's Ideas," *Journal of Negro History* 4 (October 1970), 343–47.

Hope attended school in the North and, after his father's death, worked for five years in a restaurant. With a loan from his brother, he studied at Worcester Academy, in Massachusetts, earning his way by serving meals and working in the summer as a waiter at hotels and resorts. From Worcester he went to Brown University, where he also faced financial hardships, and then taught at Atlanta Baptist College. Eventually Hope became president of Atlanta Baptist (later Morehouse College), and at Atlanta he became a close associate of W. E. B. Du Bois and other foes of Booker T. Washington.

Here is the concluding part of John Hope's speech, from the text presented in Ridgley Torrence, The Story of John Hope *(New York: Macmillan, 1948), 114–15.*

IF WE ARE NOT STRIVING for equality, in heaven's name for what are we living? I regard it as cowardly and dishonest for any of our colored men to tell white people that we are not struggling for equality. If money, education, and honesty will not bring to me as much privilege, as much equality as they bring to any American citizen, then they are to me a curse, and not a blessing. God forbid that we should get the implements with which to fashion our freedom, and then be too lazy or pusillanimous to fashion it. Let us not fool ourselves nor be fooled by others. If we cannot do what other free men do, then we are not free. Yes, my friends, I want equality. Nothing less. I want all that my God-given powers will enable me to get, then why not equality? Now, catch your breath, for I am going to use an adjective: I am going to say we demand social equality. In this republic we shall be less than free men, if we have a whit less than that which thrift, education and honor afford other free men. If equality, political, economic and social, the boon of other men in this great country of ours, of *ours,* then equality, political, economic and social, is what we demand. Why build a wall to keep me out? I am no wild beast, nor am I an unclean thing.

Rise, Brothers! Come, let us possess this land. Never say, "Let well enough alone." Cease to console yourselves with adages that numb the moral sense. Be discontented. Be dissatisfied. "Sweat and grunt" under present conditions. Be as restless as the tempestuous billows on the boundless sea. Let your discontent break mountain-high against the wall of prejudice, and swamp it to the very foundation. Then we shall not have to plead for justice nor on bended knee crave mercy; for we shall be men. Then and not until then will liberty in its highest sense be the boast of our Republic. . . . ■

137 THE AWAKENING OF THE AFRO-AMERICAN WOMAN

Victoria Earle Matthews

*Born in slavery in Fort Valley, Georgia, and largely self-educated, Victoria Earle Matthews (1861–1907) worked as a free-lance reporter and short story writer and as the editor of a collection of excerpts from the speeches of Booker T. Washington (*Black Belt Diamonds*, 1898). She was a leader in the black women's club movement and the anti-lynching campaigns of the early 1890s. But Matthews is best remembered for her social reform work in support of African American young women. Traveling through the South in 1896, Matthews was appalled at the condition and treatment of black women in employment and education. Following this trip and the death of her only child, she devoted herself to the moral and social uplift of girls and young women, both by publicizing their plight and by building institutions for their welfare.*

On July 11, 1897, Matthews addressed the annual convention of the International Society of Christian Endeavor in San Francisco. Established in 1881, the interdenominational Christian youth organization had grown to over one million members. Forty thousand, including thirty thousand young people and delegates from every state and several countries, attended the San Francisco gathering. According to the account of the San Francisco convention in Harper's Illustrated Weekly *of July 31, 1897, "there was no race line, no denominational line, no color line, no sectional line drawn" (766).*

Matthews speaks to the convention as one "to-day clothed in the garments of Christian womanhood," but who, like millions of other African American women, came out of the "horrible days of slavery." Emerging from a life in which "there was no attribute which had not been sullied," she reminds her listeners, she and others have struggled against all odds to build Christian homes and institutions. She appeals to the shared Christian principles and beliefs of her listeners to promote support for desegregation and other social reforms and services for African American women. In February 1897, six months before her speech to the Christian Endeavor convention, she had founded the White Rose Mission, which for more than eighty years provided settlement lodging and social services for homeless African American women, many of whom had migrated to New York from the South.

The text of Matthews's speech is published with the permission of the Yale Collection of American Literature, Beinecke Rare Book and Manuscript Library, at Yale University and was previously reprinted, with an introductory essay, in Shirley Wilson Logan, ed., With Pen and

Voice: A Critical Anthology of Nineteenth-Century American Women *(Carbondale: Southern Illinois University Press, 1995). For more information on Matthews and the White Rose Mission, see Floris Barnett Cash, "Radicals or Realists? African American Women and the Settlement House Spirit in New York City,"* Afro-Americans in New York Life and History *15 (1991), 7–17.*

The awakening to life of any of the forces of nature is the most mysterious as it is the sublimest of spectacles. Through all nature there runs a thread of life. We watch with equal interest and awe the transformation of the rosebud into the flower and the babe into manhood. The philosopher has well said that the element of life runs through all nature and links the destinies of earth with the destinies of the stars. This is a beautiful and ennobling thought; while it binds to earth it yet lifts us to heaven. It gives us strength in adversity, when the storms beat and the thunders peal forth their diapason and confusion reigns supreme everywhere; it tempers our joys with soberness when prosperity hedges us about as the dews of the morning hedge about with gladness the modest violet shyly concealed by the wayside. Life is the most mysterious as it is the most revealed force in nature. Death does not compare with it in these qualities, for there can be no death without life. It is from this point of view that we must regard the tremendous awakening of the Afro-American womanhood, during the past three decades from the double night of ages of slavery in which it was locked in intellectual and moral eclipse. It has been the awakening of a race from the nightmare of 250 years of self-effacement and debasement. It is not within the power of any one who has stood outside of Afro-American life to adequately estimate the extent of the effacement and debasement, and, therefore, of the gracious awakening which has quickened into life the slumbering forces and filled with hope and gladness the souls of millions of the womanhood of our land. To the God of love and tenderness and pity and justice we ascribe the fullness of our thanks and prayers for the transformation from the death of slavery to the life of freedom. All the more are we grateful to the moral and Christian forces of the world, the Christian statesmen and soldiers and scholars who were the divine instruments who made it possible for this womanhood to stand in this august presence to-day, this vast army laboring for the up-building of the Master's kingdom among men; for it is true as Longfellow said:

> *Were half the power that fills the world with terror,*
> *Were half the wealth bestowed on camps and courts,*
> *Given to redeem the human mind from error,*
> *There were no need of arsenals and forts.**

*From "The Arsenal at Springfield" (1846).

The auction block of brutality has been changed into the forum of reason, the slave mart has been replaced by the schoolroom and the church.

As I stand here to-day clothed in the garments of Christian womanhood, the horrible days of slavery, out of which I came, seem as a dream that is told, some horror incredible. Indeed, could they have been, and are not? They were; they are not; this is the sum and substance, the shame and the glory of the tale that I would tell, of the message that I would bring.

In the vast economy of nature, cycles of time are of small moment, years are as hours, and seconds bear but small relation to the problem, yet they are as the drops of rain that fall to earth and lodge in the fastnesses of the mountain from which our rivers are formed that feed the vast expanse of ocean. So in the history of a race lifting itself out of its original condition of helplessness, time is as necessary an element as is opportunity, in the assisting forces of humankind.

When we remember that the God who created all things is no respector of persons, that the black child is beloved of Him as the white child, we can more easily fix the responsibility that rests upon the Christian womanhood of the country to join with us in elevating the head, the heart and the soul of Afro-American womanhood. As the great Frederick Douglass once said, in order to measure the heights to which we have risen we must first measure the depths to which we were dragged. It is from this point of observation that we must regard the awakening of the Afro-American womanhood of the land. And what is this awakening? What is its distinguishing characteristics? It would seem superfluous to ask or to answer questions so obvious, but the lamentable truth is, that the womanhood of the United States, of the world, knows almost absolutely nothing of the hope and aspirations, of the joys and the sorrows, of the wrongs, and of the needs of the black women of this country, who came up out of the effacement and debasement of American slavery into the dazzling sunlight of freedom. My friends, call to mind the sensations of the prisoner of Chillon, as he walked out of the dungeon where the flower of his life had been spent, into the open air, and you will be able to appreciate in some sense our feelings in 1865,

> When the war drums throbbed no longer,
> And the battle flags were furled.

What a past was ours! There was no attribute of womanhood which had not been sullied—aye, which had not been despoiled in the crucible of slavery. Virtue, modesty, the joys of maternity, even hope of mortality, all those were the heritage of this womanhood when the voice of Lincoln and sword of Grant, as the expression of the Christian opinion of the land, bade them stand forth, without let or hindrance, as arbiters of their own persons and wills. They had no past to which they could appeal for anything. It had destroyed, more than in the men, all that a woman holds sacred, all that ennobles womanhood. She had but the future.

From such small beginnings she was compelled to construct a home.

She who had been an outcast, the caprice of brutal power and passion, who had been educated to believe that morality was an echo, and womanly modesty a name; she who had seen father and brother and child torn from her hurried away into everlasting separation—this creature was born to life in an hour and expected to create a home.

> Home, sweet home;
> Be it ever so humble,
> There's no place like home.

My friends, more, home is the noblest, the most sacred spot in a Christian nation. It is the foundation upon which nationality rests, the pride of the citizen and the glory of the Republic. This woman was expected to build a home for 4,500,000 people, of whom she was the decisive unit. No Spartan mother ever had a larger task imposed upon her shoulders; no Spartan mother ever acquitted herself more heroically than this Afro-American woman has done. She has done it almost without any assistance from her white sister; who, in too large a sense, has left her to work out her own destiny in fear and trembling. The color of the skin has been an almost insurmountable barrier between them, despite the beautiful lines of the gentle Cowper, that—

> Skin may differ,
> But affection
> Dwells in black and white the same.

I am not unmindful, however, of the Northern women who went into the South after the war as the missionary goes into the dark places of the world, and helped the Afro-American woman to lay the foundation of her home broad and deep in the Christian virtues. For years they did this in the schoolroom and their labors naturally had their reflex in the home life of their pupils.

Broadly speaking, my main statement holds, however, that these women, starting empty handed, were left to make Christian homes where a Christian citizenship should be nurtured. The marvel is not that they have succeeded, not that they are succeeding, but that they did not fail, *utterly fail.* I believe the God who brought them out of the Valley of the Shadow, who snatched them from the hand of the white rapist, the base slave master whose unacknowledged children are to be found in every hamlet of the Republic, guided these women, and guides them in the supreme work of building their Christian homes. The horrors of the past were forgotten in the joyous labor that presented itself. Even the ineffaceable wrongs of the past, while not forgotten, were forgiven in the spirit of the Master, who even forgave those who took His life.

If there had been no other awakening than this, if this woman who had stood upon the auction block possessed of no rights that a white man was bound to respect, and none which he did respect, if there had been no other awakening of the Afro-American woman than this, that she made a home for her race, an abiding place for husband, and son, and daughter, it would be glory enough to embalm her memory in song and story. As it is, it will be her sufficient monument through all time that out of nothing she created something, and that something the dearest, the sweetest, the strongest institution in Christian government.

But she has done more than this. The creation of a home is the central feature of her awakening, but around this are many other features which show her strong title to the countenance and respect of the sisterhood of the world. She has meekly taken her place by her husband, in the humble occupations of life as a bread winner, and by her labors and sacrifices has helped to rear and educate 50,000 young women, who are active instructors in the Christian churches of the land. In the building up of the Master's kingdom she has been and she is an active and a positive influence; indeed, in this field she has proven, as her white sister has proven, the truth of Napoleon Bonaparte's sententious but axiomatic truth, that "The hand that rocks the cradle rules the world." It is not too much to say that the 7,000,000 Afro-American church memberships would fall to pieces as a rope of sand if the active sympathy and support of the Afro-American women were withdrawn. It is demonstrable that these women who came out of slavery have done more than this. They have not only made Christian homes for their families, and educated 50,000 Sunday-school workers, but they have given to the State 25,000 educated school teachers, who are to-day the hope and inspiration of the whole race. The black women who came out of slavery in the past thirty years, have accomplished these tremendous results as farm-laborers and house servants, and they deserve the admiration of mankind for the glorious work that they have accomplished. In the past few years the educated daughters of these ex-slave women have aroused themselves to the necessity of systematic organization for their own protection, and for strengthening their race where they find it is weak, and to this end they have in the several States 243 regularly organized and officered clubs in the Afro-American women's National Association; there are besides hundreds of social clubs and temperance organizations working in their own way for a strong Christian womanhood. Indeed, the impulse of aspiration after the strong and the good in our civilization is manifest on all hands in our womanhood. It is all so grounded in Christian morality that we may safely conclude that it is built upon a rock and cannot be shaken by the fury of the storms.

The awakening of the Afro-American woman is one of the most promising facts in our national life. That she deserves the active sympathy and co-operation of all the female forces of the Republic, I think I have sufficiently shown. We need them. We have always needed them. We need them in the work of religion, of education, of temperance, of morality, of industrialism; and above all we need their assistance in combatting the public opinion and laws that degrade our womanhood because it is black and not white; for of a truth, and as a universal law, an injury to one woman is an injury to all women. As long as the affections are controlled by legislation in defiance of Christian law, making infamous the union of black and white, we shall have unions without the sanction of the law, and children without legal parentage, to the degradation of black womanhood and the disgrace of white manhood.* As one woman, as an Afro-American woman, I stand in this great Christian presence to-day and plead that the marriage and divorce laws be made uniform throughout the Republic, and that they shall not control, but legalize, the union of mutual affections. Until this shall have been done, Afro-American womanhood will have known no full and absolute awakening. As the laws now stand, they are the greatest demoralizing forces with which our womanhood has to contend. They serve as the protection of the white man, but they leave us defenseless, indeed. I ask the Christian womanhood of this great organized Army of Christ, to lend us their active co-operation in coercing the lawmakers of the land in throwing around our womanhood the equal protection of the State to which it is entitled. A slave regulation should not be allowed to prevail in a free government. A barbarous injustice should not receive the sanction of a Christian nation. The stronger forces of society should scorn to crush to earth one of the weakest forces.

Next to these degrading marriage and divorce laws which prevail in two [sic] many States of the Republic, the full awakening of the Afro-American woman to her rightful position in society, are the separate car regulations which prevail in most of the states of the South. They were conceived in injustice; they are executed with extraordinary cowardice. Their entire operation tends to degrade Afro-American womanhood. None who are familiar with their operation will dispute this statement of facts. From this exalted forum, and in the name of the large army of Afro-American women, I appeal to the Christian sentiment which dominates this organization, to assist us in righting the wrongs growing out of these regulations, to the end that our womanhood may be sustained in its dignity and protected in its weakness, and the heavenly Father, who had declared, "righteousness exalteth a nation, but sin is a reproach to any people," will give His benediction to the laws made just.

I am moved here further to invoke your patience and sympathy in the efforts of our awakening womanhood to care for the aged and infirm, for the orphan and outcast; for the reformation of the penal institutions of the Southern States, for the separation of male and female convicts, and above all for the establishment of juvenile reformatories [in] those States for both races, to the end that the shame of it may be removed that children of tender age should be herded with hardened criminals from whose life all of moral sensibility has vanished forever.

*Thirty-eight states prohibited intermarriage in the nineteenth century. In 1951, twenty-nine still had such statutes, and it was not until 1967 that the U.S. Supreme Court struck them down. See Derrick A. Bell, *Race, Racism, and American Law* (Boston: Little Brown, 1980).

I feel moved to speak here in this wise for a whole race of women whose rise or fall, whose happiness or sorrow, whose degradation or exaltation are the concern of Christian men and women everywhere. I feel moved to say in conclusion that in all Christian and temperance work, in all that lifts humanity from its fallen condition to a more perfect resemblance of Him in whose image it was made, in all that goes to make our common humanity stronger and better and more beautiful; the Afro-American women of the Republic will "do their duty as God shall give them light to do it." ∎

138 IN UNION THERE IS STRENGTH

Mary Church Terrell

Born in Memphis in 1863 and an activist until her death in 1954, Mary Eliza Church Terrell was a living link between the era of the Emancipation Proclamation and the modern civil rights movement. She was an internationally acclaimed speaker and writer, a leader in the national women's club movement, and a powerful advocate for women's suffrage, desegregation, and social justice.

She graduated from Oberlin College in 1884, having completed the "gentleman's course" of classical studies. She accepted a position on the faculty of Wilberforce College in Ohio the following year, then moved to Washington, D.C., to teach in the Latin department of the Colored High School. She received an M.A. degree from Oberlin in 1888, then toured Europe for two years on a trip funded by her father, Robert Reed Church, reputed to be the wealthiest African American in the South. Upon her return to the United States, Mary Church married Robert Heberton Terrell, a graduate of Harvard University and Howard Law School who taught at Washington's M Street High School.

She became active in public politics after the 1892 lynching of her Memphis friend Tom Moss, the grocery store owner whose murder by white competitors was described by Ida B. Wells in her famous 1893 address, "Lynch Law in All Its Phases." Terrell and Frederick Douglass, whom she had befriended while at Oberlin, met with President Benjamin Harrison but to no avail. In a burst of political activity, Terrell became active in the black women's club movement, assuming the presidency of the Colored Women's League in 1892. That same year, she became the first African American woman president of Washington's prestigious Bethel Literary and Historical Association. From 1895 to 1911, she served on the District of Columbia School Board and battled against the inequities fostered by the city's segregated system.

Terrell became a professional lecturer for the Eastern Lyceum in the 1890s and for the next three decades delivered speeches throughout the United States and Europe. Terrell memorized her speeches and used no notes during her presentations. Fluent in several languages, she delivered an address in German to the 1904 Berlin International Congress of Women. She achieved great fame as a speaker of erudition and moral courage.

Mary Church Terrell wrote in her 1952 history of the women's club movement: "The first and real reason that our women began to use clubs as a means of improving their own condition and that of their race is that they are PROGRESSIVE." When an umbrella organization, the National Association of Colored Women (NACW), was formed in 1896, Terrell was elected its first president. She was reelected to two additional terms, then named honorary president for life. The NACW became a vital force in the struggle for the rights and recognition of black women. The organization's motto, "Lifting As We Climb," became a constant theme of Terrell's oratory.

In her first presidential address to the NACW, delivered in Nashville on September 15, 1897, Terrell makes a stirring plea for unity, activism, and race pride. Seventy-three delegates from twenty-five states attended the Nashville meeting. The text of the speech appears in Beverly Eliza Jones, Quest For Equality: The Life and Writings of Mary Eliza Church Terrell, 1863–1954 *(Brooklyn, N.Y.: Carlson, 1990), 133–38, and is reproduced from the original manuscript in the Library of Congress.*

In Union there is strength is a truism that has been acted upon by Jew and Gentile, by Greek and Barbarian, by all classes and conditions alike from the creation of the universe to the present day. It did not take long for men to learn that by combining their strength, a greater amount of work could be accomplished with less effort in a shorter time. Upon this principle of union, governments have been founded and states built. Our own republic teaches the same lesson. Force a single one of the states of the United States to stand alone, and it becomes insignificant, feeble, and a prey to the rapacity of every petty power seeking to enlarge its territory and increase its wealth. But form a republic of United States, and it becomes one of the great nations of the earth, strong in its might.

Acting upon this principle of concentration and union have the colored women of the United States banded themselves together to fulfill a mission to which they feel peculiarly adapted and especially called. We have become *National*, because from the Atlantic to the Pacific, from Maine to the Gulf, we wish to set in motion influences that shall stop the ravages made by practices that sap our strength and preclude the possibility of advancement which under other circumstances could easily be made. We call ourselves an

Association to signify that we have joined hands one with the other to work together in a common cause. We proclaim to the world that the women of our race have become partners in the great firm of progress and reform. We denominate ourselves colored, not because we are narrow, and wish to lay special emphasis on the color of the skin, for which no one is responsible, which of itself is no proof of an individual's virtue nor of his vice, which neither is a stamp, neither of one's intelligence nor of ignorance, but we refer to the fact that this is an association of colored women, because our peculiar status in this country at the present time seems to demand that we stand by ourselves in the special work for which we have organized. For this reason it was thought best to invite the attention of the world to the fact that colored women feel their responsibility as a unit, and together have clasped hands to assume it.

Special stress has been laid upon the fact that our association is composed of women, not because we wish to deny rights and privileges to our brothers in imitation of the example they have set for us so many years, but because the work which we hope to accomplish can be done better, by the mothers, wives, daughters, and sisters of our race than by the fathers, husbands, brothers, and sons. The crying need of our organization of colored women is questioned by no one conversant with our peculiar trials and perplexities, and acquainted with the almost insurmountable obstacles in our path to those attainments and acquisitions to which it is the right and privilege of every member of every race to aspire.

It is not because we are discouraged at the progress made by our people that we have uttered the cry of alarm which has called together this band of earnest women assembled here tonight. In the unprecedented advancement made by the Negro since his emancipation, we take great pride and extract therefore both courage and hope. From a condition of dense ignorance. But thirty years ago, we have advanced so far in the realm of knowledge and letters as to have produced scholars and authors of repute. Though penniless as a race a short while ago, we have among us today a few men of wealth and multitudes who own their homes and make comfortable livings. We therefore challenge any other race to present a record more creditable and show a progress more wonderful than that made by the ex-slaves of the United States and that too in the face of prejudice, proscription, and persecution against which no other people has ever had to contend in the history of the world. And yet while rejoicing in our steady march, onward and upward, to the best and highest things of life, we are nevertheless painfully mindful of our weaknesses and defects [in] which we know the Negro is no worse than other races equally poor, equally ignorant, and equally oppressed, we would nevertheless see him lay aside the sins that do so easily beset him, and come forth clothed in all these attributes of mind and grace of character that claims the real man. To accomplish this end through the simplest, swiftest, surest methods, the colored women have organized themselves into this Association, whose power for good, let us hope, will be as enduring as it is unlimited.

Believing that it is only through the home that a people can become really good and truly great, the N.A.C.W. shall enter that sacred domain to inculcate right principles of living and correct false views of life. Homes, more homes, purer homes, better homes, is the text upon which our sermons to the masses must be preached. So long as the majority of people call that place home in which the air is foul, the manners bad and the morals worse, just so long is this so called home a menace to health, a breeder of vice, and the abode of crime. Not alone upon the inmates of these hovels are the awful consequences of their filth and immorality visited, but upon the heads of those who sit calmly by and make no effort to stem the tide of disease and vice will vengeance as surely fall.

The colored youth is vicious we are told, and statistics showing the multitudes of our boys and girls who fill the penitentiaries and crowd the jails appall and discourage us. Side by side with these facts and figures of crime, I would have presented and pictured the miserable hovels from which these youthful criminals come. Crowded into alleys, many of them the haunts of vice, few if any of them in a proper sanitary condition, most of them fatal to mental and moral growth, and destructive of healthful physical development as well, thousands of our children have a wretched heritage indeed. It is, therefore, into the home, sisters of the Association, that we must go, filled with all the zeal and charity which such a mission demands. To the children of the race we owe, as women, a debt which can never be paid, until herculean efforts are made to rescue them from evil and shame for which they are in no way responsible. Listen to the cry of the children, my sisters. Upon you they depend for the light of knowledge, and the blessing of a good example. As an organization of women, surely nothing can be nearer our hearts than the children, many of whose lives so sad and dark we might brighten and bless. It is kindergartens we need. Free kindergartens in every city and hamlet of this broad land we must have, if the children are to receive from us what it is our duty to give.

The more unfavorable the environments of children, the more necessary is it that steps be taken to counteract the hateful influences upon innocent victims. How imperative is it then that we inculcate correct principles, and set good examples for our own youth whose little feet will have so many thorny paths of prejudice, temptation, and injustice to tread.

Make a visit to the settlements of colored people who in many cities are relegated to the most noisome sections permitted by the municipal government, and behold the miles of inhumanity that infest them. Here are our little ones, the future representatives of the race, fairly drinking in the permissible example of their elders, coming in contact with nothing but ignorance and vice, till at the age of six evil habits are formed that no amount of civilizing and christianizing can ever completely break. As long as the evil nature alone is encouraged to develop, while the higher, nobler qualities in little ones are dwarfed and deadened by the very atmosphere which they breathe, the negligent, pitiless public is responsible for the results and is partner of their crimes.

Let the women of the National Association see to it that the little strays of the alleys come in contact with intelligence and virtue, at least a few times a week, that the noble aspirations with which they are born may not be entirely throttled by the evil influences which these poor little ones are powerless to escape. The establishment of free kindergartens! You exclaim . . . Where is the money coming from? How can we do it? This charity you advocate though beautiful in theory is nevertheless impossible of attainment. Let the women of the race once be thoroughly aroused to their duty to the children, let them be consumed with desire to save them from lives of degradation and shame, and the establishment of free kindergartens for the poor will become a living, breathing, saving reality at no distant day.

What movement looking toward the reformation and regeneration of mankind was ever proposed that did not instantly assume formidable proportions to the fainthearted. But how soon obstacles that have once appeared insuperable dwindle into nothingness, after the shoulder is put to the wheel, and united effort determines to remove them! In every organization of the Association let committees be appointed whose special mission it will be to do for the little strays of the alleys what is not done by their mothers, who in many instances fall far short of their duty, not because they are vicious and depraved, but because they are ignorant and poor.

Through mother meetings which have been in the past year and will be in the future a special feature of the Association, much useful information in everything pertaining to the home will be disseminated. Object lessons in the best way to sweep, to dust, to cook and to wash should be given by women who have made a special study of the art and science of housekeeping. How to clothe children neatly, how to make, and especially how to mend garments, how to manage their households economically, what food is the most nutritious and best for the money, how to ventilate as thoroughly as possible the dingy stuffy quarters which the majority are forced to inhabit, all these are subjects on which the women of the masses need more knowledge. Let us teach mothers of families how to save wisely. Let us have heart to heart talks with our women that we may strike at the root of evil.

If the women of the dominant race with all the centuries of education, refinement, and culture back of them, with all their wealth of opportunity ever present with them, if these women felt a responsibility to call a Mother's Congress that they might be ever enlightened as to the best methods of rearing children and conducting their homes, how much more do the women of our race from whom the shackles of slavery have just fallen need information on the same subjects? Let us have Mother Congresses in every community in which our women can be counseled. The necessity of increasing the self-respect of our children is important. Let the reckless, ill-advised, and oftentimes brutal methods of punishing children be everywhere condemned. Let us teach our mothers that by punishing children inhumanely, they destroy their pride, crush their spirit and convert them into hardened culprits—whom it will be impossible later on to reach or touch in anyway at all. More than any other race at present in this country, we should strive to implant feelings of self-respect and pride in our children, whose spirits are crushed and whose hearts saddened enough by indignities from which as victims of an unreasonable cruel prejudice it is impossible to shield them. Let it be the duty of every friend of the race to teach children who are humiliated on learning that they are descendants of slaves that the majority of races on the earth have at some time in their history been subjects to another. This knowledge of humiliation will be important when we are victims of racism.

Let us not only preach, but practice race unity, race pride, reverence and respect for those capable of leading and advising us. Let the youth of the race be impressed about the dignity of labor and inspired with a desire to work. Let us do nothing to handicap children in the desperate struggle for existence in which their unfortunate condition in this country forces them to engage. Let us purify the atmosphere of our homes till it becomes so sweet that those who dwell in them carry on a great work of reform. That we have no money to help the needy and poor, I reply, that having hearts, generous natures, willing feet, and helpful hands can without the token of a single penny, work miracles in the name of humanity and right.

Money we need, money we must have to accomplish much which we hope to effect. But it is not by powerful armies and the outlays of vast fortunes that the greatest revolutions are wrought and the most enduring reforms inaugurated. It is by the silent, though powerful force of individual influences thrown on the side of right, it is by arduous persistence and effort to keep those with whom we come in daily contact, to enlighten the heathen at our door, to create wholesome public sentiment in the communities in which we live, that the heaviest blows are struck for virtue and right.

Let us not only preach, but practice race unity, race pride, reverence, and respect for those capable of leading and advising us. Let the youth of the race be impressed about the dignity of labor and inspired with a desire to work. Let us do nothing to handicap children in the desperate struggle for existence in which their unfortunate condition in this country forces them to engage. Let us purify the atmosphere of our homes till it become so sweet that those who dwell in them will have a heritage more precious than great, more to be desired than silver or gold.■

THE ATTITUDE OF
THE AMERICAN MIND TOWARD
THE NEGRO INTELLECT

Alexander Crummell

In the last years of the nineteenth century, works of "scientific racism" purporting to deny the possibility of intellectuality among black people were used to support discriminatory policies and practices. In response, prominent African American intellectuals, led by Alexander Crummell, established the American Negro Academy in 1897 and under its auspices produced a series of important scholarly publications.

Alexander Crummell (1819–1898) was a distinguished scholar, missionary, and Pan-Africanist. Born in New York City, he attended the African Free School in Manhattan and Canal Street High School, where he studied under Theodore S. Wright and Peter Williams. He later attended the abolitionist-run Oneida Institute in Whitesboro, New York, and graduated in 1839. Rejected from New York's General Theological Seminary because of his color, Crummell studied privately with Episcopal clergy. He was ordained in 1844.

Crummell became a leader of the antislavery and black convention movements. From 1848 to 1853, Crummell lectured and studied in England. He graduated from Queen's College, Cambridge, in 1853, became a missionary and citizen of Liberia, and accepted an appointment to the faculty of Liberia College in Monrovia. Working under the auspices of the American Colonization Society, he made several trips to the United States in efforts to persuade black Americans to emigrate. But as a political opponent of the color caste system that excluded native Africans from institutional power in Liberia, Crummell himself was forced to leave the country in 1872 and returned to the United States.

Crummell was the senior African American priest in the Episcopal Church and founded and ministered to St. Luke's Church in Washington, D.C. He became a popular lecturer on college campuses, stressing the social responsibilities of educated blacks as racial leaders. While advocating a system of trade schools for most African Americans, Crummell strove to produce a class of educated black leaders who would serve as "scholar-philanthropists." From 1895 to 1897, he taught at Howard University. In the last year of his life, he helped found the American Negro Academy and, as its president, supported its efforts to sponsor and promote black scholarship and to publicize the responses of black intellectuals to racist materials that passed as scholarship. Other officers included vice presidents W. E. B. Du Bois and William Saunders Scarborough and, as treasurer, Reverend Francis J. Grimke. On December 28, 1897, Crum-

mell presented the annual address to the academy, which was entitled "The Attitude of the American Mind Toward the Negro Intellect," a topic among the basic concerns of the Academy. In it, Crummell condemns the efforts of Washington and others to limit black education to "mere industrialism" and uses the accomplishments of black intellectuals to refute widespread "scientific" claims of racial inferiority.

Crummell had a profound influence on Du Bois, whose tribute to Crummell in The Souls of Black Folk *explains that when he first heard him speak, "instinctively I bowed before this man, as one bows before the prophets of the world." "In another age," Du Bois writes, "he might have sat among the elders of the land in purple-bordered toga; in another country mothers might have sung him to the cradles."*

Further discussion of Crummell and his address to the academy appears in Henry Louis Gates, Jr., "Talking Black," in Christopher Ricks and Leonard Michaels, eds., The State of the Language *(Berkeley: University of California Press, 1990); and Alfred A. Moss, Jr.,* The American Negro Academy: Voice of the Talented Tenth *(Baton Rouge: Louisiana State University Press, 1981). The transcript of Crummell's speech appears in the* Occasional Papers of the American Negro Academy, No. 3 *(Washington, D.C., 1898). Most of the footnotes included with the speech are Crummell's own, as noted.*

For the first time in the history of this nation the colored people of America have undertaken the difficult task, of stimulating and fostering the genius of their race as a distinct and definite purpose. Other and many gatherings have been made, during our own two and a half centuries' residence on this continent, for educational purposes; but ours is the first which endeavors to rise up to the plane of culture.

For my own part I have no misgivings either with respect to the legitimacy, the timeliness, or the prospective success of our venture. The race in the brief period of a generation, has been so fruitful in intellectual product, that the time has come for a coalescence of powers, and for reciprocity alike in effort and appreciation. I congratulate you, therefore, on this your first anniversary. To me it is, I confess, a matter of rejoicing that we have, as a people, reached a point where we have a class of men who will come together for purposes, so pure, so elevating, so beneficent, as the cultivation of mind, with the view of meeting the uses and the needs of our benighted people.

I feel that if this meeting were the end of this Academy; if I could see that it would die this very day, I would nevertheless, cry out—"All hail!" even if I had to join in with the salutation—"farewell forever!" For, first of all, you have done, during the year, that which was never done so completely before,—a work which has already told upon the American mind; and next you have awakened in the Race an ambition which, in some form, is sure to reproduce both mental and artistic organization in the future.

The cultured classes of our country have never interested themselves to stimulate the desires or aspirations of the mind of our race. They have left us terribly alone. Such stimulation, must, therefore, in the very nature of things, come from ourselves.

Let us state here a simple, personal incident, which will well serve to illustrate a history.

I entered, sometime ago, the parlor of a distinguished southern clergyman. A kinsman was standing at his mantel, writing. The clergyman spoke to his relative—"Cousin, let me introduce to you the Rev. C., a clergyman of our Church." His cousin turned and looked down at me; but as soon as he saw my black face, he turned away with disgust, and paid no more attention to me than if I were a dog.

Now, this porcine gentleman, would have been perfectly courteous, if I had gone into this parlor as a cook, or a waiter, or a bootblack. But my profession, as a clergyman, suggested the idea of letters and cultivation; and the contemptible snob at once forgot his manners, and put aside the common decency of his class.

Now, in this, you can see the attitude of the American mind toward the Negro intellect. A reference to this attitude seems necessary, if we would take in, properly, the present condition of Negro culture.

It presents a most singular phenomenon. Here was a people laden with the spoils of the centuries, bringing with them into this new land the culture of great empires; and, withal, claiming the exalted name and grand heritage of Christians. By their own voluntary act they placed right beside them a large population of another race of people, seized as captives, and brought to their plantations from a distant continent. This other race was an unlettered, unenlightened, and a pagan people.

What was the attitude taken by this master race toward their benighted bondsmen? It was not simply that of indifference or neglect. There was nothing negative about it.

They began, at the first, a systematic ignoring of the fact of intellect in this abased people. They undertook the process of darkening their minds.

"Put out the light, and then, put out the light!" was their cry for centuries. Paganizing themselves, they sought a deeper paganizing of their serfs than the original paganism that these had brought from Africa. There was no legal artifice conceivable which was not resorted to, to blindfold their souls from the light of letters; and the church, in not a few cases, was the prime offender.*

---

*Baptism, for well nigh a century, was denied Negro slaves in the colonies, for fear it carried emancipation with it. Legislation on Education began at a subsequent date. In 1740 it was enacted in South Carolina: "Whereas, the having slaves taught to write suffering them to be employed in writing, may be attended with great inconvenience. Be it enacted, That all and every person or persons whatsoever who shall hereafter teach or cause any slave or slaves to be taught to write, or shall use or employ any slave as a Scribe in any manner of writing, hereafter taught to write; every such person or persons shall however, for every such offense, forfeit the sum of £, 100 current money." The next step, in South Carolina, was aimed against mental instruction of every kind, in reading and

Then the legislatures of the several states enacted laws and Statutes, closing the pages of every book printed to the eyes of Negroes; barring the doors of every school-room against them! And this was the systematized method of the intellect of the South, to stamp out the brains of the Negro!

It was done, too, with the knowledge that the Negro had brain power. There was *then*, no denial that the Negro had intellect. That denial was an after thought. Besides, legislatures never pass laws forbidding the education of pigs, dogs, and horses. They pass such laws against the intellect of *men*.

However, there was then, at the very beginning of the slave trade, everywhere, in Europe, the glintings forth of talent in great Negro geniuses,—in Spain, and Portugal, in France and Holland and England;* and Phillis Wheatley and Banneker and Chavis and Peters, were in evidence on American soil.

It is manifest, therefore, that the objective point in all this legislation was INTELLECT,—the intellect of the Negro! It was an effort to becloud and stamp out the intellect of the Negro!

The *first* phase of this attitude reached over from about 1700 to 1820:— and as the result, almost Egyptian darkness fell upon the mind of the race, throughout the whole land.

Following came a more infamous policy. It was the denial of intellectuality in the Negro; the assertion that he was not a human being, that he did not belong to the human race. This covered the period from 1820 to 1835, when Gliddon and Nott and others, published their so-called physiological work, to prove that the Negro was of a different species from the white man.

A distinguished illustration of this ignoble sentiment can be given. In the year 1833 or 4 the speaker was an errand boy in the Anti-slavery office in New York City.

On a certain occasion he heard a conversation between the Secretary and two eminent lawyers from Boston,—Samuel E. Sewell and David Lee Child. They had been to Washington on some legal business. While at the Capitol they happened to dine in the company of the great John C. Calhoun, then senator from South Carolina. It was a period of great ferment upon the ques-

---

writing. A similar law was passed in Savannah, Georgia. In 1711, in the Colony of Maryland, a special enactment was passed to bar freedom by baptism and in 1715, in South Carolina! See *"Stroud's Slave Laws."* [Speaker's note.]

*At the time when France was on the eve of plunging deeply into the slave trade and of ruining her colonies by the curse of Slavery, the ABBE GREGOIRE stept forth in vindication of the Negro, and published his celebrated work—"The Literature of Negroes." In this work he gives the names and narrates the achievements of the distinguished Negroes, writers, scholars, painters, philosophers, priests and Roman prelates, in Spain, Portugal, France, England, Holland, Italy and Turkey who had risen to eminence in the 15th century. Not long after BLUMENBACH declared that "entire and large provinces of Europe might be named, in which it would be difficult to meet with such good writers, poets, philosophers, and correspondents of the French Academy; and that moreover there is no savage people, who have distinguished themselves by such examples of perfectibility and capacity for scientific cultivation; and consequently that one can approach more nearly to the polished nations of the globe than the Negro." [Speaker's note.]

tion of Slavery, States' Rights, and Nullification; and consequently the Negro was the topic of conversation at the table. One of the utterances of Mr. Calhoun was to this effect—"That if he could find a Negro who knew the Greek syntax, he would then believe that the Negro was a human being and should be treated as a man."*

Just think of the crude asininity of even a great man! Mr. Calhoun went to "Yale" to study the Greek Syntax, and graduated there. His son went to Yale to study the Greek syntax, and graduated there. His grandson, in recent years, went to Yale, to learn the Greek Syntax, and graduated there. School and Colleges were necessary for the Calhouns, and all other white men to learn the Greek syntax.

And yet this great man knew that there was not a school, nor a college in which a black boy could learn his A, B, C's. He knew that the law in all the Southern States forbade Negro instruction under the severest penalties. How then was the Negro to learn the Greek Syntax? How then was he to evidence to Mr. Calhoun his human nature? Why, it is manifest that Mr. Calhoun expected the Greek syntax to grow in *Negro brains*, by spontaneous generation!

Mr. Calhoun was then, as much as any other American, an exponent of the nation's mind upon his point. Antagonistic as they were upon *other* subjects, upon the rejection of the Negro intellect they were a unit. And this, measurably, is the attitude of the American mind today: —measurably, I say, for thanks to the Almighty, it is not universally so.

There has always been a school of philanthropists in this land who have always recognized mind in the Negro; and while recognizing the limitations which *individual* capacity demanded, claimed that for the RACE, there was no such thing possible for its elevation save the widest, largest, highest, improvement. Such were our friends and patrons in New England in New York, Pennsylvania, a few among the Scotch Presbyterians and the "Friends" in grand old North Carolina; a great company among the Congregationalists of the East, nobly represented down to the present, by the "American Missionary Society," which tolerates no stint for the Negro intellect in its grand solicitudes. But these were exceptional.

Down to the year 1825, I know of no Academy or College which would open its doors to a Negro. In the South it was a matter of absolute legal disability. In the North, it was the ostracism of universal caste-sentiment. The theological schools of the land, and of all names, shut their doors against the black man. An eminent friend of mine, the noble, fervent, gentlemanly Rev. Theodore S. Wright, then a Presbyterian licentiate, was taking private lessons in theology, at Princeton; and for this offense was kicked out of one of its halls.

In the year 1832 Miss Prudence Crandall opened a private school for the

*As his audience was well aware, Crummell himself had mastered Greek syntax at Cambridge, as had many others present, including Vice President W. S. Scarborough, who had authored a leading college textbook in Greek used at Yale and other schools.

education of colored girls; and it set the whole State of Connecticut in a flame. Miss Crandall was mobbed, and the school was broken up.

The year following, the trustees of Canaan Academy in New Hampshire opened its doors to Negro youths; and this act set the people of that state on fire. The farmers of the region assembled with 90 yoke of oxen, dragged the Academy into a swamp, and a few weeks afterward drove the black youths from the town.

These instances will suffice. They evidence the general statement, i.e. that the American mind has refused to foster and to cultivate the Negro intellect. Join to this a kindred fact, of which there is the fullest evidence. Impelled, at times, by pity, a modicum of schooling and training has been given the Negro; but even this, almost universally, with reluctance, with cold criticism, with microscopic scrutiny, with icy reservation, and at times, with ludicrous limitations.

Cheapness characterizes almost all the dominations of the American people to the Negro:—Cheapness, in all the past, has been the regimen provided for the Negro in every line of his intellectual, as well as his lower life. And so, cheapness is to be the rule in the future, as well for his higher, as for his lower life:—cheap wages and cheap food, cheap and rotten huts; cheap and dilapidated schools; cheap and stinted weeks of schooling; cheap meeting houses for worship; cheap and ignorant ministers; cheap theological training; and now, cheap learning, culture and civilization!

Noble exceptions are found in the grand literary circles in which Mr. Howells moves—manifest in his generous editing of our own Paul Dunbar's poems. But this generosity is not general, even in the world of American letters.

You can easily see this in the attempt, now-a-days, to side-track the Negro intellect, and to place it under limitations never laid upon any other class.

The elevation of the Negro has been a moot question for a generation past. But even to-day what do we find the general reliance of the American mind in determining this question? Almost universally the resort is to material agencies! The ordinary, and sometimes the *extraordinary* American is unable to see that the struggle of a degraded people for elevation is, in its very nature, a warfare, and that its main weapon is the cultivated and scientific mind.

Ask the great men of the land how this Negro problem is to be solved, and then listen to the answers that come from divers classes of our white fellow-citizens. The merchants and traders of our great cities tell us—"The Negro must be taught to work;" and they will pour out their moneys by thousands to train him to toil. The clergy in large numbers, cry out—"Industrialism is the only hope of the Negro;" for this is the bed-rock, in their opinion, of Negro evangelization! "Send him to Manual Labor Schools," cries out another set of philanthropists. "Hic haec, hoc," is going to prove the ruin of the Negro" says the Rev. Steele, an erudite Southern Savan. "You must begin at the bottom with the Negro," says another eminent authority—as though the Negro had been living in the clouds, and had never reached the bottom. Says the Honorable George T. Barnes, of Georgia—"The kind of education the Negro should receive should not be very refined nor classical, but adapted to his present condition:" As though there is to be no future for the Negro.

And so you see that even now, late in the 19th century, in this land of learning and science, the creed is—"Thus far and no farther", i.e. for the American black man.

One would suppose from the universal demand for the mere industrialism for this race of ours, that the Negro had been going daily to dinner parties, eating terrapin and indulging in champagne; and returning home at night, sleeping on beds of eiderdown; breakfasting in the morning in his bed, and then having his valet to clothe him daily in purple and fine linen—all these 250 years of his sojourn in this land. And then, just now, the American people, tired of all this Negro luxury, was calling him, for the first time, to blister his hands with the hoe, and to learn to supply his needs by sweatful toil in the cotton fields.

Listen a moment, to the wisdom of a great theologian, and withal as great philanthropist, the Rev. Dr. Wayland, of Philadelphia. Speaking, not long since, of the "Higher Education" of the colored people of the South, he said "that this subject concerned about 8,000,000 of our fellow-citizens, among whom are probably 1,500,000 voters. The education suited to these people is that which should be suited to white people under the same circumstances. These people are bearing the impress which was left on them by two centuries of slavery and several centuries of barbarism. This education must begin at the bottom. It must first of all produce the power of self-support to assist them to better their condition. It should teach them good citizenship and should build them up morally. It should be, first, a good English education. They should be imbued with the knowledge of the Bible. They should have an industrial education. An industrial education leads to self-support and to the elevation of their condition. Industry is itself largely an education, intellectually and morally, and, above all, an education of character. Thus we should make these people self-dependent. This education will do away with pupils being taught Latin and Greek, while they do not know the rudiments of English."

Just notice the cautious, restrictive, limiting nature of this advice! Observe the lack of largeness, freedom and generosity in it. Dr. Wayland, I am sure, has never specialized just such a regimen for the poor Italians, Hungarians or Irish, who swarm, in lowly degradation, in immigrant ships to our shores. No! for them he wants, all Americans want, the widest, largest culture of the land; the instant opening, not simply of the common schools; and then an easy passage to the bar, the legislature, and even the judgeships of the nation. And they oft times get there.

But how different the policy with the Negro. *He* must have "an education which begins at the bottom." "He should have an industrial education," &c. His education must, first of all, produce the power of self-support, &c.

Now, all this thought of Dr. Wayland is all true. But, my friends, it is all false, too; and for the simple reason that it is only half truth. Dr. Wayland seems unable to rise above the plane of burden-bearing for the Negro. He seems unable to gauge the idea of the Negro becoming a thinker. He seems to forget that a race of thoughtless toilers are destined to be forever a race of senseless *boys*; for only beings who think are men.

How pitiable it is to see a great good man be-fuddled by a half truth. For to allege "Industrialism" to be the grand agency in the elevation of a race of already degraded labourers, is as much a mere platitude as to say, "they must eat and drink and sleep;" for man cannot live without these habits. But they never civilize man; and *civilization* is the objective point in the movement for Negro elevation. Labor, just like eating and drinking, is one of the inevitabilities of life; one of its positive necessities. And the Negro has had it for centuries; but it has never given him manhood. It does not *now*, in wide areas of population, lift him up to moral and social elevation. Hence the need of a new factor in his life. The Negro needs light: light thrown in upon all the circumstances of his life. The light of civilization.

Dr. Wayland fails to see two or three important things in this Negro problem:— (a) That the Negro has no need to go to a manual labor school.* He has been for two hundred years and more, the greatest laborer in the land. He is a laborer *now:* and he must always be a laborer, or he must die. But:

(b) Unfortunately for the Negro, he has been so wretchedly ignorant that he has never known the value of his sweat and toil. He has been forced into being an unthinking labor-machine. And this he is, to a large degree, to-day under freedom.

(c) Now the great need of the Negro, in our day and time, is intelligent impatience at the exploitation of his labor, on the one hand; on the other hand courage to demand a larger share of the wealth which his toil creates for others.

It is not a mere negative proposition that settles this question. It is not that the Negro does not need the hoe, the plane, the plough, and the anvil. It is the positive affirmation that the negro needs the light of cultivation; needs it to be thrown in upon all his toil, upon his whole life and its environments.

What he needs is CIVILIZATION. He needs the increase of his higher

---

*"I am not so old as some of my young friends may suspect, but I am too old to go into the business of 'carrying coals to Newcastle.' * * * * The colored citizen of the U.S. has already graduated with respectable standing from a course of 250 years in the University of the old-time type of Manual labor. The South of to-day is what we see it largely because the colored men and women at least during the past 250 years, have not been lazy 'cumberers of the ground,' but the grand army of laborers that has wrestled with nature and led these 16 States out of the woods thus far on the high road to material prosperity. It is not especially necessary that the 2,000,000 of our colored children and youth in the southern common schools should be warned against laziness, and what has always and everywhere come of that since the foundation of the world." The Rev. A.D. Mayo, M.A., LL.D. Address before State Teachers' Association (Colored)[,] Birmingham, Ala. [Speaker's note.]

wants, of his mental and spiritual needs. *This,* mere animal labor has never given him, and never can give him. But it will come to him, as an individual, and as a class, just in proportion as the higher culture comes to his leaders and teachers, and so gets into his schools, academies and colleges; and then enters his pulpits; and so filters down into his families and his homes; and the Negro learns that he is no longer to be a serf, but that he is to bare his strong brawny arm as a laborer; *not* to make the white man a Croesus, but to make himself a man. He is always to be a laborer; but now, in these days of freedom and the schools, he is to be a laborer with intelligence, enlightenment and manly ambitions.

But, when his culture fits him for something more than a field hand or a mechanic, he is to have an open door set wide before him! And that culture, according to his capacity, he must claim as his rightful heritage, as a man:—not stinted training, not a caste education, not a Negro curriculum.

The Negro Race in this land must repudiate this absurd notion which is stealing on the American mind. The Race must declare that it is not to be put into a single groove; and for the simple reason (1) that *man* was made by his Maker to traverse the whole circle of existence, above as well as below; and that universality is the kernel of all true civilization, of all race elevation. And (2) that the Negro mind, imprisoned for nigh three hundred years, needs breadth and freedom, largeness, altitude, and elasticity; not stint nor rigidity, nor contractedness.

But the "Gradgrinds" are in evidence on all sides, telling us that the colleges and scholarships given us since emancipation, are all a mistake; and that the whole system must be reversed. The conviction is widespread that the Negro has no business in the higher walks of scholarship; that, for instance, Prof. Scarborough has no right to labor in philology; Professor Kelly Miller in mathematics; Professor Du Bois, in history; Dr. Bowen, in theology; Professor Turner, in science; nor Mr. Tanner in art. There is no repugnance to the Negro buffoon, and the Negro scullion; but so soon as the Negro stands forth as an intellectual being, this toad of American prejudice, as at the touch of Ithuriel's spear, starts up a devil!

It is this attitude, this repellant, this forbidding attitude of the American mind, which forces the Negro in this land, to both recognize and to foster the talent and capacity of his own race, and to strive to put that capacity and talent to use for the race. I have detailed the dark and dreadful attempt to stamp that intellect out of existence. It is not only a past, it is also, modified indeed, a present fact; and out of it springs the need of just such an organization as the Negro Academy.

Now, gentlemen and friends, seeing that the American mind in the general, revolts from Negro genius, the Negro himself is duty bound to see to the cultivation and the fostering of his own race-capacity. This is the chief purpose of this Academy. *Our* special mission is the encouragement of the genius and talent in our own race. Wherever we see great Negro ability it is our office to light upon it not tardily, not hesitatingly; but warmly, ungrudgingly, enthusiastically, for the honor of our race, and for the stimulating self-sacrifice in upbuilding the race. Fortunately for us, as a people, this year has given us more than ordinary opportunity for such recognition. Never before, in American history, has there been such a large discovery of talent and genius among us.

Early in the year there was published by one of our members, a volume of papers and addresses, of more than usual excellence. You know gentlemen, that, not seldom, we have books and pamphlets from the press which, like most of our newspapers, are beneath the dignity of criticism. In language, in style, in grammar and in thought they are often crude and ignorant and vulgar. Not so with *"Talks for the Times"* by Prof. Crogman, of Clark University. It is a book with largess of high and noble common sense; pure and classical in style; with a large fund of devoted racialism; and replete everywhere with elevated thoughts. Almost simultaneously with the publication of Professor Crogman's book, came the thoughtful and spicy narrative of Rev. Matthew Anderson of Philadelphia. The title of this volume is *"Presbyterianism: its relation to the Negro:"* but the title cannot serve as a revelation of the racy and spirited story of events in the career of its author. The book abounds with stirring incidents, strong remonstrance, clear and lucid argument, powerful reasonings, the keenest satire; while, withal, it sets forth the wide needs of the Race, and gives one of the strongest vindications of its character and its capacity.*

Soon after this came the first publication of our Academy. And you all know the deep interest excited by the two papers, the first issue of this Society. They have attracted interest and inquiry where the mere declamatory effusions, or, the so-called eloquent harangues of aimless talkers and political wire-pullers would fall like snowflakes upon the waters. The papers of Prof. Kelly Miller and Prof. Du Bois have reached the circles of scholars and thinkers in this country. So consummate was the handling of Hoffman's "Race Traits and Tendencies" by Prof. Miller, that we may say that it was the most scientific defense of the Negro ever made in this country by a man of our own blood: accurate, pointed, painstaking, and I claim conclusive.

The treatise of Prof. Du Bois upon the "Conservation of Race," separated itself, in tone and coloring, from the ordinary effusions of literary work in this land. It rose to the dignity of philosophical insight and deep historical inference. He gave us, in a most lucid and original method, and in a condensed form, the long settled conclusions of Ethnologists and Anthropologists upon the question of Race.

This treatise moreover, furnished but a limited measure of our indebtedness to his pen and brain. Only a brief time before our assembly last year, Prof. Du Bois had given a large contribution to the literature of the nation as well as to the genius of the race. At that time he had published a work which will, without doubt, stand permanently, as authority upon its special theme.

---

*I owe Mr. Anderson an apology for omitting this references to his book on the delivery of this address.: It was prepared while its author was in a foreign land; but had passed entirely from his memory in the preparation of this address. [Speaker's note.]

"The Suppression of the Slave Trade" is, without doubt, the one unique and special authority upon that subject, in print. It is difficult to conceive the possible creation of a similar work, so accurate and painstaking, so full of research, so orderly in historical statement, so rational in its conclusions. It is the simple truth, and at the same time the highest praise, the statement of one Review, that "Prof. Du Bois has exhausted his subject." This work is a step forward in the literature of the Race, and a stimulant to studious and aspiring minds among us.

One further reference, that is, to the realm of Art.

The year '97 will henceforth be worthy of note in our history. As a race, we have, this year, reached a high point in intellectual growth and expression.

In poetry and painting, as well as in letters and thought, the Negro has made, this year, a character.

On my return home in October, I met an eminent scientific gentleman; and one of the first remarks he made to me was—"Well, Dr. Crummell, we Americans have been well taken down in Paris, this year. Why," he said, "the prize in painting was taken by a colored young man, a Mr. Tanner from America. Do you know him?"* The reference was to Mr. Tanner's "Raising of Lazarus," a painting purchased by the French Government, for the famous Luxembourg Gallery. This is an exceptional honor, rarely bestowed upon any American Artist. Well may we all be proud of this, and with this we may join the idea that Tanner, instead of having a hoe in his hand, or digging in a trench, as the faddists on industrialism would fain persuade us, has found his right place at the easel with artists.

Not less distinguished in the world of letters is the brilliant career of our poet-friend and co-laborer, Mr. Paul Dunbar.† It was my great privilege last summer to witness his triumph, on more than one occasion, in that grand metropolis of Letters and Literature, the city of London; as well as to hear of the high value set upon his work, by some of the first scholars and literati of England. Mr. Dunbar has had his poems republished in London by Chapman & Co.; and now has as high a reputation abroad as he has here in America, where his luminous genius has broken down the bars, and with himself, raised the intellectual character of his race in the world's consideration.

These cheering occurrences, these demonstrations of capacity, give us the greatest encouragement in the large work which is before this Academy. Let us enter upon that work, this year, with high hopes, with large purposes, and with calm and earnest persistence. I trust that we shall bear in remem-

---

*Henry Ossawa Tanner (1859–1937) was the first African American painter to receive substantial international recognition. He studied with Thomas Eakins at the Pennsylvania Academy of Fine Arts. After moving to Paris in 1894, Tanner placed paintings in the annual salons of the Société des Artistes Français. His biblical painting *The Raising of Lazarus* won a medal in the Paris Exhibition in 1897.

†The poet and novelist Paul Laurence Dunbar (1872–1906) received national acclaim for his second volume of verse, *Majors and Minors* (1895).

brance that the work we have undertaken is our special function; that it is a work which calls for cool thought, for laborious and tireless painstaking, and for clear discrimination; that it promises nowhere wide popularity, or, exuberant eclat; that very much of its ardent work is to be carried on in the shade; that none of its desired results will spring from spontaneity; that its most prominent features are the demands of duty to a needy people; and that its noblest rewards will be the satisfaction which will spring from having answered a great responsibility, and having met the higher needs of a benighted and struggling Race.■

140 THE FUNCTIONS OF THE NEGRO SCHOLAR

G. N. Grisham

In its issue of March 26, 1898, the Colored American, published in Washington, D.C., carried the following notice in its leading article: "Prof. G. N. Grisham, principal of the [Lincoln] high school at Kansas City, Mo., one of the ablest educators and most practical philosophers in the country, delivered an address in this city during the recent session of the Negro Academy, which was a valuable contribution to modern literature. The occasion was a reception to the Graduates Club at the residence of Prof. Kelly Miller, on College Street, December 28th, 1897." Grisham was among the leaders of the American Negro Academy, a society of prominent African American scholars and educators, including Alexander Crummell, W. E. B. Du Bois, W. S. Scarborough, and others.

Professor Grisham's address was subtitled "The Interpreter and Guide of Civilization—A Hostage to the Race's Future Greatness." It was delivered at a time of growing influence for the industrial education conception popularized by Booker T. Washington, that African Americans should be educated in industrial schools to be farmers, domestics, artisans, and craftsmen to do the more menial work in society. Professor Grisham, on the other hand, felt strongly that there was also an important place in society for the black scholar, and he urged "the thinking Negro" to "contribute to magazines, write books and cooperate with learned societies . . . investigate and discover truth . . . attack evils, devise remedies and advocate reforms." He also rejected the view that the

scholar should stand "aloof from the practical world," and he empha-
sized that "even in his own interest the Negro scholar must do some-
thing for his race."

  The text reproduced below was published in the Colored American,
Washington, D.C., March 16, 1898.

IN THE SOCIAL ORGANISM, every kind of human power has its special
place, and every grade of intelligence has its function. Men of will trace
with their swords the bounds of empire, or as statesmen enter the affairs of
nations; men of feeling fashion the cults of picture with pen or brush half-
uttered yearnings of races; men of scholarship have likewise their functions
of leadership in the higher sense of the word. The scholar is the interpreter
of civilization, as well as its guide. In him is renewed the spirit of the past;
in him are the aspirations of the future, which color the best deeds of the
present. The great schools of the world are supposed to be engaged in the
task of producing men of this higher type. But, in spite of their efforts, mental maturity is rarer than physical maturity. On every hand we meet with
intellectual dwarfs, collegiate runts standing in sorry contrast with the great
giants of intellect, whose scholarship dominates the world. The true scholar
may be a college graduate, but the college graduate is not necessarily a
scholar. He is at best, but a promise. The city of Washington is to be congratulated on having formed the first general organization of college-trained
Negroes in this country. In this graduates' club are men and women holding
degrees from the leading universities of America, men and women who recognize the fact that the power of a man in the modern world is measured
not so much by what he does in school as by what he can do and does after
he leaves school. The test of scholarship is the ability of the individual when
turned loose by his instructors to further extend his mental horizon by his
own exertions; but there is a higher scholarship which extends the world's
horizon. These two types of men have in common an unsatisfied mental curiosity, but while one ascends on ladders constructed by other men, the other
adds new rounds to the ladder of knowledge. In some ages of the world the
scholar was the man who knew books, but today the true scholar is he who,
in addition to knowing books, knows men, whose studies have led him to
comprehend the relation of man to his kind, the relation of man to the universe of matter and mind.

  The Negro graduate is here. If any one questions whether the Negro
scholar has yet been discovered we will not debate the question of fact, but
we want to insist that the function of the Negro scholar is the same as the
function of any other scholar in whom mankind thinks its highest thoughts,
preparatory to doing the grandest deed. But the Negro who today ought to
be a scholar is in peculiar danger by virtue of the novelty of his situation.
He, therefore, needs to be warned in advance, lest his claims to real scholarship prove baseless. In almost every community the general grade of scholarship is so low that it takes far less knowledge to make a Negro conspicuous

than would give prominence to a man of another race. "He is a smart man for a Negro," is a compliment that has stunted the growth of many a smart person. The cheap compliments of the press and a yearning for prominence leads men to overlook the claims of genuine merit, and resort to the familiar tricks of charlatanry. The plagiarism of Chatterton;* the scientific hoax of the age, the Cardiff giant;† and now, recently, the visionary claims of young Edison, who pretends to be able to photograph a man's thoughts‡—these are samples of the things to be avoided by the Negro who would be a scholar; remembering the words of Goethe:

> What glitters, of the moment,
> As with the moment passed,
> Ages to come will know true worth,
> For it alone can last.

It is no less important that he avoid the error of attempting too much. Many a young man leaves college with the honest intention of attempting to keep up his studies. The sooner he learns it cannot be done the better for him. For much of the university work served no purpose in generating a certain amount of power, in giving the student mental perspective, in coordinating his faculties, in supplying material for reflection, in creating habits of thought, in refining the taste and biasing the individual in favor of the work he can best do for the world. These purposes served, he would be by no means poor if he forgets, as he certainly will, the major portion of all that his professors thought. Let him single out one great task and do it. Bacon took all knowledge for his province, but no man of our age can hope to do more than reach excellence in some one department. The medieval scholar undertook to know and discuss all questions of culture. The modern scholar is content to be ignorant of much. The young aspirant for fame often feels conscious of enormous powers of acquisition, but he will not have gone far before discovering the evil of sacrificing depth to extent of research. Said Goethe to Eckerman: "It is a great thing to be able to do one thing well." He who attempts more may illustrate the sad picture drawn by Schiller:

---

*The reference is to the "Thomas Rowley" poems, which Thomas Chatterton, a young British poet, attempted to pass off as a work of a medieval cleric. It was actually a case of literary forgery rather than one of plagiarism. [Speaker's note.]

†The Cardiff giant was a famous hoax of the nineteenth century. In 1868 George Hall, of Binghamton, New York, obtained a block of gypsum from the deposits in Fort Dodge, hauled it overland to Chicago, had it carved in the shape of a human figure, and buried it near Cardiff, Onondaga County, in New York, where it was discovered by men digging a well in 1869. The Cardiff giant was exhibited in various parts of the country, as a petrified man or a statue dating from prehistoric times. The hoax was exposed by Othniel C. Marsh, of Yale, and the perpetrator confessed his part in it.

‡It is interesting that at a time when the press was busily engaged in the creation of a wide number of fantasies associated with Thomas A. Edison, Grisham expressed a skeptical attitude toward one of these claims.

"With a thousand sails spread to the winds, the youth embarks upon the ocean; calmly the old man enters the harbor in a lifeboat."

There was a time when the scholar stood aloof from the practical world, as if he formed no part of it. Scholarship cannot create and breathe an atmosphere all its own. It is commendable to search for truth as the thing best worth knowing, but not much is justified in directing his energies altogether without reference to the needs of the great world in which he lives. Man and society eventually condition each other. The maximum of individual power is attained only in the best social organization, and society is best only when the individual has a chance to become his best. No man can well refuse to raise the platform on which he, himself, must stand. There is a charge today that the better-favored Negro is disposed to desert his kind and dwell apart from the masses, but even in his own interest the Negro scholar must do something for his race. He can and should offer defense against unjust criticism and wrong. He should in his exalted personality, furnish a standard for budding aspiration, and his superior intelligence and keen foresight should offer guidance over the thousands of moral, social and political difficulties that throng the dark and devious pathway of the people. The race has a right to look to him for helpful suggestions, for kindly, sympathetic criticism, for a clear outline of policy and for the inspiration which can come alone from those whose lofty reaches of thought enable them to contemplate the depths from the standpoint of the heights.

This is no mean or narrow task, for it can be best performed only by those who clearly recognize the fact that the Negro scholar must form the connection between his race and civilization. In him they breathe its spirit, think its thought, grapple with its difficulties, and aid in the solution of its problems. The Negro scholar must not confine himself to Negro questions. He must, in action, manifest the breadth of Terence, who, in one famous utterance, identified himself with mankind—"I am a man and deem nothing that concerns humanity foreign to me." The greatest unifying social principle is intelligence that lifts men above littleness and fixes attention upon those intrinsic qualities of soul which make a man valuable to another. If Dante and Tasso in Italy united ancient and modern scholarship, the new nationalities of Europe—France, England, Spain, Germany and America—vitally connected themselves with that common center of thought in the persons of their thinkers, who saw world problems in their own national embarrassments. The Commission of international scholarship has removed the harshness of national boundaries and softened the asperities of native prejudices. Erasmus and Moore, Newton and Descartes, Galileo and Kepler, Tennyson and Victor Hugo, Carlyle and Emerson are but examples of the unifying principles of modern scholarship. Let the thinking Negro join them. Let him contribute to magazines, write books and cooperate with learned societies, let him investigate and discover truth, let him attack evils, devise remedies and advocate reforms, let him withal manifest that sympathetic approach leading him to sacrifice no realized good for any imaginary excellence. The world's work is increasingly great. It calls for brain power, and men stand ready to crown with distinction any one of whatever race, who with ability and courage will address himself successfully to the task of settling questions that arise from age to age. The Negro scholar, untrammeled by traditional modes of thought and undazzled by glittering errors of the past, may be peculiarly fitted for that clear thinking and intellectual daring now demanded in the solution of the great problems of civilization.■

141 REMARKS TO PRESIDENT MCKINLEY

Ida B. Wells-Barnett

In February 1898, a mob of whites murdered the African American postmaster of Lake City, South Carolina, and a child his wife was holding in her arms. The mob then shot his wife and other children and burned their home to the ground. Postmaster Baker's appointment had occasioned much protest because of his color, and calls for his removal had been issued by South Carolina senators Tillman and McLauren. Baker had refused to resign. At one o'clock on the morning of Washington's birthday, the murderers set fire to the post office and Baker's home. More than one hundred bullets were fired into the house. As the Cleveland Gazette *of February 28 reported:*

> *The postmaster was the first to reach the door and he fell dead just within the threshold, being shot in several places. The mother had the baby in her arms and reached the door over her husband's body, when a bullet crashed through its skull, and it fell to the floor. She was shot in several places. Two of the girls had their arms broken close to the shoulders and will probably lose them. Another of the girls is fatally wounded. The boy was also shot.*

Although a coroner's jury surveyed the sight, the editors of the Gazette *made it clear that "Nothing will be done to apprehend the infernal brutes and murderers."*

Postmaster Baker's murder was but one of thousands of lynchings that disgraced the nation. Because Baker was a federal employee, however, antilynching activists seized the opportunity to demand federal intervention and prosecution. On March 21, the great journalist, lecturer, and antilynching leader Ida B. Wells-Barnett was escorted to the White House by the Illinois congressional delegation in an effort to persuade President McKinley to take action. After she was introduced by Senator Mason of Illinois, Wells-Barnett offered a brief but powerful plea for federal action. Just one week after the sinking of the Maine *and on the eve of war with Spain, Wells-Barnett drew upon McKinley's expressed outrage at the treatment of Americans abroad and willingness to go to war to address these wrongs in order to justify federal action against lynching at home.*

As with the earlier entreaties of Mary Church Terrell and Frederick Douglass to President Harrison to intervene against lynching, Wells-Barnett received professions of sympathy but no action. McKinley told the delegation that he was "in hearty accord" with their sentiments and promised that the Justice Department and the Postal Service would take the necessary action. Nothing was done.

The text of Wells-Barnett's remarks was printed in the Cleveland Gazette *of April 9, 1898, and was republished in Herbert Aptheker, ed.,* A Documentary History of the Negro People of the United States *(New York: Citadel, 1951), 798.*

M r. President, the colored citizens of this country in general, and Chicago in particular, desire to respectfully urge that some action be taken by you as chief magistrate of this great nation, first, for the apprehension and punishment of the lynchers of Postmaster Baker, of Lake City, S.C.; second, we ask indemnity for the widow and children, both for the murder of the husband and father, and for injuries sustained by themselves; third, we most earnestly desire that national legislation be enacted for the suppression of the national crime of lynching.

For nearly twenty years lynching crimes, which stand side by side with Armenian and Cuban outrages, have been committed and permitted by this Christian nation. Nowhere in the civilized world save the United States of America do men, possessing all civil and political power, go out in bands of 50 to 5,000 to hunt down, shoot, hang or burn to death a single individual, unarmed and absolutely powerless. Statistics show that nearly 10,000 American citizens have been lynched in the past 20 years. To our appeals for justice the stereotyped reply has been that the government could not interfere in a state matter. Postmaster Baker's case was a federal matter, pure and simple. He died at his post of duty in defense of his country's honor, as truly as did ever a soldier on the field of battle. We refuse to believe this country, so powerful to defend its citizens abroad, is unable to protect its citizens at home. Italy and China have been indemnified by this government for the lynching of their citizens. We ask that the government do as much for its own.■

142

WE MUST HAVE A CLEANER "SOCIAL MORALITY"

Margaret Murray Washington

One of ten children born to her sharecropper parents in Mississippi, Margaret Murray Washington (1865–1925) played a significant role in the Tuskegee Institute enterprises and was active and
influential in the women's club movement. Murray graduated from Fisk
University in 1889 and the following year became "Lady Principal" of
Tuskegee, where she met the recent widower Booker T. Washington.
They married in 1892. She advised him on his speeches and occasionally accompanied him on lecture tours as he gained increasing fame.
Margaret Murray Washington served on the executive board of Tuskegee
and later became its dean of women.

In February 1892, she initiated a program of "mother's meetings"
that provided child care for working mothers, literacy training, and information and training for women in household management and hygiene.
This organization was an important forerunner of the black women's
club movement. Margaret Murray Washington attended the July 1895
meeting in Boston that resulted in the organization of the National Federation of Afro-American Women. The following year, she was elected its
president, and helped the organization unite with the Colored Women's
League to form the National Association of Colored Women, which she
served as secretary of the executive board. Washington was elected president of the NACW in 1914.

A stirring speaker, Washington often addressed women's clubs and
sometimes shared the program with her husband on his lecture tours. On
September 12, 1898, the Washingtons visited Charleston, South Carolina.
Her husband addressed a large audience in the church that morning and
a community gathering in the evening. During the afternoon, Margaret
Murray Washington offered a "plain, earnest talk" to "a very large assemblage" of black women at the Old Bethel A.M.E. Church. She draws attention to statistics of disproportionate infant mortality and general morbid-
ity among the African American population, as well as the problem of
unwanted pregnancy. Her answer is self-improvement in habits and hygiene. The task of moral uplift she lays upon those in her audience who
have enjoyed greater advantages in education or social opportunity.
"Stoop down now and then and lift up others," she admonishes.

The text of the speech was published in the Charleston News and
Courier (September 13, 1898) and was reprinted in volume 4 of Louis R.
Harlan, ed., The Booker T. Washington Papers (Urbana: University of Illi-
nois Press, 1975), 461–68. For further information, see Wilma King

Hunter, "Three Women at Tuskegee, 1825–1925: The Wives of Booker T. Washington," Journal of Ethnic Studies *4 (September 1976), 76–89.*

I want to say in the beginning that I do not come before you to criticize or find fault especially, but you know that a great deal of harm has been done us as a race by those who have told us of our strong points, of our wonderful advancement, and have neglected to tell us at the same time of our weak points, of our lack of taking hold of the opportunities about us. Praise a child always and he soon gets to the point where he thinks it impossible for him to make mistakes.

If we wish to help each other let us not only praise ourselves, but also criticize.

Plain talk will not hurt us. It will lead each woman to study her own condition, that of her own family and so that of her neighbor's family.

If I can do anything to hasten this study, I shall feel repaid for any effort I may put forth.

In consenting to come before you women-to-day I am influenced by this thought more than anything else: We need, as a race, a good, strong public sentiment in favor of a sounder, healthier body, and a cleaner and higher-toned morality. There is no use arguing; we do not think enough of these two conditions; we are too indifferent; too ready to say: 'O, well, I keep well, my girls and boys behave themselves, and I have nothing to do with the rest of the race!' No nation or race has ever come up by entirely overlooking its members who are less fortunate, less ambitious, less sound in body and hence in soul, and we cannot do it. We must not do it. There are too many of us down. The condition of our race, brought about by slavery, the ignorance, poverty, intemperance, ought to make us women know that in half a century we cannot afford to lose sight of the large majority of the race who have not, as yet, thrown off the badge of the evils which I have just mentioned.

You are not, I know, surprised to hear me say that the women, young and older, among us, who most need to take caution in the matter of health and character, are the last to take any personal hold. It is no longer a compliment to a girl or woman to be of a frail and delicate mold. It is no longer an indication of refinement in woman to possess a weak and fastidious stomach.

It was the great French Emperor who declared that the greatest need of France was mothers. And to-day all who are willing to study facts with reference to our growth and strength in this country declare also that the most serious drawback to the race is its lack of a careful, moral and healthy motherhood.

You have already noticed that I speak of health, then morals; morals, then health; my sisters, these two things go hand in hand, they are interdependent. They must go thus. They must be studied together at this time. They must be corrected at the same time.

To be a stronger race physically we have got to be a more moral one. We do not want to lose our tempers when we discuss these conditions either. Now that, as women, we may be able to make a move in the direction of improving the race, we have got to take certain facts regarding our health and morals. They are not all from the standpoint of the Southern white man, either, nor are they all from the Northern white man with a Southern soul. You know that we often feel that every white man and woman south of the Mason and Dixon line is a real devil. It is pretty bad down here, I will admit, but there are many very fine and noble Southern white people, women as well as men. It is a Southern man, an Alabama man, at that, who, in part at least, makes it possible for us to be here together to-day to study our own shortcomings and to try to find a way out of them. I say it is not Southern whites alone who have felt that we should make a move upward, who feel that we are weak in these directions; nor is it the white man alone at all, but our own medical men, our own educators, who also feel and know that there is too great a laxity amongst us. It is not an easy thing to secure accurate data with reference to the race in these particulars, for, in making up the statistics, especially in Southern localities, the health boards have entirely ignored us; of course many places in the South have had health boards only recently. However, we have evidence sufficient on each of these subjects to condemn us, to make us feel that something must be done; that some step, and that quick, must be made to stay the awful death rate and the alarmingly increasing illegitimate birth rate among our women and girls. This may not apply to a single woman under the sound of my voice, but it does apply to the race, and so far it comes home to you and to me. We cannot separate ourselves from our people, no matter how much we try; for one, I have no desire to do so.

I do not mean to tell you, or leave the impression, that all of the disease and immorality in the race are confined to what we are pleased to call our poorer classes or second-class folks. There is too much in our higher classes, especially in the case of too many men who as fathers of the girls and boys who, in their turn, will be fathers and mothers of other girls and boys.

And does hereditary influence count for nothing? Study your own family as far back as your great grandparents and you will agree with me when I say hereditary influence is a mighty power in the formation of character, physical, as well as moral.

I give you now these facts for five of our large Southern cities: these relate especially to the death rate of colored people in excess of white people: Rate per thousand in city No. 1, colored 36, white 19; city No. 2, colored 36, white 22; city No. 3, colored 37, white 22; city No. 4, colored 32, white 18; city No. 5, colored 35, white 17. This gives us a decrease in race by death rate in these five cities, in excess of the white people, who already so far outnumber us, respectively 100, of a fraction, 68 and over, 77 and over, and 106 per cent. In one of the large Western cities, and this is not Chicago, either, the death rate of colored people is more than twice that of the white people. Pneumonia and consumption are our most deadly foes. They are not standing still, but are on the increase in every city I have mentioned. In one Northern city alone, in one year, out of ten thousand, there was an excess of deaths, caused by pneumonia and consumption, of 135 per cent of colored people over whites; colored dying, 225, and whites, 126.

The death rate of our children is something to make us tremble. As long as it is so high we cannot hope for much. Numbers count for a great deal in this country. For five years, in one of our largest Southern cities alone, the excess in death rate among colored children under 5 years of age was 163 per cent, while that of the whites was only 32 per cent and a fraction over. In another large Southern city the death rate per cent in excess for colored children over whites is 883.4 per cent. The diseases which are undermining the life of our babies and robbing the race of its future men and women are, cholera infantum, convulsions and still-born. There is an excess in this last disease, still-born, of colored infants over white of 149 per cent per thousand. What a terrible tribute to our womanhood and to our motherhood this is. In another Southern city, not a thousand miles from here, over half the colored children die before they are 12 months old. We are very often inclined to treat this subject lightly by saying that we are a great reducing race, but I have no patience with this indifference, for it is simply impossible for any race to balance any such loss at this. And now, more than this, women, we are not so productive as we used to be. I do not know why, I wish I did. I would count no sacrifice too great to bring about a change in this respect. My grandmother had thirteen sons and daughters, every one of whom lived to rear large families. My mother had ten, most of whom have lived long enough, but they have no children. In the whole ten of us, all grown, there are only two children, and they are the children of the youngest girl, who is now 27 years of age, and there has never been more than these, and what is worse, there never will be. Study this race question, this phase of it, and you will find what I say to be true. We have got to change this state of things. Our educated women will not or do not become mothers and our less intelligent mothers let their little ones die, and thus our numbers are each year growing less and less.

In every city in the country where you observe it you find that we are losing by death more than we are gaining by birth. Immorality, as well as poverty and ignorance, bears its share of the blame for this low state of vitality. It makes us susceptible to all forms of disease and death. We must have a cleaner 'social morality.' A man who has given thought to the moral life of the race claims that over 25 per cent of the colored children born in one city alone are admittedly illegitimate. In a certain locality, in a certain State, another man states that there were during one year 300 marriage licenses taken out by white men. According to the population 1,200 licenses should have been bought by colored men. How many do you suppose were in reality taken out? Twelve hundred should have been secured and only 3 per cent were taken out. Twelve hundred colored men and women, for whom there is no excuse, living immoral lives, handing down to their offspring disease and crime, and only three living in such a way as to advance the race. No spectacle can be more appalling.

In a certain Northern city only 2 per cent of the people are colored, yet we furnish 16 per cent of male prisoners and 34 per cent [of] female criminals. In another Northern or Northwestern city we make up 1 1/3 per cent of the whole city, and yet 10 per cent of the arrests fall on us. Immorality is directly responsible for these crimes, and hence punishment. Immorality is also directly responsible for physical inability to resist crime. Go North or South, East or West, and the numbers of the dens of abandoned women, of profligate men is too large. These are the breeders of disease and the millstone of the race.

You say there are causes for all these, causes for which we are not responsible. I admit this much, but there are also causes for which we are responsible. And the fact that there are causes ought to make us hopeful, because we have it in our power to remove these causes. It will take time, however, and it will take wise and consecrated women to effect a change along these lines.

Not only are poverty, ignorance and intemperance the cause of all this misery, but downright negligence, too, plays a large part in these matters. Colored men drive, cut wood, unload ships, etc., all day in the pouring rain, at night they throw themselves onto a bed and sleep without removing their wet clothes. Our women are little or no better. What is a better feeder for pneumonia and all forms of tuberculosis? The men clean streets, sweep and dust great buildings, with no effort to keep the throat clear of dust and dirt. The majority of cases of consumption are not inherent, but are contracted through lack of thought and interest in one's own self.

How many of our women during their pregnancy make nothing of lifting from one bench to another heavy tubs of clothes, drawing buckets of water, lift great sticks of wood, run up and down stairs, and a dozen other similar things entirely against them. They do not know the laws of health, and they will not learn them. No, I do not say do not work during the months of unborn motherhood; work, even hard work, is good for one, but the manner in which labor is performed is what I criticize.

As women can we not do something to correct our condition physically and morally? I think we can.

The average colored person dislikes water, and he won't keep himself clean. He bathes, if at all, once a week—Saturday night—and changes his clothes in the same indifferent way. He seldom uses a tooth brush. He often even neglects to comb his hair, except on Sunday. There is no excuse for this. Bathe at least twice a week, and change the clothes as often, and be sure to clean the teeth at least once a day, and do not forget to comb the hair each day.

We eat too little or too poor food. We are ready to buy showy clothing, but we stint our stomachs too often. They call us great eaters. Let us eat more and better food. There is very little vitality in grits and gravy. Get fresh fruit, fresh eggs, good meat, etc. These things give strength not only to women, but to their offspring.

Keep regular hours. Do not stay in church till 12 and 1 o'clock at night. Go to bed at 10, especially if you labor through the day. When you get up in the mornings air the bedding, open up things for a while and let the sunshine in. When the little child comes do not have an ignorant granny, secure a good physician in addition to at least a clean nurse. Apply your lessons of bathing, feeding, sleeping to these little ones, remembering, of course, their age.

Teach the boys as well as the girls respect for the marriage tie and home. Be companions for your sons and daughters if you would stop the tide of immorality. A young girl has no business out to a party or church or picnic without some older member of her family or woman friend. Teach the boys to come home at night. Teach them the sin of ruining some man's daughter. These lessons can be taught around the fireside at night, from the pulpit, in the school room, in mothers' meetings; and there should be a mothers' meeting in every community. They can be instilled in many ways. Help secure a minister and teacher who will take an interest in the physical and moral improvement of our families, and together with what we women can do and our ministers and teachers, we shall be able to make some progress in the coming ten or fifteen years which will prove to our enemies that our condition physically and morally is nothing inherent or peculiar to race, but rather the outcome of circumstances over which we can and will become masters. In this way and only in this way will [we] satisfy the men and women, both North and South, who still have faith in us. Let us teach our boys and girls some useful occupations, let us insist upon an intelligent and moral ministry, let us employ teachers only who are above reproach, and above all let those of us who have had an opportunity, who have educational advantages, modify our cause lines—stoop down now and then and lift up others.■

143 THE CANCER OF RACE PREJUDICE

Booker T. Washington

After his "Atlanta Compromise" speech of 1895, Booker T. Washington rarely argued in public for African American civil rights or against racist violence and discrimination. "In my addresses I very seldom refer to the question of prejudice," he explained, "because I realize that it is something to be lived down not talked down." One no-

table exception was Washington's highly publicized speech at the National Peace Jubilee in Chicago, Illinois, on October 18, 1898, for "at that great meeting which marked in a large measure the end of all sectional feeling I thought it an opportune time to ask for the blotting out of racial prejudice as far as possible in 'business and civil relations.' "*

The Chicago Jubilee was perhaps the largest of several observances across the United States designed to celebrate the close of the Spanish American War. William R. Harper, president of the University of Chicago, invited Washington to address a gathering including President William McKinley, members of his cabinet, and numerous members of the U.S. Senate and House of Representatives. In his letter of September 21, 1898, Harper offered Washington "the largest liberty in the choice of subjects and length of treatment" and predicted that Washington would face an audience of two to four thousand people.† In fact, more than sixteen thousand jammed the auditorium—the largest audience Washington ever addressed—and many more were turned away. Washington twice repeated his speech to overflow audiences elsewhere that evening.

To Washington, as to many African Americans, the Spanish-American War raised issues of domestic as well as foreign policy. Black service in the war, as well as the ostensible purpose of the war to secure the liberties of the Spanish colonists, were premises from which Washington argued for the rights of African Americans at home. At the Chicago Jubilee, Washington seized the extraordinary opportunity both to link these two subjects and to address his appeal directly to the leaders of the nation. "We have succeeded in every conflict, except the effort to conquer ourselves in the blotting out of racial prejudices," he admonishes. "Until we conquer ourselves . . . we shall have, especially in the Southern part of our country, a cancer gnawing at the heart of the Republic, that shall one day prove as dangerous as an attack from an army without or within."

Washington's speech was a rousing success with the Chicago audiences. "At the Auditorium the applause given him made the very columns of the massive building tremble," according to the report of the Chicago Times-Herald. *"It sounded more like a roar than cheers and clapping of hands. And it would not cease. Again and again it was repeated." But Washington's uncharacteristic speech provoked a furor among white Southerners, particularly editors of newspapers such as the* Atlanta Constitution *and the* Birmingham Age-Herald *who had previously supported Washington's accommodationist policies. They bridled at his condemnation of southern prejudice (seemingly a switch from his 1895 advice to African Americans to "cast down your bucket" in the*

---

*"To the Editor of the Birmingham *Age-Herald* (November 10, 1898)," in Louis R. Harlan, ed., *The Booker T. Washington Papers*, vol. 4 (Urbana: University of Illinois Press, 1972–1989), 508–9.

†"From William Rainey Harper" (September 21, 1898), in Harlan, *The Booker T. Washington Papers*, vol. 4, p. 473.

South, where "the Negro is given a man's chance in the commercial world") and, more vehemently, at Washington's suggestion that whites and blacks should bury "all that which separates us in our business and civil relations," which they understood as an effort to promote "social equality."

When the editor of the Birmingham Age-Herald *wrote to him asking that he clarify his statements, Washington retreated. In his response of November 10, Washington reassured his white supporters that he never intended to single out the South or to urge "social equality" in defiance of racial prejudice ("What is termed social recognition is a question I never discuss") and that he still adhered to the belief expressed in the Atlanta address that "agitation of questions of social equality is the extremist folly." When he reprinted the speech in* The Story of My Life and Work *(1901), he omitted the line denouncing southern prejudice.*

The speech text is taken from volume 4 of Louis Harlan, ed., The Booker T. Washington Papers *(Urbana: University of Illinois Press, 1975), 490–92. For relevant correspondence, see pp. 389, 472–73, 502–3, 508–9. See also Louis Harlan,* Booker T. Washington: The Making of a Black Leader, 1856–1901 *(New York: Oxford University Press, 1972), 236–38.*

Mr. Chairman, Ladies and Gentlemen: On an important occasion in the life of the Master, when it fell to Him to pronounce judgment on two courses of action, these memorable words fell from His lips: "And Mary hath chosen the better part." This was the supreme test in the case of an individual. It is the highest test in the case of a race or nation. Let us apply this test to the American Negro.

In the life of our Republic, when he has had the opportunity to choose, has it been the better or worse part? When in the childhood of this nation the Negro was asked to submit to slavery or choose death and extinction, as did the aborigines, he chose the better part, that which perpetuated the race.

When in 1776 the Negro was asked to decide between British oppression and American independence, we find him choosing the better part, and Crispus Attucks, a Negro, was the first to shed his blood on State street, Boston, that the white American might enjoy liberty forever, though his race remained in slavery.

When in 1814 at New Orleans, the test of patriotism came again, we find the Negro choosing the better part; Gen. Andrew Jackson himself testifying that no heart was more strong and useful in defense of righteousness.

When the long and memorable struggle came between union and separation, when he knew that victory on the one hand meant freedom, and defeat on the other his continued enslavement, with a full knowledge of the portentous meaning of it all, when the suggestion and the temptation came to burn the home and massacre wife and children during the absence of the master in battle, and thus insure his liberty, we find him choosing the better part, and for four long years protecting and supporting the helpless, defence-less ones entrusted to his care.

When in 1863 the cause of the Union seemed to quiver in the balance, and there was doubt and distrust, the Negro was asked to come to the rescue in arms, and the valor displayed at Fort Wagner and Port Hudson and Fort Pillow, testify most eloquently again that the Negro chose the better part.

When a few months ago, the safety and honor of the Republic were threatened by a foreign foe, when the wail and anguish of the oppressed from a distant isle reached his ears, we find the Negro forgetting his own wrongs, forgetting the laws and customs that discriminate against him in his own country, and again we find our black citizen choosing the better part. And if you would know how he deported himself in the field at Santiago, apply for answer to Shafter and Roosevelt and Wheeler. Let them tell how the Ne-gro faced death and laid down his life in defense of honor and humanity, and when you have gotten the full story of the heroic conduct of the Negro in the Spanish-American war—heard it from the lips of Northern soldiers and Southern soldiers, from ex-abolitionist and ex-master, then decide within yourselves whether a race that is thus willing to die for its country, should not be given the highest opportunity to live for its country.

In the midst of all the complaints of suffering in the camp and field, suffering from fever and hunger, where is the official or citizen that has heard a word of complaint from the lips of a black soldier? The only request that has come from the Negro soldier has been that he might be permitted to replace the white soldier when heat and malaria began to decimate the ranks of the white regiment, and to occupy at the same time the post of greatest danger.

This country has been most fortunate in her victories. She has twice measured arms with England and has won. She has met the spirit of a rebel-lion within her borders and was victorious. She has met the proud Spaniard and he lays prostrate at her feet. All this is well, it is magnificent. But there remains one other victory for Americans to win—a victory as far-reaching and important as any that has occupied our army and navy. We have suc-ceeded in every conflict, except the effort to conquer ourselves in the blot-ting out of racial prejudices. We can celebrate the era of peace in no more effectual way than by a firm resolve on the part of the Northern men and Southern men, black men and white men, that the trench which we together dug around Santiago, shall be the eternal burial place of all that which sepa-rates us in our business and civil relations. Let us be as generous in peace as we have been brave in battle. Until we thus conquer ourselves, I make no empty statement when I say that we shall have, especially in the Southern part of our country, a cancer gnawing at the heart of the Republic, that shall one day prove as dangerous as an attack from an army without or within.

In this presence and on this auspicious occasion, I want to present the deep gratitude of nearly ten millions of my people to our wise, patient and brave Chief Executive for the generous manner in which my race has been recognized during the conflict. A recognition that has done more to blot out sectional and racial lines than any event since the dawn of freedom.*

I know how vain and impotent is all abstract talk on this subject. In your efforts to "rise on stepping stones of your dead selves," we of the black race shall not leave you unaided. We shall make the task easier for you by acquiring property, habits of thrift, economy, intelligence and character, by each making himself of individual worth in his own community. We shall aid you in this as we did a few days ago at El Caney and Satiago, when we helped you to hasten the peace we here celebrate. You know us; you are not afraid of us. When the crucial test comes, you are not ashamed of us. We have never betrayed or deceived you. You know that as it has been, so it will be. Whether in war or in peace, whether in slavery or in freedom, we have always been loyal to the Stars and Stripes.■

144 THE NEGRO WILL NEVER ACQUIESCE AS LONG AS HE LIVES

Reverend Francis J. Grimké

On November 20, 1898, Reverend Francis J. Grimké, pastor of the Fifteenth Street Presbyterian Church of Washington, D.C., delivered a sermon in which he denounced those African Americans who insisted that this was a time for conservatism and accommodation. Grimké called such people traitors and vowed that as long as black Americans were deprived of their full rights as citizens, they would continue to protest and agitate. He concluded with a slashing attack on white clergy who shut their eyes and closed their mouths while black Americans were being brutally oppressed. His sermon was published in the Richmond (Virginia) Planet, *a black weekly, in its issue of November 26, 1898. The* Planet *praised the sermon for "the spirit of independence shown and the plea for all of the rights guaranteed by the laws of the land."*

---

* "The President was sitting in a box at the right of the stage. When I addressed him I turned toward the box, and as I finished the sentence thanking him for his generosity, the whole audience rose and cheered again and again, waving handkerchiefs and hats and canes, until the President arose in the box and bowed his acknowledgements. At that the enthusiasm broke out again, and the demonstration was almost indescribable" (Booker T. Washington, *Up from Slavery* [New York: Dial Press, 1937], 255).

Grimké (1850–1937), threatened as a child with enslavement by his white half brother, served as a valet to Confederate officers in the Civil War. He entered Lincoln University in 1866 and graduated as valedictorian in 1870. After graduating from Princeton Theological Seminary in 1878, he assumed the pastorate of Washington's prestigious Fifteenth Street Church. Grimké's sermons often attacked segregation (especially in the church) and were widely distributed in pamphlet form. He was among the founders of the American Negro Academy in 1897 and was a trustee of Howard University for over forty years. The four-volume Works of Francis James Grimké, *edited and with a biographical essay by Carter G. Woodson, was published in 1942.*

For a discussion of Reverend Grimké's militant views, see Henry Justin Ferry, "Racism and Reunion: A Black Protest by Francis James Grimké," Journal of Presbyterian History *50 (Summer 1972), 77–88.*

L AWLESSNESS is increasing in the South. After thirty-three years of freedom our civil and political rights are still denied us; the fourteenth and fifteenth amendments to the Constitution are still a dead letter. The spirit of oppression and injustice is not diminished but increasing. The determination to keep us in a state of civil and political inferiority, and to surround us with such conditions as will tend to crush out of us a manly and self-respecting spirit, is stronger now than it was at the close of the war. The fixed purpose and determination of the Southern whites is to negative these great amendments, to eliminate entirely the Negro as a political factor. And this purpose is intensifying, is growing stronger and stronger each year.

The sentiment everywhere is: This is a white man's government. And that means, not only that the whites shall rule, but that the Negro shall have nothing whatever to do with governmental affairs. If he dares to think otherwise, or aspires to cast a ballot, or to become anything more than a servant, he is regarded as an impudent and dangerous Negro; and according to the most recent declarations of that old slave-holding and lawless spirit, all such Negroes are to be driven out of the South, or compelled by force, by what is known as the shot-gun policy, to renounce their rights as men and as American citizens.

This is certainly a very discouraging condition of things, but the saddest aspect of it all is that there are members of our race—and not the ignorant, unthinking masses, who have had no advantages, and who might be excused for any seeming insensibility to their rights, but the intelligent, the educated—who are found condoning such offenses, justifying or excusing such a condition of things on the ground that in view of the great disparity in the condition of the two races, anything different from that could not reasonably be expected. Any Negro who takes that position is a traitor to his race, and shows that he is deficient in manhood, in true self-respect. If the time ever comes when the Negro himself acquiesces in that condition of things, then his fate is sealed and ought to be sealed. Such a race is not fit to be free.

But, thank God, the cowardly, ignoble sentiment to which I have just alluded, while it may find lodgment in the breast of a few weak-kneed, time-serving Negroes, is not the sentiment of this black race. No, and never will be. During all these terrible years of suffering and oppression, these years of blood and tears, though he has been shot at, his property destroyed, his family scattered, his home broken up; though he has been forced to fly like the fugitive for his life before the hungry bloodhounds of Southern Democracy; although everything has been done to terrorize him, to keep him from the polls, he still stands up for his rights. In some cases he has stayed away; in others he has gone straightforward in the face of the bullets of the enemy, and has been shot down.

Hundreds of the men of our race have laid their lives down on Southern soil in vindication of their rights as American citizens. And shall we be told, and by black men, too, that the sacred cause for which they poured out their life's blood is to be relinquished; that the white ruffians who shot them down were justified; that in view of all the circumstances it was just what was to have been expected, and therefore that virtually we have no reasonable grounds of complaint? Away with such treasonable utterances; treason to God; treason to man; treason to free institutions, to the spirit of an enlightened and Christian sentiment. The Negro is an American citizen, and he never will be eliminated as a political factor with his consent. He has been terrorized and kept from the polls by bloody ruffians, but he has never felt that it was right; he has never acquiesced in it, and never will, as long as he lives. As long as there is one manly, self-respecting Negro in this country, the agitation will go on, will never cease until right is triumphant. It is one thing to compel the Negro by force to stay away from the polls; it is a very different thing for the Negro himself, freely of his own accord, to relinquish his political rights. The one he may be constrained to do; the other he will not do.

Another discouraging circumstance is to be found in the fact that the pulpits of the land are silent on these great wrongs. The ministers fear to offend those to whom they minister. We hear a great deal from their pulpits about suppressing the liquor traffic, about gambling, about Sabbath desecration, and about the suffering Armenians, and about polygamy in Utah when that question was up, and the Louisiana lottery. They are eloquent in their appeals to wipe out these great wrongs, but when it comes to Southern brutality, to the killing of Negroes and despoiling them of their civil and political rights, they are, to borrow an expression from Isaiah, "dumb dogs that cannot bark." Had the pulpit done its duty, the Southern savages, who have been sinking lower and lower during these years in barbarism, would by this time have become somewhat civilized, and the poor Negro, instead of being hunted down like a wild beast, terrorized by a pack of brutes, would be living amicably by the side of his white fellow-citizen, if not in the full enjoyment of all his rights, with a fair prospect, at least of having them all recognized. This is the charge which I make against the Anglo-American pulpit today; its silence has been interpreted as an approval of these horrible outrages. Bad

men have been encouraged to continue in their acts of lawlessness and brutality. As long as the pulpits are silent on these wrongs it is in vain to expect
the people to do any better than they are doing.■

145 THE WILMINGTON MASSACRE

Reverend Charles S. Morris

*In 1894 a coalition of Populists and African American Republi-
cans gained control of the government of North Carolina. During
the next four years, legislation was passed aiding education, eliminating restrictions upon the suffrage, granting African Americans a number
of public offices, reducing interest charges, and equalizing the taxation
system.*

*In 1898 the Democrats, assisted by defections from Fusionists, re-
gained control in a campaign characterized by James W. Bassett, of
Trinity College, who witnessed the events, as "a great deal of intimidation and a great deal of fraud." The high point in the intimidation came
in Wilmington and resulted in a riot in which between nine and eleven
African Americans were killed and twenty-five wounded. (Charles W.
Chesnutt's novel,* The Marrow of Tradition, *includes a vivid description
of the Wilmington massacre.) White supremacists justified the massacre
on the grounds that it was necessary to end "Negro domination," but
this claim was effectively answered by Reverend Charles S. Morris, a refugee from Wilmington, in a speech delivered in January 1899, before the
International Association of Colored Clergymen in Boston. Reverend
Morris also notes that the United States was inconsistent in ostensibly
seeking to establish a republican government in the Philippines while refusing to maintain one in Wilmington, North Carolina.*

*The speech is preserved in a three-page printed leaflet in "Writing of
Charles H. Williams," Wisconsin State Historical Society Library, Madison, Wisconsin. The leaflet, entitled* The Race Problem: A Story of Cruel
Wrongs Suffered by Colored People of the South, told by One of That
People, *was issued by Charles H. Williams, Baraboo, January 21, 1899.
Williams appended to Morris's speech his own comment, which concluded: "When will this people, this nation, take up this grave question,
as they did the Spanish barbarities against the Cubans, as they do those
of the Turks against the Armenians? Here is a call that should come
home to every justice-loving man and woman in the land, North and*

*South, causing them to act promptly, act at once, demanding of the na-
tional government that these long-oppressed people should be protected
and secured in all rights as citizens."*

NINE NEGROES massacred outright; a score wounded and hunted like
partridges on the mountain; one man, brave enough to fight against
such odds would be hailed as a hero anywhere else, was given the privilege
of running the gauntlet up a broad street, where he sank ankle-deep in the
sand, while crowds of men lined the sidewalks and riddled him with a pint
of bullets as he ran bleeding past their doors; another Negro shot twenty
times in the back as he scrambled empty-handed over a fence; thousands of
women and children fleeing in terror from their humble homes in the darkness of the night, out under a gray and angry sky, from which falls a cold
and bone-chilling rain, out to the dark and tangled ooze of the swamp amid
the crawling things of night, fearing to light a fire, startled at every footstep,
cowering, shivering, shuddering, trembling, praying in gloom and terror;
half-clad and barefooted mothers, with their babies wrapped only in a shawl,
whimpering with cold and hunger at their icy breasts, crouched in terror
from the vengeance of those who, in the name of civilization, and with the
benediction of the ministers of the Prince of Peace, inaugurated the reformation of the city of Wilmington the day after the election by driving out
one set of white officeholders and filling their places with another set of
white officers—the one being Republican and the other Democrat. All this
happened, not in Turkey, or in Russia, nor in Spain, not in the gardens of
Nero, nor in the dungeons of Torquemada, but within three hundred miles
of the White House, in the best state in the South, within a year of the twentieth century, while the nation was on its knees thanking God for having
enabled it to break the Spanish yoke from the neck of Cuba. This is our civilization. This is Cuba's kindergarten of ethics and good government. This is
Protestant religion in the Union States that is planning a wholesale missionary crusade against Catholic Cuba. This is the golden rule as interpreted by
the white pulpit of Wilmington.

Over this drunken and bloodthirsty mob they stretch their hands and
invoke the blessing of a just God. We have waited two hundred and fifty years
for liberty, and this is what it is when it comes. O Liberty, what crimes are
committed in thy name! A rent and bloody mantle of citizenship that has
covered as with a garment of fire, wrapped in which as in a shroud, forty
thousand of my people have fallen around Southern ballot boxes. A carload
of workingmen, whose only crime is their color, halted at the border of the
state of Lincoln and Grant by a governor who ought to be in a penitentiary.*

*The reference is to the attacks on black strikebreakers by white miners in the Pana
and Virden area of Illinois in 1898. The miners were supported by Governor John B. Tanner.
Although the Afro-American Labor and Protective Association of Alabama denounced "the
action of the black miners in going to Pana, remaining at Pana or participating in any
manner in carrying out their tyrannical design against labor," many black papers and

A score of intelligent colored men, able to pass even a South Carolina election officer, shot down at Phoenix, South Carolina, for no reason whatever, except, as the Charleston *News and Courier* said, because the baser elements of the community loved to kill and destroy. The pitiful privilege of dying like cattle in the red gutters of Wilmington, or crouching waist-deep in the icy waters of neighboring swamps, where terrified women gave birth to a dozen infants, most of whom died of exposure and cold. This is Negro citizenship! This is what the nation fought for from Bull Run to Appomattox!

What caused all this bitterness, strife, arson, murder, revolution and anarchy at Wilmington? We hear the answer on all sides—"Negro domination." I deny the charge. It is utterly false, and no one knows it better than the men who use it to justify crimes that threaten the very foundation of republican government; crimes that make the South red with blood, white with bones and gray with ashes; crimes no other civilized government would tolerate for a single day. The colored people comprise one third of the population of the state of North Carolina; in the legislature there are one hundred and twenty representatives, seven of whom are colored, there are fifty senators, two of whom are colored—nine in all out of a hundred and seventy. Can nine Negroes dominate one hundred and sixty white men? That would be a fair sample of the tail wagging the dog. Not a colored man holds a state office in North Carolina; the whole race has less than five percent of all the offices in the state. In the city of Wilmington, the major was white, seven out of ten members of the board of aldermen, and sixteen out of twenty-six members of the police force were white; the city attorney was white, the city clerk was white, the city treasurer was white, the superintendent of streets was white, the superintendent of garbage was white, the superintendent of health was white, the superintendent of city hospitals was white, and all the nurses in the white wards were white; the superintendent of the public schools was white, the chief and assistant chief of the fire department, and three out of five fire companies were white; the school committee has always been composed of two white men and one colored; the board of audit and finance is composed of five members, four of whom were white, and the one Negro was reported to be worth more than any of his white associates. The tax rate under this miscalled Negro regime was less than under its predecessors. This is Negro domination in Wilmington. This is a fair sample of that Southern scarecrow—conjured by these masters of the black art everywhere.

The Good Samaritan did not leave his own eldest son robbed and bleeding at his own threshold, while he went 'way off down the road between Jerusalem and Jericho to hunt for a man that had fallen among thieves. Nor can America afford to go eight thousand miles from home to set up a republican government in the Philippines while the blood of citizens whose an-

---

speakers attacked Governor Tanner for not condemning the murder of blacks during antiscab riots. Since African Americans were excluded from most trade unions, they argued, they had a right to obtain work as strikebreakers. See Philip S. Foner and Ronald Lewis, *The Black Worker*, vol. 4 (Philadelphia: Temple University Press, 1979), 216–17.

cestors came here before the Mayflower is crying out to God against her from
the gutters of Wilmington.■

146 THE FALLACY OF INDUSTRIAL EDUCATION AS THE SOLUTION OF THE RACE PROBLEM

Reverend Charles S. Smith

The vast majority of the public opponents of Booker T. Washington were centered in the North, and the strongest critics were black intellectuals, for the most part graduates of leading northern universities. Yet Washington did not entirely lack vocal black critics in the South. Bishop Henry M. Turner was one of these critics, and another was the Reverend C. S. Smith (1852–1923), of Tennessee, national secretary of the A.M.E. Sunday School Union. In a speech delivered in Nashville to a meeting of African Americans on January 28, 1899, the Reverend Mr. Smith criticized Washington's thesis that African Americans should be educated in industrial institutions and that industrial training which would produce black craftspeople and scientific farmers was the only real solution to the race problem in the United States. By making themselves useful to white Southerners, Washington insisted, African Americans would in time gain from them their civil and political rights; hence they should concentrate on industrial education until that time came.

Without specifically mentioning Washington by name, Smith makes unmistakable reference to the "chief revivalist" of industrial education and attacks his fundamental concept of black education. The cause of the "race problem" and black poverty and unemployment, Smith argues, is not a lack of skilled black laborers, but the "enforced idleness of reason colorphobia." The solution lies not in limiting African Americans to one field of education or labor, he insists, but rather in breaking down the color line.

The Reverend Mr. Smith's speech appeared in the Nashville American, *January 29, 1899. In 1900, he was elected bishop of the A.M.E. Church.*

I am heartily in favor of the industrial and mechanical training for such Negroes as may feel that their calling is on the farm or in the factory, but

I challenge the assertion of those who claim that the only solution of the so-called race problem lies in the direction of the industrial and mechanical training of the Negro.

Surprisingly strange, perhaps, but nevertheless true, slavery itself furnished the race with valuable lessons in industrial and mechanical training, and produced a race of high-class mechanics, skilled workers in wood and iron and metals of all kinds, many of whom remain until this day, and, I regret to say, far more than can obtain employment, caused by the unreasonable and unfriendly attitude of the trade-unions toward colored mechanics.* How, then, can the multiplication of Negro mechanics help to solve the so-called race problem, when those who are already skilled cannot obtain employment? In this city, to my personal knowledge, there are a score or more of skilled Negro mechanics who are subject to enforced idleness by reason colorphobia which dominates the trade-unions. Those who are disposed to advance the Negro's best interests can render him invaluable services by demanding, in tones of thunder loud and long, that the trade-unions shall cease to draw the color line, and that fitness and character shall be the only passport to their fellowship. When this barrier shall have been removed, the time for the multiplication of Negro mechanics, on anything like a large scale, will have become opportune, but not until then.

I know full well the argument of the contra-contendents—how that an appreciable increase in the present number of Negro mechanics would make a white contractor independent of white mechanics when his interests might warrant the employment of Negro tradesmen. But it cannot be justly claimed that this argument rises to the force and dignity of an argument. It is at the very best but a mere theory, and one shorn of plausibility for the reason that it apparently overlooks the fact that the trade-unions, by the power of the boycott, could influence the dealers both in raw and manufactured material not to sell to said contractor, and thus abort his designs to defy them by the employment of Negro artisans. The trade-unions constitute a most potent organization, and it is very difficult to thwart its will. Therefore, the primal and essential accomplishment is to influence its directors to abandon the cruel and frigid color line.

But then, it can be answered that if the Negro mechanic cannot find employment for his skilled hands, let him go to the farm and engage in agricultural pursuits—learn how to scientifically raise sweet potatoes, as the present chief revivalist of the industrial training for the Negro is wont to urge.

When in the unregistered aeons of the genesis of creative development—when prehistoric man roamed at will, and before God had fixed the bounds of man's habitation—in what recorded cycle of time was it written on the

---

*By the late 1890s most of the unions affiliated with the American Federation of Labor and all of the Railroad Brotherhoods barred blacks from membership either through constitutional barriers or specific restrictive clauses in their rituals. Black mechanics in the South were organized in a few unions affiliated with the A.F. of L. into separate Jim Crow locals, but their conditions were inferior to the white members of the unions and their numbers were limited.

tablet of divine fiat that the universal position of the Negro should be that of a tiller of the soil? It may not be a self-evident truth that all men are created free and equal, but it is an axiomatic verity that all men, other than imbeciles and idiots, are endowed with mental and spiritual capacities capable of varied and illimitable expansion; and the Negro, being a man, is irremovably within the sphere of this axiomatic verity. Hence, unless it can be established that the Negro is not an integral and component part of the original plan of man's creation, but the increment of a mere accident, the crystallization of the particles of the surplus dust that marked the creative place of generic man, it must be accepted as the corollary of the axiomatic verity that the Negro, in common with all the other race varieties, is endowed with mental and spiritual capacities, capable of varied and illimitable expansion; and that, as a whole, his sphere of operation cannot be limited to the tilling of the soil; but that his development will be marked by variety of attainments and accomplishments, thus proving himself to be an originator as well as an imitator.

Moreover, the acquisition of scientific agriculture cannot possibly profit the masses of the Negroes to any great extent, seeing that they are not the owners of the soil. By this I refer to the diversification of crops as the result of a knowledge of scientific agriculture. The diversification of crops is not dictated and controlled by the tillers of the soil, but by the owners. The plantation hand in the South exercises no choice whatever as to the number of acres he shall plant in cotton or the number he shall plant in corn or wheat or any other cereal. In this regard he must obey the mandates of his employer. In view of this, is the suggestion valueless that so far as the utility of a diversification of crops is concerned, that this advice should be pressed upon the owner of the soil rather than upon the tiller? It is the owner alone who can change the existing conditions of things. The advice which Secretary of Agriculture Wilson gave to the young white men of the South, in his address at the McKinley banquet in Savannah, Georgia, was most opportune and should impress the present chief revivalist of industrial training for the Negro with the fact that in insisting on the study of scientific agriculture by the masses of the Negroes, he is building a cage for a bird that is yet to be caught; unless, perchance, the Negroes should become the owners of the soil. There can be no doubt that the practical application of the principles of scientific agriculture will increase the yield of a given crop in a stated area; but if by this it is meant that a knowledge of scientific agriculture is essential to teach the Negro how to hoe cotton and plant corn, such is as far from the reality as the east is from the west; as the Negro has long since graduated in the accomplishment of hoeing cotton and planting corn, and his diploma was stamped on the great majority of the ten million bales of cotton which were marketed in this country last year. Therefore aspire to add to the Negro's present limited fund of knowledge by teaching him how to do something which he does not now know how to do.

The necessity of the Negro's training in industrial pursuits, either as a theory or a dictum, did not originate with this generation, but is coeval with his existence on the American continent. With equal propriety might one term John Wesley the apostle of Christianity as to term the Master of Tuskegee the apostle of industrial training for the Negro. The former was simply the revivalist of a long-existing doctrine; the latter is merely the revivalist of an ancient dictum, "Teach the Negro how to work,"* and in reechoing this dictum has struck a popular chord in the minds, if not the hearts, of a large element of the American people, some of whom emphasize their approval by throwing dollars into his open hands. . . .

When the present chief advocate of industrial training for the Negro as the speediest and most effective solution of the so-called race problem shall have gone outside of his own bailiwick, as I have; when he shall have placed himself in a position to observe the present status of the various elements of mankind, notably in Europe, West and Southwest Africa, South America, and the Caribbean Archipelago; when he shall have seen a woman and a dog hitched together and drawing a loaded cart through the streets of Antwerp, Belgium; when he shall have seen Hungarian women digging coal in the mines of their own native land; when he shall have looked upon the peasantry of Europe, so poorly fed, poorly clad, poorly housed, and poorly paid; when his attention shall have been directed to the fact that three fifths of the inhabitants of the earth live in a one-room hut, that scientific agriculture is as little known to the peasantry of Europe as it is to the plantation hands of the Southland, and that the farmer has no more to do with the diversification of the crops than do the latter, he may at least find some of his views modified thereby, come to realize that the doctrine of the survival of the fittest will shape and govern the destiny of the Negro as it does that of all other race societies, that the Negro cannot be limited to any one sphere of physical or mental operation, but will ramify every nook and corner of Americanism and add his quota to its strength, perpetuity and adornment.■

---

*For evidence that industrial education had a long history in this country prior to the appearance of Booker T. Washington as its leading exponent, see August Meier, "The Beginning of Industrial Education in Negro Schools," *Midwest Journal* 7 (Spring 1955), 23–44.

147 SOME FACTS ABOUT SOUTHERN LYNCHINGS

Reverend D. A. Graham

As the nineteenth century drew to a close, the wave of racist vio-lence continued unabated. In Palmetto, Georgia, in April 1899, a cheering crowd of two thousand white men, women, and children watched Sam Hose burn alive, then rushed forward to tear apart his body for souvenirs. Pieces of his crushed bones sold for a quarter; slices of his liver cost a dime. In response to the lynching of Sam Hose, the Na-tional Afro-American Council (established in 1898) issued a public ap-peal to southern leaders to maintain the rule of law and called for na-tionwide observances by black communities.

In May 1899, the council issued a proclamation calling upon African Americans to set apart Friday, June 2, "as a day of fasting and prayer." Special exercises were to be held in black churches across the nation the following Sunday, as a protest against oppression and, especially, lynch-ing. On June 4, the Reverend D. A. Graham delivered the following ser-mon at the Bethel A.M.E. Church in Indianapolis. The statistics on lynch-ing in his sermon were obtained from the Chicago Record, *a white daily paper, and the* Richmond Planet, *a black weekly.*

Below is the Reverend Mr. Graham's sermon, reprinted from the Re-corder, *a black weekly published in Indianapolis, June 10, 1899.*

THE AMERICAN NEGRO is afflicted, and the cause of his affliction is a most unreasonable and silly prejudice in the white Americans. If the hatred were reversed it would seem more reasonable, since the Caucasian has suffered nothing from the Negro, while the latter has suffered everything at the hands of the Caucasian. While this prejudice is greatest in the South, it also manifests itself greatly to the affliction of the colored man in the North.

When he wants to buy property or rent a house he is often turned away because of his color. When he seeks employment where help is advertised for, he is told that "Negroes need not apply." Our girls cannot get employ-ment in shops, stores or factories, no matter how well educated, refined and good-looking. Naturally, this causes many to fall into evil ways and makes dishonest men of youth who with a man's chance would have become hon-orable and industrious citizens.

But when we cross Mason and Dixon's line the evil shows itself at every turn. Separate waiting rooms, separate ticket windows, separate cars, noth-ing to eat at any lunch counter. Refused admission to churches, cemeteries and even parks. Parks and cemeteries are placarded "Negroes and dogs not admitted." The effect of such proscription is most baneful as well as inconvenient. How can the colored youth ever learn to look upon himself as a man when he is constantly treated as a brute? This is one of the greatest causes of vice and drunkenness among the Negroes.

To the Southern whites the manly, refined Negro is the most despicable because "he tries to act white," while the ignorant, servile fellow who dances jigs and acts the monkey on the street is the "good old darkey of antebellum days." The disfranchisement of the Negroes in the South is not the worst evil. If they would require an educational qualification for all voters, we would see no evil in it whatever.

The greatest affliction we have to suffer is the lack of trial by jury when accused of crime. Lynching of Negroes is growing to be a Southern pastime. When reproved for their barbarity they say, "The only way to stop lynching is to stop the crime which leads to lynching." Many Northern people are influenced by this cry and talk about lynching as if it were always for crimes against women. Even some colored people up here have fallen into this error. You will pardon me, therefore, while I give you some plain facts to set you right about this. Since January 1, 1892, 1,226 people have been lynched in this country, principally Negroes. Not one third of these persons were accused of assaulting women.

In 1892, out of 241 lynched, only 46 had such charge against them. In 1893, out of 159 lynched, 39 were so charged. Last year, out of 131 lynched, 24 were charged either with assault or attempted assault. In the face of these figures who can say that we can stop lynching by stopping one crime? The very next day after Sam Hose was roasted and his charred remains divided among the white savages of Georgia for souvenirs,[*] a Negro, Willis Sees, at Osceola, Arkansas, was hung on suspicion of barn burning. In 1894, 10 were lynched for barn burning. Three women were lynched the same year in three different states. Again, I beg you to consider carefully these charges of assault. How many of them are guilty? What is the proof against them?

One year ago yesterday in the town of Dorcyville, Louisiana, a man named Will Steak was burned alive upon the charge of assault of one Mrs. Parrish. The *Times Democrat* of New Orleans in its account of the affair said: "Mrs. Parrish identified the Negro almost positively." He died protesting his innocence, but because he was almost identified he was burned alive.

William Offet, of Elyria, Ohio, was fortunate because he was in a Northern state. Being identified by Mrs. J. C. Underwood, the wife of a minister, he was sent to the penitentiary for fifteen years. When he had been in prison four years, this "respectable white lady," conscience smitten, confessed to her husband that she was equally guilty with the Negro. The husband had the prisoner pardoned, and secured a divorce from his depraved wife. There are many such cases.

[*]For further information on the lynching of Sam Hose (Holt), see Stewart E. Tolnay and E. M. Beck, *A Festival of Violence: An Analysis of Southern Lynchings, 1882\1930* (Urbana: University of Illinois Press, 1995).

Ed Coy, who was burned at Texarkana, Arkansas, was another instance exactly similar to that of Offet, and Judge Tourgee* obtained the proof that the relatives and husband of the woman who made the charge were fully cognizant of the fact that she was equally guilty with Coy. They compelled her to make the charge and then to set fire to her paramour. Again, white men often black themselves and commit crime, then lead a mob to lynch some Negro who may happen to be in the neighborhood. In Atlanta, Georgia, about four years ago a black man was discovered in the room of a young white girl of high standing. While attempting to escape he was shot and captured. The black man was found to be the son of a prominent white neighbor with his face and hands blacked. Had he not been captured some poor Negro would have been seized, identified "almost positively" and hung to the nearest tree. A similar case happened in Tennessee a few years ago. Many innocent men are thus hanged or burned alive just because American prejudice refuses them a trial by their peers.

And some court trials are little better than mob trials. The present governor of Georgia, Mr. Candler, while district judge three years ago, sent Ed Aikin, a boy of nineteen years, to the chain gang for ten years on the charge of attempted assault. The only evidence the girl offered against him was that she met him coming down a path and as he did not get out of the path she was afraid and ran. She swore that he was not within ten feet of her, did not speak to her, and did not follow her, but she would make an example of him so that young darkies would get out of the path when they saw white girls coming. Thereupon he sentenced him to ten years in the chain gang. This is an example of attempted assault.

Now, we want it distinctly understood that we are not trying to excuse crime. We contend that the death penalty should be inflicted upon every man who assaults a woman, without regard to the color of the victim or the criminal. This is more than the whites ask or will allow. In fact, there are twenty colored women assaulted by white men for every white woman assaulted by Negroes. Such cases are countless in every community in the South, but there is no redress for the colored women, either by law or by custom. Colored women are absolutely at the mercy of white men in the South, and a man does not lose social prestige or church relationship for ruining colored girls. I compelled a white Southern minister to acknowledge this fact before the ministers' meeting of Minneapolis a few years ago. And yet they talk about the immorality of the Negroes!

Under all these afflictions we have a great work to perform. We must not allow the injustice and cruelty of the whites to divert our attention from

---

*Albion W. Tourgée, a reformist judge in North Carolina during Reconstruction and author of two Reconstruction novels, *A Fool's Errand* (1879) and *Bricks Without Straw* (1880), was a leading white champion of black equality in the post-Reconstruction era. In October 1891, Tourgée founded the National Citizens' Rights Association, an interracial organization, to combat lynching and disfranchisement and uphold black rights.

our own weaknesses and shortcomings. More attention must be given to the cultivation of Christian character. The morals of the race must be improved. Our women must spend more time in mothers' meetings and clubs for intellectual and moral culture and less on parties, receptions and balls. More money should be spent for good literature and in support of Christian Endeavor, Y.M.C.A., and kindred organizations instead of on Sunday excursions and theaters.

If American justice and Christianity have decreed that we must lift ourselves by our own bootstraps let us set ourselves heroically to the task. Measured by the depth from which we have come, we have much to encourage us; casting our eyes to the summits yet to be gained, let us thank God and press on.■

148 THE BURDEN OF THE EDUCATED COLORED WOMAN

Lucy Craft Laney

Hailed by the New York Age *(November 11, 1933) shortly after her death as "one of the greatest Negro women of the twentieth century," Lucy Craft Laney was born in Macon, Georgia, in 1854. She was one of ten children. Taught to read and write by her mother, a domestic worker, she graduated from Macon's Lewis High School and entered Atlanta University at the age of fifteen, graduating in 1873 as a member of the first class of the Higher Normal Department.*

Laney taught in the Georgia public schools for ten years and in 1883, with the aid of the Presbyterian Board of Missions, opened her own school in Augusta. Women principals were a rarity and many doubted her ability to sustain the school. By 1914, Haines Normal School boasted over thirty teachers and nine hundred pupils and had gained a reputation as an outstanding liberal arts institution. Mary McLeod Bethune began her teaching career under Laney's tutelage at Haines. Among the distinguished graduates was Morehouse College president John Hope, who credited Laney with his love of the classics. Laney developed programs to educate black teachers and nurses and, inspired by the innovations of German educator Friedrich Froebel, opened Augusta's first kindergarten. W. E. B. Du Bois pronounced her "the dark vestal virgin who kept the *fires of Negro education fiercely flaming in the rich but mean-spirited city of Augusta, Georgia."**

    A talented orator, Laney often spoke to the need for greater support for education. In her address to the Hampton Negro Conference in July 1899, she stressed the need for more black women teachers at every level of the educational system, from kindergarten to college. "Only those of character and culture can do successful lifting," she explained, "for she who would mould character must herself possess it." Laney envisioned the public lecture platform as presenting an opportunity to extend the teacher's reach beyond the classroom, because "as a public lecturer she may give advice, helpful suggestions, and important knowledge that will change a whole community and start its people on the upward way."

    The text of Laney's address was published in the Report of the Hampton Negro Conference No. 111, July 1899, 37–42, *and was reprinted in Bert James Loewenberg and Ruth Bogin, eds.,* Black Women in Nineteenth-Century American Life *(University Park, Pa.: Pennsylvania State University Press, 1976). A testimonial essay on Laney by A. C. Griggs of the Haines Normal and Industrial Institute appeared in the* Journal of Negro History *19 (January 1934), 97–102.*

If the educated colored woman has a burden,—and we believe she has—what is that burden? How can it be lightened, how may it be lifted? What it is can be readily seen perhaps better than told, for it constantly annoys to irritation; it bulges out as did the load of Bunyan's Christian—ignorance—with its inseparable companions, shame and crime and prejudice.

    That our position may be more readily understood, let us refer to the past. . . . During the days of training in our first mission school—slavery—that which is the foundation of right training and good government, the basic rock of all true culture—the home, with its fire-side training, mother's moulding, woman's care, was not only neglected but utterly disregarded. There was no time in the institution for such teaching. We know that there were, even in the first days of that school, isolated cases of men and women of high moral character and great intellectual worth, as Phillis Wheatley, Sojourner Truth, and John Chavers [Chavis?], whose work and lives should have taught, or at least suggested to their instructors, the capabilities and possibilities of their dusky slave pupils. The progress and the struggles of these for noble things should have led their instructors to see how the souls and minds of this people then yearned for light—the real life. But alas! these dull teachers, like many modern pedagogues and school-keepers, failed to know their pupils—to find out their real needs, and hence had no cause to study methods of better and best development of the boys and girls under

*Quoted in Casper LeRoy Jordan, "Lucy Craft Laney," in Jessie Carney Smith, ed., *Notable Black Women* (Detroit: Gale Research, 1992), 651.

their care. What other result could come from such training or want of training than a conditioned race such as we now have?

For two hundred and fifty years they married, or were given in marriage.
Oft times marriage ceremonies were performed for them by the learned minister of the master's church; more often there was simply a consorting by
the master's consent, but it was always understood that these unions for
cause, or without cause, might be more easily broken, than a divorce can be
obtained in Indiana or Dakota. Without going so long a distance as from
New York to Connecticut, the separated could take other companions for
life, for a long or short time; for during those two hundred and fifty years
there was not a single marriage legalized in a single southern state, where
dwelt the mass of this people. There was something of the philosopher in
the plantation preacher, who, at the close of the marriage ceremony, had the
dusky couple join their right hands, and then called upon the assembled congregation to sing, as he lined it out, "Plunged in a gulf of dark despair," for
well he knew the sequel of many such unions. If it so happened that a husband and wife were parted by those who owned them, such owners often
consoled those thus parted with the fact that he could get another wife; she,
another husband. Such was the sanctity of the marriage vow that was taught
and held for over two hundred and fifty years. Habit is indeed second nature.
This is the race inheritance. I thank God not of all, for we know, each of us,
of instances, of holding most sacred the plighted love and keeping faithfully
and sacredly the marriage vows. We know of pure homes and of growing old
together. Blessed heritage! If we only had the gold there might be many
"Golden Weddings." Despair not; the crushing burden of immorality which
has its root in the disregard of the marriage vow, can be lightened. It must
be, and the educated colored woman can and will do her part in lifting this
burden.

In the old institution there was no attention given to homes and to
home-making. Homes were only places in which to sleep, father had neither
responsibility nor authority; mother, neither cares nor duties. She wielded
no gentle sway nor influence. The character of their children was a matter
of no concern to them; surroundings were not considered. It is true, house
cleaning was sometimes enforced as a protection to property, but this was
done at stated times and when ordered. There is no greater enemy of the race
than these untidy and filthy homes; they bring not only physical disease and
death, but they are very incubators of sin; they bring intellectual and moral
death. The burden of giving knowledge and bringing about the practice of
the laws of hygiene among a people ignorant of the laws of nature and common decency, is not a slight one. But this, too, the intelligent women can
and must help to carry.

The large number of young men in the state prison is by no means the
least of the heavy burdens. It is true that many of these are unjustly sentenced; that longer terms of imprisonment are given Negroes than white persons for the same offences; it is true that white criminals by the help of

attorneys, money, and influence, oftener escape the prison, thus keeping small the number of prisoners recorded, for figures never lie. It is true that many are tried and imprisoned for trivial causes, such as the following, clipped from the *Tribune*, of Elberyon, Ga.: "Seven or eight Negroes were arrested and tried for stealing two fish-hooks last week. When the time of our courts is wasted in such a manner as this, it is high time to stop and consider whither we are driving. Such picayunish cases reflect on the intelligence of a community. It is fair to say the courts are not to blame in this matter." Commenting on this *The South Daily* says: "We are glad to note that the sentiment of the paper is against the injustice. Nevertheless these statistics will form the basis of some lecturer's discourse." This fact remains, that many of our youth are in prison, that large numbers of our young men are serving out long terms of imprisonment, and this is a very sore burden. Five years ago while attending a Teacher's Institute at Thomasville, Ga., I saw working on the streets in the chain gang, with rude men and ruder women, with ignorant, wicked, almost naked men, criminals, guilty of all the sins named in the decalogue, a large number of boys from ten to fifteen years of age, and two young girls between the ages of twelve and sixteen. It is not necessary that prison statistics be quoted, for we know too well the story, and we feel most sensibly this burden, the weight of which will sink us unless it is at once made lighter and finally lifted.

Last, but not least, is the burden of prejudice, heavier in that it is imposed by the strong, those from whom help, not hindrance, should come. They are making the already heavy burden of their victims heavier to bear, and yet they are commanded by One who is even the Master of all: "Bear ye one another's burdens, and thus fulfil the law." This is met with and must be borne everywhere. In the South, in public conveyances, and at all points of race contact; in the North, in hotels, at the baptismal pool, in cemeteries; everywhere, in some shape or form, it is to be borne. No one suffers under the weight of this burden as the educated Negro woman does; and she must help to lift it.

Ignorance and immorality, if they are not the prime causes, have certainly intensified prejudice. The forces to lighten and finally to lift this and all of these burdens are true culture and character, linked with that most substantial coupler, cash. We said in the beginning that the past can serve no further purpose than to give us our present bearings. It is a condition that confronts us. With this we must deal, it is this we must change. The physician of today inquires into the history of his patient, but he has to do especially with diagnosis and cure. We know the history; we think a correct diagnosis has often been made—let us attempt a cure. We would prescribe: homes—better homes, clean homes, pure homes; schools—better schools; more culture; more thrift; and work in large doses; put the patient at once on this treatment and continue through life. Can woman do this work? She can; and she must do her part, and her part is by no means small.

Nothing in the present century is more noticeable than the tendency of women to enter every hopeful field of wage-earning and philanthropy, and attempt to reach a place in every intellectual arena. Women are by nature fitted for teaching very young children; their maternal instinct makes them patient and sympathetic with their charges. Negro women of culture, as kindergartners and primary teachers have a rare opportunity to lend a hand to the lifting of these burdens, for here they may instill lessons of cleanliness, truthfulness, loving kindness, love for nature, and love for Nature's God. Here they may daily start aright hundreds of our children; here, too, they may save years of time in the education of the child; and may save many lives from shame and crime by applying the law of prevention. In the kindergarten and primary school is the salvation of the race.

For children of both sexes from six to fifteen years of age, women are more successful as teachers than men. This fact is proven by their employment. Two-thirds of the teachers in the public schools of the United States are women. It is the glory of the United States that good order and peace are maintained not by a large, standing army of well trained soldiers, but by the sentiment of her citizens, sentiments implanted and nourished by her well trained army of four hundred thousand school teachers, two-thirds of whom are women.

The educated Negro woman, the woman of character and culture, is needed in the schoolroom not only in the kindergarten, and in the primary and the secondary school; but she is needed in high school, the academy, and the college. Only those of character and culture can do successful lifting, for she who would mould character must herself possess it. Not alone in the schoolroom can the intelligent woman lend a lifting hand, but as a public lecturer she may give advice, helpful suggestions, and important knowledge that will change a whole community and start its people on the upward way. To be convinced of the good that can be done for humanity by this means one need only recall the names of Lucy Stone, Mary Livermore, Frances Harper, Frances Willard and Julie Ward Howe. The refined and noble Negro woman may lift much with this lever. Women may also be most helpful as teachers of sewing schools and cooking classes, not simply in the public schools and private institutions, but in classes formed in neighborhoods that sorely need this knowledge. Through these classes girls who are not in school may be reached; and through them something may be done to better their homes, and inculcate habits of neatness and thrift. To bring the influence of the schools to bear upon these homes is the most needful thing of the hour. Often teachers who have labored most arduously, conscientiously, and intelligently have become discouraged on seeing that society had not been benefited, but sometimes positively injured by the conduct of their pupils.

The work of the classroom has been completely neutralized by the training of the home. Then we must have better homes, and better homes mean better mothers, better fathers, better born children. Emerson says, "To the well-born child all the virtues are natural, not painfully acquired."

But "The temporal life which is not allowed to open into the eternal life becomes corrupt and feeble even in its temporalness." As a teacher in the Sabbath school, as a leader in young people's meetings and missionary societies, in women's societies and Bible classes our cultured women are needed to do a great and blessed work. Here they may cause many budding lives to open into eternal life. Froebel urged teachers and parents to see to the blending of the temporal and divine life when he said, "God created man in his own image; therefore man should create and bring forth like God." The young people are ready and anxiously await intelligent leadership in Christian work. The less fortunate women already assembled in churches, are ready for work. Work they do and work they will; that it may be effective work, they need the help and leadership of their more favored sisters.

A few weeks ago this country was startled by the following telegram of southern women of culture sent to Ex-Governor Northern of Georgia, just before he made his Boston speech: "You are authorized to say in your address tonight that the women of Georgia, realizing the great importance to both races of early moral training of the Negro race, stand ready to undertake this work when means are supplied." But more startled was the world the next day, after cultured Boston had supplied a part of the means, $20,000, to read the glaring head lines of the southern press, "Who will Teach the Black Babies?" because some of the cultured women who had signed the telegram had declared when interviewed, that Negro women fitted for the work could not be found, and no self-respecting southern white woman would teach a colored kindergarten. Yet already in Atlanta, Georgia, and in Athens, Georgia, southern women are at work among Negroes. There is plenty of work for all who have the proper conception of the teacher's office, who know that all men are brothers, God being their common father. But the educated Negro woman must teach the "Black Babies;" she must come forward and inspire our men and boys to make a successful onslaught upon sin, shame, and crime.■

149 THE STATE OF THE COUNTRY FROM A BLACK MAN'S POINT OF VIEW

Reverend D. P. Brown

The annual sessions of the conference of the African Methodist Episcopal Church usually featured the presentation of an address on the state of the country. In August 1899, at the height of white supremacist crimes against black people, the Reverend D. P. Brown deliv-

ered a lengthy and moving analysis of the state of the country as seen by a black man, in an address to the New England Conference of the African Methodist Episcopal Church. No keener summing-up of the status of African Americans at this time was presented, and few more effective indictments of the indifference of the national administration to the plight of black citizens had been set forth.

Brown begins and concludes his address by expressing the skepticism of many African Americans regarding U.S. aims in the Spanish-American War. Although the United States claimed to be fighting a war of liberation on behalf of the Cubans and Filipinos, Brown argues, "it was difficult to make many believe that a government which had shown so little concern for the lives and liberties of ten millions of its most loyal citizens should so suddenly become . . . imbued with a love of liberty for our brothers in black in another country." Like Booker T. Washington in his Chicago speech in 1898, Brown employs the service and bravery of African American soldiers in the war against Spain as a basis for arguing for the entitlement of full citizenship rights. Unlike Washington, Brown holds no illusion that these rights will be recognized. The closing portion of the address includes a scorching attack on American imperialist policy in the Philippine Islands.

The speech of the Reverend Mr. Brown is presented here as excerpted from the text published in the Christian Recorder, *August 17, 1899. For further information on African American views of the Spanish-American War, see Willard B. Gatewood, Jr.,* "Smoked Yankees" and the Struggle for Empire: Letters from Negro Soldiers, 1899–1902 *(Fayetteville: University of Arkansas Press, 1987).*

W HEN THIS annual conference was in session about one year ago, our country was just entering upon a war, the purpose of which was declared to be the independence of Cuba, to assist that people struggling for freedom to throw off the Spanish yoke of oppression and to assist them in driving from their borders the last trace of Spanish tyranny and misrule from their fair land, made red with the blood of their fathers fighting for their independence.

This on the part of the Americans was a most laudable purpose, for it was in the cause of humanity, in behalf of a brave people who deserved, and ought, to be free; and yet we cannot yield the fact that there were many persons who believe then, as many do now, that the war on the part of the Americans was not so much in the interest of humanity as it was for territorial expansion—a war to open up to this country greater commercial interest and advantages. It was difficult to make many believe that a government which had shown so little concern for the lives and liberties of ten millions of its most loyal citizens should so suddenly become interested in and imbued with a love of liberty for our brothers in black in another country. I believe I express the wish of this conference that only good should come to this people and that this war should be the indirect means for wiping the prejudice and bitterness that has become so firmly rooted against the black man in this country. That we have emerged from this war a greater and more powerful nation in the eyes of the civilized world, no one will deny. Our wonderful resources have been shown in that we were in a day able to man a navy from nothing, that astonished the civilized nations of the earth and compelled us to wonder at our own powers.

Our formidable position among the great nations has, as never before, become recognized. This much at least has been accomplished. When the bugle sounded "to arms," white men were not the only men to answer and obey that call, but men of our race, whose ancestors have felt the wrongs of human slavery, were most eager to shoulder the musket, that they might, if need be, give their lives to the cause, if thereby freedom should come to brave Maceo and his devoted followers.*

Strange as it may appear, it was difficult to convince those in authority that men of our race should be permitted to bare their breasts to Spanish shot and shell, to give their lives in the cause of humanity.

This war was felt to be the "white man's burden," freeing this dark-hued race, a war in which the black man was not wanted. A strange thing! The bravery which our ancestors had shown at Fort Wagner, Fisher, Port Hudson, Nashville, and a hundred other battlefields where they fought and shed their blood for the preservation of the Union, was, it would seem, no guarantee that in this war for humanity they would make fit soldiers. It seemed to have been the policy, even after they were accepted, not to permit them to go to the front and take an active part in the conflict. But for the black heroes of the 9th and 10th Cavalry and of the 24th and 25th Infantry, who immortalized themselves when they marched up San Juan Hill, even over the bodies of our own white troops who could not stand the Spanish bullets and who fought as soldiers had never before in their gallant charge at El Caney, virtually and forever crushing Spanish rule in Cuba, winning for themselves the plaudits of the civilized world, the black soldiers would not have been known in the American-Spanish war.† This gallant charge has left the impression that he has no superior and few equals as a soldier, and yet for this daring bravery in saving the day rescuing the Rough Riders from certain death, how many of these immortal heroes have received commissions in the regular Army? Not a man. On the other hand, how many hundred white men have been commissioned for bravery with a life term in the regular Army, who have never been in a battle? Why this discrimination against these heroes?

---

*Antonio Maceo, "the Bronze Titan," was the black leader of the guerrilla independence fighters in Cuba during the Ten Years' War (1868–1878) and the Second War for Independence, which began in 1895. He was killed in battle by the Spaniards in 1896.

†One southern white officer said: "If it had not been for the Negro cavalry the Rough Riders would have been exterminated. I am not a Negro lover. My father fought with Mosby's Rangers, and I was born in the South, but the Negroes saved the fight, and the day will come when General Shafter will give them credit for their bravery." *Literary Digest* (August 27, 1898), 248.

Has the war wiped out the color line as we had hoped it would? On the contrary has it not more clearly drawn the lines? Has not the bravery of these black heroes opened the eyes of the white man to the fact that there is in his midst a race of people capable of furnishing soldiers equal to, if not in many respects superior to, his own? Even if, before his election as Governor of New York, Roosevelt called our soldiers brave men, and spoke in the highest terms of them, yet since his election he calls these same soldiers cowards; shame on such a man who would contradict himself, which shows to the world his only desire was to secure the black man's vote.*

The picture we have seen fit to paint may not be such a one as many would like to gaze upon. It is far better that we should deal with the facts as we see them, than to cover them up. No wrong was ever righted that was not at first exposed. To discuss the "State of the Country" in the usual way might indicate a different line from the one I have seen fit to follow. I go out of the beaten track because I believe it is right to do so. Our prosperity, our commercial relations, our wonderful resources, our material growth might seem proper, but imbued with and impelled by a love of humanity broader than mere material wealth and prosperity and filled with a race pride for our fellow men, we are under the circumstances compelled to speak out in "open meeting" and discuss "The State of the Country" from a black man's point of view, as I think I see it, to cry down from the house tops and spare not, until righteousness shall prevail in all parts of this country and man shall do justice to his fellow man. What does the greatness or prosperity of our country amount to, to us as a race, if at the same time it shows to the civilized world either its weakness or unwillingness to protect ten millions of its most loyal citizens in the enjoyment of the simplest rights set forth in the Declaration of Independence that gave birth to this country and is supposed to be the fundamental principles and cornerstone upon which this fabric rests? What is it to us if the wages of the factory employees are increased, if over the door of each of them the sign hangs out, "No Black Man Wanted Here," no black boy or girl shall enter here that they may become skilled artisans? Why should we shout for prosperity that means much to the white

---

*When campaigning for the governorship of New York in October 1898, Roosevelt said, "As I heard one of the Rough Riders say after the charge at San Juan, 'Well, the Ninth and Tenth men [the Negroes in the Ninth and Tenth Cavalry] are all right. They can drink out of our canteens.'" He expressed the highest praise for the blacks who charged up San Juan with his Rough Riders and concluded, "I don't think that any Rough Rider will ever forget the tie that binds us to the Ninth and Tenth Cavalry" ("Roosevelt to Colored Men," *New York Times*, October 15, 1898, p. 2). But writing in *Scribner's Magazine* in April of the following year, months after he had been elected governor, Roosevelt said that the blacks behaved well, *but* "they are, of course, peculiarly dependent on their white officers. . . . None of the white regulars of Rough Riders showed the slightest sign of weakening; but under the strain the colored infantrymen began to get a little uneasy and to drift to the rear" ("The Rough Riders," *Scribner's Magazine* 23 [April 1899], 435–36). Roosevelt added that he could not permit this drifting and drew his revolver in order to halt the retreating blacks and threatened that he would shoot any man who went to the rear under any pretense whatever.

man and but little to his brother in black, when we know that it is the fixed purpose and determination to drive us from every favored avenue where we may earn our daily bread? What is all this to us if the courts in many sections are closed against us, meting out to us only injustice and cruelty? Why should we shout for a seeming prosperity,* when those high in authority sit silently by and see us murdered without cause, and robbed of every right guaranteed in the Constitution and laws, and utter not a single protest against these outrages? I am not a pessimist, my whole nature is the opposite, but the better part of me rebels, and all else is forgotten when I know the wrongs and injustices meted out to us as a race. A condition of things that makes me quake with fear for the safety of my country, when I remember that God is just. As a nation we are sowing to the wind, and we must certainly, ultimately reap the whirlwind and the question is, And what shall that harvest be?

Where shall we seek for relief? Shall we seek it in the commercial or industrial avenues? Shall we hope to find it in the ordinary walks of life? Are we not being excluded almost wholly from each and all of these?

At one time it was said "get wealth and education and all else will follow." Have we not in a single generation, beginning without capital, gathered in material wealth and landed possessions, more than four hundred million and set forth from our best colleges hundreds of cultured men and women, and given more than three millions of our boys and girls the rudiments of a common-school education such as is enjoyed by the masses of the whites? And yet, equipped along these lines as we are, instead of these solving the problem in our favor they seem to operate against us, and but add fuel to the flames and have made the white man more determined to oppress us in all the avenues. What is the cause of this? Some say that it is prejudice, but I cannot lead myself to so believe. Better call it friction or competition. The greater our attainments the greater the desire to enter the more favored avenues and the more we like to compete with our white brother in these.

Does not this grow out of the fact that we have demonstrated to the white man that under the same favorable conditions we are capable of the same development along the favored lines that he treads? We are competing and, handicapped as we are, winning; and in this lies the secret of the oppression which is daily being heaped upon the race. Is it not to crush out the manhood in us, well knowing if that can be accomplished all else they wish to our detriment will follow? If in one generation these wonderful strides have been made, is it probable that with a capital of culture and wealth to the credit side of the ledger, that this will be greatly increased? Is not this wonderful progress the real cause underlying this antagonism? In short, have we not become too great competitors? Is not this the secret? Shall we, however, become less ambitious? Shall we cease to gather wealth and

---

*The Republican Party boasted that it had restored prosperity after the economic depression of 1893 to 1897, and McKinley campaigned for reelection in 1900 on the "full dinner pail" platform as well as in favor of overseas expansion.

culture to our stock already in hand? On the contrary, should we not redouble our efforts as never before? Wealth and education will not lessen the friction of the oppression heaped upon us—not for the present at least. The wealthiest among the race, who may count his thousands by the hundreds, receives the same treatment as the most ordinary black man who represents no material wealth, when the question arises as to his enjoyment of his rights as a man, to which he is entitled. He must be driven into the same Jim Crow car with the most degraded, however cultured he may be. After all, there is but one thing needed by the Negro in this country, and that is absolute liberty. Grant him that and there will be no so-called Negro problem to solve. Grant him all the rights enjoyed by the most degraded Anglo-Saxon and we would ask for nothing more. Give us an even chance along these lines is all we ask. How shall this be accomplished, do you ask? By molding sound, healthy public sentiment against these outrages and injustices. By whom, do you ask? The churches of the Anglo-Saxon are dumb, just as they were when the slave trade made and held public sentiment for their peculiar institution, American slavery. We can, therefore, hope for but little from that source. Our own churches cannot do it alone. Would I venture too far to say that there is no more powerful factor for this, than the head of this nation, the Chief Executive?

We do not forget certain limitations contained in the Constitution, which may, in some instances, hamper him; and yet one word from him condemning these outrages, lynchings, burnings, and the denial of our rights as American citizens, would do more to further this end and correct these evils than anything else. One word, said officially to these wrongdoers, would do more to mold this public sentiment than any other. A word to Congress condemning this wholesale slaughter of our race, and pointing out to that body wherein we are denied our civil and political rights, would compel that body to take judicial notice of them. A word in his message to Congress, last December, touching upon the slaughter of our people in North and South Carolina, for no other reason than that the black man wished to exercise his right of suffrage, would have done much good. But, like the Anglo-Saxon church, he was silent upon *this* class of American citizens. He *must* be aroused, and it is the duty of *our* church, with more than a half million of members, who are marching up the hill of progress, to remind him that we are not asleep and that he must see to it that the laws are faithfully executed in all sections of this country, in protecting the lives and property of the citizens. This very silence on his part has encouraged these Southern murderers in their cruelty. As an evidence of this, only a short while ago he was visiting in Georgia, virtually for the time the guest of the state; a score of colored men were lynched in Georgia and Mississippi, not for the usual crime with which they are accused, rape, but in the former state only accused of house burning, with evidence that was not conclusive of their guilt; and yet not a word condemning them for these outrages. His very silence is taken as a license to continue this dastardly work.

Let us as Christian brethren, arouse the head of the nation. The politicians, the officeholders among us, dare not speak out for fear of offending the appointing power. We can no longer look to them for a protest. Let us say to the country that we are opposed to any expansion or extension of territory, extending the power to rule over other dark-hued people, so long as this government demonstrates either its weakness or unwillingness to protect our people in this country in the enjoyment of their civil and political rights. Governments are created for this purpose, and when it does not perform this sacred duty, it should not be permitted to extend its weakness and dominion over other people. Let us speak out, in no uncertain language, and enter our protest against this further murdering of an inoffensive people in the Philippines, struggling for their independence. Let us protest against this sham of taking to these people the Christian religion and civilization, with the Bible in one hand, and the bayonet and torch in the other. Until this government shall have demonstrated its ability or willingness to protect the humblest of its citizens at home, in all the enjoyment of all his rights under the law, it is the duty of every black man to protest, even with his vote, against any further expansion or extending its weakness over other black people beyond the seas. We can do this by properly organizing.

We cannot disguise the fact that the Anglo-Saxon cares but little for appeals or protests unless there is something behind them. He cares more for the power contained in the little bit of white paper called the ballot, when it is judiciously handled than all the conventions and resolutions we can hold or send forth. Let every colored man make up his mind to withhold his vote from any man who is named for Congressional honors, until he shall pledge them that he will do all in his power in the lawmaking body, to see that laws are enacted to correct these evils, if they are not already upon the statute books, and to refuse to seat any man who comes with his certificates of election, bringing with it the blood of his fellow man. I repeat, let colored men so organize as to compel the Chief Executive and Congress, to see that every American citizen shall enjoy all the rights guaranteed to him in the Constitution, however humble he may be, whether his face be black or white.

Let us, then, send forth from this conference in no uncertain sounds our grievances, and continue to do so from year to year, until the blackest and humblest citizen shall stand forth a man, enjoying all the rights to which every American citizen is entitled. Until we shall have done this, we shall have failed in our duty to ourselves and our fellow man, and shall fail to receive from God the righteous judge, "Well done thou good and faithful servant." And as we go to our respective fields of labor let us pray:

> God give us men. A time like this demands
>   Strong minds, great hearts, true faith and ready hands;
> Men whom the lust of office does not kill;
>   Men whom the spoils of office cannot buy;
> Men who possess opinions and a will;
>   Men who have honor, men who will not lie;
> Men who can stand before a demagogue,

and scorn his treacherous flatteries without winking,
Tall men, sun-crowned, who live above the fog
In public duty and private thinking.∎

150 MY MOTHER AS I RECALL HER

Rosetta Douglass Sprague

"Too often," writes Fredericka Douglass Sprague Perry, grand-daughter of Frederick and Anna Murray Douglass, "are the facts of the great sacrifices and heroic efforts of the wives of renowned men overshadowed by the achievements of the men and the wonderful and beautiful part she has played so well is overlooked."* This was certainly the case with Anna Murray Douglass (c. 1813–1882), who funded Frederick Douglass's escape from slavery, labored as a shoe binder to support their family while he lectured abroad for two years, and who, in forty-four years of marriage, her daughter Rosetta explained, guarded "as best she could every interest connected with [her husband], his lifework, and the home." She was an active participant in the women's antislavery fair movement and the Underground Railroad. Yet she is almost entirely absent from Douglass's three autobiographies and received little public attention during her lifetime despite her husband's immense celebrity. As Henry Louis Gates, Jr., has written, "Douglass had made of his life story a sort of political diorama in which she had no role" ("A Dangerous Literacy," 16).

After the Douglass family moved to Rochester, New York, Anna Douglass became increasingly reclusive, deprived of her own social contacts, uncomfortable with her husband's widening circle of affluent white friends, and wounded by the public scandals over her husband's affairs with other women. After the death of their youngest child in 1860, her health deteriorated, and she died of a stroke in 1882. Frederick Douglass may have suffered a breakdown following her death.

Five years after her father's death, on May 10, 1900, Rosetta Douglass Sprague paid tribute to her mother in an address before the Anna Murray Douglass Union of the W.C.T.U. in Washington, D.C. Sprague (1839–1906), born in New Bedford, Massachusetts, shortly after Douglass's es-

---

*Foreword to Rosetta Douglass Sprague, *My Mother As I Recall Her* (Washington, D.C.: NACW, 1923), 4.

cape from slavery, was the eldest of the five Douglass children. Although very close to her father, she had long served as her illiterate mother's scribe and had intermittently lived as an adult with her parents.

Sprague offers a portrait of her mother as an archetypal nineteenth-century woman, self-sacrificing and devoted to home and husband yet also strong and highly complex. "She could not be known all at once," Sprague observes; "she had to be studied." Tensions between her parents are buried in Sprague's public recollection. Although unlettered and "not well versed in the polite etiquette of the drawing room," Sprague maintains, her mother possessed such wisdom, virtue, culture, and strength of character that she, too, should be remembered.

The text of Sprague's speech was reprinted as a pamphlet by her daughter, Fredericka Douglass Sprague Perry, for the National Association of Colored Women on February 14, 1923. An abbreviated version, omitting the first paragraphs presented here, was published in the Journal of Negro History *8 (January 1923), 93–101. For further information, see Miriam DeCosta Willis, "Smoothing the Tucks in Father's Linen: The Women of Cedar Hill," in Patricia Bell-Scott, ed.,* Double-Stitch: Black Women Write About Mothers and Daughters *(Boston: Beacon Press, 1991), 131–36; Dorothy Sterling, ed.,* We Are Your Sisters *(New York: Norton, 1984), 134–44; William S. McFeely,* Frederick Douglass *(New York: Norton, 1991); and Henry Louis Gates, Jr., "A Dangerous Literacy: The Legacy of Frederick Douglass,"* New York Times Book Review, *May 28, 1995, p. 16.*

T HE traveler standing at the base of a high mountain viewing for the first time its lofty peak as it towers above him feels his insignificance. He scans its rugged sides with an irresistible desire to know what is hidden at its summit. Not content to stand looking upward, feeding his imagination by silently gazing, he must mount and explore and with no realization of the obstacles to be encountered, but with a determined purpose, he prepares to ascend.

This but epitomizes life. Real life is a struggle, an activity, a will to execute. Desire precedes effort. Life with no desire, no effort is merely an existence, and is void of the elements that make life worth the living.

There have been many who have iterated and re-iterated this idea in as many forms of expression as the individuality of the writers themselves. Life is as the mountain, it may be said to have its base, its rugged sides and its summit.

Looking backward over a space of fifty years or more, I have in remembrance two travelers whose lives were real in their activity; two lives that have indelibly impressed themselves upon my memory; two lives whose energy and best ability was exerted to make my life what it should be, and who gave me a home where wisdom and industry went hand in hand; where instruction was given that a cultivated brain and an industrious hand were the twin conditions that lead to a well balanced and useful life. These two lives were embodied in the personalities of Frederick Douglass and Anna Murray his wife.

They met at the base of a mountain of wrong and oppression, victims of the slave power as it existed over sixty years ago, one smarting under the manifold hardships as a slave, the other in many ways suffering from the effects of such a system.

The story of Frederick Douglass' hopes and aspirations and longing desire for freedom has been told—you all know it. It was a story made possible by the unswerving loyalty of Anna Murray, to whose memory this paper is written.

Anna Murray was born in Denton, Caroline County, Maryland, an adjoining county to that in which my father was born. The exact date of her birth is not known. Her parents, Bambarra Murray and Mary, his wife, were slaves, their family consisting of twelve children, seven of whom were born in slavery and five born in freedom. My mother, the eighth child, escaped by the short period of one month, the fate of her older brothers and sisters, and was the first free child.

Remaining with her parents until she was seventeen, she felt it time that she should be entirely self-supporting and with that idea she left her country home and went to Baltimore, sought employment in a French family by the name of Montell whom she served two years. Doubtless it was while with them she gained her first idea as to household management which served her so well in after years and which gained for her the reputation of a thorough and competent housekeeper.

On leaving the Montells', she served in a family by the name of Wells living on S. Caroline Street. Wells was Post-master at the time of my father's escape from slavery. It interested me very much in one of my recent visits to Baltimore, to go to that house accompanied by an old friend of my parents of those early days, who as a free woman was enabled with others to make my father's life easier while he was a slave in that city. This house is owned now by a colored man. In going through the house I endeavored to remember its appointments, so frequently spoken of by my mother, for she had lived with this family seven years and an attachment sprang up between her and the members of that household, the memory of which gave her pleasure to recall.

The free people of Baltimore had their own circles from which the slaves were excluded. The ruling of them out of their society resulted more from the desire of the slaveholder than from any great wish of the free people themselves. If a slave would dare to hazard all danger and enter among the free people he would be received. To such a little circle of free people—a circle a little more exclusive than others, Frederick Baily was welcomed. Anna Murray, to whom he had given his heart, sympathized with him and she devoted all her energies to assist him. The three weeks prior to the escape were busy and anxious weeks for Anna Murray. She had lived with the Wells family so long and having been able to save the greater part of her earnings was willing to share with the man she loved that he might gain the freedom he yearned to possess. Her courage, her sympathy at the start was the mainspring that supported the career of Frederick Douglass. As is the condition of most wives her identity became so merged with that of her husband, that few of their earlier friends in the North really knew and appreciated the full value of the woman who presided over the Douglass home for forty-four years. When the escaped slave and future husband of Anna Murray had reached New York in safety, his first act was to write her of his arrival and as they had previously arranged she was to come on immediately. Reaching New York a week later, they were married and immediately took their wedding trip to New Bedford. In "My Bondage of Freedom,"* by Frederick Douglass, a graphic account of that trip is given.

The little that they possessed was the outcome of the industrial and economical habits that were characteristic of my mother. She had brought with her sufficient goods and chattel to fit up comfortably two rooms in her New Bedford home—a feather bed with pillows, bed linen, dishes, knives, forks, and spoons, besides a well filled trunk of wearing apparel for herself. A new plum colored silk dress was her wedding gown. To my child eyes that dress was very fine. She had previously sold one of her feather beds to assist in defraying the expenses of the flight from bondage.

The early days in New Bedford were spent in daily toil, the wife at the wash board, the husband with saw, buck and axe. I have frequently listened to the rehearsal of those early days of endeavor, looking around me at the well appointed home built up from the labor of the father and mother under so much difficulty and found it hard to realize that it was a fact. After the day of toil they would seek their little home of two rooms and the meal of the day that was most enjoyable was the supper nicely prepared by mother. Father frequently spoke of the neatly set table with its snowy white cloth— coarse tho' it was.

In 1890 I was taken by my father to these rooms on Elm Street, New Bedford, Mass., overlooking Buzzards Bay. This was my birth place. Every detail as to the early housekeeping was gone over, it was splendidly impressed upon my mind, even to the hanging of a towel on a particular nail. Many of the dishes used by my mother at that time were in our Rochester home and kept as souvenirs of those first days of housekeeping. The fire that destroyed that home in 1872, also destroyed them.

Three of the family had their birthplace in New Bedford. When after having written his first narrative, father built himself a nice little cottage in Lynn, Mass., and moved his family there, previously to making his first trip to Europe. He was absent during the years '45 and '46. It was then that mother with four children, the eldest in her sixth year, struggled to maintain the family amid much that would dampen the courage of many a young woman of to-day. I had previously been taken to Albany by my father as a

*My Bondage and My Freedom (1855).

means of lightening the burden for mother. Abigail and Lydia Mott, cousins of Lucretia Mott, desired to have the care of me.

During the absence of my father, mother sustained her little family by binding shoes. Mother had many friends in the anti-slavery circle of Lynn and Boston who recognized her sterling qualities, and who encouraged her during the long absence of her husband. Those were days of anxious worry. The narrative of Frederick Douglass with its bold utterances of truth, with the names of the parties with whom he had been associated in slave life, so incensed the slaveholders that it was doubtful if ever he would return to this country and also there was danger for mother and those who had aided in his escape, being pursued. It was with hesitancy father consented to leave the country, and not until he was assured by the many friends that mother and the children would be carefully guarded, would he go.

There were among the Anti-Slavery people of Massachusetts a fraternal spirit born of the noble purpose near their heart that served as an uplift and encouraged the best energies in each individual, and mother from the contact with the great and noble workers grew and improved even more than ever before. She was a recognized co-worker in the A. S. Societies of Lynn and Boston, and no circle was felt to be complete without her presence. There was a weekly gathering of the women to prepare articles for the Annual A. S. Fair held in Faneuil Hall, Boston. At that time mother would spend the week in attendance having charge, in company of a committee of ladies of which she was one, over the refreshments. The New England women were all workers and there was no shirking of responsibility—all worked. It became the custom of the ladies of the Lynn society for each to take their turn in assigning mother in her household duties on the morning of the day that the sewing circle met so as to be sure of her meeting with them. It was mother's custom to put aside the earnings from a certain number of shoes she had bound as her donation to the A. S. cause. Being frugal and economic she was able to put by a portion of her earnings for a rainy day.

I have often heard my father speak in admiration of mother's executive ability. During his absence abroad, he sent, as he could, support for his family, and on his coming home he supposed there would be some bills to settle. One day while talking over their affairs, mother arose and quietly going to the bureau drawer produced a Bank book with the sums deposited just in the proportion father had sent, the book also containing deposits of her own earnings—and not a debt had been contracted during his absence.

The greatest trial, perhaps, that mother was called upon to endure, after parting from her Baltimore friends several years before, was the leaving her Massachusetts home for the Rochester home where father established the "North Star." She never forgot her old friends and delighted to speak of them up to her last illness.

Wendell Phillips, Wm. Lloyd Garrison, Sydney Howard Gay and many more with their wives were particularly kind to her. At one of the Anti-Slavery conventions held in Syracuse, father and mother were the guest of Rev.

Samuel J. May, a Unitarian minister and an ardent Anti-Slavery friend. The spacious parlors of the May mansion were thrown open for a reception to their honor and where she should meet her old Boston friends. The refreshments were served on trays, one of which placed upon an improvised table made by the sitting close together of Wendell Phillips, Wm. Lloyd Garrison and Sydney Howard Gay, mother was invited to sit, the four making an interesting tableaux.

Mother occasionally traveled with father on his short trips, but not as often as he would have liked as she was a housekeeper who felt that her presence was necessary in the home, as she was wont to say "to keep things straight." Her life in Rochester was not less active in the cause of the slave, if anything she was more self-sacrificing, and it was a long time after her residence there that she was understood. The atmosphere in where she was placed lacked the genial cordiality that greeted her in her Massachusetts home. There were only the few that learned to know her, for, she drew around herself a certain reserve, after meeting her new acquaintances that forbade any very near approach to her. Prejudice in the early 40's in Rochester ran rampant and mother became more distrustful. There were a few loyal co-workers and she set herself assiduously to work. In the home, with aid of a laundress only, she managed her household. She watched with a great deal of interest and no little pride the growth in public life of my father, and in every possible way that she was capable aided him by relieving him of all the management of the home as to know that when he stood up before an audience that his linen was immaculate and that she had made it so, for, no matter how well, the laundry was done for the family, she must with her own hands smooth the tucks in father's linen and when he was on a long journey she would forward at a given point a fresh supply.

Being herself one of the first agents of the Underground Railroad she was an untiring worker along that line. To be able to accommodate in a comfortable manner the fugitives that passed our way, father enlarged his home where a suite of rooms could be made ready for those fleeing to Canada. It was no unusual occurrence for mother to be called up at all hours of the night, cold or hot as the case may be, to prepare supper for a hungry lot of fleeing humanity.

She was greatly interested in the publication of the "North Star" or Frederick Douglass' paper as it was called later on, and publication day was always a day for extra rejoicing as each weekly paper was felt to be another arrow sent on its way to do the work of puncturing the veil that shrouded a whole race in gloom. Mother felt it her duty to have her table well supplied with extra provisions that day, a custom that we, childlike, fully appreciated. Our home was two miles from the center of the city, where our office was situated, and many times did we trudge through snow knee deep, as street cars were unknown.

During one of the summer vacations the question arose in father's mind as to how his sons should be employed, for them to run wild through the streets was out of the question. There was much hostile feeling against the colored boys and as he would be from home most of the time, he felt anxious about them. Mother came to the rescue with the suggestion that they be taken into the office and taught the case. They were little fellows and the thought had not occurred to father. He acted upon the suggestion and at the ages of eleven and nine they were perched upon blocks and given their first lesson in printer's ink, besides being employed to carry papers and mailing them.

Father was mother's honored guest. He was from home so often that his home comings were events that she thought worthy of extra notice, and caused renewed activity. Every thing was done that could be to add to his comfort. She also found time to care for four other boys at different times. As they became members of our home circle, the care of their clothing was as carefully seen to as her own children's and they delighted in calling her Mother.

In her early life she was a member of the Methodist Church, as was father, but in our home there was no family altar. Our custom was to read a chapter in the Bible around the table, each reading a verse in turn until the chapter was completed. She was a person who strived to live a Christian life instead of talking it. She was a woman strong in her likes and dislikes, and had a large discernment as to the character of those who came around her. Her gift in that direction being very fortunate in the protection of father's interest especially in the early days of his public life, when there was great apprehension for his safety. She was a woman firm in her opposition to alcoholic drinks, a strict disciplinarian—her *no* meant *no* and *yes, yes,* but more frequently the *no's* had it, especially when I was the petitioner. So far as I was concerned, I found my father more yielding than my mother, altho' both were rigid as to the matter of obedience.

There was a certain amount of grim humor about mother and perhaps such exhibitions as they occurred were a little startling to those who were unacquainted with her. The reserve in which she held herself made whatever she might attempt of a jocose nature somewhat acrid. She could not be known all at once, she had to be studied. She abhorred shames. In the early 70's she came to Washington and found a large number of people from whom the shackles had recently fallen. She fully realized their condition and considered the gaieties that were then indulged in as frivolous in the extreme.

On one occasion several young women called upon her and commenting on her spacious parlors and the approaching holiday season, thought it a favorable opportunity to suggest the keeping of an open house. Mother replied: "I have been keeping open house for several weeks. I have it closed now and I expect to keep it closed." The young women thinking mother's understanding was at fault, endeavored to explain. They were assured, however, that they were fully understood. Father, who was present, laughingly pointed to the New Bay Window, which had been completed only a few days previous to their call.

Perhaps no other home received under its roof a more varied class of people than did our home. From the highest dignitaries to the lowliest person, bond or free, white or black, were welcomed, and mother was equally gracious to all. There were a few who presumed on the hospitality of the home and officiously insinuated themselves and their advice in a manner that was particularly disagreeable to her. This unwelcome attention on the part of the visitor would be grievously repelled, in a manner more forceful than the said party would deem her capable of, and from such a person an erroneous impression of her temper and qualifications would be given, and criticisms sharp and unjust would be made; so that altho she had her triumphs, they were trials, and only those who knew her intimately could fully understand and appreciate the enduring patience of the wife and mother.

During her wedded life of forty-four years, whether in adversity or prosperity, she was the same faithful ally, guarding as best she could every interest connected with my father, his lifework and the home. Unfortunately an opportunity for knowledge of books had been denied her, the lack of which she greatly deplored. Her increasing family and household duties prevented any great advancement, altho' she was able to read a little. By contact with people of culture and education, and they were her real friends, her improvement was marked. She took a lively interest in every phase of the Anti-Slavery movement, an interest that father took full pains to foster and to keep her intelligently informed. I was instructed to read to her. She was a good listener, making comments on passing events, which were well worth consideration, altho' the manner of the presentation of them might provoke a smile. Her value was fully appreciated by my father, and in one of his letters to Thomas Auld, (his former master,) he says, "Instead of finding my companion a burden she is truly a helpmeet."

In 1882, this remarkable woman, for in many ways she was remarkable, was stricken with paralysis and for four weeks was a great sufferer. Altho' perfectly helpless, she insisted from her sick bed to direct her home affairs. The orders were given with precision and they were obeyed with alacrity. Her fortitude and patience up to within ten days of her death were very great. She helped us to bear her burden. Many letters of condolence from those who had met her and upon whom pleasant impressions had been made, were received. Hon. J. M. Dalzell of Ohio, wrote thus:

"You know I never met your good wife but once and then her welcome was so warm and sincere and unaffected, her manner altogether so motherly, and her goodby so full of genuine kindness and hospitality, as to impress me tenderly and fill my eyes with tears as I now recall it."

Prof. Peter H. Clark of Cincinnati, Ohio,* wrote: "The kind treatment given to us and our little one so many years ago won for her a place in our hearts from which no lapse of time could move her. To us she was ever kind and good and our mourning because of her death, is heartfelt."

There is much room for reflection in the review in the life of such a woman as Anna Murray Douglass. Unlettered tho' she was, there was a

---

*Clark was principal of the black high school in Cincinnati and among the first African American Socialists. He served as a correspondent for *Frederick Douglass' Paper.*

strength of character and of purpose that won for her the respect of the noblest and best. She was a woman who strove to inculcate in the minds of her children the highest principles of morality and virtue both by precept and example. She was not well versed in the polite etiquette of the drawing room, the rules for the same being found in the many treatises devoted to that branch of literature. She was possessed of a much broader culture, and with discernment born of intelligent observation, and wise discrimination she welcomed all with the hearty manner of a noble soul.

I have thus striven to give you a glimpse of my mother. In so doing I am conscious of having made frequent mention of my father. It is difficult to say any thing of mother without the mention of father, her life was so enveloped in his. Together they rest side by side, and most befittingly, within sight of the dear old home of hallowed memories and from which the panting fugitive, the weary traveler, the lonely emigrant of every clime, received food and shelter.■

151 TO THE NATIONS OF THE WORLD

W. E. B. Du Bois

Discussing "The Concept of Race" in Dusk of Dawn, *Du Bois writes*, "Africa is of course my fatherland. . . . On this vast continent were born and live a large portion of my direct ancestors going back a thousand years or more." But he adds, "The physical bond is least and the badge of color relatively unimportant save as a badge; the real essence of this kinship is its social heritage of slavery; the discrimination and insult; and this heritage binds together not simply the children of Africa, but extends through yellow Asia and into the South Seas. It is this unity that draws me to Africa."* It was also this sense of unity that brought Du Bois (1868–1963), at the turn of the twentieth century, to the First Pan-African Conference in London and that led to his prominent and continuing role in the Pan-African movement.

The term "Pan-Africanism" had been coined just the year before by conference organizer and London barrister Henry Sylvester Williams, a native of Trinidad. Thirty-three delegates from various nations responded to the call for the convention (promoted and partly sponsored by Booker

*Dusk of Dawn: Essay Toward an Autobiography of a Race (New York: Harcourt, Brace, 1940), 116.

T. Washington) and gathered in London's Westminster Hall on July 23–
25, 1900. The conference, among other things, appointed the Committee
on Address to the Nations of the World with Du Bois as its chair. Du
Bois drafted the "Address" and read it to the conference in its closing ses-
sion. It was adopted and "sent to the sovereigns in whose realms are sub-
jects of African descent."

Although the meeting did not lead to immediate action, it, in
Du Bois's words, "attracted attention" and "put the word 'Pan-African'
in the dictionaries for the first time." In Du Bois's address, it also pro-
duced a prescient call for the self-government of African nations and the
first reference to one of Du Bois's most famous statements (later used in
The Souls of Black Folks*): "The problem of the twentieth century is the*
problem of the color line, the question as to how far differences of race—
which show themselves chiefly in the color of the skin and the texture of
the hair—will hereafter be made the basis of denying to over half the
world the right of sharing to utmost ability the opportunities and privi-
leges of modern civilization."

The text was published in Alexander Walters, My Life and Work
(New York: Fleming H. Revell, 1917), 257–60, and reprinted with an intro-
duction in Philip S. Foner, ed., W. E. B. Du Bois Speaks: Speeches and Ad-
dresses, 1890–1919 *(New York: Pathfinder, 1970), 124–27. See also David*
Levering Lewis, W. E. B. Du Bois: Biography of a Race, 1868–1919 *(New*
York: Henry Holt, 1993).

In the metropolis of the modern world, in this the closing year of the nineteenth century, there has been assembled a congress of men and women
of African blood, to deliberate solemnly upon the present situation and outlook of the darker races of mankind. The problem of the twentieth century
is the problem of the color line, the question as to how far differences of
race—which show themselves chiefly in the color of the skin and the texture
of the hair—will hereafter be made the basis of denying to over half the world
the right of sharing to their utmost ability the opportunities and privileges
of modern civilization.

To be sure, the darker races are today the least advanced in culture according to European standards. This has not, however, always been the case
in the past, and certainly the world's history, both ancient and modern, has
given many instances of no despicable ability and capacity among the blackest races of men.

In any case, the modern world must remember that in this age when the
ends of the world are being brought so near together the millions of black
men in Africa, America and the Islands of the Sea, not to speak of the brown
and yellow myriads elsewhere, are bound to have a great influence upon the
world in the future, by reason of sheer numbers and physical contact. If now
the world of culture bends itself towards giving Negroes and other dark men

the largest and broadest opportunity for education and self-development, then this contact and influence is bound to have a beneficial effect upon the world and hasten human progress. But if, by reason of carelessness, prejudice, greed and injustice, the black world is to be exploited and ravished and degraded, the results must be deplorable, if not fatal—not simply to them, but to the high ideals of justice, freedom and culture which a thousand years of Christian civilization have held before Europe.

And now, therefore, to these ideals of civilization, to the broader humanity of the followers of the Prince of Peace, we, the men and women of Africa in world congress assembled, do now solemnly appeal:

Let the world take no backward step in that slow but sure progress which has successively refused to let the spirit of class, of caste, of privilege, or of birth, debar from life, liberty and the pursuit of happiness a striving human soul.

Let not color or race be a feature of distinction between white and black men, regardless of worth or ability.

Let not the natives of Africa be sacrificed to the greed of gold, their liberties taken away, their family life debauched, their just aspirations repressed, and avenues of advancement and culture taken from them.

Let not the cloak of Christian missionary enterprise be allowed in the future, as so often in the past, to hide the ruthless economic exploitation and political downfall of less developed nations, whose chief fault has been reliance on the plighted faith of the Christian church.

Let the British nation, the first modern champion of Negro freedom, hasten to crown the work of Wilberforce, and Clarkson, and Buxton, and Sharpe, Bishop Colenso, and Livingstone, and give, as soon as practicable, the rights of responsible government to the black colonies of Africa and the West Indies.

Let not the spirit of Garrison, Phillips, and Douglass wholly die out in America; may the conscience of a great nation rise and rebuke all dishonesty and unrighteous oppression toward the American Negro, and grant to him the right of franchise, security of person and property, and generous recognition of the great work he has accomplished in a generation toward raising nine millions of human beings from slavery to manhood.

Let the German Empire, and the French Republic, true to their great past, remember that the true worth of colonies lies in their prosperity and progress, and that justice, impartial alike to black and white, is the first element of prosperity.

Let the Congo Free State become a great central Negro state of the world, and let its prosperity be counted not simply in cash and commerce, but in the happiness and true advancement of its black people.

Let the nations of the world respect the integrity and independence of the free Negro states of Abyssinia, Liberia, Haiti, and the rest, and let the inhabitants of these states, the independent tribes of Africa, the Negroes of the West Indies and America, and the black subjects of all nations take courage, strive ceaselessly, and fight bravely, that they may prove to the world their incontestible right to be counted among the great brotherhood of mankind.

Thus we appeal with boldness and confidence to the Great Powers of the civilized world, trusting in the wide spirit of humanity, and the deep sense of justice of our age, for a generous recognition of the righteousness of our cause.■

INDEX OF SPEECHES BY AUTHOR

SUBJECT INDEX

Abolitionists, 71–72, 74, 124, 130, 157,
166–67, 184, 194, 197, 256, 275–76,
308, 310, 313, 328, 352–54, 373–74,
382, 395, 411, 452, 718; persecution of,
131–35, 157, 158, 160, 164–65, 186–87,
208, 355–57, 565; and temperance movement, 146; racial discrimination among,
168–73, 309–10; women, 158, 178, 564
Abolition of slavery, 165, 202–5, 339, 395,
410–25, 439, 441–42, 539, 718; gradual
versus immediate, 159; in Brazil, 717;
in Cuba, 517–20; in New York, 105–9;
in Tunis, 212. *See also* Emancipation;
Emancipation Proclamation; Great Britain; Thirteenth Amendment; West Indies
Abraham, 593
Accommodationism, 872–73
Adam, 666
Adams, E. J., 460–61, 463
Adams, John, 342
Adams, John Quincy, 169, 207, 278, 342
Africa, 675, 781; agriculture in, 448; as
point of human origin, 92, 93; before
European slave trade, 67, 93; biblical references to, 30–33, 43, 587, 820–21; colo-
nialism in, 907; cultural practices, 390–
92, 828–30; "degradation" of, 93, 743,
816, 817; geography, 91–92, 390, 821;
history and accomplishments of, 36,
587, 682, 821; ignorance of, 820, 825;
importance for African Americans, 817,
822, 831–32, 905; languages, 390, 828;
manhood in, 790, 821, 826; missionaries in, 156, 825–27; misconceptions of,
390–91; mixed races in, 824; oratory in,
1–2; peoples of, 826–30; religions, 825;
slavery in, 314, 828, 829; slave trade,
46, 66–73, 76, 81, 94–95, 149–50, 436,
447, 565, 822–23; writers on, 830. *See
also* Emigration, to Africa; Missionaries
African Free School (New York), 8, 66, 98–
99, 198, 589, 846
African Methodist Episcopal Church, 7,
56–57, 66, 86, 384–85, 403, 426, 443,
475–76, 506, 624, 626–27, 632, 725,
754, 797, 863, 878, 882, 890–91
Afro-American Bank, 723–24
Afro-American Council, 714
Afro-American League, 586, 713–14, 722–
25, 734

Alabama, 396, 549, 551, 553, 554, 561–
62, 616, 627, 645, 664, 676, 701
Alcohol, consumption of, 24–25, 27, 109,
145–54, 317, 647–48, 690, 711–12, 883
Allen, Richard, 56–57, 105
Allen, William Grant, 1, 2, 229–30
A.M.E. Zion Church, 224, 403, 725, 734
"America," 746, 760, 776
American Anti-Slavery Society, 5, 9, 158,
189, 205, 274, 331–32, 392–93, 463
American Colonization Society, 4–5, 57,
114, 117–18, 125, 130–35, 156–57, 404,
539–40, 586. *See also* Colonization
Americanization, 500, 610, 713, 816
American Missionary Association, 285,
452
American Moral Reform Society, 143, 158
American National Baptist Convention,
664
American Negro Academy, 846–47, 854–
55, 857, 873
American Revolution, 203, 291, 307, 350–
51, 677; African American service in,
20, 27, 39, 56, 59, 144, 158, 311, 315,
383, 521–22, 682, 777–78, 806, 870;
principles of, 58, 59, 71, 187, 196, 200,
250–52, 326, 355, 538, 643, 810
Amherst College, 331
Amistad, 204, 311
Amnesty for Confederates, 424, 705
Anarchism, 655–60, 709, 711
Andersonville prison, 697
Andrew, John A., 408, 429
Andrews, Charles C., 98–99
Anglo-African Magazine, The, 322, 358
Anthony, Susan B., 328, 463–64, 688
Antislavery societies, 5, 6
Arkansas, 474, 883, 884
Armed resistance: to disfranchisement,
876; to racist violence, 398, 707–8, 786–
87, 874; to slavery, 308, 311–12, 314,
367, 447, 449. *See also* Brown, John;
Civil War; Slave rebellions
Armenia, 863, 875
Arnold, Benedict, 521, 684
Asante, Molefi, 1–2, 11
Ashmun, Jehudi, 113
Asians, 319, 498.
Aspasia, 674
Athens, 665

About the Editors

The late PHILIP S. FONER was Professor Emeritus of History at
Lincoln University, Pennsylvania, and recipient of the New York
Labor History Association's Special Award for Lifetime
Achievement. He earned his master's and doctorate degrees from
Columbia University and wrote numerous books, including *The
Voice of Black America: Major Speeches by Negroes in the
United States, 1797–1971* (1972), *The History of the Labor
Movement in the United States* (10 volumes), and *The Life and
Writings of Frederick Douglass* (5 volumes).

ROBERT JAMES BRANHAM is Professor of Rhetoric at Bates College,
Maine. He earned his bachelor's degree from Dartmouth College,
his master's degree from The University of North Carolina at
Chapel Hill, and his doctorate degree from the University of
Massachusetts-Amherst. Among his many publications are
Debate and Critical Analysis (1991), numerous journal articles,
and documentary films and videos.